THE DEVELOPMENT OF CHILDREN

To our families, to whom we owe
a debt of gratitude for our own development.

THE DEVELOPMENT OF CHILDREN

SEVENTH EDITION

CYNTHIA LIGHTFOOT
Pennsylvania State University, Brandywine

MICHAEL COLE
University of California, San Diego

SHEILA R. COLE

WORTH PUBLISHERS

Vice President, Editorial and Production: Catherine Woods
Associate Publisher: Jessica Bayne
Senior Acquisitions Editor: Christine Cardone
Developmental Editor: Peter Deane
Editorial Assistant: Lukia Kliossis
Marketing Manager: Lindsay Johnson
Marketing Assistant: Stephanie Ellis
Director of Print and Digital Development: Tracey Kuehn
Associate Managing Editor: Lisa Kinne
Project Editor: Kerry O'Shaughnessy
Media and Supplements Editor: Sharon Prevost
Photo Editor: Christine Buese
Photo Researcher: Donna Ranieri
Art Director and Text Designer: Babs Reingold
Cover Designer: Lyndall Culbertson
Illustration Coordinator: Bill Page
Illustrations: Kim Martens, Chris Notarile, Northeastern Graphic, Inc.
Production Manager: Barbara Seixas
Supplements Production Manager: Stacey Alexander
Supplements Project Editor: Julio Espin
Composition: Northeastern Graphic Inc.
Printing and Binding: Quad/Graphics

Credit is given to the following sources for permission to use the part- and chapter-opening photos:
cover, Vstock/Getty Images; p. 0, Greg Elms/LPI; p. 46, Dr. David Phillips/Visuals Unlimited;
p. 48, Asian Specialists/Alamy; p. 78, Neil Bromhall/Photo Researchers; p. 120, Lev Dolgatshjov/
Dreamstime.com; p. 122, Tim Gainey/Alamy; p. 160, Tetra Images/Getty Images; p. 198, Shehzad
Noorani/age fotostock; p. 232, Dan Dalton/Getty Images; p. 234, Andy Andrews/Getty Images;
p. 270, blue jean images/Getty Images; p. 304, Robert Seitz/age fotostock; p. 342, Suzy Bennett/
Alamy; p. 386, Angelo Cavalli/age fotostock; p. 388, Floresco Productions/Getty Images; p. 428,
Stuart Fox/Getty Images; p. 464, R. Ian Lloyd/Masterfile; p. 504, Rafael Campillo/age fotostock;
p. 506, Clint Lucas/LPI; p. 550, Tom Cockrem/LPI.

Library of Congress Control Number: 2012932234

ISBN-13: 978-1-4292-4328-5
ISBN-10: 1-4292-4328-7

Worth Publishers
41 Madison Avenue
New York, NY 10010
www.worthpublishers.com

About the Authors

CYNTHIA LIGHTFOOT is Professor of Human Development and acting head of Psychology at the Pennsylvania State University, Brandywine. Her published works focus on the sociocultural contexts of child and adolescent development, most recently on teen pregnancy, risk-taking, identity development, and youth culture. Lightfoot currently serves on the editorial board of *Culture and Psychology*, and the executive board of the Jean Piaget Society. She became interested in developmental psychology as an undergraduate student, when she worked with emotionally troubled and autistic children in school settings, and became engaged in research focused on language development, communication, and culture.

MICHAEL COLE is an all-University of California Professor of Psychology, Communication, and Human Development. His home base is University of California, San Diego, where he is the Director of the Laboratory of Comparative Human Cognition. For many years he spent his afternoons participating with children and undergraduates in development-enhancing after-school programs. He is an editor of the journal *Mind, Culture and Activity*. He has published widely on the role of culture and schooling in development, for which he has been awarded honorary degrees at Copenhagen University and the University of Helsinki. He is a member of the American Academy of Arts and Sciences and the National Academies of Education (of the United States and Russia).

SHEILA COLE is a former journalist who specialized in writing about families, children, development, and education. She also writes books for children. Her most recent book offers a history of American childhood and is written for young people. She has also authored picture books, historical fiction, and novels for young adults. She participates in literacy programs for homeless adolescents.

The Coles have three grandchildren with whom they like to spend their summers.

Brief Contents

Preface   xix

Chapter 1: The Study of Human Development   1

PART I In the Beginning

Chapter 2: Biocultural Foundations   49

Chapter 3: Prenatal Development and Birth   79

PART II Infancy

Chapter 4: The First 3 Months   123

Chapter 5: Physical and Cognitive Development in Infancy   161

Chapter 6: Social and Emotional Development in Infancy   199

PART III Early Childhood

Chapter 7: Language Acquisition   235

Chapter 8: Physical and Cognitive Development in Early Childhood   271

Chapter 9: Social and Emotional Development in Early Childhood   305

Chapter 10: Contexts of Development   343

PART IV Middle Childhood

Chapter 11: Physical and Cognitive Development in Middle Childhood   389

Chapter 12: School as a Context for Development   429

Chapter 13: Social and Emotional Development in Middle Childhood   465

PART V Adolescence

Chapter 14: Physical and Cognitive Development in Adolescence   507

Chapter 15: Social and Emotional Development in Adolescence   551

Appendix   A-1

Glossary   G-1

References   R-1

Name Index   NI-1

Subject Index   SI-1

Contents

Preface.. xix

Chapter 1 The Study of Human Development 1

Developmental Science.. 2

Periods of Development   3

Domains of Development   3

Contexts of Development   4

Children, Society, and Science... 4

Historical Beliefs About Children and Childhood   5

The Emergence of Developmental Science   7

The New Field of Developmental Science   9

The Central Issues of Developmental Science............................... 10

Questions About the Sources of Development   10

Questions About Plasticity   10

Questions About Continuity/Discontinuity   12

Questions About Individual Differences   14

Theories of Development... 15

Theory in Developmental Science   15

Grand Theories   16

Modern Theories   22

Methods for Studying Development... 29

The Goals of Developmental Research   29

Criteria for Developmental Research   31

Methods of Data Collection   32

Research Designs   37

Ethical Standards   42

Looking Ahead... 43

Summary.. 44

Chapter 1 Boxes

In the Field: Probing the Mysteries of Learning   24

Observing the Living Brain   33

Understanding Causes and Correlations   36

PART I IN THE BEGINNING

Chapter 2 Biocultural Foundations 49

Inheriting Culture... 51

The Tools of Culture   52

Processes of Cultural Inheritance   54

The Complexity of Culture   55

Chapter 2 Boxes

In the Field: Doctor of the Plain People   67

Biological Inheritance 57

   Genes and Traits   57

   Evolution's Process of Natural Selection   58

   Genetic Inheritance Through Sexual Reproduction   59

   Laws of Genetic Inheritance   62

   Mutations and Genetic Abnormalities   63

   The Phenotype: From Genes to Traits   68

   Heritability   69

   Genotypes, Phenotypes, and Human Behavior   71

The Coevolution of Culture and Biology 73

   Lactose Tolerance   73

   Sickle-Cell Anemia   74

Retracing the Laetoli Footsteps 75

Summary 76

Chapter 3 Boxes

Cultural Traditions and Infant Care: From Spirit Village to the Land of Beng   106

In the Field: Midwifery in the Inuit Villages of Northern Canada   109

Chapter 3 Prenatal Development and Birth 79

The Periods of Prenatal Development 81

   The Germinal Period   81

   The Embryonic Period   82

   The Fetal Period   85

Maternal Conditions and Prenatal Development 89

   Maternal Stress   89

   Nutritional Influences   91

Teratogens: Environmental Sources of Birth Defects 94

   Drugs   96

   Infections and Other Health Conditions   99

Birth 104

   The Stages of Labor   105

   Cultural Variations in Childbirth   106

   Childbirth in the United States   107

The Newborn's Condition 111

   Assessing the Baby's Viability   111

   Problems and Complications   113

   Developmental Consequences   114

Beginning the Parent–Child Relationship 115

   The Baby's Appearance   116

   Social Expectations   116

Summary 118

PART II INFANCY

Chapter 4 The First 3 Months 123

Physical Growth 124

Measuring Body Growth   124

Growth of the Skull   125

Brain Development 126

Neurons and Networks of Neurons   126

The Structure of the Central Nervous System   127

Experience and Development of the Brain   128

Sensing the Environment 130

Methods of Evaluating Infant Sensory Capacities   131

Hearing   132

Vision   133

Taste and Smell   137

Intermodal Perception   138

The Organization of Behavior 140

Reflexes   140

From Reflex to Coordinated Action   141

Reaching   144

Piaget's Theory of Developing Action   144

Learning Theories of Developing Action   146

Temperament 148

Becoming Coordinated with the Social World 150

Sleeping   151

Feeding   153

Crying   155

Summing Up the First 3 Months 157

Summary 158

Chapter 5 Physical and Cognitive Development in Infancy 161

Physical Growth 162

Size and Shape   162

The Musculoskeletal System   164

Brain Development 165

Brain and Behavior   165

Brain and Experience   166

Motor Development 168

Fine Motor Skills   168

Gross Motor Skills   171

Chapter 4 Boxes

In the Field: Baby-Friendly Hospital Care   143

Sleeping Arrangements   151

Sudden Infant Death Syndrome   154

Chapter 5 Boxes

Bringing Up Brainy Babies   167

In the Field: The Diaper-Free Movement   176

The Role of Practice in Motor Development   174

Control of Elimination   175

Cognitive Development: The Great Debate 177

Sensorimotor Development   178

Reproducing Interesting Events (Substage 3)   178

The Emergence of Intentionality (Substage 4)   179

Exploring by Experimenting (Substage 5)   179

Representation (Substage 6)   180

Conceptual Development 181

Understanding the Permanence of Objects   181

Understanding Other Properties of the Physical World   187

Reasoning About Objects   189

The Growth of Attention and Memory 192

Developing Attention   193

Developing Memory   194

Implications 195

Summary 196

Chapter 6 Boxes

Attachment to Fathers and Others   213

In the Field: Children with Reactive Attachment Disorder   217

The Moral Life of Babies   227

Chapter 6 Social and Emotional Development in Infancy 199

The Nature of Infant Emotions and Emotional Expressions 200

Theories of Emotional Development   201

Infant Emotions and Social Life   203

Intersubjectivity and the Brain   205

The Infant–Caregiver Emotional Relationship 207

Explanations of Attachment   207

Phases of Attachment   209

Patterns of Attachment   210

The Causes of Variations in Patterns of Attachment   214

Attachment Patterns and Later Development   220

The Changing Nature of Communication 221

Social Referencing   222

Following a Caregiver's Signs of Interest   222

The Beginnings of Language Comprehension and Speech   223

A Sense of Self 224

Self-Recognition   225

The Self as Agent   226

The Emergence of Self-Conscious Emotions   226

Developing Trust and Autonomy 228

Implications 229

Summary 230

PART III EARLY CHILDHOOD

Chapter 7 Language Acquisition 235

The Power of Language 236

Keys to the World of Language 238

The Biological Key to Language   238

The Environmental Key to Language   241

The Basic Domains of Language Acquisition 247

Phonological Development   248

Semantic Development   250

Grammar Development   255

Pragmatic Development   257

Explanations of Language Acquisition 261

Biological Explanations   262

Social and Cultural Explanations   263

Cognitive Approaches   264

Reconsidering the Keys to Language 267

Summary 268

Chapter 7 Boxes

Children Creating a Language   243

Learning Two Languages   244

In the Field: A Speech–Language Pathologist in Vietnam   249

Chapter 8 Physical and Cognitive Development in Early Childhood 271

Physical and Motor Development 272

The Changing Body   272

Motor Development   273

Health   274

Brain Development   276

Preoperational Development 277

Centration   279

The Problem of Uneven Levels of Performance   284

Information-Processing Approaches to Cognitive Development 285

Cognitive Development in Privileged Domains 288

The Domain of Physics   289

The Domain of Psychology   290

The Domain of Biology   291

Explaining Domain-Specific Cognitive Development   293

Cognitive Development and Culture 298

Cultural Scripts   298

Cultural Context and the Unevenness of Development   300

Reconciling Alternative Approaches 301

Summary 302

Chapter 8 Boxes

Bearing Witness: Can Young Children Tell the Truth?   286

In the Field: Supporting Siblings of Children with Autism   296

Chapter 9 Boxes

In the Field: Coping with Chronic
Illness Through Play   324

The Spanking Controversy   333

Chapter 9 Social and Emotional Development in Early Childhood 305

Identity Development 306

Sex-Role Identity   307

Ethnic Identity   313

Personal Identity   315

A New Moral World 317

The Psychodynamic View   318

The Cognitive-Developmental View   318

The Social Domain View   319

Developing Self-Regulation 320

Regulating Thought and Action   321

Self-Regulation and Play   322

Regulating Emotions   326

Understanding Aggression 329

The Development of Aggression   329

What Causes and Controls Aggression?   331

Developing Prosocial Behaviors 336

Empathy   336

Sympathy   337

Taking One's Place in the Social Group 338

Summary 340

Chapter 10 Boxes

Fathers   354

In the Field: Louisiana Swamp
Nurse   364

Children and War   372

Chapter 10 Contexts of Development 343

The Family Context 344

The Biocultural Origins of Family   345

Parenting Practices   347

The Role of Siblings   351

Family Diversity   353

Distressed Families   358

Nonparental Child Care 364

Varieties of Child Care   365

Developmental Effects of Child Care   367

Neighborhoods and Communities 369

Community and Culture   369

Distressed Communities   370

Media Contexts 372

Print Media   374

Television   375

Interactive Media   378

Contexts, Risk, and Resilience 380

Summary 384

PART IV MIDDLE CHILDHOOD

Chapter 11 Physical and Cognitive Development in Middle Childhood 389

Physical and Motor Development 390

Patterns of Growth   391

Motor Development   393

Brain Development   398

Concrete-Operational Development 400

Conservation   402

Classification   404

Planning   405

Metacognition   406

Limitations of Concrete Operations   408

Information-Processing Approaches 409

The Role of Memory   409

Thinking About Memory   412

Increased Control of Attention   413

Executive Function   413

The Role of Social and Cultural Contexts 414

Is the Acquisition of Conservation Universal?   415

Cultural Variations in the Use of Memory Strategies   417

Cultural Variations in Planning   418

Individual Differences in Cognitive Development 419

Measuring Intelligence   420

Persistent Questions About Intelligence   420

Reconsidering the Cognitive Changes in Middle Childhood 425

Summary 426

Chapter 12 School as a Context for Development 429

The Contexts of Learning 431

School Readiness 433

Precursors to Reading and Writing   434

Precursors to Learning Mathematics   434

Chapter 11 Boxes

In the Field: Let's Move! A National Campaign to Battle Childhood Obesity   394

Chapter 12 Boxes

In the Field: Learning After School in the Fifth Dimension   444

Comparing Mathematics Achievement Across Cultures   456

The Role of Family   435

Preschools   437

In the Classroom 439

Social Organization of the Classroom and Instructional Design   439

Barriers to School Success   444

The Cognitive Consequences of Schooling 449

The School-Cutoff Strategy   449

Comparing Schooled and Nonschooled Children   450

Assessing the Second-Generation Impact of Schooling   453

Contemporary Challenges in a Globalizing World 454

The Culture of School   455

The Language of School   459

Culturally Responsive Classroom Strategies   460

Outside the School 461

Summary 462

Chapter 13 Boxes

Children's Ideas About God   474

Bullies and Their Victims   482

In the Field: Gender Politics on the Playground   490

Chapter 13 Social and Emotional Development in Middle Childhood 465

A New Sense of Self 466

Changing Conceptions of the Self   466

Self-Esteem   468

Moral Development 471

Piaget's Theory of Moral Development   472

Kohlberg's Theory of Moral Development   473

Prosocial Moral Reasoning   477

Social Domain Theory   478

Moral Reasoning and Theories of Mind   479

Peer Relationships 481

Peer Relations and Social Status   481

Competition and Cooperation Among Peers   485

Relations Between Boys and Girls   489

Friendship: A Special Type of Relationship   493

The Influence of Parents 496

Changing Expectations   496

Parents and Peers   498

Divorce   499

Reconsidering Middle Childhood 501

Summary 502

PART V ADOLESCENCE

Chapter 14 Physical and Cognitive Development in Adolescence...........507

Adolescents and Society...........507

Historical Views   508

Adolescents in Modern Society   508

Biological Theories of Adolescent Development...........510

G. Stanley Hall   510

Sigmund Freud   511

Modern Theories of Biological Development   511

Puberty...........512

The Growth Spurt   512

Sexual Development   514

Brain Development   517

The Neuro-Hormonal System   520

The Timing of Puberty   522

Puberty and Health   526

Cognitive Development...........530

Piaget's Theory of Formal Operations   530

Information-Processing Approaches   536

Sociocultural Approaches   537

Moral Development...........539

Kohlberg's Theory of Moral Reasoning   539

Gilligan's Theory of Moral Reasoning   542

Parent and Peer Contributions to Moral Development   543

Cultural Variations in Moral Reasoning   544

The Relation Between Moral Reasoning and Moral Action   546

Implications...........547

Summary...........548

Chapter 15 Social and Emotional Development in Adolescence...........551

Emotional Development in Adolescence...........552

The Experience of Emotions   553

Regulating Emotions   554

Relationships with Peers...........557

Friendships   557

Cliques and Crowds   559

Chapter 14 Boxes

Early Maturation and Reproductive Success: The Case of the Pumé Foragers   513

ICONS: Peacekeeping in a Virtual Classroom   535

Chapter 15 Boxes

In the Field: Friends with Benefits   563

Teenage Pregnancy   569

From Diaries to Facebook   576

Suicide Among Native American Adolescents   588

Peer Pressure and Conformity   560

Romantic Relationships   562

Sexual Relationships 564

Learning About Sex   565

The Sexual Debut   567

Relationships with Parents 570

Adolescent–Parent Conflicts   570

Parental Influences Beyond the Family   571

Identity Development 573

The "I" and the "Me"   574

Achieving a Mature Identity   574

Forming an Ethnic Identity   578

Forming a Sexual Identity   581

Identity and Culture   583

Adolescent Health and Well-Being 585

Emotional Health   585

Sexual Health   593

Positive Youth Development   595

Reconsidering Adolescence 597

Summary 598

Appendix A-1

Glossary G-1

References R-1

Name Index NI-1

Subject Index SI-1

Preface

Welcome to the seventh edition of *The Development of Children*. If you are new to the book, we hope you will find it a thorough yet streamlined and lively review of developmental theory and research that engages the interest and intellect of today's students. If you have used previous editions, we think you will be pleased with how we have continued to integrate recent advances in developmental science with central themes that have characterized *The Development of Children* since its debut in 1989: the interaction of cultural and biological processes throughout development; the integration of theory, research, and practice; and the child as situated within a dynamically changing set of contexts.

Our interest in children's development is the result of years of personal and professional experience. My own interest was sparked during my undergraduate years when I worked in classrooms and programs for autistic and developmentally delayed children. Later, between graduate degrees, I worked in a program for teen mothers and their children, many of whom were Vietnamese and Cambodian refugees. Having spent my adolescence in Japan, I had developed an early interest in the relationship between culture and behavior. Over time, my professional interests focused on development, culture, and issues affecting minority and immigrant children and families.

Similarly, Michael and Sheila Cole's personal interest in children's development extends back to their youth when they worked together as camp counselors. Their years of experience first as parents raising children and now as grandparents have deepened their appreciation for children's development and the changing contexts in which it occurs. Both have also committed their professional lives to children's development: Michael Cole specializes in the study of the role of culture in children's learning and cognitive development; Sheila Cole is a journalist who has written articles about children and books for children.

Beyond our interest in children's development, the Coles and I share a long-standing devotion to undergraduate education. Michael Cole has spent most of his professional life at a "research 1" university; I have spent most of mine at a small college that is part of a large state university system. He and I alike see our book as a tool for promoting cultural literacy and critical thinking as well as an appreciation for how research can improve the lives of children by leading to evidence-based programs and policies. The goal of making a positive contribution to our students' development, as well as to the development of the children that they will someday go on to educate, counsel, study, and/or parent, was a high priority for us as we worked on this book. In the sections that follow, we explain how we have pursued this goal through the book's central themes and by strengthening these themes and making other changes in this new edition.

Theoretical Orientation

A Biocultural Approach

As mentioned, culture and biology have been focuses of this book from the first edition. Integrating some of the most influential and respected work in contemporary developmental sciences, the *biocultural perspective,* which was introduced in the sixth edition and is further emphasized in this edition, is true both to the direction of the field and to our general pedagogical priorities. Regarding the direction of the field,

it is clear that the theories and methods of developmental science are expanding to embrace more synthetic conceptions of how culture and biology are intertwined in ontogenetic development. In contrast to past paradigms that asked, for example, "What part nature, what part nurture?" contemporary work increasingly recognizes that universality and variation are inherent to both cultural and biological processes, which are jointly manifested over the course of development. Regarding our pedagogical priorities, the biocultural perspective reflects our conviction that students' understanding of diversity—of culture, gender, ethnicity, class, religion—is essential to their own development in a rapidly globalizing world. In Chapter 2, we formally present the biocultural perspective as a conceptual framework for learning about how cultural processes and the biological processes of inheritance relate to each other and to the development of individual children. Biocultural foundations are underscored throughout the book in numerous discussions and illustrations, further advancing students' understanding of their relevance to developmental pathways. For highlights of the book's thoroughgoing coverage of culture as a mediator of development, please see Table 1.

In addition to its relevance to students' understanding of the world around them, the diversity focus inherent to the biocultural perspective speaks directly to our students' personal lives and histories. It is obvious to all that, like our neighborhoods, places of work, and society in general, our student populations are becoming increasingly multiethnic and multilingual. It is equally clear that students naturally seek connections between course material and their own life experience. The diversity focus of our book encourages and rewards such relevance-seeking exploration. As our many years in the classroom have shown us, when students succeed in anchoring course content to their own experience, they are more likely to understand and remember.

table 1

Highlights of the Coverage of Culture in the Seventh Edition

Culture as a context of development, p. 4
Cultural variations about managing fussiness in children, p. 5
Japanese and American understandings of aggression in children, p. 16
Vygotsky and sociocultural theory, p. 21
Ethnography, p. 33
Cultural inheritance, pp. 54–55
Coevolution of culture and biology, pp. 73–74
Cultural variations in prenatal care, pp. 89–94
Cultural variations in childbirth, pp. 106–108
Newborn functioning in different cultures, p. 113
Parental responses to infants by culture, pp. 116–117
Sleeping arrangements around the world, pp. 151–153
Symbolic cultural tools, p. 196
Cultural and universal emotional expressions, pp. 201–205
Imitative games across culture, p. 206
Cultural variations in attachment, pp. 216–218
Learning two languages, p. 244
Culture and sustained processing of spatial relations, p. 277
The role of language in culture, pp. 293, 297
Cultural scripts, p. 298
Culturally organized context of children's developing competence, p. 301
The cultural view, p. 312
Cultural variations in the age at which children mask emotion, p. 327
The influence of culture on emotional regulation, p. 328

Family and culture, p. 346
Immigrant families, pp. 354–356
Community and culture, p. 370
Children's literature and culture beliefs, pp. 369–370
Social stereotypes, p. 378
Culture and athleticism in girls and boys, p. 396
Cultural influences on the acquisition of conservation, pp. 415–417
Cultural variations in planning, p. 418
Are IQ tests culturally biased? p. 424
Cultural variations in school, pp. 429, 431
Cultural variations in preschools, p. 437
Contemporary challenges in a globalizing world, p. 454
The culture of school, p. 455
Culturally responsive classroom strategies, p. 460
The role of culture in competitive vs. cooperative play, pp. 487–489
Cultural issues in emerging adulthood, pp. 509–510
Cultural influences on epistemic development, p. 536
Cultural variations in moral reasoning, pp. 544–546
Cultural expectations and emotion regulation, pp. 555–556
Cultural variations in support for adolescent dating, the transmission of sexual knowledge and values, the sexual debut, and teen pregnancy, pp. 564–569
Ethnic identity, pp. 578–579
Culture and identity, pp. 583–585

Integrating Practice, Theory, and Research

As part of challenging students to look at information critically, we promote the understanding that information arises in the context of particular theories and particular research questions and methods of inquiry, and that it should be held to standards of science. However, along with wanting students to understand the connections among information, theory, and research, we want them to understand that child development research—its questions and methods—is significantly tied to meaningful matters of practice—that is, to the issues, problems, plans, and concerns of the day. To give practice its proper place, as well as for pedagogical reasons, we make certain not to allow the story of development to be overwhelmed and obscured by seemingly disconnected facts and figures and by theoretical disputes of interest only to people in the field. Our goal is to provide students with the essential information they need to acquire meaningful, connected, and relevant *knowledge* of development, and to present that information in a way that is accessible, transparent, and engaging from beginning to end.

The focus on practice is also consistent with our own scholarly work. We are all actively interested in discovering practical approaches for fostering the development of children, and in involving our students in this enterprise. Michael Cole's development of the Fifth Dimension after-school program is an example, as is my work with teenage mothers, immigrant families, and nutrition education programs for inner-city children. In all cases, our students are actively involved in the research process, carrying knowledge from the classroom to the contexts in which children live and develop.

Our belief in the importance of linking practical, theoretical, and research orientations in studying development comes not only from our own experience but also as a response to the current concerns of developmental science, as well as to the increasing interest in practice and service that we see in our students. It is therefore natural that our book should focus on research as an ethical enterprise, underscoring its implications for defining and creating healthy contexts of development, and preventing or solving problems that threaten children's well-being. Among the many issues we discuss are the benefits of special nutrition programs for children who have experienced malnutrition early in life, methods for assessing the quality of out-of-home care for young children, the importance of extended families in ameliorating the problems facing poor children, the special hazards of teenage pregnancy, the risk factors that may lead to depression or anxiety, approaches to parenting teenagers that are more or less effective in different contexts, and factors that contribute to positive youth development. Indeed, "In the Field" boxes, a special feature of the book, showcase developmentalists whose applied work is being recognized for its important impact on developmental and child-welfare and social justice issues. We also include many examples drawn from the everyday lives of children to show how a society's beliefs influence its children's development by shaping both the laws and the social norms that govern child-rearing practices.

A Focus on Dynamic Interaction

The Development of Children combines traditional chronological and topical approaches to the study of development in a deliberate attempt to make as clear as possible the idea that development is a process involving the whole child situated within multiple, interacting contexts. Although the book is chronological in its overall structure and adopts traditional age boundaries for each of its major sections, its organization is topical in two important respects. First, within the traditionally defined age periods, it describes development in physical, cognitive, social, and emotional

domains, emphasizing the interaction among domains. Second, it includes several chapters devoted to underscoring the role of dynamic contexts in general, and of the special context of school in particular, in shaping developmental pathways.

Our emphasis on development in context is meant to inspire students to look more closely at children in order to understand their developmental needs and how they experience the world—their peers and parents, their schools and playgrounds, their toys and games, and the monsters under their beds. After all, in their personal, professional, and civic lives, our students will influence the contexts of children's development, thereby affecting children's potential for success and happiness. Our goal as teachers is to ensure that they do so mindfully and with purpose.

New to the Seventh Edition

The overarching goals of this edition of *The Development of Children* are to introduce new material that represents the most recent significant advances in the field and to build on the radically restructured sixth edition to make sure that every discussion has earned its place and is anchored securely to other relevant aspects and domains of development. With students *and* instructors in mind, both new and reorganized chapter sections provide deeper knowledge of interactions across physical, cognitive, social, and emotional domains of development. These macro-level changes were made to help students better understand the complexity of development and to help the book fit even more comfortably into a standard course structure. The new coverage and thorough updating throughout enhance the book's characteristic focus on research and culture, while micro-level, sentence-by-sentence revisions to facilitate students' interest in and command of every discussion make this edition the most lively and student-friendly yet. We have also retained from the sixth edition several highly praised pedagogical features, including compelling vignettes that open each chapter and focus on children from a range of cultures. Another well-received pedagogical feature is the "Apply-Connect-Discuss" exercises at the end of each major chapter section. The exercises ask students, individually or in groups, to reflect and draw on what they have just read—for example, by comparing and contrasting theoretical viewpoints, creating an experiment or intervention, conducting online research, or applying what they have learned to a scenario or their own personal experience.

High points of the revision include several improvements, which we describe below.

Stronger Focus on Developmental Plasticity within Dynamic Contexts

New and expanded material underscores the interrelationship between children and the multiple, interacting contexts of their development. For instance, we explore how maternal anxiety and nutrition can affect the physical health and behavior of the developing fetus and child; how sibling interactions mediate children's resilience to the trauma of war and violence; and how immigrant children and families adapt to radically new cultural contexts, including the cultural context of school.

Updated Coverage of the Brain

The burgeoning of developmental neuroscience is reflected in expanded coverage of the brain—from prenatal and infant brain development and the emergence of executive function in middle childhood to the role of various brain structures in the triggering of puberty and the significance of the prefrontal cortex in adolescent risk-taking and decision-making. Engaging examples and illustrations help students

table 2
Highlights of the Coverage of the Brain in the Seventh Edition
High-tech research on brain function, development and disorders, p. 33
Brain activity during prenatal development, p. 87
Impact of prenatal nutrition on brain development, p. 91
Impact of teratogens, including marijuana, on brain development, pp. 97–98
Relationship between low birth weight and brain development, p. 114
Neonatal brain development, p. 126
Neurons and neural networks, pp. 126–127
The structure of the central nervous system, p. 128
Experience and development of the brain, pp. 128–130
Infant brain development, pp. 165–166
Implications of infant brain development, p. 195
Intersubjectivity and the brain, p. 205
A brain for language, pp. 239–241
Brain function and fast mapping, p. 254
Brain development and scale errors during early childhood, pp. 276–277
Brain development during early childhood, p. 398
Brain involvement in specific learning disabilities, pp. 445–447
Brain development in adolescence, including its role in the onset of puberty and its influence on behavior, pp. 517–521

make sense of recent research on brain development and its effects on other developmental domains. For highlights of the coverage of the brain in the seventh edition, see Table 2.

Increased Focus on Health, Resilience, and Well-Being

Responding to a groundswell of research seeking to elaborate an alternative to traditional "deficit models" of child health, we have included new material on the resilience of families and children in the face of stress and challenges, research on the effectiveness of preventive programs, and expanded coverage of positive youth development.

Detailed Chapter Changes

Chapter 1 The Study of Human Development

- Added information and research example on "babyness" in the section on evolutionary theories.
- Reorganization of the section on theories helps students understand some shared conceptual and historical foundations and better prepares them for later discussions.

Chapter 2 Biocultural Foundations

- The role of shared knowledge in cultural evolution is richly highlighted by a new discussion of the cultural consequences arising from the depletion of the Tasmanian cultural tool kit after rising seas millennia ago cut Tasmania off from its pool of social learners in Australia.
- The discussion of recessive gene inheritance has been revised to highlight the significance of this pattern primarily with regard to certain disorders, and to emphasize that behavioral traits of interest are polygenic.

- Reorganized discussion of canalization, along with a new figure, offers a crisper delineation of Waddington's epigenetic landscape.

Chapter 3 Prenatal Development and Birth

- New discussion of the effects of high levels of testosterone on prenatal female brain development and their possible links to congenital adrenal hyperplasia (CAH).
- New discussion of the importance of certain fetal activities that support breathing, sucking, and swallowing after birth.
- Reorganized section on the effects of prenatal maternal stress begins with research showing a consistent pattern of low birth weight for infants whose mothers lived through major disasters (e.g., the ten-week bombing of Belgrade during the Kosovo war, Hurricane Katrina) while pregnant. Section also contains new discussion of "pregnancy anxiety."
- New material on maternal overnutrition, which also features animal research on the relationship between high levels of fat in the mother's diet and a child's risk for obesity and other diseases.
- New discussion examines how poor maternal nutrition may lead to permanent "compensatory" alteration in the fetus's metabolism, creating risk for developing stroke, diabetes, and obesity.
- New discussion of methamphetamine use during pregnancy cites the rapidly rising rates of hospitalization of expectant mothers for meth-related problems and the possible effects that the mother's use may have on her fetus.
- New box, "Cultural Traditions and Infant Care: From Spirit Village to the Land of the Beng," colorfully illustrates the intertwining of cultural beliefs and practices surrounding childbirth.
- New discussion treats how fetal growth may be affected by social factors such as maternal education and family environment.

Chapter 4 The First Three Months

- Expanded discussion of brain development includes coverage of recent brain-imaging research that traced changes in overall brain volume, gray matter, and white matter from birth to adulthood. Discussion includes charts depicting these changes and a new figure showing decreases in gray matter as a result of synaptic pruning during childhood and adolescence.
- New discussion of young infants' increasing tendency to better discriminate between different faces of their own ethnic group than between those of other groups.
- Revised discussion of Rothbart's delineation of the dimensions of temperament, illustrated with a new table of Rothbart's scale definitions.
- Box on sudden infant death syndrome includes revised discussion of the possible culprit factors and a new chart of the international decline in the incidence of SIDS associated with the "back-to-sleep" campaign.

Chapter 5 Physical and Cognitive Development in Infancy

- Coverage of *infant growth restriction* and its relationship to such factors as diet and SES is expanded.
- New account presents Karen Adolph's research into infants' use of both social referencing and their own risk assessment in deciding whether or not to attempt walking down slopes that may be too steep for them.

- Coverage of Piaget's concept of object permanence has been reorganized for greater clarity and cohesion.

Chapter 6 Social and Emotional Development in Infancy

- Discussion of the still-face procedure includes fascinating new photos from Tronick's lab.

- New box, "The Moral Life of Babies," presents Hamlin, Wynn, and Bloom's intriguing research on the possibility of infants' having a rudimentary sense of morality, as evidenced by their responses to the "good" and "naughty" behaviors of puppets.

Chapter 7 Language Acquisition

- New research is presented on infants' preference for infant-directed speech and the extent to which it draws infants' attention to particular social partners.

- New discussion in the section "The Vocabulary Spurt" considers research suggesting that the rate of fast-mapping may be related to baseline vocabulary size and changes in the way the brain processes language.

- New discussion of a cross-cultural comparison of the working vocabularies of 2-year-olds living in Berkley, California, and in a Mayan mountainside village vividly illustrates how culture influences which objects become the focus of mother–child interactions.

- New discussion in the section on cognitive accounts of language development explains how Vygotsky's conception of children's egocentric speech differs from Piaget's and presents Vygotsky's idea of inner speech and its function.

Chapter 8 Physical and Cognitive Development in Early Childhood

- New section titled "The Changing Body" examines bone development and its relation to the child's changing proportions.

- New research is presented on young children's inclination to be curious about and to try to explain events that are inconsistent with their current knowledge.

Chapter 9 Social and Emotional Development in Early Childhood

- New research, table, and chart expand the discussion of gender differences in aggression.

- New discussion of the differences in acceptability of spanking internationally and, demographically, in the United States has been added to the box on "The Spanking Controversy," along with evidence that children who are spanked frequently are at risk for high levels of future aggression.

- New research on types of affiliative behaviors in preschoolers is featured in Table 9.1.

Chapter 10 Contexts of Development

- The discussion of parenting styles has been reorganized to immediately pair the styles with the behavior patterns of children exposed to them, making it easier for students to draw connections between the two.

- Expanded coverage of parenting styles includes a new discussion of recent research that compared the different parenting goals of German mothers (development of self-confidence) and Indian mothers (development of self-control) and suggests how these different goals are manifested in mothers' interactions with their children.

- New research on the effects of sibling conflict and rivalry on children's mental health and adjustment is highlighted by a study of sibling interactions and adjustment in the context of war-related trauma.

Chapter 11 Physical and Cognitive Development in Middle Childhood

- Expanded discussion of childhood obesity includes explanation of the calculation and significance of BMI, current data for the percentage of U.S. children of various ages who are overweight or obese, and detailed presentation of Harrison's (2011) Six-Cs ecological model of risks for obesity (cell, child, clan, community, country, culture).

- New box focuses on the "Let's Move!" campaign to promote healthy eating and exercise for children.

- New section on the role of practice in motor development features a study that employed a high-tech biking simulator to track the effects of practice on children's and adults' ability to navigate through traffic in a virtual town environment.

- New section, "Executive Function," explains the role of executive function and its connection to increasing maturation of the frontal cortex. It includes a discussion of research on the effects of various levels of aerobic exercise on the executive function and prefrontal-cortex activity of overweight children.

- The section "Is the Acquisition of Conservation Universal?" includes a new discussion of research that used contextually appropriate tasks to compare the concrete-operational thinking of Los Angeles schoolchildren and young nonschooled Mayan backstrap-loom weavers.

Chapter 12 School as a Context for Development

- New discussions of Head Start and the Perry Preschool Program.

- New section, "School Engagement," discusses recent research on school liking/avoidance and cooperative/resistant classroom participation.

- Section "The Culture of School" features two recent related studies, one by Cavajay, the other by Rogoff, that explore the implications that local cultural style may have for success in a classroom setting.

Chapter 13 Social and Emotional Development in Middle Childhood

- Chapter has been reorganized to begin with the section "A New Sense of Self."

- New research is presented on the increased importance of being popular with peers during middle childhood.

- Updated section, "Bullies and Their Victims," includes current research on cyberbullying in Facebook and other social media.

Chapter 14 Physical and Cognitive Development in Adolescence

- Chapter has undergone a major reorganization to accommodate a burgeoning literature on the biocultural processes affecting pubertal timing and brain development and their effects on adolescent behaviors and experience.

- Major reorganization and expansion of the section "Brain Development" includes three new subsections dealing with changes in the cerebral cortex, changes in the limbic system, and the relation between brain development and adolescent behavior, particularly risk-taking behavior.

- Major new section, "The Neuro-Hormonal System," discusses the role of the hypothalamic-pituitary-gonadal (HPG) axis in the activation of puberty. The discussion focuses on the interplay of the hypothalamus, the endocrine system, and sex hormones, and it includes a look at kisspeptin, a protein that may trigger the interplay.

- New section, "Individual Variation," discusses genetic and ethnic differences that may influence early and late maturation, as well as precocious puberty. This section also discusses the emotions and behavior often associated with "off-time" maturation.

- New box, "Early Maturation and Reproductive Success: The Case of the Pumé Foragers," examines the idea that Pumé girls' early attainment of reproductive capacity in the absence of a growth spurt may be an evolutionary adaptation for early childbearing in conditions of regular periods of nutritional stress and a short life expectancy.

- New data added on the continuing worrisome decline in age of pubertal onset in the United States that is thought to be related to obesity.

- Expanded coverage in the "Nutrition" section includes discussions of the reasons for many adolescents' poor dietary choices, the eating patterns of food-insecure families, and research suggesting the benefits of a midmorning "nutrition break" in schools.

- New material on adolescents' sleep examines the decline of nonrapid eye movement sleep in conjunction with synaptic pruning.

Chapter 15 Social and Emotional Development in Adolescence

- New research is included on gender-socialization differences in the expression of depressed emotion.

- Section "Sexual Relationships," moved from Chapter 14, now includes data from the largest study of sexual behavior ever conducted in the United States; 2010 data on adolescents' feelings about their first experience of sexual intercourse; and evidence that a large majority of adolescents practice safe sex. This section also includes updated "Teenage Pregnancy" box.

- Reflecting the rapid shifts in teenagers' digital networking, the box "From Diaries to Blogs" has been updated and accordingly retitled "From Diaries to Facebook."

- A new major section, "Adolescent Health and Well-Being," has two main sections covering emotional health and sexual health and a third that introduces the topic of positive youth development. "Emotional Health" fully addresses, in separate subsections, depression and anxiety, eating disorders, and delinquency and other externalizing problems. "Sexual Health" discusses the major STIs in various adolescent populations, with updated data on infection rates. The final section explores the idea of plasticity in adolescent development as it is reflected in the concept of positive youth development, and presents the factors that some developmentalists have identified as helping youth contribute to their psychological health as well as to the welfare of their community.

Pedagogy

This edition uses two useful pedagogical elements—the "In the Field" boxes and the "Apply–Connect–Discuss" activities, both designed to connect students with the material. In addition, we've tried to highlight high-interest topics in boxes (on everything from correlation and causation to spanking). Each part begins with a prose introduction and a milestone table, which includes relevant sociocultural factors. Each chapter begins with an outline, designed to orient students to the text material that is to come, and ends with a summary and a list of key terms designed to help them review what they've learned.

Media and Supplements

The seventh edition of *The Development of Children* is accompanied by a number of supplementary materials designed to amplify the themes of the text.

NEW! *Developing Lives:* An Interactive Simulation

The study of child development fully enters the digital age with *Developing Lives.* Using this interactive program, each student raises his or her own unique "child," making decisions about common parenting issues (nutrition choices, parenting style, type of schooling) and responding to realistic events (divorce, temperamental variations, and social and economic diversity) that shape a child's physical, cognitive and social development.

At the heart of this program is interactivity—between students and the simulation as well as among classmates. While the core experience happens on the computer, students can get notices or check in with their child "on the go" on a variety of mobile devices; they can even share photos of their baby with friends, family, and classmates. *Developing Lives* has a student-friendly, "game-like" feel that not only engages students in the program but also encourages them to learn. It features these helpful resources to reinforce and assess student learning: integrated links to the eBook version of the Worth text; readings from *Scientific American;* more than 400 videos and animations, many of them newly filmed for *Developing Lives;* and links to easy-to-implement assessment tools, including assignable quizzes on core topics, discussion threads, and journal questions.

Video Tool Kit for Human Development

The kit spans the full range of topics for the child development course, with 200 brief clips of research and news footage on topics ranging from prenatal brain development and the experience of child soldiers to empathy in adolescence. All the video clips can be assigned to students outside the classroom. Several of these clips are integrated into 45 predesigned interactive activities that are easily assignable and assessable. The student activities are available exclusively online for this edition. More than 200 clips for instructors are available for download online and a subset of more than 100 are available on DVD in the Worth Publishers Video Collection.

Development Portal

PsychPortal is the complete online gateway to all the student and instructor resources available with the textbook. It brings together all the resources of the video tool kits, integrated with an eBook and powerful assessment tools to complement your course.

The ready-to-use course template is fully customizable and includes all the teaching and learning resources that go along with the book, preloaded into a ready-to-use course; sophisticated quizzing, personalized study plans for students, and powerful assessment analyses that provide timely and useful feedback on class and individual student performance; and seamless integration of student resources, eBook text, assessment tools, and lecture resources. The quiz bank features more than 100 questions per chapter.

Instructor's Resource Manual

The *Instructor's Resource Manual* by Jennifer Coots and Ruth Alfaro Piker, California State University, Long Beach, features chapter-by-chapter previews and lecture guides, learning objectives, topics for discussion and debate, handouts for student projects, and supplementary readings from journals. Course planning suggestions and ideas for term projects are also included.

Study Guide

The carefully crafted *Study Guide* by Stephanie Stolarz-Fantino, University of California, San Diego, helps students to read and retain the text material at a higher level than they are likely to achieve by reading the text alone. Each chapter includes a variety of practice tests and exercises to help integrate themes that reappear in various chapters. Each chapter also includes a review of key concepts, guided study questions, and section reviews that encourage students' active participation in the learning process.

Test Bank

Thoroughly revised, the *Test Bank* by Jennifer Jipson, California Polytechnic State University, and Rocio Rivadeneyra, Illinois State University, includes approximately 60 multiple-choice and 70 fill-in, true-false, matching, and essay questions for every chapter. Each question is keyed to the textbook by topic, page number, and level of difficulty.

Computerized Test Bank CD-ROM

This computerized test bank CD-ROM, on dual platform for Windows and Macintosh, offers an easy-to-use test-generation system, allowing instructors to add an unlimited number of questions, select specific questions, edit or scramble questions, format a test, and include pictures, equations, and multimedia links over a secure network. The CD-ROM is also the access point for online testing, as well as for Blackboard- and WebCT-formatted versions of the Test Bank.

The accompanying gradebook enables instructors to record students' grades throughout the course, and it includes the capacity to track student records and view detailed analyses of test items, and to curve tests, generate reports, and add weights to grades.

Online Testing and Quizzing

Online testing, powered by Diploma (www.brownstone.net), gives instructors the ability to create and administer secure exams over a network and over the Internet, with questions that incorporate multimedia and interactive exercises. The program allows instructors to restrict tests to specific computers or time blocks, and includes a suite of gradebook and result-analysis features.

Online quizzing, powered by Questionmark, can be accessed via the companion Web site at www.worthpublishers.com/thedevelopmentofchildren7e. Instructors can quiz students online using prewritten multiple-choice questions for each text chapter (not from the test bank), which were written and revised by Beth Trammell, Ball State University. Students receive instant feedback and can take the quizzes multiple times. Instructors may then view results by quiz, student, or question, or get weekly results via email.

Companion Web Site

The companion Web site, www.worthpublishers.com/thedevelopmentofchildren7e, offers a variety of study aids organized by chapter. In addition to the online testing, syllabus posting, and Web site building services, the Web site offers Chapter Outlines; Online Quizzes; and Interactive Flashcards.

A password-protected Instructor Site offers a full array of teaching resources, including multiple sets of Presentation slides and an online quiz gradebook.

For Instructors

Readings on the Development of Children, Fifth Edition, edited by Mary Gauvain, University of California, Riverside, and Michael Cole, University of California, San Diego, works as a thought-provoking supplement in a development course. With material ranging from theoretical to empirical, from classic to cutting-edge, this reader provides depth and focus for classroom discussion. The new edition offers 36 articles, 14 new to this edition. New articles were chosen to expose readers to recent research in rapidly changing areas of the field, such as brain development, cognition, socioemotional development, and adolescent well-being.

Acknowledgements

A book of this scope and complexity could not be produced without the help of others. A great many people gave generously of their time and experience to deepen our treatment of various areas of development, particularly the many scholars who consented to review drafts of our manuscript and make suggestions for improvement. The remaining imperfections exist despite their best efforts.

For this edition, we thank **Gina Abbott**, Quinnipiac University; **Phyllis Adcock**, University of Nebraska at Omaha; **Nameera Akhtar**, University of California, Santa Cruz; **Kimberly Alkins**, Queens College; **Kristine Anthis**, Southern Connecticut State University; **Sumi Ariely**, Massachusetts Institute of Technology; **Melissa Atkins**, Marshall University; **Melissa Atkinson**, Surry Community College; **Mita Banerjee**, Pitzer College; **David Baskind**, Delta College; **Joann Benigno**, University of Florida; **Cheryl Beverly**, James Madison University; **Aviva Bower**, College of Saint Rose; **Chris Boyatais**, Bucknell University; **Dilek Buchholz**, Weber State University; **Holly Buckley**, University of La Verne; **Daniel Budak**, University of New Hampshire; **Jean Burr**, Hamilton College; **Emily Cahan**, Wheelock College; **Joseph Campos**, University of California, Berkeley; **Caroline Cooke Carney**, Monterey Peninsula College; **David Carroll**, University of Wisconsin; **Renia E. B. Cobb**, Virginia State University; **Claudia Cochran**, El Paso Community College; **Jennifer Coffman**, University of North Carolina; **Juanita Cole**, University of California, San Diego; **Lisa Comparini**, Clark University; **Theresa Coogan**, Bridgewater State College; **Dina Cook**, Gainesville College; **Ramie Cooney**, Creighton University; **Jennifer Coots**, California State University, Long Beach;

Brian Cox, Hofstra University; **Ron Craig**, Edinboro University of Pennsylvania; **Victoria Cross**, University of California; **Rob Currie**, Judson University; **Agnes DeWitt**, North Carolina Central University; **Christine Diamond-Hallam**, University of Western Florida; **Tina Durand**, Wheelock College; **Carol Eliot**, National Cathedral School; **Beth Engel**, Ball State University; **Chrysoula Fantaousakis**, Kean University; **L. Mickey Fenzel**, Loyola College; **Kate Fogerty**, University of Florida; **Krista Forrest**, University of Nebraska at Kearney; **Brandy Frazier**, University of Hawaii at Manoa; **Jean Louis Gariepy**, University of North Carolina; **Maria Gartstein**, Washington State University; **Katarina Guttmannova**, Washington University; **Amie Hane**, Williams College; **Elizabeth A. Henderson**, University of Evansville; **Michael Himle**, University of Utah; **Suzy Horton**, Mesa Community College; **Abraham Hwang**, Messiah University; **Jennifer Jipson**, California Polytechnic State University; **Margaret Kasimatis**, Carroll College; **Keri Brown Kirschman**, University of Dayton; **Julie Klunk**, University of Massachusetts, Boston; **Maria Korogodsky**, University of New Hampshire; **Marva Lewis**, Tulane University; **Kathleen McCluskey-Fawcett**, University of Kansas; **Christine McCormick**, Eastern Illinois University; **Roseanna McLeary**, California State University, Bakersfield; **Gerald McRoberts**, Quinnipiac University; **Winnie Mucherah**, Ball State University; **Judy Neale**, Cameron University; **Amanda O'Dell**, Loyola University Chicago; **Janet Oh**, Macalester College; **Harriet Oster**, New York University; **Martin Packer**, Duquesne University; **Behnaz Pakizegi**, William Patterson University; **Michelle Perfect**, University of Arizona; **Laura Ann Petitto**, Dartmouth College; **Justina Powers**, Cameron University; **Linda Raasch**, Normandale Community College; **Christopher Rand**, Atlantic Cape Community College; **Christine Pegorraro Schull**, University of Maryland; **Lisa Scott**, University of Massachusetts, Amherst; **Julia Sluzenski**, Stockton College; **Bryan Sokol**, St. Louis University; **Stephanie Stolarz-Fantino**, University of California, San Diego; **Dennis Thompson**, Georgia State University; **Wadiya Udell**, University of Washington, Bothell; **S. Stavros Valenti**, Hofstra University; **Deborah Vilas**, Bank Street College of Education; **Sheila Walker**, Scripps College; **Kresha Warnock**, Ball State University; **Henriette Warren**, University of Minnesota; **Sandra Wiebe**, University of Alberta.

We are grateful to Jessica Bayne, Peter Deane, Stacey Alexander, Sharon Prevost, Anna Paganelli, Alexandra Nickerson, John Harlacher, Jean Erler, Lukia Kliossis, Babs Reingold, Lyndall Culbertson, Barbara Seixas, Christine Buese, Donna Ranieri, Ramón Rivera-Moret, Tracey Kuehn, and Kerry O'Shaughnessy of Worth Publishers.

Cynthia Lightfoot
Exton, Pennsylvania
March, 2012

The Study of Human Development

Developmental Science
Periods of Development
Domains of Development
Contexts of Development

Children, Society, and Science
Historical Beliefs About Children and Childhood
The Emergence of Developmental Science
The New Field of Developmental Science

The Central Issues of Developmental Science
Questions About the Sources of Development
Questions About Plasticity
Questions About Continuity/Discontinuity
Questions About Individual Differences

Theories of Development
Theory in Developmental Science
Grand Theories
Modern Theories

Methods for Studying Development
The Goals of Developmental Research
Criteria for Developmental Research
Methods of Data Collection
Research Designs
Ethical Standards

Looking Ahead

Early one morning during the cold winter of 1800, a dirty, naked boy wandered into a hut at the edge of a tiny village in the French province of Aveyron in search of food. In the months before this appearance, some of the people in the area had caught glimpses of the boy digging for roots, climbing trees, swimming in a stream, and running rapidly on all fours. They thought he was inhuman, perhaps a wild beast. When the boy appeared in the village, word spread quickly and everyone went to see him.

Among the curious was a government commissioner, who took the boy home and fed him. The child, who appeared to be about 12 years old, seemed ignorant of the civilized comforts that the people offered to him. When clothes were put on him, he tore them off. He refused meat and would eat only raw potatoes, roots, and nuts. He rarely made a sound and seemed indifferent to human voices. In his report to the government, the commissioner concluded that the boy had lived alone since early childhood, "a stranger to social needs and practices. . . . [T]here is . . . something extraordinary in his behavior, which makes him seem close to the state of wild animals" (quoted in Lane, 1976, pp. 8–9).

The commissioner's report caused a public sensation when it reached Paris. Newspapers hailed the child as the "Wild Boy of Aveyron." In the climate that prevailed following the French Revolution, many hoped that, with instruction, the boy could rapidly develop intellectually and socially to demonstrate that even the poor and outcast of a society could be as capable as the wealthy if they were provided with a proper education. The Wild Boy seemed a perfect test case because his life had been so devoid of supportive human contact.

Unfortunately, plans to help the Wild Boy soon ran into trouble. The first physicians to examine him concluded that he was mentally deficient and speculated that he had been put out to die by his parents for that reason. (In France in the late eighteenth century, as many as one in three normal children, and a greater percentage of abnormal children, were abandoned by their parents, usually because the family was too poor to support another child [Heywood, 2001].)

Most of the doctors recommended that the boy be placed in an asylum, but one young physician, Jean-Marc Itard (1774–1838), disputed the diagnosis of retardation. Itard proposed that the boy appeared to be mentally deficient only because he had been isolated from society and thereby prevented from developing normally. In support of his view, Itard argued that if the boy had been mentally retarded, he certainly could not have survived on his own in the forest.

Itard took personal charge of the boy, with the goal of teaching him to become fully competent, to master the French language, and to acquire the best of civilized knowledge. To test his theory that the social environment has the power to shape children's development, Itard devised an elaborate set of experimental training procedures to teach the Wild Boy how to categorize objects, to reason, and to communicate (Itard, 1801/1982).

Victor, the Wild Boy of Aveyron.

Jean-Marc Itard, who tried to transform the Wild Boy into a civilized Frenchman.

At first, Victor, as Itard named the Wild Boy, made rapid progress. He learned to communicate simple needs as well as to recognize and write a few words. He learned to use a chamber pot. He also developed affection for the people who took care of him. But Victor never learned to speak or interact with other people normally.

After 5 years of intense work, Victor had not made enough progress to satisfy Itard's superiors, and Itard was forced to abandon his experiment. Victor was sent to live with a woman who was paid to care for him. Still referred to as the Wild Boy of Aveyron, he died in 1828, leaving unanswered the question of what factors prevented him from developing normally. Some modern scholars believe that Victor suffered from autism, a pathological mental condition whose symptoms include a deficit in language and an inability to interact normally with others (Frith, 1989). Others think that Itard may have been right in his belief that Victor was normal at birth but was permanently stunted in his development as a result of his social isolation (Lane, 1976). It is also possible that Itard's teaching methods failed where different approaches might have succeeded. We cannot be sure.

Victor's case became a focal point for debating fundamental questions about human nature and development: To what extent is development determined from birth? To what extent is it influenced by the surrounding environment? What is the role of early experience in shaping later development? Can the effects of negative experience be undone? Although more than 200 years have passed since the Wild Boy wandered into the village of Aveyron, these questions remain at the forefront of research on children's development.

Developmental Science

This book will introduce you to **developmental science**, a field of study that focuses on the range of children's physical, intellectual, social, and emotional developments. It is a rich and varied field, encompassing a wide array of theories and methods of study, and covering a broad range of children's characteristics. However, as Victor's story makes clear, the study of children's development has always been driven by two overarching goals. One goal is to understand the basic biological and cultural processes that account for the remarkable complexities of human development. The second goal is to devise effective methods for safeguarding children's health and well-being. These two goals come together in the popular idea, held by developmentalists and the public alike, that scientific research can make the world a better place by shedding light on the nature and conditions of children's development (Hulbert, 2003).

The field of developmental science has advanced and broadened considerably since Itard's day. As we discuss below, for much of its history, the study of children's development was dominated by psychologists. In recent decades, however, the study of development has become increasingly *interdisciplinary,* profiting from the insights of a wide range of disciplines, including psychology, anthropology, biology, linguistics, neuroscience, and sociology. The study of development has also become increasingly *international,* reflecting a growing appreciation of the many ways developmental processes are influenced by cultural contexts. In recognition

developmental science The field of study that focuses on the range of children's physical, intellectual, social, and emotional developments.

of the broad scope of modern studies of development, we use the term *developmentalist* to refer to those who contribute to a growing knowledge of children's development, regardless of their specific discipline or area of expertise.

As the scope of developmental science widened, the pace and complexity of research increased. Part of the reason for this is important advances in technology. The ability to record children's behaviors with video cameras, to obtain images of their brain activity, and to analyze data with powerful computers has revolutionized the way developmentalists do research. Concerns about the welfare of children have also fueled the pace and complexity of research. These concerns have created new questions for researchers—questions on such wide-ranging topics as the influence of maternal stress and nutrition on fetal brain growth, the effects of neighborhoods on family dynamics, the risks attached to medicating hyperactive children who experience difficulty staying focused in school, and the special challenges facing children of immigrant families in their attempts to deal with an alien culture and an unfamiliar language.

In addition to their roles as researchers looking for answers to such complex questions, developmentalists are often practitioners who strive to promote the healthy development of children. Developmentalists work in hospitals, child-care centers, schools, recreational facilities, and clinics. They assess children's development and make suggestions for helping children who are in difficulty. They design special environments, such as high-tech incubators that allow premature babies to develop normally outside the womb. They devise therapies for children who have trouble controlling their tempers, and they develop techniques to help children learn more effectively (Lerner, Almerigi, Theokas, & Lerner, 2005).

New technologies have expanded opportunities for studying children's development. This mother and her 5-year-old son, a child with autism, are participating in a study of social-emotional interaction, a typical problem area for children with autism. Each wears a net containing sensors that measure brain activity and sends signals to a complex of computers. The researchers hope to shed light on what goes on in the brains of mother and child as they are engaged in tasks and play requiring communication.

Periods of Development

In their research, theorizing, and practice, developmentalists divide the time between conception and the start of adulthood into five broad periods: the prenatal period, infancy, early childhood, middle childhood, and adolescence. Each period is marked by major changes in children's bodies and in how children think, feel, and interact with others. Each is also marked by significant changes in how children are treated by members of their society as a consequence of cultural assumptions and expectations about what children can and should be doing at different ages. Despite broad cultural differences in the particular tasks that children are expected to master, the institutions (such as school) that they are required to attend, and the rituals that they are made to undergo, most cultures organize the course of childhood in ways that recognize these five general developmental periods.

Domains of Development

As individuals move through each period of development, they undergo remarkable changes in several *domains,* or major areas of development: social, emotional, cognitive (intellectual), and physical. Although developmentalists are interested in the changes that take place within each of these four domains, they also recognize that development in any one of these domains is influenced by, and influences, development in the others. Consider, for example, how changes in the child's body,

Children's development is profoundly affected by the contexts in which they live and grow. For these children living in Tibet, Chad, and Israel, such influences as their culture's religious beliefs, educational system, and exposure to the consequences of war will significantly affect the paths of their development.

including size, strength, and coordination, permit increasingly efficient ways of moving around, exploring, and learning about the world. At the same time, the child's developing knowledge and interest in objects and people in the environment encourage even more exploration, providing additional opportunities for the body to develop greater strength and better coordination.

Contexts of Development

Those who work in the developmental sciences have never been more aware of the relationships between children's development and the *contexts* in which children live. As you will learn throughout this book, contexts of development, including physical environments, cultural beliefs and practices, families and peers, neighborhoods and communities, and institutions such as schools and governments, present children with both resources and risks that profoundly shape the course of their development. Does a child live with a single parent or in a large group of siblings, parents, grandparents, and other kin? Is the neighborhood clean and orderly, or impoverished, disorganized, and dangerous? Will the child attend school, or master skills through apprenticeship? Is it acceptable to spank children when they misbehave, or is physical punishment considered a form of violence that can result in severe psychological and emotional injury to both child and parent? Answers to such questions begin to define the contexts of the child's development.

To help get at the answers, researchers often compare children who experience or grow up under different conditions in order to understand the risks and resources provided by various contexts and how they affect children's development. However, the effects of context are also apparent when children experience radical changes of context, as when divorce leads to family reorganization and a move to a new neighborhood and school, or when war, poverty, or oppression leads to emigration to an entirely new country with a new language, culture, and lifestyle. Thus, although developmentalists remain interested in the fundamental questions raised in Itard's day, it is clear that contemporary researchers, teachers, counselors, and other developmental practitioners are also responding to questions and concerns raised by social forces of our time.

Children, Society, and Science

In order to appreciate contemporary developmental science fully, it is important to understand the cultural and historical forces that have shaped it (Valsiner, van Oers, Wardekker, Elbers, & van der Veer, 2009). We begin our discussion by exploring beliefs about children and the way these beliefs changed over the course of time and set the stage for the emergence of developmental science. We then trace the history of developmental science from its early stages to its current state.

Historical Beliefs About Children and Childhood

Societies abound with different beliefs about the nature of children and their development. Such beliefs affect every aspect of children's lives, from what behaviors are expected of them at different ages to how they are disciplined, what skills and values they are taught, how they spend their time each day, and with whom they are allowed to socialize (Apple, 2006; Mintz, 2004). Beliefs about children and childhood also differ from one historical era to another. Even within the relatively short span of decades, the pendulum can swing from one view to another about what is good or bad for children, what they should or should not do, and how adults should treat them. For example, not long ago in North America, it was thought that picking up crying or fussy babies would make them "spoiled" and demanding, whereas today such practice is considered a sign of positive and responsive caregiving. Likewise, until fairly recently, children's play was thought to be important mostly because it promoted physical development. Consequently, children's playgrounds featured gymnastic equipment—ladders, climbing bars, swings. Now, however, play is believed to have much broader implications for development, and playgrounds are built to stimulate the mind and imagination as well as the body (Solomon, 2005).

For historians interested in how social beliefs about children have changed in recent centuries, there is a wealth of information to be found in child-care manuals, books, parent magazines, and all sorts of child-rearing paraphernalia (clothing, cradles, toys, feeding utensils, baby-carrying devices, and the like). But such information is much more difficult to come by when it involves reaching back into bygone centuries before social beliefs could be easily preserved in print and before the mass production of child-related objects.

Historians seeking to unearth beliefs about childhood during medieval times, for example, have had to rely largely on two unlikely kinds of sources: art and coroners' reports. Each yields a somewhat different picture of how people viewed children and childhood.

In general, portraiture and other art suggest that before the sixteenth century, people did not give much thought to children or their special needs. Many historians have concluded that during medieval times there was no understanding of childhood as a unique period of the life course, and children were considered miniature adults (Ariès, 1965). Accordingly, children were not provided with special toys or clothes and were not educated or cared for in ways that took into account their intellectual abilities and limitations. As illustrated in Figure 1.1, the miniature-adult view was

Ever since developmental science came to public attention, parents have relied on advice books to help them deal with the uncertainties of parenting. Shifting cultural fashions as well as new scientific knowledge have resulted in many changes in the advice parents receive (Hulbert, 2003.)

Although merry-go-rounds, slides, see-saws, and swings remain popular, early playgrounds (a) emphasized physical play and motor development to the exclusion of all other developmental domains. In contrast, modern playgrounds such as the one shown here in Germany (b) often include design features intended to foster creativity and social interaction.

(a)

(b)

FIGURE 1.1 Artwork before the sixteenth century depicts children with adultlike body proportions and clothing, rarely engaged in play or youthful activities. Because age differences between adults and children, and even between younger and older children, are represented simply in terms of relative size, historians describe the period as embracing a "miniature adult" view of childhood.

Cultural beliefs about children's development influence whether or not certain activities are encouraged. This child is wearing a special glove manufactured to prevent thumb-sucking, which once was thought to be overly arousing and harmful to children's development.

expressed in the typical depiction of children as having adultlike body proportions, wearing elegant and fine, adultlike clothing, and engaging in serious-minded activities. In *Centuries of Childhood,* one of the best-known books on the history of childhood, Philippe Ariès notes that artists of the time seemed "unable to depict a child except as a man on a smaller scale" (p. 33). The belief that adultlike capacities, desires, interests, and emotions are present in early childhood is known as **preformationism**. (This centuries-old belief gained force in the 1600s, when the first microscopes allowed scientists to magnify sperm and "discover" that each sperm cell contained a miniature person.) You will see in our discussion below that this belief persisted for hundreds of years, influencing scientists as well as the general public.

Coroners' reports about the circumstances of children's deaths are a rare exception to the dearth of written documents hinting at social beliefs about children. Using them as part of her research, Barbara Hanawalt, an expert on family life in medieval England, found that it was not uncommon for little babies to be entrusted to the care of children as young as 3 (Hanawalt & Kobialka, 2000). Needless to say, 3-year-olds make poor caregivers, and infants in their charge sometimes died due to their inattention or inability to intervene appropriately when problems arose. It was also relatively common for parents to leave infants and young children entirely alone and unsupervised for extended periods of time while they themselves did chores or worked in their fields. Although reflecting the miniature-adult cultural belief, these common practices drew criticism in coroners' reports that described young children as "bad custodians" of infants and explained the accidental deaths of unsupervised toddlers as caused by "being left without a caretaker" or being without "anyone looking after" them (p. 177).

A major turning point in the history of Western beliefs about children and childhood came in the sixteenth century with the Protestant Reformation, a religious movement of considerable scope. This movement swept through Europe and crossed the ocean to the "New World," beginning with the Puritans' voyage on the *Mayflower* in 1620. It was associated with harsher child-rearing practices, which followed from the belief that children are born in original sin. In contrast to the medieval Catholic Church, Protestant denominations generally held that original sin could not be washed away by baptism and that salvation would be possible only through obedience and submission to authority—first to one's elders, then to God. Because obedience naturally requires the suppression of individual goals and desires, parents were advised to adopt practices that would hold children's innate sinfulness in check and replace their willful impulses with humility and compliance.

The legacy of Puritan ideas about children persisted for hundreds of years, as Martha Wolfenstein (1953) discovered when she analyzed manuals on infant care written in the early 1900s. The manuals urged mothers to wage war on their children's sinful and rebellious nature. Masturbation and thumb-sucking were of special concern because they involved "dangerous pleasures" that "could easily grow beyond control." Mothers were encouraged to use a variety of physical restraints, such as tying their children's feet to opposite sides of the crib to prevent their thighs from rubbing together and pinning the sleeves of their nightshirts to the bed to prevent their touching themselves. Stiff arm cuffs were sold through stores and catalogues for the purpose of eliminating thumb-sucking. It was even recommended that rocking cradles be replaced by stationary cribs in order to further reduce experiences that might be stimulating or pleasurable.

Although evidence indicates that the idea of childhood as a unique period in development was already taking root in many societies, most historians agree that the modern notion of childhood emerged on a large scale in the late eighteenth and early nineteenth centuries as a consequence of the Industrial Revolution (Stearns, 2006). Taking shape initially in Western Europe and the United States, industrialization transformed the contexts in which children developed in three major ways. First, consistent with a shift from predominantly rural to more urban living conditions, schooling and/or factory work (depending on the family's social and economic status) came to replace family farm work as the child's primary social obligation. Second, the birthrate dropped significantly, altering family relationships both between parents and their children and between siblings. Finally, the child death rate plummeted, also with impacts on family relationships.

As historian Peter Stearns points out, these three changes were interconnected and had considerable implications for children's lives and experience. With increased schooling, for example, children were removed from the workforce and became economic burdens rather than assets, so family size began to shrink. Increased schooling for girls, by helping to make possible new opportunities for women to work outside the home, played a special role in reducing family size. Beyond reducing the birthrate, girls' education contributed to declining child death rates, because it resulted in mothers being more knowledgeable about how to ensure the healthy development of their infants and children. The schooling of all children reduced the authority of home and family, bringing children into more contact with other children and increasingly under the influence of peers and nonfamilial adults.

By the late nineteenth century, the industrial age was well under way throughout the world, and children and childhood had begun to receive considerable attention from parents, educators, and scientists.

The Emergence of Developmental Science

An effect of industrialization was to drive millions of children to labor in textile factories. The conditions under which they worked became a matter of social concern and soon sparked the attention of the scientific community. The Factories Inquiries Committee in England, for instance, conducted a study in 1833 to discover whether children could work 12 hours a day without being harmed. The majority of the committee members decided that 12 hours was an acceptable workday for children. Others who thought a 10-hour workday would be preferable were concerned less with children's physical, intellectual, or emotional well-being than with their morals. They recommended that the remaining 2 hours be devoted to the children's religious and moral education (Hindman, 2002). Despite its dismal conclusion, this early committee was a start, and concern for children's welfare increased throughout the century as children became ever more visible to both the social and scientific communities.

preformationism The belief that adultlike capacities, desires, interests, and emotions are present in early childhood.

The sweeping changes of industrialization during the nineteenth century contributed to lengthening the years that most children spend in school, challenging educators to design developmentally appropriate and intellectually engaging curricula.

American Museum of Natural History Library

Charles Darwin and his son, William, who helped inspire his father's interest in the relationship between evolution and human development.

FIGURE 1.2 Early evolutionists scrutinized the motor development of children for evidence that it recapitulated evolutionary stages. Here an infant (a) crawls about on all fours like many animals, (b) uses its feet for grasping as primates do, and (c) sleeps in an animal-like crouch. This line of research was found to be overly simplistic.

Also crucial to the rise of scientific interest in children was the work of Charles Darwin. The publication of Darwin's *The Origin of Species* in 1859 set the scientific community on fire and ultimately led to fundamental changes in beliefs about children's development. If human beings had evolved from earlier species, then might not the different stages of children's behavior offer clues to stages of human evolution? It became fashionable, for example, to compare the behavior of children with the behavior of higher nonhuman primates to see if children went through a "chimpanzee stage" similar to the one through which the human species was thought to have evolved (see Figure 1.2). Although such parallels proved oversimplified, the idea that the study of human development is crucial to an understanding of human evolution won general acceptance (Bjorklund & Pellegrini, 2002). Because Darwin's theory of evolution continues to have far-reaching consequences for the way children's development is thought about and studied, we devote considerable attention to it in Chapter 2.

In the exciting aftermath of the publication of *The Origin of Species,* the study of child development grew by leaps and bounds. Some early developmentalists emphasized the importance of using scientific methods of observation to understand fully how the human mind changes over time. William Preyer (1841–1897), for example, wrote the first textbook on child development, proposing that the development of emotion, intention, mind, and language could be studied scientifically by applying strict rules of observation (see Table 1.1). He was particularly eager to identify *sequences of behavior,* because he believed that they would show how new forms of behavior emerge from earlier forms; for example, how walking emerges from crawling. Preyer was also interested in understanding how the child's development is influenced by biological and environmental factors.

Whereas Preyer's greatest contributions to developmental science were his *methods of study,* other developmentalists focused directly on the *nature of development.* James Mark Baldwin (1861–1934), for example, challenged scientists who believed in the preformationist view that adult abilities are present and fully formed in the child, just waiting "off stage" for their cue to emerge. In a striking reversal of this notion, Baldwin argued that children's abilities progress through a series of specific stages, taking on different forms and undergoing systematic changes before reaching their mature state. Baldwin's proposal represented the first of many *stage theories* of development that would emerge over the next century.

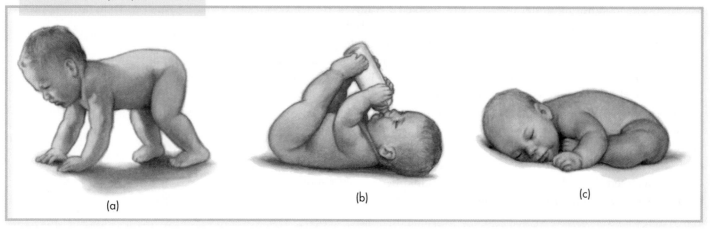

(a)   (b)   (c)

table 1.1
Preyer's Rules of Observation
• Rely only on direct observations; avoid the reports of "persons not practiced in scientific observing."
• Record observations immediately so that details are not forgotten.
• Make every effort to be unobtrusive, to "observe without the child's noticing the observer at all."
• Avoid any "training" of the young child in order to observe "unadulterated mental development."
• If regular observations are interrupted for more than 1 day, another observer must be substituted, and his or her observations should be checked for accuracy. (Preyer observed and recorded his child's behavior two to three times every day!)
• Everything should be recorded, even behaviors that seem uninteresting at the time.
Source: Preyer, 1890, pp. 187–188.

Still other developmentalists directed their efforts to practical applications. One such effort was Alfred Binet's (1857–1911) devising of methods of "mental testing" that eventually resulted in the first widely used intelligence test—the Stanford-Binet. Binet firmly believed that careful testing could reveal individual differences in children's mental abilities and identify schoolchildren who could benefit from special instruction. His work clearly established the role of developmental science in addressing practical problems and issues.

The New Field of Developmental Science

By the early twentieth century, owing in no small measure to the efforts of these pioneers, the study of development had become a recognized field of scientific inquiry. Special institutes and departments devoted to the study of development began to spring up in major universities in the United States. As argued by Cora Bussey Hillis, a child advocate of the time, if research can improve the way we grow corn and raise hogs, why should it not also be used to improve the way we bring up our children (Sears, 1975)? Agreeing with this kind of logic, government agencies and philanthropic foundations began to support research on child development. Much of this work focused on exploring basic developmental changes over the course of infancy and childhood. But some research involved "special mission" projects on a wide range of topics, including highly gifted children and the effects that watching motion pictures might have on children.

To this day, research on children's development continues to be motivated by the twin goals that were present at the discipline's origins: the scientific and philosophic goal of understanding how our biological and cultural heritages combine to shape our development as humans, and the practical goal of understanding how best to promote the health and well-being of children. We now turn to the central issues that continue to guide and inspire developmental science.

⏏ APPLY :: CONNECT :: DISCUSS

Thumb through some magazines containing images of children (you will likely find a lot of such images in magazines focused on parenting and infant care). How are the children depicted? Describe their clothing, the activities in which they are engaged, and the people and objects they are shown with. What do the images suggest regarding current conceptions of children and childhood?

The Central Issues of Developmental Science

Despite great variety in the work they do, developmentalists share an interest in four fundamental issues concerning the process of development:

1. *Sources of development.* How do the forces of biology, the environment, and the child's own activities interact to produce new ways of thinking, feeling, and behaving?

2. *Plasticity.* To what extent and under what conditions is the course of development plastic, that is, malleable and subject to change as the result of either deliberate intervention or chance experience?

3. *Continuity/discontinuity.* Is development a gradual, continuous process of change, or is it punctuated by periods of rapid change and the sudden emergence of new ways of thinking and behaving?

4. *Individual differences.* No two human beings are exactly alike. How does a person come to have characteristics that make him or her different from all other people, and how stable are these characteristics over time?

Developmentalists' answers to these questions provide insight into principles of development, as well as guidelines for promoting adaptive developmental outcomes.

Questions About the Sources of Development

What drives development? What, for example, ensures that virtually every human infant will develop the ability to walk on two feet? To use words to communicate with others? To form emotional bonds? What part of these processes is written in our genetic code, and what part is determined by our social and cultural environment? Such questions about the sources of development are often posed as a debate about the relative importance of "nature" and "nurture." **Nature** refers to the individual's inherited biological predispositions. **Nurture** refers to the influences of the social and cultural environment, particularly the family and the community, and of the individual's experiences. Much of the argument about Victor, the Wild Boy of Aveyron, was about the relative influences of nature and nurture: Was Victor incapable of speech and other behaviors normal for a boy his age because of a defective biological endowment (nature) or because of his social isolation (nurture)?

Modern developmentalists emphasize that development cannot be understood by considering nature and nurture in isolation from each other because the two are so closely intertwined, continually interacting and mutually influencing each other. Nevertheless, as you shall see, debates about the relative importance of genetic inheritance and experience as sources of development continue to preoccupy developmental science.

nature The inherited biological predispositions of the individual.

nurture The influences exerted on development by the individual's social and cultural environment and personal experiences.

plasticity The degree to which, and the conditions under which, development is open to change and intervention.

Questions About Plasticity

The second major question about development concerns **plasticity**, the degree to which, and the conditions under which, development is open to change and intervention. Plasticity enables individuals to adapt to a wide range of different environments (Causey, Gardiner, & Bjorklund, 2008). An important question for developmentalists concerns the limits of plasticity in children's responses to different environments and experiences: For different aspects of development, does our experience influence our development significantly or not much at all?

Early ideas about plasticity were influenced by the identification of certain "critical periods" of development in several nonhuman species. A **critical period** is a period of growth—in some cases only a few hours long—during which a specific kind of experience must occur for a particular ability or behavior to develop. If the critical period passes without the occurrence of the experience, the developmental "window" closes, and the ability or behavior will not develop. In other words, for the particular aspect of development in question, there is a high degree of plasticity only during this period. For example, in certain species of birds, chicks have a critical period just after hatching during which they become attached to the first moving object they see (usually their mother), which they will thereafter follow wherever it goes (see photo below). This process is called *imprinting*. If the chicks are prevented from seeing any moving object for a certain number of hours after hatching so that imprinting does not occur, they fail to become attached to anything at all and may wander around alone. As you can imagine, chicks on their own have little chance for survival (Izawa, Yanagihara, Atsumi, & Matsushima, 2001).

Examples of such "all-or-nothing" critical periods in any species are rare; in our own species they tend to be limited to specific periods of prenatal development. During the ninth week after conception, for example, the presence or absence of certain hormones will determine whether the fetus becomes male or female. Although there is little evidence of "critical" periods in human development after birth, there is abundant evidence pointing to "sensitive" periods (Gottlieb, 2002; Lickliter, 2007). **Sensitive periods** are defined as times in an organism's development during which a particular experience (or lack of it) has a more pronounced effect on the organism than does exposure to that same experience at another time (Bruer, 2001). For example, children seem to be most sensitive to learning language in the first few years of life, easily acquiring any language to which they are regularly exposed. But even if they are not regularly exposed to language until the age of 6 or 7, it appears that they are still capable of acquiring it. Thereafter, however, the risk of failing to acquire language increases (Newport, Bavelier, & Neville, 2001).

As with sources of development, questions about plasticity have important real-world implications. The answers are essential to understanding whether and how a child's development can be modified through deliberate intervention, such as therapy or education, or affected by particular experiences, from the everyday to the traumatic.

critical period A period during which specific biological or environmental events are required for normal development to occur.

sensitive period A time in an organism's development when a particular experience has an especially profound effect.

Ethologist Konrad Lorenz proposed the existence of a critical period in the development of newly hatched geese during which they form an attachment to the first moving thing they see. These goslings, which were allowed to see Lorenz rather than an adult goose when they hatched, follow him in the water as he swims.

continuity/discontinuity Addresses the extent to which development tends to be *continuous*, consisting of the gradual accumulation of small changes, and the extent to which it is *discontinuous*, involving a series of abrupt, radical transformations.

developmental stage A qualitatively distinctive, coherent pattern of behavior that emerges during the course of development.

Questions About Continuity/Discontinuity

Questions about **continuity/discontinuity** have to do with the extent to which development tends to be *continuous*, consisting of the gradual accumulation of small changes, and the extent to which it is *discontinuous*, involving a series of abrupt, radical transformations.

As a rule, developmentalists who believe that development is primarily a process of continuous, gradual accumulation of small changes emphasize *quantitative* change, such as growth in the number of connections among brain cells, in memory capacity, or in vocabulary. Those who view development as a process punctuated by abrupt, discontinuous changes emphasize *qualitative* change, or new patterns of behavior emerging at specific points in development, such as the change from babbling to talking or from crawling to walking, or from the ability to reason only in terms of one's own experience to the ability to reason hypothetically. Qualitatively new patterns that emerge during development are referred to as **developmental stages.** The contrast between the continuity and discontinuity views is illustrated in Figure 1.3.

The psychologist John Flavell (1971) suggests four criteria that are central to the concept of a developmental stage, illustrated below by the transition from crawling to walking.

1. *Stages of development are distinguished by qualitative changes.* The change in motor activity associated with the transition from crawling to walking upright is qualitative in that walking does not arise from the perfection of the movements used to crawl; instead, it involves a total reorganization of movement, using different muscles in different combinations.

FIGURE 1.3 (a) The contrasting courses of development of starfish and insects provide idealized examples of continuous and discontinuous development. In the continuity view, development is a process of gradual growth (small starfish, medium-size starfish, large starfish). In the discontinuity view, development is a series of stagelike transformations (larva, pupa, adult). (b) Human development includes elements of both continuity and discontinuity.

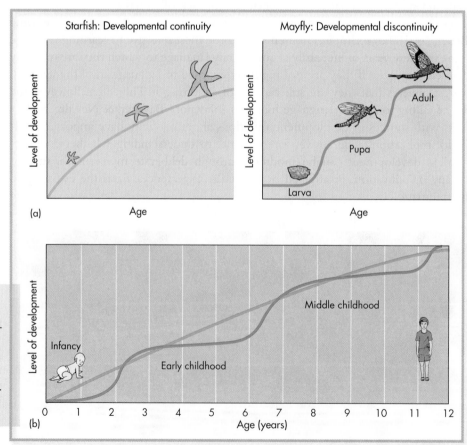

2. *The transition from one stage to the next is marked by simultaneous changes in a great many, if not all, domains of the child's development.* The transition from crawling to walking is accompanied by a new quality of emotional attachment between children and their caregivers as well as the new forms of child–caregiver relations that the child's greater mobility requires. Similarly, the transition to biological maturity during puberty takes place in concert with a rising interest in romantic peer relationships and the emergence of more adultlike thinking and reasoning skills.

3. *When the change from one state to the next occurs, it is rapid.* The transition from crawling to walking typically takes place within the space of about 90 days.

4. *The numerous changes across developmental domains form a coherent pattern.* Walking occurs at about the same time as pointing, the ability to follow the gaze of another, the child's first words, and a new relationship between children and their parents.

Supporters of discontinuity and the stage concept argue that the qualitative changes the child undergoes in each new stage alter the way the child experiences the world and the way the world influences the child. For example, before infants have any understanding of language, their learning about the world comes primarily through their actions on it. Once they begin to understand and produce language themselves, the way they learn about the world appears to change fundamentally, and so does the nature of their interaction with others. The discontinuity represented by the child's active participation in conversation is so notable that in many societies it marks the boundary between infancy and early childhood.

Supporters of the continuity view maintain that even when development appears to make an abrupt shift, continuity prevails in the underlying processes. For example, although very young children and adults appear to reason about the world in radically different ways, Tamar Kushnir and Alison Gopnik argue that there is nevertheless considerable continuity in reasoning between early childhood and adulthood. In particular, Kushnir and Gopnik believe that, regardless of age, individuals reason much the way scientists do; that is, they have *theories* that allow them to explain, predict, and understand events and behavior, and they modify their theories when their predictions prove incorrect (Kushnir & Gopnik, 2005).

One major problem for supporters of the stage concept is that, contrary to their depiction of qualitatively consistent, across-the-board shifts in behavior and thinking, children often appear to be in one stage on one occasion and in a different stage on another. According to one influential stage theory of cognitive development, for example, 4-year-olds are in a stage in which their thinking is largely egocentric, making it difficult for them to see anything from a point of view other than their own. Consider 4-year-old Nyia, who wanted to give her mother a Bitty Kitty for her birthday. Nyia's birthday present choice indicates that she is, in this case, limited to her own perspective: She wants to give her mother what she herself would enjoy as a present, failing to see that her mother might rather have breakfast in bed. Yet when Nyia talks to her 2-year-old brother, she simplifies her speech, apparently taking the younger child's perspective and realizing that he might otherwise have difficulty understanding her. The fact that at a given point in development a child can exhibit behaviors associated with different stages seems to undercut the idea that being in a particular stage defines the child's capabilities and psychological makeup.

Questions About Individual Differences

Although in some respects you are like all other human beings, in many ways you are psychologically and physically unique, like no one else in the world. What makes you different from everyone else? And will the features that make you different endure throughout your life? When we try to understand the nature of development, we must take into account these two questions about individual differences: (1) What makes individuals different from one another, and (2) to what extent are individual characteristics stable over time?

The question of what makes individuals different from one another is really another form of the question about the plasticity of development (Boyce & Ellis, 2005). The ways in which you are like all other human beings are a reflection of how certain developmental traits—the ability to walk, talk, and form close attachments to others—are highly constrained by evolution and have little plasticity. In contrast, the features that make you unique from everyone else reflect the capacity of certain traits to be more easily modified by experience.

The question of stability over time involves the extent to which the features that make you special endure throughout your life. Parents often remark that their children have been friendly or shy since infancy, but scientifically demonstrating the stability of psychological characteristics like these—at least from an early age—has proved difficult. One problem is that measures that seem appropriate for assessing psychological traits during infancy are not likely to be appropriate for assessing the same traits in an 8-year-old or in a teenager. Perhaps for this reason, many studies have found only moderate stability of individual characteristics in childhood (Caspi, Roberts, & Shiner, 2005). There is evidence that, for example, children who were shy and uncertain at 21 months of age still tend to be so at age 12 or later. Similarly, infants who rapidly processed visual information at 7 months of age still tend to be rapid visual processors at age 11 (Emde & Hewitt, 2001).

The extent of the stability of children's psychological characteristics over time depends in part on the extent of stability in their environment. Studies have found, for example, that children raised in an orphanage that provides adequate physical care but little emotional and intellectual stimulation tend to be lethargic and low in IQ. But if their environment changes—if they are adopted into caring families in their early years—their condition improves markedly, and many of them become intellectually normal adults (Clarke & Clarke, 2000).

The four major issues of developmental sources, plasticity, continuity/discontinuity, and individual differences have endured for decades and continue to focus the research efforts of developmentalists. In the next section, we explore the major theories that developmentalists have used to help address these issues.

▲ APPLY :: CONNECT :: DISCUSS

The central questions of developmental science are reflected in the ways parents and practitioners (teachers, counselors, and doctors) interpret children's behavior. Identify the central question (nature/nurture, continuity/discontinuity, individual differences, or plasticity) associated with each of the following common phrases.

"Oh, those terrible twos!"

"Don't worry. It's just a phase. She'll grow out of it."

"He's 2 going on 20," or "He's 20 going on 2."

"She's her own little person."

"Of course he's having trouble—his parents work all day and are never home."

"He's been moody since he hit puberty."

Now, drawing on your own experience, think of one or more similar phrases for each of the central questions.

Theories of Development

Many students roll their eyes at the idea that theories are needed to understand children's development. "What's so complicated?" they wonder. "Just observe children and let the facts speak for themselves." But, contrary to popular belief, facts do not speak for themselves. The facts that developmentalists collect add to our understanding of development only when they are brought together and interpreted in terms of a **theory**, a framework of ideas or body of principles that can be used to guide the collection and interpretation of a set of facts. Without the lens of theory through which to observe, we would not know what we were looking at, much less how to characterize it or what to make of it. At the same time, of course, data can be used to test theories, and theories are constantly being revised to better fit the data. In this way, data and theories go hand in hand, each shaping the other.

To appreciate the role of theory, consider a hypothetical example: You are a developmentalist observing a little boy running around a preschool classroom, hitting the other children and grabbing toys away from them. How would you interpret this instance of misbehavior? If you were framing your explanation with a theory focused on antisocial behavior, you might see the child's actions as uncontrolled aggression, whereas if you were framing it with a theory focused on the interdependency of group members, you might see those same actions as a symptom of the child's having failed to develop a sense of his dependency on others for his well-being. (In fact, for cultural reasons, Americans might tend toward the first interpretation, whereas Japanese people might tend toward the second.) Not only would your specific observations be likely to be influenced by the theory you used, but your prescriptions for dealing with the child's behavior would be as well.

The preceding example also illustrates a point made by Albert Einstein, namely, that theory is present even when we think that we are "objectively observing" the world. We think of our theories as founded on observations, when "[i]n reality the very opposite occurs. It is the theory which decides what we can observe" (quoted in Sameroff, 1983, p. 243).

Einstein's point underscores the importance of theory. A deeper understanding of human development will not automatically come from the continuous accumulation of facts. Rather, it will come through new attempts to make sense of this accumulating evidence in the light of relevant theories. It also raises a caution: Developmental scientists, like all scientists, need to keep in mind that their theories can bias, or distort, their observations. Throughout this book, you will see examples of both the power and potential problems of theories.

Theory in Developmental Science

There is no single broad theoretical perspective that unifies the entire body of relevant scientific knowledge on human development. Instead, development is approached from several theoretical perspectives that differ in a number of important ways:

1. *Domains of development under investigation.* A theory may be most appropriate for understanding the ways in which children develop cognitively, socially,

theory A broad framework or set of principles that can be used to guide the collection and interpretation of a set of facts.

psychodynamic theories Theories, such as those of Freud and Erikson, that explore the influence on development and developmental stages of universal biological drives and the life experiences of individuals.

emotionally, or physically, or it may explore some combination of these domains.

2. *Research methods used.* As you will learn in the next section, particular theories are often associated with particular research methods—observational, experimental, and so forth.

3. *Central issues addressed.* The major theories also differ in their approach to the four central issues we discussed above—the relative contributions of nature and nurture, the degree of plasticity and openness to change, the extent of continuity or discontinuity, and the stability of individual differences.

We will begin our discussion of developmental theories by reviewing the "grand theories" that were developed when the field was relatively young. We will then examine several modern theoretical perspectives that the grand theories inspired.

Grand Theories

Most developmentalists would consider four theoretical perspectives to fall into the category of "grand theories"—the psychodynamic, behaviorist, constructivist, and sociocultural perspectives. These perspectives are "grand" not only because they laid the foundation for the modern theories of development that followed them, but also because they are "grand" in scope, each presenting a sweeping view of various domains of development.

Psychodynamic Theories **Psychodynamic theories** claim a significant place in the history of developmental science, having shown how universal developmental processes and stages can be understood by exploring the specific life experiences of particular individuals. Sigmund Freud was the first to develop a psychodynamic theory. Over the years, his theory has been adopted and modified by numerous developmentalists, the most prominent of them being Erik Erikson, who, as you will see, combined the primarily biological approach taken by Freud with the view that culture plays a leading role in shaping the path of development.

Sigmund Freud. Trained as a neurologist, Freud (1856–1939) sought to create a theory of personality that would enable him to cure the patients who came to him with such symptoms as extreme fears and anxiety, hysteria, and an inability to cope with everyday life. Although many of these symptoms initially appeared similar to those of neurological disorders, Freud believed that they were rooted in unresolved traumatic experiences in early childhood.

On the basis of the clinical data he gathered from his patients, including their recollections of the past and their current dreams, Freud constructed a general theory of psychological development that gave primacy to the ways in which children satisfy their basic biological drives. The theory also gave rise to the method of treatment known as *psychoanalysis.* Influenced by Darwin's theory of evolution, Freud reasoned that, whatever their significance for the individual, all biological drives have but a single goal: the survival and propagation of the species. Since reproduction, the necessary condition for the continuation of the species, is accomplished through sexual intercourse, it followed for Freud that all biological drives must ultimately serve the fundamental sex drive.

Freud shocked his contemporaries by arguing that the behavior of children—even infants—is motivated by a need to satisfy the fundamental sex drive. As indicated in Table 1.2, Freud proposed that, beginning in infancy and moving

Austrian Press and Information Service

Sigmund Freud

table 1.2		
Freud's Psychosexual Stages and Erikson's Psychosocial Stages Compared		
Approximate Age	Freud (Psychosexual)	Erikson (Psychosocial)
First year	*Oral stage* The mouth is the focus of pleasurable sensations as the baby sucks and bites.	*Trust versus mistrust* Infants learn to trust others to care for their basic needs, or to mistrust them.
Second year	*Anal stage* The anus is the focus of pleasurable sensations as the baby learns to control elimination.	*Autonomy versus shame and doubt* Children learn to exercise their will and to control themselves, or they become uncertain and doubt that they can do things by themselves.
Third to sixth year	*Phallic stage* Children develop sexual curiosity and obtain gratification when they masturbate. They have sexual fantasies about the parent of the opposite sex and feel guilt about their fantasies.	*Initiative versus guilt* Children learn to initiate their own activities, enjoy their accomplishments, and become purposeful. If they are not allowed to follow their own initiative, they feel guilty for their attempts to become independent.
Seventh year through puberty	*Latency* Sexual urges are submerged. Children focus on mastery of skills valued by adults.	*Industry versus inferiority* Children learn to be competent and effective at activities valued by adults and peers, or they feel inferior.
Adolescence	*Genital stage* Adolescents have adult sexual desires, and they seek to satisfy them.	*Identity versus role confusion* Adolescents establish a sense of personal identity as part of their social group, or they become confused about who they are and what they want to do in life.
Early adulthood		*Intimacy versus isolation* Young adults find an intimate life companion, or they risk loneliness and isolation.
Middle age		*Generativity versus stagnation* Adults must be productive in their work and willing to raise a next generation, or they risk stagnation.
Old age		*Integrity versus despair* People try to make sense of their prior experience and to assure themselves that their lives have been meaningful, or they despair over their unachieved goals and ill-spent lives.

through adolescence and the advent of adult sexuality, the form of sexual gratification changes, passing through an orderly series of *psychosexual stages* related to the parts of the body through which gratification is achieved. According to Freud (1920/1955), each stage is associated with conflicts between the child's desires and social prohibitions and expectations that militate against the expression of those desires. The way children experience the conflicts at each stage, and whether or not they successfully resolve them, affects their later personality. Freud maintained, for example, that failure to resolve the conflicts of any given stage can result in the individual's becoming fixated with the issues related to that stage. Perhaps the best-known of such conflicts occurs during the anal stage, when the child is socially required to control elimination. Unresolved conflicts related to overly strict toilet training can, in the Freudian view, lead to an "anal retentive" fixation and a personality marked by emotional rigidity and an extreme need for cleanliness and order.

Another important contribution to understanding development was Freud's belief that the personality is made up of three mental structures: (1) the primitive *id,* which is present from birth and consists of biological drives that demand immediate gratification; (2) the *ego,* which begins to emerge in early childhood and is the rational component of the personality that attempts to mediate a practical reconciliation between the demands of the id and the contraints imposed on those demands by the outside world; and (3) the *superego,* which emerges last and, acting as one's conscience, attempts to suppress the forbidden demands of

behaviorism Theories that focus on development as the result of learning, and on changes in behavior as a result of forming associations between behavior and its consequences.

the id and force the ego to make choices that are morally acceptable (we will return to a discussion of these structures in Chapter 9; see p. 318). According to Freud, these three structures are rarely, if ever, in perfect balance. The constant battle among them is the engine of developmental change, which Freud spoke of as *ego development*.

Central to Freud's psychodynamic view of development is his idea of the *unconscious*, a storehouse of hidden motives that drive much of the individual's behavior. These motives, according to Freud, are associated with the unresolved conflicts experienced during the psychosexual stages of childhood and are kept from conscious awareness because they are threatening. As you will see below, most other major theories pay less attention to the idea of the unconscious, focusing instead on the individual's conscious behaviors, purposes, and goals. Interestingly, recent advances in neuroscience have rekindled interest in the unconscious, particularly with regard to how unconscious brain processes influence the way individuals think, experience emotions, and make decisions.

Erik Erikson

Erik Erikson. Whereas Freud's training was in medicine, Erik Erikson's (1902–1994) was eclectic, combining his experience in psychoanalysis with a background in art, teaching, and anthropology. Erikson built on many of Freud's basic ideas of development but departed from them in two significant ways. First, Erikson emphasized social and cultural factors, rather than biological drives, as the major force behind development. Second, he viewed the developmental process as continuing throughout the life span rather than ending in adolescence (the age of sexual maturity).

Erikson believed that the main challenge of life is the quest for identity. Throughout their lives, people ask themselves "Who am I?" and at each stage of life they arrive at a different answer (Erikson, 1963, 1968b). For Erikson, each *psychosocial stage* is associated with a particular main task, as shown in Table 1.2. Erikson referred to these tasks as "crises" because they are sources of conflict within the person. The person must in some way accomplish the task, or resolve the conflict, in order to move on to the next stage. The resolution may be more on the positive side or more on the negative side—for example, for the first stage, more toward trust or more toward mistrust. A person's personality and sense of identity are formed in the resolution of these crises.

According to Erikson, each individual's life cycle unfolds in the context of a specific culture. While physical maturation determines the general timetable according to which the components of our personality develop, our culture provides us with the contexts in which we must resolve the crises and the tools with which we can resolve them.

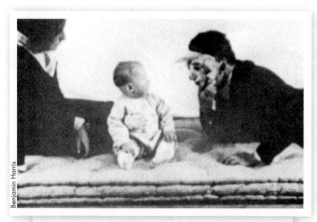

John B. Watson and Rosalie Rayner conducted early experiments in which they induced fear in infants, which they subsequently sought to eliminate through learning. Such research is no longer considered ethically acceptable because it puts the infant at risk should the experimenters fail to extinguish the infant's fears.

Behaviorism **Behaviorism** promotes the basic idea that personality and behavior are shaped by the individual's learning experiences. This learning process involves modifying behavior by forming associations between observable behavior and its consequences, favorable and unfavorable. In this respect, behaviorism is radically different from psychodynamic theories and their focus on universal biological drives, the development of internal personality structures, and the resolution of inner conflicts. Indeed, according to John B. Watson (1878–1958), behaviorism entirely transformed how human behavior should be understood and studied because it shifted the focus from the inner workings of the mind and personality to external, observable behaviors and their consequences (Watson, 1930). This shift in focus, according to Watson and other behaviorists, made the science of human behavior and development more "objective" than it had been in the past.

An early proponent of behaviorism, Edward Thorndike (1874–1949), captured the general principle of the theory in his *law of effect*. In essence, the **law of effect** states that behaviors that produce a satisfying effect in a given situation are likely to be repeated in the same or a similar situation, whereas behaviors that produce an uncomfortable effect are less likely to be repeated.

Thorndike's law of effect is readily apparent in efforts to explore how certain experiences such as rewards, punishments, and other reinforcers change the likelihood of a child's engaging in a particular behavior. According to behaviorism, rewards and punishments gradually shape children to become walkers, talkers, readers, and friends. Indeed, some theorists held the extreme position that development is overwhelmingly the product of learning alone. John B. Watson, for example, was so certain of the primary role of learning in human development, and of the insignificance of other factors, that he boasted that he could use learning principles to train any infant, regardless of talents, abilities, or family history, to become whatever he wished—doctor or lawyer, even beggarman or thief (1930, p. 104)!

In the view of development as occurring through learning, developmental change is seen as being gradual and continuous. B. F. Skinner, another leading learning theorist, whose theory of *operant conditioning* is discussed on p. 147, compared development to the creation of a sculpture: The sculptor begins with a lump of clay and gradually shaves away material until the object is complete. In Skinner's words, "the final product seems to have a special unity or integrity of design, but we cannot find a point at which this suddenly appears" (1953, p. 91).

B.F. Skinner designed his famous and controversial "baby box" to make infancy easier for parents and infants by providing a soundproof, climate-controlled environment in which clothes were not necessary. His own daughter was raised in the box until the age of 2.

Piaget's Constructivist Theory One of the most influential theories in the history of developmental science is Jean Piaget's theory of children's cognitive, or intellectual, development. Piaget (1896–1980) asserted that cognitive development is driven by the interaction of nature and nurture. In this view, nature refers to children's innate motivation to learn and explore, as well as to the maturation of their brain and body. Nurture refers to all the experiences that children learn from. The hallmark of Piaget's theory is its emphasis on children's active role in shaping their own cognitive development. He argued in particular that children do not *discover* the world and the way it works but, rather, *actively construct* an understanding of the world on the basis of their experiences with it. In Piaget's **constructivist theory**, children construct successively higher levels of knowledge by actively striving to master their environments.

Piaget believed that children progress through a series of stages of cognitive development (see Table 1.3), and he supported this idea through observation of, and interviews and experiments with, children of all ages. Each stage reflects a unique age-related way of understanding or organizing reality. Imagine, for instance, a 6-month-old baby playing with a set of wooden blocks. She may attempt to chew on some and bang them on the floor. The knowledge she constructs about the blocks—that they are better for banging than for chewing—is entirely different from the knowledge she will construct about them when she is 6 years old and can stack them or throw them at her brother. Another example of how children's stage of cognitive development affects their understanding involves age-related differences in how they tend to explain their parents' divorce. Younger children who, as noted, have a difficult time understanding the perspectives of others, may

law of effect Thorndike's notion that behaviors that produce a satisfying effect in a given situation are likely to be repeated in the same or a similar situation, whereas behaviors that produce an uncomfortable effect are less likely to be repeated.

constructivist theory Piaget's theory, in which cognitive development results from children's active construction of reality, based on their experiences with the world.

table 1.3

Piaget's Stages of Cognitive Development

Age (years)	Stage	Description
Birth to 2	Sensorimotor	Infants' achievements consist largely of coordinating their sensory perceptions and simple motor behaviors. As they move through the six substages of this period, infants come to recognize the existence of a world outside themselves and begin to interact with it in deliberate ways.
2 to 6	Preoperational	Young children can represent reality to themselves through the use of symbols, including mental images, words, and gestures. Still, children often fail to distinguish their point of view from that of others, become easily captured by surface appearances, and are often confused about causal relations.
6 to 12	Concrete operational	As they enter middle childhood, children become capable of mental operations, internalized actions that fit into a logical system. Operational thinking allows children to mentally combine, separate, order, and transform objects and actions. Such operations are considered concrete because they are carried out in the presence of the objects and events being thought about.
12 to 19	Formal operational	In adolescence, the developing person acquires the ability to think systematically about all logical relations within a problem. Adolescents display keen interest in abstract ideas and in the process of thinking itself.

Jean Piaget, whose work has had a profound influence on developmental psychology.

Bill Anderson / Photo Researchers, Inc.

believe that they themselves were somehow at fault. Older children, in contrast, have reached a stage of development that allows them to understand the divorce from their parents' perspective; that is, in terms of their parents' relationship with each other. As you will learn in later chapters, the ability to detach ourselves from our personal, idiosyncratic points of view in order to understand other perspectives takes place throughout childhood and adolescence and is key to the development of objectivity and advanced forms of reasoning. Indeed, believing that scientific reasoning is the pinnacle of cognitive development, Piaget devoted much of his work to understanding how less mature forms of objectivity and reasoning are transformed over time to become more scientific.

On the basis of data from various cultures, Piaget (1966/1974) believed that development can be speeded up or slowed down by variations in the environment (such as the presence or absence of formal schooling) but that all children go through the same basic stages. In this important sense, a constructivist approach assumes that the processes of developmental change are universal, the same in all human groups.

In Piaget's view, the most basic unit of cognitive functioning is the *schema,* a general framework that provides a model for understanding some aspect of the world (Piaget & Inhelder, 1969). Over time, as children interact with their environment, they change—strengthen or transform—their schemas through *adaptation* to new information, which involves processes Piaget termed *assimilation* and *accommodation*.

In *assimilation,* individuals incorporate new experiences into their existing schemas, strengthening those schemas. For example, in Piaget's view, infants have a primitive schema of sucking that enables them to draw milk from a nipple. However, sucking does not remain strictly bound to milk-yielding nipples. Soon, babies are likely to find, say, a pacifier, instead of a nipple, touching their lips, and to start sucking on the pacifier—and in much the same way, since a pacifier is designed to be similar to a nipple. In other words, they assimilate the pacifier, a new object, into their existing sucking schema, which is thereby strengthened.

But pacifiers are not the only objects besides nipples that infants are likely to encounter. And many of these other objects cannot be assimilated into the infant's existing sucking schema. At this point, accommodation becomes relevant. In *accommodation,* individuals modify a schema so it can be applied to both old and new experiences. If an infant encounters her father's shoulder while she is being held, for instance, she may try to suck on it. However, because the qualities of Dad's shoulder are so unlike the qualities of a nipple or a pacifier, she is unable to assimilate the shoulder into her sucking schema, and must make some accommodation to this new object. That is, she must modify the way she sucks, perhaps by choosing a bit of his shirt and sucking on that, using approximately but not exactly the same schema she had used to suck on a nipple. This transformation of her sucking schema makes it more effective, expanding the universe of suckable objects.

To summarize Piaget's theory, development occurs as the child acts on the world and searches for a fit between new experiences and existing schemas. A lack of fit leads to an imbalance, or disequilibrium, which is corrected through assimilation and accommodation. Piaget believed that this back-and-forth process of the child's search for a fit between existing schemas and new experiences creates a new balance in the child's understanding, which he referred to as **equilibration**. This process of achieving equilibrium between the child's present understanding of the world and his or her new experiences of it creates a more inclusive, more complicated form of knowledge, eventually bringing the child to a new stage of development. Of course, this new balance cannot last for long because the process of biological maturation and the accumulation of experience/knowledge lead to new imbalances and to a search for a new equilibrium and a still higher, more inclusive level of adaptation.

As you will see in later chapters, contemporary developmentalists who follow in the tradition established by Piaget have refined or amended a number of his ideas. Nevertheless, these investigators agree with Piaget's emphasis on the central role of children's active engagement with the world and with his insistence that biology and the environment interact in contributing to developmental change.

Vygotsky's Sociocultural Theory

At the same time that Piaget was building the foundation of constructivism, Lev Vygotsky (1896–1934), a Russian psychologist, was at work developing a sociocultural theory of development. Vygotsky agreed that biological and social factors both play a role in development and, like Piaget, believed that children construct their own development through active engagement with the world. But Vygotsky differed from other theorists by claiming that a third force—culture—is part of the mixture. According to Vygotsky's **sociocultural theory**, nature and nurture shape development, not by interacting directly, but by interacting indirectly through culture (Greenfield, Keller, Fuligni, & Maynard, 2003; Rogoff, 2003; Valsiner, 1998; Vygotsky, 1978).

The influence of culture on development can be seen in children's acquisition of mathematical understanding. The kinds of mathematical thinking children develop do not depend only on their innate ability to deal with abstractions (nature) and on adults' socializing efforts to arrange for them to learn mathematical concepts (nurture). They also depend on the children's cultural heritage. For example, children growing up among the Oksapmin, a group living in the jungles of New Guinea,

equilibration The main source of development, consisting of a process of achieving a balance between the child's present understanding and the child's new experiences.

sociocultural theory The theory associated with Vygotsky that emphasizes the influence of culture on development.

According to Piaget, as a consequence of experience mouthing variously shaped objects, the infant's inborn sucking reflex is transformed into a more general schema. This results in more efficient nursing, and allows the baby to suck happily and well on other objects, such as pacifiers.

Lev Vygotsky, a prominent theorist of the role of culture in development, and his daughter.

Consistent with the mathematical system of his culture, the Oksapmin child on the left is indicating a number by pointing to a specific place on his body.

appear to have the same universal ability to grasp basic number concepts as do children growing up in Boston or Berlin or Beijing. However, instead of using a formal number system to count, the Oksapmin use a system that refers to 27 specific parts of their bodies. To indicate given amounts, they point to their wrist, their elbow, their ear, and so on. This system would obviously be unwieldy if the Oksapmin had to solve arithmetic problems in school and later in a money economy like those of modern cultures, but it is perfectly adequate for dealing with the tasks of everyday life in traditional Oksapmin culture (Saxe, 2002). Thus, culture contributes to the course of development because it is through culture that biological and environmental factors interact.

One of Vygotsky's most important contributions to understanding children's development is his concept of the **zone of proximal development**, defined as the gap between what children can accomplish independently and what they can accomplish when they are interacting with others who are more competent. The term "proximal" (nearby) indicates that the assistance provided goes just slightly beyond the child's current competence, complementing and building on the child's existing abilities. Consider the following scenario:

> Amy, almost 4 months old, is sitting [o]n her father's lap in a booth at the coffee shop. He is talking to a friend, and she is teething on a hard rubber ring. The father holds Amy with his left arm, keeping his right hand free. Twice he uses that hand to catch the ring when it falls from her grasp. When Amy dropped the ring for the third time, her father interrupts his conversation, rolls his eyes and says, "Good grief; not again." He retrieves the ring, puts it on the table, and resumes his conversation. Amy leans forward, reaching excitedly, but both her hands and the ring are covered in drool, and her baby hands and fingers are not yet well coordinated. Her father, still talking to his friend while watching Amy's lack of progress, tilts the ring upward so Amy can get her thumb under it. She grasps the ring, pulls it away from her father, and returns to her enthusiastic chewing. (Adapted from Kaye, 1982, pp. 1–2).

Here you see that, even with an infant, adults can provide help that enables children to function effectively and learn. Notice that, in keeping with Vygotsky's notion of the zone of proximal development, Amy's father did not put the teething ring in her hand or hold it up to her mouth but, instead, tilted it upward so that she could grasp it herself. To help a child appropriately, the adult must know what the child is trying to do and be sensitive to the child's abilities and signals. Vygotsky attributed great significance to such finely tuned child–adult interactions throughout development. Indeed, as shown in Table 1.4, Vygotsky's theory is unique in its emphasis on social interaction as the primary source of development.

Modern Theories

The grand theories just described continue to exert tremendous influence on thinking about children and their development. At the same time, modern theories of development have generated new and distinctive insights into the fundamental issues that have concerned developmentalists since the field was established. Although the number of developmental theories has expanded significantly in recent decades, four kinds of theories have been particularly influential: evolutionary, social learning, information-processing, and systems. Because we will explore these theories in greater detail later in the book, we provide only brief sketches of each here.

zone of proximal development For Vygotsky, the gap between what children can accomplish independently and what they can accomplish when interacting with others who are more competent.

table 1.4				
Thumbnail Sketch of Grand Theories				
	Psychodynamic Theories	Behaviorism	Piaget's Constructivism	Vygotsky's Sociocultural Theory
What develops	Freud: Personality structures of id, ego, superego Erikson: Personality, sense of identity	Patterns of behavior	Knowledge structures (schema)	Cultural knowledge and practices
Source of development	Freud: Biological drives Erikson: Social and cultural factors; tasks, or "crises"	Learning through social consequences (rewards, punishments)	Lack of fit between existing schemas and new experience (disequilibration)	Social interaction within zone of proximal development
Goal of development	Freud: Survival through sexual reproduction Erikson: Identity; moving through psychosocial stages	Socially appropriate patterns of behavior	Adaptation through balancing schemas and experience (equilibration)	Participation in cultural activities and practices
Main developmental domains addressed	Physical, social, emotional	Cognitive, social	Cognitive	Cognitive, social
Main research methods used	Clinical interview	Experimental	Clinical interview	Naturalistic
Main research designs used	Longitudinal	Microgenetic	Longitudinal, cross-sectional	Microgenetic
Special topics and applications	Sexuality, aggression, identity	Self-efficacy, gender roles, behavior-modification therapies	Reasoning and scientific thinking	Problem solving, education

Evolutionary Theories **Evolutionary theories** attempt both to explain human behavior in terms of how it contributes to the survival of the species and to address the ways in which our evolutionary past continues to influence individual development (Causey, Gardiner, & Bjorklund, 2008; Konner, 2010). As you will see in Chapter 2, according to evolutionary theory, species develop as they do because individuals with characteristics that favor survival in a particular environment are more likely to reproduce and pass those characteristics on to their offspring. Thus, human characteristics—physical, behavioral, and other—can be understood in terms of their role in contributing to the survival of individuals and, in turn, to the survival and evolution of the species. Of course, evolutionary theorizing about children's development has been around since Darwin. But it has recently emerged as a dominant perspective in the discipline, owing in part to advances in sophisticated technologies and research methods that permit more direct measurements of biological processes (see the box "Observing the Living Brain," p. 33).

An evolutionary approach is central in **ethology**, which grew from the field of zoology and studies behavior in different animal species in their natural environments (see the box "In the Field: Probing the Mysteries of Learning"). For this reason, naturalistic observation, which we will discuss later, is a major research method ethologists use. In its evolutionary approach, ethology focuses on how behaviors of various species are adapted to the environment in ways that increase the likelihood that individuals will reach reproductive maturity to have offspring of their own. Ethologists look both at the adaptive behaviors of the young and at the behaviors they elicit in others, asking how both types of behaviors contribute to survival. *Imprinting,* discussed earlier, is an example of such behaviors: By becoming attached

evolutionary theories Theories that explain human behavior in terms of how it contributes to the survival of the species and that look at how our evolutionary past influences individual development.

ethology An interdisciplinary science that studies the biological and evolutionary foundations of behavior.

In The Field   Probing the Mysteries of Learning

Name:	Elizabeth Vinson Lonsdorf
Education:	Undergraduate degrees at Duke University, including summer internships in Hawaii and Florida to study whales and dolphins; Ph.D. at the Jane Goodall Institute Center for Primate Studies at the University of Minnesota
Current Position:	Director of the Lester E. Fisher Center for the Study and Conservation of Apes, Lincoln Park Zoo in Chicago
Career Objectives:	Participate in and support worldwide animal conservation projects

VIDEO CAMERA IN HAND, ELIZABETH VINSON Lonsdorf crouches in a clearing of the Gombe National Park in Tanzania. The target of her attention is a mother–daughter pair of wild chimpanzees working to extract termites—a delicacy—from a termite mound. Chimpanzees use tools to gather their food—something that is exceedingly rare among animal species. From vegetation found nearby, they fashion a long tool that can be inserted into the depths of the mound. When the termites attack and cling to the "intruder," the chimpanzees carefully withdraw the tool and feast on the clinging insects. Primatologists refer to this process of foraging as "termite-fishing."

It has been known for some time that chimpanzees engage in tool-assisted foraging. What Elizabeth Lonsdorf wants to know is how chimpanzees learn to use tools in this distinctive way. Her interest is motivated by the understanding that, because chimpanzees are our closest genetic kin, their behavior may shed light on the activities of our earliest evolutionary ancestors (Lonsdorf, 2007). In her words:

I've always been interested in animal learning and tool use—especially the way young animals grow up and learn their way in the world. When you look at chimpanzees, it's so easy to see the link between humans and the rest of the animal kingdom. They make and use tools, conduct warfare, and have very similar mother–child relationships as humans. By studying chimpanzees, we can gain insight into what the activities of our earliest ancestors might have been like.

Her studies of chimpanzee behavior in natural environments suggest that young chimps learn termite-fishing by watching their mothers, much as an apprentice acquires skills by observing a master. Although chimp mothers model succesfully fishing for termites, and seem remarkably tolerant when youngsters interrupt their foraging with awkward efforts of their own, at no time were the mothers observed to deliberately teach their children how to fish. According to many evolutionary theorists, the deliberate teaching of the young may be a distinctively human trait (see Chapter 2).

(a) The chimpanzee perched on this termite mound has just slurped termites from the stick used to "fish" them from the mound. (b) Elizabeth Lonsdorf is interested in learning how this tool-using practice, exceedingly rare in the animal kingdom, is transmitted to the young.

Anup Shah / npl / Minden Pictures

Courtesy of Lincoln Park Zoo

to the mother and following her around (and by the mother's allowing this behavior), the baby chick is able to survive.

How do human infants and children, like baby chicks, elicit care from their parents? Clearly, human infants and children require considerable parental care and investment if they are to survive to maturity. From an evolutionary perspective, it makes good sense that caregiving should have a strong biological component. A question raised by ethologists is, "What products of evolution do children possess that ensure they will be cared for?" One answer to this question (you will learn of others in later chapters) is found in the infant's appearance. Babies, as we all know, are *cute.* And this cuteness applies not only to our own babies but to those of many other species as well. Kittens are cute; puppies are cute; baby lions and tigers and bears are all cute. What we consider cute, however, boils down to several highly specific physical characteristics that distinguish newborns of many animal species from mature individuals and that seem key to eliciting care. As noted by the famous German ethologist, Konrad Lorenz (1943), these characteristics include a relatively large head; large eyes set low on the forehead; short, heavy limbs; big, round cheeks; a button nose (see Figure 1.4).

Evidence in support of the idea that babyness evokes positive adult responses comes from a study by Willian Fullard and Ann Reiling (1976). These researchers asked people ranging in age from 7 years to young adulthood which of matched pairs of pictures—one depicting an adult and the other depicting an infant—they preferred. Some of the pictures were of human beings; others were of nonhuman animals. They found that adults, especially women, were most likely to choose the pictures of infants. Children between the ages of 7 and 12 preferred the pictures of adults. Between the ages of 12 and 14, the preference of girls shifted quite markedly from adults to infants. A similar shift was found among boys when they were between ages 14 and 16. These shifts in preference coincide with the average age at which girls and boys undergo the physiological changes that make them capable of reproducing.

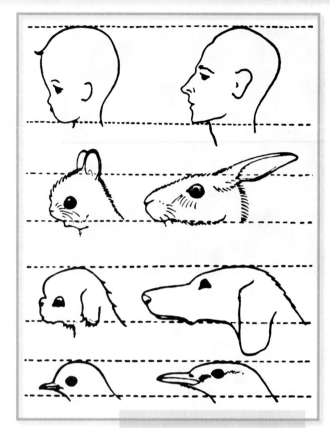

FIGURE 1.4 Side-by-side sketches of the heads of infants and adults of four species make clear the distinguishing features of "babyness." (Lorenz, 1943)

Social Learning Theories

Social Learning Theories Rooted in behaviorism, social learning theories explain development in terms of the associations that children make between behaviors and their consequences. However, unlike behaviorism, **social learning theories** emphasize the behavior–consequence associations that children learn by observing and interacting with others in social situations. Social learning theories have made a number of important contributions to the study of human development, two of which are generally associated with the work of Albert Bandura. One contribution is the concept of *modeling,* the process by which children observe and imitate others. As you will see in later chapters, the concept of modeling has proven to be particularly valuable for understanding children's gender-role development. Another key concept proposed by Bandura is *self-efficacy,* people's beliefs about their own abilities to effectively meet standards and achieve their goals (Bandura, 1974/1997). You probably know people who avoid taking on difficult tasks because they don't believe they are capable of doing them well. Or maybe you know people who have a huge amount of faith in their ability to master just about any challenge. Bandura would describe the first group of people as having

social learning theories Theories that emphasize the behavior–consequences associations that children learn by observing and interacting with others in social situations.

Among Albert Bandura's significant contributions to the discipline is his concept of modeling, in which children observe and imitate others. In the background, you can see a photograph of a child from one of Bandura's studies. After observing a model engage in similar behavior, the boy strikes a Bobo doll with a mallet.

low self-efficacy and the second group as having high self-efficacy. As we will discuss in Chapter 9, a child's self-efficacy can have a dramatic effect on learning.

Social learning theorists maintain that many aspects of personality, including personality problems such as aggression and dependency, are learned and therefore can be unlearned. This idea led to the development of *behavior modification,* a technique for breaking the associations between the behaviors and the environmental consequences that maintain them. For example, if a child engages in overly aggressive behavior in the home, a therapist might look into whether the parents were inadvertently rewarding the aggression, perhaps by giving the child a lot of attention. In order to break the association between the behavior and its rewarding consequences, the therapist might then set up a behavior-modification program in which the child's aggression results in being isolated in a "time out," thereby taking away the reward and substituting a punishment.

Information-Processing Theories

The enormous magnitude of data processed through high-speed computer technologies and communications systems leaves no doubt that we live in an information age. In addition to introducing significant changes in the ways that people work, live, and learn, the information age has inspired changes in how developmentalists think about the mind. In particular, some developmentalists describe mental functioning in terms of the workings of a digital computer—that is, they take an information-processing approach to cognition and its development. **Information-processing theories** are concerned with how information flows through the child's developing mental system—how the child comes to process, store, organize, retrieve, and manipulate information in increasingly efficient ways.

As we discuss in more detail in Chapter 9, information-processing approaches distinguish between the "hardware" and "software" of intellectual functioning. In the case of a computer, hardware includes specific *structural* components where data can be stored and retrieved. These structural features set limits on information processing, including storage capacity and speed of processing. The software, on the other hand, includes all those various programs that have been written and loaded for the purpose of moving data through the hardware components, as happens in the process of storing and retrieving data. In the case of the mind, the hardware consists of certain brain structures and neural features, whereas the software consists of problem-solving strategies and methods that individuals intentionally use to help them process and remember information. Examples of such strategies include rehearsing new information over and over for the purpose of remembering it and skimming a textbook for boldfaced key terms that might be useful to include in a term paper.

As you will learn in later chapters, information-processing theories have been especially useful in understanding such topics as how attention and memory develop, how children build information into systems of knowledge, and how children develop and use problem-solving strategies.

Systems Theories

As the name suggests, **systems theories** envision development in terms of complex wholes made up of parts—that is, *systems*—and look at how these wholes and their parts are organized and interact and change over time. The particular systems of interest vary. Some systems theorists focus on how specific behaviors of the child, such as walking, become organized and coordinated over

information-processing theories Theories that look at cognitive development in terms of how children come to process, store, organize, retrieve, and manipulate information in increasingly efficient ways.

systems theories Theories that envision development in terms of complex wholes made up of parts and that explore how these wholes and their parts are organized and interact and change over time.

time; for these theorists, the behaviors are the systems. Other theorists focus on more general systems, such as systems made up of the contexts in which children live (the family, the community, and so on) and of interrelationships among these contexts. Two types of systems theories have been particularly influential in the past few decades—*dynamic systems theory* and *ecological systems theory*. Despite the considerable differences between them, they share the view that development is best understood as a complex and unified system that is organized and reorganized over time. In the words of Esther Thelen, who devoted her career to exploring the application of systems theory to children's development, a complete understanding of development requires recognizing "the multiple, mutual, and continuous interaction of all levels of the developing system, from the molecular to the cultural" (Thelen & Smith, 1998, p. 563).

Dynamic Systems Theory. **Dynamic systems theory** addresses how new complex systems of behavior develop from the interaction of less complex parts. Consider, for example, baby Ryan's ability to reach and grasp a toy that his older brother dangles in front of him. Ryan's reaching-and-grasping system emerged from the development and interaction of several visual and motor (movement) components. First, the visual component of the system had to have developed to a point that allows Ryan's eyes to follow and fix the toy in his field of vision. In addition, his perceptual system had to have been sufficiently honed by experience for Ryan to accurately judge whether the toy is reachable and graspable. Further, his motor system must have developed the muscle coordination that allows him to engage in smooth reaching movements with his arms and effective grasping movements with his hands. Finally, all these components must interact in a unified system so that what Ryan *sees* (the toy) is successfully coordinated with what he *does* (reaches and grasps).

With development and experience, the components of Ryan's reaching and grasping will be coordinated into a stable and balanced system, and his reaching and grasping will become second nature, as it is for most of us. However, as you will learn in Chapter 4, reaching and grasping, as well as many other systems, are initially disorganized and sloppy approximations of what they will become. Dynamic systems theorists are interested in what sparks the beginnings of new systems and in how these new systems develop from initial disorganization and instability to become smoothly functioning and stable.

Ecological Systems Theory. The field of biology has been an important source of inspiration to ecological systems theory. *Ecology* is the subfield of biology that studies the relationship between organisms (plants and animals) and their environments. In developmental science, **ecological systems theory** focuses on the organization of the multiple environmental contexts within which children develop.

One of the most influential models of ecological systems was devised by Uri Bronfenbrenner. According to his model, shown in Figure 1.5, the developing child is at the center of a set of four nested, interacting systems:

1. The innermost system, the *microsystem,* includes all of the various settings that the child inhabits on a daily basis—the "face-to-face" settings of home, school, and peer groups.

2. The *mesosystem* is the connective tissue that links the face-to-face settings to one another, such as parents' involvement in their child's school. The strength and nature of these connections are important to children's development. For example, parents, teachers, and peers might be consistent

dynamic systems theory A theory that addresses how new, complex systems of behavior develop from the interaction of less complex parts.

ecological systems theory A theory focusing on the organization and interactions of the multiple environmental contexts within which children develop.

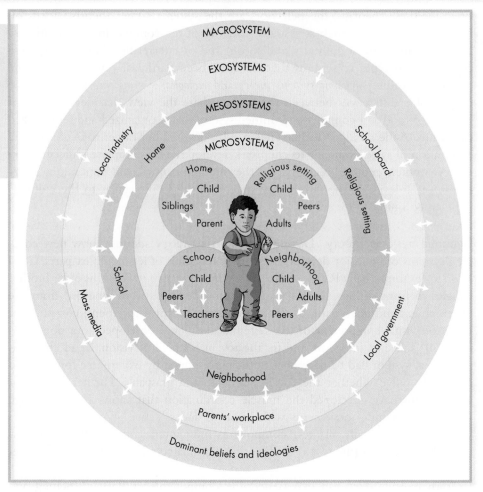

FIGURE 1.5 The ecological approach sees children in the context of all the various settings they inhabit on a daily basis (microsystems). These settings are related to one another in a variety of ways (mesosystems), which are in turn linked to settings and social institutions where the children are not present but which have an important influence on their development (exosystems). All of these systems are organized in terms of the culture's dominant beliefs and ideologies (the macrosystem).

with one another in supporting the child's academic success—or might be in conflict, as would be the case if the parents and teachers were pushing the child toward college but the peers wanted to form an indie-rock band and move to L.A. to play music full time.

3. Part three of Bronfenbrenner's model is the *exosystem,* which consists of settings that affect but do not usually include the child. An example would be the parent's workplace. If a parent's workplace provides a decent wage, security, satisfaction, and good benefits, including good medical benefits and paid leave when children are born or are ill, the parent may be more likely to provide quality care. If, on the other hand, a parent's workplace is one of stress, frustration, anxiety, and poor pay and benefits, quality of care may suffer.

4. The fourth and final part of the model is the *macrosystem*—the values, customs, hazards, and resources of the larger culture that shape what happens in all the settings of the systems nested within. The macrosystems of some cultures are very supportive of children's needs, and this may be evident from, for example, child-protection laws and resources devoted to providing quality educational and child-care facilities and to ensuring access to health care. As we will see, values regarding such characteristics as race and ethnicity, socioeconomic status, and gender may seriously diminish the quality of care, nurturing, and interaction that children experience.

As in all other systems theories, the four systems here are understood to interact and influence one another. For example, a famous study of the Great Depression found that when the unemployment rate in the United States skyrocketed and parents lost jobs, relationships among family members deteriorated, parenting skills declined, and children's development and well-being were placed at considerable risk (Elder, 1998; Modell & Elder, 2002).

hypothesis A possible explanation based on theory that is precise enough to be shown to be true or false.

None of the theories outlined above is sufficiently comprehensive to provide a full picture of all the complexities of human development. But each provides an important and unique frame for looking at certain aspects of development and for formulating **hypotheses**, or possible explanations precise enough to be shown true or false, regarding why children behave as they do, why they change over time, and what practitioners can do to support their health and well-being. In the next section, we explore the research methods typically used to test theoretical hypotheses.

⏏ APPLY :: CONNECT :: DISCUSS

Little Parminder is playing intently with wooden blocks. She puts one on top of another, and looks at her mother, who smiles, claps her hands, and exclaims, "Oh, aren't you clever? You got it on top! Are you a proud little girl?!" Parminder grasps another block and repeats her performance. She smiles broadly at her mother, who again responds with happy excitement. On the third try, however, Parminder topples her tower, and bursts into tears, scattering the blocks. "Poor baby! They fell down and now you're angry," says her mother. "Here, let me help you make the tower."

This scenario can be explored from several different theoretical perspectives. Considering the theories of Erikson, Vygotksy, and Piaget, what would you focus on? How would you interpret the scenario?

Methods for Studying Development

We mentioned previously that different theories tend to rely on different research methods for addressing questions and collecting information about human development. Indeed, the relationship between theory and method is of fundamental importance, and developmentalists take great care to ensure that one follows from the other (Valsiner, 2005). For example, it makes little sense to research children's memory development by collecting only quantitative information (e.g., changes in the number of words remembered from a long list) if, according to your theory, memory development proceeds through a sequence of qualitative stage transitions that are reflected in how memories are organized. Individual research methods, like the theories with which they are associated, provide only limited views that are often specific to particular developmental periods or domains. In the sections below, we examine the various goals of conducting research and the different methods by which those goals are accomplished.

The Goals of Developmental Research

Like any other scientists, developmentalists begin their research with particular goals in mind. The goals can range widely, from the "purely scientific" to the practical, often with a good deal of overlap. It is therefore helpful to consider three categories of research—*basic, applied,* and *action*—that differ according to the particular goals that motivate the researcher.

Margaret Beale Spencer conducts basic research on how contextual factors such as minority-group status, poverty, and neighborhood dangers influence the learning attitudes of African American youth. She then tries to identify the coping mechanisms that underlie youths' success in important learning activities.

The goal of *basic research* is to advance scientific knowledge of human development—for example, to determine whether the ability to perceive depth is inborn or learned, or to determine whether basic emotions develop universally in all children or emerge differently for children in different cultures. Although its results might be used to help solve practical problems, basic research is undertaken for the simple goal of gaining new knowledge, and it often explores major theoretical issues, such as questions of developmental continuity, plasticity, and sources of development.

In contrast to basic research, *applied research* is designed to answer practical questions related to improving children's lives and experiences—for example, assessing the effectiveness of different kinds of violence-prevention programs in schools or determining whether immigrant children learn better if they are instructed in their native language or in the language of their adopted country. In many cases, applied research also extends basic scientific knowledge. Its primary goal, however, is to benefit society by generating knowledge that can be used in solving specific problems.

Action research is a close cousin of applied research. Also known as "mission-oriented research," action research is designed primarily to provide data that can be used in making social-policy decisions (Coghlan & Jacobs, 2005). For example, action research has played an instrumental role in programs and policies ranging from the Head Start school-readiness program for disadvantaged children to federal regulations regarding the education of children with special needs; toy safety standards; requirements for foster care; and legislation concerning the prosecution of minors who have committed crimes. In contrast to basic and applied research, whose intended audience usually includes scientists and other developmental practitioners, action research is aimed at legislators and government officials and is often meant to sway their opinions.

In recent years, developmentalists have been increasingly drawn to action research. To some extent, this is the result of a growing commitment and sense of social obligation on the part of universities to recognize and serve the needs of their communities better (Greenberg & Kusché, 2006; Thomas, Donovan, Sigo, Austin, & Marlatt, 2009). Universities and communities across the United States and other nations are forging *university–community partnerships* around specific local issues. For

Sallie Motch is a psychologist with Doctors Without Borders, an organization that won the Nobel Peace Prize. She addresses mental stress and trauma issues with Palestinian youths in the area of Hebron in the West Bank. Developmentalists like Motch engage in action research to help governments and other organizations develop scientifically based programs that protect children from harm and promote their well-being (Motch, 2009).

example, the University of California at San Diego has created a charter school both to assist children from poor families that have never had access to higher education and to determine which instructional formats are most helpful to these children (Jones et al., 2002).

Although categorizing research can be helpful, it is important to remember that basic, applied, and action research often overlap in their goals. For example, a research study on the effectiveness of Head Start programs is *basic* in the sense of addressing questions of plasticity such as whether intervention with disadvantaged preschoolers can have lasting effects on IQ, *applied* in the sense of seeking knowledge to improve the lives of socially disadvantaged children, and *action*-oriented in that its data may influence social-policy decisions on program funding and development.

Criteria for Developmental Research

Whether engaged in basic, applied, or action research, developmentalists usually begin their work with commonsense observation and speculation. In this respect, they are like anyone else who might be trying to understand some interesting or puzzling aspect of children's behavior. The difference is that developmental researchers go beyond commonsense observation and speculation—as researchers, their approach to understanding children's behavior must meet certain specific criteria that have been determined by the scientific and scholarly community to which they belong. The criteria will vary to some extent, depending on the researcher's theory and method of data collection, as we discuss below. Four of the most common criteria used to judge scientific research are *objectivity, reliability, replicability,* and *validity.* Let us look at each in turn.

In a research study, data should be collected and analyzed with **objectivity**; that is, the gathering and analyzing of data should not be biased by the investigators' preconceptions. Total objectivity is impossible to achieve in practice because developmentalists, like everyone else, have beliefs that influence how they interpret what they see. But objectivity remains an important ideal to strive for.

Reliability refers to the consistency of the research findings. Research data should be reliable in two senses. First, investigators should get the same results each time they collect data under the same set of conditions. Second, the descriptions of independent observers' results should be in agreement with each other. Suppose, for example, that investigators want to determine how upset infants become when a pacifier is taken from them while they are sucking on it (Goldsmith & Campos, 1982). The findings about the degree of an infant's distress are considered reliable in the first sense if the level of distress (measured in terms of crying or thrashing about) is found to be the same when the baby's sucking is interrupted under the same conditions on successive occasions. The findings are considered reliable in the second sense if independent observers agree on how distressed the baby becomes each time the pacifier is taken away.

Replicability, the third criterion, means that if other researchers independently create the same procedures as an initial investigator did, they will obtain the same results. In studies of newborns' ability to imitate, for example, some researchers report that newborns will imitate certain exaggerated facial expressions that they see another person making directly in front of them. However, using the same methods, other investigators have failed to find evidence of such imitation in newborns (see Chapter 6, p. 206). Only if the same finding, under the same conditions, is obtained repeatedly by different investigators is the scientific community likely to regard it as firmly established.

objectivity The requirement that scientific knowledge not be distorted by the investigator's preconceptions.

reliability The scientific requirement that when the same behavior is measured on two or more occasions by the same or different observers, the measurements be consistent with each other.

replicability The scientific requirement that other researchers can use the same procedures as an initial investigator did and obtain the same results.

Of the criteria of scientific evidence, validity is in certain respects the most important. **Validity** means that the data being collected actually reflect the phenomenon that the researcher is attempting to study. A study may meet all the other criteria—it may be objective, reliable, and replicable—but still may not meet the criterion of validity, in which case it is of no value. Imagine, for example, a study of infant intelligence. The researchers may be using a particular scale to measure intelligence that is not biased by the researcher's preconceptions (it is objective), that produces the same results when given under similar conditions or when scored by different raters (it is reliable), and that can be used by other researchers to yield the same results (it is replicable). However, imagine that the scale used to measure intelligence is based on hair color. Obviously, hair color has no bearing on intelligence, so the study lacks validity and has no meaning, even though the other criteria have been met. Our example is extreme for purposes of illustration. A vast array of other examples that developmental scientists deal with regularly are much more subtle and controversial. There are, for example, researchers who claim that many laboratory studies of development lack validity because laboratory conditions are artificial and foreign to children's experience. Memory development, they might argue, is best studied in the everyday contexts in which it is used—contexts in which, for example, children remember their phone number or their friends' birthdays or their favorite team's vital statistics—not in sterile laboratory conditions in which they are required to memorize lists of random digits.

Methods of Data Collection

Over the past century, developmentalists have refined a variety of methods for gathering information about the development of children. Among the most widely used have been *naturalistic observations, experiments,* and *clinical interviews.* (For a research method that has come to the fore more recently, see the box "Observing the Living Brain.") No single method can answer every question about human development. Each has a strategic role to play, depending on the topic and the goal of the researcher, and each has its advantages and disadvantages (Table 1.5). Often researchers use a process called *triangulation,* in which two or more methods are combined to confirm their conclusions.

table **1.5**

Methods of Data Collection			
Method	Description	Advantages	Disadvantages
Naturalistic observation	Observing and recording the behavior of people in the course of their everyday lives	Direct way to gather objective information revealing the full complexity of behavior	People might behave differently under observation; expectations may shape observations; information may be lost or time-consuming to analyze
Experiment	Introducing a change in a group's experience and measuring the effects of the change	Best method of testing causal hypotheses	People may behave differently in the experimental setting, distorting the validity of the results
Clinical interview	Asking questions tailored to the individual	Possible to probe the child's way of thinking, in order to discover patterns	Reliance on verbal expression makes the method inappropriate with very young children

Observing the Living Brain

IN THE NOT-SO-DISTANT PAST, THE ONLY way to examine the brain was to surgically remove it from the skull. Neuroscientists, who study the brain and the rest of the nervous system, have been conducting postmortem research for more than a century in an effort to discover how the brain is designed, how it changes as we grow and age, and how it responds to injury. Although this research has generated a wealth of information on the anatomy of the brain, it has not revealed much about the functions of the living brain and their links to behavior (Anderson, Damasio, & Damasio, 2005). The recent development of brain-imaging techologies has begun to supply scientists with that information (Nelson, Moulson, & Richmond, 2006).

One such technology is magnetic resonance imaging (MRI), which allows scientists to see brain structures in living patients. A scan using magnetic fields and radio waves provides input to a computer that converts the data into a three-dimensional image of the brain. The MRI has led to important advances in understanding the development and functions of different structures of the brain (Choudhury, Charman, & Blakemore, 2009). For example, MRI technology has lead to fascinating insights into brain development during adolescence, particularly with regard to how changes in the frontal cortex, which is associated with higher levels of reasoning and decision making, may affect a number of behaviors, including risk taking. In addition, MRIs have aided in the early diagnosis of certain disorders, ranging from brain tumors to attention deficit/hyperactivity disorder (ADHD) and childhood psychosis (Serene, Ashtari, Szeszko, & Kumra, 2007; Rapoport et al., 2001). More recent technologies, including positron emission tomography (PET) scans and functional magnetic resonance imaging (fMRI) scans, have enabled neuroscientists to track the ebb and flow of brain activity under different experimental or disease conditions.

Neuroscience has been described as the "rising star" of developmental science, partly because of its contribution to the nature–nurture debate (Miller, 2002). For example, Helen Neville (2005) studied the brains of deaf children and found that areas of the brain typically devoted to processing auditory information gradually shift their function to the processing of visual information. Likewise, in blind children, areas of the brain that would normally process visual information shift their function to auditory processing. Neville's work demonstrates how the brain responds and adapts to different forms of sensory experience.

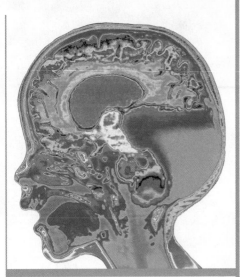

Mehan Kulyk / Photo Researchers

This brain scan of an 11-month-old child clearly reveals a large kidney-shaped cyst (the large red area) in the center of the baby's cerebral cortex. Seeing the cyst helps developmentalists to pinpoint its location and size and determine if surrounding brain structures are injured. Developmentalists then use this information to devise a plan for treating the child.

Naturalistic Observation The most direct way to gather objective information about children is to study them through **naturalistic observation**, that is, to watch them in the course of their everyday lives and record what happens.

For example, in a study of the role of play in the lives of young Mayan children in a remote farming village in southeastern Mexico, Susan Gaskins (1999) made "spot observations," recording what the children were doing at different times of the day in order to make sure that she captured the full range of their activities. She found that compared with children in the United States, young rural Mayan children spend a great deal of time observing the routine activities of adults and that at an early age they begin to take an active role in daily chores—gathering wood, hauling water, and helping to prepare food. As a result, Mayan children spend considerably less time engaged in pretend play, which is perhaps the dominant activity of young children in industrialized societies.

A special form of naturalistic observation is **ethnography**, which attempts to go beyond children's naturally occurring behaviors to explain the *meanings* of those behaviors in light of the customs, beliefs, and values of their culture. For example, researchers have documented how young infants born to the Efe foragers of the Congo's Ituri forest are routinely cared for by many people and are likely to be nursed by several women (Ivey, 2000). This pattern, which seems so at odds with Western ideas about child-rearing, is essential to the Efe's foraging way of life and is accepted by Efe children as natural (Ivey, 2000). For the Efe, as well as all other

naturalistic observation Observation of the actual behavior of people in the course of their everyday lives.

ethnography The study of the cultural organization of behavior.

Russell Gordon / Danita Delimont

Because Mayan children spend so much time helping adults with chores, they rarely engage in pretend play. However, as illustrated by the two Mayan girls above, children have ways of being playful, even when working.

cultural groups, nursing is not just a behavior that feeds an infant; it is a meaningful activity that expresses cultural customs and patterns of life (see Chapter 4 for a more detailed discussion of the relationship between culture and infant feeding practices).

Like all methods of data collection, observational research has limitations. It has been demonstrated, for example, that when people know they are being watched, they often behave differently than they normally would (Hoff-Ginsberg & Tardiff, 1995). In addition, despite their best intentions to be objective, research observers often have expectations about what they are going to see and may observe selectively in accordance with those expectations. Another limitation is that an observer cannot write down everything, so information is inevitably lost. Some studies therefore use prearranged note-taking schemes to specify what to look for and how to report it. Recordings of behavior on videotape or film can help preserve information, but they are extremely time-consuming to analyze. Despite their limitations, observational studies are a keystone of child development research and a crucial source of data about children's development.

Experiments A psychological **experiment** is used to study cause–effect relationships; that is, how changing one factor or variable (the *independent variable*) causes a change in another factor or variable (the *dependent variable*). Often the independent variable takes the form of a treatment condition or intervention, and the dependent variable takes the form of some behavioral change. To ensure that the change in the dependent variable is in fact caused by a change in the independent variable, and not some other extraneous factor, researchers randomly assign individuals to two different groups. One group, called the **experimental group**, is exposed to the treatment condition; the other, called the **control group**, is not. The two groups are then compared on the dependent variable(s) of interest to determine the effects of the independent variable.

Suppose, for example, that a researcher is interested in whether observing friendly behavior in others can increase children's friendliness. To test the hypothesis, the researcher could go to a school, give all fourth-graders a test of friendliness, and randomly assign each child into either the experimental group, which will view a film of children engaged in friendly interactions, or the control group, which will view a film of children engaged in solitary reading. After a predetermined period of time, the children will again be given the test of friendliness. If the researcher's hypothesis is correct, then the experimental group of children should show significantly higher friendliness scores on the second test than they did on the first test. In contrast, there should be no change in the test scores of children in the control group.

Another example of how developmentalists can apply the experimental method is provided by a study that tested the hypothesis that premature babies kept in skin-to-skin contact with their mothers—a practice dubbed "kangaroo care"—develop more successfully than premature babies kept in bassinets. The latter practice is currently the most common way of caring for premature newborns in locales where sophisticated incubators and highly trained nursing are scarce.

In this study, Nathalie Charpak and her colleagues (Charpak et al., 2001) worked with 764 low-birth-weight infants in a Colombian hospital serving primarily poor and working-class mothers. The infants had weighed 4.5 pounds (2000 grams) or less at

experiment In psychology, research in which a change is introduced into a person's experience and the effect of that change is measured.

experimental group The group in an experiment whose experience is changed as part of the experiment.

control group The group in an experiment that is treated as much as possible like the experimental group except that it does not participate in the experimental manipulation.

birth and by definition were at risk for a variety of developmental problems. Half of the infants were randomly assigned to the experimental group, which received kangaroo care. The other half were assigned to the control group, which received the traditional care of being placed in a bassinet in warm, sanitary conditions.

In the short term, the babies assigned to the experimental group showed more regular breathing and quicker mastery of breast feeding compared with babies in the control group. In the long term, the experimental-group babies showed significantly shorter hospital stays, less likelihood of illness or death, and faster growth rates. They were also quicker than the control group to reach important developmental milestones, such as raising their head spontaneously while lying on their stomach. These results help confirm the benefits of kangaroo care, which is increasingly being used in many countries around the world, including the United States (Tessier et al., 2009).

The clear strength of the experimental method is its unique ability to isolate causal factors. (For a discussion of the challenges to determining causation, see the box "Understanding Causes and Correlations.") However, experiments also have limitations. One major drawback is that the very control of the environment that the experiments require may distort the validity of the results obtained. As we noted earlier, people sometimes behave differently in an artificial, experimental situation than they would normally. Children are particularly likely to behave unnaturally in an unfamiliar laboratory setting with researchers they have never met before. This, of course, raises doubts about the value of experimental results. When an experimental setting diverges so completely from children's natural environment that children behave differently than they would ordinarily, the experiment is said to lack **ecological validity**, and the results cannot be put to proper use.

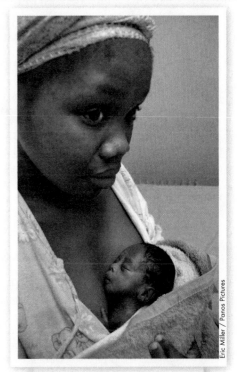

This South African mother is practicing kangaroo care, which, according to experimental research, increases the likelihood that her premature infant will develop normally.

Clinical Interviews Whereas the experimental method is designed to apply uniform procedures of data collection to every person in the study, the essence of the **clinical interview** is to tailor procedures to each individual. For example, each question the researcher asks the participant depends on the answer to the one that precedes it, allowing the researcher to follow up on any given issue or insight that emerges, verify his or her understanding of the participant's responses, and probe more deeply into the participant's thoughts and feelings.

The advantages of the clinical interview are particularly evident in the work of Jean Piaget, whose use of the procedure laid a foundation for an entirely new way of understanding the intellectual development of the child. Piaget's goal was to provide an account of how children's thinking becomes organized over time. In one of his early studies, he used the clinical method to focus on how children's understanding of internal mental processes, such as "thinking" and "dreaming," changes as they grow older. In the examples that follow, note how Piaget adapted his questions to the flow of the conversation:

7-YEAR-OLD
Piaget: . . . You know what it means to think?
Child: Yes.
Piaget: Then think of your house. What do you think with?
Child: With the mouth.

11-YEAR-OLD
Piaget: Where is thought?
Child: In the head.
Piaget: If someone opened your head, would he see your thought?
Child: No.

ecological validity The extent to which behavior studied in one environment (such as a psychological test) is characteristic of behavior exhibited by the same person in a range of other environments.

clinical interview A research method in which questions are tailored to the individual, with each question depending on the answer to the preceding one.

Understanding Causes and Correlations

WHEN A WINDOW SHATTERS AFTER we have thrown a rock at it, we say that the rock caused the window to break. When a light comes on after we have flipped a switch on the wall, we say that the switch (or the electric current it activates) caused the light. **Causation** refers to a relationship in which one event (or factor) depends upon the occurrence of a prior event (or factor). In the physical and mechanical worlds of rocks and windows, switches and lights, causal relationships can be identified with relative ease and certainty. In the developmental and behavioral worlds of children, in contrast, identifying causal relationships presents real challenges.

To see the problem, suppose that children who get good grades (do well on a measure of school performance) also have high IQ scores (do well on a measure of intelligence). It might be tempting to conclude that there is a causal relationship between children's intelligence and their school performance—that

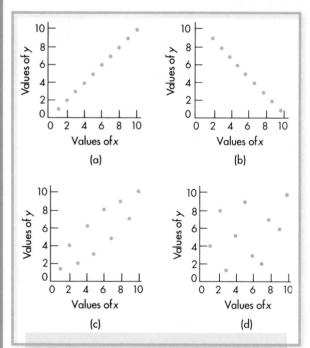

Four possible relationships between two variables: (a) As values of x increase, values of y increase, producing a correlation of 1.00. (b) As values of x increase, values of y decrease, producing a correlation of −1.00. (c) As values of x increase, values of y often increase, but there are some exceptions, producing a correlation of .84. (d) As values of x increase, values of y show a weak but noticeable tendency to increase, producing a correlation of .33.

is, that high intelligence is the prior factor that causes the exceptional school performance. However, another possibility is the opposite causal relationship—that is, working hard to get good grades might cause children's intelligence to rise. Yet another possibility is that some third factor—say, parents providing an intellectually simulating home environment and setting high expectations for academic performance—is causing both children's high intelligence and their school achievement.

As you can see, identifying the causes of behavior and development is not as straightforward as one might expect. Just because two factors occur together does not mean that one caused the other. Indeed, causation is often confused with **correlation**, a relationship in which differences in one factor (intelligence, for example) are associated with differences in another factor (school performance). Although experiments designed specifically to identify causal relationships are used to study children's development (see p. 34), the most frequent type of study by far is one that makes use of correlational methods.

Correlational methods involve measuring two or more factors and then analyzing whether variations in one factor are linked systematically to variations in another factor. If, for example, we are able to measure the quality of a child's relationship with his or her parents, as well as the quality of the child's relationship with peers, we would be able to analyze whether variations (from high to low) in the quality of parent and peer relationships correlate with each other—that is, whether having good (or bad) relationships with parents correlates with having good (or bad) relationships with peers. The degree of association between factors is represented as a **correlation coefficient** (symbolized as *r*), a number that ranges from −1.0 to +1.0 and expresses both the strength (strong or weak) and direction (positive

or negative) of the relationship. When *r* = 1.00, there is a perfect positive correlation between the two factors; that is, when one factor changes, the other factor changes in the same direction. In our example, a perfect positive correlation would exist when children who have good relationships with their parents also always have good relationships with their peers, and children who have bad relationships with their parents also always have bad relationships with peers. When *r* = −1.00, in contrast, there is a perfect negative correlation between the two factors, meaning that as one factor changes in one direction, the other factor always changes in the opposite direction. Thus, a perfect negative correlation between parent and peer relationships would mean that when the parent relationship is good, the peer relationship is inevitably poor, and vice versa. When two factors are uncorrelated, *r* = 0. Correlations, like people, are rarely perfect, and most correlation coefficients fall somewhere between 0 and +1.0 or −1.0, with weak associations producing coefficients that are close to 0 and strong associations producing coefficients closer to +1 or to −1.

Although correlational methods do not identify causal relationships, they do permit predictions, and for this reason they are highly valuable. For instance, correlational methods have generated a wealth of information regarding relationships between infant development and maternal behavior during pregnancy (diet, stress, smoking, etc.). The ability to predict developmental outcomes accurately from knowledge of maternal behavior makes it possible to identify "at-risk" infants and thus to initiate appropriate interventions early on.

causation When the occurrence of one event depends upon the occurrence of a prior event.

correlation The condition that exists between two factors when changes in one factor are associated with changes in the other.

correlation coefficient The degree of association between factors, symbolized as *r* and ranging between −1.0 and +1.0.

[At this point Piaget changes his line of questioning to get at the child's conception of thinking from a different direction.]

Piaget: What is a dream?
Child: It's a thought.
Piaget: What do you dream with?
Child: With the head.
Piaget: Are the eyes open or shut?
Child: Shut.
Piaget: Where is the dream whilst you are dreaming?
Child: In the head.
Piaget: Not in front of you?
Child: It's as if (!) you could see it.

(Adapted from Piaget, 1929/1979, pp. 39, 54)

Piaget's probing interviews of these and other children revealed two age-related patterns of understanding what thinking is. For the younger child, thinking is a bodily process—the act of speaking. You can see it happening. In contrast, the older child conceives of thinking as a mental process, something invisible and unobservable. Piaget used such data to support his contention that children go through stage-like changes in the way they understand and experience the world. He believed that not until the age of 10 or 11 are children able to understand thinking as an internal mental process. Younger children, even when given explicit hints and leading suggestions, are not able to express such an understanding:

5-YEAR-OLD
Piaget: When you are in bed and you dream, where is the dream?
Child: In my bed, under the blanket.
Piaget: Is the dream there when you sleep?
Child: Yes, it is in my bed beside me.
[Piaget writes: "We tried suggestion:"]   Is the dream in your head?
[The child forcefully rejects the possibility]: It is I that am in the dream: it isn't in my head.

(From Piaget, 1929/1979, p. 97)

The strength of clinical interviews is that they allow the researcher to follow, probe, and challenge the child's way of thinking in order to discover developmental patterns. But the clinical interview method has its limitations, most notably its reliance on verbal expression, which makes it inappropriate for use with very young children. This is especially the case in trying to assess children's cognitive abilities, since young children often understand things well before they can explain or even express their understanding.

Research Designs

Before conducting research, developmentalists must not only select a method of data collection but also develop an overall plan. This plan, referred to as the **research design**, describes how the study is put together—who will be included in the study, how and when data will be gathered from them, and how the data will be analyzed. A wide range of designs is used in the social sciences, although developmentalists tend to favor those that are best suited to the complexities of studying age-related change over time.

Here we will describe the four most basic designs that developmentalists use— *longitudinal, cross-sectional, cohort sequential,* and *microgenetic* (in later chapters you will be introduced to a few other designs). As illustrated in Table 1.6, each design takes the passage of time into account in a different way, and accordingly, each has certain advantages and disadvantages.

research design The overall plan that describes how a study is put together; it is developed before conducting research.

table 1.6			
Research Designs			
Design	Description	Advantages	Disadvantages
Longitudinal	Collects information about a group of people over time	Possible to discover patterns of continuity and change over time	Expense; long-term commitment may lead to selective dropout; risk of confounding age differences with cohort differences
Cross-sectional	Collects information about groups of various ages at one time	Relatively less time-consuming and expensive	Disconnected snap-shots, requiring inferences about processes of change; if groups differ other than in age, risk of confounding age differences with those differences
Cohort sequential	Combines longitudinal and cross-sectional approaches by studying several cohorts over time	Age-related factors in change can be separated from cohort factors	To a lesser extent, disadvantages of the longitudinal and cross-sectional designs
Microgenetic	Focuses on development over short periods, especially when children are on the threshold of a change	Provides a record of change, revealing change processes	Limited to changes occurring over short periods of time

The Longitudinal Design The **longitudinal design** collects information about a group of people as they grow older. For example, in a study of the stability of shyness, Jerome Kagan (2001) led a research team at Harvard University that traced the behavior of a group of children from shortly after birth into early adolescence. This study provided evidence that children who are shy and uncertain at 21 months are likely to show similar traits in their behavior at 12 to 14 years of age. Without such longitudinal measurements, it would be impossible to discover if there is continuity in behavior patterns and personality traits as children grow older. Other longitudinal studies have dealt with such varied topics as personality, mental health, temperament, intelligence, language development, and social adjustment (Hussong et al., 2005; Troop-Gordon & Ladd, 2005; Shapka & Keating, 2005).

Because it examines development over time, the longitudinal design would seem to be an ideal way to study development. Unfortunately, several drawbacks of the longitudinal design restrict its use. To begin with, longitudinal studies are expensive to carry out. They also require the researcher's long-term commitment to ventures that can be highly uncertain: Some parents, for example, decide that they do not want their children to continue in a lengthy study, or they may relocate, making it

Longitudinal designs follow the same persons through the years as they age.

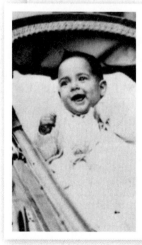

difficult for the researchers to stay in touch with the children for later assessments. Such difficulties may be more common with one social, economic, or ethnic group than with others, resulting in *selective dropout,* which creates a biased sample that can greatly reduce the validity of longitudinal work.

Another weakness of longitudinal designs is that they are at risk of confusing differences related to age with differences related to cohort. A **cohort** is a group of persons who were born about the same time and who are therefore likely to share certain experiences that differ from those of people born earlier or later. In longitudinal research, these shared experiences may actually underlie differences that appear to be related to age. Suppose, for example, that a longitudinal study of the development of children's fears from birth onward began in London in 1932. In their early years, the children in this study would have been living through the economic hardships of the Great Depression. At the age of 9 or 10, many of these children would have lost one or both parents in World War II, and many others would have been sent away from their parents to the countryside in an effort to keep them safe from nightly air-raid bombings of the city. If this study found that the children feared mainly hunger in their early years and later, at around age 9, began to fear losing their parents, it would be impossible to determine whether these age trends reflected general laws of development, true at any time and in any place, or were the result of these particular children's experiences in this particular time and place, or both (Elder, 1998).

The Cross-Sectional Design The most widely used method for studying development is the **cross-sectional design**, which collects information about people of various ages at one time. (Figure 1.6 highlights the basic differences between the

longitudinal design A research design in which data are gathered about the same group of people as they grow older over an extended period of time.

cohort A group of persons born about the same time who are therefore likely to share certain experiences.

cross-sectional design A research design in which individuals of various ages are studied at the same time.

FIGURE **1.6** The difference between longitudinal and cross-sectional research designs.

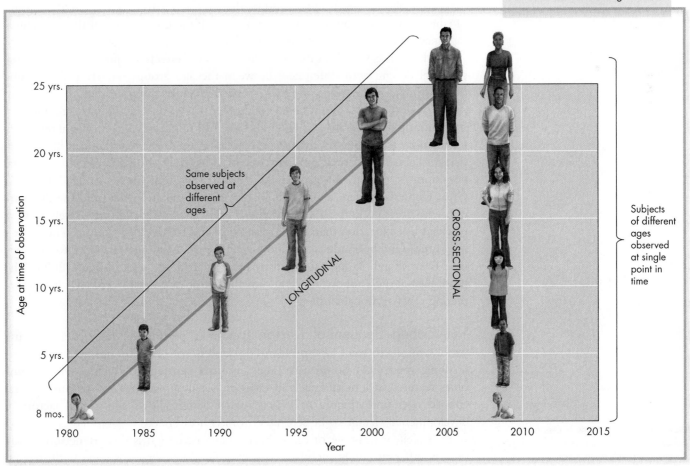

cross-sectional and longitudinal designs.) To study the development of memory, for example, a researcher might test 4-year-olds, 10-year-olds, 20-year-olds, and 60-year-olds to see how well they remember a list of familiar words. By comparing how people in the four age groups go about the task and what the results of their efforts are, the researcher could then make inferences about developmental changes in memory processes. In fact, researchers have carried out a great many cross-sectional studies of memory development demonstrating both quantitative and qualitative developmental changes that we will examine in later chapters.

Because it gathers data on several different ages at once, the cross-sectional design is less time-consuming and less expensive than the longitudinal design. The short time commitment required of the participants also makes it more likely that a representative sample will be recruited and that few participants will drop out of the study.

Despite these advantages, cross-sectional studies also have drawbacks. First, by looking at the behavior of different-age people at one time, cross-sectional studies slice up the ongoing process of development into a series of disconnected snapshots, and this is limiting. For example, although researchers can contrast the general ways in which 4- and 10-year-olds remember a list of words, they cannot gain direct insights into the developmental process by which memory abilities and strategies change over time because their study is not following the same children over time. Consequently, when theorists make inferences about development on the basis of cross-sectional designs, they must engage in a good deal of extrapolation and guesswork about processes of change.

A second drawback to the cross-sectional design is that, for studies to be properly conducted, all relevant factors other than age must be kept constant. That is, the makeup of all the age groups should be the same in terms of sex, ethnicity, amount of education, socioeconomic status, and so on. If the groups are not the same, findings may reflect these differences rather than age-related change.

In addition, as with longitudinal studies, cohort effects are possible in the cross-sectional design, with differences between the age groups reflecting the groups' different experiences rather than age-related changes. Suppose that, in a study of memory development conducted in 2000, 70-year-olds performed significantly more poorly than did 20-year-olds. These results might reflect a universal tendency for memory to decline with age, but they also might reflect differences in the participants' childhood nutrition. Early nutrition has been shown to affect intellectual development (Pollitt, 2001), and the 70-year-olds who were young during the Great Depression were likely to have had poorer nutrition than did the 20-year-olds who grew up in the 1980s. Furthermore, the 70-year-olds were likely to have received less education than the 20-year-olds and to have been out of school for a long time—and both education and practice committing new material to memory have been shown to increase performance on memory tests (Rogoff, 2003). The possibility of such cohort effects means that great care must be taken when interpreting cross-sectional studies.

The Cohort Sequential Design Resources permitting, researchers can use various means to minimize problems associated with the longitudinal and cross-sectional approaches. Some have used a **cohort sequential design**, which combines features of longitudinal and cross-sectional approaches by studying several cohorts over time (Figure 1.7). This mixed design allows age-related factors in developmental change to be separated from cohort effects.

An excellent example of the cohort sequential design is Vern Bengtson's study of how different family members as well as family generations cope with stressful

cohort sequential design A research design in which the longitudinal method is replicated with several cohorts.

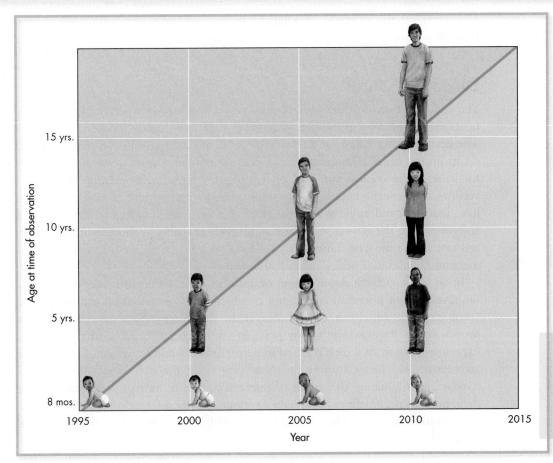

FIGURE 1.7 By combining features of longitudinal and cross-sectional approaches, the cohort sequential design allows researchers to distinguish between developmental effects and cohort effects.

life transitions such as aging, divorce, and remarriage, and changes in work and the economy (Bengtson, 2005). The study began in 1971 with 300 families, including grandparents, middle-aged parents, and grandchildren, and now includes great-grandchildren as well. The longitudinal component allows Bengtson to explore how individuals cope with life transitions over time, and the cross-sectional component, in the form of different generations, allows him to examine how these different cohorts adjust to the various transitions.

The Microgenetic Design

To try to get closer to observing change processes, developmentalists sometimes use the **microgenetic design**, which focuses on children's development over relatively short periods of time, sometimes only a few hours or days (Lawrence & Valsiner, 2003; Flynn & Siegler, 2007; Vygotsky, 1978). As a rule, the microgenetic design is used to study children on the threshold of a significant developmental change, such as being able to use a new memory strategy or a new adding strategy (e.g., calculating 6 + 2 by counting up from 6 instead of starting at 1 and counting all the way to 8). If researchers give the children concentrated experience in activities that are thought to facilitate the developmental change in question (such as playing games that involve simple addition), they are sometimes able to observe the change as it actually occurs, thereby learning what factors contributed to it.

Robert Siegler (2005) offers a useful analogy for understanding the advantage of the microgenetic design. Whereas cross-sectional designs provide us with discontinuous snapshots of development, microgenetic designs provide us with a movie, a more or less continuous record of change. In later chapters we will

microgenetic design A research method in which individuals' development is studied intensively over a relatively short period of time.

institutional review boards (IRBs) Groups responsible for evaluating and overseeing the ethical soundness of research practices at an institution.

encounter specific examples of what can be learned about children's development through microgenetic designs.

Ethical Standards

You can see from our discussion above that, in conducting research, developmentalists make a number of important decisions regarding theory, method, and design. The decisions they make have a bearing on the quality and value of their work and on its impact on developmental science. Research, however, is evaluated not only for its scientific quality but also for its ethical soundness. Worldwide, many universities and governmental agencies that conduct research with human participants have **institutional review boards (IRBs)**, which are responsible for evaluating and overseeing the ethical soundness of research practices at their institutions. This was not always the case. Until fairly recently, such decisions were left to the judgment and conscience of the individual scientist.

In no small part, the development of uniform ethical standards was prompted by the revelation of horrific experiments conducted in concentration camps by Nazi German physicians during World War II. In the name of science, thousands of Jewish, Polish, Russian, and Gypsy prisoners were forced to participate in medical experiments, most of which resulted in permanent disability or death. After the war, an international council wrote the *Nuremberg Code,* the first formal international standard for evaluating the ethics of research involving human participants. Since then, numerous guidelines have been developed at the international, national, state, and institutional levels. Most of the ethical guidelines address certain fundamental concerns:

- *Freedom from harm.* Above all, scientists need to ensure that study participants will not be physically or psychologically harmed through their involvement.

- *Informed consent.* Participants must voluntarily agree to be in the study. This means that they must be given a reasonable understanding of what their participation entails, and that their participation must not have been forced, coerced, or based on inappropriate incentives (e.g., the offer of money to low-income participants or higher grades to students). With children, "informed" consent becomes more difficult because young children cannot really understand what their participation entails. Usually, parental consent is required, as well as consent from other child advocates, such as school officials.

- *Confidentiality.* Personal information obtained in the course of research must be kept confidential; that is, confined to scientific uses and not made publicly available in a way that might embarrass or harm the participant. Often, investigators will assign code numbers to the participants to ensure the participants' anonymity. However, investigators sometimes uncover a serious problem that threatens the well-being of the participant, as when a child reports abuse or seems suicidal. Under such circumstances, the higher ethic of the participant's welfare requires that the researcher break confidentiality and inform authorities who are in a position to intervene and protect the child.

Freedom from harm, informed consent, and confidentiality are not accomplished easily. This is particularly true in the case of children. For example, what may be psychologically harmful for a 2-year-old is quite different from what might be harmful for a 12-year-old. In recognition of the unique issues involved in conducting research with child participants, a special set of ethical standards has been devised by the Society for Research in Child Development (see www.srcd.org). Institutional review boards in the United States use these guidelines to determine the ethical soundness of all research on children conducted at their universities or agencies.

▲ APPLY :: CONNECT :: DISCUSS

Your little brother brought home the following letter from school. Evaluate the scientific and ethical merits of the study described. Propose an alternative study that will address the issues.

Dear Parent or Guardian:

In response to the mayor's proposal to re-route a major highway past our elementary school, we will conduct a study of the relationship between road noise and learning in our students. With the assistance of Dr. Heezrite of Baloney University, your child, *Jonathan*, has been randomly assigned to the following group:

☑ During a lesson in mathematics, your child will be exposed to unexpected loud noises, similar to truck horn blasts, after which he/she will be given a test covering the content of the lesson.

☐ After a lesson in mathematics, your child will be given a test covering the content of the lesson.

Thank you for your cooperation in our effort to provide the best learning environment for our children.

Sincerely,

The Principal

Looking Ahead

In the chapters ahead, you will encounter many of the basic theories, methods, questions, and issues that we have outlined in this chapter. Across the five broad periods of child development—the prenatal period, infancy, early childhood, middle childhood, and adolescence—we will trace development in the physical, social, emotional, and cognitive domains. You will also come to understand how development throughout each period and within each domain is shaped by the child's interactions in a range of physical, family, neighborhood, and institutional contexts. To help organize the vast diversity of children's development, we will take a *biocultural approach,* emphasizing how biological and cultural processes intertwine over the course of childhood. Through it all, we will remain true to the two goals that have inspired developmentalists for centuries: the quest for knowledge and the desire to improve children's lives and well-being.

SUMMARY

- One of the earliest efforts in the study of child development involved Jean-Marc Itard's work with the Wild Boy of Aveyron. This unusual case posed fundamental questions: To what extent is development determined from birth, and to what extent is it influenced by the environment? What is the role of early experience in shaping development, and can the effects of negative experiences be undone?

Developmental Science

- Developmental science is an interdisciplinary field of study that focuses on the changes that children undergo from conception onward. Its two goals are to understand the basic biological and cultural processes that account for the complexities of development and to devise ways of safeguarding children's health and well-being.

- Developmentalists divide the time between conception and adulthood into five periods: the prenatal period, infancy, early childhood, middle childhood, and adolescence.

- Developmentalists look at the changes children undergo in several closely interrelated domains—social, emotional, cognitive (intellectual), and physical.

- Children's development is profoundly shaped by the contexts in which they live, including physical environments, cultural beliefs and practices, families and peers, neighborhoods and communities, and institutions such as schools and governments.

Children, Society, and Science

- Developmental science emerged and developed within historical and cultural contexts, including that of changing beliefs about children. In medieval Europe, children evidently were considered miniature adults. In the sixteenth century, the Protestant Reformation led to the view of children as willful, sinful creatures whose disobedient acts called for harsh treatment. Nineteenth-century industrialization fundamentally altered family life, education, and work, and these changed conditions contributed to a protectionist view of children and to the rise of developmental science.

- Darwin's theory of evolution sparked scientific interest in children; by the early twentieth century, developmental science had become a recognized field.

The Central Issues of Developmental Science

- Developmentalists' research is focused on four fundamental issues:

  1. *Sources of development.* How do nature and nurture interact to produce development? Developmentalists continue to debate the relative importance of biology and environment.

  2. *Plasticity.* To what degree, and under what conditions, is development open to change and intervention? Plasticity is greatest during sensitive periods.

  3. *Continuity/discontinuity.* To what extent does development consist of the gradual accumulation of small changes, and to what extent does it involve abrupt transformations, or stages?

  4. *Individual differences.* What combination of nature and nurture makes individuals different from one another? To what extent are individual characteristics stable?

Theories of Development

- Theory plays an important role in developmental science by providing a broad conceptual framework to guide the collection and interpretation of facts.

- The grand theories laid the foundation for developmental science, and each covers various domains. The grand theories include:

  - Psychodynamic theories—Freud's theory, in which psychosexual stages are associated with the changing focus of the sex drive, and Erikson's theory, in which psychosocial stages are associated with tasks or crises shaped by social and cultural factors.

  - Behaviorist theories, which focus on development through learning, emphasize behavioral changes resulting from the individual's forming associations between behavior and its consequences.

  - Piaget's constructivist theory, in which children, by striving to master their environments and searching for fits between their existing schemas and new experiences, progress through universal stages of cognitive development.

  - Vygotsky's sociocultural theory, which focuses on the role of culture in development and on children learning through finely tuned interactions with others who are more competent.

- Influential modern theories of development include:

  - Evolutionary theories, which look at how human characteristics contribute to the survival of the species and at how our evolutionary past influences individual development.

  - Social learning theories, which, like behaviorist theories, focus on the learning of associations between behaviors and their consequences but emphasize learning that occurs through the observation of, and interaction with, others.

  - Information-processing theories, which, using computer analogies, look at how children process, store, organize, retrieve, and manipulate information in increasingly efficient ways.

  - Systems theories—dynamic systems theory, which focuses on the development of new systems of behavior from the interaction of less complex parts, and ecological systems theory, which focuses on the organization of the environmental contexts within which children develop.

Methods for Studying Development

- Research—whether basic, applied, or action research—must be designed to meet the criteria of objectivity, reliability, replicability, and validity. Research must also be ethically sound.

- Depending on their topic and goal, researchers use one or more methods of data collection, each with advantages and disadvantages:
    - Naturalistic observation involves watching children in the course of their everyday lives and recording what happens.
    - Experiments consist of introducing some change into a group's experience and measuring the effects of the change on the group's members, who are compared with a similar group that did not undergo the experience.
    - Clinical interviews allow researchers to tailor data collection to each research participant.

- Researchers also use several designs, or overall plans, intended to capture the complexities of age-related change:
    - The longitudinal design studies the same children repeatedly over a period of time.
    - The cross-sectional design studies children of different ages at a single time.
    - The cohort sequential design combines the longitudinal and cross-sectional approaches by studying several cohorts over time.
    - The microgenetic design studies the same children over a short period, often one of rapid change.

Looking Ahead

- Taking a biocultural approach, which emphasizes how biological and cultural processes intertwine, the book will trace development in the physical, social, emotional, and cognitive domains across the periods of childhood.

Key Terms

developmental science, p. 2
preformationism, p. 6
nature, p. 10
nurture, p. 10
plasticity, p. 10
critical period, p. 11
sensitive period, p. 11
continuity/discontinuity, p. 12
developmental stage, p. 12
theory, p. 15
psychodynamic theories, p. 16
behaviorism, p. 18
law of effect, p. 19
constructivist theory, p. 19
equilibration, p. 21
sociocultural theory, p. 21

zone of proximal development, p. 22
evolutionary theories, p. 23
ethology, p. 23
social learning theory, p. 25
information-processing theories, p. 26
systems theories, p. 26
dynamic systems theory, p. 27
ecological systems theory, p. 27
hypothesis, p. 29
objectivity, p. 31
reliability, p. 31
replicability, p. 31
validity, p. 32
naturalistic observation, p. 33
ethnography, p. 33
experiment, p. 34

experimental group, p. 34
control group, p. 34
ecological validity, p. 35
clinical interview, p. 35
causation, p. 36
correlation, p. 36
correlation coefficient, p. 36
research design, p. 37
longitudinal design, p. 38
cohort, p. 39
cross-sectional design, p. 39
cohort sequential design, p. 40
microgenetic design, p. 41
institutional review boards (IRBs), p. 42

Each main section of this book begins with a table, similar to the one shown below, that lists some of the major developments you will learn about in the chapters that follow.

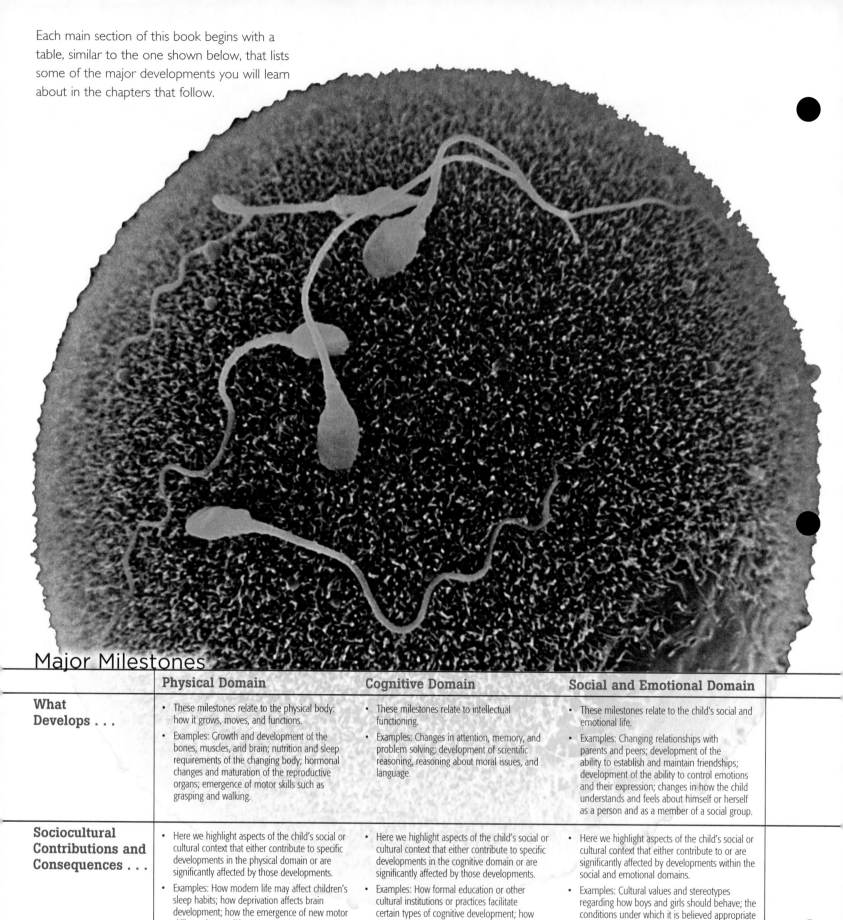

Major Milestones

	Physical Domain	Cognitive Domain	Social and Emotional Domain
What Develops . . .	• These milestones relate to the physical body: how it grows, moves, and functions. • Examples: Growth and development of the bones, muscles, and brain; nutrition and sleep requirements of the changing body; hormonal changes and maturation of the reproductive organs; emergence of motor skills such as grasping and walking.	• These milestones relate to intellectual functioning. • Examples: Changes in attention, memory, and problem solving; development of scientific reasoning, reasoning about moral issues, and language.	• These milestones relate to the child's social and emotional life. • Examples: Changing relationships with parents and peers; development of the ability to establish and maintain friendships; development of the ability to control emotions and their expression; changes in how the child understands and feels about himself or herself as a person and as a member of a social group.
Sociocultural Contributions and Consequences . . .	• Here we highlight aspects of the child's social or cultural context that either contribute to specific developments in the physical domain or are significantly affected by those developments. • Examples: How modern life may affect children's sleep habits; how deprivation affects brain development; how the emergence of new motor skills, such as walking, may require caregivers to modify the child's environment for safety reasons; how the development of breasts or facial hair affects the way others treat the child.	• Here we highlight aspects of the child's social or cultural context that either contribute to specific developments in the cognitive domain or are significantly affected by those developments. • Examples: How formal education or other cultural institutions or practices facilitate certain types of cognitive development; how the social context can affect decision making; how parents and others respond to intellectual growth by providing the child with increasing responsibilities; how cultural values support various forms of moral reasoning.	• Here we highlight aspects of the child's social or cultural context that either contribute to or are significantly affected by developments within the social and emotional domains. • Examples: Cultural values and stereotypes regarding how boys and girls should behave; the conditions under which it is believed appropriate or not appropriate to express particular emotions; cultural support for developing an ethnic or sexual minority identity.

In the Beginning

The development of every human being starts with the formation of a single cell at the time of conception, a cell that carries genetic information stretching across millennia. At the same time, every individual is part of a vast stream of human social life that reaches back through thousands of generations. As a result, every human being is a product of the evolutionary past of our species—a past that includes both biological and cultural aspects.

Science views life as a process involving the constant interplay of forces that create order and pattern, on the one hand, and forces that create diversity and variation, on the other. The interaction of these competing forces is the engine of developmental change for the species.

What forces create order and diversity in human development? In Chapter 2, you will see that part of the answer to that question can be found in our biological and cultural heritages. Order arises, on the biological side, from the fact that all human beings share a finite pool of genetic possibilities, and, on the cultural side, from the fact that we all share general ways of learning, communicating, and forming social relationships. Diversity is ever present in the fact that each human being is genetically unique (except in the case of identical twins) and in the fact that each human develops through a unique sequence of experiences associated with the specific features of the individual's family life, peer relationships, local environments, such as neighborhoods, and cultural values and traditions.

Whereas Chapter 2 focuses on the basic mechanisms of genetic and cultural transmission that enable both order and diversity in the ongoing evolution of our species, Chapter 3 narrows the focus to individual development from conception to birth. The process of prenatal development illustrates many of the basic questions about development discussed in Chapter 1. For example, gene–environment interaction in prenatal development relates to questions about sources of development; changes that distinguish the developing organism 5 months following conception from the organism at 5 weeks or 5 days following conception relate to questions about developmental continuity and discontinuity; critical periods of development, in which the organism is highly sensitive to hormonal secretions and to such external agents as drugs and toxins, relate to questions about plasticity.

After 9 months, during which the organism has grown and been nurtured within the mother's body, chemical changes initiate birth—and a radical transformation of the context of development. From the warm, dark womb, the baby crosses into a much richer and more varied environment, filled with new and constantly changing sights, sounds, and smells, and requiring new ways of moving, sensing, and behaving. Thus the cultural and biological forces that have shaped our species begin to orchestrate the development of a single individual, assuring that the newly born infant, while becoming like all other members of the species, will also be unique.

2

Biocultural Foundations

Inheriting Culture

The Tools of Culture

Processes of Cultural Inheritance

The Complexity of Culture

Biological Inheritance

Genes and Traits

Evolution's Process of Natural Selection

Genetic Inheritance Through Sexual Reproduction

Laws of Genetic Inheritance

Mutations and Genetic Abnormalities

The Phenotype: From Genes to Traits

Heritability

Genotypes, Phenotypes, and Human Behavior

The Coevolution of Culture and Biology

Lactose Tolerance

Sickle-Cell Anemia

Retracing the Laetoli Footsteps

The volcano to the east was active. Its fires dominated the night sky and held the African savannah woodland in an eerie twilight. By day, the sun barely penetrated the thick fog of smoke and ash, and the details of the landscape were muted by inches of ash that had settled on everything. Then a light rain fell, turning the ash underfoot into a firm, moist clay. Across this surface moved several figures—short, sturdy gray ghosts, their fur caked with ash, surveying the world through dark eyes set deeply under thick, protruding brows. The footprints the passersby left behind hardened and were preserved and obscured by the falling ash of the volcano's continuing eruptions. They remained hidden for 3.5 million years, until they were uncovered by natural erosion and then discovered by a paleontologist named Andrew Hill (Leakey & Hay, 1979).

The discovery of these footprints at the Laetoli site in Tanzania is one of archeology's most fascinating finds (Figure 2.1). As any criminologist will tell you, footprints can provide crucial information about the people who left them. Here is what we know about those who left the famous Laetoli prints. Two individuals walked side by side at an unhurried pace. One was about 4 feet tall (1.2 meters) and weighed about 62 pounds (28 kilograms); the other was about 4 feet 8 inches (1.4 meters) and weighed approximately 100 pounds (45 kilograms). Perhaps they were adults, or perhaps an adult and a child. The smaller of the two apparently was burdened on one side by a small load (an infant?). At one point, the larger individual turned east, toward the volcano, and then continued on with his or her companion. According to some analysts, there are traces of what may have been a child walking in the prints of the larger two. The most striking feature of the footprints is their resemblance to those of humans: They reveal a forward-pointing great toe, a well-rounded heel, a pronounced arch, and a striding bipedal gait. In short, the makers of these footprints walked upright, much as we do.

Although it is impossible to determine exactly *who* the walkers were, there is little controversy about *what* they were—members of the small-brained, apelike hominid species *Australopithecus afarensis,* the same species that produced Lucy, the celebrity skeleton discovered in Ethiopia that has helped scientists piece together our human evolutionary past. *A. afarensis* lived from about 4 million years ago until about 3 million years ago and may be one of the most ancient ancestors of our species. Recently, a team of Ethiopian scientists undertook a painstaking process of unearthing another remarkable find—a nearly complete fossil of an *A. afarensis* infant that confirms what scientists have inferred from the Laetoli footprints and from bone fragments: *A. afarensis* had lower limbs much like ours and were capable of walking upright. Their upper body and upper limbs, however, had many apelike characteristics, including broad shoulders and long curving fingers that would have made them effective tree climbers.

Thinking about the baby fossil and the individuals who left their footprints in volcanic ash 3.5 million years ago raises a host of questions that extend well beyond an interest in their physical bodies. Were these ancestors of humans generally

The illustration of a female *Australopithecus afarensis* carrying an infant is consistent with archeological evidence provided by the Laetoli footprints and skeletal remains of this ancient hominid species.

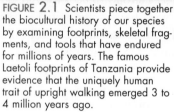

FIGURE 2.1 Scientists piece together the biocultural history of our species by examining footprints, skeletal fragments, and tools that have endured for millions of years. The famous Laetoli footprints of Tanzania provide evidence that the uniquely human trait of upright walking emerged 3 to 4 million years ago.

peaceful or aggressive, solitary or sociable? If sociable, did they live in extended or nuclear family groups? How did they communicate with each other? How did they care for their young? How did they acquire and prepare their food? What risks did they face, and how did they protect themselves? How did they think? What emotions did they feel? And how, from these early beginnings, did biological and cultural processes lead to modern humans and to the developmental path we take from childhood to adulthood?

This chapter will focus on the biocultural foundations of children's development—foundations that were laid in distant times and have left little but bone fragments, cave paintings, primitive tools, and an occasional footprint from which we try to piece together the cultural and biological history of our species and how it is contained within each one of us. As you will discover, understanding these foundations can tell us a great deal about how and why all children tend to follow similar paths of physical, intellectual, social, and emotional development. Indeed, the fact that they do so is something of a miracle when you consider the wildly different and fluctuating environments in which children grow up. Pierre lives in Paris, France; Apatite lives in a Pygmy hunter-gatherer group in the Ituri forest of South Africa. These two children move through their worlds in similar bodies, use language and tools, solve complex problems, and develop social relationships and strong, lasting emotional attachments. Notwithstanding these commonalities, Apatite and Pierre also are different from each other in notable ways—from their height and skin color to the languages they speak, the specific skills they learn, the cultural values and beliefs they adopt, and the types of knowledge about the world they acquire. As you will learn in this chapter, in addition to giving us insight into those aspects of development that all children share, an understanding of the biocultural foundations of children's development sheds light on the sources and significance of developmental diversity.

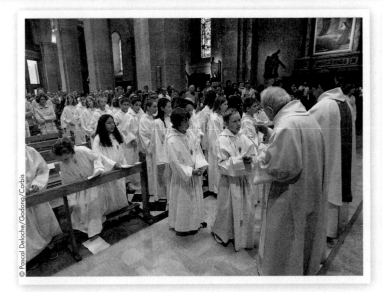

These two photographs record dramatically different cultural rituals in vastly different parts of the world: Holy Communion in France, and a Mbuti pygmy initiation ceremony in the Congo's Ituri forest. The biocultural foundations of children's development include aspects of diversity as well as features that are universal to all members of our species.

We begin this chapter by defining and discussing human culture and how it is inherited by each child. We then address the child's genetic heritage and its expression in the particular traits and behaviors the child develops over time. Throughout our discussion, you will see how culture and biology interact in the life of the child, contributing both to the universal pathways of development shared by all children and to the diverse developmental patterns that unfold in relation to the particular circumstances and life experiences of each individual child.

Inheriting Culture

Years ago, a team of researchers traveled to a small island in Japan to study macaque monkeys. Their work was difficult because the monkeys spent so much time in the forest, where they were hard to observe. In order to lure the macaques into open space, the researchers scattered sweet potatoes on the beach. The bribe worked well, but more remarkably, this seemingly innocent ploy initiated a cascade of new behaviors that entirely changed the monkeys' patterns of daily life. First, a young female named Imo began to wash her potatoes in a nearby stream (apparently, she objected to the dirt that clung to them). Before long, her potato-washing behavior was picked up by other individuals in the group. As more time passed, the monkeys began washing the potatoes in the sea, rather than carrying them to the stream, and would even bite the potatoes first, presumably so the salt would penetrate and season them better (Figure 2.2).

FIGURE 2.2 This Japanese macaque is washing sand from a sweet potato, a practice that has become part of the culture of everyday life for macaques on Koshima Island.

There were other effects as well, and this is where the story gets really interesting. Mothers would carry their babies with them when they went to the sea to collect and wash the food. The babies began to play in the water—swimming, jumping, and diving. The males tended to hang out at the beach but did not participate much in the food preparation activities. They did, however, begin to eat fish discarded by the local fishermen and later began to collect fish and octopi from pools.

culture Material and symbolic tools that accumulate through time, are passed on through social processes, and provide resources for the developing child.

material tools Cultural tools, including physical objects and observable patterns of behavior such as family routines and social practices.

symbolic tools Cultural tools, such as abstract knowledge, beliefs, and values.

Thus, the simple act of washing dirt from a sweet potato led to an entirely new pattern of life—a pattern that persists to this day. And while baby macaques from this small Japanese island learn how to wash their food and play in water, human observers of their activities are learning much about the meaning of culture and how it influences development.

In simple fashion, the story of the macaques highlights the fact that culture is rooted in everyday activities such as acquiring and preparing food, caring for children, and children's play. It also shows that these activities are interconnected and organized over time, forming complex networks: Once the macaques were drawn out of the forest where they had previously spent most of their time, a whole range of activities gradually emerged related to the beach and the water. But while many developmentalists are willing to grant that nonhuman primate species, including macaques, have evolved some of the rudiments of culture, it is clear that the human species is highly distinctive in how it has developed culture and the means by which it passes culture on to subsequent generations. Although there is a lot of debate about how to best define **culture**, most developmentalists agree that it consists of *material and symbolic tools that accumulate through time, are passed on through social processes, and provide resources for the developing child* (Cole, 2005; Rogoff et al., 2007; Valsiner & Rosa, 2007). In the following sections, we will explain the meaning of this complex definition.

The Tools of Culture

Several nonhuman primate species are known to use tools of various sorts to reach food, to use for grooming, or to wield as weapons, and it has even been reported that some have *made* tools (Savage-Rumbaugh, Toth, & Schick, 2007). However, no other species even remotely compares to humans in the complexity of their tools and the extensiveness of their tool use. We are indeed a remarkable species in the extent to which tools and technology organize our behavior and modify our relationship to the environment. The briefest reflection should enable you to realize how infused with tools and machines your life is. In fact, there is probably not a moment in the day when you are not using or being affected by them.

Developmentalists recognize that all cultural tools include two principle features: the *material* and the *symbolic* (Cole, 2005) (Table 2.1). Although all tools

Participating in a documentary focused on cultural differences, these two families—one from Japan, the other from Mali—have assembled all their material possessions in front of their homes. As you can see, the material tools of culture reflect enormous differences in how the two families spend their time.

table 2.1

Examples of Cultural Tools

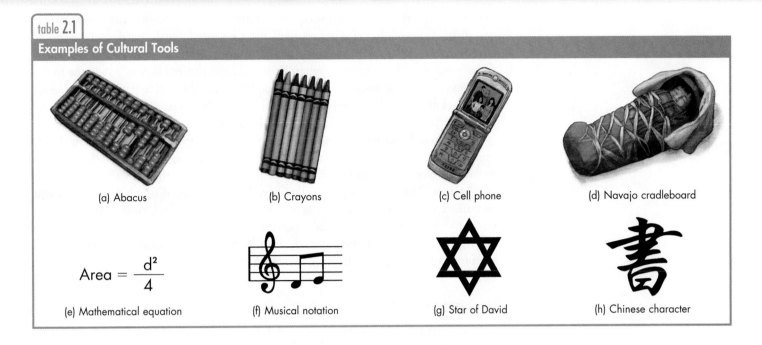

(a) Abacus (b) Crayons (c) Cell phone (d) Navajo cradleboard

$$\text{Area} = \frac{d^2}{4}$$

(e) Mathematical equation (f) Musical notation (g) Star of David (h) Chinese character

contain both features, developmentalists may refer to **material tools** when the focus is on *physical objects* (everything from abacuses and Androids to zithers and Zipcars) or on *observable patterns of behavior,* such as family routines (how children are "put to bed," how the family organizes dinnertime) and social practices (how children are educated, how they celebrate their birthdays). The environment of each and every child is saturated with material tools, which vary from one culture to the next. Born in the countryside of Japan, Kojima lives in a small house with paper walls (shoji screens) separating the rooms. As an infant, he is tightly wrapped in swaddling clothes and sleeps on a mat with his parents; he will never be placed in a crib. During mealtimes, he will not be put in a high chair or use a "sippy cup" but will sit in his mother's or older sister's lap and be helped to use "adult" eating utensils. His mother will never use an electronic baby monitor to keep tabs on him during his naptime but will carry him on her back most of the day while she works in the house and the garden. Clearly, the material tools of Kojima's culture influence his behavior and how he interacts with others (Jenkins, 1998; Enfield & Levinson, 2006).

In contrast to focusing on the concrete, material aspects of tools, developmentalists may refer to **symbolic tools** when they want to explore how abstract knowledge, beliefs, and values affect development. For example, Kojima will spend much of his time in school learning mathematics, a symbol system that he ultimately will use in a variety of ways—from measuring the wood for a new tool shed to eventually keeping the books for his family's business. Kojima will also learn his culture's expectations for masculinity and sexuality, including how certain ways of acting and speaking symbolize that he is "male." Raised within the Shinto spiritual tradition, he will come to believe that nature is sacred, that family should be honored, and that physical cleanliness is essential to the purity

This father and son are participating in a Shinto festival. One of the rituals involved in the day-long festival requires fathers to carry their 1- to 3-year-old sons over a steep and difficult mountain pass. It is said that as they participate in the rituals, the boys will become messengers of the local mountain deity.

Everett Kennedy Brown/epa/Corbis

of spirit. All of these symbolic tools of Kojima's culture—mathematics, gender expectations, religious belief systems—will affect his intellectual, social, and emotional development. As should now be clear, all tools of culture are material and symbolic at the same time. For example, when Kojima accompanies his family to bathe in the river several times a week, he is both engaging in an observable pattern of behavior (an aspect of material culture) and expressing his belief that, as he cleanses his body, he is purifying his spirit (an aspect of symbolic culture).

The material and symbolic tools of a culture have pronounced effects on development because they *organize children's activities and the way they relate to their environments*. Developmentalists call the organization of activity through the use of tools **mediation**. The idea that material and symbolic tools mediate children's behavior and affect their development is at the heart of debates that range from whether violent video games promote aggressive behavior and Barbie dolls promote poor body image to whether the increase in students' disruptive classroom behavior is a symptom of a culture's collapsing educational values.

Processes of Cultural Inheritance

When developmentalists say that material and symbolic tools accumulate over time and are passed on through social processes, thus providing resources for the developing child, they are making claims about how culture is transmitted and transformed from one generation to the next (Rogoff et al., 2007).

Social Processes of Cultural Inheritance Children inherit culture—that is, they learn to use their culture's material and symbolic resources—through several *social processes*. The most basic of these processes is **social enhancement**, in which children use cultural resources simply because the activities of others have "enhanced" the immediate environment by making these resources available (Richerson & Boyd, 2005). For example, when 18-month-old Tahira, who has never seen a crayon before, finds one on the family room floor and rubs it on the wall, she is learning through social enhancement that crayons are tools for marking surfaces. The other two processes through which children inherit culture are more complex forms of learning. When children learn by observing and copying the behaviors of others, they are using the social process of **imitation**, which we will describe in more detail in later chapters. When children are purposefully taught to use the material and symbolic resources of their culture, they are learning by **explicit instruction**.

Explicit instruction is the most complex way of inheriting culture, for two related reasons. First, unlike social enhancement and imitation, explicit instruction uses *symbolic communication*. The most obvious examples of symbolic communication are written and spoken language, but it also includes drawing, art, and music. Second, because it uses symbolic communication, explicit instruction makes it possible to teach children about things that are not present in their immediate environments. We use history books to teach children about the past; we use stories to teach them moral lessons to apply in the future; we use math to teach children calculations that they later can use to figure everything from how to find the area of geometric shapes to the number of minutes remaining in their cell phone accounts. Without the ability to use explicit instruction, our human culture might not be a great deal different than that of Imo and her clan.

The Special Role of Symbols and Language In addition to making it possible to teach children about things that are not immediately present in the environment, symbolic communication permits the expression of abstract ideas,

mediation The process through which tools organize people's activities and ways of relating to their environments.

social enhancement The most basic social process of learning to use cultural resources, in which resources are used simply because others' activities have made them available in the immediate environment.

imitation The social process through which children learn to use their culture's resources by observing and copying the behaviors of others.

explicit instruction The social process in which children are purposefully taught to use the resources of their culture.

desires, ambitions, and emotions. With astronomical diagrams, for example, we can chart the locations and movement of planets; through music, art, and poetry, we can express an infinite range of thoughts and feelings, both real and imagined; and through our stories and myths, we can learn and convey cultural values and beliefs and an understanding of our relationships to one another and the worlds in which we live. Clearly, symbols and symbolic systems are of tremendous importance to the culture-acquiring child. Symbols in the form of diagrams and stories, no less than video games and pencils, are cultural tools. Like all cultural tools, they mediate children's activities and relationships in ways that are central to the process of development (Wells, 2007).

A striking demonstration of how symbols mediate children's activities is provided in a study of young children's self-control (Carlson, Davis, & Leach, 2005). Three-year-olds are famous for acting on impulse rather than thinking things through. Consider the following example: Maria, a typical 3-year-old, is presented with two trays of candy, one of which plainly has more pieces of candy than the other. She is told to pick one tray, with the caution that the tray she chooses will be given away and that it is the other tray that she can keep for herself. According to a fascinating study conducted by Stephanie Carlson and her colleagues (2005), Maria is very likely to impulsively choose the tray with more candy—and she will continue to do so again and again, even though she sees that her choices leave her with fewer candies. However, Carlson's research suggests that Maria's behavior can be mediated by the use of symbols. In her experiment, the candies were presented in closed boxes instead of on trays (Figure 2.3), with a picture of a mouse placed on top of the box with fewer candies and a picture of an elephant placed on the box with more candies. After being told what the mouse and elephant symbolized (fewer and more candies, respectively), 3-year-olds had little trouble choosing the box with fewer candies. The symbols helped them to control their impulses and to organize their behavior to get what they wanted.

Carlson's research illustrates how symbols mediate young children's behavior in the carefully controlled environment of an experiment. In the real world, symbols and symbolic systems are a pervasive and complex part of children's lives and development.

The Complexity of Culture

There is often a tendency to think about culture as a thing of the past that is simply handed from one generation to the next. As we discussed above, it is certainly the case that culture is transmitted through specific social processes and shapes the development of individuals. However, it is also the case that individuals modify their cultures as they become users of cultural tools in the course of ongoing interactions with the people in their communities. In the words of Barbara Rogoff:

> people of each generation, as they engage in sociocultural endeavors with other people, make use of and extend cultural tools and practices inherited from previous generations. As people develop through their shared use of cultural tools and practices, they simultaneously contribute to the transformation of cultural tools, practices, and institutions" (Rogoff, 2003, p. 52).

In short, cultures continue to evolve because individuals produce *variations* in the material and symbolic cultural tools that they use. This dynamic process of cultural change through variation is known as **cumulative cultural evolution** (Tomasello & Herrmann, 2010).

Developing technologies provide straightforward examples of how cultural resources—in this case, material resources—are modified and accumulate over

FIGURE 2.3 (a) When asked to choose a tray of candy that will be given away, 3-year-olds impulsively choose the tray with more candies. (b) However, when the task is modified so the candies are hidden in boxes, one box with a mouse indicating fewer candies, the other with an elephant indicating many candies, children will choose the box with fewer candies, suggesting that their behavior can be symbolically mediated.

cumulative cultural evolution The dynamic ongoing process of cultural change that is a consequence of variation that individuals have produced in the cultural tools they use.

time. For example, 150 years ago, personal communication was limited to either talking face-to-face or writing and reading letters. The harnessing of electricity in the nineteenth century led to the telegraph and the telephone, and then to the age of computers, fax machines, cell phones, and video conferencing.

In the same way that variations in the material resources of a culture accumulate over time, so too do variations in its symbolic resources—its systems of knowledge, beliefs, and values. In many cultures, social beliefs and values about women, marriage, and family have undergone significant changes over time, as has the scientific understanding of everything from the movement of planets and the nature of light to how the brain works and affects behavior.

The nature of cumulative cultural evolution is an intriguing puzzle for developmentalists. If cultural evolution is all about accumulating new ideas, skills, technologies, and so on, where do these new things come from? According to anthropologists who study both ancient and modern cultures, a key ingredient is the shared knowledge that humans construct in groups (Powell, Shennan, & Thomas, 2009; Kline & Boyd, 2010). In particular, when groups are relatively large, complex, and connected to other groups, new ideas and technologies are more easily sparked, and culture is likely to thrive. On the other hand, when groups are small and isolated, variation is more limited, and culture is likely to stagnate or deteriorate. Michelle Kline and Robert Boyd found evidence supporting this argument when they studied several traditional societies from the islands in Oceania. All of these societies use a variety of tools to gather food from the ocean. Kline and Boyd analyzed the number and complexity of the tools, finding that larger societies had a greater variety of tools compared with the smaller societies.

Significantly, other research has indicated that aspects of culture can be lost when societies become isolated from other groups. Such was the case for Tasmanian societies (Henrich, 2004/2006) that once inhabited a region on the southern coast of Australia. According to archeologists, at least 18,000 years ago, Tasmanians interacted with other Australian Aborigine groups and crafted tools from bones and made special clothing to protect them from the winter cold. Then, 10,000 to 12,000 years ago, glaciers caused the sea level to rise, cutting off Tasmania from the rest of Australia. Across the next several thousand years, the Tasmanian cultural tool kit eroded and became less complex: Coarse stone tools replaced finely made bone tools, impeding the Tasmanians' ability to hunt, fish, and make cold-weather clothing. Joseph Henrich, who conducted the study, argued that the erosion of Tasmanian culture was a direct result of the dramatic reduction in the "pool of social learners" that would have otherwise transformed and transmitted the cultural tool kit to the next generation.

From the rather simple cases of Tasmanian societies and the Oceania islanders, you can imagine the vast possibilities for creative innovation available in large, technologically advanced societies in which the flow of ideas and opportunities for learning new skills are facilitated by modern communications and the ease of travel. Through variations, culture is, in the words of Patricia Greenfield, "constantly reinventing itself through the addition of new ethnic groups to multicultural societies, through changes in educational practices, through widening effects of the mass media, and through transformations in economy and technology" (Greenfield, Suzuki, & Rothstein-Fisch, 2006, p. 655). As you will see below, variation, inherent in culture and essential to cumulative cultural evolution, is also inherent to the child's biological inheritance and is an essential ingredient of biological evolution.

⏏ APPLY :: CONNECT :: DISCUSS

As usual, 3-year-old Star is the first in her family to awaken on this Saturday morning. She grabs her teddy bear, kicks off her Barbie-print covers, climbs out of bed, and pads down the hallway to the kitchen. She puts Teddy on a chair, instructing, "You wait right here, honey, and be quiet." Next, she moves a stepstool to the food cupboard, climbs up, and retrieves a box of cereal. She then takes the cereal and the bear to the family room, where she settles on the sofa and clicks on the TV. The annual MTV Spring Break program fills the screen. Star watches intently, crunching cereal, snuggled up with her bear.

What are some of the material and symbolic tools described in this scene? How do they organize—that is, mediate—Star's behavior? What cultural beliefs, values, and practices might she be learning by using these cultural tools? How might her environment be organized differently to reflect a different set of cultural values and beliefs?

Biological Inheritance

In the preceding sections, we made the point that cultural activities are interconnected and organized over time, forming complex networks. The tradition of washing potatoes in the ocean, for instance, emerged as a thread in a complex web of related cultural changes that involved such things as infant play (swimming) and foraging for food (scavenging from fishers, collecting octopi from pools). Like cultural evolution, biological evolution produces amazing networks in which things often, although not always, go together. As an example, think back to the story of our upright-walking *A. afarensis* ancestors. Walking upright was associated with a pelvic structure and a birth canal that were narrower than those of the knuckle-walking primates that preceded them. Over the several million years following the emergence of upright walking, however, the brain size of hominid species tripled and the skull enlarged considerably (Brunet et al., 2002; Washburn, 2004). Consistent with this interlocking network of changes in locomotion, pelvic structure, birth canal, brain size, and skull size was a change in the length of pregnancy such that infants were born earlier, in a less developed state.

In order to appreciate how this worked, and its implications for modern children's development and behavior, you need to understand two fundamental issues. The first issue concerns how an individual's genetic endowment is actually expressed in all the physical and psychological traits that he or she displays. The second fundamental issue concerns the way that an individual's genetic endowment and corresponding traits enter into the process of evolution. We will address each of these issues in the following sections.

Genes and Traits

Evolution is made possible by **heredity**, the transmission of biological characteristics from one generation to the next. **Genes**—the basic units of heredity—contain instructions that guide the formation of all the individual's traits—both physical traits (sex, skin and eye color, susceptibility to certain diseases, and so on) and behavioral and psychological traits, including how the individual attends to and responds to the environment, communicates with others, and expresses needs and desires.

The fundamental question for developmentalists is how these instructions become expressed. In addressing this question, developmentalists begin by distinguishing between the individual's *genotype* and his or her *phenotype*. An individual's **genotype** is the exact genetic makeup—the particular set of genes—that the individual has inherited. The **phenotype** represents all the observable physical,

heredity The biological transmission of characteristics from one generation to the next.

genes The segments on a DNA molecule that act as hereditary blueprints for the organism's development.

genotype The genetic endowment of an individual.

phenotype The organism's observable characteristics that result from the interaction of the genotype with the environment.

behavioral, and psychological traits that the individual actually develops. The distinction between the genotype and the phenotype is important for three reasons. First, knowledge of an individual's genotype and phenotype comes from different sources of information. Knowledge of the genotype comes from studying the individual's genetic material, whereas knowledge of the phenotype comes from studying the individual's body and behavior. Second, although an individual's genotype and phenotype are related, they do not necessarily coincide. Identical twins, for example, have precisely the same genotype, but their phenotypes—even their fingerprints—are never completely identical, and indeed become increasingly different as the twins age (see p. 61). This is because the phenotype is influenced by the individual's environment, in addition to being influenced by the individual's genotype. Third and finally, the genotype and phenotype enter the process of evolution in distinctive ways, as we discuss below.

Evolution's Process of Natural Selection

Across vast tracts of time, the survival of species, including our own, has been continually threatened by shifting climates and food supplies, natural disasters such as earthquakes and floods, and attacks by other species ranging from microscopic viruses to mighty predators. According to Charles Darwin's famous argument, species survive because of the process of **natural selection**. Through this process, individuals with phenotypes that are adaptive to their particular environmental conditions (that is, whose traits are well fitted to the environment) have an increased chance of surviving and reproducing. In contrast, individuals whose phenotypes are not adaptive either do not survive or are less reproductively successful. (The fact that the odds of survival are greater for species better fitted to their environment gave rise to the well-known phrase "survival of the fittest.") Thus, those who are phenotypically well adapted to their environment are "selected" by natural conditions to survive and reproduce, passing on to the next generation the genotypes that contribute to the development of adaptive phenotypes.

As Darwin described the process, natural selection requires *phenotypic variation,* that is, heritable variations of particular phenotypic traits that have survival value for the individual and species. Consider, for instance, the phenotypic trait of height in trees growing in a crowded forest. Taller trees may get more sun than shorter trees and are therefore likely to produce more seeds (offspring). You can see that, over the course of many generations, trees with genes for more height will greatly outnumber those with genes for less height. Thus, *variations* of phenotypic traits that are adaptive in the existing environmental conditions will increase in the species as a whole while those that are maladaptive will quite literally die out.

The Emergence of Shorter Pregnancies
The phenotypic trait of pregnancy duration provides an excellent example of how this process works. In our species, shorter pregnancies evolved as a part of an integrated network of changes related to bipedalism, a smaller birth canal, a larger brain, and increased skull size. The natural selection process resulting in shorter pregnancies probably went something like this. Genotypic variations among females contributed to phenotypic variations in the length of their pregnancies. Females with longer pregnancies, who consequently gave birth to larger infants, were more likely to be damaged during the birth process, less likely to survive, and therefore less likely to have additional offspring than were females with shorter pregnancies. Likewise, the infants of

natural selection The process through which species survive and evolve, in which individuals with phenotypes that are more adaptive to the environmental conditions survive and reproduce with greater success than do individuals with phenotypes that are less adaptive.

those with longer pregnancies were more likely to be harmed during difficult deliveries, reducing their chances for reaching reproductive maturity. And those that did live to reproduce were likely to have inherited their mothers' genetic tendency for longer pregnancies, placing both themselves and their offspring at greater risk. In contrast, females whose genotypes favored the development of "shorter pregnancy" phenotypes would have given birth earlier to smaller infants. The mothers would have been more likely to survive and have additional offspring who would inherit the genetic tendency for shorter pregnancies. You can see that over the course of thousands of years, even tens of thousands of years, the average length of pregnancy for the entire species would have shortened as natural selection favored this adaptive phenotypic trait from one generation to the next.

In addition to affecting the evolution of physiological processes such as the length of pregnancy, natural selection works on phenotypic traits that are more behavioral in nature. For example, evolutionary theorists argue that our species' behavioral capacities for learning and socialization are due to the natural selection of adaptive phenotypes. It is important to note, however, that arguments regarding the selection of adaptive phenotypes are always tentative, especially in instances involving behavioral phenotypes. In all instances, scientists make inferences about how particular behavioral phenotypes affect the survival of species, inferences that are based on the best available fossil evidence and on the survival value of comparable behaviors in species that are highly similar to humans, such as chimpanzees and bonobos.

You now have a grasp of genotypes and phenotypes, and how together they define the biological foundations of each member of our species. In the sections below, we explore in more detail the processes that determine the formation of individual genotypes and the development of specific phenotypes.

Genetic Inheritance Through Sexual Reproduction

To ask about the process of genetic inheritance is to ask about how an individual's genotype is formed. The *genotype,* you remember, refers to the individual's genetic endowment, which remains constant over the individual's lifetime. An individual's genotype contains information that defines the individual's membership in the human species, as well as information unique to that individual. All of this information is transmitted in the course of sexual reproduction, through the combination of the mother's egg and the father's sperm.

You may remember from your high school biology class that every human sperm and ovum (egg) contains 23 chromosomes and that a **chromosome** is a single molecule of **DNA (deoxyribonucleic acid)**. The DNA molecule takes the form of two long, connected strands that spiral around each other—the famous double helix (Figure 2.4). Every chromosome contains thousands of genes, each of which is a small segment of DNA.

chromosome A threadlike structure made up of genes. In humans, there are 46 chromosomes in every cell except sperm and ova.

DNA (deoxyribonucleic acid) A long, double-stranded molecule that makes up chromosomes.

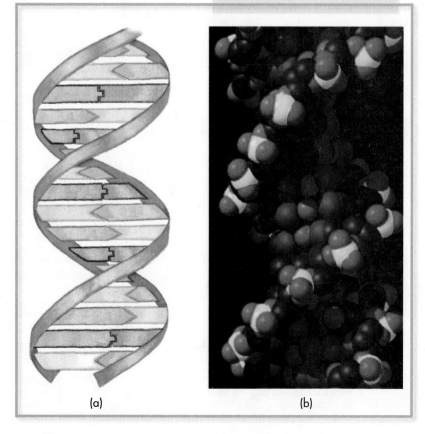

FIGURE **2.4** (a) DNA molecules include two long strands that spiral around each other in a double helix. DNA is a vast database containing all the genetic information a cell will need to develop. (b) A computer-generated, color-coded model of DNA allows researchers to rotate the image and study it from various angles.

(a)

(b)

zygote The single cell formed at conception from the union of the sperm and the ovum.

germ cells The sperm and ova, which are specialized for sexual reproduction and have half the number of chromosomes normal for a species.

somatic cells All the cells in the body except for the germ cells (the ova and sperm).

mitosis The process of cell duplication and division that generates all the individual's cells except sperm and ova.

meiosis The process that produces sperm and ova, each of which contains only half of the parent cell's original complement of 46 chromosomes.

monozygotic (MZ) twins Twins who come from one zygote and therefore have identical genotypes.

dizygotic (DZ) twins Twins who come from two zygotes.

X chromosome One of the two chromosomes that determine sex; in females, both members of the 23rd pair of chromosomes are X, and in males, one member of the 23rd pair is.

Each gene carries a particular set of instructions for manufacturing the proteins that are used to create the body's cells and that control how the cells function. The 23 chromosomes in the ovum carry half the genes necessary for the development of a new individual. The other half are carried by the chromosomes in the man's sperm. When conception occurs, the ovum and sperm fuse to form a **zygote**, a single cell containing 46 chromosomes—23 from the mother and 23 from the father—that are arranged in 23 corresponding pairs. This single cell, with its 23 pairs of chromosomes, is the foundation for all the cells that will ever develop in the individual.

Creating New Cells Our cells are of two types: germ and somatic. **Germ cells** are the sperm and ova, which contain 23 unpaired chromosomes, as described above. **Somatic cells** (or *body cells*) are all the other cells of the body (skin cells, blood cells, bone cells, nerve cells, and so on). Each somatic cell contains 46 chromosomes in 23 pairs, identical to the chromosomes in the zygote. New somatic cells are created through a process called **mitosis**. The process of creating germ cells is called **meiosis**.

Mitosis: A Process of Making New Somatic Cells. The process of mitosis begins with the 46 chromosomes in a cell replicating, that is, producing exact copies of themselves (Figure 2.5). These chromosomes then move to the middle of the cell, where they separate into two identical sets, which migrate to opposite sides of the cell. The cell then divides in the middle to form two daughter cells, each of which contains a set of 46 chromosomes. These two daughter cells go through the same process of replication and division to create two new cells each, which themselves replicate and divide as the process repeats itself again and again.

This process continues throughout the life of the individual, constantly creating new somatic cells and replacing those that die off. Each new somatic cell contains an exact copy of the original 46 chromosomes inherited by the zygote at conception. Thus, under the ordinary conditions of life, our chromosomes and the genes they carry are not altered by the passage of time or by the experiences that shape our minds and bodies; that is, as mentioned earlier, our genotype remains constant.

Meiosis: A Process of Making Germ Cells. Mitosis works very well as a process of creating new somatic cells, each with 46 chromosomes identical to those inherited by the zygote. Germ cells, however, must have only 23 chromosomes each, so that when an ovum and sperm fuse, they create a zygote with 46 chromosomes. This is accomplished through the special cell-division process of meiosis.

In the first phase of this process, the 23 pairs of chromosomes in the cells that produce sperm or ova duplicate

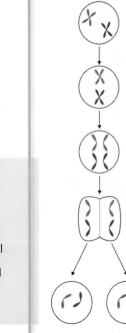

FIGURE 2.5 Mitosis is the process of cell division that generates new somatic cells. First, all the chromosomes in the cell replicate, producing a new set of chromosomes identical to the first. The two sets then separate and the cell divides, producing two daughter cells. Mitosis ensures that identical genetic information is maintained in the somatic cells over the life of the organism.

Somatic cell

Replication of chromosomes

Movement to middle of cell

Chromosomes separate into two identical sets

Chromosomes migrate to opposite sides of cell; cell begins to divide

Cell divides into two daughter cells, each identical to original cell

themselves, just as in mitosis. But then the cell divides not once, as in mitosis, but twice, creating four daughter cells (Figure 2.6). Each of these daughter cells contains only 23 unpaired chromosomes—half the original set from the parent cell. Thus, when the ovum and sperm fuse at conception, the zygote receives a full complement of 46 chromosomes (23 pairs).

Meiosis represents the initial stage of shuffling genetic material from the parent generation to produce new genetic variations in the offspring. Although we receive 23 chromosomes from each of our parents, it is a matter of chance which member of any pair of chromosomes ends up in a given germ cell during meiosis. According to the laws of probability, there are 2^{23}, or about 8 million, possible genetic combinations for each sperm and ovum. Consequently, the probability that siblings will inherit exactly the same genes from both parents is, at best, 1 chance in 64 trillion! This extreme improbability shows the importance of meiosis as a source of variation, a means of introducing new genetic combinations in the species.

There is one exception to the odds of genetic variability—the special case of **monozygotic (MZ) twins**, who come from a single fertilized egg that, for reasons still not understood, divides and develops into two separate individuals. Because they originate from the same zygote, monozygotic twins have identical genetic material, so they potentially could have the same physical and psychological makeup. However, as a result of their encounters with their environments, "identical twins" are never exactly alike in every detail and may even appear far from identical. (Twins who come from two ova that were fertilized at the same time are referred to as **dizygotic [DZ] twins**, or "fraternal twins," and are no more likely to resemble each other than are any other two siblings.)

Sex Determination

Like many other species on the planet, the human species has evolved two sexes—male and female. But what determines whether a given individual is one or the other? In 22 of the 23 pairs of chromosomes found in a human cell, the two chromosomes are of the same size and shape and carry corresponding genes. For chromosomes of the 23rd pair, however, this is not necessarily the case. This pair of chromosomes determines a person's genetic sex. In females, both members of the 23rd pair of chromosomes are of the same type, called an **X chromosome** (Figure 2.7). Males, however,

FIGURE 2.6 Meiosis is the process of cell division that generates new germ cells (in this case, sperm). Like mitosis, meiosis begins with replication of the cell's chromosomes, but the cell then divides twice. The result is sperm cells, each with just 23 chromosomes.

Because they developed from two separate ova, these dizygotic, or fraternal, twins look no more alike than nontwin siblings.

Despite apparently similar environments and identical genetic material, these monozygotic twin boys have distinguishably different facial features. This suggests that an individual's phenotype can be influenced by subtle variations in the environment.

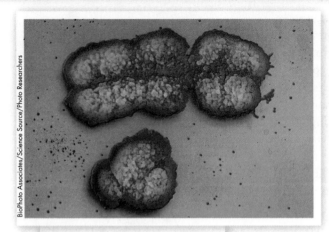

FIGURE 2.7 Human X (above) and Y (below) chromosomes. Note how much larger the X chromosome is. Males have both an X and a Y chromosome, and females have two X chromosomes.

Y chromosome One of the two chromosomes that determine sex; in males, one member of the 23rd pair of chromosomes.

allele The specific form of a gene that influences a particular trait.

homozygous Having inherited two genes of the same allelic form for a trait.

heterozygous Having inherited two genes of different allelic forms for a trait.

dominant allele The allele that is expressed when an individual possesses two different alleles for the same trait.

recessive allele The allele that is not expressed when an individual possesses two different alleles for the same trait.

carriers Individuals who are heterozygous for a trait with a dominant and recessive allele and thus express only the characteristics associated with the dominant allele but may pass the recessive allele, including for a recessive disorder, on to their offspring.

codominance Outcome in which a trait that is determined by two alleles is different from the trait produced by either of the contributing alleles alone.

have just one X chromosome, which is paired with a different, much smaller chromosome, called a **Y chromosome**. Since a female is XX, each of her eggs contains an X chromosome. Since a male is XY, half of his sperm carry an X chromosome and half carry a Y chromosome. If a sperm containing an X chromosome fertilizes an egg, the resulting child will be XX, a female. If the sperm contains a Y chromosome, the child will be XY, a male. The genetic determination of a person's sex is controlled by a single chromosome; however, other aspects of biology and behavior have more complex origins.

Laws of Genetic Inheritance

The laws of genetic inheritance describe several different ways in which genetic material transmitted by parents can be expressed in the child. In the simplest form, a single pair of corresponding genes, one from each parent, contributes to a particular inherited characteristic. A gene that influences a specific trait (for example, the presence or absence of a cleft in the chin) can have different forms. The specific form of a gene is called an **allele**. When the corresponding genes inherited from the two parents are the same allele (both "cleft" or both "uncleft"), the person is said to be **homozygous** for the trait. When the alleles are different (one "cleft" and one "uncleft"), the person is said to be **heterozygous** for the trait.

Whether the allele pairings are homozygous or heterozygous affects the characteristics of the phenotype. If a child is homozygous for a trait that is affected by a single pair of alleles, only one outcome is possible: The child will display the particular characteristics associated with that allele. If a child is heterozygous for such a trait, one of three outcomes is possible:

- The child will display the characteristics associated with only one of the two alleles. In such cases, the allele whose associated characteristics are expressed is referred to as a **dominant allele**, and the allele whose associated characteristics are not expressed is referred to as a **recessive allele**. Even though individuals who are heterozygous for a recessive trait do not express that trait, they are nevertheless **carriers** of the recessive allele, meaning that they can pass the allele on to their offspring. When a child inherits a recessive allele for a recessive trait from both parents, the child will exhibit the trait.

- The child will be affected by both alleles and will display characteristics that are intermediate between those associated with the two alleles. Thus, with skin color, for example, the offspring of a dark-skinned parent and a light-skinned parent may have skin tones in between those of the parents.

- Rather than displaying intermediate characteristics, the child will fully express the characteristics associated with each of the two alleles, an outcome that is called **codominance** (Figure 2.8). For example, children with type AB blood may have a type-A mother and a type-B father. The blood type of each parent is fully expressed in the AB blood type of the child.

It is important to note that although most recessive traits are of little consequence for the health and development of the child (e.g., cleft chin, attached earlobes,

FIGURE 2.8 In this illustration of codominance, Mom's horizontal stripes and Dad's vertical stripes are expressed equally in their youngster's stylish plaid phenotype.

straight hairline), there are a number of recessive disorders that can occur when a child inherits a recessive allele for the disorder from both parents (Figure 2.9). Among these *recessive disorders* are phenylketonuria and sickle-cell anemia, both of which we discuss below (see Table 2.2 for other examples).

It is also important to reiterate that the patterns we have just outlined represent the simplest form of genetic inheritance. Most traits, especially behavioral traits—from empathy and intelligence to aggression and risk-taking—involve **polygenic inheritance**, in which a variety of genes—sometimes a great many—contribute to the development of the phenotype. In addition, some genes can influence a number of traits.

Mutations and Genetic Abnormalities

Sexual reproduction is a fantastic source of genetic diversity in human beings, but it is not the only one. Diversity also arises from **mutation**, which involves an alteration in the structure of an individual's DNA. Mutations can occur for a variety of reasons, including errors in chromosome replication during either meiosis or mitosis and exposure to external agents such as certain chemicals and certain forms of radiation.

When mutations occur in germ cells, the changed genetic information may be passed on to the next generation and, over time, to the human **gene pool**, the total variety of genetic information possessed by a sexually reproducing population. Geneticists assume that spontaneous mutations have been occurring in germ cells constantly and randomly for millions upon millions of years, introducing new genes into the gene pool of every species and providing a source of variation for the process of natural selection.

The fact that mutations are a natural and fundamental part of life does not, however, mean that they usually benefit the individual organisms in which they occur. Most mutations are lethal, rather than adaptive, and in humans and other mammalian species, result in early miscarriage (Biancotti et al., 2010).

It is estimated that about 3.5 percent of all babies are born with some kind of genetic abnormality (Ward, 1994). Some of the more commonly occurring disorders related to genetic abnormalities are listed in Table 2.2. These disorders are of two main types. Some are a consequence of the specific genetic material inherited by the individual by means of normal processes of inheritance. For example, recessive disorders such as phenylketonuria and sickle-cell anemia, as mentioned above, occur through ordinary processes when both parents transmit the relevant allele. The second type of disorder occurs as result of a breakdown in the process of genetic transmission—the normal process of meiosis, for example,

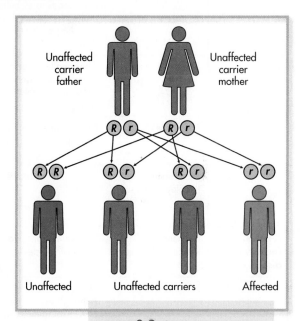

FIGURE 2.9 If both parents carry the recessive allele (*r*) for a disorder, a child who receives that allele from both parents (*rr*) will have the disorder; alternatively, a child may receive the dominant allele (*R*) from both parents (*RR*) and be unaffected, or may receive a dominant and recessive allele (*Rr*) and be unaffected but be a carrier.

polygenic inheritance Refers to the contribution of a variety of genes—sometimes very many—to a particular trait.

mutation An alteration in the molecular structure of an individual's DNA.

gene pool The total variety of genetic information possessed by a sexually reproducing population.

Common Genetic Disorders

	Disorder	Description	Incidence	Prenatal/Carrier Detection?	Treatment and Prognosis
Recessive disorders	Cystic fibrosis	Lack of an enzyme causes mucus obstruction, especially in lungs and digestive tract	1 in 3000 Caucasian births in U.S.; 1 in 17,000 African American births	Yes/Yes	Medications, treatments, diet used to clear airways, loosen mucus, aid digestion. In U.S., most survive into 30s
	Phenylketonuria (PKU)	Inability to metabolize phenylalanine, an amino acid, leads to its buildup in the bloodstream, retarding brain-cell development	1 in 10,000–15,000 U.S. infants	Yes/Yes	Treatment by diet beginning in infancy and continuing throughout life can reduce severity of brain damage and mental retardation
	Sickle-cell anemia	Abnormally shaped blood cells cause circulatory problems and severe anemia	8–9% of African Americans; more than 20% of West Africans	Yes/Yes	Organ damage and severe pain can result. Treatment by medication can reduce symptoms and complications.
	Tay-Sachs disease	Lack of an enzyme causes buildup of waste in brain	1 in 3600 among Ashkenazi Jews in United States	Yes/Yes	Neurological degeneration leads to death before age 4
	Thalassemia (Cooley's anemia)	Abnormal red blood cells	1 in 500 births in populations from subtropical areas of Europe, Africa, Asia	Yes/Yes	Listlessness, enlarged liver and spleen, occasionally death; treatable by blood transfusions
X-linked recessive disorders	Duchenne muscular dystrophy	Weakening and wasting away of muscles	1 in 3500 males under age 20	Yes/Yes	Crippling, often fatal by age 20
	Hemophilia	Blood does not clot readily. Although usually the result of X-linked gene, also occurs by spontaneous mutation	1 in 10,000 live births of males	Yes/Yes, if not spontaneous mutation	Possible crippling and death from internal bleeding. Transfusions ameliorate effects
Dominant disorders	Neurofibromatosis	Nervous system disorder, causing tumors on nerves and other abnormalities. Usually inherited, but 30–50% of cases arise through spontaneous mutation	1 in 3000 births	Yes/Yes, if not spontaneous mutation	Symptoms are highly variable and may include café au lait spots, benign tumors on peripheral nerves, optic nerve tumors, learning disabilities. Treatment by surgery may be possible
Chromosomal disorders	Down syndrome	Extra copy of chromosome 21 results in mental and physical retardation, distinctive physical characteristics, and susceptibility to certain medical conditions	1 in 1000 live births in U.S.	Yes/N.A.	Medical conditions monitored and treated; special education to develop skills and independence. Depending on severity and complications, survival into 60s is possible
	Klinefelter syndrome	Extra X chromosome in males (XXY) results in incomplete development of sex organs and secondary sex characteristics	1 in every 500–1000 males born in U.S.	Yes/N.A.	Treatment by testosterone replacement therapy at puberty can be beneficial. Most lead normal lives, although with increased risk for certain cancers and heart disease
	Turner syndrome	Lack of an X chromosome (XO) in females. Common symptoms include short stature, failure to develop secondary sex characteristics	1 in 2500 females	Yes/N.A.	Growth hormone and estrogen therapies can facilitate growth and development. Most women lead normal lives, but are infertile

is disrupted for some reason, affecting the structure of chromosomes in the germ cell. Various abnormalities can result, such as Down syndrome and Klinefelter syndrome.

Phenylketonuria: A Recessive Disorder *Phenylketonuria (PKU)* is an example of a recessive disorder caused by specific genetic material inherited by the individual through the normal process of genetic transmission. PKU is a particularly debilitating condition that leads to severe mental retardation if it is not treated. It is caused by a defective recessive allele that, when inherited from both parents, reduces the body's ability to metabolize phenylalanine, an amino acid that is highly concentrated in foods such as milk, eggs, bread, and fish. When too much phenylalanine builds up in a baby's bloodstream, brain-cell development is retarded (Enns et al., 2010). About 1 in every 10,000 to 15,000 infants born each year in the United States has PKU, and about 1 in 100 people of European descent is a carrier of the recessive allele (Guttler, 1988). The incidence of PKU is lower among Blacks than among Whites (Connor & Ferguson-Smith, 1993). (For another example of a recessive disorder, see the discussion of GA1 in the box "In the Field: Doctor of the Plain People.")

PKU can be tested for prenatally (Fan et al., 1999), and most states require that all newborns be tested for the disorder. Infants who test positive are treated with diets that are low in phenylalanine. While such treatment significantly reduces the severity of mental retardation, it does not prevent the effects of PKU entirely (Enns et al, 2010). The timing of the treatment is crucial. If phenylalanine intake is not restricted by the time an infant with PKU is 1 to 3 months of age, the brain will already have suffered irreversible damage. Genetic testing can identify people who carry the recessive PKU allele, allowing prospective parents who are both carriers to decide whether they want to risk having a child with the disease.

Down Syndrome: A Chromosomal Disorder In contrast to disorders, such as PKU, that are caused by the inheritance of specific genetic material, Down syndrome is a consequence of a disruption in the normal process of genetic transmission. In the vast majority of cases, it results from an error during meiosis that creates extra genetic material on chromosome 21. Indeed, more than 95 percent of the children born with Down syndrome have three copies of chromosome 21 instead of two. (For this reason, the disorder is sometimes called *trisomy 21*.) The effects of this disorder, which occurs at the rate of about 1 of every 1000 births in the United States, include varying degrees of mental and physical retardation, as well as several distinctive physical characteristics: slanting eyes and a fold on the eyelids; a rather flat facial profile; ears located lower than normal; a short neck; a protruding tongue; dental irregularities; short, broad hands; a crease running all the way across the palm; small curved fingers; and unusually wide-spaced toes. Children with this disorder are more likely than other children to suffer from heart, ear, and eye problems, and they are more susceptible to leukemia and to respiratory infections (Steiner et al., 2005). Although the trigger for the meiotic error that causes Down syndrome is unknown, the disorder is strongly associated with conceptions involving older parents, particularly older mothers (Saltvedt et al., 2005; see Figure 2.10.).

How effectively children with Down syndrome function as they grow up depends not only on the severity of their disorder but also on the environment in which they are raised. Supportive intervention that includes special education by concerned adults can markedly improve the intellectual functioning of some

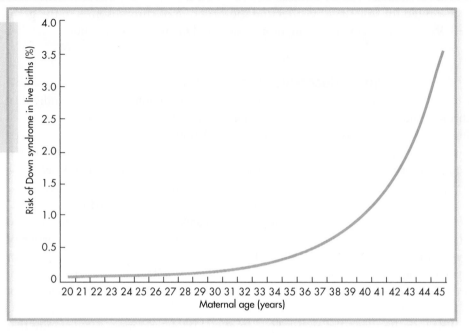

FIGURE 2.10 The risk of Down syndrome is closely associated with maternal age. As shown here, babies born to women in their 20s are highly unlikely to have the chromosomal disorder, whereas the risk rises dramatically for those born to women in their 40s. (Adapted from Newberger, 2000.)

Although this young girl's intellectual development will be limited by Down syndrome, the enriched environment provided at home and school will have a significant impact on what she is able to accomplish as she grows up.

children with Down syndrome, especially when it is begun at an early age (Guralnick, 2005). As you will learn below, even in the case of serious genetic abnormalities such as Down syndrome, variations in the environment can lead to a range of possible phenotypic outcomes.

Klinefelter's Syndrome: A Disorder of the Sex Chromosomes

Half of all chromosomal abnormalities in newborns involve the X and Y chromosomes. Occasionally, a boy is born with an extra X or Y chromosome—that is, with an XXY or XYY genotype. Girls are sometimes born with only one X chromosome (XO genotype) or with three X chromosomes (XXX genotype). Both males and females can be affected by a condition in which the X chromosome, which carries many genes, is brittle and breaks into two or more pieces. Each of these chromosomal abnormalities has different implications for development.

The most common sex-linked chromosomal abnormality is *Klinefelter's syndrome,* the condition in which males are born with an extra X chromosome (XXY). This abnormality occurs in about 1 of every 500 to 1000 males born in the United States (Geschwind & Dykens, 2004). Males who have Klinefelter's syndrome appear to develop normally until adolescence, when they fail to show the typical signs of sexual maturation because they have low levels of testosterone, the hormone that is key to sexual development in males. They do not acquire facial hair, their voices do not deepen, and their sex organs do not develop, making them sterile. In addition, most have speech and language problems and, as a result, have problems in school (Temple & Sanfilippo, 2003).

The most prevalent treatment for Klinefelter's syndrome is to begin testosterone replacement therapy at age 11 or 12, when testosterone levels normally begin to rise in males. The syndrome is not often diagnosed that early, but even if therapy is started later, it can have positive effects. The benefits include increased

In the Field   Doctor of the Plain People

Name:	D. Holmes Morton
Education:	High school dropout; undergraduate degree at Trinity College; M.D. from Harvard Medical School; pediatric residency at Children's Hospital of Boston; genetic researcher at Children's Hospital of Philadelphia
Current Position:	Pediatrician; genetic researcher
Career Objectives:	Understand and treat genetic disorders affecting Amish and Mennonite communities

DR. D. HOLMES MORTON PRACTICES MEDICINE IN the farmlands of Pennsylvania, home to the nation's largest communities of Amish and Mennonites, collectively called the Plain People because of a lifestyle that shuns technology. The traditions of the Plain People include marrying within their communities, which limits opportunities to introduce genetic variation. As a consequence, children of the Plain People are beset with unusually high rates of rare genetic disorders, making their communities of great interest to genetic researchers. Despite their general aversion to modern technologies, the Plain People welcome the assistance of medicines and treatments that can help their children lead healthy, fulfilling lives. And so, using traditional materials of wooden beams and pegs, the Plain People "raised" Dr. Morton's Clinic for Special Children in an alfalfa field. Outside is a hitching post; inside is the most advanced medical machinery available for analyzing children's DNA.

Most of the children treated by Dr. Morton suffer from recessive disorders that interfere with their ability to metabolize proteins, fats, or sugars. An example is GA1, so named because it results in the buildup in the brain of glutaric acid, a by-product of protein. Children who inherit GA1 appear to be healthy at birth. It is only when they contract some common childhood illness like chicken pox or even a common cold that a strokelike event is triggered in their brains, causing severe physical and intellectual damage and sometimes death.

Dr. Morton's research has identified the defective gene responsible for GA1. As with other metabolic disorders, the defect limits the production of an enzyme that the body needs to break down proteins. Dr. Morton has discovered that the best chance of avoiding the most serious health consequences associated with GA1 is for children born with the defect to have the condition diagnosed at birth, before the newborn is nursed or given protein-rich foods, such as milk. Several procedures can be used to diagnose GA1 in newborns, including analyzing urine for high concentrations of glutaric acid. The preferred procedure, however, is to sample amniotic fluid when labor begins and the water breaks. The amniotic fluid contains fetal skin cells that can be used to analyze the baby's genotype. The advantage of this procedure is that GA1 can be diagnosed before the newborn is damaged by ingesting protein.

In addition to developing diagnostic procedures, Dr. Morton has found several ways to keep children with GA1 healthy during the first 2 years of life, when their growing brains are most vulnerable to damage. For example, when children become ill in ways that can trigger strokelike episodes, infusions of sugar can reverse the buildup of toxic glutaric acid in the brain.

Like many scientist–practitioners engaged in applied research, Dr. Morton is committed to creating knowledge that can improve children's lives and development. There are many ways to gauge his success. For example, when he first began practicing medicine in the Amish and Mennonite communities, 95 percent of the children with GA1 suffered devastating physical and intellectual disabilities as a consequence of the disease. Now, in contrast, only 25 percent are severely affected. But the most inspiring measure of his success is found in the exuberant play of healthy toddlers attending the parties that Dr. Morton gives for his 2-year-old GA1 patients. For them, "it truly is a new birth day." (Adapted from Belkin, 2005.)

As a geneticist and physician, Dr. Morton is dedicating his work to improving the lives of children with genetic disorders.

Eugene Richards

phenotypic plasticity Refers to the degree to which the phenotype is open to influence by the environment, rather than determined by the genotype.

canalized A trait that is canalized follows a strictly defined path, regardless of most environmental and genetic variations.

facial and pubic hair, a more masculine distribution of body fat, increased strength and bone density, and increased sexual functioning (Smyth & Bremner, 1998).

The Phenotype: From Genes to Traits

Notwithstanding the enormous power of the genotype to influence human development, the genotype does not account for how development actually takes place for each individual; that is, how all the phenotypic traits and characteristics that together define the individual emerge over time. For example, although Down syndrome substantially affects development, the care and support of family members, as well as educational and vocational services provided in schools and communities, can have an enormous impact on the skills and abilities the individual will acquire.

The most important question that developmentalists ask about the development of phenotypic traits concerns **phenotypic plasticity**; that is, the extent to which traits are determined by the genotype or are open to influence by the environment. In traits with *low plasticity,* such as eye color, the genotype is strongly influential, and the phenotype develops in a highly predictable manner, irrespective of environmental factors. In contrast, in traits with *high plasticity,* the genotype exerts less pressure, so the phenotype is easily influenced by the environment and develops less predictably, as in the case of intellectual skills and abilities.

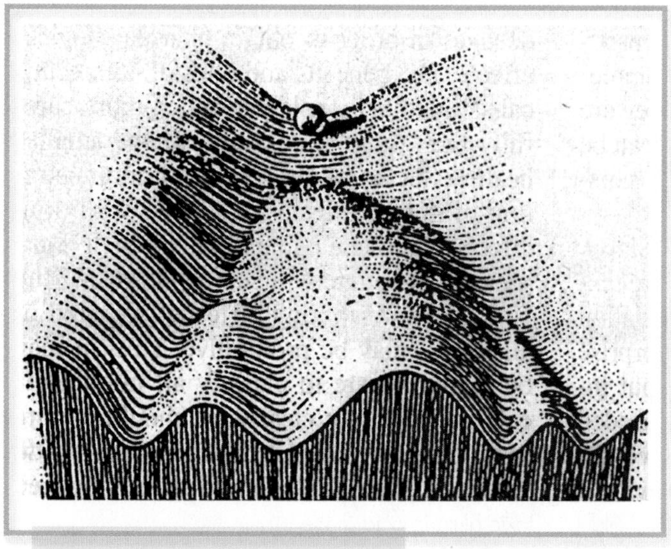

Conrad Waddington, a British geneticist, brilliantly captured the basic principles of phenotypic plasticity in his famous landscape of phenotypic development (Figure 2.11). He imagined the development of a phenotypic trait as a journey across a vast landscape of hills and intersecting valleys flowing downward from a high plateau. As shown in the figure, the ball that is rolling down from the top of the plateau represents the particular phenotypic trait in its "infancy"; the valleys represent the possible developmental pathways that lead to various phenotypic outcomes. You can see from the figure that as the ball rolls downward, it sometimes encounters "forks in the road" where more than one valley is available for continuing the journey, as is the case for traits with high plasticity. You can also see that some valleys are narrow and deep, as is the case for low-plasticity traits. Waddington referred to these latter traits, which follow confined courses, as being **canalized**.

FIGURE 2.11 Waddington's landscape. The rolling ball represents a trait of the developing organism. At each fork in the road, development of the trait can proceed along one of several diverging pathways. (From Waddington, 1957.)

The particular shape of the landscape—the forks, the hills, the depth of the valleys—is the result of a complex system of interactions between genes and the environment. And because the gene–environment system of interaction changes over the course of a lifetime, *the landscape is not stable over the life course of the individual.* Rather, it changes its shape, sometimes dramatically, according to the individual's particular experiences. Exposure to toxins during the prenatal period, for example, can substantially alter the landscape in ways that change the course of developing phenotypes, resulting in physical deformities, mental retardation, and other disorders (see Chapter 3).

We noted earlier in this chapter that development is astonishing in its capacity to generate common developmental outcomes in children despite vast differences in how and where they grow up. In part, this similarity is due to the tight control that the genotype exerts over the developing phenotype. Indeed, canalization ensures that the development of certain essential traits—walking, speaking, and forming friendships, for example—is not easily diverted by environmental variations. On the other hand, the high plasticity of some traits ensures that each individual is able to adapt to changes in the environment. Together, high plasticity and canalization are tremendously powerful forces in organizing children's development.

In the next section, we will continue to explore the genotype–phenotype relationship by considering whether and how certain phenotypic traits of parents are likely to occur in the development of their offspring.

Heritability

You have no doubt often seen news reports announcing the discovery of links between certain genes and this or that physical or psychological trait. Although it is tempting to look for genetic causes to explain human characteristics—from physical traits such as height and weight to behavioral traits such as aggressiveness, thrill-seeking, musical talent, intelligence, and so on—developmentalists know that the gene–behavior relationship is usually more complex. In particular, they know that any trait that shows a large range of individual differences—shyness, say—is almost certainly influenced by multiple genes, as well as by characteristics of the environment. Consequently, their conclusions about the role of genes with respect to phenotypic traits are likely to use the phrase "genetically influenced" rather than "genetically caused."

Estimating Heritability

In the broadest sense, the **heritability** of a particular trait is the amount of phenotypic variation in a population that is due to genetic variation. Geneticists who study heritability often use statistical methods to calculate correlations between measures of a given characteristic among a specific population and the genetic relatedness of the individuals being studied (Haworth & Plomin, 2010). High correlations reflect high heritability for the characteristic; low correlations reflect low heritability.

Using this method, behavioral geneticists have calculated estimations of heritability for a number of characteristics. Consider the example of height. For North Americans, height has a heritability of about 90 percent, meaning that for the population as a whole, 90 percent of the variation in height is the result of genetic factors. Keep in mind that heritability estimates are for populations; in another population the heritability of height might be considerably lower. The reason for the high heritability of height in the United States is the relative lack of environmental diversity: Most of the population has access to adequate nutrition and health care, so environmental differences play relatively less of a role in height differences, and genetic differences relatively more of a role (Tanner, 1990).

Studying Heritability

To study the heritability of a given trait, developmentalists use **kinship studies** to determine the extent to which relatives of varying degrees of genetic closeness are similar on the trait in question (Emde & Hewitt, 2001). Children share 50 percent of their genes with each parent; siblings (except for identical twins) share 50 percent of their genes with each other; half-siblings share 25 percent of their genes; and so on. As noted, if the extent of similarity on a particular trait correlates strongly with the degree of genetic closeness, it can be inferred that the trait is highly heritable, while weaker correlations indicate lower heritability. The three main types of research designs used in kinship studies are family studies, twin studies, and adoption studies.

In the typical **family study**, relatives who live together in a household—parents, children, stepchildren, half-siblings—are compared with one another to determine how similar they are on a given trait. The shortcoming of family studies

heritability A measure of the degree to which a variation in a particular trait among individuals in a specific population is related to genetic differences among those individuals.

kinship studies Studies that use naturally occurring conditions provided by kinship relations to estimate genetic and environmental contributions to a phenotypic trait.

family study A study that compares members of the same family to determine how similar they are on a given trait.

These Japanese teenagers are clearly enjoying this interactive video game. Research suggests that their enthusiasm may be due to both genetic and environmental factors. Genetic factors may contribute to good eye–hand coordination, enhancing their enjoyment of, and leading them to seek out, experiences requiring such skill. At the same time, repeated exposure to such experiences results in even greater skill and, consequently, greater pleasure in challenging experiences.

for estimating the degree of genetic influence is the obvious fact that relatives who live together not only share genes but also, to a large degree, participate in the same family environment. Thus, whatever similarities are found among them could be attributable to environmental influences as well as to hereditary ones.

In order to obtain more precise estimates of genetic and environmental contributions to individual differences, researchers capitalize on the other two designs. In a **twin study**, monozygotic twins and dizygotic twins of the same sex are compared with each other and with other family members for similarity on a given trait (Segal & Johnson, 2009). Since MZ twins have 100 percent of their genes in common, MZ twins raised together should, to the degree that the trait in question is genetically influenced, show greater similarity on the trait than do DZ twins or other siblings. By the same logic, DZ twins and siblings should be more similar than half siblings.

In an **adoption study**, researchers compare children who have been reared apart from their biological parents. Some adoption studies compare twins or other siblings who have been adopted into different families; others compare children and their adoptive and biological parents. The basic purpose of this strategy is to determine whether adopted children are more similar to their biological parents and siblings, who share their genes, or to their adoptive parents and siblings, with whom they share a family environment.

Many family, twin, and adoption studies have shown that the degree of similarity among kin correlates with the degree of genetic similarity. This pattern has been shown for such varied characteristics as attention deficit/hyperactivity disorder (McLoughlin et al., 2007), intelligence (Harden, Turkheimer, & Loehlin, 2007), cheerfulness (Robinson, Emde, & Corley, 2001), antisocial behavior (Viding et al., 2008), and susceptibility to schizophrenia (Edvardsen et al., 2008). Table 2.3, for example, shows results from a massive study of the correlations between the personalities of family members of differing degrees of genetic relatedness (Loehlin, 1992). The correlations in the table are for the personality trait referred to as "extroversion," which includes general sociability, impulsiveness, and liveliness.

Both genetic and environmental influences are evident in the table. If you focus first on genetic influences, you will see that the correlations for MZ twins are markedly greater than those for DZ twins or other siblings, whether the set of twins is raised together in a single family or apart in different families. You can also see that the degree of correlation between personality scores decreases consistently as the degree of genetic relatedness decreases. Environmental influences clearly play a role as well. The correlation between scores for the MZ twins is well below 1.0, although these twins share 100 percent of their genes. In addition, the correlation between biological relatives who are raised together is higher than that between biological relatives raised apart.

Like family studies, twin and adoption studies are not without problems (Richardson & Norgate, 2006). It is possible, for example, that MZ twins may receive more similar treatment from parents and others than do DZ twins or other siblings, and to the extent that they do, MZ twins may be more alike than DZ twins for environmental rather than genetic reasons (Segal, 1999). In addition,

table 2.3

Family and Adoption Results for Extroversion

Type of Relative	Actual Correlation	Percentage of Shared Genes
MZ twins raised together	.51	100
DZ twins raised together	.18	50
MZ twins raised apart	.38	100
DZ twins raised apart	.05	50
Parents/children living together	.16	50
Adoptive parents and children	.01	00
Siblings raised together	.20	50
Siblings raised apart	−.07	50

Source: Loehlin, 1992.

when siblings are adopted by different families and raised apart, the rearing environments may be similar because adoption agencies generally attempt to place children with adoptive parents whose social and cultural backgrounds match those of the biological parents (Joseph, 2001). Thus, the extent to which adopted children are similar to their biological families might not be entirely attributable to the similarity of their genes but may also be due to environmental similarities.

A further complication for kinship studies is that children within a family do not share the same family environment. Age, birth order, and gender can all affect how children within the same family experience family life, and differences in family-linked experiences may create differences between the siblings (McGuire, 2002; Segal & Johnson, 2009). For example, not only do parents treat each of their children differently, but siblings offer different environments for each other. In addition, siblings are likely to have different teachers at school, different friends, and different experiences outside the home. The fact that the distinctive environments experienced by different children in the same family can lead to differences in their development in no way minimizes the importance of genetic factors. Rather, it affirms the principle that genes and the environment make essential contributions to phenotypic development.

An excellent illustration of this principle comes from a study of identical twins, conducted by Manel Esteller at the Spanish National Cancer Center in Madrid (Poulsen, Esteller, Vaag, & Fraga, 2007). At birth, identical twins are on their way to developing identical phenotypes. However, as you already know, even genetically identical individuals develop phenotypic differences. Focusing largely on cellular processes associated with the development of particular diseases, Esteller found that the phenotypic traits of identical twins become increasingly different as the twins grow older, and become greater still as the twins live apart in adulthood. The increasing divergence of their phenotypic characteristics is due in part to increasing differences in the twins' exposure to environmental and social factors assumed to influence phenotypic development, such as toxins, stress, and nutrition.

Genotypes, Phenotypes, and Human Behavior

At this point, you should have a fairly good idea about how phenotypes develop in response to genetic and environmental factors. But Waddington's image of a ball rolling down a landscape, drifting across valleys, and falling into canals is limited in two ways, both of which relate to how the landscape is formed and reformed over the course of development. First, Waddington's account can suggest that developing individuals themselves play but a small role in the process of their own development, when this is far from the case. Second, Waddington's ideas fail to adequately capture how the individual's cultural and social environments form and transform the landscape over the lifetime of the individual. We will now explore these issues in more detail.

Niche Construction

Developmentalists are becoming increasingly aware of how children actively contribute to their own development. **Niche construction** is the term that developmentalists use to refer to how the behaviors, activities, and choices of individuals actively shape the environments (*niches*) in which they live. Take the example of an unusually quiet and nondemanding infant girl who may receive little social interaction and stimulation from her busy family simply because she seems content to be by herself. When she enters school, her social and communication skills may be lacking, making it hard for her to join group play and contributing to her further social withdrawal and isolation. Or think about a 10-year-old boy who wants to be just like his big brother—a gang member. He follows his brother around and hangs out on the fringe of the group, trying to talk, dress, and act in

twin study A study in which groups of monozygotic (identical) and dizygotic (fraternal) twins of the same sex are compared to each other and to other family members for similarity on a given trait.

adoption study A study that focuses on children who have been reared apart from their biological parents.

niche construction The active shaping and modification of individuals' environments by the individuals' own behaviors, activities, and choices.

co-construction The shaping of environments through interactions between children and their caregivers, siblings, neighbors, and friends.

ecological inheritance Environmental modifications, as a result of niche construction, that affect the development of offspring and descendants.

ways that would please them. Naturally, because his time and attention are spent in this way, he is not exposed to alternate contexts that may provide other, healthier avenues for his development.

In different ways, the behaviors of both these children dramatically affect the very environments in which they are developing. In this respect, the children play active roles in the process of niche construction (Laland et al., 2000; Lewontin, 2001; Parker, 2005). It is important to note, however, that niche construction is a social, not an individual, process. The quiet baby, for example, may have fared quite differently in a less busy family, in which a parent, grandparent, or other caregiver took a great deal of pleasure and time interacting with the quiet, companionable baby. Developmentalists use the term **co-construction** to capture the way that environments are shaped and reshaped through interactions between developing individuals and their caregivers, siblings, neighbors, and playmates.

Ecological Inheritance You know from Chapter 1 that Bronfenbrenner used the term *ecology,* which refers to the relationship between individuals and their environments, to explain how children develop at the center of nested, interacting social systems. Developmentalists interested in the biological foundations of human development have found it useful to return to a more expansive definition of ecology, one that includes not only children's social environments but their physical environments as well. This broader definition has encouraged scientists to explore the complex relationships between children and the environments in which they develop.

The term **ecological inheritance** refers to how niche construction can result in environmental modifications that affect the development of offspring and descendants. Such modifications take place when individuals or families elect to move to new places or when large groups of people migrate from one area to another—a behavior that ecologists refer to as *selection of habitat.* For example, if a young couple moves from a rural to an urban environment (habitat), they reconstruct the niche in which their children, and perhaps many future generations, will live and develop. This reconstruction occurs on a larger level when groups of people migrate to a new land in order to escape environmental disaster, oppression, or violence, or to seek economic, educational, or political opportunities.

The modifications that descendants inherit may also come about through *changes to the existing habitat.* Some examples include structural changes, such as building homes, subway systems, or schools. Other examples include depleting resources or introducing toxins—frequent consequences of human activity (for example, cutting down forests for building materials or polluting water sources with industrial waste).

Whether through selection of habitat or changes to the existing habitat, it is the niche-constructing behaviors and lifestyles of individuals that bring about the modified environments that are passed on to offspring and descendants through the process of ecological inheritance. Recent research undertaken from an ecological perspective has demonstrated the remarkable and sensitive connections between human behavior and the developing individual's genotype and phenotype. These connections become especially apparent in light of arguments regarding how our biological and cultural inheritances have coevolved.

▲ APPLY :: CONNECT :: DISCUSS

If you could clone a child from your own exact genes and thereby create a genetic twin, how would this twin be the same as or different from you? Why?

In what ways does your own behavior shape your environment? How might this affect your children?

In human beings, language is a highly canalized trait, whereas intelligence appears to have greater plasticity. Why does this make sense from an evolutionary standpoint?

coevolution The combined process that emerges from the interaction of biological evolution and cultural evolution.

Baldwin effect The role of cultural factors in determining which phenotypes are adaptive.

The Coevolution of Culture and Biology

For many years it was believed that the biological and cultural characteristics of humans developed in a strict sequence: The biological capacities we associate with humanity evolved to a critical point at which humans became capable of developing language and generating culture. Now, however, the situation is believed to have been far more complicated. Contemporary studies of human origins have found evidence that rudimentary forms of culture were already present during early phases of human evolution. *Australopithecus* relatives of those who left the famous Laetoli footprints domesticated fire, built shelters, engaged in organized hunting, and used tools—flint knives, cooking utensils, and notation systems.

Developmentalists are becoming increasingly aware of how culture and biology interact in a process of **coevolution** (Parker, 2005; Richerson & Boyd, 2005; Henrich & Henrich, 2006). Interestingly, the idea is a rather old one in the developmental sciences. James Mark Baldwin, whom we introduced in Chapter 1, proposed that cultural factors may influence the likelihood that people with various mental and physical qualities will survive and reproduce. His idea has been recently resurrected and dubbed the **Baldwin effect** (Wozniak, 2009). Cultural evolution and transmission of information about how to obtain and preserve food, how to make shelters, and how to heal the sick and injured are obvious examples of how cultural practices contribute to reproductive success. Individuals who have access to these types of cultural tools are more likely to live to reproductive maturity and to pass on both their genes and their cultural knowledge to the next generation. Insofar as the capacity to engage in cultural activities and make use of culture's material and symbolic tools confers a selective reproductive advantage, it is probable that the more effective users of culture have been more successful in passing on their genes to succeeding generations. In short, the two forms of evolution, biological and cultural, have interacted and coevolved, as we illustrate below with two famous examples.

Art Wolfe/Photo Researchers

Quechua child-care practices illustrate the coevolution of culture and biology. In their extremely cold environment, parents who use the cultural practices of infant swaddling and carrying are more likely to have surviving offspring, and thus are more likely to pass both their genes and their cultural knowledge to the next generation.

Lactose Tolerance

Our first example of the coevolution of biology and culture comes from a study of *lactose tolerance*—that is, the ability to digest fresh milk (Durham, 1991; Jablonka & Lamb, 2005). Following the domestication of cattle some 6000 years ago, humans began to use milk, cheese, and other dairy products for food. However, despite the popular notion that milk is the "perfect food," most adults in the world are unable to profit from its nutritional content and get indigestion and diarrhea if they drink it. This is because they cannot produce a sufficient amount of lactase, an enzyme that is needed to break down the milk sugar lactose. The ability to produce lactase is present in virtually all newborn mammals, including humans, but it normally declines after weaning. Nevertheless, some adults can digest milk because they have

Pastoral nomads of the Middle East, such as this Bedouin woman and her child, probably evolved the ability to digest milk as a consequence of selection pressure; in a land of food and water scarcity, milk provides both good nutrition and hydration.

a variant allele of the gene responsible for producing lactase, and this allele overrides the normal postweaning shutdown of lactase production. The variant allele occurs commonly among those of European descent, as well as those from cultures in which there is a selection pressure for adults to benefit from milk consumption. Pastoral nomads of the Middle East and Africa are an example. Hunger and thirst were probably very common among these groups, so animals that had been originally domesticated for meat became a source of food and drink in the form of fresh milk. In these "dairying cultures," those with the variant lactase allele were more likely to survive and have children, thus passing on the genetic capacity for digesting milk.

In Scandinavian countries, more than 90 percent of the adult population has the variant lactase allele. But in this case, the selective advantage is related to the fact that lactose, like vitamin D, aids in the absorption of calcium. In sunny regions, exposure to the sun produces enough vitamin D to ensure that people absorb sufficient calcium to avoid rickets and other bone diseases. However, in the northern climes of Scandinavia, where the hours of sunlight are scant and people are well-bundled against the cold, lactose enables people to absorb vitamin D without much exposure to the sun. Interestingly, many Scandinavian myths and legends feature cows as sacred creatures and milk as a food of the gods and a source of strength.

Sickle-Cell Anemia

Another example of the coevolution of biology and culture involves the recessive-gene disorder known as *sickle-cell anemia*. People who inherit the recessive gene for this disorder from both parents, and thus are homozygous for it, have seriously abnor-

FIGURE 2.12 A normal, round, red blood cell (bottom) and a sickle-shaped red blood cell (top) from a person with sickle-cell anemia.

mal red blood cells. Normally, red blood cells are disc-shaped, smooth, and flexible, but in people with sickle-cell anemia, they are more rigid and sticky, with a curved, sickle shape (Figure 2.12). Particularly when the supply of oxygen to the blood is reduced, as it may be at high altitudes, after heavy physical exertion, during a fever, or while under anesthesia, these abnormal blood cells tend to clump together and clog the body's smaller blood vessels, damaging affected organs and causing severe pain (Chang, Ye, & Kan, 2006). Because of their characteristics, sickle cells are prone to rupturing and die off much more quickly than normal red blood cells do, often resulting in chronic anemia. Complications of sickle-cell anemia may also lead to early death. People who are heterozygous for the sickle-cell gene are said to have the *sickle-cell trait* and usually do not suffer symptoms.

Sickle-cell anemia is found most prominently among people of African descent. In the United States, the incidence of the sickle-cell trait among African Americans is about 8 to 9 percent. But in West Africa, the incidence of the sickle-cell trait is greater than 20 percent (Serjeant & Serjeant, 2001). This difference is explained in large part by the fact that carriers of the sickle-cell trait are highly resistant to the parasite that causes malaria. Much of the West African coast is infested with malaria-carrying mosquitoes because the cultural practice of cutting down vast forests has radically increased their habitat and reproductive success. Needless to say, West Africans who carry the sickle-cell gene are at a selective advantage because they are less likely to suffer from malaria, which can be deadly, and are more likely to survive to reproduce. Because of this selective advantage, the frequency of the sickle-cell gene has been maintained in the West African population despite the losses caused by the deaths of homozygous carriers. In the United States, where the sickle-cell trait confers no advantage, it is gradually being eliminated from the gene pool.

▲ APPLY :: CONNECT :: DISCUSS

Think of some examples from your own cultural practices that may contribute to our species' evolution.

Retracing the Laetoli Footprints

We began this chapter by piecing together a scene from an ancient world. We asked how our evolutionary forebears experienced that world and how their lives and experiences were similar to yet different from our own. An understanding of our biocultural foundations, we argued, provides insight into both why all children follow a common path of biological and cultural development, and why each child is nevertheless distinct from all others. Indeed, as we explained throughout the chapter, the complex interplay between commonality and distinctiveness, similarity and diversity, assures that our biological and cultural heritages are passed on to subsequent generations but continue to evolve through time.

Although we have no way of knowing what happened to the individuals whose footprints on the world would survive for 3 million years, it is interesting to speculate about their fate in light of contemporary knowledge of the coevolution of our biological and cultural inheritances. The thick ash that recorded their steps suggests that volcanic activity was affecting their physical habitat, probably limiting food and water resources. So why was their pace so unhurried? Perhaps they, and others like them, were used to volcanic eruptions, and were able, for a time at least, to eke out a life with the food and water resources available to them. We know, however, that under such circumstances their reproductive success would be more restricted than it would be in resource-rich environments, and their contributions to the human gene pool and cultural toolkit more limited. But perhaps they were in the process of migrating to a new habitat with better resources and more opportunities to reproduce—biologically and culturally. If so, was this because the particular individuals were phenotypically uncommonly intelligent or had personality traits that encouraged their migration in the face of environmental destruction?

We may never know the answers to these questions. However, the accumulating knowledge of the ways in which biology and culture interact inspires us to consider ourselves in light of our biocultural foundations. The complex interactions between biology and culture are present at the very beginning of each life, when genes in the zygote start to express themselves and guide the creation of new cells that will ultimately result in a unique human being. Chapter 3 follows the course of this development from the moment the genetic material of the mother and father come together. In later chapters, as we follow the general patterns of the development of children, you will encounter many instances of the elegant dance between biology and culture.

SUMMARY

Inheriting Culture

- Culture is defined by the use of material and symbolic tools that accumulate over time, are passed on through social processes, and provide resources for the developing child. Material tools are observable, and include manufactured objects and patterns of behavior. Symbolic tools are more abstract, and include systems of knowledge, beliefs, and values. Both types of tools provide resources for development by mediating children's behavior—that is, by organizing children's activities, including how children relate to their environment.

- Culture is inherited through social processes whereby children learn to use their culture's tools. These processes include social enhancement, in which children make use of tools simply because they are available; imitation, in which children copy the tool-using behaviors of others; and explicit instruction, which uses language and other symbolic communication. The use of symbolic communication, which is claimed to be uniquely human, allows children to learn about things not immediately present in the environment and about abstractions such as spiritual belief systems.

- Cultures change through the process of cumulative cultural evolution, as individuals produce variations in both material tools (e.g., the production of new technologies) and symbolic tools (e.g., modification of belief systems and the introduction of new knowledge). This process of change is complex and messy, not a harmonious pattern of progress.

Biological Inheritance

- Biological evolution is made possible by heredity—the transmission of genes from parents to offspring. Genes contain instructions that guide the formation of the individual's traits. The genotype (the individual's particular set of genes) strongly influences the phenotype (the individual's actual traits) but does not completely determine the phenotype, which is also strongly influenced by the individual's environment.

- Natural selection is the process whereby individuals with phenotypes well adapted to the local environment survive and reproduce to a greater extent than do individuals with less well-adapted phenotypes, preferentially passing on the genotypes associated with the better-adapted phenotypes. Over many generations, the more adaptive variations of phenotypic traits increase in the species as a whole, while the less adaptive variations decrease. The emergence of shorter pregnancies in our prehuman ancestors is an example of the process of natural selection.

- Humans reproduce through sexual reproduction: The 23 chromosomes in the mother's ovum and the 23 chromosomes in the father's sperm are combined at conception, when ovum and sperm fuse to form a zygote with 23 pairs of corresponding chromosomes, 46 in all. A chromosome is a molecule of DNA; a gene is a segment of a chromosome, a working subunit of DNA.

- The sperm and ova are called germ cells; all the other cells of the body are called somatic cells. New somatic cells, each with 46 chromosomes in 23 pairs identical to those in the zygote, are constantly formed through mitosis. New germ cells, each with only 23 chromosomes, are formed through meiosis.

- A child's sex is determined by the chromosomes of the 23rd pair—females have two X chromosomes, males an X and a Y chromosome.

- A person who inherits the same form of a gene (the same allele) from both parents is homozygous for the trait influenced by that gene; a person who inherits different alleles is heterozygous. When a person is heterozygous for a particular trait, three outcomes are possible:
  - One allele is dominant (the person fully expresses the characteristics associated with that allele), and the other is recessive (the person does not express the characteristics associated with the allele but can pass the allele on to offspring); if the person mates with a carrier of the same recessive allele, the offspring have 1 in 4 chances of inheriting the recessive trait.
  - The person expresses characteristics intermediate between those associated with each allele.
  - The alleles are codominant (the person fully expresses the characteristics associated with each allele).

- Mutations—alterations in the structure of an individual's DNA—can be passed on to the next generation if they occur in germ cells. Mutation is the only process that can add new genes to the gene pool and thus is an important source of variation of genotypes. However, most mutations are harmful or even lethal, not adaptive.

- Disorders related to genetic abnormalities may result from genes inherited through normal processes of inheritance (for example, phenylketonuria) or from a breakdown in the process of genetic transmission affecting the chromosomes in a germ cell (for example, Down syndrome and Klinefelter's syndrome).

- The extent to which the genotype determines any specific phenotypic trait depends on the plasticity of the trait: Traits with high plasticity are easily influenced by the environment, whereas traits with little plasticity develop in much the same way regardless of the environment. Traits, such as language acquisition, that are extremely resistant to environmental influences are said to be canalized.

- The heritability of a trait is the amount of phenotypic variation on a trait in a given population that is due to genetic differences. Statistical methods are used to estimate heritability, which is assessed through several types of kinship studies—namely, family, twin, and adoption studies.

- Traits are also influenced by the individual's own activities, as can be seen in the phenomena of niche construction, in which individuals actively shape their environments, and ecological inheritance, in which niche construction results in modified environments that affect the development of subsequent generations.

The Coevolution of Culture and Biology

- Culture and biology interact in the process of coevolution, whereby cultural factors influence the likelihood that people with certain genetically influenced mental and physical traits will survive and reproduce. For example, in certain populations, coevolution has favored the survival of individuals with the genes responsible for lactose tolerance and for sickle-cell anemia, which are advantageous because of cultural and environmental factors.

Retracing the Laetoli Footprints

- The complex interplay of culture and biology ensures that both heritages are passed on to subsequent generations and that both continue to evolve.

Key Terms

culture, p. 52

material tools, p. 53

symbolic tools, p. 53

mediation, p. 54

social enhancement, p. 54

imitation, p. 54

explicit instruction, p. 54

cumulative cultural evolution, p. 55

heredity, p. 57

genes, p. 57

genotype, p. 57

phenotype, p. 57

natural selection, p. 58

chromosome, p. 59

DNA (deoxyribonucleic acid), p. 59

zygote, p. 60

germ cells, p. 60

somatic cells, p. 60

mitosis, p. 60

meiosis, p. 60

monozygotic (MZ) twins, p. 61

dizygotic (DZ) twins, p. 61

X chromosome, p. 61

Y chromosome, p. 62

allele, p. 62

homozygous, p. 62

heterozygous, p. 62

dominant allele, p. 62

recessive allele, p. 62

carriers, p. 62

codominance, p. 62

polygenic inheritance, p. 63

mutation, p. 63

gene pool, p. 63

phenotypic plasticity, p. 68

canalized, p. 68

heritability, p. 69

kinship studies, p. 69

family study, p. 69

twin study, p. 70

adoption study, p. 70

niche construction, p. 71

co-construction, p. 72

ecological inheritance, p. 72

coevolution, p. 73

Baldwin effect, p. 73

3

Prenatal Development and Birth

The Periods of Prenatal Development
The Germinal Period
The Embryonic Period
The Fetal Period

Maternal Conditions and Prenatal Development
Maternal Stress
Nutritional Influences

Teratogens: Environmental Sources of Birth Defects
Drugs
Infections and Other Health Conditions

Birth
The Stages of Labor
Cultural Variations in Childbirth
Childbirth in the United States

The Newborn's Condition
Assessing the Baby's Viability
Problems and Complications
Developmental Consequences

Beginning the Parent–Child Relationship
The Baby's Appearance
Social Expectations

Foua Lee is pregnant for the 10th time. Raised in the Hmong community of Laos, Foua knows that she must pay careful attention to her food cravings to ensure the health of her unborn child. If she craves ginger and fails to eat it, the child may be born with an extra finger or toe; if she craves but does not eat chicken flesh, the child may have a blemish near its ear; and if she craves but does not eat eggs, the child may have a lumpy head. When she feels the first pangs of labor, Foua will hurry to her house, or at least to the house of her husband's cousins, because if she gives birth anywhere else, she may be injured by an evil spirit. Foua will give birth without an attendant, delivering the baby into her own hands by reaching between her legs to ease out the head and then letting the rest of the body slip out onto her bent forearms. Soon after the birth, the father, Nao Kao, will dig a deep hole in the dirt floor of their home and bury the placenta. The Hmong believe that the placenta is a "jacket" for the soul. When a Hmong person dies, his or her soul must travel back to the burial place of the placenta, put on the jacket in which it was born and, thus protected, continue its dangerous journey to the land of ancestors from which it will one day be summoned to be reborn as the soul of a new baby. Indeed, a few days after their child is born, Foua and Nao Kao will sacrifice a pig and invite family and friends to witness the soul-calling ritual. Attracted by the sacrifice, as well as by the promises and prayers from parents and elders, an ancestor will be reborn in their infant's body.

(Adapted from Fadiman, 1998.)

Foua's beliefs about how to ensure a healthy pregnancy and successful delivery, and her experiences giving birth to her children, sound both foreign and familiar to those of us who have been raised in technologically advanced societies. Foua worries that unmet food cravings may result in particular malformations; we worry that nutritional deficiencies or environmental toxins may harm the developing fetus. Foua gives birth at home, where she feels protected from malevolent spirits; we give birth in hospitals or birthing centers where we feel protected from potential medical problems. Foua and her family engage in ritual practices that link her newborn to a spiritual ancestral world; we participate in a variety of ritual practices (circumcision, baptism) to welcome, celebrate, and proclaim our babies as members of specific religious communities.

However they may differ in terms of particular beliefs and practices, these examples make clear that, around the globe, bringing children into the world is regarded as a matter of enormous weight and is approached with great care. The special consideration given to pregnancy and childbirth is understandable in light of the fact that some of the most eventful and vulnerable periods of human growth and development occur during the prenatal months and the hours of transition between the womb and the outside world.

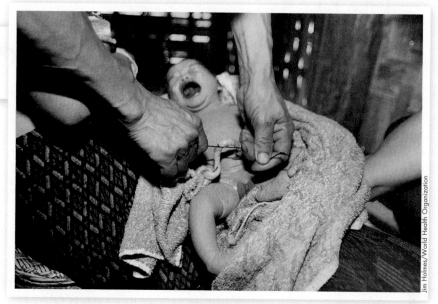

In a traditional Laotian practice, the umbilical cord of this newborn is being cut with a razor-sharp piece of bamboo.

Jim Holmes/World Health Organization

As humans, we begin our development as a zygote, a single cell the size of a period on this page, weighing approximately 15 millionths of a gram. At birth only 9 months later, we consist of at least a trillion cells and weigh, on average, 7 pounds (3.2 kilograms). Along with these remarkable changes in size are truly astonishing changes in form (Figure 3.1) and in behavior. The first few cells to develop from the zygote are all identical, but within a few weeks, many different kinds of cells will be arranged in intricately structured, interdependent organs. Within a few months, the baby-to-be will move and respond actively to its environment.

The study of prenatal development seeks to explain how these changes in size, form, and behavior take place. This goal is important for both theoretical and practical reasons. On the theoretical side, many scholars believe that development in the prenatal period reflects principles of development that apply in all subsequent periods, from birth to death. For example, development throughout life is characterized by changes both in the form of the organism and in the kinds of interactions the changing organism has with its environment. Following our discussion of prenatal development, we will outline these principles in Table 3.4 (see p. 103).

On the practical side, understanding the prenatal period is important because the developing organism can be positively or adversely affected by the mother-to-be's nutritional status, health, and habits, including whether or not she uses drugs or alcohol. Considerable research is devoted to promoting healthy prenatal development and preventing damage to the growing organism.

In order to make clear the relation of development in the womb to later development in the world, we first must trace the changes that take place as the organism progresses from zygote to newborn and examine the environmental factors that support or threaten development. Then we can consider the circumstances surrounding the newborn's entrance into the world.

FIGURE 3.1 Changes in the size and form of the human body from 14 days to 15 weeks after conception. (Adapted from Arey, 1974.)

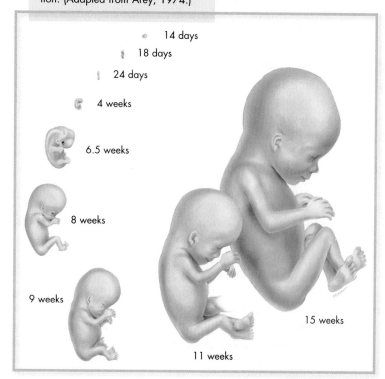

14 days

18 days

24 days

4 weeks

6.5 weeks

8 weeks

9 weeks

11 weeks

15 weeks

The Periods of Prenatal Development

The transformations that occur during prenatal development are nothing short of amazing. Through a microscope, the fertilized ovum, or zygote, appears to be made up of small particles inside larger ones. The chromosomes bearing the genes are contained within the nucleus at the center of the cell. Surrounding the nucleus is the cell matter, which serves as the raw material for the first few cell divisions. Within the first few weeks after conception, this single cell subdivides many times to form many kinds of cells with vastly different destinies. In approximately 266 days, these cells will have been transformed into a wriggling, crying infant.

Developmental scientists often divide prenatal development into three broad periods, or trimesters, each characterized by distinctive patterns of growth and interaction between the organism and its environment: the germinal period, the embryonic period, and the fetal period.

1. The **germinal period** begins at conception and lasts until the developing organism becomes attached to the wall of the uterus, about 8 to 10 days later.

2. The **embryonic period** extends from the time the organism becomes attached to the uterus until the end of the 8th week, when all the major organs have taken primitive shape.

3. The **fetal period** begins the 9th week after conception, with the first signs of the hardening of the bones, and continues until birth. During this period, the primitive organ systems develop to the point where the baby can exist outside the mother without medical support.

At any step in these prenatal periods, the process of development may stop. One study estimates that approximately 25 percent of all pregnancies end before the woman even recognizes that she is pregnant (Wilcox, Baird, & Weinberg, 1999). If all goes well, however, the creation of a new human being is under way.

The Germinal Period

During the first 8 to 10 days after conception, the zygote moves slowly through the fallopian tube, where fertilization occurred, and into the uterus (Figure 3.2). The timing of this journey is crucial. If the zygote enters the uterus too soon or too late, the uterine environment will not be hormonally prepared and the organism will be destroyed.

The First Cells of Life Recall from Chapter 2 (p. 60) that all body cells reproduce through the process of duplication and cell division known as *mitosis*. About 24 hours after conception, as the zygote travels down the fallopian tube, **cleavage** begins—the zygote divides by mitosis into two cells, which then divide into four, and those four divide into eight, and so on (see Figure 3.3). Thanks to this repeated duplication, the developing organism will already consist of hundreds of cells by the time it reaches the uterus. An important characteristic of cleavage is that the cells existing at any given moment do not all divide at the same time. Instead of proceeding in an orderly fashion from a two-cell stage to a four-cell stage and so on, cells divide at different rates (Tokita, Kiyoshi, &

germinal period The period that begins at conception and lasts until the developing organism becomes attached to the wall of the uterus about 8 to 10 days later.

embryonic period The period that extends from the time the organism becomes attached to the uterus until the end of the 8th week of pregnancy, when all the major organs have taken primitive shape.

fetal period The period that begins in the 9th week after conception, with the first signs of the hardening of the bones, and continues until birth.

cleavage The series of mitotic cell divisions that transform the zygote into the blastocyst.

FIGURE 3.2 Development of the human embryo in the mother's reproductive tract from fertilization to implantation. (Adapted from Tuchmann-Duplessis, David, & Haegel, 1971.)

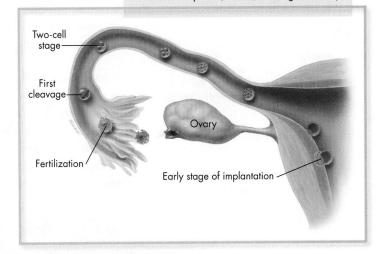

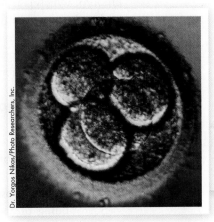

FIGURE 3.3 A zygote after two cleavages, resulting in four cells of equal size and appearance.

heterochrony Variability in the rates of development of different parts of the organism.

heterogeneity Variability in the levels of development of different parts of the organism at a given time.

totipotent stem cells Cells that have the potential to grow into a complete embryo and, ultimately, to become a normal, healthy infant.

implantation The process by which the developing organism becomes attached to the uterus.

amnion A thin, tough, transparent membrane that holds the *amniotic fluid,* and surrounds the embryo.

chorion A membrane that surrounds the amnion and becomes the fetal component of the placenta.

placenta An organ made up of tissue from both the mother and the fetus that serves as a barrier and filter between their bloodstreams.

umbilical cord A flexible helical structure containing blood vessels that connects the developing organism to the placenta.

ectoderm Cells of the inner cell mass that develop into the outer surface of the skin, the nails, part of the teeth, the lens of the eye, the inner ear, and the central nervous system.

endoderm Cells of the inner cell mass that develop into the digestive system and the lungs.

mesoderm The cells of the inner cell mass that give rise to the muscles, the bones, the circulatory system, and the inner layers of the skin.

Armstrong, 2007). This is the first instance of developmental **heterochrony**, whereby different parts of the organism develop at different rates. (*Heterochrony* literally means "variability in time.") This unevenness in rates of development gives rise to **heterogeneity**—variability in the levels of development of different parts of the organism at a given time. The fact that newborns' sense of hearing is more advanced than their ability to see, for example, means that they will recognize their mothers more readily by the sound of her voice than by the way she looks. Both kinds of variability play an important role in the process of development throughout the life of the child.

As illustrated in Figure 3.3, cells formed during the first several cleavages resemble Ping-Pong balls crowded into a balloon. At this very early stage of development, all these cells are **totipotent** ("totally potent") **stem cells**, meaning that each has the potential to grow into an embryo and, ultimately, to become a normal, healthy baby (Do, Han, & Schöler, 2006). In fact, identical twins develop when this single mass of totipotent cells separates into two cell masses, which then develop into two individual, genetically identical human beings. Such developmental freedom at the cellular level—the ability to develop into virtually any type of human cell and, consequently, into an entirely distinct human being—is unique to this very early period of cell division. Thereafter, the development potential of stem cells becomes limited. Stem cells are harbored in various tissues and organs for making repairs, and they can only develop into cells related to the specific tissues and organs they are part of. A stem cell in the brain, for instance, can become different sorts of neural cells (a neuron or glial cell) but not a bone or liver cell. Because they are capable of becoming different types of cells only within a closely related family of cells, adult stem cells are referred to as *multipotent stem cells.* As you are probably aware, many scientists believe that stem cells (both totipotent and multipotent) have the potential to be used therapeutically to replace damaged cells associated with myriad diseases, including heart disease, leukemia and other cancers, Parkinson's disease, and Type I diabetes.

Implantation As the developing cell mass moves farther into the uterus, the outer cells put out tiny branches that burrow into the spongy wall of the uterus until they come into contact with the mother's blood vessels. This is the beginning of **implantation**, the process by which the developing organism becomes attached to the uterus. Implantation marks the transition between the germinal and the embryonic periods. Like many other transitions, such as birth itself, implantation is hazardous for the organism, and the spontaneous termination of pregnancy during this process is common.

The Embryonic Period

If the developing organism is successfully implanted, it enters the period of the embryo, which lasts for about 6 weeks. During this time, all the basic organs of the body take shape, and the organism begins to respond to direct stimulation. The organism's rapid growth during this period is facilitated by the efficient way in which the mother now supplies nutrition and protects the organism from harmful environmental influences.

Sources of Nutrition and Protection Early in the embryonic period, the **amnion**, a thin, tough, transparent membrane that holds the *amniotic fluid,* surrounds the embryo (the amnion and the fluid are often called the "bag of waters"). The amniotic fluid cushions the organism as the mother moves about, provides liquid support for its weak muscles and soft bones, and gives it a medium in which it can move and change position.

Surrounding the amnion is another membrane, the **chorion**, which later becomes the fetal component of the **placenta**, a complex organ made up of tissue

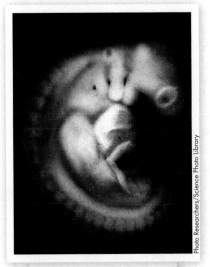

The human embryo at 3 weeks after conception.

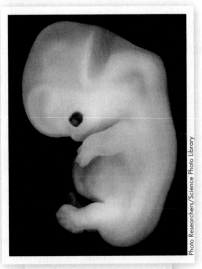

The human embryo at 5 weeks after conception.

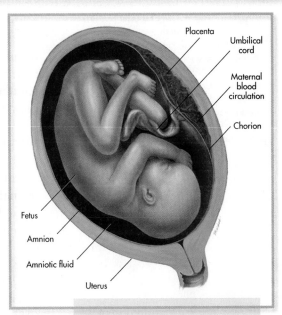

FIGURE **3.4** The fetus in its protective environment. (Adapted from Curtis, 1979.)

from both the mother and the embryo (Figure 3.4). Attached to the uterine wall, the placenta acts simultaneously as a barrier and a filter, preventing the bloodstreams of the mother and the embryo (and later the fetus) from coming into direct contact with each other, while at the same time allowing critical exchanges to occur between them. By means of this barrier/filter system, the placenta provides the embryo with nutrients and oxygen carried by the mother's blood and also enables the embryo's waste products to be absorbed by the mother's bloodstream, from which they are eventually extracted by her kidneys. These exchanges take place through the **umbilical cord**, a flexible, helical structure with a vein for carrying oxygen- and nutrient-rich blood from the placenta to the embryo and two main arteries for carrying depleted blood from the embryo back to the placenta (Heifetz, 1996). The umbilical cord is approximately 20 inches (51 centimeters) long and is filled with a gelatinous substance called *Wharton's jelly,* which contributes to its flexibility, allowing it to twist and turn as the fetus moves and grows.

Embryonic Growth While the outer cells of the developing organism are forming the placenta and the other membranes that will supply and protect the embryo, the growing number of cells in the inner cell mass begin to differentiate into the various kinds of cells that eventually become all the organs of the body (Figure 3.5). The first step in this process is the separation of the inner cell mass into two layers. The **ectoderm**, the outer layer, gives rise to the outer surface of the skin, the nails, part of the teeth, the lens of the eye, the inner ear, and the central nervous system (the brain, the spinal cord, and the nerves). The **endoderm**, the inner layer, develops into the digestive system and the lungs. Shortly after these two layers form, a middle layer, the **mesoderm**, appears, eventually becoming the muscles, the bones, the circulatory system, and the inner layers of the skin (Gilbert, 2001).

One of nature's greatest mysteries is the process through which a few identical stem cells with unlimited developmental capacity evolve into a highly differentiated cell community composed of specialized parts. What causes a cell to act like part of the endoderm rather than the exoderm or mesoderm and, later, to form liver tissue rather than pancreas or colon tissue? Scientists estimate that each cell contains something on the order of 25,000 genes, the vast majority of which remain inactive as the cell develops into its specialized

FIGURE **3.5** Within days of fertilization, a highly organized cell community develops. Distinct parts of the community are identified according to their location and the specialized functions they will take on. The ectoderm (outer layer) will develop functions associated with the growth of the skin, nails, and nervous system. The endoderm (inner layer) will develop functions associated with the digestive system and lungs. The mesoderm (middle layer) will develop functions associated with the growth of the muscles, bones, the circulatory system, and the inner layers of the skin.

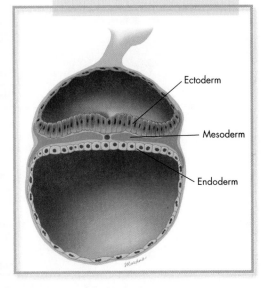

epigenesis The process by which a new phenotypic form emerges through the interactions of the preceding form and its current environment.

cephalocaudal pattern The pattern of development that proceeds from the head down.

proximodistal pattern The pattern of development that proceeds from the middle of the organism out to the periphery.

phenotypic role—as part of the pancreas, liver, or colon, for example. Current explanations emphasize the idea that each new phenotypic form emerges as a result of the interactions that take place between the preceding form and its environment, a process called **epigenesis** (from the Greek, meaning "at the time of generation") (Gottlieb & Lickliter, 2007). And what is the environment of a cell? In part, a cell's environment consists of surrounding cells, which exchange information and regulate each other's gene activities. Thus, a stem cell "knows" it should act like part of the endoderm because surrounding endoderm cells have "told" it to do so through the release of special signaling proteins. Interestingly, the signals from the surrounding cells do not appear to communicate which genes should be turned on; rather, they indicate which genes—those relevant to forming liver or pancreas tissue, for instance—should remain inactive (Boyer et al., 2005). According to the epigenetic explanation of embryonic development, the different interactions that cells have with their environmental conditions (including each other) is what leads to the creation of new kinds of cells and subsequent new forms of interactions between the organism and the environment (Gilbert, 2001).

The embryo develops at a breathtaking pace, as you can see in Table 3.1. The table also reflects two patterns of body development that are maintained until the organism reaches adolescence. In the first, the **cephalocaudal pattern**, development proceeds from the head down. The arm buds, for instance, appear before the leg buds. In the second, the **proximodistal pattern**, development proceeds from the middle of the organism out to the periphery. Thus, the spinal cord develops before the arm buds; the upper arm develops before the forearm; and so on. In general, the process of organ formation is the same for all human embryos, but in one major respect—sexual differentiation—it varies.

table 3.1

Growth and Development of the Embryo

Days 10–13
Cells separate into ectoderm, endoderm, and mesoderm layers. The neural plate, which eventually will become the brain and the spinal cord, forms out of the ectoderm.

Third Week
The three major divisions of the brain—the hindbrain, the midbrain, and the forebrain—begin to differentiate by the end of the third week. Primitive blood cells and blood vessels are present. The heart comes into being, and by the end of the week it is beating.

Fourth Week
Limb buds are visible. Eyes, ears, and a digestive system begin to take form. The major veins and arteries are completed. Vertebrae are present, and nerves begin to take primitive form.

Fifth Week
The umbilical cord takes shape. Bronchial buds, which eventually will become the lungs, take form. Premuscle masses are present in the head, trunk, and limbs. The hand plates are formed.

Sixth Week
The head becomes dominant in size. The halves of the lower jawbone meet and fuse, and the components of the upper jaw are present. The external ear makes its appearance. The three main parts of the brain are distinct.

Seventh Week
The face and neck are beginning to take form. Eyelids take shape. The stomach is taking its final shape and position. Muscles are rapidly differentiating throughout the body and are assuming their final shapes and relationships. The brain is developing thousands of nerve cells per minute.

Eighth Week
The growth of the gut makes the body evenly round. The head is elevated and the neck is distinct. The external, middle, and inner ears assume their final forms. By the end of this week, the fetus is capable of some movement and responds to stimulation around the mouth.

Sexual Differentiation As we described in Chapter 2 (pp. 61–62), the genes that influence sexual determination are located on the X and Y chromosomes inherited at conception. Zygotes with one X and one Y chromosome are genetically male, and zygotes with two X chromosomes are genetically female. For the first 6 weeks after conception, there is no structural difference between genetically male and genetically female embryos. Both males and females have two ridges of tissue, called *gonadal ridges,* from which the male and female sex organs (*gonads*) will develop. Initially, these ridges give no clue to the sex of the embryo. Then in the 7th week, if the embryo is genetically male (XY), the process of sexual differentiation begins with the gonadal ridges beginning to form testes (Ostrer, Huang, Masch, & Shapiro, 2007). If the embryo is genetically female (XX), no changes are apparent in the gonadal ridges until several weeks later, when ovaries begin to form.

It is not genes, however, but hormones that determine whether the embryo subsequently develops male or female external genitalia. The male gonads produce high levels of hormones called *androgens,* chief among which is *testosterone.* (Females also produce testosterone, but in much smaller quantities.) If enough testosterone is present, a penis and scrotum develop; otherwise, female external genitalia are formed. Very rarely, errors in sex development (for example, too little testosterone in males or too much in females) result in a baby's having sex organs that show characteristics of both sexes.

Interestingly, the influence of prenatal androgens is not limited to the gonads and the genital tract, nor is it limited to the prenatal period. For example, female embryos that produce higher levels of testosterone tend to have slower brain growth, as measured by head circumference at birth, compared with those that produce lower levels (Whitehouse, Maybery, Hart, & Sloboda, 2010). Moreover, some studies have suggested that the effects of prenatal androgens can extend well into childhood to affect sex-typed play (Auyeung, Baron-Cohen, Ashwin, & Knickmeyer, 2009; Knickmeyer, Wheelwright, Taylor, Raggatt, Hackett, & Baron-Cohen, 2005; van de Beek, van Goozen, Buitelaar, & Cohen-Kettenis, 2009). For example, compared with other girls, those with congenital adrenal hyperplasia (CAH)—a genetic disorder that causes the production of high levels of fetal testosterone—may be somewhat more likely to choose boys as playmates and to prefer the rough-and-tumble play that occurs more typically in boys than in girls. Girls affected by CAH also may be more likely than unaffected girls to play with cars, trucks, and toy weapons. Later in the chapter, we will discuss several other ways in which childhood and even adulthood behaviors and conditions may have their origins in fetal development. For now, it is important to note that the process linking fetal testosterone exposure and later "masculinized" play preferences is far from clear and very likely includes substantial input from the child's social environment (Jordan-Young, 2010).

The Fetal Period

The fetal period begins once all the basic tissues and organs exist in rudimentary form and the tissue that will become the skeleton begins to harden, or *ossify* (Gilbert, 2001; Figure 3.6). During the fetal period, which lasts from the 8th or 9th week of pregnancy until birth, the fetus increases in length from approximately 1½ inches to 20 inches (4 centimeters to 51 centimeters) and in weight from approximately 0.02 to 7.1 pounds (0.09 kilograms to 3.2 kilograms).

FIGURE 3.6 This fetus is approximately 9 weeks old. It is attached to the placenta and the mother's blood circulation by the umbilical cord and floating in an amniotic sac filled with fluid. The round, red structure is the remnant of the yolk sac. The embryo's eye and limbs are visible, as is its male sex.

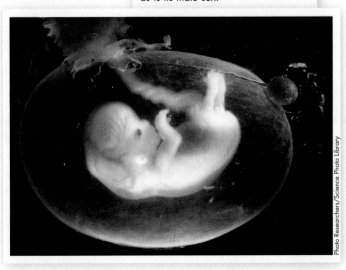

Photo Researchers/Science Photo Library

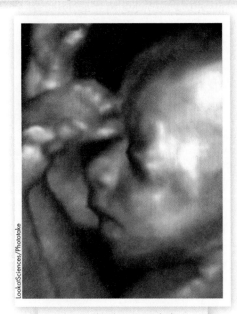

Modern technologies, including the fetal ultrasound used here, produce such high-quality images of the fetus that a variety of disorders can be identified and, in some cases, surgically corrected long before birth.

Over the course of the fetal period, each of the organ systems increases in complexity. By the 10th week after conception, the intestines have assumed their characteristic position in the body. Two weeks later, the fetus's external sexual characteristics are clearly visible, and its neck is well defined. By the end of 16 weeks, the head is erect, the lower limbs are well developed, and the ears, which began to take form in the 4th week, migrate from the neck to the sides of the head. By the end of the 5th month, the fetus has almost as many nerve cells as it will ever have as a person. By the end of the 7th month, the lungs are capable of breathing air, and the eyes, which have been closed, open and can respond to light. Consequently, the 7th month is often described as the **age of viability**, that is, the age at which the fetus is able to survive outside the uterus. By the end of the 8th month, many folds of the brain are present, enabling brain cells to be packed more efficiently within the skull, and during the 9th month, the brain becomes considerably more wrinkled. In the final weeks before birth, the fetus doubles in weight.

The fetal period marks a critical stage during which the baby-to-be becomes responsive to its environment in new ways and is developmentally influenced by factors both inside and outside the uterus. We will now take a look at some of the events that affect fetal development and experience.

Sensory Capacities Using modern techniques of measurement and recording, researchers have begun to produce a detailed picture of the development of sensory capacities before birth (Lecanuet, Graniere-Deferre, & DeCasper, 2005). This information is essential for determining how the fetus is influenced by the uterine environment. Scientists have discovered the following about the fetus's sensory capacities:

- *Sensing motion.* The vestibular system of the middle ear, which controls the sense of balance, begins to function in the human fetus about 5 months after conception and is fully mature at birth (Lecanuet & Jacquet, 2002). This early maturity means that the fetus is capable of sensing changes in the mother's posture and orienting itself as it floats inside the fluid-filled amniotic sac.

- *Seeing.* Little is known for certain about the extent of the fetus's visual experience. At 26 weeks following conception, if a bright light is held against the mother's abdomen, the fetus may respond with changes in heart rate and movement (Lecanuet & Schaal, 1996). Aidan Macfarlane (1977) suggested that the fetus's visual experience of light that has penetrated the mother's stretched stomach wall may be similar to the glow seen when the palm of the hand covers the lens of a flashlight.

- *Hearing.* The fetus responds to sound at 5 to 6 months after conception (Abrams, Gerhardt, & Antonelli, 1998). Studies in which tiny microphones have been inserted into the uterus adjacent to the fetus's head reveal that the average sound level inside the womb is approximately 75 decibels, about the level at which we hear the outside world when we ride in a car with the windows up. When sounds of moderate or loud intensity are presented in laboratory situations, it is possible to detect changes in the fetus's heart rate (Morokuma et al., 2008; Kisilevsky & Hains, 2010). Background noise from the outside world is punctuated by the sound of air passing through the mother's stomach and, every second or so, by the more intense sound of the mother's heartbeat. Of all such sounds, the mother's voice is heard best because it is also transmitted as vibrations

age of viability The age at which the fetus is able to survive outside the uterus.

through her body. In what will prove essential to language acquisition, the fetus recognizes *changes* in sound between 6 and 7 months after conception (Draganova et al., 2007).

Fetal Activity Just about any woman who has been pregnant will tell you that the fetus does not float passively in its amniotic fluid. By the end of the 4th month, the mother-to-be can feel her fetus moving around, bumping and rolling against the uterus and sometimes kicking and elbowing—in later weeks, with enough force to make her uncomfortable. By midpregnancy, the movements of the fetus can be felt by placing a hand on the pregnant woman's belly, enchanting expectant parents, as well as brothers- and sisters-to-be.

Actually, movement in the womb occurs long before the mother can detect it. Modern technologies, such as ultrasound, have revealed that embryos become active within 8 weeks following conception. As the embryo enters the fetal stage, its body movements become increasingly varied and coordinated (Table 3.2; Robinson & Kleven, 2005). At 15 weeks of age, the fetus is capable of all the movements observable in newborn infants, such as head turning and leg flexing (James, Pillai, & Smoleniec, 1995). Evidence indicates that spontaneous fetal activity plays a significant role in development (Smotherman & Robinson, 1996). Experiments with chick embryos, for example, suggest that prenatal activity is crucial to normal limb development. Under normal circumstances, the spinal cord sends out neurons, or nerve cells, to connect the limbs to the brain—many more neurons than the animal will need when it is fully coordinated. Many of these neurons die off, while the remainder are connected to muscles in an efficient way. If chick embryos are treated with drugs that prevent them from moving, the elimination of excess neurons that ordinarily accompanies neuromuscular development does not occur. The results are disastrous. In as little as 1 or 2 days, the failed elimination of all but the neurons compatible with coordinated movement causes the joints of the chick embryos to become fixed into rigid structures, a result showing that movement is necessary for normal limb development (Pittman & Oppenheim, 1979). Fetal movements are believed to play a similar role in establishing basic neuronal connections in humans (Robinson & Kleven, 2005).

Other prenatal activities that are important to later development include breathing, swallowing, and sucking The fetus, of course, does not breathe in utero; as noted, it obtains oxygen through the placenta. But it makes certain "breathing" movements with its chest and lungs that help develop the muscles necessary for respiration after birth (Wilson, Olver, & Walters, 2007). Sucking and swallowing, which will be needed for feeding after birth, begin to occur by 15 weeks and become well coordinated with each other by the third trimester (Miller, Macedonia, & Sonies, 2006). In fact, shortly before birth, the fetus may be swallowing as much as 2 to 4 cups (0.5 to 1 liters) of amniotic fluid per day (Ross & Nyland, 1998). The extensive "practice" of breathing, sucking, and swallowing that occurs in the womb is vital, given that without these behaviors, the newborn cannot survive.

Research has also shown that fetal *inactivity* provides important clues to development. From 24 to 32 weeks after conception, the relatively high rate of fetal activity begins to alternate with quiet periods, and there is a gradual overall decrease in the fetus's movements (Kisilevsky & Low, 1998). This shift is believed to reflect the development of neural pathways that inhibit movement. The appearance of these inhibitory pathways is related to maturation in the higher regions of the brain (Figure 3.7). By 38 to 40 weeks after conception, four behavioral states can be identified: quiet and active sleep, and quiet and active awake (Nijhuis, Prechtl, Martin, & Bots, 1982).

table 3.2

Appearance of Fetal Movements in Early Pregnancy

Movement	Gestational Age (weeks)
Any movement	7
Startle	8
Generalized movements	8
Hiccups	8
Isolated arm movements	9
Head retroflexion	9
Hand–face contact	10
Breathing	10
Jaw opening	10
Stretching	10
Head anteflexion	10
Yawn	11
Suck and swallow	12

Source: De Vries et al., 1982. Adapted by permission.

FIGURE 3.7 The primitive parts of the brain are present very early in prenatal development. The cerebral hemispheres, with their characteristic convolutions, do not make their appearance until the middle of pregnancy. (Adapted from Cowan, 1979.)

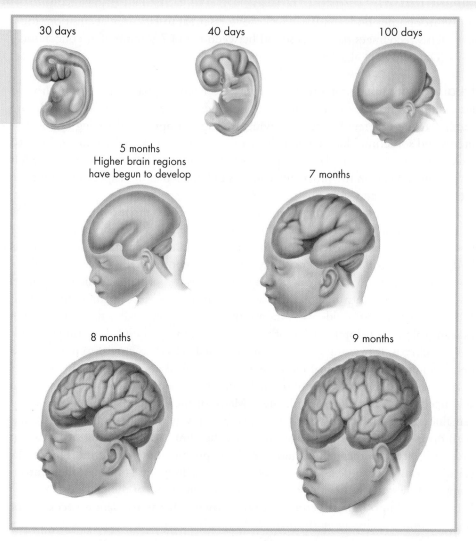

30 days

40 days

100 days

5 months
Higher brain regions have begun to develop

7 months

8 months

9 months

FIGURE 3.8 This baby is listening to a recording of its mother telling a story. The apparatus records changes in sucking to determine how newborns react to stories read to them while they were in the womb.

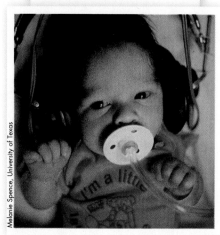

Melanie Spence, University of Texas

Learning in the Womb The folklore of many societies includes the belief that the fetus can learn the sound patterns of stories and songs while in the womb (Lefeber & Voorhoeve, 1998). Although scientists were once highly skeptical of such beliefs, there is now considerable evidence that the fetus comes to recognize at least some aural events both inside the mother (her heartbeat and intestinal gurgles, for example) and outside, in the mother's environment (voices and music, for example) (James, 2010; Lecanuet, Granier-Deferre, & DeCasper, 2005).

In a particularly well-known study, Anthony DeCasper and Melanie Spence (1986) asked 16 pregnant women to read aloud a particular passage from *The Cat in the Hat,* a rhyming children's story by Dr. Seuss, twice a day for the last month and a half before their babies were due. By the time the babies were born, the passage had been read to them for a total of about 3½ hours.

Two or three days after the babies were born, DeCasper and Spence tested them with a pacifier that had been wired to record sucking rates (Figure 3.8). First the babies were allowed to suck for 2 minutes to establish a baseline sucking rate. Afterward, changes in the rate of sucking turned on or off a tape recording of their mothers reading a story. For half of the babies, increasing their sucking rates turned on the passage from *The Cat in the Hat* that their mothers had previously read aloud, while decreasing their sucking rate turned on a story their mothers had not read. For the other half, increased sucking turned on the new story, while decreased sucking produced *The Cat in the Hat*. The key finding was that the infants modified their rates of sucking to produce *The Cat in the Hat*. The investigators concluded that the babies had indeed heard the stories being read to them by their mothers and that their learning in the womb influenced the sounds they found rewarding after birth. Later research has also shown that in the weeks before birth, fetuses prefer the sounds of their native language, indicating that they had learned its particular sounds and could discriminate them from those of a nonnative language (Lecanuet et al., 2000).

In addition to showing evidence of learning from auditory input, research indicates that human fetuses also learn through other sensory modalities, including smell and taste, and that such prenatal learning experiences may have consequences for postnatal experiences, including food preferences. We will examine this research in detail in Chapter 4.

⏏ APPLY :: CONNECT :: DISCUSS

After reviewing the distinction between continuity and discontinuity presented in Chapter 1 (p. 12), discuss the ways in which prenatal development and activity are both continuous and discontinuous.

Maternal Conditions and Prenatal Development

Although the mother's womb provides a protective and supportive environment for prenatal growth, the baby-to-be is influenced both positively and negatively by the larger world. Certain outside influences reach the developing organism by way of the placenta either directly or through changes they cause in the mother. This section focuses on how fetal development may be affected by maternal stress, nutrition, and general health. Then, in a separate section, we will discuss the effects of specific environmental toxins and substances known to adversely affect the developing fetus.

Maternal Stress

During the Kosovo war in 1999, NATO bombs rained down on the Yugoslav city of Belgrade for 10 solid weeks. Two years later and an ocean away, the World Trade Center collapsed in a terrorist attack. In 2005, the Mississippi Gulf coast and New Orleans were devastated by Hurricane Katrina. Although each of these disasters was unique, they all had a similar consequence: a spike in the rate of low-birth-weight babies born to mothers who lived through one of the disasters (Maric, Dunjic, Stojiljkovic, Britvic, & Jasovic-Gasic, 2010; Lederman et al., 2004; Xiong et al., 2008).

Studies have shown that a mother who is under stress or becomes emotionally upset secretes hormones, such as adrenaline and cortisol, that pass through the placenta and can have a measurable effect on the fetus's motor activity (Relier, 2001). These effects can be long-lasting (Weinstock, 2005). Elizabeth Susman and her colleagues found that mothers who were in more stressful environments during pregnancy produced elevated levels of cortisol, and that at 3 years of age, their children were more aggressive than children of mothers who had less stressful environments and produced lower levels of cortisol while pregnant (Susman, Schmeelk, Ponirakis, & Gariepy, 2001; Susman, 2006).

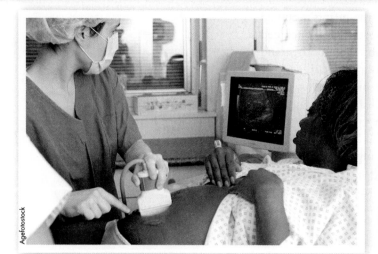

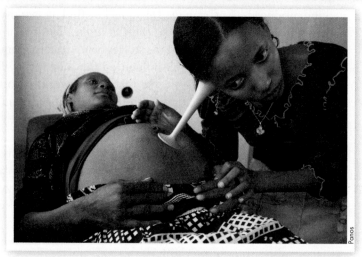

All cultures have evolved tools and practices that are believed to contribute to the well-being of the fetus. While some societies have high-tech machinery with which to monitor neonatal health, others, such as the Ethiopian midwife shown on the right, monitor the growing fetus with traditional tools.

Less dramatic forms of stress can also have prenatal effects. Many physicians who care for pregnant women and newborn infants have long suspected that a woman's having negative feelings about her pregnancy can negatively affect the well-being of the fetus and of the child after birth. This idea is supported by a variety of research, including findings of a strong relationship between a mother's negative attitudes toward her pregnancy and her infant's risk of low birth weight (Suzuki, Minai, & Yamagata, 2007). Perhaps the clearest evidence that a mother-to-be's negative attitudes can affect her baby's development comes from an extensive investigation conducted in Czechoslovakia in the 1960s and 1970s. Henry David (1981) studied the lives of 220 children whose mothers indicated strong negative attitudes toward having them by twice asking for an abortion. The refusal by medical authorities to grant the abortion indicated they believed these women to be capable of carrying through the pregnancy and raising the child.

The unwanted children were compared with a carefully matched control group of children whose mothers either had planned their pregnancies or had accepted them after they occurred. The mothers in the two groups were matched for socio-economic status and age; the children were matched for sex, birth order, number of siblings, and date of birth. At birth, the unwanted children weighed less and needed more medical help than did the children in the control group, even though their mothers had ready access to medical care and were judged to be in good health themselves.

Even when a child is wanted and a pregnant woman has a supportive family, a moderate amount of stress can be expected during pregnancy. The mother-to-be has to adjust her life to accommodate new responsibilities. One who decides to quit her job may have to cope with a reduced income. Another may be working so hard that she feels she does not have enough time to take care of herself, let alone her expected child. One recent study explored the relationship between brain development and *pregnancy anxiety*. Pregnancy anxiety was measured by a 4-point scale on which pregnant women indicated how much they agreed or disagreed with statements such as "I am fearful regarding the health of my baby," "I am concerned or worried about losing my baby," and "I am concerned or worried about developing medical problems during my pregnancy" (Buss, Davis, Muftuler, Head, & Sandman, 2010). The researchers found that when assessed between ages 6 to 9 years, children born to mothers who had been rated as high in pregnancy anxiety at 19 weeks after conception showed reduced volume in gray matter in certain areas of the brain, including the prefrontal cortex and other regions that are associated with cognitive performance. Interestingly, no such reductions were found for children whose mothers had reported high anxiety at 25 or 31 weeks after conception. The researchers suggest that fetal exposure to high levels of stress hormones in early prenatal development may interfere with the development of new neural cells. As you will later see, timing plays a crucial role in many aspects of prenatal development.

neural tube An embryonic structure that later develops into the brain and spinal cord.

Nutritional Influences

What nutrients a fetus receives obviously depends on the nutrients its mother consumes. By eating the right foods—in the right amounts—a mother can contribute to her baby's healthy development. In contrast, a mother's poor diet or overnourishment can have adverse consequences that are difficult or impossible to overcome.

Good Nutrition Research indicates that, whether pregnant or not, a woman who exercises a moderate amount needs to consume between 2000 and 2800 calories daily, in a well-balanced diet that includes all the essential vitamins and minerals (Christian, 2002). In addition, pregnant women are advised to increase their intake of folic acid (a member of the vitamin B–complex group commonly found in green vegetables and fruit), calcium, and iron to ensure healthy development and prevent certain birth defects (Van Der Put et al., 1997).

Folic acid, for example, is essential to the normal development of the fetus's **neural tube**, an embryonic structure that later develops into the brain and spinal cord (Yang et al., 2007). Neural-tube development takes place between 3 and 4 weeks after conception, often before a woman realizes that she is pregnant. In the absence of enough folic acid, the neural tube may develop serious defects, including *spina bifida,* in which the spinal cord fails to close completely, and *anencephaly,* a fatal disorder in which large portions of the brain and skull are missing. Because the neural tube develops so soon after conception, and because like many other vitamins, folic acid needs time to build up in the woman's system, it is important that women have sufficient folic acid in their diet *before* they become pregnant, in order to maximize protection against these conditions. A nationwide study found that most nonpregnant women of childbearing age in the United States reported consuming less than the recommended amount of folic acid, with non-Hispanic Black women and Hispanic women reporting higher deficiencies than non-Hispanic White women (Yang et al., 2007).

Loading a cart with fresh veggies; attending a health clinic for pregnant women. Although from vastly different cultures (the United States and Sierra Leone), these two women have access to resources necessary to help ensure healthy pregnancies.

Undernourishment, Malnutrition, and Overnourishment Pregnant women with deficient diets often suffer from *undernourishment*—food intake insufficient to develop or function normally—or *malnutrition*—the imbalance between the body's needs and the intake of nutrients even when calorie intake is within the normal range. The effects of these dietary deficiencies on prenatal development can be profound.

The clearest evidence of these effects comes from studies of sudden periods of famine. During World War

II, for example, Leningrad (now St. Petersburg) was encircled by the German army in September 1941, and no supplies reached the city until February 1942. The standard daily food ration in late November 1941 was 250 grams of bread (four slices) for factory workers and 125 grams (two slices) for everybody else. The bread was 25 percent sawdust. The number of infants born in the first half of 1942 was much lower than normal, and stillbirths doubled. Very few infants were born in the second half of 1942, all of them to couples who had better access to food than did the rest of the population. These newborns were, on average, more than a pound lighter than babies born before the siege, and they were much more likely to be premature. They were also in very poor condition at birth; they had little vitality and were unable to maintain body temperature adequately (Antonov, 1947). Because the onset of the famine was so sudden and its duration precisely known, it was easy to link the timing of severe prenatal malnutrition with its consequences. Severe nutritional deprivation during the first 3 months of pregnancy was most likely to result in abnormalities of the central nervous system, premature birth, and death. Deprivation during the last 3 months of pregnancy was more likely to retard fetal growth and result in low birth weight.

Studies of the relationships between maternal nutrition, prenatal development, and neonatal health suggest that lesser degrees of undernourishment and malnourishment also increase risks to the fetus. Poor maternal nutrition can lead to low birth weight and even miscarriage (Mora & Nestel, 2000; Morton, 2006). Research conducted in a number of countries, including Finland, Norway, Sweden, the United Kingdom, and the United States provides ample evidence that poor prenatal nutrition can also have long-term effects, such as increased risk for heart disease, diabetes, strokes, and other illnesses in later life. This association is thought to result from the fetus's adaptation to an inadequate supply of nutrients during a sensitive period in early prenatal life that leads to permanent changes in physiology and metabolism and makes the body extremely efficient in processing nutrients. The body is thus prepared for surviving in a calorie-poor environment. When it instead encounters a persistently normal or rich dietary environment, its fetally reset metabolism becomes a liability that can lead to the aforementioned diseases, which are typically associated with obesity and overweight (Thompson & Einstein, 2010; Egeland, Skajareven, & Irgens, 2000; Forsen, Eriksson, Tuomilehto, Reunanen, Osmond, & Barker, 2000; Lawlor, Smith, Clark, & Leon, 2006).

However, it is often difficult to isolate the effects of poor nutrition, because undernourished and malnourished mothers frequently live in impoverished environments where housing, sanitation, education, and medical care, including prenatal care, are also inadequate. Expectant mothers with low incomes are also more likely to suffer from diseases or simply to be in a weakened state than are women who live in better material circumstances. Their babies are more likely to suffer from a wide variety of birth defects and illnesses and to be born prematurely (Vintzileos, Ananth, Smulian, Scorza, & Knuppel, 2001, 2002). According to a variety of studies conducted in many parts of the world, including the United States, low-income mothers are also more likely to have babies who die at birth or soon after birth (UNICEF, 2003).

Several studies demonstrate that it is possible to prevent or reduce the damaging effects of malnutrition and an impoverished environment. One of the largest intervention programs designed to assess the effects of a massive supplemental food program for women, infants, and children—dubbed WIC—was initiated by the U.S. government in 1972. Low-income women in the program are given vouchers for such staples as milk, eggs, fruit juices, and dried beans. Women who have participated in the WIC program have been found to lose fewer babies during infancy than do comparable women who have not participated in the program (Moss

& Carver, 1998). Food supplements during pregnancy have also been found to be important to the baby's postnatal intellectual development. In a study carried out in Louisiana, schoolchildren whose mothers had participated in the WIC program were evaluated on a variety of intellectual measures when they were 6 or 7 years old. Those children whose mothers had received food supplements during the last 3 months of their pregnancy—the period in which the fetal brain undergoes especially rapid development—outperformed the children of mothers who did not receive food supplements until after their children were born (Hicks, Langham, & Takenaka, 1982). Similar results were obtained in studies of food supplement programs in rural Guatemala and Zanzibar (Pollitt, Saco-Pollitt, Jahari, Husaini, & Huang, 2000; Stoltzfus et al., 2001).

Although developmentalists have focused most of their attention on how babies' health suffers when their mothers do not get enough nutrients during their pregnancies, they have recently begun to emphasize that fetuses are also at risk when pregnant mothers are *overnourished*, usually as a result of their consuming a high-fat diet (Baker, Olsen, & Sorensen, 2008). At birth, these babies are often **large for gestational age**; that is, their weight is above the 90th percentile of babies of the same sex who are the same **gestational age** (the amount of time since conception). Usually born to mothers who are diabetic and obese, overweight babies are likely to develop diabetes and obesity themselves.

You may well be thinking that the development of these diseases could be due, not to the mother's diet during pregnancy, but rather to the child's diet after birth. If so, you would be partially correct: Research has demonstrated that a mother's postnatal eating behavior can affect how much food her child consumes (Gluck, Venti, Lindsay, Knowler, Salbe, & Krakoff, 2009). However, other research suggests that the uterine environment is at least partly implicated. Studies of non-human mammals (rats, mostly) find that mothers who are fed diets high in fat during pregnancy have offspring at risk for overweight, diabetes, and high blood pressure (Khan, Dekou, Hanson, Poston, & Taylor, 2004; Taylor, et al., 2005). And a convincing study conducted with the Pima Indians, who have extremely high rates of obesity and diabetes, found that children whose mothers were diabetic while pregnant had higher rates of diabetes than did children whose mothers developed diabetes after their pregnancy (Pettitt et al., 1988). In general, populations with high adult obesity rates also have higher rates of large-for-gestational-age babies (Chu, 2005).

Developmentalists have expressed concern about the problem of overweight babies in future generations (Thompson & Einstein, 2010). In particular, while the rate of underweight babies has been generally stable, the rate of overweight babies has increased substantially. In the United States, for example, the number of large-for-gestational-age babies increased from 9.3 percent to 11.7 percent between 2000 and 2006. This is a distressing change that foreshadows a number of health problems as these individuals mature (Martin et al., 2008).

These conclusions concerning poor maternal and fetal nutrition must be considered with some caution because they are correlational. However, the overall evidence strongly suggests that millions of children throughout the world are damaged by undernourishment, malnutrition, or overnourishment before birth. Moreover, many of the children who are undernourished or malnourished prenatally also have nutritional and other deprivations in childhood: most do not receive food supplements, and even fewer receive high-quality medical and educational help. Thus, they tend to have a cascade of risk factors, of which poor maternal and fetal nutrition is only one (Figure 3.9). Together, such conditions lead to high rates of infant mortality and shorter life expectancies (Pollitt, 2001).

large for gestational age Babies whose weight at birth is above the 90th percentile of babies of the same sex who are the same gestational age.

gestational age The amount of time between conception and birth. The normal gestational age is between 37 and 43 weeks.

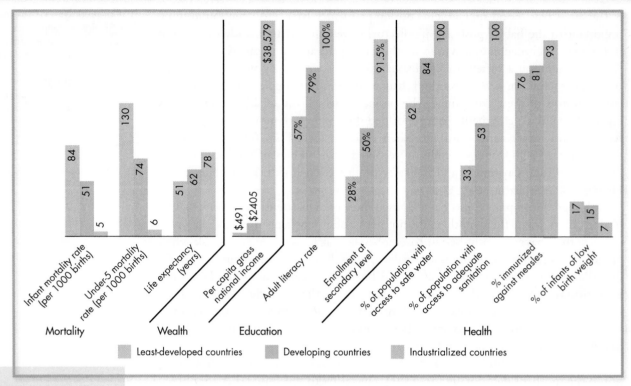

FIGURE 3.9 In many countries of the world, poor economic conditions create a set of risk factors. For example, poor health conditions and parents' lack of education negatively influence child health and welfare. (Adapted from UNICEF, 2008.)

▲ APPLY :: CONNECT :: DISCUSS

Along with the famine in Leningrad during World War II, the famous Dutch famine of 1944 has provided a wealth of information for scientists interested in the effects of fetal malnourishment on subsequent development. Conduct some online research and explore some of the projects associated with the Dutch Famine Birth Cohort Study. What are some of the questions currently addressed by the study? What are some of the most recent findings?

Teratogens: Environmental Sources of Birth Defects

Other threats to the prenatal organism come from **teratogens**—environmental agents such as toxins, disease, drugs, and alcohol that increase the risk of deviations in normal development and can lead to serious abnormalities or death. Although the effects of teratogens on the developing organism vary with the specific agent involved, six general principles apply to all of them (Moore & Persaud, 1998):

1. A developing organism's susceptibility to a teratogenic agent depends on its developmental stage at the time of exposure. Overall, the gravest danger to life comes during the first 2 weeks, before the cells of the organism have undergone extensive differentiation and before most women are even aware that they are pregnant (Figure 3.10). During this critical period, a teratogenic agent may completely destroy the organism. Thereafter, the various body systems are most vulnerable during the initial stages of their formation and development. As Figure 3.10 indicates, the most vulnerable period for the central nervous system is from 15 to 36 days after conception, whereas the upper and lower limbs are most vulnerable from 24 to 49 days after conception.

teratogens Environmental agents that can cause deviations from normal development and can lead to abnormalities or death.

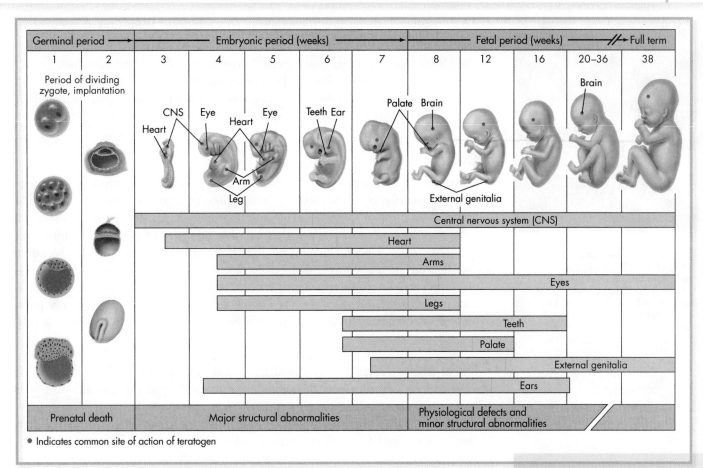

Germinal period →		Embryonic period (weeks) →					Fetal period (weeks) → // Full term				

• Indicates common site of action of teratogen

FIGURE 3.10 The critical periods in human prenatal development occur when the organs and other body parts are forming and therefore are most vulnerable to teratogens. Before implantation, teratogens either damage all or most of the cells of the organism, causing its death, or damage only a few cells, allowing the organism to recover without developing defects. In the figure, the blue portions of the bars represent periods of highest risk of major structural abnormalities; the peach portions represent periods of reduced sensitivity to teratogens. (Adapted from Moore & Persaud, 1993.)

2. A teratogenic agent's effects are likely to be specific to a particular organ. Therefore, each teratogen causes a particular pattern of abnormal development. The drug thalidomide, for example, causes deformation of the legs and arms, and mercury compounds cause brain damage that is manifested as cerebral palsy.

3. Individual organisms vary in their susceptibility to teratogens. The way a developing organism responds to teratogenic agents depends to some degree on its genetic vulnerability to these agents. For example, while maternal exposure to air pollution *increases the risk* of malformations in all fetuses, among fetuses equally exposed to a given air pollutant, some will be severely affected, others will be only slightly affected, and some will develop normally.

4. Susceptibility to teratogenic agents also depends on the mother's physiological state. The mother's age, nutrition, uterine condition, and hormonal balance all influence the effects that teratogens can have on the developing organism. The risk of malformation is highest, for example, when the mother is younger than 20 or older than 40 (the precise reasons for this are not known). Nutritional deficiency in the mother intensifies the adverse effects of some teratogens. The impact of teratogens also appears to increase if the mother suffers from diabetes, a metabolic imbalance, or liver dysfunction, among other disorders.

FIGURE 3.11 The deformed hand of this 13-year-old boy may have been caused by toxic materials released by a steel plant and inhaled and ingested by his mother when she was pregnant with him. A number of other children born around the same time to mothers in his London community were similarly affected with serious birth defects.

5. In general, the greater the exposure to teratogenic agents, the greater the risk of abnormal development.

6. Some teratogens, such as rubella ("German measles"), that have little or only a temporary effect on the mother can lead to serious abnormalities during prenatal development. The most common such teratogens include certain drugs and infections, radiation, and pollution (Figure 3.11).

Drugs

Most pregnant women in the United States take some medication during pregnancy, primarily over-the-counter pain relievers, antinauseants, or sleep aids. Fortunately, most of these drugs do not appear to harm the fetus, but there are some that do. It is also estimated that a sizable minority of women use nonmedical substances during pregnancy, ranging from caffeine, alcohol, and tobacco to "hard" drugs such as cocaine and heroin. While most of these drugs appear harmful to prenatal development, it is often hard to isolate the effects of specific drugs because drug-abusing mothers often abuse multiple drugs or are generally poor, undernourished, and unlikely to receive proper prenatal care (Orioli & Castilla, 2000).

Prescription Drugs The potential teratogenic effects of prescription drugs first came to light with the drug thalidomide. From 1956 until 1961, thalidomide was used in Europe as a sedative and to control nausea in the early stages of pregnancy. The women who took the drug were unharmed by it, and many of the children they bore suffered no ill effects. Some children, however, were born without arms and legs; their hands and feet were attached directly to their torsos like flippers. Some had defects of sight and hearing as well. About 8000 children with deformities were born before their problems were traced to the drug and it was removed from the market (Persaud, 1977).

Since the disastrous effects of thalidomide were discovered, other prescription drugs have been found to cause abnormalities in the developing organism, including the antibiotics streptomycin and tetracycline; anticoagulants; anticonvulsants; most artificial hormones; Thorazine (used in the treatment of schizophrenia); Valium (a tranquilizer); and Accutane (used to treat difficult cases of acne).

Caffeine Found in coffee, tea, and many soft and "energy" drinks, caffeine is the most common drug used by pregnant women. There is no evidence that caffeine causes malformations in the fetus (Clausson et al., 2002). However, some studies have found that caffeine in large doses is associated with low birth weight and impaired bone growth (Bakker, Steegers, Obradov, Raat, Hofman, & Jaddoe, 2010). On this basis, women are advised to limit their caffeine intake during pregnancy.

Tobacco Smoking tobacco is not known to produce birth defects, but it has been found to harm the fetus in a variety of ways. Smoking is related to an increase in the rate of spontaneous abortion, stillbirth, and neonatal death (Chan, Keane, & Robinson, 2001). Nicotine, the addictive substance in tobacco, causes abnormal growth of the placenta, resulting in a reduction in the transfer of nutrients to the fetus. It also reduces the oxygen, and increases the carbon monoxide, in the bloodstream of both the mother and the fetus. As a result, mothers who smoke usually have babies whose birth weights are lower than those of infants born to women who do not smoke. The effects of cigarette smoke seem to be dose related: pregnant women who smoke more have babies who weigh less (Hindmarsh et al., 2008; Wang et al., 2002). Research suggests that even if a pregnant woman does not smoke herself, the health of her baby can be significantly affected by the cigarette smoke of others (Ashford, Hahn, Hall, Rayens, Noland, & Ferguson, 2010). Consistent with the fact that nicotine is a stimulant, prenatal nicotine exposure has also been associated with sleep problems throughout the first 12 years of life (Stone et al., 2010).

Alcohol About 4 percent of all U.S. women of childbearing age suffer from alcoholism, and many more are "social drinkers" who consume alcohol on a regular basis (Stratton, Howe, & Battaglia, 1996). Women who drink substantial amounts of alcohol while they are pregnant, especially during the first trimester, are in danger of having a baby with serious birth defects (O'Leary et al., 2010).

Many studies have found that a large proportion of infants born to mothers who were heavy drinkers during pregnancy—that is, who drank at least 14 standard drinks per week on average, or engaged in binge drinking (4 or more drinks on a single occasion)—were abnormal in some way (see Molina et al., 2007, for a review). Many of these babies suffered from **fetal alcohol syndrome**, a set of symptoms that includes an abnormally small head and underdeveloped brain, eye abnormalities, congenital heart disease, joint anomalies, and malformations of the face (Figure 3.12). The physical growth and mental development of children with this syndrome are likely to be retarded. Women who drink heavily during the first trimester of pregnancy and then reduce their consumption of alcohol during the next 3 months do not reduce the risk of having children with this affliction. Binge drinking early in pregnancy has been associated with a subtle impairment of learning and behavior in adolescence (Kesmodel, 2001). As adults, individuals who were exposed to excessive amounts of alcohol prenatally (that is, whose mothers consumed more than 20 drinks per week, on average) perform more poorly on measures of learning and memory, and have significantly smaller brains, than do nonexposed individuals (Coles et al., 2011).

The effects of lower levels of alcohol consumption on development are not entirely clear, to some extent because they have not been thoroughly studied (Huizink & Mulder, 2006). Research has found that, in some cases, the equivalent of one or two glasses of wine, either occasionally or daily, causes no discernible harm to the fetus. In other cases, such drinking results in effects that include subtle but measurable deficits in cognitive and motor functioning. Notwithstanding some mixed results, a comprehensive review of the effects of alcohol on human and nonhuman fetal development indicates that alcohol exposure places fetuses at risk for defects—defects that will vary with both the amount of prenatal exposure to alcohol and the timing of the exposure.

Marijuana According to a recent report, approximately 4 percent of women in the United States acknowledge using illegal drugs while pregnant, with marijuana (cannabis) being the one most commonly used (see Figure 3.13 and SAMHSA, 2006). Marijuana has not been definitively found to cause birth defects, but its use is associated with low birth weight, as well as with certain neurological differences that may persist throughout childhood (Smith et al., 2004; Willford, Chandler, Goldschmidt, & Day, 2010). Some researchers have also found an increase in

Heather was born with fetal alcohol syndrome. At 22 years of age, she is autistic, has cerebral palsy, a seizure disorder, and the mental capacities of a 3-year-old.

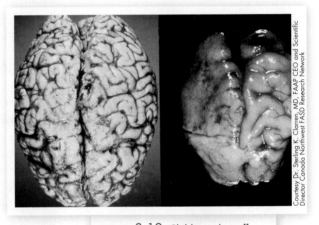

FIGURE 3.12 Children who suffer from fetal alcohol syndrome have underdeveloped brains and often severe retardation. When severely affected by alcohol, the brain (above right) lacks the convolutions characteristic of the brain of a normal child (above left). Such an affected brain will result in the death of the fetus.

fetal alcohol syndrome A syndrome found in babies whose mothers were heavy consumers of alcohol while pregnant. Symptoms include an abnormally small head and underdeveloped brain, eye abnormalities, congenital heart disease, joint anomalies, and malformations of the face.

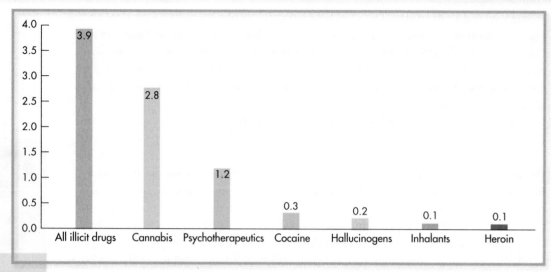

FIGURE 3.13 Nearly 4% of women in the United States report using illicit drugs, most commonly, marijuana. (Source: SAMHSA, 2006.)

premature delivery among women who use marijuana more than once a week. However, it is uncertain whether these effects can be attributed solely to the use of marijuana because U.S. women who use marijuana during pregnancy tend to be poorer, less educated, younger, single, and more likely to use other illegal drugs than mothers who do not use marijuana. They also receive less prenatal care and gain less weight. Nonetheless, since it is estimated that approximately one-third of the psychoactive compound present in the marijuana-smoking mother's bloodstream crosses the placenta to the fetus, there is obvious cause for concern about possible short-term and long-term effects on development (Hurd, Wang, Anderson, Beck, Minkoff, & Dow-Edwards, 2005).

Cocaine A stimulant that rapidly produces addiction in the user, cocaine may result in numerous medical complications for the mother-to-be, including heart attacks, strokes, rupture of the aorta, and seizures (Cunningham et al., 2001). Babies of cocaine-addicted mothers are at elevated risk for a variety of problems, including stillbirth or premature birth, low birth weight, strokes, and birth defects (Ursitti, Klein, & Koren, 2001). They are also described as being irritable, excessively reactive to environmental stimulation, uncoordinated, and slow learners (Schuetze, Eiden, & Edwards, 2009).

Residual effects of cocaine exposure during the prenatal period may last for several years. For example, preschool-age children prenatally exposed to cocaine exhibit subtle delays in language development and are likely to experience difficulty regulating their emotions when frustrated (Morrow et al., 2003; Schuetze, Eiden, & Danielewicz, 2009).

Despite the justified concern about the effects of prenatal exposure to cocaine, some researchers have been critical of claims that cocaine itself is the cause of the problems just described (Lester & Tronick, 1994). These researchers note that, as we saw in the case with marijuana, many mothers who use cocaine also are likely to drink alcohol and use other drugs. In addition, many of the mothers are poor and live in stressful circumstances. All these factors are known to contribute to symptoms such as those attributed to prenatal cocaine exposure. Consequently, while more recent research on prenatal cocaine exposure continues to show negative impacts on later development, a causal link between such exposure and later behavior is still not considered ironclad (Hurt et al., 2009; Morrow et al., 2003).

Methamphetamine The use of methamphetamine (also known as "meth" or "crystal") during pregnancy is on the rise in the United States, with the rate of hospital admissions of expectant mothers for methamphetamine-related problems tripling between 1994 and 2006 (Terplan, Smith, Kozlosk, & Pollack, 2009). A *longitudinal study* (see p. 38) found that babies whose mothers had used the drug during their pregnancy were significantly smaller than babies whose mothers were nonusers (Nguyen et al., 2010). The study included nearly 4000 women and statistically controlled for (that is, took into account) a number of other factors associated with deficient fetal growth, including prenatal care, maternal age, maternal weight gain, family income, and other drug use. Although this study provides strong evidence that methamphetamine exposure interferes with normal fetal growth, the precise mechanism of fetal growth retardation is not clear. One possibility is that the drug restricts the mother's blood flow, consequently restricting the nutrition that reaches the fetus. Regardless of the specific mechanism involved, fetuses exposed to methamphetamine very likely are at risk for problems known to affect other babies who are unusually small, as we discuss later in the chapter (Barker, Osmond, Simmonds, & Wield, 1993).

Heroin and Methadone Babies of mothers who are addicted to the opium derivatives heroin or methadone are born addicted themselves and must be given heroin or methadone shortly after birth to avoid the often life-threatening ordeal of withdrawal. These babies are at risk of being premature, underweight, and vulnerable to respiratory illnesses (Kaltenbach et al., 1998).

While these babies are being weaned from the drugs to which they were born addicted, they are irritable and have tremors, their cries are abnormal, their sleep is disturbed, and their motor control is diminished. The effects of the addiction are still apparent in their motor control 4 months later, and even after a year, their ability to pay attention is impaired (Yanai et al., 2000).

Several studies have also reported long-term developmental problems in children exposed in utero to heroin, methadone, or other opium derivatives. But as with marijuana and cocaine, whether these problems can be solely attributed to the mother's drug use is still open to question (Jones, 2006).

Infections and Other Health Conditions

A variety of infection-causing microorganisms can endanger the embryo, the fetus, and the newborn. Most infections spread from the mother to the unborn child across the placental barrier. In a few instances, however, the baby may become infected during the passage through the birth canal. Some of the more common infections and other maternal conditions that may affect the developing human organism are summarized below; Table 3.3 summarizes others.

Rubella Rubella (sometimes called the 3-day measles) is a mild condition with symptoms that include a rash, swollen lymph glands, and a low fever. If contracted by a mother-to-be early in pregnancy, however, the consequences can be devastating for her baby. Research has found that half of all children born to women who had the disease during the first 16 weeks of pregnancy exhibit a syndrome of congenital heart disease, cataracts, deafness, and mental retardation (Centers for Disease Control, 2010). (Exposure to rubella infections after 16 weeks of pregnancy is less likely to have these effects.) The development of a vaccine for rubella in 1969 has greatly reduced the incidence of the disease, but it has not been eradicated, and several U.S. states require a blood test of immunity to rubella before issuing

table 3.3

Some Maternal Diseases and Conditions That May Affect Prenatal Development

Sexually Transmitted Diseases

Genital herpes	Infection usually occurs at birth as the baby comes in contact with herpes lesions on the mother's genitals, although the virus may also cross the placental barrier to infect the fetus. Infection can lead to blindness and serious brain damage. There is no cure for the disease. Mothers with active genital herpes often have a cesarean delivery to avoid infecting their babies.
Gonorrhea	The gonococcus organism may attack the eyes while the baby is passing through the infected birth canal. Silver nitrate or erythromycin eyedrops are administered immediately after birth to prevent blindness.
Syphilis	The effects of syphilis on the fetus can be devastating. An estimated 25 percent of infected fetuses are born dead. Those who survive may be deaf, mentally retarded, or deformed. Syphilis can be diagnosed by a blood test and can be cured before the fetus is affected, since the syphilis spirochete cannot penetrate the placental membrane before the 21st week of gestation.

Other Diseases and Maternal Conditions

Chicken pox	Chicken pox may lead to spontaneous abortion or premature delivery, but it does not appear to cause malformations.
Cytomegalovirus	The most common source of prenatal infection, cytomegalovirus produces no symptoms in adults, but it may be fatal to the embryo. Infection later in intrauterine life has been related to brain damage, deafness, blindness, and cerebral palsy (a defect of motor coordination caused by brain damage).
Diabetes	Diabetic mothers face a greater risk of having a stillborn child or one who dies shortly after birth. Babies of diabetics are often very large because of the accumulation of fat during the third trimester. Diabetic mothers require special care to prevent these problems.
Hepatitis	Mothers who have hepatitis are likely to pass it on to their infants during birth.
Hypertension	Hypertension (chronic high blood pressure) increases the probability of miscarriage and infant death.
Influenza	The more virulent forms of influenza may lead to spontaneous abortion or may cause abnormalities during the early stages of pregnancy.
Mumps	Mumps is suspected of causing spontaneous abortion in the first trimester of pregnancy.
Toxemia	About 5 percent of pregnant women in the United States are affected during the third trimester by this disorder of unknown origin. The condition occurs most often during first pregnancies. Symptoms are water retention, high blood pressure, rapid weight gain, and protein in the urine. If untreated, toxemia may cause convulsions, coma, and even death for the mother. Death of the fetus is not uncommon.
Toxoplasmosis	A mild disease in adults with symptoms similar to those of the common cold, toxoplasmosis is caused by a parasite that is present in raw meat and cat feces. It may cause spontaneous abortion or death. Babies who survive may have serious eye or brain damage.

Sources: Moore & Persaud, 1993; Stevenson, 1977.

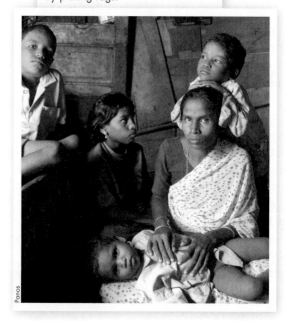

This mother with AIDS, living in Mumbai, India, sits with her four HIV-positive children. Her husband died of AIDS, and she supports her family by picking rags.

Panos

a marriage license. Women are advised to avoid becoming pregnant for at least 6 months after they receive the vaccine.

HIV and AIDS Worldwide in 2008, approximately 430,000 babies, nearly 90 percent of whom are in sub-Saharan Africa, were born with *human immunodeficiency virus* (HIV) (UNICEF, 2009). The virus, which can lead to *acquired immune deficiency syndrome* (AIDS), may be transmitted from the mother to her baby by passing through the placental barrier, by the baby's exposure to the mother's infected blood during delivery, or through breastfeeding. About half of all children infected with HIV from their mothers will die before their 2nd birthday (Newell, Coovadia, Cortina-Borja, Rollins, Gaillard, & Dabis, 2004). The risk of transmission increases with the length of time the mother has been infected.

There is no known cure for AIDS, now the seventh-leading cause of death in children under the age of 4. However, if HIV-positive women receive HIV-inhibiting antiretroviral drugs during pregnancy and at the time of delivery, and their baby receives treatment immediately after birth, the chances of the baby's contracting the virus are substantially reduced (World Health Organization/UNAIDS/UNICEF, 2010). Therefore, there are two challenges to preventing mother-to-child transmission of HIV. The first is to identify HIV-infected mothers through testing; the second is to provide them, and their newborns, with antiretroviral drugs and infant-feeding alternatives.

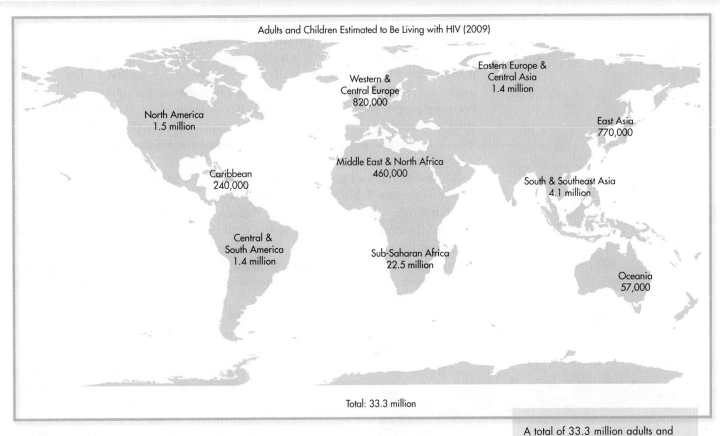

Adults and Children Estimated to Be Living with HIV (2009)

Eastern Europe & Central Asia
1.4 million

Western & Central Europe
820,000

North America
1.5 million

East Asia
770,000

Middle East & North Africa
460,000

Caribbean
240,000

South & Southeast Asia
4.1 million

Central & South America
1.4 million

Sub-Saharan Africa
22.5 million

Oceania
57,000

Total: 33.3 million

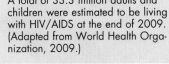

A total of 33.3 million adults and children were estimated to be living with HIV/AIDS at the end of 2009. (Adapted from World Health Organization, 2009.)

Unfortunately, the challenges have proved difficult to meet. A scant 24 percent of pregnant women in countries with the highest HIV rates are tested. And, as shown in Figure 3.14, only 53 percent of HIV-infected pregnant women, and 35 percent of their newborns, receive antiretrovirals.

Rh Incompatibility Rh is a complex substance on the surface of the red blood cells. One of its components is determined by a dominant gene, and people who have this component are said to be Rh-positive. Fewer than 1 in 10 people inherit the two recessive genes that make them Rh-negative (de Vrijer et al., 1999).

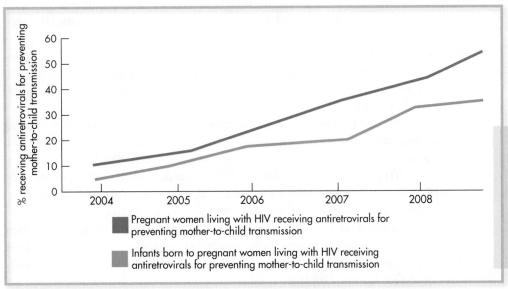

% receiving antiretrovirals for preventing mother-to-child transmission

2004 2005 2006 2007 2008

■ Pregnant women living with HIV receiving antiretrovirals for preventing mother-to-child transmission

■ Infants born to pregnant women living with HIV receiving antiretrovirals for preventing mother-to-child transmission

FIGURE 3.14 Although the number of pregnant women and infants receiving antiretrovirals to prevent mother-to-child transmission of HIV has increased significantly since 2004, nearly half of pregnant women and two-thirds of infants in need of such drugs do not receive them. (Source: World Health Organization, UNAIDS, & UNICEF, 2010.)

When an Rh-negative woman conceives a child with an Rh-positive man, the child is likely to be Rh-positive. During the birth of the baby, some of the baby's blood cells usually pass into the mother's bloodstream while the placenta is separating from the uterine wall. To fight this foreign substance, the mother's immune system creates antibodies, which remain in her bloodstream. If she becomes pregnant again with another Rh-positive child, these antibodies will enter the fetus's bloodstream and attack its red blood cells. (Firstborn children are usually unharmed because they are born before the mother has produced many antibodies.)

Rh disease can lead to serious birth defects and even death. Fortunately, physicians can prevent Rh disease by giving the Rh-negative mother an injection of anti-Rh serum within 72 hours of the delivery of an Rh-positive child. The serum kills any Rh-positive blood cells in the mother's bloodstream so that she will not develop antibodies to attack them. Alternatively, the fetus can be given blood transfusions, usually through its umbilical chord (Somerset et al., 2006). Children who are born with Rh disease can be treated with periodic blood transfusions (Fanaroff & Martin, 1997).

Radiation Massive doses of radiation often lead to serious malformations of the developing organism and, in many cases, cause prenatal death or spontaneous abortion (Douple et al., 2011). Somewhat lower doses may spare the life of the organism but may have a profound effect on its development. Many of the pregnant women who were within a mile (1500 meters) of the atomic bomb blasts at Hiroshima and Nagasaki in 1945 and survived later lost their babies. Of the babies who appeared to be normal at birth, 64 percent were later diagnosed as mentally retarded.

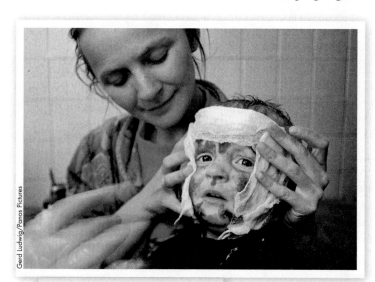

This Ukrainian boy is being treated for a skin disease associated with exposure to radiation caused by the famous Chernobyl nuclear plant explosion which, decades later, continues to pollute his community.

The effects of low doses of radiation on human beings have not been firmly established. Because X-rays may cause malformations in the embryo, women who need to be X-rayed should inform their doctor if they are or may be pregnant.

Pollution Most of the thousands of chemicals that are present in our environments—in our homes, in the air we breath, in the food and water we consume—have never been tested to see if they are harmful to prenatal development, even though some of these substances reach the embryo or fetus through the placenta (Jones, 1997). Many environmental toxins that have been studied, however, are associated with dramatic disruptions and disorders in fetal development, including birth defects, growth retardation, premature birth, and fetal death (Wigle et al., 2008; Yanai et al., 2008).

In 1956, the consumption of large quantities of fish from Minamata Bay in Japan was discovered to be associated with a series of neurological and other symptoms, which have come to be known as Minamata disease (Yorifuji, Tsuda, Inoue, Takao, & Harada, 2011). It was later determined that mercury waste discharged from an industrial plant had polluted the bay, and that the mercury had passed, in increasingly concentrated amounts, through the bay's food chain to fish eaten by humans. Pregnant women who ate the contaminated fish passed the mercury on to their unborn babies. Symptoms in these babies included cerebral palsy (a disorder of the central nervous system), deformation of the skull, and sometimes an abnormally small head (Tuchmann-Duplessis, 1975).

The incidence of birth defects is also known to be abnormally high in areas of heavy atmospheric pollution. In the Brazilian industrial city of Cubatão, for instance, the air pollution from petrochemical and steel plants alone once exceeded that generated by all the combined industries in the Los Angeles basin of California. During the 1970s, 65 of every 1000 babies born in Cubatão died shortly after birth because their brains had failed to develop—double the rate of this defect in neighboring communities that were not so heavily polluted (Freed, 1983). Fortunately, strong environmental safety efforts have greatly reduced the pollution in Cubatão, and the death rate of infants there has declined remarkably (Brooke, 1991).

In China, the recent dramatic increase in birth defects, which has been reported as having jumped 40 percent between 2001 and 2006, is largely due to pollutants associated with the country's explosive industrial growth. According to a 2007 report by the Chinese government's National Population and Family Planning Commission, a child with a birth defect is born every 30 seconds in mainland China (Yinan, 2007).

In many U.S. cities, atmospheric pollution is severe enough to cause concern about effects on prenatal development. One recent study found a strong relationship between rates of air pollution and infant death rates (Ritz, Wilhelm, & Zhao, 2006). There is also a good deal of concern about the risk chemical dumps pose to the fetuses of pregnant women who live nearby. Unfortunately, much more research is required before the risks that these and other such environmental hazards pose for prenatal development can be accurately assessed.

We have now come to the end of our survey of prenatal development. As we noted, many developmentalists view the prenatal period as a model for all subsequent development because certain principles that apply to prenatal development also appear to explain development after birth. Before moving on to our discussion of birth, you might find it helpful to review these principles, summarized in Table 3.4. Because

table 3.4

Principles of Prenatal Development
Sequence is fundamental. One cell must exist before there can be two. Muscles and bones must be present before nerves can coordinate movement. Gonads must secrete testosterone before further sexual differentiation can occur.
Timing is crucial to development. If the ovum moves too rapidly or too slowly down the fallopian tube, pregnancy is terminated. If exposure to a particular teratogen occurs during a particular stage of development, the impact on the organism may be devastating, whereas if it occurs before or after this stage, there may be little or no impact—a difference that implies the existence of sensitive periods for the formation of organ systems.
Development consists of a process of differentiation and integration. From the single cell of the zygote, division leads to many identical cells, which eventually differentiate into the distinct kinds of cells of all the organs of the body, with the specifics likely the result of cells' interactions with surrounding cells. Arm buds differentiate to form fingers, which will differ from each other in ways that make possible the finely articulated movements of the human hand.
Development proceeds unevenly. From the earliest steps of cleavage, the various subsystems that make up the organism develop at their own rates. An important special case of such unevenness is physical development, which follows cephalocaudal (from the head down) and proximodistal (from the center to the periphery) sequences.
Development is characterized by changes both in the form of the organism and in the ways it interacts with its environment. The embryo not only looks altogether different from the fetus but also interacts with its environment in a qualitatively different way.
Development is epigenetic. Although the development of new phenotypic forms is constrained by genetic materials coded in the zygote, the phenotypic forms emerge out of the ongoing organism–environment interactions that sustain and propel development.

the principles have been found useful for characterizing development during other periods, you will see them recur throughout our study of child development.

⏏ APPLY :: CONNECT :: DISCUSS

Visit the Web site of the Centers for Disease Control and Prevention. Explore their "One Test. Two Lives." initiative. What is the goal of the initiative? How does the CDC hope to implement the initiative? What materials and tools have they developed to move the initiative forward?

Birth

DELLA'S STORY

everything out of sync
  lights on and off
  contractions on top of each other . . .
  nurse never really there—and when she was, she wasn't, reprimanding . . .
  everybody talked to me while I'm blind—increasingly frozen with pain. Even Dr. A trying to extricate himself from my grasp: "you're breaking my hand and if you don't let go I won't be able to deliver your baby. . . ."
  then the order to move my legs "square up your knees" the giant operating lights suddenly descending from the ceiling behind Dr. A's head. where am I? my head won't talk to my legs—can't make them move—can't breathe for the pain. . . .
  blue rubbery wet doll on my chest—I wish this gown was off. much to my amazement you are blond! (From Pollock, 1999.)

NISA'S STORY

Mother's stomach grew very large. The first labor pains came at night and stayed with her until dawn. That morning, everyone went gathering. Mother and I stayed behind. We sat together for a while, then I went and played with the other children. Later, I came back and ate the nuts she had cracked for me. She got up and started to get ready. I said, "Mommy, let's go to the water well, I'm thirsty." She said, "Uhn, uhn, I'm going to gather some mongongo nuts." I told the children that I was going and we left; there were no other adults around. We walked a short way, then she sat down by the base of a large nehn tree, leaned back against it, and little Kumsa was born. (From Shostak, 1981.)

These two descriptions of giving birth are from two vastly different cultures. The first describes the experience of Della, a highly educated, middle-class, urban American woman. The second is provided by Nisa, a woman of the !Kung, a hunting-and-gathering society living in the Kalahari Desert of southern Africa. Each story is unusual in its own way, but neither is unique. In some societies, giving birth unassisted is treated as a cultural ideal that displays the mother's fearlessness and self-confidence. In other societies, birthing has become highly medicalized, while in still others the process is supported by other members of the community, particularly the women in the mother-to-be's family.

Of all life's transitions, birth may be the most radical. Before birth, the amniotic fluid provides a wet, warm environment, and the fetus receives continuous oxygen and nourishment through the umbilical cord. At birth, the lungs inflate to take in oxygen and exhale carbon dioxide for the first time. The first breath of oxygen acts to shut off the bypass that shunts blood away from the lungs to the placenta. It also causes the umbilical arteries to close down, cutting off fetal circulation to the placenta. Now the baby must obtain oxygen through the lungs, must work for nourishment by sucking, and no longer has the placenta to provide protection against disease-causing organisms.

The social and behavioral changes that occur at birth are no less pronounced than the biological ones. The newborn encounters other human beings directly for the first time, and the parents get their first glimpse of their child. From the moment of birth, infants and parents begin to construct a social relationship.

The Stages of Labor

The biological process of birth begins with a series of changes in the mother's body that force the fetus through the birth canal. It ends when the mother expels the placenta after the baby has emerged. Labor normally begins approximately 280 days after the first day of a woman's last menstrual period, or 266 days after conception. It is customarily divided into three overlapping stages (Figure 3.15).

The first stage of labor begins when uterine contractions of sufficient frequency, intensity, and duration begin to cause the cervix (the narrow outer end of the uterus) to dilate. This initial stage continues until the opening of the uterus into the vagina is fully dilated and the connections between the bones of the mother's pelvis become more flexible (Cunningham et al., 2001). The length of this stage varies from woman to woman and from pregnancy to pregnancy: It may last anywhere from less than an hour to several days. The norm for first births is about 14 hours. At the beginning of labor, contractions come 15 to 20 minutes apart and last anywhere from 15 to 60 seconds. As labor proceeds, the contractions become more frequent, more intense, and longer in duration.

The second stage of labor begins as the baby is pushed headfirst through the fully dilated cervix into the vagina. (This passage is facilitated by the fact that the baby's head is comparatively soft because the bones of the skull have not yet fused.) The contractions now usually come no more than a minute apart and last about a minute. The pressure of the baby in the birth canal and the powerful contractions of the uterus typically cause the mother to bear down and push the baby out.

Usually the top of the baby's head and the brow are the first to emerge. Occasionally, babies emerge in other positions, the most common being the breech position, with the feet or buttocks emerging first. In cases in which the baby is born in a breech position, which occurs in 3 to 4 percent of single births, both mother and fetus are at considerably increased risk of serious complications or death (Nkata, 2001).

The third stage of labor, the final one, occurs when the baby has emerged from the vagina and the contractions of the uterus cause the placenta to buckle and

FIGURE 3.15 During the first stage of labor, which usually lasts several hours, the cervix dilates, often to 9 or 10 centimeters in diameter. During the second stage, the birth canal widens, permitting the baby to emerge. The final stage (not shown) occurs when the placenta is delivered. (Adapted from Clarke-Stewart & Koch, 1983.)

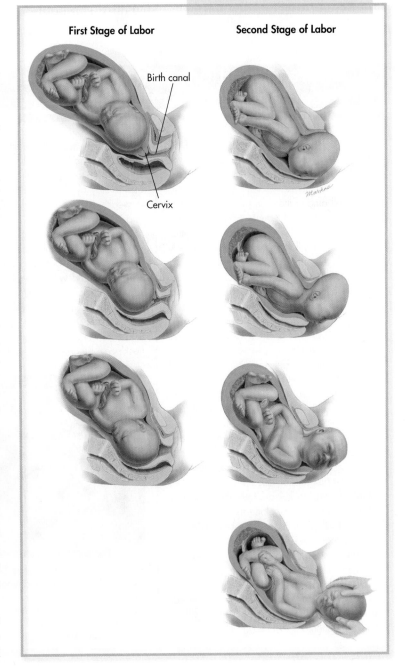

First Stage of Labor **Second Stage of Labor**

Birth canal

Cervix

separate from the uterine wall, pulling the other fetal membranes with it. Contractions quickly expel them, and they are delivered as the afterbirth.

Cultural Variations in Childbirth

As a biological process, labor occurs in roughly the same way everywhere. However, as you encountered in our descriptions of childbirth in various cultures—the !Kung, the Hmong, and Western cultures such as the United States—there are wide cultural variations in childbirth practices. One striking example concerns the presence of birth attendants who assist the mother as she labors. Although relatively rare, women in some cultures are expected to give birth unassisted. During childbirth, women in the remote Bajura district of eastern Nepal stay alone in an animal shed that is separate from the main home and is usually small and dirty. This isolation is based on the traditional Nepalese view that the blood

Cultural Traditions and Infant Care: From Spirit Village to the Land of Beng

AT THE EDGE OF A RAIN FOREST IN West Africa, villagers engage in the daily activities of farming, housekeeping, and communicating with the many spirits that dwell among them and are the source of both good and bad fortune. According to anthropologist Alma Gottlieb (2005), the spiritual beliefs of the villagers, who are collectively known as the Beng, pervade infant care practices and the early life experiences of babies. The Beng believe that babies are reincarnations of dead ancestors currently dwelling in the "spirit village," where they enjoy rich and full social lives. The invisible spirit world exists side by side with the earthly world of the living, and the boundary between them is fluid and permeable, permitting easy movement from one to the other. Ancestors are believed to visit the world of the living on a daily basis, and some adults are known to have visited the spirit world in their dreams, where they communicate with their ancestors.

Against the backdrop of this complex spiritual belief system is an equally complex system of infant care. Babies are believed to occupy a precarious and risky place as they pass from the spirit village to the world of the living—a journey that does not begin until the umbilical stump drops off (a special drying salve is applied frequently to the stump to hurry the process along) and can take up to 7 years to complete. During this time, it is believed, there is a possibility that the infants will return permanently to the spirit village, usually

because they miss the wealth, comforts, and friends they had there. Much of Beng infant care is therefore focused on convincing babies to stay by showering them with symbols of wealth. Because cowry shells are believed to be the primary form of wealth in the ancestral village, infants are adorned with cowry shell jewelry as a symbol of their wealth in the land of the living and are promised that they are valued and will be well cared for. They may also be provided with special jewelry or elaborate face paint to combat diseases and disabilities inflicted by ancestral spirits. Gottlieb noted that some babies wear "so many necklaces, bracelets, anklets, knee bands and

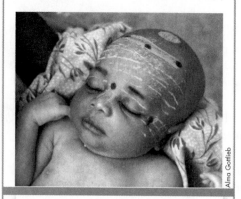

Beng mothers paint elaborate designs on their babies' faces every day to protect them and keep them healthy. The large orange dot on the "soft spot" ensures that the baby can nurse and eat well.

waist bands that an outside observer might well wonder how the weighed-down infant ever manages to crawl" (p. 113). Infant bathing is highly ritualized, involving symbolic objects and washes, and lasts about an hour. Newborns are bathed 4 times a day; toddlers, twice daily. The purpose is to cleanse the residue of "dirt" from the spirit world. Special care is taken to keep infants and young children away from corpses, which might entice them to join their journey back to the spirit world. Beng infant care illustrates some of the same aspects of culture that are referred to in our discussion of the macaques, including the way that it is rooted in daily life and behavior and the way it forms a complex network of interconnected activities. But it also leads us to recognize that human culture involves other layers of complexity arising from a vast network of beliefs, values, and practices that reflect common human concerns and problems. Like many communities in developing nations, the Beng suffer from high infant mortality rates; about 11 percent of all infants die before the age of 1 year, and about 17 percent die before age 5 (in contrast, the infant mortality rate for infants under 1 year in the United States is about 0.64 percent; see also p. 94, regarding international infant mortality rates). It makes sense, then, that Beng child-care practices are oriented toward infant survival through cultural practices that follow from their beliefs about the spiritual relationship between life and death.

and body fluids associated with childbirth are pollutants. During the delivery, no one helps or touches the mother, who must cut and tie the umbilical cord and then care for the baby herself. The villagers further believe that if a woman gives birth to a baby inside her home, God will be displeased and will cause family members and cattle to be become sick and die (Sreeramareddy et al., 2006). Similar childbirth practices and beliefs that divine will dictated birth outcomes were common in rural France as late as the end of the nineteenth century (Gelis, 1991). (For a detailed account of the intertwining of beliefs and practices surrounding childbirth, see the box on the Beng.)

Far more common is the practice of having several people attend the mother during labor and delivery, although there is cultural variation in who is expected to do the attending. Among the Ngoni of East Africa, for example, women regard men as "little children" in matters related to pregnancy and totally exclude them from the birth process. (Read, 1960/1968, p. 20). When a woman learns that her daughter-in-law's labor has begun, she and other female kin move into the woman's hut, banish the husband, and take charge of the preparations. They remove everything that belongs to the husband—clothes, tools, and weapons—and all household articles except old mats and pots to be used during labor. Men are not allowed back into the hut until after the baby is born. By contrast, among the Maya of the Yucatán peninsula, a trained midwife is present and the husband is expected to be present as well, both to help his wife and to bear witness to the pain she feels (Jordan, 1993). If the husband is absent and the child dies, the death is likely to be attributed to his failure to participate.

In all industrialized countries, a large proportion of births take place in hospitals, where the process is assisted by a physician or a trained midwife (Gelis, 1991). However, there are wide cultural variations in the place of delivery, in the extent to which midwives rather than physicians assist, and in such matters as the use of medication. For example, in Holland, roughly one-third of births take place at home, and the rate of infant mortality is actually lower for home births than for hospital births (Jordan, 1993). Moreover, practices are changing, not least in the areas where traditional practices had once been replaced by a more medical model (see the box "In the Field: Midwifery in the Inuit Villages of Northern Canada").

Childbirth in the United States

Ninety-nine percent of all babies in the United States are born in hospitals, and 92 percent are delivered by a physician (Centers for Disease Control and Prevention, 2006a). Nevertheless, the United States ranks 29th in the world in infant mortality, with 6.7 deaths per 1000 live births in 2006 (MacDorman & Mathews, 2008). In the late 1960s and 1970s, when nurse-midwives became more common in U.S. hospital birth centers, several studies compared physician-assisted with nurse-midwife-assisted deliveries (MacDorman & Singh, 1998; Levy, Wildinson, & Marine, 1971), In general, the studies found that nurse-midwife-assisted deliveries were much less likely to involve babies who had low birth weights or who died at birth or within the first weeks of life. Differences in outcomes between births attended by physicians and those attended by nurse-midwives may be due in part to labor and delivery practices, as well as to differences in prenatal care. Compared with physicians, nurse-midwives typically spend more time with women during their prenatal appointments and place more emphasis on education and counseling. They are also more likely to view themselves as an important source of emotional support during the labor and delivery process.

Given the relative success rates of home births and deliveries by nurse-practitioners, one might wonder why these practices aren't more common in the United States. Three major factors may contribute to the high rates of physician-assisted hospital birth. First, hospitals staffed by trained physicians and nurses are better equipped to provide both antiseptic surroundings and specialized help to deal with any complications that might arise during labor and delivery. Second, many drugs have been developed to relieve the pain of childbirth, and by law such drugs can be prescribed only by physicians. Third, most health insurance policies will not pay for services performed outside hospital settings.

There is no doubt that the lives of thousands of babies and mothers are saved each year by the intervention of doctors and nurses using modern drugs and special medical procedures. However, research indicates that typical labor and delivery practices in the United States may lean too heavily on medical procedures and actually place mothers and babies at risk for health problems, especially when medical interventions are used during normal, uncomplicated births (Centers for Disease Control, 2007). In general, concerns center on two questions: What is the safest method for dealing with pain during childbirth, and What precautions are necessary to ensure the health of the mother and the baby?

Childbirth Pain and Its Medication In industrialized nations, three types of drugs are primarily used to lessen the pain of labor and delivery during hospital births: *anesthetics* (which dull overall feeling), *analgesics* (which reduce the perception of pain), and *sedatives* (which reduce anxiety). These medications seldom threaten the lives of healthy, full-term babies, but in the first days after birth, the newborns of mothers who received one or another of such drugs during labor and delivery are less attentive and more irritable, have poorer muscle tone and less vigorous sucking responses, and are weaker than are those whose mothers received no medication (Jones, 1997).

Because of their concern about the possible adverse effects of drugs on the newborn, many women use alternative methods of controlling the pain of labor. Typically, these methods include educational classes that give the mother-to-be an idea of what to expect during labor and delivery and teach her relaxation and breathing exercises to help counteract pain. Often they also involve having someone—the baby's father or a sympathetic friend—be at the woman's side during labor to provide comfort and emotional support.

Medical Interventions In addition to administering drugs to ease the pain of labor, doctors may use medical procedures to safeguard the well-being of the mother and child. For example, when the baby is significantly overdue or when the mother is confronted with some life-threatening situation, physicians commonly induce labor, either by rupturing the membranes of the amniotic sac or by giving the mother some form of the hormone oxytocin, which initiates contractions. However, over the past two decades, the rate of induced labors more than doubled, rising from 9.5 percent in 1990 to 22 percent in 2006, with much of the increase being due not to medical or obstetric conditions that threaten the baby or mother but to physician practice patterns or maternal choice (Centers for Disease Control, 2006a; American Congress of Obstetricians and Gynecologists, 2009). Of special concern is the fact that induced labors are associated with higher rates of cesarean delivery (surgical removal of the baby from the uterus by making an incision through the mother's belly), exposing both mother and child to increased health risks.

In the Field Midwifery in the Inuit Villages of Northern Canada

Name:	Akinisie Qumaluk
Education:	Trained in both traditional and scientific approaches to pregnancy, childbirth, and infant care
Current Position:	Inuit elder and midwife
Career Objectives:	Preserve and integrate traditional knowledge of health care for the purpose of increasing infant, family, and community well-being.

AKINISIE QUMALUK IS AN INUIT MIDWIFE WHO LIVES in a remote community in the far north of Quebec, Canada. Her craft of assisting women while they are pregnant, delivering their babies, and caring for their newborns draws from modern medical approaches as well as traditional Inuit knowledge. The blending of medical science with Inuit birthing and newborn care traditions is a major innovation in the education and practice of Inuit midwives. But what may be most remarkable is the fact that Akinisie is allowed to practice her craft in the local community. Although midwifery once was an integral part of traditional Inuit culture, in the 1970s the Canadian government began to insist that at 36 weeks gestation, women be flown to a major city in the south in order to deliver their babies in modern medical facilities. As described by a member of the Inuit community, "This intimate, integral part of our life was taken from us and replaced by a medical model that separated our families, stole the power of the birthing experience from our women, and weakened the health, strength, and spirit of our communities" (Van Wagner et al., 2007).

Inuit women did not allow this invasion of their cultural heritage to go unchallenged. A community organization was formed for the purpose of reviving cultural practices, including midwifery, and establishing self-government. As a consequence of the organization's efforts, the first community birth center was opened in 1986. The philosophy of the center was to provide care for pregnant Inuit women by educating health-care workers in the community in ways that integrated traditional midwifery skills and knowledge with modern approaches to care. Today, future midwives are recruited from the local villages to participate in an apprenticeship-style educational program rooted in Inuit teaching methods such as observation and storytelling.

Throughout the process of "returning childbirth to the villages," there was much discussion by women's groups, leaders, elders, and local health-care providers about the capacity and limitations of care in remote village locations and the potential for adverse outcomes should medical complications arise so far from emergency medical services. In response to such concerns, an Inuit elder explains: "I can understand that some of you may think that birth in remote areas is dangerous. (But) you must know that a life without meaning is much more dangerous." Indeed, taking birth out of the community is generally understood as disrespectful of Inuit culture and knowledge and harmful to women and families. In Akinisie's words:

> With all the changes and women going south, the common knowledge—the things everyone knew about childbirth and health—began to disappear. . . . People became very dependent on health-care services. . . . We knew birth had to come back to the north. Our aim was to revitalize that common knowledge and community involvement around the birth process—to put the responsibility back in the hands of the Inuit.

Interestingly, when pregnant Inuit women undergo "risk screening" to determine whether they might need to be evacuated to southern medical facilities equipped to deal with complications, the screening includes not only biomedical assessments but social, cultural, and community considerations as well. Conceptualizing risk within this broader context is consistent with Inuit beliefs that good health is not simply an absence of disease but also includes positive mental, emotional, and spiritual features and is related to health in the family and community as a whole.

Analyses indicate that the policy of allowing Inuit women to give birth in their own communities, assisted by midwives trained in both modern and traditional approaches, results in fewer labor and delivery complications than did the past practice of automatic evacuation. It is, of course, more difficult to gauge additional benefits such as mental, emotional, and spiritual well-being. But according to Inuit midwife Nellie Tukalak, "the midwives have become a voice for our families and our way of life."

(Adapted from Van Wagner, Epoo, Nastapoka, & Harney, 2007)

The cesarean procedure is typically used in cases of difficult labor, when the baby is deemed to be in distress during delivery or is not in the headfirst position. Starting in the 1970s, the number of cesarean sections performed in the United States began to increase significantly. By 2008, nearly a third of all births were by cesarean section, an increase of 56 percent since 1996 (Centers for Disease

Control, 2010). Critics argue that many of the cesarean operations performed in the United States not only are unnecessary (for example, cesearean sections that are initiated at the first sign of complications to avoid malpractice suits or to comply with the mother's wishes) but also raise the cost of childbirth, expose the mother to the risk of postoperative infection, cause mothers to be separated from their infants while they heal from surgery, and may be detrimental to the babies' well-being. For example, Herbert Renz-Polster and his colleagues report increased susceptibility of children delivered by cesarean section to hay fever and asthma (Renz-Polster & Buist, 2002), while others report increased chances of maternal death (Kusiako, Ronsmans, & Van der Paal, 2000).

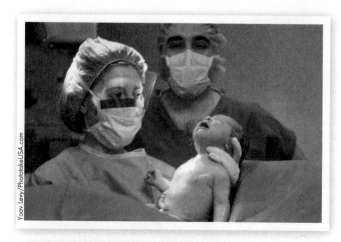

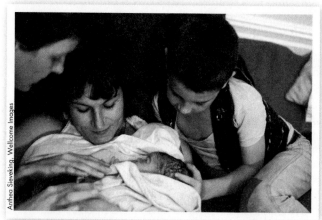

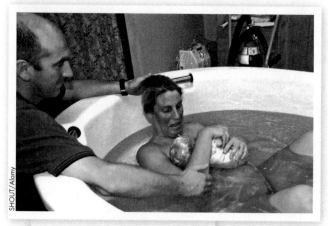

In many countries, families have choices regarding the context in which their babies will be born. Some prefer highly medical contexts, believing them "safer" in the event of trouble. Other families choose the intimacy of home birth. Still others choose alternatives such as water births, believing that they will relieve some of the stress typically associated with the birth process.

Concerns about unnecessary medical intervention extend to other procedures, such as highly sensitive electronic monitoring of the vital signs of the fetus during labor, which has been associated with an increase in cesarean sections, perhaps because it overestimates potential problems (Martin, 1998). In part because of such concerns, there has been more interest in alternative ways of giving birth that range from birthing at home with the assistance of a midwife to the use of special birthing centers where family members can also be present. Such centers are often located in or near a hospital in case serious complications arise. Alternative measures are especially popular when prenatal examinations find no indications that the birth will be especially complicated. Moreover, in such cases, the involvement of midwives does in fact appear to reduce the use of medical interventions such as those we have mentioned. For example, a study carried out in the state of Washington found that in low-risk pregnancies, certified nurse-midwives were less likely to use fetal monitoring or induce labor than were physicians. Their patients also were less likely to have spinal injections of anesthesia and cesarean sections than were the patients of family physicians and obstetricians (Rosenblatt et al., 1997).

The Baby's Experience of Birth There is no doubt that the process of being born is stressful for babies, even if all proceeds normally. The baby must squeeze through a very narrow opening, placing a great deal of pressure on the head; and if the umbilical cord becomes constricted in the process, the baby's supply of oxygen is reduced. A number of studies document a surge in the fetus's production of stress hormones around the time of birth. In fact, it seems that stress hormones may contribute to initiating the process of labor and delivery. Hugo Lagercrantz and Theodore Slotkin have proposed that the stress hormones are of vital importance because these hormones prepare the infant to survive outside the womb (Lagercrantz & Slotkin, 1986). In particular, they argue that high levels of the stress hormones in the hours before birth facilitate the absorption of liquid from the lungs and the production of surfactin, both of which allow the lungs to function well. In support of their hypothesis, they point out that breathing difficulties are common among infants delivered by cesarean section, a procedure they believe deprives infants of the experiences leading to the hormonal surge.

Lagercrantz and Slotkin also believe that the stress hormones raise the newborn's metabolic rate and are instrumental in increasing blood flow to the heart, lungs, and brain, thereby enhancing the chances of survival for a baby who is having breathing difficulties. Furthermore, they speculate that the hormonal surge puts the newborn in a state of alertness. Immediately following birth, most normal newborns have a prolonged period of quiet alertness, lasting as long as 40 minutes, during which their eyes are open in a wide-eyed gaze (Klaus, Kennell, & Klaus, 1995).

⏏ APPLY :: CONNECT :: DISCUSS

When it comes to prenatal care, labor, delivery, and newborn care, technologically advanced societies rely heavily on medical science. How would you characterize the culture of medical science (you may want to review the definition of culture presented in Chapter 2, p. 52)? What are some of the costs and benefits of medical science for pregnant women and newborns?

The Newborn's Condition

To first-time parents, especially those who imagine that newborns look like the infants pictured on jars of baby food, their neonate's actual appearance may cause disappointment, even alarm. A newborn's head is overly large in proportion to the rest of the body, and the limbs are relatively small and tightly flexed. Unless the baby has been delivered by cesarean section, the head may be misshapen because of the tight squeeze through the birth canal. (The head usually regains its symmetry by the end of the 1st week after birth.) Adding to this less than ideal appearance, the baby's skin may be covered with *vernix caseosa,* a white, cheesy substance that protects against bacterial infections, and it may be spotted with blood.

In the United States, neonates weigh an average of 7 to 7½ pounds (3.2 to 3.4 kilograms), although babies weighing anywhere from 5½ to 10 pounds (2.5 to 4.5 kilograms) are within the normal range. During their first days of life, most babies lose about 7 percent of their initial weight, primarily because of loss of fluid. They usually gain the weight back by the time they are 10 days old.

The average neonate is 20 inches (51 centimeters) long. To a large extent, the length of the newborn is determined by the size of the mother's uterus, and thus does not reflect the baby's genetic inheritance for height. The genes that regulate height begin to express themselves shortly after birth (Tanner, 1990).

Assessing the Baby's Viability

In professionally assisted births, health-care practitioners (midwives, doctors, or nurses) check the neonate for indications of danger so that immediate action can be taken if something is wrong. They check the baby's size and vital signs and look for evidence of normal capacities. A variety of scales and tests are used to assess the neonate's physical state and behavioral condition (Singer & Zeskind, 2001).

Physical Condition In the 1950s, Virginia Apgar (1953), an anesthesiologist who worked in the delivery room of a large metropolitan hospital, developed a quick and simple method of determining whether a baby requires emergency care. The **Apgar scale**, which is now widely employed throughout the United

Apgar scale A quick, simple test used to diagnose the physical state of newborn infants.

table 3.5			
The Apgar Scoring System			
	Rating		
Vital Sign	0	1	2
Heart rate	Absent	Slow (below 100)	Over 100
Respiratory effort	Absent	Slow, irregular	Good, crying
Muscle tone	Flaccid	Some flexion of extremities	Active motion
Reflex responsivity	No response	Grimace	Vigorous cry
Color	Blue, pale	Body pink, extremities blue	Completely pink

Source: Apgar, 1953.

States, is used to rate babies at 1 minute and again at 5 minutes after birth using five vital signs: heart rate, respiratory effort, muscle tone, reflex responsivity, and color. Table 3.5 shows the criteria for scoring each of the signs. The individual scores are totaled to give a measure of the baby's overall physical condition. A baby with a score of less than 4 is considered to be in poor condition and requires immediate medical attention. According to a recent nationwide study, the proportion of newborns with Apgar scores indicating excellent health declined from 91.1 percent in 2003 to 88.6 percent in 2006, with non-Hispanic Black infants having the highest percent of very low Apgar scores (0–3 points), more than twice the level of Hispanic and non-Hispanic White infants (Martin, Hamilton, Sutton, Ventura, et al., 2009).

Behavioral Condition During the past half century, many scales have been constructed to assess the more subtle behavioral aspects of the newborn's condition (Singer & Zeskind, 2001). One of the most widely used is the **Brazelton Neonatal Assessment Scale**, developed by pediatrician T. Berry Brazelton and his colleagues in the late 1970s (Brazelton, 1984). A major purpose of this scale is to assess the neurological condition of newborns who are suspected of being at risk for developmental difficulties. It is also used to assess the developmental progress of infants, to compare the functioning of newborns of different cultures, and to evaluate the effectiveness of interventions designed to alleviate developmental difficulties (Lundqvist & Sabel, 2000).

The Brazelton scale includes tests of infants' reflexes, motor capacities, muscle tone, capacity for responding to objects and people, and capacity to control their own behavior (such as turning away when overstimulated) and attention. When scoring a newborn on such tests, the examiner must take note of the degree of the infant's alertness and, if necessary, repeat the tests when the baby is wide awake and calm. Here are some typical items on the Brazelton scale:

- *Orientation to animate objects—visual and auditory.* The examiner calls the baby's name repeatedly in a high-pitched voice while making up-and-down and side-to-side head movements in front of the baby. The goal is to see if the baby focuses on the examiner and follows the examiner's movements with smooth eye movements.

- *Pull to sit.* The examiner puts a forefinger in each of the infant's palms and pulls the infant to a sitting position, testing to see if the baby tries to adjust the posture of his or her head when in a seated position, and if so, how well the baby succeeds.

Brazelton Neonatal Assessment Scale A scale used to assess a newborn's neurological condition.

- *Cuddliness.* The examiner holds the baby in a cuddling position, checking to see whether the baby resists being held, is passive, or cuddles up.

- *Defensive movements.* The examiner places a cloth over the baby's face to see if the baby tries to remove it, either by turning away from it or by swiping at it.

- *Self-quieting activity.* The examiner notes whether the baby exhibits self-quieting behavior (such as thumb-sucking or looking around) during an episode of fussing.

In addition to their primary function of screening for infants at risk, neonatal assessment scales are used to predict aspects of newborns' future development, such as their temperament or their typical rate of learning. Research with neonates thought to be at risk has shown that these scales are, in fact, satisfactory guides for determining when medical intervention is necessary, and that they are also fairly good at characterizing whether the baby is developing normally in the period following birth (Hart et al., 1999; Schuler & Nair, 1999). They are less useful when it comes to predicting later intelligence or personality, however.

Problems and Complications

Though most babies are born without any serious problems, some are in such poor physical condition that they soon die. Others are at risk for later developmental problems. Newborns are considered to be at risk if they suffer from any of a variety of problems, including brain damage resulting from asphyxiation or a head injury during delivery, acute difficulty breathing after birth, or difficulty digesting food because of an immature digestive system (Korner & Constantinou, 2001). These are the kinds of problems that are likely to result in low scores on the Apgar scale. Most of the newborns who are at risk are premature, abnormally underweight, or both (Singer & Zeskind, 2001).

Prematurity Prematurity is measured in terms of gestational age—in this case, the time that has passed between conception and birth. The normal gestational age is 37 to 43 weeks. Babies born before the 37th week are considered to be **preterm**, or premature (Figure 3.16). In the United States, after climbing 18 percent between 1990 and 2004, the rate of preterm births dropped slightly to stand at 12.3 percent of all births in 2008 (Centers for Disease Control, 2010). Disorders related to premature birth are the fourth-leading cause of infant mortality. However, with the expert care and technology now available in modern hospitals (Figure 3.17), mortality rates for premature infants are declining in the United States.

The leading cause of death among preterm infants is immaturity of the lungs (Lee et al., 2010). The other main obstacle to the survival of preterm infants is immaturity of their digestive and immune systems. Even babies of normal gestational age sometimes have difficulty coordinating sucking, swallowing, and breathing during the first few days after birth. The difficulty is likely to be more serious for preterm infants, who may need additional help with all of these functions. Their coordination may be so poor that they cannot be fed directly from breast or bottle, so special equipment must be used

preterm The term for babies born before the 37th week of pregnancy.

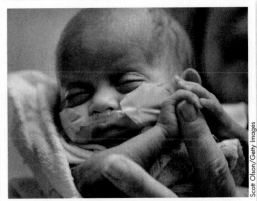

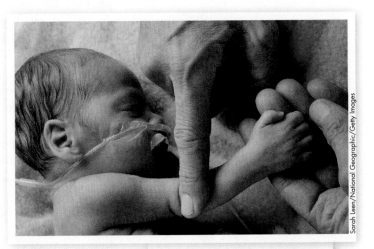

FIGURE 3.16 At the time of her birth in 2004, Rumaisa Rahman (whose first name means "white as milk" in India) weighed 8.6 ounces (0.24 kilograms), making her the smallest known surviving baby in the world. After nearly 5 months of extensive medical care at the Loyola University Medical Center in Illinois (U.S.), Rumaisa, then weighing 5.5 pounds (2.5 kilograms), was discharged with a prognosis of normal development.

FIGURE 3.17 The care provided for premature infants in modern hospitals now includes gentle massage in addition to sophisticated medical technologies.

low birth weight The term used to describe babies weighing 5 pounds, 8 ounces (2500 grams) or less at birth, whether or not they are premature.

small for gestational age Newborns whose birth weight falls in the lowest 10 percent for their gestational age because they have not grown at the normal rate.

to feed them. Moreover, their immature digestive systems often cannot handle normal baby formulas, requiring that they be fed special formulas.

There are many potential contributors to prematurity, some of them known. Twins are likely to be born about 3 weeks early; triplets and quadruplets, even earlier. Very young women whose reproductive systems are immature and women who have had many pregnancies close together are more likely to have premature babies. So are women who smoke, who are in poor health, or who have infections of the uterus. The chances of giving birth to a premature infant also vary with socioeconomic status (Joseph et al., 2007). Even in countries with universal health coverage, such as Canada, poor women are significantly more likely than affluent women to give birth to small or preterm infants, or to infants who die in the first months of life. This disparity can be explained in part by the fact that poor women are more likely to be undernourished or chronically ill, to smoke, to be overweight, and to experience complications during pregnancy. Cultural factors such as the use of fertility drugs and fasting can also play a role.

Many other causes of prematurity are still not well understood. At least half of all premature births are not associated with any of the identified risk factors and occur after otherwise normal pregnancies to healthy women who are in their prime childbearing years and have had good medical care.

Low Birth Weight Newborns weighing less than 5 pounds, 8 ounces (2500 grams) are said to have **low birth weight**. Often, low-birth-weight babies are preterm, but this is not necessarily the case. They may also be **small for gestational age**, meaning that their birth weight falls in the lowest 10 percent for their gestational age. Small-for-gestational-age infants have usually experienced intrauterine growth restriction; in other words, they have not grown at the normal rate. Multiple births, intrauterine infections, chromosomal abnormalities, maternal smoking or use of narcotics, maternal malnutrition, and abnormalities of the placenta or umbilical cord have all been identified as probable causes of intrauterine growth restriction (Meara, 2001).

Interestingly, it seems that birth weight may also be affected by social factors such as maternal education and the family environment. Fetal growth, for example, especially growth of the head, tends to be significantly slower when mothers are less educated, probably because less educated women tend to receive poor health care and have less knowledge regarding what is required for healthy prenatal development (Silva et al., 2010). Regarding family environment, in rural South Africa, where multigenerational households are common, pregnant women who live with other family members, but without a husband or nonmarital partner, are more likely to give birth to small babies than are women who reside with a husband or partner (Cunningham, Elo, Herbst, & Hosegood, 2010). The researchers who studied this population controlled for a number of factors, including family income, and speculated that the social and emotional support provided by a husband or partner made a significant contribution to successful pregnancy outcomes.

Developmental Consequences

Intensive research has been conducted on the developmental consequences of prematurity and low birth weight. Both put babies at risk for later developmental problems, including delays and disorders in intellectual and language development, attention, and neurological functioning (Aylward, 2006).

Low-birth-weight infants are at increased risk for developmental difficulty, even if they are full term. Two-thirds of the deaths that occur in the period immediately following birth are among low-birth-weight infants. In addition, low-birth-weight infants are 3 times more likely to have neurologically based developmental handicaps than are other babies, and the smaller the baby, the greater the risk (Holcroft, Blakemore, Allen, & Graham, 2001).

Common outcomes for low-birth-weight babies are a decrease in coordination and intellectual capacities. For example, one study that compared 7- to 11-year-olds who had a very low birth weight with children born at a normal weight found that the low-birth-weight children performed more poorly on tests of motor coordination, intelligence, and arithmetic (Holsti, Grunau, & Whitfield, 2002).

The long-term outcome of prematurity appears to be influenced by various factors. Premature babies who are small for gestational age and have medical complications are most likely to have future developmental difficulties. Those premature babies who are of normal size for their gestational age may stand a much better chance of catching up with full-term babies (Lorenz, 2001). However, there is some evidence that even in the absence of any clinically detectable disability, when compared with full-term children, children born prematurely have problems with maintaining attention and with visual–motor coordination when they are of school age (Foreman et al., 1997).

The importance of a supportive environment in overcoming these potential risks is underscored by research on the social ecology of premature and low-birth-weight infants. Babies who are raised in comfortable socioeconomic circumstances with an intact family and a mother who has had a good education are less likely to suffer negative effects from their condition at birth than are children who are raised without these benefits (Liaw, Meisels, & Brooks-Gunn, 1995). Low-birth-weight or premature babies who live in impoverished homes or have neglectful parents are more likely to suffer serious developmental problems in later years (Strathearn, Gray, O'Callaghan, & Wood, 2001).

▲ APPLY :: CONNECT :: DISCUSS

Low birth weight is one of the leading causes of infant mortality. According to Dr. Alan Brann, a professor of pediatrics at Emory University, birth weight is an important indicator of a community's overall health status. In particular, Dr. Brann argues that low birth weight signals an unhealthy community. In recent years, many Southern states have seen a shocking rise in the number of infant deaths. Have birth weights and infant deaths in your community/state/province/nation changed in recent years? How does your community/state/province/nation compare with others on measures of infant birth weight and mortality? What community/state/provincial/national efforts are underway to increase birth weight and/or decrease infant death?

Beginning the Parent–Child Relationship

Because human infants are dependent on the active support and protection of their caregivers for their very survival, the development of a close relationship between infants and their parents is crucial to infants' well-being. However, love and caring between parent and child is neither inevitable nor automatic. The large numbers of infants who are neglected, abused, abandoned, or murdered each year should convince even the most sentimental and optimistic observer of this harsh fact. In 2007, for example, approximately 5.8 million children in the United States were involved in child abuse reports and allegations (U.S. Department of Health & Human Services, 2009). How, then, is the bond between parent and child formed? And when no strong attachment develops, what has gone wrong? These are broad questions that you will encounter again and again in subsequent chapters, because a close parent–child relationship is not formed in an instant; it develops over many years. Here we will examine two factors that come into play immediately after birth and help set the stage for future parent–child relations: parents' initial reaction to their newborn's appearance, and the expectations they have for their babies.

The Baby's Appearance

In their search for the sources of attachment between mother and infant, some developmentalists have turned to *ethology*—the study of animal behavior and its evolutionary bases. These developmentalists believe that examination of what causes nonhuman mothers to protect or reject their young can shed light on the factors that influence human mothers. As noted in Chapter 1 (p. 25), one important factor that seems to influence animals' responses to their young is their offsprings' appearance (Koyama, Takahashi, & Mori, 2006). Parents tend to pay more attention to, and respond more positively to "cute" infants, perhaps because their attractiveness signals physical fitness and a good prospect for survival. You may recall from our discussion in Chapter 1 that ethologist Konrad Lorenz referred to the unique physical features of newborns—large head and eyes, full cheeks, and so forth—as "babyness."

Desires and expectations for their children's futures affect parenting practices and children's experiences from the first days of life. This mother is having her newborn blessed by a leader in her religious community.

James Estrin/The New York Times/Redux

Appearance may also be an explanation for parental rejection of offspring. Mothers in certain species, including dogs, cats, and guinea pigs, will kill malformed offspring. Though human parents usually do not kill their malformed babies, they do interact less frequently and less lovingly with infants they consider unattractive than they do with those they consider attractive. They also attribute less competence to unattractive babies (Langlois et al., 2000). This pattern is particularly noticeable for baby girls. While still in the hospital with their newborn girls, mothers of less attractive babies directed their attention to people other than their babies more often than did mothers of attractive babies (Langlois et al., 1995).

Social Expectations

During pregnancy, most parents-to-be develop specific expectations about what their babies will be like, and no sooner does a baby emerge from the womb than the parents begin to examine the neonate's looks and behaviors for hints of his or her future. Will she have her grandmother's high, round forehead? Does his lusty cry mean that he will have his father's quick temper?

One of the most significant characteristics affecting parents' expectations is the sex of the baby (Basow, 2006). One study found that when parents were shown ultrasound pictures of their babies-to-be, they tended to rate female fetuses as softer, littler, cuddlier, calmer, weaker, more delicate, and more beautiful than male fetuses (Sweeney & Bradbard, 1988). In another study, first-time mothers and fathers were asked to choose words that described their newborn babies within 24 hours after their birth (Rubin, Provezano, & Luria, 1974). Although the babies did not differ in length or weight or in their Apgar scores, the parents described daughters as "little," "beautiful," "pretty," or "cute," and as resembling their mother, whereas they described sons as "big" and as resembling their father. Fathers, the researchers found, were especially likely to sex-type their babies in these ways. Thus, beliefs and expectations shape the way that the parents see the child right from the start.

There is every reason for their baby's sex to be important to the parents. Children's sex determines what they are named, how they are dressed, how they are treated, and what will be expected of them in later life. Many of these expectations are based on cultural ideas about the experiences that males and females are likely to encounter as they grow from infancy to adulthood. In turn, these expectations shape the way parents perceive infants and the way they construct the contexts within which children develop. Thus, when differences are found in how boys and girls are treated, they occur not just because parents think that infant boys and girls are different to begin with but, perhaps more significantly, because they believe that their infants will develop into men and women with different roles to play in their society.

Within the context of culture, then, parents organize their infants' activities and environments with an eye to the future (Lyra, 2007). This orientation is expressed in clear symbolic form by the Zincantecos of south-central Mexico (Greenfield, Brazelton, & Childs, 1989). When a son is born, he is given, in expectation of his adult role, a digging stick, an ax, and a strip of palm used in weaving mats. When a daughter is born, she is given a weaving stick. Such future orientation is not only present in ritual; it is coded in a Zincantecan saying: "For in the newborn baby is the future of our world."

Ultimately, parents' organization of the present in terms of the future contributes to the powerful role that culture has in development (Valsiner, 2006). Just as infants are born with a set of genetically built-in capacities to learn about and to act upon the world, parents come to this moment with their tendencies to respond in certain ways that have developed through their experience as members of their culture. These tendencies help shape the relationship between child and parents that begins at birth—itself an essential part of the foundation upon which development builds.

▲ APPLY :: CONNECT :: DISCUSS

Provide some examples of how the relationship between the newborn's characteristics and the care he or she receives is mediated by cultural beliefs and values (see Chapter 2, p. 54).

SUMMARY

The Periods of Prenatal Development

- Prenatal development is often divided into three broad periods:

  1. The germinal period begins at conception and lasts until the zygote enters the uterus and becomes implanted there about 8 to 10 days later. Through repeated division, the organism has grown from a single cell into hundreds of cells by the time it reaches the uterus.

  2. The embryonic period extends from implantation to the end of the 8th week. With cell differentiation, by the end of this period, all major organs have taken primitive shape and sexual differentiation has begun. This rapid growth is facilitated by the efficient way the placenta allows the exchange of nutrients and waste products between the mother and the embryo.

  3. The fetal period goes from the 9th week, with the beginning of ossification, until birth. The fetus grows dramatically in size, and the brain and all organ systems increase in complexity to the point where the baby can exist outside the mother. The fetus is subject to environmental influences originating from outside as well as inside the mother. Basic sensory capacities (for sensing motion, light, and sound) develop during this period, enabling fetal learning. By 15 weeks, the fetus exhibits all movements observable at birth; fetal activity is crucial to neuronal development.

Maternal Conditions and Prenatal Development

- A mother's negative attitudes toward a pregnancy, or stress during pregnancy, may be associated with problems such as low birth weight and certain longer-term developmental risks. The problems may stem from the mother's elevated levels of the hormone cortisol during pregnancy.

- A mother's nutrition is an important factor in fetal development. Pregnant women are advised to consume 2000–2800 calories a day in a well-balanced diet and to increase their intake of folic acid, calcium, and iron. Extreme maternal undernourishment and malnutrition are associated with low birth weight, prematurity, abnormalities, and death. Lesser degrees also increase risk, although the effects can be difficult to isolate. Maternal overnutrition is also associated with negative outcomes, including overweight in babies, who may be at later risk for health problems such as obesity and diabetes.

Teratogens: Environmental Sources of Birth Defects

- Teratogens (environmental agents that can cause deviations from normal fetal development) take many forms. Six general principles apply to all:

1. The susceptibility of the organism depends on its developmental stage.

2. A teratogen's effects are likely to be specific to a particular organ.

3. Individual organisms vary in their susceptibility to teratogens.

4. The mother's physiological state influences susceptibility to teratogens.

5. The greater the concentration of a teratogenic agent, the greater the risk.

6. Teratogens that have little or no effect on the mother can seriously affect the developing organism.

- Among the common teratogens are drugs, including prescription drugs, caffeine, tobacco, alcohol, marijuana, cocaine, and heroin and methadone. Their effects vary considerably; heavy drinking, for example, is associated with fetal alcohol syndrome. Other teratogenic agents are infections, including rubella and HIV, and radiation or pollution at high levels.

Birth

- Labor begins approximately 266 days after conception and proceeds through three stages, in which contractions cause the cervix to dilate, the baby is pushed through the birth canal and is delivered, and the afterbirth is delivered.

- There are marked cultural variations in childbirth, such that a woman may give birth unassisted, be assisted by a midwife and/or others at home, or be assisted by a physician or midwife in a hospital.

- In the United States, concern about the possible adverse effects of pain medication on the newborn and about the overuse of medical interventions (induced labor and cesarean sections, for example) has led to interest in alternatives, such as the use of midwives and birthing centers.

- Birth is a stressful experience for the baby, but research suggests that a surge of stress hormones as the process begins protects the baby from the adverse conditions and prepares the baby for survival outside the womb.

The Newborn's Condition

- The Apgar scale is used to assess the newborn's physical condition by measuring heart rate, respiratory effort, reflex responsivity, muscle tone, and color. Babies with a low Apgar score require immediate medical attention. Other scales have been developed to assess behavioral aspects of the newborn's condition.

- Risks are associated with prematurity (birth before the 37th week) and low birth weight (less than 5 pounds, 8 ounces [2500 grams]). They are especially great for premature infants who are small for their gestational age and have medical complications.

Beginning the Parent–Child Relationship

• A newborn's appearance plays a significant role in the parents' response to the baby, with "babyness" evidently evoking caregiving behaviors.

• From birth, parents' expectations, influenced by the culture, influence the child's environment in ways that shape the child's development.

Key Terms

germinal period, p. 81

embryonic period, p. 81

fetal period, p. 81

cleavage, p. 81

heterochrony, p. 82

heterogeneity, p. 82

totipotent stem cells, p. 82

implantation, p. 82

amnion, p. 82

chorion, p. 82

placenta, p. 82

umbilical cord, p. 83

ectoderm, p. 83

endoderm, p. 83

mesoderm, p. 83

epigenesis, p. 84

cephalocaudal pattern, p. 84

proximodistal pattern, p. 84

age of viability, p. 86

neural tube, p. 91

large for gestational age, p. 93

gestational age, p. 93

teratogens, p. 94

fetal alcohol syndrome, p. 97

Apgar scale, p. 111

Brazelton Neonatal Assessment Scale, p. 112

preterm, p. 113

low birth weight, p. 114

small for gestational age, p. 114

Major Milestones of Infancy

	Physical Domain	Cognitive Domain	Social and Emotional Domain
What Develops…	• Rapid growth to about 30–34 inches (76–86 centimeters) and 22–27 pounds (10–12 kilograms) by end of second year. • Ossification of bones; beginning of ongoing changes in proportions; increase in muscle strength. • Development of cerebral cortex areas, including prefrontal cortex and language-related areas. • Myelination of neurons, including neurons of language-related areas and neurons linking areas of the brain. • Most brain structures present by 2 years of age, with neurons in the cerebral cortex similar to those of adults in length and branching. • Increasing coordination of and control over gross and fine motor behaviors. • Gross motor developments include crawling (around 8–9 months) and walking (around 1 year). • Fine motor developments include perfecting reaching and grasping, and by 2 years, performing movements needed to feed and dress self, etc.	• Behavior becomes increasingly intentional and goal-directed. • Emergence of object permanence and representational thinking. • With ability to represent objects and experiences mentally, increased problem solving, symbolic play, deferred imitation, and language use. • Development of understanding of cause–effect relationships. • Development of ability to categorize objects according to common features. • Increased ability to control and sustain attention; increased speed of processing information. • Improved memory.	• Basic emotions are present at birth or soon after. • Emergence of primary intersubjectivity. • Increased ability to regulate emotions. • Development of attachment to caregivers (7–9 months); fear of strangers emerges with attachment. • Emergence of secondary intersubjectivity, including social referencing, gaze following, pointing. • Emergence of language comprehension and speech, including recognizing common words and expressions (6–9 months), babbling (7 months), and first words (1 year). • Greater ability to share and communicate knowledge, desires, and interests. • Emerging sense of self, including self-recognition by 18 months and associated sense of independence. • Emergence of self-conscious emotions. • In first year, stage of basic trust versus mistrust; in second year, stage of autonomy versus shame and doubt.
Sociocultural Contributions and Consequences…	• Factors such as socioeconomic status and diet can contribute to variations in growth. • Cultures vary in how they restrict or encourage specific motor actions, affecting the sequence and timing of attainment of gross motor milestones. • Culture influences age of control of elimination. • Child begins to participate in feeding and dressing.	• Motor development coupled with interest in exploring can be risky; parents respond by "baby-proofing" the environment.	• Basic emotions emerge across cultures, facilitating ties to members of the community and, in this way, acquisition of culture. • Cultures differ in ideas about what constitutes sensitive caregiving, including in infancy. • Emotionally warm and responsive interactions generate sense of trust and exploration.

Infancy

assing from the birth canal into the hands of the mother or her birth attendant marks the transition from fetal life to infancy. Preparations for this event—perhaps the most radical in the life course of the individual—have been underway for 9 months or for millennia, depending on whether they are viewed through the lens of ontogeny (the individual's development) or in terms of the evolution of human species and culture. In either case, the transition from the intrauterine to the extrauterine environment takes place in the context of a facilitating or supportive environment. The birth canal, for example, the channel formed by the mother's cervix, vagina, and vulva, is not simply a physical structure through which the baby passes; it also plays a dynamic role in the transition by exerting pressure on the fetus's chest, forcing fluid from airways in preparation for the drawing of the first breath of life. Then the umbilical cord is cut, often with great ceremony, and the infant enters into a fundamentally new relationship with the environment.

The chapters in Part II are organized to highlight the nature of this new relationship and how it continues to change over the course of infancy. Chapter 4 traces development from birth to about 3 months of age, exploring infants' earliest capacities for perceiving and acting on the world and highlighting the ways in which infants' behavior becomes increasingly organized and integrated. The most obvious requirement of this earliest postnatal period is that infants receive enough nourishment and protection to support their continued growth. This requirement is met through a wide variety of cultural systems of infant care that call upon and promote infants' basic capacities to signal their needs and learn from experience. A key element in this process is infants' increasing ability to co-ordinate their actions with those of their caregivers, helping to ensure that their basic needs are met.

Chapter 5 examines the marked changes in physical and cognitive development that take place between 3 months and 2 years of age. Increases in infants' physical size and strength are accompanied by increases in their motor coordination and control, opening up entirely new opportunities for exploring the world. Both memory and problem-solving abilities improve, providing infants with a finer sense of their environment and how to act upon it. The emergence of imitation and symbol use lays a foundation for new ways of communicating and connecting with others.

The processes through which infants are drawn into the lives of others are the focus of Chapter 6, where we examine the developmental course of infant emotions and emotional expressions, infants' attachments to their caregivers, and the beginnings of language. We discuss why infants become wary of strangers and become upset when left alone. We also explore the budding sense of self, the first glimmer of independence (sometimes described as the "terrible twos"), and the dawning ability to distinguish between "good" and "bad."

Throughout this section, we underscore how interacting domains of development (physical, cognitive, social, and emotional) and the sociocultural contexts in which development occurs jointly contribute to the increasing organization and coordination of the infant's behavior.

CHAPTER

4

Physical Growth
Measuring Body Growth

Growth of the Skull

Brain Development
Neurons and Networks of Neurons

The Structure of the Central Nervous System

Experience and Development of the Brain

Sensing the Environment
Methods of Evaluating Infant Sensory Capacities

Hearing

Vision

Taste and Smell

Intermodal Perception

The Organization of Behavior
Reflexes

From Reflex to Coordinated Action

Reaching

Piaget's Theory of Developing Action

Learning Theories of Developing Action

Temperament

Becoming Coordinated with the Social World
Sleeping

Feeding

Crying

Summing Up the First 3 Months

The First 3 Months

On the second day: *M'ama Afwe, a 16-year-old first-time mother, is dozing on her bed with her 2-day-old daughter. They are recovering from the delivery and waiting for the baby's umbilical cord to fall off, the sign in Afwe's West African culture that it is safe to take the newborn outside. When her daughter starts to fuss and cry, Afwe leans over her, trying to get her breast close to the baby's mouth. But her breasts are large and full of milk, and this leaning-over position makes it difficult for the baby to latch onto the nipple. The hungry baby is frustrated and frets. Afwe's grandmother observes the scene and offers some advice: Why not try lying down next to the baby? Perhaps Afwe's nipple will fit into the little mouth that way. Afwe tries out the new position. It works: The baby nurses eagerly.*

In the second week: *After some hours of cycling between fussing and nursing, Afwe's baby girl is sleeping in her grandmother's arms while Afwe naps, tired in the way that new mothers often are. A neighbor comes in to admire the latest addition to the community. She takes the baby from the grandmother to hold and look at her, which rouses the infant from her slumber, and initiates a new bout of fussing. When the baby is returned to her grandmother's arms, she begins to cry vigorously. The grandmother speaks to her in a soft and soothing tone, but the infant is highly agitated, and cries all the more, so the grandmother, who has a nursing toddler of her own, offers the baby her breast. Her granddaughter eagerly accepts it, nurses for a few moments, and then drops off to sleep.*

(Adapted from Gottlieb, 2000.)

Compared with other animals, many of which are fairly able to take care of themselves at birth, human beings are born in a state of marked immaturity and dependence. As Afwe quickly learned, she must help her baby to accomplish even such an elementary act as feeding. The relative helplessness of human babies at birth has several obvious consequences. Babies require extensive care and attention. This limits the mother's ability to provide for herself and her other children, and consequently increases the importance of child-care assistance from her mate and others in her community. In Afwe's West African culture, extended kin, such as Afwe's grandmother, provide help with infant care. In other cultures or communities, babysitters or day-care providers may give comparable levels of assistance. Moreover, the survival of human offspring depends on the efforts of their parents and other adults for many years. As we discussed in Chapter 2, in order to survive on their own and become integrated into the activities of their community, human children must learn a vast repertoire of knowledge, skills, traditions, and patterns of living that they do not possess at birth.

In this chapter, we describe the initial phase of this integrative learning process, which begins immediately after birth and ends approximately 3 months later. Examining capacities and characteristics that babies bring with them into the world, we will see the ways in which newborns' brains and sensory systems allow them to experience the world, the ways in which their specific reflexes and temperamental

growth charts Charts that show average values of height, weight, and other measures of growth, based on large samples of normally developing infants; the charts are used to evaluate an infant's development.

styles influence how they respond to their experiences, and the ways in which certain innate learning capacities come to affect their early behavior.

In addition to exploring what babies bring with them into the world, we will examine how the world interacts with the newly born through the contexts of family, community, and cultural traditions, and how these contexts and traditions affect the young infant's development. The story of early infancy, as you will see, is a story about organization and coordination: how the brain becomes organized into a highly efficient communication network; how newborn reflexes and sensory systems become organized into more complex systems of behavior; and how these brain and behavioral developments are coordinated with the particular social and cultural environment into which the child is born.

Physical Growth

During the infant's first 3 months, physical growth progresses at an astonishing pace. In just 12 short weeks, the baby will gain approximately 6 pounds and grow more than 4 inches in length. As a consequence of the rapid development of the brain, the circumference of the head will increase by more than an inch. Keeping in mind that the average baby weighs a bit more than 7 pounds (3 kilograms) at birth, is just 19.5 or so inches (50 centimeters) long, and has a head circumference of about 14 inches (36 centimeters), these changes to the physical body are truly remarkable!

Measuring Body Growth

Pediatricians and other health-care providers for infants closely monitor infants' early physical growth for reassuring signs of normal development—or for early warnings that a problem might exist. Typically, the baby's development is evaluated by using **growth charts**, which depict average values of height, weight, and other measures of growth that have been compiled by studying large samples of normally developing infants. Growth charts, such as those in Figure 4.1, indicate the average values as well as various degrees of deviation from the average.

Because growth charts are an integral tool for assessing a baby's health status, developmentalists are highly invested in assuring their validity. The problems that otherwise can ensue became apparent in recent years when many pediatricians became concerned that some breast-fed babies were malnourished because, according to growth chart averages, they were gaining weight relatively slowly. To compensate for what they believed was inadequate nutrition, some doctors advised mothers to supplement their infants' diets with formula and solid foods. Such advice goes against the recommendation of many infant-health organizations that babies be exclusively breast-fed throughout the first year to optimize healthy development. (Among other long-term benefits, breast-feeding is associated with decreased risk for immune-related diseases, childhood cancers, and obesity, and possibly with improved cognitive functioning [Schack-Neilson, Larnkjaer, & Michaelson, 2005]). As you can see, the pediatricians faced a conflict. On one hand, many breast-fed babies appeared underweight; on the other hand, a trove of evidence indicates that breast-fed babies are generally healthier than their formula-fed peers. The conflict was resolved when it was realized that breast-fed babies typically gain less weight during the first year because, compared with formula-fed babies, they voluntarily take in less milk, due to the fact that it is easier to control the flow of milk from a breast than from a bottle (World Health Organization, 2006). However, the growth charts were calculated with data from both breast- and formula-fed babies, so the averages were raised by the heavier, faster-growing (but not necessarily healthier) formula-fed babies.

Perhaps because they have greater control over the amount of milk they drink, breastfed babies tend to gain less weight during the first year compared with their bottle-fed counterparts.

Giacomo Pirozzi / Panos Pictures

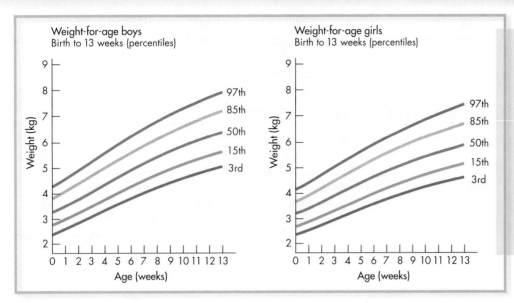

Weight-for-age boys
Birth to 13 weeks (percentiles)

Weight-for-age girls
Birth to 13 weeks (percentiles)

FIGURE 4.1 Growth charts show age-specific averages as well as variations from averages, helping health-care providers assess whether a child's development is on track or is a cause for concern. The figures to the left illustrate changes in weight averages for boys and girls between birth and 13 weeks of age. As shown in the chart for boys, at 8 weeks of age, 50 percent of all boys weigh more than 5.5 kilograms (12.1 pounds), and 50 percent weigh less (purple line). An 8-week-old boy weighing 4 kilograms (8.8 pounds), would be in the 3rd percentile (blue line), suggesting possible malnutrition and health problems. (WHO, 2006.)

Faced with mounting evidence that breast-fed and formula-fed babies grow differently during the first year, the World Health Organization (WHO) launched a massive international study to determine optimal standards of physical growth when children are being breast-fed through the first year of infancy and raised in a healthy environment (for example, with adequate health care and with mothers who do not smoke). Nearly 8500 children growing up in such healthy environments in Brazil, Ghana, India, Norway, Oman, and the United States participated in the study, which resulted in new international standards for evaluating the physical growth of infants and young children. The study indicates that when raised in a healthy environment, babies everywhere, regardless of ethnicity or socioeconomic status, show comparable patterns of physical growth (World Health Organization, 2006).

Growth of the Skull

Health-care providers for infants track changes to the baby's head circumference because the primary determinant of the growth and shape of the head is the development of the brain. If you have ever stroked a baby's head, you know that a newborn's skull is considerably different than that of an older child or adult. The infant's skull is composed of seven flat, membranous bones that are relatively soft and elastic (Margulies & Thibault, 2000). Early in development, the bones are separated by **fontanels**, also known as the "soft spots." Because the bones of the skull are separated, rather than fused together, they are capable of moving in response to external or internal pressure. This allows the skull to "mold" during birth in response to external pressure exerted by the relatively narrow birth canal and to expand in response to

fontanels "Soft spots," or spaces, that separate the bones of the skull prenatally and in early infancy.

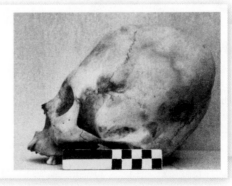

Illustrating how flexible the skull is in infancy is considerable evidence that certain indigenous cultures in the Americas used a variety of methods and devices to intentionally and permanently alter the shape of their infants' skulls as a way of indicating the child's community or kinship ties and family wealth (Hoshower et al., 1995).

neuron A nerve cell.

axon The main protruding branch of a neuron; it carries messages to other cells in the form of electrical impulses.

dendrite The protruding parts of a neuron that receive messages from the axons of other cells.

synapse The tiny gap between the axon of one neuron and the dendrite of another.

neurotransmitter A chemical secreted by a neuron sending a message that carries the impulse across the synaptic gap to the receiving cell.

synaptogenesis The process of synapse formation.

myelin An insulating material that forms a sheath around certain axons and speeds the transmission of nerve impulses from one neuron to the next.

spinal cord The part of the central nervous system that extends from below the waist to the base of the brain.

brain stem The base of the brain, which controls such elementary reactions as blinking and sucking, as well as such vital functions as breathing and sleeping.

internal pressure exerted by a rapidly developing brain—an illustration of evolution's marvelous web of adaptations. During the first months of infancy, the growing brain pushes against the bones of the skull, expanding the infant's head circumference and contributing to its relatively round shape.

▲ APPLY :: CONNECT :: DISCUSS

In societies in which mothers have the option of breast- or bottle-feeding their newborns, their choice is often influenced by cultural norms and expectations. Interview your mother and your grandmother about newborn feeding practices common in their generation. (If your mother or grandmother is not available, find another mother of the same generation.) Ask about how newborns were fed, why women might have chosen one method over another, what their own choices were, and so forth. Compare the two women's experiences and assess them in light of what is now known regarding feeding practices and infants' physical development.

Brain Development

Changes in the brain are associated with many of the developmental changes you will encounter in this chapter. As you saw in Chapter 3 (pp. 86–87), well before full-term babies are born, their brains and central nervous systems support elementary sensory and motor functions. These basic capacities are sufficient to allow them to learn to recognize the sound of their mother's voice and the language spoken around them and to prepare them physically for their earliest adaptations to their new environment.

At birth, the brain contains the vast majority of all the information-transmitting cells it will ever have—around 100 billion, by most estimates. Nevertheless, it will become 4 times larger by adulthood, with most growth occurring during the first few years after birth (Groeschel, Vollmer, King, & Connelly, 2010). To understand this growth requires looking more closely at the nerve cells that transmit information, referred to as **neurons**, and at the brain structures into which neurons are organized.

Neurons and Networks of Neurons

The brain is an enormously complex communication system of neuron networks. Its complexity begins with how neurons transmit information. A neuron accomplishes its basic communication task in two ways: (1) by sending information via small electrical impulses along its **axon**, a branch that reaches out to connect with other brain cells, and (2) by receiving information from the axons of other cells through spiky protrusions called **dendrites** (Figure 4.2).

FIGURE 4.2 The neuron receives information from other neurons through its dendrites and feeds that information to other neurons through its axon. The photograph shows a neuron in the cerebellum, a part of the brain that plays an important role in motor control.

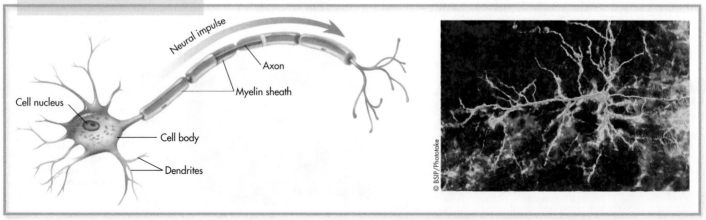

Neural impulse

Axon

Myelin sheath

Cell nucleus

Cell body

Dendrites

© BSIP/Photolake

Between the axons and dendrites of communicating neurons is a tiny gap called a **synapse**. When an electrical impulse from the axon of the sending neuron arrives at the synapse, the sending neuron secretes a chemical, called a **neurotransmitter**, that carries the impulse across the synaptic gap, setting off a reaction in the receiving neuron.

The combination of a sending neuron and a receiving neuron represents the simplest form of a neuronal network. More complex networks are formed as multiple dendrites and axons interconnect. Many networks are established initially during the second half of gestation, although after birth they may change considerably in size and organization as a consequence of biological growth processes and the—baby's experiences (Kostovic & Jovanov-Milosevic, 2006; Smyser et al., 2010). Such multiple forms of connectivity—and the fact that there are billions and billions of neurons—make possible a virtually infinite variety of patterns of brain activity and behavior.

The basic architecture of neurons and neuronal networks suggests two of the reasons for the astonishing growth in brain size that occurs during infancy. Brain size is typically measured in terms of volume, which is estimated from brain scans (see the box "Observing the Living Brain" in Chapter 1, p. 33). Some of the growth in brain volume is due to an increase in the size and complexity of *gray matter*—that is, the information-receiving dendrites, which develop new branches, and the information-transmitting axons, which become longer. As a result of this increase, many new synapses are formed in a process called **synaptogenesis**, which we discuss in more detail below. In addition to the increase in gray matter, brain volume grows as a consequence of increases in *white matter*, which includes **myelin**, an insulating material that forms a sheath around certain axons, speeding the transfer of information from one neuron to the next. Myelinated axons transmit signals anywhere from 10 to 100 times faster than unmyelinated axons, making possible more effective interconnections and communication among various parts of the brain, and more complicated forms of thought and action (Lenroot et al., 2009). Using magnetic imaging technology, a team of developmental neuroscientists was able to chart changes in overall brain volume, gray matter, and white matter from birth to adulthood (Groeschel, Vollmer, King, & Connelly, 2010). As you can see in Figure 4.3, there is substantial growth during the first years of life, with gray matter making a particularly significant contribution to total brain volume.

The Structure of the Central Nervous System

Because of its association with the most complex behaviors of our species, the system of neural connections of greatest interest to developmentalists is the central nervous system. The central nervous system is conventionally divided into three major sections—the spinal cord, the brain stem, and the cerebral cortex. The **spinal cord**, a tubelike bundle of nerves, is encased in the spinal bones that extend from the base of the brain to below the waist. The nerves of the spinal cord carry messages back and forth from the brain to the spinal nerves that branch out from the spinal cord and communicate with specific areas of the body. Some of these nerves carry messages to the brain from the skin and other body parts and organs; others carry messages from the brain to the various body parts to initiate actions such as muscle movement.

The brain itself grows out of the top of the spinal cord (Figure 4.4). At its base is the **brain stem**, which controls such vital functions as breathing and sleeping, as well as such elementary reactions as reflexive blinking and sucking. All these capacities are established in at least rudimentary form during the later stages of prenatal development. At birth, the brain stem is one of the most highly developed areas of the central nervous system.

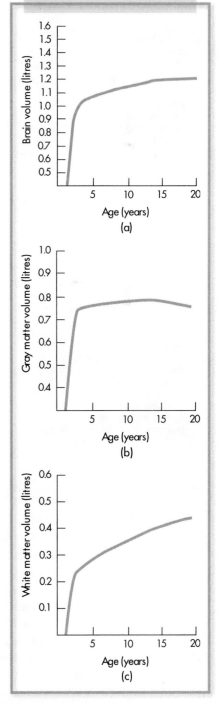

FIGURE 4.3 Magnetic imaging technology reveals substantial growth in brain volume during the early years of childhood (a). Much of this growth is a consequence of rapidly increasing gray matter, or *synaptogenesis* (b). White matter, or *myelin*, also increases rapidly during infancy, and more gradually throughout childhood and adolescence (c). (Groeschel et al., 2010.)

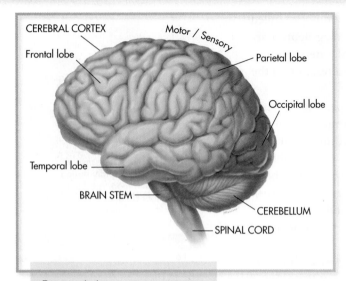

FIGURE 4.4 This schematic view of the brain shows the major lobes, or divisions, of the cerebral cortex (including the areas where some functions are localized); the brain stem, the cerebellum; and the spinal cord. (Adapted from Tanner, 1978.)

The **cerebral cortex** is the brain's outermost layer and most complex system, the processing center for the perception of patterns, the execution of complex motor sequences, and planning, decision making, and speech. The cerebral cortex is divided into two hemispheres, each of which is divided into four sections, or lobes, separated by deep grooves. Under ordinary conditions of development, the *occipital lobes* are specialized for vision; the *temporal lobes,* for hearing and speech; the *parietal lobes,* for spatial perception; and the *frontal lobes,* for control and coordination of the other cortical areas to enable complex forms of behavior and thought.

Despite the specialization of areas of the cortex for these functions, many of the functions involve considerable interplay among areas. In addition, the human cortex, unlike that of other animals, has large areas that are not "prewired" to respond directly to external stimulation in any discernible way (Figure 4.5). These "uncommitted" areas provide infants with the capacity to develop brain circuits that grow and change depending upon the experiences they have as they develop, a capacity we referred to in Chapter 1 (p. 10) as *plasticity.* (We will discuss plasticity in greater detail below.)

At birth, the circuitry of the cerebral cortex is less mature than that of the spinal cord and brain stem (that is, it has fewer dendritic branches and is less myelinated) and is poorly connected to the lower-lying parts of the nervous system that receive stimulation from the environment. Because of their relative maturity, the spinal cord and brain stem enable movement, responses to visual stimuli, and even elementary forms of learning without cortical involvement (Woodruff-Pak, Logan, & Thompson, 1990). As the nerve fibers connecting the cortex with the brain stem and spinal cord become myelinated, the infant's abilities expand.

Experience and Development of the Brain

FIGURE 4.5 In these six mammalian species, the proportions of the brain mass that are devoted to different functions vary widely. The areas designated "uncommitted cortex" are not dedicated to any particular sensory or motor functions and are available for integrating information of many kinds. (Adapted from Fishbein, 1976.)

Although brain development in large measure takes place according to strictly internal biological processes, the environment also plays a major role in shaping the brain's structures. Developmentalists distinguish two major classes of brain development, which they refer to as *experience-expectant* and *experience-dependent* (Bruer & Greenough, 2001; Marshall & Kenney, 2009).

As the name implies, **experience-expectant** processes of brain development are those that seem to *anticipate* experiences that are universal in all normally developing

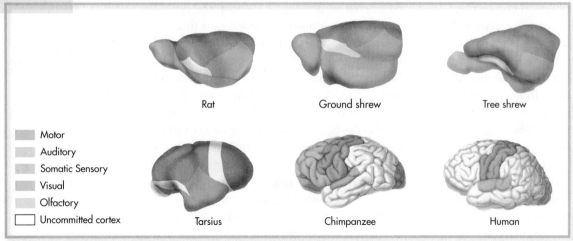

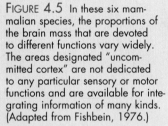

Motor
Auditory
Somatic Sensory
Visual
Olfactory
Uncommitted cortex

Rat   Ground shrew   Tree shrew

Tarsius   Chimpanzee   Human

members of our species (Greenough et al., 1987). In other words, the brain is prewired for these experiences, with the relevant synapses in place at birth. For example, the evolution of the visual cortex prepares the baby for certain types of visual experiences such as seeing patterns and borders between light and dark. Likewise, the part of the brain associated with language has evolved in a way that prepares the baby to process and learn language (see Chapter 7). All human environments are infused with visual patterns and light–dark borders that help us distinguish one object from another. And, of course, virtually all human environments are rich with language. Experience-expectant processes of brain development allow infants to take advantage of their exposure to these features of the environment and use them to acquire the related basic human behaviors and abilities. When such expected experiences are lacking during sensitive periods of brain development, as may happen in the case of blind infants or of babies who have been severely deprived of human contact, the brain will fail to develop normally (Hubel & Weisel, 2004; Fox, Levitt, & Nelson, 2010).

Evidence for experience-expectant brain development is found in an interesting pattern of synaptic proliferation and elimination. At several points during development (including adolescence), different portions of the brain undergo an explosive increase in synapse formation, called **exuberant synaptogenesis**, which produces far more synapses than would be required by the particular experiences the growing organism is likely to encounter. In other words, the profusion of synapses, at different points in development, would seem to prepare the brain for a range of possible experiences. Over time, in something like a "use it or lose it" process, synapses that are not used atrophy and die off, a phenomenon referred to as **synaptic pruning** (Webb, Monk, & Nelson, 2001). It has been estimated that fully 70 percent of the neurons in the human cortex are pruned between the 28th week after conception and birth. Other intensive periods of synaptic pruning have been found in infancy, middle childhood, and adolescence (Giedd & Rapoport, 2010) (see Figure 4.6).

cerebral cortex The brain's outermost layer. The networks of neurons in the cerebral cortex integrate information from several sensory sources with memories of past experiences, processing them in a way that results in human forms of thought and action.

experience-expectant Processes of brain development that seem to *anticipate* experiences that are universal in all normally developing members of our species.

cerebral cortex The brain's outermost layer. The networks of neurons in the cerebral cortex integrate information from several sensory sources with memories of past experiences, processing them in a way that results in human forms of thought and action. **exuberant synaptogenesis** A rapid growth in synaptic density that prepares the brain for a vast range of possible experiences.

synaptic pruning The process of selective dying-off of nonfunctional synapses.

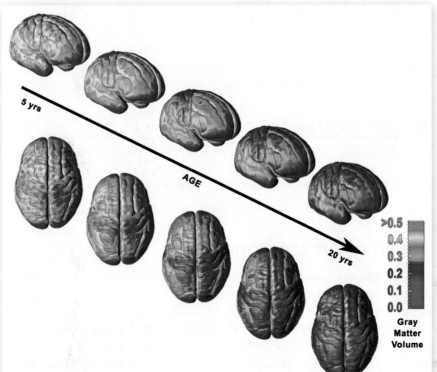

FIGURE 4.6 Decreases in the amount of gray matter reflect a process of *synaptic pruning* in which synapses that are not used by the developing brain atrophy and die off. (From Gogtay et al., 2004.)

experience-dependent Development of neural connections that is initiated in response to experience.

In contrast to the synapses involved in universal experience-expectant brain development, those involved in **experience-dependent** brain development synapses are not created in advance of species-universal experiences; instead, they are generated in response to the specific experiences of specific individuals. Experience-dependent processes have evolved to allow the organism to take advantage of new and changing information in the environment. It is this experience-dependent brain–environment relationship that allows humans to learn from experience.

An example of experience-dependent brain development comes from pioneering studies by Mark Rosenzweig and his colleagues (Rosenzweig, 1984), in which groups of young male laboratory rats from the same litter were raised in three different environments. Rats in the first two groups were housed individually or together in standard laboratory cages equipped with only food and water dispensers. In contrast, rats in the third group were provided with enriched conditions. They lived together in a large cage furnished with a variety of playthings that were changed daily to keep their lives interesting. They were also given formal training in running a maze or were sometimes placed in an open field filled with toys.

At the end of the experimental period, which lasted anywhere from a few weeks to several months, behavioral tests and examinations of the animals' brains revealed superior development in the animals raised in enriched conditions. Compared with the other two groups, these rats demonstrated:

- Increased rates of learning in standard laboratory tasks, such as learning a maze

- Increased overall weight of the cerebral cortex, the part of the brain that integrates sensory information

- Increased amounts of acetylcholinesterase, a brain enzyme that enhances learning

- Larger neuronal cell bodies and larger glial cells (cells that provide insulation, support, and nutrients to neuronal cells)

- More synaptic connections

These findings have been replicated and extended in numerous experiments (Nelson & Bloom, 1997). As you will see in Chapter 6, they are also consistent with what is known about how the quality of the environment of human infants can affect their brain development as well as their development in other domains.

▲ APPLY :: CONNECT :: DISCUSS

It is widely believed that the developing brain benefits from an enriched environment and suffers in an environment of deprivation. Using the language and concepts presented in this section, explain what it means for an environment to be "enriched" or "deprived."

Sensing the Environment

Baba is Qalandar, born to a nomadic tribe of entertainers who travel from town to town in Pakistan, exhibiting their dancing bears and monkeys, singing, juggling, and performing magic. As a newborn, when Baba wasn't in the arms of his mother or another tent member, he was placed in a *jhula*, a patchwork cloth hammock suspended a few feet off the ground from the tent ridgepole. Swinging gently in his *jhula*, he would be exposed to the smiling faces of other tent members as they kissed and tickled him, the smells of food and animals, and the sounds of language and laughter, music and chattering monkeys, and the jingling bells tied to his own ankles and wrists (Berland, 1982).

To what extent was Baba aware of the kaleidoscope of sights, sounds, and smells that surrounded his *jhula*? Did he perceive his surroundings as a "buzzing confusion," as the philosopher-psychologist William James (1890) believed all infants do—a perceptual jumble that would only gradually become clear with time and experience? Or was Baba born with fairly sophisticated, even adultlike, capacities that allowed him to perceive order and consistency in the world? Did he understand, for example, the connection between the jingling sounds he heard and the movement of his arms and legs?

At present, developmentalists are divided on how to answer such questions (Wang, Baillargeon, & Patterson, 2005; Cohen, 2002). This difference of opinion about what perceptual abilities and understandings infants start out with strongly influences the kind of theory needed to explain subsequent processes of developmental change. The idea that infants' perceptions initially amount to total confusion suggests that the world becomes an ordered and predictable place to infants only as they gain experience and learn about the environment. In contrast, the idea that infants are highly competent suggests that biology may play a critical role, endowing infants with special abilities that allow them to tune in to specific features of the environment—certain visual patterns or the sound of the human voice, for example. As you will see, most developmentalists take a middle ground, maintaining that initial sensory capacities are biologically determined, but only to the extent that they guide how experience shapes later development.

As Qalandar custom dictates, this infant lies in a cloth hammock called a *jhula*, safe from snakes and insects and close to the faces of older siblings.

electroencephalography (EEG) A common physiological method used to evaluate infant sensory capacities, which involves attaching sensors to the baby's head and measuring changes in brain waves in response to the presentation of different stimuli.

Methods of Evaluating Infant Sensory Capacities

You do not have to spend much time with a newborn to understand the difficulties researchers face in assessing infants' initial capacities. Babies sleep a lot—about three-quarters of every day in the first month. When they are awake, they may be drowsy or upset. Even when they appear to be alert and calm, they often do not seem to be paying attention to anything in particular; occasionally something seems to catch their interest, but only fleetingly. These constant fluctuations in newborn states make it difficult for developmentalists to provide reliable and replicable evidence regarding particular newborn capacities.

Normal full-term newborns enter the world with all sensory systems functioning. However, not all of these systems have developed to the same level. For example, newborns' senses of touch and smell are considerably more advanced than their sharpness of vision. This is not surprising, given the relative importance of touch and odor for finding a food source—the breast—and the relative unimportance of vision to the newborn's survival. In addition, this unevenness illustrates the general rules of development of heterochrony and heterogeneity that we remarked on in Chapter 3 (p. 84). Different parts of an organism develop at different rates and are therefore at different levels of development at a given time.

The basic method developmentalists use to evaluate infant sensory capacities is to present infants with a stimulus and observe their overt behavioral or physiological responses to it. For example, an investigator might sound a tone or flash a light and watch for an indication—a turn of the head, a variation in brain waves, a change in heart rate—that the newborn has sensed it. One of the most common physiological methods used in this type of procedure is **electroencephalography (EEG)**, which involves attaching sensors to the baby's head and measuring changes

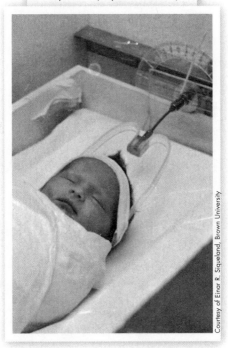

This newborn has on a specially designed headpiece that records head turning. In operant-conditioning experiments, head turns of more than 10 degrees are reinforced by the opportunity to suck on a pacifier (Siqueland, 1968).

visual preference technique A common behavioral method used to evaluate infant sensory capacities, which involves presenting two different stimuli at once to determine if the baby displays a preference by looking at one longer than the other.

habituation The process in which attention to novelty decreases with repeated exposure.

dishabituation The term used to describe the process in which an infant's interest is renewed after a change in the stimulus.

phonemes The smallest sound categories in human speech that distinguish meanings. Phonemes vary from language to language.

in brain waves in response to the presentation of different stimuli (Grossman et al., 2007). A widely used behavioral method, the **visual preference technique**, involves presenting two different stimuli at once to determine if the baby displays a preference by looking at one longer than the other. If so, the baby must be able to tell the stimuli apart.

Yet another technique for assessing sensory capacities exploits a process known as **habituation**, in which an infant's attention to a novel stimulus decreases following continued exposure to it. Using this technique, an investigator presents an infant with a novel stimulus that captures the infant's attention, such as a musical tone or a pictorial arrangement of simple geometric figures, and then continues presenting it until the infant gets bored and stops paying attention to it. The next step is to change some aspect of the stimulus, such as the pitch of the musical tone or the arrangement of the geometric figures, for example. If the infant shows renewed interest after the change in the stimulus, the infant is said to exhibit **dishabituation**, and the investigator can conclude that the infant perceived the change. The use of such subtle indicators of infants' attention to sensory stimuli provides developmentalists with essential tools for understanding developmental processes at a time when infants are still too immature to make their experiences known through coordinated movement or speech.

Hearing

Since fetuses respond to sounds outside the mother's womb, it is no surprise that newborns respond to sound immediately after birth. Make a loud noise, and infants only minutes old will startle and may even cry. They will also turn their head toward the source of the noise, an indication that they perceive sound as roughly localized in space (Morrongiello et al., 1994). However, newborns' hearing is not as acute for some parts of the sound spectrum as it will be when they are older (Fernald, 2001). (Sensitivity to sound improves dramatically in infancy and then more slowly until the age of 10, when it reaches adult levels.) Significantly, newborns can distinguish the sound of the human voice from other kinds of sounds, and they seem to prefer it over any other. They are especially attuned to the sounds of language. Newborns all over the world are particularly interested in speech directed to them that has a high pitch and slow, exaggerated pronunciation—speech known as "motherese," "baby talk," or "infant-directed speech" (Schachner & Hannon, 2011). This preference for motherese appears even when the speaker is speaking a foreign language (Werker, Pegg, & McLeod, 1994). By the time they are 2 days old, however, babies would rather hear the language that has been spoken around them than a foreign language (Moon et al., 1993).

One of the most striking discoveries about the hearing of very young infants is that it is sensitive to the smallest sound categories in human speech that distinguish meanings (Sato, Sogabe, & Mazuka, 2010). These basic language sounds are called **phonemes**, and they vary from language to language. In Spanish, for example, /r/ and /rr/ are different phonemes (linguists use slashes to denote phonemes); thus, "pero" and "perro," for example, which sound different—"perro" has a rolling *r*—have different meanings. In English, however, there is no such distinction. Similarly, /r/ and /l/ are different phonemes in English but not in Japanese.

In a pioneering study, Peter Eimas and his colleagues demonstrated that 2-month-olds can distinguish among a variety of phonemes (Eimas, 1985). The researchers began by having the infants suck on a nipple attached to a recording device similar to the one shown in Figure 4.7. After establishing a baseline rate of sucking for each

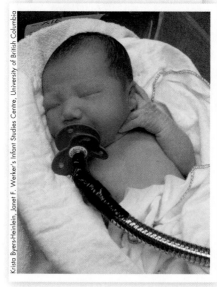

FIGURE **4.7** This photo shows an apparatus used to register young infants' responses to artificially manipulated speech sounds. The baby sucks on a pacifier connected to recording instruments as speechlike sounds are presented. The recording instruments register changes in the baby's rate of sucking as different sounds are presented.

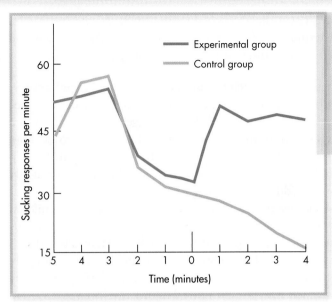

FIGURE 4.8 When two groups of infants were repeatedly presented with a single consonant over a 5-minute period, their rates of sucking decreased to just over 30 sucks per minute. For half of the infants (the experimental group), the consonant was changed at the time marked 0. Note that their rate of sucking increased sharply. For the remaining infants (the control group), who continued to hear the same consonant, the rate of sucking continued to decrease. (Adapted from Eimas, 1985.)

baby, they presented the speech sound /pa/ to the babies each time they sucked. At first, the babies' rate of sucking increased, as if they were excited by each presentation of the sound, but after a while they settled back to their baseline rates of sucking. When the infants had become thoroughly habituated to the sound of /pa/, some of them heard a new sound, /ba/, which differed from the original sound in its initial phoneme—/b/ versus /p/. Others were presented with a sound that was different but remained within the /p/ phoneme category. The babies began sucking rapidly again only when they heard a sound that belonged to a different phoneme category, an indication that they were especially sensitive to the kinds of differences that languages use to distinguish phonemes (Figure 4.8).

Follow-up studies have shown that very young infants are able to perceive all the categorical sound distinctions used in all the world's languages. Adults, in contrast, perceive only those of their native language. Japanese babies, for example, can perceive the difference between /r/ and /l/; adult speakers of Japanese cannot (Yoshida et al., 2010). Infants' ability to make phonemic distinctions apparently begins to narrow to just those distinctions that are present in their native language at about 6 to 8 months of age, the same age at which an infant's first halting articulations of languagelike sounds are likely to begin (Kuhl et al., 2006; Weikum et al., 2007) (Figure 4.9). Given the pattern of infant brain growth during this time, some developmentalists have speculated that the narrowing of the ability to make phonemic distinctions is an example of how cultural experience interacts with the biological process of synaptogenesis and pruning that we discussed earlier (see pp. 128–129; Munakata et al., 2004).

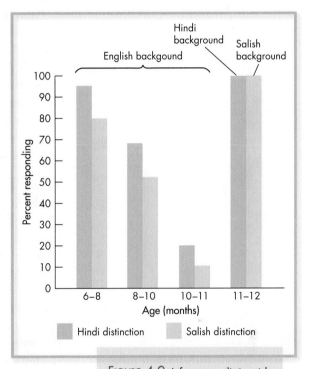

FIGURE 4.9 Infants can distinguish among language sounds that do not occur in their native language, but this capacity diminishes during the first year of life. Note the decrease in the proportion of infants from an English-speaking background who respond to consonants in Hindi and Salish (a Native American Indian language). In contrast, at 1 year, Hindi and Salish infants retain the capacity to distinguish sounds in their native languages. (Adapted from Eimas, 1985.)

Vision

The basic anatomical components of the visual system are present at birth, but they are not fully developed. The lens of the eye and the cells of the retina are somewhat immature, limiting visual sharpness. In addition, the movements of the baby's eyes are not coordinated well enough to align the images on the two retinas to form a clear composite image. The result is that the baby's vision is blurry. The immaturity of some of the neural pathways that relay information from the retina to the brain

visual acuity Sharpness of vision.

further limits the newborn's visual capacities (Atkinson, 1998). Numerous studies have been conducted to determine exactly what, and how well, infants can see, and how the visual system changes over time (Maurer et al., 2007).

Visual Acuity A basic question about infants' vision concerns their **visual acuity**, that is, their sharpness of vision. Estimates of newborns' visual acuity differ somewhat according to the particular measure used, but all suggest that newborns are very nearsighted, with a visual acuity in the neighborhood of 20/300 to 20/600. In other words, they can see at 20 feet (6 meters) what an adult with normal vision can see at 300 to 600 feet (91 to 182 meters) (Martin, 1998). (Figure 4.10 roughly indicates what infants can see at different ages.)

Poor visual acuity is probably less troublesome to newborns than to older children and adults. After all, newborns are unable to move around on their own and they cannot hold their heads erect without support. Still, their visual system is tuned well enough to allow them to see objects about a foot (30 centimeters) away—roughly the distance of the mother's face when they are nursing. This level of acuity allows them to make eye contact, which is important in establishing the social relationship between mother and child (Stern, 2002). Between 2 and 3 months of age, infants can coordinate the vision of both their eyes (Atkinson, 1998). By 7 or 8 months of age, when infants are able to crawl, their visual acuity is close to the adult level.

Visual Scanning Despite their nearsightedness and their difficulty in focusing, newborns actively scan their surroundings from the earliest days of life (Bronson, 1997). Marshall Haith and his colleagues developed recording techniques that allowed them to determine precisely where infants were looking and to monitor their eye movements in both light and dark rooms. They discovered that even in a completely darkened room, neonates scan with short eye movements. Since no light is entering their eyes, this kind of scanning cannot be caused by the visual environment. It must therefore be *endogenous,* originating in the neural activity of the central nervous system. Endogenous eye movements seem to be an initial, primitive basis for looking behavior (Haith, 1980).

Haith's studies also revealed that neonates exhibit an early form of *exogenous* looking, that is, looking that is stimulated by the external environment. When the lights are turned on after infants have been in the dark, they pause in their scanning

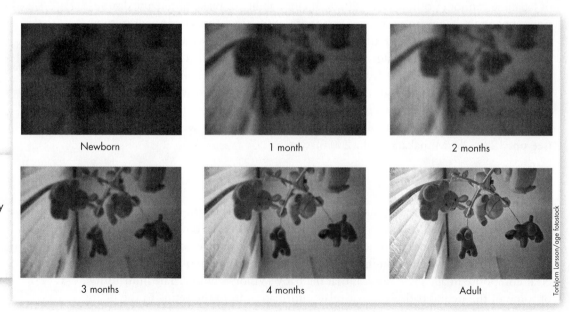

FIGURE 4.10 Infants' visual acuity increases dramatically over the first few months of life. By the age of 4 months, a baby can see nearly as distinctly as an adult, as seen in this photographic conception of the appearance of a visual scene for infants of different ages.

Newborn   1 month   2 months

3 months   4 months   Adult

Torbjorn Larsson/age fotostock

when their gaze encounters an object or some change of brightness in the visual field. This very early sensitivity to changes in brightness, which is usually associated with the edges and angles of objects, appears to be an important component of the baby's developing ability to perceive visual forms (Haith, 1980).

Color Perception Newborns seem to possess all, or nearly all, of the physiological prerequisites for seeing color in a rudimentary form. When two colors are equally bright, however, they do not discriminate between them. By 2 months of age, infants' ability to perceive different colors appears to approach adult levels (Kellman & Banks, 1998).

Perception of Patterns and Objects What do babies see when their eyes encounter an object? Until the early 1960s, it was widely believed that neonates perceive only a formless play of light. Robert Fantz (1961, 1963) disproved this assumption by demonstrating that babies less than 2 days old can distinguish between visual forms. The technique he used was very simple. Babies were placed on their back in a specially designed "looking chamber" and shown various forms (Figure 4.11). An observer looked down through the top of the chamber and recorded how long the infants looked at each form. Because the infants spent more time looking at some forms than at others, presumably they could tell the forms apart and looked longest at the ones they preferred. Fantz found that neonates would rather look at patterned figures, such as faces and concentric circles, than at plain ones (Figure 4.12). Fantz's findings set off a search to determine the extent of newborns' capacity to perceive objects and the reasons they prefer some forms over others. That research has confirmed that infants visually perceive the world as more than random confusion, as well as that infants' ability to perceive objects is far from adult-like and continues to develop over the first months of life (Johnson et al., 2003; Bornstein, Mash, & Arterberry, 2011).

By 2 months of age, infants begin to show that in some circumstances they see the boundaries between objects and recognize that objects are three-dimensional (Arterberry & Yonas, 2000). These abilities are by no means as elementary as you may think. How, for example, does a newborn who is staring at a cat on a chair know that the cat is not part of the chair? Is it easier for the infant to distinguish between cat and chair if the cat meows, or licks its paw? In a later section we will address the importance of vocalization and movement as important cues in the baby's visual perception of objects. Here we will focus on another important cue, contrast: The baby's ability to tell the cat from the chair is enhanced if the cat is black and the chair is white.

A number of studies have shown that the vision of young infants is best under conditions of high contrast, such as when a visual field is divided clearly (like the cat on the chair) into parts that are black and parts that are white (Kellman & Banks, 1998). Gordon Bronson (1991, 1994, 1997) used this property of newborn vision to study the way 2-week-old and 12-week-old babies scan outline drawings of simple figures, such as a cross or a V, on a lighted visual field. When adults are shown such figures, they scan the entire boundary. Two-week-old babies appear to focus only on areas of high contrast, such as black lines and angles on a

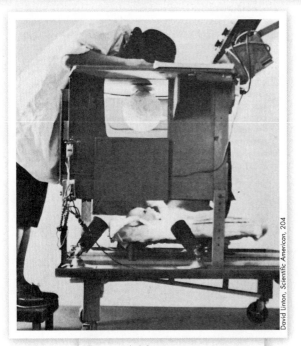

David Linton, *Scientific American*, 204

FIGURE 4.11 The apparatus in this photo is the "looking chamber" that Robert Fantz used to test newborns' visual interests. The infant lying under the chamber is looking up at the stimuli attached to the chamber's ceiling. The observer, watching through a peephole, is determining how long the infant looks at each stimulus.

FIGURE 4.12 Infants tested during the first weeks of life show a preference for patterned stimuli over plain stimuli. The length of each bar indicates the relative amount of time the babies spent looking at the corresponding stimulus. (Adapted from Fantz, 1961.)

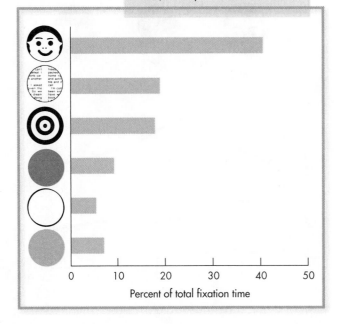

Percent of total fixation time

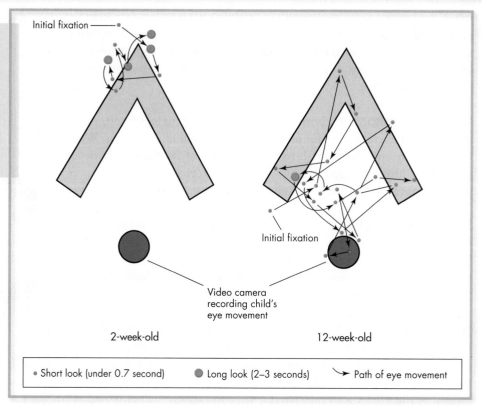

FIGURE 4.13 The diagram depicts the visual scanning of a triangle by young infants. The triangle was mounted on a wall. A video camera was mounted just beneath it, positioned to record the eye movements of infants as they gazed at the triangle. Note that the 2-week-olds concentrated their gaze on only one part of the figure, whereas the 12-week-olds visually explored the figure more fully. Large dots indicate long fixation times; small dots represent short ones. (Adapted from Bronson, 1991.)

FIGURE 4.14 Visual preferences of infants for (a) a schematic face, (b) a scrambled schematic face, and (c) a nonfacelike figure, all having equal amounts of light and dark area. The infants preferred both facelike forms over the non-facelike form, and they paid slightly more attention to the "real" than to the scrambled face. (Adapted from Fantz, 1961.)

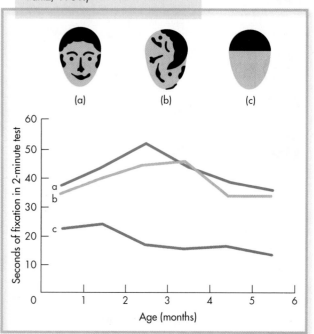

white background (Figure 4.13). This kind of looking behavior is clearly not random; it shows that infants are born with the ability to perceive basic patterns. At 12 weeks of age, as Figure 4.13 indicates, infants scan more of the figure than at 2 weeks, although their scanning movements are sometimes off the mark and may still be arrested by areas of high contrast. In one of his studies, Bronson (1994) found that 13-week-old infants scanned more rapidly and extensively than did infants 10 weeks of age and under. The developmental change was so marked that Bronson concluded that "by 3 months of age [the] infants appear[ed] to be quite different organisms, at least with respect to their scanning characteristics" (p. 1260). He suggested that as the nervous system matures, it becomes more sophisticated and can begin to control visual scanning.

Perception of Faces In some of his early studies, Fantz presented newborns with a schematic diagram of a human face and a diagram of a facelike form in which facial elements had been scrambled (Figure 4.14; Fantz, 1961, 1963). He found that the infants could distinguish the normal face from the jumbled face, and preferred the normal one. Although the preference was small, the possibility that newborns have an unlearned preference for a biologically significant form like a face naturally attracted developmentalists' interest.

More recent work has shown that a crucial factor in newborns' preference for faces is the presence of more elements in the upper part of the configuration than in the bottom half. This imbalance corresponds to the fact that there are more visual elements in the top half of actual faces, and babies show that they are sensitive to this imbalance. Even a facelike stimulus is not preferred over a scrambled stimulus unless it has more visual elements in the upper half (Turati, Di Giorgio, Bardi, & Simion, 2010).

Another key finding is that motion critically influences newborns' perception of faces. In Fantz's studies and other early work, researchers used only stationary schematic representations of faces. In real life, people's heads move and their facial expressions change. Research suggests that young infants, like adults, may discriminate and remember dynamic faces more easily than they do still faces (Lander, Chuang & Wickham, 2006; Bahrick, Moss, & Fadil, 1996). This may help account for why newborns only 2 to 7 hours old recognize, and show a preference for, their mother's face when it is contrasted with that of a stranger, even after a delay as long as 15 minutes between the time that the infant sees the mother's face and the time that test is begun (Bushnell, 2001).

Indeed, as we learned in the case of the auditory system, the developing visual system is highly sensitive to the baby's individual experiences (Mondloch & Desjarlais, 2010). Thus, by 3 months of age, babies tend to look more at faces with ethnic features (for example, Asian, Caucasian, African) similar to those with which they are most familiar (Liu et al., 2010). Likewise, over the course of the first year, infants become able to discriminate between faces of their own ethnicity better than they can discriminate between faces of some other ethnic group. Chinese babies, for example, become better at discriminating between faces with Asian features than between faces with African or Caucasian features (Kelly et al., 2009).

Taste and Smell

Neonates have a built-in capacity to discriminate between different tastes and odors, and show strong preferences for things that taste and smell sweet, as does their first natural source of food, breast milk. The newborn's reaction to sweetness, however, extends well beyond simple preference. Research shows that a sweet taste has a calming effect on crying babies, and diminishes indications of pain, both physiological (for example, heart rate and brain excitation) and behavioral, helping babies cope with aversive situations (Fernandez et al., 2003).

Beyond their capacity to distinguish sweet from not-sweet, to what extent do newborns discriminate between different tastes and odors, and why might it be important for them to do so? An influential study conducted by Diana Rosenstein and Harriet Oster (1988) found that babies only 2 hours old produce different facial expressions in response to bitter, sour, and salty tastes. The characteristic facial expressions they make in response to specific tastes, especially those that are bitter and sour, look remarkably like the expressions made by adults when they encounter the same tastes, evidence that these expressions are innate and may have important evolutionary implications (Figure 4.15). Oster, who has done extensive studies of infant facial expressions, suggests that when the face puckers in response to a sour taste (see Figure 4.15c), it stimulates the production of saliva, which has the effect of diluting the pungency of a potentially edible substance. In contrast, in response to bitter tastes (see Figure 4.15b), newborns' mouths (like adults') tend to "gape," or open widely, as though in readiness to eject the food, an adaptive response given that bitter substances are more likely to be inedible and potentially harmful (Oster, 2005).

Infants' taste responses go beyond the innate capacity to make general distinctions between edible and inedible foods. They also involve cultural factors. For example, it has been known for some time that the flavors of the

FIGURE **4.15** Newborns respond to different tastes with distinctive facial expressions that have significant adaptive value. In these photographs, newborns react to tastes that are (a) sweet, (b) bitter, (c) and sour.

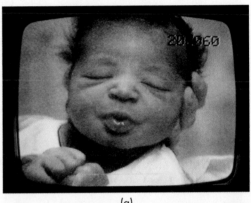
(a)

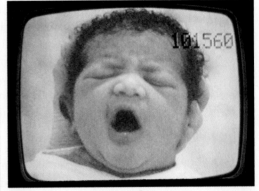
(b)

(c)

Diana Rosenstein

intermodal perception The ability to perceive an object or event by more than one sensory system simultaneously.

mother's diet during pregnancy are transmitted to the fetus by way of the amniotic fluid it swallows (Hauser et al., 1985). Similarly, flavors from the mother's diet are transmitted to her newborn by way of her breast milk (Mennella & Beauchamp, 1999). A carefully controlled study suggests that these forms of indirect exposure to the flavors of food common in the mother's culture affect the newborn's taste preferences (Mennella, Jagnow, & Beauchamp, 2001).

In this study, pregnant women who planned on breast-feeding their infants were randomly assigned to experimental and control groups. Those in the experimental group drank a specified amount of carrot juice several times a week in their last trimester of pregnancy and/or during the period in which they breast-fed their newborns. Those in the control group drank water instead. The babies' taste preferences were tested several weeks after they had begun to eat cereal but before they had any direct exposure to the flavor of carrots. The test involved comparing the babies' reactions to cereal mixed with water and to cereal mixed with carrot juice. Compared with infants in the control group, the infants who had been exposed to carrot-flavored amniotic fluid or breast milk exhibited fewer negative facial expressions when being fed carrot-flavored cereal than when being fed cereal mixed with water, and they tended to eat more of the flavored cereal. The babies in the control group showed no such preferences.

This research is consistent with that conducted with nonhuman species (rabbits, for example) and suggests that the mother's prenatal diet prepares offspring for the particulars of the nutritional environment into which they will be born (Jablonka & Lamb, 2005). Interestingly, studies have shown that young children's food preferences can be influenced even by the flavors of the specific formulas they were fed as infants. More specifically, when 4-year-olds were exposed to an array of tastes, they preferred the tastes that were reminiscent of the formula they had been fed as infants, even when the formula tasted a bit like overcooked broccoli (Mennella & Beauchamp, 2005)!

In addition to reacting differently to various tastes, newborns are known to discriminate between different odors. Within just minutes of being born, infants will turn their head preferentially toward maternal breast odors, which help guide them toward the nipple (Porter & Winberg, 1999). One test of newborns' capacities for odor discrimination involved holding either an odorless cotton swab or a swab soaked in one of various aromatic solutions under their nose. The infants showed no reaction to the odorless swab but reacted to unpleasant odors, such as garlic or vinegar, by pursing their lips or wrinkling their nose; and when they smelled something sugary, they smiled. Like gaping and puckering in response to bitter and sour tastes, newborn (and adult) facial reactions to foul odors have the adaptive consequence of reducing the individual's contact with the unpleasant and potentially unhealthy stimulus. The common reaction of wrinkling the nose is a case in point. Take a deep breath through your nose and notice how freely the air flows into your lungs. Now do it again, but with your nose wrinkled up as though you smell something foul. See how the airflow is restricted? Pursing the lips has the same general effect of inhibiting airflow (try it!).

Intermodal Perception

One of the most intriguing areas of research on infants' perceptual capacities focuses on their **intermodal perception**—that is, their ability to simultaneously process various kinds of sensory information from an object or event and perceive them as interconnected. When seeing the mother's face while feeling her warmth, smelling her, and hearing her voice, for example, to what degree does the infant perceive these stimuli in a unitary way? Recent research suggests that infants may be born prepared to perceive certain stimuli as inherently connected to each other (Johnson, Amso, Frank, & Shuwairi, 2008).

An early demonstration of intermodal perception was provided by a study in which, in a series of trials, 29-day-old infants were given a tiny rubber shape to feel with their mouth (Meltzoff & Borton, 1979). After they had "explored" the shape for 90 seconds, the shape was removed carefully so the babies could not see it. When the infants were then shown a pair of shapes (Figure 4.16), they looked longer at the one that they had felt in their mouth, suggesting that they had made an intermodal connection between what they had felt and what they were seeing.

FIGURE 4.16 In a study of intermodal perception, infants were given one of two rubber shapes, like those depicted here, to feel with their mouth. When they were later shown the pair of shapes, the infants looked longer at the shape that matched the one they had felt in their mouth.

Further research has examined how intermodal perception may be a vehicle for learning in the first hours of life (Sai, 2005). You know from our previous discussion that within hours of birth, babies learn the features of their mother's face and prefer looking at their mother's face to looking at a stranger's. However, since in the first few hours of interacting with the mother, the baby not only sees her face but also hears her voice, developmentalists have wondered whether hearing the mother's voice somehow contributes to the baby's ability to learn about the visual features of her face. To tackle this question, researchers compared preferences for the mother's face in two groups of babies 2 to 12 hours after birth. In one group, the infants did not hear their mother's voice prior to the preference tests (a condition ensured by a researcher who stayed with the mother from the birth of the baby until the experimental test). Mothers in the second group interacted with their newborns normally, including talking and cooing to them. A standard preference test, in which the infant is presented with the mother and a female stranger, was used to determine whether the babies recognized their mother (Figure 4.17). (The mother and the stranger were both draped in a white cloth to conceal clothing and body features; the stranger's hair length and color matched the mother's; strong air freshener was used to mask body odors.) It was discovered that the babies who had been prevented from hearing their mother's voice were unable to recognize their mother's face in the experimental test, suggesting that the intermodal perception of the maternal face and voice is essential for newborns to learn the unique visual features of their mother's face.

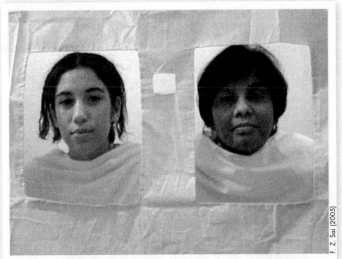

F. Z. Sai (2005)

FIGURE 4.17 To test whether newborns can distinguish between their mother's face and that of a female stranger, researchers attempt to mask as many nonfacial cues as possible, and then compare the amount of time newborns spend looking at each face.

Overall, there is extensive evidence that babies come into the world with sensory capacities in good working order and far more organized than were once thought. (Infants' sensory capacities are summarized in Table 4.1.) The next question is: What capacities do infants have for acting on the world? This is a crucial question, because over the first 3 months of life, infants' growing ability to act in an organized way toward the people and objects in their environment fundamentally changes the nature of their interactions in the world and marks the starting point of postnatal psychological development.

table 4.1

Early Sensory Capacities	
Sense	**Capacity**
Hearing	Ability to distinguish phonemes
	Preference for native language
Vision	Slightly blurred, slight double vision at birth
	Color vision by 2 months of age
	Ability to distinguish patterned stimuli from plain
	Preference for moving, facelike stimuli
Smell	Ability to differentiate odors well at birth
Taste	Ability to differentiate tastes well at birth
Touch	Responsive to touch at birth
Temperature	Sensitivity to changes in temperature at birth
Position	Sensitivity to changes in position at birth

This section has introduced you to several different research methods that developmental-ists use to answer questions about the newborn's sensory systems. Identify and briefly describe four of these methods. Choose one or two of them to design a study addressing some facet of infant sensory capacity.

The Organization of Behavior

As a midwife in a small, rural Turkish village, Fulya is highly knowledgeable about, and experienced in, newborn care. In addition to giving advice on feeding, clean-ing, and protecting infants from the evil eye, Fulya tells new mothers how impor-tant it is to keep their babies wrapped tightly in cloth:

> Indeed, we continue to swaddle for several months until the baby seems strong and healthy. Swaddling makes the baby feel protected and helps it to sleep. I was shocked when the anthropologist who lived in our village told me how Americans dress their babies—it seems that in summertime the little ones are almost naked, wearing little more than a tiny shirt and diaper. Poor little things with their arms and legs flailing around, they must feel quite unprotected. (Delaney, 2000, pp. 131–132.)

The practice of swaddling is very common across cultures and is thought to have a number of benefits. Consistent with Fulya's observation that swaddling helps in-fants sleep, research indicates that newborns who are swaddled tend to be calmer than those who are not swaddled (Giacoman, 1971). Although it is hard to know whether swaddled babies "feel protected," as Fulya believes, it is clear that swaddling reduces opportunities for "arms and legs flailing around," a sign that the baby's behavior has become disorganized, as it does in states of fussiness and agitation.

Developing and maintaining behavioral organization is important for infants because it allows them to interact more effectively and adap-tively with the world around them. At birth, babies possess a number of inborn behaviors (reflexes) that provide highly organized ways of responding adaptively to the environment. As development progresses during the early months of infancy, new forms of behavioral organiza-tion emerge, expanding infants' capacities for engagement with people and objects in their world. By the age of 3 months, for example, infants' physical control and coordination enable them to raise their head to look around, smile in response to the smiles of others, and perform deliberate actions, such as shaking a rattle to make a noise. A major goal of the developmental sciences is to explain how biological and cultural processes contribute to the emergence of these new forms of orga-nized behavior. We begin first with infant reflexes, evolution's contribution to the newborn's behavioral organization. We then explore how more complex forms of behavioral organization arise and become coordinated with the particular social world in which the child develops.

The cultural practices of swaddling and providing pacifiers help this Mongolian baby to maintain behav-ioral organization and be calm and quiet.

Reflexes

Newborn babies come equipped with a variety of **reflexes**—specific, well-integrated, automatic (involuntary) responses to specific types of stimulation (see Table 4.2). Some reflexes are clearly adaptive throughout life. One of these is the *eyeblink re-flex,* which protects the eye from overly bright lights and foreign objects that might damage it. Other reflexes are adaptive during infancy but disappear over time. For example, the *sucking reflex,* of obvious adaptive value to newborn feeding, can be

reflex A specific, well-integrated, auto-matic (involuntary) response to a specific type of stimulation.

table 4.2			
Reflexes Present at Birth			
Reflex	**Description**	**Developmental Course**	**Significance**
Babinski	When the bottom of the baby's foot is stroked, the toes fan out and then curl	Disappears in 8 to 12 months	Presence at birth and normal course of decline are a basic index of normal neurological condition
Crawling	When the baby is placed on the stomach and pressure is applied to the soles of the feet, the arms and legs move rhythmically	Disappears after 3 to 4 months; possible reappearance at 6 to 7 months as a component of voluntary crawling	Uncertain
Eyeblink	Rapid closing of eyes	Permanent	Protection against aversive stimuli such as bright lights and foreign objects
Grasping	When a finger or some other object is pressed against the baby's palm, the baby's fingers close around it	Disappears in 3 to 4 months; replaced by voluntary grasping	Presence at birth and later disappearance is a basic sign of normal neurological development
Moro	If a baby experiences a sudden dropping sensation while being held or hears a loud noise, the baby will throw the arms outward while arching backward and then bring the arms together as if grasping something	Disappears in 6 to 7 months (although startle to loud noises is permanent)	Disputed; its presence at birth and later disappearance are a basic sign of normal neurological development
Rooting	When touched on the cheek, the baby turns head in the direction of the touch and opens mouth	Disappears between 3 and 6 months	Component of nursing
Stepping	When held upright over a flat surface, the baby makes rhythmic leg movements	Disappears in first 2 months but can be reinstated in special contexts	Disputed; it may be only a kicking motion, or it may be a component of later voluntary walking
Sucking	The baby sucks when something is put into his or her mouth	Disappears and is replaced by voluntary sucking	Fundamental component of nursing

elicited by a touch on the baby's lips. Needless to say, this particular reflex disappears with time.

There are also some reflexes that seem to serve no apparent function. An example is the *Moro reflex,* in which infants make a grasping motion with their arms in response to a loud noise or when suddenly experiencing a feeling of being dropped. Some developmentalists believe that these reflexes currently serve no purpose but were functional during earlier evolutionary stages, allowing infants to cling to their mothers in threatening situations, as do infants of most nonhuman primate species (Jolly, 1999). Others believe that such seemingly useless reflexes may still be functional because they promote a close relationship between mother and infant (Bowlby, 1973; Prechtl, 1977).

Infant reflexes are an important window into the infant's developing brain and can, therefore, be used to diagnose the functioning of the central nervous system. For example, the *absence* of a neonatal reflex, such as sucking, often indicates that the infant suffers some form of brain damage. Brain damage is also indicated when a reflex *persists* beyond the age at which it should have disappeared. For example, the Moro reflex typically disappears in the months after birth. It is seen again only in the event of injury to the central nervous system (Zafeiriou et al., 1999).

From Reflex to Coordinated Action

Virtually all developmentalists agree that reflexes are important building blocks for constructing more complex and coordinated behaviors, often referred to as **action** (Valsiner, 2007). For example, one new action that appears in early infancy is nursing.

action Complex, coordinated behaviors.

When we compare the way newborn infants feed with the nursing behavior of 6-week-old infants, a striking contrast is evident. Newborns possess several reflexes that are relevant to feeding: rooting (turning the head in the direction of a touch on the cheek), sucking, swallowing, and breathing. These component behaviors are not well integrated, however. Newborns tend to root around for the nipple in a disorganized way and may lose it as soon as they find it. They also have trouble coordinating breathing with sucking and swallowing, and must frequently break away from sucking to come up for air.

By the time infants are 6 weeks old, a qualitative change is evident in their feeding behavior. For one thing, infants anticipate being fed when they are picked up and can prepare themselves to feed by turning toward the nipple and making sucking movements with their mouths—all without direct stimulation on their cheek or lips from the breast or bottle. Equally significant, they have worked out the coordination of all the component behaviors of feeding—sucking, swallowing, and breathing—and they can now perform them in a smooth, integrated sequence (Meyers, 2001). In short, feeding has become nursing. In fact, babies become so efficient at nursing that they can get as much milk in 10 minutes as it once took them up to an hour to get. In the language of *dynamic systems theory* (see Chapter 1, p. 27), the stable and balanced behavioral system of nursing has emerged as its component parts (sucking, swallowing, breathing) interacted over time, became increasingly coordinated with each other, and ultimately unified into a complex system of action. However, as we discuss below, the emergence of nursing as an organized system of action does not happen in a vacuum but is facilitated by the active efforts of the caregiver. (See also the box "In the Field: Baby-Friendly Hospital Care" for procedures used to promote nursing and other aspects of developing behavioral organization in premature infants who are in intensive care units.)

Whereas the connection between the sucking reflex and the emergence of nursing is readily discernible, the developmental path between other reflexes and subsequent action is less apparent and more controversial. For example, when newborn babies are held in an upright position with their feet touching a flat surface, they make rhythmic leg movements as if they were walking, a form of behavior often referred to as a "stepping reflex" (see Figure 4.18). But they stop doing so at around 3 months of age. Around 1 year of age, babies use similar motions as a component of walking, a voluntary activity that is acquired with practice.

There are competing explanations for the developmental changes in these rhythmic leg movements. According to Philip Zelazo (1983), the newborn's movements are a genuine (that is, involuntary) reflex, probably controlled by subcortical brain processes. In the first months after birth, the brain undergoes a period of reorganization as the cortex, the seat of voluntary behavior, develops, and many lower-level reflexes, including the stepping reflex, disappear. Zelazo maintains that the old stepping behavior reappears in a new form as a voluntary component of walking after this period of brain reorganization.

Esther Thelen and her colleagues rejected this explanation (Thelen, 1995). According to these researchers, early stepping disappears, not because of changes in the cortex, but because of changes in the baby's muscle mass and weight that make stepping difficult. In other words, for a period of time, babies' legs are just too heavy for their muscles to lift. In support of their view, Thelen and her colleagues hypothesized that if infants were partially submerged in water and supported in a standing position, stepping would reappear because the buoyancy of the water would counterbalance the infant's increased weight and relative lack of leg strength. They were correct: When infants who had stopped exhibiting

FIGURE 4.18 Babies held upright with their feet touching a flat surface move their legs in a fashion that resembles walking. Experts have debated the origins and developmental history of this form of behavior, called the stepping reflex.

Elizabeth Crews

In the Field | Baby-Friendly Hospital Care

Name:	Heidelise Als
Education:	M.S. in education and Ph.D. in human learning and education from University of Pennsylvania; additional training at the Child Development Unit at Children's Hospital Boston
Current Position:	Director, Neurobehavioral Infant and Child Studies, Children's Hospital, Harvard Medical School
Career Objectives:	Develop procedures to minimize premature newborns' trauma while being treated in hospital intensive care units

HEIDELISE ALS, A DEVELOPMENTAL PSYCHOLOGIST AT Harvard Medical School and Children's Hospital, has spent years trying to understand how premature babies experience the world of the traditional newborn intensive care unit (NICU), which may be their home for weeks or even months after their birth (Raeburn, 2005). Emerging from a warm, dark amniotic pool where they had bobbed in warmth, relative quiet, and constant physical and hormonal contact with their mothers, preterm babies are thrust into the high-tech environment of the NICU, where they lie on their back, with their nose, hands, chest, or feet often pinned with gauze and adhesive tape to hold medical monitors and equipment in place. It is an environment dominated by constant bright lights, the noisy hum and whir of life-support machines, the continual chatter of NICU personnel, and a daily series of by-the-clock feedings, diaper changes, and medical procedures, often painful, in which the fragile newborns are handled on average more than 200 times in a 24-hour period (Sizun & Westrup, 2004). All this, from Als's perspective, overwhelms their immature brains.

Indeed, although it is well known that premature infants are at risk for a number of neurological problems and have more difficulty maintaining alert states and behavior organization than do full-term infants (see Chapter 3, pp. 114–115), recent research has suggested that the stress of traditional NICUs may actually contribute to babies' difficulties. For example, preterm babies often experience episodes in which the oxygen in their blood drops to dangerous levels. It now appears that routine nursing procedures trigger many of these episodes, as well as increase concentrations of stress hormones in the baby's system (reviewed in Sizun & Westrup, 2004). Moreover, this stress of the NICU is experienced at a critical time in the development of the brain's neuronal circuitry. More specifically, the preterm baby's brain is undergoing the radical synaptic pruning characteristic of the final weeks of pregnancy, and it is thus particularly vulnerable to lasting effects from abnormal sensory input and pain.

Fortunately, as a consequence of Als's impassioned efforts to improve the early experiences of the prematurely born, NICUs throughout the world are beginning to change the way they operate. The busy, stimulus-intense, and medically oriented

Heidelise Als

Stephanie Mitchell/Harvard News Office

NICU is being replaced by a NICU that is decidedly more baby friendly. In this new NICU, lights are dimmed and varied to suggest day–night cycles, nurses whisper, and, rather than being kept on a strict schedule, babies are watched for cues that they are hungry or need changing. Stethoscopes are warmed before they are placed on the baby's chest; incubators look more like cozy nests than sterile platforms (see photo); and family members are included in the baby's care.

The individualized developmental care adopted by many modern NICUs also includes procedures used to support developing behavioral organization. For example, babies are given pacifiers to suck, even though, because of their prematurity, many are fed by a tube that delivers nutrients directly into their stomachs. Interestingly, when babies are given pacifiers for sucking, they not only make an easier transition from tube to breast- or bottle-feeding than babies who are not given pacifiers but they also digest the tube-fed nutrients better, sleep better, and have shorter hospital stays (Pinelli & Symington, 2001). Other procedures used to promote behavioral organization include wrapping babies tightly (swaddling) in order to reduce disorganized motor behavior, such as the frequent occurrence of the Moro (startle) reflex, which often disrupts the baby's sleep.

According to Als, "the neurological disability that many preterms are left with when they leave the NICU may in some ways be preventable" (Cassidy, 2005). It may be, then, that the new medical and nursing practices intended to decrease babies' stress may have significant, long-lasting benefits for the developing brain and neurological health of preterm babies (Symington & Pinelli, 2003).

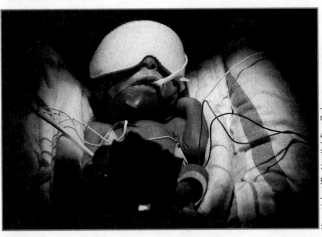

Vincent Laforet/The New York Times/Redux

Although the stepping reflex seems to disappear around 3 months of age, Esther Thelen and her colleagues demonstrated that it would reappear if babies were given proper support. Here, a baby who no longer exhibits a stepping reflex under normal conditions makes the same stepping motions when partially submerged in water.

stepping were held upright in water up to their waists, the stepping behavior reappeared.

Instead of invoking complex explanations about brain development in order to account for the relationship between early stepping and later walking, Thelen and her colleagues took a dynamic systems approach. In their view, infant walking is a new complex form of behavior that emerges from the interaction of a variety of less complex parts, including the infant's weight and muscle mass.

Reaching

Even from the earliest days of postnatal life, babies' arms are often moving, sometimes allowing them to bring their fingers to their mouth to initiate sucking, and sometimes bringing their hands into contact with objects in the world around them. At first, their contact with objects appears to be totally accidental. Nevertheless, research initiated by Claus von Hofsten (1982, 1984) identified an early form of movement he termed *prereaching,* which he elicited by showing very young infants a large, colorful, slow-moving object such as a ball of yarn. As the object passed in front of them, they reached toward it. However, they were unable to grasp an object even after repeated attempts because the movements of reaching with the arm and grasping with the hand are uncoordinated in the newborn, and the babies were unable to get their fingers to close around the object.

At about 3 months of age, a time of maturational changes in the visual and motor areas of the cerebral cortex, *visually guided reaching* emerges. Now, once infants locate an object by either seeing or hearing it, they can use feedback from their own movements to adjust the trajectory of their reach and get their hands close to the object. They are also able to open their fingers in anticipation of grasping the object. Remarkably, they can do this even when a bright object is presented in a darkened room so that they cannot see their own arms, clear evidence that it is feedback from their movement relative to the object that is controlling their reaching and grasping (McCarty, Clifton, Ashmead, Lee, & Goubet, 2001).

In an ingenious experiment, Amy Needham and her colleagues demonstrated that the process of infants' reaching and grasping can be accelerated if infants are given support (Needham, Barrett, & Peterman, 2002). The researchers put specially designed Velcro-covered mittens on the hands of a group of 3-month-old infants, and placed Velcro-covered objects within their reach. The infants' successful experiences connecting their Velcro-covered mittens with objects had fascinating consequences. Compared with a control group of infants who did not have such mittens, those in the experimental group showed greater interest in objects, as well as greater skill in grasping objects when they were later tested without the special mittens.

Piaget's Theory of Developing Action

Jean Piaget, one of the "grand theorists" described in Chapter 1 (see p. 19), provided an impressively comprehensive explanation for the infant's transition from reflexive behavior to coordinated action. As you may recall, Piaget believed that children actively organize an understanding of the world through their engagement with it and that their understanding develops in distinct stages. According to Piaget, the *schema* is the most elementary form of understanding—a mental structure that provides a model for understanding the world. Piaget argued that schemas develop through *adaptation,* a twofold process involving *assimilation* and *accommodation* (see pp. 20–21).

Piaget referred to infancy as the **sensorimotor stage** of cognitive development because during this period, the process of adaptation through which infants gain

sensorimotor stage Piaget's term for the stage of infancy during which the process of adaptation consists largely of coordinating sensory perceptions and simple motor behaviors to acquire knowledge of the world.

table 4.3

Piaget's Stages of Cognitive Development and the Sensorimotor Substages

Age (years)	Stage	Description	Characteristics of Sensorimotor Substages
Birth to 2	Sensorimotor	Infants' achievements consist largely of coordinating their sensory perceptions and simple motor behaviors. As they move through the six substages of this period, infants come to recognize the existence of a world outside themselves and begin to interact with it in deliberate ways.	**Substage 1 (0–1½ months)** *Exercising reflex schemas:* involuntary rooting, sucking, grasping, looking
			Substage 2 (1½–4 months) *Primary circular reactions:* repetition of actions that are pleasurable in themselves
2 to 6	Preoperational	Young children can represent reality to themselves through the use of symbols, including mental images, words, and gestures. Still, children often fail to distinguish their point of view from that of others, become easily captured by surface appearances, and are often confused about causal relations.	**Substage 3 (4–8 months)** *Secondary circular reactions:* dawning awareness of the effects of one's own actions on the environment; extended actions that produce interesting change in the environment
6 to 12	Concrete operational	As they enter middle childhood, children become capable of mental operations, internalized actions that fit into a logical system. Operational thinking allows children to mentally combine, separate, order, and transform objects and actions. Such operations are considered concrete because they are carried out in the presence of the objects and events being thought about.	**Substage 4 (8–12 months)** *Coordination of secondary circular reactions:* combining schemas to achieve a desired effect; earliest form of problem solving
			Substage 5 (12–18 months) *Tertiary circular reactions:* deliberate variation of problem-solving means; experimentation to see what the consequences will be
12 to 19	Formal operational	In adolescence, the developing person acquires the ability to think systematically about all logical relations within a problem. Adolescents display keen interest in abstract ideas and in the process of thinking itself.	**Substage 6 (18–24 months)** *Beginnings of symbolic representation:* images and words come to stand for familiar objects; invention of new means of problem solving through symbolic combinations

knowledge about the world consists largely of coordinating sensory perceptions and simple motor responses. Piaget saw the sensorimotor stage as consisting of six substages (Table 4.3). During the first few months of life, infants are said to progress through substages 1 and 2, *exercising reflex schemas* and *primary circular reactions* (substages 3–6 are covered in Chapter 5, on pp. 178–181).

Substage 1: *Exercising reflex schemas.* Piaget believed that in the first 4 to 6 weeks, infants learn to control and coordinate the reflexes present at birth, which provide them with their initial connection to their environment. However, these initial reflexes add nothing new to development because they undergo very little accommodation (they are largely unchanged). In this sense, infants seem to accomplish little more than exercising inborn reflexes.

Substage 2: *Primary circular reactions.* Accommodation first appears in this substage, which occurs from about 1 to 4 months of age. The first hints of new forms of behavior are that existing reflexes are extended in time (as when infants suck between feedings), or are extended to new objects (as when infants suck their thumb). Piaget acknowledged that babies may suck their thumb as early as the first day of life (we now know they may do so even before birth), but he believed that the thumb sucking seen during substage 2 reflects a qualitatively new form of behavior. That is, in substage 1, infants suck their thumb only when they accidentally touch their mouth with their hand. During substage 2, in contrast, if a baby's thumb falls from her mouth, the baby is likely to bring the thumb back to her mouth so that she can suck it some more. In other words, infants in this substage repeat pleasurable actions for their own sake. Piaget used the term **primary circular reaction** to characterize such behavior. Behaviors of this type are considered *primary* because the objects toward which they are directed are parts of the baby's own body; they

primary circular reaction The term Piaget used to describe the infant's tendency to repeat pleasurable bodily actions for their own sake.

Blowing bubbles is an early instance of a primary circular reaction in which an accidental aspect of sucking is prolonged for the sheer pleasure of continuing the sensation.

age fotostock / SuperStock

are called *circular* because they circle back to themselves (sucking leads to more suck-ing, which leads to more sucking, and so on).

Over the course of substage 2, primary circular reactions undergo both differentia-tion and integration. *Differentiation* occurs as actions become increasingly fine-tuned and flexible and infants modify them in response to variations in the environment (for example, sucking on a thumb differently than on a nipple). *Integration* occurs as separate actions become coordinated into new patterns of behavior (for example, reaching becomes coordinated with grasping). Piaget believed that primary circular reactions are important because they offer the first evidence of cognitive develop-ment. "The basic law of dawning psychological activity," he wrote, "could be said to be the search for the maintenance or repetition of interesting states of consciousness" (Piaget, 1977, p. 202). By the end of substage 2, infants are ready to direct their at-tention to the external world.

Learning Theories of Developing Action

Learning theorists argue that new forms of behavioral organization emerge as a consequence of **learning**, a relatively permanent change in behavior brought about when the infant makes associations between behavior and events in the environment. Several types of learning are believed to operate throughout development, including *habituation* (described previously) and *imitation* (which we will explore in Chapter 6), as well as two processes referred to as *classical conditioning* and *operant conditioning*.

Classical Conditioning **Classical conditioning** is learning in which previously existing behaviors come to be associated with and elicited by new stimuli. The ex-istence of this very basic learning mechanism was demonstrated in the early part of the twentieth century by the Russian physiologist Ivan Pavlov (1849–1936). Pavlov (1927) showed that after several experiences of hearing a tone just before food was placed in its mouth, a dog would begin to salivate in response to the tone before it received any food. In everyday language, Pavlov had caused the dog to learn to expect food when it heard the tone, and its mouth watered as a result.

In the terminology of learning theories, Pavlov elicited the dog's response by pairing a **conditional stimulus (CS)**—a tone—with an **unconditional stimulus (UCS)**—food in the mouth. The food is called an unconditional stimulus because it "unconditionally" causes salivation, salivation being a reflex response to food in the mouth. Salivation, in turn, is called an **unconditional response (UCR)** because it is automatically and unconditionally elicited by food in the mouth. The tone is called a conditional stimulus because the behavior it elicits depends on (is conditional on) the way it has been paired with the unconditional stimulus. When the unconditional response (salivation in response to food in the mouth) occurs in response to the CS (the tone), it is called a **conditional response (CR)** because it depends on the pair-ing of the CS (the tone) and the UCS (the food). The key indicator that learning has occurred is that the CS (tone) elicits the CR (salivation) before the presentation of the UCS (food) (Figure 4.19).

A number of developmentalists seized on Pavlov's demonstrations as a possible model for the way infants learn about their environment. One of Pavlov's coworkers demonstrated conditioned feeding responses in a 14-month-old infant based on the principle of classical conditioning (Krasnogorski, 1907/1967). The baby opened his mouth and made sucking motions (CRs) at the sight of a glass of milk (CS). When a bell (a new CS) was sounded on several occasions just before the glass of milk was presented, the baby began to open his mouth and suck at the sound of the bell, an indication that classical conditioning built expectations in the infant by a process of

learning A relatively permanent change in behavior brought about by making associations between behavior and events in the environment.

classical conditioning Learning in which previously existing behaviors come to be elicited by new stimuli.

conditional stimulus (CS) In classical conditioning, a stimulus that elicits a behavior that is dependent on the way it is paired with the unconditional stimulus (UCS).

unconditional stimulus (UCS) In classical conditioning, the stimulus, such as food in the mouth, that invariably causes the unconditional response (UCR).

unconditional response (UCR) In clas-sical conditioning, the response, such as salivation, that is invariably elicited by the unconditional stimulus (UCS).

conditional response (CR) In classical conditioning, a response to the pairing of the conditional stimulus (CS) and the unconditional stimulus (UCS).

operant conditioning Learning in which changes in behavior are shaped by the consequences of that behavior, thereby giving rise to new and more complete behaviors.

association. The crucial point of these observations is that there is no biological connection between the sound of a bell and the mouth-opening and sucking responses it elicited. Rather, the fact that the new stimuli elicited these responses shows that learning has occurred.

Operant Conditioning

Classical conditioning explains how infants begin to build up expectations about the connections between events in their environment, but it does little to explain how even the simplest new behaviors come into being. According to learning theorists, new behaviors, both simple and complex, arise from a different kind of conditioning: *operant conditioning* The basic principle of **operant conditioning** is that behaviors are shaped by their consequences; that is, organisms will tend to repeat behaviors that lead to rewards and will tend to give up behaviors that fail to produce rewards or that lead to punishment (Skinner, 1938). A consequence (such as receiving a reward) that increases the likelihood that a behavior will be repeated is called a *reinforcement*. Operant conditioning in young infants has been experimentally demonstrated with a variety of reinforcers, such as milk, sweet substances, the opportunity to suck on a pacifier, the sound of a heartbeat or the mother's voice, and the appearance of an interesting visual display (Rovee-Collier & Giles, 2010).

An elegant procedure designed by Rovee-Collier and her colleagues demonstrates how infants will repeat behaviors in order to produce interesting visual effects. The researchers tied one end of a ribbon around an infant's ankle and attached the other end of the ribbon to a mobile hanging above the infant's crib (Figure 4.20). Within just a few minutes the infant learned that kicking would animate the mobile, causing the shapes to shake and spin. The interesting visual effects of the mobile thus acted as a positive reinforcer, prompting the infant to organize her kicking behavior in order to produce additional reinforcements.

Further support for the argument that learning is an important contributor to the development of behavioral organization comes

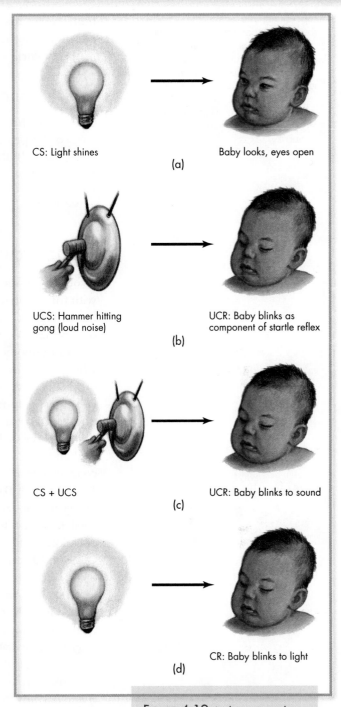

CS: Light shines   Baby looks, eyes open
(a)

UCS: Hammer hitting gong (loud noise)   UCR: Baby blinks as component of startle reflex
(b)

CS + UCS   UCR: Baby blinks to sound
(c)

CR: Baby blinks to light
(d)

FIGURE 4.19 In the top panel, (a) the sight of a light (CS) elicits no particular response. In (b), the loud sound of a gong (UCS) causes the baby to blink (UCR). In (c), the sight of the light (CS) is paired with the sound of the gong (UCS), which evokes an eyeblink (UCR). Finally, in (d), the sight of the light (CS) is sufficient to cause the baby to blink (CR), demonstrating that learning has occurred.

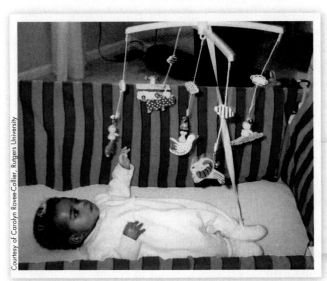

Courtesy of Carolyn Rovee-Collier, Rutgers University

FIGURE 4.20 This baby has learned that her kicking produces the interesting effect of moving the objects dangling from the mobile. Such operant conditioning is an important process in the organization of infant behavior.

temperament The term for the individual modes of responding to the environment that appear to be consistent across situations and stable over time. Temperament includes such characteristics as children's activity level, their intensity of reaction, the ease with which they become upset, their characteristic responses to novelty, and their sociability.

from studies that show that even very young infants are capable of remembering what they have learned from one testing session to the next, a capacity that improves markedly during the first few months of life (Bearce & Rovee-Collier, 2006).

⏏ APPLY :: CONNECT :: DISCUSS

Suppose you have been hired by a local health clinic to lead a class on newborn behavioral organization for expecting parents. How would you describe "behavioral organization" to these parents? How would you explain its importance for development? What sorts of activities or interactions would you recommend to parents for promoting the development of behavioral organization in their newborn?

Temperament

In our discussion of how newborns learn about and become increasingly engaged with the features of their environment, we have focused on universal capacities inherited by each individual infant as a consequence of the evolutionary history of our species. We know, however, that infants are also born with individual differences in how they respond to their environment. Some infants seem to fuss a lot, while others are usually cheerful; some wake at the slightest noise, whereas others seem able to sleep through fireworks. Individual differences such as these relate to variations in **temperament**, an individual's emotional and behavioral characteristics that appear to be consistent across situations and to have some stability over time (Calkins & Degnan, 2005).

Pioneering longitudinal studies of temperament and its role in development were conducted by Alexander Thomas, Stella Chess, and their colleagues (Chess & Thomas, 1996; Wachs & Bates, 2001). They began their research in the late 1950s with a group of 141 middle- and upper-class White children in the United States, and later broadened their study to include 95 working-class Puerto Rican children and several groups of children suffering from diseases, neurological impairments, and mental retardation. Chess and Thomas began their study by conducting structured clinical interviews of the children's parents shortly after the children's birth. They questioned parents about such matters as how the child reacted to the first bath, to wet diapers, to the first taste of solid food. As the children grew older, these interviews were supplemented by interviews with teachers and by tests of the children themselves.

From their data, Chess and Thomas identified nine key traits of temperament: *activity level, rhythmicity* (the regularity or irregularity of the child's basic biological functions), *approach–withdrawal* (the child's response to novelty), *adaptability, threshold of responsiveness* (the minimum intensity of stimulation required to evoke a response), *intensity of reaction, quality of mood* (negative or positive), *distractibility,* and *attention span* or *persistence.* After scoring the children on each of these nine traits, they found that most of the children could be classified in one of three broad temperament categories:

- *Easy babies* are playful, are regular in their biological functions, and adapt readily to new circumstances.

- *Difficult babies* are irregular in their biological functions, are irritable, and often respond intensely and negatively to new situations or try to withdraw from them.

- *Slow-to-warm-up babies* are low in activity level, and their responses are typically mild. They tend to withdraw from new situations, but in a calm way, and require more time than easy babies to adapt to change.

Although the three categories of temperament described by Chess and Thomas are widely used by developmentalists, a number of researchers have tried to create a more refined set of temperament types. For example, Mary Rothbart and her colleagues created a child-behavior questionnaire that provided scores on 195 questions divided into 15 different scales. Parents were asked to decide how well each item applied to their child during the past half year. The results suggested three dimensions of temperamental variation, providing a profile of each child's temperament (see Table 4.4; Rothbart, 2007):

- *Effortful control*—control over what one attends to and reacts to.
- *Negative affect*—the extent of negative emotions.
- *Extraversion*—the extent to which one engages eagerly and happily with people and activities.

There is widespread agreement that genetic factors provide the foundation for temperamental differences (Emde & Hewitt, 2001). For example, working with monkeys, Stephen Suomi (2000) found that an allele on a specific gene is associated with a highly reactive temperament, while a different allele is associated with a calmer temperament. A genetic basis to temperamental traits implies that one should expect to find relatively stable "biases" in the way given individuals respond to their environment, and that it should thus be possible to predict the characteristic style with which they will behave at later stages of development. Indeed, studies conducted in several different societies find evidence of stability

table **4.4**

Definitions of Temperament in the Children's Behavior Questionnaire

Broad dimensions/ Temperament scales	Scale definitions
Effortful control	
Attention control	The capacity to focus attention as well as to shift attention when desired
Inhibitory control	The capacity to plan future action and to suppress inappropriate responses
Perceptual sensitivity	Detection or perceptual awareness of slight, low-intensity stimulation in the environment
Low-intensity pleasure	Pleasure derived from activities or stimuli involving low intensity, rate, complexity, novelty, and incongruity
Negative affectivity	
Frustration	Negative affect related to interruption of ongoing tasks or goal blocking
Fear	Negative affect related to anticipation of distress
Discomfort	Negative affect related to sensory qualities of stimulation, including intensity, rate, or complexity of light, movement, sound, or texture
Sadness	Negative affect and lowered mood and energy related to exposure to suffering, disappointment, and object loss
Soothability	Rate of recovery from peak distress, excitement, or general arousal.
Extraversion	
Activity	Level of gross motor activity including rate and extent of locomotion
Low—shyness	Behavioral inhibition to novelty and challenge, especially social
High-intensity pleasure	Pleasure derived from activities involving high intensity or novelty
Smiling and laughter	Positive affect in response to changes in stimulus intensity, rate, complexity, and incongruity
Impulsivity	Speed of response initiation
Positive anticipation	Positive excitement and anticipation for expected pleasurable activities

Source: Adapted from Rothbart, 2007.

in temperamental traits such as irritability, persistence, and flexibility (Emde & Hewitt, 2001).

At the same time, researchers have found ethnic and national differences related to temperamental traits. Comparing large groups of children from several countries, including the People's Republic of China and the United States, for example, Mary Rothbart and her colleagues found that their three basic dimensions emerged from the data within both countries but also found salient differences (Gartstein et al., 2006). For example, the Chinese children were less active than the American children, a fact the researchers attributed to Chinese child-rearing practices. Chinese culture places a high value on interdependence, and this leads parents to discourage high levels of activity and impulsiveness in their children that might be disruptive to others.

In addition to examining the degree of innate temperamental stability, researchers have also tried to determine whether certain adjustment problems in childhood or adolescence may be related to temperament in infancy. They have indentified several dimensions of early temperament reflective of fearfulness, withdrawal, distress, and lack of adaptability that appear to be linked to later problems with anxiety, depression, and social withdrawal (see Calkins & Degnan, 2005, for a review of this research). Suppose, for example, that an infant tends to react negatively to new people, objects, and situations with screaming and crying. Because the infant's reactions create a state of behavioral disorganization that severs connections to the baby's environment, the baby loses opportunities to practice more adaptive coping skills such as looking away from the source of distress, sucking a pacifier, or seeking comfort from someone. And because of this failure to develop adaptive coping skills, the world continues to overwhelm the child, who may grow up generally anxious and depressed.

Although evidence supports the idea that temperamental traits are stable over time and that certain of them may contribute to adjustment problems later in childhood and adolescence, it needs to be emphasized that most studies find only modest correlations of temperament at different ages, indicating that temperament is a complex trait that can be influenced by a variety of factors (Wachs, 2000).

▲ APPLY :: CONNECT :: DISCUSS

How would your characterize your own temperament in light of the discussion above? In what ways have your temperamental characteristics influenced who you are?

Becoming Coordinated with the Social World

The indisputable fact that human infants are enormously dependent on others for their survival may often obscure babies' own contributions to the care they receive. Infants' survival and continued development depend not only on the actions of responsive caregivers but also on infants' ability to coordinate their actions with those of their caregivers. This ability is essential because caregivers have their own rhythms of life and work and cannot always be hovering over their infant, anticipating his or her every need. Most parents, whether they work the land or work in an office, need to sleep at night, and this need is often in direct conflict with their infant's sleep and hunger patterns. As a result, parents may attempt to modify their infant's patterns of sleeping and feeding so that they will fit into the life patterns of the household and the community. In this and other ways, infants become coordinated with their social world. (The box "Sleeping Arrangements" shows the variety of sleeping practices that are typical in different cultures.)

Sleeping Arrangements

LULLABIES, ROCKING CHAIRS, MUSIC boxes, and cuddly stuffed toys are common features of many infants' bedtime routines. But cross-cultural research shows that the use of such objects in bedtime rituals, as well and where and with whom the baby sleeps, are steeped in cultural beliefs, values, and traditional practices.

In a study of 120 societies around the world, 64 percent of the mothers surveyed reported that their infants sleep in the same bed with them (a practice referred to as co-sleeping). Co-sleeping is widely practiced in highly urban, modern communities in countries such as Japan and Italy, as well as in rural communities in many countries including Mexico and China (Lozoff, Askew, & Wolf, 1996). In only a few countries, such as the United States and Germany, are infants expected to sleep in their own beds in a separate room (Valentin, 2005). Within the United States, the practice of having infants sleep separately, while particularly common among college-educated, middle-class families, is far from universal across regions and groups. A study in eastern Kentucky, for example, found that 48 percent of newborns share their parents' room, and 36 percent, their parents' bed, with available space not seeming to be the issue (Abbott, 1992). African American babies are more likely than European American babies to have a caregiver present when they fall asleep, to sleep in their parents' room, and to spend at least part of the night in their parents' bed (Lozoff, Askew, & Wolf, 1996).

Sleeping practices are related to broad cultural themes regarding the organization of interpersonal relations and the moral ideals of the community (Shweder et al., 1998; Yang & Hahn, 2002). Whereas middle-class U.S. and German mothers emphasize the values of independence and self-reliance, mothers in societies where co-sleeping is the norm emphasize the need for babies to learn to be interdependent and to be able to get along with others and be sensitive to their needs. In Korea, for example, where nearly all infants

Sleep arrangements vary considerably both within and across cultures. The co-sleeping of this mother and baby is somewhat uncommon in England, where they live.

Peter Marlow/Magnum Photos

sleep with their parents, that practice is considered a natural part of child-rearing and an important step in developing family bonds (Yang & Hahn, 2002).

These different underlying values are reflected in a study by Gilda Morelli and her colleagues, who interviewed middle-class mothers in the United States and rural Mayan mothers in Guatemala about their infants' sleeping arrangements (Morelli et al., 1992). None of the U.S. parents in the study allowed their infants to sleep with them. Many parents kept the sleeping child in a nearby crib for the first few months but soon moved the baby to a separate room. They gave such reasons for their arrangements as "I think he would be more dependent . . . if he was constantly with us like that," and "I think it would have made any separation harder if he wasn't even separated from us at night." In contrast, the Mayan mothers always had each new child

sleep in the bed with them until the next baby was born. They insisted that this was the only right thing to do. When they were told about the typical U.S. practice, they expressed shock and disapproval at the parents' behavior and pity for the children. They seemed to think that the U.S. mothers were neglecting their children. Similar sentiments have been voiced by mothers from other societies where co-sleeping is a common practice.

Some researchers have tried to determine whether one arrangement or the other is better or worse for infants. For example, Melissa Hunsley and Evelyn Thoman (2002) report that co-sleeping infants spend more of their time in quiet sleep, which has been associated with slower development. Likewise, a great deal of concern has been raised regarding the possible relationship between co-sleeping and sudden infant death syndrome (see the box "Sudden Infant Death Syndrome" on pp. 156–157) because of accidental suffocation (Perrizo & Pustilnik, 2006). In contrast, on the basis of cross-cultural evidence, James McKenna (1996) reports no ill effects associated with co-sleeping and concludes that "infant–parent co-sleeping is biologically, psychologically, and socially the most appropriate context for the development of healthy infant sleep physiology." On balance, it appears that except in rare cases, whether infants sleep in a bed alone or with their mother does not seem to make a great deal of difference (Okami, Weisner, & Olmstead, 2002). All cultural systems are relatively successful in seeing that infants get enough sleep and grow up normally.

However, while co-sleeping or solitary sleeping may not make a big difference, describing cultural differences in family sleeping arrangements highlights the fact that all such arrangements are organized with a view toward ways in which children will be expected to act at a later time—for example, in a way that emphasizes independence or sensitivity to others' needs.

Sleeping

As with adults, the extent of newborns' arousal varies from deep sleep to frantic activity. The patterns of their rest and activity are quite different from those of adults, however, particularly in the first weeks after birth. To find out about the range and cycles of newborns' arousal patterns, developmentalists use a variety of methods, including direct observation, video recordings, and sophisticated electronic monitoring devices (Salzarulo & Ficca, 2002). In a classic study in which babies' eye movements and

table 4.5

States of Arousal in Infants

State	Characteristics
Nonrapid eye movement (NREM) sleep	Full rest; low muscle tone and motor activity; eyelids closed and eyes still; regular breathing (about 36 times per minute)
Rapid eye movement (REM) sleep	Increased muscle tone and motor activity; facial grimaces and smiles; occasional eye movements; irregular breathing (about 48 times per minute)
Periodic sleep	Intermediate between REM and NREM sleep—bursts of deep, slow breathing alternating with bouts of rapid, shallow breathing
Drowsiness	More active than NREM sleep but less active than REM or periodic sleep; eyes open and close; eyes glazed when open; breathing variable but more rapid than in NREM sleep
Alert inactivity	Slight activity; face relaxed; eyes open and bright; breathing regular and more rapid than in NREM sleep
Active alert	Frequent diffuse motor activity; vocalizations; skin flushed; irregular breathing
Distress	Vigorous diffuse motor activity; facial grimaces; red skin; crying

Source: Wolff, 1966.

muscle activity were observed over the first several weeks following birth, Peter Wolff (1966) was able to distinguish seven states of arousal (Table 4.5). Each state has since been associated with a distinctive pattern of brain activity (Estevez et al., 2002).

Neonates spend most of their time asleep, although the amount of sleep they need gradually decreases. Several studies have shown that babies sleep about 16½ hours a day during the first week of life. By the end of 4 weeks, they sleep a little more than 15 hours a day, and by the end of 4 months, they sleep a little less than 14 hours a day (Thoman & Whitney, 1989).

If babies sleep most of the time, why do their parents lose so much sleep? The reason is that newborns tend to sleep in snatches that last anywhere from a few minutes to a few hours. Thus they may be awake at any time of the day or night. As babies grow older, their sleeping and waking periods lengthen and coincide more and more with the night/day schedule common among adults (Salzarulo & Ficca, 2002; Jenni, Deboer, & Achermann, 2006) (Figure 4.21).

Although babies' adoption of the night/day sleep cycle seems natural to people who live in industrialized countries and urban settings, studies of infants raised in other cultures suggest that it is at least partly a function of cultural influences on the infant (Meléndez, 2005). In a widely cited example of the role of social pressure in rearranging newborns' sleep, the development of the sleep/wake behavior of infants in the United States was compared with that of Kipsigis babies in rural Kenya. In the United States, parents typically put their infants to bed at certain hours—often in a separate room—and try not to pick them up when they wake up crying at night, lest they become accustomed to someone's attending to them whenever they make a fuss. In rural Kenya, infants are almost always with their mother. During the day they sleep when they can, often while being carried on their mother's back as the mother goes about her daily round of farming, household chores, and social activities. During the night, they sleep with their mother and are

FIGURE 4.21 These recordings from electronic monitoring devices document significant differences in the activity of a newborn compared with that of a 4-month-old. Notice how the 4-month-old has both periods of more intense activity and longer stretches of quiet and sleep.

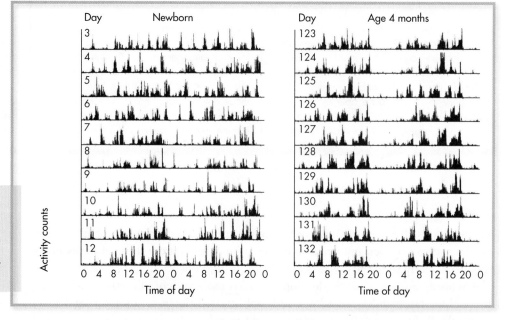

permitted to nurse whenever they wake up. Among Kipsigis infants, the longest period of sleep reported at 1 month is only about 3 hours; many shorter periods of sleep are sprinkled throughout the day and night. Eventually Kipsigis infants begin to sleep through the night, but not until many months later than American infants begin to do so. Even as adults, the Kipsigis are more flexible than Americans in their sleeping hours (Super & Harkness, 1972).

In the United States, the length of the longest sleep period is often used as an index of the infant's maturation. Charles Super and Sara Harkness (1972) suggest that parents' efforts to get babies to sleep for long periods of time during the early weeks of life may be pushing the limits to which young infants can adapt. They believe that the many changes that occur in a newborn's state of arousal in every 24-hour period reflect the immaturity of the infant's brain, which sets a limit on how quickly the child can conform to an adult routine. This may be the explanation for the failure of some infants in industrialized countries to adopt a night/day pattern of sleeping and waking as quickly and easily as their parents would like them to. (Cultural differences in sleeping practices may also be relevant to differences in rates of infant deaths from sudden infant death syndrome; see the box "Sudden Infant Death Syndrome.")

Feeding

As you saw in the description of Afwe's awkward first efforts to feed her baby at the beginning of this chapter, a new mother's initial nursing behavior frequently may not be much more coordinated than her infant's (Page-Goertz, McCamman, & Westdahl, 2001). She must learn how to hold the baby and adjust herself so that her nipple is placed at exactly the right spot against the baby's mouth to elicit the sucking reflex, but not press so tightly that the infant's breathing is disrupted.

The coordination of infant and maternal behavior during feeding is also apparent in the physical movements mothers make while they are feeding their infants by either breast or bottle. Kenneth Kaye (1982) and his colleagues found that even during the very first feeding, mothers occasionally jiggle the baby or the bottle. These jiggles come not at random intervals but during the pauses between the infant's bursts of sucking. The jiggles increase the probability of sucking and prolong the feeding session, thereby increasing the amount of milk the neonate receives. Researchers are not certain how such adaptive patterns originated. Kaye calls them "preadapted responses," implying that they may have arisen in the course of human evolution.

Like many other developments that you have encountered in this chapter, the newborn's feeding behaviors are affected by culture as well as by biology. In many parts of the world, such as sub-Saharan Africa, where artificial means of birth control are unavailable, breast-feeding babies for 2 or more years is an essential birth-control strategy in that it can suppress menstruation for up to 2 years (although not reliably in all women), increasing the intervals between the birth of children (LeVine et al., 1994). The Sukuma of Tanzania, for example, try to space pregnancies by 24 to 30 months and describe someone who does not breast-feed for this length of time as a woman who "gives birth like a chicken." The Baganda of Uganda traditionally forbade sexual activity by a new mother because if she has another child too soon, the first child might be deprived of breast milk and be in danger of contracting **kwashiorkor**, an often-fatal form of protein-calorie malnutrition.

Yet another example of culture influencing infant feeding behaviors involves pediatricians' recommendations regarding when babies should be fed. Today, pediatricians in the United States often tell parents to feed their newborn baby whenever they think the baby is hungry, perhaps as often as every 2 to 3 hours. But from the early 1920s through the 1940s, pediatricians advised parents to feed their

kwashiorkor A potentially fatal form of malnutrition in which the diet is extremely low in protein.

Sudden Infant Death Syndrome

AMONG INFANTS 1 TO 6 MONTHS OF age, sudden infant death syndrome, often referred to as SIDS, is the most common cause of death in the United States, as well as a major cause of infant death in many other countries in the world (Nagler, 2002). In the typical case of SIDS, an apparently healthy infant is put to bed and a few hours later is dead. The infant may be found with clenched fists, discharge from the nose or mouth, and mottled skin, but based on the infant's prior health conditions, the family and its medical history, and the surrounding circumstances, the death is inexplicable.

The first medical report about SIDS was published more than 50 years ago (Garrow & Werne, 1953); since that time there has been an increasingly intense research program to discover its causes and ways to prevent it. Early research suggested that some infants are prone to a condition referred to as sleep apnea, that is, irregular breathing due to the brain's periodic failure to activate the muscles controlling the lungs. The most effective prevention for sleep apnea in babies involves using an electronic monitoring device that sounds an alarm whenever an infant has an episode of apnea, so that an adult can come and revive the baby in time.

Postmortem studies of infant brains have suggested that sleep apnea and SIDS are associated with insufficient development of a key area in the brain stem, the medulla, which is involved in the regulation of involuntary motor behaviors, including breathing and arousal from sleep

(Matturri et al., 2002; Lavezzi, Corna, Mingrone, & Matturri, 2010). However, research has also shown that episodes of apnea are relatively common in early infancy, and that most babies are startled awake and experience no lasting harm from such incidents. This suggests that the maturity of the medulla may not be the only factor involved in sleep apnea and SIDS.

In addition to sleep apnea, researchers have considered whether SIDS may result from accidental smothering when a baby's nose is obstructed by a soft pillow, blankets, or a stuffed animal, or when a baby is sleeping in bed with an adult. Lewis Lipsitt (2003) noted that most deaths from SIDS occur when babies are 2 to 5 months of age. Babies this age are especially vulnerable, he suggested, because they have lost the reflex that causes them to turn their head when they cannot breathe (the reflex disappears prior to 2½ months) but have not yet developed firm voluntary control of their head movements.

An important turning point in the quest to eliminate SIDS came in 1994 when the American Academy of Pediatrics, in conjunction with the National Institutes of Health and other organizations, began informing parents about SIDS through a campaign called the "Back to Sleep" movement. This clever phrase identified the major strategy upon which the campaign was based: placing babies on their back to sleep instead of having them sleep on their stomach, which greatly increased the chances of accidentally obstructing their breathing. Since the

inauguration of this campaign, the rate of SIDS in the United States has been cut in half, from 1.5 per 1000 births to approximately 0.7 per 1000 births. Reductions in the incidence of SIDS have occurred in other countries where awareness of the back-to-sleep practice has been increased (see figure; Blair et al., 2006).

To the alarm of some parents, infants who spend most of their sleep time lying on their back are prone to developing "positional skull flattening" from ongoing external pressure to the same part of the head. However, the condition is not believed to harm the baby and tends to disappear during the second 6 months of infancy, as babies become capable of moving around more and their brain continues to expand, reshaping the skull (Piatt, 2003).

Despite the success of the Back to Sleep campaign, SIDS clearly remains a serious threat, so research is currently underway to discover what additional factors might, either singly or in combination, increase infants' risk. A number of prenatal and postnatal risk factors have been identified (Hauck et al., 2003), including the following:

- Maternal malnutrition and smoking during pregnancy, which increase the risk of prematurity (immaturity of the brain stem is almost certainly involved in apnea episodes)
- Other teratogens
- Postnatal exposure to secondary tobacco smoke—the greater the exposure to tobacco smoke, the greater the risk of SIDS

babies only every 4 hours, even if the babies showed signs of hunger long before the prescribed time had elapsed.

For a very small infant, 4 hours can be a long time to go without food, as was demonstrated by a study of mothers and infants in Cambridge, England. The mothers were asked to keep records of their babies' behaviors and their own caregiving activities, including when they fed their babies and the time their babies spent crying. All of the mothers were advised to feed their babies on a strict 4-hour schedule, but not all followed the advice. The less experienced mothers tended to stick to the schedule, but the more experienced mothers sometimes fed their babies as soon as 1 hour after a scheduled feeding. Not surprisingly, the reports of the less experienced mothers showed that their babies cried the most (Bernal, 1972).

What happens if babies are fed "on demand"? In one study, the majority of newborn babies allowed to feed on demand preferred a 3-hour schedule (Aldrich & Hewitt, 1947). The interval gradually increased as the babies grew older. At 2½ months of age, most of the infants were feeding on a 4-hour schedule. By age 7 or 8 months, the majority had come to approximate the normal adult schedule and were

- Formula-feeding of babies, which is associated with a higher SIDS rate than is breast-feeding
- Placing infants to sleep on their stomach on a soft mattress with stuffed animals or other toys in the crib

A great many studies have found different rates of SIDS for different ethnicities (Pollack & Frohna, 2002). For example, Native Americans have a higher rate of SIDS than do European Americans, while Latinos have a lower rate. The incidence of SIDS also varies widely across countries (Bajanowski et al., 2007). Current research strongly suggests that these variations result from cultural differences in eating habits, alcohol and cigarette consumption, and sleeping patterns, not from any group differences in a genetic predisposition for SIDS. Thus, preventive measures are focused on informing local populations about the factors they can change to help reduce the possibility of their babies dying from SIDS.

In the developed world, SIDS is the leading cause of death among infants between 1 and 12 months of age. Its incidence has been reduced radically—well over 50 percent in most countries—due to national campaigns launched in the early 1990s that urged caregivers to avoid the prone position for sleeping infants. The "back to sleep" message resulted in an 81 percent decline in infants' prone-sleeping rates in the United States between 1992 and 2005. (From Hauck & Tanabe, 2008.)

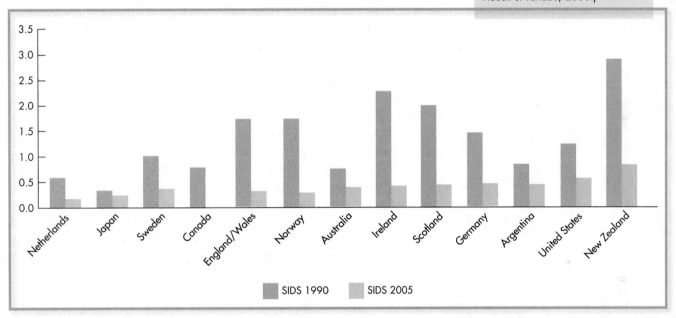

choosing to feed about 4 times a day. (Some parents reported the four feedings as "three meals and a snack.") A more recent study found no difference in growth rate between babies fed on demand and those fed on a strict schedule (Saxon, Gollapalli, Mitchell, & Stanko, 2002).

Crying

One of the most difficult problems parents face in establishing a pattern of care for their babies is how to interpret their infants' needs. Infants obviously cannot articulate their needs or feelings, but they do have one highly effective way of signaling that something is wrong—crying.

Crying is a complex behavior that involves the coordination of breathing and movements of the vocal tract. Initially it is coordinated reflexively by structures in the brain stem, but within a few months, the cerebral cortex becomes involved, enabling babies to cry voluntarily (Zeskind & Lester, 2001). This change in the neural organization of crying is accompanied by physical changes in the vocal tract that lower the pitch of infants' cries. At this point, parents in the United States begin to report that their infants are "crying on purpose," either to get attention or because they are bored (Lester et al., 1992). Across cultures, and even in chimpanzees, there is a peak in the frequency of infant crying at 6 weeks of age, followed by a decline at approximately 12 weeks (Bard, 2004) (Figure 4.22).

Developmentalists with an evolutionary perspective believe that human crying evolved as a signal to promote caregiving when the infant is hungry, in pain, or separated from its caregiver (Zeifman, 2001). Indeed, cross-cultural evidence suggests that infants cry less when their culture's caregiving practices include proximal care—that is, prolonged holding, frequent breast-feeding, rapid response to infant frets and cries, and co-sleeping with infants at night—all found, for example, in several African cultures, including the !Kung and the Aka (Hewlett et al., 1998; Barr et al., 1991; Kruger & Konner, 2010). These practices have been found to different extents in Western cultures, and the differences have similar repercussions for infant crying (St. James-Roberts et al., 2006). As shown in Figures 4.23 and 4.24, compared with mothers in London, those in Copenhagen spent significantly more time holding their infants, and in the course of a day, their babies cried and fretted significantly less.

Certainly babies' cries have a powerful effect on those who hear them. Experienced parents and childless adults alike respond to infants' cries with increases in heart rate and blood pressure, both of which are physiological signs of arousal and anxiety (Stallings et al., 2001; Out, Pieper, Bakermans-Kranenburg, & van IJzendoorn, 2010). When nursing mothers hear babies' cries, even on recordings, their milk may start to flow (Newton & Newton, 1972).

The problem for anxious parents who hear their newborns cry is to figure out the source and seriousness of their baby's discomfort. Research shows that adults are in fact able to make certain distinctions among cries. According to Phillip Zeskind and his colleagues, the higher-pitched the cries and the shorter the pauses between them, the more urgent—and unpleasant—adults perceive them to be. In addition, listeners in a variety of cultures can distinguish the cries of normal infants

FIGURE 4.22 Crying decreases substantially between birth and 1 year of age. (From Bard, 2004.)

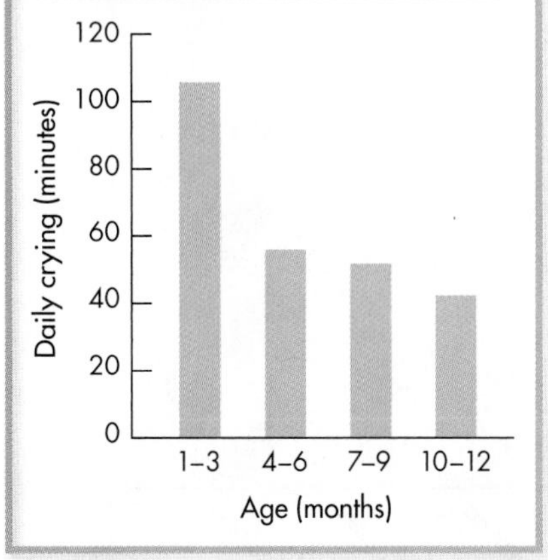

FIGURE 4.23 There are considerable differences within and across cultures in the amount of time that babies are held. In general, those babies who are held more spend less time fussing and crying. (From St. James-Roberts et al., 2006.)

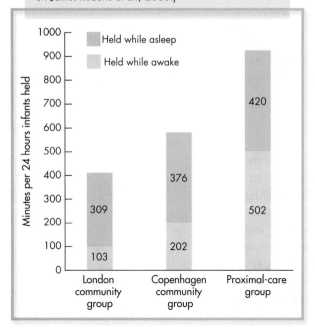

FIGURE 4.24 Although many people continue to believe that infants who are held a lot will cry more than those who are held less, research indicates just the opposite. As shown here, the amount of distress during the first 12 weeks of life of infants who are held less (the London group) is significantly higher than that of infants who are held more (the Copenhagen group).

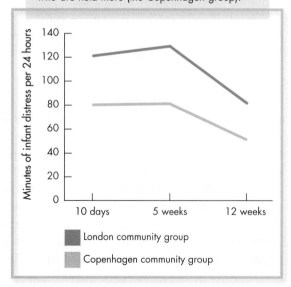

from the higher-pitched cries of low-birth-weight babies and babies who have been exposed prenatally to alcohol or the chemicals from cigarette smoke (Worchel & Allen, 1997).

It is widely believed that some children suffer from an unexplained medical condition called *colic,* which causes them to cry excessively. Indeed, excessive infant crying is the most common complaint heard by pediatricians from mothers with infants under 3 months of age (Forsyth, 1989). However, while there are marked individual differences in the amounts that infants cry, the cries of babies thought to suffer from colic are not distinguishable from those of others who cry frequently. Thus, it would appear that it is not the specific sounds of the colicky infant's crying that troubles parents but rather "its unpredictable, prolonged, hard to soothe, and unexplained nature" (St. James-Roberts, Conroy, & Wilshir, 1996, p. 375).

Caregivers' efforts to get babies on a schedule for sleeping and feeding and to comfort them when they are distressed continue as the months go by. Infants' adaptations to these parenting activities are so commonplace that it is easy to overlook their significance. They are, however, the first instances of infants' coordination and active participation in the social world.

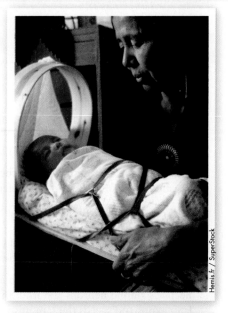

▲ APPLY :: CONNECT :: DISCUSS

How would you respond to a new parent who takes an operant conditioning approach to newborn crying, believing that babies will cry more if their crying is "reinforced" by the parents' always responding to it?

Summing Up the First 3 Months

Looking back over the first 3 months of postnatal life, you can see a remarkable set of changes in the organization of infants' behaviors and how they become coordinated with social life.

Babies are born with a rudimentary ability to interact with and learn about their new environment. They have reflexes that enable them to take in oxygen and nutrients and expel waste products. They are able to perceive objects, including people, although they tend to focus on only a part of the entire stimulus. They are sensitive to the sounds of human language, and they quickly develop a preference for the sound of their mother's voice. Although they sleep most of the time, they are occasionally quite alert.

From the moment of birth, infants interact with and are supported by their parents or other caregivers. Initially, the first interactions of babies and their caregivers are tentative and somewhat uncoordinated, but within a matter of days a process of behavioral coordination has begun that will provide an essential framework for later development.

The developmental changes that characterize the first 3 months of infancy have clear origins in biology and in the physical and sociocultural environment. In the domain of biology, there is rapid maturation of the central nervous system, particularly in the connections between the brain stem and the cerebral cortex. Physically, babies become bigger and stronger; behaviorally, reflexes make way for more sophisticated actions that are increasingly coordinated and responsive to variations in the environment. This responsiveness is assisted by shifts in the infants' arousal states: Less time is spent sleeping and crying, and more time is spent in alert states, where babies can profit from and learn through active engagement with the world. All of these accomplishments converge to position the newborn at a new threshold of cognitive, social, and emotional development.

Parents throughout the world employ a variety of methods to deal with infant cries and fussiness. Holding the baby close, rocking, patting, or making rhythmic sounds such as clapping, are common. Some child-care practices, including swaddling and carrying, reduce the amount and intensity of fussiness, making it easier for caregivers to soothe their infants.

SUMMARY

Physical Growth

- As growth charts reveal, early physical growth is rapid, with the infant gaining about 6 pounds (2.7 kilograms) and growing more than 4 inches (10 centimeters) in just 12 weeks.

- The growing brain pushes against the bones of the skull, expanding the infant's head circumference.

Brain Development

- At birth, the brain contains most of the cells (neurons) it will ever have, but it will become 4 times larger by adulthood.

- Increased size results primarily from an increase in the connections among neurons and from myelination, which insulates axons and speeds the transmission of impulses.

- At birth, the cerebral cortex is less mature than the brain stem, which controls reflexes such as sucking and vital functions such as breathing. Development of the cortex occurs through both experience-expectant and experience-dependent processes.

Sensing the Environment

- Although newborns' sensory systems are all functioning, some are more developed than others. Newborns are able to perceive an object or event with more than one sensory system.

- Newborns are sensitive to the differences that distinguish the various sounds of human languages and, although they are initially able to hear and discriminate between sounds made in all the world's languages, they are soon able to perceive only those made in the language they hear around them.

- Because of immaturity of the eye's structures, newborns are very nearsighted, but visual acuity soon improves. Newborns are able to visually scan their surroundings, are able to perceive patterns and discern among forms, show a preference for faces, and have the ability to distinguish their mother's face.

- Newborns can distinguish various tastes and smells. They prefer tastes and smells that are sweet, like breast milk, and make characteristic facial expressions in response to sour and bitter tastes and foul odors.

The Organization of Behavior

- Developing and maintaining behavioral organization is important for infants because it allows them to interact more effectively and adaptively with the world around them.

- At birth, reflexes give newborns highly organized ways of responding to the environment.

- Reflexes are building blocks for more complicated, coordinated forms of behavioral organization—for example, nursing develops from reflexes such as rooting and sucking. With maturational changes in the cerebral cortex, infants become able to coordinate reaching and grasping.

- According to Jean Piaget, infants gain knowledge largely by coordinating sensory perceptions and simple motor responses. During the first few months, they progress through the first two of the six substages of the sensorimotor stage:
  - In substage 1, infants learn to control and coordinate inborn reflexes.
  - In substage 2, accommodation first appears, and infants prolong pleasant sensations arising from reflex actions.

- According to learning theorists, learning, as evidenced by a change in behavior, occurs when the infant makes associations between his or her behavior and events in the environment. Learning may take various forms:
  - In classical conditioning, previously existing behaviors come to be associated with, and elicited by, new stimuli.
  - In operant conditioning, new behaviors may come about as a result of the reinforcement and punishment of behaviors.

Temperament

- Infants differ in temperament, the emotional and behavioral characteristics that show consistency across situations and some stability over time. Temperament includes such traits as activity level, quality of mood, and attention span. It is genetically based but is also subject to environmental influences.

- The same temperamental traits appear to be found in all cultures, but the strength of their expression may be influenced by cultural factors.

Becoming Coordinated with the Social World

- Infants' survival depends not only on the actions of caregivers but also on infants' ability to coordinate their own actions with those of caregivers.

- Newborns sleep approximately two-thirds of the time, but their periods of sleep are relatively brief, so they may be awake at any time. They tend to adapt gradually to adults' night/day sleep cycle, but the specifics of their sleep cycle depend in part on cultural patterns.

- The maternal–infant coordination that nursing requires has a biological underpinning. However, culture influences the age at which infants breast-feed and their feeding schedules. Newborns tend to prefer a 3-hour schedule, moving to a 4-hour schedule by 2½ months and approximating an adult schedule by 7 or 8 months.

- Infants' crying is a primitive means of communication that evokes a strong emotional response in adults and alerts them that something may be wrong. Infants tend to cry less in cultures with caregiving practices such as prolonged holding and frequent feeding. Certain distinctive patterns of early cries may indicate difficulties.

Summing Up the First 3 Months

- From birth, infants have a wide range of abilities and interact with their caregivers. Developmental changes in the first 3 months, originating in biology and depending also on the environment, include rapid physical growth and maturation of the central nervous system and a shift from reflexes to complex actions. The 3-month-old is at a new threshold of cognitive, social, and emotional development.

Key Terms

growth charts, p. 124

fontanels, p. 125

neuron, p. 126

axon, p. 126

dendrite, p. 126

synapse, p. 127

neurotransmitter, p. 127

synaptogenesis, p. 127

myelin, p. 127

spinal cord, p. 127

brain stem, p. 127

cerebral cortex, p. 128

experience-expectant, p. 128

exuberant synaptogenesis, p. 129

synaptic pruning, p. 129

experience-dependent, p. 130

electroencephalography (EEG), p. 131

visual preference technique, p. 132

habituation, p. 132

dishabituation, p. 132

phonemes, p. 132

visual acuity, p. 134

intermodal perception, p. 138

reflex, p. 140

action, p. 141

sensorimotor stage, p. 144

primary circular reaction, p. 145

learning, p. 146

classical conditioning, p. 146

conditional stimulus (CS), p. 146

unconditional stimulus (UCS), p. 146

unconditional response (UCR), p. 146

conditional response (CR), p. 146

operant conditioning, p. 147

temperament, p. 148

kwashiorkor, p. 153

Physical and Cognitive Development in Infancy

Physical Growth

Size and Shape

The Musculoskeletal System

Brain Development

Brain and Behavior

Brain and Experience

Motor Development

Fine Motor Skills

Gross Motor Skills

The Role of Practice in Motor Development

Control of Elimination

Cognitive Development: The Great Debate

Sensorimotor Development

Reproducing Interesting Events (Substage 3)

The Emergence of Intentionality (Substage 4)

Exploring by Experimenting (Substage 5)

Representation (Substage 6)

Conceptual Development

Understanding the Permanence of Objects

Understanding Other Properties of the Physical World

Reasoning About Objects

The Growth of Attention and Memory

Developing Attention

Developing Memory

Implications

Two neighbors—Jake, who is about to celebrate his first birthday, and Barbara, his mother—have been out for a walk and have stopped by the house of two of your authors, Mike and Sheila Cole. Sheila is in the kitchen preparing dinner. Jake sits on his mother's lap at the kitchen table, drinking apple juice from a plastic cup while the two women chat. Jake finishes his juice, some of which has dribbled onto his shirt, and puts the cup down on the table with a satisfied bang. He squirms around in his mother's lap so that he is facing her. He tries to get her attention by pulling at her face. When Barbara ignores him, Jake wriggles out of her lap to the floor, where he notices the dog.

"Wuff wuff," he says excitedly, pointing at the dog.

"Doggie," Barbara says. "What does the doggie say, Jake?"

"Wuff wuff," Jake repeats, still staring at the dog.

Following his pointing finger, Jake toddles toward the dog. His walk has a drunken, side-to-side quality, and he has a hard time bringing himself to a stop. Barbara grabs hold of Jake's extended hand, redirecting it from the dog's eyes.

"Pat the doggie, Jake."

Jake thumps the dog's head with a flat hand.

The dog does not like the attention and escapes into the living room. Jake toddles after her like a pull toy on an invisible string. The dog leads him back into the kitchen, where Jake bumps into Sheila's legs and falls to a sitting position.

"Well, hello, Jake," Sheila says, as she bends over and picks him up. "Did you fall down? Go boom?"

Jake, who until now hasn't taken his eyes off the dog, turns, looks at Sheila with a smile, and points at the dog. "Wuff wuff," he repeats.

At almost 1 year of age, Jake behaves far differently than he did as a typical 3-month-old. At that earlier age, Jake's main activities were eating, sleeping, and gazing around the room. He could hold his head up and turn it from side to side, but he could not readily reach out and grasp objects or move around on his own. He took an interest in mobiles and other objects when they were immediately in front of him, but he quickly lost interest in them when they were removed from his view, as though they no longer existed for him. His communications were restricted to cries, frowns, and smiles.

The contrast between Jake's behavior then and his behavior at 1 year gives you a hint of some of the amazing changes that occur during the overall period of infancy. Perhaps most obvious are the outwardly visible physical changes: Infants become markedly larger and stronger between 3 and 24 months of age. Essential maturation has also taken place in the central nervous system, particularly the cerebral cortex and other parts of the brain.

Related to these biological changes are the enormous gains that infants make in being able to move their bodies. At 3 months of age, infants are just beginning to be able to roll over, and their parents can be confident that they will remain more or less wherever they are put down. That soon changes. At about 7 to 8 months, infants begin to crawl; at about 1 year, they begin to walk in the toddler's drunken, uncoordinated fashion demonstrated by Jake; and by the time they are 2, they can run, take a few steps backward, and walk up stairs (with a helping hand). During this period, infants also become much more adept at manipulating objects. At 1 year of age, babies prod, bang, squeeze, push, and pull almost anything they can get their hands on, including the neighbor's dog, and they often put objects into their mouths to learn about them; at 2 years of age, they possess enough control to feed themselves with a spoon, to toss a large ball, to open cabinets, drawers, and boxes, and to pet, rather than poke at or thump, the dog. As infants' mobility, motor control, and curiosity about the world increase, their parents must constantly be on the watch to keep them out of harm's way.

Important changes also occur in infants' cognitive abilities. Older babies learn more rapidly and remember what they have learned for longer periods of time. By the end of infancy, babies can remember actions they have observed others perform, in person or on television, and can imitate them days later in play. They can follow simple directions, and they laugh when someone does something silly like wear a cooking pot for a hat. They also begin to use symbols, turning a banana into a telephone or a wooden block into a race car. Of special significance is their emerging mastery of that uniquely human symbol system, language.

These changes in biological makeup, motor behavior, and cognitive capacities interact throughout infancy. We will focus on them in this chapter, and in the next, we will turn to the substantial social and emotional developments that they help make possible.

Physical Growth

FIGURE 5.1 As is apparent in this photograph, the child's body undergoes remarkable changes over the course of infancy, enabling a host of new actions and behaviors, including climbing on Mom's back and giving her a hug.

The physical differences between a 3-month-old and a 2-year-old are so striking that it's hard to believe that so much could have changed in a scant 21 months (Figure 5.1). There are changes in body size and proportions and in the muscles and bones, as well as in the brain. These changes are connected both with each other and with the development of the new behavioral capacities babies display. For example, their greater weight requires larger and stronger bones to support them and stronger muscles to enable movement. Their developing cognitive capacities make them want to explore new aspects of the world, but to explore the world they must coordinate their constantly changing size and strength in new ways.

Size and Shape

During their 1st year, most healthy babies triple in weight and grow approximately 10 inches; in the United States, the typical 1-year-old weighs 20 to 22 pounds (9 to 10 kg) and stands 28 to 30 inches (71 to 76 cm) tall. During the second year of life, children's bodies continue to grow rapidly, though at a much slower rate (Bogin, 2001); in the United States, children on average gain 5 pounds (2.2 kg) and grow 4 inches (10.6 cm), to about 27 pounds and about 34 inches (12.2 kg and 86.3 cm). (This tapering off of the growth rate, apparent in Figure 5.2, continues until adolescence, when there is a noticeable growth spurt.) Also by 2 years of age, most children will have all their baby teeth.

Increases in babies' height and weight are accompanied by changes in their body proportions (see Figure 5.3). At birth, the baby's head is 70 percent of its adult size and accounts for about 25 percent of the baby's total length. By 1 year of age, the head will account for 20 percent of body length, and by adulthood, 12 percent.

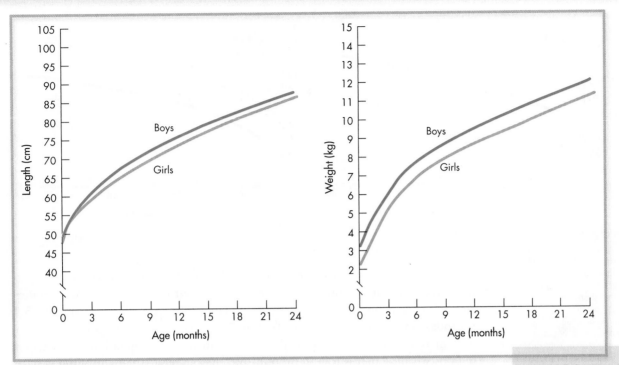

FIGURE 5.2 U.S. babies' lengths roughly double and their weights increase 5 or 6 times during the first 2 years of life. Note that at this stage, boys tend, on average, to be heavier and taller than girls. (Adapted from the Centers for Disease Control and Prevention, 2009)

Infants' legs at birth are not much longer than their heads; by adulthood the legs account for about half of a person's total height. By 12 months, the changes in body proportions have led to a lower center of gravity, making it easier for the child to balance on two legs and begin to walk (Thelen, 2002). As their bodies stretch out, most babies will lose the potbellied look so characteristic of early infancy; they begin to look more like children than infants.

It should be noted that norms for children's growth, such as those depicted in Figure 5.2, are derived by averaging large samples of children and that individual children normally grow at widely varying rates (Tanner, 1998). Many factors contribute to these variations, including not only genetic factors but also, for example, diet, socioeconomic status, and maternal health (Ruel & Menon, 2002; Pelletier & Frongillo, 2003). Sometimes these factors can lead to significantly slower growth rates, known as *infant growth restriction*. Infant growth restriction is associated with a number of serious problems, including SIDS, developmental delay, infections, and poor psychological health. One study of several thousand

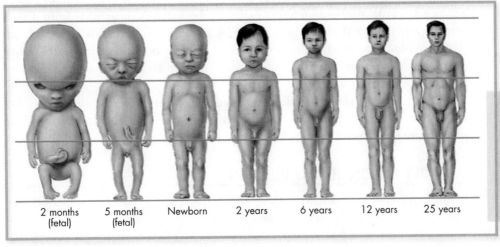

2 months (fetal)   5 months (fetal)   Newborn   2 years   6 years   12 years   25 years

FIGURE 5.3 These drawings show the proportions of body length accounted for by the head, trunk, and legs at different stages of development. During the fetal period, the head accounts for as much as 50 percent of body length. The head decreases from 25 percent of body length at birth to 12 percent in adulthood. (From Robbins et al., 1929.)

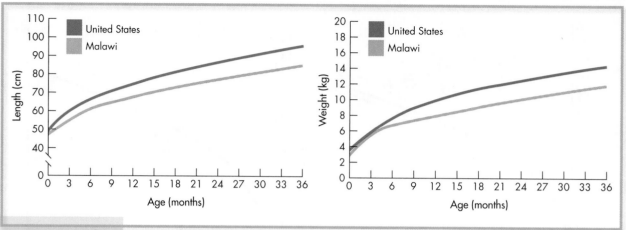

FIGURE 5.4 Environmental conditions play an important role in infant growth. Babies born in Malawi, a country in southeast Africa, face conditions such as widespread malnutrition, chronic poverty, disease, and a rising HIV/AIDS infection rate. As a result of this complicated array of factors, Malawian infants grow at a slower rate than do their American counterparts. These graphs show height and weight curves for the 50th percentile of Malawian and American children. Compared with their American counterparts, the Malawian children were on average 1 inch (2.5 cm) shorter and 1.12 pounds (510 g) lighter. (Adapted from Maleta et al., 2003.)

babies born in a rural area of Malawi found that infant growth was significantly restricted if mothers contracted malaria during their pregnancies, or were illiterate and presumably less educated about infant and maternal health (Figure 5.4; Kalanda, van Buuren, Verhoeff, & Brabin, 2005). The researchers note that infant growth restriction poses a special challenge in less developed countries where the postweaning diet is low in protein, and they suggest that controlling malaria during pregnancy and educating girls and young women may help curb the incidence of this serious threat to children's health and development.

The Musculoskeletal System

As babies grow, the bones and muscles needed to support their increasing bulk and mobility undergo corresponding growth. Most of a newborn's bones are relatively soft, and they harden (ossify) only gradually as minerals are deposited in them in the months after birth. The bones in the hand and wrist are among the first to ossify. They harden by the end of the 1st year, making it easier for a baby to grasp objects, pick them up, and play with them. At the same time, infants' muscles increase in length and thickness, a process that continues throughout childhood and into late adolescence. In infancy, increases in muscle mass are closely associated with the development of the baby's ability to crawl, stand alone, and walk.

Although boys are generally larger than girls, as Figure 5.2 clearly indicates, research supports the common wisdom that girls mature faster than boys. In fact, sex differences in growth rates are apparent even before birth: Halfway through the prenatal period, the skeletal development of female fetuses is some 3 weeks more advanced than that of male fetuses. At birth, the female's skeleton is from 4 to 6 weeks more mature than the male's, and by puberty it is 2 years more advanced. (Girls are more advanced in the development of other organ systems as well. They get their permanent teeth, go through puberty, and reach their full body size earlier than boys do [Bogin, 1999].)

The physical changes of infancy described above open wholly new ways of exploring and learning about the environment. Equally significant in making these possible are the changes taking place in the brain.

⏏ APPLY :: CONNECT :: DISCUSS

Provide some concrete examples of how socioeconomic status may affect infants' physical growth.

Brain Development

The development of the baby's brain is as fascinating as it is important. As discussed in Chapter 4 (pp. 128–129), the brain has evolved in such a way that it develops through both experience-expectant and experience-dependent processes. In *experience-expectant* processes, the brain expects that the world will present particular, species-universal experiences—patterns of light and dark, various kinds of tastes and odors, language, and the like—and develops in response to those experiences. In *experience-dependent* processes, development occurs in response to specific experiences—hence the brain's amazing capacity to be changed by the unique experiences of each individual child.

In their efforts to understand infant brain development, researchers have focused on answering two interconnected questions. One concerns the relationship between brain and behavior: What is the relationship between developments in certain parts of the brain and the onset of new skills or abilities? The other key question concerns the relationship between brain and experience: To what extent does experience or the lack thereof (that is, deprivation) enhance or impede brain development and function?

Brain and Behavior

As we discussed in Chapter 4, the brain undergoes substantial development throughout infancy, although different parts grow at different times and rates. The *cerebral cortex,* as you may recall, is very immature at birth. Because the cortex is associated with such complex functions as voluntary (as opposed to reflexive) behavior, abstract thought, problem solving, and language, its development has been of special interest to researchers eager to understand brain–behavior relationships.

The **prefrontal area** of the cortex, located behind the forehead, plays a particularly important role in the development of voluntary behavior. It begins to function in a new way sometime between 7 and 9 months of age. With this change in functioning comes an increase in infants' ability to regulate themselves (Posner et al., 2007). Infants can stop themselves from grabbing the first attractive thing they see; they can cuddle their teddy bear to keep from being upset when they are put down for a nap. With the emerging ability to inhibit action, they can also better control what they attend to. In effect, they begin to be able to stop and think (Diamond, 2000; Stevens, Quittner, Zuckerman, & Moore, 2002).

Another important development, revealed by brain-imaging techniques, involves the language-related areas of the cortex. These areas, in the frontal and temporal lobes, undergo significant myelination shortly before a characteristic spurt in toddlers' vocabulary (myelin, remember, is the fatty substance that covers axons, speeding the brain's communications) (Pujol et al., 2006; see Chapter 7, p. 240).

At least as important as the growth of different brain areas is that the different areas increasingly function together (Bruer & Greenough, 2001; Fox, Levitt, & Nelson, 2010). Once again, myelination plays an important role. For example, myelination of the neurons that link the prefrontal cortex and frontal lobes to the brain stem, where emotional responses are partially generated, creates a new potential for interaction between thinking and emotion. In general, the greater synchrony among brain areas appears vital to the emergence of functions that define late infancy, including more systematic problem solving, the voluntary control of behavior, and the acquisition of language (Richmond & Nelson, 2007).

prefrontal area Part of the cortex that is located directly behind the forehead and is important to the development of voluntary behaviors.

Toward the end of infancy, the length and the degree of branching of the neurons in the cerebral cortex approach adult magnitudes: Each neuron now has connections with other neurons, usually numbering in the thousands. Although brain structures mature at different rates, those that eventually will support adult behavior are present, and the pace of the brain's overall growth becomes slower and steadier until adolescence.

Brain and Experience

When we think of how experiences can affect the brain's structures and functions, we are likely to think of intense and traumatic experiences—a blow to the head, high levels of exposure to drugs or toxins, extreme malnourishment, chronic abuse. However, as we discussed in Chapter 4, everyday experience can also affect the brain's structures and functions. Thus, in discussing *exuberant synaptogenesis* and *synaptic pruning* (p. 129), we described how the infant's normal everyday experiences, such as exposure to a specific language, can affect which synapses are strengthened and which are eliminated, or "pruned." (As detailed in the box "Bringing Up Brainy Babies," the idea that brain development is highly sensitive to the baby's experiences has fueled a multimillion-dollar industry aimed at making babies smarter.)

If brain development is so readily influenced by the infant's daily experience, how might it be affected by situations in which an infant endures prolonged periods of deprivation? The effects of such deprivation have been studied extensively in children from Romanian orphanages who were adopted into families in Western Europe and North America. The adoptions occurred during the early 1990s, after the collapse of a repressive regime, under which the country's orphanages had been little more than human warehouses. Together, the numerous studies of Romanian orphans tell a heart-wrenching story about the conditions that they endured and the severe developmental effects of these conditions. The orphans received basic physical care with little social and intellectual stimulation. Typically, they were confined to cribs for most of each day, with no social interaction and nothing to look at but bare walls. At the time of their adoption, most of the children were physically, cognitively, and emotionally impaired. The question developmentalists were interested in was whether the experience of a normal adoptive home could make up for their previous deprivations.

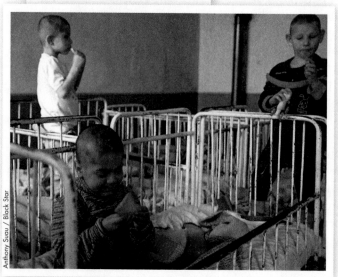

The conditions in orphanages such as this one in Romania provide insufficient stimulation for normal mental development.

The most recent research finds that even after the children have spent 7½ or more years in adoptive families and schools, the marks of early deprivation remain, unless the children were adopted in early infancy (Nelson et al., 2007). In particular, the researchers found that babies who were rescued before 6 months of age seemed to recover fully from their experiences, but that those who remained in the orphanages beyond the age of 6 months showed significant impairments in intellectual functioning—the older they were when rescued, the greater the impairments.

What accounts for these age differences in recovery, and how exactly did deprivation affect the brain development of the orphans? In answering these questions, the researchers point out that the infant brain undergoes considerable development between 6 and 24 months of age and that during such phases of rapid growth, brain structures are particularly sensitive to the infant's experiences. In Chapter 1, we described such phases as *sensitive periods,* or periods of *plasticity,* during which a

Bringing Up Brainy Babies

PARENTS IN MANY PARTS OF THE world believe that just as nature takes its course, children will develop at their own pace, and there is no need to push nature along (Rogoff, 2003). But American parents have a seemingly unstoppable desire to speed up their offsprings' rate of development. Piaget referred to this parental desire as "the American problem."

One by-product of modern research on infant development has been the creation of a major industry producing toys, books, DVDs, and computer programs designed to speed up various aspects of young infants' cognitive development, in the belief that such acceleration will give children an advantage over their peers in later life. The range and ingenuity of the products that have been created to speed infants' cognitive growth are matched only by the claims their manufacturers have made about their effectiveness and by the enormous amounts of money that have been raked in by this "growth industry." But do these products deliver on their promise to educate babies and promote their development? The consensus of the scientific community is that they do not (Jones & Zigler, 2002; Courage & Setliff, 2010).

Although the idea that environmental stimulation can enhance young infants' cognitive and social competence has been around since the middle of the twentieth century, the current craze in providing special stimulation for very young infants received a significant boost from various lines of research conducted in the 1980s. First, there were studies showing that fetuses learn from the environment outside of their mother's womb (such as the preference for listening to *The Cat in the Hat*) (see Chapter 3). Second, research began to appear on experience-dependent brain growth, showing that animals raised in enriched environments had more brain development and showed improved problem-solving abilities (see Chapter 4). Third, data appeared showing that young infants learned to categorize alphabet letters

and that this learning was retained for sometimes surprisingly long intervals.

Then, in 1993, Frances Rauscher and her colleagues published an article in the prestigious scientific journal *Nature* in which they reported that listening to a Mozart sonata enhanced IQ by an average of 8 to 9 points (Rauscher, Shaw, & Ky, 1993). This report attracted extensive attention and was followed in 1997 by a book, written by a former choral conductor, entitled *The Mozart Effect* (Campbell, 1997). The book was a best seller and was convincing enough for the then-governor of Georgia to propose giving every newborn in the state a classical music CD to enhance the baby's cognitive development. The "brainy baby" movement was well on its way. Not surprisingly, the movement has taken a decidedly electronic turn in recent years, producing video game consoles like the V.Smile, Leapster, and Baby Einstein, marketed with such catchy claims as "Turn game time into brain time."

However, subsequent scientific research has not been kind to the "Mozart effect." When positive effects on intelligence have been reported, they have generally involved very short-term increases (on the order of a dozen minutes or so), and there have been a large number of failures to obtain any effect at all, leading many researchers to conclude that it's "curtains for the Mozart effect" (McKelvie & Low, 2002). Public outcry about false advertising, as well as the threat of a class-action lawsuit for unfair and deceptive marketing practices, spurred one of the biggest manufacturers of brainy-baby products to offer full refunds to parents who are unsatisfied with the effectiveness of their product.

Critics of the brainy-baby movement note that the American Academy of Pediatrics recommends no screen time at all for children under age 2, mainly because it may displace human interaction—a source of essential experiences for infant brain growth and emerging cognitive, social, and emotional development. Indeed, at least one study supports

A multimillion-dollar toy industry has provided children with an array of high-tech toys, including tablet computers. Despite parents' enthusiasm for such toys, there is little evidence that they are effective in stimulating children's brain functioning or intellectual development.

this conclusion. Dan Anderson and his colleagues showed 12- to 15-month-olds how to use a puppet (Anderson & Kirkorian, 2006). One group of babies saw the demonstration live, while another group saw it on a video. Those who saw the live demonstration learned to imitate the action much more quickly than did their video-trained counterparts.

At present it appears clear that environmental stimulation can speed up certain aspects of children's development. But whether or not it provides any lasting benefits for children depends strongly on the nature of the extra stimulation and the cultural context of the infants' later lives.

particular experience (or lack of it) has a more pronounced effect on development than it would at another point in time (see p. 10). It is likely that during sensitive periods of brain development, the orphans lacked the species-universal experiences required for strengthening and fine-tuning normal experience-expectant neural connections. In addition, the infants' experience-dependent brain development may have been adversely affected by the deprived conditions of the orphanage.

Adopted from Romania, Vasile (right) is playing with his friend, Lauren. Research on the development of Romanian orphans who were severely deprived indicates that those adopted before 6 months of age usually are able to recover from their early deprivation.

Aided by new brain-imaging technologies (see Chapter 1, p. 33), developmentalists are gaining spectacular new insights into the relationships between the developing brain and the experiences and behaviors of infants. Indeed, brain scans of a group of these orphans showed significant deficits in the functioning of certain areas in the limbic system, which is involved in emotion and motivation (Chugani et al., 2001). Interestingly, work with rats and other animals indicates that the specific limbic areas affected are especially vulnerable to stress, particularly when it is experienced early in development. As the findings involving the orphans suggest, advances in developmental neuroscience hold great promise for exploring how biological and environmental processes interact in the life of the developing child.

▲ APPLY :: CONNECT :: DISCUSS

Review the four central issues of developmental science that were discussed in Chapter 1 (pp. 10–14). How does current knowledge of infant brain development shed light on these issues?

Motor Development

One of the most dramatic developments between 3 and 24 months of age is the enormous increase in infants' ability to explore their environment by grasping and manipulating objects and by moving about. These changing motor abilities have widespread consequences for cognitive, social, and emotional development (Campos et al., 2000; Lejeune et al., 2006). As their motor skills advance, babies gain important information about features of the world and how it is put together—for example, how objects feel to the touch and how they behave when they are poked, pulled, dropped, or banged together. Importantly, advances in motor skills give babies new opportunities to pursue people (quite literally) and to communicate to them and get feedback from them about interesting objects in the environment—from odd bits of trash ("No, don't touch—that's *dirty*") to the tail of the family dog ("Be careful, don't pull—that might *hurt*"), to a toy on a chair that was out of reach just a few months before ("What a big girl to reach that teddy bear!").

Developmentalists who study motor development typically distinguish between **fine motor skills**, which involve the development and coordination of small muscles, such as those that move the fingers and eyes, and **gross motor skills**, which involve the large muscles of the body and make locomotion possible.

Fine Motor Skills

We pointed out in Chapter 2 that human beings are highly distinctive in their ability to make and use tools. Such tool use would be impossible without the development of fine motor skills that allow us to grasp and manipulate objects. From the perspective of parents and caregivers, increasing fine motor control and coordination means that their baby can participate more fully in such daily activities as feeding and dressing. It also means that the baby can get into drawers, cupboards, and

fine motor skills Motor skills related to the development and coordination of small muscles, such as those that move the fingers and eyes.

gross motor skills Motor skills related to the development and coordination of large muscles; important for locomotion.

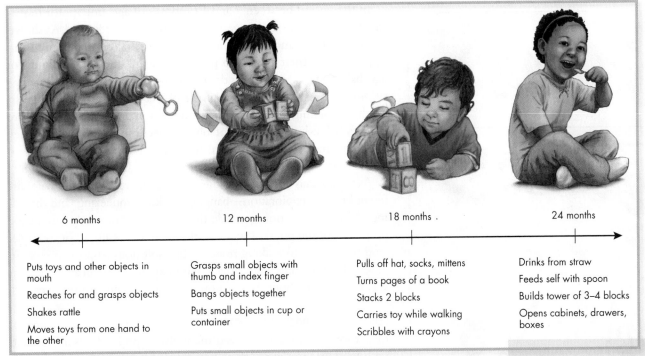

6 months	12 months	18 months	24 months
Puts toys and other objects in mouth	Grasps small objects with thumb and index finger	Pulls off hat, socks, mittens	Drinks from straw
Reaches for and grasps objects	Bangs objects together	Turns pages of a book	Feeds self with spoon
Shakes rattle	Puts small objects in cup or container	Stacks 2 blocks	Builds tower of 3–4 blocks
Moves toys from one hand to the other		Carries toy while walking	Opens cabinets, drawers, boxes
		Scribbles with crayons	

FIGURE 5.5 The development and coordination of the small muscles that control the fingers and hands are associated with a variety of important skills and follow a fairly predictable timetable.

other spaces that may contain dangerous objects. Figure 5.5 provides a summary of the major milestones of the infant's fine motor skills.

Early Skills: Reaching and Grasping

Remember from Chapter 4 (p. 144) that very young infants reach for an object moving in front of them, a reflexlike motion we referred to as *prereaching*. As we discussed, at this initial stage, the perceptions and actions involved in reaching and grasping are not yet coordinated. Infants may reach for an object but fail to close their hands around it, usually because they close their hands too soon. Then, around 3 months of age, babies begin to gain voluntary control over their movements, so reaching and grasping occur in the proper sequence. At first, their reaching and grasping is pretty much hit or miss (von Hofsten, 2001). With practice, their fine motor coordination gradually improves, although there are marked individual differences in the rapidity and vigor of their reaching movements (Figure 5.6). At about 5 months of age, infants can gauge when an object is beyond their reach, and they no longer attempt to reach for it. By the time they are 9 months old, most babies can guide their reaching and grasping movements with a single glance and execute them in a manner that looks well integrated and automatic (Smitsman, 2001). This is the time when caretakers need to "baby proof" their homes by putting dangerous or fragile objects out of the infant's reach. They also have to watch out for the sudden appearance of unexpected items in the grocery cart if the baby is along for the ride!

FIGURE 5.6 At 3 months of age, the baby's reaching and grasping are not yet well coordinated, making it difficult to seize the object of interest (a). In contrast, by 8 months of age, motor skills are so advanced that the baby can not only grasp the object easily but also explore it intently (b).

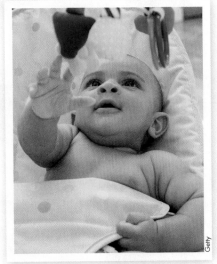

(a)

(b)

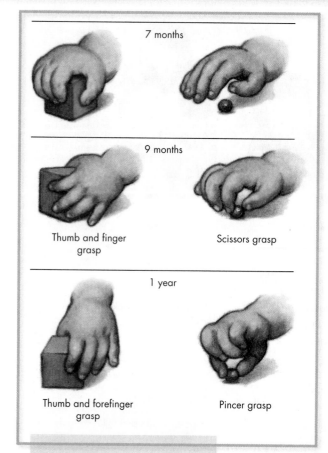

7 months

9 months

Thumb and finger grasp   Scissors grasp

1 year

Thumb and forefinger grasp   Pincer grasp

FIGURE 5.7 Babies find ways to grasp objects from an early age, but good coordination of the thumb and forefinger requires at least a year to achieve. (Adapted from Halverson, 1931.)

In the period between 7 and 12 months of age, fine motor movements of the hands and fingers become better coordinated. As shown in Figure 5.7, 7-month-olds are still unable to use their thumbs in opposition to their fingers to pick up objects, but by 12 months of age, babies are able to move their thumbs and other fingers into positions appropriate to the size of the object they are trying to grasp. As their reaching and grasping become better coordinated and more precise, babies' explorations of objects become more refined. They are increasingly able to do such things as drink from a cup, eat with a spoon, and pick raisins out of a box (Connolly & Dalgleish, 1989).

As babies gain control over their hands, different objects invite different kinds of exploration—banging, shaking, squeezing, and throwing. All of these actions provide the baby with knowledge about the properties of the physical world (Gibson, 1988). Rattles, for example, lend themselves to making noises, while soft dolls lend themselves to pleasurable touching. Perceptual-motor exploration is an all-important way to find out about the environment and to gain control over it.

Later Skills: Manual Dexterity A lot of parents keep pictures of their babies' first efforts to feed themselves—pudgy faces all smeared with food. As amusing as these pictures can be, they illustrate the difficulty of mastering an act as elementary as using a spoon. Figure 5.8 depicts the variety of ways in which infants between 10 and 23 months of age attempt to hold a spoon, and suggests the incredibly precise coordination the effective use of a spoon entails. At 10 to 12 months of age, babies can do only simple things with a spoon, such as bang it on the table or dip it repeatedly into their bowl. Slightly older children can coordinate the action of dipping, opening their mouth, and bringing the spoon to it, but as often as not, the spoon is empty when it arrives. Once the baby masters the sequence of getting

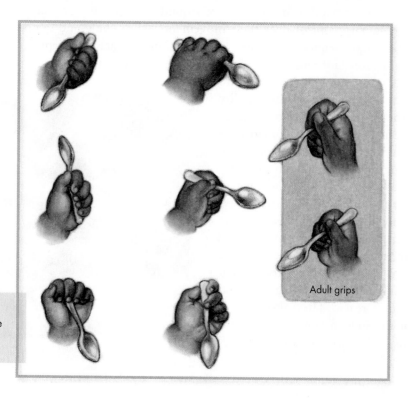

Adult grips

FIGURE 5.8 Babies initially grip a spoon in many different ways. As they accumulate experience and gain motor control, they eventually adopt an adult grip.

food on the spoon, carrying it to the mouth without spilling, and putting the food in the mouth, the sequence is adjusted until it is smooth and automatic.

Coordination of fine motor movements increases significantly during the second year of life. At age 1, infants can only roll a ball or fling it awkwardly; by the time they are age 2, they are more likely to throw it. By age 2, they can also turn the pages of a book without tearing or creasing them, snip paper with safety scissors, string beads with a needle and thread (although the bead hole usually has to be pretty big!), build a tower six blocks high with considerable ease, hold a cup of milk or a spoon of applesauce without spilling it, and dress themselves (as long as there are no buttons or shoelaces) (Bayley, 1993). Each of these accomplishments may seem minor in itself, but infants' growing ability to manipulate objects with their hands relates to one of the most sophisticated accomplishments of our species and the most effective way of transmitting and transforming culture—using and making tools.

Gross Motor Skills

Progress in **locomotion**, the ability to move around on one's own, is a central developmental change that occurs toward the end of the 1st year. As we have noted, the development of gross motor skills greatly expands infants' opportunities to learn about the world and decreases their dependence on caregivers. Although there is wide variation in the age at which the various gross motor milestones are achieved, most babies throughout the world move through the same sequence of development, which begins with reflexive creeping and ends with purposeful walking, that uniquely human form of locomotion (Figure 5.9).

Creeping and Crawling During the 1st month of life, when their movements appear to be controlled primarily by subcortical areas of the brain, infants may occasionally creep short distances, propelled by the rhythmic pushing movements of their toes or knees (Figure 5.10). At about 2 months of age, this reflexive pushing disappears, and it will be another 5 or 6 months before babies can crawl about on their hands and knees (World Health Organization, 2006).

By the time they are 8 to 9 months of age, most infants can crawl on flat, smooth surfaces with some skill. The onset of crawling allows babies to explore their environment in a new way and acquire new information about it, thus changing how they respond to the world.

Using a spoon is a lot more complicated than you might think. It will take this baby many more months of practice before the fine motor skills involved in spoon use become smooth and automatic.

locomotion The ability to move around on one's own.

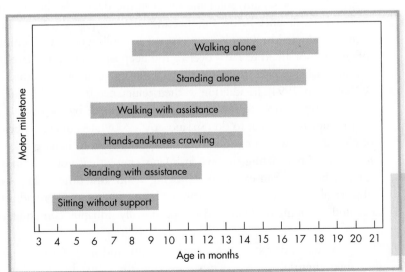

FIGURE 5.9 Despite wide variation in the ages at which specific gross motor skills are acquired, most children follow the same sequence of motor milestones, from sitting without support to independent walking.

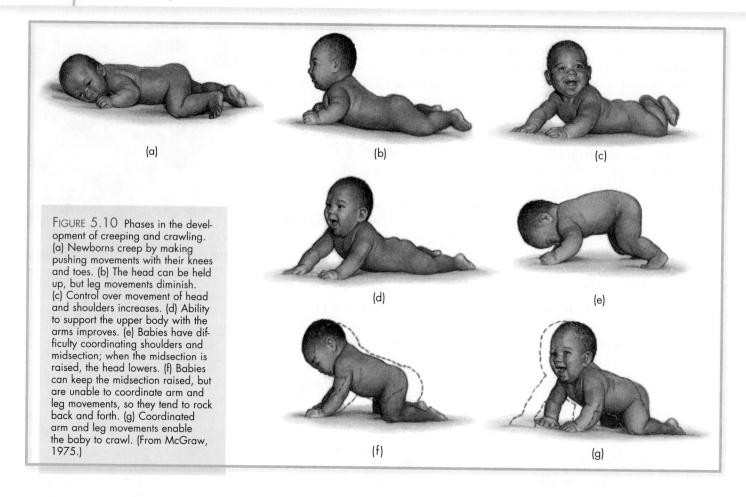

FIGURE 5.10 Phases in the development of creeping and crawling. (a) Newborns creep by making pushing movements with their knees and toes. (b) The head can be held up, but leg movements diminish. (c) Control over movement of head and shoulders increases. (d) Ability to support the upper body with the arms improves. (e) Babies have difficulty coordinating shoulders and midsection; when the midsection is raised, the head lowers. (f) Babies can keep the midsection raised, but are unable to coordinate arm and leg movements, so they tend to rock back and forth. (g) Coordinated arm and leg movements enable the baby to crawl. (From McGraw, 1975.)

FIGURE 5.11 Despite being encouraged to do so, this little boy is hesitant about crossing the transparent surface of the visual cliff. Associated with learning to crawl, his behavior indicates a fear of heights typical of 7- to 9-month-olds.

One manifestation of infants' new exploration of and response to the environment is the emergence of wariness of heights, typically, among children in the United States, between 7 and 9 months of age, about the same time that they begin to crawl (Scarr & Salapatek, 1970). This wariness is demonstrated by infants' behavior on a "visual cliff," a specially constructed apparatus that gives the illusion of a dangerous drop-off. As shown in Figure 5.11, the apparatus includes a strong sheet of clear acrylic that extends across two sides—one "shallow," and one "deep." On the shallow side, a checkered pattern is placed directly under the acrylic sheeting, so the surface seems solid and safe. On the deep side, the checkered pattern is placed at a distance below the sheeting, suggesting a cliff. A number of experiments conducted by Joseph Campos and his colleagues have demonstrated that infants are not afraid to cross over to the deep side until they have had a certain amount of experience trying to crawl about on their own (Bertenthal, Campos, & Kermoian, 1994). In addition to their reluctance to cross the cliff, infants with crawling experience express their wariness of depth by looking to their mothers for cues about what to do (Striano et al., 2009). (As discussed below, this kind of checking-in with a caregiver for cues about how to behave is known as *social referencing.*) Appreciating that when infants crawl, they not only move across flat surfaces but also gain experience moving—and sometimes falling—over various objects, obstacles, and steps, you can see how crawling may provide children with a clearer understanding of depth and its occasionally unhappy consequences.

Walking A baby's first steps are a source of joy and marvel for caregivers as well as the babies themselves. As infants approach their first birthday, many become able to stand up and walk, which soon allows them to cover more distance than

Mark Richards/Photo Edit

crawling did, and frees their hands for carrying, exploring, and manipulating objects (Garciaguirre, Adolph, & Shrout, 2007). At first they need assistance of some kind in order to walk. This assistance can come in several forms. Many babies grasp onto furniture to pull themselves into a standing position (Berger & Adolph, 2003). Seeing such attempts, caregivers often help by holding both the baby's arms to support the initial hesitant steps.

Of course, it's a long road from a baby taking his or her first steps to being able to walk with ease around obstacles, up and down stairs, and on surfaces that are uneven or slippery. In addition to receiving a lot of assistance and encouragement from others throughout this process, babies become quite adept at responding to communications from others about their motor behavior. Karen Adolph's research shows an example of the ways infants use social referencing when walking down slopes that may put them at risk of falling (Adolph, Karasik, & Tamis-LeMonda, 2010). As noted above, **social referencing** refers to infants' tendency to look to their caregiver for an indication of how to feel and act in unfamiliar circumstances. Placing infants on a walkway with an adjustable slope (see Figure 5.12), Adolph and her colleagues found that even when the slope was shallow and posed little risk of falling, babies proceeded with caution (if at all) when their mother discouraged them from walking. On the other hand, they refused to walk when the slope was steep and dangerous, even when their mother encouraged walking. The researchers concluded that when social signals from the caregiver conflict with the baby's own assessment of risk, the latter generally wins the day, which is probably good news. As the researchers point out:

> In everyday situations, parents cannot be so vigilant that they can protect infants from every potential danger. With the advent of independent locomotion comes increasing autonomy. Although mothers' advice can often be useful, especially under conditions of uncertainty, infants must eventually learn to navigate the world on their own (p. 1041).

No one factor can be considered the key to walking; rather, as dynamic systems theorists point out, walking becomes possible only when all the component motor skills—upright posture, leg alternation, muscle strength, weight shifting, and sense of balance—have developed sufficiently and when the child has been able to practice

Usually emerging around 8 to 9 months of age, crawling is a very effective form of locomotion. This photograph was taken at a crawling competition in Hong Kong. The babies are dressed up like panda bears because the competition was part of a celebration of two new pandas arriving at a Hong Kong zoo.

social referencing Infants' tendency to look to their caregiver for an indication of how to feel and act in unfamiliar circumstances.

FIGURE 5.12 The transition from crawling to walking changes the way babies approach the task of going down a ramp. The younger baby (left) sees that there is a slope but plunges down it just the same. The toddler (right) looks much more unsure, despite being lured by a toy.

combining them (Thelen, Fisher, & Ridley-Johnson, 2002). These new motor skills must then be combined with an increased sensitivity to perceptual input from the environment and social information from others about where, when, and how to walk.

The Role of Practice in Motor Development

Studies of motor development were among developmentalists' earliest strategies for investigating the relative roles of nature and nurture. During the 1930s and 1940s, it was commonly believed that the attainment of such motor milestones as sitting and walking were dictated by maturation, with learning and experience playing little or no role.

One of the studies cited to support this view was conducted by Wayne and Margaret Dennis among Hopi families in the southwestern United States (Dennis & Dennis, 1940). In traditional Hopi families, babies in the first several months after birth are tightly swaddled and strapped to a flat cradle board. They are unwrapped only once or twice a day so that they can be washed and their clothes can be changed. The wrapping allows infants very little movement of their arms and legs and no practice in such complex movements as rolling over. The Dennises compared the motor development of traditionally raised Hopi babies with that of the babies of less traditional Hopi parents who did not use cradle boards. They found that the two groups of babies did not differ in the age at which they began to walk by themselves, which is consistent with the notion that this basic motor skill does not depend on practice for its development.

However, observations of babies from other cultural settings provide evidence that practice can affect the age at which babies reach motor milestones and may even alter the sequence of the milestones. Charles Super (1976) reported that among the Kipsigis people of rural Kenya, parents begin to teach their babies to sit up, stand, and walk not long after birth. To teach their children to sit up, for example, Kipsigis parents seat their babies in shallow holes in the ground that they have dug to support the infants' backs, or they nestle blankets around them to hold them upright. They repeat such procedures daily until the babies can sit up quite well by themselves. Training in walking begins in the 8th week after birth. The babies are held under the arms with their feet touching the ground and are gradually propelled forward. On average, Kipsigis babies reach the developmental milestones of sitting 5 weeks earlier, and walking 3 weeks earlier, than do babies in the United States. (Similar results have been reported among West Indian and Cameroonian children, whose mothers put them through a culturally prescribed sequence of motor exercises during the early months of infancy [Hopkins & Westen, 1988; Keller, 2003]). At the same time, Kipsigis infants are not advanced in skills they have not been taught or have not practiced. They learn to roll over or crawl no faster than children in the United States, and they lag behind children in the United States in their ability to negotiate stairs.

Further evidence about the impact that practice—or lack of it—can have on early motor development comes from the Ache, a nomadic people living in the rain forest of eastern Paraguay. Hilliard Kaplan and Heather Dove (1987) reported that Ache children under 3 years of age spend 80 to 100 percent of their time in direct physical contact with their mothers and are almost never seen more than 3 feet away from them. A major reason is that Ache hunter–gatherer groups do not create clearings in the forest when they stop to make camp. Rather, they remove just enough ground cover to make room to sit down, leaving roots, trees, and bushes more or less where they found them. For safety's sake, mothers either carry their infants or keep them within arm's reach.

As a result of these cultural patterns, Ache infants are markedly slower than U.S. infants in acquiring gross motor skills such as walking. In fact, they begin walking,

Babies who are just beginning to stand up find other people and furniture to be handy aids. This Filipino baby who lives in a house on stilts is being trained at an early age in the essential skill of climbing a ladder.

Martha Cooper

on the average, at about 23 months of age, almost a full year later than children in the United States. At about the age of 5, however, when Ache children are deemed old enough to be allowed to move around on their own, they begin to spend many hours in complex play activities that serve to increase their motor skills. Within a few years they are skilled at climbing tall trees and at cutting vines and branches while they balance high above the ground in a manner that bespeaks normal, perhaps even exceptional, motor skills.

The influence of practice, and of cultural norms, on physical development is further highlighted by the recent "back-to-sleep" movement in the United States to eradicate SIDS (see Chapter 4, p. 154–155). The widespread success of getting parents to put their infants on their back to sleep rather than on their belly has had the unexpected effect of delaying the onset of crawling in babies in the United States by as much as 2 months (Majnemer & Barr, 2005). Since time spent in the prone position (face down) provides babies with their earliest experiences of bearing their body weight with their arms, shifting their weight to reach for a toy, and trying out coordinated movements of their arms and legs, children who spend their waking as well as sleeping hours on their back miss out on developmentally appropriate experiences. As a consequence, pediatricians in the United States are urging parents to provide their young infants with "tummy time to play" so that they can practice pushing themselves up as a precursor to crawling (Pontius et al., 2001). Indeed, researchers are finding that babies with more tummy time tend to roll, crawl, and sit at earlier ages than do those who spend less time in the prone position (Kuo, Liao, Chen, Hsieh, & Hwang, 2008).

Intended to prevent sudden infant death syndrome, the practice of putting babies to sleep on their back has had the unexpected effect of delaying the onset of crawling. Pediatricians now encourage parents to provide young infants with plenty of "tummy time" in which to gain experiences important for learning to crawl.

Control of Elimination

Another significant development in the lives of babies, not to mention their families, is the ability to control the muscles that govern elimination. In the early months of life, elimination is an involuntary act—a reflex. When full, the baby's bladder or bowels stimulate the appropriate sphincter muscles, which open automatically, causing elimination. Before a baby can control these muscles voluntarily, the sensory pathways from the bladder and bowels must be mature enough to transmit signals to the brain. Children must then learn to associate these signals with the need to eliminate. They must also learn to "hold it" by tightening their sphincter to prevent elimination and to loosen their sphincter when they want to "go."

As the box about the diaper-free movement makes clear, learning to control elimination takes place within a historical and cultural context. Until the 1950s, toilet training in many countries was begun as early as possible, not only for convenience in an era before washing machines and disposable diapers but also because early training was believed to ensure bowel regularity, which was considered important for good health. (*Infant Care*, published by the U.S. Children's Bureau in 1914, advised mothers to begin bowel training by the 3rd month or even earlier [Wolfenstein, 1953].) With the advent of washing machines and disposable diapers in the latter half of the twentieth century, parental practices began to change. For example, Remo Largo and his colleagues found that 96 percent of Swiss parents in the 1950s began toilet training before their infants were 12 months old, but by the mid-1970s, the vast majority of Swiss parents did not begin the training until their children were 36 months of age. Significantly, the toilet training of the earlier generation succeeded only in the sense that young infants learned to eliminate when placed on the potty; there was no change at all in the ages at which they gained sufficient control over their bladder and bowel functions to stay dry at night

In the Field The Diaper-Free Movement

AT 7 MONTHS, LITTLE HANNAH HAS CHUBBY THIGHS and a dimpled bottom but lacks her peers' familiar hind-end bulge. She is diaper-free. Her mother, Melinda, has joined a growing number of parents who are starting their children's toilet training at surprisingly early ages—early, that is, by modern, Western standards. Belonging to Internet groups and e-mail lists, and poring over how-to books with such titles as *Diaper Free! The Gentle Wisdom of Natural Infant Hygiene* (Bauer, 2001), these parents are learning about techniques that encourage their babies—too young to walk or talk—to eliminate in toilets, sinks, or pots. They are also bucking historical trends in the United States, according to which the onset of toilet training has been increasingly delayed (see the table).

The Trend in the United States for Beginning Toilet Training

Time period	Starting age
1920–1940	12 months
1940–1960	18 months
1960–1980	2 years
1980–1990	2½ years
1990–present	3 years

Adapted from Bakker & Wyndaele, 2000

At a "diaper-free baby" meeting in New York, 7-month-old Neshama is sitting on a potty.

Andrea Mohin/The New York Times/Redux

The training begins with parents holding the diapered baby by the thighs in a seated position against their stomach and making encouraging grunts or "pss-wss-wss" sounds. With time, the parent learns the baby's elimination rhythms (babies often go after eating or bouts of activity); meanwhile, the baby learns to eliminate at the sound of the parent's cues. In Hannah's case, at least, the training was highly effective: She can sleep all night without a diaper and goes in a plastic potty as her mother encourages her. Melinda is pleased. She's also saving her mother a bundle in diaper costs, which can reach $3,000 per child, and is helping the environment, which currently sags under the accumulating weight of 22 billion dirty diapers per year. In addition, Hannah is free of diaper rash, and her nursery doesn't smell like a diaper pail.

Although toilet training at such a young age may seem unusual, if not impossible, it used to be common practice in the United States, and it continues to be embraced in many countries across the globe, including India, China, Kenya, and Greenland. Some parents in the United States who adopt children from these countries are startled to discover that that their babies arrive toilet-trained. Indeed, it has been estimated that more than 50 percent of the world's children are toilet-trained by 1 year of age (de Vries & de Vries, 1977).

Not surprisingly, there is a great deal of controversy regarding the effectiveness of early toilet training, and what, exactly, it means to be "trained." One way of interpreting the difference between reports of early training success and evidence that children are not capable of voluntary control until much later is to argue that it is the parents, not the babies, who have been trained. According to this interpretation, parents become adept at picking up their babies' signals and rhythms and learn when it is time to put their children on the pot. On the other hand, it might be that early training draws upon a different learning mechanism than does later training. Specifically, early training may take advantage of *classical conditioning*, in which a conditional stimulus (Melinda's "pss-wss-wss") is paired with an unconditional stimulus (Hannah's full bladder or bowel) such that over time Melinda's cue is enough to produce the desired response (see p. 146 for a review of classical conditioning). In contrast, later training involves deliberate, voluntary control, requiring the development of sensory pathways in the brain and higher cognitive processes.

Regardless of whether the diaper-free movement is a passing fad or a signal that the historical pendulum of toilet training is about to reverse its direction, it provides an excellent example of how children's development is culturally organized. It also reflects the variety of developmental mechanisms (classical and operant conditioning, for example) that allow children to adapt to radically different rearing conditions.

(Adapted from Kelley, 2005)

(Largo et al., 1996). Similar trends were found in a study conducted in Belgium (Bakker & Wyndaele, 2000). These results provide strong evidence that the processes of gaining voluntary control over bowel and bladder are under maturational control.

By the time they are 2 years old, some children are able to remain dry during the day, owing in large measure to the watchfulness of adults who place them on the potty when they show signs of needing it. Many children in the United States and Europe today, however, do not achieve this milestone until sometime later, and most do not manage to stay dry while they are asleep until they are 3½ to 4 years old (Schum, Kolb, McAuliffe, Simms, Underhill, & Marla, 2002). The successful completion of toilet training is an important milestone because it allows children a noticeably greater degree of independence.

The presence of friends no doubt encourages these young children in their attempts to learn to use the potty.

▲ APPLY :: CONNECT :: DISCUSS

Imagine two children—one an early walker, walking well at 9 months of age, the other a late walker, walking well at 15 months. Suppose both children live in the same neighborhood or village and have parents with similar resources and with similar child-rearing practices and beliefs. Explain how the difference in onset of walking may have significant implications for each child's development.

Cognitive Development: The Great Debate

As the physical body, and the ability to control it, continue to mature across the first 2 years after birth, so too does the mind. As we shall see in the following sections, developmentalists are engaged in a great debate about how thinking progresses during the first 2 years.

For some developmentalists, such as Piaget, the mind undergoes a radical, discontinuous shift at the end of infancy (Müller, 2009). According to Piaget's stage theory, young infants are limited to *sensorimotor intelligence;* that is, they understand the world only through their own actions and perceptions. They, therefore, cannot think about people and objects that are not immediately present to be seen, heard, or felt, and acted upon. All this changes fundamentally at age 18 or so months of age, when infants become capable of *representational thinking,* forming mental pictures or images of the world. The ability to form such mental images, and to reason about them, is a significant turning point in cognitive development. Knowledge is no longer tied to the immediate here and now. Instead, infants can hold in mind past experiences, compare and contrast them with each other and with present circumstances, and use them to anticipate the future and guide their actions. Developmentalists who take this view claim that the emergence of the ability to represent the world mentally results in a mind that is truly *conceptual,* rather than simply "sensorimotor."

On the other side of the debate are developmentalists who maintain that mental development is more continuous than Piaget supposed—that the ability to represent and understand the world conceptually is present very early in development, if not from birth. According to this view, conceptual understanding does not emerge out of sensorimotor knowledge, as Piaget claimed. Instead, young babies are believed to possess at least a rudimentary conceptual system. This system is thought to develop separate from, although in close association with, the sensorimotor system (Mandler, 2007; Moore & Meltzoff, 2004). As you will see below, there is much at stake in the debate about the nature and development of the human mind.

Sensorimotor Development

Piaget referred to infancy as the stage of *sensorimotor development* because of his belief that at this early age, infants acquire knowledge exclusively through motor actions that are directed at their immediate environment and guided by their sensory organs. He combined the terms "sensory" and "motor" to emphasize the intimate relationship between sensing the world and acting upon it. Each influences the other: What infants perceive depends on what they are doing, and what they do depends on what they are perceiving at the moment (Piaget, 1973). As noted above, Piaget maintained that infants are bound to this moment-to-moment, here-and-now form of understanding until the final stage of sensorimotor development, when they begin to think representationally.

You may recall from our previous discussions (Chapter 1, p. 20; Chapter 4, pp. 144–146) that Piaget divided the sensorimotor period into six substages (Table 5.1). During the first substage, the newborn learns to control and coordinate reflexes, and during the second, the newborn begins to modify and repeat behaviors, such as thumb-sucking, simply because they are pleasurable (primary circular reactions). The following sections provide an overview of the four remaining substages of sensorimotor development. As you read through the sections, notice how infants become increasingly flexible, purposeful, and inventive.

Reproducing Interesting Events (Substage 3)

In contrast to the first two substages, in which infants' actions primarily involve their own body, in the third substage, 4- to 8-month-olds begin to direct their attention and their actions to the external world—to objects and outcomes. This new interest in external things gives rise to a characteristic behavior observed in infants during this substage—the repetition of actions that produce interesting changes in the environment. For example, when babies in this substage accidentally discover that a particular action, like squeezing a rubber toy, produces an interesting effect, such as squeaking, they repeat the action again and again to produce the effect. Similarly, when babies vocalize by cooing or gurgling and a caregiver responds, they repeat the sound they made. Piaget termed these new, object-oriented actions

table **5.1**		
Piaget's Sensorimotor Substages		
Substage	**Age (months)**	**Characteristics of Sensorimotor Substage**
1	0–1½	*Exercising reflexive schemas:* involuntary rooting, sucking, grasping, looking
2	1½–4	*Primary circular reactions:* repetition of actions that are pleasurable in themselves
3	4–8	*Secondary circular reactions:* dawning awareness of relation of own actions to environment; extended actions that produce interesting changes in the environment
4	8–12	*Coordination of secondary circular reactions:* combining schemas to achieve a desired effect; earliest form of problem solving
5	12–18	*Tertiary circular reactions:* deliberate variation of problem-solving means; experimentation to see what the consequences will be
6	18–24	*Beginning of symbolic representation:* images and words come to stand for familiar objects; invention of new means of problem solving through symbolic combinations

secondary circular reactions. They are "secondary" because they apply to something outside the infant, in contrast to primary circular reactions, which apply to the infant's own body (see p. 145).

The change from primary circular reactions to secondary circular reactions indicated to Piaget that infants are beginning to realize that objects are more than an extension of their own actions, that objects have their own, separate identities. In this substage, however, babies still have only a rudimentary understanding of objects and space, and their discoveries about the world seem to have an accidental quality.

The Emergence of Intentionality (Substage 4)

The hallmark of the fourth sensorimotor substage, which occurs between 8 and 12 months of age, is the emergence of the ability to engage in behaviors directed toward achieving a goal. Piaget called this ability **intentionality**. He believed goal-directed behavior to be the earliest form of true problem solving.

Piaget's son, Laurent, provided a demonstration of intentional problem solving of this kind when he was 10 months old. Piaget had given him a small tin container, which Laurent dropped and picked up repeatedly (a secondary circular reaction characteristic of behavior in substage 3). Piaget then placed a washbasin a short distance from Laurent and struck it with the tin box, producing an interesting sound. From earlier observations, Piaget knew that Laurent would repeatedly bang on the basin to make the interesting sound occur (another typical secondary circular reaction). This time Piaget wanted to see if Laurent would combine the newly acquired "dropping the tin box" schema with the previously acquired "make an interesting sound" schema. Here is his report of Laurent's behavior:

> Now, at once, Laurent takes possession of the tin, holds out his arm and drops it over the basin. I moved the latter as a check. He nevertheless succeeded, several times in succession, in making the object fall on the basin. Hence this is a fine example of the coordination of two schemas of which the first serves as a "means" whereas the second assigns an end to the action. (Piaget, 1952b, p. 255)

In Piaget's view, then, over the course of substages 3 and 4 of sensorimotor intelligence, infants become capable of intentional action directed at objects and people around them, but these abilities come fully into play only when infants can directly perceive the objects and people in question. Piaget maintained that this is because infants lack **object permanence**, that is, the understanding that objects exist even when they are out of view. Until substage 4 of sensorimotor development, according to Piaget, infants live in a world in which objects come and go from their line of sight, each "a mere image which reenters the void as soon as it vanishes, and emerges from it for no apparent reason" (1954, p. 11). Piaget's classic test of object permanence was to put a cloth over a young infant's favorite toy as the infant watched and then observe whether or not the infant searched for the hidden toy. Unfailingly, infants under 8 months of age not only did not search for the vanished toy, they also showed no interest or surprise in its vanishing—as though it had never existed. Thus, Piaget believed that for young babies, out of sight is literally out of mind. In stage 4, infants begin to demonstrate some degree of object permanence (they will lift the cloth off the hidden toy), but until substage 6, it is rudimentary and fragile.

Exploring by Experimenting (Substage 5)

The fifth substage of the sensorimotor period, **tertiary circular reactions**, emerges between 12 and 18 months of age and is characterized by an ability to vary the actions of substage 4 systematically and flexibly. This ability makes explorations of the

secondary circular reactions The behavior characteristic of the third substage of Piaget's sensorimotor stage, in which babies repeat actions to produce interesting changes in their environment.

intentionality The ability to engage in behaviors directed toward achieving a goal.

object permanence The understanding that objects have substance, maintain their identity when their location is changed, and ordinarily continue to exist when out of sight.

tertiary circular reactions The fifth stage of the sensorimotor period, characterized by the deliberate variation of action sequences to solve problems and explore the world.

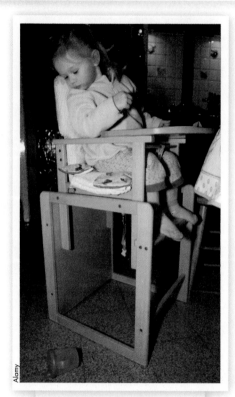

Experimenting with objects, including dropping cups from one's high chair in order to watch them fall and bounce, is typical of Piaget's sensorimotor substage 5.

At 22 months of age, this little girl engages in deferred imitation, giving her bear a drink in imitation of how she herself is helped to drink from a cup.

world more complex. Indeed, Piaget (1952b) referred to tertiary circular reactions as "experiments in order to see," because children seem to be experimenting in order to find out about the nature of objects and events (p. 272). Here is Piaget's description of this kind of behavior in Laurent, at 10 months and 11 days, lying in his crib:

> He grasps in succession a celluloid swan, a box, etc., stretches out his arm and lets them fall. He distinctly varies the positions of the fall. . . . Sometimes he stretches out his arm vertically, sometimes he holds it obliquely, in front of or behind his eyes, etc. When the object falls in a new position (for example, on his pillow), he lets it fall two or three times more on the same place, as though to study the spatial relations; then he modifies the situation. (Piaget, 1952b, p. 269)

According to Piaget's observations, infants in substage 5 seem unable to reason systematically about actions and anticipate their probable consequences. As suggested in Laurent's behavior of trying different ways of dropping the object for the sheer purpose of seeing what might happen, infants in substage 5 live in a here-and-now, trial-and-error world. The ability to mentally plan, organize, and otherwise envision their actions and foresee their possible consequences does not begin until the arrival of *representational thinking*.

Representation (Substage 6)

According to Piaget, the hallmark of substage 6, the final stage of the sensorimotor period, between 18 and 24 months of age, is that babies begin to base their actions on internal, mental symbols, or **representations**, of experience. When they can *re-present* the world to themselves—that is, when they can present it to themselves over again mentally—they can be said to be engaging in true mental actions.

The infant's ability to represent people, objects, events, and experiences mentally has been a central focus for researchers because it has enormous ramifications in other areas of development. For example, once infants are able to represent a sequence of events, they can *solve problems* more systematically, rather than by trial and error. Similarly, once babies become capable of representation, they begin to engage in **symbolic play** (also known as *pretend play* or *fantasy play*), in which one object is used to stand for (represent) another, as when a child combs a baby doll's hair with a twig or gives it a drink from a small plastic block. Representation also enables **deferred imitation**, the imitation of actions observed in the past, which is of tremendous importance to children's learning and socialization. A child who observes a parent having coffee and reading the paper and then hours or days later pretends to be drinking coffee and reading is engaged in deferred imitation. Finally, of special significance is the role of representation in *language,* in which words are used to stand for (represent) people, objects, and events.

There is little disagreement about the importance Piaget attached to representation as a foundation for the development of problem solving, symbolic play, deferred imitation, and language. Nor do developmentalists disagree with Piaget's descriptions of the sequence of behavioral changes that occurs as children progress through the early stages of dealing with objects. Indeed, his observations have been widely replicated, not only in Europe and the United States but in traditional societies as well. For example, Baule infants living in rural areas of the West African country of Côte d'Ivoire have been found to proceed through the same sequence of object-related behaviors on almost exactly the same timetable as European children do, despite vast differences in their cultural environments (Dasen, 1973). In fact, research conducted with infant great apes reveals the same pattern of sensorimotor development (Parker & McKinney, 1999). The sequence and timing of sensorimotor stages are so reliable that Piaget's procedures were long ago standardized for assessing the development of children who are at risk because of disease, physical impairment, or extreme environmental deprivation (Uzgiris & Hunt, 1975).

However, in the past two decades there have been challenges both to Piaget's theory and to his methods. In general, these challenges attack the idea that infants are unable to represent objects they cannot see, arguing instead that infants are born with, or quickly develop, a conceptual system with representational powers. As we discuss below, critics argue that young infants have the competence to form representations of objects but lack various skills needed to demonstrate that ability on traditional Piagetian tests. Using a variety of ingenious methods, the critiques suggest that infants' mental lives are more complex than Piaget believed.

▲ APPLY :: CONNECT :: DISCUSS

Imagine that you have been hired by a company to develop a line of toys appropriate to the ongoing sensorimotor development of infants through age 2. Prepare a presentation of some of your ideas for products, including arguments for how your products will appeal to infants at the various substages of sensorimotor development.

Conceptual Development

As we have seen, Piaget maintained that before the onset of representations, infants have no knowledge that endures beyond the immediate here and now. Although they can form primitive associations as, for example, in classical and operant conditioning (see Chapter 4, pp. 146–147), it is not until the end of the sensorimotor stage of intelligence that infants gain a conceptual understanding of the characteristics of objects and events. The distinction between sensorimotor and conceptual intelligence was cleverly highlighted by Jean Mandler when she characterized the sensorimotor infant as an "absent-minded professor" who, finding herself in the kitchen unable to remember what she wanted there, searches around for a clue and, upon seeing a cup by the sink, thinks, "Aha, I came for coffee!" (2004, p. 21). From Piaget's perspective, the sensorimotor infant can be similarly cued by perceptual features of the immediate environment to "remember" past associations but cannot grasp them conceptually in the absence of such prompts.

In the sections below, we explore the ways that infants demonstrate capacities to understand the world in more conceptual, abstract terms. As you will see, there is strong evidence that Piaget underestimated the conceptual intelligence of infants. As yet, however, there is no unifying theory that accounts for conceptual development during the first 2 years. Should such a unifying theory take shape, the accumulating evidence indicates that it will need to account for the infant's biological preparedness to construct a typically "human" understanding of the world as well as for the consequences of the infant's experiences in specific contexts.

Understanding the Permanence of Objects

- Observation 1. A baby seated at a table is offered a soft toy. He grasps it. While he is still engrossed in the toy, the experimenter takes it from him and places it on the table behind a screen. The baby may begin to reach for the toy, but as soon as it disappears from sight, he stops short, stares for a moment, and then looks away without attempting to move the screen (Figure 5.13) (Piaget, 1954).

Courtesy of A. Meltzoff

Studies by Andrew Meltzoff (1988) have shown that young infants imitate live models and will also imitate actions they have seen on television. This child observes a televised adult model manipulate blocks, and then immediately the child imitates the adult's actions. Meltzoff also demonstrated that infants who watch a televised model on one day are able to reproduce the model's behavior 24 hours later.

representations Internal, mental symbols of experience; according to Piaget, the ability to form mental symbols emerges during sensorimotor substage 6.

symbolic play Play in which one object stands for, or represents, another.

deferred imitation The imitation of an action observed in the past.

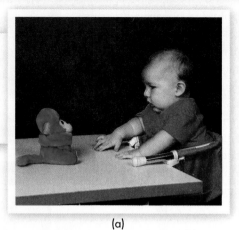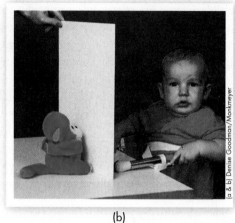

FIGURE 5.13 Instead of searching behind the screen when his toy disappears, this infant looks dumbfounded. This kind of behavior led Piaget to conclude that objects no longer in view cease to exist for infants younger than 8 months of age.

(a)   (b)

(a & b) Denise Goodman/Monkmeyer

- Observation 2. A baby is placed in an infant seat in a bare laboratory room. Her mother, who has been playing with her, disappears for a moment. When the mother reappears, the baby sees three of her, an illusion the experimenter has created through the use of carefully arranged mirrors. The baby displays no surprise as she babbles happily to her multiple mothers (Bower, 1982).

- Observation 3. A baby watches a toy train as it chugs along a track (Figure 5.14). When the train disappears into a tunnel, the child's eyes remain

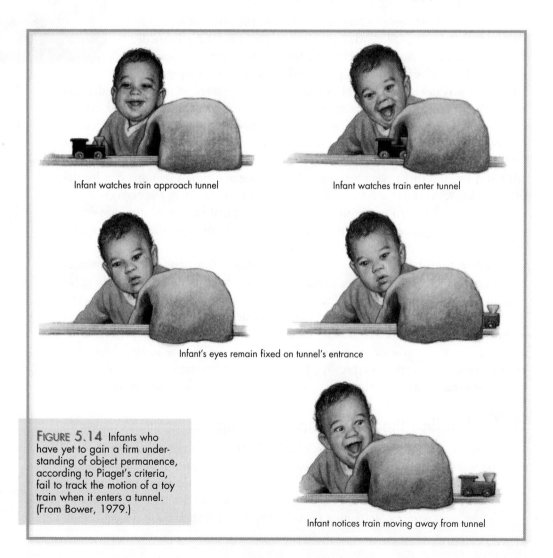

Infant watches train approach tunnel

Infant watches train enter tunnel

Infant's eyes remain fixed on tunnel's entrance

Infant notices train moving away from tunnel

FIGURE 5.14 Infants who have yet to gain a firm understanding of object permanence, according to Piaget's criteria, fail to track the motion of a toy train when it enters a tunnel. (From Bower, 1979.)

fixed on the tunnel's entrance rather than following the train's expected progress through the tunnel. When the train reappears at the other end of the tunnel, it takes the child a few seconds to catch up with it visually, and the child shows no surprise when the train that comes out of the tunnel is a different color or shape (Bower, 1982).

A-not-B error A pattern of reacting in the object permanence task, in which the infant looks for the hidden object in location A, where the infant had previously found the object, instead of location B, where the infant has just observed it being hidden.

Each of these observations was recorded in the context of studying *object permanence,* a full and stable grasp of which is, according to Piaget, a clear indicator that the development of mental representation and conceptual thinking is underway. As noted, Piaget contended that babies demonstrate object permanence only when they begin to search actively for an absent object, as when they uncover a toy they have just seen the experimenter hide under a cloth or behind a barrier. His own research indicated that although this active searching behavior first appears at around 8 months of age, infants' mastery of object permanence is incomplete until the second half of their 2nd year. He discovered, for example, that babies between 8 and 12 months tend to make a characteristic mistake when searching for objects: If, after they have successfully searched for an object hidden in one location, A, the object is then hidden, *right before their eyes,* in a new location, B (Figure 5.15), they will still search for the object in location A where they previously found it!

Piaget interpreted this pattern of responding—referred to as the **A–not-B error**—as evidence that the child remembers the existence of the object but cannot reason systematically about it. He believed that true representation requires the ability both to keep in mind the existence of an absent object and to reason about that absent object mentally, an achievement he did not think occurs until late in the 2nd year, during the sixth substage of the sensorimotor period.

Alternative Explanations of Infants' Difficulties
Other developmentalists have disagreed with Piaget's interpretation of young infants' A-not-B error. They believe that the error is due not to a failure to represent and reason about the object but to other developmental limitations, including limitations of memory or motor skills.

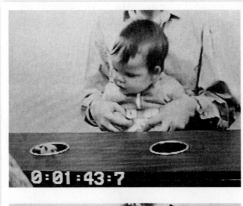
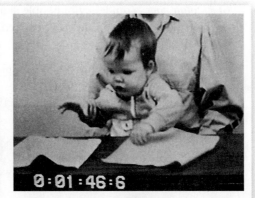
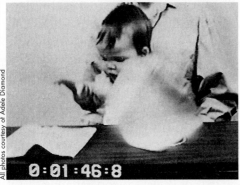

All photos courtesy of Adele Diamond

FIGURE 5.15 In this movie sequence, an object is placed in the circle on the left (position B), and then both circles (positions A and B) are covered with a cloth while the baby watches. In a previous trial, the object had been placed in the right-hand circle (position A), and the baby had correctly retrieved it. This time, while remaining oriented toward the hidden object at position B, the baby nonetheless picks up the cloth at position A, where the object was hidden before.

The Role of Memory. In an influential series of studies, Adele Diamond (1991) suggested that young infants may be capable of representation but fail Piaget's A–not–B task because they simply do not remember where the object was hidden. Diamond varied the time between the switching of an object from location A to location B and the moment when children were allowed to reach for the hidden object (Diamond, 1991, 2000). She found that, if they were allowed to reach immediately, 7½-month-old babies correctly located the object at position B, but if they were prevented from reaching for as little as 2 seconds, they exhibited the A–not–B error. By 9 months of age, infants could withstand a delay of 5 seconds before beginning to make mistakes, and by 12 months of age, they could withstand a delay of 10 seconds. These results suggest that young infants are capable of representing objects they cannot see but quickly forget their location and become confused (this may explain the behavior of the baby in Figure 5.15). Other studies documenting a relationship between the delay of reaching and successful searching (Bremner et al., 2005; Ruffman, Slade, & Redman, 2005) further suggest that the A–not–B task may impose significant demands on infants' memory system, masking their representational abilities.

The Role of Perseveration. *Perseveration* refers to the persistent repetition of a particular behavior. Diamond believed that young infants may exhibit the A–not–B error not only because of their memory limitations but also because of their tendency to engage in *motor perseveration,* in which they repeat a movement rather than modify it to fit new events. She noted that some infants who make the A–not–B error in fact look at location B but reach toward location A. Research suggests that such perseveration (which could also explain the behavior of the baby in Figure 5.15) may be due to the tendency of certain motor behaviors to become habits (Clearfield et al., 2009) or may be related to immature brain development that makes it difficult for infants to inhibit responses (Diamond & Amso, 2008).

The A–not–B error may also involve another type of perseveration that is not specifically linked to motor behavior: Babies may reach incorrectly for the object at location A because of their previous success in finding it there. This is an example of a *capture error,* a tendency of people at all ages to continue using a once-successful solution whenever possible, as illustrated in the following task that Renée Baillargeon (1993) conducted with her 2-year-old son:

> Mother: What is an animal with a hump?
> Son: A camel.
> Mother: What is something warm you wear on your feet during the winter?
> Son: Boots.
> [A bit later]
> Mother: What is an animal with a hump?
> Son: A camel.
> Mother: What is something warm you wear on your head during the winter?
> Son: Boots.

Memory limitations, motor perseveration, and capture errors are all explanations for why infants may fail the A–not–B task, even though they may possess the ability to form mental representations. In other words, many developmentalists believe that infants have representational *competence* but lack the *performance* skills required to successfully demonstrate that competence on the task (Hespos & Baillargeon, 2008).

Alternative Approaches to Measuring and Understanding Object Permanence Prompted by evidence that the performance demands of the A–not–B task obscure the young infant's representational competence about objects, several developmentalists have proposed alternative ways of measuring and understanding object permanence. Some designed new tests of Piaget's theory, arguing that if infants were not required to demonstrate their understanding by reaching for and manipulating things, it might be possible to show that infants are capable of representational thought at or near birth. Others have taken a much more radical stance, proposing that the whole idea of competence in the absence of performance is irrelevant to infants' performance on the A–not–B test. As you will see, these developmentalists do not call for new measures of object permanence as much as for a new theory about how infants behave in various testing situations.

Violation-of-Expectations Method.   To challenge Piaget's theory of when representation develops, Renée Baillargeon and her colleagues devised an object permanence test that exploits the well-known tendency of infants (in fact, of everyone) to stare at events that violate their expectations (Hespos & Baillargeon, 2008; Wang, Baillargeon, & Brueckner, 2004). This test, the **violation-of-expectations method**, involves a bit of research trickery. Basically, babies are habituated to a particular event and then presented two variants of the event—one that is "possible" under normal circumstances, and one that is "impossible" and comes about only through an illusion created by the researcher. The premise is that if infants are capable of mentally representing their experiences, they should develop specific expectations during the habituation phase and then look longer at events that violate those expectations, that is, at the impossible events.

   In one study, infants were habituated to two events. In one, a short carrot moved behind a screen and reappeared on the other side; in the other, a tall carrot moved behind the screen and likewise reappeared (Figure 5.16). Once the infants were habituated to these two events, they were presented with two test events in which a window had been cut out of the screen.

1. In the *possible event,* a short carrot again moved behind the screen and reappeared on the other side. The window in the screen was high enough that the small carrot was hidden from view as it passed behind the screen.

2. In the *impossible event,* a tall carrot moved behind the screen and reappeared on the other side. In this case, the tall carrot *should* have appeared in the window as it passed behind the screen—but, in violation of anyone's expectations, it did not (thanks to the experimenter's secret manipulations).

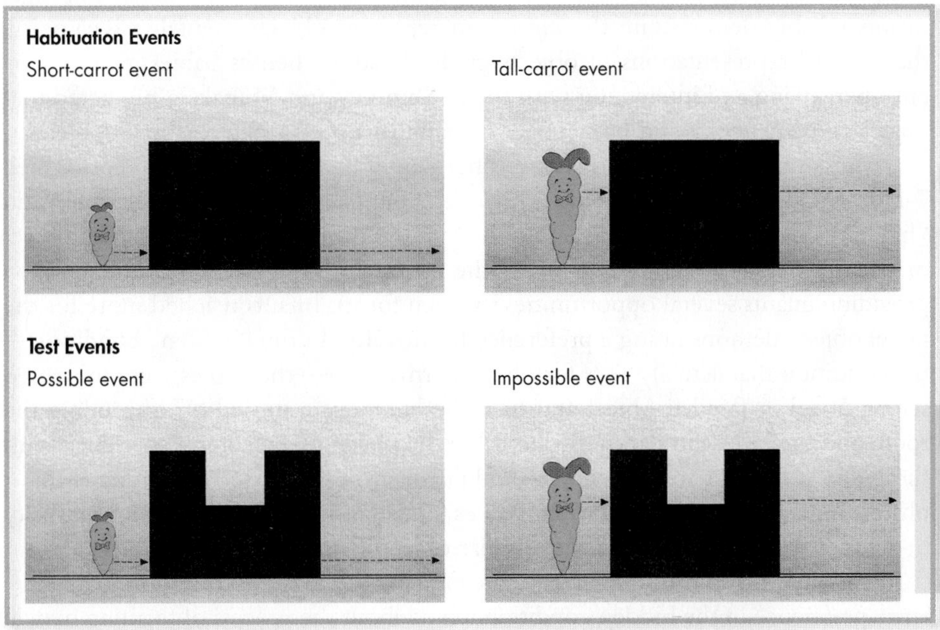

violation-of-expectations method A test of mental representation in which the child is habituated to an event and then presented with possible and impossible variants of the event.

FIGURE 5.16 Using this version of the violation-of-expectations method, researchers find that infants as young as 2½ months of age look longer at the impossible event, suggesting that they are capable of mentally representing their past experiences.

Using this method, Baillargeon demonstrated that infants as young as 2½ months of age looked longer at the impossible event than at the possible event, suggesting that they had, indeed, formed mental representations of their past experiences with the habituation events. As you will see later in this chapter, developmentalists have used similar tricks to figure out what infants do and do not understand about the physical world.

Dynamic Systems Approach. While many developmentalists have focused on untangling infants' underlying conceptual competence from the performance demands of the tasks, Esther Thelen and her colleagues have offered an entirely different approach to thinking about the nature of knowledge and its development in infants (Thelen, Schoener, Scheier, & Smith, 2001). According to their *dynamic systems* perspective (see Chapter 1, p. 27), it is unnecessary to invoke the idea of performance limitations to explain infants' failures on the A-not-B task, or to invoke the idea of mental concepts such as object permanence to account for their ultimate success. In their view infants' behaviors on tests of object permanence—indeed, all human action in any context—are the result of the dynamics that emerge from the "immediate circumstances and the [individual's] history of perceiving and acting in similar circumstances" (p. 34). Thus, infants' experiences with specific objects, their current memory of those experiences, and their current motor skills all interact in their solving the specific problems posed by whatever task faces them. From this perspective, the critical developmental process is not, as Piaget contended, a shift from sensorimotor intelligence to conceptual intelligence. Rather, it is infants' growing abilities to better coordinate all the various systems involved in both sensorimotor and conceptual intelligence (looking, reaching, perceiving, remembering, and so on) required by the task at hand (Clearfield et al., 2006).

The Role of Experience. Noting that infants' performance on tests of object permanence is highly sensitive to the particulars of the test itself—such as the search method (reaching or looking) and the amount of time between hiding and searching—Jeanne Shinskey and Yuko Munakata (2005) wondered if infants gradually develop stronger representations of objects through their experience with them, and if stronger representations are required for some tasks than for others. In line with the dynamic systems approach, the researchers focused on the *process* through which infants build mental representations rather than on whether, and at what age, infants reliably demonstrate the *capacity* to represent objects mentally. Reasoning that infants' representations of objects gradually strengthen as babies gain experience perceiving and interacting with them, Shinskey and Munakata predicted that object permanence would be stronger for familiar objects than for novel objects.

To test their prediction, the researchers used an inventive method in which 7-month-olds were presented with novel and familiar objects under "visible" and "hidden" conditions (Figure 5.17). In the "visible" condition, either a novel object or a familiar object was set in front of the babies (an object was made familiar by providing infants several opportunities to reach for it). Infants reached more for the novel object, demonstrating a preference for novelty. In the "hidden" condition—the condition that actually tests for object permanence—the babies were presented with a novel or familiar object and then the lights were turned off, shrouding the room and the object in darkness (the babies had been given some experience with the lights going out so that they wouldn't be surprised or scared during the test phase). In this hidden condition, the babies tended to reverse their previous novelty preference, reaching more for the familiar object than for the novel object.

What does this shift from a novelty preference in the visible condition to a familiarity preference in the hidden condition tell us about the process of forming mental representations? As Shinskey and Munakata point out, once infants have mastered information contained in one stimulus, seeking the novelty of a new stimulus is an adaptive strategy for acquiring new information about the world—a strategy that has likely evolved in our species because of its useful role in helping us explore, learn about, and respond to changes in our environments. When the infants in their study showed a preference for the novel object in the visible condition, they were demonstrating that they had processed the familiar object sufficiently well that it had become less interesting to explore, so they were more inclined to reach for the novel object. Furthermore, the fact that the infants were more inclined to reach for the familiar object in the hidden condition suggests that their experience with the object had helped them develop a stronger representation of it than of the novel object. It is evidence such as this that leads some developmentalists to argue that the formation of mental representations depends heavily on experience (Wang & Baillargeon, 2008; Johnson, Amso, & Slemmer, 2003; Kochukhova & Gredebäck, 2007). Thus, it seems likely that infants' developing representations and knowledge of the world is a joint consequence of human evolutionary processes and experiences available to babies in the specific cultural contexts in which they are brought up.

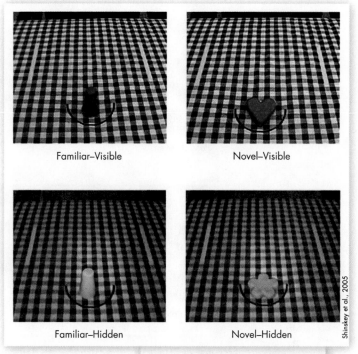

FIGURE 5.17 Illustrating that mental representations become stronger with experience, 7-month-olds reach for a novel, rather than a familiar, object when both are visible, but reach for the familiar object when both are "hidden" by turning out the lights (the pictures of the hidden objects shown in the lower panels were taken with infrared technology).

Developmentalists continue to debate questions about when object permanence emerges in development, and whether it is innate, learned through experience, or is some combination of the two. As you will now see, these fundamental questions also inspire research on how infants understand other properties of the physical world.

Understanding Other Properties of the Physical World

There are, of course, properties of the physical world other than objects' continuing existence when out of sight. As adults, we are so thoroughly familiar with the properties of our physical world that is it easy for us to overlook their significance for our behavior and development. We walk around obstacles rather than attempting to walk through them; we expect an apple that falls from a tree to land on the ground and not fly around crazily and hit someone on the nose; we may playfully smack a friend with a pillow but would never do so with a brick; when we reach into the back of a closet, we expect to find a wall, not the land of Narnia.

Where does our knowledge of the physical world come from? Are we born with the knowledge that objects are solid and conform to physical laws, such as the law of gravity, or does that knowledge emerge from experience? By what process do we come to reason about objects, recognizing, for example, that they can be counted, that there are often cause-and-effect relationships between them, or that certain objects share some of their features with other objects and can be categorized accordingly? As they have done in their research on object permanence, developmentalists have turned to infants to explore these fundamental questions. And, as they do in their research on object permanence, developmentalists often employ the violation-of-expectations method, generally in the form of research trickery, to good advantage.

A number of such experiments found that between 3 and 9 months of age, and sometimes earlier, infants appear to have at least an initial grasp of a wide variety of physical laws concerning the behavior of objects. An early experiment in a series carried out by Renée Baillargeon and her colleagues (Baillargeon, 2001) tested

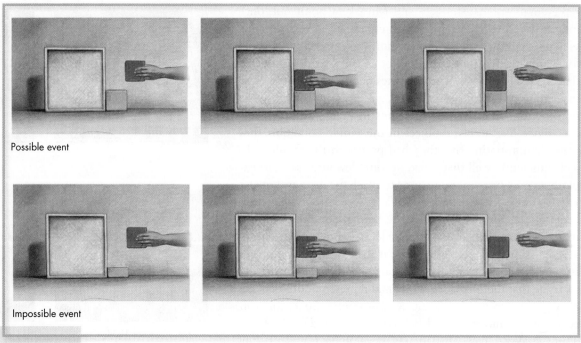

Possible event

Impossible event

FIGURE 5.18 Evidence that very young infants have some appreciation of the laws of gravity is demonstrated by the fact that they stare longer at impossible "gravity" events, such as a block remaining suspended in air, than at possible events, such as a block being supported by a block underneath it.

whether young infants would expect an object that is suspended unsupported in midair to fall (Needham & Baillargeon, 1993). The experimenters repeatedly presented 4½-month-old infants with the habituation event shown at the top of Figure 5.18 in which a hand reaches out and places one block on another before withdrawing. Then they presented either an event that defies the law of gravity, in which the top block is left dangling in midair as the hand withdraws (bottom part of Figure 5.18), or a control event (not shown), in which the hand withdraws part-way and continues holding the top block, which is not supported by the bottom block. Infants looked longer when the block appeared to be suspended in midair without any visible support, indicating to the researchers that the babies expected the block to fall. Similar studies have demonstrated that by 4 months of age, infants appear to believe that objects cannot move behind one screen and reappear from a separate screen without appearing in the space between screens, and to believe that if a container with an object inside is moved, the object will move with it (Figure 5.19) (Spelke, Breinlinger, Macomber, & Jacobson, 1992; Baillargeon, 2004).

FIGURE 5.19 Studies using the violation-of-expectations method find that infants as young as 4 months of age look longer at events that violate certain physical laws. The first sequence shown here depicts the impossible event of an object passing behind a screen, then reappearing from behind a separate screen, without showing up in the space between the screens. The second sequence shows the impossible event of an object inside a container failing to change position when the container is moved.

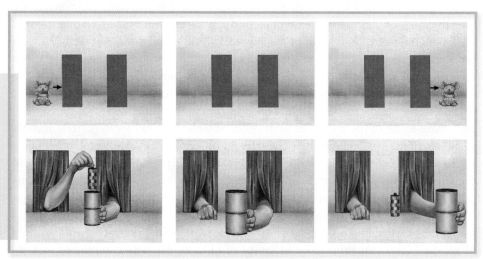

Reasoning About Objects

An important part of Piaget's theory about knowledge of objects is that even after children begin to be aware of the physical properties of objects, they cannot reason about those objects; for example, they cannot count them, understand cause–effect relations between them, or categorize them according to some feature they have in common.

Counting The question of whether young babies can count was addressed by Karen Wynn (1992), who showed 4-month-old infants the events depicted in Figure 5.20. First, a mouse doll was placed on an empty stage while the baby watched. Then a screen was raised to hide the doll from the baby's view. Next, the baby saw a hand holding a doll identical to the first one go behind the screen and then reappear without the doll. The screen was then lowered, in half the trials revealing two dolls (the possible event) and in the other half revealing only one doll (the impossible event). The infants looked longer when there was only one doll, suggesting that they had mentally calculated the number of dolls that ought to be behind the screen. Similarly, when the experiment began with two dolls on the stage and the hand removed one doll from behind the screen, the infants seemed surprised when the screen was lowered to reveal two dolls.

Interestingly, babies seem to "match" number across sensory modalities (see the discussion of intermodal perception, Chapter 4, pp. 138–139). For example, when 7-month-olds hear a recording of three voices speaking, they will look longer at a video that shows three faces than at a video that shows only two (Jordan & Brannon, 2006; Figure 5.21). Such experiments appear to demonstrate that infants are

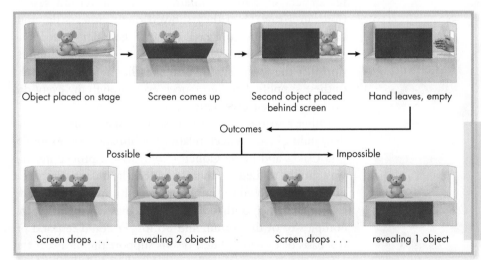

Object placed on stage   Screen comes up   Second object placed behind screen   Hand leaves, empty

Outcomes

Possible   Impossible

Screen drops . . .   revealing 2 objects   Screen drops . . .   revealing 1 object

FIGURE 5.20 After 4-month-olds observe the sequence of events depicted at the top of the figure, they show surprise when the screen is removed and only one mouse remains. Apparently the babies not only remember the presence of the first mouse hidden behind the screen but mentally add the second mouse and expect to see two mice. (After Wynn, 1992.)

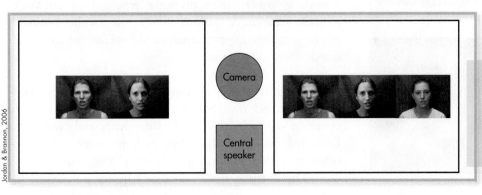

Jordan & Brannon, 2006

Camera

Central speaker

FIGURE 5.21 When 7-month-old infants hear a recording of three voices speaking (coming through the central speaker), they look longer at a video showing three people speaking than at a video showing two people speaking, suggesting that they are capable of simple mathematical calculations.

capable of making simple arithmetical calculations far ahead of Piaget's timetable regarding their ability to reason about objects.

However, as with other research suggesting precocious, possibly innate, infant abilities (such as whether infants understand the permanence of objects), research claiming to demonstrate that infants can count has not gone unchallenged. For example, Leslie Cohen and Kathryn Marks (2002) found that the infants looked longer the more objects there were and that they looked longer at a familiar display, no matter how many objects were in it. Developmentalists are still trying to reach conclusions about competence based on performance, wondering whether young babies are truly able to count objects or whether they only appear to do so in the context of specific tasks (Cordes & Brannon, 2009).

Cause–Effect Relationships

Another way of reasoning about the physical world is through cause–effect relationships. Alan Leslie and his colleagues have contended that primitive knowledge about physical causality is innate and does not require prior experience of the world to develop (Leslie, 1994, 2002). In an experiment to test this idea, they presented 6-month-olds (the youngest infants they could test reliably) with two computer displays in which one small square appeared to bump into a second square, which then moved. In one, *causal* version, the second square moved immediately, an event that adults perceive as the result of its being bumped by the first square. In the other, *noncausal* version, there was a delay in the movement of the second square, suggesting that its movement was not caused by its being bumped. The researchers showed the infants the causal version several times in a row. Then they showed them either a different causal event or the noncausal version. The infants stared longer at the noncausal event, thus supporting Leslie's contention that they were sensitive to causality as it is manifested in these simplified circumstances, even though the event did not involve their own actions.

Other research calls into question Leslie's claim that understanding cause-effect relations is innate. For example, Lisa Oakes and Leslie Cohen (1990) used a procedure that was similar to Leslie's but presented the infants with real objects (as opposed to simple squares). In this version of the experiment, 6-month-olds appeared overwhelmed by the complexity of the stimuli and no longer could respond on the basis of causality. Such results support the idea that the infants are learning to infer causality and will display such knowledge only under properly arranged circumstances (Cohen, Chaput, & Cashon, 2002)—yet another reminder of the competence–performance debate so central to research on infant cognition.

Categorizing

Imagine 2-year-old Sylvie playing "bedtime" with her toys. She has put her Dora doll under a cover on the table, along with Bitty Kitty and Pooh Bear. Excluded from the makeshift bed, however, are several other toys that she had just been playing with, among them Dora's truck and Pooh Bear's honey pot. Sylvie has

Figure 5.22 When 3-month-olds are shown a sequence of pictures of cats, they are surprised at the presence of a dog in the sequence, indicating that they are sensitive to the category of cats.

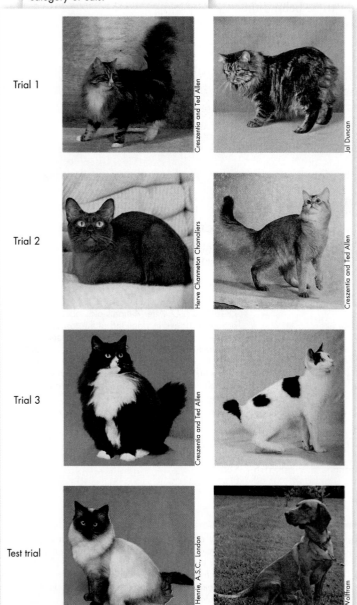

Trial 1

Trial 2

Trial 3

Test trial

Creszentia and Ted Allen
Jal Duncan
Herve Chamelon Chamaliers
Creszentia and Ted Allen
Creszentia and Ted Allen
Marc Henrie, A.S.C., London
Karl Wolfframm

appropriately categorized her toys into two groups: those that need sleep and those that do not.

The process of categorizing—that is, of seeing similarities in different objects and events—is an essential feature of how we make sense of the world. Without the ability to categorize, we would need to learn about each new detail of our experience from scratch. We would not be able to take knowledge gained in one situation and apply it to another, similar situation, and this would make learning about the world a very slow and inefficient process. The adults of our species, however, are incredibly adept at categorization. Developmentalists are interested in when this ability emerges and how it changes over time.

Infants display an ability to form categories remarkably early in life. For example, if 3-month-olds are shown a series of pairs of pictures of different cats and then shown a pair consisting of a picture of a cat and a picture of a dog, the infants will look longer at the picture of the dog than they will at the picture of the new cat (Figure 5.22). This preferential looking indicates that the infants had formed a category for what they had been viewing and that a dog did not fit it (Quinn, Eimas, & Rosenkrantz, 1993; Quinn & Eimas, 1996). Brain studies have shown that when young babies form categories, the electrical activity of their brains changes in ways that suggest that basic neurological processes have evolved that support early categorizing abilities (Quinn, Westerland, & Nelson, 2006).

Most research on categorization, however, has been conducted with somewhat older infants and has focused on the bases infants use to form categories. Do they rely primarily on perceptual similarities—that is, on similarities in how objects look, feel, or sound—or are they able to categorize according to more abstract, conceptual features, such as how objects function or behave? The framing of this question may remind you of the general theme that has permeated much of our discussion of infant intelligence: the extent to which an infant's knowledge is primarily perceptual and sensorimotor in nature, and the extent to which it is also abstract and conceptual.

In an early effort to identify the features babies use when they categorize, Jean Mandler and Laraine McDonough (1993) found that 7-month-olds, but not 9- to 11-month-olds, responded to toy birds and toy airplanes as if they were members of the same category. The 9- to 11-month-olds responded to toy birds and airplanes as members of different categories despite the perceptual similarities—the toy birds all had outstretched wings and looked like the airplanes (Figure 5.23). Although this research suggests a developmental shift from infants' reliance on perceptual cues to an ability to use more general object features, it nevertheless challenges Piaget's view that infant intelligence is of a sensorimotor nature until 18 or so months of age.

Further evidence that infants form conceptual categories before the 1st year comes from an intriguing study of "generalized imitation" (Mandler & McDonough, 1996; Mandler, 2004). In this study, 9- and 11-month-old babies observed an adult model performing an action that would be appropriate either for animals as a category or for vehicles as a category—for example, giving a toy dog a drink from a cup or turning a key in a toy car door (Figure 5.24). Then, in the imitation phase, either the dog or the car was put away and the infants were presented with a different item that was placed next to the prop (the cup or the key).

This baby is learning to categorize objects according to their shapes.

FIGURE 5.23 Seven-month-old babies respond to plastic toy birds and airplanes, which are perceptually similar, as if they were members of the same category. Babies 9 to 11 months old respond to them as members of different categories, despite their perceptual similarity.

FIGURE 5.24 Illustrating infants' ability to categorize objects is the finding that when 7- to 11-month-olds (a) observe an adult give a toy dog a drink, they (b) will not imitate the action with a toy truck but (c) will imitate the adult's action with a toy bunny.

Sometimes the new item was from the same category as the previous one (a bunny was placed next to the cup or a truck was placed next to the key); sometimes it was from the other category (the bunny was placed next to the key or the truck was placed next to the cup). The researchers found that the babies would give a drink to the bunny but not to the truck, and likewise would use the key with the truck but not with the bunny. That is, while the babies were likely to imitate the action with the appropriate object, they rarely performed the action on the item from the incorrect category.

There is still uncertainty among developmentalists about the basis for the changes in categorization observed across infancy. Some researchers believe that perceptual similarity remains fundamental to category formation for the entire period. Thus, older infants show improved categorization skills because their sensory systems are more developed and they have greater experience, making them sensitive to more subtle cues (Quinn, 2002). Others believe that before the end of the 1st year, infants become capable of forming genuine conceptual categories—categories based on such meaningful features as what things do and how they come to be the way they are—in addition to perceptual categories (Mandler, 2004). Taking an information-processing approach, Leslie Cohen and his colleagues have argued that young infants form categories on the basis of specific object features or parts (for example, objects go together because they have wings) but that at around 10 months of age they become capable of processing *relations* among features (objects with wings and feathers are one category; objects with wings and no feathers are another) (Cohen & Cashon, 2006).

Although developmentalists are continuing to test different theories about how infants form categories, it is clear that by the end of infancy, babies are able to use them to organize their own behavior in relation to their environments, as did Sylvie when she put some of her toys to bed but not others.

▲ APPLY :: CONNECT :: DISCUSS

Design an experiment to test whether infants understand the difference between "natural" objects (trees, fish, people, etc.), and "artificial" objects (cars, watches, buildings, etc.).

The Growth of Attention and Memory

Although we have not yet discussed it specifically, a baby's ability to pay attention to, and remember, specific aspects of the environment clearly plays an important role in many of the developments described above. Obviously, before babies can figure out whether an object with wings has feathers or a different surface, they first need to attend to the object. And it would be impossible for babies to understand cause–effect relationships if, as they were watching some effect, they could not remember the earlier event that caused it.

Developing Attention

The process of attention appears to involve four distinct phases that can be distinguished by changes in infants' heart rates (Figure 5.25) (Courage, Reynolds, & Richards, 2006).

Phase I: Stimulus-Detection Reflex. The stimulus-detection reflex signals the baby's initial awareness of some change in the environment. In this phase (not labeled in the figure), there is a very brief slowing and then quickening of the heart rate.

Phase II: Stimulus Orienting. During the second phase, the baby's attention becomes fixed on the stimulus. As you can see in the figure, the heart rate slows considerably during this period.

Phase III: Sustained Attention. In the third phase, the heart rate remains slow as the baby cognitively processes the stimulus. The baby's entire body may become still, and it is relatively more difficult to distract the baby with a new stimulus (Reynolds & Richards, 2007). Sustained attention is believed to be a voluntary state; that is, the baby purposefully controls and focuses his or her attention on the stimulus. At this point, the baby is truly *paying attention.*

Phase IV: Attention Termination. In this phase, the baby is still looking at the object but is no longer processing its information (it takes a moment to break contact with the stimulus). The heart rate begins to return to prestimulus levels.

From the descriptions of these phases, you can imagine why developmentalists are particularly interested in the development of sustained attention. It is during the attention phase that babies actively learn about and remember their experiences. At 3 months of age, babies can sustain their attention only for periods of 5 to 10 seconds. Certainly, one of the most significant developments in the first 2 years is infants' increasing ability to focus their attention in a sustained way.

In addition to getting better at focusing their attention over the course of the first 2 years, babies get faster at processing information about the targets of their attention. Show 1-year-olds a picture of a bunny and they are likely to stare with rapt attention for a long period of time. Show the same picture to 2-year-olds and they may look at it for a few seconds and be done with it. They have processed it, recognized it, and are ready to turn their attention elsewhere. Clearly, it is not the case that 1-year-olds have better sustained attention than the 2-year-olds. Rather, 1-year-olds need more time to process the information. Indeed, research indicates that with increasing age, there is a decrease in the amount of time that babies spend looking at simple patterns or figures (Figure 5.26a). It has even been found that 6-month-olds who spend relatively long periods of time looking at simple patterns tend to have lower IQs when they are tested at the age

FIGURE 5.25 Attention is a process involving four phases that can be distinguished by changes in the infant's heart rate. As shown here, the heart rate drops considerably when the infant is engaged in sustained attention. (From Courage, Reynolds, & Richards, 2006)

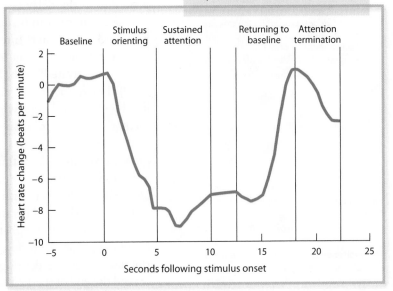

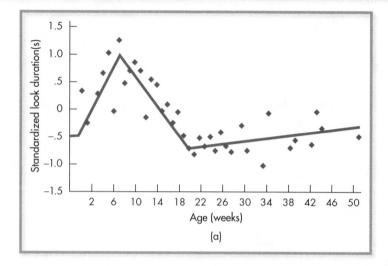

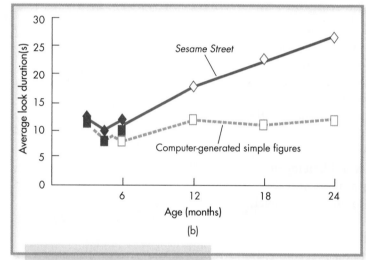

FIGURE 5.26 (a) Between 6 and 22 weeks of age, there is a significant decline in the amount of time that infants will look at simple geometric figures. (b) Between 6 and 24 months of age, however, there is a significant increase in the amount of time that infants will look at complex stimuli, such as *Sesame Street* videotapes, while the amount of time they spend looking at simple figures remains stable. (From Rose, Feldman, & Jankowski, 2004.)

implicit memory The type of memory that is used to recognize objects and events that have been previously experienced.

explicit memory The type of memory that is used to recall, without any clear reminder, absent objects and events.

of 11 (Rose, Feldman, & Jankowski, 2004, 2009). Among other things, all of this means that care must be taken not to confuse *visual attention* (how the baby processes information) with *visual fixation* (the amount of time the baby looks at an object).

While infants' attention to simple visual displays decreases after the first few months of life, attention to complex stimuli increases (Rose, Feldmen, & Jankowski, 2009). Figure 5.26b illustrates the amount of time babies of different ages, ranging from 6 to 24 months, looked at two different videotapes. One videotape showed a computer-generated display of simple geometric patterns. The other showed a segment from *Sesame Street*. The time spent watching the computer-generated film was about the same for all babies, whereas the time spent watching the *Sesame Street* segment increased with age.

As we mentioned earlier, the development of attention, especially focused, sustained attention, is of enormous significance to the infant's emerging ability to remember past events and learn about the environment, a topic that we address next.

Developing Memory

Carolyn Rovee-Collier and her colleagues have demonstrated that infants' memory increases rapidly during the 1st year of life (Rovee-Collier & Giles, 2010). Using the operant-conditioning procedure described in Chapter 4 (p. 147), the researchers trained babies between ages 2 and 6 months of age to kick in order to make an overhead mobile move. (One of the infants' ankles, you will recall, was connected to the mobile by a ribbon; Figure 5.27.) Following the training, the babies were returned to the lab after delays of various durations to see if they remembered how to make the mobile move. The researchers found that 2-month-olds started kicking immediately following a 24-hour delay but seemed to forget the procedure if the delay lasted 3 days. Memory for the task was better in 3-month-olds and better yet in 6-month-olds, who remembered their training 2 weeks later but not 3 weeks later. Interestingly, if infants are permitted to observe the experimenter pulling the string to shake the mobile, their apparently forgotten memories can be "reactivated" (Joh, Sweeney, & Rovee-Collier, 2002; Rovee-Collier et al., 1999). However, as the researchers point out, such reactivation is significantly limited by the infant's age, with younger babies needing more exposure to the experimenter's "reminder" than do older babies.

In an extension of this research, infants from 6 to 18 months of age learned to press a lever to make a train move. As shown in Figure 5.28, with age there was a steady increase in the number of days that the infants could remember the train task, just as there was with the mobile task (Hartshorn et al., 1998).

Rovee-Collier and her colleagues believe that the improvement in infant memory is a continuous process that does not involve any new principles of learning or remembering (Joh, Sweeney, & Rovee-Collier, 2002; Rovee-Collier & Giles, 2010). But just as there are developmentalists who believe that categorization skills expand at around the end of the 1st year to include conceptual categories, so there are those who believe that a qualitative shift in memory occurs at the same time. According to this view, young infants move from relying on **implicit memory**, which allows them to *recognize* what they have experienced before, to acquiring the ability to use **explicit memory**, which allows them to *recall* ("call to mind") absent objects and events without any clear reminder (Bauer et al., 2003; Mandler, 1998).

Explicit, or recall, memory is considered an especially important cognitive achievement because it seems to require the conscious generation of a mental representation for something that is not present to the senses. However, as with perceptual and conceptual categories, the task of distinguishing between implicit and explicit remembering in young infants is a tricky one. What is clear in any case is that developments in memory and attention are intertwined with the other cognitive achievements of the baby's first 2 years.

⏶ APPLY :: CONNECT :: DISCUSS

In what ways might the changes in the brain discussed on pp. 165–168 contribute to the development of attention and memory during infancy?

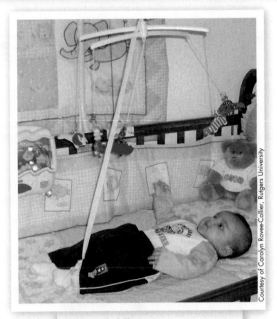

FIGURE 5.27 Because of the ribbon tied between his ankle and the mobile overhead, this 3-month-old will learn that kicking causes the mobile to move. Research indicates that he is likely to remember what he learned about the mobile for several days. However, he will probably be at least 6 months old before he can remember the task for 2 or more weeks.

Implications

It is truly astonishing that babies undergo such enormous physical and cognitive changes in such a brief period of time. Equally amazing are the implications that these changes have for future development. Already, as a consequence of synaptogenesis and selective pruning, the baby's neural pathways are taking shape according to both species-universal and individual experiences. Whereas the crucial biological events during the newborn period (Chapter 4) involve changes in the connections between the sensory cortex of the brain and the brain stem, the remaining months of infancy are marked by increased myelination of the prefrontal cortex, which is associated with voluntary behavior and language, and myelination of pathways connecting different areas of the brain, which allows the brain to work in a more integrated way. Equally important are increases in height and weight, increases in the strength of muscles and bones, and a change in body proportion that shifts the baby's center of gravity—all of which are necessary to support developing motor skills.

As we noted earlier, motor development appears to orchestrate the reorganization of many other functions that have been developing in parallel during infancy. For one thing, the acquisition of new motor skills leads infants to discover many properties of objects in their immediate environment. They become capable of reaching for objects efficiently and picking them up, feeling them, tasting them, moving around them, carrying them, and using them for various purposes of their own. Their growing autonomy and ability to explore the world advances further as gross motor skills emerge, especially the uniquely human form of locomotion—walking.

These experiences would not amount to much, however, if babies were not able to represent them mentally or to remember them. The capacity to represent objects, people, events, and experiences mentally exerts a powerful influence on other areas of development that we explore in detail in later chapters, including symbolic play, imitation, and language. Indeed, as you will learn in later chapters, mental representation plays a pivotal role in how children make use of the material and symbolic tools of their culture. In the next chapter, we address the social and emotional domains of infancy and how they enter into the biocultural equation of children's development.

FIGURE 5.28 The number of weeks that infants can remember the train and mobile tasks climbs steadily and continuously between 2 and 18 months of age. (From Hartshorn et al., 1998.)

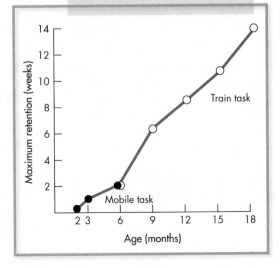

SUMMARY

Physical Growth

- Height and weight increase rapidly throughout infancy, especially during the 1st year. Body proportions shift, too, with the head coming to account for relatively less of the infant's length, and the legs, for relatively more. Soft bones gradually ossify, and muscle mass increases. Although boys tend to be larger than girls, girls tend to develop more quickly.

Brain Development

- Increased myelination of axons, along with other changes, leads to substantial development of the cerebral cortex, including the prefrontal and language-related areas, and to greater synchrony among the brain areas. These changes appear vital to the emergence in late infancy of more systematic problem solving, voluntary control of behavior, and the acquisition of language. By late infancy, most of the brain structures that will support adult behavior are present.

- As shown by studies of Romanian orphans who were adopted, prolonged deprivation in infancy leads to ongoing impairments in intellectual functioning. Because the brain undergoes considerable development between 6 and 24 months of age, lack of experiences during this sensitive period appears to affect both experience-expectant and experience-dependent brain development.

Motor Development

- Made possible by physical changes, the development of fine and gross motor skills enables infants to reduce their dependence on caregivers to get around and allows them to increasingly explore their environment.

- As the movements of their hands and fingers become better coordinated during the 1st year, infants perfect their reaching and grasping. With continuing increases in coordination of fine motor movements, by age 2 infants can do much in the way of feeding and dressing themselves and can turn book pages, cut paper, string beads, and stack blocks.

- Progress in locomotion leads to the emergence of crawling by 8 to 9 months of age, at which time wariness of heights appears. Walking begins at around 1 year, and is made possible by the development of component motor skills and by practice. Studies in different cultures reveal that practice or lack of it can affect the age at which infants reach motor milestones.

- Cultural factors affect the timing of learning to control elimination, but, although young infants can learn to eliminate when placed on the potty, for maturational reasons, gaining overnight control of bowel and bladder functions generally is not possible before age 3½.

Cognitive Development: The Great Debate

- For some developmentalists, including Piaget, young infants are limited to sensorimotor intelligence until about 18 months of age, when they become capable of representational thinking—thinking that is truly conceptual.

- For other developmentalists, very early in development, if not from birth, infants are capable of representing and understanding the world conceptually. A rudimentary conceptual system develops separately from, although in close association with, the sensorimotor system.

- In Piaget's stage of sensorimotor development, infants acquire knowledge exclusively through motor actions directed at their immediate environment and guided by their senses.

- Following the first two of Piaget's substages, in which infants learn to control reflexes and then to modify and repeat actions involving their bodies, infants move through four additional sensorimotor substages:

  - In substage 3, infants 4 to 8 months of age become capable of secondary circular reactions, repeating actions that involve objects, not simply those that involve their own body.

  - In substage 4, at 8 to 12 months of age, infants begin to display intentionality, engaging in goal-directed behavior.

  - In substage 5, the stage of tertiary circular reactions, infants 12 to 18 months of age deliberately vary their actions, thus experimenting in order to explore the world.

  - In substage 6, which occurs between 18 and 24 months of age, infants begin to base their actions on representations. The ability to represent mentally is crucial to problem solving, symbolic play, deferred imitation, and the use of language.

- The sequence and timing of the behaviors associated with Piaget's sensorimotor stages have been replicated with infants in a wide range of societies. However, critics of Piaget argue that young infants have representational competence that traditional Piagetian tests do not enable them to reveal.

Conceptual Development

- For Piaget, object permanence—the understanding that objects continue to exist when out of sight—emerges only gradually, beginning at about 8 months. Thus, 8- to 12-month-olds continue to search for an object in a location where they discovered it even when they have then seen it rehidden in a different location. Piaget claimed that these infants still did not have true representations. Other developmentalists have argued that the infants' behavior reflects not a lack of representational competence but performance problems—specifically, memory limitations or a tendency to perseverate, repeating the same movement or the same successful strategy.

- Using the violation-of-expectations method, in which babies are habituated to an event and then presented with possible and impossible variants, researchers have obtained results suggesting that infants as young as 2½ months old are capable of representations.

- According to the dynamic systems approach, cognitive development in infancy involves not a shift from sensorimotor to conceptual intelligence but the growing abilities to coordinate all the various systems involved in sensorimotor and conceptual intelligence.

- The formation of representations may depend heavily on experience. In experiments, infants' typical preference for a novel object over a familiar object is reversed when the room is darkened, perhaps because experience with an object leads to a stronger representation of it.

- Experiments using the violation-of-expectations method suggest that infants as young as 3 months of age have an initial grasp of various physical laws concerning the behavior of objects, such as the law of gravity.

- Other experiments using simplified tests suggest that, contrary to Piaget's view, young infants may be capable of understanding basic numbers and cause–effect relationships. Of particular interest is infants' abilities to categorize, evident as early as 3 months of age. Developmentalists are uncertain whether changes in categorization abilities during infancy simply reflect improved perceptual abilities or signal a change from categorization based only on perceptual features to categorization that is also conceptually based.

The Growth of Attention and Memory

- Developments in attention and memory are crucial to all the other cognitive changes of infancy.

- Infants are increasingly able to sustain their attention; in addition, they are increasingly fast at processing information about the targets of their attention. These changes are reflected in experiments showing that attention to simple visual displays decreases after the first few months but attention to complex stimuli increases.

- Memory increases rapidly during the 1st year, as shown by the increase in the length of time over which infants are able to remember procedures such as how to make a mobile move. Some developmentalists believe that the improvement may involve simply a continuous process of memory growth; others believe that it may reflect a shift from reliance on implicit memory (recognizing what has been experienced before) to explicit memory (recalling absent objects and events without a reminder). Explicit memory is an important cognitive achievement because it requires generating a mental representation for something not present to the senses.

Implications

- Infancy is a brief period of enormous physical and cognitive changes with enormous implications for development in other domains and for future development. Brain development and increases in height and weight support developing motor skills, which help make the cognitive changes possible. Among cognitive changes crucial to development are the growing capacity to represent mentally and to remember.

Key Terms

prefrontal area, p. 165
fine motor skills, p. 168
gross motor skills, p. 168
locomotion, p. 171
social referencing, p. 173
secondary circular reactions, p. 179

intentionality, p. 179
object permanence, p. 179
tertiary circular reactions, p. 179
representations, p. 180
symbolic play, p. 180
deferred imitation, p. 180

A-not-B error, p. 183
violation-of-expectations method, p. 185
implicit memory, p. 195
explicit memory, p. 195

CHAPTER

6

Social and Emotional Development in Infancy

The Nature of Infant Emotions and Emotional Expressions

Theories of Emotional Development

Infant Emotions and Social Life

Intersubjectivity and the Brain

The Infant–Caregiver Emotional Relationship

Explanations of Attachment

Phases of Attachment

Patterns of Attachment

The Causes of Variations in Patterns of Attachment

Attachment Patterns and Later Development

The Changing Nature of Communication

Social Referencing

Following a Caregiver's Signs of Interest

The Beginnings of Language Comprehension and Speech

A Sense of Self

Self-Recognition

The Self as Agent

The Emergence of Self-Conscious Emotions

Developing Trust and Autonomy

Implications

In a creaky bus bumping along the highway from the airport to the city of Changsha, China, Jeff and Christine take in the passing scenes of marshy rice paddies and smokestacks. They want to remember this landscape so they can describe it someday to their 2-year-old daughter, Jin Yu, whom they are about to meet for the first time. They arrive at a hotel with 25 other new parents from America, all waiting to receive their children. One by one the children are handed over. And one by one they wail in protest. But not Jin Yu. And this disturbs Jeff and Christine. In preparing for this life-altering moment, they learned that such tears are a sign that the child has formed attachments to his or her orphanage caregivers and is therefore capable of forming new attachments to the adoptive parents. Jeff and Christine take Jin Yu to their hotel room, where she sits on the bed, silent and lethargic. They talk to her in soothing tones, stroke her, smile, and reassure her that all is well. But Jin Yu seems untouched and is unresponsive. Jeff and Christine become increasingly concerned. How long has she been like this—so socially and emotionally disconnected? Is her condition temporary or permanent? Then Jeff and Christine discover a ragged scar running across her head. They are frightened—for Jin Yu and for themselves. But she is their daughter now, and committed to this fact, they brace themselves for the unknowable. Back in the United States, doctors relieve their fears; the scar was probably a wound that became infected, but there is no evidence of permanent damage. Most reassuring, however, is Jin Yu's own rapid development. Within 6 months, she has grown 5 inches and gained 5 pounds, and she is taking an avid interest and obvious joy in her toys and playmates. If she becomes frustrated because her parents won't let her handle a cup of hot coffee or a steak knife, she makes an angry face, slams down her hand, and scolds them in Chinese. She has begun speaking in English, too. She requests, "Fries, please," and exclaims, "All done!" And she hums little melodies to herself. Jeff and Christine take great comfort in knowing that someone took time to sing to their baby. Perhaps a caregiver they would never know gave them and Jin Yu the foundation for building loving relationships in their new life together.

(Adapted from Gammage, 2003.)

F aced with Jin Yu's initial lack of social and emotional responsiveness, Jeff and Christine were rightly distraught. The ability to respond to others socially and emotionally is crucial to human development because it draws children into the lives of others—and into contact with their knowledge and values, goals and desires, and cultural activities and practices (Trevarthen & Reddy, 2007). Although we cannot be sure why Jin Yu was so unresponsive and "disconnected" at first, it is clear that within months of her adoption, she developed a rich emotional life that included feelings such as interest, joy, anger, and frustration. It is equally clear that she communicated these feelings effectively to others through gesture, facial expression, and language. She had become actively engaged in a social and emotional world that is, most importantly, *shared*.

Jeff, holding Jin Yu, age 6, and Christine, holding their other adopted daughter, Zhao, age 4.

This chapter explores fundamental developments in the social and emotional lives of babies. We will discuss the range of infants' emotions and their origins, as well as infants' emotional attachments to caregivers and the ways in which those attachments can be affected by experience. We will also examine the changing nature of communication—how babies share their emotions, needs, and interests with others and become interactive partners in an ever-widening sphere of social life. As you will see, the fundamental social and emotional developments of the first 2 years are nurtured and shaped by interacting biological and cultural processes. Thus, some of these developments are universal and deeply rooted in the evolution of our species, and others are specific to the local contexts of children's development.

The Nature of Infant Emotions and Emotional Expressions

When in everyday conversation we talk about emotions, we are usually referring to the feelings aroused by an experience—feelings of happiness and excitement on unexpectedly winning a prize, of sadness on saying good-bye to a loved one whom we will not see for some time, of frustration and anger on being prevented from achieving a goal. But when we think deeply about what it is like to truly *feel* an emotion, it becomes clear that we are dealing with a process of enormous complexity. Our heart pounds; we catch our breath; our palms sweat; we shout or moan; we run away from or rush toward the source of our arousal. Recognizing the complexity of emotion, developmentalists typically define it in terms of the following features (Saarni, Campos, Camras, & Witherington, 2006):

- *A physiological aspect.* Emotions are accompanied by identifiable physiological reactions such as changes in heart rate, breathing, and hormonal functioning.

- *A communicative function.* Emotions communicate our internal feeling states to others through facial expressions, vocalizations, and other distinctive forms of behavior.

- *A cognitive aspect.* The emotions we feel depend on how we appraise what is happening to us.

- *An action aspect.* Emotions are a source of action. When something causes joy, for example, we laugh or cry or do both at once. When we are scared, we withdraw.

Despite the ease with which we express and share our feelings, developmentalists recognize that emotions are remarkably complex.

Technically speaking then, **emotion** can be defined as a feeling state that involves distinctive physiological responses and cognitive evaluations that motivate action (Saarni et al., 2006). But even this technically comprehensive definition of emotion fails to capture the complexity of the phenomenon fully. Emotions, for example, can emerge slowly, as when a feeling of pleasure blossoms into full-blown elation, or they can emerge rapidly, as in an explosive rage. Emotions can vary in their intensity, as indicated by the different smiles shown in Figure 6.1. Sometimes emotions mix together, as in the excitement and apprehension that many parents feel when their children go off to college. Complicating things further is the fact that people have ways of controlling the emergence and intensity of their own and others' emotions. When an older brother tries to distract his fussy baby sister with a toy, he is attempting to control

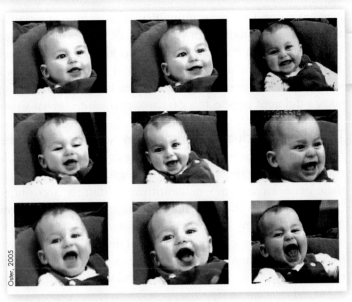

FIGURE 6.1 Various emotional intensities are clearly apparent in the different smiles shown by this baby.

Oster, 2005

her emotions; when the baby sister soothes herself by sucking on her pacifier, she is controlling her own emotions, although probably not intentionally. **Emotion regulation** is the term used by developmentalists to describe how people act to modulate and control their emotions. In the sections below, we explore developmental changes in infants' emotions, their expression, and how they are regulated.

Theories of Emotional Development

Most developmentalists agree that there are universal **basic emotions**—joy, fear, anger, surprise, sadness, and disgust—that are expressed in similar ways in all cultures. For example, adults from vastly different cultures, including isolated, pre-literate cultures, generally agree on which facial expressions represent happiness, sadness, anger, and disgust. In addition, research finds that, across cultures, babies' smiles, expressions of distaste, and cry faces are comparable to those of adults (Camras et al., 2007).

Taken together, such findings are considered strong evidence for the widely held belief that the basic emotions represent universal adaptive responses that are generated by, and contribute to, the biological and cultural evolution of our species (Panksepp, 2010). From a biological perspective, the basic emotions and their expression both protect children from potential sources of danger and ensure that their basic needs are met, largely by eliciting care and protection. From a cultural perspective, these emotions facilitate social connections to family and community members—connections that are vital to learning about the world and acquiring cultural knowledge and values (Trevarthen, 2009; Tronick & Reck, 2009). Indeed, according to Vygotsky's sociocultural theory, introduced in Chapter 1 (pp. 21–22), all complex forms of reasoning and understanding develop as a consequence of the connections formed between individuals (1978).

Although there is consensus on the biological and cultural significance of human emotions generally, developmentalists disagree on several fundamental issues regarding the nature of emotion and its development during infancy. One controversy concerns whether infants' emotions are, from early on, similar to those of adults, or whether they become increasingly adultlike over time. In other words, do infants, like adults, experience distinct emotions such as joy, sorrow, fear, anger, and so on, or does the capacity to feel these specific emotions emerge in the course of infancy and childhood? The second controversy concerns the source of

emotion A feeling state that involves distinctive physiological reactions and cognitive evaluations, and motivates action.

emotion regulation Ways of acting to modulate and control emotions.

basic emotions Joy, fear, anger, surprise, sadness, disgust—universal emotions, expressed similarly in all cultures and present at birth or in the early months.

theory of gradual differentiation The view that infants are born only with general emotional reactions, which differentiate into basic emotions over the first 2 years.

differential emotions theory The view that basic emotions are innate and emerge in their adult form, either at birth or on a biologically determined timetable.

new emotions. That is, assuming that at least some emotions experienced by adults are not present from birth (shame, guilt, and pride are clear examples), do new emotions emerge from more global positive or negative feeling states, or do they emerge full-blown, without precursors, at specific periods of development? We will now consider three different views of early emotional development, each of which takes a different perspective on these two controversial issues.

Theory of Gradual Differentiation

According to the **theory of gradual differentiation**, infants are born with the capacity to express only general emotional reactions that are simply positive or negative. Over the course of the first 2 years, these general reactions—contentment or distress, according to one early theorist (Bridges, 1932)—gradually differentiate into the basic emotions described above. Note that this view emphasizes the *discontinuity* of emotional expression: A young baby's crying signals a general feeling of distress, whereas that of an older infant may be expressing sadness or anger (Sroufe et al., 2010). The theory of gradual differentiation held sway for many years until it was challenged by a new theory called *differential emotions theory*.

Differential Emotions Theory

Rejecting the view that distinct emotions gradually emerge from general emotional states, Carroll Izard and his colleagues proposed that the basic emotions are biologically innate and present at birth in essentially adultlike form (Izard et al., 2010). They called their theory **differential emotions theory** to highlight the idea that infants' early emotions represent a set of distinct emotions comparable to those experienced by adults. In support of their argument, they point to the cross-cultural studies described above, which find that people from widely different cultures use similar facial expressions to signal basic emotions, and to research suggesting that many infant facial expressions are similar to those of adults and can be fairly reliably identified as such by untrained adult observers (Figure 6.2; Izard et al., 1980). In this view, biology dictates the presence of distinct emotions at birth and the timing at which new, adultlike emotions such as guilt and shame emerge during infancy and childhood. Biology also underlies the increasing ability to regulate emotions; for example, emotion regulation is associated with prefrontal-cortex development, which, as you may recall from Chapter 5,

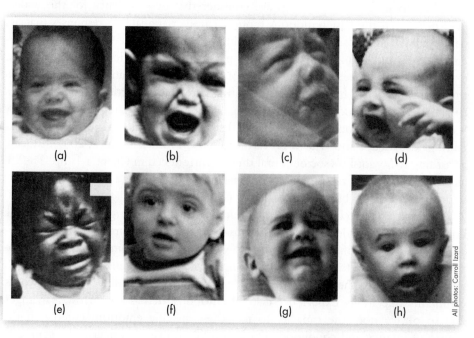

FIGURE 6.2 These images are from a video-taped recording of infants' facial expressions used by Carroll Izard and his colleagues to assess the identifiability of infants' basic emotions by having untrained adult observers classify the images according to their perceived emotional content. What emotion do you think each facial expression represents? The responses most of Izard's adult observers gave (Izard et al., 1980) are printed upside down below:

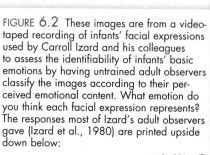

(a) joy; (b) anger; (c) sadness; (d) disgust; (e) distress/pain; (f) interest; (g) fear; (h) surprise.

All photos: Carroll Izard

is believed to affect a variety of voluntary behaviors (Panksepp & Smith-Pasqualini, 2005; Trevarthen, 2005).

Emotions as Ontogenetic Adaptations A third view of infants' emotions proposes that they are **ontogenetic adaptations**, meaning that they have evolved because they contribute to infants' survival and development. Therefore, developmentalists who take this view focus on the circumstances or situations in which babies experience and express different emotions (for example, on the sorts of situations that provoke feelings of fear or joy), and on the ways infants' emotional expressions affect their interactions with their caregivers (Oster, 2005). An illustrative example is the changing nature of the infant's smile.

During the first weeks of life, the corners of a baby's mouth often curl up in a facial expression that looks just like a smile. Most likely to occur when the infant is asleep or very drowsy, these early smiles are called *endogeneous smiles* because they seem to be associated with internal, physiological fluctuations rather than with external stimulation from the environment. However, between 1 and 2 months of age, infants begin to smile in response to mild perceptual stimulation, such as when a caregiver talks softly to them or lightly strokes their skin. Then, between 2 and 3 months of age, the infant's smile becomes truly social, both responding to and eliciting the smiles of others. At this point, parents report a new emotional quality in their relationship with their child. The significance of the emergence of the social smile as a marker of a new level of development is reflected in a special celebratory ritual traditionally practiced by the Navajo. When an infant first displays the smile,

> the baby's hands are held out straight by the mother, and some member of the family (usually a brother or a sister) puts a pinch of salt with bread and meat upon them. . . . The person who sees the baby smile first should give a present (with salt) to all members of the family. The father or mother will kill a sheep and distribute this among relatives along with a bit of salt for each piece. (Leighton & Kluckhohn, 1947/1969, p. 29)

According to the theory of emotions as ontogenetic adaptations, the changing nature of smiling during these early months of postnatal life demonstrates both continuities and discontinuities in infants' emotions, their origins, and the meanings they have for social interaction.

Infant Emotions and Social Life

> *His eyes locked onto hers for a silent and almost motionless instant, until the mother said "Hey!" opened her eyes wider, raised her eyebrows further, and tossed her head up and toward the infant. Almost simultaneously the baby's eyes widened, his head tilted up, his smile broadened. Now she said, "Well hello! . . . hello . . . heeelloooo!" so that her pitch rose and the "hellos" became longer and more stressed on each successive repetition. With each phrase the baby expressed more pleasure, and his body resonated almost like a balloon being pumped up. (From Stern, 1977, p. 3)*

We mentioned that infants' emotions play a key role in connecting infants to their social world. The coordination of movement and mood apparent in the interaction described above—the emotional expression of one partner eliciting similar responses from the other—indicates that the mother and baby are each able to recognize and share the emotional state of the other. Colwyn Trevarthen (1998) labeled this kind of well-organized, reciprocal social interaction **primary intersubjectivity**. (It is "primary" in the sense that it is direct face-to-face interaction whose focus is the interaction itself.) The importance of maintaining primary

ontogenetic adaptation Refers to a trait or behavior that has evolved because it contributes to survival and normal development; in one view, infant emotions are ontogenetic adaptations.

primary intersubjectivity Organized, reciprocal interaction between an infant and caregiver with the interaction itself as the focus.

This very young Congolese infant is demonstrating an endogeneous smile, which was probably a reaction to internal physiological fluctuations.

Around 2 months of age, babies begin to smile in response to the smiles of others. An example of such social smiling is illustrated by this Chinese infant.

intersubjectivity is nowhere more apparent than in circumstances in which it breaks down, as when interactions between the baby and caregiver are disorganized and out of synch. As we discuss below, the interruption of this synchronous, or coordinated, interaction can take place for a variety of reasons. Mothers who suffer from depression, for example, often have difficulty being emotionally responsive to their babies. But before we discuss such "naturally occurring" influences on primary intersubjectivity, let us first consider what has been found in laboratory settings, when developmentalists experimentally disrupt the emotional connection between babies and their interactive partners.

Manipulating Intersubjectivity in the Laboratory

Developmentalists have experimentally manipulated the synchrony of social interactions in two ways. One of these involves a procedure known as the *still-face method* (Tronick et al., 2005; Tronick, 2007). In this procedure, after a few minutes of normal synchronous interaction with her infant, the mother is cued to pose a neutral "still face" and to stop responding to the baby (Figure 6.3). The other way of disrupting synchrony is by *delayed transmission,* a method that involves the use of TV monitors (Murray & Trevarthen, 1986; Tremblay et al., 2005). In this method, the mother and baby interact naturally and synchronously but they are seeing and hearing each other on the monitors. Periodically, the experimenters make transmissions from the mother's monitor run several seconds behind the baby's, so that her responses are out of synch with the infant's behavior. In both the still-face and delayed-transmission methods, babies as young as 2 months of age react to the loss of synchrony by averting their gaze and ceasing to smile. Frequently, the babies become agitated and fussy. These negative emotional responses have been found in babies interacting with mothers, fathers, and even complete strangers in several countries, including the United States, Canada, France, and China (Kisilevsky et al., 1998; Mesman, van IJzendoorn, & Bakermans-Kranenburg, 2009).

Both photos: Edward Tronick

(a)

(b)

FIGURE 6.3 In the still-face method, after a few minutes of normal interaction (a), the mother is instructed to pose a "still face" (b) and stop responding to her baby. The baby shown here has become notably distressed, a typical reaction.

Maternal Depression: An Obstacle to Intersubjectivity

Disruptions in infant–caregiver synchrony, of course, are commonplace outside the lab: Caregivers can be distracted or otherwise busy; babies can be fussy or drowsy. Usually, these disruptions are fleeting, and synchrony is quickly restored. However, there are circumstances in which infant–caregiver interactions are routinely disorganized and out of synch. For example, compared with nondepressed mothers, those who suffer from depression may be less sensitive to their infants' emotional cues. In addition to missing opportunities to share emotions, they may "transfer" their unresponsiveness to their babies (Field et al., 2007a). Indeed, in the still-face procedure, infants of depressed mothers act quite differently than do those of nondepressed mothers (Field, 2010). In particular, although they will avert their gaze when their depressed mothers "still face" (as do infants of nondepressed mothers), they do not fuss and protest. Helene Tremblay and her colleagues believe this reaction suggests not that the babies are undisturbed by their mothers' lack of responsiveness but that they have learned over time to disengage from stressful, unresponsive interactions with their mother (Tremblay et al., 2005). Developmentalists speculate that many problems frequently observed in children of depressed mothers, such as anxiety and conduct disorders, are due to a history of disorganized and unresponsive emotional interactions (Pelaez et al., 2008).

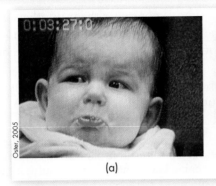
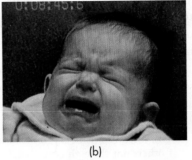

FIGURE 6.4 Pouting (a) may be one of the baby's first efforts to regulate distress by signaling to another that help is needed to avoid intense crying (b).

(a)　(b)

mirror neurons Specialized brain cells that fire when an individual sees or hears another perform an action, just as they would fire if the observing individual were performing the same action.

Emotion Regulation to Maintain Intersubjectivity

Based on evidence from the still-face and delayed-transmission methods, it seems that babies have a deeply ingrained need to be emotionally connected to others. Indeed, Harriet Oster (2005) has argued that this need for connection may account for a particularly interesting and very common infant behavior—pouting. Pouting is most common when the infant is just beginning to be upset. The pout is intriguing for two reasons. First, the facial muscles involved in pouting are diametrically opposed to the facial muscles that pull the mouth into a cry face (Figure 6.4), suggesting that pouting is not simply a component of crying. Second, pouting is typically "directed" at a social partner—that is, the baby's eyes tend to remain open and focused on the other individual. In crying, on the other hand, the eyes are usually shut, and the baby's behavior becomes too disorganized for coordinated social interaction. Oster believes that pouting reflects the baby's first efforts (not necessarily intentional) to regulate distress and thereby maintain the social contact that crying would otherwise disrupt. Advocating the position that infant emotions are ontogenetic adaptations, Oster suggests that pouting has evolved as part of an emotion-regulation process because it serves to interrupt intense crying (which can deplete oxygen and lead to physical exhaustion) and also signals the caregiver to provide comfort before the baby begins to cry uncontrollably (Oster, 2005, p. 284). Her account of the evolutionary origins of emotion regulation has its roots in Darwin's observation that some of our most characteristic facial expressions are related to crying and our efforts to control it (Darwin, 1872).

Intersubjectivity and the Brain

The growing emphasis on the evolutionary origins of emotions has led to an intensive effort to discover how the brain contributes to the experience, expression, and regulation of emotions in infancy. A breakthrough in this quest occurred in a laboratory in Italy on a hot summer day in 1991. A monkey with electrodes implanted in its brain to monitor its brain activity happened to observe a graduate student enter the lab with an ice cream cone. The monkey stared at him, and then the breakthrough moment occurred: When the student raised the cone to his lips, the monkey's brain monitor began registering as if the *monkey* were eating the cone. Subsequent research by Giacomo Rizzolatti, the neuroscientist who heads the laboratory, suggested that specialized brain cells, called **mirror neurons**, fire when an animal sees or hears another perform an action, just as they would if the animal itself were carrying out the action (Rizzolatti & Sinigaglia, 2010). Since then, neuroscientists have identified a variety of *mirror neuron systems* in the human brain that are much more complex and flexible than the systems found in monkeys and register the perceived intentions and emotions of others

Seeking evidence of mirror neurons, scientists compare how a person's brain reacts when the person has a particular experience to how it reacts when the person observes someone else having the experience. In the image shown here, the red color indicates brain activity in response to the individual feeling disgust; the blue indicates activity in response to observing another person express disgust; and the white shows areas of overlap between red and blue.

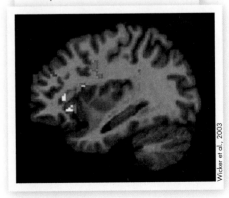

as if they were those of the person who is observing them in others. According to this evidence, we feel happy when those around us seem happy, and sad when others seem sad, because the emotional expressions of others activate our mirror neurons.

The discovery of mirror neurons has suggested a revolutionary way of understanding how infants connect emotionally with their social partners. As Rizzolatti argued,

> we are exquisitely social creatures. Our survival depends on understanding the actions, intentions, and emotions of others. Mirror neurons allow us to grasp the minds of others not through conceptual reasoning but through direct stimulation. By feeling, not by thinking. (Blakeslee, 2006)

Indeed, Andrew Meltzoff and Jean Decety have argued that mirror neurons very likely contribute to the remarkable ability of newborn infants—within 42 minutes of birth—to imitate certain facial actions or movements of others (Figure 6.5). Meltzoff and Decety consider such imitation in newborns to be innate, governed by brain processes that include mirror neurons (Meltzoff & Decety, 2003). Noting that adults across cultures play imitative games with their children, these researchers suggest that, over the period of infancy, imitation has a special role to play in establishing emotional connections between self and other. Young infants not only imitate the facial expressions of others; they also pay special attention when their own behaviors are imitated. If a young baby sticks out her tongue, for example, and an adult follows suit, the baby will act interested and generate more tongue protrusions. By 14 months of age, the neurological basis of imitation is moderated by other cognitive and social processes. At this age, infants derive a great deal of pleasure from being imitated by adults and, once the "game" is established, they will modify their behaviors to make the adult follow their lead (see also Asendorph, 2002; Nadel, 2002). Indeed, they will play such games gleefully for 20 minutes or more—a long time for a 14-month-old to do anything! Meltzoff and his colleagues argue that the joy babies derive from imitative games is a joint function of the emotional connection that comes from understanding that the adult is choosing to do "the same as me" and the sense of agency that comes from controlling the behavior of another (Meltzoff, 2007; Repacholi, Meltzoff, & Olsen, 2008). Developing a sense of agency is a key feature of an emerging sense of self, a topic we address more fully later in this chapter.

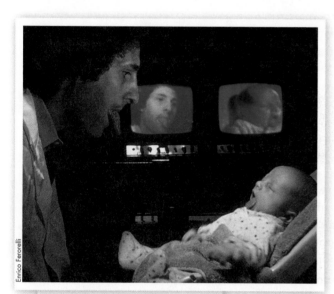

Enrico Ferorelli

FIGURE 6.5 This photo shows Andrew Meltzoff demonstrating that some newborns can imitate adult facial actions.

Although the concept of mirror neurons has inspired a great deal of research and theorizing about the relationship between brain and social behavior, it has also generated considerable controversy. Critics point out that research has yet to clearly identify specific cells as mirror neurons. Instead, the existence of mirror neurons has been inferred from brain imaging technologies that do not measure the specific activity of individual cells but, instead, measure the general activity of brain regions that include many types of neural cells. (This is why, as noted, these brain regions are referred to as "mirror neuron systems.")

All the research that we have considered in this section points to the importance of well-coordinated, responsive, and synchronous social interactions in establishing emotional connections between babies and their caregivers. In the next section, we examine in depth the development of the infant's first, and what many believe to be the infant's most significant, emotional relationship—that between the baby and his or her primary caregiver. As you will see, the interactive synchrony we have been discussing is considered an essential ingredient to the formation of this first relationship.

attachment The emotional bond that children form with their caregivers at about 7 to 9 months of age.

▲ APPLY :: CONNECT :: DISCUSS

Consider the nature of emotion regulation from a Vygotskian perspective (you may want to review p. 202) and discuss how maternal depression may complicate its development.

The Infant–Caregiver Emotional Relationship

During the second year of life, children find novelty and excitement everywhere. A walk to the corner drugstore with a 1½-year-old can take forever. Each step presents new and interesting sights to explore: A bottle cap lying by the edge of the sidewalk requires close examination; a pigeon waddling across a neighbor's lawn invites a detour; even the cracks in the sidewalk may prompt sitting down to take a closer look.

Things that attract babies and young children, however, may also cause them to be wary. Whizzing cars, strange people, and novel objects are often frightening as well as fascinating. There needs to be a balance between interest and fear as infants continue to explore and learn about the world. They cannot spend their entire lives in close proximity to their parents, but they cannot survive for long if they wander off on their own too soon.

Research with both monkey and human mothers and babies indicates how the balance between exploration and safety is created and maintained in ways that allow development to continue. A key element in this process is the emotional bond called **attachment** that develops between children and their caregivers sometime between the ages of 7 and 9 months (Ainsworth, 1982). Developmentalists generally cite four signs of attachment in babies and young children:

1. They seek to be near their primary caregivers. Before the age of 7 to 8 months, few babies plan and make organized attempts to achieve contact with their caregivers; after this age, babies often follow their caregivers closely, for example.

2. They show distress if separated from their caregivers. Before attachment begins, infants show little disturbance when their caregivers walk out of the room.

3. They are happy when they are reunited with the person to whom they are attached.

4. They orient their actions to the caregiver. When they are playing, for example, they watch the caregiver or listen for the caregiver's voice.

The special relationship with their primary caregivers that babies begin to display between 7 and 9 months of age undergoes significant changes during the remainder of infancy and beyond.

Explanations of Attachment

The fact that 7- to 9-month-old children everywhere begin to become upset when they are separated from their primary caregivers suggests that attachment is a universal feature of development (Simpson et al., 2007). This possibility has led to a

Many small children become strongly attached to a teddy bear, a blanket, or some other object. The British psychiatrist D. W. Winnicott (1971) has called such objects "transitional objects." They support children in their attempts to understand and deal with the reality that exists beyond their own bodies. The strong attachment this little girl feels for her teddy bear is written all over her smiling embrace.

Courtesy of Sheila Cole

lively debate about the evolutionary reasons for attachment, the causes of changes in attachment behaviors as children grow older, and the influence of the quality of attachment on children's later development.

Freud's Drive-Reduction Explanation

Early on, Sigmund Freud suggested that infants become attached to the people who satisfy their need for food. He believed that human beings, like other organisms, are motivated in large part by **biological drives**—the impulses of organisms to satisfy essential physiological needs, such as hunger or thirst, that create tension and a state of arousal in the organism. When such a need is satisfied, the drive is reduced as biological equilibrium is restored, and the organism experiences a sensation of pleasure. In this sense, pleasure-seeking is a basic principle of existence. With respect to attachment in particular, Freud asserted that "love has its origin in attachment to the satisfied need for nourishment" (1940/1964, p. 188). Thus, according to Freud, infants become attached to their mother because she is the one most likely to nourish them. The major problem with this explanation is that research with nonhuman primates has not substantiated Freud's notion that attachment is caused by the reduction of the hunger drive.

In one study that tested Freud's drive-reduction theory of attachment, Harry Harlow and his coworkers (Harlow, 1959) separated eight baby rhesus monkeys from their mothers a few hours after birth and placed each monkey in an individual cage with two inanimate "substitute mothers"—one made of wire, the other made of terry cloth (Figure 6.6). These substitute mothers were the monkeys' sole source of nutrition, with four babies receiving milk from the wire mothers, which had been specially equipped with milk-giving nipples, and four receiving milk from the terry cloth mothers, similarly equipped. The two types of substitute mothers were equally effective as sources of nutrition: All eight babies drank the same amount of milk and gained weight at the same rate.

FIGURE 6.6 This baby monkey spent most of its time clinging to the terry cloth substitute mother even when its nursing bottle was attached to a wire substitute mother nearby. This preference indicates that bodily contact and the comfort it gives are important in the formation of the infant's attachment to its mother.

Nevertheless, over the 165-day period that they lived with the substitute mothers, the baby monkeys showed a distinct preference for their terry cloth mother, regularly climbing on her and clinging to her. Even those who obtained their food from a wire mother would go to it only to feed and would then go back to cling to the terry cloth mother. From the perspective of drive-reduction theory, it made no sense that the four infant monkeys who received their food from a wire mother would prefer to spend their time with a terry cloth mother that might feel good but satisfied no apparent biological drive, such as hunger or thirst. Harlow (1959) concluded, "These results attest to the importance—possibly the overwhelming importance—of bodily contact and the immediate comfort it supplies in forming the infant's attachment to its mother" (p. 70).

John Bowlby's Ethological Explanation

John Bowlby's theory of attachment arose from his study of the mental health problems of British children who had been separated from their families during World War II and were cared for in institutions (Bowlby, 1969, 1973, 1980). Bowlby's observations of children in hospitals, nurseries, and orphanages, as well as his analyses of clinical interviews with psychologically troubled or delinquent adolescents and adults, indicated that when children are first separated from their mothers, they become frantic with fear. They cry, throw tantrums, and try to escape their surroundings. Then they go through a stage of despair and depression. If the separation continues and no new stable relationship is formed, these children seem to become indifferent to other people. Bowlby called this state of indifference **detachment**.

biological drives Impulses to attempt to satisfy essential physiological needs.

detachment For Bowlby, the state of indifference toward others experienced by children who have been separated from their caregiver for an extended time and have not formed a new stable relationship.

Martin Rogers/Tony Stone

In his attempt to explain the distress of young children when they are separated from their parents, Bowlby was particularly influenced by the work of ethologists, who emphasize a broad, evolutionary approach to understanding human behavior (see Chapter 1, pp. 23–25). Ethological studies of monkeys and apes revealed that infants of these species spend their initial weeks and months of postnatal life in almost continuous direct physical contact with their biological mothers. Bowlby noted that these primate infants consistently display several apparently instinctual responses that are also essential to human attachment: clinging, sucking, crying, and separation protest. After a few weeks or months (depending on the species of primate), infants begin to venture away from their mothers to explore their immediate physical and social environments, but they scurry back to the mother at the first signs of something unusual and potentially dangerous (Suomi, 1995). These primate behaviors, Bowlby hypothesized, are the evolutionary basis for the development of attachment in human babies as well.

In contrast to their conclusions regarding Freud's drive-reduction hypothesis, Harlow and his colleagues found strong support for Bowlby's evolutionary theory in their subsequent research with monkeys placed in cages with "substitute mothers" (Harlow & Harlow, 1969). Knowing that normal human and monkey babies run to their mothers for comfort when faced with an unfamiliar and frightening situation, the researchers created such a situation for the monkeys who had received milk from the wire mothers. They introduced into these monkeys' cages a mechanical teddy bear that marched forward while loudly beating a drum. The terrified babies fled to their terry cloth mother, not to the wire one, and began rubbing their body against hers (Figure 6.7). Soon their fears were calmed, and they turned to look at the bear with curiosity. Some even left the protection of the terry cloth mother to approach the object that had so terrified them only moments before.

Harlow concluded that soothing tactile sensations provide the baby with a sense of security that is more important to the formation of attachment than food. However, as Harlow's team discovered, although soothing tactile sensations appear to be necessary for healthy development, they are not sufficient. As these monkeys grew older, they showed signs of impaired development: They were either indifferent or abusive to other monkeys, and none of them could copulate normally. Noting that the substitute mother "cannot cradle the baby or communicate monkey sounds and gestures," the researchers concluded that the physical comfort provided by the cloth-covered mother in the monkey's infancy does not produce a normal adolescent or adult (Harlow & Harlow, 1962, p. 142). Applying the concept of *primary intersubjectivity* introduced earlier, it would seem that the absence of a sensitive and responsive social partner interfered with establishing the infant–mother emotional relationship considered so critical to later social and emotional development.

FIGURE 6.7 (a) This baby monkey clings to its terry cloth substitute mother when it is frightened by the approach of a mechanical teddy bear. (b) After gaining reassurance, the baby monkey looks at the strange intruder. The terry cloth mother, which does not provide nourishment, acts as a secure base, whereas the wire mother, which does provide nourishment, does not. This behavior contradicts drive-reduction theories of attachment.

Phases of Attachment

Bowlby (1969) believed that attachment normally develops through four broad phases during the first 2 years of life, eventually producing a balance between infants' need for the safety provided by the caregiver and their need to explore their world. As you read through the descriptions of each phase, notice how infants take on more responsibility for maintaining the balance of the attachment system as their capacities to act and interact become more sophisticated.

1. *The preattachment phase* (birth to age 6 weeks). In the first few weeks of life, infants remain in close contact with their caregivers and do not seem to get upset when left alone with an unfamiliar caregiver.

secure base Bowlby's term for the people whose presence provides the child with the security that allows him or her to make exploratory excursions.

separation anxiety The distress that babies show when the person to whom they are attached leaves.

internal working model A mental model that children construct as a result of their experiences with their caregivers and that they use to guide their interactions with their caregivers and others.

2. *The "attachment-in-the-making" phase* (ages 6 weeks to 6 to 8 months). Infants begin to respond differently to familiar and unfamiliar people, and by the time they are 6 or 7 months old, they start to show clear preferences for their familiar caregivers as well as signs of wariness when confronted with unfamiliar objects and people.

3. *The "clear-cut attachment" phase* (between ages 6 to 8 months and 18 to 24 months). During this period, the mother becomes a **secure base** from which babies make exploratory excursions and to which they come back every so often to renew contact before returning to their explorations. This is also the time when children display full-blown **separation anxiety**, becoming visibly upset when the mother or another caregiver leaves the room. Once this phase of attachment is reached, it regulates the physical and emotional relationship between children and those to whom they are attached. Whenever the distance between attachment figures and the child becomes too great, one or the other is likely to become upset and act to reduce that distance.

4. *The reciprocal relationship phase* (ages 18 to 24 months and older). As the child becomes more mobile and spends increasingly greater amounts of time away from the mother, the pair enter into a more reciprocal relationship, sharing responsibility for maintaining the equilibrium of the attachment system. When engaged in separate activities, the mother and the child will occasionally interrupt what they are doing to renew their contact. Among humans, this transitional phase lasts several years.

Once achieved, a firm attachment helps infants to retain feelings of security during the increasingly frequent and lengthy periods of separation from their caregivers. It is noteworthy that this phase develops at the same time that infants' powers of mental representation are on the rise (see Chapter 5). Bowlby believed that as a consequence of infants' growing symbolic capacities, parent–child attachment begins to serve as an **internal working model**, a mental model that children construct as a result of their experiences and that they use to guide their interactions with caregivers and others (we will address the implications of the model in detail below).

Patterns of Attachment

The maladaptive social behavior of Harlow's monkeys raised with inanimate substitute mothers, coupled with Bowlby's original observations of detachment in orphans, prompts a question: What kinds of interactions between primary caregivers and children provide the most effective basis for the development of healthy human social relations? (The following discussion is in terms of the mother as the attachment figure because most attachment research has focused on mother–infant pairs. Our use of the word "mother," however, is meant to refer to the person who "mothers" the child and to whom the child becomes attached [Bowlby, 1969].)

Because no two mother–infant pairs are alike and because their environments also vary enormously, developmentalists do not propose that one pattern of attachment is "right" for social development in all cases. Many believe, however, that it is possible to identify general patterns of mother–child interaction that are most conducive to positive development.

Research on such patterns of mother–child interaction has been greatly influenced by the work of Mary Ainsworth. On the basis of her observations of mother–infant pairs in Africa and the United States, she concluded that there are consistent, qualitatively distinct patterns in the ways mothers and infants relate to each other during the second and third years of infancy (Ainsworth, 1967, 1982). Most of the mother–infant pairs she observed seemed to have worked out a comfortable, secure relationship by the third year, but some of the relationships were characterized by persistent tension and difficulties in regulating joint activities.

To test the security of the mother–child relationship, Ainsworth designed a procedure called the **strange situation**. The procedure, which takes place in a toy-stocked laboratory playroom, consists of eight brief episodes, including ones in which the child is with the mother, is with the mother and a stranger, is left alone with the stranger, is left entirely alone, and is reunited with the mother after a separation. The basic purpose of this procedure is to observe how infants make use of the mother as a secure base from which to explore the playroom, how they respond to separation from the mother, and how they respond to a stranger. Ainsworth reasoned that different patterns of reactions would reflect different qualities of the attachment relationship.

On the basis of their findings, Ainsworth and her colleagues initially categorized infants' responses in the strange situation into three types that seemed to reflect the quality of the children's attachment: *secure, avoidant,* and *resistant* (Ainsworth et al., 1971, 1978). Later researchers added a fourth attachment type, *disorganized* (Main & Solomon, 1990). These types of attachment, or *attachment statuses,* and the responses they are associated with in the strange situation can be described as follows:

- **Secure attachment.** As long as the mother is present, securely attached children play comfortably with the toys in the playroom and react positively to the stranger. These children become visibly and vocally upset when their mother leaves. Although they may be consoled by the stranger, they clearly prefer the mother. When the mother reappears and they can climb into her arms, they quickly calm down and soon resume playing. This pattern of attachment, which reflects a healthy balance between wanting to be in close contact with the mother and wanting to explore the environment, is shown by about 65 percent of middle-class children in the United States.

- **Avoidant attachment.** During the time the mother and child are alone together in the playroom, avoidant infants are more or less indifferent to where their mother is sitting. They may or may not cry when she leaves the room. If they do become distressed, the stranger is likely to be as effective at comforting them as their mother is. When the mother returns, these children may turn or look away from her instead of going to her to reestablish contact. About 23 percent of middle-class children in the United States show this pattern of attachment.

- **Resistant attachment.** Resistant children have trouble from the start in the strange situation. They stay close to their mother rather than exploring the playroom and appear anxious even when she is near. They become very upset when the mother leaves, but they are not comforted by her return. Instead, they simultaneously seek renewed contact with the mother and resist her efforts to comfort them. They may demand to be picked up, cry angrily with arms outstretched, but then arch away and struggle to get free once the mother starts to pick them up. These children do not readily resume playing after the mother returns. Instead, they keep a wary eye on her. This attachment pattern is shown by about 12 percent of middle-class children in the United States.

strange situation A procedure designed to assess children's attachment on the basis of their use of their mother as a secure base for exploration, their reactions to being left alone with a stranger and then completely alone, and their response when they are reunited with their mother.

secure attachment A pattern of attachment in which children play comfortably and react positively to a stranger as long as their mother is present. They become upset when their mother leaves and are unlikely to be consoled by a stranger, but they calm down as soon as their mother reappears.

avoidant attachment The attachment pattern in which infants are indifferent to where their mother is sitting, may or may not cry when their mother leaves, are as likely to be comforted by strangers as by their mother, and are indifferent when their mother returns to the room.

resistant attachment The attachment pattern in which infants stay close to their mother and appear anxious even when their mother is near. They become very upset when their mother leaves but are not comforted by her return. They simultaneously seek renewed contact with their mother and resist their mother's efforts to comfort them.

Even a spoonful of cereal offered by a stranger may evoke wariness in young children.

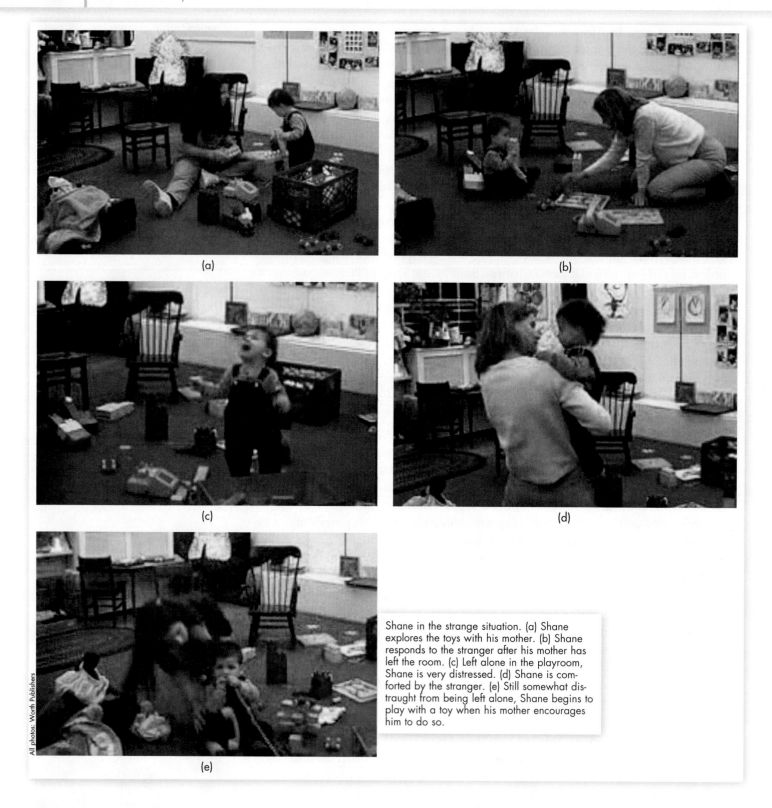

(a)

(b)

(c)

(d)

All photos: Worth Publishers

Shane in the strange situation. (a) Shane explores the toys with his mother. (b) Shane responds to the stranger after his mother has left the room. (c) Left alone in the playroom, Shane is very distressed. (d) Shane is comforted by the stranger. (e) Still somewhat distraught from being left alone, Shane begins to play with a toy when his mother encourages him to do so.

(e)

disorganized attachment The insecure attachment pattern in which infants seem to lack a coherent method for dealing with stress. They may behave in seemingly contradictory ways, such as screaming for their mother but moving away when she approaches. In extreme cases, they may seem dazed.

• **Disorganized attachment.** Children who fit this category seem to lack any coherent, organized method for dealing with the stress they experience. Some cry loudly while trying to climb onto the mother's lap; others may approach the mother while refusing to look at her; still others may stand at the door and scream while she is gone but move away from her silently when she returns. In some extreme cases, the children seem to be in a dazed state and refuse to move while in their mother's presence (Main & Solomon, 1990).

Thus, attachment may be secure or fall into one of three insecure patterns. Over the past several decades, developmentalists have conducted a good deal of research trying to understand the causes of these four basic patterns of attachment behavior (summarized in Shaver & Cassidy, 2008, and Waters & Waters, 2006). (Although most of this research has focused on the mother–infant relationship, other attachments that are important in children's lives have also been studied; see the box "Attachment to Fathers and Others.") Two major questions have dominated the study of attachment patterns. First, what are the causes of variations in the patterns of attachment? Second, do these variations have important consequences for later development?

This baby's attachment to his mother will be strongly affected by the role she plays in providing a secure base from which to explore the world.

Attachment to Fathers and Others

ALTHOUGH MOTHERS CONTINUE TO play the dominant role in rearing the family's children (Hossain et al., 2007), for a variety of social and economic reasons associated with the employment of mothers, fathers in many countries are becoming more deeply involved as parents. Fathers' sensitivity to their children's needs is increasingly recognized as important to children's well-being and attachment and emotional development (Davidov & Grusec, 2006; Ryan, Martin, & Brooks-Gunn, 2006; Stoltz, Barber, & Olsen, 2005; Hawkins et al., 2008; Lamb, 2010).

When fathers spend time with their children, they are most likely to play with them, but in some societies, they increasingly take a direct role in routine caretaking as well, a role for which they are by no means lacking in ability (Hawkins et al., 2008; Pleck & Masciadrelli, 2003). Fathers in the United States who have been observed feeding their infants, for example, respond sensitively to the babies' feeding rhythms and engage the babies in social episodes just as often as mothers do. Moreover, the infants of fathers who are judged to be sensitive caregivers are likely to be as securely attached to them as they are to their mothers (Howes, 1999), whereas infants of fathers with relatively poor parenting skills develop insecure patterns of attachment to them (Brown et al., 2010).

The specifics of family relationships play an important role in determining infant–father attachments. In nontraditional American families in which fathers have the role of primary caregiver, babies turn to their fathers, not their mothers, for comfort when they are under stress (Geiger, 1996). A similar pattern has been observed in a vastly different culture, that of the Aka pygmies, a hunter–gatherer group who live in central Africa. Aka men, women, and

Among the Aka of the Ituri forests, men play a major role in the care of their young children, promoting close emotional bonds.

children generally forage together, and Aka adult couples spend more time together than do couples in any other documented social group (Morelli et al., 1999). Hewlett (1992) reports that "Aka fathers are within an arms reach of their infants 47 percent of the day and are more likely than mothers to hug or soothe their infants while holding them than are mothers" (p. 238). In contrast with traditional patterns in the United States and many other countries, Aka fathers are more likely than their wives to pick up infants who crawl over and request to be held. On the basis of his findings, Hewlett concludes that when cultural patterns lead fathers to be closely involved in their children's upbringing,

attachment to the father occurs in the same way as attachment to the mother.

Of course, mothers and fathers are not the only people with whom infants form attachments. Babies also form attachments with nonparental caregivers, including siblings, day-care providers, teachers, and grandparents (Howes, 1999). An analysis that combined results from 40 separate studies showed that 42 percent of children were securely attached to their day-care providers. Secure attachments between children and day-care providers were more likely to develop in home-based care than in center-based care and were more prevalent among girls (Ahnert, Pinquart, & Lamb, 2006).

Many families in the United States, particularly those living close to or below the poverty line, have historically created caregiving systems that include networks of adults, such as grandparents and other kin, to whom children become attached (we will return to this topic in Chapter 10). And in some societies, such as that of the !Kung of the Kalahari Desert, babies begin to receive group care starting around the age of 1 year so that their mothers can resume their work as the society's food gatherers (Konner, 1977). In such circumstances, babies form strong attachments to many older children in the group in addition to adults.

The critical feature that seems to determine to whom infants become attached is whether the caregiving the child receives provides a safe base from which to explore the world and is a source of comfort. To the extent that such caregiving is restricted to the mother, she is the natural object of attachment. But when caregiving is distributed to include fathers and others, they also become effective attachment figures (Belsky & Pasco Fearon, 2008).

socioeconomic status (SES) An indicator of social class based on factors such as income, education, and occupation.

The Causes of Variations in Patterns of Attachment

Research on what leads to variations in patterns of attachment has focused on three types of contexts that influence the responsiveness and sensitivity of care received by infants: the family; the institutional context of orphanages, and the child-rearing patterns of the cultural group to which the mother and child belong.

The Family Context In her early studies of the antecedents of attachment, Mary Ainsworth used *ethological* methods (see Chapter 1, p. 23) to examine patterns of attachment in mother–infant pairs in Africa and the United States. Her repeated, detailed observations of mother–infant behavior throughout the first year of life indicated a link between attachment patterns and mothers' sensitivity to their infants' signals of need (Ainsworth & Bell, 1969). Specifically, it was found that 3-month-olds whose mothers responded quickly and appropriately to their cries and were sensitive to their signals of need were likely to be evaluated as securely attached at 1 year of age.

Over the past several decades, many additional studies have examined the relationship between parental sensitivity and attachment status. Michael Lamb and his colleagues reported that parents of securely attached infants are generally more involved with their infants, more in synchrony with them, and more appropriate in their responsiveness (Lamb & Ahnert, 2006). The mother's sensitivity to her infant's distress seems particularly important (McElwain & Booth-LaForce, 2006). This link is especially evident where such sensitivity is low: Maternal depression has been consistently linked to reductions in secure attachment behaviors (Diener, Nievar, & Wright, 2003; Flykt, Kanninen, Sinkkonen, & Punamäki, 2010), and, as might be expected, children raised by extremely insensitive or abusive caregivers are particularly likely to be rated as insecurely attached (Thompson, 1998).

A variety of factors that contribute to stress on parents have also been found to be associated with insecure attachment, including marital discord, and low **socioeconomic status (SES)** which is an indicator of social class based on factors such as income, education, and occupation. Researchers believe that these stressors are related to insecure attachment in two ways. First, difficult conditions within the family are likely to increase maternal depression and lower maternal sensitivity. Second, witnessing angry or violent interactions between adult caretakers or experiencing unpredictable changes in caregiving arrangements is likely to make children feel that their caregivers are not reliable sources of comfort and safety.

Although many studies support Ainsworth's hypothesis regarding a relationship between parental sensitivity and attachment, some research has found less than strong evidence for it. An analysis of 65 studies conducted in many parts of the world revealed only a modest correlation between measures of sensitivity and secure attachment, indicating that many factors linking parental behaviors to attachment are still not well understood (De Wolff & van IJzendoorn, 1997).

Out-of-Home Care In many parts of the world, one of the most common features of young children's lives is some form of out-of-home care during the first year (Greenspan, 2003). In North American society, this phenomenon is related to two trends: (1) the growing number of single-parent households, and (2) the increasing economic need for both parents to work full time. As of 2008, 64 percent of women with children under the age of 6 were in the labor force, including 56.5 percent who had an infant under the age of 1 year (U.S. Department of Labor, Bureau of Labor Statistics, 2009).

Out-of-home care for infants has been the subject of controversy among developmentalists for several decades (Ahnert, Pinquart, & Lamb, 2006). A prominent voice in this controversy has been that of Jay Belsky, who warned that out-of-home care during the first year of life carries possible developmental risks (Belsky et al., 2007). Belsky's concerns were aroused by evidence that children who had experienced extensive nonmaternal care (more than 20 hours a week) during the first year of life were more likely to exhibit insecure patterns of attachment in the strange situation, were less compliant in meeting adults' demands, and were more aggressive in interactions with peers than were children who spent less time in nonmaternal care. These concerns were supported by studies that found that firstborn children who had been placed in child-care arrangements before their first birthday were significantly more likely to display insecure forms of attachment when they were 12 to 13 months old than were children who stayed at home with their mothers (Bargelow, Vaughn, & Molitor, 1987).

At 9 months of age, both Samuel and Olivia attend Kids Unlimited, a day-care facility in Oxford, United Kingdom. The effects of out-of-home care for infants is a subject of considerable controversy and research.

These findings prompted the U.S. government to initiate a massive longitudinal study to determine what influence various kinds of child care during infancy and early childhood have on later development. The ongoing study, which was initiated in 1991, is carried out by a network of leading researchers from centers at 10 different geographical locales. Investigators collect data on the characteristics of the children's families—including their educational and income levels, ethnicity, and size—and on the quality of the care provided—including the ratio of caregivers to children, the size of the care groups, the quality of the facilities, and the quality of caregiving itself. To assess the effects of the care on the children, data are collected on the children's emotional attachment, self-control, compliance with adult demands, mental development, and language development (NICHD Early Child Care Research Network, 2010).

As you will see when we discuss the effects of child care in more detail in Chapter 10, this research indicates that an extensive amount of time in nonparental child care has slight negative effects on children's attachment relationships, as well as on their social behaviors and intellectual development. Much stronger influences on the effects of child care are the quality of mothering and the socioeconomic status of the family (NICHD, 2003b).

The stakes in assessing the effects of child care are very high. On the one hand, it is obviously in the interests not only of the children in question but also of society as a whole to ensure that children grow up to be emotionally stable and socially competent adults. On the other hand, economic and social pressures bring many mothers into the workforce and keep fathers there. The problem is how best to deal with these conflicting realities to maximize children's life chances, particularly for low-income families who are often unable to afford high-quality care. Belsky suggests that this goal could best be achieved if parents received a subsidy for staying home with their infants during their first year of life. Others argue that what is called for instead is better and more available child care. Proponents of this latter view suggest that responsive, stable, and loving environments can be provided outside the home and point to a number of recent studies indicating that infants and children establish warm, close relationships with a large variety of nonparental figures, including other family members and friends, as well as paid child-care providers (Shonkoff & Phillips, 2000).

Orphanages When Jeff and Christine adopted Jin Yu from the orphanage in China, they were particularly concerned about whether she would be able to develop strong emotional attachments to them. Indeed, a large body of research indicates that children who spend their early lives in orphanages may experience significant levels of social-emotional deprivation that impede their ability to form loving relationships with others. (In rare cases, this impeded ability can take the form of reactive attachment disorder, discussed in the box "In the Field: Children with Reactive Attachment Disorder.") The effects that institutional living can have on a child vary dramatically, depending on such factors as the severity of deprivation the child experiences, the length of time the child remained in the orphanage, and the quality of the child's environment after leaving the orphanage.

A factor of particular importance is the child's age at adoption. As you may recall, the cognitive development of children who were adopted from Romanian orphanages where they had experienced severe deprivation depended largely on how old the children were when adopted (see Chapter 5, pp. 166–168). Similarly, when Kim Chisholm (1998) followed the social and emotional development of a group of infants and young children adopted from these same orphanages into Canadian homes, he found that those who were adopted before they were 4 months of age were developmentally indistinguishable from native-born Canadian children who lived in the homes of their biological parents. However, children who were adopted after 8 months of age showed residual effects of their orphanage experiences. In particular, although all the children had formed emotional attachments to their adoptive parents, they tended to display more evidence of insecure attachment in the strange situation than did the children adopted before the age of 4 months. They also tended to be indiscriminately friendly to strangers, suggesting that they were hungry for attention.

Children's social and emotional development seems to suffer even when the orphanages are judged to be of good quality. Barbara Tizard and Jill Hodges studied 65 English children of working-class backgrounds who were raised in high-quality residential nurseries from just after birth until they were at least 2 years old (Hodges & Tizard, 1989a, 1989b; Tizard & Hodges, 1978; Tizard & Rees, 1975). (These nurseries were designed to provide both temporary and long-term care and education for children whose families could not care for them adequately, usually due to ongoing family problems or some type of crisis.) The children in the study were fed well; the staff, consisting primarily of nurses, was well trained; toys and books were plentiful. However, the turnover and scheduling of staff members discouraged the formation of close personal relationships between the staff and children. Tizard and Hodges estimated that by the time the children were 2 years old, each child had been in the care of some 24 nurses, and that by the age of 4½, each had been cared for by as many as 50 nurses. Such circumstances would certainly seem to preclude the kind of intimate knowledge and caring that presumably underlie sensitive caregiving.

Tizard and her colleagues evaluated the developmental status of the children when they were 4½ and 8 years old, and again when they were 16. They found that leaving institutional care had a positive effect on the children, as would be expected, but that how much difference it made depended on what kind of environment they entered. One of the surprising findings was that the children who were restored to their biological families did not fare as well as the children who were adopted, a pattern that persisted even at the follow-up study conducted when the children were 16 years old. Almost all the children who were adopted formed

In the Field   Children with Reactive Attachment Disorder

Name:	Lark Eshleman
Education:	B.A. in English and American literature, Utica College of Syracuse University; M.A. in library science, State University of New York at Geneseo; M.A. in psychology, Millersville University; Ph.D. in clinical psychology, Union Institute (also certified in school psychology and play therapy)
Current Position:	Psychotherapist; developed Synergistic Trauma and Attachment Therapy, Pennsylvania
Career Objectives:	Help children and families recover from the effects of early childhood trauma, including abuse, neglect, and family upheaval

LARK ESHLEMAN IS A CHILD AND ADOLESCENT PSYCHO-therapist specializing in the treatment of children who have experienced early emotional traumas such as exposure to violence, abuse, neglect, or parental separation and loss (Eshleman, 2003). Such children are at risk for reactive attachment disorder (RAD), a severe psychological disorder linked to a disruption in the development of the parent–child attachment relationship (Chaffin et al., 2006).

According to the *Diagnostic and Statistical Manual of Mental Disorders,* the main feature of RAD is extremely inappropriate social relating that takes one of two forms: (1) The child engages in indiscriminate and excessive efforts to receive comfort and affection from any adult, even strangers, or (2) the child is extremely reluctant to seek or accept comfort and affection, especially when distressed, even from familiar adults. Other symptoms used to diagnose this rare disorder include onset before 5 years of age, a history of significant neglect, and lack of a reliable, consistent primary caregiver (APA, 2000). Barbara Braun-McDonald, another attachment therapist, explains that "if a baby cries and he's ignored, and it happens over and over again, at some level he begins to tell himself, 'I can't trust that the people who are in charge are going to meet my needs'" (in Meltz, 2004, p. H1).

Eshleman came into the international spotlight for her therapeutic interventions with orphans in Croatia and her advice to parents seeking to adopt them (Eshleman, 2003). Not surprisingly, children who have spent considerable time in orphanages, especially those of poor quality, are at special risk for developing RAD. Significantly, therapies that are specifically linked to attachment theory have been found most effective in healing children whose attachment process has been seriously disrupted by various emotional traumas. As concluded in a major review of research into various therapies for RAD,

Services for children described as having attachment problems should be founded on the core principles suggested by attachment theory, including caregiver and environmental stability, child safety, patience, sensitivity, consistency, and nurturance. (Chaffin et al., 2006, p. 87)

Especially important to therapeutic success, according to the review, is to focus on the parent–child relationship, rather than on the individual child's pathology, and to teach positive parenting skills that promote a secure attachment relationship between parent and child.

mutual attachments with their adoptive parents, no matter how old they were when they were adopted. This was not the case for the children who returned to their biological parents. The older they were when they left the orphanages, the less likely it was that mutual attachment developed.

One reason that outcomes were better in the adoptive homes than in the biological homes may have been that many of the families who took back their children were not altogether happy to do so. Many of the mothers expressed misgivings, but they accepted the responsibility because the children were their own. Often the children returned to homes in which there were other children who required their mother's attention or a stepfather who was not interested in them. Most of the adoptive parents, by contrast, were older, childless couples who wanted the children and gave them a good deal of attention. Also, most of the adoptive families

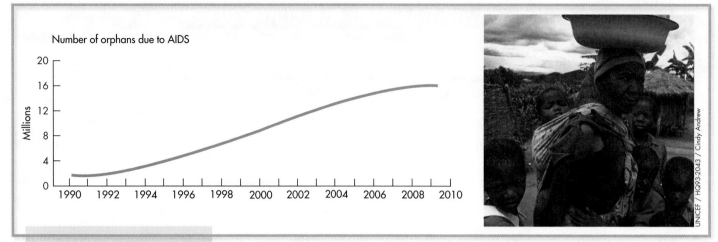

Number of orphans due to AIDS

FIGURE 6.8 More effective and more effectively distributed anti-viral medications have slowed the pace of children being orphaned as a consequence of parental death from HIV-AIDS. Nevertheless, in some areas of sub-Saharan Africa, more than 15 percent of all children have been orphaned because of the disease. The crisis has put terrible pressure on the African extended family system, which has traditionally been a refuge for family members in need. The woman in this photograph is the grandmother and now the primary caregiver and provider for six grandchildren whose parents died from AIDS. (From WHO/ UNAIDS/UNICEF, 2010.)

were financially better off than the children's biological families had been (Tizard & Hodges, 1978).

Research on the emotional development of children raised in institutions has become especially important in light of the millions of children worldwide who are orphaned because of the HIV-AIDS epidemic. In sub-Saharan Africa alone, there are estimated to be more than 14 million children living as orphans because one or both of their parents have died from AIDS (Figure 6.8) (WHO/ UNAIDS/UNICEF, 2010; Liddell, 2002). In African cultures, orphaned children traditionally would be cared for by extended family. However, the vast and exponentially growing number of parents killed by AIDS has overburdened the extended family system, and the need for orphanages is quickly outpacing the supply (Liddell, 2002; Abebe & Aase, 2007). As you might expect, many AIDS orphans suffer the same effects of institutional care that have been documented in past studies of orphaned children.

Cultural Contexts At present there is sharp disagreement among developmentalists concerning the extent to which the process of attachment is influenced by cultural variations. Many have argued that attachment is a universal feature of human development and that the emotionally sensitive interactions that nourish attachment are similar across cultures (Posada et al., 2004). Others have argued that there are important cultural variations in attachment and that the very notions of what constitutes sensitive caregiving and secure human relationships are culturally specific (Rothbaum, Weisz, Pott, & Morelli, 2000; Rothbaum & Kakinuma, 2004). Research has produced data that support both positions (Figure 6.9; see van IJzendoorn & Sagi, 2001, for a review of the conflicting evidence).

One of the earliest studies of cultural influences on attachment examined children who from an early age were raised communally on Israeli collective farms called *kibbutzim*. Although these children saw their parents daily, the adults who looked after them were usually not family members, and the children slept together in dormitories. When at the age of 11 to 14 months, such communally raised children were placed in the strange situation with either a parent or a caregiver, only 56 percent were classified as securely attached, and 37 percent were classified as resistant (Sagi-Schwartz et al., 2005; Aviezer & Sagi-Schwartz, 2008).

Abraham Sagi and his colleagues suspected that the high rate of insecure attachment among these children was caused by the fact that the communal

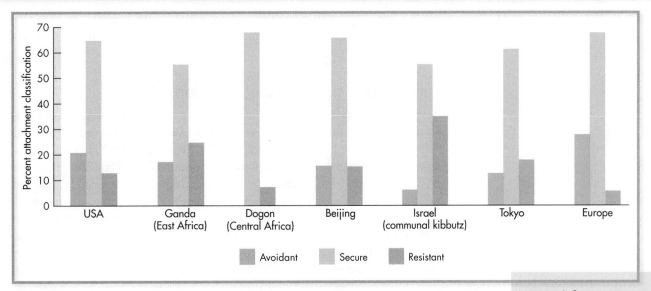

FIGURE 6.9 Secure attachments predominate across cultures, but the percentage of different forms of insecure attachments varies. (As summarized in IJzendoorn & Sagi-Schwartz, 2008.)

caregiving, along with staffing rotations, did not allow the caregivers to provide the children with prompt individualized attention. To test this hypothesis, the researchers used the strange situation to compare the attachment behaviors of children raised in the traditional kibbutzim arrangement described above with those of children raised in kibbutzim in which they returned to sleep in their parents' home at night (Sagi et al., 1995). They once again found a low level of secure attachments among the children who slept in communal dormitories. Those who slept at home displayed a significantly higher level of secure attachments, supporting the idea that cultural differences in the opportunities for sensitive caregiving accounted for cultural differences in attachment quality.

While evidence indicates that interactive sensitivity is necessary to the development of secure attachments, it seems that the very nature of "sensitive caregiving" differs depending on the values, beliefs, and socialization goals of the culture (Driessen, Lyenedecker, Scholmerich, & Harwood, 2010). In a study that illustrates this point, Vivian Carlson and Robin Harwood (2003) examined maternal sensitivity in mothers from the United States and Puerto Rico, and found that the Puerto Rican mothers exerted significantly more control over their infants—a form of behavior typically judged as "insensitive." Paradoxically, however, the infants of highly controlling mothers were not more likely to be insecurely attached. Carlson and Harwood explained that maternal control is consistent with Puerto Rican cultural values that emphasize the importance of obedience and respect. Mothers who exert this control in order to foster calm, attentive, and well-behaved infants are acting in predictable and meaningful ways that promote their babies' successful integration into the community. Noting that in Ainsworth's description, a sensitive mother is one who establishes a harmonious relationship with her infant, Carlson and Harwood argue that harmonious mother–infant relationships may be best established "by caregiving practices designed to produce culturally valued traits in the growing infant" (p. 69). Thus, while attachment may be universal, this does not exclude the possibility that the development of attachment behaviors, and the caregiving practices that affect their development, differ depending on the

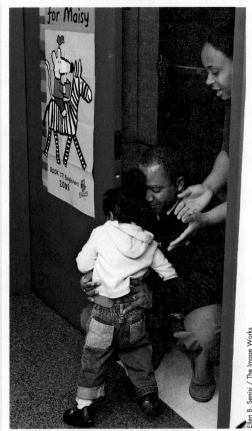

This child is clearly distressed at the prospect of being separated from her father when he goes to work.

Ellen B. Senisi / The Image Works

nature of the community in which the child is becoming engaged as an active participant (Yaman, Mesman, van IJzendoorn, Bakermans-Kranenburg, & Linting, 2010; Belsky, 2005).

Attachment Patterns and Later Development

Many developmentalists agree that establishing a secure attachment relationship is crucial not only to infants' emotional well-being but also to the quality of their future relationships (Osofsky & Fitzgerald, 2000; Zeanah, Egger, Smyke, Nelson, et al., 2009). Supporting this idea, early studies conducted by Alan Sroufe and his colleagues reported that when children who are judged to be securely attached at 12 months of age are assessed at age 3½, they are more curious, play more effectively with their age-mates, and have better relationships with their preschool teachers than do children who were insecurely attached as infants (Erikson, Sroufe, & Egeland, 1985; Frankel & Bates, 1990; Sroufe & Fleeson, 1986). In follow-up observations conducted when the children were 10 years old, and then again when they were 15, researchers found that those who had been assessed as securely attached in infancy were more skillful socially, had more friends, displayed more self-confidence, and were more open in expressing their feelings (for a summary, see Sroufe et al., 2005).

More recent longitudinal studies also suggest the continuity of attachment from infancy to adulthood. For example, a 20-year longitudinal study conducted by Everett Waters and his colleagues indicated that, as adults, 72 percent of the sample received the same attachment classification (secure or insecure, as assessed through interviews) that they had received as infants (Waters, Hamilton, & Weinfield, 2000a; Waters et al., 2000b).

Researchers who see patterns of attachment as tending to remain consistent throughout development emphasize that such continuity depends on one key factor—how well the individual's *internal working model* functions over time and across situations (Bretherton & Munholland, 1999; Grossmann et al., 2008). As discussed earlier (p. 209), Bowlby (1969) proposed that on the basis of their interactions with their primary caregiver, infants build up an internal working model of the way to behave toward other people. Enlarging on Bowlby's idea, Inge Bretherton and colleagues (2005) argue that internal working models provide expectations about how others are likely to respond to the child's own behavior and emotional expressions—whether the child will be comforted or rejected, and whether others will be emotionally available to respond when the child expresses his or her feelings. These expectations influence how the child acts in new situations and with new people. The child's actions, in turn, can provoke either positive or negative reactions in others, which can confirm the child's expectations and perpetuate patterns of behavior. Changing a child's internal working model is not accomplished easily and may require an adult who provides experiences that disconfirm the child's expectations. Thus, change and continuity depend on the cumulative outcomes of everyday transactions between children and their environments (Main et al., 2005).

In addition to the effects of the child's internal working model, research also indicates that major changes in the child's life can affect attachment status. In Waters's research cited above, for example, interviews with the mothers of the minority of participants who changed classification from secure to insecure reported at least one of the following negative life experiences:

- loss of a parent
- parental divorce

- life-threatening illness of a parent or child
- parental psychiatric disorder
- physical or sexual abuse by a family member

These and other traumatic events, such as isolation and deprivation, can have a significant impact on a child's attachment status.

secondary intersubjectivity A form of interaction between infant and caregiver, emerging at about 9–12 months, with communication and emotional sharing focused not just on the interaction but on the world beyond.

⏏ APPLY :: CONNECT :: DISCUSS

In light of research suggesting that extensive out-of-home care during the first year of life may pose a risk for developing insecure attachments, some developmentalists and family advocacy groups have argued for public policy that would grant parents leave for a year after the birth of a child. How acceptable would this policy be to fathers or mothers with strong career goals? Would it be good for infants from low-SES families where mothers might have several small children at home? What other options besides parental leave would serve family needs and be sensitive to the infant's attachment needs?

The Changing Nature of Communication

Seated in his stroller, 12-month-old Juan is enjoying a beautiful spring day with his father. As they stroll through the park, Juan points excitedly and exclaims, "Da!" at a dog, at a bicycle, at another baby in a stroller, each time looking over his shoulder and smiling at his father, who smiles back and says, "Yes, that's a doggie [bicycle, baby]." They come across a small crowd gathered around street performers who are dressed in colorful costumes, entertaining the audience with jokes, juggling, and antics. The performers invite the children to join them—throwing or catching balls, chasing each other around, acting like various animals, and just being generally silly. Juan seems to be enjoying the spectacle—until one of the performers slinks toward him on hands and knees, like a stalking lion. First, Juan leans back into his stroller, stares warily, and looks up at his father, who is scowling at the insensitive performer. The lion-man continues his approach and begins to make growling vocalizations. Then, obviously frightened, Juan bursts into tears and raises his arms toward his father, who picks him up and gives him a reassuring hug.

As you know from our earlier discussions, by 3 months of age, infants and their caregivers are jointly experiencing pleasure in simple interactions. This early form of communication, which we referred to as *primary intersubjectivity,* is limited to direct face-to-face interactions and is supported mainly by the efforts of the caregiver (Trevarthen, 1998). Between 9 and 12 months of age, babies begin to interact with their caregivers in a new and more complex way. This new form of connection is referred to as **secondary intersubjectivity**, because now the infant and the caregiver communicate with each other about the world that extends beyond themselves, such as their pleasure in seeing a passing puppy or their concern over an approaching threat.

The emergence of secondary intersubjectivity marks a major turning point in the infant's development because it brings a new dimension to the communicative process, serving as a foundation for sharing one's thoughts, feelings, and expectations about the world.

The pleasure this child and mother take in their interaction using a fork is an example of the kind of emotional sharing referred to as secondary intersubjectivity.

Rick Gomez / Masterfile

Social Referencing

An important form of secondary intersubjectivity in infancy is *social referencing,* in which, as you saw in Chapter 5, babies look to their caregiver for an indication of how they should feel and act when they encounter some unfamiliar object or event. (Juan's looking up at his father as the street performer slunk toward him was a clear instance of social referencing.) Social referencing becomes a common means of communication as soon as babies begin to move about on their own (Campos et al., 2000; Thompson & Newton, 2010). When approaching an unfamiliar object, for example, if they notice that their caregiver is looking at the object and appears to be concerned, they typically hesitate and become wary. If, instead, the caregiver smiles and looks pleased, they continue their approach. (Perhaps if Juan's father had not been scowling at the advancing performer, Juan would not have burst into tears.) As they grow more experienced, babies become increasingly sensitive to where their caregiver is looking and will even check back to see how the caregiver responds to an object after they have made their own appraisal of it (Rosen, Adamson, & Bakeman, 1992; Striano & Rochat, 2000).

In a wonderful illustration of social referencing, this baby checks in with mom before deciding how to react to the medical exam. Mom's reassuring smile will greatly influence how the baby interprets and emotionally responds to this unusual event.

Between approximately 9 and 12 months of age, infants' contributions to secondary intersubjectivity become more sophisticated. For example, Tricia Striano and Philippe Rochat (2000) compared the way 7- and 10-month-old infants in a laboratory playroom reacted to the appearance of a remote-controlled toy dog that barked intermittently. An experimenter in the room was instructed either to look at the infant when the dog barked or to look away. The 7-month-olds kept checking with the adult even if the adult ignored them, while the 10-month-olds immediately stopped checking with the adult unless the adult looked at them when the dog barked. Striano and Rochat believe that the 10-month-olds were beginning to engage in "selective social referencing" because the infants knew they could obtain information from the adult only if the adult was attending to them.

Following a Caregiver's Signs of Interest

Another way in which infants communicate with their caregivers is by following the caregiver's gaze to see what the caregiver is looking at and to look at what the caregiver is pointing at. If a mother and her 5-month-old are looking at each other and the mother suddenly looks to one side, the infant will not follow the mother's gaze. And if the mother points at some object in the room, the baby is more likely to stare at the end of the mother's finger than to look in the direction the mother is pointing. A few months later, in similarly simple circumstances, the infant will look in the direction of the mother's gazing or pointing (Butterworth, 2001).

Like social referencing, an infant's abilities to use a caregiver's pointing and gazing strengthen and provide more reliable means of communication after their initial appearance between 7 and 9 months of age (Liebal, Behne, Carpenter, & Tomasello, 2009). A baby's ability to look in the direction of a caregiver's pointing increases rapidly between 10 and 12 months (although the baby's own ability to use pointing will not appear for another several months), while the more subtle form of communication involved in following another's gaze continues to improve well into the second year. As you will now see, both abilities are associated with the infant's growing vocabulary (Slaughter & McConnell, 2003).

The Beginnings of Language Comprehension and Speech

As babies become more mobile and more likely to wander out of their caregivers' sight and reach, a new means of interaction, one that will allow babies and caregivers to communicate at a distance, becomes an urgent necessity. That new means, of course, is language.

To some extent, all languages are "foreign languages" to young infants. Think about what it is like for you to hear an unfamiliar foreign language. Very probably, it seems like an uninterrupted sound stream; that is, it is difficult to tell where one word ends and another begins. Indeed, one of the first tasks of learning a language is to segment its sounds into distinct words and phrases. Infants are able to recognize their own names and distinguish them from names with similar stress patterns, such as "Amy" versus "Suzie," as early as 4 months of age (Jusczyk, 2001; Nazzi, Kemler Nelson, Jusczyk, & Jusczyk, 2000). By 6 months of age, they begin to show the first signs of comprehending words for highly familiar objects, such as "mommy" or "daddy." These new abilities are interesting in their own right, but they also have implications for developing the ability to segment language. In particular, Roberta Golinkoff and her colleagues have found that when babies hear a familiar word—their own name, or "mommy" or "daddy"—the familiar word serves as an anchor for learning the words that immediately precede or follow the familiar word (Bortfeld et al., 2005; Pruden et al., 2006). Thus, it is easier for the baby to learn the word "cup" if it is used in the sentence "Here's your cup, Amy" than if it is used in the anchorless "Here's your cup." Developmentalists use the term **perceptual scaffolding** to refer to the process through which the sound of a familiar word serves as an anchor for learning new words.

At about 9 months of age, children begin to understand some common expressions such as "Do you want your bottle?" "Wave bye-bye," and "Cookie?" when they are used in highly specific, often routine, situations. One little girl observed by Elizabeth Bates and her colleagues would bring her favorite doll when she was asked to "bring a dolly," but she did not understand the word "doll" as referring to any doll other than her own (Bates et al., 1979; see Chapter 7 for more details on this common error of "underextension," and others, in language acquisition).

The ability to produce language follows several months behind the ability to understand it. Its origins can be traced back to the cooing and gurgling noises babies begin to make at 10 to 12 weeks of age (Butterworth & Morisette, 1996). Soon thereafter, babies with normal hearing not only initiate cooing sounds but also begin to respond with gurgles and coos to the voices of others. When their cooing is imitated, they will answer with more coos, thereby engaging in a "conversation" in which turns are taken at vocalizing. They are most likely to vocalize with their caregivers and other familiar people.

Babbling, a form of vocalizing that combines a consonant and vowel sound, such as "dadadadadadada" or "babababababa," begins at around 7 months of age (Adamson, 1995). Recent research indicates that babbling is controlled by the left hemisphere of the brain; thus, well before recognizable language has begun, the brain areas that will support language are already active and behaving in language-specific ways (Baker, Golinkoff, & Petitto, 2006). At first, babbling amounts to no more than vocal play, as babies discover the wealth of sounds they can make with their tongue, teeth, palate, and vocal cords. They practice making these sound combinations endlessly, much as they practice grasping objects.

perceptual scaffolding The way in which a familiar word serves as an anchor for learning new words that come immediately before or after it.

babbling A form of vocalizing, beginning at around 7 months, in which infants utter strings of syllables that combine a consonant sound and a vowel sound.

This father and his baby girl appear to be engaged in a "conversation" in which they take turns vocalizing about a picture that has captured their attention.

Early babbling is the same the world over, no matter what language the baby's family speaks; babies produce syllables they have never heard before and will not use when they learn to speak (Blake & De Boysson-Bardies, 1992). At about 9 months of age, however, babies begin to narrow their babbling to the sounds produced in the language that they hear every day (Davis, MacNeilage, Matyear, & Powell, 2000). Since babies often babble when they play alone, early babbling does not seem to be an attempt to communicate. It is almost as if children are singing to themselves using repeatable parts of their language.

Toward the end of the first year, babies begin to babble with the intonation and stress of actual utterances in the language they will eventually speak. Such vocalizations are called *jargoning*. At this point, as Lauren Adamson (1995) describes it, "a stream of babbling often flows like speech, following its distinctive intonational patterns of declarations, commands, and questions" (p. 163). At about the same time, babies start to repeat particular short utterances in particular situations, as if their utterances have some meaning.

By about 12 months of age, infants are able to comprehend a dozen or so common phrases, such as "Give me a hug," "Stop it!" and "Let's go bye-bye." At about this same time, the first distinguishable words make their appearance, although their use is restricted to only a few contexts or objects (Fenson et al., 1994).

It used to be thought that deaf children babbled, beginning at the same age as hearing children (Lenneberg, 1967). Research has shown, however, that, although deaf infants in their early months do vocalize, they will only progress to babbling if the infants have some residual hearing (Koopmans-van Beinum, Clement, & van den Dikkenberg-Pot, 2001). In the case of totally deaf infants, vocalizations become rare by 1 year of age. However, if their caregivers communicate with each other in sign language, these infants "babble" with their hands—that is, just as hearing infants' babbling comes to have the sounds and sound patterns of the language they hear, so these infants make the movements that will become the elements of sign language (Cormier, Mauk, & Repp, 1998).

After the first year, the baby's ability to understand and produce language accelerates at an astonishing pace. Given the special significance of language development for our species, as well as its importance to advances in various developmental domains, we will devote all of the next chapter to examining the emergence and growth of language competence.

▲ APPLY :: CONNECT :: DISCUSS

Social referencing emerges during infancy and persists throughout life. Give examples of events that might prompt social referencing in an 8-year-old, a 15-year-old, and a 50-year-old. What similarities are there across your three events? What differences are there? How might social referencing have important biocultural implications?

A Sense of Self

Strapped securely in the grocery-cart seat with a bit of a pout on her face, 10-month-old Nadia watched her mother, who had turned away from her to read the nutritional content of a cereal box. All of a sudden, Nadia let out a piercing, heart-stopping screech that could be heard throughout the store. Everyone in the cereal aisle looked at her—and Nadia looked back at them, grinning at the attention she was getting. For weeks afterward, Nadia would shriek like that whenever she wanted attention, and acted happy and self-satisfied when she got it. It was as though she were saying, "Look at me!"

Nadia's emotional life has changed considerably since she was a newborn, when her internal feeling states seemed to trigger certain facial and other non-verbal behaviors—smiles, frowns, agitated crying, and so forth. At 10 months of age, she is aware that her emotional expressions affect those around her, and she uses her expressions intentionally to elicit predictable social responses. Clearly, Nadia's ability to intentionally draw attention her way, and her delight in showing off, indicate that she has developed a sense of self, that is, of being an entity separate from the people and objects around her. However, as vivid as her expressions of self-awareness are, they represent only the the early phase of a long process in the development of the ability to think about oneself.

By the time they are 6 months old, infants have acquired a great deal of experience interacting with objects and other people and have developed an intuitive sense of themselves as a result (Rochat, 2009). The ability to locomote provides them with still further experience of their separateness from their caregivers. Having a more explicit sense of self as separate from others promotes new forms of social relations. Infants at that age begin to learn that they can share their own experiences and compare their own reactions with those of others, especially through their emerging use of language (Trevarthen, 1998).

Self-Recognition

Consciousness of self has been proposed to be among the major characteristics distinguishing human beings from other species. This is an interesting idea, but finding a way to demonstrate it convincingly has been a problem.

Several decades ago, Gordon Gallup (1970) argued that a form of self-consciousness is apparent in the ability to recognize one's image in a mirror. He reported an ingenious series of experiments using mirrors with chimpanzees, experiments that have since been replicated with chimpanzees and also used with children. Gallup showed adolescent wild-born chimpanzees their images in a full-length mirror. At first the chimps acted as if they were looking at another animal: They threatened, vocalized, and made conciliatory gestures to the "intruder." After a few days, however, they began to use the mirror to explore themselves; for example, they picked bits of food from their faces, which they could see only in the mirror.

To make certain of the meaning of his finding, Gallup anesthetized several chimps and painted a bright, odorless dye above one eye and on the ear on the opposite side of the head. When they woke up and looked in the mirror, the chimps immediately began to touch their faces and ears, where the mirror showed the appearance of spots. Gallup concluded that they had learned to recognize themselves in the mirror.

This kind of self-recognition is by no means universal among primate species. Gallup gave a wild-born macaque monkey more than 2,400 hours of exposure to a mirror over a 5-month period, but the monkey never showed any sign of self-recognition. The problem was not simply dealing with the mirror image, because the monkey quickly learned to find food that it could see only in the mirror. The monkey simply could not recognize itself.

Gallup's procedure has been used in modified form with human infants between the ages of 3 and 24 months (Inoue-Nakamura, 2001; Rochat & Striano, 2002; Bard et al., 2006). The results indicate that there are several stages in learning to recognize oneself in a mirror (Bigelow, 1998). When held up to a mirror

This baby seems delighted to see his own image in the mirror. Developmentalists use infant reactions to mirror images as a way to study the emerging understanding of self.

Charles Gullung / Getty Images

self-conscious emotions Emotions such as embarrassment, pride, shame, guilt, and envy, which emerge after 8 months with infants' growing consciousness of self.

in the first few months of life, infants show little interest in their own image or in anyone else's. At about 3 months of age, however, babies begin to engage in long bouts of cooing and smiling at, and reaching for their images. An interesting question is whether infants at this age respond differently to their own mirror image than they do to images of other babies, which would suggest that they are able to distinguish between self and other. According to a study conducted by Tiffany Field, the answer is yes. Specifically, while the infants tended to look longer at themselves in a mirror than at images of other babies, they tended to smile and vocalize more at the images of other babies (Field, 1979). One interpretation of this intriguing finding is that the infants recognize and find their own images interesting, while behaving as if images of other babies may be potential interactive partners.

Some researchers have argued that infants' interest in their own mirror images may be due not to self-recognition but, rather, to their fascination with the fact that the movement of the image is exactly contingent with their own movements (Lewis & Brooks-Gunn, 1979). In an effort to explore this possibility, Philippe Rochat and Tricia Striano showed 4- and 9-month-olds a live video image of either themselves or an adult who mimicked their every move (Rochat & Striano, 2002). Their results indicated that even the 4-month-olds discriminated between their own images and those of the mimicking adult. While this suggests some early awareness of self/other discrimination, even 10-month-olds do not react to the sight of a red spot that has been surreptitiously applied to their nose. Not until children are 18 months old will they reach for their own nose or ask "What's that?" when they see the red spot. Within a few months, whenever someone points to the child's mirror image and asks, "Who's that?" the child will be able to answer unhesitatingly, "Me" (Rochat, 2000).

The Self as Agent

When speech first emerges, it mostly consists of one-word utterances naming objects the child is looking at. Children point at or pick up an object and say its name. These first descriptions include no explicit reference to the self. Between the ages of 18 and 24 months, about the same time that children begin to use two-word utterances, they also begin to describe their own actions. A child completing a jigsaw puzzle exclaims, "Did it!" or "Becky done." When a tower of blocks falls down, a child exclaims, "Uh-oh. I fix." In these utterances we see not only children's ability to refer to themselves explicitly but also their ability to assert themselves as *agents* who exert control and power over their environments. Recall from our discussion earlier in the chapter that this emerging sense of control and mastery underpins the delight shown by infants when their actions are imitated by adults.

The Emergence of Self-Conscious Emotions

The sense of self that arises during infancy gives rise to a new class of emotions, including embarrassment, pride, shame, guilt, and envy (Reddy, 2005) (see the box, "The Moral Life of Babies"). These new emotions are referred to as **self-conscious emotions** because they depend on babies' newly acquired abilities to recognize, talk about,

This little girl's obvious pride in her drawing is a consequence of being able to consider her behavior in relation to the standards and expectations of others. The mother's hand-clapping signals clearly that the drawing is indeed an accomplishment of great merit.

Blend Images / Hill Street Studios / Getty

The Moral Life of Babies

ONE-YEAR-OLD NICHOLAS HAD JUST witnessed a puppet behaving badly. In the three-puppet show that he observed, one puppet rolled a ball to another, who passed it back. Then the first puppet rolled it again, this time to a different puppet, who caught the ball . . . and ran off with it. The two puppets who had received the ball were then brought off the stage and set before Nicholas. Each puppet had a pile of treats. When Nicholas was asked to take away a treat from one puppet, he took from the pile of the "naughty" one. He then leaned over and smacked the puppet on the head.

This incident took place in a study conducted by a team of researchers at the Infant Cogntion Center at Yale University. The team—Kiley Hamlin, Karen Wynn, and Paul Bloom—have been studying the moral life of babies. Their work has challenged the view, held by Freud and Piaget, among others, that human beings begin life as amoral, largely selfish animals. According to this view, babies only gradually learn about right and wrong, and only gradually develop emotions such as empathy, shame, and guilt that are associated with understanding injustice and behaving in ways that society deems are morally appropriate.

A growing body of evidence, however, suggests that humans do have a rudimentary moral sense from the very start of life (Thompson & Newton, 2010). A series of studies conducted by the research team at Yale bears this out. In one study, babies watched as geometrical objects on a miniature stage acted out "helping" or "hindering" behaviors in various situations (the objects were manipulated by behind-the-scenes experimenters). For example, the babies saw a red ball trying to

go up a hill. On some attempts, a yellow square got behind the ball and gently nudged it upward; in others, a green triangle got in front of it and pushed it down. After the babies saw each event, the experimenter presented them with the helper (yellow triangle) and the hinderer (green square) on a tray to see which object they reached for and presumably preferred. Both 6- and 10-month-old babies overwhelmingly preferred the helper to the hinderer.

Infants' responsivness to the "nice" and "naughty" behavior of others was assessed in another set of studies designed as puppet shows. In one, a puppet struggled to open a box. The box would be partly opened, but then the lid would fall back down. In some scenes, another puppet would help out by grabbing the lid and pulling it off the box. In other scenes, another puppet would jump on the box and slam it shut. The researchers found that babies as young as 5 months of age preferred the nice puppet to the naughty one. In a fascinating extension of the study, 8-month-olds saw the original helping/hindering scenes, and then witnessed two other puppets either reward or punish the good guy and the bad guy. The results were striking. The babies clearly preferred the puppet who rewarded the good-guy puppet. This finding isn't particularly suprising, however, since it had already been determined that babies like those who behave nicely. What was especially interesting is how the babies responded when they watched the bad-guy puppet being rewarded or punished. In this instance, they preferred the puppet who punished bad behavior over the one who rewarded it.

The human ability to understand and act with compassion toward others, to recognize

In addition to our own species, other highly social primate species have an apparent capacity for moral behavior, empathy, and concerns for others, as amply demonstrated by these bonobos.

and remedy harm and injustice, will undergo remarkable change across the childhood years. The capacity for this development, however, seems deeply rooted in our species, as it is in other species that depend for survival on social relationships and community.

(Adapted from Bloom, 2010.)

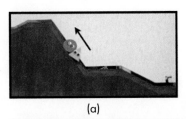
(a)

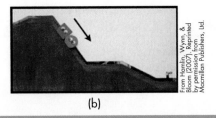
(b)

To explore early moral understanding, researchers presented young babies with different scenarios in which geometric shapes seemed to be helping or hindering each other's efforts. This particular sequence includes a "helping" scenario in which a triangle assists a circle in getting up a hill (a), and a "hindering" scenario in which a square gets in the way of a circle and pushes it back down the hill (b). When presented with the geometric shapes, the vast majority of infants reached for the helpers.

and think about themselves in relation to other people (Lewis, 2001; Thompson & Newton, 2010). That is, whereas basic emotions (joy, fear, anger, and so forth) bear a simple and direct relation to the events that elicit them, self-conscious emotions involve complex combinations of cognition and emotion and cannot appear until children are able to think about and evaluate themselves in relation to other people and the goals they desire. Take pride, for example. To feel pride, babies must be able to judge their own behavior as proper and admirable in the eyes of other people; that is, they must be able to think about other people's standards and use those standards to measure their own behavior (Tomasello, 1999).

Such measurement of one's behavior can, of course, lead to emotions other than pride. Jerome Kagan (1981) explored children's sensitivity to adult standards in a series of studies in which children were encouraged to imitate an adult who performed complex activities. For example, the adult might make one toy monkey hug another monkey, or build a stack of blocks, or enact a simple drama using toy blocks as animals. Many of these activities were too complex for the 18-month-old children to imitate. As a result, many of them started to fret, stopped playing, and clung to their mothers. Kagan concluded that their distress signaled a new ability to recognize adult standards, a sense of responsibility to live up to them, and shame or embarrassment when they failed to do so.

As infancy comes to an end, the process of developing a distinctive sense of self undergoes further change that comprises several interconnected elements: children's increasing self-awareness, their growing sensitivity to adults' standards of what is good; their new awareness of their own ability to live up to those standards; an ability to create plans of their own and judge them against adult standards; and a strong desire to see that their plans are not thwarted by adults (Harter, 1998; Kagan, 2000). This change is recognized by parents the world over. On the South Pacific island of Fiji, for example, parents say that, around their second birthday, children gain *vakayalo*—"sense"—and can be held responsible for their actions because they are supposed to be able to tell right from wrong. Similarly, the Utku of the Hudson Bay area say that the 2-year-old has gained *ihuma,* or reason. Parents in the United States tend to focus on their infants' newly acquired independence and the dwindling of their own control over them, labeling the change as the onset of the "terrible twos." However parents describe it, the distinctive pattern of infants' behavior at around the age of 2 signals to adults that a new stage of development has been entered. Key to this next stage of development is the growing sense of autonomy that Erikson (1963) says normally characterizes late infancy.

▲ APPLY :: CONNECT :: DISCUSS

In what respects might the development of a sense of self contribute to the development of emotion regulation?

Developing Trust and Autonomy

Much of what we presented in this chapter is consistent with Erik Erikson's picture of infancy. As indicated in Chapter 1 (Table 1.2, p. 17), Erikson divided infancy into two main stages. The first of these he called the stage of **basic trust versus mistrust**, in which the infant determines whether the world is a safe place

basic trust versus mistrust For Erikson, the first stage of infancy, during which children either come to trust others as reliable and kind and to regard the world as safe or come to mistrust others as insensitive and hurtful and to regard the world as unpredictable and threatening.

to explore and discover or an unpredictable and threatening one, and whether the people in the world are reliable, loving, and kind or insensitive and hurtful. Consistent with much of the research we have reviewed, Erikson believed that warm and responsive parenting fosters infants' development of trust, and that unresponsive, insensitive, or disorganized parenting fosters a mistrust of people and a wariness about exploring the world.

During the second year, babies enter the stage of **autonomy versus shame and doubt**, during which they develop a sense of themselves as competent or not competent to solve problems and accomplish tasks. In this important period of self-assertion, babies want to do things themselves, often resisting the assistance or control of another. Parents frequently hear the refrain "No! I do it!" (remember Jin Yu, who scolded her parents in Chinese when they tried to keep her from handling dangerous objects). According to Erikson, when parents structure their children's environments in ways that foster success in their early, self-initiated efforts at mastery and control, babies develop confidence in their own abilities and seek challenges. On the other hand, when parents are overly controlling, or fail to create contexts in which their children can demonstrate competence, a sense of doubt and shame may take hold and dampen the children's efforts to achieve.

autonomy versus shame and doubt For Erikson, the second stage of infancy, during which children develop a sense of themselves as competent to accomplish tasks or as not competent.

▲ APPLY :: CONNECT :: DISCUSS

Imagine that you are responsible for the infant care provided at a child-care center. Using insights from Erikson's theory, make a list of points you would cover in a training session for newly hired infant-care providers.

Implications

Infancy is a time during which babies and caregivers forge social and emotional ties that provide a foundation for infants' exploring and learning about the world. Consistent with a biocultural perspective, both biological and sociocultural processes contribute to the creation of these ties. On the side of biology, evolution provides infants with certain capacities to express and share their emotions through a variety of facial expressions and behaviors and to form early attachments to social partners. The infant is also biologically endowed with a brain that includes special cells, called mirror neurons, that seem particularly sensitive to the social and emotional behaviors of others.

On the sociocultural side, the infant's emerging emotional and social development and expressiveness are significantly shaped by the nature of early interactions. Social interactions that are well organized and responsive to the baby's cues seem essential to healthy development and to nurturing the baby's sense of trust that the world is a safe and welcoming place to explore. Furthermore, because early interactions are influenced by the values and patterns of life in the infant's culture, they serve to draw the child into the lives of others, laying the foundation for the child's engaged participation in the community.

SUMMARY

The Nature of Infant Emotions and Emotional Expressions

- Emotion can be defined as a feeling state that includes distinctive physiological responses, can be expressed to others, involves a cognitive appraisal, and can motivate action. Through emotion regulation, people modulate and control emotions.

- Certain basic emotions—joy, fear, anger, surprise, sadness, and disgust—appear to be universal and present from birth or early infancy. Several theories explain basic emotions in infancy:

  - According to the theory of gradual differentiation, newborns experience only general emotional states—contentment and distress—from which the basic emotions gradually differentiate.

  - The differential emotions theory argues that at birth or soon after, infants have distinct basic emotions similar to those of adults.

  - Theorists who see infants' emotions and emotional expressions as ontogenetic adaptations believe these evolved because they contribute to babies' development and well-being by eliciting care and protection.

- Through primary intersubjectivity, which involves face-to-face interaction, infants and their caregivers share emotions that focus on the interaction itself. In the laboratory, disruption of the synchrony between infants and their interactive partners results in negative emotional responses in infants. Maternal depression may prove an obstacle to intersubjectivity, since mothers may be less responsive to babies' emotional cues and infants may disengage from stressful, unresponsive interactions.

- Pouting, most common when an infant is beginning to be upset, may have evolved as a form of emotion regulation to maintain the intersubjectivity between infant and caregiver that crying would disrupt.

- Mirror neurons, which evidently fire in the same way when one is observing an action as when one is performing it, may register the intentions and emotions of others as if they were happening to the observer. Mirror neurons may contribute to newborns' ability to imitate facial actions and, more generally, to the importance of imitation in establishing emotional connections between infants and caregivers.

The Infant–Caregiver Emotional Relationship

- Attachment is an emotional bond between children and their caregivers, which begins to develop at around 7 to 9 months of age. According to Freud's drive-reduction explanation, attachment to the mother originates from her satisfying the infant's need for nourishment. Experiments with monkeys have failed to support Freud's explanation but do support John Bowlby's ethological explanation, according to which attachment arises from the infant's coming to feel that the mother is a source of security and a safe base from which to explore the world.

- Bowlby described attachment as developing in four phases, with infants ultimately being able to retain feelings of security during separations and developing an internal working model for relationships.

- Using a procedure called the strange situation, Mary Ainsworth and other researchers found that the infant's attachment relationship could be one of secure attachment—with a healthy balance between wanting close contact with the mother and wanting to explore—or any of three types of insecure attachment—avoidant, resistant, or disorganized.

- Variations in patterns of attachment may relate to differences in several contexts:

  - Parental sensitivity correlates with secure attachment, while maternal depression, abusive or extremely insensitive caregiving, and family stressors such as parental conflict and low SES appear to be linked to insecure attachment patterns.

  - Institutional contexts such as orphanages can negatively affect attachment, with the extent of their impact depending on factors such as severity of deprivation, age on leaving the institution, and the quality of the subsequent environment.

  - Standard procedures for measuring patterns of attachment may not be valid in some cultures.

- Establishing a secure attachment relationship may be crucial to later relationships, since there appears to be continuity of attachment status from infancy to adulthood, particularly if the internal working model developed remains unchanged.

The Changing Nature of Communication

- Toward the end of the first year, with the emergence of secondary intersubjectivity, infants and their caregivers interact and share emotions about the world beyond themselves.

- Important forms of communication include social referencing, in which babies look to their caregiver for an indication of how to feel and act on encountering something unfamiliar, and gaze-following and pointing.

- Word comprehension is in evidence by age 6 months, and by age 9 months children can understand some common expressions. The ability to produce language progresses from early vocalizations through babbling in the sounds and intonation patterns of the surrounding language to speaking some words at around 1 year, after which the pace of language learning accelerates remarkably.

A Sense of Self

- By about age 6 months, experience interacting with objects and people, along with emerging abilities to locomote and to use language, contributes to the infant's new sense of self. Infants' ability to recognize themselves in a mirror emerges gradually and is clearly evident at around 18 months. Children's two-word utterances reflect their ability to see themselves as agents.

- The emergence of a sense of self gives rise to the self-conscious emotions—for example, embarrassment, pride, shame, guilt, and envy—which require thinking about and evaluating oneself in relation to other people and their standards.

- The end of infancy is marked by patterns of behavior reflecting a sense of self and a new independence.

Developing Trust and Autonomy

- In the first of the two stages into which Erikson divided infancy—that is, basic trust versus mistrust—infants may come to see the world as safe for exploration and people as reliable and loving or they may come to see the world as dangerous and people as insensitive and hurtful.

- In the second stage—autonomy versus shame or doubt—infants may acquire a sense of their ability to accomplish tasks and tackle challenges or they may come to doubt their ability and feel shame.

Implications

- During infancy, babies and caregivers forge social and emotional ties that give infants a foundation for exploring the world. Both biological and sociocultural processes contribute to the creation of these ties.

Key Terms

emotion, p. 200
emotion regulation, p. 201
basic emotions, p. 201
theory of gradual differentiation, p. 202
differential emotions theory, p. 202
ontogenetic adaptations, p. 203
primary intersubjectivity, p. 203
mirror neurons, p. 205
attachment, p. 207

biological drives, p. 208
detachment, p. 208
secure base, p. 210
separation anxiety, p. 210
internal working model, p. 210
strange situation, p. 211
secure attachment, p. 211
avoidant attachment, p. 211
resistant attachment, p. 211

disorganized attachment, p. 212
socioeconomic status (SES), p. 214
secondary intersubjectivity, p. 221
perceptual scaffolding, p. 223
babbling, p. 223
self-conscious emotions, p. 226
basic trust versus mistrust, p. 228
autonomy versus shame and doubt, p. 229

Major Milestones of Early Childhood

	Physical Domain	Cognitive Domain	Social and Emotional Domain	
What Develops...	• Compared to infancy, growth rates of the body and brain slow considerably while ability to use and control the body increases. • Gross motor developments include running, kicking, climbing, throwing, skipping. • Fine motor developments include unbuttoning, using eating utensils, pouring liquid into a glass, coloring within the lines with crayons. • Brain grows to 90% of its full weight. • Myelination and neuronal branching increase in the frontal cortex and other areas important to advanced cognitive functions including planning and regulating behavior.	• Tendency to confuse appearance and reality. • Difficulty taking the perspectives of others. • Limitations in cause-effect reasoning. • Increased memory ability due to greater efficiency in encoding, storing, and retrieving information. • Increased knowledge of physical laws and properties of objects, such as gravity and inertia. • Development of coherent theories about mental life and activity. • Acquisition of basic vocabulary and grammar of native language.	• Stage of initiative versus guilt, with autonomy asserted but in ways that begin to conform to social roles and moral standards. • Play becomes gender-segregated. • Development of concepts of "boy" and "girl," and efforts to match own behavior to concepts. • Emergence of ethnic identity. • Moral judgments often emphasize external consequences rather than motives or intentions. • Increased ability to regulate thought, action, and emotion. • Increasing ability to feel empathy and sympathy toward others.	
Sociocultural Contributions and Consequences...	• The fast pace of modern life may interfere with children's sleep habits. • Changes in food access and eating behavior associated with globalization may increase risk for obesity, diabetes, and heart disease in children from developing countries. • Certain culturally organized activities may stimulate specific areas of the brain, facilitating growth and synaptic connections that, in turn, support further competence and learning.	• Cultural customs and routines support the development of generalized knowledge and shared understanding.	• Development of gender stereotypes is mediated by social and cultural practices that emphasize gender differences. • Increased cognitive abilities and decreased behavioral problems are associated with parents' socializing pride in ethnic background. • Cultural variations in parenting affect the emergence of self-conscious emotions. • Cultures differ in their tolerance of aggression and violence, affecting the extent to which children behave aggressively.	

part III

Early Childhood

By the age of 2½ or 3, children are no longer infants. It is clear that they are entering early childhood—the period between ages 2½ and 6. They are losing their baby fat, their legs are growing longer and thinner, and they are moving around the world with a great deal more confidence than they did only 6 months earlier. Within a short time, they can usually ride a tricycle, control their bowels, and put on their own clothes. They can help bake cookies, gather berries, and begin to participate in cultural ceremonies and rituals—as flower girls or ring bearers at a wedding, for example. Three-year-olds can talk an adult's ears off, and they are an avid audience for an interesting story. They can be bribed with promises of a later treat, but they may try to negotiate for a treat now as well. They develop theories about everything, from where babies come from to why the moon disappears from the sky, and they constantly test their theories against the realities around them.

Despite their developing independence, 3-year-olds need assistance from adults and older siblings in many areas. They cannot hold a pencil properly, cross a busy road safely by themselves, or tie their shoes. They do not yet have the ability to concentrate for long on their own. As a result, they often go off on tangents in their games, drawings, and conversations. One minute a 3-year-old may be Dora the Explorer, the next minute a unicorn, and the next a little girl in a hurry to go to the toilet.

In early childhood, children still understand relatively little about the world in which they live, and they have little control over it. Thus they are prey to fears of monsters, shadows, and things that go bump in the night. They combat their awareness of being small and powerless by wishful, magical thinking that turns a little boy afraid of ghosts into a big, brave, fighter pilot who dominates the playground.

Our discussion of early childhood development covers four chapters. Chapter 7 focuses on language and its acquisition. One of our most significant cultural tools, language is the medium through which children learn about their roles in the world, about acceptable behavior, and about their culture's assumptions about how the world works. Simultaneously, language enables children to ask questions, to explain their thoughts and desires, and to make more effective demands on the people around them.

Chapter 8 examines physical and cognitive developments during early childhood. The challenge developmentalists face is to explain how children can think and behave logically at one moment and then with complete lack of logic the next. The chapter considers different explanations for the unevenness of young children's cognition.

Chapter 9 shifts attention to social development and personality formation—to children's growing sense of a distinct identity, their ability to control their actions and feelings, their ways of thinking about rules of proper behavior, and their relations with the people around them. Topics that receive particular emphasis include the acquisition of a sense of culturally acceptable gender roles and children's increasing ability to get along with one another as they learn to balance their own desires with the demands of their social group.

With these general characteristics of early childhood as background, Chapter 10 addresses the influence of various contexts on young children's development. Among these are the family, where children first learn about who they are and what adults expect of them; community settings, including day-care centers and preschools; and the media, which link children's experiences in different settings and have important socializing effects.

Language Acquisition

Although it has been 15 minutes since her father put her down with her "baby" and gave her a good-night kiss, the sandman has yet to arrive, and 21-month-old Emily is filling her quiet room with words:

> *baby no eat dinner*
> *broccoli, soup carrots cause rice*
> *baby eat that*
> *baby no in night*
> *broccoli broccoli soup carrots cabbage*
> *no baby sleeping*

> *then baby get sick*
> *Emmy no eat dinner*
> *broccoli soup cause*
> *no baby sleeping*
> *baby sleeping all night*

One year later, Emily's bedtime monologue sounds like this:

> *actually it's Stephen's koala bear . . .*
> *when Stephen wakes up I'll have to throw his koala bear in his room*
> *'cause it's really Stephen's*
> *as a matter of fact Stephen's*
> *as a matter of fact it's sleeping with me now*

(Levy, 1989, pp. 158 and 169)

The Power of Language

Keys to the World of Language
The Biological Key to Language
The Environmental Key to Language

The Basic Domains of Language Acquisition
Phonological Development
Semantic Development
Grammar Development
Pragmatic Development

Explanations of Language Acquisition
Biological Explanations
Social and Cultural Explanations
Cognitive Approaches

Reconsidering the Keys to Language

As you can see, the first of Emily's bedtime monologues is barely interpretable. Words are missing or out of the usual order, and the monologue seems a jumble of disconnected statements with no clear meaning. The word "cause" appears in both monologues, but in the first it is next to impossible to figure out the meaning of "broccoli, soup carrots cause rice" and "broccoli soup cause." In fact, the only likely clue to what Emily might mean is the fact that many young children are not big fans of vegetables: She might be reciting her reason for not eating dinner.

By contrast, in the second monologue, Emily's words are far more grammatically organized and more clearly convey her meaning. The groups of words are longer and more like complete sentences now. The word "'cause" expresses a causal relationship ("'cause it's really Stephen's"), and possessive and temporal relationships are also expressed ("it's Stephen's"; "it's sleeping with me now"). It is also clear that Emily has picked up certain speech mannerisms, such as "actually" and "as a matter of fact." Although her language is not fully developed by any means, it is significantly more adultlike and easy to interpret.

The progress Emily has made in her ability to use language during the year separating the two monologues is amazing but by no means exceptional, and similar increases in language-using ability will continue for several years to come. Indeed, by her 6th birthday, Emily's mental and social life will be totally transformed by an explosive growth in the ability to comprehend and use language. Typically, developing children are estimated to learn several words a day during the preschool years, and by the time they are 6 years old, their vocabularies have grown to anywhere between 8,000 and 14,000 words (Anglin, 1993; Biemiller & Slonim, 2001). They can understand verbal instructions ("Go wash your face—and do not come back until it's clean"), chatter excitedly about the tiger they saw at the zoo, teach friends how to play a video game, or insult their siblings with a variety of colorful labels. In short, 6-year-old children are competent language users. Without this competence, they could not carry out the new cognitive tasks and social responsibilities that their society will now assign them, including acquiring the tools of their culture through formal education or other instruction.

We begin this chapter by reviewing the nature of language as a symbolic system and elaborating on the emerging foundations of linguistic communication that we discussed in earlier chapters. Next, we describe the two main keys—human biological structures and processes, and human social environments—that unlock the door to the world of language. We then trace the course of children's development in the four basic domains of language—*phonology* (sound), *semantics* (meaning), *grammar,* and *pragmatics* (the uses to which language is put). With the facts of language development in hand, we examine various theories about the processes that underlie this fundamental human capacity. Finally, we explore the unique role of language as a tool for creating and transforming reality.

The Power of Language

The story of Romeo and Juliet has endured for centuries. It is a tragic love, made so by the fact that one lover is a Montague, the other, a Capulet, the names of two families caught in a long and violent feud. In deep despair, Romeo challenges the idea that one's family name could stand as an obstacle to the happiness of a shared life together and asks the famous question "What's in a name? That which we call a rose by any other name would smell as sweet." Romeo suggests that names should not matter; they are just words for things. It is the things themselves that we love or despise, that move us with their sweet scent and beauty. But we know better. Names, like words in general, can carry deep and complex meanings. And when names and other words are woven together into sentences and stories, like Shakespeare's *Romeo and Juliet,* they can move and inspire people for generations.

We made the point in Chapter 2 that language is a *symbolic system* of enormous scope and power (pp. 54–55). It allows communication about the past and the future; permits the expression of abstract ideas, desires, and emotions; and is one of the most significant means of preserving and passing on—and even of challenging and transforming—a culture's knowledge, values, and beliefs. We also explained that language, like other tools of culture, profoundly affects development because it organizes or *mediates* human activities, relationships, and thinking—as "Montague" and "Capulet" did for Romeo and Juliet. Alexander Luria (1981, p. 35) beautifully summarized the power human beings possess as a consequence of language:

> In the absence of words, humans would have to deal only with those things which they could perceive and manipulate directly. With the help of language, they can deal with things which they have not perceived even indirectly and with things which were part of the experience of earlier generations. Thus, the word adds another dimension to the world of humans. . . . Animals have only one world, the world of objects and situations which can be perceived by the senses. Humans have a double world.

Although many other species make a variety of communicative sounds and gestures, none has evolved a system of communication as powerful and flexible as human language (Greenspan & Shanker, 2004; Jablonka & Lamb, 2007). Indeed, the evidence presented in previous chapters leaves little doubt that children are born predisposed to attend to language and to communicate with the people around them. At birth they show a preference for speech over other kinds of sounds and are capable of differentiating between two sounds that are distinct *phonemes* (basic sound categories) in any of the world's languages (see Chapter 6, p. 223). Within a few days after birth, they can distinguish the sounds of their native language from those of a foreign language. Well before they are able to speak intelligibly, the range of sounds they recognize as distinct becomes narrowed to those that their native language treats as distinct phonemes (Kuhl et al., 2006; Luo & Baillargeon, 2005; see p. 223). They first come to recognize their own name and words for familiar objects and people and then entire often-heard phrases. Babies make comparable strides in their capacity to produce language. Although newborns' abilities to communicate are limited initially to a small set of facial expressions and crying, soon their sound repertoire expands to include *cooing, babbling,* and then *jargoning,* with each change bringing the baby closer to producing recognizable words.

At the same time that their capacity to distinguish and produce linguistic signals increases, babies become more adept at interacting with the people and objects around them. In Chapter 6, we explained how infants and their social partners establish *primary intersubjectivity,* sharing feelings as a consequence of well-coordinated and organized face-to-face social interactions (see pp. 203–204). This ability is evident in the rounds of greeting noises and smiling that caregivers and babies engage in, to their mutual delight. We noted, moreover, that between the ages of 9 and 12 months, babies and their partners become able to establish *secondary intersubjectivity,* a crucial precursor to language acquisition because it allows babies and their caregivers to communicate their feelings about objects and events that are the focus of their joint attention (see p. 221).

Somehow, in the space of a very few years, children are launched from these early foundations and enter the world of language (see Table 7.1 for a summary of some of the early developments). We will now examine the special keys that unlock the door to this world.

The face-to-face social interaction enjoyed by this Jordanian mother and baby will expand dramatically as language develops and provides a way to communicate about the world around them.

There is no mistaking this baby's gesture to her father: "Pick me up!" In just a few more months, her gesturing will be accompanied by words.

table **7.1**	
The Progress of Language Development	
Approximate Age	**Typical Behavior**
Birth	Phoneme perception
	Discrimination of language from nonlanguage sounds
	Crying
3 months	Cooing
6 months	Babbling
	Loss of ability to discriminate between nonnative phonemes
9 months	First words
12 months	Use of words to attract adults' attention
18 months	Vocabulary spurt
	First two-word sentences (telegraphic speech)
24 months	Correct responses to indirect requests ("Is the door shut?")
30 months	Creation of indirect requests ("You're standing on my blocks!")
	Modification of speech to take listener into account
	Early awareness of grammatical categories

Keys to the World of Language

Access to the world of language is virtually guaranteed to all who hold two keys: (1) the human biological structures and systems that support language, and (2) participation in a language-using community. Let us consider the biological key first.

The Biological Key to Language

Developmentalists have used two conceptually related approaches to tackle the question of how biology unlocks the door to the world of language. The first is to inquire about the capacities and limitations of nonhuman species. If humans' abilities in producing and comprehending language depart significantly from those of other species, then evolutionary forces must have produced the uniquely human biological structures and processes that make language possible. The second, related approach is to try to discover which structures and processes of the human brain support language development and what their special contributions to it are.

Is Language Uniquely Human?
Research to determine whether language is uniquely human has a long history (Weiss & Newport, 2006). One early strategy involved experimenters' raising chimpanzees in their home as though they were human children. The hope was that these genetically close relatives (with whom it was then assumed we share 98.5 percent of our genes) would acquire oral language if they were treated just like humans. This research demonstrated that chimpanzees can, in fact, learn to comprehend dozens of spoken words and phrases (Hayes & Hayes, 1951; Kellogg & Kellogg, 1933). But the chimps never *produced* language, at least not in the form of spoken words. Subsequent research that involved manual signing instead of oral speech provided clear evidence that chimps can learn to use signs to refer to and request certain things (such as different kinds of fruit or specific toys). However, the evidence that they can acquire language is still disputed (Buttelmann, Call, & Tomasello, 2008; Fields, Segerdahl, & Savage-Rumbaugh, 2007; Greenfield, Lyn, & Savage-Rumbaugh, 2008; Tomasello, 2000).

Current enthusiasm for the idea that chimpanzees have the capacity to understand and produce language has been inspired by the work of Sue Savage-Rumbaugh and Duane Rumbaugh (Rumbaugh et al., 1994). The Rumbaughs provided chimpanzees with a "lexical keyboard"—that is, a keyboard that bore symbols that stood for words ("banana," "give," and so on)—and they used standard reinforcement learning techniques to teach the chimpanzees the meaning of these symbols. In addition, the people who worked with the chimpanzees used natural language in everyday, routine activities such as feeding.

The Rumbaughs' most successful student has been Kanzi, a bonobo ape who initially learned to use the lexical keyboard by observing his mother being trained to use it. Kanzi is able to use the keyboard to ask for things, and he can comprehend requests made of him by researchers using the lexical symbols. He has also learned to understand some spoken English words and phrases (Rumbaugh & Washburn, 2003). For example, when told to "feed your ball some tomato," Kanzi picked up a tomato and placed it in the "mouth" of a facelike soft sponge ball. He has also demonstrated some understanding of syntax: When asked to "give the shot [syringe] to Liz" and then to

Kanzi uses a specially designed keyboard composed of lexical symbols to communicate.

Courtesy of Iowa Primate Learning Sanctuary

"give Liz a shot," he correctly handed the syringe to the girl in the first instance and touched the syringe to the girl's arm in the second.

Kanzi's ability to produce language is not as impressive as his comprehension. Most of his "utterances" on the lexical keyboard are single words that are closely linked to his current actions, and they usually involve requests. He also uses two-word utterances in a wide variety of combinations and occasionally makes observations. For example, he produced the request "car trailer" on one occasion when he was in the car and wanted (or so his caretakers believed) to be taken to the trailer rather than to walk there. He has created such requests as "play yard Austin" when he wanted to visit a chimpanzee named Austin in the playyard. When a researcher put oil on him while he was eating a potato, he commented, "potato oil."

Using combinations of visual symbols or gestures, bonobos and chimpanzees can produce language at roughly the level of a 2-year-old child. In their productions, they form telegraphic utterances that encode the same semantic relations as do those of children (for example, a two-symbol combination relating an agent to its action—"Kanzi eat") (Greenfield & Lyn, 2007). Bonobos are also capable of comprehending English speech at roughly the level of a 2-year-old child (Savage-Rumbaugh, 1993). However, in contrast to human children, who acquire complex language with no formal teaching, nonhuman primates develop language ability only in the context of intense explicit instruction provided by their human caretakers. To explore what might account for this dramatic species difference in the ability to learn language, developmentalists have looked to species-unique features of the human brain.

A Brain for Language Scientists have long been aware that the left side of the human brain plays a dominant role in language ability, but it was not until the middle of the nineteenth century that the brain bases of language became an active area of research in medicine and psychology. In particular, it was the work of two physicians, each studying a different form of a speech disorder called *aphasia,* that led to the discovery of language areas of the brain (Luria, 1973).

In 1861, a French surgeon named Paul Broca treated a man who was unable to speak. When his patient died, Broca examined his brain and found damage on the outside surface of the left frontal lobe in an area that came to be known as *Broca's area.* Patients with damage to this area suffer from what is called *Broca's aphasia,* a condition in which speech is either absent or severely disrupted. Individuals with Broca's aphasia may speak with great effort in brief, meaningful phrases that omit small words such as "is," "and," and "the." For example, they might say "Walk dog" to mean "I will take the dog for a walk." (Those who recover from this disorder often report that they knew what they wanted to say but could not control their speech.) Generally, patients with Broca's asphasia are able to understand individual words but have difficulty understanding more complex structures.

A few years later, Carl Wernicke, a German physician, discovered that damage to an area slightly to the rear of Broca's area results in an inability to comprehend language. People with damage to this area, now called *Wernicke's area,* are often capable of producing language, but much of what they say makes little sense. Patients with what is known as *Wernicke's aphasia* thus often produce long sentences that include unnecessary words and even nonsense words. For example, they might say something like "You know that smoodle pinkered and that I want to get him round and take care of him like you want before" to mean "The dog needs to go out so I will take him for a walk" (National Institute on Deafness and Other Communication Disorders, 2012).

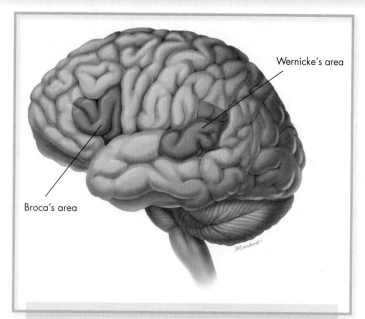

FIGURE 7.1 This view of the left hemisphere of the brain highlights two key areas for normal language processing in adults. Wernicke's area is central to processing sounds and comprehension. Damage to this area results in an inability to comprehend language. Broca's area is central to motor control and language production. Damage to this area of the brain results in the loss or severe disruption of normal speech. (From E. H. Chudler, "Neuroscience for Kids: The Brain and Language," at http://faculty.washington.edu/chudler/lang.html.)

Contemporary studies of the brain and language have shown that in adults, injuries to the left hemisphere in either Broca's or Wernicke's area are overwhelmingly more likely to cause aphasia than are injuries to the corresponding parts of the right hemisphere (Figure 7.1). This evidence appears to confirm the idea that there is indeed a part of the brain that is genetically programmed to produce and comprehend language—an idea that has gained additional support from studies using technologically sophisticated neuroimaging techniques.

Angela Friederici and her colleagues at the Max Planck Institute for Human Cognitive and Brain Sciences in Germany have been using advanced neuroimaging techniques to investigate relationships between language development and brain mechanisms (Obleser, Meyer, & Friederici, 2011). In one study, they tried to determine whether Broca's area plays a special role in processing complex language (Friederici et al., 2006). Their inquiry was inspired by increasing evidence suggesting that although some nonhuman species show at least a rudimentary capacity to process simple sentences (as did Kanzi when he distinguished the difference between "give the shot to Liz" and "give Liz a shot"), they are not able to process more complex sentences. When the researchers presented participants with both simple and complex speech sequences (for example, a simple sentence like "The song pleased the teacher" and a more complex sentence like "The song that the boy sang pleased the teacher"), they discovered that the complexity of the sequence determined which area of the brain became active. In particular, complex sequences activated Broca's area, which evolved fairly recently in the history of our species. Simple sequences, in contrast, activated only an evolutionarily older area of the brain that we share with other primates. In another line of research using neuroimaging, studies conducted at the University of Barcelona have shown that the characteristic spurt in toddlers' vocabulary (discussed in more detail below) occurs only after substantial myelination of language-related brain regions (Pujol et al., 2006).

Although Broca's and Wernicke's areas seem to play a significant role in humans' ability to acquire and use language, research with children strongly suggests that it is possible to develop normal, or near-normal, language abilities even if Broca's and Wernicke's areas are damaged, as long as the damage occurs early in life (Bates & Roe, 2001). Data in support of this conclusion come largely from studies of children who, just before, during, or after birth, suffered strokes that cut off the blood supply to the left or right hemisphere of the brain, resulting in damage to the cerebral cortex. These children still acquire language, although their performance may be at the lower end of the normal range. Most important, however, they do so even when the damage occurs in the left hemisphere, where language appears to be localized in adults! Whereas left-hemisphere damage would leave an adult considerably more language-impaired than would right-hemisphere damage, damage on either side results in little impairment for children, as Figure 7.2 shows. This is because of the plasticity of the brain in early development; in infants with left-hemisphere damage, parts of the right hemisphere become the brain center for the language.

Some researchers interpret these and similar findings to indicate that, in the absence of any interfering factors, the infant brain is predisposed to ensure the eventual emergence of an area in the left hemisphere of the brain that is specialized to process language (Bates, 2005). Indeed, a fascinating study indicates that when 5-month-old babies babble, their mouths open more on the right side than the left; since the right side of the mouth is controlled by the left side of the brain, this suggests that the left side of the brain has already begun to specialize as a center for language processing (Holowka & Petitto, 2002). On the other hand, evidence that the newborn's brain can compensate for damage caused by strokes indicates that the brain mechanisms supporting language are not fixed at birth. Indeed, recent research indicates that the brain undergoes highly specific changes as the child's language abilities progress (Brauer, Anwander, & Friederici, 2011). The extent to which brain maturation may *cause* particular language advances remains unclear. It is likely, however, that "learning itself plays a major role in organizing the brain for efficient language use" (Bates & Roe, 2001, p. 305).

The Environmental Key to Language

Sometime before her 2nd birthday, a girl named Genie was permanently locked in her room by her abusive father. For more than 11 years, she spent her days chained to a potty and her nights tied up in a sleeping bag. She lived in almost total isolation, and as far as can be determined, was never spoken to after she was confined. Every time her father came to tie her in for the night or to bring her food, he growled at her like a beast and often scratched her with his fingernails. When she was finally liberated from these horrible circumstances at the age of 13, Genie was a pitiful creature. She did not make intelligible sounds, walk normally, chew solid food, or express her emotions appropriately. David Rigler, a scientist, and his wife petitioned the Department of Social Services to become Genie's foster parents and to study her extensively, along with a team of linguists and psychologists. Genie spent 4 years in the Rigler household. During that time she was treated as much as possible like a member of the family. She was taught how to chew solid food, to behave properly at the table, to express her emotions appropriately, and to stop masturbating publicly whenever she felt the urge to. However, despite the special emphasis placed on nurturing her language development, Genie's speech resembled the language used in telegrams. There is no evidence that she ever learned to ask a real question or to form a proper negative sentence (Curtiss et al., 1974).

Genie's case tells a tragic story of unimaginable deprivation and destruction. It also underscores how participation in a normal social environment is essential to the process of language acquisition (Clark, 2008, 2010). In the course of such participation, children are not only exposed to *models* of how language is used and understood; they are also provided with opportunities to communicate with others—opportunities that *motivate* them to be better communicators, that is, to use language to express and share ideas effectively (Hoff, 2006; Tomasello, 2011). Clearly, Genie was denied both language models and communication opportunities during the years children acquire language, and these deprivations certainly contributed to her inability to develop normal language. But Genie's horrific deprivations affected every aspect of her health and development, making it impossible

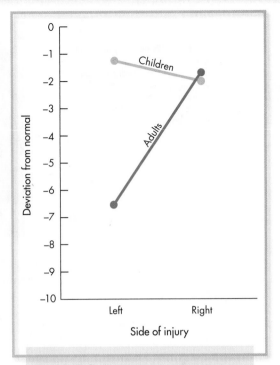

FIGURE 7.2 The figure shows the difference in the impact of brain injury to the left and right hemispheres for adults and children. When adults were presented with novel phrases, the performance of adults with left-hemisphere damage was far worse than the performance of those with right-hemisphere damage. There was no significant difference in performance between children with left-hemisphere damage and those with right-hemisphere damage. (After Bates & Roe, 2001.)

Children with hearing impairments acquire language at a comparable rate to hearing children, especially when they receive support from the environment. Here, a deaf child learns sign language at a special school in Sri Lanka.

Paul Hahn / laif / Redux

to use her case to assess the specific effects that language deprivation can have on children's language development. To do this, researchers have turned to the case of deaf children whose hearing parents do not know sign language and discourage its use (Goldin-Meadow, Mylander, & Franklin, 2007; Goldin-Meadow, Özyürek, Sancar, & Mylander, 2009).

Language-Deprived Environments The biological condition of deafness need not be an impediment to normal language acquisition: Deaf children born to deaf parents who communicate in sign language acquire language at least as rapidly and fully as hearing children born into hearing households (Morgan & Woll, 2002; Volterra et al., 2006). Thus, any delays or difficulties in deaf children's language development must result from the way the linguistic environment is organized.

Such difficulties often arise in deaf children whose parents refuse to learn or use sign language because they believe that their children can and should learn to read lips and to vocalize sounds. Although many children raised in these circumstances have significant trouble learning spoken language (Geers et al., 2002), they often develop fairly sophisticated gestural systems that allow them to communicate with others (reviewed in Schick, 2006). In particular, many deaf children raised without exposure to a signed language spontaneously begin to gesture in "home sign," a kind of communication through pantomime (Pizzuto et al., 2001).

Research by Susan Goldin-Meadow and her colleagues (Franklin, Giannakidou, & Goldin-Meadow, 2011) has determined that the home-sign gestering developed by deaf children has certain characteristics of language, even when children have no one to show them the signs. Home sign begins as pointing. Children then gesture one sign at a time—at the same age that hearing children develop single-word utterances. Home-sign gestures also seem to refer to the same kinds of objects, and to fulfill the same functions, as the early words of hearing children or of deaf children with signing parents. Remarkably, around their 2nd birthday, about the same time that hearing children begin to utter multiword sentences, home-signing children begin to make patterns of two, and sometimes three or more, signs. In addition, these patterns appear to involve complex sentence structures that are characteristic of all human languages and are absent from the communicative system of chimpanzees and other creatures even after long training—structures equivalent to the type of speech sequences that we described above as activating Broca's area, rather than the evolutionarily older part of the brain.

To explore the robustness of home sign, Goldin-Meadow and her colleagues compared its development in deaf children in the United States and in children of

Mandarin-speaking parents living in Taiwan (Goldin-Meadow & Mylander, 1998; Goldin-Meadow et al., 2007). Despite a variety of cultural differences between these two groups in child-rearing practices—including Taiwanese mothers' greater use of gesture when speaking to their young children, deaf or hearing—the researchers found the same patterns of spontaneous home-sign production, suggesting that universal processes of language creation are at work (see the box "Children Creating a Language"). However, once the children in both cultures are able to make two- to three-word "utterances" in their home sign and begin to form structurally complex sentences, their spontaneous language development appears to come to an end. Thus it seems that the mere fact of being raised in an environment where the actions of all the other participants are organized by human language is sufficient

Children Creating a Language

BEFORE THE 1970S, THERE WAS NO national education system for deaf Nicaraguans, and no Nicaraguan sign language. The deaf were socially isolated and marginalized in Nicaraguan society. But in 1977, a school for 25 deaf children was built in the capital city, Managua. Two years later, the school was expanded to admit 100 children, and the following year, a vocational school was opened for deaf adolescents. These schools served more than 400 students, mostly through lip-reading instruction. Within a few years, a community of deaf people ranging in age from childhood to adulthood developed, and with it, a new language, Nicaraguan Sign Language. The emergence of this language within the newly formed community has been studied by Ann Senghas (Senghas, 2011). Her findings illustrate that while the child's *capacity* for learning complex language is rooted in the evolutionary history of our species, the acquisition of a fully fledged grammar requires social participation.

Specifically, Senghas found that when the first children to attend the school for the deaf were together on school playgrounds and buses, they began to communicate with one another using the home signs that they had invented before coming to school. Although teachers were instructing children in lip-reading and finger-spelling in Spanish, the children largely ignored these lessons outside the classroom and instead created their very own language community. As children interacted socially, the number and variety of signs that they used increased dramatically, as did the complexity of their communication.

At the start of the second and third school years, new groups of children arrived at the school and with no deliberate instruction,

These girls are students at the Escuelitas de Bluefields, a school for the deaf in Nicaragua, where they learn sign language as well as other literacy and academic skills.

Susan Meiselas/Magnum

began combining their own individual home signs with those of their schoolmates. The new signing mix eventually became conventionalized, producing a *pidgin language*. A pidgin language is a blending of two different languages and is characterized by simplified grammar and vocabulary (pidgin languages most often emerge in situations of slave or immigrant labor). Over time, the pidgin language the deaf schoolchildren used became increasingly stylized and took on more complex grammatical forms. In short, the children began to communicate with each other in a language that exhibits the same structure as any other natural language. Significantly, it was the *youngest* children who elaborated on and enriched the pidgin language they encountered and introduced new grammatical forms that were not present in the signing of the older students (Senghas, Senghas, & Pyers, 2005; Slobin, 2005).

In his review of Senghas's work, Dan Slobin argues the point that children's creation

of home signs suggests a human capacity to create the rudiments of a language system but that, for such rudimentary systems to develop further, a community of users, as in the case of the Nicaraguan school, is needed. Slobin writes that "language is like other sorts of human technology; once it is present, it provides a 'niche'—a modified environment—creating new pressures for the refinement of that technology" (2005, p. 280).

Taken as a whole, the research on language-deprived environments suggests that even in the absence of direct experience with language, children will develop the beginnings of language during the first 2 years of life, as long they regularly have the opportunity to communicate with others. However, the language that appears under such linguistically impoverished conditions does not go beyond that of children at the two-word phase. Apparently, to fully acquire language, children must grow up in an environment that provides a language-support system.

Learning Two Languages

WE LIVE IN AN AGE IN WHICH vast numbers of people move from one language community to another, rear children among people whose native tongue is different than their own, or grow up in families in which more than one language is spoken. In fact, well over 50 percent of the world's people are *bilingual* or *multilingual*—that is, speak two or more languages (Tucker, 1999). In the United States alone, more than 3 million children are *dual-language learners (DLL)* (National Center for Education Statistics, 2004). This state of affairs poses interesting questions about language acquisition for parents as well as developmentalists. How does exposure to multiple languages affect a child's language acquisition? Is the child confused by clashing vocabularies and grammars? Is it better for a child to learn one language first before being exposed to another? Despite ample scientific evidence that young children can acquire two or more languages effortlessly (Bialystok, 2001; Petitto, 2009), it is widely believed among North American parents that early exposure to two languages might confuse children and cause them to learn language more slowly or less well than their monolingual peers. As a result of these concerns, many bilingual parents deliberately choose to withhold knowledge of one family language from their children until it is "safe" to add a second language to their repertoire (Petitto et al., 2009).

Psycholinguists who study DLL children have been divided in their interpretation of whether, and to what extent, acquiring two languages at the same time differs from acquiring one language and then another. Some adhere to the *unitary language hypothesis*, believing that children exposed to two languages from birth interpret the two languages as part of a single, fused, system. In support of this view, they point to cases where infants in the one-word stage acquire each of their words in just one or the other language. For example, a child who knows the word for dog in one language will not know the word for it in the other language. The fact that children exposed to two languages often use words from both languages in the same sentence is also taken as evidence that they do not distinguish between their two native vocabularies. According to this view, it is not until children are about 3 years old that they become capable of differentiating between two separate languages. The unitary language hypothesis supports those who recommend delaying exposure to a second language in order to avoid confusion and possible language delay.

Those who adhere to the *differentiated language hypothesis*, on the other hand, accept

In today's world, the ability not only to speak but also to read and write in a foreign language is becoming an increasingly important part of every child's development.

The Power of Forever Photography / iStockphoto

---

to allow the child to acquire the rudiments of linguistic structure, but that without access to the linguistic complexities (signed or spoken) provided by accomplished language users, the child has no opportunity to discover the more subtle features of language. Highlighting this point is the case of a hearing child raised by deaf parents (Sachs, Bard, & Johnson, 1981). This child's parents exposed him to neither conventional oral nor conventional manual language input. He heard English only on TV and during a brief time spent in nursery school. The course of this child's language development was precisely the same as for the deaf children of nonsigning, hearing parents: He developed the basic features of language but not more subtle ones. Once he was introduced to normal American Sign Language, at the age of 3 years and 9 months, he quickly acquired normal language ability.

Variations in Language Environments Research shows that, even if we look just at "normal" environments, there is enormous variety in the language environments to which children across the globe are exposed. Indeed, some children are exposed to a variety of languages (see the box "Learning Two Languages"). One significant difference concerns the amount of talk that adults direct to infants. North American mothers, for example, are known to talk to their babies from birth, if not before, even using the babies' burps, sneezes, and other noises to engage in

infant-directed speech (or motherese or baby-talk) Speech that adults use with infants, characterized by high pitch, exaggerated intonation, clear boundaries between meaningful parts of utterance, and simplified vocabulary.

the evidence that children mix two languages but emphasize that children's speech exhibits regular grammatical patterns that are appropriate to both languages they speak. In addition, the language they use is sensitive to the language used by the adults around them. For example, if young children learning Chinese and English are addressed in Chinese, they will respond in Chinese, not English, suggesting that they are able to keep straight which language is appropriate in a given context.

In an effort to find evidence against which to test the two hypotheses, a team of researchers headed by Laura-Ann Petitto looked at the language acquisition both of hearing Canadian children who had deaf parents and were acquiring sign language and French and of hearing Canadian children who were acquiring French and English (Petitto et al., 2001). The researchers found no evidence of language delay in either group; whether the combination of languages was sign and French or French and English, children reached the key milestones of acquiring their first word, their first 2-word combination, and their first 50 words at almost precisely the same age as did monolingual children. This is consistent with a number of other studies showing that vocabulary development for children under the age of 3 is comparable for DLL and monolingual children (Jia, Chen, & Kim, 2008;

Conboy & Thal, 2006). In addition, when the researchers created conditions under which children spoke with a person who knew only one of the relevant languages (French, English, or sign), the children almost always used the language that the adult knew, indicating that they differentiated the two languages.

Taken as a whole, these data appear to lay to rest the idea that there is anything harmful about children's acquiring two languages simultaneously. Indeed, DLL children reap surprising rewards. The constant need to switch between two active language systems—inhibiting one while using the other—may carry over to other areas of intellectual functioning. A case in point is DLL children's early ability to see multiple images in an ambiguous figure (Bialystok & Shapero, 2005). It is well known that children, particularly those under the age of 5, have difficulty identifying more than one image in ambiguous figures, such as the vase and the faces shown in the figure (Diamond, 2002a, 2002b; Gopnik & Rosati, 2001). Once they see the vase, it is hard for young children to reinterpret the picture and see it in a different way—as a picture of faces (see p. 252 regarding how preoperational children can be "captured" by a specific feature of an object). DLL children, however, seem to master such tasks at earlier ages than do chil-

Bilingual children are able to see both the faces and the vase in this ambiguous figure at an earlier age than can children who are learning a single language.

dren learning a single language. Ellen Bialystok and her colleagues believe that this early mastery is due to DLL children's ability to control their attention to selected aspects of the figure, an ability that stems from their experience in paying attention to and managing two different languages. Thus, in addition to the social benefits of being able to communicate in more than one language, bilingual children seem to reap cognitive rewards as well.

"conversation" with them (Snow, 1995; Hoff, 2006). In contrast, adults in cultures such as the Mayan of Mexico and the Walpiri of Australia talk very little to their babies, believing that there is no point in engaging prelinguistic children in conversation (Brown, 2002).

In some cultures, adults believe that it is important to actively teach their children how to talk (Ochs & Schieffelin, 1995). The Kaluli of New Guinea, for example, believe that children must be explicitly taught language just as they must be taught other culturally valued forms of behavior. Kaluli parents take their child's first spoken words as a signal that the child is ready to be taught language, and they begin a form of speech activity called *elema:* The mother provides the utterance she wants the child to repeat followed by the command "Elema" ("Say like this"). Eleanor Ochs (1982) described similar practices among Samoans, and Peggy Miller (1982) reported that working-class mothers in Baltimore, Maryland, follow a similar strategy with respect to teaching vocabulary.

Even in societies in which adults do not engage in deliberate language-teaching strategies, many adults are likely to use a special kind of speech when speaking to infants. Dubbed **infant-directed speech**, or more popularly, *motherese* or *baby-talk*, this speech is characterized by a high-pitched voice with exaggerated shifts in intonation, a simplified vocabulary, and an emphasis on the boundaries between

There is wide cultural variation in whether and how older children and adults engage infants in conversation. Sitting on a sidewalk in Calcutta, the older boy obviously thinks that his baby brother has something interesting to say.

table 7.2

Simplifications Used by Middle-Class U.S. Adults Speaking to Small Children

Phonological Simplifications

Higher pitch and exaggerated intonation

Clear pronunciation

Slower speech

Distinct pauses between utterances

Syntactic Differences

Shorter and less varied utterance length

Almost all sentences well formed

Many partial or complete repetitions of child's utterances, sometimes with expansion

Fewer broken sentences

Less grammatical complexity

Semantic Differences

More limited vocabulary

Many special words and diminutives

Reference to concrete circumstances of here and now

Middle level of generality in naming objects

Pragmatic Differences

More directives, imperatives, and questions

More utterances designed to draw attention to aspects of objects

Source: De Villiers & De Villiers, 1978.

meaningful parts of an utterance, all of which help to highlight what the adult wants to communicate (Fernald, 1991; Kitamura et al., 2002). Such modifications to normal speech are believed to provide a variety of clues that children can use in segmenting the flow of speech to identify words. Indeed, a study conducted by Erik Thiessen and his colleagues demonstrated that 8-month-old babies who heard a string of nonsense words presented in the pitch and intonation characteristic of infant-directed speech were able to learn the words better than were babies who heard them presented in a fashion more typical of adult speech (Thiessen, Hill, & Saffran, 2005). It also appears that infants may quickly develop preferences for individuals who use infant-directed speech. In one study, 5-month-olds were shown videos of a woman who spoke in either an adult-directed or an infant-directed manner (Schachner & Hannon, 2011). The babies were then shown two photographs simultaneously—one of the woman from the video, the other of a novel woman. After seeing the video in which the woman used infant-directed speech, babies preferred to look her photograph when it was paired with an image of a novel face. In contrast, after seeing the video of the woman using adult-directed speech, babies instead looked longer at the photograph of the novel face.

As Table 7.2 indicates, middle-class parents in the United States simplify virtually every aspect of their language when they speak to their children. In addition, studies of both English-speaking and Mandarin-speaking adults have shown that the complexity of their speech to children is graded to the level of the complexity of the individual child's speech (Liu, Tsao, & Kuhl, 2009; Rivero, 2010; Snow, 1995).

Catherine Snow (1972) showed how such tailoring processes can work in the case of a mother directing a child to put away toys: "Put the red truck in the box now. . . . The red truck. . . . No, the red truck. . . . In the box. . . . The red truck in the box." Note the sequence of the mother's directions. Snow argues that this kind of grading of language, in which statements are gradually simplified and their meaning highlighted, isolates constituent phrases at the same time that it models the whole correct grammatical structure.

In their efforts to aid children's comprehension (and perhaps to help children discover how to use language), North American adults not only simplify what they say to children but also often expand upon and reformulate what children say, putting it into a grammatically correct adult version (Brown & Bellugi, 1964). A mother whose child says "Mommy wash," for example, might respond with "Yes, Mommy is washing her face"; and to the declaration "Daddy sleep," she might respond "Yes, Daddy is sleeping. Don't wake him up." Recent research conducted by developmental psycholinguist Eve Clark and her colleagues confirmed that the practice of adults' reformulating young children's utterances is widespread, providing novice language learners feedback about the grammar of their language (Clark & Bernicot, 2008).

Developmentalists have not been able to draw firm conclusions about whether and how the reformulations adults make of childen's speech affect children's language acquisition. Indeed, several studies suggest that the extent to which such reformulations and other infant-directed speech occur very much depends on the specific cultural community involved (Ochs & Schieffelin, 1984). For example, such child-centered speech patterns are relatively rare in certain U.S. immigrant Mexican American and Puerto Rican communities (Valdes, 1996; Zentella, 1997). One thing that is clear, however, is that the development of children's vocabulary is affected by the amount of language they hear. This relation was strikingly demonstrated in a study by Betty Hart and Todd Risley (1999) that recorded the language spoken in the homes of families on welfare, working-class families, and professional families. The differences in vocabulary exposure and development were quite marked: The 1- to 3-year-old children in welfare homes heard only 33 percent as much language as the children in working-class families heard, and only 20 percent as much language as children from professional families heard. The rate at which the children acquired vocabulary closely tracked the amount of language they heard.

But again, rate of vocabulary development aside, several decades of research show that no one method of structuring children's language experience is essential and that the differences in the adults' everyday, intuitive language practices with children appear to make little difference in the rate at which children acquire language. All normally developing children become competent language users.

⏏ APPLY :: CONNECT :: DISCUSS

In describing language as an "instinct," Stephen Pinker (1994) wrote that "people know how to talk in more or less the sense that spiders know how to spin webs . . . spiders spin spider webs because they have spider brains, which give them the urge to spin and the competence to succeed." In what ways might his argument be insufficient for explaining how individual children acquire language?

The Basic Domains of Language Acquisition

The first challenge in understanding a new language is segmenting the stream of sounds into separate and recognizable words. Consider the sentence "Thomas kissed Sylvia, so she slapped his face." If someone read you this sentence aloud, your interpretation would clearly be impaired if you heard something like "To mask issed sylvias oshes lapped hisfa ce." The process through which children acquire knowledge of how to segment strings of speech sounds into meaningful units of language is part of the domain of language acquisition referred to as **phonological development**.

Beyond understanding how to segment the speech sounds of the sentence, it is necessary to understand the meaning of the words that compose the sentence. **Semantic development** refers to this process of learning the meanings of words and word combinations. We know, for example, that the word "kiss" refers to a particular type of action in which the lips are puckered and applied to some person or object. However, the fact that the action resulted in being slapped, which we understand to mean striking another with one's hand, adds another layer of meaning to the kiss: it was unwanted and resented. As this simple example illustrates, word meanings are complex and interact with each other; and as you will see, the meanings of words change for children as they learn and apply them—often in error.

Yet another challenge to interpreting the sentence about Thomas and Sylvia is to understand the rules about how the words are arranged in the sentence. For words to be combined into a comprehensible sentence, they must be related not only to objects and events but to one another. That is, they must be governed by **grammar**, the rules of a particular language for sequencing words in a sentence, and word parts within words. For example, the word sequence "Thomas kissed Sylvia" has a very different meaning from the sequence "Sylvia kissed Thomas." Rules of grammar also lead us to understand that the kissing and slapping are actions that happened in the past (as indicated by the "-ed" ending), and that one action (the kissing) led to the other (the slapping). Thus language acquisition includes the process of learning grammar.

phonological development Learning to segment speech into meaningful units of sound.

semantic development Learning meanings of words and of combinations of words.

grammar The rules of a given language for the sequencing of words in a sentence and the ordering of parts of words.

pragmatic development Learning the conventions that govern the use of language in particular social contexts.

morpheme The smallest unit of meaning in the words of a language.

Finally, a full interpretation of the sentence requires that we know something about the connections between the sentence and the social or cultural context in which it occurs. **Pragmatic development**, the process of learning the social and cultural conventions that govern how language is used in particular contexts, is an especially important challenge in children's acquisition of language. Children's failure to appreciate the connections between sentences and their contexts often leads to inappropriate utterances. Indeed, young children are famous for speaking their minds without regard for context, blurting out various facts or opinions at exactly the wrong moment. One of your authors will never forget the time her 4-year-old daughter greeted the somewhat portly chairman of her psychology department with a cheery "Hi, fatso!"

Phonological development, semantic development, grammar, and pragmatic development together represent the basic domains of language acquisition. We explore each of these domains in the sections below. For the sake of clarity, we will describe how children become competent in each domain separately. However, it is important to keep in mind that language is a system—each domain is connected to all of the others, as well as to the social world of which it is an essential part (de Lemos, 2000).

Phonological Development

As discussed in Chapter 6, in the change from babbling to pronouncing words that occurs late in the 1st year, children give up their indiscriminate play with sounds and begin to vocalize the particular sounds and sound sequences that make up the words in the language of their community (Kuhl, 2004). The process of mastering the pronunciation of the separate words of a native language takes several years (and can be complicated by, for example, malformation of structures involved in articulation; see the box, "In the Field: A Speech-Language Pathologist in Vietnam"). Children's early pronouncing efforts may be no more than crude stabs at the right sound pattern that frequently leave out parts of words (resulting in "ca" instead of "cat," for example). They may also include using a particular sound pattern for several different multisyllabic words that have sound similarities. For example, a child may use the sound pattern "bubba" to say "button," "bubble," "butter," and "baby." A long word, such as "motorcycle," can come out sounding like almost anything: "momo," "motokaka," or even "lomacity" (Preisser, Hodson, & Paden, 1988).

Children's command of their native sound system develops unevenly. Sometimes children will find a particular sound especially difficult to master, even after they understand many words that employ that sound. At the age of 2½, for example, one of our sons, Alexander, could not pronounce /l/ sounds at the beginning of words, and whenever he referred to his friend's dog, Lucky, it came out "Yucky," much to everyone's amusement.

Alexander's transformation of "Lucky" to "Yucky" generated chuckles because when he changed the phoneme from /l/ to /y/, he changed the *meaning* of the word. As noted in Chapter 6, the close connection between phonemes and meanings becomes clear when one is attempting to learn a foreign language. Some native speakers of Spanish find it difficult to hear or produce the difference between /b/ and /v/, which in English can change meaning, because Spanish has no corresponding distinction in sound. To native English speakers, "boat" and "vote" sound quite different; to Spanish speakers, these two words sound much the same. Likewise, English speakers frequently have difficulty hearing and producing the difference between the French /u/ and /ou/, because that difference, which in French can change meaning, does not exist in English.

While phonemes are the basic units of sound, **morphemes** are the basic units of meaning. Words are composed of one or more morphemes. The word *horse,* for

In the Field | A Speech–Language Pathologist in Vietnam

Name:	Charlotte Ducote
Education:	B.A. from Louisiana State University; M.A. from Vanderbilt; Ph.D. in speech and hearing sciences from Louisiana State University
Current Position:	Director of the Division of Communicative Disorders at the Ochsner Clinic; volunteer for Operation Smile
Career Objectives:	Provide education and services to improve speech and language skills for children with communication disorders

GIANG, A 6-YEAR-OLD VIETNAMESE GIRL, WAS BORN IN Ho Chi Minh City (Saigon) with a cleft lip and palate, a serious birth defect caused when the structures of the mouth form abnormally during fetal development. As a consequence of the defect, Giang had difficulty eating, communicating, and even breathing. It is estimated that clefting of the lip, palate, or both occurs in 1 to 2.5 of every 1,000 births worldwide, making it one of the most common birth defects (McLeod, Arana-Urioste, & Saeed, 2004). Fortunately for Giang and other children from impoverished areas of the world, a number of humanitarian groups have formed to provide affected children with reconstructive surgery and speech and language therapy.

Charlotte Ducote, a speech-language pathologist, has devoted considerable time to one such group—Operation Smile, a private, not-for-profit medical services organization that has helped tens of thousands of indigent children in more than 20 countries, including Bolivia, Brazil, China, the Gaza Strip and the West Bank, Russia, the United States, and Vietnam. In addition to volunteering on medical teams that include plastic surgeons, anesthesiologists, pediatricians, nurses, and dentists, Ducote cofounded the Speech Therapy–Vietnam Project, which aims to expand speech therapy services in the country by teaching health-care providers how to screen, evaluate, and treat communication disorders.

Ducote studied Vietnamese and its phoneme system and acquainted herself with the country's customs and culture. Armed with this knowledge and the assistance of a translator, Ducote met Giang, who was brought to the clinic by her mother for speech problems that interfered with her being accepted into first grade.

Charlotte Ducote, a speech and language pathologist with Operation Smile.

Giang's cleft palate and lip had been surgically corrected the previous year, and her mother was convinced that additional surgery would help her daughter speak better. Ducote's evaluation, however, showed otherwise: Rather than requiring additional surgery, Giang's speech difficulties could be drastically improved with daily speech therapy. Her mother was skeptical but finally agreed, at the urging of a Vietnamese surgeon. Ducote reports the following instantaneous improvement:

> Within minutes of beginning treatment and having success with the child imitating a word that began with a phoneme with which she had particular difficulty, her mother was in tears. "I never thought my child would be able to say that word. How did you do that? It is like magic!"

Over the course of the next week, Ducote met regularly with Giang and her mother, teaching them how to form phonemes and breathe properly during speech (her mother was to work with Giang every day at home). Ducote also encouraged Giang to open her mouth wider while talking to facilitate airflow and reduce the nasal tone of her voice. Her mother resisted this particular intervention, because she worried that speaking with the mouth more open would make Giang unattractive to future suitors. She relented, however, once she witnessed the dramatic improvement in her daughter's speech.

At last report, Giang is in school and doing very well. Ducote, for her part, continues to volunteer in Vietnam and to mobilize financial and educational resources to help children with communication disorders throughout the world.

One of the most common birth defects, cleft lip and palate is caused by abnormal development of the structures of the mouth during the prenatal period. Without surgery, this baby's health and development would have been seriously affected. Fortunately, a surgical team associated with Operation Smile corrected the cleft when the baby was 5 months of age.

example, consists of one morpheme, which means "a member of the equine family." *Horses,* on the other hand, includes two morphemes: *horse,* meaning "a member of the equine family," plus "-s" meaning "more than one." Until the rules are pointed out, we rarely stop to think about the parts of words or the way we put these parts together. Yet every child must acquire the ability to decipher and reproduce just such intricate interweaving of sound and meaning. By the time they are 8 or 9 years old, children can use knowledge about morphemes to figure out the meanings of made-up words such as "treelet" (Anglin, 1993).

Semantic Development

Semantic development, as you may recall, refers to the process of learning the meanings of words and word combinations. As we described previously through the example of Romeo and Juliet, words refer to something beyond themselves (Hoff, 2001). Indeed, for a child acquiring language, a significant and surprisingly difficult part of the process of learning a new word involves what Sandra Waxman described as "mapping words to the world" (Waxman & Leddon, 2011). Key to this process is the ability to identify the object to which the word refers; for example, knowing that the fluffy creature with the wet nose and wagging tail is the object referred to when the mother exclaims, "Look! It's a *puppy!*"

To get an intuitive feel for just how difficult it may be for a young child to learn the relationship between a word and its referent, examine Figure 7.3. Imagine that you are the child in the picture, and try to decide what the Russian father is saying. It's a puzzle, isn't it? Suppose you know all the words except one: "Look, son, there sits a *ptitsa.*" The word *ptitsa* still has various possible referents—the cat, the bird, the helicopter on the roof. At first you may think that the example is unfair because the utterance is in a foreign language. But remember that a baby's native language *is* "foreign" in the beginning and, moreover, that babies must somehow figure out that the sounds they hear are in fact meant to refer to something in the ongoing flow of experience—to indicate an actual object, event, or feeling. According to Eve Clark (2006), the process of identifying a word's referent depends critically on the child's ability to establish joint attention with the speaker and to understand that the object or event of joint attention is what the speaker is talking about. As we will see, it takes some years before the child is fully able to appreciate the *referential intentions* of a speaker, which may account for why the child's vocabulary development is initially fairly slow but undergoes a substantial growth spurt during toddlerhood.

"Vot, sinochik, tam sidit ptitsa."

FIGURE 7.3 For children just beginning to acquire language, the problem of learning what words refer to is particularly acute. (This father is telling his son to look at the bird.)

It is useful to think of the process of learning the meanings and referents of words as a special sort of joint effort (Tomasello, 2011). Neither the adult nor the child really knows what the other is saying. Each tries to gather in a little meaning by supposing that the other's utterance fits a particular sound pattern that corresponds to a particular meaning. This joint effort may eventually result in something common, a word that both can understand. This process may also fail. As the following examples make clear, the process of learning words can proceed in a variety of ways, depending on how the parent interprets the relation between the child's sounds and actions.

At 8 months of age, Pablo began to say "dahdee." Although this "first" word sounds like "daddy," Pablo used "dahdee" for commands and requests when his father was nowhere to be seen, so it must have had some other meaning for him. Adults interpreted "dahdee" to mean either "Take it from me" (when Pablo said it while he offered something to someone) or "Give it to me"; they ignored the fact that Pablo's first word sounded like "daddy." At about the age of 12 months, "dahdee" disappeared from Pablo's vocabulary (Shopen, 1980).

A different fate befell Brenan's first word, "whey." Around 1 year of age, Brenan began to say "whey" after one of his parents had spoken. In this case, "whey" not only sounded something like "why" but also came at a position in normal conversational turn-taking where "why" would be a possible (if not always appropriate) thing to say. Brenan's parents therefore responded to "whey" as if Brenan had asked a question and rephrased what they had said in order to "answer his question," expanding on their original utterance. Over time, Brenan pronounced and used "whey" more and more like a true "why" until it became a genuine "why" in the English language (Griffin, 1983).

In both of these examples, the child uses a sound pattern that adults might interpret on the basis of its similarity to a word with which they are familiar. But in Pablo's case, the use of "dahdee" did not fit the patterns of usage for its soundalike, "daddy," so his parents simply ignored it. Brenan's use of "whey" both sounded like "why" and was basically consistent with his parents' guess that he meant "why," so they provided the feedback necessary for Brenan to adjust his pronunciation and use of the sound pattern to fit adult norms. Each illustrates the general point that adults collude with each other and their children to create word meanings.

The Earliest Vocabulary Much of the evidence concerning children's earliest words has come from having parents keep records of their children's vocabulary development or by making recordings of children's speech in their homes or in organized play facilities (Dromi & Zaidman-Zait, 2011). A number of studies have shown that children typically begin to produce their first comprehensible words around their 1st birthday and continue to utter single words for several months or more. Although there is a great deal of variation in the ages at which children reach particular levels of language production (Figure 7.4), infants, on average,

FIGURE 7.4 There are wide variations in the rates at which young children acquire new words. Each curve indicates the number of words that the designated child spoke while in the one-word phase. Note that despite the variability, each child shows the growth spurt in vocabulary that typically begins shortly before children start to produce utterances of two or more words. (After Dromi, 1999, p. 104.)

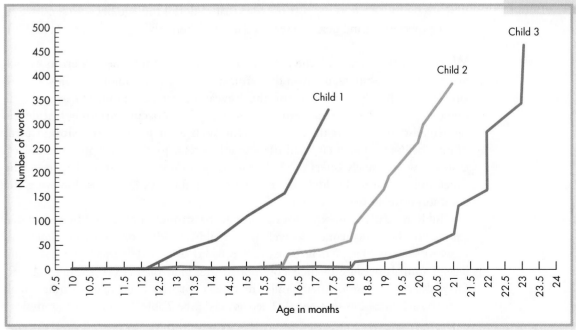

are able to use approximately 10 words by 13 to 14 months of age, 50 words by the time they are 17 to 18 months old, and approximately 300 words by the time they reach their second birthday. More impressive still is children's *receptive vocabulary*—that is, the vocabulary they understand—which is considerably larger. For example, when they can produce 10 words, they can understand over 100 (Fenson et al., 1994).

The first 100 or so words in young children's vocabularies are predominantly nouns used to label objects; this is true for children who speak languages as diverse as Spanish, Dutch, French, Hebrew, Italian, Korean, and American English (Bornstein et al., 2004). Many of these nouns refer to objects that young children can manipulate or somehow act upon (Mandler, 2006). For example, "hat" and "sock" are common in the initial vocabularies of American children, but "sweater" and "diapers" are not, presumably because little children can put on and take off hats and socks more or less effectively, but cannot do the same with sweaters and diapers. In addition, objects that can change and move and thus capture children's attention (such as cars and animals) are likely to be named; large, immobile objects that are "just there" (such as trees and houses) are not.

As young children's vocabularies grow, there is a rapid increase in the proportion of verbs and adjectives they contain, and by age 2, nouns usually account for less than half of children's vocabularies. Toddlers' growing vocabularies also include a variety of relational words that are used to communicate about changes in the state or location of an object (Gopnik & Meltzoff, 1997). "Gone" and "here," for example, may be used to announce the disappearance and appearance of objects. One of the most useful relational words in children's early vocabularies is "no," which can serve such important communicative functions as rejection, protest, and denial. "No" can also be used to comment on unfulfilled expectations (for example, "no play" when a planned trip to the park is cancelled because of rain) and on an object's absence (for example, "no teddy" when a favorite toy goes missing). Given these multiple functions, it is little wonder that "no" is among the earliest and most frequently used words in a child's budding vocabulary (Bloom, 1973).

Alison Gopnik and Andrew Meltzoff (1997) identified an additional class of words that children begin using around the age of 2 years—words used to comment on their successes ("There!" "Hooray!") and failures ("Uh-oh"). The appearance of these words seems to support the idea that children this age become sensitive to social expectations and begin to set standards for themselves (see Chapter 6, p. 226).

Word Errors
Along with the first words of language come the first errors of language use. Interestingly, many of the errors made by young children as they acquire language are highly systematic and thus reveal a great deal about language development (Jaeger, 2005). Some errors are so typical and occur so reliably that developmentalists have given them names. One such error is **overextension**, a form of mislabeling in which children use a word to refer to a broader group of objects than the word usually refers to. A 2-year-old who points to a strange man on the street and exclaims "Daddy!" or sees the ocean and says "bath" is displaying the common error of overextension.

Children's early overextensions appear to be strongly influenced by perceptual features of the items named, as well as by children's ideas of the items' functions. A word such as "kitty" may be extended to cover a wide variety of small four-legged animals because of their common shape, or it may cover a variety of soft, furry objects because of their similar texture, or it may even refer to other small animals such as rabbits that people keep as pets. (See Table 7.3 for other examples.)

overextension The error of applying verbal labels too broadly.

table **7.3**			
Typical Overextensions in the Speech of Young Children			
Child's Word	**First Referent**	**Extensions**	**Possible Common Property**
Dog	Dogs	Lambs, cats, wolves, cows	Four-legged animal
"Peca"	Wound	Cuts, wounds, Scotch tape, spots on fabric, balloons	Uncertain, partial defect or injury of some kind
Kick	Kicking ball	Cartoon turtles doing the cancan, pushing chest against mirror, watching a butterfly	Common movement pattern
"Tik"	Handbag	Folders, nylon bags, plastic sacks, box, hat upside down, pockets	Containing object

Source: Dromi, 1999.

Another reliably occurring error is **underextension**, in which children use words in a narrower way than they are usually meant (Barrett, 1995). It is common, in fact, for children's early words to have a unique referent, often closely associated with a particular context (Golinkoff et al., 1994). For example, a child may use the word "bottle" to label only his or her favorite yellow plastic bottle, not other kinds of bottles; or use "biddie" to refer to only a special blanket clutched at bedtime and naptime, not to other kinds of blankets. Likewise, it is not uncommon for young children to believe that "cat" applies only to their family's cat, not to cats in the neighborhood or on television.

The Vocabulary Spurt One of the most remarkable features of children's early vocabulary development is the astonishing *growth spurt* of new words that typically occurs during toddlerhood (see Figure 7.4, p. 251). What makes this rapid acquisition possible?

Elsa Bartlett and Susan Carey made use of the normal routine of a preschool classroom to find out what happens when a totally new word is introduced into conversation with children (Bartlett, 1977; Carey, 1978). They chose to study the acquisition of color terms. Pretesting had revealed that none of the 14 children in the classroom knew the name of the color that adults call olive, so the researchers chose olive as the experimental color but instructed the children's teacher to refer to it with the implausible name "chromium," just in case some children had partial knowledge of the real name that they had not revealed.

The researchers then arranged to have a cup and tray that had been painted "chromium" paired in the classroom with a cup and a tray of a primary color, such as red or blue. While preparing for snack time, the teacher, as instructed, created an opportunity to ask each child, "Please bring me the chromium cup; not the red one, the chromium one," or "Bring me the chromium tray; not the blue one, the chromium one." Despite the fact that the children had never heard the word "chromium" before, all of them picked the correct cup or tray, although they were likely to ask for confirmation ("You mean this one?"). Some of the children could be seen repeating the unfamiliar word to themselves.

One week after this single experience with the new word, the children were given a color-naming test with an array of color chips. Two-thirds of them showed that they had learned something about this odd term and its referents—when asked for chromium, they chose either the olive chip or a green one. Six weeks later, many of the children still showed the influence of this single experience.

underextension The error of applying verbal labels too narrowly.

As in this experiment, it appears that when children hear an unfamiliar word in a familiar, structured, and meaningful social interaction, they form a quick, "first-pass" idea of the word's meaning (Clark & Wong, 2002). Developmentalists refer to this form of rapid word acquisition as **fast mapping**. Fast mapping has been observed in children as young as 15 months of age in controlled experiments (Schafer & Plunkett, 1998).

An important question for researchers is why fast mapping occurs in toddlerhood but not before. Some research suggests that a tipping point occurs once children have achieved a vocabulary of 50 to 75 words (Bates, Thal, Finlay, & Clancy, 2002; von Koss Torkildsen et al., 2009). For example, a study conducted with Norwegian 20-month-olds found that children with more than 75 words in their vocabulary learned new words significantly faster than did children with smaller vocabularies, perhaps because of changes in how the brain processes language. In particular, the children's brain activity was monitored as they were presented with five repeat pairings of nonsense words and pictures of fantasy objects. In the small-vocabulary group, brain activity associated with attention persisted across all five presentations; in the large-vocabulary group, attention peaked during the third presentation and then declined. This finding suggests that children with larger vocabularies processed the word-object associations more efficiently than did the children with smaller vocabularies (von Koss Torkildsen et al., 2009). Other research, however, suggests that fast mapping is due not to brain changes but to toddlers' increased abilities to use social cues to infer a speaker's intentions. For example, Shannon Pruden and her colleagues devised an experiment in which two groups of younger babies were presented with two objects, one boring (like a kitchen cabinet latch) and one interesting (like a sparkle wand), neither of which the infants would know the name of. With one group, the experimenter repeated a nonsense label like "blicket" several times while looking at the boring object; with the other group, the experimenter repeated the same label several times while looking at the interesting object. Subsequent testing in which the infants were told to look at the blicket revealed that they had applied the "blicket" label to the interesting object regardless of which object the experimenter had been looking at while repeating the label. Thus, unlike the word learning of toddlers that takes into account the speaker's intention, word learning in younger children seems to be indifferent to the social intent of the speaker, and driven instead by the children's own interest and point of view (see also Golinkoff & Hirsh-Pasek, 2006; Poulin-Dubois & Forbes, 2006). The researchers speculate that this form of word learning is necessarily slower than the fast mapping of toddlers because it probably requires repeated word-to-object pairings and may often leave infants with wrong names to unlearn. On the other hand, the pace of word learning should be considerably faster once children are able to use social information to infer a speaker's labeling intent.

Figurative Language Not long after children start to name objects, they begin to use figurative language, specifically, metaphors. A **metaphor** involves the use of a word or a phrase in a way that draws a direct comparison between the thing it ordinarily refers to and some other, seemingly unrelated, thing. When hip-hop artist Big Boi raps about being "cooler than a polar bear's toenails," and Lauryn Hill claims to be "sweet like licorice," they are using metaphors. Likewise, a 2½-year-old may point at his yellow plastic baseball bat and say "Corn!" or throw Styrofoam bits in the air and shout "Snow!" Children's use of metaphor provides evidence that language production is a creative process, not simply an imitative one. To generate a metaphor, children must recognize a similarity between two unrelated things and express that similarity in a way that they have never heard before (Dent-Read, 1997; Winner, 1998).

fast mapping The way in which children quickly form an idea of the meaning of an unfamiliar word they hear in a familiar and highly structured social interaction.

metaphor Use of a word in a way that draws a comparison between the thing the word usually refers to and some other, unrelated thing.

At the same time that young children appear extraordinarily creative in inventing metaphors, they can be very limited in understanding metaphors used by others. An example is the following exchange one of your authors observed at a birthday party: As one 4-year-old girl sat at the table eating cake, another child's mother, evidently a stranger to the girl, reached over and wiped chocolate frosting from the girl's cheek. "Thank you," said the little girl. "I've got your back, sister," said the mother. Obviously shaken by the mother's statement, the little girl replied, "I'm not your sister!" (We can only imagine what she made of "I've got your back.")

The ability to understand and use metaphors develops throughout childhood. During middle childhood, for example, children still have difficulty understanding metaphors that compare people to objects. Metaphors such as "That kid is a bulldozer" are confusing to them because they lack knowledge about personality traits and thus fail to understand the similarity proposed by the metaphor. Not until adolescence will children be able to understand and create metaphors of this nature (Pan & Snow, 1999).

Grammar Development

As noted earlier, a watershed of language development is reached toward the end of infancy, when children begin to produce utterances consisting of two or more words. Significantly, two-word utterances carry more than twice as much information as a single word alone because of the meaning conveyed by the relationship between the two words. With as few as two words, children can indicate possession ("Daddy chair"), nonexistence ("Gone cookie"), and a variety of other meanings. They can also create different meanings by varying the order of words ("Chase Daddy" and "Daddy chase"). This new potential for creating meaning by varying the arrangement of linguistic elements marks the birth of grammar.

Grammar and Meaning
As we indicated previously, the rules of grammar play a critical role in interpreting the meaning of sentences. Evidence that children have some grasp of grammatical rules fairly early in their language development comes from studies in which young children are asked to interpret grammatically correct sentences that contain nonsense words (Fisher et al., 2006). One such study tested early understanding of syntax by seeing if 2-year-olds could use word order to correctly interpret transitive sentences that had nonsense verbs. In one experiment, the children were shown two pictures of a duck and a bunny interacting (Gertner, Fisher, & Eisengart, 2006). One picture showed the bunny acting on the duck; the other showed the duck acting on the bunny (Figure 7.5). As the children viewed the pictures, they were told "The duck is *gorping* the bunny! See?" Even though "gorping" is a nonsense word, English grammar dictates that if the duck is gorping

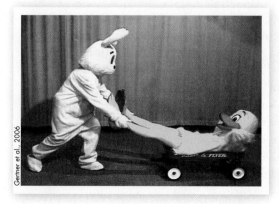

FIGURE 7.5 Despite the fact that "gorping" is a nonsense word, 2-year-olds associate the sentence "The duck is gorping the bunny!" with the second photo, demonstrating the importance of grammar in learning and understanding language.

syntactic bootstrapping Use of knowledge of grammar to figure out the meaning of new words.

grammatical morphemes Words and parts of words that create meaning by showing the relations between other elements within the sentence.

the bunny, the duck is the active agent and the bunny is the object being acted upon. The 2-year-olds presented with this sentence indicated their knowledge of grammar by looking significantly longer at the picture in which the duck was acting on the bunny. Developmentalists interpret results like this as evidence of an innate universal grammar that helps children interpret the language they hear (Chang, Dell, & Bock, 2006). The process of using grammar to learn the meaning of new words—as the children do with "gorp" in the study—is referred to as **syntactic bootstrapping** (Fisher et al., 2006; Landau & Gleitman, 1985).

Young children also demonstrate their knowledge of grammar through the errors they make when they string words together. Between ages 2 and 3, English-speaking children often make statements like "My doggy runned away" or "Mommy, Johnny camed late." Such errors are so common that it is easy to overlook their significance. Children cannot have been taught to say such things, nor could they have learned them by simple imitation, because they virtually never hear such incorrect sentences uttered. Rather, they are revealing their knowledge of the general rule for forming the past tense with regular verbs by misapplying it to irregular verbs.

Increasing Complexity At the same time that children begin to string more and more words together to form complete sentences, they increase the complexity and the variety of words and grammatical devices they use. These changes are illustrated by the following prodigious sentence spoken by an excited 2-year-old girl: "You can't pick up a big kitty 'cos a big kitty might bite!" (De Villiers & De Villiers, 1978, p. 59).

This sentence is by no means typical of 2-year-olds, but it provides a good opportunity to assess how more complex utterances communicate more explicitly. The sentence communicates not only that the little girl does not want to pick up a big cat but also that no one should pick up a big cat; it also conveys her understanding that big cats sometimes bite but do not invariably do so. Such complex sentences communicate shades of meaning that help adults to respond sensitively to children's experiences.

As Figure 7.6 indicates, the length of the utterances of most 2- and 3-year-olds grows explosively (Eve being a bit earlier than most), along with their vocabularies and grammatical abilities (Devescovi et al., 2005). Note that the growth in the length of utterances (or the *mean length of utterance*) is indicated by the average number of morphemes per utterance rather than by the average number of words. The phrase "That big bad boy plays ball," for example, contains six words and seven morphemes, whereas the phrase "Boys aren't playing" contains only three words but six morphemes ("boy," "s," "are," "not," "play," "ing"). Assessing linguistic complexity by counting morphemes rather than words provides an index of a child's total potential for making meaning in a particular utterance.

The complexity of the 2-year-old girl's long sentence about picking up cats is attributable in large measure just to her use of those little words and word parts that are systematically absent in two-word utterances. The article "a" ("a big kitty") indicates that it is big cats in general, not just this particular big cat, that are worrisome. The word "'cos" connects two propositions and indicates the causal relationship between them. The contraction "can't" specifies a particular relationship of negation. These elements are a special type of morpheme called **grammatical morphemes** because they create meaning by showing the relations between other elements within the sentence.

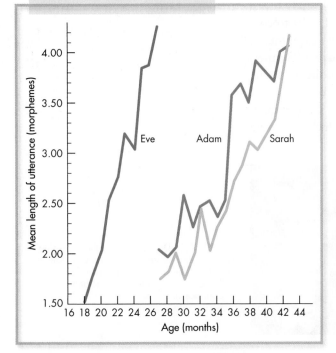

FIGURE 7.6 This graph shows the rapid increase in the mean length of utterances made by three children from 18 months to 3½ years of age. (From Brown, 1973.)

table 7.4		
Usual Order of Acquiring Grammatical Morphemes		
Morpheme	**Meaning**	**Example**
Present progressive	Temporary duration	I walk*ing*
In	Containment	*In* basket
On	Support	*On* floor
Plural	Number	Two balls
Past irregular	Prior occurrence	It *broke*
Possessive inflection	Possession	Adam's ball
To be without contraction	Number	There it *is*
Articles	Specific/nonspecific	That *a* book
		That *the* dog
Past regular	Prior occurrence	Adam walk*ed*
Third person regular	Number	He walk*s*
Third person irregular	Number	He *does*
		She *has*
Uncontractible progressive auxiliary	Temporary duration; number	This *is going*
Contraction of *to be*	Number; prior occurrence	That's a book
Contractible progressive auxiliary	Temporary duration	I'm walking

Source: Brown, 1973.

Whether the rate of language acquisition is fast or slow, grammatical morphemes appear in roughly the same sequence in the speech of all children who acquire English as a first language. As Table 7.4 indicates, the grammatical morpheme likely to appear first in children's language production is *ing*, used to indicate the present progressive verb tense. This verb form allows children to describe their ongoing activity. Morphemes indicating location, number, and possession make their appearance next. Morphemes that mark complex relations, such as the contraction *'m* in "I'm going" (which codes a relation between the first person singular subject of the action and the present time of the action), are generally slower to emerge.

The appearance of grammatical morphemes is a strong indicator that children are implicitly beginning to distinguish nouns and verbs, because their speech conforms to adult rules that specify which morphemes should be attached to which kinds of words in a sentence. Thus, for example, children do not apply past-tense morphemes to nouns ("girled"), nor do they place articles before verbs ("a walked").

Evidence collected by a number of language-development researchers shows that although children begin to produce grammatical morphemes relatively late in the language acquisition process, they recognize and understand the significance of grammatical morphemes in the language they hear at least by the time they are starting to produce their first multiword utterances (Golinkoff et al., 1999).

Pragmatic Development

Many of us have observed a mother trying to talk to a friend while her child pulls on her pant leg, impatiently intoning "Mommy, Mommy, Mommy." "Not now," the mother may say, or "I'm talking; you need to wait until I'm done." Whether interrupting a conversation or using language that is inappropriate for the context (remember the little girl who greeted her mother's psychology department head with "Hi, fatso!"), young language learners are famous for saying the wrong thing at the wrong time simply because they have not yet mastered *pragmatics,* which include social and cultural conventions of language use in particular contexts. These

conversational acts Actions that achieve goals through language.

protoimperatives Early conversational acts whose purpose is to get another person to do something.

protodeclaratives Early conversational acts whose purpose is to establish joint attention and sustain a dialogue.

conventions may vary markedly from one culture to another. In many cultures, children are expected to say "please" when they request something and "thank you" when they are given something. But in certain Colombian communities, such verbal formulas are frowned upon in the belief that "please" and "thank you" signal the speaker's inferiority; obedience, not formulaic politeness, is what these adults expect of their children (Reichel-Dolmatoff & Reichel-Dolmatoff, 1961).

Conversational Acts One important aspect of pragmatics is the use of language as **conversational acts**, actions to achieve goals performed through language and gesture. According to Elizabeth Bates and her colleagues (Bates, Camaioni, & Volterra, 1975), children's earliest conversational acts fall into two categories, *protoimperatives* and *protodeclaratives*. Using **protoimperatives** is an early way of engaging another person to achieve a desired goal; for example, holding up a cup and saying "More" to get a refill on juice. Using **protodeclaratives** is a way of establishing joint attention and sustaining a dialogue. Perhaps the earliest form of a protodeclarative is the act of pointing, which may be accompanied by words, as when a baby points to a dog and says "Doggie." Young children will often use a succession of protodeclaratives for the purpose of sustaining a dialogue. A common gestural example of this is a child's bringing all of his or her toys, one after another, to show to a visitor if each presentation is acknowledged by a smile or a comment (Bates, O'Connell, & Shore, 1987).

In the process of acquiring pragmatics, children also come to understand that a single sequence of words may accomplish several alternative goals and that linguistic and other contexts can be crucial to interpretation. An amusing example of this occurs in a series of incidents in *Higglety, Pigglety, Pop,* Maurice Sendak's tale of an adventurous dog who accepts a job as nanny for Baby, a child caught in the grip of the "terrible twos." At first the dog attempts to get the baby to eat, and the baby says, "No eat!" When the dog decides to eat the food himself, the baby again says, "No eat!" Finally the baby and dog find themselves confronted by a lion, and the baby says for the third time, "No eat!"

In addition to using the same words to convey different meanings, children must also gain competence in using social cues in order to get the meaning intended by the speaker. For example, the sentence "Is the door shut?" has the grammatical form of a request for information. But it may be functioning as a request for action or as a criticism—that is, pragmatically equivalent to "Please shut the door" or "You forgot to shut the door again." Marilyn Shatz (1978) found that children as young as 2 years old responded correctly to their mother's indirect commands, such as "Is the door shut?" That is, instead of responding to the surface grammatical form and answering "Yes" or "No," Shatz's toddlers went to shut the door. This finding is consistent with work we described earlier linking toddlers' sensitivity to social cues to the fast mapping of vocabulary growth.

At the same time that children are recognizing that a single phrase can have multiple meanings or goals, they develop the ability to express a single meaning or goal in multiple ways. For example, a 3-year-old observed by John Dore (1979) used three different grammatical forms to achieve a single goal: "Get off the blocks!" "Why don't you stay away from my blocks?" and "You're standing on my blocks."

Viewing communications as conversational acts in which a single phrase can have more than one meaning, and a single meaning can be conveyed in many ways, exposes the complex relationship between the world of language and the world of objects, events, and direct experience. There is no simple and direct correspondence between the two worlds, making the child's apparently easy acquisition of

The conversational skills of these 4-year-olds allow them to tell each other stories about memorable events.

language all the more wondrous. As they get older, children will become increasingly skilled in their use and understanding of the subtleties of conversational acts—eventually knowing, for example, that despite the difference in language and tone, "I think I need some time to myself to sort things out" and "I'm dumping you" mean the same thing.

Developing Narratives As children's conversational skills develop, so too does their capacity to tell stories or *narratives* about their experiences. In a seminal study of developing storytelling abilities, Peterson and her colleagues (2004) asked children to tell them about memorable events such as going to the doctor's office. They found that the stories of young children followed the very simple structure of **chronology**, in which they present a sequence of concrete events. For example, 3½-year-old Paul describes a visit to the doctor's office to get stitches as "I get a needle. I get stitches, like first I got a needle, then I got stitches and then go home." As children's narrative abilities mature, their stories become more elaborate and more dramatic in emotional tone, as shown in the following story about a younger brother getting stung by a bee (Peterson & McCabe, 2004, p. 29):

> Mark [brother] got a big sting when he was just first born. I, I was walking with him and, and I just and he falled and he didn't know that he falled right on a bee. And he, and his knee was on a bee and stung, he got stung on a bee. I tried to pick him up but, but he didn't want me to but I had to call my Mommy. My Daddy and everybody who I knowed who was a grown-up came. And then I, I told them and I looked down at his knee and there it was, stung.

When children first begin to produce narratives, their stories can be hard to follow because they leave out essential information. A teacher who is approached by a tearful preschooler saying only "He broked it" does not have much to work with without asking the child to elaborate ("What was broken?" "Who broke it?"). Indeed, adults will often ask young children to expand their stories in an effort to make them more organized and coherent, as the following dialogue between a mother and her 3½-year-old child demonstrates (Nelson & Shaw, 2002, p. 51):

Child: You know something?
Mother: What?
Child: Let me think . . . . What's her name again?
Mother: Who?
Child: That girl.

chronology In language development, a simple story structure used by young children, in which they present a sequence of concrete events.

cultural modeling Culturally specific ways of telling stories.

Mother: Who?

Child: Don't you remember her? You've seen her before.

Mother: Where is she?

Child: I don't know. I don't know her name. Somebody has a rocket. That can turn into a big rocket.

Mother: Who is this person?

Child: I don't know her.

Mother: Where'd you meet her?

Child: At our house!

Mother: Was I home for this?

Child: (shakes head)

Mother: So how would I know who this is?

Although the mother is working hard to help her child develop her story, the child has difficulty understanding that her mother's knowledge of the girl is necessarily limited by the fact that she was not home to meet her, a cognitive limitation we discuss in more detail below.

As they grow older, children's narrative development is also influenced by **cultural modeling**, that is, culturally specific ways of telling stories. Carol Lee's work with African American children has done much to advance our understanding of how children use the storytelling traditions of their culture to form stories of their own (Lee et al., 2004a; Lee, 2010). For example, common features of African American narratives include the following (Lee et al., 2004a, p. 47):

- Use of dramatic language

- Use of or description of body language and gesture

- Sermonic tone (a dramatic tone of voice typically used during African American church services)

- References to culturally specific objects, events, and behaviors

To illustrate the cultural modeling of African American children's narratives, Lee and her colleagues showed pictures to 8- to 10-year-old children and asked the children to tell stories about them. One picture, "Jumping the Broom" (Figure 7.7), depicts a custom of great significance in the history of African Americans, dating back to the time of slavery, when African Americans were not legally allowed to marry. To mark their marital commitment, couples would jump over a broom in front of witnesses, a custom that is still enacted in some African American weddings. One girl who participated in Lee's study told the following story about the picture, giving names to the man and woman being married, and creating a dialogue between them. Notice how she incorporates several of the features of African American narratives described above:

> The wedding looked so pretty. There was dancing [and] Mr. Johnson said to his wife, "I love you." "I love you, too," Ms. Sara Lee said. Mr. Johnson threw up his Bible and said, "Thank you Jesus! For giving me a wonderful ceremony," and Ms. Sara said, "Amen to that." They were both happy. They jumped over the broom. (Lee et al., 2004a, pp. 52–53)

Annie Lee

FIGURE 7.7 Developmentalist Carol Lee studies cultural modeling—that is, the ways that children draw from cultural traditions to construct meaningful stories of life and experience. To facilitate children's storytelling, Lee makes use of culturally relevant artifacts, such as Annie Lee's painting "Jumping the Broom," which depicts African American marriage traditions.

⏏ APPLY :: CONNECT :: DISCUSS

Consider the two exchanges on the next page between a mother and her son, Richard, while they were looking at a book, the first when Richard was about 1 year old; the second when he was nearly 2 years old (Bruner, 1983, cited in Clark, 2003). Analyze each in terms of concepts presented in this section.

First exchange:

Mother: Look!

Richard: (touches pictures)

Mother: What are those?

Richard: (vocalizes a babble string and smiles)

Mother: Yes, there are rabbits.

Richard: (vocalizes, smiles, looks up at mother)

Mother: (laughs) Yes, rabbit.

Richard: (vocalizes, smiles)

Mother: Yes. (laughs)

　Second exchange:

Mother: What's that?

Richard: *Mouse.*

Mother: Mouse, yes. That's a mouse.

Richard: (pointing at another picture) *More mouse.*

Mother: No, those are squirrels. They're like mice but with long tails. Sort of.

Richard: *Mouse, mouse, mouse.*

Mother: Yes, all right, they're mice.

Richard: *Mice, mice.*

Explanations of Language Acquisition

During much of the twentieth century, two widely divergent theories dominated explanations of how children acquire language. These theories correspond roughly to the polar positions on the sources of human development—nature versus nurture. Social learning theorists, for example, once attributed language acquisition largely to nurture, especially to the language environment and teaching activities provided by adults. Biological theorists, in contrast, attributed language acquisition largely to nature, assuming that as children mature, their innate language capacity enables acquisition to occur naturally, with only minimum input from the environment and without any need for special training.

In recent decades, both theoretical positions have been modified. On the nurture side, there has been a growing consensus that such mechanisms as learning by association, classical and operant conditioning, and imitation are insufficient to account for how children acquire language. Contemporary theorists who emphasize the role of the environment now focus on how social and cultural contexts are organized in ways that draw children into language-using communities. Likewise, theorists who emphasize the biological foundations of language acquisition agree that it is important to specify the ways in which the environment, however minimally, contributes to the developmental process. Thus, as we indicated at the beginning of this chapter, virtually all developmentalists agree that both biology and the environment provide important keys to the world of language. At the same time that these two dominant approaches were undergoing modification, a third approach gained attention—one that places emphasis on the distinct role of cognition in language development. We will review each of three approaches in the sections below.

**language acquisition device
(LAD)** Chomsky's term for an innate
language-processing capacity that is
programmed to recognize the universal
rules that underlie any particular language that a child might hear.

Biological Explanations

For half a century, biological explanations of language acquisition have been dominated by the work of the linguist Noam Chomsky (Chomsky, 2006; Hauser &
Chomsky, 2002). According to Chomsky, the fact that children acquire language
quickly and effortlessly without any direct instruction and that they produce a vast
array of sentences that they have never before heard makes it impossible to claim
that language could be acquired primarily through learning mechanisms. Rather,
language is innate and develops through a universal process of maturation. Chomsky (1988, p. 134) phrased this idea as follows:

> Language learning is not really something that the child does; it is something that
> happens to the child placed in an appropriate environment, much as the child's body
> grows and matures in a predetermined way when provided with the appropriate nu-
> trition and environmental stimulation.

In likening the acquisition of language to the maturation of the body, Chomsky
also emphasized that language is a "mental organ." Just as the functions of a physical organ such as the liver are specific, so are the functions of the "mental organ"
of language (Chomsky, 1980, p. 52). This view is echoed by psycholinguist Steven
Pinker in a book pointedly titled *The Language Instinct*. In Pinker's words, language
is a "distinct piece of the biological makeup of our brains . . . distinct from more
general abilities to process information or behave intelligently" (2007). The fact
that Chomsky describes language as a distinct process does not mean that he denies
its connection to other psychological processes or to the environment. Indeed, he
explicitly acknowledges that "children acquire a good deal of their verbal and non-
verbal behavior by casual observation and imitation of adults and other children"
(Chomsky, 1959, p. 49). But such factors, he argues, cannot fully account for language acquisition.

In certain formulations of this theory, Chomsky proposed that children learn
language as a result of a mental mechanism he dubbed the **language acquisition
device (LAD)**. Through the LAD, the child is, in essence, hardwired to recognize
the abstract grammatical rules (for example, for the order of elements in sentences)
of whatever language the child is regularly exposed to. According to Chomsky, at
birth, the LAD is in an embryonic state, but as children mature and interact with
the environment, maturation of the LAD enables them to use increasingly complex language forms. The eventual result of this process is the adult capacity to use
language.

Like Chomsky, those who believe that there must be some preexisting linguistic mechanism that guides children's language acquisition argue that the feedback
children get on their early utterances provides insufficient information for them to
induce the rules of grammar (Pinker, 2002). One strategy for evaluating this argument is to document how much feedback children actually receive about their
use of language. The answer, based on several decades of research, is "very little"
(Valian, 1999). Furthermore, even when parents do attempt to correct erroneous
grammar, the effort is likely to fail, as shown in a classic exchange reported by David
McNeill (1966, pp. 106–107):

> Child: Nobody don't like me.
> Mother: No, say "nobody likes me."
> Child: Nobody don't like me.
> [This interchange is repeated several times. Then:]
> Mother: No, now listen carefully; say "nobody likes me."
> Child: Oh! Nobody don't likes me.

Sequences like this, which are commonplace, seriously undermine the idea that specific teaching is important to language acquisition and bolster the biological view that language acquisition depends only minimally on the environment.

In summary, biological theorists contend that the essential structures that make language acquisition possible—the universals of grammar—are determined far more by the evolutionary history of our species than by the experiential history of particular children. Experience does of course determine which of the many possible human languages a child actually acquires. Children who never hear Chinese spoken will not grow up speaking Chinese, even though they are genetically capable of learning that (or any other) language. According to Chomsky's theory, however, the experience of hearing a particular language does not modify the LAD; it only triggers the innate mechanisms designed for language acquisition and implements the particular language features it encounters.

Social and Cultural Explanations

While acknowledging that innate features of the human brain play an important role in the acquisition of language, many developmentalists stress the fact that language is necessarily a social process. They argue that children acquire language in the process of using it in a particular sociocultural environment (Karmiloff & Karmiloff-Smith, 2001; Ochs & Schieffelin, 1995; Tomasello, 2011; Vygotsky, 1978).

In an early and influential statement of this position, Jerome Bruner (1982) proposed that the earliest social structures for language development involve what he calls **formats**—recurrent socially patterned activities in which adult and child do things together. In the United States and other cultures, for example, simple formatted activities include such games as peekaboo and the routines surrounding bathing, bedtime, and meals, which provide a structure for communication between babies and caregivers even before babies have learned any language. In this way, formats serve as "crucial vehicles in the passage from communication to language" (Bruner, 1982, p. 8). Bruner argued that, viewed as a whole, the formatted

formats Recurrent socially patterned activities in which adult and child do things together.

A great deal of language learning takes place in casual interactions among family members as they talk, joke, and even sing.

language acquisition support system (LASS) Bruner's term for the patterned behaviors and formatted events within which children acquire language. It is the environmental complement to the innate, biologically constituted LAD.

events within which children acquire language constitute a **language acquisition support system (LASS)**, which is the environmental complement to the innate, biologically constituted LAD emphasized by Chomsky.

In a series of studies, Michael Tomasello and his colleagues (summarized in Tomasello, 2000) revealed that a key element in such language-learning support systems is the finely tuned and well-timed interaction of the participants. These researchers videotaped mothers interacting with their young children in order to identify the precise moment at which the mothers referred to objects in the immediate environment. They found that the mothers talked mostly about objects that were already a part of the child's current actions and the focus of the child's and mother's joint attention, thus greatly reducing the child's problem in figuring out the referents of the mother's words. As you recall from a previous discussion, children are much more likely to learn new words for objects they find interesting (see p. 254).

Importantly, culture often influences whether and how particular objects become a focus of mother-child joint attention. This was nicely illustrated in Jeremy Anglin's comparison of two studies that explored how children learn the names for plants (Anglin, 1995). One study was conducted in a small Mayan hamlet in a highland region of central Mexico; the other, in the urban area of Berkeley, California (Stross, 1973). The Mayans live on a mountain slope covered by lush and varied vegetation, including both cultivated and wild trees, bushes, grasses, and herbs. The Mayan community depends on this botanical environment for food and fuel, as well as for material with which to make their houses. In contrast, the residents of Berkeley, like most urban-dwelling Americans, generally do not interact directly with the botanical world. As you might imagine, compared with that of the children in the Berkeley study, the language environment of the Mayan children contained far more words specific to the botanical world. Indeed, as early as 2½ years of age, most Mayan children knew as many as 30 different plant names and could appropriately describe a variety of ways that the different plants were used. In contrast, 2-year-olds in Berkeley had acquired just a few, very general plant words, usually labels for fruits and vegetables used in the home (for example, "banana," "spinach").

This young Aboriginal Australian boy lives in a community that depends heavily on the natural environment for food, shelter, and other basic needs. Compared with his non-Aboriginal peers, his vocabulary likely includes many more terms relevant to his important relationship to nature.

Penny Tweedie / Corbis

Cognitive Approaches

Another approach to understanding language development emphasizes how the child's emerging language abilities follow from the child's increased ability to think and process information (Clark, 2004). Many theorists, including Alison Gopnik and Andrew Meltzoff (1997), suggest that changes in the way children use language arise as a consequence of the kind of cognitive developments described by Piaget. For example, as you saw in Chapters 5 and 6, sometime around 18 months of age, children begin to reason systematically about hidden objects; deliberately vary their actions to achieve a goal; and display increasing awareness of social standards. Correspondingly, before 18 months of age, children are restricted to words that reflect what they are experiencing at the moment, "social words" such as "Bye-bye" (when Mother is leaving for work) and "Hereyare" (when discovering a searched-for toy). After the age of 18 months, however, they can articulate knowledge of absent objects ("Gone"), describe their own activities ("Done it"), and comment on their perceived failure to meet social expectations ("Uh-oh").

Cognitive development also influences children's emerging conversational skills. Consider the following "conversation" between two preschoolers:

Jenny: My bunny slippers . . . are brown and red and sort of yellow and white. And they have eyes and ears and these noses that wiggle sideways when they kiss.

Chris: I have a piece of sugar in a red piece of paper. I'm gonna eat it but maybe it's for a horse.

Jenny: We bought them. My mommy did. We couldn't find the old ones. These are like the old ones. They were not in the trunk.

Chris: Can't eat the piece of sugar, not unless you take the paper off. (Stone & Church, 1957, pp. 146–147)

Clearly, Jenny and Chris are not having a true conversation. Instead, each is voicing his or her own thoughts without regard for the utterances of the other, a form of communication that Piaget referred to as **collective monologues**. According to Piaget, preschool-age children engage in such talk because they are egocentric and lack the cognitive ability to take into account another person's knowledge, interests, and activities. We encountered a similar example of this cognitive limitation in the dialogue between the mother and the child who were trying to figure out the name of the girl that the mother had never met (pp. 259–260). This particular cognitive limitation, called *egocentrism,* is discussed in detail in Chapter 8 (279–280). As cognitive development progresses, collective monologues eventually give way to **true dialogue**, in which the utterance of one person takes into account the utterance of another.

In what would become a famous counterargument to Piaget's analysis, Vygotsky (1943/1986) claimed that young children's egocentric talk has an entirely different source. Rather than being rooted in an inability to take into account another person's perspective, as Piaget posited, Vygotsky suggested that children use egocentric speech to help in their early efforts to organize their thoughts and regulate their behavior. In other words, egocentric speech is a form of "thinking out loud," a prelude to the ability to think entirely internally, as amply demonstrated in this preschool boy's verbalizations during solitary play with action figures and objects:

Caught him! Whoops! Got him. He fell down. He's dead. Whoopsey! What's that? I caught her. Hey, you get, you get back up here. I got ya, I got her. Look what you did to the building. Stop! There you go! Show you. Argh! Pow! Boom! I got you now. I pull you. Oww, that hurt! You guys are dead. Hahaha. Boom! I'll cut that thing off. Haha. Hey what's wrong with you? Haha. You're dead! . . . What's that handcuff doing on me? Haha. You're still handcuffed on. We need the key, where's the key? Right here? Where's the key? Lock him up. We can't. Lock him up. Lock him up. I locked him. I'm the cops. Thanks. You're welcome. (Bergen, 2011, p. 237)

Vygotsky also differed from Piaget regarding the developmental course and outcome of egocentric speech. Piaget argued that egocentric speech is simply replaced by socialized speech as the child matures cognitively. In contrast, Vygotsky believed that egocentric speech never truly disappears. Instead, it is gradually internalized as **inner speech**, the internal mental "talk" that we all engage in as we think about our experiences, plan our daily activities, and solve problems Thus, although the

collective monologues Communications in which young children each voice their own thoughts without attending to what the others are saying.

true dialogue A communication in which each person's utterances take into account the utterances of others.

inner speech According to Vygotsky, the internalization of egocentric speech that occurs during early childhood and allows individuals to mentally plan activities and solve problems.

Marko MacPherson / Masterfile

Despite their shared delight in sand, sea, and shells, it will be several years before these two toddlers develop the cognitive and language skills necessary to engage in true dialogue about their day at the beach.

FIGURE 7.8 When the size of children's vocabulary is plotted against the degree of grammatical complexity of their utterances, there is a clear, positive relationship. These data are used by Elizabeth Bates and her colleagues to argue that grammar emerges from the need to use many words to convey complex messages. Note that there is an acceleration of grammatical complexity that begins when children's vocabularies reach approximately 400 words. (From Bates, 1999.)

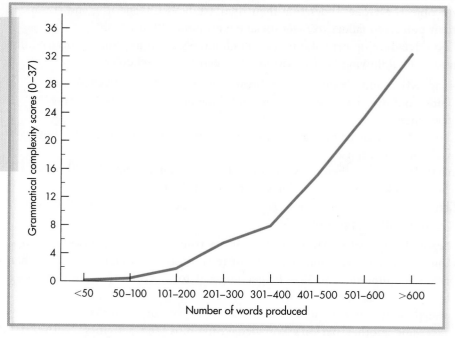

form of egocentric speech becomes transformed with development (that is, internalized as inner speech), the *function* of egocentric speech in regulating thought and action is developmentally invariant.

Explaining Grammar

Because they deny that language acquisition is driven primarily by biological processes, a major challenge for those who adopt a cognitive approach is to explain how children acquire grammar, with its complex rules and structures. As we noted earlier, as children's vocabulary increases, so too does the complexity of the grammar they use. Elizabeth Bates and her colleagues propose that children's growing mastery of grammatical structures is, in fact, a by-product of the growth of their vocabulary and of their attempts to express increasingly complex thoughts (Elman et al., 1996). Evidence supporting this view comes from research demonstrating a direct link between the size of children's vocabularies and the degree of complexity of the grammatical utterances they can make (Fernald, Perfors, & Marchman, 2006). As was illustrated in Figure 7.4 (p. 251), individual children vary greatly in the rates at which they acquire vocabulary. The same is true for their acquisition of grammar (Fenson et al., 1994). However, when grammatical complexity is compared directly with the number of words that children know, there is an almost perfect relationship between vocabulary size and grammatical complexity, regardless of how old the children are. Bates and her colleagues argue that such data clearly demonstrate that grammar develops to deal with a growing vocabulary (Figure 7.8).

Language and Cognitive Impairments

Given the extent to which cognitive development is understood to influence language development, researchers and practitioners are naturally interested in how children with various cognitive impairments acquire language. In Chapter 2 (pp. 65–66), we briefly described Down syndrome, a genetic disorder that produces moderate to severe mental retardation. Although children with Down syndrome are able to hold a conversation, their vocabulary is relatively restricted and their talk is grammatically simple. When tested for the ability to produce and comprehend complex linguistic constructions, they fail. Such results suggest that normal language development requires normal cognitive functioning.

This broad conclusion is brought into question, however, by research on children who suffer from a rare genetic disorder called *Williams syndrome*. Children afflicted with Williams syndrome are also mentally retarded, yet their language is much less impaired than their cognitive abilities would suggest. Although initial language acquisition is often delayed, many children with Williams syndrome eventually produce sentences that are grammatical, clearly pronounced, and understandable. They are also able to tell stories that are meaningful and display considerable subtlety in their portrayal of human feelings (Thomas & Karmiloff-Smith, 2003). A much smaller proportion of children with Down syndrome reach this level of sophisticated language use, even when their level of mental retardation is relatively mild (Fowler, 1990).

Overall, data on children who have some form of genetic disease indicate that children are capable of developing some degree of language competence even in the face of intellectual impairment and that at least some aspects of language develop independently of general cognitive functioning.

▲ APPLY :: CONNECT :: DISCUSS

Review the discussion of primary and secondary intersubjectivity presented on p. 237. In what ways are they similar to Bruner's concept of a language acquisition support system (LASS)?

Reconsidering the Keys to Language

At the beginning of this chapter we argued that although research with nonhuman animals continues to raise the question of whether language is uniquely human, there is no doubt that humans are unique because of language. Language is the foundation of a symbolic universe that is distinctively human, a universe where music is made, mathematical equations are imagined and solved, cathedrals are built, books of poetry and law are written, and genetic codes are cracked and even changed (Jablonka & Lamb, 2007).

Not all the mechanisms of children's acquisition of language are fully understood. However, there appear to be two keys that give children entrance to the world of language: normal human biological structures and processes and active participation in a language-using community. Or, as Jerome Bruner whimsically suggested, language is born from the union of the LAD and the LASS. That is, equipped with an innate acquisition device, children may acquire normal linguistic competence without special instruction, merely by having access to language (either oral or sign) and participating in routine, culturally organized activities that serve as a language acquisition support system. Indeed, Goldin-Meadow's work with deaf children in hearing households suggests that participation in normal cultural routines can be sufficient for the rudiments of language to appear.

Although children 2½ to 3 years of age can properly be considered language-using human beings, their language development is obviously incomplete. Language continues to develop during childhood; indeed, some aspects of language develop into adulthood (Clark, 1995). Moreover, as children begin to acquire the specialized skills they will need to cope with adult life in their culture, deliberate teaching may begin to play a conspicuous role in language development. Such specialized activities as reciting nursery rhymes, acting in a play, and writing an essay are all forms of language activity that require practice and instruction. We shall return to examine some of the more specialized language developments associated with middle childhood in Chapter 11.

SUMMARY

The Power of Language

- Language is a cultural tool, a symbolic system of enormous scope and power. As such, it profoundly affects development by mediating human activities, relationships, and thinking. Children are born predisposed to attend to language and to communicate. They move rapidly from cooing, babbling, and jargoning into the world of language.

Keys to the World of Language

- The two keys to language acquisition are the biological structures and systems that support language, and participation in a language-using community.

- Humans differ dramatically from nonhuman primates in their ability to acquire language. Bonobos and chimpanzees can be taught to understand and (with symbols and gestures) produce simple utterances, abilities at roughly the level of 2-year-old children.

- Studies of patients with Broca's and Wernicke's aphasia have shown the importance of the left frontal lobe in acquiring and using language. Neuroimaging studies confirm the involvement of Broca's area in the processing of complex speech. Although the left hemisphere appears to have evolved as the brain center for language, when infants suffer left-hemisphere damage, the right hemisphere can take over language functions.

- A community of language users provides children with models of, and opportunities for, language acquisition, as is clear from studies of children in language-deprived environments. Deaf children of hearing parents who refuse to use sign develop home sign and reach but do not progress beyond early stages of producing complex sentences.

- Cultural variations in language environments—for example, whether and how much adults talk to infants, use motherese, and attempt deliberate instruction—generally do not have much effect on children's overall acquisition of language.

The Basic Domains of Language Acquisition

- As part of phonological development, young children learn to segment sequences of speech into meaning units of language and to master the pronunciation and rules of their native sound system.

- Semantic development brings increasing understanding of the meaning of words and strings of words. With the help of adults, children learn to pair words to their referents, overcoming problems of overextension (using words too broadly) and underextension (using words too narrowly).

- Infants' first words tend to be nouns, but these are soon supplemented by verbs, adjectives, and relational words. A vocabulary spurt occurs at about 2 or 3 years of age, when young children's new ability to understand speaker intent makes possible fast mapping, in which children form quick first-pass ideas of word meanings.

- With two-word utterances, the acquisition of grammar (or the rules for sequencing words) is evident. Children's utterances become increasingly long and complex, with more units of meaning, or morphemes, including grammatical morphemes.

- Pragmatic development enables children to understand and employ social and cultural conventions of language use, to use communications as conversational acts to achieve goals, and to use context to interpret communications.

- Young children increasingly understand and use figurative language such as metaphors and produce increasingly sophisticated narratives.

Explanations of Language Acquisition

- Biological explanations of language acquisition argue that children are able to acquire language on the basis of limited input because the human brain is hardwired to learn a language that follows certain universal rules.

- Social and cultural explanations emphasize the role of the sociocultural environment, through, for example, formats (routine, patterned activities that adult and child do together) and through interactions generally.

- Cognitive approaches focus on the way emerging language abilities follow from children's increased ability to think and process information. For example, as egocentrism wanes, collective monologues give way to true dialogue.

Reconsidering the Keys to Language

- Questions about the specifics remain, but it is clear that with the two keys to the world of language—a brain for language and participation in a language-using community—young children enter a symbolic universe that is distinctively human.

Key Terms

infant-directed speech, p. 245

phonological development, p. 247

semantic development, p. 247

grammar, p. 247

pragmatic development, p. 248

morpheme, p. 248

overextension, p 252

underextension, p. 253

fast mapping, p. 254

metaphor, p. 254

syntactic bootstrapping, p. 256

grammatical morphemes, p. 256

conversational acts, p. 258

protoimperatives, p. 258

protodeclaratives, p. 258

chronology, p. 259

cultural modeling, p 260

language acquisition device (LAD), 262

formats, p. 263

language acquisition support system (LASS), p. 264

collective monologues, p. 265

true dialogue, p. 265

inner speech, p. 265

Physical and Cognitive Development in Early Childhood

Physical and Motor Development

The Changing Body

Motor Development

Health

Brain Development

Preoperational Development

Centration

The Problem of Uneven Levels of Performance

Information-Processing Approaches to Cognitive Development

Cognitive Development in Privileged Domains

The Domain of Physics

The Domain of Psychology

The Domain of Biology

Explaining Domain-Specific Cognitive Development

Cognitive Development and Culture

Cultural Scripts

Cultural Context and the Unevenness of Development

Reconciling Alternative Approaches

A group of 5-year-old children has been listening to their teacher read the folktale "Stone Soup," which tells the story of three hungry soldiers who trick some peasants into giving them food by pretending to make soup out of stones. "We've made some stone soup to share with everyone," say the soldiers, "but of course it would taste better with some cabbage and meat . . . ." Rose, one of the children listening to the story, asks, "Do stones melt?" The teacher, Vivian Paley, decides to help the children answer this question by having them make some stone soup of their own. Here is her report of the conversation surrounding their classroom experiment:

"Do you think they melt, Rose?"

"Yes."

"Does anyone agree with Rose?"

"They will melt if you cook them," said Lisa.

"If you boil them," Eddie added.

No one doubted that the stones in the story had melted and that ours, too, would melt.

"We can cook them and find out," Ms. Paley said. "How will we be able to tell if they've melted?"

"They'll be smaller," said Deana.

The stones are placed in boiling water for an hour and then put on the table for inspection.

Ellen: They're much smaller.

Fred: Much, much. Almost melted.

Rose: I can't eat melted stones.

Ms. Paley: Don't worry, Rose. You won't. But I'm not convinced they've melted. Can we prove it?

Ms. Paley suggests weighing the stones to see if they will lose weight as they boil. The children find that the stones weigh 2 pounds at the start. After they have been boiled again, the following conversation ensues:

Eddie: Still 2 [pounds]. But they are smaller.

Wally: Much smaller.

Ms. Paley: They weigh the same. Two pounds before and 2 pounds now. That means they didn't lose weight.

Eddie: They only got a little bit smaller.

Wally: The scale can't see the stones. Hey, once in Michigan there were three stones in a fire and they melted away. They were gone. We saw it.

Deana: Maybe the stones in the story are magic.

Wally: But not these.

(Adapted from Paley, 1981, pp. 16–18.)

T his discussion among a group of kindergarten children and their teacher illustrates both the fascination developmentalists feel, and the challenges they face, as they study the cognitive changes that occur in the years following infancy. When the teacher prompts the children to reconcile the world of the folktale and the world of their senses, the children exhibit a pattern of thinking that is typical for their age—a mixture of sound logic and magical thinking. The children correctly believe that when things are "cooked down," they grow smaller and that small stones should be lighter than big ones. At the

Like kindergartners everywhere, the children in this Dayton, Ohio, class probably give their teacher plenty of examples of how the young mind wobbles back and forth between logic and magic.

same time, they are willing to believe that there really are such things as magical stones that melt, and so they miss the point of "Stone Soup." Their way of thinking appears to wobble back and forth between logic and magic, insight and ignorance, the reasonable and the irrational.

A similar mixture of cognitive competence and incompetence can be found in the youngsters' ability to remember objects and events. Young children can often recall the names and descriptions of their favorite dinosaurs, details of trips to the doctor's office, or where they last left their favorite toy with an accuracy that astounds their parents (Nelson & Fivush, 2000). But if an adult asks them to remember a short list of words or a set of toy objects—a task that is easy for older children and adults—they find it difficult to do so, even just a few minutes later (Tulving & Craik, 2000).

The variability of young children's intellectual performances highlights in a special way the unevenness of development, one of the key principles discussed in Chapter 3 (see p. 103 for the list of principles). At the same time, it raises important questions: Can early childhood be considered a distinct stage of development? If it can, then what explains the uneven and variable quality of thought during the years between 2 and 5?

As you probably expect from your reading thus far, theorists' answers to these questions depend on whether they view development as discontinuous and stage-like or continuous and gradual. Stage theorists see young children as being at a certain stage, that is, at a certain level of cognitive *competence,* which they have attained as a result of general processes of change—physical maturation and the universal experiences children have with a variety of people, objects, and other features of their environments. According to these theorists, the unevenness of thought in early childhood is of little significance or consequence: In their view, it is largely a matter of variability in *performance* resulting from such factors as the variations in children's familiarity with a particular task or the specific way in which the task is presented (see also p. 181). In contrast, theorists who emphasize the continuity of development see the unevenness as consequential and as inconsistent with a stage view. These theorists tend to maintain that cognitive change and its unevenness arise either from (1) gradual increases in various general psychological mechanisms such as short-term memory capacity or (2) from changes within various isolated domains of psychological functioning, with changes in different domains occurring at different rates. In this chapter, we will examine each of these views in turn, looking at Piaget's preoperational stage, at information-processing approaches to cognitive development, and at cognitive development in specific domains.

Physical and Motor Development

Growth rates of the body and brain are considerably slower during early childhood than they were in infancy. At the same time, the ability of children to use and control their bodies grows by leaps and bounds. As you will see, these changes affect children's health and nutritional needs—needs that are not always met, for various cultural, social, and economic reasons.

The Changing Body

By the time children enter early childhood, around the age of 2½, their body proportions have changed substantially. Gone are the dimpled bottoms, pudgy thighs, and sumo-wrestler bellies so typical of the infant build. Much of the change in the

ossification A process through which new bone tissue is formed at the growth plates of long bones.

motor drive The pleasure young children take in using their new motor skills.

body's proportions and appearance is due to the lengthening of the long bones of the arms, legs, and fingers (Olsen, Reginato, & Wang, 2000). This bone development occurs when new bone tissue is formed through a process of **ossification**. In general, ossification takes place at the ends of long bones, around areas of cartilage known as *growth plates* (see Figure 8.1). In addition to generating new bone tissue, ossification is associated with bones' becoming harder and stronger (Kalkwarf et al., 2007; Rauch & Schoenau, 2001). Until a bone becomes fully mature and ossified, it is vulnerable to fracture, especially the area of the growth plate, which is the last part to ossify and harden. It is estimated that 15 to 30 percent of all childhood fractures are growth-plate fractures (Sullivan & Anderson, 2000). Because they may affect future bone growth, growth-plate fractures should be treated immediately and followed over time to best prevent consequences such as crooked or uneven limbs.

Motor Development

Watching little children on a playground is a lesson in the extraordinary physical and motor developments that separate early childhood from infancy. As shown in the Table 8.1 column on gross motor skills, at 2 years of age, children can run, kick a ball, and climb the ladder of the slide, and at 3 years they can ride a tricycle. The ability to throw a ball overhand emerges at around age 4, as does skipping—that quintessentially childlike way of moving through the world. By the time they are 5, children have achieved a great deal of mastery over their bodies; they have good balance and can ride a scooter and climb nimbly on a jungle gym.

Just as impressive as these gains in motor development is the exuberance with which children practice them. Have you ever been at the grocery store or mall and noticed a young child hopping around or gyrating goofily for no apparent reason other than the sheer joy of doing so? Indeed, young children seem to take great pleasure in their newfound abilities to control their bodies, an aspect of motor development described as **motor drive**.

In addition to advances in their gross motor skills, young children's fine motor skills improve notably—to the point that 5-year-olds can fully dress themselves and tie their shoes, use eating utensils effectively, pour water into a glass more or less reliably, and

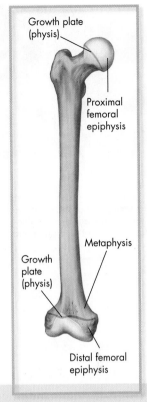

FIGURE 8.1 Growth plates (physes) are located between the widened part of the shaft of the bone (the metaphysis) and the end of the bone (the epiphysis). This diagram of a femur (thighbone) shows the location of the growth plates at both ends of the bone. (Adapted from Sullivan, 2000.)

table **8.1**

Motor Milestones of Early Childhood		
Age, in Years	**Gross Motor Skills**	**Fine Motor Skills**
2	Walks well	Uses spoon and fork
	Runs	Turns pages of a book
	Goes up and down stairs alone	Imitates circular stroke
	Kicks ball	Builds tower of 6 cubes
3	Runs well	Feeds self well
	Marches	Puts on shoes and socks
	Rides tricycle	Unbuttons and buttons
	Stands on one foot briefly	Builds tower of 10 cubes
4	Skips	Draws a person
	Standing broad jump	Cuts with scissors (not well)
	Throws ball overhand	Dresses self well
	High motor drive	Washes and dries face
5	Hops and skips	Dresses without help
	Good balance	Prints simple letters
	Skates	Ties shoes
	Rides scooter	

The enormous gains in gross motor development that characterize early childhood provide good reasons for South Korean parents to enroll their children in martial arts classes.

This young boy's colorful drawing of his family demonstrates some of the remarkable advances in fine motor control that emerge in early childhood.

wield crayons with enough control to stay within the lines when they want to. Taken together, the growth and refinement of young children's gross and fine motor capacities markedly increase their abilities to explore their environments and add significantly to the variety of experiences they can have, providing ample occasions for the development of new ways to think and act.

Health

The slowed pace of physical growth during early childhood is reflected in the decreased and occasionally finicky appetites of young children (Dubois et al., 2006). Nevertheless, new levels of physical activity enabled by increased motor development and control place significant demands on the young body for appropriate amounts of both sleep and nutrition. It is fairly well known that older children and adolescents often do not get enough sleep or eat as well as they should (see Chapter 11, pp. 394–395, and Chapter 14, pp. 526–530), but research indicates that this is also often true for young children. As any parent can attest, children who do not get enough sleep or have not been eating well can be grumpy, overemotional, and easily frustrated, and may have trouble concentrating (Dahl & Lewin, 2002; El-Sheikh et al., 2006).

Sleep Despite pediatricians' recommendations that young children get 12 to 15 hours of sleep in a 24-hour period (naps included), a study conducted by Christine Acebo and her colleagues found that children between 2 and 5 years of age typically sleep only about 8.7 hours at night and less than 9.5 hours in the course of 24 hours (Acebo et al., 2005). The researchers collected their data by placing activity monitors on the children's ankles or wrists to record their sleep and by asking mothers to report their children's sleep habits in detailed diaries. In addition to finding that children sleep much less than recommended, the researchers discovered that more than 80 percent of the children in the study were not taking naps on some or all days. Furthermore, although most children woke frequently during the night, this was particularly true for children from low-income families, who also spent more time in bed compared with children from higher-income families. The effects of early sleep deprivation on later development have yet to be determined. However, the researchers expressed concern that the fast pace of modern life may be taking a toll on the sleep patterns of young children.

Childhood obesity rates continue to rise throughout the world, including China, due in part to increased access to diets high in fats and sugars.

Nutrition In many parts of the world, breast-feeding continues well into the third and even fourth year of life (Whiting & Child, 1953; Konner, 2005). In most industrial societies, however, children usually have been fully weaned from the breast or bottle by the time they are 2 years of age. How parents meet the energy needs of young children has become a major source of concern for developmentalists, particularly in light of the obesity epidemic affecting an estimated 42 million children under the age of 5 throughout the world (WHO, 2010). In the United States, a nationwide longitudinal study found that children identified as overweight between 2 and 4 years of age were 5 times more likely than their normal-weight peers to be overweight as adolescents, placing them at risk for a variety of health problems, including diabetes, high blood pressure, and heart disease (Nader et al., 2006). Interestingly, it appears that in addition to the amount of weight gained, the velocity of weight gain during early childhood poses significant health risks. A large study conducted in France found that young children who gained weight quickly relative to their peers were at greater risk of being overweight (Péneau, Rouchard, Rolland-Cachera, Arnault, Herc-berg, & Castetbon, 2011).

A similar national study of Finnish children found an interesting growth pattern associated with the emergence of heart disease in adult-hood (Alastalo et al., 2009). Specifically, indi-viduals most at risk for cardiovascular disease as adults were those who were actually un-derweight during the first 2 years of life and then underwent a period of rapid weight gain through early and later childhood. This par-ticular pattern has worrisome implications for children in third-world countries where globalization is creating major changes in access to food and in eating behavior, with an increase in calories and in fats and sugar in the diet. In fact, a study of children in China, India, Guatemala, Brazil, and the Philippines—all of which are experiencing the "nutrition transition" associated with globalization—found evidence for the pattern described in the Finnish study, that is, growth failure in the first few years of postnatal life followed by overweight in early and later childhood and elevated risk for diabetes and heart disease in adult-hood (Stein et al., 2005).

Young children rely on parents to provide them with nutritious meals and snacks. For economic reasons, some parents may have difficulty meeting the nutritional needs of their children. This is especially true in developing countries, where an es-timated 195 million children under the age of 5 have stunted growth because their parents cannot afford to feed them adequately (UNICEF, 2009). Even in the United States, 21.3 percent of households with children (8.4 million) are considered **food-insecure** (Fiese et al., 2011; Nord et al., 2010), meaning that they do not have access to enough food to ensure good health for all family members (Figure 8.2). Table 8.2 lists items that are included in a national survey completed by parents in the United States to assess the food security of their children. Children who suffer food insecu-rity are at risk for a number of problems, including developmental delays and poor academic achievement (Cook & Frank, 2008; Jyoti, Frongillo, & Jones, 2005).

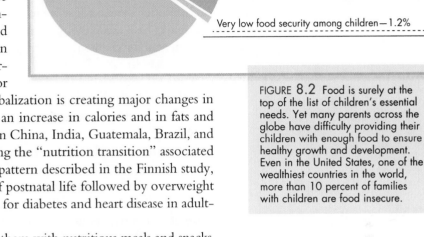

FIGURE 8.2 Food is surely at the top of the list of children's essential needs. Yet many parents across the globe have difficulty providing their children with enough food to ensure healthy growth and development. Even in the United States, one of the wealthiest countries in the world, more than 10 percent of families with children are food insecure.

table 8.2
Questions Used in a Survey to Assess the Food Security of Children

1. "We relied on only a few kinds of low-cost food to feed our children because we were run-ning out of money to buy food." Was that often, sometimes, or never true for you in the last 12 months?

2. "We couldn't feed our children a balanced meal, because we couldn't afford that." Was that often, sometimes, or never true for you in the last 12 months?

3. "The children were not eating enough because we just couldn't afford enough food." Was that often, sometimes, or never true for you in the last 12 months?

4. In the last 12 months, did you ever cut down the size of any of the children's meals because there wasn't enough money for food? (Yes/No)

5. In the last 12 months, were the children ever hungry but you just couldn't afford more food? (Yes/No)

6. In the last 12 months, did any of the children ever skip a meal because there wasn't enough money for food? (Yes/No)

7. (If you answered yes to question 6) How often does this happen—almost every month, some months but not every month, or in only 1 or 2 months?

8. In the last 12 months did any of the children ever not eat for a whole day because there wasn't enough money for food? (Yes/No)

Source: Adapted from Nord et al., 2010.

food-insecure Lacking enough food to ensure good health.

Parental attitudes about food and eating can also take a toll on children's nutrition. A series of studies conducted by Thomas Joiner and his colleagues found that parents of 3-year-olds worried that their sons but not their daughters were underweight and did not eat enough, despite the fact that there was no difference in the actual average weight of boys and girls in the study (Holm-Denoma et al., 2005). This finding prompted the researchers to speculate that body-image stereotypes—specifically, that girls should be thin, and boys big and strong—may be affecting the diet of very young children and possibly increasing the risk of eating disorders in the future (see Chapter 15, p. 590). And, although parents today are increasingly concerned about early-childhood obesity, researchers have made the point that these concerns must be carefully balanced with the potential for children's undernutrition (Allen & Myers, 2006).

Brain Development

As we discussed in Chapter 5, after infancy, the brain's development slows considerably until adolescence, when it undergoes another growth spurt. At the start of early childhood, the brain has attained about 80 percent of its adult weight; by age 5, it has grown to 90 percent of its full weight (Huttenlocher, 1994). Despite this modest growth rate, several noteworthy changes occur in the brain during early childhood (Lenroot & Giedd, 2006; Shaw et al., 2008). For example, the overall enlargement in size results from the continuing process of *myelination,* which speeds the transmission of neural impulses within and among different areas of the brain (Sampaio & Truwitt, 2001). During early childhood, myelination is most prominent in brain areas such as the frontal cortex that are important for more advanced cognitive functions, including planning and regulating behavior (Pujol et al., 2006). In addition to increased myelination, there is an increase in the length and branching of neurons that connect different areas of the brain, as well as a continuation of *synaptic pruning,* in which nonfunctional synapses die off (see Chapter 4, p. 129).

Even with these changes, the brain, of course, is still relatively immature, which may account for the limitations of children's problem-solving abilities. For example, myelination in parts of the brain that support memory (the hippocampus and frontal cortex) is still far from complete, which likely contributes to young children's difficulties in keeping several things in mind at once. In addition, various areas of the brain are developing, and connecting, at different times and at different rates, and this variability may account for the unevenness of cognitive development evident during this age period. When one part of the brain develops more rapidly than others, or when the neural pathways connecting a particular combination of cortical areas undergo a spurt in myelination, the psychological processes supported by the brain area or areas can be expected to undergo rapid change as well. High levels of performance are expected to occur when a given task calls on brain systems that are highly developed, and, correspondingly, low levels of performance are expected to occur when a given task calls on brain systems that are not yet mature.

A fascinating example of what happens when areas of the brain that will eventually communicate with each other are not yet connected is the *scale errors* made by toddlers. In older children and adults, the perception of the size, or scale, of an object is seamlessly integrated into the person's actions with the object. You would not, for example, try to put a really large peg into a really small hole. Children between 18 and 30 months of age, on the other hand, very well might. This is because they frequently commit **scale errors**; that is, they fail to integrate information about the size of an object into their decisions about how to use it (Ware et al., 2006). The result is serious and often amusing attempts to perform impossible actions, such as trying to sit in a dollhouse chair or get into a miniature toy car (Figure 8.3). On the basis of their research, Judy DeLoache and her colleagues

scale errors Young children's inappropriate use of an object due to their failure to consider information about the object's size.

argue that scale errors in young children involve a "disconnect" between children's use of visual information and their ability to plan and control their actions (2005; 2011). The dissociation of perception and action, they speculate, may be due to the immature cortical functioning of the brain, particularly in the prefrontal cortex (see also Barsalou, 2008, and Diamond et al., 2002).

Some of the changes that occur in brain development during early childhood are influenced by the cultural context: Different culturally organized activities promote *experience-dependent* brain growth in the form of increased synaptic development and connections (see Chapter 4, p. 130). For example, if a young child lives in a culture that emphasizes hunting or weaving, both of which require concentrated and sustained processing of spatial relations, it can be expected that the child's brain will undergo increased growth of cells in the area responsible for processing spatial information (the parietal cortex). By contrast, if the child's culture places a heavy emphasis on verbal expression, the language centers of the child's brain are likely to undergo additional development. The influence of culturally organized activities on brain development is intriguingly illustrated in a recent study indicating that when children take music lessons between the ages of 4 and 6, brain processes associated with attention and memory become more active when they listen to music, and their general memory capacity and IQs improve compared with those of children who do not receive music training (Fujioka, Trainor, & Ross, 2008).

▲ APPLY :: CONNECT :: DISCUSS

Armed with the information in Table 8.1, and your understanding of *motor drive*, visit a playground where you can observe young children engaged in motor play. What examples of motor skills and motor drive can you identify? Focusing on one or two children, can you guess their ages based on the motor skills they exhibit?

Preoperational Development

Adult: Why is it cold in winter?
Child: Because there is snow.
Adult: What is it that makes the cold?
Child: The snow.
Adult: If there were no snow would it be cold?
Child: No.
Adult: It is the snow which makes the cold, or the cold which makes the snow?
Child: The cold makes the snow.
Adult: And where does the cold come from?
Child: From the snow.
(Piaget, 1929/1979, p. 323.)

As we discussed in Chapter 5, Piaget believed that when children complete the final sensorimotor substage of infancy, they are able to think symbolically, using one thing to stand for ("re-present") another. This newfound ability to use one thing to stand for another is the foundation for developing language. It is also the bridge to the next stage of intellectual development, which Piaget called *preoperational* and considered a transitional stage between the sensorimotor intelligence of infancy and the fully *operational* intelligence of middle childhood (Piaget & Inhelder, 1969). In order to explain what Piaget meant by *preoperational thinking,* we need first to say a bit about the meaning of operational thought (which we will discuss in more detail in Chapter 11).

 (a)

 (b)

 (c)

all: DeLoache et al., 2004

FIGURE 8.3 Three examples of scale errors. (a) This 21-month-old child has committed a scale error by attempting to slide down a miniature slide; she has fallen off in this earnest effort to carry out what is an impossible act. (b) This 24-month-old child has opened the door to the miniature car and is repeatedly trying to force his foot inside the car. (c) This 28-month-old child is looking between his legs to precisely locate the miniature chair that he is in the process of sitting on. (From DeLoache, Uttal, & Rosengren, 2005.)

The extensive knowledge that young children acquire when they become engrossed in subjects like dinosaurs may only be a passing phase. But children's expertise about such matters is scientifically important because it shows that even young children, when they accumulate an extensive knowledge base in a specific domain, will display cognitive abilities more like those of adults.

According to Piaget, operational thinking involves **mental operations**, that is, mental "actions" in which children combine, separate, and transform information in a logical manner. Examples of mental operations include mathematical processes such as adding and subtracting, as well as arranging objects in particular orders (from smallest to largest, or alphabetically, and so on) or putting objects into categories based on some feature they have in common. The ability to engage in such mental actions and think operationally emerges around 7 to 8 years of age, making it possible for children to arrange their stamp collections according to country of origin and estimated value, for example, or to assemble a complex new toy right out of the box. They are better able to formulate explicit problem-solving strategies because they can think through alternative actions and modify them mentally before they actually act. Piaget believed that until children are able to engage in mental operations, their thinking is subject to fluctuations of the kind Ms. Paley's class demonstrated when answering questions about "Stone Soup," and to the type of circular reasoning illustrated in the above dialogue, in which a child explains the relationship between snow and the cold of winter.

Piaget's belief that young children often fall into error and confusion because they are still unable to engage in true mental operations is what led him to call the period of cognitive development in early childhood the **preoperational stage**. In his view, cognitive development during early childhood involves a process of overcoming the limitations that stand in the way of operational thinking. (These limitations, discussed in the next several sections, are outlined in Table 8.3.)

Although fluctuations and errors are typical of early childhood thought, Piaget insisted that preoperational thinking is not random or unsystematic. Indeed, as you

table 8.3

Piaget's Stages of Cognitive Development: Preoperational

Age (years)	Stage	Description	Characteristics and Examples
Birth to 2	Sensorimotor	Infants' achievements consist largely of coordinating their sensory perceptions and simple motor behaviors. As they move through the 6 substages of this period, infants come to recognize the existence of a world outside of themselves and begin to interact with it in deliberate ways.	Centration, the tendency to focus (center) on the most salient aspect of whatever one is trying to think about. A major manifestation of this is egocentrism, or considering the world entirely in terms of one's own point of view. • Children engage in collective monologues, rather than dialogues, in each other's company. • Children have difficulty taking a listener's knowledge into account in order to communicate effectively. • Children fail to consider both the height and width of containers in order to compare their volumes. • Children confuse classes with subclasses. They cannot reliably say whether there are more wooden beads or more brown beads in a set of all wooden beads.
2 to 6	Preoperational	Young children can represent reality to themselves through the use of symbols, including mental images, words, and gestures. Objects and events no longer have to be present to be thought about, but children often fail to distinguish their point of view from that of others; become easily captured by surface appearances; and are often confused about causal relations.	
6 to 12	Concrete operational	As they enter middle childhood, children become capable of mental operations, internalized actions that fit into a logical system. Operational thinking allows children to mentally combine, separate, order, and transform objects and actions. Such operations are considered concrete because they are carried out in the presence of the objects and events being thought about.	Confusion of appearance and reality. • Children act as if a Halloween mask actually changes the identity of the person wearing it. • Children may believe that a straight stick partially submerged in water actually does become bent. Precausal reasoning, characterized by illogical thinking and an indifference to cause-and-effect relations.
12 to 19	Formal operational	In adolescence, the developing person acquires the ability to think systematically about all logical relations within a problem. Adolescents display keen interest in abstract ideals and in the process of thinking itself.	• A child may think a graveyard is a cause of death because dead people are buried there. A form of moral reasoning that sees morality as being imposed from the outside and that does not take intentions into account.

will see below, the errors children make in the preoperational stage are remarkably consistent, and this may reveal much about the nature of cognition and its development. On the other hand, as you learned in Chapter 5, many developmentalists disagree with Piaget's conclusions, and argue that his interview methods make it difficult for children to demonstrate their competence on various tasks, thereby obscuring their level of actual understanding.

Centration

Imagine that we show you two beach balls. One is red with blue stripes; the other is red with yellow stripes. If we then ask you to point to the red ball, you would very likely want clarification: "Which red one? The one with yellow stripes or the one with blue stripes?" In contrast, a preoperational child would most likely point to one or the other of the balls with total confidence. According to Piaget, the source of such an error, and the greatest limitation to early childhood thinking, is **centration**, the tendency of young children to be "captured" by a single, usually perceptual, feature of whatever they are trying to think about, and to focus on that one feature to the exclusion of all others. In the case of the beach balls, the child focuses on the perceptual feature of color (red, in this case) and consequently ignores the other feature of stripes. As you can imagine, centration results in thinking and knowledge that are highly biased and limited to the particular perceptions that happen to have captured the child's attention at a given point in time. The opposite of centration—and the key to cognitive growth beyond the preoperational stage—is **decentration**, that is, the ability to mentally pull away from focusing on just one aspect of an object or problem in order to consider multiple aspects of it simultaneously. Decentration allows children's thinking and knowledge to be less subjective and reflect a broader point of view. For this reason, Piaget argued that the *consequence* of the mental distancing enabled by decentration is **objectivity**—that is, an understanding of reality as separate from one's subjective perceptions, thoughts, and actions—which Piaget regarded as the full flowering of cognitive development. Indeed, as you will see in later chapters, Piaget held that cognitive development from infancy through adolescence involves a steady march toward increasing objectivity, the hallmark of scientific reasoning.

Preoperational children, however, have just begun this journey toward objectivity. Their tendency to be captured by a single aspect or dimension of an object or event is at the root of what Piaget identified as the three most common errors in early childhood reasoning: (1) egocentrism, (2) the confusion of appearance and reality, and (3) precausal reasoning. In the sections that follow, we will look at these three errors, first summarizing the evidence that led Piaget to his conclusions about each one and then presenting findings that challenge his interpretations.

Egocentrism If you and some friends were to walk together down a road in the dark of night, you all might notice that the moon seemed to be following you. You would all know, of course, that the moon was not *really* coordinating its movement with your own. To think otherwise, you would have to account for the fact that if each of you suddenly set off in different directions, each of you would still have the sense of being followed by the moon. The contradiction here no doubt seems obvious to you. Preoperational children, on the other hand, have no sense of such a contradiction. They will steadfastly maintain that the moon follows them around and fail to appreciate that it cannot possibly follow someone heading west at the same time it follows someone heading east.

In the context of Piaget's general concept of centration, **egocentrism** refers to the tendency to "center on oneself," or, in other words, to be captive to one's own point of view and unable to take another person's perspective. The child who

mental operations In Piaget's theory, the mental process of combining, separating, or transforming information in a logical manner.

preoperational stage According to Piaget, the stage of thinking between infancy and middle childhood in which children are unable to decenter their thinking or to think through the consequences of an action.

centration Young children's tendency to focus on only one feature of an object to the exclusion of all other features.

decentration The cognitive ability to pull away from focusing on just one feature of an object in order to consider multiple features.

objectivity The mental distancing made possible by decentration. Piaget believed the attainment of objectivity to be the major achievement of cognitive development.

egocentrism In Piaget's terms, the tendency to "center on oneself," that is, to consider the world entirely in terms of one's own point of view.

FIGURE 8.4 Preschool children shown this diorama of three mountains, each with a distinctive feature on its top, were unable to say how the scene might look from perspectives other than the one they had at the moment. (From Piaget & Inhelder, 1956.)

FIGURE 8.5 In Borke's modification of Piaget's three-mountain perspective-taking task, with a diorama that contains familiar objects, preschoolers are more likely to be able to say how it looks from a point of view other than their own.

wants to give Daddy a Care Bear or an action hero for his birthday and the child who believes that he or she is being followed around by the moon are both demonstrating egocentrism.

A famous example of egocentrism as a failure to take another person's perspective is found in young children's performance on Piaget's classic "three-mountain problem." In this procedure, young children were shown a large diorama containing models of three mountains that were distinctively different in size, shape, and landmarks (Piaget & Inhelder, 1956) (Figure 8.4). First, the children were asked to walk around the diorama and become familiar with the landscape from all sides. Once the children had done this, they were seated on one side of the diorama. Next, a doll was placed on the opposite side of the diorama so that it had a "different view" of the landscape. The children were then shown pictures of the diorama from several perspectives and were asked to identify the picture that corresponded to the doll's point of view. Even though they had seen the diorama from the doll's location, the children almost always chose the picture corresponding to their own spatial perspective, not the doll's. Preoperational children's poor performance on Piaget's three-mountain problem has been widely replicated and long assumed to demonstrate the perspective-taking limitations of young children.

Speculating that the complexity of Piaget's task might affect children's performance, Helen Borke (1975) first replicated the classic three-mountain experiment with children between 3 and 4 years of age. She then presented the same children with an alternative form of the problem—a farm scene that included such landmarks as a small lake with a boat on it, a horse and a cow, ducks, people, trees, and a building (Figure 8.5). In this alternative version, Grover, a character from *Sesame Street,* drove around the landscape in a car, stopping from time to time to take a look at the view. The child's task was to indicate what that view looked like from Grover's perspective.

Children as young as 3 years old performed well on this perspective-taking problem, despite the fact that, as would be expected, their performance on the three-mountain version of the problem was poor. These contrasting levels of performance between the two forms of a logically identical problem led Borke to conclude that when perspective-taking tasks involve familiar, easily differentiated objects, and when care is taken to make it easy for young children to express their understanding, young children demonstrate that they are able to take spatial perspectives other than their own. In other words, young children have the *competence* to take the perspectives of others, but their *performance* may be affected by the demands of the task.

Confusing Appearance and Reality

First child: Pretend there's a monster coming, okay?
Second child: No. Let's don't pretend that.
First child: Okay. Why?
Second child: 'Cause it's too scary, that's why.
(Garvey & Berndt, 1977, p. 107.)

The tendency to confuse appearance and reality is another common error of early childhood that Piaget attributed to centration. Difficulty distinguishing between appearance and reality would explain why 2½-year-olds often become

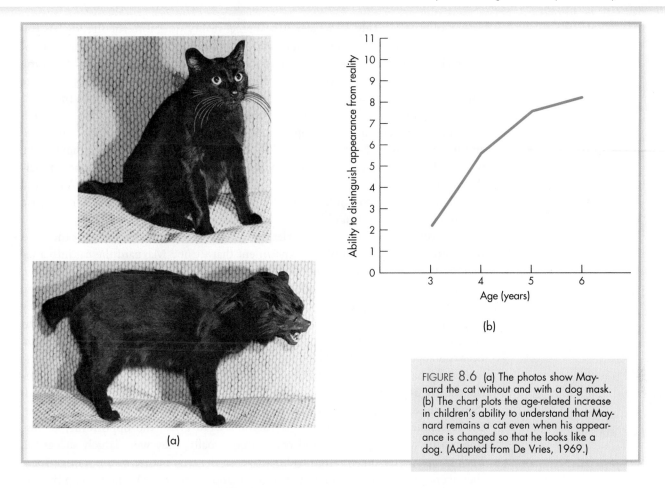

FIGURE 8.6 (a) The photos show Maynard the cat without and with a dog mask. (b) The chart plots the age-related increase in children's ability to understand that Maynard remains a cat even when his appearance is changed so that he looks like a dog. (Adapted from De Vries, 1969.)

frightened when someone puts on a mask at Halloween, as if the mask had actually changed the person into a witch or a dragon. In a classic study of this form of behavior, Rheta De Vries (1969) studied the development of the appearance–reality distinction with the help of Maynard, an unusually well-behaved black cat. At the start of the experiment, all the children said that Maynard was a cat. After they played with Maynard for a short while, De Vries hid Maynard's front half behind a screen, while she strapped a realistic mask of a ferocious dog onto his head (Figure 8.6a). As she removed the screen, De Vries asked a set of questions to assess the children's ability to distinguish between the animal's real identity and its appearance: "What kind of animal is it now?" "Is it really a dog?" "Can it bark?"

By and large, the 3-year-olds focused almost entirely on Maynard's appearance (Figure 8.6b). They said he had actually become a ferocious dog, and some were afraid he would bite them. Most of the 6-year-olds scoffed at this idea, understanding that the cat only looked like a dog. The 4- and 5-year-olds showed considerable confusion. They did not believe that a cat could become a dog, but they did not always answer De Vries's questions correctly.

Similar confusions between appearance and reality have been reported by John Flavell and his colleagues, who showed young children various objects that appeared to be one thing but were really another: a sponge that appeared to be a rock, a stone that appeared to be an egg, and so on. After each object was presented, the children were asked, "What does that look like?" (the appearance question) and "What is it really?" (the reality question) (Flavell et al., 1986; Melot & Houde, 1998). The researchers found that

At 2 years of age, Riley can hardly be blamed for bursting into tears when she meets the Easter Bunny for the first time. Her age-typical confusion between appearance and reality can make such encounters truly scary.

3-year-olds were likely to answer appearance–reality questions incorrectly. As expected, the children initially thought that the sponge "rock" was a rock because it was realistic enough to fool even adults. But once children discovered by touching it that the "rock" was really a sponge, they began to insist that it not only felt like a sponge but also looked like a sponge! Four-year-olds seemed to be in a transition state; they sometimes answered correctly, sometimes incorrectly. Five-year-olds had a much firmer grip on the appearance–reality distinction in these circumstances and usually answered the experimenters' questions correctly. These findings have been replicated in several countries, including China, Germany, and France (Huelsken et al., 2001; Melot & Houde, 1998). Thus, research like that of De Vries and Flavell would seem to confirm Piaget's view that centration can make it difficult for preschoolers to distinguish appearance from reality.

However, modifications of De Vries's and Flavell's experiments suggest otherwise. In an interesting variation of the experiment that turned Maynard the cat into a ferocious dog, Carl Huelsksen and his colleagues demonstrated that young children can make appearance–reality distinctions with regard to adults dressed up in a costume (Huelsken et al., 2001). In four out of five cases, 3- to 4-year-olds indicated that they knew the person in the costume was the same as the person in his or her regular clothing, although a majority had difficulty providing an explicit verbal distinction between appearance and reality.

Felicity Sapp and her colleagues also determined that the main difficulty experienced by 3-year-olds is formulating the appearance–reality distinction in words (Sapp, Lee, & Muir, 2000). In a variation of Flavell's deceptive-objects experiment, the researchers found that when 3-year-olds were given the opportunity to distinguish between appearance and reality nonverbally, they were largely successful. For example, after the children had discovered the true nature of the sponge rock, they were presented with a number of items and asked to pick one to help the experimenter wipe up some water. Nearly all the children picked the sponge rock.

In a different approach, Catherine Rice and her colleagues (1997) repeated and extended Flavell's study by using a procedure that engaged 3- and 4-year-olds as co-conspirators in the fake-object deception. After tricking a child with a fake object such as a sponge rock, the experimenter asked the child to help in pulling the same trick on an adult visitor who would soon be arriving. The experimenter and child displayed the trick object on a table, and then, while waiting for the adult to arrive, the experimenter asked the child to help in pulling the same trick on an adult visitor who would soon be arriving. What does it appear to be? What will the adult visitor think it is? In this playlike context, the children were able to say that the object was a sponge but that it looked like a rock—and that the adult would think it was a rock. Thus, they were clearly able to distinguish reality from appearance. The findings of the Sapp and Rice experiments illustrate just how careful experimenters must be to create appropriate versions of their tasks so that they are meaningful for young children and give them ample opportunity to reveal what they know (see Deák, 2006, for a review).

Precausal Reasoning Nothing is more characteristic of 4- to 5-year-old children than their love for asking questions: "Why is the sky blue?" "What makes clouds?" "Where do babies come from?" Clearly, children are interested in the causes of things. Piaget believed, however, that because young children are not yet capable of true mental operations, they cannot engage in genuine cause-and-effect reasoning. He claimed that instead of reasoning from general premises to particular cases (deduction) or from specific cases to general principles (induction), young children think *transductively,* from one particular to another. As an example, he described how his young daughter missed her customary nap one afternoon and remarked, "I haven't had a nap, so it isn't afternoon." As a consequence of such reasoning, young children are likely to confuse cause and effect. Because he believed that transductive reasoning precedes true causal reasoning, Piaget referred to this aspect of young children's thinking as **precausal thinking** (Piaget, 1930).

A splendid demonstration of how transductive reasoning can lead a young child to confuse cause and effect was provided by one of the authors' daughters. At the age of 3½, Jenny happened to walk with her parents through an old graveyard. Listening to her father read the inscriptions on the gravestones, she realized that somehow the old moss-covered stones represented people. "Where is she now?" she asked when he finished reading the inscription on one stone.

"She's dead," said her father.

"But where is she?"

Jenny's father tried to explain that when people die, they are buried in the ground, in cemeteries. After that, Jenny steadfastly refused to go into cemeteries and would become upset when she was near one. At bedtime every evening, she repeatedly asked about death, burial, and graveyards. Jenny's parents answered her questions as best as they could, yet Jenny kept repeating the same questions and was obviously upset by the topic. The reason for her fear became clear when the family was moving to New York City. "Are there any graveyards in New York City?" she asked anxiously. Exhausted by her insistent questions, her parents' belief that they should be honest was crumbling.

"No," her mother lied. "There are no graveyards in New York City."

At this response, Jenny visibly relaxed. "Then people don't die in New York," she said.

Jenny had reasoned that since graveyards are places where dead people are found, graveyards must be the cause of death. This reasoning led her to the comforting but incorrect conclusion that if you can stay away from graveyards, you are not in danger of dying.

As with the other two errors we have described, research on cause-and-effect reasoning suggests that under certain, carefully crafted conditions, young children are capable of greater cognitive sophistication than Piaget credited them with. Merry Bullock and Rochel Gelman, for example, used the apparatus shown in Figure 8.7 to demonstrate the causal reasoning abilities of 3- to 5-year-olds, specifically, their understanding that causes precede effects. (Bullock, 1984; Bullock & Gelman, 1979). Children observed two sequences of events. First, a steel marble was dropped into one of two slots in a box, both of which were visible through the side of the box. Two seconds after the marble disappeared at the bottom of the slot, a Snoopy doll popped out of the hole in the middle of the apparatus. Then, at that moment, a second ball was dropped into the other slot. It too disappeared, with no further result. The children were then asked to say which of the balls had made Snoopy jump up and to provide an explanation.

Even children as young as 3 years old usually said that the first ball had caused Snoopy to jump up, and the 5-year-olds had no difficulty with the task at all. However, as was the case in young children's explanations for the difference between appearance and reality, there was a marked difference between the age groups in their ability to verbally explain what had happened. Many of the 3-year-olds could give no explanation or said something completely irrelevant ("It's got big teeth"). Almost all the 5-year-olds could provide an explanation related to the principle that causes

precausal thinking Piaget's description of the reasoning of young children that does not follow the procedures of either deductive or inductive reasoning.

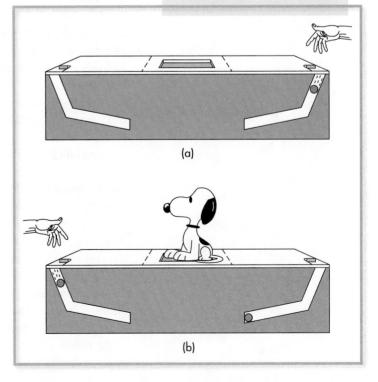

FIGURE 8.7 This illustration depicts the apparatus used by Bullock and Gelman to test preschoolers' understanding that cause precedes effect. (a) A marble was dropped into one of the slots. (b) Two seconds after the marble disappeared, a Snoopy doll popped out of the hole in the middle of the apparatus. At the same moment, a second marble was dropped into the other slot, where it disappeared, with no further result. Preschoolers are generally able to indicate which marble caused Snoopy to jump up. (Based on Bullock & Gelman, 1979.)

(a)

(b)

Introduction to task: blue object is a "starter" (turns on light box); green object is a "do-nothing" (does not turn on light box)

Test Trial A: both objects turn on light box

Test Trial B: neither object turns on light box

FIGURE 8.8 This apparatus was designed to test young children's understanding of cause-effect relationships. First, children are taught that the blue cube turns on a light box, while the green cone has no effect. Then, they are presented with different test trials in which the blue and green objects either work as expected, or violate the children's expectations. (Adapted from Legare, Gelman, & Wellman 2010.)

precede effects. Subsequent research has shown that if the problem is slightly complicated, 3-year-olds become confused and cannot understand, much less explain, what appear to be relatively simple mechanical cause-and-effect relationships (Frye, 2000).

Given children's unflagging curiosity about the world around them and their persistent attempts to understand it, a team of researchers wondered what might trigger children to reason about the causes of events they observe (Legare, Gelman, & Wellman, 2010). The researchers presented preschoolers with events that included two objects, one blue, one green, and two special "light boxes." The blue object was called a "starter" and, when placed on top of one of the light boxes, activated a light causing the box to glow. The green object was called a "do-nothing" and would not activate a light box when placed on top of it (see Figure 8.8). After observing how the objects and light boxes worked, the children were shown the two light boxes again, and then watched as the blue object was placed on top of one box and the green object on top of the other. The boxes, however, did not always behave as the children had come to expect them to. In particular, the light boxes had been rigged so that, in one test trial, both were activated when the objects were placed on top of them, and, in a second test trial, neither box was activated by the objects. The researchers found that the preschoolers were much more likely to look first at the inconsistent events. That is, on Test Trial A, they tended to look first at the box being activated by the "do-nothing" green object, whereas on Test Trial B, they tended to look first at the unlit box with the "starter" blue object. When the experimenter asked, "Why did that happen?", the children were also much more likely to offer explanations for the inconsistent events than for events that were consistent with their prior knowledge. Thus, it appears that young children are most likely to look for causes and reasons when their current knowledge is challenged by new information.

The Problem of Uneven Levels of Performance

The examples of preoperational thinking that we have provided thus far (summarized in Table 8.3 on p. 278) are only a sample of the phenomena supporting the idea that there is a distinctive mode of thought associated with early childhood. But they are sufficient to give the flavor of the sorts of evidence collected by Piaget and others to argue that an inability to decenter one's thought pervades the preoperational stage of cognitive development, making it difficult for young children to consider multiple aspects of a situation simultaneously or to think through a problem systematically (for an example of the real-world challenges presented by young children's cognitive limitations, see the box "Bearing Witness: Can Young Children Tell the Truth?" on p. 286).

On the other hand, we have also discussed various studies that cast doubt on certain specifics of Piaget's tasks and on his reliance on interviews, which led him to judge young children as particularly vulnerable to errors of reasoning. Much of this new evidence indicates that cognitive development in early childhood is a good deal more uneven and less stagelike than Piaget suggested. Under some circumstances, children show evidence of cognitive abilities well before Piaget believed they emerge (Goswami, 2008; Inagaki & Hatano, 2006; Rosengren & Brasswell, 2001). Piaget himself argued that certain types of tasks may be more difficult for children to solve than others, even though the tasks require the same type of reasoning skills (we discuss this in more detail in Chapter 11).

As noted earlier, some developmentalists believe that uneven levels of performance within a specific Piagetian stage are not particularly surprising. Others suggest that such unevenness poses a significant challenge to Piaget's fundamental idea that development proceeds through a sequence of qualitatively distinct, discontinuous stages (Feldman, 2004). Those in the latter camp propose two kinds of approaches that offer alternatives to Piaget's concept of a preoperational stage as characteristic of early childhood. These alternative approaches take different paths but share the twin goals of understanding the sources of unevenness in children's performance and the extent to which developmental change is general or piecemeal and stagelike or gradual (Case, 1999; Rose & Fischer, 2009; Goswami, 2008). As you will see in the next section, information-processing approaches propose *general psychological mechanisms,* such as increases in short-term memory capacity and knowledge, to account for the process of cognitive change and the unevenness of young children's cognitive performances. A competing set of theories, which we examine later, relegates general mechanisms to a secondary role and focuses on the ways in which cognitive development builds on *domain-specific psychological processes,* such as the ability to distinguish between living things and non-living objects.

▲ APPLY :: CONNECT :: DISCUSS

When young children are asked where they live, they often confuse the name of the city with the name of the state. How is this confusion an example of preoperational thinking?

Information-Processing Approaches to Cognitive Development

As discussed in Chapter 1, information-processing models of development depict the workings of the mind as analogous to the workings of a digital computer (Siegler, 2000). According to such models, the neural features of the human brain are analogous to the hardware of a computer—that is, its *structural* components— whereas the activities and practices that individuals engage in for the purpose of re- membering and using information are analogous to the computer's software—that is, the programs that are written to *process* information through the system.

An overview of the essential components of this view of the mind is illustrated in Figure 8.9. The three boxes labeled "sensory register," "short-term storage," and "long-term storage" represent the basic system for attending to, interpreting, and storing information. The box at the top of the figure, labeled "control processes," represents the systems that, in effect, monitor and modify the results of the ongoing processes of the basic system.

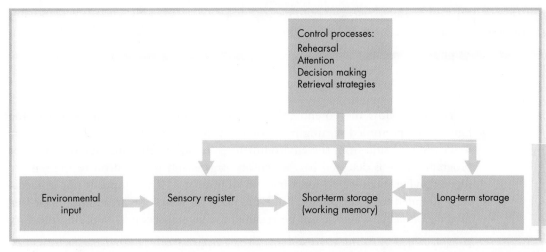

FIGURE 8.9 This figure shows the major components of an information-processing model of mental actions. (Adapted from Atkinson & Schiffrin, 1968.)

Bearing Witness: Can Young Children Tell the Truth?

IT IS A SAD FACT THAT CHILDREN OF ALL ages are victims of crimes or witness crimes committed against others. Psychologists have traditionally viewed children's eyewitness testimony concerning such events as unreliable—especially in cases involving sexual abuse and other traumatic events—because young children have been considered suggestible (Stern, 1910), incapable of distinguishing fantasy from reality (Piaget, 1926), and prone to fantasizing sexual events (Freud, 1905/1953). Judges, lawyers, and prosecutors have also expressed reservations about children's reliability as witnesses (Bottoms et al., 2002; Goodman & Melinder, 2007). Legal rulings on the admissibility of children's testimony continue to reflect these longstanding doubts. In many states, for example, it is left up to the judge to determine whether a child below a certain age is competent to testify.

Owing to a growing concern about the prevalence of sexual and physical abuse of children in recent years, the scientific and legal communities are particularly interested in determining when and under what conditions young children can testify reliably about past events (Goodman, 2006; Lyon, Carrick, & Quas, 2010). Children's behavior both in actual criminal trials and in experimental psychological studies reveals a complex picture in which a child's memories and testimony about an event are affected by the child's age, the nature of the event being recalled, and a number of socioemotional factors.

A concern that has spurred considerable research is whether very young children may be unreliable witnesses because either their long-term memory is less reliable than older children's and adults' or they are particularly susceptible to misremembering events when they are coached or presented with misleading questions (Goodman & Melinder, 2007; Klemfuss & Ceci, 2009). Indeed, several studies have demonstrated that preschool-age children are more susceptible to false suggestions

In an effort to put young children at ease during testimony, some courts are using child witness rooms. The one shown here uses a two-way, closed-circuit television system that both displays the courtroom to the child and uses a camera to transmit the child's testimony to the court.

Ron Thompson / ZUMA Press / Newscom

than are older children and adults (Poole & Lindsay, 2001). For example, when researchers asked young children misleading, even strange questions about what happened when they went to the doctor's office ("Did the doctor cut off your hair?" or "Did the nurse lick your knee?"), the youngest children were much more likely than the older children to say that these things happened even though they did not (Ornstein et al., 1997).

On the other hand, Gail Goodman and her colleagues have found that children can be remarkably resistant to misleading questions if they are interviewed soon after an event, when it is still fresh in their minds (Quas et al., 2007; Malloy & Quas, 2009). Moreover, their memory is improved when the event in question is emotionally intense. In one study, for example, when children were asked about their experiences getting vaccinated at the doctor's office, those who were more upset and cried more recalled more information (Goodman et al., 1991). In a long-term study of memory for child sexual abuse, it was found that sexual-abuse victims who had more posttraumatic stress symptoms remembered the abuse particularly well, suggesting that such trauma leads to "fear net-

works" that foster hypervigilance to trauma cues and reactivation of traumatic memories (Alexander et al., 2005).

Although much of the research on children's eyewitness testimony has focused on how unreliable children can be, Gail Goodman has turned her attention to finding out how to help children tell the truth about the frightening events they have witnessed or personally experienced. She has, for example, identified techniques that help children make accurate face identifications in photo lineups and that limit their suggestibility in interviews (such as the interviewer's telling children things like "I may try to trick you" and "It's OK to say 'I don't know'"). As she has pointed out,

the legal system makes numerous assumptions about children's abilities and needs. For instance, the criminal justice system assumes that "confrontation" of victims in open court is the best way to reach the truth—even if the victim is a young, traumatized child. Psychological science has the potential to test many of those assumptions and, in the process, to help create a more scientifically based jurisprudence concerning children. (Goodman, 2005, p. 873.)

You can follow the potential flow of information by starting at the left of the figure. The presumed starting point of any problem-solving process is the *sensory register*. Stimulation from the environment—"input," in the language of computer programming—is detected by the sensory organs and is passed on to the sensory register, where it is stored for a fraction of a second. If the input is not immediately attended to, it disappears. If it is attended to, it may be "read into" *short-term (working) memory*, where it can be retained for several seconds. Working memory is the part of the information-processing system where active thinking takes place. Working memory combines incoming information from the sensory register with memory of past experiences, or *long-term memory,* changing the information into new forms. If the information in working memory is not combined with information in long-term memory, it is easily forgotten.

Figure 8.9 also shows the way in which the flow of information between sensory register, working memory, and long-term memory is coordinated by *control processes.* These control processes determine how the information temporarily held in working memory is applied to the problem at hand. Important control processes include attention, rehearsal, and decision making. The "software" that implements the control processes determines the particular information that must be attended to, whether long-term memory must be searched more thoroughly, or whether a particular problem-solving strategy should be used. Control processes also determine whether a piece of information in short-term memory needs to be retained or can be forgotten.

You can get an overall idea of the information-processing approach by considering what occurs when a mother tries to teach her 4-year-old daughter to remember the family phone number. The mother sits with the child at the phone and shows her the sequence of buttons to push—say, 543-1234. The child watches what her mother does and hears what her mother is saying. First, the set of numbers enters the child's sensory register as images and a sequence of sounds, and is transferred to working memory. Next, meanings corresponding to those images and sounds are retrieved from long-term memory and matched with the images and sounds in working memory. The child recognizes each number and applies control processes in order to "try to remember," perhaps by using the strategy of repeating each number to herself. Remembering occurs when the information concerning the numerical sequence enters long-term memory so that it is retrievable at a later time.

The young child in our example may experience difficulty at any phase of this process. She may pay insufficient attention to what her mother is saying, in which case the information will not enter her sensory register. Being young, she has a small (immature) working-memory capacity and may not be able to hold all the numbers in working memory as she tries to remember them. The speed with which she can transfer information from the sensory register to working memory and to long-term memory may be relatively slow, causing her to forget some of the numbers before they can be enduringly stored in long-term memory. Lastly, she may have little experience with intentional memorization and hence no repertoire of strategies for holding information in working memory for an extended period or for manipulating numbers in working memory.

Developmentalists who study children's memory find striking changes across the years of early childhood. To a large extent, the dramatic increase in young children's ability to remember is due to "software" changes, that is, changes in the way information flows through the memory system as a consequence of changes in the processes by which it is encoded, stored, and retrieved (Ornstein & Light, 2010). Moreover, two factors can be key in contributing to children's increasing success: children's prior knowledge about the events or materials being remembered, and adults' assisting children in remembering. In general, children are better at remembering when they have substantial prior knowledge on which to "hang" the new information. In the absence of prior knowledge, their memory can be greatly improved if adults talk with them about the new event or experience as it unfolds (Boland, Haden, & Ornstein, 2003; Haden et al., 2001). Studies of mother–child interactions (Ornstein, Haden, & Hendrick, 2004) have found that children's

Using a host of information-processing skills involving the sensory register, working memory, long-term memory, and retrieval processes, this boy takes a picture of a rooster contest being held in the Saudi city of Qatif.

AFP / Getty Images

elaborative style A form of talking with children about new events or experiences that enhances children's memories for those events and experiences.

privileged domains Cognitive domains that call on specialized kinds of information, require specifically designated forms of reasoning, and appear to be of evolutionary importance to the human species.

memories improve when mothers (and presumably other caregivers) use an **elaborative style**, which includes

- *wh- questions* (What's happening? Who is that?);
- *associations* that relate the new information to the child's prior knowledge;
- *follow-ins* that follow and discuss aspects of the events that the child finds interesting;
- *positive evaluations* that praise the child's verbal and nonverbal contributions to the interaction.

Intervention studies in which mothers were trained to use a more elaborative style when interacting with their children likewise found an increase in children's memory for specific events and experiences (Boland et al., 2003; Peterson et al., 1999).

In sum, from an information-processing perspective, young children's cognitive difficulties are caused by general cognitive factors including limitations in knowledge, memory, attentional control, and the speed of processing information, as well as by limited strategies for acquiring and using information (Thompson & Siegler, 2010). Difficulties may be less in situations in which children have prior knowledge or caregivers' elaborative style encourages remembering. As children grow older, their performance improves and its unevenness diminishes because the cognitive limitations are gradually reduced through maturation of their brain ("hardware") and the development of more effective information-processing strategies ("software").

▲ APPLY :: CONNECT :: DISCUSS

Suppose that two children are presented with the same set of unrelated pictures and told to remember the pictures because they will be given a memory test shortly.

Picture presented	Child 1 says	Child 2 says
Cat	cat, cat, cat	cat, cat
Shoe	shoe, shoe, shoe	cat, shoe, cat, shoe
Truck	truck, truck, truck	cat, shoe, truck
Pen	pen, pen, pen	cat, shoe, truck, pen

According to material presented in this section, why is Child 2 likely to outperform Child 1 on the memory test?

Cognitive Development in Privileged Domains

The teddy's arm fell off because you twisted it too far.

I talking very quiet because I don't want somebody to wake me up.

He needs more meat because he is growing long arms.

Each of these statements was made by a young child offering an explanation of an event encountered in daily life—a physical event (a broken object), a psychological event (an internal desire), and a biological event (physical growth) (Hickling & Wellman, 2001). In contrast to Piagetian and information-processing theorists, who emphasize how general intellectual processes such as centration or information storage and retrieval affect virtually all aspects of the young child's thinking, developmentalists taking another approach to cognition focus on changes within specific areas of knowledge acquisition, known as **privileged domains** (Chen & Siegler, 2000; Goswami, 2008). These domains are "privileged" in that they involve specific kinds of reasoning that have evolutionary significance for our species. The most frequently studied privileged domains relevant to early childhood thinking are the domains of physics, psychology, and biology. Although these domains obviously are rudimentary in early childhood, they nevertheless direct children to attend to and respond to highly specific and important features of the environment, in particular, the way in which objects and people and other biological organisms behave under various conditions.

The Domain of Physics

In arguing that stones melt when they are boiled, the children in Vivian Paley's class seemed to demonstrate an intuitive understanding of the effect that intense heat has on physical materials. Of course, for stones to melt, much greater heat would be needed than that provided by a stove. Moreover, by the time the stones would start to melt, there would not be any water left in the pot. Nevertheless, children's reasoning about melting stones indicates that they have ideas about the physical properties of objects. Indeed, Rose's question "Do stones melt?" indicates that children are interested in learning about such features of their environments. Because young children, like most adults, are not physicists but nevertheless harbor "everyday ideas" about how the physical world works—for example, about motion, the consequences of objects colliding, gravity, and changes of material state such as water turning into ice or stones melting—developmentalists refer to their reasoning as *naïve,* or *intuitive, physics* (Baillargeon, 2002; Wilkening & Cacchione, 2011). As you saw in Chapter 5, it appears that within months after birth, children have some grasp of at least a few very basic physical principles, including expectations that two objects cannot occupy the same location at the same time and that an object cannot pass through physical obstructions. Clearly, the foundations of a naïve physics are laid down in infancy.

Much research on the naïve physics of young children has used the *violation-of-expectations* method—the research trickery you learned about in Chapter 5 in our discussion of research on the cognitive capacities of infants (see pp. 185–186). For example, Kyong Kim and Elizabeth Spelke used the violation-of-expectations method to study developmental changes in children's understanding of gravity and inertia (Kim & Spelke, 1999). They showed infants and young children video animations in which a ball rolled along a board and went off the end in one of three ways: (1) moving in a straight line and at the same speed that it had traversed the board—in defiance of the laws of gravity and inertia (Figure 8.10b); (2) plummeting straight down—in accordance with the law of gravity but in defiance of the law of inertia (Figure 8.10c); or (3) falling in a gradual arch—in accordance with the laws of both inertia and gravity (Figure 8.10d).

In these experiments, the infants showed no understanding of gravity or inertia, reacting no differently to one sequence than to another. The results for 2-year-olds were mixed: They generally seemed unsurprised when the ball rolled off the end of the board and kept moving in a straight line or fell in a natural curve to the ground, but they stared longer when the ball fell straight down after leaving the end of the board, indicating that they were beginning to develop some understanding of inertia. In contrast, 6-year-olds displayed sensitivity to both inertia and gravity, although they were not entirely consistent in their reactions, indicating that they had not fully mastered these concepts (Spelke, 2000).

Terry Au and her colleagues (1993) demonstrated that young children also have a reasonably good grasp of the physical makeup of objects. She showed middle- and working-class children as young as 3 years of age various natural and artificial substances, including wood and playdough, which she then transformed in one of three

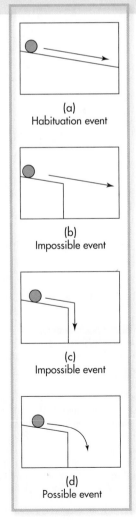

FIGURE 8.10 In this test used by Kim and Spelke to explore children's knowledge of the physical principles of gravity and inertia, all the children saw the ball roll across a smooth surface (a) and then were tested with events such as those in (b)–(d), to see which of the test events violated their expectations and thus revealed awareness of the relevant physical laws. (Adapted from Kim & Spelke, 1999.)

(a)
Habituation event

(b)
Impossible event

(c)
Impossible event

(d)
Possible event

ways while they watched. Large chunks of a substance were broken into smaller chunks; chunks of the substance were broken down into a powder; the powder made from the substance was dissolved in water! Even when confronted with the most drastic transformation—a physical substance's being dissolved in water—the 3-year-olds correctly insisted that the substance continued to exist. As Wellman and Gelman (1998, p. 534) point out, "These data show that even quite young children know that larger objects are composed of smaller pieces and these pieces, even if invisible, have enduring physical existence and properties."

There is a great deal more to be learned about physical laws, as everyone who has taken an introductory physics course knows. But by the age of 5 to 6 years, children have developed a serviceable set of ideas about the physical world that appear to be shared by people all over the world.

The Domain of Psychology

Just as children reason about their everyday physical world, they also reason about people, specifically, about how people's actions are affected by their internal mental states. Children's early understanding of the relationship between mental states and behavior is referred to as *naïve psychology*.

In the transition from infancy to early childhood, and all during early childhood, children gain a more comprehensive idea about how other people's desires, beliefs, and knowledge are related to how they act in the world. As you learned in Chapter 6, by the end of the first year, infants possess at least an intuitive understanding that other people's actions are caused by their goals and intentions. Even at the age of 2, children are able to distinguish between their own desires and those of others (Wellman, 2011). If the child's own preference is for strawberry ice cream but a character in a story prefers chocolate ice cream, the child will predict that, given a choice between the two, the storybook character would choose chocolate ice cream. Children's ability to reflect on and understand the mental states of others continues to develop throughout early childhood. As you will see, during this period children construct coherent *theories* about how people's beliefs and desires combine to shape their actions—that is, they develop a **theory of mind**.

To determine when children develop a mature theory of mind, developmentalists use a technique called the **false-belief task**, which assesses a child's ability to recognize that others can have, and act according to, beliefs that are contrary to the facts as the child knows them. In one version of this task, the child is presented with a brief story in which one of the characters comes to have a false belief. After hearing the story, the child is asked questions designed to reveal his or her understanding about what goes on in another person's mind. Here are a typical story and a follow-up question:

> **Story:** Once there was a little boy who liked candy. One day he put a chocolate bar in a drawer and went out to play for a while. While he was gone, his mother came. She took the candy out of the drawer and put it in the kitchen. When the little boy came back, he was hungry and went to get his candy.

> **Question:** Where do you think the little boy will look for his candy?

When 3-year-olds are asked this question, they say that the boy will look in the kitchen, where they themselves know the candy to be, and not in the drawer, where the boy left it. In short, they respond as if the boy had the same information that they do. Five-year-olds are far more likely to say that the boy will look

theory of mind Coherent theories about how people's beliefs, desires, and mental states combine to shape their actions.

false-belief task A technique used to assess children's theory of mind; children are tested on their understanding either of stories in which a character is fooled into believing something that is not true or of situations in which they themselves have been tricked into a false belief.

in the drawer, presumably because they understand that he has a false belief about the current location of the candy.

A second version of the false-belief task involves tricking children themselves into a false belief. In one task of this type, children are shown a box covered with pictures of candy and are asked what they think is in the box. All, of course, answer, "Candy." Then they are shown that they are wrong—the box actually contains something else, such as a pencil. Next, the children are asked what a friend who has not yet seen inside the box would think it contains. Even though they have just gone through the process of being deceived themselves, most 3-year-olds say that the friend will think the box contains a pencil despite the fact that it has pictures of candy on it. In contrast, 5-year-olds realize that the friend will be tricked into a false belief (Astington, 1993).

In addition, 3-year-olds will often ignore their own false belief held just minutes earlier. If asked what they first thought was in the box, they will declare that they knew all along that it contained a pencil (Wimmer & Hartl, 1991). This kind of result supports the idea that young children still experience difficulty thinking of things separately from the way they have represented them mentally.

However, just as there is evidence that young children's performance on Piagetian tasks differs according to how the problem is posed for them, so there is evidence that, in some circumstances, 3-year-olds can appreciate the false-belief states of others (Carpenter, Call, & Tomasello, 2002). One way to induce children this young to solve false-belief tasks is to make them codeceivers in the experiment. Using a variation of the pencil-in-the-candy-box task, Kate Sullivan and Ellen Winner (1993) arranged for an adult accomplice to be present together with the child while the experiment was in progress. In their procedure, the experimenter first pulls the standard candy-box trick on the child and then leaves the room. Next, the adult accomplice suggests to the child that the two of them play a trick on the experimenter just like the trick that the experimenter played on the child. Making a great display of being a co-conspirator in the plot to fool the experimenter, the adult produces a crayon box and helps the child remove the crayons and replace them with something else. Then, just before the experimenter returns to the room, the adult, in a hushed, secret-sharing tone, asks the child what the experimenter's response will be when asked what the box contains. In this gamelike situation, 75 percent of 3-year-olds predicted that the experimenter would mistakenly say that the box contains crayons. This result indicates that the children were, at least in these circumstances, able to think about the thought processes of others. By comparison, only 25 percent were correct in the standard false-belief task, a rate that was in line with the typically reported results. The researchers suggest that their version of the task engaged the children in the familiar scripted activity of fooling someone else, which primed the children to think about other people's mental states.

This and a range of corroborating evidence from false-belief tasks conducted in various industrialized countries indicate that although the exact timing of acquiring a theory of mind may vary from one culture to another, the child's developing theory of mind is in a transition around 3 years of age and becomes more-or-less solidified when children are 4 or 5 years old (Liu et al., 2008).

The Domain of Biology

Inquisitive developmentalist: How did the baby happen to be in your mommy's tummy?

Child: It just grows inside.

Developmentalist: How did it get there?

Child: It's there all the time. Mommy doesn't have to do anything. She waits until she feels it.

Developmentalist: You said the baby wasn't in there when you were there.

Child: Yeah, then he was in the other place. In . . . in America.

Developmentalist: America?

Child: Yeah, in somebody else's tummy.

Developmentalist: In somebody else's tummy?

Child: Yes, and then he went through somebody's vagina, then he went in, um, in my Mommy's tummy.

Developmentalist: In whose tummy was he before?

Child: Um, I don't know, who his, her name is. It's a her.

(Cowan, 1978, p. 86.)

Young children's ideas about conception, as well as other biological processes are, well, different from ours, and arise in the privileged domain referred to as *naïve biology*.

An important starting point for developing biological understandings is making the distinction between animate and inanimate things. Christine Massey and Rochel Gelman (1988) demonstrated that 3- to 4-year-olds are able to make this distinction, associating self-initiated movement with living creatures. They showed the children drawings of unfamiliar animate and inanimate objects and, for each, asked if the object could walk uphill "all by itself" (Figure 8.11). The drawings included unfamiliar animals (for example, a marmoset, a tarantula) and artifacts (statues of animals; objects with wheels, such as a golf caddy; complex rigid objects, such as a camera).

Many of the 3-year-olds and most all of the 4-year-olds knew that only the animals, and not the artifacts, could move uphill on their own. Even though the animals were not seen in motion, the children's comments often focused on feet and "little legs" (Gelman, 1990). Especially interesting were their responses to drawings such as those in Figure 8.11: Although no "little legs" are visible for the echidna, the children said that it could walk uphill but that the statue of the four-footed animal could not.

In addition to knowing that only living things can move themselves, young children know that living things grow and change their appearance, whereas artifacts may change in appearance due to wear or damage but do not grow. Moreover, as illustrated by Kayoko Inagaki and Giyoo Hatano's interviews with Japanese children, they also recognize that if neglected, living things may die. Upon seeing a sweet potato drooping, a 3-year old boy exclaimed, "Poor thing! Are you thirsty? I give lots of water (to you). So, cheer up." When asked what would happen to a tulip if it went without water for a day, a 5-year-old girl replied, "The tulip will wither. 'Cause if the tulip doesn't drink water, it won't become very lively" (Inagaki & Hatano, 2002, p. 19).

At present, developmentalists who support the idea of a privileged domain of naïve biology are uncertain about when and how it originates. Some believe that it slowly differentiates itself from naïve psychology, as young children gain greater experience with living things. Others believe that as children come into contact with different kinds of living creatures, they draw analogies between themselves and other living creatures to reason about the biological world. This tendency is clearly shown in the response of a Japanese boy interviewed by Inagaki and Hatano close to his 6th birthday. Asked if it was inevitable that a baby rabbit would grow, the child replied, "We can't keep

FIGURE 8.11 Massey and Gelman used pictures of unfamiliar creatures and artifacts such as these to determine if young children distinguish between animate things (which move on their own) and inanimate things (which do not). Children judged that the clay figure on the top would not move on its own but that the echidna on the bottom would, even though its legs are hidden.

Drawings by Mary McManus; images courtesy of Dr. Rachel Gelman, Rutgers University it [the rabbit] forever the same size. Because, like me, if I were a rabbit, I would be 5 years old and become bigger and bigger" (Inagaki & Hatano, 2002, p. 51). In drawing such analogies, children sometimes overlook important differences between living things, including the fact that not all living things have goals and intentions (Figure 8.12).

Explaining Domain-Specific Cognitive Development

Although it is clear that young children have an intuitive understanding of physics, psychology, and biology, there are questions about where these privileged domains come from and how they develop. There are three major approaches to explaining the source and development of privileged domains. One, *modularity theory,* views each domain of reasoning as a distinct and separate set of mental processes that has evolved to handle domain-specific information and that changes very little over the course of development. The second approach, *theory theory,* holds that children are biologically endowed with basic notions about each domain but modify their ideas as they learn more about the world. Finally, the third approach emphasizes the special role of language and culture in weaving together the contributions of biological and general cognitive factors.

Modularity Theory Modularity theory's approach to understanding domain-specific intelligence is to conceive of it in terms of **mental modules**, innate mental faculties that are dedicated to receiving information from, and processing information about, particular types of objects in the environment, such as physical objects, people, and biological organisms (Atran, 1998; Fodor, 1983). Each module is distinct and separate from all others; there is very little interaction among them. In addition, because they are coded in the genes, such psychological processes do not need special tutoring in order to develop. They are present "at the beginning" in the normal human genome and only need to be "triggered" by the environment.

An intriguing line of research with autistic children provides strong evidence for modularity theory. **Autism** is a poorly understood, genetically induced condition that is defined primarily by an inability to relate normally to other people (Frith, 2003). Young autistic children rarely use language to communicate; they do not engage in symbolic, pretend play; and they often engage in unusually repetitive movements such as rocking, spinning, or flapping their hands (see the box "In the Field: Supporting Siblings of Children with Autism" on p. 296).

What makes autism so interesting for modularity theorists is that autistic children, who often exhibit high ability in some specific domains, routinely score poorly on false-belief tasks such as the one involving a story about a mother who, while her son was outside playing, moved a candy bar from the drawer, where the son had put it, to another location (Schroeder et al., 2010; Pellicano, 2010). When autistic children of various ages are asked where the boy will look for the candy when he returns and how he will feel when he looks there, they perform like typical 3-year-olds, failing to realize that the boy has a false belief about the candy's present location and that he will be disappointed when he acts on his belief. These same children may be very clever at solving mechanical puzzles such as putting together blocks to make a racing car, or they may have unusual abilities in music, art, math, memory, or some other specific area. The extreme difference in performance suggests that autism may affect a specific module—a theory-of-mind module, perhaps—leaving other modules unaffected.

In an early study to demonstrate the domain-specific nature of autism, Simon Baron-Cohen and his colleagues (1986) asked groups of 4-year-olds to arrange

Siegal & Peterson, 1999

FIGURE 8.12 Children often attribute humanlike properties, including goals and intentions, to all living things. This drawing of a germ depicts an organism with humanlike arms, legs, and eyes, as well as sharp fangs and spiky hair suggesting evil intent.

mental modules Hypothesized innate mental faculties that receive inputs from particular classes of objects and produce corresponding information about the world.

autism A biologically-based condition that includes an inability to relate normally to other people and low scores on false-belief tasks.

scrambled sequences of picture cards into stories. There were three types of stories, each depicted with four cards:

Mechanical sequences depicting physical interactions between people and objects—for example, a man kicks a rock, which rolls down a hill and then splashes in the water (Figure 8.13a).

Behavioral sequences depicting interactions among people—for example, a girl takes an ice cream cone from a boy and eats it, and the boy cries (Figure 8.13b).

Mentalistic sequences depicting stories that involve mental events—for example, a girl puts a toy down behind her while she picks a flower; another person sneaks up and takes the toy; the girl looks surprised when she turns around and finds the toy gone (Figure 8.13c).

Some of the children in this study were autistic; others were not autistic but were mentally retarded; and others were developing typically. The autistic children outperformed the typically developing children in arranging mechanical sequences and were just as proficient as typically developing children when arranging behavioral sequences in which the emotions of the figures in the story were obvious. But they were unable to create meaningful mentalistic sequences that reflected an understanding of thoughts or inner emotions, such as the surprise experienced by the girl whose toy disappeared (see Figure 8.13c). In addition, when asked to verbally tell the story of the mentalistic sequences, the autistic children's narratives tended to be purely descriptive, with no reference to mental states. Of the last card in Figure 8.13c, for example, they might say something like "The girl held the flower" rather than "The girl wondered where her toy went."

Studies of naïve physics and biology have also found evidence for the domain-specific nature of autism (Binnie & Williams, 2003; Peterson, 2005). For example, a study of Australian children conducted by Candida Peterson found that when asked

FIGURE 8.13 These drawings illustrate some of the stimuli used to assess autistic children's ability to think about mental states. At the top of the figure is a *mechanical sequence* (a) showing a man kicking a rock, which rolls down a hill; the middle *behavioral sequence* (b) shows a girl taking an ice cream cone away from a boy; the bottom *mentalistic sequence* (c) shows a boy taking a girl's teddy bear when her back is turned.

(a)

(b)

(c)

questions about biological functions ("What does your heart do?" "What does your brain do?"), autistic children performed at least as well as typically developing children. On the other hand, most of the autistic children failed the false-belief task. Interestingly, in another study focused on the domains of physics and psychology, autistic children performed better than did typically developing children—but they also tended to explain psychological events in terms of physical causation (Binnie & Williams, 2003). For example, when presented with a picture of a flower with a cut stem, autistic children indicated that the wind blew the flower over, whereas normally developing children indicated that the flower had been cut by a person. Findings like this, along with the fact that autistic children perform very well in some privileged domains but routinely fail false-belief tasks, lead many developmentalists to argue for the existence of isolated modules, and to speculate that autism is due to a cognitive defect in a theory-of-mind module (Baron-Cohen, Leslie, & Frith, 2007).

Theory Theory Despite the link between autism and difficulty with the false-belief task, not all developmentalists agree that there is a theory-of-mind module that is present at birth and that a defect in this module explains autism (Tager-Flusberg, 2007). Those who disagree with modularity theory point out that, when placed in intensive therapeutic programs, many autistic children show significant improvement in their social behavior and communication skills. They can learn, for example, to interact with other children and to carry out simple household routines, and some are eventually able to hold jobs (Scheuermann, 2002). Such facts naturally raise a question that modularity theory does not address: How does experience influence domain-specific development?

An influential theory that does address this question is somewhat playfully referred to by developmentalists as the **theory theory**. According to this approach, young children, from birth or shortly thereafter, have primitive theories of how the world works. These theories direct the child's attention to domain-specific features of the environment and influence the child's actions in particular domains. Over time, the child modifies the theories in light of his or her experience (Gopnik, Wellman, Gelman, & Meltzoff, 2010).

Children's thinking within privileged domains is like scientific theorizing in at least two important respects. First, children's ideas are accompanied by causal explanations. If asked why a little girl who climbs a tree and hangs from a branch soon falls to the ground, they provide a reasonable biological explanation: "She is not strong enough, so her arms get tired and she eventually has to let go." If asked why a little boy who declares that he is going to step off a stool and float in the air actually falls to the ground, they provide explanations such as "He is too heavy to float in the air," or "Gravity brings him down." Second, their ideas generate reasonable predictions, as a theory should. They will predict that the little girl who drops from the tree will hurt herself if the branch is high off the ground and that the little boy who fails to float will be disappointed. Although 3-year-olds may sometimes confuse biological and psychological explanations, by the time they are 4 years old, American children invoke the right kinds of theory to fit what it is that needs explaining (Wellman, Hickling, & Schult, 1997).

An important source of information for children's developing theories is their interactions and conversations with their parents (Hughes et al., 2005). For example, a study of Mexican American parents and their children attending an agricultural

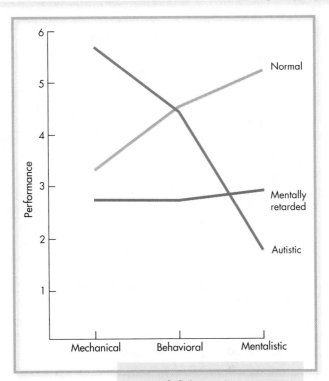

FIGURE 8.14 The graph shows the level of performance achieved by normal, mentally retarded, and autistic children when asked to create meaningful mechanical, behavioral, and mentalistic sequences. Note that the autistic children are especially good at creating mechanical sequences but have even greater difficulty than retarded children do when asked to create mentalistic sequences.

theory theory The theory that young children have primitive theories about how the world works, which influence how children think about, and act within, specific domains.

Name: Charley Moskowitz

Education: Master's of Social Work, Fordham University; additional experience at various agencies with infants with HIV, pediatric hospice, special-needs preschoolers

Current Position: Director of Special Needs Academic and Arts Center at the Jewish Community Center of Mid-Westchester, New York; private practice counseling children and families

Career Objectives: Provide enrichment programs for children with disabilities and their families

"MY BROTHER'S BEEN HAVING A BIG PROBLEM," began 6-year-old Ruthie in a quiet and anxious voice. "He's been having a hard time with beeping noises. When he goes to school, there's a little beep, but you can hardly hear it, but he can hear it, but he still comes in the door and then he runs out of the other door and right into the classroom, and he's scared."

Ruthie continued to talk in sad pensive tones about her brother's terror of beeping noises until she was interrupted by Charley Moskowitz, a social worker who runs Sib Connection, a support group for siblings of children with disabilities: "Let me ask you a question, O.K.? Why are you so sad about this?"

"Because I don't want my brother to be like this, and it makes me feel sad that he has to be afraid of that."

"Can anybody help her?" Moskowitz asked the other children in the group.

Thomas raised his hand. "Well, a lot of times what autistic kids do, is like—my brother will go through a phase. This could just be, like, one month he might be afraid of beeps, and then next month he'll love beeps."

Then Nick chimed in. "The reason your brother might be doing that is because autistic kids, they have almost better senses. I know it sounds weird, but, like, my brother, he can hear things that are really low. It's nothing really bad; it's just something that happens." (Adapted from Olson, 2007.)

Most of the children in Ruthie's support group have siblings with an autism spectrum disorder (ASD). ASDs are a group of highly heritable developmental disabilities that include autistic disorder, pervasive developmental disorder, and Asperger syndrome, all of which are characterized by significant impairments in social interaction and communication, and the presence of unusual behaviors and interests—a fear of beeps, or a fascination with the whirl of electric fans, for example (CDC, 2007). ASD usually appears before the age of 3, and it affects the person throughout life. While some individuals with ASD may have severe intellectual deficits, others may be highly gifted in certain areas of functioning. According to a recent

estimate by the Centers for Disease Control and Prevention, ASD in the United States is far more common than once supposed, affecting 1 out of every 110 children (CDC, 2011). It is four times more common in boys than in girls.

The Autism Genome Project, a massive international study involving scientists who are collecting genetic data in 19 countries, is shedding increasing light on the chromosomal changes and mutations that contribute to ASD phenotypes (Ylisaukko-oja et al., 2006; Karsten et al., 2006), including abnormalities in the number of copies of specific genes (Pinto et al., 2010). In the meantime, children like Ruthie, Thomas, and Nick struggle to make sense of their siblings' behavior. Fortunately, some of them will do so with the help of peers who have similar experiences and of people like Charley Moskowitz who are aware of the unique issues and challenges facing siblings of special-needs children.

Charley Moskowitz

"Ruthie, you know what? There are some things that we can't change," Moskowitz said. "One of the things that we can't change is the way your brother reacts to things. What else is she doing, Nick?"

"Responsibility. You're having too much responsibility for your brother."

The sense of obligation weighs heavily on siblings of special-needs children. As Moskowitz says, "These are the kids who are going to be taking care of their siblings when their parents die. These are the kids that are going to have all the responsibility, and if they don't get help now, who's going to help them? They have to work through this before they graduate from high school so that they can have the courage to go off to college and have a life and still be connected to their sibling when it comes time to make a decision about what they have to do" (Olson, 2007, pp. 46–47).

Nick, who has an autistic sibling and participates in Sib Connection, designed this pin to help people better understand the behavior of autistic children.

Mark Plage, 15, right, shares a quiet moment with his 13-year-old autistic brother, Derek. Sib Connection was designed to help children like Mark cope with the stress of having autistic siblings.

science exhibition found that the context prompted children to ask questions that fall within the domain of biology, and that parents offered domain-appropriate causal explanations. For instance, when one child asked, "Why can't I water the plants too much?" his mother answered, "Because they are going to drown; they don't need that much water." Another parent used an analogy to provide a basis for the child's theory development. When asked "Why do insects eat each other?" the mother answered, "Because insects are food for other animals just like other animals are food for us" (Tenenbaum, Callanan, Alba-Speyer, & Sandoval, 2002, p. 237). Sometimes parents spontaneously offered up explanations of puzzling phenomena, providing a rich source of information that confirmed or denied children's initial theories. This study highlights the important role that parents play in the process of children's theory-testing; teachers, peers, and personal experience also contribute to children's construction of their knowledge base.

The Special Role of Language and Culture The third approach to explaining domain-specific development focuses primarily on how language and culture influence the emergence and growth of various domains. Considerations of language and culture are important for thinking about the nature of privileged domains because cultures vary dramatically in their use of domain-specific language. As an example, take the domain of psychology. Language, as Janet Astington and Eva Filippova point out, helps the young child figure out what other people might think, want, or feel (Astington & Filippova, 2005). Ample evidence from cultures around the world suggests that there is enormous variety in the extent and ways that mental states and actions are conceived (Lillard, 2006; Vinden, 2002). In terms of sheer number, English is at one extreme of the continuum, possessing more than 5,000 words for emotions alone. By contrast, the Chewong people of Malaysia are reported to have only five terms to cover the entire range of mental processes, translated as "want," "want very much," "know," "forget," "miss or remember" (Howell, 1984).

At present, it is unclear whether the lack of mental terms in a culture's language slows down, or even eliminates altogether, the development of the kind of naïve psychology found in cultures where such language is prevalent. In some cases, there appears to be no lag in performance, for example, on standard false-belief tasks (Avis & Harris, 1991). In other cases, there does seem to be a significant delay, and in still other cases, it appears that the sort of theory of mind assumed to be universal by privileged-domain theorists does not appear at all (Vinden, 1998, 2002). In cultures where talk about minds and mental processes is prevalent, positive correlations have been found between the pace at which children demonstrate competence on standardized tests for theory of mind and the amount of conversation parents devote to mental processes in the course of their daily interactions with their children (Nelson et al., 2003).

The influence of language and cultural variation on privileged domains is not restricted to the domain of naïve psychology. Among the Tainae of Papua New Guinea, for example, Penelope Vinden found that it is common for people to believe that that certain individuals can literally change themselves into a pig or other animal, and that such changelings can, and occasionally do, physically assault young children. Such beliefs defy the distinction we ordinarily make between human beings, other animals, and inanimate natural objects, calling into question the extent to which naïve biology and naïve psychology are distinct domains.

Indeed, the very idea that knowledge can be compartmentalized into distinct domains has been challenged by some developmentalists on the grounds that it represents a specifically Western perspective at odds with the belief systems of many

scripts Event schemas that specify who participates in an event, what social roles they play, what objects they are to use during the event, and the sequence of actions that make up the event.

non-Western cultures. It has been found, for example, that certain African societies have a more integrated view of knowledge. According to Bame Nsamenang, who studies African beliefs about knowledge, the knowledge, skills, and values children learn are not "compartmentalized into this or that activity, knowledge, or skill domain, but are massed together as integral to social interaction, cultural life, economic activity, and daily routines" (Nsamenang, 2006, p. 296).

⏏ APPLY :: CONNECT :: DISCUSS

Of *modularity theory* and *theory theory,* which is more consistent with Piaget's understanding of development? Why?

Cognitive Development and Culture

As you may recall from Chapter 1, Vygotsky's sociocultural theory has had a significant impact on understanding how development in general, and cognitive development in particular, are influenced by the cultural contexts in which children live. As we have noted on numerous occasions, children's active participation in cultural activities, especially their interactions and communications with others, appears essential to their developing knowledge of the world (Nelson, 2003; Rogoff, 2003). One aspect of these cultural activites that has received much attention is *cultural scripts,* which are said to account for both the acquisition and unevenness of knowledge during early childhood.

Cultural Scripts

Katherine Nelson (2009) suggested that as a result of their participation in routine, culturally organized events, children acquire *generalized event representations,* or **scripts**. These scripts, which are also referred to as *cultural scripts,* specify who participates in an event, what social roles they play, what objects they are to use during the event, and the sequence of actions that make up the event. Scripts exist both as external, material tools of culture—observable patterns of behavior expressed in the words and the customary practices of daily life—and as internal representations of those tools (see Chapter 2, pp. 52–54). Scripts are, in both their internal and external aspects, *resources* for cognitive development that affect the child's thinking and reasoning skills.

Initially, cultural scripts are a good deal more external than internal. Anyone who has made the attempt to bathe a 2-month-old knows that "taking a bath" is something the adult does to the baby. The adult fills a sink or appropriate basin with warm water, lays out a towel, a clean diaper, and clothing, and then slips the infant into the water, holding on firmly to keep the infant's head above water. The infant's contribution consists of squirming around. Gradually, however, as they become stronger and more familiar with the script of bath taking (and their caregivers perfect their role as bath-givers), babies acquire more competence in parts of the activity and assume a greater role in the process.

By the age of 2 years, most children have "taken" many baths. Each time, roughly the same sequence is followed, the same kinds of objects are used, the same cast of characters participates, and

As she participates in basket-weaving lessons over time, this young Palauan girl will develop a generalized script of what it means to "have a lesson," including the guidance of a teacher, the use of particular materials, and the sequence of activities performed.

Tim Rock / Lonely Planet Images

the same kinds of talk accompany the necessary actions. Water is poured into a tub, clothes are taken off, the child gets into the water, soap is applied and rinsed off, and the child gets out of the water, dries off, and gets dressed. There may be variations—a visiting friend may take a bath with the child or the child may be allowed to play with water toys after washing—but the basic sequence has a clear pattern to it.

During early childhood, adults still play the important role of "bath-giver" in the scripted routine called "taking a bath." Adults initiate children's baths, scrub their ears, wash their hair, or help them dry off. Not until adulthood will the child be responsible for the entire event, including scouring the tub and worrying about clean towels, hot water, and the money to pay for them.

Nelson points out that, as in the "taking a bath" script, children grow up inside other people's cultural scripts. As a consequence, human beings rarely, if ever, experience the natural environment "raw." Rather, they experience the world, including such simple activities as taking a bath and eating a meal, in a way that has been prepared (cooked up!) according to the scripts prescribed by their culture.

Nelson and her colleagues have studied the growth of scripted knowledge by interviewing children and by recording the conversations of children playing together. When Nelson asked children to tell her about "going to a restaurant," for example, she obtained reports like the following:

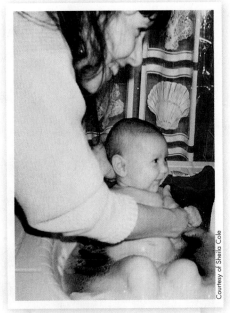

This is one version of an infant's "taking a bath."

> Boy aged 3 years, 1 month: Well, you eat and then go somewhere.
> Girl aged 4 years, 10 months: Okay. Now, first we go to restaurants at nighttime and we, um, we, and we go and wait for a while, and then the waiter comes and gives us the little stuff with the dinners on it, and then we wait for a little bit, a half an hour or a few minutes or something, and, um, then our pizza comes or anything, and um, then when we're finished eating the salad that we order, we get to eat our pizza when it's done, because we get the salad before the pizza's ready. So then when we're finished with all the pizza and all our salad, we just leave.
> (Nelson, 1981, p. 103.)

Even these simple reports demonstrate that scripts represent generalized knowledge. For one thing, the children are describing general content: They are clearly referring to more than a single, unique meal. The 3-year-old uses the generalized form "you eat" rather than a specific reference to a particular time when he ate. The little girl's introduction ("First we go to restaurants at nighttime") indicates that she, too, is speaking of restaurant visits in general.

Besides containing general content, children's cultural scripts are organized into a general structure, similar to that of adult scripts. Even very young children know that the events involved in "eating at a restaurant" do not take place haphazardly but, rather, occur sequentially: "First we do this, then we do that." Children evidently abstract the content of a script and its structure from many events and then use that knowledge to organize their behavior.

Cultural scripts are guides to action. They are mental representations that individuals use to figure out what is likely to happen next in familiar circumstances. Until children have acquired a large repertoire of scripted knowledge from which they can generalize in unfamiliar circumstances, they must pay attention to the details of each new activity. As a consequence, they may be less likely to distinguish between the essential and the superficial features of a novel context. The little girl interviewed by Nelson, for example, seemed to think that eating pizza is a basic part of the "going to a restaurant" script, whereas paying for the meal was entirely absent. However, because the little girl has grasped a small part of the restaurant

Even a script such as "taking a bath" can vary considerably from one culture to another. This image shows a pilgrim and a child bathing in a sacred waterfall near a temple in India.

This particular cultural script for celebrating a birthday, common in Mexico, involves taking turns batting at a swinging piñata until it breaks, spilling its candies and toys on the ground for the children to collect.

script, and going to restaurants is a routine activity in her family, she will be free to attend to new aspects of the setting the next time she encounters it. Over time, she will gain a deeper understanding of the events she participates in and the contexts of which they are a part.

Cultural scripts also allow people within a given social group to coordinate their actions with each other because, in a very important sense, scripts are *shared*. That is, they are a source of common meanings, expectations, and ways of understanding how and why people behave as they do in particular contexts. For this reason, Nelson argued that "the acquisition of scripts is central to the acquisition of culture" (Nelson, 1981, pp. 109, 110). Knowing the script, especially its variants and nuances, is an important marker of maturity and adaptation. For example, when children go to a "sit-down" restaurant in the United States, they learn that first you are seated by a host or hostess and later you tell a server what you want to eat. However, a different script applies to fast-food establishments, where you first go to the counter and place your order and then seat yourself. If someone were to take the sit-down script to a fast-food establishment, they would go hungry. Likewise, someone who took the fast-food script to a sit-down restaurant would be viewed as very peculiar.

Cultural Context and the Unevenness of Development

Once children leave the confines of their cribs and their caregivers' arms, they begin to experience a great variety of contexts that compel them to acquire a variety of new scripts, as well as refine those with which they are already familiar. Thus, it is natural that cognitive development during early childhood should appear to be so uneven. In familiar contexts, where they know the expected sequence of actions and can properly interpret the requirements of the situation, young children are most likely to behave in a logical way and adhere to adult standards of thought. But when the contexts are unfamiliar, they may apply inappropriate scripts and resort to magical or illogical thinking.

Overall, cultures influence the unevenness of children's development in several basic ways (Laboratory of Comparative Human Cognition, 1983; Rogoff, 2003; Super & Harkness, 2002):

1. *By making specific activities available:* One cannot learn about something without observing or hearing about it. A 4-year-old growing up among the !Kung of the Kalahari Desert is unlikely to learn how to use a TV remote, and children growing up in Seattle are unlikely to learn how to find water-bearing roots.

2. *By determining the frequency of basic activities:* Dancing is an activity found in all societies, but with varying degrees of emphasis. Owing to the importance placed on traditional dancing in Balinese culture, many Balinese children become skilled dancers by the age of 4 (McPhee, 1970), whereas Norwegian children are likely to become better skiers and skaters than dancers.

3. *By relating different activities to each other:* If pottery-making is a valued cultural activity, children are likely to not only become skilled pottery makers but also to learn a variety of related skills, such as digging clay from a quarry, firing clay, glazing clay, painting designs, and selling the

products. Molding clay as part of a nursery school curriculum will be associated with a distinctively different pattern of experiences, skills, and knowledge.

4. *By regulating the child's role in the activity:* Children enter most activities as novices who bear little responsibility for the outcome. As their roles and responsibilities change, so do the specialized abilities they develop.

▲ APPLY :: CONNECT :: DISCUSS

In arguing against the notion that knowledge can be compartmentalized into separate domains, Bame Nsamenang asserts that, according to African beliefs, knowledge is integrated into social life and daily routines. To what extent is this consistent with Katherine Nelson's theory of cultural scripts?

Reconciling Alternative Approaches

By this point, you should be convinced that the exceedingly uneven and complex picture that emerges from studies of childhood thought in the first few years following infancy cannot be explained by any single approach. Indeed, there have been a number of attempts to formulate more inclusive theories that are capable of accounting for both general and domain-specific changes in young children's competence and performance and for the fact that cognitive development sometimes appears to occur in discontinuous leaps and at other times as a process of gradual change. For example, Kurt Fischer has proposed that whether change appears continuous and gradual or abrupt and stagelike depends crucially on the relationship between the specific cognitive process being investigated and the context in which it occurs (Fischer & Yan, 2002). Fischer has demonstrated that under conditions of optimal support from the context, increases in the level of children's performance go through a series of stagelike changes. But when support is low (and a child has many distracting problems to deal with simultaneously), change is continuous. Thus, the culturally organized context of children's developing competence and performance is an element that must always be taken into account.

Whether she is pretending to be a monster, a character peering out from a television set, or both, this young Japanese girl has created an imaginary "play space" within a highly supportive cultural context that provides her with play materials, a play room, a vast variety of TV monster characters, and cultural expectations that pretend play is appropriate behavior for young children. According to Kurt Fischer, the specific cognitive processes used in such play, and supported by the culture, should result in stagelike changes in her development.

Toshi Kawano / Getty Images

SUMMARY

Physical and Motor Development

- Early childhood is marked by impressive gains in both gross and fine motor skills.

- Young children's sleep needs often are not adequately met. Nutrition is also a common problem, with undernourishment and obesity both causes for concern.

- Brain development, which is slower than in infancy, includes myelination of the frontal cortex, as well as increases in the length and branching of neurons connecting different areas of the brain. Variability in the development of different areas may contribute to the unevenness of early childhood cognition.

Preoperational Development

- According to Piaget, children in the preoperational stage are in the process of overcoming limitations that stand in the way of their attaining mental operations, that is, the ability to perform logical transformations of information. He considered the greatest such limitation to be centration, in which the child focuses on one aspect of an object or problem to the exclusion of others. Centration explains three common early childhood errors:

  - Egocentrism, the tendency to be captive to one's own perspective and unable to take that of another.

  - The tendency to confuse appearance and reality.

  - Precausal reasoning, the tendency to reason from one particular to another rather than engaging in cause-and-effect reasoning.

- Contemporary research suggests that under certain circumstances—for example, with tasks involving familiar objects—children do not commit these errors, showing evidence of cognitive abilities well before Piaget thought possible and hence more unevenness of cognitive development.

Information-Processing Approaches to Cognitive Development

- Information-processing approaches explore the workings of the mind through analogy to the digital computer, with the brain's neural features being likened to a computer's hardware, and the practices that people engage in to process information likened to its software.

- Input from the environment goes to the sensory register and may be read into short-term (working) memory, where it may combine with information from long-term memory. The flow of information among these components is coordinated by control processes, which include attention, rehearsal, and decision making.

- As children grow older, their cognitive performance improves as a result of both the maturation of their brains and their devel-opment of more effective information-processing strategies. Prior knowledge and caregivers' elaborative style in interactions with children can help children encode and store memories.

Cognitive Development in Privileged Domains

- Another approach to early childhood cognitive development focuses on changes within privileged domains, specific areas of knowledge that may have evolutionary significance.

  - Naïve physics traces to infancy and, in early childhood, extends to an understanding of laws such as gravity and inertia and of properties of objects.

  - Within naïve psychology, young children develop a theory of mind, as is reflected by their improving performance on false-belief tasks.

  - Naïve biology includes an understanding of differences between living things and inanimate objects.

- Several approaches seek to explain domain-specific cognitive development.

  - Modularity theory holds that distinct and separate mental modules—mental processes present from birth—are dedicated to the different privileged domains. Autistic children's having difficulties in the psychological domain while being normal or even exceptional in some others is seen as support for this approach.

  - Theory theory holds that from birth or shortly thereafter, children have primitive theories about how the world works—theories that direct their attention to domain-specific features of the environment and that they modify over time in light of their experience.

  - A third approach focuses on the influence of language and other aspects of culture on the emergence and development of domains. The idea of domains of knowledge may be a Western construct.

Cognitive Development and Culture

- As children participate in routine events of their culture, they acquire increasingly accurate scripts, or generalized representations, of these events.

- Cultures influence cognitive development by determining the frequency of basic activities, the specific activities that are available, and children's roles in activities.

Reconciling Alternative Approaches

- Studies of cognition in early childhood yield a picture, not of a homogeneous stage, but of complexity and unevenness. More inclusive theories are probably needed in order to account for processes that are both domain-specific and general, and for developmental changes that are both continuous and discontinuous (stagelike).

Key Terms

ossification, p. 273

motor drive, p. 273

food-insecure, p. 275

scale errors, p. 276

mental operations, p. 278

preoperational stage, p. 278

centration, p. 279

decentration, p. 279

objectivity, p. 279

egocentrism, p. 279

precausal thinking, p. 283

elaborative style, p. 288

privileged domains, p. 288

theory of mind, p. 290

false-belief task, p. 290

mental modules, p. 293

autism, p. 293

theory theory, p. 295

scripts, p. 298

Identity Development

Sex-Role Identity

Ethnic Identity

Personal Identity

A New Moral World

The Psychodynamic View

The Cognitive-Developmental View

The Social Domain View

Developing Self-Regulation

Regulating Thought and Action

Self-Regulation and Play

Regulating Emotions

Understanding Aggression

The Development of Aggression

What Causes and Controls Aggression?

Developing Prosocial Behaviors

Empathy

Sympathy

Taking One's Place in the Social Group

Social and Emotional Development in Early Childhood

Didi, a 2-year-old Chinese boy, is talking with his mother and older sister about an event in which he cried and made a scene at his sister's music lesson, causing his mother to lose face:

Mother to Didi: *That day when you went to music lesson with Mama and older sister. Was that fun?*

Didi: *It was fun.*

Mother: *What didn't the teacher give you?*

Didi: *Didn't give me a sticker.*

Mother: *Didn't give you a sticker. . . . Then what did you do?*

Didi: *Then I cried.*

Sister: *Cried loudly! "Waah! Waah! Waah!"*

Mother: *Oh, then you cried? Yeah, you constantly went, "Waah! Why didn't you give me a sticker?" (Mother says in a whining tone, rubbing her eyes with her fists). "Why didn't you give me a sticker? Why didn't you?"*

Didi looks up from a picture book he's holding, looks at his mother and smiles, and looks back at the book.

Sister: *Yes, you said, "Why didn't you give me a sticker?"*

Mother to Didi, with a sigh: *"A sticker. Ai, you made Mama lose face. I wanted to dig my head into the ground! Right?*

Didi points to the picture book.

Sister: *Mommy wanted to faint! She almost began to faint!*

(Adapted from Miller, Fung, & Mintz, 2010)

A s they do for children everywhere, Didi's lessons in proper behavior and emotional expression begin early. And as they are for children everywhere, his lessons are steeped in cultural values and expectations. In Chinese culture, personal desire is expected to be carefully controlled. Indeed, individual goals and needs are considered secondary to those of the group, and children's behaviors are believed to reflect strongly on the family. Didi's outburst about not getting a sticker was consequently not only contrary to his culture's values about containing one's emotions but also an embarrassment to his mother—a fact not lost on his older sister. In chastising Didi for his behavior, his mother and sister are providing him a lesson in the importance of regulating his feelings, as well as in being a member of Chinese society. This chapter explores how children learn to act appropriately and how they develop a sense of themselves in relation to the societies in which they live.

During early childhood, children's social and emotional lives develop along two closely connected paths. One is the path of **socialization**, which leads children toward the standards, values, and knowledge of their society. The second is that of **personality formation**, on which children will develop their own unique patterns of feeling, thinking, and behaving in a wide variety of circumstances.

socialization The process by which children acquire the standards, values, and knowledge of their society.

personality formation The process through which children develop their own unique patterns of feeling, thinking, and behaving in a wide variety of circumstances.

initiative versus guilt According to Erikson's theory, the stage in early childhood during which children face the challenge of continuing to declare their autonomy and existence as individuals, but in ways that begin to conform to the social roles and moral standards of society.

In addition to fulfilling a traditional role in a wedding ceremony, these little flower girls are learning about many important aspects of the social roles and behaviors expected of them when they grow up.

Children begin their trek down the paths of socialization and personality formation as soon as they are born, and with plenty of help from the significant people in their lives. It is not just idle talk when a father says of his newborn daughter, "She could be a concert pianist with these long fingers," and her mother adds, "Or a basketball player." The beliefs that give rise to such statements lead parents to shape their child's experience in a variety of ways, some obvious, others quite subtle. Socialization is apparent in the ways parents communicate to children about how they should and should not behave ("Ai, you made Mama lose face"). Socialization is also apparent in the ways parents—and their social and economic circumstances—influence the neighborhoods children live in, the day-care centers or preschools they attend, and a variety of other contexts in which they become conversant with their culture's funds of knowledge and rules of behavior.

But children do not automatically or passively absorb adults' lessons. They interpret and select from the many socializing messages they receive according to their budding and unique personalities. The early origins of personality formation are present in infancy. As we saw in Chapter 4 (p. 151), neonates display individual differences in characteristic levels of activity, responses to frustration, and readiness to engage in novel experiences. We referred to these patterns of responsivity and associated emotional states as *temperament,* and noted that it tends to be moderately stable over time: Children who draw back from novel experiences in infancy, for example, are more likely to behave shyly when they first enter a nursery school. Personality formation expands as children's initial temperamental styles of interacting with people and objects in their environments are integrated with their developing cognitive understanding, emotional responses, and habits (Sanson, Hamphill, & Smart, 2002).

Thus, the paths of socialization and personality formation are closely connected. In traveling these paths, children, along with the significant others in their lives, play an active role in *co-constructing* the course of development (Hutto, 2008; Valsiner, 2007). That is, as we learned in Chapter 2, the behaviors, activities, and choices both of children and of the people with whom they interact, shape and modify the environments in which children develop. In this chapter, we will examine the social and emotional development of young children as they gain experience interacting with a variety of people, develop a more explicit sense of themselves and their abilities, and come to understand the ways in which they can (and cannot) use the rules and tools that society attempts to press upon them. These changes in social and emotional development do not, of course, occur independently of the biological and cognitive changes discussed in Chapter 8. Socialization, personality formation, biological maturation, and cognitive development occur simultaneously.

Identity Development

Erik Erikson (1950) claimed that the path of identity takes a sharp and fateful turn in early childhood. As discussed in Chapter 6 (p. 229), in the previous stage of *autonomy versus shame and doubt* (associated with the "terrible twos"), children acquire, and confidently declare, their sense of free will and their ability to control their environment: "*I* do it!" "No! I don't want that one; I want *that* one!" During early childhood, in contrast, children face the challenge of **initiative versus guilt**—that is, the challenge of continuing to declare their autonomy and existence as individuals, but in ways that begin to conform to the social roles and moral standards of society. According to Erikson, we see evidence of this in children's initiative and eagerness to join both peers and adults in constructing, planning, and making things. From building "forts" in which to play to baking cookies or repairing broken toys, children of this age take special delight in cooperating with others for the purpose of accomplishing specific goals and tasks. In Erikson's words, "the child is at no time more ready to learn quickly and avidly, to become bigger in the sense of sharing obligation and performance" (1950, p. 258). Such enthusiasm during early childhood underscores identity development as a process by which children come to express and believe in their own value as social participants—as individuals who can contribute to the plans and goals of a group.

One factor that is essential to socialization is **identification**, a psychological process in which children try to look, act, feel, and be like significant people in their social environment. The development of identification can be studied with respect to almost any social category—a family, a religious group, a neighborhood clique, or a nationality. We could ask, for example, how a boy goes about identifying with his father, his Hindu religion, his soccer team, or his country, India. The overwhelming majority of studies on identification in early childhood, however, focus on the acquisition of sex-role identity and ethnic identity. As the social categories and role expectations regarding gender and ethnicity become increasingly visible in our rapidly globalizing world, developmentalists are eager to understand the processes of identification through which children come to understand themselves as members of various social categories, and adopt behaviors consistent with various social roles. In this section we look at sex-role and ethnic identity in turn and then at the sense of self of which they are part. As you will see, there is much disagreement about the processes through which identification in these areas is achieved.

Sex-Role Identity

If an infant wearing nothing but a diaper and a bright-eyed smile were placed in your arms, you would probably have a hard time determining the baby's sex. But you wouldn't have that problem with a 3-year-old! In the short span of 3 years, children come to behave in ways that give clear signals about whether they are boys or girls (Golombok & Hines, 2002). These signals begin as early as age 2, when both girls and boys tend to produce more same-gender-typed words ("boy," "girl," "truck," "dress") than other-gender-typed words (Stennes, Burch, Sen, & Bauer, 2005). By the time children enter preschool, boys and girls differ in both what they play and how they play. They have distinctly different toy preferences, and boys are more active and rough-and-tumble, whereas girls tend to be more verbal and nurturing. Even their selection of playmates becomes gender-typed. In a study of 95 children ages 1 to 3 years, researchers found distinct gender-typed patterns in *affiliative behaviors*—that is, behaviors involving seeking and establishing friendly contact with peers (Blicharski, Bon, & Strayer, 2011. Examples of the affiliative behaviors measured in the study are shown in Table 9.1.). As shown in Figure 9.1, by age 2, girls affiliated with other girls rather than with boys, and by age 3, boys affiliated with other boys rather than with girls. The phenomenon of same-gender preference in young children has been observed throughout the world and is known as **gender segregation**.

Because sex-role identity is so central to adult experience, the question of how children acquire their sex-role identity and how they interpret that sex role* is of

---

*Some developmentalists recommend the use of the word "gender" instead of "sex" when this topic is discussed because they believe that the term "sex" implies that all sex-typed behavior is ultimately determined by biology. Others argue against the term "gender," which they think implies that sex-linked behavior is ultimately determined by the environment. We will use both "sex" and "gender" in contexts where they appear most appropriate, without implying either that sex/gender roles are basically biological or that they are basically environmental.

identification A psychological process in which children try to look, act, feel, and be like significant people in their social environment.

gender segregation The term for the preference of girls to play with other girls, and of boys to play with other boys.

table 9.1

Types of Affiliative Behaviors in Preschoolers

Category	Examples
Look	Glance, observe, look toward
Signal	Point, show, wave, talk, offer, smile, take, play face
Approach	Walk to, run to, follow
Contact	Touch, kiss, hug, caress

Source: Blicharski, Bon, & Strayer, 2011

FIGURE 9.1 Gender segregation in children's play is clearly established by 3 years of age, with boys tending to affiliate with other boys, and girls tending to affiliate with other girls.

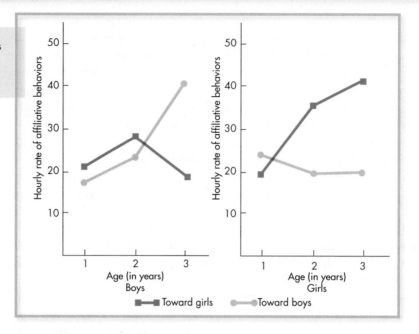

Many young boys are fascinated by their father's typical activities, just as many young girls are fascinated by the typical activities of their mother. Less often, however, do children become fascinated with the gender-related activities of the other-sex parent. Why this is the case would be explained differently by each of the major theoretical perspectives.

great interest to developmental psychologists (Eckes & Trautner, 2000). Here we will explore five major views of sex-role identity development—the psychodynamic, social learning, cognitive-developmental, gender schema, and cultural views (see Table 9.2 for a summary).

The Psychodynamic View By far the best-known account of sexual identity formation is that of Sigmund Freud (1921/1949, 1933/1964). Although many of Freud's specific hypotheses about development have not been substantiated, his theories remain influential. Certainly, many parents can tell stories of "Freudian moments" when their own young children began to test the boundaries between their personal desires and culturally accepted behavior, as reflected in the following conversation:

> "When I grow up," says [4-year-old] Jimmy at the dinner table, "I'm gonna marry Mama."
> "Jimmy's nuts," says the sensible voice of 8-year-old Jane. "You can't marry Mama and anyway, what would happen to Daddy?"

table 9.2	
Paths to Sex-Role Identity	
View	**Process**
Psychodynamic	**Differentiation and identification:** Boys differentiate from their mothers and identify with their fathers through resolution of the Oedipus complex. Girls' resolution of the Electra complex results in identification with their mother, with the attempt to differentiate from her being short-circuited.
Social learning	**Modeling and differential reinforcement:** Boys and girls observe and imitate sex-typed behaviors of males and females, respectively, because they are rewarded for doing so.
Cognitive developmental	**Conceptual development:** Children develop sex-role constancy (an understanding that their sex remains the same no matter what), and sex-role identity then begins to guide their thoughts and actions.
Gender schema	**Gender schemas and observation and imitation:** As in cognitive-developmental theory, children form concepts—gender schemes, which they use to process gender-relevant information. As in social learning theory, observation and imitation play a role.
Cultural	**Mediation:** The acquisition of gender roles occurs as children's activities are organized (media ted) by cultural conceptions and stereotypes of gender.

"He'll be old," says [Jimmy], through a mouthful of string beans. "And he'll be dead."

Then, awed by the enormity of his words, [Jimmy] adds hastily, "But he might not be dead, and maybe I'll marry Marcia instead."
(Fraiberg, 1959, pp. 202–203)

By Freud's account, when Jimmy says that he wants to "marry Mama," he is playing out the universal predicament of boys around the age of 3 or 4, who have moved beyond the oral and anal stages to the **phallic stage** of development, at which children have become capable of deriving pleasure from their genitals. Jimmy's feelings toward his mother and father cause him a lot of mental anguish. He is old enough to know that feelings like wanting your father to die are bad, and he is young enough to believe that his parents, who are powerful figures in his life, are always aware of what he is thinking. So he lives in fear of being punished and feels guilty about his bad thoughts.

Freud called this predicament the **Oedipus complex**, referring to the ancient Greek tragedy in which Oedipus, king of Thebes, unknowingly kills his father and marries his mother. To resolve these feelings, little boys, as they leave infancy and enter childhood, must mentally reorder their emotional attachments by *differentiating,* or distancing, themselves from their mothers and becoming closer to their fathers, identifying with them and taking on their characteristics, beliefs, and values. This process is driven by complex social emotions such as guilt and envy.

According to Freud, girls go through a very different process of sex-role identity development. The key event in the development of a girl's sex-role identity is her discovery that she does not have a penis: The girl is "mortified by the comparison with boys' far superior equipment" (Freud, 1933/1964, p. 126). She blames her mother for this "deficiency" and transfers her love to her father. Then she competes with her mother for her father's affection. This process was dubbed the **Electra complex** by Freud's student, Carl Jung (1915, in reference to another Greek tragedy, in which Electra persuades her brother to kill their mother in order to avenge the murder of their father).

As it does for boys, girls' wish to replace the same-sex parent results in guilt. The girl is afraid that her mother knows what she is thinking and that she will be punished by loss of her mother's love. She overcomes her fear and guilt by repressing her feelings for her father and intensifying her identification with her mother. Freud believed that this pattern of identity formation, in which girls affiliate with their mothers, renders women "underdeveloped" versions of men because their attempts to differentiate themselves from their mothers are short-circuited.

Not surprisingly, Freud's argument has been strongly attacked, on numerous grounds. For example, critics reject Freud's belief that females are somehow underdeveloped compared with males. Indeed, if any priority were to be given to one sex, it would more plausibly be given to the female. As we saw in Chapter 3 (p. 85), the sex organs of all human embryos initially follow a female path of development, becoming male only if modified through the action of male hormones. Moreover, modern research indicates that there is more to children's achievement of sex-role identities than identifying with the same-sex parent around the age of 4 or 5, because aspects of identity formation can be discerned well before this age (Ruble & Martin, 1998). Freud's ideas, however criticized, continue to influence both popular and scholarly thinking about the acquisition of sex roles. The challenge facing those who dispute his theories is to provide a better account of the processes at work.

The Social Learning View

Freudian theories of identification assume that young children are caught in hidden conflicts between their fears and their desires. Identification with the same-sex parent is their way of resolving those conflicts. The

phallic stage In Freudian theory, the period beginning around the age of 3 or 4 years when children start to regard their own genitals as a major source of pleasure.

Oedipus complex In Freudian theory, the desire young boys have to get rid of their father and take his place in their mother's affections.

Electra complex In Freudian theory, the process by which young girls blame their mother for their "castrated" condition, transfer their love to their father, and compete with their mother for their father's affection.

Dressed in a traditional costume, this little Swedish girl learns to clap and dance at a midsummer festival by observing and imitating the behavior of adults.

Caring for others is an important component of socialization. Here, Michael and Sheila Cole's grand-daughter (left) cuddles her doll in imitation of how her mother comforts the newest addition to the family.

FIGURE 9.2 These girls are participating in a modeling contest—the first of its kind in their province in south China. Like many young girls from Western countries, they are learning that physical appearance in girls is valued and rewarded in their community.

social learning view differs from this in two fundamental ways. First, social learning theories emphasize entirely different developmental processes. Second, they assume that parents are not the only ones responsible for the child's sex-role development (Eagly & Koenig, 2006).

Social learning theory proposes that identification arises through two related processes. The first is **modeling**, in which children observe and imitate others; the second is **differential reinforcement**, in which children are rewarded for engaging in specific types of behavior. In the particular case of gender identification, social learning theorists believe that children model the behavior of individuals of the same sex as themselves, and receive differential reinforcement for engaging in gender-appropriate behavior.

Social learning theory also proposes that it is simplistic to think that children acquire gender-role identity primarily by imitating their same-sex parents. Instead, in coming to understand their gender role, children rely also on peers, siblings, and other adults in their lives, as well as on the gender stereotypes communicated in their cultures through television and other media (Sadovsky & Troseth, 2000) (Figure 9.2).

Siblings, for example, are known to be important resources in the child's construction of gender roles. In a major longitudinal study, John Rust and his colleagues (2000) examined the gender development of more than 5,000 preschoolers. Some of the preschoolers had an older sister, some had an older brother, and some had no siblings. They found that boys with older brothers and girls with older sisters showed the greatest amount of sex-typed behavior—that is, behavior traditionally considered characteristic of one's gender. In contrast, boys with older sisters and girls with older brothers were the least sex-typed. Those without siblings were somewhere in the middle. Clearly, older siblings exert significant influence on the gender-role development of their little brothers and sisters.

The Cognitive-Developmental View The belief that a child's own conceptions are central to the formation of sex-role identity is implied by Piaget's theory of cognitive development and is the cornerstone of the *cognitive-developmental approach* to sex-role acquisition proposed by Lawrence Kohlberg (1966). In contrast to the social learning theorists' assumption that children passively absorb the gender-relevant information around them, Kohlberg argues that "the child's sex-role concepts are the result of the child's active structuring of his own experience" (p. 85). In contrast to Freud, Kohlberg claimed that the "process of forming a constant sexual identity depends less on guilt and fear than on the general process of conceptual development" (p. 85).

Kohlberg believed that sex-role development has three stages:

1. Basic sex-role *identity*. By the time children are 3 years old, they are able to label themselves as boys or girls.

2. Sex-role *stability*. During early childhood, children begin to understand that sex roles are stable over time, recognizing that boys grow up to be men and girls grow up to be women.

3. Sex-role *constancy*. Young children may believe that their sex can be changed by altering their outward appearance in some way. Their sex-role development is completed when they understand that their sex remains the same no matter what the situation. They know that even if they dress up as a member of the opposite sex for Halloween, they will not turn into a member of the opposite sex.

There is a good deal of evidence that the development of sex-role identity goes through the general sequence proposed by Kohlberg (Szkrybalo & Ruble, 1999). However, psychologists remain divided about how this sequence interacts with the emergence of sex-role concepts and sex-appropriate behaviors. Kohlberg himself believed that sex-role identity begins to guide thoughts and actions only after children attain sex-role constancy, because only then are they "categorically certain" that their sex is unchangeable (Kohlberg, 1966, p. 95). Current data, however, do not support Kohlberg's strict idea of sex-role constancy as the critical turning point. For example, well before they attain sex-role constancy as defined by Kohlberg's criteria, children prefer the same toys as other members of their sex and, for the most part, imitate the behavior of same-sex models (Maccoby, 2003).

The Gender Schema View

To many developmentalists it appears that an adequate explanation of how children's sex-role identity develops must include features of both social learning and cognitive-developmental theories. One approach that attempts this inclusion is *gender schema theory*.

Gender schema theory is similar in some respects to Kohlberg's cognitive-developmental theory. Adherents of both approaches believe that the environment affects the child's understanding of gender indirectly, through a *schema,* or cognitive structure. Once formed, this schema guides the way the child selects and remembers information from the environment, and leads the child to act in ways that are considered gender-appropriate in the child's culture (Martin & Ruble, 2010). A **gender schema**, then, can be considered a mental model containing information about males and females that is used to process gender-relevant information, such as which types of toys, clothing, activities, and interests are "male" or "female" (Liben & Bigler, 2002).

Children form gender schemas not only for objects ("boy things" and "girl things") and people but also for familiar events and routines, such as how Daddy barbecues or how Mommy shops for groceries. Accordingly, at the same time that they are discovering how to classify people and objects in terms of gender, gender information is becoming a part of the scripts that boys and girls will draw upon and apply—so that their barbecuing script features a male, for example, and their grocery shopping script features a female.

Gender schema theorists depart from Kohlberg's cognitive-developmental theory in two ways. First, they believe that children's developing schematic knowledge motivates and guides their gender-linked interests and behavior even prior to the onset of Kohlberg's stages. Second, these theorists often employ an information-processing approach, rather than a stage approach, to describe how the cognitive and learning elements of the system work together.

modeling In gender identification, the process by which children observe and imitate individuals of the same sex as themselves.

differential reinforcement In gender identification, the process by which girls and boys are rewarded for engaging in ways that are considered gender-appropriate in their culture.

gender schema A mental model containing information about males and females that is used to process gender-relevant information.

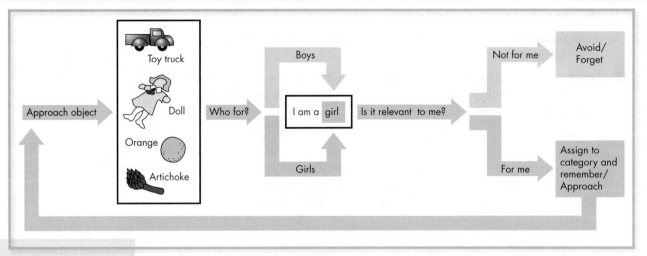

FIGURE 9.3 An example of an information-processing sequence associated with gender-schema formation. In this case, the child is a girl who has been offered four objects with which to play. (Adapted from Martin & Halverson, 1981)

Trucks and little boys just seem to go together, as they do here in Indonesia. Understanding the source of gender-specific toy preferences is an important focus of developmental research.

Figure 9.3 provides an illustration of how gender schemas work (Martin & Ruble, 2004). A little girl who can say that she is a girl and that her brother is a boy is presented with four objects with which to play. Two of the objects are gender-neutral—an orange and an artichoke—and two are stereotypically male or female—a truck and a doll. When the girl is presented with the doll, she must first decide if it is specifically relevant to her. She will think "Dolls are for girls" and "I am a girl" and thus conclude that dolls are relevant to her. As a result of this decision, write Martin and Halverson (1981), "she will approach the doll, explore it, ask questions about it, and play with it to obtain further information about it" (p. 1121). (This sequence is depicted by the green arrows in the diagram.) In contrast, when the little girl is presented with a truck, she will think "Trucks are for boys" and "I am a girl" and thus conclude that the truck is not relevant to her. As a result, she will avoid the truck and not be interested in knowing anything else about it. (This sequence is depicted by the orange arrows.) Asked about these toys later on, she will remember more about the doll than about the truck.

Naturally, children's ability to associate particular objects, such as toy trucks and dolls, with one gender or the other depends on the presence and use of such objects in the child's environment. Indeed, our understanding of gender-role development would be incomplete without exploring the impact of culture—the gender-specific objects, expectations, values, and beliefs that *mediate* children's activities and experiences from very early in life.

The Cultural View The acquisition of gender roles provides an excellent illustration of how the tools of culture (in this case, gender categories) organize children's activities and the way children relate to their environment. Evidence that such mediation may have significant consequences for children's gender-role development comes from studies of children's responses to various contexts in which the amount of emphasis on gender varies. For example, preschool teachers may differ widely in their emphasis on gender in classroom activities. One preschool teacher may greet her class with an enthusiastic "Good morning, boys and girls!" During circle time, she may say, "All the boys with blue socks stand up! Now, all the girls wearing sweaters stand up!" Later, when it is time to go outside, she may say, "Okay, let's line up boy-girl-boy-girl." In her classroom, gender categories organize activities, and gender-typed language is used frequently. Another teacher may make an effort to establish the classroom as a gender-neutral environment. Children who spend time in pre-school classrooms that emphasize gender have higher levels of gender stereotyping than do children in classrooms that are more gender-neutral (Biggler, 1995).

Children's behavior is mediated not only by the *content* of gender categories (what sorts of behaviors count as specifically "male" or "female") but also by the rigidness of the categories and the consequences of crossing category boundaries (Ruble & Martin, 2002). In many Western cultures, the stereotype of the male is defined more clearly—and more rigidly—than the stereotype of the female. In the United States, for example, this difference is reflected in the relative permissiveness toward girls' en-gaging in typically male-identified behaviors and much greater intolerance toward boys' engaging in typically female-identified behavior. One young mother told us of a time when her 2-year-old son snuggled up to her on the sofa while she was painting her fingernails, extended his hand, and said, "Me, too, Mommy." This mother took great pride in her efforts to raise her son to be as affectionate and gentle as he was assertive and independent and made sure that he had dolls as well as trucks to play with. Yet after she had painted one of his stubby fingernails a pearly pink, she had to stop, concerned that she might be going too far. It seems that crossing from male into female territory may be difficult even for parents who are trying hard to break down gender stereotypes.

Thus, it is no surprise that while girls and women will readily admit to being "tomboys," very few boys and men will confess to being "sissies." Interestingly, the extent to which cultures tolerate (or fail to tolerate) individuals behaving in ways that are more typical of the other gender may influence children's developing knowledge about gender. For example, a study by Marion O'Brien and her colleagues (2000) found that preschool-age boys and girls are equally knowledgeable about male ste-reotypes but that girls are considerably more knowledgeable about female stereotypes than are boys. It may be that the male stereotype, being more rigid than the female stereotype, is easier for boys and girls to learn. It is also possible that girls know both stereotypes well because they are allowed to experiment with both, whereas boys are confined to behaviors that are consistent with what society defines as the "male domain."

Ethnic Identity

Jean Phinney (2001) defines **ethnic identity** as "a subjective sense of belonging to an ethnic group, and the feelings and attitudes that accompany this sense of group membership" (p. 136). In a society populated by many ethnic groups, children's developing sense of their own ethnic identity* has a host of social, psychological, and economic implications (Phinney & Baldelomar, 2011). These implications range from whether there are ethnic grocery stores in particular communities and whether ethnically relevant after-school clubs and activities are available for students to whether ethnic-minority youth are at elevated risk for suicide (see Chapter 15, pp. 578–581). As a consequence, researchers have studied how children identify their own ethnic group and how they form stable attitudes toward their own and other groups (Cross & Cross, 2008; Phinney, 2008). Studies have explored the dif-ferent kinds of feelings and attitudes that children might associate with their ethnic

---

*The difference between "racial identity" and "ethnic identity" is highly controversial, largely because of the difficulty of distinguishing between "race" and "ethnicity." Although it was once believed that race could be defined in terms of genetic makeup, whereas "ethnicity" applied to cultural heritage, scientists now widely agree that there are no discernable biological differences that can be used to distinguish reli-ably between people of different "racial" backgrounds. Many researchers deal with the ambiguity by using "race" and "ethnicity" interchangeably, as we have done here.

ethnic identity A sense of belonging to an ethnic group, and the feelings and attitudes that accompany the sense of group membership.

Photograph by Gordon Parks, © The Gordon Parks Foundation

Kenneth and Mamie Clark conducted groundbreaking research in the 1930's and 1940's indicating that African American children of that era tended to make more positive attributions to light-colored rather than dark-colored dolls.

identity and the possible effects such feelings and attitudes might have on children's self-esteem.

Perhaps the most famous research on the development of ethnic identity was carried out by Kenneth and Mamie Clark (1939, 1950), who asked African American and European American children to indicate their preferences between pairs of dolls. The children, who were 3 years old and older, were presented with pairs of dolls representing the two ethnic groups and were asked to choose "which boy would you would like to play with" or "which girl you don't like." The Clarks reported that most of the youngest children could distinguish between the categories of dolls and, more important, that African American children of all ages seemed to prefer the white dolls, a phenomenon that has come to be called "the white bias" (Justice et al., 1999). On the basis of this research, many psychologists concluded that African American children define themselves entirely in terms of the majority group, thereby denying the importance of their own families and communities in shaping their identities (Jackson, McCullough, & Gurin, 1997).

Studies conducted since the 1950s have confirmed the Clarks' findings (Justice et al., 1999; Spencer & Markstom-Adams, 1990) and have extended them to children of other minority groups, including Native Americans (Annis & Corenblum, 1987) and Bantu children in South Africa (Gregor & McPherson, 1966). However, these studies have also cast doubt on the notion that minority-group children acquire a negative ethnic self-concept (Spencer, 2006). Margaret Spencer (1988), for example, showed that while many of the 4- to 6-year-old African American children she interviewed said that they would prefer to play with a white doll, 80 percent of these children displayed positive self-esteem. Several other studies confirm that the "white bias" is not connected to the way that children think about and evaluate themselves (Justice et al., 1999). Ann Beuf (1977) reported incident after incident in which Native American children who chose white dolls made evident their understanding of the economic and social circumstances that make their lives difficult in contrast to the lives of White people. In one study, 5-year-old Dom was given several dolls representing Caucasians and Native Americans (whose skins were depicted as brown) to put into a toy classroom:

> Dom: (holding up a white doll) The children's all here and now the teacher's coming in.
> Interviewer: Is that the teacher?
> Dom: Yeah.
> Interviewer: (holding up a brown doll) Can she be the teacher?
> Dom: No way! Her's just an aide.
> (Beuf, 1977, p. 80)

In Beuf's view, the children's choices are less a reflection of their sense of personal self-worth than of their desire for the power and wealth of the White people with whom they had come in contact. Her views are echoed by James Jackson (2006), whose review of existing data provided little support for the idea that minority-group children's recognition that they are members of a less powerful group translates into a negative personal sense of themselves.

Decades of research on ethnic-identity development make clear that understanding oneself as a member of a particular ethnic group emerges in the first years of life. An important question is how ethnic identity is affected by children's social experiences. To address this question, developmentalists have explored how parents communicate with their children about issues of ethnicity. **Ethnic socialization**

ethnic socialization Ethnic-based messages communicated to children.

Despite an early awareness that White Americans are more likely than Black Americans to have wealth and power, African American children generally display positive self-esteem. These young girls are participating in an international parade in Florida that celebrates their African heritage, which may contribute to their sense of ethnic pride.

refers to the ethnicity-related messages communicated to children. Several categories of messages have been identified (Hughes & Chen, 1999, p. 473), including:

1. *Cultural socialization,* which emphasizes ethnic heritage and pride.

2. *Preparation for bias,* which stresses ethnic discrimination and prejudice.

3. *Promotion of ethnic mistrust,* which encourages mistrust of the majority ethnicity.

4. *Egalitarianism,* which emphasizes the equality of members of all ethnicities.

In a study of African American preschoolers, Margaret Caughy and her colleagues (2002) discovered that the vast majority of parents in their sample routinely incorporated a variety of ethnic socialization messages when interacting with their young children. Nearly all of the parents (88 percent) communicated messages that emphasized cultural heritage and pride; the majority also had Afrocentric items in their homes. In contrast, a notably smaller proportion of parents (65 percent) communicated messages promoting ethnic mistrust. The greater emphasis placed on socializing ethnic pride over mistrust and preparation for bias has also been found in studies of Puerto Rican and Dominican parents in the United States (Hughes, 2003).

As demonstrated by Caughy and her colleagues, differences in the form of ethnic socialization bear importantly on children's cognitive abilities and behavioral adjustment. In their study, children whose parents promoted ethnic pride and provided a home that was rich in African American culture had stronger cognitive abilities and problem-solving skills, and fewer behavior problems, than did children whose parents provided other forms of ethnic socialization, such as "preparation for bias" or "promotion of mistrust." Although similar findings have been reported in older school-age children (Johnson, 2001), Caughy's study indicates that the process of forming an ethnic identity is well under way in early childhood.

Personal Identity

I'm 3 years old and I live in a big house with my mother and father and my brother, Jason, and my sister, Lisa. I have blue eyes and a kitty that is orange and a television in my own room. I know all my ABC's, listen: A, B, C, D, E, F, G, H, L, K, O,

M, P, Q, X, Z. I can run real fast. I like pizza and I have a nice teacher at preschool. I can count up to 100, want to hear me? I love my dog Skipper. I can climb to the top of the jungle gym, I'm not scared! I'm never scared! I'm always happy. I have brown hair and I go to preschool. I am really strong. I can lift this chair, watch me! (Harter, 1999, p. 37)

The preceding monologue is a composite of the kinds of statements 3- to 4-year-olds typically make when describing themselves, revealing their sense of personal identity. Traditionally, developmentalists define **personal identity** as consisting of two parts, the *I-self* and the *me-self*. The I-self is the person's subjective sense of being a particular individual who exists over time and who acts and experiences the world in a particular way. The me-self, in contrast, is the person's sense of his or her objective characteristics, such as physical appearance, abilities, and other personal features that can be objectively known ("I live in a big house. I have blue eyes and a kitty.") The "I" and the "me" are two sides of the same coin; they shape each other continuously over the course of development (see also Chapter 15).

For reasons of cognitive immaturity, young children's descriptions of themselves focus mainly on the objective self and typically list highly specific, loosely connected behaviors, abilities, and preferences that are usually seen in an unrealistically positive way. These self-descriptions are rarely combined into generalized traits such as "being shy" or "being smart." That is, young children's self-descriptions are not well integrated into a *personality structure*. Instead, they tend to be fluid and shifting, as well as disjointed. As you learned in Chapter 8, reasoning that proceeds from particular to particular (transductive reasoning) is characteristic of preoperational thought. The integration of the self system is a gradual process that continues in step with cognitive development throughout childhood and adolescence (see Chapter 15, p. 574).

Cognitive limitations also contribute to young children's tendency to see themselves in the most favorable light. Their self-evaluations tend to be unrealistically positive because they have difficulty distinguishing between what they want to do and what they actually are able to do. For example, a child will say, "I know all my ABCs," and "I can swim the whole way across the pool," when he or she can do neither of these things. One reason young children describe themselves in such glowing and unrealistic terms is that they are not yet capable of distinguishing between a "real" self and an "ideal" self—a cognitive ability that doesn't emerge until middle childhood (Chapter 13, p. 466).

The continuing process of developing personal identity is greatly influenced in early childhood by children's increasingly sophisticated use of language. Recall from Chapter 7 (pp. 263–264) that language is acquired in routine, scripted activities during which young children interact with their caregivers. The same routine activities in family settings are crucial contexts for further development of the self. Not only do caregivers tell children that they are boys or girls, good or bad, Black or White, Japanese or Irish, but they also help them acquire an enduring sense of themselves by helping them to create a personal narrative about themselves. This personal narrative is referred to as **autobiographical memory**.

Adults typically contribute to children's development of autobiographical memory by helping children recall and interpret events in which they have participated (Bauer & Fivush, 2010; Fivush & Nelson, 2006). Initially, adults carry the burden of helping the child remember. Gradually, with increasing age and growing facility with language, the child assumes a more active role, as one of our daughters, Jenny, did when she was about 2 years old. "Tell me what Jenny did," she would say every night at bedtime, and her parents would oblige her by recounting the events of the day in a schematic way that highlighted events that were particularly interesting or worrisome to her. These conversations would go like this: "Do you remember this morning, when we went to pick up Michael, and Mandy [the dog] came running out?" and Jenny would say,

personal identity A person's sense of his or her self as persisting over time (*I-self*), as well as a sense of personal characteristics such as appearance and abilities that can be objectively known (*me-self*).

autobiographical memory A personal narrative that helps children acquire an enduring sense of themselves.

"Doggie go wuff, wuff, wuff." "And what did Mandy do?" her parents would prompt. "Wagged her tail," Jenny would respond. "And what else did Mandy do?" they would ask, and she would laugh remembering, "She kissed me!" Although her parents continued to guide the narrative, as Jenny grew older, she increasingly corrected them and added details of her own until she stopped asking them to tell her what happened and started telling them the events of her day (or refusing to tell, as she often did).

Like all parents in such interactions, Jenny's parents were not simply mirrors reflecting their child's experiences. As participants in creating the stories of children's experience, parents strongly influence their children's autobiographical memories and are themselves influenced by the larger culture as well as by their own personal histories, values, and interests. What is more, as illustrated in Jenny's case, parents are not necessarily objective in their contributions to the stories. Some parents may tend to embellish and exaggerate to heighten the stories and make them more exciting, or to play down children's incompetence or fears and exaggerate their capabilities and bravery. Other parents might stay closer to the objective facts in recounting the events in their children's lives. Yet others might tend to structure the stories of prior events so that they teach moral lessons. There are great variations among parents in what events they remember and include in these narratives, as well as in how they structure the narratives (Nelson, 2003). Despite this variation, by the time most children are 4 years old, they have internalized the narrative structures appropriate to their culture and can recount their personal experiences by themselves, a significant step in developing personal identity.

▲ APPLY :: CONNECT :: DISCUSS

Visit a major toy store and look for evidence of social categories of gender and ethnicity. What sorts of toys are marketed for boys, girls, or children of specific ethnic backgrounds? How might these toys mediate children's behavior?

Visit the children's section of a public library and look for similar evidence of social categories in books appropriate for 3- to 5-year-olds (you might enlist the help of the librarian). What similarities and differences do you note between books and toys?

A New Moral World

Eddie: Sometimes I hate myself.
Teacher: When?
Eddie: When I'm naughty.
Teacher: What do you do that's naughty?
Eddie: You know, naughty words. Like "shit." That one.
Teacher: That makes you hate yourself?
Eddie: Yeah, when my dad washes my mouth with soap.
Teacher: What if he doesn't hear you?
Eddie: Then I get away with it. Then I don't hate myself.
(Paley, 1981, p. 54)

Children's early ideas of what is good and bad come from the ways in which the significant people in their lives respond to their behavior. In the conversation above, it is clear that for Eddie, as for young children generally, "[b]ad and good depended on the adult response. . . . An angry parent denoted a naughty child" (Paley, 1981, p. 55). As you learned in Chapter 6, the seeds of this moral development are apparent at the end of infancy when children acquire sensitivity to adult standards and become frustrated or disappointed when they fail to meet them.

To get a sense of the vast territory between these early beginnings and fully mature moral reasoning, take a moment to think about your own moral standards—what you consider right, just, and fair. It is very likely that you believe these standards are not based on the dictates of authority. That is, although you may share your parents' or community's moral values, it is unlikely that you embrace your moral standards because you were told to do so or because you worry about what will happen if you get caught violating a moral standard. Instead, you probably have a deeply *personal* sense of right and wrong. Developmentalists are intent on discovering how such personally felt moral standards are acquired. In the sections below, we examine three perspectives that have dominated research on children's moral development: psychodynamic theory, cognitive-developmental theory, and social domain theory.

The Psychodynamic View

According to psychodynamic theory, we acquire a personal sense of what is right and wrong because we have *internalized* the moral standards of our parents, especially those of our same-sex parent. Indeed, our previous discussion of Freud's views on sexual identity development contains the kernel of his thinking about the development of moral reasoning.

According to Freud, the internalization of moral standards that occurs as a consequence of identifying with a same-sex parent is responsible for the creation of the last of the three mental structures that he said develop in early childhood (previewed in Chapter 1). The first, the **id**, which is present at birth, functions unconsciously, and operates on the basis of the *pleasure principle;* that is, it strives for the immediate satisfaction of bodily drives and does so impulsively (Freud, 1933/1964). Over the first few years of life, the id comes gradually to be held in check by the emergence of the second mental structure, the **ego**. The ego serves as the intermediary between the demands of the id and the demands of the social world, enabling children to control and regulate their behavior. The ego is said to operate on the basis of the *reality principle*—that is, it is concerned with how bodily drives can be satisfied while taking reality into account. Sometime later, around age 5, children internalize adult standards, rules, and admonitions, resulting in the formation of the **superego**. In Freud's words, the superego "continues to carry on the functions which have hitherto been performed by the [parents]: it observes the ego, gives it orders, judges it and threatens it with punishments, exactly like the parents whose place it has [partially] taken" (1940/1964, p. 205). The emergence of the superego, and all its associated emotions of shame and guilt, is fundamental to children's abilities to regulate their behaviors according to their personal sense of right and wrong.

The Cognitive-Developmental View

Consider two scenes. In one, a young child named Luke is warned by his mother to stay away from the freshly baked cookies cooling on the kitchen counter. When she leaves the room, Luke snitches a cookie and, in his clumsy haste, knocks over a cup that falls to the floor and breaks. Now consider the second scene, in which young Zack is helping his mother set the dining room table for dinner. With hands full of napkins and silverware, he pushes open the door leading from the kitchen to the dining room. When the door swings open, it hits a tray on which are stacked a dozen cups, all of which fall to the floor and break. Who, in your judgment, is the naughtier child—Luke, who broke one cup while snitching a cookie, or Zack, who broke a dozen while helping his mother set the table?

When Piaget presented similar contrasts to children of different ages, he found that young, preoperational children considered Zack the naughtier of the two because he broke more cups. Older children, in contrast, chose Luke because he was

id In Freudian theory, the mental structure present at birth that is the main source of psychological energy. It is unconscious and pleasure-seeking and demands that bodily drives be satisfied.

ego In Freudian theory, the mental structure that develops out of the id as the infant is forced by reality to cope with the social world. The ego mediates between the id and the social world, allowing children to control and regulate behavior.

superego In Freudian terms, the conscience. It represents the authority of the child's parents and sits in stern judgment of the ego's efforts to hold the id in check. It becomes a major force in the personality in middle childhood.

deliberately violating his mother's order, whereas Zack was trying to do good and simply had an unfortunate accident.

As you might predict from previous discussions of preoperational thinking, when young children reason about moral issues, they tend to focus on objective consequences—how much damage is done (in the case of Luke and Zack) or whether the person gets caught and in trouble (as when Eddie's father washed his mouth out with soap). Jean Piaget (1932/1965) called this pattern of thinking **heteronomous morality**, that is, morality defined in terms of externally imposed controls and objective consequences. According to Piaget, as children enter middle childhood and begin to interact increasingly with their peers outside of situations directly controlled by adults, heteronomous morality gives way to an *autonomous morality,* in which one's moral judgments are freely and personally chosen. (This idea and its extension by Lawrence Kohlberg and other contemporary researchers will be discussed further in Chapter 14.)

As you can see, the cognitive-developmental and psychodynamic views both focus on how children move past their reliance on external authority and objective consequences to define right and wrong. But whereas the psychodynamic view emphasizes processes such as identification, internalization, and the development of the superego, the cognitive-developmental view links changes in moral reasoning to broader cognitive developments that are supported by the expansion of children's social lives.

The Social Domain View

The social domain view of moral development stands apart from the other two views we have considered because it emphasizes that there are different *types* of "right" and "wrong" (Killen & Smetana, 2007). For example, jaywalking is a very different type of transgression than pushing someone off a bridge. According to **social domain theory**, rules that dictate right and wrong fall into three domains, which are at different levels of generality: Some rules are *moral rules,* others are *social conventions,* and yet others are rules within the *personal sphere* (Lagattuta, Nucci, & Bosacki, 2010; Turiel, 2008) (Table 9.3).

Moral rules are the most general; they are based on principles of justice and the welfare of others. Thus, moral rules specify, for example, that others be treated

heteronomous morality Piaget's term for young children's tendency to define morality in terms of objective consequences and externally imposed controls.

social domain theory The theory that the moral domain, the social conventional domain, and the personal domain have distinct rules that vary in how broadly the rules apply and in what happens when they are broken.

table 9.3

Social Domain Theory Approach to Rules and Infractions

Rule Type	Sample Infractions
Moral Rules—rules related to	
Physical harm	Hitting, pushing
Psychological harm	Hurting feelings, ridiculing
Fairness and rights	Refusing to take turns
Social Conventions—rules related to	
School behavior	Chewing gum in class, talking back to the teacher
Forms of address	Calling a physician "Mr." when he is working
Attire and appearance	Wearing pajamas to school
Sex roles	Boy wearing barrette to keep hair out of eyes while playing football
Personal Sphere—rules related to	
Personal habits	Making loud noises while eating
Hygiene	Not brushing teeth
Social events	Not sending a thank-you card for a gift

fairly, in a way that preserves their rights and avoids causing them harm. Often believed to derive from a divine source (for example, to be God's law), and found in all societies, moral rules are obligations that are not to be transgressed.

At the next level of generality are social conventions—rules that are important for coordinating social behavior in a given society, such as rules about how men or women should act, or what constitutes appropriate dress at a house of worship or on the beach, or who has authority over whom. Social conventions are important aspects of the cultural scripts that young children are acquiring. Social conventions vary tremendously, not only among societies but also among subcultural groups within a society. This variation can contribute to difficulties children may have in knowing whether a rule they have broken is a moral rule or a social convention. For example, some families may treat cursing as violating a social convention ("That's not a nice word; you definitely shouldn't say it in front of your grandmother"), but when Eddie says "shit" and gets his mouth washed out with soap, he might well believe that he has broken a moral rule!

At the most specific level are rules that govern the personal sphere, in which children can make decisions on the basis of their personal preferences. They are allowed to choose whether to call or send a note to thank an uncle for a birthday gift. It is in the personal sphere that children are able to develop what is unique about the way they deal with the world (Nucci & Turiel, 2009; Helwig, 2008).

Several studies have found that children as young as 3 or 4 years old from a variety of cultures can distinguish among moral, social, and personal rules (Yau & Smetana, 2003). For example, they respond quite differently to moral rule violations, such as hurting another child or taking another's favorite toy, than they do to violations of a social convention, such as wearing inappropriate clothes to school (Turiel, 2006).

As already suggested, the borders between the three levels of rules are not easy to learn and keep straight. Parents, for example, may treat their young children's wearing a bathing suit at the beach as a matter of social convention. Their young children, however, may treat wearing a bathing suit as a matter of personal choice, so they take it off to play naked in the water. It takes children many years to acquire their culture's normative separations, and even then, deciding which rules should be applied in which situations often require a good deal of thought and flexibility (Nucci, 2004; Smetana, 2006).

⏏ APPLY :: CONNECT :: DISCUSS

Erikson believed that identity development and moral development are closely related. Using material presented in this chapter, pull together evidence for his argument.

Developing Self-Regulation

In the process of learning about basic social roles and rules and developing their sense of self, children are also learning to act in accordance with the expectations of their caregivers, even when they do not want to and are not being directly monitored. Learning to control one's thoughts, emotions, and behaviors, an ability referred to as **self-regulation**, spans various developmental stages and involves all the developmental domains (Kochanska & Aksan, 2006; Kochanska, Philibert, & Barry, 2009). As you have seen in previous chapters, the capacity for self-regulation begins to emerge early in development, as infants first acquire the ability to regulate their sleep/wake cycles, their crying, and later, to a certain degree, their behavior. As

self-regulation The ability to control one's thoughts, emotions, and behaviors.

they get older, children's regulatory capacities expand and deepen, allowing them, for example, to increasingly control their attentional state and tune out distractions in order to complete a task; to put aside hurt feelings in order to patch up a friendship; and to keep secrets.

Infants and young children require a great deal of assistance with regulation. They are soothed by caregivers when they cry; their interpersonal relationships are often orchestrated by others ("Tell him you're sorry and make up"); and their emotional expressions are monitored and managed ("No hitting! Use words!"). Even the large and simple figures contained in young children's coloring books reflect the culture's response to children's need for assistance in regulating their attention and behavior (in this case, their fine motor behavior).

Because the ability to regulate one's own thoughts, emotions, behaviors, and attentional states is such an important part of what it means to function independently, many developmentalists consider self-regulation to be a cornerstone of children's development (Cunningham & Zelazo, 2010; Shonkoff & Phillips, 2000).

This girl's culture helps her regulate her immature motor skills by making extra big shovels for filling buckets with sand.

Regulating Thought and Action

To intentionally focus one's attention, or remember to do something, or map out a plan to solve a problem involves the regulation of cognitive processes. Consider a preschooler who is stringing beads (after Shonkoff & Phillips, 2000, p. 116). Accomplishing this task requires that she regulate her thoughts in order to:

- Generate and maintain a mental representation that directs her behavior: "I need to hold up the string and put the end through the hole in the bead."

- Monitor her own progress: "I got one on; now I'll try another."

- Modify her problem-solving strategies: "This bead won't go on; I need one with a bigger hole."

The simple act of stringing beads calls on a host of skills that require the child to select certain actions (holding the bead to the string), eliminate actions that do not fit the goal (throwing the bead), and inhibit actions as the task requires (stop trying the bead with the too-small hole). The inhibition of an action that is already under way, also called **effortful control**, can be particularly difficult for young children, as anyone knows who has observed a game of "Red Light, Green Light" or "Simon Says" (Shonkoff & Phillips, 2000). Once a behavior has been initiated, especially in a highly exciting situation, it can be difficult to stop.

In addition to exploring how children come to regulate their thoughts and actions in solving problems and accomplishing tasks, developmentalists have asked how children regulate themselves in order to achieve social goals such as pleasing a parent or teacher. The most common way of studying this form of self-regulation is to examine children's ability to resist temptation and comply with adult norms. For example, Grazyna Kochanska and Nazan Aksan (1995) videotaped and analyzed the behavior of more than 100 children between the ages of 2 and 5 while they interacted with their mother in two situations. In the first, the mother and child were given a large number of attractive toys to play with in their own home. After the child played with the toys for a while, the mother asked the child to put them away. Only 10 percent of the children overtly disobeyed. Of the others, some exhibited what the researchers called "committed compliance"—that is, they wholeheartedly embraced their mother's agenda. Most, however, engaged in "situational compliance," meaning that they had to be continually prompted by their mother to do as they were told. Consistent with what we know about effortful control,

effortful control The inhibition of an action that is already under way.

The ability to share requires that children control their own desires and regulate their behaviors in order to comply with social norms and the expectations of friends.

the children clearly found it difficult to put away the attractive toys with which they were still playing.

In the second situation, which took place in a laboratory playroom, the mothers were instructed to tell their children not to touch a set of especially attractive

Many adults have childhood memories about the difficulty of sitting quietly and respectfully during religious ceremonies that seemed to last forever. As illustrated by these Iranian girls reading the Qu'ran in a mosque, children are able to regulate their behavior to comply with adult expectations when consistently prompted to do so.

toys on a shelf. After the children had been playing for a while, the researchers asked each mother to leave the playroom so that they could see if her child would continue to obey her instructions even when she was not watching. In this situation, which did not involve effortful control because the children had not been actively engaged with the forbidden toys, most of the children complied wholeheartedly with their mother's instructions. Some of the children were heard to say to themselves such things as "We don't touch these." Their use of the word "we" in such circumstances was a clear sign that they identified with their mother and accepted her rules.

You have probably recognized that children's ability to control themselves in this manner is an example of internalization. In addition to being a key component of Freud's theory of moral development, internalization is central to the developmental theory of Lev Vygotsky. Vygotsky's view of the internalization process was both broader and more benevolent than Freud's. For Freud, internalization is a response to an ongoing battle against parental authority, a battle that the child will ultimately lose. Vygotsky, in contrast, saw internalization as the process through which external social regulations, which may originate from parents, other adults, or even peers, are transferred to the child's internal psychological system. Once the social regulations are internalized, the child is capable of self-regulation without the assistance of others. A particularly interesting example of this process can be observed in children's play.

Self-Regulation and Play

Play occupies a conspicuous role not only in young children's physical development but also in their cognitive and social development. According to Vygotsky and those who have followed in his footsteps, the development of self-regulation is a crucial function of play (Hirsh-Pasek, Golinkoff, Berk, & Singer, 2009; Goncu & Gaskins, 2011).

Key to Vygotsky's theory about how play leads to self-regulation are his ideas regarding children's ability to separate the objects they play with from their thoughts about those objects. Remember that early in development, children have

sociodramatic play Make-believe play in which two or more participants enact a variety of related social roles.

difficulty separating their thoughts and actions from the objects and situations that they think about and act upon. For example, before they are 2 years old, children can pretend to talk on a telephone only if the toy really looks and acts like a telephone, complete with buttons to push and a shape that allows it to be held up to the mouth and ear. Not until age 2 can children let one object substitute for another; at 2, for instance, they might play "telephone" with a rectangular block that has the general shape of a real telephone. The ability to detach the *idea* of the telephone from the *object itself* increases through the next year, and by the age of 3, the attributes of the play symbol can be entirely independent of the object that it represents. So, for example, children can play "telephone" using a ball or a stuffed animal or any other object. Their ability to separate thought—which carries the *idea* or *meaning* of the object—from the object that is thought about indicates that they are regulating their thoughts and actions. They are making themselves imagine that an object that is not a telephone is a telephone and are acting on it accordingly. Vygotsky believed that children's self-regulation is most required in, and hence most developed through, this type of imaginary play.

Play provides an important opportunity for acquiring self-control. These young children are regulating their behavior so that it is coordinated with that of their playmates.

A particularly important and complex type of imaginary play is **sociodramatic play**—make-believe play in which two or more participants enact a variety of related social roles. Sociodramatic play requires a shared understanding of what the play situation involves, which often must be negotiated as part of the play. As an example, consider the following scene involving several children in preschool. The girls in the group have just agreed upon the roles they will play: mother, sister, baby, and maid.

Karen: I'm hungry. Wa-a-ah!
Charlotte: Lie down, baby.
Karen: I'm a baby that sits up.
Charlotte: First you lie down and sister covers you and then I make your cereal and then you sit up.
Karen: Okay.
Karen: (to Teddy, who has been observing) You can be the father.
Charlotte: Are you the father?
Teddy: Yes.
Charlotte: Put on a red tie.
Janie: (in the "maid's" falsetto voice) I'll get it for you, honey. Now don't that baby look pretty? This is your daddy, baby.
(Adapted from Paley, 1984, p. 1)

The sociodramatic play of these two little girls involves enacting the roles of doctors or nurses. According to Vygotsky, such play is fundamental to the emergence of self-regulation.

This transcript illustrates several features of young children's sociodramatic play. The children are enacting social roles and using scripts that they have encountered numerous times in their daily lives, on television, or in stories. Babies make stereotypic baby noises, maids get things for people, and fathers wear ties. At the same time that they are playing their roles in the pretend world, the children are also outside of it, giving stage directions to one another and commenting on the action. The "baby" who sits up has to be talked into lying down, and the boy is told what role he can play. The children here are clearly acting against immediate impulse and regulating their thoughts and behaviors according to the imaginary situation as it evolves in the course of interacting with their playmates.

In the Field | Coping with Chronic Illness Through Play

Name:	Cindy Clark
Education:	B.A. in international relations, University of Pennsylvania; M.A. and Ph.D. in human development, University of Chicago
Current Position:	Visiting associate professor, Rutgers University.
Career Objectives:	Use research to learn about and reduce the stress and anxiety of children with chronic illnesses

THE SIGHT OF A CHILD UNABLE TO BREATHE CARRIES unspeakable anxiety. Life begins with the first breath and ends when breathing does. Children's connection to life is only as reliable as inhaling and exhaling. Against this fact of life, asthma stalks, specterlike.

(Cindy Clark, 2003, p. 89)

A parent's letter to Mr. Rogers:

Our 5½-year-old daughter has an inoperable brain tumor. Our only hope to remove the tumor is radiation. On the first day of her radiation treatment, she screamed and cried when she found out that she would have to be in the room all by herself. . . . We kept saying that it would only take a minute. . . . Finally, she asked me, "What is a minute?" . . . I looked at my watch and started singing, "It's a beautiful day in this neighborhood, a beautiful day for a neighbor," and before I could finish the song I said "Oops, the minute's up. I can't even finish Mr. Rogers' song." Then Michelle said, "Is that a minute? I can do that." And she did. She laid perfectly still for the entire treatment; but there was a catch to it. I have to sing your song every time over the intercom.

From an interview with a child living with chronic asthma:

If I had a magic wand, all asthma medicine would taste good, not like the yucky stuff. And my inhaler and breathing machine would work as fast as I can snap my fingers, so I could start breathing and go play. My breathing machine takes 10,000 years. That's how slow it seems to me. Sometimes, I play games with myself when I do my breathing machine. I pretend I have a friend who is a dragon, and the dragon breathes smoke. You know the steam coming from the machine? That's dragon smoke. Another game is, I have a toy airplane. I fly my airplane through the steam. I pretend to fly away, to a place away from this. That's really fun to pretend, getting up and away.

Children afflicted with serious illness and disease face a number of challenges. The disease itself can be painful and physically exhausting—and terribly frightening. It can also be socially isolating, as when children need to stay home or in hospitals, away from their friends and schoolmates.

Beyond the physical, psychological, and social costs of the disease itself, chronically ill children pay a heavy toll as a consequence of the medical procedures required to heal them. As expressed in the stories above, the procedures can be scary and seem to make time stand still. Medical procedures can also unnerve the very people on whom sick children count for support, friendship, and comfort. That is, children with chronic illness are often shunned inadvertently by peers, and even family members, who may be squeamish in the face of the diabetic child's insulin shots and blood tests, the hair loss that typically accompanies chemotherapy, or the disfigurement of surgery.

Cindy Clark

Bill Clark

How do children cope with chronic illness? According to Cindy Clark's intensive study (2003), they cope surprisingly well, particularly when they are allowed to play. In her interviews with children living with chronic severe asthma or diabetes, Clark found that play has an important role in altering the meanings of medical procedures and devices, and symbolically

Recently, developmentalists have sought empirical evidence for the link between sociodramatic play and the more general ability of children to regulate their actions. An example is a study conducted by Cynthia Elias and Laura Berk (2002), in which they observed 51 children aged 3 and 4 in their preschool classrooms. Elias and Berk recorded and assessed the children's involvement in sociodramatic play, and they assessed their level of self-regulation by observing how well they participated

recasting what it means to be ill. Play provides children with a sense of control and empowerment over conditions and circumstances that are otherwise forced upon them by doctors, parents, and the medical regimens that keep them alive.

Thus, Clark found that parents and children often develop games and playful routines that transform unpleasant medical experiences into something fun, or at least endurable. The examples above of singing Mr. Rogers's song or imagining smoke-breathing dragons are cases in point. Parents of children with asthma described a variety of playful ways of counting off the breaths their children needed to take on their inhalers (also known as puffers)—they counted in French, in pig Latin, in the voice of the Count from *Sesame Street*. Some parents got their children inhalers that look like toys (see the figure). Sometimes, children themselves transformed the medical devices into toys. Certain types of inhalers make a whistling sound to signal to patients that they are inhaling too quickly, so, as you might imagine, a lot of asthmatic children get the giggles by using their inhalers (improperly) as musical instruments. One mother recounted how her daughter played with a breathing mask used with the nebulizer (a machine that delivers asthma medication automatically as a breathable aerosol, often to children too young to manipulate the more complicated puffer). The mother had intentionally acquired a second mask, thinking that using it in the context of play might facilitate her daughter's coping with asthma. Sure enough, the girl "played asthma" with her friends, placing the mask on their faces, instructing them to sit quietly, and promising that mommy would read stories to pass the time.

Clark also found playful approaches adopted with chronic illness in other contexts. At an "illness camp" for children with diabetes, syringes and paint were used to create art; at an asthma camp, some of the children put on a "Three Little Pigs" skit in which the big, bad wolf was unable to blow the house down because he had life-threatening asthma. He was taken to

Puffa Pals introduce a playful dimension to asthma inhalers, making them more attractive to the young children who must use them to manage the symptoms of their disease.

the hospital, received a lung transplant, and, to the delight of the audience, was thereafter able to blow down just about anything.

In her child-centered approach to understanding chronic illness, Clark attempts to reveal how children attach meaning to their illness and to the medical procedures and devices that they endure and use on a daily basis. What she found is a child's world in which fear, pain, embarrassment, and confusion are ordered and controlled through song, jokes, art, pranks, and funny stories. From a Vygotskian perspective, the blending of fantasy play and medical treatment creates a zone of proximal development through which the child gains a sense of control over the uncontrollable and frightening. Much of the play is spontaneously generated by children. However, some is encouraged by adults—parents in particular—who are sensitive to how children can regulate their thoughts and feelings in the context of play.

Increasingly, the therapeutic value of play is recognized by the medical community. At one hospital, the pediatric blood-testing machine is named "Herbie"; his most distinctive characteristic is his inclination to "suck your blood." One of Herbie's child "victims" claimed that his encounter with blood-sucking Herbie was the best part of his hospital stay, and that Herbie made the procedure seem like it did not hurt quite so much. Other hospitals have systematically incorporated play into children's treatment regimens. Many now employ *child life specialists* whose primary duties involve familiarizing children with the treatment they will be undergoing and facilitating their coping and adjustment to it through the use of play and games.

Currently, developmentalists such as Clark are seeking new ways of using the functions of play to help children deal with debilitating diseases and medical procedures. Clark is now engaged in a study that incorporates inhalers that are shaped like toys, as in the photo above. And you can bet that if they whistle, it is not when they are being used improperly.

in cleanup and how attentive they were when they gathered in a circle to listen to the teacher. They used a short-term longitudinal design, assessing both play and self-regulation in the fall and assessing self-regulation again several months later.

Their findings support Vygotsky's main idea regarding the role of play in facilitating self-regulation (see also the box "In the Field: Coping with Chronic Illness Through Play"). In particular, children who engaged in a lot of sociodramatic play in the fall showed high levels of self-regulation several months later, even though there was no correlation between the two variables at the time of the first assessment. Interestingly, the correlation was especially strong for the most impulsive children, indicating that they benefited more from opportunities to engage in sociodramatic play than did their less impulsive peers. On the basis both of their findings and on what is known about the social and academic difficulties that go along with poor self-regulation skills (a matter we will address below), Elias and Berk argued that sociodramatic play deserves a significant place in preschool curricula and may provide an important form of early intervention for highly impulsive children.

Although sociodramatic play provides an important context for the development of self-regulation, it is but one of many contexts through which children come to master themselves. Children encounter a vast array of social norms, parenting practices, school curricula, and work demands, which vary according to the child's culture, gender, and age. All provide possible contexts in support of the child's journey toward independence in thought and action.

Regulating Emotions

To be competent members of society, children must learn how to control their emotions as well as their thoughts and actions. As we noted in Chapter 6 (pp. 226–227), the development of self-conscious emotions—pride, shame, guilt, envy, and embarrassment—is one of the key changes associated with the transition from infancy to early childhood. In combination with anger, joy, and the other basic emotions, self-conscious emotions enable children to participate in new and more complex social relationships (Mascolo, Fischer, & Li, 2003). Children must now begin to understand how their emotional states and expressions affect others and learn to manage their emotions and, when necessary, to mask their true feelings.

Controlling Feelings Most of us know what it feels like to carry a chip on one's shoulder, to stew over a negative experience, or to react explosively to a frustrating situation. Such feelings present special challenges to children's developing self-regulation abilities. However, between 2 and 6 years of age, children develop a number of strategies to help them keep their emotions under control (Grolnick, McMenamy, & Kurowski, 1999; Saarni, 2007; Thompson & Newton, 2010). For example, they avoid or reduce emotionally charged aversive information by closing their eyes, turning away, and putting their hands over their ears. They also regulate negative emotions by distracting themselves with pleasurable activities. Further, they use their budding language and cognitive skills to help them reinterpret events to create a more acceptable version of what is occurring ("I didn't want to play with her anyway; she's mean"), to reassure themselves ("Mommy said she'll be right back"), and to encourage themselves ("I'm a big girl; big girls can do it"). At the age of 3, one of our daughters displayed a useful strategy for regulating her fright when hearing Maurice Sendak's tale, *Where the Wild Things Are:* She hid the book so her parents could not read it to her.

The emerging ability to control emotions helps the preschool-age child deal with the disappointments, frustrations, and injured feelings that are so common at this stage. In addition, emotional regulation can be helpful in the increasingly important realm of social behavior. For example, when children observe a playmate fall down and get hurt, they will likely feel anxious themselves. Children who can moderate their personal distress are more likely to show sympathy toward the playmate and offer help than are children who cannot manage their own emotional reactions (Eisenberg, 2010). Indeed, in order to sustain play with each other, children must create and maintain a delicate balance of emotional expression and regulation (Halberstadt et al., 2001). As you will see, the skills associated with this balance are significantly related to children's altruistic, or *prosocial,* behaviors.

Controlling and Understanding Emotion Expressions Young children must
learn not only to control their feelings but also to express their feelings in a socially appropriate way. Young infants display no such ability. They communicate their emotions directly, regardless of the circumstances. A 1-year-old who starts to fidget and fuss during a wedding because she's hungry and tired is not going to settle down until she's been fed and had a nap. It takes several years for children to learn to control their emotional expressions. Likewise, it takes time before children are able to appreciate that the emotional expressions of others may not correspond to their true feelings—that they may hide or even fake their emotions in order to be polite or achieve particular social goals (acting brave to avoid teasing, for instance). The ability to control one's emotional experiences, and to understand that others do so as well, requires the cognitive capacity to distinguish between emotional *expressions* and emotional *experiences* (Lightfoot & Bullock, 1990).

In many cultures, for example, it is considered socially inappropriate to express disappointment when someone gives you a present you don't like. You are expected to thank the giver and say something nice, masking your true feelings. A social or cultural group's informal conventions regarding whether, how, and under what circumstances emotions should be expressed are known as **display rules**. Several researchers have studied the ability of children to use display rules and to understand their use by others. In some studies, children were asked to interpret stories about a child who expects an exciting present and gets something undesirable instead. In other studies, the children themselves were led to expect a desirable object but received a disappointing one (as when, for example, they were led to expect a toy car as a prize for playing a game but got a picture book instead).

Several general results come from this type of research in different cultures (summaries are provided in Saarni et al., 2006, and Thompson, 1998). First, during early childhood, children around the world appear to gain the ability to recognize when someone is masking his or her feelings. Second, girls tend to be better than boys at recognizing and displaying masked emotions. Third, there are wide cultural variations in the age at which children learn about masking emotion. For example, one study found that young English children acquired display rules for masking negative emotions earlier than did young Italian children (Manstead, 1995). In accounting for this difference, the researcher speculated that English children are likely socialized to be more reserved in expressing their feelings because English culture is less tolerant of the open display of extreme emotions, especially negative ones, and that Italian children, correspondingly, experience less pressure to mask their feelings. Similarly, another study found that 4-year-old girls from India were more sensitive to the need to mask negative emotions than were their English counterparts, perhaps because of cultural

Caught in the act of making a big mess, the signs of guilt are unmistakable on this girl's face. Self-conscious emotions, including guilt, first emerge during early childhood.

display rules A social or cultural group's informal conventions regarding whether, how, and under what circumstances emotions should be expressed.

socioemotional competence The ability to behave appropriately in social situations that evoke strong emotions.

differences placed on the importance of respecting the needs and feelings of others (Joshi & MacLean, 1994).

Children's increasing ability to control their own emotional expression, as well as to read the emotions of others, are considered forms of **socioemotional competence**, the ability to behave appropriately in social situations that evoke strong emotions. Carolyn Saarni (2007) proposed that socioemotional competence involves a variety of skills, most of which are acquired in early childhood. The skills include an awareness of one's own emotional state and the emotional states of others, as well as the realization that outward expressions of emotion do not necessarily reflect inner emotional states. It should come as no surprise that preschool children who display the characteristics of socioemotional competence are better liked by both their peers and their teachers (Eisenberg, Losoya, & Spinrad, 2003; Saarni, 2011).

The Influence of Culture on Emotion Regulation

As you know from the previous section on regulating thought and action, the developmental task of self-regulation is not a solitary accomplishment. The child receives a great deal of social and cultural assistance. Developmentalists are just beginning to explore how children's emotions and emotion regulation are affected by their culture's values, meanings, and belief systems.

For example, Michael Mascolo, Kurt Fischer, and Jin Li (2003) have explored differences in the emotional development of children growing up in China and the United States. The two cultures embrace vastly different values and beliefs. In the United States, great emphasis is placed on individualism and hence on personal achievement. Children are socialized to express themselves and take pleasure in their own accomplishments. Accordingly, U S. parents act to bolster their children's pride, and in this way their self-esteem, when they succeed ("Good girl! You did it all by yourself!"). Because failure is associated with children's incompetence and feelings of self-reproach ("I'm not smart enough to do this"), parents may act to protect their children from feelings of shame and failure by emphasizing the difficulty of the task in relation to the competence of the child ("That puzzle is too hard for you; let's do this one instead"). In contrast, the Chinese embrace the philosophy of Confucianism, which emphasizes harmony with others as a principal goal. When a child succeeds at a task, the culturally appropriate response is not self-celebration but modesty and praise for others. Accordingly, parents might respond to their child's achievement with a caution like, "You did all right, but now you need more practice. Play down your success." When a child fails, the failure is viewed as a discredit to the family and to the child's larger social group. Chinese parents thus often utilize a variety of "shaming techniques" to promote good behavior and effortful performance. Mascolo and his colleagues report that if a child does poorly in school, a parent might say things like "Shame on you!" "You didn't study hard enough!" "Everyone will laugh at you!" Because of such use of shame as a strategy of control, Mascolo and his colleagues argue, shame emerges for Chinese children at an earlier point in development than it does for American children. As shown in Figure 9.4, children's emotional responses to their accomplishments follow radically different pathways as a consequence of their cultural traditions.

Consistent with the philosophy of Confucianism, Chinese parents commonly play down their children's successes and use "shaming techniques" when their children perform poorly.

©Yang Liu / Corbis

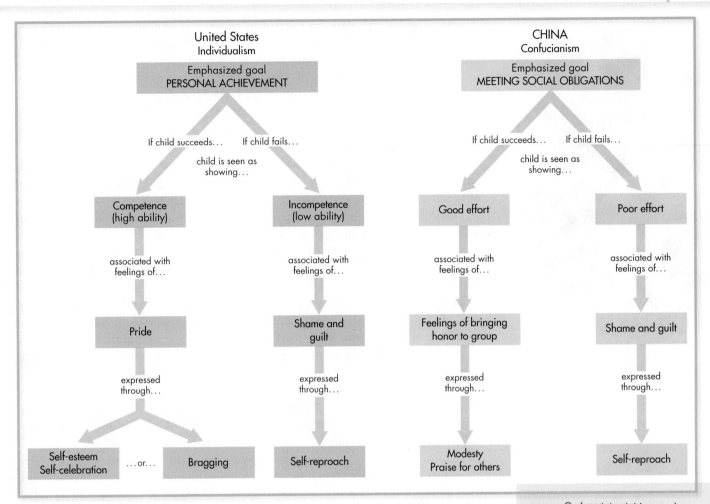

FIGURE 9.4 While children in the United States are socialized to strive for, and take pride in, personal achievements, children in China are encouraged to strive to meet social obligations and to feel honor in doing so. This figure shows the emotional outcomes for children who are successful or unsuccessful in meeting their culture's expectations.

▲ APPLY :: CONNECT :: DISCUSS

We argued in Chapter 6 that one of the earliest purposes of emotion regulation is to maintain intersubjectivity. Review pages 203–207 and discuss the similarities and differences between infancy and early childhood in the purposes and consequences of emotion regulation.

Understanding Aggression

In order to be accepted as members of their social group, young children must learn not only to subordinate their personal desires to the good of the group when the situation demands it but also to regulate their anger when their goals are thwarted. Such anger can lead to aggression, and learning to control aggression is one of the most basic tasks of young children's social development. Indeed, researchers have argued that early childhood holds the key to understanding both the origins of aggressive behavior and the ways to control such behavior (Tremblay, 2011).

The Development of Aggression

There are two main categories of aggression during early childhood that can be easily identified, each of which follows its own developmental path (Berkowitz, 2003). **Hostile aggression** is intended to injure the victim, physically or otherwise.

hostile aggression Aggression that is aimed at hurting another person physically, psychologically, or socially.

Playground fights, especially among boys, is a common scene in preschools.

Instrumental aggression, in contrast, is directed at achieving a particular goal—for example, threatening or hitting another child in order to obtain a toy or to gain peer approval. A study of sibling interactions found that instrumental aggression rose sharply between the ages of 1 and 2, just at the time when children typically begin to develop a distinctive sense of self and worry about "ownership rights" regarding their toys (Dunn, 1988).

Whether hostile or instrumental, children's aggressive behavior can take a variety of forms. And, as with other types of behaviors, the form of aggression may change as a consequence of the child's development. For example, as children develop cognitive and language skills, they become capable of teasing. Teasing is a subtle form of aggression requiring the ability to understand something about the mental states and desires of another—how destroying a favorite toy, or calling someone a name, may be hurtful. Until the age of about 18 months, teasing and physical aggression occur with equal frequency. But as children approach their 2nd birthday, teasing increases enormously, and they are much more likely to tease their siblings than to hurt them physically.

Many studies of childhood aggression from around the world have reported that boys are more aggressive than girls in a wide variety of circumstances (Segall et al., 1999). Boys are more likely than girls to hit, push, hurl insults, and threaten to beat up other children (Dodge, Cole, and Lynham, 2006). When asked to pretend about conflict situations that might happen to them in preschool (for instance, a peer's knocking over a block tower or refusing to share a toy), boys are more likely than girls to offer aggressive rather than positive solutions (Walker et al., 2002). This difference seems to emerge during the 2nd and 3rd years of life (Underwood, 2002). The same study that looked at affiliative behaviors in preschoolers (p. 307) also examined patterns of aggressive behavior like those shown in Table 9.4 (Blicharski, Bon, & Strayer, 2011). As you can see in Figure 9.5, the researchers found that aggressive behaviors in girls drop markedly as they approach their 2nd birthday, while overall aggression in boys increases. Consistent with our earlier discussion of *gender segregation,* while boys' aggression toward girls declines between the ages of 1 and 3, boys' aggression toward other boys increases dramatically (Blicharski, Bon, & Strayer, 2011). On the other hand, as we will discuss in detail in Chapter 13,

FIGURE 9.5 The physical aggression of girls toward both boys and other girls declines between 1 and 3 years of age. In contrast, although the physical aggression of boys toward girls decreases, the physical aggression of boys toward other boys increases dramatically between 1 and 3 years of age.

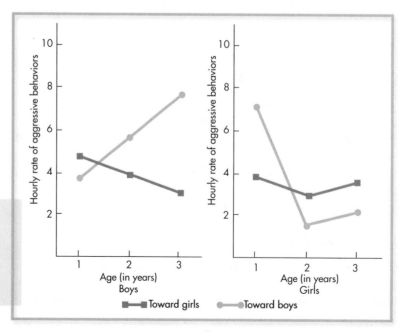

table **9.4**	
Categories of Aggressive Behavior Observed in Preschoolers	
Category	**Behavioral examples**
Attack	Hit, grab, bite, pull, push, kick
Threat	Pretend hit, pretend throw object, chase, postural/facial display
Competition	Grab object, object struggle, position struggle

Adapted from Blicharski, Bon, & Strayer, 2011.

preschool- and school-age girls are more likely than boys to engage in **relational aggression**, an indirect form of aggression intended to harm another child's friendships or exclude that child from the group (Ostrov & Crick, 2006).

What Causes and Controls Aggression?

Patterns of aggressive behavior often emerge during early childhood as personality becomes more defined. There is substantial evidence that 3-year-old children who behave defiantly and disobediently with adults, act aggressively toward their peers, and are impulsive and hyperactive are likely to still have these problems during middle childhood and adolescence (Campell et al., 2006). A number of longitudinal studies have found that, for boys in particular, the earlier the age at which children begin to exhibit such problem behaviors, the greater the likelihood that they will continue to behave in those ways later in life (Baillargeon et al., 2007). But what initiates these behaviors in young children? And how can such aggression be controlled? In studying aggression—both problematic patterns of aggressive behaviors and aggression more generally—developmentalists have tended to focus on one of three sets of factors: biological, social and cultural, or emotional and cognitive factors.

Biological Contributions Those who emphasize the role of biology in the development of aggression base their arguments on evolutionary factors (Ellis & Bjorklund, 2005). Noting that no group in the animal kingdom is free of aggression, many students of animal behavior have proposed that aggression is an important force in animal evolution (Lorenz, 1966). According to Darwin (1859/1958), individuals compete with each other for the resources necessary for survival and reproduction. Consequently, evolution favors individuals with more aggressive phenotypes. In many species, including our own, phenotypic characteristics such as territoriality, which ensures that a mating pair will have access to food, are believed to contribute to survival (Wilson, 1975). According to this interpretation, aggression is natural and necessary and appears automatically in the development of the young.

While aggression is widespread among animal species, so are mechanisms that limit it. The aggressive behavior in litters of puppies, for example, changes in accordance with a maturational timetable (James, 1951). At about 3 weeks, puppies begin to engage in rough-and-tumble play, mouthing and nipping one another. A week later, the play becomes rougher; the puppies growl and snarl when they bite, and the victims may yelp in pain. Once injurious attacks become really serious, however, a hierarchical social structure emerges, with some animals dominant and others subordinate. After such a dominance hierarchy is formed, the dominant puppy needs only to threaten in order to get its way; it has no need to attack. At this point, the frequency of fighting diminishes (Cairns, 1979). Throughout the animal kingdom one finds such hierarchies, which regulate interactions among members of the same species (Figure 9.6).

instrumental aggression Aggression that is directed at obtaining something.

relational aggression Indirect aggression intended to harm someone's friendships or exclude an individual from the group.

FIGURE 9.6 Many species of animals have innate behaviors for signaling defeat to allow the establishment of a social dominance hierarchy without bloodshed. One such behavior is reflected in the crouching posture of the wolf on the left.

The developmental history of aggression and its control among puppies is similar in some interesting ways to the development of aggression in human children. F. F. Strayer (1991) and his colleagues observed a close connection between aggression and the formation of dominance hierarchies among 3- and 4-year-olds in a nursery school. They identified a specific pattern of hostile interactions among children: When one child would behave aggressively, the other child would almost always submit by crying, running away, flinching, or seeking help from an adult. Dominance encounters like these led to an orderly pattern of social relationships within the group. Once children knew their position in such a hierarchy, they challenged only those whom it was safe for them to challenge and left others alone, thereby reducing the amount of aggression within the group. As you will see in Chapter 13 (p. 481), the formation of dominance hierarchies may explain the increase in bullying that is associated with children's transitions into the new social environment of middle school.

Social and Cultural Contributions

A second explanation for the causes of aggression, and for different levels of aggression, is that people learn to behave aggressively because aggression is sanctioned in their families, peer groups, or cultures. According to this perspective, children learn aggression because they observe aggressive behaviors in others and imitate it, or because they are in some way rewarded for behaving aggressively (Côté, 2009). For example, in studies of aggression in nursery school children, Gerald Patterson and his colleagues found that in well over 75 percent of the cases, aggressive acts were followed by positive consequences for the aggressor: The victim either gave in or retreated (Patterson et al., 1967). Likewise, parents of aggressive children have been found to reward their children's aggressive behaviors by paying more attention to them, laughing, or otherwise signaling approval (Dishion et al., 2006).

Cross-cultural studies have yielded evidence both that children model the aggressive behavior of adults and that societies differ markedly in the levels of interpersonal violence they consider normal (Segall et al., 1997; see also the box, "The Spanking Controversy"). For example, Douglas Fry (1988) compared the levels of aggression of young children in two Zapotec Indian towns in central Mexico. On the basis of anthropological reports, Fry chose one town that was notable for the degree to which violence was controlled and a second town that was notable for the fact that people often fought at public gatherings, husbands beat their wives, and adults punished children by beating them with sticks.

Fry and his wife established residences in both towns so that they could get to know the people and develop enough rapport to be able to make their observations unobtrusively. They then collected several hours of observations of 12 children in each town as they played in their houses and around the neighborhood. When the researchers compared the aggressive acts of the children in the two towns, they found that those in the town with a reputation for violent behavior performed twice as many violent acts as did the children in the other town.

Emotional and Cognitive Contributions

Another way to explore the development of aggression is to focus more particularly on how children feel and think about social situations that might provoke aggressive responses. Children's

The Spanking Controversy

"THIS IS GONNA HURT ME MORE than it hurts you."
—Prelude to a whuppin'

Two-year-old Mairin is starting to get the upper hand in her house—but not the kind of upper hand she had in mind. She throws her food across the kitchen, pitches tantrums when anyone touches "her" television, and recently got up and marched out the door when asked to sit still at the dinner table. So how is her mother responding? With a firm swat on the backside. "I know some people think it's awful," says her mother, "But how many of them have a 2-year-old?" (as reported by Costello, 2000).

A national survey in 2005 indicated that 72 percent of U.S. parents approve of spanking at least occasionally (Straus, 2009). In addition, although there has been a notable decrease in the rate of parental use of corporal punishment on children 12 years and older over the past few decades, the rate of decrease for younger children, especially toddlers, has been relatively minor. Further, in the face of international efforts to discourage spanking, several states have recently passed laws explicitly granting parents the right to spank their children. The right to spank, moreover, extends well beyond the home front. As of 2010, 20 states permitted the practice in public schools.

In addition to being one of the more common forms of discipline in the United States, spanking is also one of the most controversial. Most parents do not like to hit their children and resort to spanking only after other tactics, such as reasoning and time-outs, fail to produce the desired results. However, the argument made by those who oppose spanking is that it can damage children psychologically and emotionally. In fact, the practice has been outlawed in many European countries, where public opinion takes a much dimmer view of its effectiveness.

In the United States, most spanking is done by mothers, largely because they spend more time with their children than fathers do (Dietz,

Spanking is outlawed in many countries because it is thought to contribute to the development of aggression in children.

David Strickler/The Image Works

2000). The acceptability and frequency of spanking also varies by ethnicity, family income, and geographic region. Spanking is most commonly practiced in African American families (Straus, 2009). Researchers have speculated that African American parents may use spanking as a means of tightening their control over their children because they worry that highly active behavior in their children, particularly in boys, may draw negative attention from others who harbor racial stereotypes regarding aggression in African American youths. Spanking is also more common among low-income families and is most acceptible in southern regions of the United States (Straus, 2009).

Is spanking an effective form of discipline? This question is at the heart of developmental research on the effects of spanking, as well as of the advice given to parents by pediatricians and other child-care experts. In general, developmentalists discourage the practice. A host of studies link physical discipline to increased aggression and low self-esteem in children and adolescents (Simons & Wurtele, 2010; Baumrind, Larzelere, & Owens, 2010). For example, a large study of nearly 2,500 children found that 3-year-olds who are spanked frequently are at increased risk for high levels of aggressiveness as 5-year-olds (Taylor, Manganello, Lee, & Rice, 2010). In another study, Vonnie McLoyd and Julia Smith (2002) followed more than 2,000 children from three different ethnic groups over a period of 6 years and found that spanking predicted an increase in children's problem behaviors over time. In addition, abusive parents are known to spank their children more than nonabusive parents, prompting speculation that relying on spanking may increase parents' risk for using more severe forms of punishment (Walsh, 2002).

On the other hand, some studies suggest that physical discipline does not inevitably place children at risk for later problems. The consequences of spanking seem to depend on other dimensions of parenting that tend to be associated with spanking. For example, many parents who spank are also more emotionally rejecting and less involved with their children. In the study described above, McLoyd and Smith (2002) found that the negative effects of spanking are particularly pronounced when parents provide low levels of emotional support. However, when parents provide high levels of warmth and emotional support, the negative effects typically associated with spanking disappear. Similar results have been found in a sample of families in the Netherlands (Verhoeven, Junger, van Aken, Deković, & van Aken, 2010). Nevertheless, most research, as well as most professional opinion, suggests that parents should seek alternatives to spanking.

emotional reactions to events and their ability to regulate their emotional reactions depend to a great extent on how they interpret social contexts and on their ability to understand the emotions and intentions of others. It is known, for example, that aggressive children often misinterpret social interactions in negative ways—taking a joking remark as an intentional insult, or an accidental bump as a

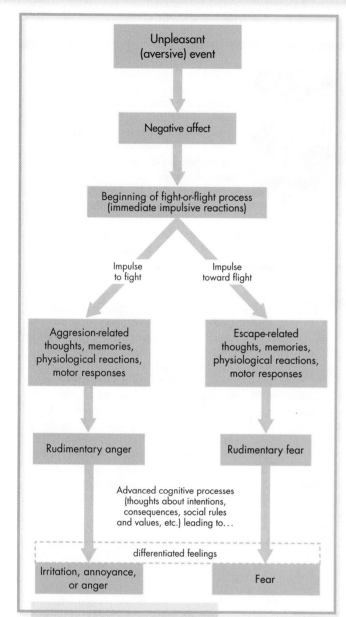

FIGURE 9.7 According to Len Berkowitz, aggression has its source in the negative feelings aroused by an unpleasant event, but these feelings can be significantly modified by cognitive processes.

challenge or threat—and retaliate aggressively (Coie & Dodge, 1998).

According to one view, aggression has its origins in the negative affect that arises in frustrating or otherwise unpleasant (aversive) situations (Berkowitz, 2003). These general negative feelings might come about when a child fails to achieve a goal, encounters a parent's disapproval, or is rejected by a peer. The negative feelings initiate a fight-or-flight process, an impulsive reaction to be aggressive or to withdraw. The impulse to fight is associated with aggression-related thoughts, memories, physiological reactions, and motor responses; the flight impulse has corresponding escape-related associations. In this way, the initial general negative feelings become the more specific emotions of rudimentary, or basic, anger (in the case of the fight impulse) or fear (in the case of the flight impulse). These rudimentary emotions can be significantly modified by cognitive processes, including the child's anticipation of consequences or thoughts about what he or she understands to be acceptable behavior. As a result, the child experiences more differentiated feelings— feelings different from and more complex than the rudimentary anger or fear—and the response of the child whose initial impulse was aggressive may or may not be aggression.

Suppose, for example, that a preschooler is playing with a toy and a playmate takes it away. According to the model shown in Figure 9.7, children in such a situation will experience negative feelings, and, depending on their temperament and past social experiences, may be inclined to act aggressively. However, if they have internalized the "no hitting" rule of the classroom and know that violating the rule carries the consequence of a time-out, they may, as a result of their thought processes, refrain from using physical confrontation to get the toy back and enlist the help of the teacher instead.

Developmentalists are building a strong case for the role of thought processes in children's aggressive behavior. A major influence on young children's aggressive tendencies is their understanding of their own and others' emotions, goals, and behaviors, and of how these are all linked together. The general argument is that children who have a more advanced understanding of emotions, including what causes them and how they are expressed, are less likely to behave aggressively (Halberstadt et al., 2001; Lemerise & Arsenio, 2000; Arsenio, 2006).

Susanne Denham and her colleagues (Denham et al., 2002) tested this argument in a longitudinal study that followed 127 children between preschool and kindergarten. To assess children's emotional knowledge, the researchers used puppets that had several attachable faces depicting different emotions. The procedure involved asking children questions about a puppet's emotions in a variety of circumstances— its basic emotions ("What does she look like when she's sad?"), its emotions in particular situations ("What does she look like when she's had a nightmare?"), and its emotions in social situations that require masking emotions ("What does she look like if she's getting teased, but if she shows she's upset, she'll get teased even more?"). The children responded by choosing and attaching a face to the puppet. Children's anger and aggressive behaviors were assessed through both naturalistic observation of their play and through teacher reports. In general, the researchers found that both boys and girls who, as preschoolers, had less advanced knowledge of emotions and their expression were, as kindergarteners, more likely to behave aggressively toward their peers.

Another study of preschoolers looked at how beliefs about aggression—specifically, the belief that aggression is an enduring trait rather than a changeable behavior—might contribute to children's use of aggression (Giles & Heyman, 2003). Jessica Giles and Gail Heyman argued that children who take an *essentialist* view of aggression—that is, believe that individuals who are aggressive in one situation will very likely be aggressive in the future—may be more likely to jump to conclusions about the hostile intention of a peer who behaves aggressively and, therefore, may be more likely to endorse the use of aggressive solutions.

To test preschoolers' essentialist beliefs about aggression, Giles and Heyman presented a group of 100 children with brief scenarios such as "Imagine there is a new girl in your class. She steals things from people, calls people mean names, and trips kids at recess. Do you think this new girl will always act this way?" Some children tended to believe that aggressiveness would endure over time, whereas others rejected this idea.

Children rely on adults to help them regulate the expression of emotions.

The children's endorsement of aggressive solutions was tested by presenting scenarios such as "Renee scribbled all over Belinda's art project. So Belinda hit Renee. What else could Belinda have done to solve the problem?" Some children said things such as "Well, she could kick her instead"; others, however, provided more socially appropriate solutions such as "She could tell the teacher." Consistent with their hypothesis, Giles and Heyman found that children who believed in aggressiveness as an enduring trait were more likely to endorse aggressive solutions.

Using testing methods such as those described above, developmentalists are amassing significant evidence that aggression must be understood in light of children's thoughts and beliefs about their own and others' emotional lives. This general idea suggests the possibility of controlling aggression by using reason. Though it is sometimes difficult to hold a rational discussion with a 4-year-old who has just grabbed a toy away from a playmate, discussions that emphasize how aggression hurts another person, and how conflicts can be resolved by sharing and taking turns, have been found to reduce aggression even at this early age (Erdley & Asher, 1999).

In contrast to employing cognitive strategies to help children select nonaggressive solutions, many people believe that aggression can best be controlled by providing children with harmless ways to be aggressive. This belief is based on the assumption that unless aggressive urges are "vented" in a safe way, they build up until they explode violently. There is little convincing evidence to support this belief (Bemak & Young, 1998). Nonetheless, the idea that venting releases negative emotions continues to be widely applied in psychotherapy with young, troubled children.

⏏ APPLY :: CONNECT :: DISCUSS

Based on evidence presented in this section, design an activity for preschoolers that might reduce their aggressive behavior.

prosocial behavior Behavior such as sharing, helping, caregiving, and showing compassion.

empathy Sharing another person's emotions and feelings.

Developing Prosocial Behaviors

David: I'm a missile robot who can shoot missiles out of my fingers. I can shoot them out of everywhere—even out of my legs. I'm a missile robot.
Josh: (in a teasing tone) No, you're a fart robot.
David: (defensively) No, I'm a missile robot.
Josh: No, you're a fart robot.
David: (hurt, almost in tears) No, Josh!
Josh: (recognizing that David is upset) And I'm a poo-poo robot.
David: (in good spirits again) I'm a pee-pee robot.

(From Rubin, 1980, p. 55)

As suggested in the dialogue above between two 4-year-olds, young children can be remarkably sensitive to the emotional needs of their playmates. Josh not only recognized his friend's distress at being teased but was able to remedy the situation by making similar deprecating remarks about himself. Such diplomacy becomes relatively common during early childhood as children acquire a number of sophisticated prosocial skills.

Prosocial behavior is defined as voluntary action intended to benefit others (Eisenberg et al., 2006). Sharing, helping, caregiving, and showing compassion are all examples of prosocial behaviors. Two psychological states—*empathy* and *sympathy*—correspond to prosocial behavior in the way that anger corresponds to aggression.

Empathy

Empathy, the sharing of another person's emotions and feelings, is widely believed to provide the essential foundations for prosocial behavior (Eisenberg, 2010). According to Martin Hoffman, a child can feel empathy for another person at any age. As children develop, however, their ability to empathize broadens and they become better able to interpret and respond appropriately to the distress of others.

Hoffman has proposed that empathy develops in four stages significantly linked to stages in the child's self-development. The first stage occurs during the 1st year of life. As we noted earlier, babies as young as 2 days old become stressed and cry at the sound of another infant's cries (Dondi, Simion, & Caltran, 1999). Hoffman calls this phenomenon *global empathy*. This early form of empathic crying is reflexive, since babies obviously can have no understanding of the feelings of others. Yet they respond as if they were having those feelings themselves.

During the 2nd year of life, as children develop a sense of themselves as distinct individuals, their responses to others' distress change, and *egocentric empathy* emerges. Now when babies are confronted by someone who is distressed, they are capable of understanding that it is the other person who is upset. This realization allows children to turn their attention from concern for their own comfort to comforting others. Since they have difficulty keeping other people's points of view in mind, however, some of their attempts to help may be inappropriate and *egocentric* (see p. 279), such as giving a security blanket to an adult who looks upset.

The third stage of empathy occurs in early childhood, when role-taking skills increase. Being able to distinguish one's own emotional needs from those of another allows the child to respond in a way that is less egocentric and more sensitive to the other. In addition, the growing command of

Sensitive to the needs of others, this girl from the Hazara ethnic group in Afghanistan provides care for her young sibling.

The increasing capacity to separate her own emotional state from that of others contributes to this preschooler's effectiveness in responding empathetically to her distressed friend.

language vastly increases the contexts in which children can behave empathically. Language allows children to empathize with people who are expressing their feelings verbally, without visible emotions, as well as with people who are not present. Information gained indirectly through stories, pictures, or television permits children to empathize with people whom they have never met. (The fourth stage of empathy emerges in middle childhood, when the child understands that emotional responses may be tied to an individual's unique history of past experiences.)

Note that Hoffman's theory of empathy is linked to Piaget's theory of cognitive development. Each new stage of empathy corresponds to a new stage of cognitive ability in which decreasing egocentrism and increasing *decentration* (see p. 279) allow children to understand themselves better in relation to others.

Perhaps because it is linked so closely to what children understand, Hoffman's explanation of the development of empathy tends to leave out their own personal feelings. It is tacitly assumed that the more children understand, the more intensely they adopt the feelings of the person in distress. The catch, as Judy Dunn (1988) has pointed out, is that children may understand perfectly well why another child is in distress and feel glad as a result.

Sympathy

Other researchers have been more attentive to the emotional component of empathy, particularly with regard to its role in prosocial behaviors. One of the best examples is found in the work of Nancy Eisenberg and her colleagues (Eisenberg et al., 2007). Like Hoffman, Eisenberg sees empathy as an emotional reaction that stems from, and is similar to, what is experienced by another. However, she proposes that empathy can turn into either sympathy or personal distress. **Sympathy** involves feelings of sorrow or concern for another person. A child who is being sympathetic is not feeling the same emotion as the other person. Instead, he or she feels "other-oriented concern." In contrast, **personal distress** is a self-focused emotional reaction in the face of another's distress.

Eisenberg argues that it is important to distinguish between sympathy and personal distress because they have entirely different consequences for prosocial behavior. For example, when shown films that depict characters who are distressed,

sympathy Feelings of sorrow or concern for another.

personal distress A self-focused emotional reaction to another person's distress.

children who exhibit concern or sadness are more likely to engage in prosocial behaviors than are children who exhibit personal distress (Eisenberg, Spinrad, & Sadovsky, 2006).

Personal distress, according to Eisenberg, stems from empathic overarousal in response to the negative emotions of another (Eisenberg, 2010). When another person's distress generates too much negative emotion in the child, the result is a focus on the self rather than the other-directed focus that underlies sympathy. Not surprisingly, personal distress is associated with poor social skills.

A deciding factor in whether the child's initial empathic response becomes personal distress or sympathy is the child's capacity to regulate his or her emotions. The relationship between emotional regulation and sympathy is illustrated in a series of studies involving 6- to 8-year-olds. The studies focused on three variables: (1) general emotional intensity—the children's personal tendencies to respond to another's distress with strong feelings; (2) emotional regulation—the ability to modulate their negative feelings; and (3) sympathy—the expression of concern for the other. The first study found that children who were rated low in regulation were also low in sympathy, regardless of their general emotional intensity (Eisenberg et al., 1996). However, for those children who could regulate their emotions, greater emotional intensity was associated with greater levels of sympathy.

The second study went one step further and examined how the ability to focus one's attention—another form of self-regulation—might enter into the picture (Eisenberg et al., 1998). The researchers argued that children who are more capable of focusing their attention may take in more information about other people and their circumstances, leading to increased perspective-taking and, by extension, greater sympathy. They found that children who were low in emotional intensity and attention-focusing were also low in sympathy. However, children who were low in emotional intensity but high in attention-focusing were relatively high in sympathy.

All of this suggests that sympathy results from an optimal level of emotional arousal but that an optimal level can be achieved by different routes. Children who are inclined to extreme emotional reactions need to be able to regulate their emotions in order to be sympathetic. For children who are not as emotional, the ability to focus attention on others may enhance their understanding of others' needs.

▲ APPLY :: CONNECT :: DISCUSS

From a Vygotskian perspective, what might account for whether children react to someone's distress with their own personal distress or with sympathy?

Taking One's Place in the Social Group

The kindergartners in Vivian Paley's classroom are discussing the story of Tico, a wingless bird who is cared for by his black-winged friends. In the story, the wishingbird visits Tico one night and grants him a wish. Tico wishes for golden wings. When his friends see his golden wings in the morning, they are angry. They abandon him because he wants to be better than they are. Tico is upset by his friends' rejection and wants to gain readmission to the group. He discovers that he can exchange his golden feathers for black ones by performing good deeds. When at last he has replaced all the golden feathers with black ones, he is granted readmission by the flock, whose members comment, "Now you are just like us" (Leoni, 1964).

> **Teacher:** I don't think it's fair that Tico has to give up his golden wings.
> **Lisa:** It is fair. See, he was nicer when he didn't have any wings. They didn't like him when he had gold.
> **Wally:** He thinks he's better if he has golden wings.
> **Eddie:** He is better.
> **Jill:** But he's not supposed to be better. The wishingbird was wrong to give him those wings.
> **Deana:** She has to give him his wish. He's the one who shouldn't have asked for golden wings.
> **Wally:** He could put black wings on top of the golden wings and try to trick them.
> **Deana:** They'd sneak up and see the gold. He should just give every bird one golden feather and keep one for himself.
> **Teacher:** Why can't he decide for himself what kind of wings he wants?
> **Wally:** He has to decide to have black wings.
>
> (Paley, 1981, pp. 25–26)

This conversation shows that the children understand that by wishing for golden wings, Tico has wished himself a vision of perfection. Each child has done the same thing countless times: "I'm the beautiful princess"; "I'm Superman; I'll save the world." For the blissful, magical moments when the world of play holds sway, perfection is attainable, even by a lowly bird or a preschool child. Wally and his friends also appreciate the dilemmas of perfection. In their eyes, Tico not only thinks he is better but is better—yet he is not supposed to be. Try as they may to conceive of a way for Tico to retain his prized possessions, the children realize that conformity is unavoidable. Wally's summary is difficult to improve upon: Tico has to choose to conform.

The children's discussion of Tico and his community of birds reveals more than an appreciation of the pressure of group norms as it is experienced by children everywhere. It also shows the children's awareness that individuals have a responsibility for regulating social relations. They understand that it is the wishingbird's job to grant wishes and therefore not the wishingbird's fault that Tico wished to be better than the others. Tico should have been able to control himself and make a reasonable wish.

This story returns us to the theme with which this chapter began—that socialization and personality development are two aspects of a single process. When children engage in acts of sharing and comforting, they reveal their ability to know another person's mental state. At the same time, they are displaying their own ways of thinking and feeling—in other words, their personalities.

Before we turn in Part IV to the wide range of new roles and rules that children encounter in middle childhood and the corresponding changes that take place in their sense of themselves, we need to round out the discussion of early childhood by investigating the range of contexts that make up the world of young children and structure their everyday experiences. As you will see in Chapter 10, the many different social influences and cultural prescriptions that children encounter in these contexts play a key role in the processes through which their personality and sense of personal and social identity develop.

This little girl's ability to understand her younger brother's mental state helps her draw him into the storybook, providing an opportunity for sharing a happy emotional experience.

SUMMARY

- Children's social and emotional lives develop along two paths—that of socialization, through which they acquire the standards, values, and knowledge of their society, and that of personality formation, through which they develop their own unique patterns of feeling, thinking, and behaving in a wide variety of situations.

Identity Development

- Crucial to socialization is identification, a psychological process in which children try to look, act, feel, and be like significant people in their social environment. Identification includes acquisition of sex-role and ethnic identities.

- Sex-role identity development has been explained in various ways:
  - In Freud's psychodynamic view, during the phallic stage, boys experience the Oedipus complex and girls experience the Electra complex, both of which are resolved by the child's identifying with the same-sex parent, at around the age of 4 or 5.
  - According to the social learning view, identification occurs through modeling, in which children observe and imitate people of their gender, and through differential reinforcement, in which they are rewarded for gender-appropriate behavior.
  - In Kohlberg's cognitive-developmental approach, sex-role development goes through three stages—labeling oneself as a boy or girl, understanding the stability of sex roles, and finally, understanding sex-role constancy—following which, sex-role identity guides thoughts and actions.
  - According to gender schema theory, children form mental models containing information about males and females that are used to process gender-relevant information, such as which types of toys, clothing, activities, and interests are "male" or "female."
  - In the cultural view, gender categories are tools of culture, mediating children's behavior by organizing their activities and the ways they relate to the environment as "boys" or "girls."

- Ethnic identity is the sense of belonging to an ethnic group and having the feelings and attitudes associated with being a member of that group. Young children show awareness of the status of their own ethnic group and those of others. Parents can communicate different sorts of ethnicity-related messages.

- Young children's personal identity, or sense of self, tends to be fluid and, as reflected in self-descriptions, focused on disconnected concrete attributes, which the children often see in an unrealistically positive light. Caregivers contribute to children's developing sense of self by helping them create an autobiographical memory, or personal narrative.

A New Moral World

- According to Freud's psychodynamic view, children's internalization of adult standards and rules results, at about age 5, in the formation of the superego, a third personality structure (along with the already existing id and ego). The superego functions within the child to regulate the child's behavior.

- The cognitive-developmental view held by Piaget maintains that, as part of broader cognitive developments, children's moral reasoning moves from a focus on external authority and objective consequences to, in middle childhood, a sense of morality as personally chosen.

- According to social domain theory, young children can distinguish among three categories of rules—moral rules, social conventions, and personal sphere rules. The boundaries between these categories vary across and within cultures.

Developing Self-Regulation

- The ability to control one's thoughts, behaviors, and emotions, referred to as self-regulation, is considered a cornerstone of children's development. Children must regulate myriad thoughts and actions to solve problems or achieve social goals.

- According to Vygotsky, play is important in the development of self-regulation, in part because it requires control of thoughts and actions. Sociodramatic play is particularly important in that children must negotiate a shared understanding of the evolving situation and control their thoughts and actions to enact their roles.

- To function socially, young children must learn to interpret the emotional states of others, manage their own emotions, and mask their feelings when necessary—all part of socioemotional competence, the ability to behave appropriately in social situations that evoke strong emotions.

- Cultures can influence the development of children's emotions and of their regulation of emotions.

Understanding Aggression

- Aggression can be categorized according to its purpose. Hostile aggression is intended to hurt someone in some way; instrumental aggression is intended to achieve a particular goal. Along with having different purposes, aggression can take different forms—for example, teasing and physical aggression.

- Boys' and girls' expression of aggression differs after age 2, with boys being more likely to use direct, physical aggression and girls being more likely to use relational aggression, a kind of indirect aggression aimed at excluding a child or harming the child's friendships.

- Developmentalists studying causes and control of aggression have focused on:
  - Biological contributions: Aggression is evident across animal species, a natural consequence of competition for resources. In groups of human children, as in other species, the development of dominance hierarchies can control aggression.
  - Social and cultural contributions: Children learn aggression through imitation of adults or by being rewarded for aggressive behaviors. Cross-cultural studies have found a correlation between levels of adult violence and children's aggressive behaviors.
  - Emotional and cognitive contributions: Negative feelings in frustrating situations may or may not lead to violence, depending on factors including the child's cognitions. Children who have a better understanding of emotions and their expression are less likely to behave aggressively.

Developing Prosocial Behaviors

- Prosocial behavior, or voluntary action intended to benefit others, may have as its foundation empathy, the sharing of another person's emotions and feelings. Development of empathy in early childhood may correspond to decreasing egocentrism.

- According to some developmentalists, empathic feelings may, depending on emotional regulation, become sympathy (feelings of sorrow or concern for another) or personal distress, with sympathy being more likely to lead to prosocial behavior.

Taking One's Place in the Social Group

- Young children are increasingly able to understand others' mental states and to be aware that individuals have a responsibility for regulating social relations. They also increasingly display their own ways of thinking and feeling.

Key Terms

socialization, p. 305

personality formation, p. 305

initiative versus guilt, p. 306

identification, p. 307

gender segregation, p. 307

phallic stage, p. 309

Oedipus complex, p. 309

Electra complex, p. 309

modeling, p. 310

differential reinforcement, p. 310

gender schema, p. 311

ethnic identity, p. 313

ethnic socialization, p. 314

personal identity, p. 316

autobiographical memory, p. 316

id, p. 318

ego, p. 318

superego, p. 318

heteronomous morality, p. 319

social domain theory, p. 319

self-regulation, p. 320

effortful control, p. 321

sociodramatic play, p. 323

display rules, p. 327

socioemotional competence, p. 328

hostile aggression, p. 329

instrumental aggression, p. 330

relational aggression, p. 331

prosocial behavior, p. 336

empathy, p. 336

sympathy, p. 337

personal distress, p. 337

10

Contexts of Development

Africa is the continent of drums. Formed from the wood of special trees and animal skins, drums are slapped or beaten with sticks to celebrate birth, mourn the dead, and coronate kings. When beaten with special skill and grace, the drums of the Republic of Burundi resemble rolling thunderclaps; they are to be heard "not with your ear, but your heart-beat." For 13-year-old Thierry, beating the drums with his friends, all orphans of Burundi's genocidal war, is a source of pride and honor. Thierry and his friends are among 823,000 war orphans, 20,000 of whom lead desperate lives on the streets. Although such a dire existence places children at considerable risk for a number of physical, emotional, and intellectual problems, the lives of Thierry and his friends have taken a decided turn for the better. They have been recruited to a special program sponsored by UNICEF, which provides war orphans, including former child soldiers, with homes, education, and life skills, while also promoting Burundi's cultural traditions, such as beating the sacred drums. The newfound hope of young Thierry and his friends was apparent when they met with an international peace delegation and explained how young people must avoid the mistakes of their elders and work together in beating the drums and rebuilding their country. Education, Thierry emphasized, is essential to Burundi's children, as well as to its future as a nation.

(Adapted from Ajia, 2007.)

The Family Context
The Biocultural Origins of Family
Parenting Practices
The Role of Siblings
Family Diversity
Distressed Families

Nonparental Child Care
Varieties of Child Care
Developmental Effects of Child Care

Neighborhoods and Communities
Community and Culture
Distressed Communities

Media Contexts
Print Media
Television
Interactive Media

Contexts, Risk, and Resilience

t is hard to imagine what it might be like growing up on the street in Burundi, where "family" may be nothing more than a few other child associates with whom you steal food; where "education" involves learning how to avoid being captured by soldiers who would force you to fight in a war you do not understand; where "neighborhood" is a territory scarred by burned and abandoned buildings; and where "government"—including the policies and programs meant to provide a safety net in times of strife—has been brought to its knees by years of civil war. The importance of these contexts for children's health and well-being is recognized by developmental scientists and practitioners, and inspires the efforts of international organizations such as UNICEF to help children like Thierry by repairing the damaged contexts of their lives and development, or by creating new ones.

Families, neighborhoods, schools, governments, the media—these and other settings constitute the contexts of children's development. As we shift our attention to these contexts, it is helpful to remember Urie Bronfenbrenner's idea that children's development occurs within nested, interacting ecosystems (see Figure 1.5, p. 28). The innermost system is the *microsystem*, which includes the various settings children experience directly in their daily lives, such as the home, the church, the neighborhood, and the child-care center. The *mesosystem* comprises connections among these microsystem settings; for example, parents' involvement with their children's school. Elements of the *exosystem*, such as caregivers' workplaces, government agencies, and mass media, may influence children either

These Burundi children, displaced by genocidal violence, engage in the traditional practice of beating drums.

directly, as television does, or indirectly, through their impact on parents and other family members. The outermost *macrosystem* includes cultural values and beliefs that infuse the entire ecology, affecting everything from the content of television, to educational programs and health-care policies, to beliefs parents have about how to raise their children.

Our discussion of the major contexts of children's development begins with the more immediate and personal contexts of *family* and *child care*. We then move to consider the broader contexts of *neighborhoods and communities* before discussing what may be the broadest context that directly influences children—the *media*. As you read this chapter, you will come to appreciate how each context can provide children with resources for positive growth and development, or present significant challenges and risks to their health and well-being.

The Family Context

According to an ancient Latin proverb, "the hand that rocks the cradle rules the world." Although each child's development is shaped by many hands—teachers, coaches, and playmates and other peers—the hand of the family is the first influence on the child and remains one of the most significant. Through their traditions, routines, stories, and cultural artifacts, families communicate their perceptions and values about the world to their children, and shape their children's behavior and how they relate to the world (Pratt & Fiese, 2004).

A classic study by Beatrice and John Whiting (1975) illustrates how differences in family life influence children's development. The Whitings organized teams of anthropologists to observe child-rearing in six communities from vastly different cultures. A comparison of two of the groups, the Gusii of Nyansongo, Kenya, and Americans in a small New England town, demonstrates how cultural belief systems, practices, and economics are expressed in family contexts, affecting the way parents treat and socialize their children.

In many cultures, children care for younger children. This responsibility requires both nurturance and control.

At the time of the Whitings' work, the 1950s, the Gusii were agriculturalists living in the fertile highlands of western Kenya. The basic family unit was large, commonly including three generations headed by a grandfather. Polygyny was the traditional marriage form, with several wives living in a compound that included a separate house for the husband. Women, who did most of the farm work, often left their infants and toddlers in the care of older siblings and elderly family members. As is typical of farming societies, children's labor was important in the production of food, in the care of younger children, and in household maintenance. Beginning at the age of 3 or 4, Gusii children were expected to start helping their mothers with simple domestic tasks. By the age of 7, their economic contributions to the family were indispensable.

The small New England town, referred to as "Orchard Town" by the researchers, represented the opposite extreme in family organization and social complexity. Most of the men of Orchard Town were wage earners who lived with their wives and children in single-family dwellings. A few of the mothers had part-time jobs, but most were full-time homemakers. The children of Orchard Town divided their time between playing at home (they were rarely asked to do chores) and attending school.

The Whitings' observations of children's behavior patterns in these two cultures documented notable overall differences. The Gusii children, for example, were more likely to offer help and support and to make responsible suggestions to others. At the same time, they were more likely to aggressively reprimand other children. Both of these tendencies were consistent with their child-tending duties: They needed to be nurturing and responsible, but they also needed to exert high levels of control both for safety's sake and to communicate the cultural value of respecting one's elders.

Orchard Town children, in contrast, were more often observed seeking, rather than giving, help and attention, and were more often observed engaging in sociable horseplay, touching others, and joining groups in an amiable way. According to the Whitings, children of industrialized societies, such as those in Orchard Town, are less nurturing and responsible because they do not contribute economically to the family, and because they spend most days in school competing with other children rather than helping them. On the other hand, the higher level of intimacy shown by the Orchard Town children is likely a reflection of the close bonds that develop between individuals living in small families. Gusii, in contrast, socialize attachments to the broader group, consistent with a family living pattern that includes many members from several generations.

The Biocultural Origins of Family

Cultural comparisons like the one conducted by the Whitings show that families can differ in many ways that affect children's lives and development. Take a moment to think about your own family. Were you raised by one parent, or two, or even three, or perhaps by a grandparent? Do you have brothers and sisters? Half-siblings or step-siblings? Did other people or relatives live with you while you were growing up? An important feature that defines your family is the members it includes and their relationships to you and each other. Developmentalists use the term **family structure** to refer to how a family is organized socially. There are two major forms of family structure—**nuclear families**, which consist of parents (including single parents) and their children, and **extended families**, which consist of parents (again including single parents) and their children as well as other kin, who may include grandparents, cousins,

family structure The social organization of a family. Most commonly, the structure is nuclear or extended.

nuclear families Families consisting of parents (including single parents) and their children.

extended families Families in which not only parents and their children but other kin—grandparents, cousins, nieces and nephews, or more distant family relations—share a household.

This extended family from a remote Bhutan village in the Himalaya mountains gathers in the prayer room of their earthen house, around the food they will prepare and eat over the course of a week.

aunts, uncles, and others. Why are some families nuclear, while others are extended? And what difference does family organization make in the lives and development of children? As you will see below, answers to these questions hinge on the cultural and evolutionary processes that influence how families are socially organized.

Family and Culture A major source for understanding the origins and significance of family is the historical work of Philippe Ariès (1962). According to Ariès, the nuclear family is a highly private structure unique to modern societies. Especially in the late eighteenth and early nineteenth centuries, large migrations from rural areas into newly industrialized cities contributed to a shift from extended-family farm life to nuclear-family patterns. In the relative isolation of nuclear families, close, intimate relationships between parents and children took on greater importance than the less personal relationships that are central to the extended-family pattern and bind children to their ancestral line. The greater isolation of nuclear families had other repercussions for children's lives. For example, Ariès contrasts the private nuclear family with the more sociable families of premodern times, in which "people lived on top of one another, masters and servants, children and adults, in houses open at all hours." Children reared in these conditions were exposed to an enormous diversity of roles, relationships, and patterns of interacting—experiences quite different from those of children growing up in nuclear families.

Despite the predominance of the nuclear-family structure in the United States, the proportion of extended families has been steadily increasing in recent decades. According to a recent national study, approximately 12 percent of all U.S. children live in extended families (Taylor et al., 2010; see Figure 10.1). This arrangement is more common when families are experiencing economic stress, when the mother is young and single, or when cultural traditions and values are consistent with extended-family living arrangements, as they are among those of Asian or Hispanic descent and African Americans (Goodman & Satya, 2007; Taylor et al., 2010; see Figure 10.2). A strong grandparenting tradition is also apparent in African American families, in which grandmothers have been esteemed as the "guardian of the generations" (Crewe, 2003; Goodman & Silverstein, 2006).

Many scholars see the extended family as a natural strategy for dealing with the combined handicaps of low income and low social standing (Goodman & Silverstein, 2006). Young, economically disadvantaged minority children are particularly likely to benefit from the problem-solving and stress-reducing resources provided by the extended family (Smith, 2002). Moreover, for children living in a single-parent nuclear family, grandparents and other members of the extended family often appear to be an important source of support. Indeed, a nationwide study conducted in Sweden found that in the absence of help from extended family members, children in single-parent homes are at heightened risk for injury and death (Weitoft et al., 2003). Interestingly, recent studies of hunter–gatherer societies in the Amazon forest of Peru and in Tanzania found that children with only one biological parent were more likely to live with extended family than those with two parents (Sugiyama & Chacon, 2005; Marlowe, 2005).

Family and Evolution Extended kin make a difference in the lives of children because they provide essential *resources,* including food, income, child care, and help in maintaining the household, as well as less tangible assistance in the form

FIGURE 10.1 The number of people in the United States who live in extended families has grown dramatically over the past three decades. Today, approximately 12 percent of all children in the United States live in multi-generational family homes. (Adapted from Taylor et al., 2010.)

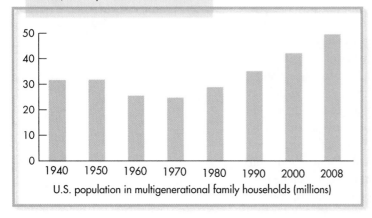

U.S. population in multigenerational family households (millions)

FIGURE 10.2 In the United States, Asians, Blacks, and Hispanics are much more likely than Whites to live in extended families. (Adapted from Taylor et al., 2010.)

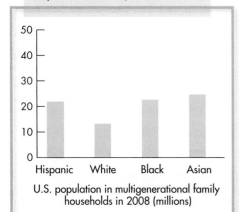

U.S. population in multigenerational family households in 2008 (millions)

of emotional support and counseling, and in some cultures, opportunities for the mother to improve the family's economic situation by furthering her education (Jarrett, 2000). Such significant contributions to child and family well-being have been recognized by anthropologists and evolutionary theorists who study **allocare-giving**, that is, child care and protection provided by group members other than the parents (Hewlitt & Lamb, 2005; Kruger & Konner, 2010). Allocaregivers may include a child's siblings, uncles, aunts, and grandmothers, as well as non-kin such as foster children who live within the group. Several studies of highly diverse cultures have found that the presence of allocaregivers increases the likelihood that mothers will have more children (see Hrdy, 2009, for review). Some of these studies have shown the advantages of having a grandmother living with the family; others have pointed to the importance of having a big sister. For example, in villages in Micronesia, the Caribbean, and Gambia, West Africa, it has been found that women whose firstborn child is a daughter tend to have more births, and more *surviving* children, than do women whose firstborn is a son.

Evidence that allocaregiving increases mothers' reproductive success has also been documented in nonhuman species. In addition to humans, many species of birds, as well as wild dogs, lions, and elephants, form networks of support in which nonparental individuals contribute resources toward rearing the young—that is, networks of allocaregivers—a practice referred to as **cooperative breeding** (Heinsohn & Double, 2004; Kaptijn, Thomese, Van Tilburg, & Liefbroer, 2010). Cooperative breeding is rather rare in the animal kingdom (estimates are that 8 to 17 percent of bird species, and only 3 percent of mammalian species, breed cooperatively). However, when it occurs, it results not only in more numerous births and larger, healthier offspring but also in prolonged periods of childhood dependency, since offspring can take longer to mature without becoming too burdensome to their mothers, who are busy producing new offspring (Hrdy, 2009; McDonald et al., 2008).

With respect to our own species, evidence regarding the effects of cooperative breeding has ignited a fascinating controversy about why human offspring take so long to mature. According to the traditional view, an extended childhood evolved in our species because it provides the time necessary for the maturation of large, complex brains and the development of cognitive, symbolic, and linguistic skills, as well as other tools of culture, that are important to children's survival and success. In Darwinian terms, *natural selection* assures that individuals with *phenotypically* large and complex brains, and the spectacular cognitive, social, and linguistic skills that go along with them, are more likely to reproduce than are individuals with less complex brains (presumably due to shorter childhoods; see Chapter 2, pp. 58–59). From this perspective, delayed maturation is a by-product of brain evolution; we have long childhoods because we grow big brains. Evolutionary theorists who study cooperative breeding, however, have turned this perspective on its head, arguing that we grow big brains because we have long childhoods, and we have long childhoods because we have families. More specifically, the lengthy childhood enabled by the resources of extended family networks opened the door that allowed brain evolution to occur.

Parenting Practices

Regardless of who raised you, or how, there can be little doubt that the caregiving you received growing up has had a powerful impact on who you are today. As you will see in the next section, virtually all people who raise children share a common set of goals. Efforts to reach these goals, however, vary considerably depending on the family's ecological context, cultural values, and beliefs about how children should behave.

From bandaging toes and braiding hair to providing educational resources that allow his daughter to read a letter, the parenting practices of this father will profoundly affect the development of his offspring.

allocaregiving Child care and protection provided by group members other than the parents, usually other relatives.

cooperative breeding In humans and certain other species, a system involving networks of support in which individuals other than parents contribute resources toward rearing the young.

Parenting Goals On the basis of his study of child-rearing practices in diverse cultures, the anthropologist Robert LeVine (1988) has proposed that three major goals are shared by parents the world over:

1. *The survival goal:* To ensure that their children survive, by providing for their health and safety.

2. *The economic goal:* To ensure that their children acquire the skills and other resources needed to be economically productive adults.

3. *The cultural goal:* To ensure that their children acquire the basic cultural values of the group.

These goals form a hierarchy. The most urgent goal for parents is their children's physical survival. It is not until the safety and health of their children appear secure that parents can focus on the other two goals, passing on the economically important skills and cultural values the children will need as adults to ensure the continued existence of their family and community.

LeVine found that the way parents raise their children reflects the extent to which any of these goals is threatened by the local ecology. For example, child-care practices in places with high infant-mortality rates look fairly uniform throughout the world. In places as different as Africa, South America, and Indonesia, when there is a general threat to children's physical survival, parents tend to keep their infants on their bodies at all times, respond quickly to infants' cries, and nurse their babies often. Under such threat conditions, parents show little concern for the emotional and behavioral development of their infants and young children, rarely attempting, for instance, to elicit smiles from their babies or engage them in vocal play. In contrast, in places where children's physical survival is more or less guaranteed, parents are more likely to focus on ensuring their children's future economic success. In industrialized societies, for example, where education is crucial to earning a living wage, many child-care practices are oriented toward enhancing cognitive development and supporting "school readiness" and children's achievement in the classroom. Indeed, as you may recall from Chapter 5, this trend in the United States has led to the development of a highly profitable industry devoted to toys and games that supposedly foster intellectual development in infants and young children.

Thus, LeVine's research contributes to understanding both the universality of parental goals and the diversity of parenting practices observed throughout the world. For example, it gives insight into the "no-nonsense parenting" often practiced by African American single mothers (Brody & Murry, 2001; Steele et al., 2005). **No-nonsense parenting** is characterized by a mixture of high parental control, including physical restraint and punishment, and warm affection. Developmentalists who study no-nonsense parenting in African American families find that it is used more frequently by mothers who live in urban areas than by those in rural areas, and by mothers who are better educated. This pattern is consistent with LeVine's conclusions, which would suggest that no-nonsense parenting, with its mix of control and warmth, is a protective response to the threats—social as well as physical—that urban life poses for children, especially in inner cities. Similarly, better-educated mothers may have higher aspirations for their children and consequently exert high levels of control over their behavior to see that they do what is needed to succeed.

Parenting Styles Research in the United States has shown that while child-rearing practices vary widely, they can be analyzed using measures of parental warmth and control. This research addresses the question: What mix of control, autonomy, and expression of affection contributes most to healthy development?

no-nonsense parenting Parenting characterized by a mix of high parental control—including punishment—and warmth, and associated especially with African American single mothers.

authoritative parenting pattern Parenting style identified by Baumrind in which parents set standards and limits for children but also encourage discussion and independence, and express warmth.

authoritarian parenting pattern Parenting style identified by Baumrind that focuses on enforcing obedience and conformity to traditional standards, including by use of punishment, and that is lacking in verbal give-and-take with children and in expressions of warmth.

permissive parenting pattern Parenting style identified by Baumrind in which parents express warmth but do not exercise control over their children's behavior.

In the early 1970s, Diana Baumrind (1971, 1980) launched what would become one of the best-known research programs on the developmental consequences of *parenting styles*. On the basis of interviews and observations of predominantly White, middle-class preschoolers and their parents, Baumrind and her colleagues found that parenting behaviors in 77 percent of their families fit one of three patterns— *authoritative, authoritarian,* and *permissive*. Baumrind also found that each parenting pattern tended to be associated with a different pattern of children's behavior in preschool (see Table 10.1).

This mother disciplines her son by attempting to explain why his behavior was wrong.

- **Authoritative parenting pattern**: Parents who follow an authoritative pattern set high standards for their children's behavior and expect them to respect established limits, but they also recognize that their children have needs and rights. They tend to be warm and also responsive, willing to consider their children's point of view, even if they do not always accept it. Authoritative parents are less likely than authoritarian parents to use physical punishment and less likely to stress obedience to authority as a virtue in itself. Instead, these parents attempt to control their children by explaining the basis for their rules or decisions and by reasoning with them. Authoritative parents encourage their children to be independent but socially responsible.

  Children of authoritative parents appear more self-reliant, self-controlled, and willing to explore than do children raised by permissive or authoritarian parents. Baumrind believes that this difference is a result of the fact that authoritative parents explain the standards and limits they set for their children, and when they punish them, they make clear why. Such explanations improve children's understanding and acceptance of social rules.

Authoritarian parents emphasize obedience and tend to favor punitive measures in response to misbehaviors.

- **Authoritarian parenting pattern**: Parents who follow an authoritarian parenting pattern try to shape, control, and evaluate the behavior and attitudes of their children according to a set traditional standard. They stress the importance of obedience to authority and discourage their children from engaging them in verbal give-and-take. Comparatively lacking in the expression of warmth and responsiveness, they tend to favor punitive measures to curb their children's behavior whenever it conflicts with what they believe to be correct.

  Children of authoritarian parents tend to lack social competence in dealing with other children. They frequently withdraw from social contact and rarely initiate social interaction. In situations of moral conflict, they tend to look to outside authority to decide what is right. These children are often characterized as lacking spontaneity and intellectual curiosity.

- **Permissive parenting pattern**: Parents who exhibit a permissive pattern exercise less explicit control over their children's behavior than do authoritarian and authoritative parents, either because they believe children must learn how to behave through their own experience (*permissive parenting*) or because they do not take the trouble to provide discipline (*neglectful parenting*). They give their children a lot of leeway to determine their own schedules and activities and often consult them about family policies. Although they tend to be warm, these parents do not demand the same levels of achievement and mature behavior from their children that either authoritative or authoritarian parents demand from theirs.

  Children of permissive parents tend to be relatively immature; they have difficulty controlling their impulses, accepting responsibility for social actions, and acting independently.

table 10.1		
Baumrind's Parenting Styles		
Parenting Style	**Description**	**Typical Children's Characteristics**
Authoritative	• Demanding but reciprocal relationship • Favor reasoning over physical punishment • Encourage independence	• Self-reliant • Self-controlled • Display curiosity • Content
Authoritarian	• Demanding and controlling • Favor punitive methods over reasoning • Stress obedience over independence	• Other-directed • Lack social competence • Lack curiosity • Withdrawn
Permissive	• Undemanding and little control exercised • Allow children to learn through experience as a result of indulgence or neglect • Neither independence nor obedience stressed	• Dependent on others • Poor impulse control • Relative immaturity

Baumrind's pioneering work inspired hundreds of studies on how parenting practices affect children's development. In more recent research, however, developmentalists have attempted to view patterns of parenting from a broader, more dynamic perspective. Some developmentalists have examined how children's behavior may elicit different styles of parenting (Caspi, 1998; Collins, 2005; Maccoby, 2007). A particularly active and easily frustrated child, for instance, may elicit an authoritarian style from a parent, whereas an easygoing or timid child might elicit an authoritative style from that same parent. Similarly, parents may change their style over time in response to developmental changes in their child's behavior. For example, as their children move out of the "terrible twos" and are better able to understand and comply with their parents' verbal directives, some parents may become less controlling and physically coercive.

A broader, more dynamic approach to parenting styles is also apparent in research focused on the cultural contexts of parenting practices. A team of researchers headed by Heidi Keller compared parenting styles in two countries with very different cultural beliefs and values—Germany and India (Keller et al., 2010). German culture cherishes independence, personal freedom, and autonomy; India embraces the interdependence of family and social connections and relationships. The researchers studied mother–child interactions when the babies were 3 months old, and then again when they were 19 months old. The researchers found significant cultural differences in the mothers' parenting goals, as well as in how they talked to and played with their babies. To a greater extent than German mothers, Indian mothers emphasized the importance of learning self-control and talked more often to their babies about other people's feelings and needs and the social consequences of their actions. German mothers, in contrast, tended to emphasize the importance of developing self-confidence and talked more about their babies' own internal states and personal needs. These differences were apparent when the babies were both 3 and 19 months of age. Cultural differences in parenting styles have been identified in other cultures as well, including in China (Wu et al., 2002).

The Role of Siblings

Our friend Laureen is the oldest of three siblings. Reflecting on her experiences growing up with two younger brothers, she remembers a lot of fighting (but does not remember what was being fought about), babysitting (when she would rather have gone out with her friends), and sticking up for her brothers when they got into trouble with peers or parents (which was often). In her words, "it was fine for *me* to push them around, but everyone else had better keep their hands off my little brothers!" Laureen also vividly remembers when her brothers overtook her in physical size and strength. "After that, my power as the 'big sister' was entirely psychological." Despite the fact that all three of them are now in their 50s and fairly good friends, Laureen still considers herself the big sister. Her relationships with her brothers, which have existed longer than any other relationships in her life, still bear the mark of their early experiences.

Studies indicate that, across cultures, siblings are influential in one another's development (Carpendale & Lewis, 2004; Whiteman, McHale, & Crouter, 2007). The socializing role of siblings is most obvious in agricultural societies, like the Gusii, discussed earlier in the chapter, in which much of the child care is performed by older siblings. It is through these child caregivers, who are sometimes no more than 4 years older than their charges, that many of the behaviors and beliefs of the social group are passed on (Zukow-Goldring, 1995). In many industrialized societies, including the United States, the role of siblings as socializers has become more prominent in recent years. With more mothers working, more children are being called upon to provide care for their younger siblings (McHale & Crouter, 1996). Within African American families, reliance on siblings for child care and socialization is commonplace, perhaps a reflection of African family traditions (Brody & Murry, 2001).

As suggested by Laureen, sibling relationships are often ambivalent, sometimes loving and supportive, sometimes hostile and competitive. Indeed, siblings provide children with opportunities to learn about sharing and trust, as well as about conflict and negotiation. The degree of intimacy and conflict in sibling relationships depends on a variety of factors, including the sex and age of the children. In a longitudinal study of U.S. siblings between 9 and 20 years of age, there appeared to be higher levels of intimacy between sisters than between brothers or between brothers and sisters (Kim et al., 2007). In addition, whereas the intimacy of same-sex sibling pairs remained fairly stable over time, that of mixed-sex pairs declined during middle childhood, perhaps as a consequence of *gender segregation* (see Chapter 9, p. 307), and then increased in mid-adolescence, when siblings may turn to each other for advice and support on matters of peer and dating relationships (Figure 10.3).

Overall, and as Laureen recalls, sibling conflict declines throughout adolescence (Figure 10.4). One factor that reliably affects the siblings' relationship is the emotional climate of their family (Brody, 1998; Modry-Mandell, Gamble, & Taylor, 2007). Siblings are more likely to fight when their parents are not getting along well together, when their parents divorce, and when a stepfather enters the family, especially if one or both of the siblings are boys (Hetherington, 1988).

Hugh Sitton / Corbis

Of all the relationships an individual may ever have, those with siblings may be the longest lasting. Developmentalists are just beginning to understand the complexity of these relationships and how they are affected by the ages and gender mix of the sibling pair.

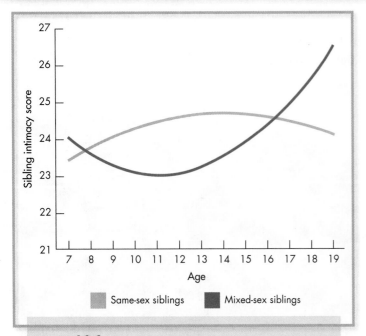

FIGURE 10.3 Intimacy between siblings varies depending on the age and gender mix of the sibling pair. Intimacy of same-sex sibling pairs is fairly constant over time, whereas the intimacy of mixed-sex pairs declines during middle childhood, then increases throughout adolescence and early adulthood. (Adapted from Kim et al., 2006, p. 1753.)

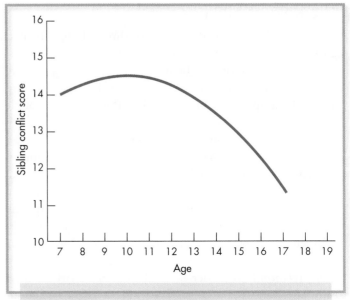

FIGURE 10.4 Conflicts between siblings peak during middle childhood and decline throughout adolescence. (Adapted from Kim et al., 2006, p. 1753.)

Sibling intimacy and conflict have been associated with children's mental health and adjustment. In general, warmth and intimacy in sibling relationships tend to be associated with emotional understanding and sharing in later childhood (Howe et al., 2001). In contrast, negative sibling relationships are associated with later adjustment problems (Waldinger, Vaillant, & Orav, 2007). An interesting case in point is a study that examined the relationship between adjustment to war-related trauma and sibling relationships in a group of Palestinian schoolchildren in the Gaza Strip (Peltonen, Qouta, El Sarraj, & Punamäki, 2010). Palestinian boys and girls aged 10 to 14 years were asked to report their exposure to war-related trauma (such as the shelling of their home, being wounded, or losing a family member) and were assessed for depression and psychological distress. Relationships with their siblings were also analyzed, including their degree of intimacy, conflict, and rivalry. Specifically, the children used a 5-point scale to indicate how well specific sentences applied to their own sibling relationships. Some of the sentences that the children were asked to rate on a scale ranging from 1 ("not at all") to 5 ("very well") were:

- "We usually laugh and joke together."

- "I usually tell him/her about my secrets."

- "He/she annoys and teases me."

- "I feel jealous of him/her when he/she takes all of my mother's attention."

The researchers found that children who witnessed or were themselves the target of military violence had higher levels of sibling rivalry than children exposed to lower levels of trauma. As the researchers point out, increased sibling rivalry under life-threatening conditions makes sense from an evolutionary perspective in which siblings may be competing for limited parental attention and resources. On the other hand, the researchers also found that higher levels of sibling intimacy appeared to provide some protection against depression and psychological distress in children exposed to the traumatizing conditions of war (see Figure 10.5; see also p. 381 for a discussion of "protective factors").

While most studies of siblings have focused on emotional factors such as intimacy and conflict, researchers have also examined cognitive dimensions of sibling relationships, including the ways that the sibling relationship may provide a context for teaching and learning (Strauss & Ziv, 2004). When Margarita Azmitia and Joanne Hesser (1993) had young children play with building blocks while their older sibling and an older friend, both of whom were approximately 9 years old, played with blocks nearby, the younger children spent more time imitating and consulting with their sibling than with the friend. Their older sibling, in turn, offered more spontaneous help than did the friend. When the older sibling and the friend were asked to help the younger sibling build a copy of a model out of blocks, the older sibling again provided more explanations and encouragement. Others studies find that older siblings are particularly helpful (provide more demonstrations and feedback) as tasks become more difficult or when siblings are significantly younger (Howe, Brody, & Recchia, 2006). These findings suggest that close relationships encourage individuals to create a *zone of proximal development*, which, according to Lev Vygotsky, is key to the acquisition of new knowledge (see Chapter 1, pp. 22–23).

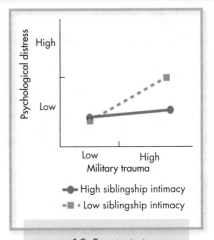

FIGURE 10.5 A high degree of intimacy with a sibling may protect children from the psychological distress associated with exposure to military violence. (Adapted from Peltonen, Qouta, El Sarraj, & Punamäki, 2010.)

Family Diversity

Changes in values, politics, economies, and transportation technologies have altered the face of "family" in many parts of the globe, bringing to it a wide diversity of ethnic backgrounds, cultural heritages, and lifestyles. As immigrant populations swell across the globe, family ethnicity has become a special focus of developmentalists' attention. Likewise, research on families with single parents or sexual-minority parents has increased in recent years, owing to ever-growing numbers of single parents and of gay and lesbian couples raising children. Another area of growing research attention is the role of fathers in children's development, a role that, until fairly recently, had largely been relegated to the back-burner of scientific inquiry (see the box, "Fathers").

Immigrant Families

When I was in Korea, I did everything for my kids. But, since I came here [to the United States], I had to completely change my parenting style; I make my kids take care of themselves. Well, when I was in Korea, I was not working, and I enjoyed my life. But, here in America, I have to do lots of physical work. It is very hard because my husband and I are not used to doing this kind of labor [running a discount store]. My husband had a white-collar job [CPA] in Korea, so his doing this kind of labor is very hard for him as well. I can do very little for my kids. So, I asked them to do what they need. My daughter cooks for us, and we eat the food that she made. Sometimes, she cooks special food for us, and she is taking care of her little brother very well. She prepares food for him, and she does whatever he asks. . . . She also comes to our shop on every Saturday and during the summer and winter breaks. She works at our shop. While she was in Korea, she was like a princess. She did not do anything that she does now before, but now she is different. (Kim, Conway-Turner, Sherif-Trask, & Wolfolk, 2006, p. 51)

In 2005, 191 million people (3 percent of the world population) lived outside their country of birth (United Nations Department of Economic and Social

Fathers

IN "FATHER OF MINE," EVERCLEAR SINGS of desertion, when the whole world disappeared because "Father of mine . . . gave me a name . . . then he walked away." In "Dance with My Father," Luther Vandross describes a different childhood, one colored by an image of his father lifting him high, dancing with his mother and him, spinning him around until he fell asleep: "Then up the stairs he would carry me, and I knew for sure I was loved."

Whether of loss and pain, or love and security, the lyrics by Everclear and Vandross capture the importance of fathers in the lives of their children. Nonetheless, research on fathers and fathering is just beginning to make a significant mark in the developmental sciences (McKinney & Renk, 2008). Part of the recent interest in fathers may be due to evidence of their increasing involvement in bringing up their children. In the past 30 or 40 years, as more mothers have gone to work, fathers have provided more direct child care. There has also been a sharp rise in the number of children being raised by single fathers. In the United States, 2.5 million children were living in father-only households in 2010—a sharp contrast to the 745,000 children being raised by single fathers in 1970 (U.S. Bureau of the Census, 2011). Even in two-parent families in which the mother does not work, today's fathers appear to be interacting with their children in a way that distinguishes them from fathers of the past. Rather than being regarded primarily as the "breadwinner," the "new father" is expected to provide daily physical care, be emotionally connected to his children, and be more attuned to their

This father and son are clearly enjoying each other's company. Research is increasingly focusing on the role fathers play in children's development.

experiences and concerns than in the past (Yeung et al., 2001).

Indeed, one of the most significant new developments in research on fathers is an expanded notion of paternal involvement (Dufur, Howell, Downey, Ainsworth, & Lapray, 2010). Instead of focusing simply on the amount of time that fathers spend with their children, contemporary researchers are looking in detail at the different types of activities in which they engage. It seems, in fact, that the sheer amount of time that fathers devote to their children is less important to children's well-being than how that time is spent. For

example, going out together to dinner or to the movies is unrelated to children's levels of life satisfaction, whereas talking over problems and sharing and encouraging accomplishments are associated with high levels of satisfaction (Young et al., 1995). In general, fathering practices typically associated with authoritative parenting—providing emotional support, monitoring children's behaviors, and using noncoercive discipline—seem to be most beneficial to children (Marsiglio et al., 2000; Simons & Conger, 2007). Other research demonstrates that the influence of fathers extends well beyond the quality of their interactions with children. Fathers who know their children's friends, maintain contact with teachers and coaches, and are generally connected to individuals and institutions in the community can help their children develop and maintain important social networks. Fathers, in other words, can play a decisive role in developing their children's social ecologies (Furstenberg, 1998).

Interestingly, at the same time that fathers are gaining more attention, studies suggest that at least in some respects, the proportion of men experiencing fatherhood may be diminishing (Eggebeen, 2002). In the mid-1960s, nearly 60 percent of U.S. men were living with children, compared with only 45 percent today. Developmentalists are beginning to ask questions regarding men's images of fathering and what it means to men to be fathers (Eggebeen, Dew, & Knoester, 2010). Probing the identity issues surrounding the role of father, and the emotional and subjective experiences of fathering, may shed additional light on how much, and how well, fathers parent their children.

Affairs, 2009). As shown in Figure 10.6, the number of people who emigrated to the United States far exceeds the number who emigrated to any other country.

Ethnic diversity has been present in the United States throughout its history as a result of the colonization of Native Americans, the importation of slaves from Africa, and a continuous stream of immigrants, mostly from Europe. Moreover, in the past few decades, the United States has had an enormous influx of families from other parts of the globe. As shown in Figure 10.7, the vast majority of U.S. immigrants now come from Mexico, followed by Asia and Europe. Currently, approximately 22 percent of all children in the United States are from immigrant families, a number projected to increase to 33 percent by 2020, making immigrant children the fastest-growing group of children in the United States (Mather, 2009). Similar changes in the influx of immigrants have also occurred in Canada, Australia, and

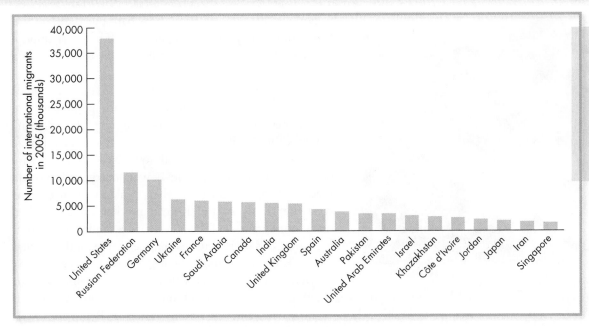

FIGURE 10.6 A report issued by the United Nations shows that in 2005, vastly more people emigrated to the United States than to any other country. (Adapted from United Nations Department of Economic and Social Affairs, 2006.)

Germany and other European countries (United Nations Commission on Population and Development, 2005).

One of the most common ways of exploring diversity in families is to examine differences in parenting style. However, developmentalists have discovered that the patterns of parenting originally formulated by Baumrind on the basis of her research with middle-class White parents may not apply to other ethnic populations, as you saw in the case of African American no-nonsense parenting (Creveling, Varela, Weems, & Corey, 2010). Indeed, the very categories and language that U.S. researchers use to describe differences in styles may be culturally specific (Parke & Buriel, 1998).

For example, research comparing Chinese American and European American parents has found that "authoritarian" does not have the same meaning for the two groups (Russell, Crockett, & Chao, 2010; Wu & Chao, 2005). According to Ruth Chao (1996), although Chinese American families might typically seem to have an authoritarian style, the English word "authoritarian"—with its negative connotations of hostility, aggressiveness, mistrust, and dominance—does not apply to the core methods of parenting in the Chinese family. While it is true that Chinese parents place high value on controlling their children and on requiring their obedience, the preferred Chinese pattern of parenting is more aptly characterized by a Chinese notion that Chao translates as "training." Chao maintains that Chinese parents exercise control over their children and demand their obedience "in the context of a supportive, highly involved, and physically close mother–child relationship" (Chao, 1996, p. 112).

Just as parenting styles vary across cultures, so do the values that parents seek to instill in their children. Many recent immigrants to the United States come from cultures that place great value on education as a means to achieving a successful life. Indeed, immigrant parents tend to emphasize the importance of education more than do native-born Americans. In his ethnographic case study of a Hispanic immigrant family, Gerardo Lopez (2001) reported that the parents would often take their children with them as they worked in the fields in order to underscore

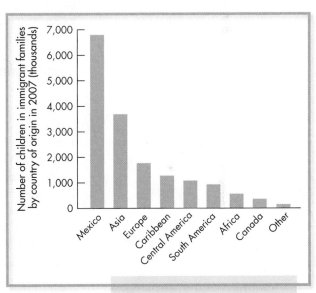

FIGURE 10.7 In the United States, about two-fifths of all children in immigrant families were born in Mexico or had a parent who was born in Mexico. (Adapted from Mather, 2009.)

A significant proportion of emigrant families to the United States come from Asia. This Cambodian family has made their new home in Long Beach, California.

important "life lessons" about how hard they worked and how poorly they were compensated. The most important lesson, however, was that education is the key to a better life.

What accounts for this difference in the valuing of education? Many developmentalists have pointed to the "ideologies of opportunity" and "cultures of optimism" that motivate families to migrate in the first place (Suárez-Orozco, Suárez-Orozco, & Todorova, 2008). In short, parents believe that life in the new country will provide increased opportunities for their children. However, as with the family of the Korean mother quoted earlier, many immigrant families experience a significant drop in economic and social status when they arrive in the United States (Kim et al., 2007). Sadly, and perhaps counterintuitively, research indicates that, among immigrant Asian and Latino children alike, length of residence in the United States is associated with declines in health, school achievement, and aspirations (Portes & Rumbaut, 2001; Suárez-Orozco, Bang, & Onaga, 2010). Carola Suárez-Orozco and her colleagues (2008) suggests that the "Americanization" of foreign-born children often includes exposure to persistent forms of racism and to peer influence that together undermine their initial sense of optimism and regard for education.

Single-Parent Families It is estimated that half of all children born in the United States today will spend at least some portion of their childhood in a single-parent home. Studies of children from single-parent families report a number of behavioral, social, and academic problems. One explanation for this pattern is that when a single parent has to assume the role of sole breadwinner, caregiver, and household manager, that parent's contact with, and supervision of, the children is reduced, giving the children more unregulated time. According to this explanation, the very structure of the family places children at risk.

Other researchers argue that the presence of only one parent is not itself a problem; rather, other factors that often correlate strongly with single-parenthood are to blame. For example, with only one wage earner, single-parent families have fewer material resources and have greater financial stress than do two-parent families. According to this view, whether there is one parent or two in the household is not the issue; exposure to poverty is the critical factor.

Yet another explanation associates the problems of children from single-parent families with the traumatic effects of divorce (you will learn more about the effects of divorce in Chapter 13). From this perspective as well, single-parent families are not a problem in and of themselves. Rather, the crisis of divorce generates behavioral, social, and academic problems for children, problems that can be expected to decline over time as the family learns to cope with the divorce and its effects.

In an effort to untangle these competing explanations, Gunilla Weitoft and her colleagues (2003) launched a nationwide study comparing health outcomes for children in single-parent and two-parent families in Sweden. They identified almost 1 million children who were living with the same single parent or the same two opposite-sex adults in both 1991 and 1999. Using national records of child deaths, social welfare benefits, and hospital discharges, they found that, compared with their peers in two-parent homes, children in the single-parent homes fared less well on a variety of physical and mental health indicators. Although the researchers found that socioeconomic status was the most important factor in accounting for a number of differences between the two groups, children in single-parent families, regardless of SES, remained at greater risk for psychiatric disorders, suicide, injury, and addiction.

The results of such large-scale studies can provide important information about populations of individuals in general, as Weitoft and her colleagues suggest. However, they reveal little about family dynamics, family communication patterns, child-rearing practices, the reasons for single-parenthood, kin relationships outside the immediate family, and other factors that may influence the well-being of children in single-parent families.

Another problem with conclusions about children in single-parent families is that most of the relevant research has been conducted primarily with Caucasian families, raising the question of whether the results apply as well to ethnic-minority families. To address this question, John Kesner and Patrick McKenry (2001) studied 68 preschool children and their parents living in a large city in the southeastern United States. Most of the families were African American (66 percent) or Hispanic (10 percent). Sixty-six percent of the children lived with both parents, and 34 percent lived with their mothers who had never been married. There were no differences between the single- and two-parent families in terms of ethnicity or socioeconomic level.

Kesner and McKenry examined the children's social skills and styles of conflcit management and found no differences between children from single-parent families and those from two-parent families. In discussing their results, the researchers note that compared with European Americans, African Americans are more supportive of single-parent families and attach less stigma to them. In addition, the extended-family pattern characteristic of the Hispanic and African American cultural traditions (as discussed earlier) may mean that children have a network of kin that provides additional support. Finally, Kesner and McKenry point out that because the single mothers in their study had never been married, their families were not exposed to the sudden emotional and financial changes typically experienced by divorced families. These mothers may also have had stronger commitments to their nonconventional family structure than mothers who may have been divorced against their choice.

Gay and Lesbian Parents

Gay and Lesbian Parents Another significant change in the nature of families is the increasing number of gay and lesbian parents (Patterson & Riskind, 2010). Estimates of both the number of same-sex parents and the number of children they are raising vary considerably. According to one, widely cited study, there were 116,000 same-sex couples raising approximately 250,000 children in the United States in 2008 (Gates & Romero, 2009). Although research on gay- and lesbian-parent families has increased in recent years, it has a number of limitations that complicate interpretations of its findings. Some of these limitations stem from the reluctance of many gay and lesbian parents to discuss their sexual orientation and their families for fear of discrimination. Other limitations, however, stem from a lack of reliable demographic information regarding gay- and lesbian-parent families. For example, the U.S. Census has not collected data on how many parenting couples are gay and lesbian, or how many single parents are gay and lesbian. Moreover, studies of gay- and lesbian-parent families have tended to involve small numbers of families that may or may not be representative.

The families of gay and lesbian couples are diverse in size, ethnicity, religion, and socioeconomic status.

Mark Ralston / AFP / Getty Images

Like families in general, those with gay and lesbian parents are diverse in size and structure, ethnicity, religion, and socioeconomic class. Some gay and lesbian parents come out after having their children in a heterosexual relationship. More recently, openly gay and lesbian couples and individuals are choosing to raise children that they have adopted or conceived by means of artificial insemination or surrogacy (Ariel & McPherson, 2000). In the United States, adoption is often a difficult process for gay and lesbian couples because traditional family law does not recognize such couples as constituting a legal marriage and because many adoption agencies and some states do not allow gays and lesbians to adopt (Patterson, 2009; Herek, 2006). Thus, co-parents who wish to adopt their partners' legal or biological children often must convince judges to reinterpret adoption statutes in ways that are inclusive of gay and lesbian unions (Ryan, 2000).

A number of studies have sought to determine whether children raised in gay and lesbian households are different from children raised in heterosexual families. Although most of these studies have been limited in size, they paint a generally positive picture of children's development and adjustment in gay and lesbian families (Patterson, 2006; Biblarz & Sevci, 2010). For example, on measures of psychological well-being, peer relationships (number and quality of friendships), and behavioral adjustment, a number of studies find no differences between children raised by heterosexual parents and those raised by gay or lesbian parents (Bos et al., 2007; Wainright & Patterson, 2008; MacCullum & Golombok, 2004). On the other hand, children of same-sex parents are often teased about their parents' sexual orientation, as documented by research in several countries, including the United States, the Netherlands, and Belgium (Bos & van Balen, 2008; Gartrell, Deck, Rodas, Peyser, & Banks, 2005; Vanfraussen, Ponjaert-Kristoffersen, & Brewaeys, 2002). Interestingly, a rare cross-national study found that peer teasing about parents' sexual orientation is more likely to take place in the United States than in the Netherlands (Bos, Gartrell, van Balen, Preyer & Standfort, 2008). Not surprisingly, children of gay and lesbian parents seem to be more tolerant of same-sex experimentation and may be somewhat more likely to develop a gay or lesbian identity than are children growing up with heterosexual parents (Biblarz & Sevci, 2010; Bos, Standfort, de Bruyn & Hakvoort, 2008).

Distressed Families

Because the family is the first and perhaps the most important developmental context, *distressed families*—that is, families facing significant social, economic, and/or psychological challenges—are of special concern to those interested in children's well-being. According to developmentalists who study distressed families, the most significant family factors that impede children's development are poverty, parenthood in adolescence, abuse, and divorce. We will look at the first three of these factors below (and at divorce in Chapter 13).

Families in Poverty One of the most consistent findings in research on families is the relationship between economic hardship and children's well-being. As you will recall from Chapter 6, socioeconomic status includes education level and occupation as well as income. It therefore serves as a predictor of the amount of hardship experienced by families, especially those in poverty.

Poverty touches all aspects of family life: the quality of housing and health care, access to education and recreational facilities, and even safety when walking along the street (Fauth, Leventhal, & Brooks-Gunn, 2007; Shonkoff, Boyce, & McEwen, 2009). Interest in the influence of poverty on children's development has increased in recent years, due in part to the increasing numbers of poor children in the United States. According to the National Center for Children in Poverty (NCCP), approximately 22 percent of all children in the United States live in poverty, part of the approximately 42 percent who live in low-income families (National Center for Children in Poverty, 2011; see Figure 10.8). As we discussed in Chapter 8, nearly 11 percent of children in the United States are considered *food insecure*, meaning that they do not have access to enough food to ensure their good health; and 1.2 percent are considered to have "very low food security," meaning that they have so little food that they are often hungry. In addition, it is estimated that 1.5 million children in the United States currently become homeless at some point each year (National Center for Family Homelessness, 2009).

Contrary to popular belief, only half of all poor children and families in the United States are chronically and persistently poor. In a nationwide study, Duncan and his colleagues found that family income fluctuates significantly across the family's life cycle and tends to increase as children age (Duncan & Raudenbush, 1999). However, they also found that being poor during early childhood presents a greater challenge to children's well-being, particularly to their academic achievement, than does being poor during later stages of development. Considering that the family's SES is the most powerful predictor of intellectual skills when children enter school, and that early school success forecasts lifelong achievement and adjustment, the effects of poverty are particularly serious (Stipek, 2001).

Poverty-stricken children are at elevated risk for mental health problems, but this risk can be significantly reduced if their family's income rises above the poverty level. This was demonstrated by Jane Costello and her colleagues (2003) in an 8-year study of Native American children growing up on an Indian reservation. Some of the children lived in poverty; others did not. Halfway through the study, a casino opened on the reservation, lifting many of the poor families out of poverty. Overall, children in these families subsequently showed a significant decrease in mental health disorders, whereas the children whose families remained in poverty showed no improvement in their mental health. A similar effect was found in a study of very poor rural Mexican families who participated in a program that gave them access to cash resources (Fernald & Gunnar, 2009). Preschool-age children whose families were assigned to participate in the program had lower levels of the stress hormone cortisol than did children whose families were not assigned to participate.

In addition to mental health problems, poverty is also associated with physical health problems and problems in intellectual development. For example, environmentally induced illnesses such as tuberculosis and asthma are all observed at higher rates in poor children than in nonpoor children (Shonkoff, Boyce, & McEwen, 2009). Lead poisoning, which is associated with learning disabilities and impaired intellectual functioning, is also a significant threat to impoverished children, who tend to live in rundown housing where they may be exposed to contaminated chips and dust from deteriorating lead-based paint.

Poverty may also affect parents' approach to child-rearing. In particular, studies have found that in families experiencing economic hardship, parents are likely to be more harsh and controlling, in some cases to discourage children's curiosity and restrict their movements because of the dangerous circumstances of their daily lives (McLoyd, 1998b). However, this pattern may also arise because of the stress

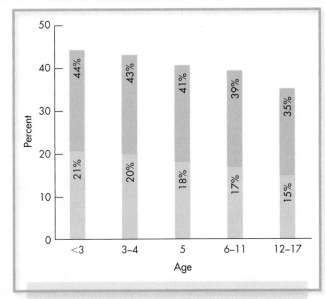

FIGURE 10.8 This figure shows the percentages of children in the United States living in low-income (green) or poor (peach) families (NCCP, 2010). The National Center for Children in Poverty defines "poor" families as those with incomes below the federal poverty level ($22,050 for a family of 4 in 2010). It defines "low income" families as those with incomes at or below twice the federal poverty level. Defining low-income families is important because research indicates that families cannot meet their basic needs of food, clothing, shelter, transportation, and medical care unless their income is at least 200 percent higher than the federal poverty level (Berstein, Brocht & Spade-Aguilar, 2000).

that poverty creates for parents. Compared with parents of higher SES, low-income parents have higher rates of depression, negative feelings of self-worth, and negative beliefs about the extent to which they have control over their own life circumstances (summarized in Shonkoff & Phillips, 2000). Parents who are under stress are less nurturing, more likely to resort to physical punishment, and less consistent when they interact with their children (Sameroff et al., 1998).

The studies reviewed here indicate that poverty has far-reaching and long-lasting effects on children's development. Another risk associated with poverty arises in adolescence—that of becoming a teenage parent.

Families with Teen Mothers

Many women who are raising children are still teenagers. In contrast to older mothers, teen mothers are less knowledgeable about child development, less confident in their ability to parent their children, and have less positive attitudes about parenting (Bornstein & Putnick, 2007). As Figure 10.9 indicates, between 1991 and 2005 there was a dramatic drop in the proportion of adolescents giving birth in the United States. Since then, teen birth rates have been fairly stable and among the lowest ever recorded (Ventura & Hamilton, 2011).

Despite the decline of the past two decades, the teen birth rate in the United States is still among the highest in the industrialized world (Figure 10.10). This situation is of grave concern because research has shown that children of unmarried teenage mothers suffer significant deficits in several developmental areas. In general, they tend to be more aggressive, less self-controlled, and less intellectually advanced than the children of older, married mothers (Jaffe et al., 2001). In one study of more than 100 children born to unmarried teenage mothers, less than one-third scored within normal ranges on tests of intelligence, language, and socioemotional functioning (Sommer et al., 2000).

Frank Furstenberg and his colleagues (1992) believe that two factors contribute to the negative developmental effects of being raised by a young unmarried mother. First,

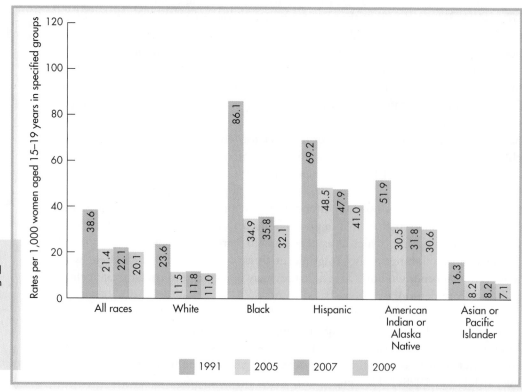

FIGURE 10.9 The proportion of adolescents giving birth in the United States dropped dramatically between 1991 and 2005, particularly among Black teens. Overall, this downward trend has continued for younger and older adolescents across all groups. (Adapted from Ventura & Hamilton, 2011.)

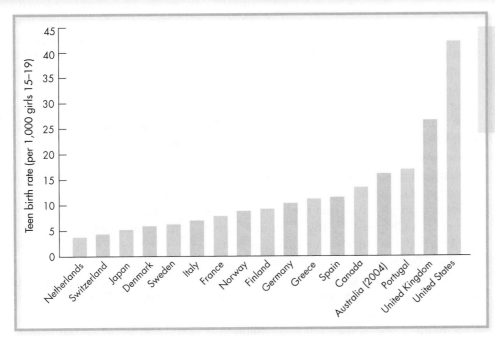

FIGURE 10.10 In the industrialized world, birth rates for teenagers 15 to 19 years of age are particularly high in the United States. Teenage mothers, as well as their children, face a number of developmental challenges. (Adapted from United Nations Statistics Division, 2006.)

young mothers often are less prepared to bring up children and have little interest in doing so. One consequence is that they tend to vocalize less with their babies than older mothers do. As we discussed in Chapter 6, mother–infant communication is an important source of intellectual stimulation. Second, young mothers, especially those without husbands, are likely to have very limited financial resources. As a consequence, they are likely to be poorly educated, to live in disadvantaged neighborhoods, to lack quality health care, and to be socially isolated.

It is important to recognize that not all children born to teenage mothers have negative developmental outcomes. Tom Luster and his colleagues (2005) compared "more successful" and "less successful" children of adolescent mothers. Children who were most successful, as measured by a standardized test of intellectual and language functioning, were likely to live in environments that were more intellectually stimulating and less stressful than those of their less successful peers. In addition, the mothers of the most successful children had received more years of education, were more likely to be employed, had fewer children, resided in more desirable neighborhoods, and lived with a male partner. Likewise, a study of adolescent mothers' participation in welfare-reform programs indicates that highly involved mothers—those who take advantage of center-based child care, educational opportunities, and job-training programs—have children with more developed cognitive abilities than do children whose mothers are less involved (Yoshikawa et al., 2001). Social programs for teen mothers, such as the one described in the box "In the Field: Louisiana Swamp Nurse" (pp. 364–365), aim to decrease risks and increase protective factors for children by encouraging teen mothers to continue their education, pursue job opportunities, and read to their babies.

Despite the stresses of teen parenting, this young mother takes time to play with her toddler in the park.

Abusive Families

Scarcely a day goes by without a story in the media about a child who has been neglected, maltreated, or even murdered by a parent or other relative. Add to this the stories about children from around the world who are forced into prostitution, made to work long hours at grueling and sometimes dangerous tasks, commandeered to serve as soldiers, or killed simply because they are female or members of a particular ethnic group and you begin to get a sense of the enormity of child abuse and maltreatment across the globe.

Researchers interested in tracking the worldwide incidence of child maltreatment face a number of difficulties. One of the most common difficulties relates to how "maltreatment" is defined in different cultures. As you can see in Table 10.2, with the exception of extreme physical and sexual abuse, there is wide regional variation in the sorts of behaviors that are recognized as abusive (ISPCAN, 2006). Definitional problems arise because what is deemed appropriate and inappropriate treatment of children, including the frequency and severity of physical punishment, varies dramatically from one family and community to the next (Holden, 2002). As noted in Chapter 9, nearly 3 out of 4 parents in the United States approve of spanking, a practice that is viewed as unacceptable in countries such as Sweden (see the box "The Spanking Controversy," Chapter 9, p. 333). Clearly, the borders between culturally acceptable physical punishment and physical punishment that is defined as maltreatment depend very much on parents' beliefs about children and the modes of interaction sanctioned in the children's families and communities.

Why do parents abuse their own children? It is generally believed that parents who were physically abused by their parents are more likely to abuse their own children than are parents who were not themselves abused (Ammerman et al., 1999). However, only 30 percent of those who were abused become child abusers themselves; 70 percent do not (Kaufman & Zigler, 1989). Hence, a history of abuse may be associated with later abuse but cannot be considered a simple cause. Rather, a complex interplay of factors seems to set the stage for maltreatment (Zielinski & Bradshaw, 2006).

table 10.2

What Constitutes Abuse? Views from across the Globe

	Percent Agreement by Region			
	Africa	Americas	Asia	Europe
Sexual abuse (e.g., incest, sexual touching, pornography)	100.0	100.0	100.0	100.0
Physical abuse (e.g., beating, burning)	90.9	100.0	100.0	100.0
Failure to provide adequate food, clothing, or shelter (neglect)	72.7	100.0	91.7	92.0
Abandonment by parent or caretaker	81.8	100.0	83.3	92.0
Emotional abuse (e.g., repeatedly belittling or insulting a child)	63.6	100.0	62.5	88.0
Failure to secure medical care for child based on religious beliefs	72.7	80.0	60.9	84.0
Psychological neglect (e.g., failure to provide emotional support/attention)	63.6	80.0	54.2	79.2
Parental substance abuse	63.6	70.0	45.8	88.0
Domestic violence	63.6	60.0	41.7	76.0
Parental mental illness	36.4	40.0	37.5	64.0
Physical discipline (e.g., spanking)	45.5	60.0	37.5	60.0
Nonorganic failure to thrive (FTT)	36.4	50.0	37.5	56.0
Child prostitution	100.0	100.0	100.0	96.0
Children living on the street	100.0	100.0	83.3	92.0
Physical beating of a child by any adult	72.7	90.0	83.3	96.0
Forcing a child to beg	63.6	90.0	87.5	84.0
Female/child infanticide	72.7	70.0	82.6	88.0
Child labor	63.6	80.0	70.8	68.0
Abuse by another child	63.6	80.0	62.5	76.0
Children serving as soldiers	60.0	66.7	59.1	50.0
Female circumcision	60.0	60.0	45.0	60.9

This table reflects results from a 2006 mail survey of key informants identified by the International Society for the Prevention of Child Abuse as knowledgeable about child maltreatment issues within their respective countries. The number of informants from each region ranged from 10 (Americas) to 25 (Europe).

There is a good deal of evidence that one major contributor to abuse is stress on the family, including chronic poverty, recent job loss, marital discord, and social isolation (Gordon et al., 2003). The likelihood of abuse is also higher when the mother is very young, is poorly educated, abuses drugs or alcohol, or receives little financial support from the father (Goodman et al., 1998; Gordon et al., 2003).

Any child may be neglected or abused, but some characteristics seem to put certain children at greater risk (HHS, 2003). Factors that affect risk for children in the United States include the following:

- *Age:* Infants and children under the age of 3 are at special risk.

- *Gender:* Girls are slightly more likely than boys to be maltreated.

- *Ethnicity:* Pacific Islander, Native American, and African American children have the highest rates of maltreatment. For example, the rate of maltreatment for European American children is 11.0 per 1,000, compared with rates of 21.4 per 1,000 for Pacific Islanders, 21.3 for Alaska Natives, and 20.4 for African Americans.

Many scholars who have studied the physical abuse of children in the United States see it as a social disease that accompanies the acceptance of violence by families, local communities, and society at large. Two kinds of evidence support this position. First, most child abuse occurs when parents set out to discipline their children by punishing them physically and then end up hurting them (Zigler & Hall, 1989). Second, countries in which the physical punishment of children is frowned upon, such as Sweden and Japan, have very low rates of physical abuse of children (Belsky, 1993; Cicchetti & Toth, 1993).

Although adults who have been maltreated as children are more likely to be depressed, abuse drugs and alcohol, have sexual problems, and engage in criminal behavior, nearly one-fourth of maltreated children show no long-term problems (McGloin & Widom, 2001). Factors that seem to buffer children from long-term consequences of abuse include having a warm relationship with at least one adult, having a fairly stable family residence (not moving around a lot), having positive experiences in school, and participating in extracurricular activities (Zielinski & Bradshaw, 2006). The multiple cultural, family, parent, and child factors that operate together in cases of child maltreatment suggest that broad-based, systematic intervention campaigns would offer the best hope for reducing the problem in the long run (Hughes, Graham-Bermann, & Gruber, 2001).

Family Affluence As surprising as it may seem, another family factor that may place children at risk for behavioral and emotional problems is wealth (Racz, McMahon, & Luthar, 2011). Suniya Luthar and Bronwyn Becker (2002) studied middle-school students living in one of the most affluent suburban communities in the United States. Their results showed high levels of depression, particularly among girls, as well as high levels of substance abuse. What might cause this pattern of distress among affluent young? According to the findings, many children of wealth feel themselves to be under a great deal of pressure to achieve—in school, in sports, socially, and financially. They also tend to be isolated from adults and feel emotionally distant from their mothers. Luthar and Becker's study supports recent concerns voiced in the popular press that wealthy families have become overly invested in performance and achievement issues and that their children are suffering as a consequence. Their children's time is overscheduled, especially with activities driven by the need to succeed. Such free time as children do have is often spent in the company of peers who endorse the use of drugs and alcohol as a means of "letting off steam." The study stands as a cautionary note against the assumption that children of means lack for nothing.

In the Field — Louisiana Swamp Nurse

Name:	Luwana Marts
Education:	B.S. in nursing
Current position:	Nurse Visitor for the Nurse-Family Partnership of Louisiana

LUWANA MARTS IS ONE OF EIGHT NURSES WHO WORK with teen mothers living in a swampy, isolated region southwest of New Orleans. In Louisiana, 30 percent of all children are poor, almost half of all children are born to single mothers, and the proportion of people unable to read or write is among the highest in the nation. Myths about children and their development abound: Formula is healthier than breast milk; babies held by menstruating women will become constipated; the baby's brain will be damaged if his or her hair is cut before the first birthday. In this context, a beautiful young woman named Alexis became pregnant with her first child, and became part of Luwana's caseload.

Until her 8th month of pregnancy, Alexis lived with her parents, but their constant fighting became more than she could bear, so she moved out. She made other changes as well. At Luwana's urging, Alexis gave up drinking and smoking, and had regular medical checkups. When her son, Daigan, was born, Luwana visited regularly to educate Alexis about her son's development, and how to be a good parent.

Alexis: One thing that I learned already is how he cries different when he's hungry than when he's wet.

Luwana: (with a dazzling smile) Making that distinction is important. You're listening to him, and in his own way he's explaining what he needs. Pretty soon now he'll be making other sounds,

and when he does you'll want to make that noise right back. He'll babble, and then you'll talk to him, and that's how you'll develop his language. Now, what you may also find, around 5 to 8 weeks, is that he'll be crying even more—it's a normal part of his development, but it can also stress out the mom, so we'll want to be prepared for it. The main things will be keeping calm—if you find yourself getting all worked up and frustrated—well, then what?

Alexis: Put him down? So I don't hurt him, shake him, make him brain-dead?

Luwana: Put him down and . . . ?

Alexis: Call someone who isn't upset? Let the baby be, and get help.

Luwana: (talking sweetly to Daigan) See, your mama is getting it. She's surely going to figure you out.

On another occasion, Luwana takes up the subject of infant attachment, which she skillfully tailors to Alexis's limited education on such matters. "The love link," she explains, "(i)t's a cycle. When there's no safe base for the baby—when you're not meeting his basic needs, satisfying his hunger, keeping him out of harm's way—there will be no trust, no foundation for love. . . . It's on you now to comfort him, earn his trust, because that's how Daigan is going to learn how to love."

It is clear that families have pronounced effects on children's development. In addition to exerting influence through the ways they are structured (nuclear or extended) and the styles of care and interaction they provide, families influence children by linking them to other developmentally important contexts, including nonparental child–care settings.

▲ APPLY :: CONNECT :: DISCUSS

Using Bronfenbrenner's model (Chapter 1, pp. 27–29), analyze the ecology of Alexis and her baby as described in the box about the Louisiana swamp nurse. Describe features of the microsystems, exosystems, mesosystems, and macrosystems. If you lack specific information about the features of a system, try to speculate on the basis of features in the other systems.

Nonparental Child Care

Nonparental child care is a fact of life for nearly all children in the United States. In 2010, 86 percent of children between birth and 4 years of age with employed mothers spent some time in nonparental child care (Forum on Child and Family

Luwana Marts, visiting nurse, with two of her clients.

Alec Soth/Magnum Photos

Luwana is part of a growing legion of visiting nurse practitioners whose work is dedicated to helping families raise healthy children. They bring their skills, knowledge, and resources to where they are most needed in the first few years of children's lives: the home. Visiting nurse practitioners focus on improving mothers' prenatal care, educating parents about how to provide sensitive and competent child care, and helping parents to plan future pregnancies, complete their education, and find work (Zielinski, Eckenrode, & Olds, 2009). In addition to making intervention programs more accessible to families who are unable or unlikely to attend programs offered elsewhere in the community, home visits provide rich detail about the often-changing characteristics and needs of specific families. Consequently, nurse practitioners are able to individualize their interventions, as well as provide critical feedback regarding program effectiveness.

Research on the effectiveness of visiting nurse programs is mixed (Pinquart & Teubert, 2010). In general, the programs are somewhat effective in promoting positive parenting practices, reducing parents' stress, increasing children's social and cognitive development, and reducing risk for child abuse and children's later criminal behavior, although their effectiveness tends to decline over time in what is commonly described as a "fade-out" effect (Olds, 2006; Pinquart & Teubert, 2010). These modest results apply, of course, only to families who persist in the programs. Sadly, Alexis and Daigan did not. But despite the odds, visiting nurse practitioners such as Luwana continue delivering intervention programs to families in need.

(Adapted from Katherine Boo, 2006)

Statistics, 2011). These numbers alone suggest the importance of nonparental child care as a context for young children's development. In this section we focus on the varieties and general developmental consequences of nonparental care. (In Chapter 12, we will take up the more particular case of academically focused care such as preschools.)

Varieties of Child Care

One of the most popular child-care arrangements for children younger than 5 is **home child care**—care provided for children in their own homes, primarily by their grandmothers or other relatives, while their mothers are at work. (Nearly half of all children in nonparental care are cared for by other family relatives.) Children cared for at home experience the least change from normal routine: They eat food provided by their parents and take naps in their own beds. They also come in contact with relatively few children their own age.

Child care provided in someone else's home, that of either a relative or nonrelative, is called **family child care** (U.S. Bureau of the Census, 2003). Family child care often exposes children not only to caretakers from outside the family circle

home child care Child care provided in the child's own home, primarily by a grandmother or other family member, while the parents are at work.

family child care Child care provided in someone else's home, that of either a relative or a stranger.

High-quality child-care centers offer children a variety of educational and social experiences.

but also to new settings and to children of other families. The children in a family-child-care setting may range widely in age, forming a more diverse social group than is likely to exist in the children's own home. The routine of activities in family child care, however, is usually very similar to the routine at home.

Child-care centers—organized child-care facilities supervised by licensed professionals—provide care for 24 percent of children receiving nonparental care, and have attracted the most public attention. The programs available vary in style and philosophy. Some offer an academic curriculum, emphasize discipline, and have a school-like atmosphere. Others emphasize social development and allow children to exercise more initiative in their activities. Programs vary widely in quality as well. An important task many parents face is selecting the high-quality child-care facility or preschool that they feel best meets their children's needs (see Table 10.3 for questions that parents should ask about the quality of a child-care program they may be considering). Because licensed child-care centers often receive public financing, they have been more accessible than other nonparental care settings to researchers, who have studied both their characteristics and the way these characteristics affect children's development.

child-care center An organized child-care facility supervised by licensed professionals.

---

table 10.3

Determining the Quality of Child-Care Centers

Questions About the Program:

- Is the program licensed by the state or local government?
- Is the program accredited by the National Association for the Education of Young Children or the National Association of Family Child Care?
- Does the program offer staff medical benefits and leave? Does it support caregivers' continuing education through tuition reimbursement programs and/or sponsoring attendance at professional conferences and workshops?
- Does the staff-to-child ratio conform to state-regulated guidelines for the age group?
- Does the program encourage parent involvement through volunteering in the classroom or participating on the board of directors or other committees?

Questions About the Environment:

- Is the environment safe and sanitary?
- Is the place appealing, with comfortable lighting and an acceptable noise level?
- Does the environment accommodate the child who may have special needs?
- Are toys and materials well organized so children can choose what interests them?

Questions About the Caregivers:

- Are the caregivers certified by the Council for Early Childhood Professional Recognition with a Child Development associate degree credential for infant/toddler caregivers or an equivalent credential that addresses comparable competencies (such as an A.A./A.S. or a B.A./B.S.)?
  - Are the caregivers responsive, showing the following characteristics?
  - Playful partners who introduce new ideas and games?
  - Supportive of children in their social contacts with other children and adults?
  - Respectful of the child's individual development, rhythms, style, strengths, and limitations?
  - Respectful of the child's native culture or ethnicity?

Source: Adapted from Zero to Three, 2003.

Preschool provides an important context for developing "children's culture." Hand-clapping games, like the one shown in this Malaysian preschool, are but one example of the many games and rituals that children learn from each other.

Developmental Effects of Child Care

The effects of child care during the first 2 years of life depend primarily on the quality of the care provided and not on the mere fact of parent–child separation during the day. Nevertheless, concerns about the later effects of early child care continue to be raised, primarily regarding children's intellectual development, social development, and emotional well-being.

Physical and Intellectual Effects When children enter care outside the home, they enter a whole new world. There are new routines and expectations, new toys and children to play with, new adults who will provide care and comfort, and, as any parent will tell you—new germs. In fact, children under 3 years of age in care arrangements with more than six other children are at increased risk for upper respiratory infections, gastrointestinal illnesses, and ear infections (NICHD, 2003a). Although cold and flu bugs make regular rounds in child-care facilities, and often follow children home to their families, there is no evidence that increased illness takes a toll on children's overall development or school readiness (NICHD, 2003a).

Stress is another physical consequence of time spent in child care. Sarah Watamura and her colleagues (2003) assessed stress—as measured by levels of salivary cortisol—in groups of infants and toddlers who received care either in their homes or in child-care centers. Of those in child-care centers, 35 percent of the infants and 71 percent of the toddlers showed a rise in cortisol across the day. Of those receiving care in their homes, however, 71 percent of the infants and 64 percent of the toddlers showed *decreases* in cortisol levels. At this point, any conclusion about the long-term consequences of elevated cortisol in infants and toddlers in child care can only be speculative. However, as you learned in Chapter 5 (p. 168), animal studies indicate that the quality of "mothering" that offspring receive can have both immediate and lasting effects on their stress levels and the way they respond to new and challenging environments (Brotman et al., 2007; Parent et al., 2005). In these studies, animals with high stress levels due to inadequate care early in life engaged in fewer exploratory behaviors and showed higher levels of anxiety when faced with unfamiliar settings compared to animals with lower stress levels who had received adequate early care.

Despite the evidence that children in child care may have higher levels of stress, research conducted in Europe as well as the United States indicates that intellectual development of children in high-quality child-care centers is at least as good as that of children raised at home by their parents (Campbell et al., 2001; Jaffe, Van Hulle, & Rodgers, 2011). For children of low SES, being in a high-quality child-care program can lessen or prevent the decline in intellectual performance that is sometimes seen in their counterparts who remain at home after the age of 2 and whose parents are poorly educated (NICHD, 2003b). Of special importance in the quality of child-center care is the caregivers' level of training and having appropriate child-to-staff ratios (NICHD, 2002).

Impact on Social and Emotional Development

Children who attend child-care centers in the United States tend to be more self-sufficient and more independent of parents and teachers, more verbally expressive, more knowledgeable about the social world, and more comfortable in new situations than are children who do not attend child-care centers. They are also more enthusiastic about sharing toys and participating in fantasy play. This development of greater social competence is not simply a matter of the children's learning how to get along by interacting with a variety of playmates. Caregivers play a crucial role as well. Children's social play and peer interactions become more complex and skilled when they are monitored and facilitated by warm, responsive caregivers (NICHD, 2001).

Not all the social and emotional effects of child care are positive, however. Children who attend child-care centers tend to be less polite, less agreeable, less compliant with adults, and more aggressive than those who do not attend. These effects seem to be related to the number of years a child spends in full-time nonparental care, with more extensive time being associated with more aggressive behavior and a greater likelihood of behavior problems in kindergarten (NICHD, 2003c). These negative behavioral effects, however, tend to be mild and are likely to be associated with additional factors such as maternal insensitivity and low family SES.

Indeed, research suggests that children's home life is critical in determining adjustment to child care. Lieselotte Ahnert and Michael Lamb (2003) argue that children in child care are likely to have trouble adjusting if their working mothers are stressed and have little time and energy to engage them in high-quality interactions. In contrast, children are more likely to adjust well to child care when experiences at home are nurturing and positive. For example, a study of middle-class German children in child care found that their mothers compensated for being away during the day with intense bouts of interaction and intimacy during the early morning and evening hours (Ahnert & Lamb, 2000).

Other developmentalists have also taken issue with those who suggest that child-center care may adversely affect children's social behavior and emotional well-being. Some have reasoned that the quality, not the quantity, of child-center care exerts the biggest influence on children's adjustment. For example, a controlled study of children from low-income families (who would be expected to be at special risk for behavioral problems) found that those who received high-quality child care benefited in many ways and had fewer aggressive behavior problems than did similar children who received lesser-quality care (Love et al., 2003).

Next we turn to research that goes well beyond the typical focus on parental versus nonparental child care.

By attending Head Start, a federally funded preschool program, these preschoolers from low-income families acquire learning skills and attitudes designed to help them succeed in school in the years ahead.

Yana Paskova / The New York Times / Redux

In particular, this research calls attention to the ways in which other features of the ecology—the neighborhood and the community and its culture—contribute to how children experience and adapt to different contexts of care.

▲ APPLY :: CONNECT :: DISCUSS

Imagine that you are preparing to have or adopt your first baby, and you are debating about when to return to work. To help you decide, outline the arguments for and against enrolling your baby in a child-care center. Based on the evidence of your arguments, what do you decide to do?

Neighborhoods and Communities

As children mature, their spheres of action expand beyond the microsystem settings of home and child care to include other developmentally important microsystem settings within the neighborhood and community. From the ecological perspective that we have been emphasizing throughout this chapter, these microsystem settings not only influence each other but also can be affected by other systems—for example, by local politics and the mass media (elements of the exosystem), as well as by the dominant beliefs and values of the culture (elements of the macrosystem).

Neighborhoods and communities differ substantially in the resources they provide to children and families, including whom they interact with, the activities they engage in, the health services available to them, and even the food they eat. Researchers use the term **social capital** to refer to such resources, which also include a community's social structures, its expectations for behavior, and the levels of trust and cooperation of its members (Franzini et al., 2006). These features of social capital are associated with children's quality of life and mental health outcomes (Drukker et al., 2003).

Community and Culture

Like families and other child-care settings, communities play an important role in transmitting the values and beliefs of culture. An excellent illustration of this is provided by Donna Marie San Antonio's (2004) study of children from two neighboring but vastly different communities in the rural northeastern United States. One community, Hillside, is a working-class community with one of the lowest levels of education and median family income in the state. The other, Lakeview, is more affluent, a white-collar community built around a thriving tourist industry. Beyond social class differences, San Antonio found that the two communities have profoundly divergent perspectives on what constitutes a good life and how to secure it for one's children. For example, the people of Hillside cherish tradition, community, and family ties, with social status being determined "more by social and civic connections than by material wealth" (p. 87). In contrast, the people of Lakeview embrace the values of independence, family privacy, achievement, and upward mobility. San Antonio's study revealed that these two very different sets of beliefs and values are reflected in children's language and social interaction. Her observations of the children's behavior as she rode with them on school buses makes the point:

> [On Lakeview buses], most students spaced out in separate seats. Students were polite, but I was not drawn into conversations as I was on the Hillside–Two Rivers buses. The words spoken between students [on the Lakeview buses] seemed fragmented; they were not conversations I could follow. Conversations between friends sitting together were whispered privately. In some instances, the communication seemed intended for power and position rather than for peer connection. On the Hillside bus,

social capital The resources that communities provide children and families, including not only schools, health services, and so on, but also social structures, expectations for behavior, and levels of trust and cooperation among community members.

I heard students talk to each other in whole sentences—they included others, they said hello and good-bye to each other; on the Lakeview buses, I had an entirely different experience. (p. 170)

San Antonio's observations demonstrate how the values and beliefs of communities are expressed in children's behaviors and interactions. As we emphasized in Chapter 2, culture affects children's development so profoundly precisely because it is rooted in the everyday activities of families and peers.

Distressed Communities

Jasmine's elementary school is just two short blocks from her home. Nevertheless, her mother walks her back and forth each day because she worries about Jasmine's safety. The street and sidewalk between the steps of their small row house and the school is strewn with litter and garbage; a street intersection they have to cross is a hang-out for mean-looking older kids who harass passersby for spare change. A few weeks ago, a boy was shot and killed in front of the school—an innocent victim caught in the crossfire of a drug-related shootout. How will Jasmine be affected by growing up in such a neighborhood?

The past several years have seen an explosion in research on the impact that distressed neighborhoods and communities have on children's development (Franzini et al., 2008). This work has focused on economic disadvantage and physical and social disorder.

Economic Disadvantage You know from our previous discussion that children growing up in poverty-stricken families often suffer a variety of health, intellectual, social, and emotional problems. As you also know, most poverty-stricken families live in economically disadvantaged neighborhoods, which themselves contribute risk factors, including lack of decent housing and health care services, lack of grocery stores with fresh fruits and vegetables, and lack of recreational facilities. Plagued by excessive noise, crowding, and street traffic, economically disadvantaged neighborhoods generally have few parks or natural settings where children can play.

Research on communities indicates that neighborhood economic disadvantage profoundly affects children's development and well-being, over and above

The ways that families cope with economic misfortune can dramatically affect their children's risk for developmental problems. If the children living in this railroad car are cared for as well as their beautiful garden suggests, they may escape many of the usual consequences of poverty.

© Phil Schermeister / Corbis

These two neighborhoods, both in New York, demonstrate the stark differences between clean and organized physical environments and those that are disordered and deteriorating.

the effects of the income levels of their families. For example, a number of studies show that low-SES children living in substandard housing are at greater risk for emotional and academic problems, get sick and injured more often, and miss more school compared with low-SES children living in better housing (Evans, 2006). Not surprisingly, children show significant improvements in school when their families move from substandard to better-quality housing.

Physical and Social Disorder In addition to their poor economic conditions, distressed neighborhoods and communities are often ugly, congested, and confusing. One problem associated with such conditions is referred to as **neighborhood physical disorder**, which includes both *physical deterioration,* such as abandoned buildings and cars, garbage on the streets, broken windows, and graffiti on buildings, and *chaotic activity,* such as crowding, heavy street traffic, and high noise levels. Overall, children growing up in physically disordered environments are at risk for a variety of developmental problems. Compared with their peers in nondisordered environments, they are more likely to do poorly in school, be easily frustrated, have less motivation to master difficult tasks, and suffer health problems such as being overweight (Haines et al., 2001; Maxwell & Evans, 2000; Slater et al., 2010).

Another problem associated with the conditions of distressed neighborhoods is **social disorganization** (Wen et al., 2005), which includes weak *social cohesion* (the sense of trust and connection between people), poor *neighborhood climate* (the level of fear related to crime and violence), and *perceived racism*. Children growing up in socially disorganized communities are at risk for a poor quality of life and poor mental health (Drukker et al., 2003).

Although most studies of physical and social disorganization have been conducted in North America, the effects of chaotic environments on children's development and well-being can be found everywhere. Recently, researchers have turned their attention to a particularly troubling source of community disorganization that affects children in many parts of the world—the disruptive and destructive consequences of war (see the box "Children and War").

⬥ APPLY :: CONNECT :: DISCUSS

A newly elected mayor campaigned on promises to tackle the problems affecting a distressed community in his city. He has put you in charge of a task force and wants you to develop a plan for reducing social disorganization. Generate a list of possible community programs that you think might help reduce social disorganization and explain why and how they would improve the lives of children in the community.

neighborhood physical disorder A problem in distressed communities, including both physical deterioration (garbage on the streets, rundown buildings, etc.) and chaotic activity (crowding, high noise levels, etc.).

social disorganization A problem in distressed communities, including weak social cohesion (lack of trust and connection among community members), poor neighborhood climate (fear related to crime and violence), and perceived racism.

Children and War

POLITICAL VIOLENCE HAS BEEN IDENTIfied as a major risk that threatens the lives and well-being of children across the globe (Daiute, 2010; Wainryb, 2010). A United Nations General Security Council (2011) report catalogs a list of horrifying traumas and rights violations suffered by children and their families. Children are recruited as soldiers and forced to commit murder and other atrocities (including suicide bombings); they are exposed to disease and malnutrition when they are forced to flee their homes or while living in refugee camps; their access to education and health care is severely curtailed due to relocation, or because their schools and hospitals have been destroyed; children are injured, permanently disabled, or killed in conflict, often intentionally, sometimes by stumbling on unexploded land mines; they are raped and otherwise exploited sexually; they witness the murder of family members and neighbors; and they are orphaned.

In light of these horrors, it is no surprise that children exposed to war often show symptoms of traumatic stress, including irritability, sleep difficulties, separation anxiety, and nightmares (Klasen et al., 2010). However, studies on the long-term effects of war on children present a complex picture. While some children suffer greatly, becoming depressed and developing psychosocial problems, many others appear to be relatively resilient and cope reasonably well in everyday life (Betancourt, Brennan, Rubin-Smith, Fitzmaurice, & Gilman, 2010). In try-

ing to identify the factors that may contribute to children's successful coping with the traumas of war, developmentalists have focused on two particular factors—quality of parenting and the cultural traditions in which the child develops.

The importance of parenting in helping children cope with the devastations of war has been suggested by parenting-intervention programs especially designed for wartime conditions. Because of the significant stress warfare places on families, parenting may deteriorate, with parents often becoming less emotionally supportive in their interactions with their children (Miller, 1996). Intervention programs focused on supporting good parenting skills in the face of wartime conditions have been shown to benefit children's adjustment and overall well-being. In one study, mothers and children who were refugees from the Bosnian War in the 1990s were randomly assigned either to a control group or to an experimental group that was counseled on the importance of emotionally responsive communication with their children and of providing an emotionally warm and supportive environment (Dybdahl, 2001). (The war experiences faced by the parents and children who participated in the study are shown in the table.) Compared with the control group, mothers in the experimental group showed fewer trauma symptoms and greater life satisfaction. On the basis of the mothers' reports, the children of mothers in the experimental group appeared less anxious and sad, and had fewer nightmares compared with

War Experiences of Children and Families Participating in Parenting Program

Type of Event	n	%
Had to flee from my home	76	100
Thought I would die	70	92
Experienced war activities	68	90
Been shot at	64	84
Separated from close family	57	75
Family members missing	50	66
Family members wounded	49	65
Serious food deprivation	48	63
Saw dead bodies of victims	46	61
Family members killed	44	58
Witnessed home destroyed	23	30
Wounded	16	21
Forced to do things against own will	22	17
Witnessed torture	17	13
Abused, tortured	9	12
Been in concentration camp	6	8

Data were collected during the war in Bosnia and Herzegovina (1992–1995); n = 76.

Source: Dybdahl, 2001, p. 1221.

the children whose mothers were in the control group. In addition, they gained more weight, showed higher levels of improvement on tests of

Media Contexts

The term **media** refers to forms of mass communication, such as newspapers, books, magazines, comic books, radio, television, film, video games, and the Internet. Needless to say, children in technologically advanced societies are immersed in modern communications media to a staggering degree. As you can see from Table 10.4 and Figure 10.11 (p. 374), children spend considerable amounts of time using media, especially between the ages of 11 and 14, when media use occupies an astonishing 8½ hours on a typical day (Rideout & Hamel, 2006; Rideout, Foehr, & Roberts, 2010). What children see on TV, read in books, and learn from video games influences their behavior in other contexts. Research from Germany, Israel, South Korea, and the United States indicates that children across cultures take themes and characters from media and fold them into their play and make-believe worlds (Gotz, Lemish, Aidman, & Moon, 2005). Concerns about how children are affected by media are apparent in movie ratings and television V-chips and in the way parents worry about their children's vulnerability to everything from nightmares induced by fairy tales to Internet sexual predators.

media Forms of mass communication, including newspapers, magazines, books, comic books, radio, television, films, video games, and the Internet.

Children who experience the horrors of war firsthand often show psychological and emotional symptoms that are similar to those associated with post-traumatic stress disorder. This child's drawing illustrates the frightening effects of war on home and village life.

One of the most disturbing ways that children become victims of war is by being recruited into armies and other militant groups as armed combatants.

cognitive reasoning, and perceived their mothers as more emotionally supportive.

Cultural traditions can also help children cope with the trauma of war. An example of this is provided in studies of child soldiers (Honwana, 2000; Summerfield, 1999). In many African nations torn by war over the years—including Zimbabwe, Mozambique, Angola, and Ethiopia, among others—children have been recruited to fight. Part of the process of

their recovering from the emotional effects of war involves participating in ritualized cleansing ceremonies. In contrast to Western traditions that view dealing with trauma as a personal matter, African traditions view it as a process that involves the entire community. Thus, when child soldiers return home from fighting, they must undergo ceremonies that symbolically purge them of the contaminating ancestral spirits of their victims, which would

otherwise spread from the soldiers to the entire social body (Honwana, 2000). The children are forbidden to speak of their war experiences, since this would "open a door" for the harmful spirits to infect the community. Instead, the former child soldiers proclaim a complete break from the past, often burning anything associated with their role as warriors, and through reintegration rituals, are welcomed back into their community of origin.

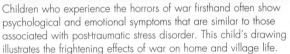

Time Spent Using Media and in Other Activities

	Average time among all children			
	Total	0–1	2–3	4–6
Reading or being read to	0:40	0:33	0:42	0:42
Listening to music	0:48	0:57	0:50	0:41
Watching TV	0:59	0:34	1:11	1:02
Playing outside	1:22	0:56	1:26	1:34
Watching a video or DVD	0:24	0:13	0:32	0:25
Reading an electronic book	0:05	0:05	0:06	0:04
Using a computer	0:07	0:01	0:05	0:12
Playing video games	0:06	0:00	0:03	0:10
Total used any screen media+	1:36	0:49	1:51	1:50

Source: Rideout and Hamel, 2006.

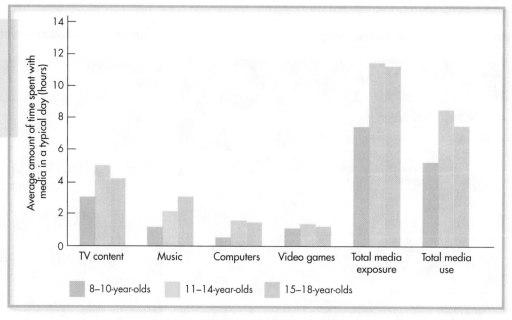

FIGURE 10.11 As shown here, media exposure between the ages of 8 and 18 varies according to the type of media, with television being the most common. It also varies according to the age of the child, with 11- to 14-year-olds being the most frequent users overall. (From Rideout, Foehr, & Roberts, 2010.)

Research on how the various media affect children's development focuses on two general issues. The first concerns whether the *physical form* of the medium affects development. For example, could the vivid images on television confuse young children regarding differences between reality and make-believe? Does excessive Internet use contribute to social isolation from one's peers and interfere with developing social skills? The second issue concerns whether the *content* of the medium affects development. Does Mr. Rogers really teach children that "you are special; you are the only one like you"? Does a steady diet of violent television teach children that aggression is an appropriate way to solve problems?

It is clear from the nature of these questions that considerable controversy surrounds the subject of media effects on children. Below we outline the controversies as they have surfaced in research on the effects of print media, television, and interactive media.

Learning to read involves understanding how to hold a book and turn pages, and what to look for on the page.

One common purpose of children's books is to help parents discuss significant family events and experiences, such as adoption.

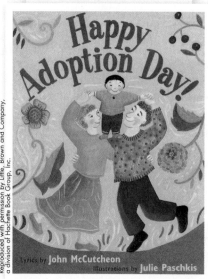

Print Media

As shown in Table 10.4, children's exposure to print media—books, comics, magazines, and newspapers—is relatively small, and fairly stable throughout childhood, compared with their exposure to the other media forms (see Figure 10.12 for examples of print media for children). Nevertheless, we can reasonably conclude that many children read, or are read to, just about every day (Comstock & Scharrer, 2007). Certainly, this is consistent with the fact that children's literature is a growing multimillion-dollar industry. In general, developmentalists have approached children's literature from two directions. One direction, which we examine in Chapter 12, considers children's literature as a means of fostering intellectual development and "school readiness"—in particular, the development of

FIGURE 10.12 Children's literature takes many forms and serves many purposes—from helpful instructions on how to work a toilet, to moral lessons conveyed through the antics and adventures of popular comic strip characters.

language, reading, and writing skills. The other direction, which we examine here, explores why certain types of literature—adventures, mysteries, fantasies, and fairy tales, in particular—appeal to children and what functions they may serve in children's emotional development.

One of the most famous analyses of the role of fairy tales in children's emotional development is that of the psychoanalyst Bruno Bettelheim (1977). Noting that many fairy tales include symbolic representations of universal childhood anxieties, such as abandonment and aggression, Bettelheim argued that children need fairy tales in order to find solutions to their own inner conflicts and fears. Consider, for example, Maurice Sendak's wonderful tale, *Where the Wild Things Are.* You may remember that naughty Max is sent to his room, where he imagines sailing to an enchanted land and becoming king of the wild things. From a psychoanalytic perspective, the story traces Max's feelings of anger and aggression as they are projected into the forms of imaginary "wild things." When Max masters his emotions—that is, tames and becomes king of the wild things—he returns to the reality of his room, his mother, and his dinner, which is, comfortingly, "still hot."

In addition to serving as a tool of emotional control and development, children's literature has been used as a therapeutic device to help children cope with and communicate about a variety of emotionally troubling events, such as divorce, illness, and death, or even the birth of a sibling (Malchiodi & Grinns-Gruenberg, 2008).

Whether intended to delight, instruct, or comfort, children's literature reflects a centuries-old cultural belief that children's thoughts and emotions can be affected by exposure to specific types of print media.

Television

Do you remember the TV images of airplanes slicing into the Twin Towers on 9/11, the plumes of smoke, the towers collapsing into clouds of dust? Do you remember the sight of people leaping from 80 floors up to escape the inferno and of the streets filled with people running in panic, or sitting, confused or hurt, on sidewalk curbs? Perhaps you also remember the flurry of concern about how children might be harmed by viewing—over and over again—the television replays of 9/11. In fact, research suggests that children who were exposed to extensive television

The Muppet Kami is a newcomer to the cast of *Sesame Street* in South Africa. She likes nature, collecting stuff, and telling stories. She is also HIV-positive.

replays of the World Trade Center attack were more likely to show symptoms of separation anxiety and posttraumatic stress disorder than were children who had less television exposure to the event (Gershoff & Aber, 2004; Hoven et al., 2004).

Television is powerful. It communicates information, sways opinions, and moves viewers emotionally. And, clearly, young children are exposed more to television than to any other medium. Between birth and 6 years of age, children watch nearly one hour of television each day, while between ages 8 and 10, the amount of viewing time jumps to just under 4 hours per day. Extensive research has focused on television as a potentially positive or destructive influence on children's development (Pecora, Murray, & Wartella, 2006).

Television Form

> The Count von Count: (with a bad Transylvanian accent) I am the Count, and I *love* to count. Today I will count my bats. I see *one* bat. Now I see *two* bats. Now there is another. That makes how many bats?
> Tens of thousands of children watching the Count on TV respond as one: *Three bats!!!!*
> The Count: Yes! There are *three bats*.

Before asking how television viewing affects children's thoughts, feelings, and behavior, it is necessary to understand how children make sense of television sounds, images, and plots. For example, a special concern about television viewing is that young children easily confuse TV make-believe and reality. Consistent with our earlier discussion of preoperational thinking (see Chapter 8, p. 278), research suggests that young children have little comprehension of the boundary between what they see on television and the rest of their perceptual environment (Troseth, 2003). They are likely to think, for example, that a bowl of popcorn shown on TV would spill if the TV set were turned upside down (Flavell et al., 1990). Even 4- and 5-year-olds may display such difficulty, believing that Sesame Street is a real place or that television characters can see and hear the people who are watching them. This no doubt contributes to the enthusiasm with which young children enter into conversations with TV characters such as the Count and to how special they may really feel when Mr. Rogers looks them right in the eye and says, "*You are my special friend; I like you.*"

In addition to problems distinguishing between appearance and reality, young children often fail to comprehend what they watch, especially if understanding requires linking together fast-paced scenes (Juston et al., 2007). Consequently, they may fail to appreciate the overarching meaning of a TV story, not recognizing, for example, that the point of a typical police drama is that even if a character's bad behavior results in short-term gains, it does not pay off in the long run. Problems understanding the relationship between one scene and another may also contribute to the difficulty children have distinguishing between television programs and advertisements. Indeed, not until they are 7 or 8 years of age do children both distinguish between TV programs and advertisements and appreciate the persuasive intent of the latter (Gunter, Oates, & Blades, 2005). Concerns that children who do not understand the persuasive intent of advertising may be highly susceptible to it have led some countries, including Sweden, to ban television advertising to children under the age of 12 (Bjurström, 1994).

Television remains the most popular form of media among children.

vario images GmbH & Co.KG / Alamy

Television Content Television exposes children to a great range of content. The Count teaches counting; Mr. Rogers counsels on the importance of caring for others; cartoon characters meet violent ends (sometimes more than once); prime-time dramas, as well as the evening news, depict sexuality, violence, and aggression, but also empathy and tenderness. For decades, developmentalists have been deeply interested in how television content affects children's behavior, attitudes, and development—both positively and negatively.

Violence. The aggressive and violent content of children's television in the United States has received considerable attention from researchers, as well as from society at large. Little wonder, given that nearly 70 percent of children's television shows contain acts of physical aggression, averaging 14 violent acts per hour, compared with fewer than 4 in programming not aimed at children (Wilson et al., 2002). Researchers estimate that by the age of 18, children have witnessed 200,000 acts of television violence and 16,000 television murders. To be sure, a large portion of these images are in the form of cartoons, in which the likes of Road Runner and Wile E. Coyote commit mayhem on each other, only to recover miraculously to fight another day. But there is a great deal of graphic and realistic violence as well.

Compared with children who watch less television violence, children who watch a lot of programs with fantasy violence, such as *Power Rangers,* or reality-based violent programs, such as *Cops,* tend to show lower levels of moral reasoning and are more likely to believe that violence is acceptable in certain circumstances (Krcmar & Vieira, 2005; Funk et al., 2004). Research into how violence is actually depicted in children's programming provides some clues as to why this might be the case. For one thing, violence goes unpunished in a vast majority of cases and is often perpetrated by characters that children may find attractive and identify with. In addition, the consequences of violence, such as pain and injury, are played down or overlooked much of the time (Wilson et al., 2002). For the most part, violence takes the form of "good guys" combating "evil," conveying the moral lesson that violence is an acceptable means to a greater good.

As we have pointed out on many occasions, children are not passive recipients of what goes on around them but actively select and interpret particular messages and information from their environments, including their television sets. This was demonstrated by Jamie Ostrov and his colleagues, who conducted a longitudinal study of 78 preschoolers whose parents reported on their children's three favorite TV and video shows and assessed how violent and how educational the shows were (Ostrov, Gentile, & Crick, 2006). For this group of children, who were from families of relatively high SES, educational shows (mostly from PBS) were significantly preferred over violent shows. Interestingly, the children who watched the most television were rated by teachers and observers as engaging in more prosocial behaviors than children who watched less. Furthermore, although no gender differences were found in the type of programs watched by boys and girls, results suggested that boys and girls were learning different behaviors from the shows. In particular, for boys, greater exposure to violent shows predicted higher levels of future physical, verbal, and relational aggression. In girls, however, higher levels of exposure to violent shows were associated only with future verbal aggression. On the basis of this gender difference, the researchers speculated that boys and girls might be keying in on different forms of aggression depicted on TV. Additional support for this idea comes from the provocative finding that high levels of exposure to educational shows predict future relational aggression in girls but not in boys. These results suggest that even educational programs may be exposing children to relational aggression and, further, that gender socialization processes may be influencing how the content of television affects children's behavior (see Chapter 9, pp. 309–310, to review gender socialization in young children).

Social Stereotypes. Another area of special concern to researchers and society is the social stereotypes in children's television programming, especially the stereotypes pertaining to gender and to ethnic minorities.

Regarding gender stereotyping, throughout the history of television in North America, the people who dominate the television screen have tended to be strong, powerful, and resourceful European American men, with women playing more passive and less visible roles. Although this is changing to some extent, gender stereotypes remain, even in children's programming. For example, a study of the gender content of such former and contemporary favorites as *Rugrats, Pokemon, Arthur,* and *CatDog* indicates that male characters are still more likely than female characters to answer questions, boss or order others around, show initiative and ingenuity, achieve their goals, and eat (Aubrey & Harrison, 2004). Gender stereotypes also abound in music videos, and studies indicate that adolescents who watch a lot of music videos tend to hold more traditional attitudes toward gender roles than do peers who are less frequent viewers (Ward, Hansbrough, & Walker, 2005).

In light of the changing demographics of American society, developmentalists have become increasingly interested in TV ethnic stereotypes and their impact on the multicultural awareness of children. Research examining the presence and characteristics of ethnic-minority televison characters finds ample evidence of negative stereotyping. Ethnic minorities tend to be underrepresented on network television programs, and when they do appear on the screen, they are more often depicted as behaving immorally compared with White characters (Monk-Turner, Heiserman, Johnson, Cotton, & Jackson, 2010). The misrepresentation of ethnic minorities on television is of concern because it may both create or maintain negative attitudes toward minority groups and influence young minority children's attitudes about their own group and place in society.

Interactive Media

Although the television set continues to claim the lion's share of children's leisure time, interactive media, in which the actions of the user—clicking the mouse, turning the joystick, tapping the keyboard—are closing in quickly. The new media are appealing to children because of both their form and their content, and as you will see, many of the issues and controversies surrounding children's television viewing loom equally large in the case of children's use of interactive media.

Interactive media is having a pronounced effect on children's experiences in the classroom. This preschooler is using an iPad to look at pictures of schools in a country half-way around the world—Australia.

William DeShazer / Chicago Tribune / MCT via Getty Images

The Form of Interactive Media From your own experience, you probably have a good sense of how exciting and mentally challenging playing interactive video games can be. The amazing special effects of computer games provide children with highly sophisticated cartoonlike scenes that they can interact with, controlling the characters' actions and engaging in active problem solving at the same time. In general, computer games call upon a number of cognitive skills, including divided attention, spatial imagery, and representation (Subrahmanyam, Garcia, Harsono, Li, & Lipana, 2009).

In addition to stimulating cognitive and intellectual processes, interactive media can stimulate emotional responses in children beyond excitement. An example is *Tamagotchi,* a game toy created in Japan. The *Tamagotchi* is an artificial life form that communicates its needs for food, sleep, or play by beeping its owner. The goal of the game is to keep the *Tamagotchi* alive as long as possible, which requires the child's constant attention. As you can imagine, *Tamagotchis* are dropping like flies; there have even been virtual Internet "cemeteries" available in which to "bury" them. One researcher observed a young girl in a restaurant burst into tears when her own *Tamagotchi* bit the dust (Richards, 1998; reported in Subrahmanyam et al., 2001). The appearance–reality phenomenon associated with children's interpretation of television is clearly just as operative in the case of interactive media.

One concern about new media technologies—games, as well as e-mail, text messaging, blogging, and so forth—is how they affect relationships with peers. In a report on the state of young people throughout the world, the United Nations addressed the argument that electronic networks have begun to replace face-to-face networks in many parts of the world, leading to an erosion of social cohesion and trust (U.N. Department of Economic and Social Affairs, 2005). It has been suggested, for example, that spending time on a machine necessarily cuts into time that otherwise would be spent interacting with friends. However, research does not entirely support this concern. Indeed, studies indicate that Internet communication is positively related to both the number and quality of adolescent friendships, perhaps because it encourages a form of behavior long associated with intimacy: self-disclosure (Valkenberg & Peter, 2007).

Another concern is about the ways that new interactive media affect family relationships. An early study found that new computer games brought families together for shared play and interaction (Mitchell, 1985). However, now that games and computers are common, and children are often more knowledgeable than their parents about how to operate them, such sharing may be less frequent (Subrahmanyam & Šmahel, 2010). Indeed, most parents are fairly ignorant about the interactive games that appeal to their children, perhaps because many games, including "Bloody Day," "Sniper Assassin 2," and "Beat Me Up," are available free on computers, tablets, and cell phones, and children play them away from the watchful eyes of parents. Despite all the public controversy over violent video

The ability to use technology is considered key to success in an increasingly wired world. This 11-year-old, who lives in a remote village outside of Mumbai, is using a laptop provided through a special project funded by a non-governmental organization.

HEART OF THE CITY   *BY MARK TATULLI*

© 2003 Mark Tatulli/Distr. by Universal Press Syndicate

email: heartofthecity@hotmail.com   www.ucomics.com/heartofthecity

Interactive computer games have introduced entirely new ways of playing ball.

games, one national survey found that only 17 percent of parents check their children's video game ratings (Rideout et al., 2005), and only 30 percent set rules about the type of video games their children are allowed to play (Rideout, Foehr, & Roberts, 2010).

The Content of Interactive Media Like TV content, the content of interactive media, particularly that of violent interactive games, has received a huge amount of attention in the popular press. It has also received increased attention from the scientific community. For the most part, research finds strong support for the conclusion that violent video game play is associated with an increase in aggressive, antisocial behavior (Anderson et al., 2010). Interestingly, more recent studies find stronger associations than did earlier research, perhaps reflecting the fact that video games have become increasingly graphic, explicit, and realistic (Comstock & Scharrer, 2007). In addition to their association with aggression and antisocial behavior, violent video games would appear to affect children's perceptions of real-world crime. For instance, a study of more than 300 Flemish 3rd- through 6th-graders found that children who played a lot of violent video games tended to overestimate the amount of violent crime occurring in the real world (Van Mierlo & Van den Bulck, 2004). This finding contributes to the concern that repeated exposure to video game violence may desensitize children to actual violence, making it seem normal and acceptable and reducing children's capacity to respond empathically to the emotional distress of others (Funk et al., 2004). Although this concern about the effects of repeated exposure arises with other violent media as well, it is heightened in the case of interactive media because children are actively and constantly making violent choices and being rewarded (receiving more points, getting to the next level) for making these choices.

All told, research on the effects of media on children's development paints a consistent, if complex, picture. Children are immersed in media, and the media can have pronounced effects on how and what children think and feel. At the same time, however, children are active agents in the process; their individual differences and preferences shape how they are affected.

▲ APPLY :: CONNECT :: DISCUSS

Some argue that exposure to violent and aggressive interactive games causes children to be more aggressive. Others believe that such games are a symptom, not a cause, of the fact that our species and/or society is inherently aggressive, and that children's exposure to these games is unlikely to make much difference. What is your own position on this classic chicken-or-egg debate? What evidence supports your position?

Contexts, Risk, and Resilience

prevention science An area of research that examines the biological and social processes that lead to maladjustment as well as those that are associated with healthy development.

risk factors Personal characteristics or environmental circumstances that increase the probability of negative outcomes for children. Risk is a statistic that applies to groups, not individuals.

Questions about the impact of different contexts on children's development are motivated by a desire to protect children from harm and to promote their health and well-being. In recent years, a new area of research called **prevention science** has emerged to examine the biological and social processes that lead to maladjustment, as well as those that are associated with healthy development (Wandersman & Florin, 2003).

Developmentalists working within this field are particularly interested in identifying **risk factors**, personal characteristics or environmental circumstances that increase the probability of negative outcomes for children. Risk is a statistic that applies to groups, not individuals. One can say, for example, that children who have parents who are depressed are more likely than the general population to become depressed themselves, but one cannot say that a particular child whose father or mother is depressed is necessarily at risk for becoming depressed. Most risk factors are not the direct cause of the developmental problems or disorders with which they are associated but, instead, interact in complex ways with other risk factors in contributing to a problem (Roosa, 2000). For example, having a poorly educated mother is a risk factor for school failure—but not a cause of it. Rather, if a child with a poorly educated mother is failing in school, despite being of normal intelligence, the failure can be seen as a large puzzle in which one piece is the mother's lack of education and of familiarity with the demands of school (for example, the need for the child to spend time at home studying), with other pieces possibly including a peer group that does not value academic achievement, a school with limited resources due to its location in an economically distressed community, and other risk factors such as poor nutrition and exposure to environmental pollutants.

Many studies have demonstrated that most serious developmental problems are associated with a combination of biological, social, and environmental risk factors interacting over a considerable period of time (Cicchetti & Toth, 1998; Luthar et al., 2000; Sameroff et al., 1998; Shaw et al., 1998). Thus, an increase in the number of risk factors increases the likelihood of problems (see Figure 10.13 for a related example involving IQ scores). However, all of these studies have also demonstrated marked individual differences in outcome among children who live in highly stressful circumstances. Many children who grow up in the face of adversity—who are raised by alcoholic parents, attend substandard schools, have siblings who belong to gangs, experience dislocation due to war or homelessness due to poverty—are able to rise above their circumstances and lead healthy, productive lives. That is, they seem to have **resilience**—the ability to recover quickly from the adverse effects of early experience or to persevere in the face of stress with no apparent negative psychological consequences. Such cases have led developmentalists to search for the sources of children's resilience, referred to as **protective factors** (Luthar et al., 2000; Robinson, 2000). Table 10.5 summarizes risk and protective factors that have been identified.

At this point, you are well aware of how children's development can be impaired by risks present in family, community, and media contexts. When children are harmed by social chaos, poverty, abuse, hunger, or disease, responsible adults look for ways to reduce their suffering. This is, in fact, the goal of prevention science. A question that reaches deeply to address this goal is: What fundamental needs must be met to assure that children will develop into healthy, well-adjusted adults? In an effort to answer this question, the General Assembly of the United Nations in 1959 produced a document called the "United Nations Declaration of the Rights of the Child" (see Table 10.6). This document reflected governments' recognition of the importance of coming together for the sake of protecting and nurturing the world's children (Colon & Colon, 2001). The declaration was followed, in 1989, by the "United Nations Convention on the Rights of the Child," a binding resolution to provide children with specific protections. As of this writing, it has been ratified by all countries except two—Somalia and the United States.

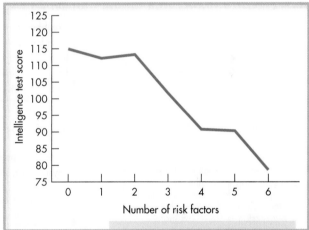

FIGURE 10.13 The average IQ scores for 13-year-olds decrease markedly when their development is affected by more than two risk factors. (From Sameroff et al., 1993.)

resilience The ability to recover quickly from the adverse effects of early experience or persevere in the face of stress with no apparent special negative psychological consequences.

protective factors Environmental and personal factors that are the source of children's resilience in the face of hardship.

public policies Governmental laws and programs designed to promote the welfare of children and families.

Cliff Volpe / Getty Images

table 10.5

Examples of Risk and Protective Factors Associated with Childhood Problems

Risk Factors	Protective Factors
Child Characteristics	
Difficult infant temperament	Easy infant temperament
Limited cognitive abilities	High intelligence
Insecure attachments	Secure attachments
Low self-esteem	High self-esteem
Poor peer relations	Positive peer relations
School difficulties	Positive adaptation to school
Psychopathology	Good mental health
Family	
Domestic violence	Good marital relations
Financial hardship	Consistent employment
Hostile family environment	Positive family relations
Parental psychopathology	Good parental mental health
Maladaptive child-rearing skills	Positive child-rearing skills
Neighborhood and Community	
High levels of community violence and crime	Low levels of community violence and crime
Impoverished community	Economically thriving community
Lack of community services	Extensive, easily accessed community services
Little or weak church presence	Supportive church
Society	
Lack of child-centered programs and policies	National support of education and children's rights
Social acceptance of violence	Social intolerance of violence
Physical punishment of children acceptable	Physical punishment unacceptable as a disciplinary practice
Economic recession	Strong economy with low unemployment

Source: Adapted from Cicchetti et al., 2000.

These young Uzbek children are helping each other wash in preparation for a meal. Violent ethnic clashes that took place in Kyrgyzstan in 2010 left many families, including this one, living outdoors in the ruins of what once were their homes.

In addition to international organizations such as the United Nations, individual governments have worked to develop programs to optimize children's development. **Public policies** are governmental laws and programs designed to promote the welfare of children and families. In the United States, public policies range from nutritional and education programs such as Women, Infants, and Children (WIC) and Head Start to policies regarding children's television programming and advertising and laws that govern the age at which children can be employed, married, vote, admitted to military service, or required to attend school.

This chapter has by no means surveyed all the contexts that influence the lives and development of children. Many children also spend considerable time in peer-group contexts and the special contexts created by religious or ethnic traditions and backgrounds. Indeed, children's ecologies include a great variety of interacting systems that can be mutually supportive, mutually damaging, or present a mixture of risk and protective factors. Each child finds, and responds to, a myriad of meanings across a vast array of contexts according to his or her unique characteristics and past experiences, underscoring the incredible diversity of developmental pathways and outcomes.

table 10.6

United Nations Declaration of the Rights of the Child

Proclaimed by General Assembly Resolution 1386(XIV) of 20 November 1959

Principle 1

The child shall enjoy all the rights set forth in this Declaration. Every child, without any exception whatsoever, shall be entitled to these rights, without distinction or discrimination on account of race, color, sex, language, religion, political or other opinion, national or social origin, property, birth or other status, whether of himself or of his family.

Principle 2

The child shall enjoy special protection, and shall be given opportunities and facilities, by law and by other means, to enable him to develop physically, mentally, morally, spiritually and socially in a healthy and normal manner and in conditions of freedom and dignity. In the enactment of laws for this purpose, the best interests of the child shall be the paramount consideration.

Principle 3

The child shall be entitled from his birth to a name and a nationality.

Principle 4

The child shall enjoy the benefits of social security. He shall be entitled to grow and develop in health; to this end, special care and protection shall be provided both to him and to his mother, including adequate pre-natal and post-natal care. The child shall have the right to adequate nutrition, housing, recreation and medical services.

Principle 5

The child who is physically, mentally or socially handicapped shall be given the special treatment, education and care required by his particular condition.

Principle 6

The child, for the full and harmonious development of his personality, needs love and understanding. He shall, wherever possible, grow up in the care and under the responsibility of his parents, and, in any case, in an atmosphere of affection and of moral and material security; a child of tender years shall not, save in exceptional circumstances, be separated from his mother. Society and the public authorities shall have the duty to extend particular care to children without a family and to those without adequate means of support. Payment of State and other assistance towards the maintenance of children of large families is desirable.

Principle 7

The child is entitled to receive education, which shall be free and compulsory, at least in the elementary stages. He shall be given an education which will promote his general culture and enable him, on a basis of equal opportunity, to develop his abilities, his individual judgement, and his sense of moral and social responsibility, and to become a useful member of society. The best interests of the child shall be the guiding principle of those responsible for his education and guidance; that responsibility lies in the first place with his parents.

The child shall have full opportunity for play and recreation, which should be directed to the same purposes as education; society and the public authorities shall endeavor to promote the enjoyment of this right.

Principle 8

The child shall in all circumstances be among the first to receive protection and relief.

Principle 9

The child shall be protected against all forms of neglect, cruelty and exploitation. He shall not be the subject of traffic, in any form.

The child shall not be admitted to employment before an appropriate minimum age; he shall in no case be caused or permitted to engage in any occupation or employment which would prejudice his health or education, or interfere with his physical, mental or moral development.

Principle 10

The child shall be protected from practices which may foster racial, religious and any other form of discrimination. He shall be brought up in a spirit of understanding, tolerance, friendship among peoples, peace and universal brotherhood, and in full consciousness that his energy and talents should be devoted to the service of his fellow men.

▲ APPLY :: CONNECT :: DISCUSS

Visit the Web site of the United Nations Children's Fund (UNICEF) at www.unicef.org. What are the priorities of the organization (see "What We Do")? Explore the most recent *State of the World's Children* report.

SUMMARY

- The contexts of children's development can be thought of as nested, interacting ecosystems. Each context can provide resources for positive growth or present significant challenges to health and well-being.

The Family Context

- Families are the first influence on development and one of the most important. The culture affects the way parents treat and socialize their children.

- The two major forms of family structure are nuclear families (parents and their children) and extended families (parents and their children and other kin), each with different implications for children's socialization. Although industrialization brought a shift to the nuclear family, the extended family prevailed for most of human history and remains important as a strategy for dealing with low income. From an evolutionary perspective, caregiving by extended kin may have made possible humans' extended childhood and large brain.

- Parents the world over have three goals: first, ensuring their children's survival; second, ensuring that their children will be economically productive adults; and third, ensuring that their children will share the group's values. Parenting practices reflect this hierarchy of goals.

- Research initiated by Diana Baumrind found three patterns of parenting:
  - Authoritative—parents exert some control, explain the reasoning behind standards and punishments, and express warmth
  - Authoritarian—parents focus on obedience and control, use physical punishment, and tend not to express warmth.
  - Permissive—parents express warmth but fail to set standards or exert control.

- The authoritative parenting pattern style is associated with more self-reliant and self-controlled child behavior.

- Siblings play important roles in one another's social and cognitive development, with their relationship influenced by culture and by factors such as age and gender and the family's emotional climate.

- In many of the world's countries, families are becoming increasingly diverse, through immigration and through changes in family composition.

- Approximately 22 percent of children in the United States have immigrant parents. Parenting styles and values vary across cultures, with education, for example, being more highly valued by new U.S. immigrant parents than by those who have been established in the United States for a generation or more.

- About half of all children born in the United States today will spend at least some of their childhood in a single-parent home. Children from single-parent families have more behavioral, social, and academic problems. Various explanations have been offered, and it appears that cultural contexts may mitigate problems.

- Research on the increasing number of children in gay and lesbian households, while limited, paints a generally positive picture of the children's development.

- Various family factors may impede children's development. The most significant of these factors are poverty, having an adolescent parent, and abuse.
  - Poverty, affecting approximately 1 in 5 children in the United States, touches all aspects of life—housing, health care, education, even safety. Poverty in early childhood is associated with mental and physical health problems and problems in intellectual development.
  - Despite a recent dramatic drop, the teen birth rate in the United States remains among the highest in the industrialized world. Children of unmarried teenage mothers tend to be more aggressive, less self-controlled, and less intellectually advanced than other children.
  - Definitions of abuse vary widely across cultures. Causes of abuse by parents are not clear, but a parent's childhood experience of abuse, stresses on the family, certain maternal and child characteristics, and cultural acceptance of violence may increase its likelihood.

Nonparental Child Care

- By age 4, eighty-six percent of children in the United States spend time in regular nonparental care, which takes three forms: home child care (in the children's own home), family child care (in someone else's home), and care in child-care centers (organized facilities supervised by licensed professionals).

- The effects of early child care depend largely on the quality of the care. Children in child-care centers may be subject to higher levels of stress than are children who receive care in their own homes. Nevertheless, if they are in high-quality child-care centers, their intellectual development is at least as good as that of their peers being cared for in the home. Social and emotional effects appear to be both positive (e.g., more self-sufficiency and verbal expressiveness) and negative (e.g., more aggressive behavior), with maternal sensitivity and family SES playing a role. With ethnic-minority children in particular, an understanding of the effects of child care requires an understanding of the larger context.

Neighborhoods and Communities

- Neighborhoods and communities differ substantially in the resources they provide children and families, with consequences for children's quality of life and mental health outcomes. Communities may also differ in the values and beliefs transmitted to children.

- Children are often adversely affected by living in distressed communities—communities characterized by economic disadvantage, physical disorder, and social disorganization.

Media Contexts

- Children in technologically advanced societies are extensively exposed to a wide range of media. Research has investigated how the form and content of different media affect development.

- Children's literature may help children with emotional control and development.

- Young children are exposed more to television than to any other medium. A concern about TV viewing is that young children have trouble distinguishing between appearance and reality. Other causes for concern are TV violence, which is especially common in children's shows, and stereotyping,

evident in the somewhat limited roles of female and ethnic-minority characters.

- Increasingly important, interactive media such as video games help children develop cognitive skills. Like television, interactive media raise various concerns, including regarding the effects on relationships with peers and with family and the effects that playing games with violent content may have on children's thinking and behavior.

Contexts, Risk, and Resilience

- Prevention science seeks to protect children from harm and promote their well-being by identifying risk factors—personal and environmental characteristics that increase the probability of negative outcomes—as well as protective factors—factors that may be sources of children's resilience.

- International organizations such as the United Nations, and individual governments through public policies, work to optimize children's development.

Key Terms

family structure, p. 345

nuclear families, p. 345

extended families, p. 345

allocaregiving, p. 347

cooperative breeding, p. 347

no-nonsense parenting, p. 348

authoritative parenting pattern, p. 349

authoritarian parenting pattern, p. 349

permissive parenting pattern, p. 349

home child care, p. 365

family child care, p. 365

child-care centers, p. 366

social capital, p. 369

neighborhood physical disorder, p. 371

social disorganization, p. 371

media, p. 372

prevention science, p. 380

risk factors, p. 380

resilience, p. 381

protective factors, p. 381

public policies, p. 382

Major Milestones of Middle Childhood

	Physical Domain	Cognitive Domain	Social and Emotional Domain	
What Develops...	• Increase in muscle mass results in greater strength for boys and girls. • Increase in fat tissue changes overall shape of the body. • Sex differences in motor skills increase, with boys excelling in strength and girls in agility. • Continued brain growth and synaptic pruning, especially in late-maturing areas of the brain (frontal and prefrontal cortex). • Electrical activity in different brain areas becomes more synchronous, suggesting greater coordination between areas.	• Emergence of mental operations allows sorting, classification, experimentation with variables. • Increased memory and attention abilities. • Acquisition of memory strategies. • Increased memory ability due to greater efficiency in encoding, storing, and retrieving information. • Increased knowledge of cognition and memory and of own limitations in both.	• Stage of industry versus inferiority; success in coping with increased expectations for maturity result in positive self-esteem. • Emergence of playing games with rules. • Moral behavior regulated less by fear of authority, more by social relationships. • Emergence of clearly defined peer social structures. • Gender-typed behaviors increase. • Increasing proficiency at making and keeping friends, and dealing with interpersonal conflicts. • Emergence of social comparison through which self is defined in relation to peers.	
Sociocultural Contributions and Consequences...	• Access to healthy food influences changes in height and weight • Cultures provide different opportunities for boys and girls to engage in sports and physical activities.	• School experience is associated with development of specific intellectual skills and memory abilities. • Different cultures may support the development of different memory and planning strategies. • Cultural and socioeconomic factors affect whether families encourage school-related activities. • Different instructional methods affect the rate and effectiveness of learning.	• Cultural differences in whether particular behaviors are seen as matters of morality or just convention. • Transition from elementary to middle school may contribute to increase in bullying as children reorganize social relationships. • Cultures may support development of different forms of aggression in girls and boys. • Sociocultural contexts may support development of cooperation or competition between children. • Cultural differences affect parental expectations for mature behavior and degree of parental supervision.	

part

Middle Childhood

IV

Anthropological descriptions of a wide variety of cultures indicate that as children reach the age of 5 to 7 years, they are no longer restricted to the home or to settings where they are carefully watched by adults. Instead, they become responsible for behaving themselves and are given responsibilities in a variety of new contexts, including contexts where they are alone or interacting with peers. The new activities they engage in vary from one society to the next. Among some of the Mayan people in the highlands of Guatemala, for example, boys go out to gather wood, a solitary activity that takes them well beyond the range of watchful adults, while girls spend more time doing domestic work in the company of their mothers and the older women of the village (Rogoff, 2003). In the United States, by contrast, boys and girls alike spend long hours in school receiving formal education; both in and out of school, their interactions with peers increase.

All these shifts prove important to children. Thus, solitary activities, such as gathering wood or chasing birds away from a growing rice crop, and peer interactions, such as playing games, exchanging secrets, or simply hanging out, can be as significant for development as time spent in the classroom. Being in charge of the family cornfield or a younger sibling or engaging in informal interaction with peers provides children with important opportunities to learn what it means to take responsibility, to explore social relationships, and to develop moral understanding and personal identity.

The fact that cultures everywhere give children greater autonomy and responsibility as they enter middle childhood both reflects and supports the significant expansion of children's physical and cognitive capacities. For example, as you shall see, evidence from experiments, naturalistic observations, and clinical interviews makes it clear that during middle childhood children are increasingly able to think more deeply and logically, to follow through on a task once it is undertaken, and to keep track of several aspects of a situation at one time.

Our discussion of middle childhood is divided into three chapters. Chapter 11 focuses on the changes in children's physical and cognitive capacities between the ages of 6 and 12 that support the new freedoms and responsibilities that adults place upon them. Chapter 12 examines the influence of schooling on development, with particular attention to the organization of school activities and to the intellectual capacities that schooling both demands and fosters. Chapter 13 focuses on emotional development and on the significance of the new social relations that emerge during middle childhood, particularly among peers. The influence of physical, cognitive, and social factors, as they are woven together in different cultural contexts, creates the particular tapestry of middle childhood as it is encountered around the world.

387

Physical and Cognitive Development in Middle Childhood

Physical and Motor Development

Patterns of Growth

Motor Development

Brain Development

Concrete-Operational Development

Conservation

Classification

Planning

Metacognition

Limitations of Concrete Operations

Information-Processing Approaches

The Role of Memory

Thinking About Memory

Increased Control of Attention

Executive Function

The Role of Social and Cultural Contexts

Is the Acquisition of Conservation Universal?

Cultural Variations in the Use of Memory Strategies

Cultural Variations in Planning

Individual Differences in Cognitive Development

Measuring Intelligence

Persistent Questions About Intelligence

Reconsidering the Cognitive Changes in Middle Childhood

A girl from the Kukatja community, a hunter-gatherer society in the desert of Western Australia, provides the following description of life in her camp:

Mothers and fathers gone out hunting and leave us kids in camp. When we got hungry we go hunting for little lizard, get him and cook it and eat him up. Me little bit big now, I go hunting myself, tracking goanna [a type of lizard] and kill him. . . . Soon as mother leave him, little ones go hunting, kill animals, blue tongue, mountain devil [both lizards], take them home before mother and father come back, cook and eat it. Mothers, they bring him goannas and blue tongue and father one still long way. Mother come back and feed all them kids. . . . After lunch mother and father go hunting for supper, all the little kids walk and kill little lizard, take him home, cook and eat him. . . .

Morning again, father one he go hunting. All little kids go hunting self. . . . Mother go out separate from father and come back with big mob of animals. Me big enough to hunt around self. . . . Morningtime, father one bin for hunting long way way. He bin get and kill an emu, bring and cook him. Everyone happy, they bin say he good hunter. Mother and father sometime bin come back late from hunting. They bin go long way.

(Kapanankga, 1995; cited in Bird & Bird, 2005, p. 129).

Despite being a "little bit big now," and able to track, kill, and cook goanna, the Kukatja girl quoted above remains dependent on her mother and father to provide adequate nutrition and care throughout the years of middle childhood. As we have discussed in earlier chapters, our species is unique in its prolonged period of childhood dependency; once weaned, children in all societies rely on their elders for care and protection for well over a decade (Kaplan et al., 2003; Bird & Bird, 2005).

On the other hand, research conducted in many societies shows that adults begin to have new expectations when their children approach 6 years of age. Among the Ngoni of Malawi, in central Africa, for example, adults believe that the loss of milk teeth and the emergence of second teeth (starting around the age of 6) signal that children should begin to act more independently. They are supposed to stop playing childish games and start learning skills that will be essential when they grow up. They are also expected to understand their place and are held accountable for being discourteous. The boys leave the protection and control of women and move into dormitories, where they must adapt to a system of male dominance and male life. Margaret Read (1983) describes the difficulties that this transition to a new stage of life causes for Ngoni boys:

There was no doubt that this abrupt transition, like the sudden weaning [several years earlier], was a shock for many boys between six-and-a-half and seven-and-a-half. From having been impudent, well fed, self-confident, and spoiled youngsters among the women many of them quickly became skinny, scruffy, subdued, and had a hunted expression. (p. 49)

Although children begin to hunt and work at early ages in the Kukatja community of Western Australia, they also have time to play together in the mud after a rare rainstorm in their desert home.

Observations of life among the Ifaluk of Micronesia provide a similar picture. The Ifaluk believe that at the age of 6 years, children gain "social intelligence," which includes the ability to acquire important cultural knowledge and skills, as well as the ability to work, to adhere to social norms, and to demonstrate compassion for others—all valued adult behaviors (Lutz, 1987). In Western Europe and the United States, this same transition has long been considered the beginning of the "age of reason" (White, 1996).

Adults' expectations that their children will begin to behave more maturely at around the age of 6 or 7 arise from a combination of cultural traditions, ecological circumstances and demands (for example, whether children must learn to cross busy streets or fast-moving streams), and their observations of how well their children now cope with new demands (Sameroff & Haith, 1996). At the age of 6, children are strong and agile enough to catch a runaway goat or to carry their little sisters on their hips. They become more proficient at hunting and gathering food and know not to let a baby crawl near an open fire (Bock et al., 2005; Bird & Bird, 2005). They can wait for the school bus without wandering off. They can, sometimes under duress, sit still for several hours at a time while adults attempt to instruct them, and they are beginning to be able to carry out their chores in an acceptable manner. In short, they can perform tasks independently, formulate goals, and resist the temptation to abandon them.

In this chapter, we focus on the physical and cognitive changes of middle childhood that lead to these advances and might justify adults' new demands and expectations of children. The physical changes of middle childhood—continued growth, improved motor skills, and increased brain maturation and activity—are readily measurable. Changes in children's cognitive functioning, however, are more difficult to measure and, as you might expect, have been addressed by different theoretical approaches.

Physical and Motor Development

An obvious reason that children can do more on their own is that they are bigger, are stronger, and have more endurance than they had when they were younger. Size and strength increase significantly during middle childhood, although more

The transition to middle childhood is often marked by new responsibilities, privileges, and rituals. These young Nicaraguan children are walking to church for their first Communion.

slowly than in earlier years. Motor development shows marked improvement as children perfect the skills needed for running, throwing, catching, and turning somersaults.

Patterns of Growth

Children in the United States are on average about 39 inches tall and about 36 pounds at age 4; by the time they are 6 years old they are about 45 inches tall and weigh about 45 pounds. At the start of adolescence, 6 or 7 years later, their average height will have increased to almost 5 feet, and their weight, to approximately 90 pounds (Cameron, 2002). During middle childhood, increases in muscle mass contribute to increased strength in both boys and girls (Figure 11.1). In addition, beginning at approximately age 7 for girls and age 8 for boys, there is a gradual increase in fat tissue that contributes to the changing appearance of the body (Figure 11.2). Like all aspects of development, children's growth during middle childhood continues to depend on the interaction of environmental and genetic factors.

Height Now fully grown, Amita just barely reaches the 5'3" mark on the measuring stick. There would be nothing remarkable about her small stature except for the fact that she comes from a very tall family. Growing up with jokes that question her mother's relationship with the milkman, Amita is good-natured about defying what we know regarding how genetic factors influence one's height: Tall parents tend to have tall children. Monozygotic twins reared together are very similar in their patterns of growth, and those reared apart still tend to resemble each other more than do dizygotic twins. Yet environmental conditions also play a significant role, as attested to by the existence of many cases in which one monozygotic twin is significantly smaller than the other because of the effects of illness (Amita attributes her shortness to several severe infections suffered during infancy) or a poor environment, as when, in the case of twins reared apart, one twin is raised in a healthy environment and the other is raised in impoverished conditions.

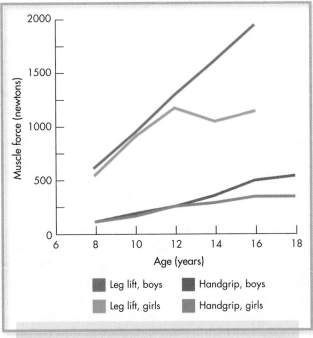

FIGURE 11.1 Developmental changes in strength for boys and for girls.

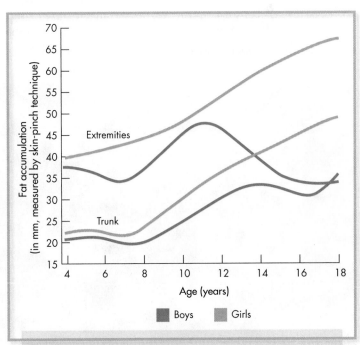

FIGURE 11.2 Developmental changes in fat distribution for boys and for girls.

The environmental contribution to size can also be seen in the variations in the height and rate of growth typical of populations that undergo changes in living conditions. From the late 1970s to the early 1990s, Mayan families from Guatemala migrated to the United States in record numbers (Bogin et al., 2002). Barry Bogin and his colleagues measured the height of more than four hundred 5- to 12-year-old Mayan American children in 1999 and 2000. These data were compared with data for a sample of more than 1000 Mayan children living in Guatemala at the time. The Mayan American children were about 4½ inches taller, on average, than their Mayan peers living in Guatemala. These results illustrate how the heights of human populations can be sensitive indicators of the quality of the environment for growth.

One of the key environmental factors that moderates genetic growth potential is nutrition. Poor children, who have less access to nutritious food and good health care than do children in well-off families, are usually smaller than their well-off peers. This difference is especially evident if the lack of access is extreme. For example, in a study of the physical development of North Korean children whose families fled to South Korea because of North Korea's chronic food shortages, the children's malnourishment was so severe that, by the time they reached their 14th birthdays, the boys were approximately 6 inches shorter, and the girls, 3 inches shorter, than their South Korean counterparts (Pak, 2010).

As indicated, health also plays a role in a child's growth. Growth slows during illnesses, even mild illnesses. When children are adequately nourished, this slow-down is usually followed by a period of rapid "catch-up growth," which quickly restores them to their genetically normative path of growth (Georgieff & Raghavendra, 2001). When nutritional intake is inadequate, however, the children never do catch up, and their growth is stunted (deRegnier et al., 2007).

Weight Body weight, like height, is influenced by genetic factors. A study of 540 Danish adoptees found a strong correlation between the adoptees' weight as adults and the weight of their biological parents, especially their mothers (Stunkard et al., 1986). Yet environmental factors—including the quantity and quality of food available—play a significant role in determining weight (Whitaker et al., 1997). For example, the number of calories consumed in an average day can have long-term effects for a child's growth. The consumption of as few as 50 extra calories a day can lead to an excess weight gain of 5 pounds over a course of a year (Kolata, 1986). Given that the average 12-ounce can of soda contains 150 calories and that soda has replaced bread as a major source of calories in the diets of American children and adults, you will not be surprised to learn that scores of studies have implicated the consumption of soft drinks as a major contributor to childhood obesity (reviewed in Vartanian, Schwartz, & Brownell, 2007).

Because of the growing problem of obesity among American children, increasing attention has been focused on the factors that contribute to it (Harrison et al., 2011). (See the box "Let's Move! A National Campaign to Battle Childhood Obesity," pp. 394–395) While obesity is commonly measured by weight, many researchers have argued that it can be diagnosed earlier and more accurately by measuring *body mass index* (*BMI*), the ratio of weight to

Rising rates of obesity among children throughout the world have spurred efforts to prevent it, including the exercise program in which these children participate.

AP Photo / Charlie Riedel

height (American Academy of Pediatrics, 2003). BMI can be calculated by multiplying a person's weight in pounds (or kilograms) by 705 and dividing by the person's height in inches (or meters) squared. A BMI above the 95th percentile for age and sex is considered obese; a BMI between the 85th and 95th percentile is considered overweight and at risk for obesity. An analysis of the National Health and Nutrition Examination Survey 2007–2008 revealed that among children between the ages of 2 and 19 years, nearly 17 percent were at or above the 95th percentile (with close to 12 percent at or above the 97th percentile) and 31.7 percent were at or above the 85th percentile. Within specific age brackets, 10 percent of 2- to 5-year-olds, 19.6 percent of 6- to 10-year-olds, and 18.1 percent of 12- to 19-year-olds were at or above the 95th percentile (Ogden & Flegal, 2010).

A vast variety of biological and environmental factors are known to contribute to childhood overweight and obesity. In an effort to organize these factors into a "big picture," Kristen Harrison and her colleagues proposed the Six-Cs developmental ecological model (Harrison et al., 2011). As indicated in the following list, the six Cs range from the microscopic level of genes to the most general level of culture.

- Cell: biological and genetic characteristics, such as the inheritance of genes that contribute to fat storage.

- Child: behaviors, attitudes, and knowledge relevant to weight gain, including eating patterns, exercise, and the ability to control behavior (self-regulation).

- Clan: family characteristics, such as parents' encouragement to exercise and eat healthy foods, family media use, and whether the child was fed breast or artifical milk during infancy.

- Community: factors within the local community, including school meal programs and vending-machine options, availability of grocery stores, and access to recreational activities.

- Country: state and national characteristics such as government funding for nutrition programs, healthy-eating media campaigns, and state or federal dietary guidelines.

- Culture: cultural and social beliefs and practices, including gender-role expectations concerning eating and activity, cultural standards for beauty, and norms regarding portion sizes served in restaurants.

Given that the risk of childhood obesity resides at multiple levels, Harrison and her colleagues are not surprised that most intervention efforts to reduce overweight and obesity have been unsuccessful, because such efforts are narrowly focused at a single level. For example, one approach may target the *child level* by engaging childen in physical activity programs, whereas another may target the *community level* by introducing healthier lunch menus at schools. Ecological models such as the Six-Cs underscore the importance of comprehensive interventions that tackle childhood overweight and obesity from multiple levels simultaneously.

Motor Development

Walking along the beach one day, we saw a girl about 7 years old and her little brother, who was about 4 years old, following their father and their older brother, who was 10 or 11 years old. The father and older brother were tossing a ball back and forth as they walked. The girl was hopping along the sand on one foot, while

In the Field   Let's Move! A National Campaign to Battle Childhood Obesity

Name:	Michelle Obama
Education:	B.A. in sociology, Princeton University; J.D., Harvard University
Profession:	Lawyer
Current Objectives:	Use resources of position as First Lady of the United States to promote initiatives to reduce childhood overweight and obesity

MICHELLE OBAMA IS ON A MISSION TO ELIMINATE childhood obesity in a generation. To this end, she recently launched a nationwide campaign called "Let's Move!", which targets four areas regarded as key to children's healthy nutrition and weight: parental knowledge about nutrition and exercise; the quality of food in schools; accessibility and affordability of healthy food in communities; and physical education.

Since 1980, the incidence of childhood obesity has tripled among school-age children (Ogden, Carroll, Curtin, Lamb & Flegal, 2010). The consequences of becoming obese during childhood and adolescence are severe. Obese children are often rejected by their peers, causing many of them to become withdrawn and suffer from a loss of self-esteem. Obese children are also more vulnerable to a variety of serious health problems such as asthma, heart disease, diabetes, respiratory disease, and orthopedic disorders (Davies & Fitzgerald, 2008). In recent years, there has been an alarming increase among obese minority children in the incidence of Type II diabetes, a serious condition that can lead to kidney disease, eye disorders, and nervous system problems as well as heart disease and stroke.

There appear to be three important periods during which there is an increased risk for developing obesity that persists into adulthood (Strauss, 1999). The first is the prenatal period, during which

Bob Daemmrich/The Image Works

Although many school cafeterias are now offering a greater variety of fruits and vegetables, children often bypass the salads and reach for the fries. It is also common for children to supplement their lunches with unhealthy foods that they bring from home, such as potato chips and sports drinks.

maternal overnutrition or maternal undernutrition (see pp. 91–93), as well as smoking during pregnancy, raise the risk that the child will become overweight (Tabacchi, Giammanco, La Guardia, & Giammanco, 2007). The second important period is related to what is known as the adiposity rebound period, during which children's body fat begins to increase again after a period of decreasing. Normally, the adiposity rebound period occurs at around age 6. Longitudinal studies have found that children whose body fat increases before the age of 5½ are significantly more likely than other children to become and remain obese (Centers for Disease Control and Prevention, 2009; McCarthy et al., 2007). The third important period for the development of persistent obesity is adolescence, when there are changes in the quantity and location of body fat. This period is especially critical for girls. In boys, the quantity of body fat normally decreases by about 40 percent, whereas in girls, the quantity of body fat increases by about 40 percent, putting girls at elevated risk for becoming and staying obese.

Obviously, children's risk of obesity is influenced substantially by the family, including its mealtime habits, food preferences, and leisure activities—how much time is spent watching television or going for walks, for example (Galloway, Fiorito, Lee, & Birch, 2005; Larson, Neumark-Sztainer, Hannan, & Story, 2007). It is also influenced by parents' knowledge of nutrition and access to healthy food in the community.

her younger brother scrambled to keep up with her. Suddenly the little girl threw her arms up in the air, leaned over, threw her feet up, and did a cartwheel. She then did another cartwheel. Her younger brother stopped to watch her. Then he tried one. He fell in a heap in the sand, while she continued doing one perfect cartwheel after another. He picked himself up and ran ahead so that he was now between his father and his older brother. His father tossed the ball to him. He missed it, and when he picked it up and tried to throw it back, it flew off to the side. His older brother retrieved it and made a perfect throw.

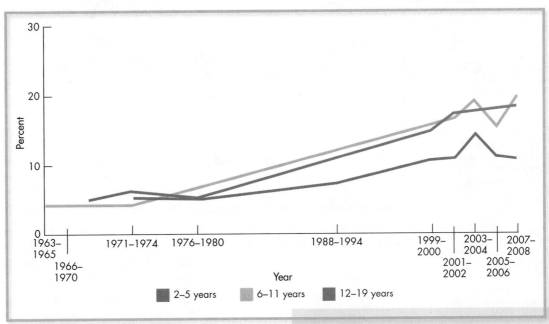

Since the late 1970s, there have been dramatic increases in the percentages of children and adolescents in the United States who are overweight and obese. (Adapted from Ogden & Carroll, 2010.)

Michelle Obama's Let's Move! campaign helps families make informed choices at the supermarket by working with governmental agencies to improve nutrition labeling on food packages.

Social institutions, including schools, bear significant responsibility for children's eating behavior. For example, sugary drinks and snacks high in fat, sugar, and salt once were regular fare in school cafeterias and vending machines (Prentice & Jebb, 2003). Increasingly, however, many new school programs have tackled the obesity epidemic by including a greater variety of fresh fruits and vegetables, reducing the amount of soda and candy sold in vending machines, and educating children about the importance of a healthy diet. Nutritionists and other health care professionals agree that to combat childhood obesity effectively, public attitudes must continue to shift responsibility from children and families to include the schools and other social institutions that provide children with meals and snacks when they are away from home. Let's Move! includes government support for schools to provide more nutritious meals. Noting that many schools are reducing or eliminating recess, physical education, and gym classes, Obama is also encouraging renewed attention to the importance of physical activity for children's health: "When we were growing up, it wasn't a choice. It wasn't either you learn how to read or you learn how to run. We did both." (Ferran, 2010).

Let's Move! is a broadly focused effort that encourages the cooperation of local, state, and federal governments, along with schools, businesses, and nonprofit agencies. As Obama explained, "We all know the numbers. I mean, one in three kids are overweight or obese, and we're spending $150 billion a year treating obesity-related illnesses. So we know this is a problem and there's a lot at stake."

In such everyday scenes you can see the increases in motor development that occur over the course of middle childhood (Figure 11.3). Children become stronger and more agile, and their balance improves. They run faster; they throw balls farther and with greater efficiency and are more likely to catch them. They also jump farther and higher than they did when they were younger, and they learn to skate, ride bikes, dance, swim, and climb trees as well as acquire a host of other physical skills during this period. Nonetheless, studies indicate that about 10 percent of 9-year-olds fail to develop skills like kicking and throwing, indicating that such

FIGURE 11.3 The physical changes of childhood make possible a range of new activities. The ability to kick a ball, for example, improves dramatically. (a) A young child learning to kick will simply push the leg forward, while (b) an older child will step forward, cock the leg, and take a limited swing at the ball. (c) By the end of middle childhood, the child is able to take a full swing at the ball while simultaneously moving arms and trunk to provide support and balance. (From Haywood & Getchell, 2005.)

In an example of how culture supports the development of fine motor skills, Michael carves a design in a clay turtle during a class focused on the pottery of Native Americans.

achievements require practice and do not develop purely as a result of maturation (Haywood & Getchell, 2005).

Gender Differences As a general rule, boys and girls differ in their physical skills. By the time they are 5 years old, boys, on average, can jump a little farther, run a bit faster, and throw a ball about 5 feet farther than the average girl. Boys also tend to be better at batting, kicking, dribbling, and catching balls than most girls. Girls, on the other hand, tend to be more agile than boys. Over the course of middle childhood, these sex differences in motor skills become more pronounced (Malina, 1998). On average, boys tend to be slightly advanced in motor abilities that require power and force, while girls often excel in fine motor skills, such as drawing and writing, or in gross motor skills that combine balance and foot movement, such as skipping and hopping and the skills needed in gymnastics (Cameron, 2002).

Boys tend to have slightly greater muscle mass than most girls do and are slightly bigger—until about the age of 10½, when girls spurt ahead in height for a few years—but these sex-related physical differences are not large enough in themselves to account for the superiority of boys in many motor skills during middle childhood. Cultural conceptions of the activities appropriate to boys and to girls also play a large role in shaping these differences in abilities. For example, being able to throw, catch, and hit a baseball is a valued set of skills for boys in U.S. culture. Correspondingly, parents usually encourage their sons, much more than their daughters, to develop these skills by buying them balls and bats, taking them to ballgames, talking about baseball with them, playing catch with them, and enrolling them in Little League. And in all cultures, it is also much truer for boys than for girls that those who are considered to be good athletes are more popular with their peers than those who show no athletic ability. While the participation of girls in such sports as baseball, soccer, and tennis has increased significantly in a number of countries in recent decades, girls are still not given the amount of encouragement and coaching that boys receive in these sports, nor are they rewarded to the extent boys are for having the abilities these sports require (Horn, 2002). Nonetheless, both boys and girls appear to profit from being active in sports. As shown in Figure 11.4, compared with peers who do not participate in sports, children who are highly involved in sports have (1) more positive friends who encourage behaviors such as doing well in school, (2) fewer negative friends who encourage behaviors such as disobeying parents, (3) higher self-esteem, (4) a greater sense of belonging at school, and (5) lower levels of depression (Simpkins et al., 2006). As we discuss a bit later, regular aerobic exercise may even increase the mathematics achievement and cognitive functioning of overweight children.

The Role of Practice. As suggested above, and as we have discussed in previous chapters, the practice of motor skills is essential to furthering motor development. A striking demonstration is provided in a laboratory study of how children bicycle across traffic-filled intersections (Plumert, Kearney, Cremer, Recker, & Strutt, 2011). As you will see, crossing the street involves considerably more than just looking both ways.

The study used a bicycling simulator, that is, a very high-tech stationary bike surrounded by enormous screens that projected a complex virtual town environment (see Figure 11.5). The participants—10-year-olds, 12-year-olds, and adults—"rode" the bicycle through the virtual town along a two-lane residential roadway with stop signs at 12 intersections. The high-tech bicycle generated data about the participant's pedal speed and steering, while video cameras recorded other behavior, such as head turns. After a short warm-up session in which the participants became acquainted with how the bike works, they were given the following instructions:

> Your job is to cross every intersection without getting hit by a car. So, when you get to an intersection, you will see a stream of cars coming from your left-hand side. Some of the spaces between the cars will be too small to get across without getting hit, and some will be big enough for you to get across without getting hit. You can wait as long as you need to before going across.

The researchers found that over the course of riding through 12 intersections, both children and adults chose to cross the street through increasingly smaller gaps between cars. This finding suggests that participants of all ages learned from their experiences in the virtual environment. In addition, there were interesting age differences in the timing of participants' riding through the intersections. At the first several intersections, the 10-year-olds had very little time to spare between clearing the intersection and the passing of the oncoming car. But by the end of their ride, they had increased their time-to-spare by an average of 25 percent. In contrast, the time-to-spare changed very little throughout the ride for 12-year-olds and adults. It seems that the 10-year-olds had much more room for improvement than did the older participants. Indeed, at later intersections, they crossed at higher rates of speed and also cut in closer behind the lead car. Their increased speed was likely due to the effects of practice on their ability to control the bike. Not only did they pedal faster, they became better able to look left for traffic without veering around like drunken sailors.

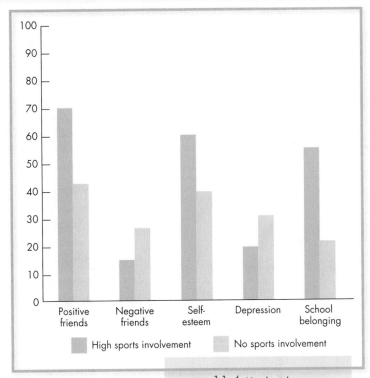

FIGURE 11.4 Youths who are highly involved in sports report more positive friends, fewer negative friends, higher self-esteem, lower levels of depression, and a greater sense of belonging at school, compared with youths who do not participate in sports. (Adapted from Simpkins, 2006, p. 298.)

FIGURE 11.5 To study the role of practice in the development of motor skills, researchers designed a high-tech bicycling simulator. Participants in the study rode a stationary bike surrounded by giant screens that made it seem as if they were riding through a town, complete with stop signs and intersections.

Brain Development

Middle childhood—particularly the early years, between ages 6 and 8—is a period of continued growth of the brain and of the development of specific kinds of brain functioning that are believed to underlie changes in cognitive skills.

1. Myelination, particularly in the frontal cortex, continues, and indeed will continue to adulthood (Janowsky & Carper, 1996; Sowell et al., 2007). (Recall from Chapter 4 that myelination provides the axon of cortical neurons with an insulating sheath of tissue that speeds transmission of nerve impulses.)

2. Synaptic pruning, the process by which unused synapses die off, continues for late-maturing areas of the brain (the frontal and prefrontal cortices), reducing the density of synapses among neurons. At the same time, connections among the remaining, utilized neurons become more stable (Sowell et al., 2002).

3. Brain activity patterns as measured by an EEG (electroencephalogram) undergo a dramatic change (Figure 11.6). Until the age of 5, EEGs recorded when children are awake display more theta activity (characteristic of adult sleep states) than alpha activity (characteristic of engaged attention). Between 5 and 7 years of age, the amounts of theta and alpha activity are about equal, but thereafter alpha activity (engaged attention) dominates (Corbin & Bickford, 1955).

4. The synchronization of electrical activity in different areas of the brain, called *EEG coherence,* increases significantly, reflecting the fact that different parts of the brain function more effectively as coordinated systems. Particularly important, according to Robert Thatcher (1994), is evidence of increased coordination between the electrical activity of the frontal lobes and the electrical activity in other parts of the brain.

This pattern of changes in brain structure and function—particularly in the frontal lobes and their connections to other parts of the brain—suggests that maturation of the brain plays an important role in the development of thinking during middle childhood, as it does in earlier periods. The pattern of brain changes following the onset of middle childhood permits the frontal lobes to coordinate the activities of other brain centers in a more complex way, enabling children to better control their attention, solve complex problems, form explicit plans, and engage in self-reflection, all behaviors that appear to undergo significant development in the transition to middle childhood. (The importance of the frontal lobes in these developments is supported by the fact that when the frontal lobes are damaged in humans and in other animals, the affected individuals are unable to maintain goals: They respond to irrelevant stimuli, they are easily thrown off track if their goal-directed activity is interrupted, and their actions become fragmentary and uncontrolled.)

One of the most convincing demonstrations that changes in brain functioning lead to changes in problem-solving processes comes from a study of changes in the brain activity of 5-year-old children being tested on a standard Piagetian task (conservation of quantity, which we will discuss later). The children wore caps that contained recording electrodes, allowing the researchers to track the changes in brain activity that accompanied their problem-solving endeavors. The children were first tested at age 5 and then

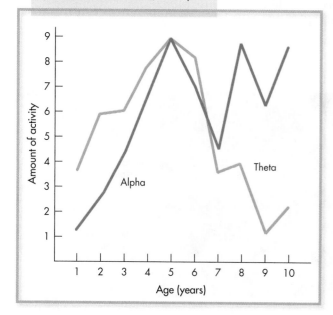

FIGURE 11.6 Changes in the amount of theta (sleeplike) and alpha (alert) EEG activity during development. Note that alpha waves come to predominate over theta waves around the age of 7. (From Corbin & Bickford, 1955.)

again at ages 6 and 7. Initially, the children did not succeed in solving the problem, but as they grew older, those who did succeed had a pattern of brain activity different from that of the children who failed at the task (Stauder et al., 1999), while the brain patterns of those who failed were similar to those observed among young children. These findings seem to support the idea that certain behavioral changes of middle childhood are linked to changes in the organization and functioning of the brain.

Another interesting example of the relationship between brain and behavior comes from a study linking differences in brain development to individual differences in children's intelligence (Shaw et al., 2006). On the basis of standardized tests of intelligence (which we discuss in detail later in this chapter), more than 300 children and adolescents were classified as being of superior intelligence, high intelligence, or average intelligence. Neuroimaging techniques were used to measure the thickness of each child's cortex. Interestingly, the researchers found that intelligence test scores correlated, not with cortical thickness per se, but with a certain *developmental pattern* of cortical thickening and thinning over the course of childhood. Specifically, as shown in Figure 11.7, children with superior intelligence tended to have thinner cortices at age 7 but then showed a marked increase

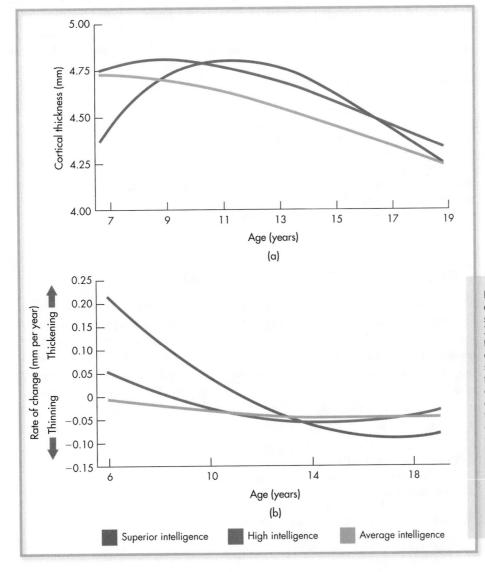

FIGURE 11.7 (a) Compared with children of high or average intelligence, children with superior intelligence have thinner cortices at 7 years of age, but thereafter their cortices thicken dramatically (by synaptogenesis) until age 11 and then begin to thin gradually (by synaptic pruning). This pattern suggests that the brains of children of superior intelligence are more flexible and better able to respond to children's experiences. (The data shown are for the right superior frontal gyrus; similar patterns are found for other parts of the cortex.) (b) The rate of change in cortical thickening (indicated by positive values) and thinning (indicated by negative values) is much more dynamic in children of superior intelligence than it is in children of high or average intelligence, suggesting more responsive experience-dependent brain processes. (Adapted from Figures 2a and 3 from Shaw et al., 2006, p. 677.)

in cortical thickening that peaked around 11 years of age, and then rapidly declined. In contrast, children with average intelligence showed a fairly steady decline in cortical thickening from age 7, while children with high intelligence demonstrated an intermediate pattern, but one more closely approximating that of the average intelligence group. Maximum cortical thickness occurred at 5.6 years for the average intelligence group, 8.5 years for the high intelligence group, and 11.2 years for the superior intelligence group.

What do we make of the waxing and waning of cortical thickness in these different groups of children? As the researchers point out, an increase in cortical thickness may be due to a proliferation of brain cells and synapses and/or an increase in myelin. Cortical thinning, in contrast, takes place as a consequence of "pruning" unused synapses. The researchers speculate that cortices of the "brainy" children, which thicken and then thin at a rapid rate through middle childhood and adolescence, are more flexible and dynamic compared with those of other children—that the pattern of cortical development provides a larger window in which neural circuitry can be laid down in response to learning experiences, a process of brain development we previously described as *experience-dependent* (see Chapter 4, p. 130). Thus, these children are smarter not because of the sheer amount of brain matter but because of the dynamic properties of cortical development.

Despite these various research findings, we must be cautious about inferring direct causal links between particular changes in the brain and specific changes in behavior. The evidence we have cited is correlational: As children grow older, we observe changes in their brains and changes in their behavior, but the direction of causation remains uncertain. As explained in Chapter 4, the development and strengthening of neural pathways in the brain both affects and is affected by the individual's experience.

▲ APPLY :: CONNECT :: DISCUSS

Discuss some of the ways that physical activity affects the physical and psychological development of girls and boys during middle childhood. In your discussion, consider how the effects are similar for boys and girls, how they may differ, and the extent to which culture may contribute to any gender differences you identify.

Concrete-Operational Development

The apparatus shown in Figure 11.8 is one that Piaget presented to children of different ages to assess their level of cognitive development. The apparatus involves a toy wagon, suspended by a cable, that can be moved up and down a slope by manipulating three variables: the number of counterweights at the end of the cable; the weight of the load being carried by the wagon; and the angle of the track on which the wagon moves (Inhelder & Piaget, 1958, pp. 182–198). When a 6-year-old was asked how the wagon could be made to move, he pushed it down the track with his hand.

Experimenter: Can you do anything else?
Child: You drive in the train.
Experimenter tried a suggestion: And with the weights?
Child adds a counterweight to the cable: I put something on.
Experimenter: Why does it go up?
Child: I don't know. Because it's heavy.
Experimenter: And to make it go down?
Child: I don't know. You could push it.

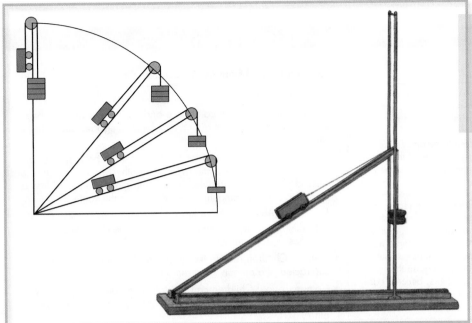

FIGURE 11.8 In this classic Piagetian task, a toy wagon, suspended by a cable, is hauled up the inclined plane by the counterweights at the other end of the cable. The counterweights can be varied and the angle of the plane is adjustable; weights placed in the wagon provide the third variable. (Adapted from Inhelder & Piaget, 1958, p. 183.)

A 10-year-old responded quite differently.

Child: To make it go up, you have to put a heavier weight here [at the end of the cable].
Experimenter: What else could you do?
Child: Unload the wagon.
Experimenter tried a suggestion: Can you do something with the rail?
Child: Maybe you could lower it; it's easier for the wagon to go forward because the track isn't as high.

In accounting for the vastly different ways in which these two children responded to the problem, Piaget points out that the 6-year-old is unable to identify the relevant variables (wagon load, counterweight, slope of incline); indeed, he is unable to separate the variables from his own actions of pushing, pulling, and "putting something on." The older child, in contrast, appreciates that the wagon's movement will depend on changes to the load, counterweight, and incline independent of the child's own actions on the apparatus.

In Chapter 8, we introduced you to Piaget's argument that the stages of cognitive development involve a process of increasing *decentration* through which thought becomes ever more *objective* (see p. 279). As we discussed, prior to middle childhood, children are in the *preoperational* stage of thinking and are vulnerable to *centration,* in which they become mentally "captured" by a single feature or attribute of experience. Centration interferes with the child's ability to engage in *mental operations,* or mental "actions" in which information is combined, separated, and transformed in a logical fashion. Emerging around 7 or 8 years of age, mental operations allow children to begin understanding how to experiment with several different variables to solve tasks such as the wagon problem. Mental operations also allow children to engage in activities such as sorting, collecting, and trading Pokémon cards according to category variables (whether they are character, energy, or trainer cards) and subcategory variables (whether they are Dark or Metal Energy). **Concrete operations** is the term Piaget applied to the new stage of development in which children begin to engage in mental operations. As suggested by the term "concrete," these mental operations typically involve concrete objects and events that children experience directly. (See Table 11.1 for a summary of concrete operations in relation to other Piagetian stages.)

concrete operations In Piaget's terms, coordinated mental actions that allow children to mentally combine, separate, order, and transform concrete objects and events that children experience directly.

table 11.1

Piaget's Stages of Cognitive Development: Concrete Operational

Age (years)	Stage	Description	Characteristics and Examples of Concrete Operations
Birth to 2	Sensorimotor	Infants' achievements consist largely of coordinating their sensory perceptions and simple motor behaviors. As they move through the 6 substages of this period, infants come to recognize the existence of a world outside of themselves and begin to interact with it in deliberate ways.	**New features of thinking** • Decentration: Children can notice and consider more than one attribute of an object at a time and form categories according to multiple criteria. • Conservation: Children understand that certain properties of an object will remain the same even when other, superficial ones are altered. They know that when a tall, thin glass is emptied into a short, fat one, the amount of liquid remains the same.
2 to 6	Preoperational	Young children can represent reality to themselves through the use of symbols, including mental images, words, and gestures. Objects and events no longer have to be present to be thought about, but children often fail to distinguish their point of view from that of others; become easily captured by surface appearances; and are often confused about causal relations.	• Logical necessity: Children have acquired the conviction that it is logically necessary for certain qualities to be conserved despite changes in appearance. • Identity: Children realize that if nothing has been added or subtracted, the amount must remain the same. • Compensation: Children can mentally compare changes in two aspects of a problem and see how one compensates for the other.
6 to 12	Concrete operational	As they enter middle childhood, children become capable of mental operations, internalized actions that fit into a logical system. Operational thinking allows children mentally to combine, separate, order, and transform objects and actions. Such operations are considered concrete because they are carried out in the presence of the objects and events being thought about.	• Reversibility: Children realize that certain operations can negate, or reverse, the effects of others. **Declining egocentrism** • Children can communicate more effectively about objects a listener cannot see. • Children can think about how others perceive them. • Children understand that a person can feel one way and act another.
12 to 19	Formal	In adolescence, the developing person acquires the ability to think systematically about all logical relations within a problem. Adolescents display keen interest in abstract ideas and in the process of thinking itself.	**Changes in social relations** • Children can regulate their interactions with each other through rules and begin to play rule-based games. • Children take intentions into account in judging behavior and believe the punishment must fit the crime.

According to Piaget, in the transition from early to middle childhood, the advent of concrete operations transforms all aspects of psychological functioning. The physical world becomes more predictable because children come to understand that certain physical aspects of objects, such as volume, weight, mass, and number, remain the same even when other aspects of the object's appearance, such as its shape, have changed (recall from Chapter 8 that preoperational children confuse appearance and reality). Children's thinking also becomes more organized and flexible, allowing them to think about alternative approaches and strategies for solving problems.

Piaget invented a number of problem-solving tasks, such as the wagon task, for assessing the presence or absence of concrete-operational thinking. In the following sections, we look at some other examples of this key Piagetian concept, which demonstrate with special clarity why Piaget believed that preoperational thinking and concrete-operational thinking represent qualitatively different stages of cognitive development (Piaget & Inhelder, 1973).

Conservation

Conservation is Piaget's term for the understanding that some properties of an object or substance remain the same even when its appearance is altered in some superficial way. Consider, for example, the **conservation of number**, that is, the ability to

conservation of number Recognition of the one-to-one correspondence between sets of objects of equal number.

conservation of volume The understanding that the amount of a liquid remains unchanged when poured from one container into another that has different dimensions.

recognize the one-to-one correspondence between two sets of objects of equal number, despite a difference in the sizes of the objects or in their spatial positions (Piaget, 1952a). To assess conservation of number, children are presented with two rows of objects, one the child's, the other the experimenter's, as shown in Figure 11.9a. Both the numbers of objects—in this case, playing cards—and the lengths of the two lines are equal, and the child is asked to affirm that they are. Then the experimenter's row is either spread out or compressed (Figure 11.9b), and the child is asked if the numbers of objects in the two rows are still equal. Unless the total number of objects is very small, children below the age of 6 or 7 rarely display conservation of number, saying, for example, that the elongated row has more. In contrast, older children realize that, on the grounds of *logic alone,* the number must remain the same. They are able to say to themselves, in effect, "There must be the same number of objects, because if the experimenter moved the objects back to where they were at the beginning, nothing would have changed." This understanding of *logical necessity*—that "it has to be that way"—is Piaget's key criterion of concrete-operational thinking.

One of Piaget's most famous studies of conservation examines children's **conservation of volume**, the understanding that the amount of a liquid remains unchanged when poured from one container into another that has different dimensions. The task used to assess conservation of volume involves presenting children with two identical glass beakers containing the same amounts of liquid (Figure 11.10). The experimenter begins by pouring the contents of one of the beakers into a third beaker that is taller and narrower. Naturally, the liquid is higher in the new beaker than it was in the one it was poured from. The experimenter then asks the child, "Does the new beaker have more liquid than the old one, does it have the same amount, or does it have less?"

Ordinarily, 3- to 4-year-old children say that the taller beaker has more. When asked why, they explain, "There's more because it's higher," or "There's more because it's bigger," or even "There's more because you poured it." Consistent with the *centration* characteristic of preoperational thinking, the children appear to focus their attention on a single aspect of the new beaker—its height. Even when the experimenter points out that no liquid was added or subtracted—and even after the experimenter pours the liquid back into the original beaker to demonstrate that the amount has not changed—3- and 4-year-olds generally stick to their claim that there was more liquid in the taller, narrower beaker.

Piaget found that around the age of 5 or 6 years, children's understanding of conservation goes through a transitional stage. At this point, children seem to realize that it is necessary to consider both the height and the circumference of the beakers, but they have difficulty keeping

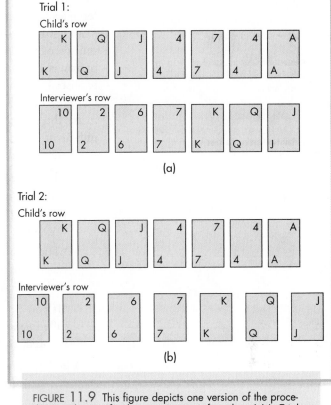

FIGURE 11.9 This figure depicts one version of the procedure used to test for the conservation of number. (a) In Trial 1, the child's and the experimenter's rows of objects—in this case, seven playing cards—are arrayed at equal intervals. (b) In Trial 2, the experimenter spreads out the cards in his or her row and asks the child if both rows still have the same number of cards. (From Ginsburg, 1977.)

FIGURE 11.10 The procedure that Piaget used to test for the conservation of quantity follows three simple steps. First, present the child with two beakers of equal size containing equal amounts of liquid. Second, present a taller, narrower beaker and pour the contents of one of the other beakers into it. Third, ask the child, "Which beaker has more liquid, or do they contain the same amount?" Like most children under age 6, this girl appears to lack an understanding of conservation of quantity.

identity A mental operation in which the child realizes that a change limited to outward appearance does not change the substances involved.

compensation A mental operation in which the child realizes that changes in one aspect of a problem are compared with and compensated for by changes in another aspect.

reversibility A mental operation in which the child realizes that one operation can be negated, or reversed, by the effects of another.

the dimensions of both beakers in mind simultaneously and coordinating the differences between them in order to make a valid comparison.

According to Piaget, children fully master the principle of conservation around the age of 8, when they understand not only that the new beaker is both taller and narrower but also that a change in one dimension of the beaker (increasing height) is offset by a change in the other (decreasing circumference). Children who have mastered conservation recognize the logical necessity that the amount of liquid remains the same despite the change in appearance. When asked the reasons for their judgment, they offer arguments such as the following, showing that they understand the logical relationships involved:

- "They were equal to start with and nothing was added, so they're the same." This mental operation is called **identity**; the child realizes that a change limited to outward appearance does not change the actual amounts involved.

- "The liquid is higher, but the glass is thinner." This mental operation is called **compensation**; changes in one aspect of a problem are mentally compared with, and compensated for, by changes in another.

- "If you pour it back, you'll see that it's the same." This mental operation is called *negation* or **reversibility**; the child realizes that one operation can be negated, or reversed, by the effects of another.

Whether they are asked to reason about number or volume, children's ability to conserve leads to the logical conclusion that a change in visual *appearance* does not change the logical *reality* of amount.

Classification

Another significant change associated with concrete operations is the ability to understand the hierarchical structure of categories, in particular, the logical *relation of inclusion* that holds between a superordinate class and its subclasses (for example, the subclass of cats is included in the superordinate class of mammals; see Chapter 5, p. 190).

When 4- to 6-year-old children are shown a set of wooden beads that includes some brown beads and a smaller number of white beads and are asked, "Are there more brown beads or more beads?" they are likely to say there are more brown beads than beads. According to Piaget, they answer this way because they cannot attend to the subclass (brown beads) and the superordinate class (beads) at the same time. Instead, they compare one subclass (brown beads) with another subclass (white beads). In middle childhood, understanding of subordinate–superordinate relations become more stable, so children realize that brown beads are a subset of the overall set of beads and answer correctly.

A more difficult classification ability that emerges during middle childhood is the capacity to categorize objects according to multiple criteria. This kind of logical classification can be seen when children begin to collect stamps, baseball cards, or Pokémon cards. Stamp collections, for example, can be organized according to multiple criteria. Stamps come from different countries. They are issued in different denominations and in different years. There are stamps depicting insects, animals, sports heroes, rock stars, and space exploration. Children who organize their stamps according to type of animal and country of origin (so that, for example, within their collection of stamps from France, all the birds are together, all the rabbits are together, and so on) are creating a multiple classification for their collections. The result is a marked increase in the number of relations among objects and events that children can think about and increased flexibility in the particular relations they choose to use in particular circumstances.

This young comic-book collector is looking for a deal at an annual fair held at the Wolfson campus of Miami-Dade College. If he is a serious collector, he will have a fairly elaborate classification system that organizes his comic books according to multiple criteria.

Jeff Greenberg / Alamy

Planning

The abilities of decentering, considering multiple variables, and thinking flexibly in new situations are all cognitive prerequisites to efficient and effective planning. Preschoolers can be heard saying things to one another like "When you come over, we'll play house and have a party," but they have no plans to achieve their goal aside from informing their parents that they want to play with the other child. During middle childhood, children begin to plan in the sense that they form cognitive representations of the actions needed to achieve a specific goal. To make a plan, they have to keep in mind what is presently happening, what they want to happen in the future, and what they need to do in order to get from the present to the future. They must also have enough self-control to keep their attention on achieving the goal (a topic we address in more detail later in the chapter).

Take, for example, the kind of planning that is required in choosing a route to a destination. William Gardner and Barbara Rogoff (1990) asked groups of 4- to 6-year-olds and 7- to 10-year-olds to solve mazes such as the one shown in Figure 11.11. A glance at this maze quickly reveals that a child who simply begins to trace a path from the nearest opening, without first scanning the maze to see what barriers lie ahead, is certain to fail. To see how children's ability to plan a solution to the maze developed, Gardner and Rogoff gave different instructions to half the children in each age group. Half were told that they should plan ahead from the start because it was most important to avoid making wrong turns. The other half were told the same thing but were also told that they had to go through the maze as quickly as possible.

When both speed and accuracy mattered, the children in both age groups planned out the beginning of their route ahead of time and thereafter planned only when they came to uncertain choice points. When accuracy in navigating the maze was the only factor that counted, many of the older children realized that a better strategy was to plan their entire set of moves before they began. In contrast, when only accuracy, not speed, mattered, 4- to 6-year-olds did not change their planning, either because they did not understand that they would make fewer errors if they planned ahead more systematically or because they could not keep this possibility in mind as they tackled the maze.

Planning is also important in reasoning tasks. Games that require children to solve logical problems, like checkers or Mastermind, become popular in middle childhood. To play these games skillfully, children have to analyze both the goals and the means of attaining them. A good example of such a game is the Tower of

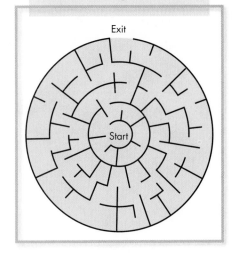

FIGURE 11.11 A maze of this kind was used by Gardner and Rogoff (1990) to assess children's ability to plan ahead. Trace the route from start to finish to get a feel for how planning is needed to avoid encountering a dead end.

From China (left) to India (right), children enjoy the intellectual challenges of board games that call on newly acquired cognitive skills.

FIGURE 11.12 To solve the Tower of Hanoi problem, this child must, using the three pegs in front of him, reorder the cans one at a time to re-create the experimenter's model stack of cans. The task requires careful planning, because it is against the rules to place a small can on top of a large can when moving the cans from peg to peg. (After Klahr, 1989.)

Child's peg board →

Experimenter's model →

Hanoi, the goal of which is to move a set of size-graded objects from one location to another in accordance with two rules: (1) only one object can be moved at a time; and (2) a larger object must go on top of a smaller one.

In an experimental form of this game shown in Figure 11.12, the child is presented with a peg board with three pegs, on one of which there are three cans of different sizes—the smallest on the bottom, the largest on the top. The task is to move the cans individually from one peg to another so that they end up on the third peg at the other end of the board in their original order, as illustrated by the experimenter's model. The solution to this problem requires a minimum of seven moves.

A variety of research (summarized in Siegler, 1998) shows that between the ages of 6 and 7 years, children become better at playing the game. This trend is not surprising, since, according to the evidence, older children are increasingly able to keep in mind both their current circumstances and the circumstances they want to create. Three-year-olds could not keep the rules in mind at all. Six-year-olds began to form subgoals that would take them part of the way to a solution, but they could not think the problem all the way through, and they still found it difficult to assemble their subgoals into an overall plan. When similar types of problems require larger numbers of moves, even 9- and 10-year-olds fail to plan their solutions all the way through (Spitz, Minsky, & Besselieu, 1985). When, however, children are given opportunities to reflect on their planning, either by watching videotapes of themselves working on the task or by being instructed in efficient problem strategies, their performance improves (Fireman & Kose, 2002).

As you might imagine, the planning skills described above are important not just to solving mazes and playing games. They are also essential to children's routine activities including, for example, their ability to safely cross busy streets (Barton & Morrongiello, 2011).

Metacognition

The fact that children's problem solving can be enhanced by calling their attention to effective strategies and ways to use them suggests that *knowledge* about how to think things through may facilitate problem-solving performance. Indeed, **metacognition**, the ability to think about and regulate one's own thoughts, allows one

metacognition The ability to think about one's own thought processes.

to assess how difficult a problem is likely to be and to be flexible in choosing strategies to solve it (Flavell, 2007). The development of metacognition has received considerable attention from researchers, who generally find large mismatches between young children's estimates of what they think they know about a problem and what they actually know. Preschoolers and kindergartners are especially prone to overestimating their knowledge. As metacognition develops over the course of middle childhood, children become more accurate in recognizing the limits of their knowledge and problem-solving skills.

An example of metacognitive development is provided by Candice Mills and Frank Keil, who asked kindergartners, second-graders, and fourth-graders to estimate their understanding of mechanical devices such as toasters, gum-ball machines, and staplers (Mills & Keil, 2004). First, the children were trained to use a 5-point scale to show how much they thought they knew about how the device worked. The low end of the scale was one star, indicating very little understanding; the high end was five stars, indicating a lot of understanding. Next, the children were asked to estimate their knowledge of how, for instance, a toaster works by pointing to the appropriate number of stars on the scale. Then they were asked to provide an explanation for how toasters toast, after which they once again used the scale to estimate their knowledge (some sample explanations from each age group are shown in Table 11.2). The idea behind this was that the children might sense the holes in their explanations and downgrade their original estimates of their knowledge. Finally, to really drive home the children's lack of knowledge, the researchers explained the workings of toasters as reported by an expert "who knows five stars about how a toaster works," after which children had one last opportunity to rate their knowledge on the star scale.

As shown in Figure 11.13, the researchers found clear overall age differences in children's ratings of their toaster knowledge: fourth-graders were significantly more conservative than kindergartners, and second-graders fell in between. Only the second- and fourth-graders significantly downgraded their estimates after they were asked to explain how the device works or were told of the "five-star" expert's explanation. Indeed, at the end of the study, several of them remarked that they were surprised at how little they knew about toasters. Kindergartners' ratings, as you can see in the figure, actually *increased* after hearing the expert's account. Why? Apparently, they believe that the expert's explanation simply reminded them of what they already knew but forgot to mention. This is a classic example of egocentrism—in this case, the youngsters' obvious difficulty separating their own perspective and knowledge from that of the expert.

table **11.2**	
Examples of Children's Explanations of How a Toaster Works	
Grade	**Explanation**
Kindergarten	"You put something in it and then you press a button and then—you press the button. Push it down and leave it there. And then it heats and then it comes up too."
Second grade	"Well, you put the bread in and you push this little lever down so then there you go. It'll heat rays inside and it'll make the bread really really hard and stuff and it'll just pop out."
Fourth grade	"Ok. A toaster is made by electricity. You plug it in. There's a cord it comes electricity and then you put bread in. And then you press a button down. When you hit that button all the way down red lights which is heat comes out which is from the electricity and it heats the bread and when it comes out it's toast."

Source: Mills & Keil, 2004, p. 13.

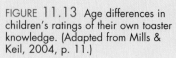

FIGURE 11.13 Age differences in children's ratings of their own toaster knowledge. (Adapted from Mills & Keil, 2004, p. 11.)

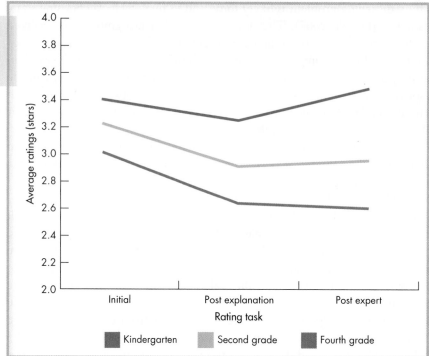

The growth of metacognitive skills provides children with important cognitive resources. As metacognitive skills increase, children are better able to keep track of how successfully they are accomplishing their goals, and this allows them to modify their strategies in order to be more successful.

Limitations of Concrete Operations

With the emergence of concrete operations, children take a significant step toward objectivity, and the ability to think logically and apply their knowledge flexibly to new problems and situations. However, as we indicated previously, children's intellectual functioning and problem solving are at their best when they involve concrete objects and events that children have experienced directly. As soon as children are asked to reason about abstract phenomena, their problem solving falters.

The difficulty children encounter when reasoning about abstract situations with which they have no direct experience is apparent in a study undertaken by Jason Low and Steve Hollis (Low & Hollis, 2003). These researchers asked groups of 6-, 9-, and 12-year-olds and college students in New Zealand to draw a portrait of themselves as they would look if they had three eyes instead of two and then to explain why they had placed the third eye where they had. Given good reasons for believing that no one in the sample had ever encountered a three-eyed person, the self-portrait task constituted a true challenge to abstract thinking.

Typical responses of each age group are shown in Figure 11.14. As you can see, all three groups of children tended to place the third eye close to the other two. In their concrete experience, this is, after all, where eyes belong. In addition to drawing similar portraits, children's reasons for their particular eye placements were fairly uniform—and concrete—emphasizing that a third eye on the forehead would help them see better or see farther. In contrast, the self-portraits of college students were much more imaginative and diverse, permitting not only better eyesight but an entirely different, 360-degree view.

6-year-old
"Just felt the best place."

9-year-old
"So the person can see further away."

12-year-old
"So I could see sideways and straight ways."

18-year-old
"So I can see behind myself as well."

© 2003 International Society for the Study of Behavioral Development. (2003). *International Journal of Behavioral Development, 27*(2), pp. 97–108.

FIGURE 11.14 Age differences in drawings of where one would put a third eye. (Low & Hollis, 2003.)

▲ APPLY :: CONNECT :: DISCUSS

Explain how Piaget's fundamental concepts of *decentration* and *objectivity* are apparent in the ability of children who are at the concrete-operational stage to solve conservation and classification tasks.

Information-Processing Approaches

In contrast to Piaget's focus on decentration as a source of increasing objectivity in reasoning, information-processing theorists account for cognitive changes during middle childhood by pointing to processes such as increased memory capacity and attention, more rapid and efficient mental operations, and the acquisition of a variety of mental strategies. According to these theorists, children's increased memory and attention abilities play a central role in allowing them to hold two or more aspects of a problem in mind while they are thinking. For example, a young soccer player racing for the goal can pay attention to, and keep in mind, the positions of teammates, the goalie's well-known difficulty blocking low shots, and an appropriate fake-out move to use on a charging defender. Younger players may have a difficult time simply remembering they are in a soccer game and may run after the ball only when it passes in front of them, or have their attention diverted by some irrelevant event taking place off the field.

The Role of Memory

Three factors, taken together, appear to bring about the memory changes characteristic of middle childhood (Schneider, 2011):

1. Increases in the speed and capacity of working memory.

2. Increases in knowledge about the things one is trying to remember.

3. The acquisition of more effective strategies for remembering.

Increased Speed and Capacity of Working Memory

Working memory has received a great deal of attention as a source of improved intellectual functioning during middle childhood because it is considered the "active" memory system that holds and manipulates information needed to reason about complex tasks and problems (Bayliss et al., 2005). Developmentalists have been particularly interested in the

memory span The number of randomly presented items of information that can be repeated immediately after they are presented.

capacity of children's working memory to "hold" larger amounts of information with age, as well as in the increases of its *speed* in manipulating (or processing) information.

A common behavioral method of measuring the changing capacity of working memory is to assess children's **memory span**, the number of randomly presented items of information children can repeat immediately after the items are presented. Most 4- and 5-year-olds can recall four digits presented one after another; most 9- and 10-year-olds can remember about six; most adults can remember about seven (Schneider, Knopf, & Sodian, 2009). Although it seems clear that the older child's memory capacity is larger than that of the younger child's, developmentalists are keenly aware that other factors also come into play. For example, in order to store several randomly presented numbers into working memory, individuals must somehow represent each number to themselves, perhaps by silently repeat-

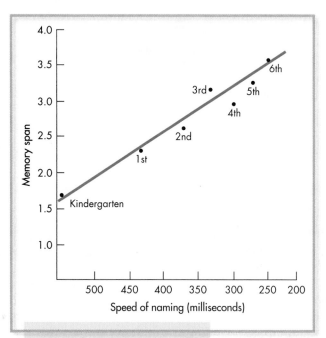

FIGURE 11.15 Relationship between memory span and speed of naming. (From Case et al., 1982.)

ing them. It takes young children longer than older children simply to repeat a number such as 10 or 2, making their memory for the numbers already presented more likely to decay and be lost. Because, by comparison, older children name individual numbers quite quickly, reducing the time interval between storing numbers, they have a greater likelihood of retaining the numbers in memory (Figure 11.15) (Case, Kurland, & Goldberg, 1982).

Cross-cultural research enriches these conclusions. When Chuansheng Chen and Harold Stevenson (1988) compared the memory spans of U. S. and Chinese children 4 to 6 years of age, they found that the Chinese children were able to recall more digits at each of the ages tested. At first, this finding might seem to suggest that the working memory of Chinese children was larger than that of the American children. However, as Chen and Stevenson pointed out, the Chinese words for the digits are shorter than their English equivalents. Thus the task was easier for the Chinese children for the same reason that it was easier for the older North American children: There was a shorter interval between repeated items. This hypothesis was supported by a study in which Stevenson and his colleagues used lists of objects whose names were equal in length in English and Chinese. When these words were presented for remembering, Chinese and American children were found to have equal memory capacities (Stevenson et al., 1985).

Not surprisingly, developmentalists have looked increasingly at brain development as a source of the change in working memory observed during middle childhood (Blair et al., 2006). EEG studies indicate that the speed with which children's brains can respond to complex stimuli increases gradually during middle childhood (Travis, 1998), and as you know from our discussion above, increased speed of processing may help prevent information from being lost. In addition to processing speed, increases in the connections between brain regions have also been directly linked to memory performance in children aged 7 to 16 years (Sowell et al., 2001; Scherf, Sweeney, & Luna, 2006).

Expanded Knowledge Base The second factor that contributes to improved memory during childhood is the greater knowledge that older children are likely to have about any given topic simply because they have accumulated more experience (Ornstein & Haden, 2009). This experience provides older children with a richer knowledge base, or store of information, with which to relate, and remember, new information.

A classic demonstration of how a rich knowledge base contributes to children's ability to remember was provided by Michelene Chi (1978), who studied the ability of 10-year-old chess experts and college-student chess novices to remember the arrangement of chess pieces that might occur in a game. She found that the 10-year-olds' memory for the positioning of chess pieces was better by far than that of the college students. However, when the two groups were compared on their ability to recall a random series of numbers, the college students' performances were far superior. A replication of this study by German researchers confirmed and extended these results by asking expert and novice participants to remember random arrangements of chess pieces rather than meaningful patterns that might occur in an actual game. With the importance of chess knowledge thus removed, the superiority of experts' performance was greatly reduced (Schneider et al., 1993).

Improved Memory Strategies A third source of improved memory ability is children's increased use of **memory strategies**, that is, their deliberate use of actions to enhance remembering (Pressley & Hilden, 2006). A large number of studies have shown that children's spontaneous use of strategies for remembering undergoes a marked increase between early and middle childhood (Ornstein & Haden, 2009). Three memory strategies that have been intensively studied are rehearsal, organization, and elaboration.

Rehearsal is the process of repeating to oneself the material that one is trying to memorize, such as a word list, a song, or a phone number. In a classic study of the development of rehearsal strategies in children, John Flavell and his colleagues (Keeney et al., 1967) presented 5- and 10-year-olds with seven pictures of objects to remember. The children were asked to wear a "space helmet" with a visor that was pulled down over their eyes during the 15-second interval between the presentation of the pictures and the test for recall. The visor prevented the children from seeing the pictures and allowed the experimenter to watch their lips to see if they repeated to themselves what they had seen. Few of the 5-year-olds were observed to rehearse, but almost all the 10-year-olds did. Within each age group, children who had rehearsed the pictures recalled more of them than did children who had not.

Marked changes are also found in **organizational strategies**, that is, strategies of mentally grouping the materials to be remembered in meaningful clusters of closely associated items so that remembering only one part of a cluster brings to mind the rest. The use of organizational strategies is often studied by means of a procedure called *free recall*. In a free-recall task, children are shown a large number of objects, or read a list of words one at a time, and then asked to remember them. This kind of memory is called *free* recall because the children are free to recall the items in any order they choose.

Research has demonstrated that 7- and 8-year-olds are more likely than younger children to group the items they have to remember into easy-to-remember categories (Schlagmüller & Schneider, 2002). The kinds of groupings that children impose on lists of things to be remembered also change with age. Younger children often use sound features such as rhyme ("cat," "sat"), or situational associations ("cereal," "bowl") to group words they are trying to remember. In middle childhood, children are more likely to link words according to categories such as animals ("cat," "dog," "horse"), foods ("cereal," "milk," "bananas"), or geometric figures ("triangle," "square," "circle"). These changes in strategy enhance the ability to store and retrieve information deliberately and systematically.

Children who do not spontaneously use rehearsal and organizing strategies can be taught to do so (Pressley & Hilden, 2006). In the "space helmet" experiment by Flavell and his colleagues, for example, those who had not rehearsed were later taught to do so and subsequently did as well on the memory task as those who had

memory strategies Specific actions used deliberately to enhance remembering.

rehearsal The process of repeating to oneself the material that one is trying to remember.

organizational strategies Memory strategies in which materials to be remembered are mentally grouped into meaningful categories.

elaboration A memory strategy that involves making connections between two or more things to be remembered.

metamemory The ability to think about one's memory processes.

rehearsed on their own. The effectiveness of such training indicates that there is no unbridgeable gap between the memory performance of 4- to 5-year-olds and that of 7- to 8-year-olds or between children who use strategies spontaneously and those who do not. Over the course of middle childhood, children become increasingly better at using various strategies to help them remember.

A third strategy, **elaboration**, is a process in which children identify or make up connections between two or more things they have to remember. In a typical study of elaboration strategies, children are presented with pairs of words and are asked to remember the second one when they hear the first. For example, they might be asked to remember the word "street" after hearing the word "tomato." An elaboration strategy for this word pair might be to think of a tomato squashed in the middle of a street. The spontaneous use of elaboration strategies emerges during middle childhood, and children's skill in using them continues to increase with age (Bjorklund, Dukes, & Brown, 2009).

Thinking About Memory

Most 7- and 8-year-olds not only know and remember more about the world in general than do 3- to 5-year-olds but they also are likely to know more about memory itself—knowledge referred to as **metamemory**, which is a particular form of *metacognition*. Even 5-year-olds have some understanding of how memory works. In a study that has stimulated a great deal of the subsequent research on memory development, 5-year-olds said they knew that it was easier to remember a short list of words than a long one, easier to relearn something you once knew than to learn it from scratch, and easier to remember something that happened yesterday than something that happened last month (Kreutzer, Leonard, & Flavell, 1975).

Nevertheless, most 8-year-olds have a better understanding of the limitations of their own memories than most 5-year-olds do. When shown a set of 10 pictures and asked if they could remember them all (something not many children at these ages can do), the majority of the 5-year-olds—but only a few of the 8-year-olds—claimed that they could. The 5-year-olds also failed to correctly evaluate how much effort they would need to remember the pictures. Told that they could take all the time they needed to commit the set of pictures to memory, the 5-year-olds announced that they were ready right away, and, of course, succeeded in remembering only a few of the items. The 8-year-olds, by contrast, knew enough to study the materials and to test themselves on their ability to remember (Flavell, Friedrichs, & Hoyt, 1970).

Not surprisingly, there seems to be a connection between children's metamemory and their use of memory strategies (Pressley & Hilden, 2006). In one study, William Fabricius and John Hagen (1984) created a memory task in which 6- and 7-year-olds were presented with approximately 60 pictures of common objects (farm animals, clothing, fruit, and so forth). In one condition, the children were instructed to place each picture on one of several stands until they had placed all the pictures. In another condition, the children were given the same instruction but were also told to do "whatever you want to help yourself remember." Some children used an organizational strategy in both conditions; that is, they placed the pictures on the stands according to category—all the farm animals on one stand, all the clothing on another, and so on. Other children used the strategy only in the condition in which the experimenter instructed them to do something to help themselves remember. The researchers found that when the children used the organizational strategy, they almost always remembered better. Yet when the researchers asked the children to tell them what they thought accounted for their better remembering efforts, some of the children did not recognize that the organizing strategy had been helpful, even though they had just used it successfully. Instead, they attributed their better recall to taking more time and being more careful or to paying more attention to the stimuli. Other children attributed their better recall to the deliberate use of the organizing strategy. When the children were brought back for a second session, in which their ability to remember was tested in a slightly different situation, 99 percent of those who had understood the helpfulness of the organizing strategy in the first session used the same strategy the second time around. By contrast, only 32 percent of the children who had attributed their better remembering efforts to some other factor used the organizing strategy. These and similar results indicate that children must acquire the ability to use metamemory knowledge in addition to acquiring useful strategies.

Increased Control of Attention

In addition to gaining greater control over memory strategies, during middle childhood children become better able to regulate their attention, staying focused on relevant aspects of a task and ignoring irrelevant distractions.

A classic study by Elaine Vurpillot (1968) illustrates the kinds of changes observed by many researchers. She recorded the eye movements of children age 3 to 10 while the children examined pairs of line drawings of houses such as those shown in Figure 11.16. In some trials, children were shown identical houses; in others, the houses differed in one or more fairly subtle ways. The children were asked to say whether or not the houses were identical.

Vurpillot found that all the children responded correctly when the houses were identical but that the younger children were more likely to make mistakes when the houses differed, especially if the houses differed in only one way. Her recordings of eye movements pinpointed the difficulty. Rather than systematically paying attention to each of the houses to see how they differed, the younger children scanned the houses in a haphazard order. By contrast, the older children paid attention to each of the houses, scanning, and sometimes rescanning, row by row or column by column. It seems from this that older children have a greater ability to select and execute an effective attentional strategy.

During early and middle childhood, better regulation of attention is also seen in children's increasing ability to ignore distractions and gain voluntary control over what they choose to pay attention to in order to obtain information more efficiently (Dossett & Burns, 2000; Huang-Pollack, Carr, & Nigg, 2002).

Executive Function

You have probably noticed that a key component of cognitive development in middle childhood is the increasing ability to *control* and *monitor* one's own thinking and behavior in order to make plans, solve problems, and pursue goals. Developmentalists use the term **executive function** to describe higher-level cognitive processes, such as planning and problem solving, that involve supervising and controlling lower-level cognitive processes, such as attention and memory (Fuhs & Day, 2011; Zelazo & Müller, 2011). For example,

executive function Higher-level cognitive processes, such as aspects of cognition associated with supervising and controlling lower-level cognitive processes.

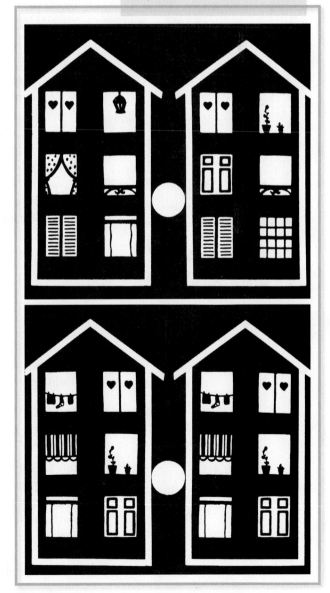

FIGURE 11.16 Stimuli like these were used by Vurpillot to assess the development of visual search strategies. It is not until middle childhood that children systematically compare the two houses of each pair in order to discover the subtle differences between them. (From Vurpillot, 1968.)

when children attempt to solve a problem—let's say a math problem—they need to utilize their executive function to keep their attention focused and avoid distractions, consider whether problem-solving strategies they've used in the past can be used in this instance, and monitor whether the strategy they are employing seems to be working or should be changed for a different strategy. As you can see, executive function is highly similar to the *self-regulation* we discussed in Chapter 9 (pp. 320–321). Indeed, developmentalists are divided on whether and where to draw the boundaries between the two (Blair, Zelazo, & Greenberg, 2005). Nevertheless, there is broad agreement that the skills involved in executive function and self-regulation are essential to academic success and are related to developing areas of the brain, especially the frontal cortex, associated with higher cognitive processes.

Given the importance of executive function to children's academic performance, developmentalists have been eager to discover whether it can be improved. An interesting study conducted by Catherine Davis and her colleagues suggests that executive function may be affected by children's health, and that improving health through exercise may benefit executive function as well as academic achievement, especially in children who are overweight (Davis et al., 2011). Their experiment included approximately 170 overweight children 7 to 11 years of age who were randomly assigned to one of three groups: *low-exercise* (20 minutes per day of aerobic exercise for approximately 3 months), *high-exercise* (same exercise for 40 minutes per day), and a *no-exercise* control group. As shown in Figure 11.17, aerobic exercise significantly improved the children's math achievement and executive function (as measured by a test of planning ability). In addition, the researchers found a significant "dose effect," meaning that children in the high-exercise group performed signficantly better than those in the low-exercise group. An especially intriguing result concerned changes in the children's brain activity over the course of the 13-week program. Specifically, neuroimaging data (fMRI) showed significant increases in prefrontal cortex activity for children in the exercise groups. These results have important implications for educational policies, suggesting that physical activity programs may pay off not only in terms of children's health but also in terms of their academic success in elementary school.

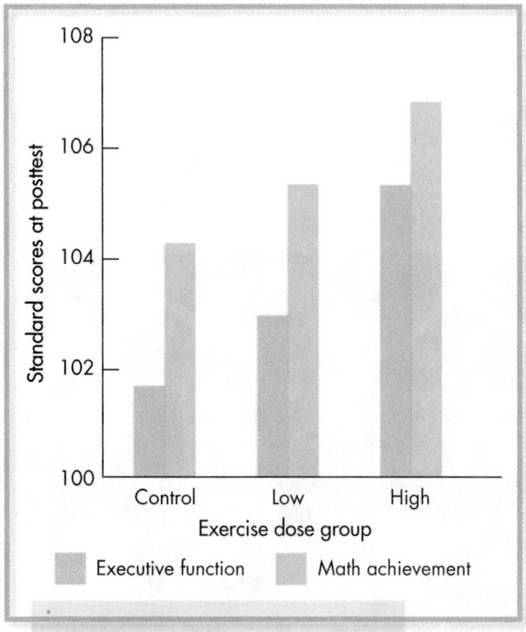

FIGURE 11.17 A study conducted with overweight children found that aerobic exercise significantly improved children's math achievement and executive function. (Adapted from Davis et al., 2011.)

▲ APPLY :: CONNECT :: DISCUSS

Many people believe that a really good memory involves the ability to store a lot of information for considerable periods of time. However, good memory is not just about the *quantity* of information stored over time; it also involves how the information is organized. In what specific ways does it seem that children's memories may be organized differently in middle childhood than in early childhood?

The Role of Social and Cultural Contexts

Thus far we have treated cognitive changes between early and middle childhood as if they were entirely determined by development of the brain and the specific internal mental processes brought to bear on the task at hand. But as Usha Goswami cautions, "the functioning of even these relatively specific developmental mechanisms . . . turns out to be influenced by the social . . . and cultural context in which learning takes place" (Goswami, 2002, p. 227). Cross-cultural research on developmental changes in cognitive ability underlines this point.

Is the Acquisition of Conservation Universal?

It was Piaget's (1966/1974) belief that the development of conservation is a universal achievement of human beings, regardless of the cultural circumstances in which they live. The only cultural variation he expected in the acquisition of conservation was that children in some cultures might acquire this form of reasoning earlier than children in others, because their culture provided them with more extensive relevant experiences.

However, cross-cultural research on the acquisition of conservation has provoked a great deal of controversy regarding its presumed universality and age of onset. Using Piaget's conservation tasks, several researchers found that children in traditional, nonindustrial societies who have not attended school lag a year or more behind the norms established by Piaget—and, in some cases, appear not to acquire this form of reasoning at all, even as adults. Reviewing the evidence available in the early 1970s, Pierre Dasen (1972) wrote, "It can no longer be assumed that adults of all societies reach the concrete operational stage" (p. 31).

This conclusion was quickly challenged because of its wide-reaching implication that traditional, nonliterate adults think like the preschool children of industrialized countries. For example, Gustav Jahoda (1980), a leading cross-cultural psychologist, rejected outright the possibility that in some cultures people never achieve the ability to think operationally. Jahoda pointed out that it is difficult to see how a society could survive if its members were indifferent to causal relations, incapable of thinking through the implications of their actions, or unable to adopt other people's points of view. He concluded that "no society could function at the preoperational stage, and to suggest that a majority of any people are at that level is nonsense almost by definition" (Jahoda, 1980, p. 116).

To resolve this issue, developmentalists who questioned nonschooled children's apparent failure to understand conservation designed new tests or otherwise modified research procedures. They sought to demonstrate that Piaget's research methods somehow misrepresented such children's mental capacities, either because the test situation was too unfamiliar to the children or because the experimenters, working in an unfamiliar culture and language, did not make their intentions clear. (Similarly, as you may recall from Chapter 8, researchers in early childhood cognition designed new tasks because they felt Piaget's tasks underestimated the thought processes of preschool-age children.) Ashley Maynard and Patricia Greenfield (2003) addressed this problem in a study comparing task performance of children growing up in a city in the United States (Los Angeles) with that of Zinacantec Mayan children growning up in a rural community in the highlands of Chiapas, Mexico.

Through their extensive field work in the Mexican community, Maynard and Greenfield noted that young girls are introduced to the cultural practice of backstrap-loom weaving when they are as young as 3 years of age. Weaving, considered an alternative to schooling, is a complex technical skill acquired by virtually all the girls in the community through apprenticeship (see Chapter 12, pp. 431–432). The girls begin weaving on relatively simple toy looms and later graduate to adult looms (see Figure 11.18). In analyzing the cognitive skills involved in using the looms, the researchers found that the adult loom, but not the toy loom, requires concrete operational reasoning. Significantly, Mayan girls

The kinds of work that children are assigned afford different kinds of learning opportunities. Young street vendors who have no formal education often acquire a variety of arithmetic skills that, in some respects, may surpass those of children of the same age who attend school.

Macduff Everton

FIGURE 11.18 Back-strap loom weaving is an important cultural practice learned through apprenticeship. Simple toy looms are used in early lessons. After the girls gain basic skills and develop physically, they graduate to adult looms.

usually begin using adult looms between the ages of 8 and 10 years. Because most girls in the study had never been to school, this finding contradicts the assertion that schooling is essential to the acquisition of concrete operations.

To further explore the results of their field observations and analyis of loom skill-level differences, Maynard and Greenfield presented 160 boys and girls from the Zinacantec community and Los Angeles with two types of concrete operational tasks. One was a traditional Piagetian task (referred to as the knots problem because it involves twisted/knotted strings of beads that study participants are required to mentally untwist/unknot); the other was based on traditional weaving practices (see Figure 11.19). Although the children in Los Angeles performed significantly better on the Piagetian task, the Zinacantec Mayan children, especially girls, performed significantly better on the weaving task.

While some developmentalists, including Maynard and Greenfield, focus on how standard Piagetian tasks may underestimate the cognitive abilities of unschooled children, others suggest that the tasks may pose special difficulties even for schooled

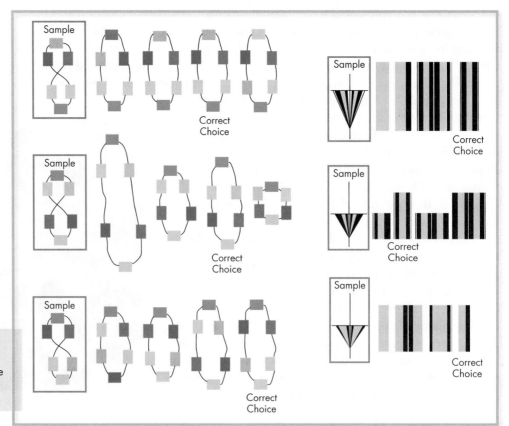

FIGURE 11.19 The knots problem is a traditional Piagetian task that measures cognitive development. (From Maynard and Greenfield, 2003.)

children, if their native language is different from that used to administer the tasks. Raphael Nyiti (1982), for example, compared the conservation performances of 10- and 11-year-old children of two cultural groups, both living on Cape Breton, Nova Scotia. Some of the children were of English-speaking European backgrounds, and some were of the Micmac Indian tribe. The Micmac children all spoke Micmac at home, but they had spoken English in school since the first grade. The children of European backgrounds were all interviewed in English by an English speaker of European background. The Micmac children were interviewed once in English and once in Micmac.

Nyiti found that when the Micmac children were interviewed on the conservation tasks in their native language, there was no difference between their performance and that of the other group. But when the Micmac children were interviewed in English, only half as many seemed to understand the concept of conservation. Nyiti (1976) obtained similar results in a study of children in his native Tanzania, as did other researchers in the West African country of Sierra Leone (Kamara & Easley, 1977).

Taken as a whole, these studies, along with others, demonstrate that when Piaget's clinical procedures are applied appropriately, using contents with which people have extensive experience, conservation (and by extension, concrete operations) is a universal cognitive achievement of middle childhood, just as Piaget assumed it was (Segall et al., 1999). However, the evidence also shows that there are quite dramatic cultural variations in children's familiarity with the contents and procedures used in standard Piagetian tests of conservation and that these variations clearly influence children's performances on the tests.

Cultural Variations in the Use of Memory Strategies

Cross-cultural research has revealed striking variations in the use of organizational strategies in free-recall studies, but these results must be interpreted with great caution. For example, Michael Cole and his colleagues studied the development of memory among people living in rural Liberia (summarized in Cole, 1996). In one set of studies, they presented groups of children of different ages with a set of 20 common objects that belonged to familiar and salient categories, such as food, clothing, and tools. Half the children at each age were attending school, while half were not because there were no schools in their villages.

The researchers found that children who had never gone to school improved their performance on these tasks very little after the age of 9 or 10. These children remembered approximately 10 items on the first trial, and managed to recall only 2 more items after 15 practice trials on the full set of 20 items. In contrast, the Liberian children who were attending school memorized the full set of materials rapidly, much the way U. S. schoolchildren of the same age do.

The unschooled children's poor performance seemed to be attributable to their failure to use organizational strategies. Schoolchildren in Liberia and the United States used categorical similarities among the items to aid their recall. After the initial trial, they clustered their responses, recalling first, say, the items of clothing, then the items of food, and so on. The Liberians who had never attended school did very little clustering, an indication that they were not using the categorical relationships among the items to help them remember.

To track down the source of this difference, the researchers varied aspects of the task. They found that if, instead of presenting a series of objects in random order, they presented the same objects in a meaningful way as part of a story, their nonschooled Liberian subjects recalled them easily, clustering the objects according to the roles they played in the story. When memory for traditional children's stories was tested, cultural differences were also absent (Mandler et al., 1980). Similar results on tests of children's memorization skills have been obtained in research among Mayan people of rural Guatemala (Rogoff, Correa-Chávez, & Navichoc-Cotuc, 2005).

The implication of these cross-cultural memory studies differs from that of the cross-cultural studies of concrete-operational thinking. The latter studies probed basic mental operations presumed by Piaget and his followers to reflect the logic underlying everyday actions and reasoning in any culture. The ability to remember is also a universal intellectual requirement, but specific strategies for remembering are not universal. Indeed, many of them—the ones most often studied by psychologists—are associated with formal schooling.

As you will see in the next chapter, schooling presents children with specialized information-processing tasks—committing large amounts of information to memory in a short time, learning to manipulate abstract symbols in one's head and on paper, using logic to conduct experiments, and performing many more tasks that have few if any analogies in societies without formal schooling. The free-recall, random-order task that Cole and his colleagues initially used to assess memory among Liberian tribal people has no precise analogy in traditional Liberian cultures, so it is not surprising that subjects who had not attended school failed to show skill at such tasks.

Cultural Variations in Planning

A cross-cultural study by Shari Ellis and Bonnie Schneiders (reported in Ellis & Siegler, 1997) shows how differences in cultural values can shape the way and extent to which children plan ahead. Using a schematic drawing of a maze representing a rural scene (Figure 11.20), Ellis and Schneiders studied the way that Navajo and European American children planned their routes to and from different parts of the maze. They were interested in contrasting these two groups because the two cultures place different values on doing things speedily. The Navajo emphasize doing things thoughtfully rather than quickly (John, 1972). By contrast, speed of mental performance is often treated as an index of intelligence among Americans of European background (Sternberg, 1990). This cultural difference in values was expressed in the children's behavior as they planned their routes through the maze. The Navajo children spent almost 10 times as long planning their movements as the European-American children did—and as a result, they made significantly fewer errors.

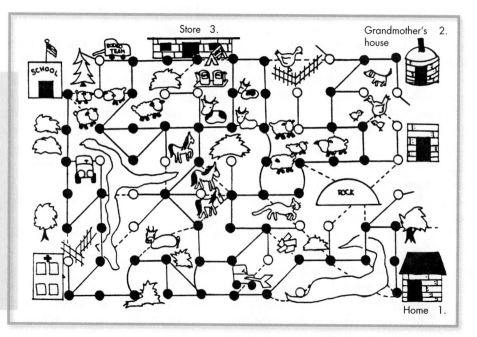

FIGURE 11.20 A schematic drawing of the battery-operated wooden apparatus used by Ellis and Schneiders to examine cultural differences in children's planning. Children were asked to find the shortest obstacle-free path from home to Grandmother's house, where they would pick up some money and then go to the store. Children chose their routes along various roads painted on the maze by inserting a probe into holes that were drilled into the roads. Each hole on a legitimate path buzzed when the probe was inserted into it. In the drawing shown here, the dotted lines and open circles indicate incorrect routes (the holes did not buzz when the probe was inserted); solid lines and solid dots are acceptable routes. (From Ellis & Gauvain, 1992. © 1992 by Lawrence Erlbaum Associates.)

▲ APPLY :: CONNECT :: DISCUSS

In what ways does Michael Cole's study of Liberian children suggest that culture contributes both to children's knowledge bases and to the type of memory strategies that children favor?

Individual Differences in Cognitive Development

If you were a hungry 10-year-old Australian Aborigine and your parents were out hunting and gathering, how would you know where to go to find the edible go-anna lizard? With all the various scratches and scuffs in the sand, how would you recognize the special tracks that would lead you to your prey? How would you catch and carry your lizards? How would you prepare them for cooking? Acquiring your afternoon snack would obviously require a good deal of knowledge and planning, characteristics of intelligent behavior. And if you nearly always returned to camp with a goanna sack brimming with lizards, while your peers rarely did, you might even be considered the most intelligent child in the village.

But all those intelligent behaviors associated with successful goanna hunting wouldn't protect you from having an empty stomach. They would, for example, get you nowhere at the corner store where you and your friends might stop for a snack on the way home from school. In this instance, your superior intelligence might be manifested by your having brought enough money with you, being able to count your change, and knowing that a granola bar and an apple are better choices than a bag of chips and a soda.

The fact that intelligence is so securely anchored to the cultural contexts in which it is used has led many developmentalists to argue that intelligence has no clear meaning outside its cultural context (Sternberg & Grigorenko, 2008). Indeed, although all languages have terms that describe individual differences in people's ability to solve various kinds of problems, the precise meanings of these terms vary among cultures, and it has proved difficult—some say impossible—to define intelligence so that individual differences in intelligence can be measured as precisely as weight or height, or the number of lizards in a goanna sack. Some cultures, including the Chewa of eastern Zambia, define intelligence largely in social terms, emphasizing cooperation and obedience (Serpell, 2000). Other cultures, including those of Europe and North America, define intelligence in mainly cognitive terms. Still others, including many Asian and African cultures, believe that intelligence includes both social and cognitive features. A case in point is the conception of intelligence of rural Kenyans, which has been studied by Elena Grigorenko and her colleagues (Grigorenko et al., 2001). These researchers report that among the Luo of rural Kenya, there are four words that people apply to different kinds of problem-solving abilities. One of these words appears to correspond to the notion of cognitive competence at the heart of European and North American conceptions of intelligence. The others refer to social qualities such as diligence or obedience, or personal qualities with social implications, such as a willingness to take initiative.

While cultural notions of intelligence vary, almost all children growing up today in industrialized countries can expect to take an intelligence test intended to assess their cognitive competence. Such tests are used to decide the kind of education they will receive and the kind of work they seem best suited for, which in turn, will influence the lives they will lead as adults. It is thus important to understand the concept of intelligence that underlies these tests, as well as intelligence-testing itself as a factor in children's development.

intelligence quotient (IQ) The ratio of mental age to chronological age, calculated as IQ = (MA/CA)100.

Measuring Intelligence

Interest in measuring intelligence became widespread at the beginning of the 20th century, when mass education was becoming the norm in industrialized countries. Though most children seemed to profit from the instruction they were given, some had considerable difficulty learning. In France, the minister of public instruction named a commission to determine how to distinguish between what he termed "defective" children, who needed special educational treatment, and children who were failing to learn in school for other reasons. The commission asked Alfred Binet, a professor of psychology at the Sorbonne, and Théodore Simon, a physician, to create a means of identifying those children who needed special educational treatment. Binet and Simon set out to construct a test for diagnosing mental subnormality that would have all the precision and validity of a medical examination. They especially wanted to avoid incorrectly diagnosing children as "mentally subnormal" (Binet & Simon, 1916).

After considerable research on various test items presented to children of various ages, Binet and Simon concluded that they had succeeded in constructing a scale of intelligence. They called the basic index of intelligence for this scale *mental age* (*MA*). A child who performed as well on the test as an average 7-year-old was said to have an MA of 7; a child who did as well as an average 9-year-old was said to have an MA of 9; and so on. The MA provided a convenient way to characterize mental subnormality. A "dull" 7-year-old child was one who performed like a normal child 1 or more years younger.

Shortly after Binet and Simon introduced their scale, psychologist William Stern recognized a serious limitation in using MA as an index of intelligence. To get a sense of this limitation, consider two children, an 18-year-old with an MA of 16 and a 5-year-old with an MA of 3. Although both children are 2 years "behind" the average, there would be reason to be much more concerned about the 5-year-old's intellectual development than about the 18-year-old's. To address the fact that 2 years of development in the life of a very young child is not equivalent to 2 years of development in the life of an older child, Stern (1912) introduced a new way of calculating intelligence. He used the simple strategy of dividing children's mental age by their chronological age (CA) to obtain a measure of their intelligence. Thus was born the unit of measurement that we use today, the **intelligence quotient (IQ)**:

$$IQ = (MA/CA) \times 100$$

Calculation of IQ in this fashion ensures that when children are performing precisely as expected for their age, the resulting score will be 100; thus 100 is an "average IQ" by definition (Figure 11.21). Applied to the two children described above, the calculation generates an IQ score of 89 for the 18-year-old and 60 for the 5-year old.

Intelligence tests, along with the manner of calculating IQs, have undergone substantial refinement since the seminal work of Binet, Simon, and Stern. Nevertheless, despite various revisions, the logic of the procedures devised by Binet and Simon—to define "average" performance for each age and compare the scores of individual children against the average—is still the basis of standardized intelligence tests.

Persistent Questions About Intelligence

The adoption and refinement of IQ testing methods by later generations of developmentalists represent only part of the contribution that Binet and Simon made to the study of intelligence. Equally

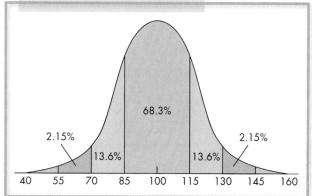

FIGURE 11.21 This figure illustrates an idealized bell-shaped curve of the distribution of IQ scores. A bell-shaped curve is a distribution of scores on a graph in which the most frequent value, the mode, is in the center, and the less frequent values are distributed symmetrically on either side. By definition, the modal IQ score is 100.

important have been the questions they brought to the fore, three of which have dominated research on intelligence ever since. The first question focuses on the nature of intelligence itself: Is it a general characteristic of a person's entire mental life, or is it a bundle of relatively specific abilities? Second is the nature–nurture question: How do biological and environmental factors contribute to variations among individuals and groups in test performance? The third question is about the nature of IQ tests and their relationship to culture: To what extent might tests be biased in their assessment of intelligence?

Despite persistent questions about the nature of intelligence and how to measure it, IQ tests are a routine part of many children's lives.

The Nature of Intelligence: General or Specific?

Although Binet and Simon (1916) were skeptical about the possibility of defining intelligence, they attempted to specify the quality of mind they were trying to test for:

> It seems to us that in intelligence there is a fundamental faculty, the alteration or lack of which is of the utmost importance for practical life. This faculty is judgment, otherwise called good sense, practical sense, initiative, the faculty of adapting oneself to circumstances. To judge well, to comprehend well, to reason well, these are the essential activities of intelligence. (p. 43)

By referring to intelligence as "a fundamental faculty," Binet and Simon signaled their belief that intelligence is a basic characteristic. Many others have followed this approach, noting, for example, that an individual's performance tends to be similar across types of intelligence-test items, a tendency consistent with the existence of a "general intelligence" (Spearman, 1927).

However, many psychologists now reject the idea of general intelligence, arguing instead that intelligence is composed of several distinct and separate abilities. Two approaches that depict intelligence in terms of distinctive capacities have been particularly influential. Howard Gardner (1983, 2006) has proposed a theory of *multiple intelligences,* each of which coincides with a different cognitive module and follows its own developmental path (Table 11.3). For example, musical intelligence often appears at an early age; logical mathematical intelligence seems to peak in late adolescence and early adulthood; and the kind of spatial intelligence on which artists rely may reach its peak much later. Gardner argues that the expression of each kind of intelligence depends upon a combination of three factors: (1) innate biological brain structures; (2) the extent to which the particular kind of intelligence

These talented young dancers display their creative intelligence in a dance competition at a ceremonial powwow in New Mexico.

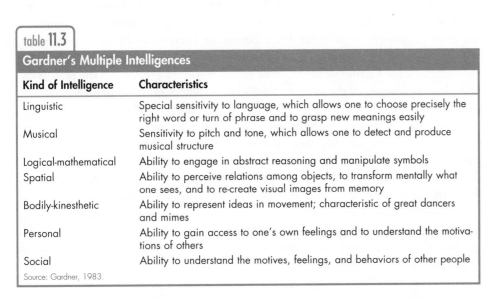

table 11.3	
Gardner's Multiple Intelligences	
Kind of Intelligence	**Characteristics**
Linguistic	Special sensitivity to language, which allows one to choose precisely the right word or turn of phrase and to grasp new meanings easily
Musical	Sensitivity to pitch and tone, which allows one to detect and produce musical structure
Logical-mathematical	Ability to engage in abstract reasoning and manipulate symbols
Spatial	Ability to perceive relations among objects, to transform mentally what one sees, and to re-create visual images from memory
Bodily-kinesthetic	Ability to represent ideas in movement; characteristic of great dancers and mimes
Personal	Ability to gain access to one's own feelings and to understand the motivations of others
Social	Ability to understand the motives, feelings, and behaviors of other people

Source: Gardner, 1983.

is emphasized in a given culture; and (3) the extent to which a child is provided deliberate instruction in activities associated with the particular kind of intelligence.

The second approach that views intelligence as consisting of distinct capacities is Robert Sternberg's (1985) "triarchic" theory of intelligence, which proposes that there are three kinds of intelligence:

1. *Analytic:* the abilities we use to analyze, judge, evaluate, compare, and contrast.

2. *Creative:* the abilities we use to create, invent, discover, and imagine or suppose.

3. *Practical:* the abilities we use to apply knowledge by putting it into practice.

Sternberg (2007) reports that an individual's performance level can vary from one kind of intelligence to another and argues that only analytic intelligence is measured by standard IQ tests.

What Explains Population Differences?

Along with their disagreements about what intelligence means and whether it is specific or general, developmentalists disagree about the significance of differences across individuals and across groups in performance on tests. The debate dates back to the beginning of World War I, when Robert Yerkes proposed that all military recruits be given an intelligence test to determine their fitness to serve in military capacities. In addition to determining individual recruits' fitness, the testing was perceived as generating data about the U.S. population as a whole (Yerkes, 1921). Approximately 1.75 million men were given IQ tests—written tests for those who could read and write English, a picture-completion test for those who could not (Figure 11.22). Never before had IQ tests been administered to such large groups of people at one time or to people for whom the language of the tests was not their native language.

Yerkes's research began a controversy that continues to the present time. Two results appeared to be particularly provocative. First, the average mental age of native-born Anglo Americans was assessed to be 13 years. Since, by the standards of the time, a mental age of 8 to 12 years was considered subnormal for an adult, it appeared that a substantial part of the Anglo population consisted of "morons." Second, there was a substantial difference between the scores obtained by recruits of European American and of African American origin. Overall, the average for recruits of European origin was a mental age of 13.7 years, whereas African Americans averaged slightly more than 10 years.

Several of the pioneer testers of intelligence interpreted such differences as the result of innate, immutable differences in natural intelligence ("nature"). According to this *innatist hypothesis of intelligence,* some people are born generally smarter than others, and no amount of training or variation in the environment can alter this fact. The generally lower test scores of members of ethnic-minority groups and the poor (who often, but not always, are the same people) were widely interpreted to mean that such groups were innately and irrevocably inferior (Herrnstein & Murray, 1994).

During the 1930s and 1940s the general-intelligence, innatist position was countered by an *environmental hypothesis of intelligence,* which asserted that intelligence is both specific—that is, includes distinct and separate abilities—and heavily dependent on experience. It was demonstrated, for example, that after people had moved from rural areas to the city, their intelligence test scores rose (Klineberg, 1935), and that when orphans were removed from very restricted early environments, their intelligence test scores improved markedly.

One of the most striking new lines of evidence for the environmental hypothesis of intelligence is the fact that worldwide there has been a steady increase in IQ test

FIGURE 11.22 In the picture-completion test used by Robert Yerkes and his colleagues to test recruits during World War I, each picture is incomplete in some way; the task was to identify what was missing. (From Yerkes, 1921.)

performance since testing began roughly 100 years ago, a trend called the **Flynn effect**, named after the scientist who discovered it (Flynn, 1984, 2007). Although the amount of improvement differs somewhat according to the kind of test that is used and the particular country in which it is administered, the general result for the 20 countries where intelligence testing has been widely carried out for many decades indicates that IQ scores have been going up an average of 10 to 20 points for every generation (Figure 11.23). This means, for example, that the average English person in 1900 would have scored at the level currently considered to indicate mental retardation.

There is no clear consensus about what environmental factors are causing IQ scores to go up, but it is certain that the change must involve the environment, since rapid change in the genetic constitution of people all over the world has not taken place, but large changes in the environment have (Dickens & Flynn, 2006). As Flynn points out, it is almost impossible to determine precisely how the environment contributes to the development of intelligence because all the possible

Flynn effect The steady increase over the past 100 years in IQ test performance, an increase believed to support the environmental hypothesis of intelligence.

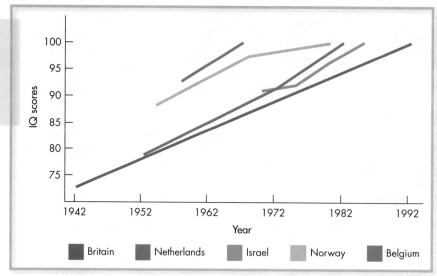

FIGURE 11.23 Countries that have been testing intelligence for decades, including the five illustrated here, find that IQ has been increasing by 10 to 20 points every generation, a phenomenon dubbed the "Flynn effect," after the scientist who discovered it. (Flynn, 1999, p. 7.)

causal factors are closely connected with each other, and all lead to changes that are in the same direction. The list of the possible causal factors ranges from improved nutrition and increasing years of education to an increase in the complexity of life, and even to the spread of interactive video games.

Are IQ Tests Culturally Biased? At the present time, no responsible scholar believes that the variation in intelligence test scores from person to person can be attributed entirely to either environmental or genetic factors. As we pointed out in Chapter 2, the attempt to tease apart the specific gene–environment interactions that shape human beings is especially difficult in relation to traits like intelligence that are *polygenic,* that is, that are shaped by several or many genes acting in combination in a given set of environmental conditions. Thus, even when it has been possible to estimate the genetic contribution to a trait, little can be said about precisely which genes are interacting with the environment in what way. Efforts to separate the various influences of nature and nurture on the phenotype are further complicated by the fact that parents contribute both to their children's genetic constitution and to the environment in which their children grow up. And then there is the final knot in untangling gene–environment interaction: Children actively shape their own environments in response to both genetic and environmental influences.

Attempts to understand how genetic and environmental factors combine to create the phenotypic behavior called "intelligence" face another, even greater difficulty. As we noted earlier, psychologists disagree profoundly about what, precisely, they are measuring when they administer an intelligence test. All they can say with any confidence is that these tests predict later school performance to a moderate degree.

At first glance, IQ tests may appear to be standard measures logically similar to a yardstick. But this appearance is an illusion. Precisely because intelligence tests derive their validity from their correlation with academic achievement, they are rooted in the schooled society in which they are developed and bound to the graphic systems of representation that are central to all schooling. But these modes of representation are generally absent in nonliterate societies. To be administered to a !Kung child, every existing intelligence test would thus require some modification—and not just translation from English to !Kung. If, for example, one of the test questions asks how many fingers are on two hands, the testers might assume that the test could be adapted to !Kung with only minimal modification—but that assumption would be wrong. The number system used by the !Kung is not the same as that used by Westerners, and it plays a different role in their lives (there is not much to count in a hunting-and-gathering society). In !Kung society, the relative importance of knowing the number of fingers on a hand is less important than knowing how to tie knots with those fingers.

When it comes to the tests that require interpretation of pictures or some form of written answer, even more serious difficulties arise. The !Kung have no tradition of either drawing or writing, and research with nonliterate peoples in several parts of the world and with young children in the United States shows that people without such experience do not automatically interpret two-dimensional pictures of objects as they would the objects themselves (Pick, 1997; Serpell & Hanes, 2004). For them, interpreting the pictures requires additional mental work. As a result, tests that use pictures or require copying figures graphically would be inappropriate, as would any tests that depend on the ability to read. We thus cannot assume that an IQ test is like a yardstick, yielding equivalent measures in all cultural environments.

Various attempts have been made to create "culture-free" tests, but no generally satisfactory approach has been found: All tests of intelligence draw on a background of learning that is culture-specific (Serpell & Hanes, 2004). The fact that intelligence cannot be tested independently of the culture that gives rise to the test greatly limits the conclusions that can be drawn from IQ testing in different social and cultural groups.

▲ APPLY :: CONNECT :: DISCUSS

IQ tests were first developed in order to identify children who needed special education. Today, the use of IQ tests in making decisions to place children on different "academic ability tracks" is hotly debated. Using concepts and research evidence presented in this section, describe the pros and cons of IQ testing and ability tracking in schools.

Reconsidering the Cognitive Changes in Middle Childhood

The changes in children's biological and cognitive abilities between early and middle childhood point to specific features of children's physical abilities and thought processes that are becoming more systematic and can be applied across a broader variety of settings. Particularly important is the extent to which children are gaining increasing understanding of, and control over, their new powers of thought and action. Considered as a whole, rather than as isolated achievements, these changes help explain why adults begin to grant their children more independence during this developmental period.

Although the cognitive skills and capacities of children everywhere change dramatically over the course of middle childhood, our discussions of cross-cultural work suggest that the specific contexts of children's daily lives support intellectual development in what can be radically different ways. To properly address the issue of how culturally organized environments exert their effects on cognitive development, we need to reach beyond the relatively narrow range of tasks that has been featured in psychologists' studies and investigate the changes that children display in a variety of social contexts, especially in classrooms and peer groups, where many children in middle childhood begin to spend so much of their time. Many developmentalists believe that experiences in both of these contexts are crucial to the cognitive changes associated with middle childhood. We will examine these contexts in the next two chapters.

Although children from traditional agricultural societies sometimes perform poorly on psychological tests, their cognitive abilities are often manifested in other ways. This Ugandan boy has constructed his toy car out of bits of wire and some wooden wheels.

David Young-Wolff / PhotoEdit

SUMMARY

- The beginning of middle childhood is recognized in cultures around the world, particularly in adults' new expectations of their 6- and 7-year-olds. These expectations relate to children's increased physical capacities and cognitive abilities.

Physical and Motor Development

- Size and strength increase significantly during middle childhood, although more slowly than in earlier years. Muscle mass and fat tissue both increase.

- Although height and weight are both influenced by genetic factors, environmental factors, such as nutrition and health, also play an important role. For example, in the United States, changes in diet in recent decades have contributed to an increase in childhood obesity.

- Strength, agility, and balance all improve in middle childhood. Boys tend to be slightly advanced in motor abilities requiring power and force; girls often excel in fine motor skills and gross motor skills combining balance and foot movement.

- Brain development in the early years of middle childhood includes:
  - Continued myelination, especially in the frontal cortex.
  - Continued synaptic pruning in late-maturing brain areas, with more stable connections among remaining neurons.
  - A shift to more alpha activity (characteristic of engaged attention) than theta activity (characteristic of sleep states).
  - A significant increase in the synchronization of electrical activity between different brain areas, among them the frontal lobes, with the areas functioning more effectively as coordinated systems.

Concrete-Operational Development

- According to Piaget, as a result of increasing decentration, at about age 7 or 8, children become capable of mental operations—of logically combining, separating, and transforming information. With the advent of this stage of concrete operations, children can think in a more organized, flexible way, and the world becomes more predictable to them.

- Concrete-operational thinking is reflected in new abilities related to:
  - Conservation, Piaget's term for the understanding that some properties of an object or substance remain the same even when its appearance is altered in some way.
  - Classification, with children now able to understand the relation between a superordinate class and its subclasses and to categorize objects according to multiple criteria.
  - Planning, which requires forming mental representations of actions needed to achieve a goal.

- Metacognition, with children better able to think about and regulate their thoughts.

- The limitations of concrete operations are apparent in the difficulty children encounter when reasoning about abstract, unfamiliar situations.

Information-Processing Approaches

- According to information-processing theorists, the cognitive changes in middle childhood are made possible by changes such as:
  - Improvements in memory arising from increased processing speed and capacity of working memory; increases in knowledge; and greater use of more effective strategies for remembering, such as rehearsal, organizational strategies, and elaboration.
  - Improvements in metamemory, or knowledge about memory, including about memory limitations and strategies.
  - Increases in children's ability to regulate their attention, which enables them to stay focused and ignore distractions.

- Developmentalists have suggested that the mechanisms for cognitive change suggested in Piaget's stage theory and those suggested by information-processing theorists may in fact work together.

The Role of Social and Cultural Contexts

- Cross-cultural studies suggest the universality of concrete operations in middle childhood as well as significant cultural variations that influence performance.

- Across cultures, memory strategies used differ significantly depending on whether children have had schooling. Cross-cultural differences in planning relate to cultural differences in values.

Individual Differences in Cognitive Development

- Definitions of intelligence differ among cultures and may focus on social, rather than cognitive, competence.

- Intelligence tests, as they have been developed since their introduction by Binet and Simon, attempt to measure cognitive competence by producing an IQ score based on a child's performance compared with that of children of the same age.

- Research on intelligence has been dominated by three questions:
  1. Is intelligence a general characteristic or are there specific kinds of intelligence? Two approaches taking the second position are Gardner's theory of multiple intelligences and Sternberg's triarchic theory of intelligence.

2. Are differences among individuals and among groups in performance on IQ tests the result of genetic or environmental factors? Evidence for an environmental role comes from the Flynn effect, the increase across generations in performance on IQ tests.

3. To what extent might IQ tests be culturally biased? All tests draw on learning that is culture-specific, limiting the conclusions that can be drawn.

Reconsidering the Cognitive Changes in Middle Childhood

• The cognitive changes of middle childhood are associated with children's increasing control over their thoughts and actions. This is consistent with the greater independence that children of this age are granted by adults.

Key Terms

concrete operations, p. 401

conservation of number, p. 402

conservation of volume, p. 403

identity, p. 404

compensation, p. 404

reversibility, p. 404

metacognition, p. 406

memory span, p. 410

memory strategies, p. 411

rehearsal, p. 411

organizational strategies, p. 411

elaboration, p. 412

metamemory, p. 412

executive function, p. 413

intelligence quotient (IQ), p. 420

Flynn effect, p. 423

School as a Context for Development

The Contexts of Learning

School Readiness

Precursors to Reading and Writing

Precursors to Learning Mathematics

The Role of Family

Preschools

In the Classroom

Social Organization of the Classroom and
Instructional Design

Barriers to School Success

The Cognitive Consequences of
Schooling

The School-Cutoff Strategy

Comparing Schooled and Nonschooled Children

Assessing the Second-Generation Impact of
Schooling

Contemporary Challenges in a
Globalizing World

The Culture of School

The Language of School

Culturally Responsive Classroom Strategies

Outside the School

Last month, I was sitting in the headmaster's office of a primary school in Samfya, in the heart of rural Zambia. Mr. Ben Charma leads 46 teachers in his school of 1,700 children, more than half of whom have been orphaned by AIDS. The son of a copper miner, Ben Charma worked hard at school and avoided the mining life that ruined his father's health. He knows what lies in store for children when educational chances are limited by poverty. The exam results were out and the final-year pupils at the primary school had done well. Yet, this is the most heartbreaking time of all for school staff. They have worked so hard to achieve a good pass rate for their pupils, yet for many children—particularly girls— this will be their very last day at school, at the age of just 11 or 12. Without money for school clothing, shoes, books, stationery, and fees, these children have no chance of going on to secondary school. And so it is that parents come to beg. They know that, without the benefits of education, their daughters will be forced to marry young and face lives of back-breaking agricultural and domestic toil with babies born into families too poor to give them more than life.

It is a scandal that more than 24 million girls in sub-Saharan Africa are still not able to go to school. This has a devastating impact, particularly on rural communities. Children die younger when their mothers do not know about basic hygiene; HIV spreads more rapidly when uneducated women do not know how to protect themselves from the disease; and earnings are lower when women do not have access to education. Send a girl to school and the opportunities are multiplied across her whole community. When women farmers have the same access to education as their brothers and husbands, crop yields rise by 22 percent. In Africa, if mothers receive just 5 years of education, their children are 40 percent more likely to live to their fifth birthday. And educated women are three times more likely to protect themselves against AIDS than those with no education. Lamentably, the world has been slow to heed the urgent message that educating girls is the key to eradicating poverty. Former United Nations Secretary-General Kofi Annan once said: "Without achieving gender equity for girls in education, the world has no chance of achieving many of the ambitious health, social and development targets it has set for itself."

(Adapted from Cotton, 2006.)

n contrast to the students of Samfya, it is unlikely that at the tender age of 11 or 12, you worried that your education might be about to end or thought about school in terms of its consequences for your future. But as Ann Cotton argues in her heartfelt plea to increase educational access for Africa's children, especially girls, going to school not only improves the life circumstances of individuals, it also contributes substantially to the health and economic well-being of local communities and to human society as a whole. Indeed, in the case of Africa, where children spend less time in school than do children anywhere else on earth (Figure 12.1), increasing access to education may provide countries with a powerful defense against the devastating epidemics of poverty and AIDS that are killing so many of their citizens.

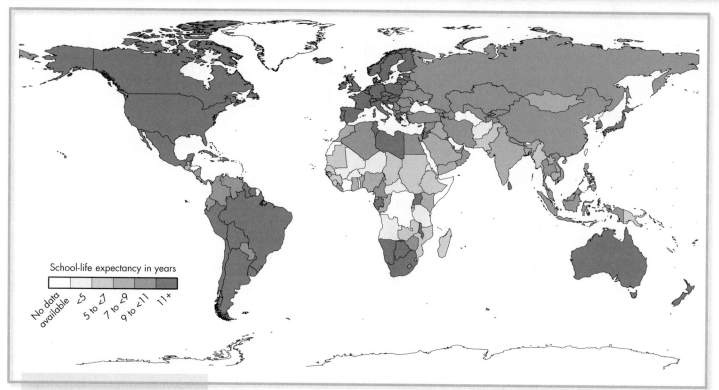

FIGURE 12.1 Compared with most other countries in the world, many African countries face significantly greater challenges in providing education to their children. (From UNESCO, 2004, p. 11.)

These Ghanaian children are ready for school. Children in many other African countries tend to leave school at earlier ages compared with those in Ghana, placing entire communities at greater risk for AIDS and poverty.

Although access to education is not nearly as restricted in the United States and other wealthier nations as it is in Africa, disparities in who has access to quality education can be quite pronounced for a number of reasons. It is well known, for example, that educational quality in the United States suffers substantially in schools located in economically impoverished neighborhoods, where large numbers of ethnic-minority children grow up. Yet conditions in such neighborhoods make educational quality all the more important. For example, living in poor neighborhoods makes it more likely not only that children will be exposed to environmental toxins that have been shown to harm cognitive development but also that they will be exposed to violence, which increases the likelihood of psychiatric disorders. To make matters more complicated, financing for schools in poor neighborhoods is often inadequate, and such schools are disproportionately assigned inexperienced teachers because experienced teachers, who often have more choice in where they teach, are reluctant to work in them. A study of nearly 4,000 African American families that moved from urban high-rise housing projects, where poverty and crime are pervasive, to new, private housing in a wealthier suburban school district found a marked improvement in several indicators of academic achievement, including a decrease in high school dropout rates and increased college attendance (Rubinowitz et al., 2000). Clearly, equal access to quality education remains an ideal to be struggled for rather than a reality for millions of American, as well as African, children.

This chapter is devoted to exploring the extraordinary impact of school as a context for children's development. We begin by discussing the unique features of school that set it apart from other contexts of learning and consider the particular contributions that school makes to intellectual development. We then examine *school readiness,* arising from the academic building blocks that children bring with them into the classroom, including those provided by family, community, and culture.

Next, we examine the different ways of "doing school," that is, the various forms of classroom instruction and their implications for learning. Finally, we confront contemporary challenges to school access and school success in our rapidly globalizing world.

The Contexts of Learning

In Chapter 2, we introduced the idea that children acquire the material and symbolic tools of culture through three fundamental social processes: *social enhancement* (making use of resources present in the immediate environment), *imitation* (observing and copying the behaviors of others), and, the process we examine here, *explicit instruction* (deliberate teaching of knowledge and skills). The most structured type of explicit instruction is **formal education**, through which adults instruct the young in the specialized knowledge and skills of their culture.

It is not known if education existed among the hunter–gatherer peoples who roamed the earth hundreds of thousands of years ago, but explicit instruction is not a conspicuous part of socialization in contemporary hunter–gatherer societies (Rogoff, 2003). Among the !Kung of Africa's Kalahari Desert, for example, basic training in the skills expected of adults is embedded in everyday activities, involving processes of social enhancement and imitation. The basic means by which adults ensure that children acquire culturally valued skills and knowledge is to include children in adult activities:

> There is . . . very little explicit teaching. . . . What the child knows, he learns from direct interaction with the adult community, whether it is learning to tell the age of the spoor left by a poisoned kudu buck, to straighten the shaft of an arrow, to build a fire, or to dig a spring hare out of its burrow. . . . It is all implicit. (Bruner, 1966, p. 59)

When societies achieve a certain degree of complexity and specialization in the roles people play, the tools they use, and the ways they secure food and housing, preparation for some occupations is likely to occur through **apprenticeship**, a form intermediate between learning through participation in family and community life and the explicit instruction of formal education. A young apprentice learns a craft or a skill by spending an extended period of time working for an adult master (Collins, 2006). The settings in which apprentices learn are not organized solely for the purpose of teaching. Rather, instruction and productive labor are combined; from the beginning, apprentices contribute to the work process.

Researchers have found that novice apprentices receive relatively little explicit instruction but, instead, are given ample opportunity to observe skilled workers and to practice specific tasks (Rogoff, 2003). In many societies, the apprentice's relationship with the master is part of a larger web of family relationships. Often the apprentice lives with the master and does farm or household chores to help pay for his or her upkeep. In this way, the tasks of education and community-building are woven together (Rogoff et al., 2007).

Formal education differs from traditional apprenticeship training (and from informal instruction in the family) in four main ways (Lave & Wenger, 1991; Singleton, 1998):

1. *Motivation.* Apprentices get to practice their craft from the beginning and see the fruits of their labor. Students in schools must work for years to perfect their skills before they can put their knowledge to use in adult

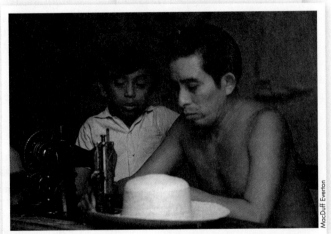

Apprenticeship arrangements in which children learn by observing adults and working alongside them are still an important form of education despite the spread of formal schools.

formal education The most structured type of explicit education, through which adults instruct the young in the specialized knowledge and skills of their culture.

apprenticeship A form of education in which a young person learns a craft or skill by spending an extended period of time working for an adult master.

work. In the meantime, the tasks they are engaged in may seem pointless to them.

2. *Social relations.* Unlike masters of apprentices, schoolteachers are rarely kin or family acquaintances, and they may not even live in the community.

3. *Social organization.* Apprentices are most likely to learn in a work setting among people of diverse ages and skill levels, so they have more than one person to turn to for assistance. At school, children typically learn in the company of other children who are about their age and one adult, who instructs them, and they are often expected to work individually (in fact, asking for assistance from their peers may be considered cheating).

4. *Medium of instruction.* Apprenticeship instruction is usually conducted orally in the context of production. Oral instruction is important in formal schooling as well, but, as we will see later, it is speech of a special kind, closely associated with the use of written symbols as a means of acquiring skills and knowledge.

Not only does schooling differ from other learning contexts in these ways but the types of problems posed to children in school differ considerably from those they encounter in other learning contexts (Table 12.1). Consider, for example, a problem in which a child needs to figure out the distance between two locations. In a school context, the child might be asked to use a scientific instrument, such as a ruler, to precisely measure abstract units (centimeters, inches) between two points. The goal of this problem solving is to learn or demonstrate mastery over a mathematical system of measurement that can be applied to measure distances in any situation. In an everyday context, in contrast, the child might be faced with a problem of finding and cutting tree saplings of sufficient length to bridge a small stream so that people can cross into crop fields without getting their feet wet. In this instance, problem solving is undertaken in the service of a highly specific goal that is important to the local community. In all likelihood, the child works with others to find saplings that are tall enough and strong enough to accomplish the task at hand. The measuring "tools" are specific to the particular, concrete problem, and may be as variable as the sense that the saplings should be "taller than my house" or "young trees of at least 4 winters." The outcomes of such measuring

table 12.1	
School Problems versus Everyday Problems	
School Problems	**Everyday Problems**
• Tend to draw on analytic intelligence.	• Tend to draw on practical intelligence.
• Abstract in nature and goals.	• Concrete in nature and goals.
• Formulated for the learner by other people.	• Must be recognized or formulated by learners themselves.
• Generally have little or no intrinsic interest to the learner.	• Are intrinsically important to the learner.
• Are clearly defined.	• Generally are poorly defined.
• Usually have a single correct answer that can be reached by a single, generalizable method.	• Usually have several acceptable solutions that can be reached by a variety of routes.
• Include all the information needed to deal with them.	• Require people to seek new information.
• Are detached from ordinary experience.	• Are embedded in ordinary experience.

will also be variable, lacking the precision of scientifically calibrated measurement instruments.

Thus, it appears that school problem solving supports the development and use of abstract reasoning, whereas everyday problem solving supports reasoning based on particular concrete experience (Cole, 2005). Indeed, Alexander Luria, a Russian developmentalist who studied the cognitive effects of literacy, found evidence of this when he presented illiterate peasants with school-type problems that required the application of abstract reasoning, as in the following (adapted from Luria, 1976, pp. 108–109):

Luria: In the North, where there is snow, all bears are white. Novaya Zemlya is in the Far North, and it always has snow. What color are the bears there?

Peasant: I don't know. I've never been to Novaya Zemlya.

Luria: But on the basis of my words [repeats the problem].

Peasant: I've only seen black bears.

Luria: But if you just think about my words [repeats the problem again].

Peasant [becoming annoyed]: Look. . . . If a king or a czar had been to Novaya Zemlya and saw a bear and told about it, then maybe he could be believed. But I have never been there, and I have not seen the bears there, so I can't say. That's my last word!

Clearly, different contexts pose different types of intellectual challenges and support the development of different forms of reasoning. Formal education, according to Luria's research, encourages the development of abstract, hypothetical reasoning crucial to success in technologically advanced societies.

▲ APPLY :: CONNECT :: DISCUSS

Using concepts presented in this section, explain some ways that going to school might contribute to the health and economic well-being of local communities and human society as a whole.

School Readiness

Four-year-olds Dawn and Heshan are coloring pictures when Dawn invites, "Let's play li-eberry." "Okay," says Heshan, agreeably. Gesturing to a collection of books stacked on a toy shelf, Dawn suggests, "You can get some books over there." Heshan chooses several books while Dawn prepares a "check-out" by clearing toys from a space on the table and assembling some crayons and paper. "I'll take these," Heshan announces. Dawn takes the books he offers, looks at each one, gives them back, and warns, "They're due in 1 week." Heshan retreats to a corner of the room and begins "reading" a book about animal babies. Meanwhile, Dawn is scratching marks on small pieces of paper. After some minutes, she approaches Heshan and hands him a piece of paper. "You owe 5 dollars," she says. "What?" asks Heshan, clearly puzzled. Dawn explains, "You're overdue 1 week. If you don't pay 5 dollars that will be 5 weeks and you have to pay 100 dollars." "Oh," says Heshan, uncertainly. "Here," says Dawn, handing him another piece of paper. "This can be 5 dollars."

It is clear from our previous discussions of development during infancy and early childhood that by the time they start school, children already possess a number of building blocks relevant to literacy and math instruction. **Emergent literacy** and **emergent numeracy** include knowledge, skills, and attitudes that are precursors to learning to read, write, and do math. In the example above, it is clear that Dawn and Heshan have had experiences relevant to developing literacy and numeracy. They know about books and libraries and enjoy them well enough to include them in their play. Dawn pretends to write; Heshan pretends to read. And Dawn expresses the rudiments of mathematical knowledge. She not only uses number words—"one,"

emergent literacy Knowledge, skills, and attitudes that provide the building blocks for learning to read and write.

emergent numeracy Knowledge, skills, and attitudes that provide the building blocks for learning how to do math.

During play time, this preschooler chose to look at a book. Early childhood teachers often mix books and toys together on shelves for the purpose of increasing children's exposure to books and promoting emergent literacy skills.

"five," "one hundred"—but also demonstrates an understanding of which words reflect larger amounts (and higher library fines). When Dawn and Heshan start school, their emergent literacy and numeracy skills will provide an important foundation for academic success. In the following sections, we will examine several emergent literacy and numeracy skills associated with school readiness, as well as a number of factors known to contribute to the development of these skills, including experiences provided by families and preschools.

Precursors to Reading and Writing

The first step children must take in learning to read and write is to realize that there is a correspondence between the marks on the printed page and the spoken language. Once they understand that each word is represented by a cluster of graphic signs, they still have to figure out how each graphic sign is related to a linguistic sound. One of the most basic reading skills is **decoding** text, that is, translating units of print, or *graphemes,* to units of sound, or *phonemes* (Tolchinsky, 2006). Obviously, before this process of translation can occur, children must be able to distinguish between letters, as well as detect and manipulate phonemes (Thompson & Nicholson, 1999). As you learned in Chapter 4 (see pp. 132–133), the capacity to discriminate between phonemes occurs very early in life. However, this infant capacity is quite different from the ability to detect and manipulate the phonemes that make up words. So, for example, your own capacity to detect and manipulate phonemes makes it easy for you to fill in the blanks below, each of which represents a phoneme:

Fuzzy Wu_y wa_ a bear.
Fuzzy Wu_y had no h_ _.
Fuzzy Wu_y wa_ n't fuzzy, wa_ he?

Research suggests that the *phonological awareness* you used to fill in the blanks of the "Fuzzy Wuzzy" ditty—your ability to detect and manipulate the phonemes in words—does not occur without deliberate instruction: Nonliterate adults in various parts of the world do not seem able to identify the phonemic units that make up individual words (Scholes, 1998).

A wealth of research conducted by Terizinha Nunes and Peter Bryant in different countries has demonstrated that children who find it difficult to break words into their constituent syllables and phonemes in a purely oral task have difficulty linking sounds and letters (Nunes & Bryant, 2009). This research has spawned special educational programs that provide children with enriched experiences in oral language analysis before they are taught to read or when they experience difficulty in reading (Sunseth & Bowers, 2002). The lessons include practice in rhyming, breaking words down into syllables, and special language games such as Pig Latin, in which the first phoneme of each word is moved to the end of the word and then followed by an "ay" (as in "igpay atinlay"). Such special instruction has been found to increase the literacy skills of poor readers substantially (Blachman et al., 2004).

The capacity to be engrossed in a storybook requires mastery of a number of precursors to reading, including understanding how each graphic sign on the page is related to a linguistic sound.

Precursors to Learning Mathematics

Like learning to read and write, learning mathematics involves a process of translation. In the case of mathematics, however, children must learn to translate their culture's number words and symbols (e.g., Arabic numerals) into an understanding

decoding The process of translating units of print into units of sound.

of specific quantities (Geary, 2006; Bryant & Nunes, 2011). Although very young babies (as well as a wide variety of nonhuman species) demonstrate the ability to discriminate between different amounts—distinguishing, for example, between a set containing 6 objects and a set containing 12 objects—the vastly more complex process of mapping symbols to quantities does not begin in earnest until 2 to 3 years of age (Gilmore & Spelke, 2008; Beran & Beran, 2004; Gordon, 2004).

As we all know, early counting efforts are prone to error, as when a child says "three, five" when asked to count two crayons, and "three, five, six" when asked to count three crayons. However, errors like this actually reveal several competencies that are central to mathematics learning. First, when asked to count, the child responded with number words, not color words, demonstrating awareness of the special language of mathematics. Furthermore, the child used each count word only once, suggesting an understanding that different number words correspond to different quantities. Finally, the word order the child used—"three, five" and "three, five, six"—indicates awareness that the sequence of words matters in counting (Sarnecka & Gelman, 2004).

With increasing age, children become more proficient at mapping number words onto specific quantities. Interestingly, research indicates that this developmental process unfolds more quickly for children who speak Chinese than for those who speak English (Geary et al., 1996). Mapping number words onto the base-10 number system can be troublesome for English-speaking children because the language includes some irregular number words such as "eleven" and "twelve" that do not carry the same structural information as words like "thirteen," "fourteen," and "fifteen." Chinese, in contrast, does not include irregular number words. Moreover, Chinese number words map very clearly onto the base-10 number system. The Chinese word for "twelve," for example, translates as "ten two," making the tens value of 1 and units value of 2 much more transparent than they are in English (Geary, 2006). It is easy to see why English-speaking first-graders make such errors as writing "203" when they mean to write "23": This representation corresponds to the way the number is said ("20-3").

As children gain mathematical experience during elementary school, they become able to envision quantities in terms of a mental number line. That is, they can imagine an abstract number line composed of discrete units and identify the placement of a particular number on the line (Figure 12.2). As we found with children's abilities to identify and manipulate the phonemic units of words, the ability to identify and manipulate numeric units seems to emerge only in the context of deliberate instruction (Siegler & Opfer, 2003). Later in the chapter, we will examine other ways in which formal education fosters the development of abstract thinking.

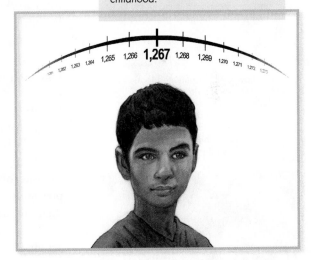

FIGURE 12.2 The ability to locate a specific number on an abstract number line emerges during middle childhood.

The Role of Family

The family's important role in supporting the child's emergent literacy and numeracy skills has long been recognized by teachers and researchers alike. In many cultures, parents provide their children with special toys, games, and activities designed to promote learning mathematics, reading, and writing (Ginsburg, 2008; Tudge et al., 2006). When Jonathan Tudge and his colleagues conducted an ethnographic study of 3-year-olds growing up in the United States, Kenya, and Brazil, they found important differences in children's school-readiness activities depending on the children's culture and socioeconomic status (Tudge et al., 2006). For example, as shown

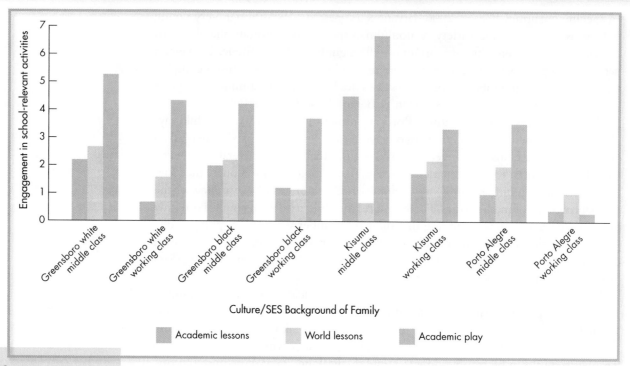

FIGURE 12.3 Ethnographic studies find that families prepare their children for school in a number of ways, emphasizing academic lessons, world lessons, and/or academic play. The extent to which a family may stress one or more of these ways depends on the specific culture and socioeconomic status of the family. (From Tudge et al., 2006.)

It is now well documented that children who are read to on a daily basis will develop larger vocabularies and, in turn, have even more reading experiences compared to children who are read to less often.

in Figure 12.3, in all cultures, children from middle-class families were more likely than their working-class counterparts to engage with their parents in academically oriented play and academically oriented lessons such as counting, spelling, and learning shapes and colors. Significantly, in Kenya, but not in the other cultures, children from working-class families were more likely than their middle-class counterparts to be engaged with their parents in "world lessons," such as learning how things work, why things happen, and how to be safe. Interestingly, Kenyan working-class children also spent considerably more time engaged in work-related activities, such as cleaning, shopping, and repairing, than did children in any of the other cultural/socioeconomic groups. As the researchers suggest, it is likely that the concentration on "world lessons" and work-related activities helps move Kenyan working-class children "on a trajectory more to do with the world of work than the world of school" (2006, p. 1463). In contrast, Kenyan middle-class children spent more time than any other group engaged in academically oriented play and academic lessons with parents. In Kenyan society, children must pass school-readiness tests to be admitted to the more prestigious schools. In preparation for these tests, most middle-class families enroll their children in preschools that provide substantial school-relevant content.

Taken together, results from Tudge's exhaustive analysis of children's everyday activities underscore the importance of family in creating contexts for children to engage in activities relevant to school readiness. There is, in fact, a wealth of research indicating that such activities have a significant bearing on children's intellectual development and academic success. Strong relationships have been found, for example, between being read to at 14 months of age and language comprehension, vocabulary size, and cognitive functioning at 2 years (Raikes et al., 2006). In addition, it seems that such early reading experience and emergent literacy skills enhance one another. Thus, when young children are read to on a daily basis, their vocabularies increase, and as their vocabularies increase, so, too, do their daily reading experiences. Helen Raikes, who discovered this relationship in a study involving more than 2,500 children and families, described it as a "snowball" effect in which reading and vocabulary lead to more opportunities to use and learn language.

Preschools

Preschools came into being early in the twentieth century, initiated by educators' and physicians' concern that the complexities of urban life were overwhelming children and stunting their development. The preschool was conceived as "a protected environment scaled to [children's] developmental level and designed to promote experiences of mastery within a child-sized manageable world" (Prescott & Jones, 1971, p. 54).

In the 1960s, a variety of scientific and social factors combined to create great interest in preschools' potential to increase the educational chances of the poor. On the scientific side was a growing belief that environmental influence during the first few years of life is crucial to all later abilities, especially intellectual ones. This belief coincided with growing political concern that social barriers between the rich and the poor and between Whites and Blacks were creating a dangerous situation in the United States. In 1963 Michael Harrington warned that the United States was creating "an enormous concentration of young people who, if they do not receive immediate help, may well be the source of a kind of hereditary poverty new to American society" (Harrington, 1963, p. 188). Commentators on the lives of poor young children issue the same warning today.

This combination of social, political, and scientific factors led the U.S. Congress to declare a "war on poverty" in 1964. One of the key programs in this "war" was Project Head Start. Its purpose was to intervene in the cycle of poverty at a crucial time in children's lives by providing them with important learning experiences that they might otherwise miss. Federal support enabled Head Start programs to offer these experiences at no charge to low-income families.

This strategy of social reform through early childhood education rested on three crucial assumptions:

1. The environmental conditions of poverty-level homes are insufficient to prepare children to succeed in school.

2. Schooling is the social mechanism that permits children to succeed in U.S. society.

3. Poor children could succeed in school, and thereby overcome their poverty, if they were given extra assistance during the preschool years.

Originally conceived as a summer program, Head Start soon began to operate year-round, serving approximately 200,000 preschool children at a time (Consortium for Longitudinal Studies, 1983). More than three decades later, Head Start programs have expanded to provide services for more than 750,000 children. Since its inception in 1965, more than 27 million children have enrolled in the program (Office of Head Start, 2010). Despite its phenomenal growth, the program serves significantly less than half of the children who are eligible to participate (Devaney, Ellwood, & Love, 1997).

In recent decades, a large number of studies have evaluated preschool programs for poor children, including Head Start and a variety of similar efforts (Zigler & Styfco, 2010; Puma et al., 2005; Yoshikawa, 2005). Some of the studies have been able to do follow-up evaluations of children as they reached their early 20s and to include broader developmental indicators such as crime rates and earned income in the assessment. These broad evaluations revealed a variety of positive findings, although success has not been uniform. On the positive side, children who attend regular Head Start or special model programs show meaningful gains in intellectual performance and socio-emotional development. Children who attend Head Start are also less likely to be assigned to remedial special-education classes when they attend school. As is the case with child-care programs, however, the success of Head

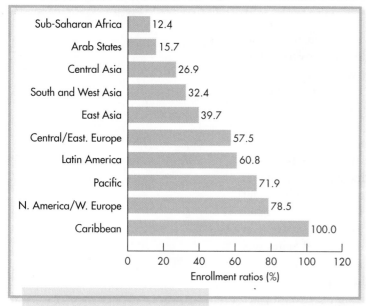

Region	Enrollment ratio (%)
Sub-Saharan Africa	12.4
Arab States	15.7
Central Asia	26.9
South and West Asia	32.4
East Asia	39.7
Central/East. Europe	57.5
Latin America	60.8
Pacific	71.9
N. America/W. Europe	78.5
Caribbean	100.0

Enrollment ratios (%)

FIGURE 12.4 There are vast differences in preschool enrollments throughout the world. Children who are most at risk for malnourishment and disease are least likely to be enrolled in preschool. (From UNESCO, 2007.)

Preschool programs can boost children's readiness for primary school, especially when children are from immigrant families.

Arthur Booker/Freudenthal Institute at Universiteit Utrecht

Start programs depends on the quality of the classroom experience; and, unfortunately, while most classrooms have been rated as adequate in quality, very few are considered to be of high quality.

Nonetheless, the success of well-run programs is now broadly accepted (Zigler & Styfco, 2008). In one of the best and most heavily studied cases, the Perry Preschool Program in Ypsilanti, Michigan, it has been possible to follow up the progress of experimental and control children for more than 35 years. The children in the experimental group had higher achievement scores than those in the control group at the ages of 9 and 14. They were more likely to graduate from high school, more likely to be employed at the age of 19, less likely to have run afoul of the law by the age of 28, and less likely to have gone on welfare. A recent cost–benefit analysis of the Perry Preschool Program showed that the money invested is more than recovered in savings on other social services and interventions (Heckman et al., 2010).

With the recognition of the importance of school readiness to academic success, and of education in general to the health and well-being of children, their communities, and society as a whole, enrollment in preschools throughout the world has tripled since 1970. Nevertheless, consistent with our earlier discussion about children's access to education, significant cross-national disparities exist in preschool enrollments (Figure 12.4). Sadly, according to a report issued by the United Nations (UNESCO, 2007), the children most likely to benefit from preschool education—for example, those at highest risk for poor health due to malnourishment and contracting preventable diseases—are the least likely to be enrolled in a preschool program (Magnuson & Shager, 2010).

In addition to cross-national differences in preschool enrollments, there are differences within countries. Several studies conducted in the United States, for example, have found that children of ethnic-minority immigrant families are less likely than their native-born ethnic-majority peers to participate in preschool (Brandon, 2004; Crosnoe, 2006). Knowing that immigrant families are overrepresented among the poor, undereducated, and underemployed (Magnuson et al., 2006; Capps et al., 2004), it might be thought that immigrant children are more likely to stay home because unemployed adult family members are available to care for them and because their families lack financial resources to pay for preschool, as well as such related costs as transportation, clothing, and supplies. Although this may well be the case for some immigrant families, research suggests that cultural factors, including cultural norms regarding whether and how to prepare children for school, are also influential in determining whether or not immigrant children attend preschool (Bainbridge et al., 2005; Liang, Fuller, & Singer, 2000). Supporting this idea, one study found that even when family income and maternal employment are held constant, children whose families speak Spanish at home remain less likely to be enrolled in preschool, perhaps because of the cultural value placed on family care (Liang et al., 2000).

As Magnuson and her colleagues (2006) point out, studies on the effects of preschool participation on school readiness rarely undertake comparative analyses of the effects for immigrant children and those for native-born, ethnic-majority children, but when they do, they generally find that preschool experience is at least as beneficial for the former as for the latter. Indeed, similar to findings that preschool participation is more effective for children who are economically disadvantaged or demonstrate lower levels of intellectual development, research indicates that children of immigrant families profit significantly from preschool experiences (e.g., NICHD Early Child Care Research Network, 2004; Magnuson & Waldfogel, 2005). In particular,

- Preschool enrollment has a larger impact on the language skills of Hispanic children than it does on those of non-Hispanic White children (Gormley & Gayer, 2005).

- Hispanic children who participate in Head Start preschools show significant gains in reading and math skills and diminished risk for having to repeat grades (Lee & Burkam, 2003; Magnuson et al., 2006).

- Participation in preschool reduces the risk for later delinquency (Welsh & Farrington, 2009).

- Participation in preschool improves the English proficiency of immigrant children, especially those whose mothers have less than a high school education (Magnuson et al., 2006).

Taken as a whole, this research presents a strong case for the role of preschool programs in boosting a variety of school-readiness indicators for children of immigrant families. This would seem to suggest that the more immigrant children enrolled in preschool, the better. But accomplishing this goal requires understanding the barriers that may exist to preschool participation and knowing how to remove them.

▲ APPLY :: CONNECT :: DISCUSS

Both phonemic awareness and the ability to identify and manipulate numeric units appear to emerge only in the context of formal education. What do these two developments have in common, and how might formal schooling stimulate their development?

In the Classroom

At this point in your education, you are no doubt aware of the vastly different ways in which school can be experienced by students. Students come to have different feelings about school and, accordingly, put more or less energy into doing well. Students also experience different types of instruction according to the educational philosophy of the particular schools they attend or the teachers they have. In your own extensive experience, you have surely encountered some teachers who rely on workbooks and tests and others who emphasize hands-on projects and papers. In this section, we explore various factors that shape students' school experiences, including the social organization of classroom instruction and personal and cultural barriers to school success.

Social Organization of the Classroom and Instructional Design

From the earliest schools of the ancient Middle East to neighborhood schools throughout the modern world, there has been controversy about how to design instruction more effectively. Opinion seems to oscillate between two extreme approaches. One approach begins with the assumption that instruction should proceed from the simple to the complex. Known as **bottom-up processing**, this approach starts with the teaching of basic skills and then, after these have been mastered, moves on to teaching skills to solve a variety of more complicated tasks. The other approach argues that such an exclusive focus on the acquisition of basic skills causes children to lose sight of the larger goal—using reading, writing, and arithmetic to accomplish interesting, important purposes—and, thus, in many cases, to lose motivation and fail to thrive in school. It urges, instead, **top-down processing**, which focuses on teaching and developing skills to accomplish specific meaningful tasks. This fundamental difference of opinion about the appropriate organization of school-based instruction can be clearly seen in the different ways that classroom instruction is organized.

The Standard Classroom Format Today, as in centuries past, the most common classroom arrangement is for the teacher to sit at a desk or stand at a blackboard facing the children, who sit in parallel rows facing front (Gallego, Cole, & LCHC, 2000). These physical circumstances reflect the assumption that the teacher is an authority figure who is there to talk to and teach children who are there to listen and learn. This assumption is also reflected in the routine use of **instructional discourse**, a unique way of talking that is typical in school but rarely encountered in everyday interactions in the community or home. A common pattern for instructional discourse is the "known-answer question." When the teacher asks a student, "What does this word say?" the teacher already knows the answer (a fact the student fully understands) and is actually seeking information about the student's progress in learning to read. Learning to respond easily to known-answer questions, in addition to learning the academic content of the curriculum, is an important early lesson of schooling (Mehan, 1984).

Alternative Forms of Classroom Instruction Although the standard classroom format is widespread in classrooms around the world, many developmentalists argue that it is not the best way of organizing instruction. Among other shortcomings, children taught in this manner are placed in the role of passive recipients of predigested information and therefore gain very little practice in formulating and solving problems for themselves. In contrast, the instructional alternatives we will consider next make children active participants in the educational process—a strategy that is closely aligned with the developmental theories of Piaget and Vygotsky.

Reciprocal Teaching One alternative to the recitation script is **reciprocal teaching**, which was designed by Ann Brown and Annemarie Palincsar as a way to integrate bottom-up and top-down processing, through small-group discussion at the time of reading. It was designed for children who are able to read in the sense that they can decode simple texts but who have difficulty making sense of what they read (Brown, Palincsar, & Armbruster, 1994).

In the reciprocal-teaching procedure, a teacher and a small group of students read silently through a text one segment at a time and take turns leading discussions about what each segment means (Palincsar et al., 2007). The discussion leader (teacher or child) begins by asking a question about the main idea of the segment and then answers the question by summarizing the content in his or her own words. If members of the group disagree with the summary, the group rereads the segment and discusses its contents to clarify what it says. Finally, the leader asks for predictions about what will come next in the text.

Reading in unison is common in classrooms throughout the world.

Dean Conger/Corbis

bottom-up processing An approach to education that starts with teaching basic skills and, once they have been mastered, moves on to more complex tasks.

top-down processing An approach to education that focuses on using skills to accomplish specific, meaningful tasks.

instructional discourse A distinctive way of talking and thinking that is typical in school but rarely encountered in everyday interactions in the community or home.

reciprocal teaching A method of teaching reading in which teachers and children take turns reading text in a manner that integrates decoding and comprehension skills.

Note that each of the key elements in reciprocal teaching—asking questions about content, summarizing it, clarifying it, and predicting narrative progression—presupposes that the purpose of the activity is comprehension, that is, figuring out what the text means. And because these strategies involve talking about (and arguing over) textual meaning, children are able to see and hear the teacher and other children model metacognitive behaviors that aid comprehension. For example, as a way of making sense of what is being read, the teacher might point to relevant information in a prior paragraph that needs to be taken into account, or might relate an idea in the text to some common experience that all the children have had. As Brown (1997) points out, reciprocal teaching is an application of Vygotsky's notion of the "zone of proximal development" (Chapter 1, p. 22) that allows children to participate in the act of reading for meaning even before they have acquired the full set of abilities that independent reading requires. A number of studies (summarized in Brown, 1997) have found that reciprocal teaching can produce rapid and durable increases in children's reading skills. Figure 12.5 shows the findings of a study in which reciprocal teaching was being used in a science class and a social studies class, not as a "reading lesson" but as a way to foster mastery of the course material. Used in this manner, the reciprocal-teaching activity increases knowledge of important subject matter at the same time that it improves reading skills.

In related research, Cathy Block and her colleagues studied the effectiveness of various instructional approaches to reading with nearly 700 elementary school students in 30 different classrooms. Over the course of an academic year, some students received standard reading instruction, while others received alternative instructional approaches. The researchers found that alternative approaches that included student-guided, teacher-led group discussion of the texts were significantly more effective than the standard approach (Block et al., 2009).

Realistic Mathematics Education Recognizing the limitations of recitation scripts and the bottom-up approach, the National Council of Teachers of Mathematics adopted a set of standards for improving mathematics education that shifts the focus of mathematics instruction from training in basic skills, procedures, and

FIGURE 12.5 (a) Reciprocal teaching proved to be more effective than traditional strategies such as explicit instruction and modeling alone: All three led to improved reading, but by far the greatest improvement was obtained through reciprocal teaching. (b) Reciprocal teaching also led to large and sustained improvement in social studies and science classes; students in a control group showed no improvement. (From Brown et al., 1992.)

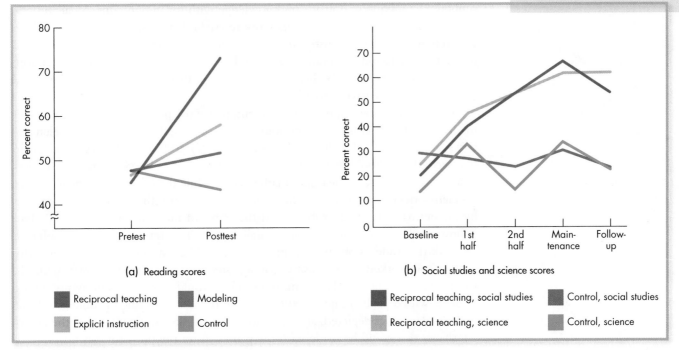

(a) Reading scores

Reciprocal teaching   Modeling
Explicit instruction   Control

(b) Social studies and science scores

Reciprocal teaching, social studies   Control, social studies
Reciprocal teaching, science   Control, science

realistic mathematics education An approach to mathematics education that focuses on developing the student's understanding of how math can be used to solve real-world problems.

memorization toward conceptual understanding and linkages between mathematics and real-world problems (National Council of Teachers of Mathematics, 2000). An example of a mathematics program designed to implement these goals is provided by the work of Paul Cobb and his colleagues, who draw on "realistic mathematics education," which is widely used in the Netherlands (Cobb et al., 1997; Hickendorff et al., 2010). According to these researchers, **realistic mathematics education** should do the following:

1. *Use meaningful activities.* For example, a first-grade teacher might introduce counting up to 20 by creating a make-believe situation in which a bus conductor has to keep track of how many people are on a double-decker bus that has 10 seats on each deck. As we have learned from the experimental research on children's problem solving discussed in previous chapters, such stories help to provide a meaningful context for carrying out cognitive operations.

2. *Support basic mathematical skills.* In the case of the double-decker bus, for example, the teacher wants children to learn how to group numbers for calculation, to realize that there are 8 people on the bus if there are 4 on top and 4 on the bottom, or 6 on the top and 2 on the bottom, or 2 on the top and 6 on the bottom, and so on. Each configuration is a different way of representing a total of 8.

3. *Employ models in educational activity.* Cobb describes a number of studies that use an "arithmetic rack," with two rows containing 10 beads each. For the conductor-on-the-bus context, the arithmetic rack provides a rather precise spatial model with each of its rows corresponding to a deck of the bus. But the beads on the rack can also be used to represent the number of cookies put in or taken out of a cookie jar and a variety of other story contexts involving similar mathematical concepts.

Over time, children gradually master the conceptual structures that the stories and models initially support, and they can carry out the needed calculations without such aids.

As in the case of reciprocal teaching, a social organization of the classroom that supports the mixing of bottom-up knowledge with top-down conceptual and utilization knowledge is key. Teachers work to establish a classroom culture in which children are expected to justify their reasoning when they answer a question and to try to understand the reasoning behind other children's answers. In addition, children are expected to be helpful to the group, to solicit help from others, and to share what they have learned.

"Problem-oriented" approaches that emphasize the processes of reasoning about mathematical problems have been found to be successful well beyond the elementary school years (Boaler, 2001; Nunes et al., 2007). Jo Boaler observed students in two secondary school classrooms in England. One class followed a traditional recitation-script approach to learning mathematics, while the other used a small-group, problem-oriented approach. In the traditional classroom, the teacher began lessons by presenting a standard problem and the standard method for solving it ("Here is how to determine the area of a parallelogram"). After observing the solution method, the students practiced it on their own. The teacher did not explain why the method worked and did not encourage students to invent their own methods. In the activity-centered classroom, the teacher would begin a lesson by presenting students with a problem designed to intrigue them. In one such problem, a fence with 36 planks was depicted, and the students were asked to figure out all the different shapes that could be made with the planks. After the problem was introduced,

Instructional methods that encourage students to work together and participate actively in the learning process, as shown here in a classroom in the United Kingdom, often result in higher levels of learning and language skills than those achieved through more traditional instructional approaches.

the students were encouraged to ask questions as a way of orienting themselves to the task. Then they worked in small groups while the teacher moved around the room, providing help when it was requested.

The teachers in both classrooms believed strongly that their approach was superior, and they passed on their enthusiasm for it to their students. They also reported that discipline problems were virtually nonexistent, but the researchers noted that the project-oriented classroom was somewhat noisier than the traditional classroom, and that the students in it more often engaged in "off-task" activities such as chatting with their friends.

When the students were tested at the end of the year on both standard tests and tests that assessed their ability to apply mathematics to new problems, there were striking differences between students in the two classrooms. Students who participated in the traditional instructional format scored better on knowledge of prespecified mathematical procedures, but students in the project-based class were significantly better on conceptual questions and on questions that required them to apply their knowledge to a novel problem, such as designing an apartment.

Playworld Practice In contrast to the recent educational trend in the United States to emphasize content that will help students pass mandatory statewide tests, several European countries are moving in the direction of integrating play and art into classroom activities. Devised on the basis of developmental theory pointing to the importance of play in children's understanding and representation of the world (see Chapter 9, pp. 324–325), **playworld practice** involves discussing, enacting, and making art about themes based on children's literature (Ferholt & Lexusay, 2010). Although playworld practice has been featured in Swedish and Finnish classrooms for some years (Sandberg & Samuelsson, 2003; Hakkarainen, 2004), only recently have efforts been made to experimentally compare playworld practice with other instructional formats. In one such effort, Sonja Baumer and her colleagues studied two classrooms of 5- to 7-year-olds who were learning about the C. S. Lewis fantasy novel *The Lion, the Witch, and the Wardrobe* (Baumer, Ferholt, & Lecusay, 2005). One classsroon used the playworld-practice approach; the other used standard instruction. In the playworld-practice classroom, the children, teacher, and researchers enacted scenes from the story; drew pictures of the scenes; and played with costumes and props used in the enactments. In the standard-instruction classroom, in contrast, the teacher read from the book, guided the students in a discussion of the story, and had the children draw

playworld practice A type of classroom activity that is based on theories regarding the importance of play in intellectual development and involves students enacting and discussing various themes in children's literature.

In the Field | Learning After School in the Fifth Dimension

Name:	Michael Cole
Education:	B.A. in psychology, University of California, Los Angeles; Ph.D. in psychology, Indiana University
Current Position:	Professor of Communication and Psychology, University of California, San Diego
Career Objectives:	Explore relationships between development and culture, and use understanding to improve contexts of children's learning

THE EARLY 1980S SAW THE INVENTION OF COMPUTERS that were affordable and accessible enough to be used beyond the high-tech, professional, and academic contexts to which they previously had been restricted. Michael Cole, a professor of communication and psychology at the University of California, San Diego, remembers the time as one of "enormous optimism about the potential of new technology to provide opportunities for individual instruction" (Rich, 2004, p. 11). It was also a time that allowed him to bring into alignment three areas that interested him deeply: his research on the acquisition of literacy and its effect on cognitive development; his concern about the poor literacy skills in the growing population of immigrant children attending San Diego schools; and his conviction that undergraduate programs focused on children, education, and development should provide hands-on experience with kids. Seizing the moment, Cole created the Fifth Dimension, an after-school program that is based on computer and other games and that has been elaborated and extended by a number of developmentalists working with schoolchildren throughout the world (Cole & Distributed Literacy Consortium, 2006).

The Fifth Dimension program is used in Brazil (above) and throughout the world to scaffold children's intellectual development by providing a context that fosters creativity and imagination.

Courtesy of the SARAH Network of Rehabilitation Hospitals, Brazil

---

pictures or write stories about the novel. Results from the study indicated that compared with standard instruction, the playworld practice format generated significantly larger increases in children's language skills, especially their abilities to tell and understand stories. (For another example of the use of play in instruction, this time in an after-school program designed to promote computer literacy and cognitive and other skills, see the box "In the Field: Learning after School in the Fifth Dimension.")

Overall, the evidence indicates that when properly organized, instructional methods that induce students to be active contributors to classroom discourse can be quite effective. But such methods are more complex to organize than the recitation script and are still used in only a minority of classrooms.

Barriers to School Success

There is, of course, more to children's school experience than the ways classroom instruction is organized and designed. Many students experience difficulty in school, regardless of instructional organization and design, often because they have learning disabilities or because they lack motivation to learn.

Although the Fifth Dimension program is intentionally flexible so that it can be fitted to the needs of the particular children enrolled—their ages, academic skill levels, languages spoken, and so on—it includes several key features. One is the use of a model wooden maze composed of 20 rooms that helps the children organize their play. Each child is represented by a token, a toy creature, that the child moves from one room to another. Each room includes a list of one to three games (usually, but not always, a computer game) that the child must complete before moving to another room in the maze. Thus, the maze is a means of self-monitoring, helping children keep track of the games they have completed and motivating future game-play that will allow them to continue their progress through the maze. Many games are structured to foster progressive skill development, from basic, through intermediate, to advanced levels. For example, at the basic level, the computer game *Space Adventure* presents the child with the following challenge: *The alien council wants to know what Earthlings know about the moon. Find out when the first men landed on the moon and what they found there.* Once children navigate through the program and discover answers to the challenge, they are presented with an "adventure task," such as *Pretend you are walking on the moon. Draw what you see, and then make a list of the things that you see or don't see.* An advanced challenge might include using Internet and video equipment to research and make a video "telling everything you know about space." Other games such as *Candy Land* and *Where in the World Is Carmen*

Michael Cole

Sandiego? reinforce counting and reasoning skills. Indeed, research on the Fifth Dimension indicates that participants score higher than nonparticipants on math and reading exams and show improved basic language skills.

Another key feature of the Fifth Dimension is its use of undergraduate college students as mentors for the children. Each child is linked with a college student whose main role is to help the child define and meet his or her own challenges and game goals. Not only do the college students gain insight into how developmental principles can be applied in interacting with children, but the children seem to profit tremendously from interacting with their mentors. In particular, spending hours and hours with college students seems to increase the children's interest in attending college someday themselves.

Cole attributes the enormous success of the Fifth Dimension to its capacity for scaffolding children's intellectual development by creating a context that engages their curiosity and imagination. Allowing children to choose their own game activities and pursue their goals with the assistance of college student mentors creates a zone of proximal development for the acquisition of literacy skills. In his junior year in high school, Ismael Castanon, who had participated in the program for more than a decade, wrote, "At first I didn't think that the program would have such a big impact on my life, but boy was I wrong. Through this program I learned most of my English and math, and about computers in general" (Rich, 2004, p. 6). Like many other Fifth Dimension "success stories," Ismael went on to college.

Specific Learning Disabilities **Specific learning disabilities** is a term used to refer to the academic difficulties of children who fare poorly in school despite having normal IQ test scores. The U.S. government defines specific learning disabilities as

> a disorder in one or more of the basic psychological processes involved in understanding or in using language, spoken or written, that may manifest itself in an imperfect ability to listen, think, speak, read, write, spell, or to do mathematical calculations, including conditions such as perceptual disabilities, brain injury, minimal brain dysfunction, dyslexia, and developmental aphasia. . . . The term does not include learning problems that are primarily the result of visual, hearing, or motor disabilities, of mental retardation, of emotional disturbance, or of environmental, cultural, or economic disadvantage. (34 Code of Federal Regulations §300.7[c][10])

Although it has been repeatedly criticized as imprecise, the most widely used method to distinguish children with a specific learning disability is to analyze their performance both on an intelligence test and on an academic achievement test that covers many parts of the curriculum (D'Angiulli & Siegel, 2003). According to this approach, to qualify as specifically learning disabled (and not retarded), a child should

specific learning disabilities A term used to refer to the academic difficulties of children who fare poorly in school despite having normal intelligence.

have an overall IQ test score in the normal range but show a large discrepancy be-tween different parts of the test (for example, a low score on a subtest that taps verbal ability but a high score on a subtest that taps quantitative ability). The profile of the child's academic performance should correspond to the pattern in the IQ test. That is, a child with a low verbal-ability score and a high quantitative-ability score would be expected to have difficulty in learning to read but not in learning arithmetic. This pattern of performance, called *dyslexia,* is the most common form of specific learning disability. Other children display a pattern of performance called *dyscalculia,* in which their verbal IQ is high and their quantitative IQ is low: Correspondingly, they do not have difficulty learning to read but have difficulty learning arithmetic. Yet another specific learning disability is *dysgraphia,* which involves special difficulties in learning to write, including poor handwriting, problems with spelling, and difficulty putting thoughts on paper. In the remainder of our discussion of special learning disabilities, we focus on dyslexia, which is not only the most common such disability but also the one about which the most is known.

The primary question regarding children with dyslexia is: Why do they have difficulty reading? As we saw earlier, phonological awareness—the ability to detect and manipulate the phonemes in words—is crucial to learning to decode text, that is, to relate graphemes (symbols of the writing system) to phonemes. More directly, phonological awareness is a crucial part of *phonological processing*—of understanding and applying the rules relating phonemes and graphemes. Like problems with pho-neme awareness, delays in the development of phonological processing skills may indicate that a child has dyslexia (Helland et al., 2008).

The leading test of phonological processing skills employs *pseudowords,* pro-nounceable combinations of letters that are not real words—for example, "shum," "laip," and "cigbet"—but can be read by following the rules for converting graph-emes into phonemes. Because they are not real words, they cannot be recognized and therefore permit an accurate assessment of phonological processing.

To demonstrate the link between deficient phonological processing and dys-lexia, Linda Siegel and her colleagues have compared normal and dyslexic read-ers in their ability to read pseudowords (Siegel, 2008; Gottardo et al., 1999). By 9 years of age, the normal readers were quite proficient in reading the pseudowords, but 14-year-old dyslexic readers were no better at reading pseudowords than were normal 7-year-old readers. Even when dyslexic readers and normal readers were matched for reading level on a standardized test (the dyslexic readers being consid-erably older than the normal readers), the dyslexic readers performed more poorly on the pseudowords task.

Current theories about the causes of dyslexia assume that the difficulties arise be-cause of anomalies in brain development. Recent brain-imagining studies have, in fact, indicated that when reading, children with dyslexia show less activation in two areas of the brain than do normal readers. One of these areas is directly involved in phonological processing, while the other plays a role in the integration of visual letters and the sounds they correspond to (Schlaggar & Church, 2009). In line with evidence pinpointing difficulties in phonological processing, Paula Tallal and her colleagues report that, when asked to identify whether letter names rhymed or did not rhyme (D–B versus M–T, for example), children diagnosed with dyslexia had much greater difficulty than did normal readers. They showed slower neural pro-cessing, with less activation in just those areas of the brain that are specialized for language (Figure 12.6a, b), supporting the idea that dyslexia involves specific brain locations (Tallal, 2003).

To help children who have this phonological processing difficulty, Tallal has cre-ated computer games that provide rich practice in making accurate discriminations

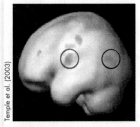

(a) Normal

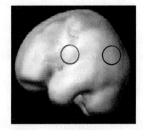
(b) Learning disabled

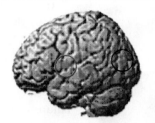
(c) Learning disabled; after training

FIGURE 12.6 Brain activation of normal and dyslexic readers. The children were given the task of providing a rhyming sound when they heard a letter pronounced. Comparison of the two groups shows significant differences in left-hemisphere activity (brightness of red indicates degree of activation) for normal and dyslexic children. (a) While the normal children display heightened activity in both the visual cortex and Broca's area (specialized for language), the dyslexic readers do not (b). However, after intense training in discriminating between phonemes, the dyslexic children display activity in the same areas as do the normal children (c).

between very brief, rapidly changing sounds—and in some cases, children become capable of such discriminations with as few as 16 hours of this therapy (Tallal et al., 1998). Moreover, as a result of this training, the brain activation patterns of the dyslexic children on tasks such as identifying rhyming letter names appear to be similar to those of normal readers (Figure 12.6c).

Motivation to Learn As we noted earlier, a distinctive aspect of formal education is that children are expected to pay attention and try to master material that may be difficult to learn and that may hold little interest for them. They must also learn to cope with the fact that they will not always be successful in their schoolwork. In such circumstances, a significant proportion of children lose their **academic motivation**—the ability to try hard and persist at school tasks in the face of difficulties. On the other hand, many children seem to thrive on the challenges presented by formal education.

What accounts for these differences? Researchers who study this question distinguish between two ways in which children approach school tasks (Anderman, Austin, & Johnson, 2001; Martin et al., 2008): **mastery orientation**, in which children are motivated to learn, to try hard, and to improve; and **performance orientation**, in which children are motivated by their level of performance, ability, and incentives for trying.

Mastery and performance orientations have consistently been associated with two different outcomes in terms of children's academic success. Children who adopt a mastery orientation are more likely to succeed in the long run, to use more advanced learning strategies, and to relate what they are trying to accomplish at the moment to relevant prior knowledge. Even if these children have just done poorly or failed at a task, they remain optimistic and tell themselves, "I can do it if I try harder next time." As a result of this kind of thinking, they tend to persist in the face of difficulties and to seek out new intellectual challenges. Over time, this kind of motivational pattern allows these children to improve their academic performance. By contrast, children who adopt a performance orientation are more likely, when failing at a task, to tell themselves, "I can't do this." They may give up trying altogether and, when they encounter similar tasks in the future, tend to avoid them.

It might be thought that more-able students would typically display the mastery-oriented pattern and that less-able students would be the ones to adopt a performance orientation, quickly giving up in the face of difficulty and avoiding challenges. However, the evidence concerning motivational orientation and school achievement is mixed. Carol Dweck and her colleagues report that these two patterns are not related to children's IQ scores or their academic achievement: Many able students give up in the face of difficulty, and many weaker students show a mastery orientation (Dweck & Master, 2009). But a large-scale review of many recent studies reports that mastery motivation does promote cognitive development (Jennings & Dietz, 2003).

academic motivation The ability to try hard and persist at school tasks in the face of difficulties.

mastery orientation A way that children approach school tasks in which they are motivated to learn, to try hard, and to improve their performance.

performance orientation A way of approaching school tasks in which students are motivated by their level of performance, ability, and incentives for trying.

This student seems to be the personification of academic motivation: If she happens to give an incorrect answer this time, she will not give up and is likely to work harder to get it right the next time.

In an extensive series of studies looking at factors that might lead to the two different motivational patterns, Carol Dweck and Allison Master have related the patterns to two different conceptions of ability, conceptions that children develop as they progress through school (Dweck & Master, 2009). According to Dweck and Master, children as young as 2½ years old are sensitive to success or failure in their problem-solving attempts and are vulnerable to becoming discouraged and unmotivated when they fail. But it is not until the onset of formal schooling, when, through grading practices, children's academic abilities are directly compared with those of their peers, that the notion of ability becomes a distinctive category that children use to evaluate themselves and their relationship to academic challenges. Children's conceptions of ability continue to change during the elementary school years, with children increasingly less likely to engage in wishful thinking about problems they can solve and increasingly more likely to see ability as a fixed characteristic of people.

Around the age of 12, when children make the transition from elementary to middle school, North American children begin to articulate theories about what it means to "be intelligent." Some children adopt an **entity model of intelligence**; that is, they see intelligence as quantitatively fixed in each individual. Other children, by contrast, adopt an **incremental model of intelligence**; they see intelligence as something that can grow as one learns and has new experiences. These theories about intelligence include ideas about how effort is related to outcome. Children who adopt the entity model see academic success as depending primarily on fixed ability and thus remaining relatively unaffected by effort; children who adopt the incremental model see academic success, along with ability, as depending on the effort expended. Dweck has found that children who adopt an entity model of intelligence are likely to develop a performance orientation to problems. When they fail, they believe that it is because they lack ability and that nothing they can do will change this. Because they view intelligence as a fixed entity, they try to avoid situations that put them at risk for failure and feel hopeless when they are confronted with challenging tasks. Children who adopt an incremental model of intelligence, on the other hand, tend to develop a mastery orientation to challenging situations. They believe that if they apply themselves and try hard enough, they will succeed and become more intelligent; and when they fail at a particular task, their response is to try harder the next time. As children encounter the more challenging environment of middle school, notable achievement gaps arise between students who have one or the other of the basic motivational patterns.

Findings such as these have led developmentalists to devise ways to assist children who develop a helpless motivational pattern. One approach has been to train teachers to provide feedback to students in ways that foster a mastery orientation. Another has been to retrain the children themselves so that they attribute their failures to a lack of effort rather than a lack of ability (Dweck, 1999).

School Engagement In addition to mastery motivation, students' *engagement* in the classroom environment may affect academic performance (Ladd & Dinella, 2009). **School engagement** refers to the thoughts, behaviors, and emotions that children have about school and learning. It makes sense that the child who likes school, cooperates willingly in classroom activities, and devotes effort to learning

entity model of intelligence The belief that intelligence is a quality of which each person has a certain fixed amount.

incremental model of intelligence The belief that intelligence is something that can grow over time as one learns.

school engagement The thoughts, behaviors, and emotions that children have about school and learning.

will perform better than the child who dislikes school, resists involvement, and invests little intellectual effort.

Gary Ladd and Lisa Dinella explored the relationship between school engagement and academic achievement in nearly 400 children as they progressed from first to eighth grade (Ladd & Dinella, 2009). They focused on two dimensions of engagement. The first dimension was *school liking/avoidance,* as measured by teacher and parent reports about factors such as whether the child "likes being in school," "complains about school," and "enjoys most classroom activities." The second dimension was *cooperative/resistant classroom participation,* as measured by teacher reports about factors such as whether the child "responds promptly to teacher requests," "breaks classroom rules," and "acts defiant." Ladd and Dinella discovered that school engagement was moderately stable over time; that is, most children maintained their degree of engagement—whether high or low—from first through eighth grade. In addition, the researchers found that children with higher levels of engagement made greater academic progress than did those with lower levels, and that children who were increasingly resistant and avoidant of school and classroom activities were at greater risk for academic problems.

▲ APPLY :: CONNECT :: DISCUSS

Write a letter to the best or worst teacher you ever had. Using concepts presented in this section, explain how the format of the classroom and method of instruction affected your motivation.

The Cognitive Consequences of Schooling

Because formal schooling is so widely available throughout the world, it is difficult to do research that directly compares groups of schooled and nonschooled children for the purpose of assessing the cognitive consequences of formal education. Given this limitation, three research strategies have generally been found useful:

1. *The school-cutoff strategy* compares 6-year-olds who have experienced formal schooling with 6-year-olds who have not yet experienced it.

2. *School–nonschool comparisons* take advantage of circumstances in which schooling has been introduced unevenly into a society, providing formal education for some children but not for others.

3. *Second-generation studies* focus on differences between children whose mothers have attended school and children whose mothers have not, looking for effects that the mothers' schooling might have on their children.

The School-Cutoff Strategy

In many countries, school boards require that children be a certain age by a particular date to begin attending school. To enter first grade in September of a given year, children in Edmonton, Alberta, Canada, for example, must have passed their 6th birthday by March 1 of that year. Children who turn 6 after that date must attend kindergarten instead, so their formal education is delayed for a year. Such policies allow researchers to use a **school-cutoff strategy** to assess the impact of early schooling while holding the factor of age virtually constant: They simply compare

school-cutoff strategy A means of assessing the impact of early education by comparing the intellectual performance of children who are almost the same age but begin schooling a year apart because of school rules that set a specific cutoff birthday date for starting school.

Because of the school-cutoff strategy, some children in this first-grade class may be just a month or so older than some children in the kindergarten class next door. Research shows that over the course of the school year, memory development of the first-graders will significantly surpass that of similar-aged kindergarteners, illustrating the importance of schooling to intellectual development.

the intellectual performances of children who turn 6 in January or February with those who turn 6 in March or April, testing both groups at the beginning and at the end of the school year (Christian, Bachnan, & Morrison, 2001).

Researchers who have used the school-cutoff strategy find that the first year of schooling brings about a marked increase in the sophistication of some cognitive processes but not others. Frederick Morrison and his colleagues (1995), for example, compared the ability of first-graders and kindergartners to recall pictures of nine common objects. The first-graders were, on average, only a month older than the kindergartners. The performances of the two groups were virtually identical at the start of the school year. At the end of the school year, however, the first-graders could remember twice as many pictures as they did at the beginning of the year, whereas the kindergartners showed no improvement in memory at all. Significantly, the first-graders engaged in active rehearsal (a memory strategy you encountered in Chapter 11, p. 411) during the testing, but the kindergartners did not. Clearly, one year of schooling had brought about marked changes in their strategies and performance. The same pattern of results was obtained in tasks such as recognizing the names of the letters of the alphabet, in standardized reading and mathematics tests, and in a variety of deliberate remembering tests. But no effects of attending a year of school were found when children were administered a standard Piagetian test of conservation (see Chapter 11, pp. 402–404), or assessed for the coherence of their storytelling or for the number of vocabulary words they understood (Christian et al., 2001). Performance in these latter tasks improved largely as a consequence of children's age. These findings both confirm the importance of schooling in promoting a variety of relatively specific cognitive abilities and support Piaget's belief that the ability to understand the conservation of number, volume, and the like develops without any special instruction at some time between the ages of 5 and 7.

Comparing Schooled and Nonschooled Children

Although the school-cutoff strategy provides an excellent way to assess the cognitive consequences of small amounts of schooling, it is, by definition, limited to only the first year. For a longer-range picture of the contribution of formal education to cognitive development, researchers have conducted studies in societies in which schooling is available to only a part of the population. We will summarize evidence from such studies that pertains to three domains emphasized in our earlier discussions of cognitive development: logical thinking, memory, and metacognitive skills.

Logical Thinking A large number of cross-cultural studies have been conducted to determine if participation in formal schooling enhances performance on Piagetian conservation tasks and other tasks created to reveal concrete-operational thinking (Keller, 2011; Maynard, 2008). In terms of results, the studies have split more or less evenly between those that found enhanced performance among schooled children and those that did not. Consistent with the evidence presented in Chapter 11 (pp. 417–418), when schoolchildren do better than their unschooled peers on the standard Piagetian tests, their greater success appears to have less to do with more rapid achievement of concrete-operational thinking than with their greater familiarity with the circumstances of test-taking. Such familiarity includes experience with the forms in which test questions are asked, greater ease in speaking to unknown adults, and fluency in the language in which the test is given when the testing is not conducted in the child's native language. When these factors are taken into account, the overall pattern of results indicates that the development of concrete-operational thinking increases with age and is relatively unaffected by schooling.

Memory In Chapter 11 (pp. 417–418), you saw that, unlike North American children, children in some cultures do not show an increase in free-recall memory performance as they grow older and that the difference related to the fact that the children did not attend school. Indeed, research comparing schooled and nonschooled children in other societies, like the research on first-graders and kindergartners presented here, has shown that schooling is the crucial experience underlying differences in performance on free-recall tasks. The performance of children in other cultures who attended school is more similar to that of their North American counterparts in the same grade than it is to that of their age-mates in the same village who have not been to school (Rogoff, 2003).

A classic study by Daniel Wagner (1974) suggests the kind of memory-enhancing information-processing skills that children acquire as a consequence of schooling. Wagner conducted his study among Mayans in Yucatán, Mexico, who had completed different amounts of schooling. He asked 248 people ranging in age from 6 years to adulthood to recall the positions of picture cards laid out in a line (Figure 12.7a). (To ensure that the items pictured on the cards would be familiar to all the participants, the pictures were taken from a local version of bingo called *Lotería,* which uses pictures instead of numbers.) On each trial, each of seven cards was displayed for 2 seconds and then turned facedown. After all seven cards had been presented, a duplicate of one of the cards was shown faceup and the participant was asked to point to the facedown card that it matched.

(a) Take a good look and turn the page

FIGURE 12.7 (a) In this test of short-term memory, seven picture cards are laid out, picture-side up, and then they are turned facedown one at a time. The person being tested is next shown a duplicate of one of the cards faceup and asked to select the card that corresponds to it from the seven that are facedown. (b) After looking at (a), test yourself on the display on p. 452. (From Wagner, 1978.)

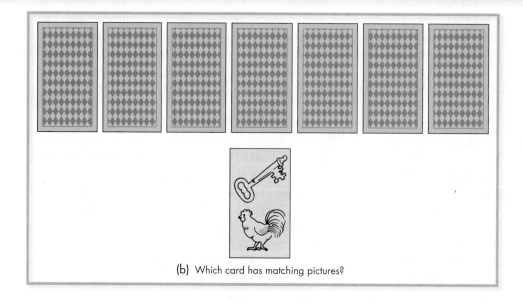

(b) Which card has matching pictures?

For participants who attended school, performance improved markedly with age (Figure 12.8), as in similar research in the United States. In contrast, among those who did not attend school, older children and adults remembered no better than young children did, leading Wagner to conclude that it was schooling that made the difference. Additional analyses of the data revealed that increasingly efficient use of the memory strategy of rehearsal (discussed in Chapter 11, p. 411) by those who attended school was largely responsible for the improvement in their performance.

Evidence such as this does not mean that memory simply fails to develop among children who have not attended school. The difference between schooled and non-schooled children's performance in cross-cultural memory experiments is most noticeable when the items to be remembered are not related to one another according to any everyday script. When the items are part of a meaningful setting, such as the animals found in a barnyard or the furniture placed in a toy house, the effects of schooling on memory performance disappear (Rogoff & Wadell, 1982). Similarly, we saw in Chapter 11 that although schooled children were better than unschooled children in a free-recall task because they used a clustering strategy for the items to be remembered, the difference between the two groups' successful recall disappeared when the items to be remembered were presented in a story context. It appears that schooling helps children to develop specialized strategies for remembering and thereby enhances their ability to commit arbitrary material to memory for purposes of later testing. There is no evidence to support the conclusion that schooling increases memory *capacity* per se.

Metacognitive Skills Schooling appears to influence children's metacognitive skills, which, as discussed in Chapter 11, involve the ability to reflect on and talk about one's own thought processes (Rogoff, 2003; Tulviste, 1991). When children have been asked to explain how they arrived at the answer to a logical problem or what they did to make themselves remember something, those who have not attended school are likely to say something like "I did what my sense told me" or to offer no explanation at all. Schoolchildren, on the other hand, are likely to talk about the mental activities and

FIGURE 12.8 This graph depicts short-term memory performance as a function of age and number of years of education. In the absence of further education (as among the rural people tested in this study), performance does not improve with age. Thus, schooling appears to be a key factor in one's ability to do well at this task. (Numbers in parentheses represent the average number of years of education for the designated group.) (From Wagner, 1974.)

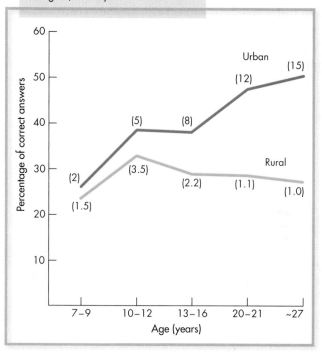

logic that led to their responses. The same pattern applies to *metalinguistic skills,* that is, the ability to think logically about, and express, the rules of grammar. Sylvia Scribner and Michael Cole (1981) asked schooled and unschooled Vai people in Liberia to judge the grammatical correctness of several sentences spoken in Vai. Some of the sentences were grammatical, some were not. The researchers reported that education had no effect on the interviewees' ability to identify the ungrammatical sentences, but schooled people could generally explain just what it was about a sentence that made it ungrammatical, whereas unschooled people could not.

Assessing the Second-Generation Impact of Schooling

The evidence from both school-cutoff and cross-cultural research supports the conclusion that the cognitive consequences of schooling are quite specific to the particular skill being tested. The clearest evidence for a general cognitive impact of schooling comes from studies of the child-rearing practices of mothers who have, or have not, gone to school and the subsequent school achievement of their children.

On the basis of evidence collected in many countries over several decades, Robert LeVine and his colleagues emphasize that, overall, children whose mothers have some degree of formal education tend to experience three major benefits over children whose mothers have had no formal schooling—a lower level of infant mortality, better health during childhood, and greater academic achievement (LeVine, LeVine, & Schnell, 2001). These researchers propose a set of habits, preferences, and skills that mothers acquire in school that might help account for these differences. Beyond rudimentary literacy and numeracy skills, this set includes the mothers':

1. Ability to understand written texts concerning, and engage in discussion about, health and educational issues involving children;

2. Use of teaching and learning models based on the scripted activities and authority structure of schooling, which they then employ in the home, talking more to their children and using less directive child-rearing methods;

3. Ability and willingness to acquire and accept information from governmental agencies and the mass media regarding their children's health and development.

LeVine and his colleagues hypothesize that girls who have been to school retain these habits of mind into adulthood and apply them in the course of raising their own children. The work of these researchers has been supported by direct observations of the teaching styles of Mayan mothers who have, or have not, been to school. Pablo Chavajay and Barbara Rogoff found that mothers who had had 12 years of schooling used school-like teaching styles when asked to teach their young children to complete a puzzle, whereas mothers who had had 2 years or less of schooling participated with their children in completing the puzzle but did not explicitly teach them (Chavajay & Rogoff, 2002). There is nothing wrong with the unschooled mothers' teaching style, but it does not prepare their children well for school, which relies heavily on instructional discourse as the primary mode of instruction.

When we consider how school affects health-related behaviors, including mothers' use of modern social welfare institutions and ways of interacting with their children, it is clear that schooling can have profound consequences for society.

Overall, extensive research on the cognitive consequences of schooling has produced a mixed picture. The idea that schooling is directly responsible for broad changes in the way the mind works is, at best, only minimally supported. When schooling has been found to improve cognitive performance, the effect appears to work in one of three ways: (1) by increasing children's knowledge base, including ways of using language; (2) by teaching specific information-processing strategies that are relevant primarily to school itself; and (3) by changing children's overall life situations and attitudes, which they later pass on to their children in the form of new child-rearing practices that promote school achievement. As we emphasized at the beginning of the chapter, it may be that the most important consequences of schooling for the majority of the world's people are not simply cognitive. Schooling is a gateway to health and nutrition, to economic power, and to social status.

▲ APPLY :: CONNECT :: DISCUSS

Your local government has earmarked a special pool of money to support services for the rising population of immigrant families in your community. Concerned about the school readiness of immigrant children, officials plan to apply most of the money to a vast preschool expansion project. You believe this focus would be too narrow and want to convince the officials to divert funds to support adult education for immigrant parents. Map out the evidence that you will use to persuade the officials to your point of view.

Contemporary Challenges in a Globalizing World

As we pointed out earlier, access to quality education continues to be a major challenge for educators and policy makers. There are vast disparities among countries in the proportions of children who are able to go to school. Within many countries, there are also vast disparities among children in the amount and quality of the schooling they receive. As we discussed previously, a child's gender, ethnicity, and socioeconomic status all can profoundly affect both the amount and the quality of schooling. (Another disparity among countries exists in children's school achievement; for a discussion of some differences in this area and possible explanations of them, see the box "Comparing Mathematics Achievement across Cultures.")

In addition to the challenge of access, schools are challenged by the increasing cultural and linguistic diversity of the students they serve. Throughout the world, large numbers of families are moving away from their native lands and cultures, seeking new lives in places where the language, cultural practices, and values and beliefs are radically different from their own. Indeed, as you may recall from our discussion in Chapter 10, children of immigrant families are the fastest-growing group of children in the United States, accounting for approximately 22 percent of all U.S. children—a figure that is projected to increase to 33 percent by the year 2020 (Mather, 2009).

Although some areas in the United States, especially border states, attract a preponderance of Spanish-speaking immigrants, an increasing number of school districts are seeing an enormous rise in the cultural and linguistic diversity of their immigrant students (for an example, see Table 12.2). Given that studies routinely find that children of immigrant families are overrepresented among students who experience academic difficulties and school failure (Schmitt-Rodermund & Silbereisen, 2008; Conchas, 2001; Capps et al., 2004), schools face a particularly difficult challenge in identifying and responding to the

Children of immigrant families are the fastest-growing group of children in the United States.

Gideon Mendel/In Pictures/Corbis

table 12.2

Languages Spoken in Head Start Classrooms near Philadelphia			
Akan	English	Laotian	Spanish
Albanian	French	Liberian English	Swahili
American Sign Language (ASL)	French Creole	Limba	Tagalog
	Fulani	Loman	Temne
Arabic	Greek	Mandarin	Twi
Bambara	Gujarati	Mandingo	Urdu
Bassa	Haitian Creole	Mende	Vietnamese
Bengali	Igbo	Nigerian	West African Creole
Cantonese	Indonesian	Oromo	Yoruba
Cherokee	Jamaican Patwa	Pali	West African
Creole	Kirio	Pashto	
Dutch	Krahn	Portuguese	
Edo	Krio	Punjabi	

Source: Delaware County Intermediate Unit, Head Start, personal communication.

unique academic needs of immigrant students who vary so widely in native language and heritage culture. Indeed, as we will see, many immigrant children and their families must adjust not only to a new culture and language but also to the unique culture and language of school.

The Culture of School

A number of scholars have proposed that every culture can be described in terms of its own particular worldview, a dominant way of thinking about and relating to the world that arises from a people's common historical experience. This dominant pattern of interpreting events is called a **cultural style** (Greenfield, Keller, Fuligni, & Maynard, 2003; Gratier, Greenfield, & Isaac, 2009). An important dimension of cultural style is that of independence–interdependence. An *independent,* or *individualistic,* cultural style emphasizes the individual and the individual's personal choices and goals; an *interdependent,* or *collectivist,* style emphasizes the group and group harmony, downplaying individual achievement (see Table 12.3 for a summary of the differences between the two styles).

Cultural style is not just a matter of abstract values and beliefs; it is embodied in daily life and patterns of social interaction. A fascinating example of this comes from Pablo Chavajay's study of how Guatemalan Maya fathers interact with their children to solve a puzzle task (Chavajay, 2008). The Mayan families all lived in a town that over the past two decades changed from a traditional agricultural lifestyle to one that is modern and technologically advanced. As a consequence of rapid modernization—including the introduction of television, cell phones, computers, and Western-style schools—some fathers are comparatively well-educated, while

table 12.3

Cultural Styles: Independent (Individualistic) versus Interdependent (Collectivist)	
Independent	**Interdependent**
Emotional detachment from group; personal goals have primacy over group goals.	Self is defined in terms of group; personal goals relate to group goals.
Behavior regulated by attitudes and by analysis of cost and benefits to self.	Behavior regulated by group norms and analysis of costs and benefits to group.
Confrontation considered OK.	Harmony within the group considered important.

Source: Adapted from Triandis et al., 1990.

cultural style A dominant way of thinking about and relating to the world that arises from a people's common historical experience.

Comparing Mathematics Achievement Across Cultures

F YOU WERE SOMEHOW ABLE TO VISIT schools throughout the world, you would find that—for all the vast differences in geographic location, languages spoken, economic resources available, religious beliefs adhered to, and so on—the world's classrooms and curricula are in many ways remarkably similar. Despite these fundamental similarities, studies of classroom life and academic performance in different societies reveal that both the process and the products of schooling vary markedly from one culture to the next (Zhou, Peverly, & Lin, 2005; Kim & Park, 2006). One noteworthy difference is the exceptionally high level of mathematics achievement in many Asian countries; for example, on standardized international tests of mathematics achievement given every 4 years to fourth- and eighth-graders, children from Asian countries consistently outperform their peers in other countries (see the figure for a sample of the 2007 mathematics results in the Trends in International Mathematics and Science Study).

Not surprisingly, developmentalists concerned with educational issues have been interested in discovering the source of such exceptional achievement and, more generally, factors responsible for variation in children's achievement from one society to the next. A series of studies initiated by psychologist Harold Stevenson in the 1980s provided a good deal of insight into the ways in which cultural differences in elementary school education may contribute to variations in children's performance (Stevenson & Stigler, 1992; Stigler,

Gallimore, & Hiebert, 2000). These studies used videotapes of actual classroom lessons in three countries—the United States, Japan, and Taiwan—to discover how differences in modes of instruction were related to overall test performance (the list of participating countries has now swelled to 38). Several results stood out when comparing the ways classroom behaviors differed among the three countries.

First, the researchers found that compared with children in other countries, including the United States, Asian children attended school more days each year and spent more hours in school each week. At the fifth-grade level, for example, Japanese children went to school 44 hours a week; Chinese students, 37 hours a week; and American children, 30 hours a week. Furthermore, on each school day the two Asian groups spent as much time on mathematics as they did on reading and writing, while the American group spent almost three times as much on language arts.

Second, the Asian classrooms were organized quite differently from classrooms in the United States. For the most part, they were centrally organized, with the teacher instructing the whole class at once. In contrast, classrooms in the United States were generally decentralized, with the teacher often devoting attention to one group at a time while the other children worked independently. As a result of this classroom organization, children in the United States spent a good deal of time being instructed by no one. This might not have mattered much if the children had been absorbed by their academic assignments and

truly working independently. But here another difference came into play: The children in the United States did not use their independent study time well, spending almost half of it out of their seats or engaged in inappropriate behavior such as gossiping with friends or causing mischief. Asian children spent far more time attending to schoolwork.

Recent studies of cultural differences in mathematical achievement have expanded their focus beyond the amount and organization of math instruction to explore cultural beliefs about education and the process of learning. An example is a study of Korean beliefs about academic achievement, conducted by Uichol Kim and Young-Shin Park (Kim & Park, 2006). Compared with most Western countries, Korea spends considerably less money per student and has larger class sizes, yet it consistently outranks most Western nations in tests of academic achievement. Kim and Park argue that the exceptional academic achievement of Korean students is due to Korean cultural values and family relationships. For instance, Koreans tend to believe that achievement is a consequence of personal effort rather than innate ability—a belief conducive to academic success, as discussed earlier in the chapter. Furthermore, they view education as an important aspect of self-growth that should be pursued for its own sake. Finally, parents are expected to play a key role in their children's academic success, largely by providing emotional (rather than informational) support, which is thought to foster a sense of indebtedness in children and a desire to repay parents by doing well in

Developmentalists point out that schools have different cultural styles that influence classroom practices and the assumptions and attitudes of teachers and students. Because of the increasing number of students from immigrant families, some U.S. schools are training their teachers to be sensitive to the possibility of "culture clashes" between the cultural style of the school and the children's culture of origin.

Christian Kober/Robert Harding/drr.net

school. Differences between the United States and Korea in after-school private mathematics tutoring also point to the significance of cultural beliefs in children's mathematics acheivement. In particular, one study discovered that while private, after-school mathematics tutoring is relatively common in both the United States and Korea, it serves very different functions for each country: In the United States, it is used primarily to help students who are performing poorly in their math classes, whereas in Korea, it is used to enrich mathematics learning for high-achieving students who are under substantial pressure to gain admission into competitive, elite universities (Lee, 2007).

Such findings underscore the fact that classroom learning is a cultural activity in which many different factors are always at work (Hiebert et al., 2005). Thus, as sociologist Merry White (2001) noted, cross-cultural research cannot provide a blueprint for improving the education of children. Rather, it provides a mirror that sharpens awareness of the influence of cultural practices and provides some hints about how they might be changed to make teaching and learning more effective.

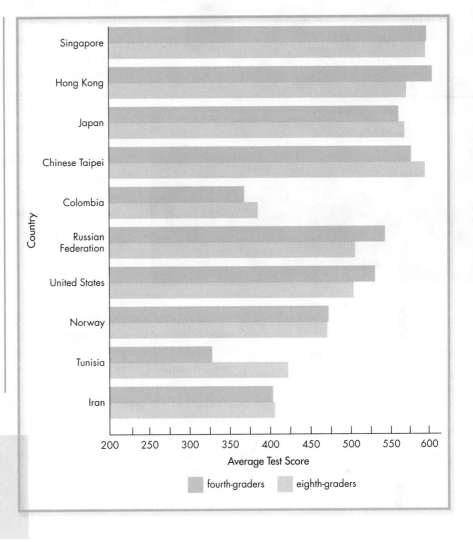

Average mathematics scores from fourth- and eighth-graders in 10 countries from different parts of the world. Adapted from Mullis, Martin, & Foy, 2008

others have little in the way of formal schooling. Chavajay found that fathers of different educational levels had very different ways of interacting with their children on a puzzle-solving task he presented them. In particular, less-educated fathers were much more likely to work with their children in a coordinated, cooperative way, while more-educated fathers were likelier to be directive, like a teacher telling a student how to solve a problem.

In related research, Barbara Rogoff and her colleagues are exploring how Guatemalan Maya cultural style may affect children's learning in the classroom (Silva, Correa-Chavez, & Rogoff, 2010). In one study, children were present when an adult showed their sibling how to make a toy. Some of the children were from middle-class European American families; some were from Guatemalan Maya families with mothers who had extensive experience with Western schooling; and some were from traditional Guatemalan Maya familes with mothers who had little exposure to school (Correa-Chavez & Rogoff, 2009). The researchers discovered that children from the

Researchers have found that Mayan parents who have at least 12 years of schooling typically use school-like teaching styles when helping their children complete a puzzle. These styles may reinforce their children's classroom learning.

traditional families were much more likely than the others to pay close attention to the interaction that was directed at their sibling. These children also demonstrated greater learning of how to make the toy. This attentiveness to the activities of others is consistent with the Guatemalan Maya cultural tradition in which children pitch in to help during ongoing events of importance in their community—an example of an interdependent or collectivist style. The Mayan collectivist style contrasts sharply with the cultural practices of most Western-style classrooms, which tend to emphasize the centrality of the teacher. But if Mayan children are socialized to focus broadly on the activities of the group, rather than on the activities of a central individual, then Western-style classroom practices may not be the most effective way for them to learn.

Patricia Greenfield and her colleagues have addressed the potentially problematic relationship between children's traditional cultural practices and the practices they encounter in school. In particular, they have proposed that, given the competitive nature of the American education system, the cultural practices of standard American classrooms favor children who come from homes that promote the prevailing American cultural style of independence, with the goal of socializing children to become autonomous individuals who enter into social relations by personal choice (an individualistic orientation). They also propose that the standard culture of American schools is correspondingly disadvantageous to children from homes that promote a cultural style of interdependence, that is, children whose parents have been socializing them to place a strong value on social networks and downplay personal achievement. To help reduce this possible disadvantage, Greenfield and her colleagues have conducted special training programs that sensitize teachers to work effectively with children and their families from cultures with an interdependent style (Turnbull, Rothstein-Fisch, Greenfield, & Quiroz, 2001).

Other researchers emphasize the point that many children who come from families with an interdependent orientation thrive in the standard American classroom. The success of these children appears to be due in large measure to the positive role the parents play in their schooling. For example, Nathan Caplan and his colleagues studied the children of refugees who fled to the United States from Vietnam, Cambodia, and Laos during the 1970s and 1980s. These children, whose home cultures are characterized by an interdependent cultural style, have been conspicuously successful in educational pursuits (Caplan, Choy, & Whitmore, 1991). Although they had lost from 1 to 3 years of formal education in refugee camps and most were unable to speak English when they entered school in the United States, 8 out of 10 students surveyed had a B average or better within 3 to 6 years. Almost half received A's in mathematics. These achievements are all the more noteworthy because they were attained in schools in low-income, inner-city areas traditionally associated with limited resources and poorly motivated, often disruptive students.

In trying to account for the spectacular success of these children, Caplan and his colleagues found parents' involvement to be crucial. Almost half of the parents surveyed said that they read to their children, many in their native language. That the parents didn't know English well evidently mattered less to the children's school performance than did the children's positive emotional associations of being read to and the connection to their culture. Indeed, it has been found that children across a variety of ethnic-minority groups profit when their families make explicit efforts to pass on to them their native language and cultural heritage: They do better in school, are more likely to attend college, have higher academic and occupational aspirations, and are less at risk for certain psychiatric disorders and behaviors, including suicide (Portes & Rumbaut, 2001; Farver, Eppe, & Ballon, 2006; Chandler & Proulx, 2008; Schwartz et al., 2011).

Aspects of culture other than an interdependent cultural style can prove to be poorly supported by, and disadvantageous in the context of, the standard American classroom culture. According to Wade Boykin, African American children inherit a rich tradition of using expressive movement as a part of their everyday communicative behavior—a tradition they are required to suppress in classrooms that emphasize sitting quietly while learning. Hypothesizing that this suppression of an important cultural asset has a negative impact on their learning, Boykin conducted experiments with African American children in which they listened to stories under different conditions and were then asked questions about the stories. The story conditions varied in terms of the activity levels of the stories' characters, whether the storytelling was accompanied by music with a lively beat, and whether children were instructed to sit quietly or were told they could clap and dance while they listened to the story. As shown in Figure 12.9, the children performed significantly better on the questions when the story involved high levels of character activity and music and they were encouraged to clap and dance, supporting Boykin's idea about the importance of this cultural factor for the children's learning (Boykin & Cunningham, 2001).

Taken together, these different studies strongly implicate home cultural values and modes of behavior as important factors in children's school success. But they also indicate that there is no "one right way" to incorporate such differences into classroom practices.

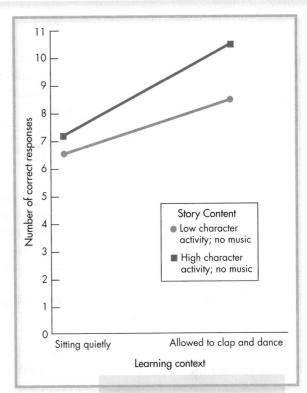

FIGURE 12.9 As indicated by the number of correct responses on a memory task, students were much better at remembering a story when it had a high level of character activity, and when the children were allowed to clap and dance while they heard the story. (Adapted from Boykin & Cunningham, 2001.)

The Language of School

Even when people speak the same language, they do not necessarily use language in the same way. As we have noted, language is used in schools in rather distinctive ways, and children's experience of oral and written language in the home will differ to some extent not only from language practices at school but also from those of other homes within the community.

In order to gain insight into how language used in the home may differ from language practices associated with school and school success, Shirley Heath (1983) conducted an ethnographic study of three populations of children and their families over a period of years. The populations she studied, all from the same geographical locale, included the families of a group of European American schoolteachers, a group of European American textile workers, and a group of African Americans engaged in farming and textile jobs.

Conducting observations both in homes and in classrooms, Heath found that the families of European American teachers experienced the least mismatch with the school. About half of the conversations she recorded in the teachers' homes included the "instructional discourse" that is a prominent feature of classrooms. In addition, these parents involved their children in labeling objects, naming letters, and reading. When reading with their children, they went well beyond the text itself to make clear the relationships between what was in the book and experiences the child might have had or might have in the future. In a sense, the teachers were being teachers at home as well as at school. Perhaps as a result, their children tended to do well in school.

The pattern in the homes of European American textile workers differed from the pattern in schools and in the teachers' homes in that the parents limited their storybook conversations to the text itself. They asked their children questions about the characters and events in stories they read to them but did not encourage their children to imaginatively link the stories to the world around them. Overall, the children from these working-class European American families tended not to do well in school. More precisely, in what may have been a reflection of the language-use pattern in their homes, they tended to perform well in the early grades of school, where a focus on the literal meaning of a text fits most tasks, but they did less well in the higher grades, where it becomes necessary to draw inferences from complex texts.

Unlike the two groups of European American parents, the African American parents rarely used the known-answer questions of instructional discourse ("What color is your jacket?"). Rather, they most often asked children questions that encouraged them to think about similarities across situations related to the children's own experience ("Do you think you can get along with your cousin on this visit?"). Such questions often served as the pretext for discussing some interesting event and helped children think about their shifting roles and responsibilities in different situations. Heath also documented many inventive uses of language in teasing and storytelling. But the children's language experience generally did not expose them to the kinds of language patterns they would be expected to use in school. Again, perhaps in part because of the mismatch, these African American working-class children tended not to perform well in school. Similar findings have been reported for Latino children (Vasquez, 2002).

These differences in academic success among the children from the three groups are understandable in terms of the relative fit between school and home language use and culture. At the same time, it is the goal of teachers to be successful with all children. So the question becomes one of how to design educational interventions to make it possible for everyone to learn effectively.

Culturally Responsive Classroom Strategies

In recognition of the importance of children's home language and culture to their success in the classroom, schools have begun to make a place for them in academic curricula and to host special events to explore and celebrate the cultural heritages of the young people they serve. Common programs such as English as a second language (ESL), bilingual education programs, and heritage language classes are intended to help immigrant students make the transition to an all-English curriculum. The overarching goal is to foster assimilation while valuing cultural diversity (Padilla, 2006).

An early and influential example of the culturally responsive approach to education occurred in a classroom of students from the Odawa Indian tribe in Canada taught by an expert Odawa teacher (Erickson & Mohatt, 1982). On the surface, the teacher appeared to adhere to a recitation-script approach, talking for most of the lessons, asking many known-answer questions, and limiting the students' role to answering her questions. But she did so in a special way consistent with the language use and cultural patterns employed in Odawa homes. When she was giving instruction, she organized students into small groups instead of rows, approximating the way the children interacted in groups at home. She generally addressed the children as a group and did not single out individual children. Instead of saying "good" when students answered her questions correctly, she signaled her acceptance of their answers by moving on to the next question. She praised but did not reprimand students in public, in accordance with Odawa norms against public criticism. This culture-sensitive way of implementing classroom lessons worked well to improve children's academic performance.

Another example of the importance of culture-sensitive instruction was provided by an experiment conducted by Carol Lee, who drew on African American high school students' familiarity with, and appreciation of, the linguistic form called *signifying* (Lee, 2010). Within the African American community, to signify means to speak in a manner that uses innuendo and words with double meanings, to play with the sounds and meanings of words, and to be quick-witted and funny, all at the same time. According to Lee, African American adolescents use signifying for a wide variety of speech functions including:

- To challenge someone in a verbal duel, but remain friendly
- To persuade someone by driving home a message in a distinctive way
- To criticize someone in a way that is difficult to pin down

Lee began by presenting students examples of signifying dialogues of the sort they were familiar with and getting the students to analyze and explain how each example of signifying worked to achieve a specific goal. Then she had them read stories and novels by African American writers that included signifying and asked them to apply the rules, which they knew intuitively, to the interpretation of complex inferential questions from the literary texts.

When Lee compared the performance of students who engaged in this kind of culturally responsive instruction with that of students who took the regular literature course, she found that they demonstrated a significantly higher level of literary understanding and active engagement with the problem of literary interpretation.

On the basis of available research, these examples could be multiplied to encompass a wide variety of ethnic and social-class groups—wide enough to make a convincing case that it is possible to organize effective contexts for education by taking into account local variations in culture and social class (Tharp, 2005). At the same time, it needs to be recognized that there is no single "right way" to connect classroom instruction to home culture. Research on this topic makes it clear that a wide variety of specific classroom strategies can successfully engage students from the vast variety of backgrounds characteristic of American society. However, culturally specific strategies are likely to be applicable only when there is a culturally homogeneous classroom (Gallego & Cole, 2000).

Learning other languages has become an important part of school curricula in many countries.

⬥ APPLY :: CONNECT :: DISCUSS

In her research with African American children, Carol Lee found that, compared with traditional instruction, culturally responsive instruction results both in a higher level of literary understanding (of how to analyze and interpret texts) and in increased engagement. Review the curriculum she developed around the concept of "signifying" and explain how it led to both these results.

Outside the School

As important as schooling is to middle childhood, it is not the only context beyond the family that influences children. Especially important is the time spent in new kinds of activities with friends and one's peer group. On weekday afternoons and evenings, on weekends and holidays, children of elementary-school age are likely to be found among other children their own age, engaged in activities of their own choosing. Some of these settings have an adult or two present, but in many cases, adults are not on the scene.

Participation in these peer groups provides a kind of preparation for adult life that is quite different from that organized by adults in classrooms or at home. At the same time, peer-group experiences influence life at home and in school. Consequently, a full understanding of the nature of middle childhood requires investigation of peer contexts as well, so we turn to this important topic in Chapter 13.

SUMMARY

The children of the world have vastly unequal access to education, yet school can have an extraordinary impact as a context for children's development.

The Contexts of Learning

- Education refers to explicit instruction of children in order to transmit a culture's knowledge and skills.

- Early hunter–gatherer societies most likely transmitted cultural knowledge and skills through social enhancement and imitation as children participated in everyday activities, rather than through explicit instruction. Increasing specialization led to the emergence of apprenticeship—an intermediate form involving some explicit instruction but relying mainly on participation—and to the emergence of education, or schooling.

- Schooling differs from traditional apprenticeship training in dimensions including motivation, social relations, social organization, and mediums of instruction. Its problems are abstract, in contrast to those of everyday life.

School Readiness

- Children often start school with knowledge, skills, and attitudes that serve as building blocks for learning to read and write and to do math.

- A basic reading skill is decoding text—translating graphemes (units of print) to phonemes (units of sound). This, in turn, requires the ability to detect and manipulate the phonemes in words, an ability that comes only with instruction.

- To learn math, children must be able to relate number words and symbols to quantities. Children learn to envision the placement of numbers on an abstract number line and to manipulate numeric units.

- Families play a key role in promoting school readiness by creating contexts for children to engage in relevant activities. School readiness promotes academic success.

- Preschools also promote school readiness. Although worldwide preschool enrollment has tripled in recent decades, there are significant disparities in enrollment across and within countries, with lower enrollments among many groups of children who might most benefit from preschool, including immigrant children in the United States.

In the Classroom

- Educators have debated the merits of a bottom-up approach, which initially focuses on basic skills, versus a top-down approach, which focuses on the big picture of which the basic skills are part.

- The standard classroom format features a teacher at the head of the class instructing students through the use of a special instructional discourse, typified by the teacher's asking known-answer questions.

- Alternative forms of classroom instruction seek to counter the passivity of students in the standard format and make them active participants in their education. Examples include:
  - Reciprocal teaching, in which a teacher and a small group of students read segments of text and take turns leading discussions of their meaning.
  - Realistic mathematics education, which encourages development of conceptual understanding as well as basic skills through the use of models and meaningful problem-oriented activities.
  - Playworld practice, which involves enacting, making art about, and playing with themes based on children's literature.

- For many children, specific learning disabilities pose a barrier to school success. These children have normal IQs but fare poorly in at least some academic areas. The most common specific learning disability is dyslexia, a reading problem that typically involves difficulties detecting phonemes and understanding the rules that relate graphemes and phonemes.

- While some students thrive on the challenges of schooling, others lose their academic motivation. Researchers exploring the reasons have found two patterns:
  - Children who adopt an incremental model of intelligence see intelligence as something that can grow as one learns. They tend to have a mastery motivation that motivates them to learn and improve.
  - Children who adopt an entity model of intelligence see intelligence as fixed. They tend to develop a performance orientation that motivates them to perform well but also to give up when they experience failure.

The Cognitive Consequences of Schooling

- The cognitive consequences of schooling have been assessed through three research strategies for comparing schooled and nonschooled children:
  - The school-cutoff strategy, which compares 6-year-olds in first grade with those in kindergarten, finds that schooling makes a difference mainly to a range of relatively specific cognitive abilities.
  - School–nonschool comparisons show few clear differences other than increased use of specialized memory strategies and increased metacognitive skills.
  - Second-generation studies, comparing schooled and unschooled mothers, suggest that habits and skills acquired in school may influence child-rearing practices in such a way as to lead to better health and educational outcomes for children. Thus, school's greatest impact may be other than cognitive.

Contemporary Challenges in a Globalizing World

- A major challenge is to increase access to quality education, reducing disparities across and within countries, including disparities related to gender, ethnicity, and socioeconomic status.

- Another major challenge in many countries is to serve student populations that are increasingly diverse in terms of language and culture.

- Home cultural values are important to children's school success. A good match between home and school language also favors success. Although the culture of U.S. schools reflects the dominant cultural style, classroom practices can be sensitive to other cultural styles, thereby benefiting a wider range of children.

Key Terms

formal education, p. 431
apprenticeship, p. 431
emergent literacy, p. 433
emergent numeracy, p. 433
decoding, p. 434
bottom-up processing, p. 440
top-down processing, p. 440

instructional discourse, p. 440
reciprocal teaching, p. 440
realistic mathematics education, p. 442
playworld practice, p. 443
specific learning disabilities, p. 445
academic motivation, p. 447
mastery orientation, p. 447

performance orientation, p. 447
entity model of intelligence, p. 448
incremental model of intelligence, p. 448
school engagement, p. 448
school-cutoff strategy, p. 449
cultural style, p. 455

Social and Emotional Development in Middle Childhood

A New Sense of Self

Changing Conceptions of the Self

Self-Esteem

Moral Development

Piaget's Theory of Moral Development

Kohlberg's Theory of Moral Development

Prosocial Moral Reasoning

Social Domain Theory

Moral Reasoning and Theories of Mind

Peer Relationships

Peer Relations and Social Status

Competition and Cooperation Among Peers

Relations Between Boys and Girls

Friendship: A Special Type of Relationship

The Influence of Parents

Changing Expectations

Parents and Peers

Divorce

Reconsidering Middle Childhood

Cassie and Becca had been best friends since first grade. When the girls were in fifth grade, Kelly moved into town. At first, the three of them were quite close. But something happened a few weeks ago. According to 10-year-old Cassie:

Becca kind of forgot me. They started to get really close and they just forgot me. And then they started ganging up on me and stuff. Like, after lunch we have a place where we meet and stuff. We get in a circle and just talk. And they'd put their shoulders together and they wouldn't let me, you know, in the circle. They would never talk to me, and they would never listen to what I had to say. I don't think I've ever done anything to them. I've always been nice to them. I feel like I don't want to go to school, because I don't know what they'll do every day. I talk to my mom but it kind of makes her mad because she says I should ignore them. But I can't. And I can't concentrate. They're like—they look at me and stuff like that. They stare at me. I can hear them saying stuff and whispering and they look right at me.

(Adapted from Simmons, 2002)

Very few of us pass through middle childhood without experiencing the sting of peer rejection. As children between the ages of 6 and 12 spend more time in the company of age-mates, and correspondingly less time with parents, peers begin to assume a more prominent place in their lives and exert more influence on their behavior and development. Indeed, one of the most significant changes of middle childhood is the emergence of peer influence as a considerable power in shaping behavior. Sometimes the rule of "might makes right" prevails, as when an especially strong child dominates group activity. At other times, the complexity of social relationships, including popularity, sets the tone, as Cassie came to experience.

The emergence of new forms of *social control*—that is, ways of organizing behavior in relation to group life and society—is also apparent in the changing nature of children's relations with their parents. Parents can no longer successfully demand blind obedience from their children, nor can they easily just pick them up and remove them from danger or from situations in which they are behaving badly. Parents can still monitor their children's whereabouts, but they must rely on their children's greater understanding of the consequences of their actions and on their desire to conform to the standards that have been set for them for behaving in ways that are safe, socially appropriate, and morally acceptable. As a result, parents' socialization techniques become more indirect, and they rely increasingly on discussion and explanation to influence their children's behavior.

As their relationships with others change, so, too, does children's sense of themselves. As long as they spend their time primarily among family members, their social roles and sense of self are more or less predefined and determined. They are little brothers or older sisters, with all the expectations and privileges that go along with those roles. When children spend more time among their peers, however, the sense of self they acquired in their families no longer suffices, and they must form

industry versus inferiority According to Erikson's theory, the stage during which children judge themselves to be industrious and successfully meeting the new challenges posed by adults at home and school, or inferior and incapable of meeting such challenges.

new identities appropriate to the new contexts they inhabit. The child who seems fearless at home and who dominates younger siblings may find that he or she needs to be more restrained on the playground with peers.

This chapter focuses on how new forms of social control are manifested in children's changing sense of self, moral development, peer interactions and friendships, and relationships with parents.

A New Sense of Self

> On our quests to create ourselves we brown girls play dress up. What is most fascinating about this ritual of imitation is what we choose to mimic—what we reach for in our mothers' closests. We move right on past the unglamorous garb of our mothers' day-to-day realities—the worn housedresses or beat-up slippers—and reach instead for the intimates. Slip our sassy little selves into their dressiest of dresses and sexiest of lingerie like being grown is like Christmas or Kwanzaa and can't come fast enough. Then we practice the deadly art of attitude—rollin' eyes, necks, and hips in mesmerizing synchronization, takin' out imaginary violators with razor-sharp tongues.
> (Morgan, 1999, pp. 29–30)

Joan Morgan's reflection on playing dress up surely resonates with anyone who remembers clomping around in their mother's high heels, with the hems of fancy dresses trailing behind. Dress-up is a common play activity toward the end of early childhood and in the first years of middle childhood. Morgan's point that it tends to reflect glamour, success, and even power is especially interesting in light of Erik Erikson's theory that the main challenge of middle childhood is to establish a sense of *competence*. As you learned in Chapter 1 (see p. 18), Erikson believed that development throughout life involves seeking answers to the question, "Who am I?" At each *psychosocial stage,* the individual faces a particular challenge in his or her quest for identity. In middle childhood, when children are expected to develop more mature forms of behavior—pitching in around the house or solving more complicated problems at school—the main challenge is that of **industry versus inferiority**. Children who emerge from middle childhood with a sense of industry believe that they are competent and effective at activities valued by adults and and peers. Those who emerge with a sense of inferiority feel inadequate, believing themselves incapable of mastering the tasks expected of them.

In addition to general feelings of competence, the transition from early to middle childhood is accompanied by equally striking developments in how children think about themselves, the emergence of a new level of sensitivity to their personal standing among their peers, and their resulting efforts to maintain their self-esteem.

Changing Conceptions of the Self

A sizable body of evidence suggests that as children move from early childhood to middle childhood and then to adolescence, their sense of self undergoes marked changes that parallel the changes occurring in their cognitive and social processes (Harter, 2006b; Mascolo & Fischer, 1998).

To understand how children's conceptions of themselves change as they grow older, William Damon and Daniel Hart (1988) asked children between 4 and 15 years of age to describe themselves. They found that all of the children referred to their appearance, their activities, their relations to others, and their psychological characteristics, but both the importance they attached to these various characteristics and the complexity of their self-concepts changed with age. As Table 13.1

table 13.1

A Developmental Model of Self-Concept

Typical Organizing Principle for Self-Concepts	Area of Evaluation			
	Physical	Activity-Based	Social	Psychological
1. Categorical identification (4–7 years)	I have blue eyes. I'm 6 years old.	I play baseball. I play and read a lot.	I'm Catholic. I'm Sarah's friend.	I get funny ideas sometimes. I'm happy
2. Comparative assessments (8–11 years)	I'm bigger than most kids. I have really light skin, because I'm Scandinavian.	I'm not very good at school. I'm good at math, but I'm not so good at art.	I'm one of the best players on my baseball team. I don't do as well in school as my sister does.	I'm not as smart as most kids. I get upset more easily than other kids.
3. Interpersonal implications (12–15 years)	I am a four-eyed person. Everyone makes fun of me.	I play sports, which is important because all kids like athletes.	I am an honest person, so people trust me.	I understand people, so they come to me with their problems.
	I have blonde hair, which is good because boys like blondes.	I treat people well so I'll have friends when I need them.	I'm very shy, so I don't have many friends.	I'm the kind of person who loves being with my friends; they make me feel good about being me.

Source: After Damon & Hart, 1988.

shows, between the ages of 4 and 7 years, children's self-concept is expressed typically through categorical statements about themselves that place them in socially recognized categories ("I'm 6 years old; I have blue eyes"). Between ages 8 and 11, their expressions of self-concept include comparative judgments relating their own characteristics to those of others ("I'm bigger than most kids"). (Descriptions of personal characteristics as significant to interpersonal relationships are, as shown in the table, uncommon until adolescence.)

Subsequent research has supported the picture of a general trend from self-concepts based on limited, concrete characteristics to more abstract and stable conceptions arrived at through **social comparison**, the process of defining oneself in relation to one's peers (Pomerantz et al., 1995; Butler, 2005; Guest, 2007).

There is no mystery about why social comparison begins to play a significant role in children's sense of themselves during middle childhood. The increased time they spend with their peers and their greater ability to understand others' points of view lead children to engage in a new kind of questioning about themselves. They must decide on answers to such questions as "Am I good at sports?" "Am I a good friend?" "Do the other kids like me?" and "Am I good at math?" Such questions have no absolute answer because there are no absolute criteria of success. Rather, success is measured in relation to the performance of others in the social group. The many comparisons children make in a wide variety of settings provide them with a new overall sense of themselves.

Children's use of social comparison becomes increasingly complex and subtle over time. When deliberate and pervasive social comparison becomes important at around 8 years of age, children are initially inclined to make overt social comparisons in interactions with their peers, saying such things as "I'm finishing the math problems a lot faster than you are," or "I bet I beat your

social comparison The process of defining oneself in relation to one's peers.

Social comparison often takes the form of asking how one's friends are doing on a school assignment.

self-esteem One's evaluation of one's own worth.

score in the video game." But they soon discover that this kind of comparison is perceived as bragging and is likely to evoke negative reactions. As a consequence, they begin to develop more subtle ways of making social comparisons, asking questions such as, "What problem are you on?" or "What was your highest score?" (Pomerantz et al., 1995). It is important to note that not all social comparison is competitive in nature. Indeed, the form taken by children's social comparison appears to depend importantly on the extent to which peer competition or social integration is valued in the culture, a topic to which we will return later in the chapter (Guest, 2007).

Sometime around the age of 7 or 8, children also begin to describe themselves in terms of more general, stable traits. Instead of saying "I can kick a ball far" or "I know my ABCs," they begin to say "I am a good athlete" or "I am smart." At the same time, they begin to assume more consistently that other people also have stable traits that can be used to anticipate what they will do in a variety of contexts (Olson & Dweck, 2009). Studies indicate that children begin to attribute stability to the psychological states of others at about the same time they begin to think about themselves as having stable traits.

Self-Esteem

Susan Harter, a developmental researcher and clinician, has been intrigued for decades by the question of children's development of **self-esteem**, that is, their evaluations of their own worth (1999). Her research has shown that self-esteem is an important index of mental health. High self-esteem during childhood has been linked to satisfaction and happiness in later life, while low self-esteem has been linked to depression, anxiety, and maladjustment both in school and in social relations.

The positive feedback this African American girl receives from her father for completing her chores will likely have an important impact on her developing self-esteem.

To study the basis on which children's evaluations of themselves change in the transition from early to middle childhood, Harter and Robin Pike (1984) presented 4-, 5-, 6-, and 7-year-olds with pairs of pictures and asked them to say whether each picture was a lot or a little like them. Each pair of pictures was selected to tap the children's judgments in one of four domains important to self-esteem: cognitive competence, physical competence, peer acceptance, and maternal acceptance. The younger and older children were given comparable but age-appropriate items. For example, an item such as "Knows the alphabet" used to assess judgments of cognitive competence in the 4- and 5-year-olds corresponded to the item "Can read alone" for the 6- and 7-year-olds.

The pattern of their responses to these self-evaluation tasks revealed that the children judged their own worth in terms of two broad categories—competence and acceptance. That is, statistical analysis revealed that the children lumped cognitive and physical competence together in a single category of competence and combined peer and maternal acceptance in the single category of acceptance. Nevertheless, the scale seemed to tap children's feelings of self-worth in a realistic way. Harter and Pike found, for example, that, as might be expected, the picture selections of children who had been held back a grade reflected a self-evaluation of low competence, while the picture selections of newcomers to a school reflected a self-evaluation of low acceptance.

In research on somewhat older children (8 to 12 years old), Harter (1982) assessed self-esteem using the written format shown in Figure 13.1. She found that these older children made more differentiated self-evaluations; for example, they

Really true for me	Sort of true for me	Some kids often forget what they learn	but	Other kids can remember things easily	Sort of true for me	Really true for me
☐	☐				☐	☐

FIGURE 13.1 In this sample item from Harter's scale of self-esteem, choices to the left of center indicate degrees of poor self-esteem. Choices to the right indicate degrees of positive self-esteem. (From Harter, 1982.)

distinguished between cognitive, social, and physical competence (Harter, 1987). At the same time that older children's self-evaluations become more differentiated, a new level of integration in the components of self-esteem appears, enabling children to form an overall sense of their general self-worth (Harter, 2006b). (Table 13.2 shows the content of sample items in each area of self-esteem included in Harter's scale for 8- to 12-year-olds.)

Another aspect of children's changing ideas about themselves in middle childhood is that they begin to form representations of the kind of person they would like to be—an "ideal self" against which they measure their "actual self," that is, the person they believe they actually are. The fact that there is likely to be a discrepancy between children's actual and ideal selves can be either a source of motivation toward self-improvement or a source of distress and discouragement, depending on the perceived degree of discrepancy.

Of course, not all discrepancies between the actual and ideal selves are equally important. If, for example, being athletic is not important to a child, then the child's self-worth will not be much affected by the realization that he or she is not a good athlete and will never become one. In contrast, if athletic ability is a core part of the child's sense of self, then the child might be devastated by the idea of never being very good at sports (Harter, 2006a).

Harter and others also report that there is an age-related change in the extent to which children's self-evaluations fit the views of others (Harter, 1999). Younger children's rating of their peers' "smartness" at school generally agrees with teachers' evaluations. Their ratings of their own smartness, however, do not correlate with either their teachers' or their peers' ratings, tending generally to be unrealistically high. Around the age of 8, children's self-evaluations begin to fit with the judgments of both their peers and their teachers. This pattern of results fits nicely with the conclusion presented earlier that an overall sense of oneself in relation to others arises around the age of 8.

Foundations of Self-Esteem Self-esteem has been linked to patterns of child-rearing (Coopersmith, 1967; Hughes et al., 2006). In an extensive study of 10- to 12-year-old boys, Stanley Coopersmith found that parents of boys with high self-esteem (as determined by their answers to a questionnaire and their teachers' ratings) employed a style of parenting strikingly similar to the *authoritative parenting*

table 13.2	
Harter Self-Esteem Scale for 8- to 12-Year-Olds	
Area of Self-Evaluation	**Content of Sample Items**
Cognitive competence	Good at schoolwork, can figure out answers, remembers easily, remembers what is read
Social competence	Have a lot of friends, popular, do things with kids, easy to like
Physical competence	Do well at sports, good at games, chosen first for games
General self-worth	Sure of myself, do things fine, I am a good person, I want to stay the same

Source: Harter, 1982.

pattern described by Diana Baumrind (see Chapter 10, p. 349). Recall that authoritative parents are distinguished by their mixture of firm control, promotion of high standards of behavior, encouragement of independence, and willingness to reason with their children. Coopersmith's data suggest that three parental characteristics combine to produce high self-esteem in late middle childhood.

1. *Parents' acceptance of their children.* The mothers of sons with high self-esteem had closer, more affectionate relationships with their children than did mothers of children with low self-esteem. The children seemed to appreciate this approval and to view their mothers as supportive. They also tended to interpret their mothers' interest as an indication of their personal importance, as a consequence of which they came to regard themselves favorably. "This is success in its most personal expression—the concern, attention, and time of significant others" (Coopersmith, 1967, p. 179).

2. *Parents' setting of clearly defined limits.* Parents' imposition and enforcement of strict limits on their children's activities appeared to give the children a sense that norms are real and significant and contributed to their self-definition (Barber, Stolz, & Olsen, 2005).

3. *Parents' respect for individuality.* Within the limits set by the parents' sense of standards and social norms, the children with high self-esteem were allowed a great deal of individual self-expression. Parents showed respect for these children by reasoning with them and considering their points of view.

Taken together, contemporary evidence suggests that the key to high self-esteem is the feeling, transmitted in large part by the family, that one has some ability to control one's own future by controlling both oneself and one's environment (Chirkov & Ryan, 2001; Harter, 2006a). This feeling of control is not without bounds. As Coopersmith's data suggest, children who have a positive self-image know their boundaries, but this awareness does not detract from their feeling of effectiveness. Rather, it sets clear limits within which they feel considerable assurance and freedom.

While several decades of study on the relationship between parenting practices and children's self-esteem provides a fairly consistent picture, most of this work has been conducted on European American families. It has recently been pointed out that other cultures and ethnic groups attach much less weight to the importance of self-esteem in their children's development. An interesting example is provided by Andrew Guest's comparison of two distinct but relatively impoverished cultural communities (2007). One was a public housing project in Chicago; the other was a group of refugee camps in the Republic of Angola. As shown in Table 13.3, adults in the Chicago community rated self-esteem as the most important developmental task of middle childhood, whereas adults in the Angolan community rated it a distant eighth.

Naturally, cultures that attach little weight to self-esteem probably do not organize their parenting practices in ways that explicitly promote it. Peggy Miller and her colleagues (2002) found evidence for this in interviews they conducted about child rearing with European American and Taiwanese mothers. For the American mothers, self-esteem played a prominent role in child-rearing practices and children's development. The Taiwanese mothers, in contrast, rarely mentioned the role of "self-respect–heart/mind" (the nearest Chinese word to "self-esteem"). When they did, they expressed concern that it would create psychological vulnerabilities. Similarly, another cross-cultural study found that the relationship between parenting practices and children's self-esteem was strong in European American families but comparatively weak in Mexican American families (Ruiz, Roosa, & Gonzales,

table 13.3

Adults' Ratings of the Importance of Developmental Tasks for Children from 6 to 12 Years Old (from most to least important)

Chicago, United States

1. Developing self-esteem (self-love)
2. Forming a good relationship with parents and adults
3. Developing basic reading, writing, and math skills
4. Building good attitudes toward hygiene, the body, and physical self-care
5. Developing values and morals
6. Learning to get along with other children
7. Developing the ability to think and be creative
8. Achieving personal independence
9. Learning teamwork (working in groups)
10. Learning physical skills for play, games, and sports

Republic of Angola

1. Building good attitudes toward hygiene, the body, and physical self-care
2. Learning physical skills for play, games, and sports
3. Developing basic reading, writing, and math skills
4. Forming a good relationship with parents and adults
5. Learning to get along with other children
6. Developing values and morals
7. Developing the ability to think and be creative
8. Developing self-esteem (self-love)
9. Learning teamwork (working in groups)
10. Achieving personal independence

Source: Adapted from Guest, 2007, p. 18

2002). That is, in Mexican American families, parenting practices appeared to have less influence on the child's level of self-esteem.

As a consequence of cultural comparative research, developmentalists are taking a close look at the possibility that the concept of self-esteem may be not a universal feature of children's sense of self but rather, that it develops in particular cultural contexts and with specific patterns of parenting practices that are common within those particular cultural contexts.

▲ APPLY :: CONNECT :: DISCUSS

- In what ways do changing conceptions of self appear related to cognitive developments characteristic of middle childhood (see Chapter 11)?

- How might self-esteem be related to the development of self-regulation discussed in Chapter 9 (see pp. 320–329)?

Moral Development

During middle childhood, the child's new ability to internalize society's rules and standards leads to significant changes in moral development, just as it does in social development generally. Remember from Chapter 9 that as children develop, their reasoning and behaviors become less dependent on external rewards and punishments and more dependent on an internal, personal sense of right and wrong. According to Freud's *psychodynamic theory* (see Chapter 9, p. 318), this transition occurs with the development of the superego. The *superego,* remember, is the part of the personality that monitors and evaluates whether the individual's actions are morally appropriate. It is the individual's conscience—the *internalization,* first, of the same-sex parent's standards and moral codes, and then of society's. Once the superego has formed, the child is able to draw upon his or her own internal notions of right and wrong in making moral judgments, rather than be driven by hope of reward or fear of reprisal.

Interest in the shift from external to internal control is also apparent in the *cognitive-developmental* view of moral development held by Piaget and those who follow in his footsteps (see Chapter 9, pp. 318–319). Much of their work has focused on exploring children's reasoning about what is morally right or wrong and the relationship between moral reasoning and moral behavior.

Piaget's Theory of Moral Development

In Chapter 9, we explained that for Piaget, moral development involves a shift from *heteronomous morality*—in which right and wrong are defined according to objective consequences of behavior—to **autonomous morality**, in which right and wrong are defined according to the person's internal motives and intentions (see p. 319). An important question for Piaget, as well as for contemporary developmentalists, is: What triggers the shift from heteronomous to autonomous moral reasoning? How is it that children who formerly had to be told what is right and wrong come to reason this out for themselves? Piaget's answer was that the shift in moral reasoning takes place in the context of peer activities—playing games, in particular.

Like 4- and 5-year-olds, children who have entered middle childhood engage in fantasy role play, with each child taking a part in an imaginary situation: Cops chase robbers; shipwrecked families take up residence in tree houses; runaway children hide in secret forts (Singer, 2006). But around the age of 7 or 8, children also engage in a new form of play—games based on rules. As you saw in Chapter 9, preschool fantasy role play may involve rules, but these rules can change on a whim. In contrast, in the rule-based fantasy role play and other games characteristic of middle childhood, the rules must be agreed upon ahead of time and consistently followed; anyone who changes the rules without common consent is considered to be cheating.

Piaget conducted some of the most famous and influential studies of how children develop an understanding of games with rules. By observing changes in how children play the game of marbles, he found that young children (6 to 8 years of age) have a "mystical respect" for the rules of the game. They believe that rules are "eternal and unchangeable" because they have been handed down by authority figures such as parents, grandparents, or even God (Piaget, 1965/1995, pp. 206–207) (see the box "Children's Ideas about God"). This way of thinking about rules corresponds, of course, to heteronomous morality. In contrast, and consistent with the onset of autonomous morality, older children (10 to 12 years of age) recognize that the rules are not mystical and unchangeable

These Yemeni boys are playing street soccer. Throughout the world, children in middle childhood begin to play games based on rules, activities that Piaget considered fundamental to developing moral reasoning.

GAMAL NOMAN/AFP/Getty Images

These members of the Long Island Gulls hockey team know that breaking the rules is cheating. According to Piaget, participating in rule-governed games such as hockey contributes to children's moral development.

but are rational; and since they have been agreed upon by the players, they can be modified with the players' consent.

Piaget (1932/1965) believed that games are models of society—that is, that rule-based games have certain fundamental characteristics of social institutions. First, rule-based games remain basically the same as they are passed from one generation to the next. Thus, like social institutions, rule-based games provide an existing structure of rules about how to behave in specific social circumstances. Second, rule-based games can exist only if people agree to participate in them. There would be no religions, for example, if there were no practicing believers; there would be no game of marbles if children stopped playing it. In order to participate in social institutions, people must subordinate their immediate desires and behavior to a socially agreed-upon system, be it the beliefs and rituals of a religion or the rules of marbles. Piaget (1932/1965) linked this ability to play within a framework of rules to children's acquisition of respect for rules and a new level of moral understanding.

In Piaget's (1932/1965) view, it is through game-playing—that is, through the give-and-take of negotiating plans, settling disagreements, making and enforcing rules, and keeping and breaking promises—that children come to understand that social rules make cooperation with others possible. As a consequence of this understanding, peer groups can be self-governing, and their members capable of autonomous moral thinking.

Kohlberg's Theory of Moral Development

The most influential attempt to build on Piaget's approach to moral development was carried out by Lawrence Kohlberg (Turiel, 2002). Whereas Piaget argued for the existence of two stages of moral reasoning, heteronomous and autonomous, Kohlberg proposed a sequence of six stages extending from childhood into adolescence and adulthood. These six stages are grouped into three levels of moral reasoning: *preconventional, conventional,* and *postconventional* (Colby & Kohlberg, 1987; Kohlberg, 1969, 1976, 1984). The stages are characterized by ideas about what is right and the reasons for doing right, all of which evolve over time as egocentrism

autonomous morality The second and final stage of Piaget's theory of moral development in which right and wrong are defined according to internal motives and intentions rather than objective consequences.

Children's Ideas About God

CAREN, AGE 9:

Once upon a time in Heaven. . . . God woke up from his nap. It was his birthday. But nobody knew it was his birthday but one angel. . . . And this angel rounds up all these other angels, and when he gets out of the shower, they have a surprise party for him. (Heller, 1986, cited in Barrett, 2001)

An adult:

God is infinite, pervasive, and man finite and limited to a locality. Man cannot comprehend God as he can other things. God is without limits, without dimensions. (Ullah, 1984, cited in Barrett, 2001)

The quotes above would seem to support the conclusion shared by many developmentalists that children's understanding of God moves from primitive, anthropomorphic conceptions—God has birthdays, naps, and showers—to abstract concepts that refer to God's infinite knowledge and power and existence beyond the realm of physical and natural laws.

This was certainly the view held by both Freud and Piaget, who believed that, early on, children's conceptions of God are similar to their conceptions of parents. Freud, for example, argued that the idea of God is a projection of our need for a protective parent figure. Piaget, as you would expect, adopted an approach that links children's changing conceptions of God to their changing cognitive systems. In particular, children initially attribute godlike properties to both God and their parents. Once they realize that their parents are fallible—vulnerable to errors in judgment and knowledge—they differentiate the divine from the merely human, granting ultimate supremacy to God alone. Not until adolescence and the advent of abstract reasoning do children begin to understand God in terms of "infinite knowledge" and being "without limits."

Children's developing conceptions of God have been studied using a variety of methods. Children have been asked to describe God, or to draw pictures of God, or the house that God lives in. In general, the studies suggest that major cognitive shifts occur across childhood. For example, Dimitris Pnevmatikos (2002) asked first- through fifth-grade Catholic and Greek Orthodox children living in Luxembourg to draw the house where God lives. He found a tendency for first- and second-graders to draw real houses or churches on Earth, sometimes next door to their own homes. Many third-graders, however, located the buildings in clouds, suggesting a more heavenly neighborhood. With increasing age, material buildings became less frequent in the drawings, which began to include symbolic elements, including heaven's gates, angels, and planets. Not until fourth grade did a very few children, perhaps on the threshold of adolescent abstract reasoning, begin to depict God as coexisting with qualities such as goodness, love, peace, and so on, rather than as residing in tangible structures.

On the other hand, some developmentalists have argued that the differences between younger and older children's views of God, or even between children's and adults', are not as robust or dramatic as once believed and depend greatly on the demands of the task used to elicit those views. Some studies have found evidence that under certain circumstances, adults are prone to anthropomorphize God, much as children do. In one such study, adults of several faith traditions in the United States and India were told a story in which a boy was swimming in a swift and rocky river. His leg became caught between two rocks, and he began to struggle and pray. Although God (or Vishnu, Shiva, Brahman, or Krishna, depending on the adult's faith) was answering another prayer in another part of the world when the boy started praying, before long God responded by pushing one of the rocks so the boy could get his leg out. The boy then struggled to the riverbank and fell over exhausted (Barrett, 2001).

When asked to interpret the story, most adults reported that God had been busy answering another prayer and attended to the drowning boy as soon as business allowed. Attributing to God such qualities as limited at-

declines and is replaced by social perspective-taking. Table 13.4 shows all six stages, and gives greater details on the first three, which we discuss below. (In Chapter 14, we will discuss moral development in adolescence and evaluate Kohlberg's view as a whole.)

Kohlberg's method for studying moral reasoning was to present children with stories about people faced with dilemmas involving the value of human life and property, people's obligations to each other, and the meaning of laws and rules. In the manner of Piaget's clinical interview technique, after reading the story, Kohlberg would ask the child for his or her opinion about how the protagonist should behave in response to the dilemma and would then probe for the reasoning behind the opinion. Kohlberg's (1969) most famous story is the "Heinz dilemma":

In Europe, a woman was near death from cancer. One drug might save her, a form of radium that a druggist in the same town had recently discovered. The druggist was charging $2,000, ten times what the drug cost him to make. The sick woman's husband, Heinz, went to everyone he knew to borrow the money, but he could get together only about half of what it cost. He told the druggist that his wife was dying

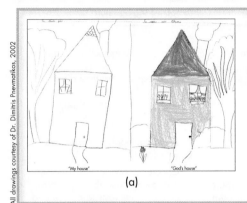

(a)

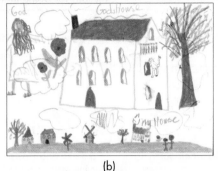

(b)

(b)

All drawings courtesy of Dr. Dimitris Pnevmatikos, 2002

(a, b) Young children's drawings of the house where God lives often depict real houses, (c) whereas older children's drawings link God's house to abstract ideas such as "goodness," "love," and "peace."

tention suggests that adults, like children, are quite capable of anthropomorphizing God. (Interestingly, when God was replaced in the story by a space alien named Mog, who had godlike properties, most adults believed that Mog could handle both problems simultaneously.) The discrepancy between the findings that in some situations adults will anthropomorphize God but in others will describe God as infinite and without limits suggests that adults' conceptions of God are complex, and depend at least in part on the context of reasoning.

Yet another challenge to the idea of a dramatic shift in conceptions of God comes from evidence that very young children, like adults, are capable of distinguishing between merely human knowledge and abilities and the infi-

nite knowledge and power associated with God. Using a version of the "false-belief task" (see Chapter 8, p. 290), Justin Barrett and his colleagues showed 3- to 6-year-old children a closed cracker box which, when opened, revealed rocks. The children were asked what their mother, in another room, would think was in the closed box if she were to come in and see it on the table. Consistent with much of the theories-of-mind research, the youngest children replied "rocks," not appreciating that their mother could have a different point of view, whereas the 5- and 6-year-olds replied "crackers." However, when asked what God would think was in the box, children of all ages were equally likely to say "rocks." Thus, the 5- and 6-year-olds seemed to under-

stand that a "God's-eye view" is much different, and less limited, than their mother's.

Evidence that children's and adults' understanding of God may not be as different as once supposed suggests that anthropomorphic and abstract conceptions of God are not mutually exclusive but interact, and remain relevant to the ways in which individuals try to make sense of the divine.

and asked him to sell it cheaper or let him pay later. But the druggist said no. The husband got desperate and broke into the man's store to steal the drug for his wife. Should the husband have done that? Why? (p. 379)

In Kohlberg's theory of moral development, individuals who are at the *preconventional level* see right and wrong in terms of external consequences to the individual for following or not following the rules. This level comprises stages 1 and 2.

Stage 1, *heteronomous morality,* coincides with the end of the preschool period and the beginning of middle childhood. The social perspective of children at stage 1 is egocentric: In making judgments about right and wrong, they do not recognize the interests of others as distinct from their own. What is right or wrong for them must be right or wrong for others. Moreover, their judgments about the rightness and wrongness of an action are based on its objective outcome, which in this case is how powerful authorities would respond to the action. In stage 1, children might assert that Heinz must not steal the medicine because he will be put in jail.

Stage 2, *instrumental morality,* ordinarily is reached at around the age of 7 or 8, with a shift in children's social perspective: Children can now recognize that different people have different perspectives and interests, and that these may conflict

table **13.4**

Kohlberg's Six Moral Stages

Level and Stage	What Is Right	Reasons for Doing Right	Social Perspective
Level I—Preconventional			
Stage 1—Heteronomous morality	• Adherence to rules backed by punishment • Obedience for its own sake • Avoidance of physical damage to persons and property	• Avoidance of punishment • Superior power of authorities	Egocentric perspective: doesn't consider the interests of others or recognize that they differ from one's own. Actions are considered in terms of physical consequences, not psychological consequences for others. Confusion of authority's perspective with one's own
Stage 2—Instrumental morality	• Following rules when doing so is in one's immediate interest • Acting to meet one's own interests and needs and letting others do the same • Fairness, seen as an equal exchange	• To serve one's own needs or interests in a world where other people have their own interests	Concrete individualistic perspective: aware that all people have their own interests to pursue and these interests conflict, so that right is relative
Level II—Conventional			
Stage 3—Good-child morality	• Living up to what is expected by people close to you • Having good motives, and showing concern about others • Keeping mutual relationships by such means as trust, loyalty, respect, and gratitude	• The need to be a good person in one's own eyes and those of others • Caring for others • Belief in the Golden Rule • Desire to maintain rules and authority that support stereotypical good behavior	Perspective of an individual in relationships with other individuals: aware of shared feelings, agreements, and expectations. Ability to relate points of view through the Golden Rule
Stage 4—Law-and-order morality	• Upholding the law	• To keep the institution going as a whole	Perspective of an individual in relation to the social group
Level III—Postconventional, or Principled			
Stage 5—Social-contract reasoning	• Being aware that people hold a variety of values and opinions	• A sense of obligation to law because of one's social contract to act for the welfare of the group	Prosocial perspective: perspective of a rational individual aware of others' values and rights
Stage 6—Universal ethical principles	• Following self-chosen ethical principles	• A belief in the validity of universal moral principles	Perspective of a moral point of view from which social arrangements derive

Source: Adapted from Kohlberg, 1976.

with their own. Consequently, they believe that what is morally right is highly individualistic; that is, it depends on the specific perspective and situation of the person who is dealing with the moral issue. In keeping with this *concrete individualistic* social perspective, morality is seen as serving one's immediate interests and needs and letting others do the same. Similarly, fairness is understood in the context of an exchange system, of giving as much as you receive. Kohlberg referred to the moral reasoning of children at this stage as instrumental morality because it assumes that what serves one's own interests is moral. Children at this stage might respond to the Heinz dilemma by saying that Heinz should steal the drug because someday he might have cancer and would want someone to steal it for him.

Stage 2 is the key transition associated with school-age children's ability to get along without adult supervision. Children no longer depend on a strong external source to define right and wrong; instead, their behavior is regulated by reciprocal relations between group members. Sometimes the resulting behaviors are desirable ("I'll help you with your model if you help me with mine"); other times, they are less so ("I won't tell Mom you got detention today if you don't tell her I failed my math quiz"). In either case, this form of thinking allows children to regulate their actions with each other.

At the *conventional level* of moral reasoning, children's focus shifts from external consequences to society's standards and rules. The first phase of this shift occurs in stage 3, *good-child morality*, which children begin to reach around the age of 10 or 11. In this stage, moral judgments are made from the social perspective of *relationships with other individuals*. Children at this stage have come to see shared feelings and agreements, especially with people close to them, as more important than individual self-interest. One child quoted by Kohlberg (1984) said, "If I was Heinz, I would have stolen the drug for my wife. You can't put a price on love, no amount of gifts make love" (p. 629). Stage 3 is often equated with the golden rule (treat others as you wish to be treated), a moral rule of reciprocity found in scriptures in all major religions.

Kohlberg's theory and interview method have been extremely influential in studies of children's moral development, although, as you will see in Chapter 14, some of his work has been criticized as being both narrowly focused on the issue of justice and lacking recognition of cultural differences in moral values and thinking.

Prosocial Moral Reasoning

Prosocial moral reasoning refers to the thinking that is involved in deciding whether to engage in *prosocial behavior,* that is, to share with, help, or take care of other people when doing so may prove costly to oneself (Eisenberg, Spinrad, & Sadovsky, 2006). According to Nancy Eisenberg (1992; Eisenberg & Fabes, 2006; Eisenberg, Eggum, & Edwards, 2010), prosocial moral reasoning goes through stagelike developmental changes similar to those proposed by Kohlberg with regard to moral reasoning.

In her research on prosocial moral reasoning, Eisenberg used story dilemmas that generally included a conflict between immediate self-interest and the interest of others. For example, in one such story, a boy is having a good time playing in his yard and sees a bully hurting another child when no adults are around. The question for children to consider is whether the boy should give up his play and try to help the other child even though he might get bullied himself. In another, the child has to choose between going to a birthday party or stopping to help a child who has injured his leg. The following contrasts between a 5-year-old's and a 10-year-old's response to the latter story illustrate the changes in reasoning typical of early and middle childhood.

> Age 5 years
> Interviewer: What do you think [Eric, the story protagonist] should do?
> Child: Go to the party.
> Interviewer: Why is that?
> Child: Because he doesn't want to be late.
> Interviewer: Why doesn't he want to be late?
> Child: 'Cause then it'd be over.
>
> Age 10 years
> Interviewer: What do you think Eric should do?
> Child: Go get the boy's parents.
> Interviewer: Why do you think he would want to get his parents for him?
> Child: Because he doesn't want him to have a broken leg and he wants him to get to the hospital real fast because he doesn't want him to get a broken leg or anything worse.
> (Eisenberg, 1992, p. 29)

prosocial moral reasoning The thinking that is involved in deciding whether to share with, help, or take care of other people when doing so may prove costly to oneself.

As children acquire more advanced forms of prosocial reasoning, they show higher levels of prosocial behavior, as illustrated by these girls who are participating in their school's annual community service event.

Although many factors are involved in determining the sophistication of children's prosocial moral reasoning, reviews of the large amount of literature on this topic show that as children get older, their reasoning reflects the trend in these two examples. Young children focus on themselves, and their decisions to help others are based on what is to be gained personally. With increasing age, children express more empathy for the person in difficulty and a greater consideration of social norms.

A question of central interest in research on prosocial moral reasoning is how such reasoning relates to real-world prosocial behavior. For example, are children who reason at advanced levels about hypothetical stories more likely to exhibit higher levels of morality in their actual behavior? In an extensive survey of studies on children's prosocial moral reasoning, Nancy Eisenberg and her colleagues (2003) found that higher levels of reasoning are indeed positively correlated with higher levels of prosocial behavior. Studies of cheating, for example, find that children who score at higher levels on tests of prosocial reasoning are less likely to cheat than children who score at lower levels. However, even children with advanced reasoning may sometimes succumb to temptation if it seems that they can get away with it (Alencar, de Oliveira, & Yamamoto, 2008; Subbotsky, 1993). Apparently, there is no guarantee that a person will engage in high levels of prosocial behavior, even though he or she may have the intellectual means to do so.

Social Domain Theory

As you have learned, Freud, Piaget, and Kohlberg all shared the view that young children rely on external consequences and authority in order to determine right and wrong. However, as we indicated in Chapter 9 (see p. 320), research within the social domain perspective has suggested that a relatively strong sense of fairness and others' welfare, as well as an ability to question the legitimacy of authority, may emerge at earlier ages than developmentalists once thought (Turiel, 2010). In this research, often children are presented with stories that create a conflict between authority on the one hand and fairness or others' welfare on the other. For example, children might be told of a situation in which two children are fighting on the school playground. A peer tells the two to stop fighting; however, a teacher says that it is okay for the fight to continue. Researchers find that children as young as 5 or 6 years of age will insist that the peer's position to stop the fight is more legitimate than the teacher's position to allow it to continue (Laupa et al., 1995).

Despite sometimes getting into fights, even young children know that fighting is generally wrong. This suggests that they are able to use concepts of harm and welfare in judging moral behavior.

The priority that children give to the morality of a particular act over the status of the authority figure has been found even in cultures, such as Korea and China, that are assumed to attach great weight to authority (Kim, 1998; Helwig, Yang, Tan, Liu, & Shao, 2011). This suggests that instead of deferring to rules and authority, children rely on concepts of harm and welfare in judging moral behavior. This fact led Elliot Turiel and his colleagues (2010) to conclude that reasoning about moral issues is quite different from reasoning about authority and social conventions.

Consider the following example, in which children from 5 to 11 years of age are presented with two different stories about school rules (Turiel, 1983, p. 62). In one story, the school allows children to take off their clothes when the weather is hot (a social conventional issue); in the other, the school permits children to hit each other (a moral issue). A child in the study gave

this response when asked whether it is appropriate to allow children to remove their clothes:

> Yes, because that is the rule. (*Why can they have that rule?*) If that's what the boss wants to do, he can do that. (*How come?*) Because he's the boss, he is in charge of the school.

On the other hand, the child was much less likely to recognize the principal's authority to dictate whether children can hurt each other:

> No, it is not okay. (*Why not?*) Because that is like making other people unhappy. You can hurt them that way. It hurts other people, hurting is not good.

Over the course of the past several decades, more than 100 studies have supported the claim that children distinguish between the moral domain and the social conventional domain when they judge how people should and should not behave (reviewed in Killen, McGlothin, & Lee-Kim, 2002; Nucci, 2009). Consequently, researchers have begun to look at the development of children's reasoning in the two separate domains. They have found that, while the bases for reasoning are different in the two domains, in both cases the pattern of reasoning develops from more concrete to more abstract.

In the moral domain, research indicates that young children's judgments are based on concepts of harm or welfare, whereas the judgments of older children and adolescents make use of the more abstract concepts of justice and rights. Children of all ages, however, are unlikely to judge moral transgressions, such as hitting or stealing, according to rules, the dictates of authority, or common practices. Hitting, for example, is wrong even if there is no rule against it, even if the school principal says it is okay, and even if hitting is a common behavior in a particular context.

In contrast to judgments in the moral domain, reasoning about social conventions takes into account rules, authority, and custom. However, whereas young children's reasoning about social conventions tends to emphasize social rules, that of older children tends to emphasize more abstract concepts such as social roles and the social order. For example, a young child might argue that it is wrong to call a teacher by her first name because there is a rule against it, but an older child might express concern that the students would begin to treat the teacher as a peer rather than as someone in authority (Turiel, 1983). Over the course of middle childhood, children become increasingly concerned with social group roles and effective group functioning (Killen & Smetana, 2010). As you will discover later in this chapter, age-related changes in reasoning in the social conventional domain influence children's interpretations of peer rejection and social exclusion.

A current controversy among the developmental psychologists who study moral reasoning concerns cultural variations in distinguishing between the moral and social conventional domains. Using culturally appropriate versions of Turiel's stories, researchers have replicated his basic findings in a wide variety of societies (summarized in Turiel, 1998). Other researchers, using slightly different methods to elicit judgments, have concluded that certain issues North Americans tend to see as matters of social convention may in some other cultures tend to be considered moral issues (Shweder et al., 2006). We will discuss the question of cross-cultural variation in this area again in Chapter 14, because most of the relevant data have been collected from adolescents and adults.

Moral Reasoning and Theories of Mind

Yet another way to look at moral reasoning is to ask how it relates to other areas of development. You learned in Chapter 8 that around 4 to 5 years of age, children develop a *theory of mind,* that is, the ability to think about other people's

objective view of responsibility An understanding that responsibility depends on objective consequences alone.

subjective view of responsibility An understanding that responsibility depends on both intentions and consequences.

mental states. Indeed, when judges and juries deliberate a criminal case, they devote a lot of time to understanding the mental state of the accused: Did he or she intend to commit the crime? Was it premeditated? What was the motive? Research indicates that the way that children judge someone's moral behavior may depend on their ability to understand the person's mental state. Bryan Sokol and Michael Chandler (2004) explored this in a series of studies that involved a *Punch and Judy* puppet theater. *Punch and Judy* is a famous slapstick puppet show that can be found at carnivals, amusement parks, and other places frequented by children. If you have ever seen it, you probably remember that Punch and Judy are comically and often literally at each other's throats, each trying unsuccessfully to "off" the other.

Two of the scenarios devised for Sokol and Chandler's studies unfolded as follows.

Scenario 1: Punch and Judy are on stage with two large boxes. One is orange. The other is green, and Punch and Judy are busily filling it with oranges. At some point Punch leaves the stage briefly. While he is gone, Judy trips and falls into the orange-colored box containing the oranges. "Help!" she cries, "I have fallen into the orange box!" Punch rushes on stage and, seeing this as his golden opportunity to be rid of Judy forever, pushes the green box—the one containing oranges—off the edge of the stage.

Scenario 2: Punch and Judy are again on stage with boxes. One is green. The other is white with a large, green number "1" painted on it. Again Punch leaves briefly, and again, in his absence, Judy accidentally falls into one of the boxes—the green-colored box. Shouting for help, she cries, "Check the green one!" This time Punch really and truly tries to rescue Judy. However, misinterpreting her cry to mean that she is in the box with the green "1," he inadvertently pushes the green box—the one that Judy fell into—off the edge in a frenzied effort to reach her in the other box.

Punch and Judy, a famous slapstick puppet show in which the characters are continually trying to kill each other, provides a context for studying the relationship between children's developing theories of mind and the ways that children reason about moral issues. Here, Punch believes that Judy is inside the box of oranges (green) rather than in the orange box and is preparing to shove her off the stage.

When children were asked to rate the "badness" of Punch's behavior in the two scenes, the youngest commonly claim that he behaves more badly in scenario 2 because it ends with Judy being jettisoned off the stage. The children maintain what Sokol and Chandler describe as an **objective view of responsibility**, in that they assess responsibility based on objective consequences alone. Older children and adults, in contrast, demonstrate a **subjective view of responsibility** in that they consider Punch's intentions. They therefore rate the failed attempted murder of scenario 1 much more negatively than the accidental manslaughter of scenario 2.

Thus, with increasing age, children become more competent at interpreting a person's objective behavior in light of the person's subjective mental state. In suggesting that moral deliberations are tied importantly to children's developing theories of mind, Sokol and Chandler offer an alternative explanation for the shift, documented by Piaget and Kohlberg, from children's reliance on external consequences to their reliance on internal motives.

▲ APPLY :: CONNECT :: DISCUSS

Academic integrity is a "hot button" issue on many high school and college campuses. Review your school's definition of academic integrity.

■ To what extent does it emphasize academic integrity as a moral issue rather than a social conventional issue?

■ Do you think middle school children are more or less likely to view cheating as a moral or social conventional issue? Why?

■ Drawing on the theoretical insights of Piaget and Kohlberg, describe how middle schools might encourage the development of academic integrity in their students.

social structures Complex organizations of relationships between individuals.

dominant children In reference to social hierarchies, those children who control "resources" such as toys, play spaces, and decisions about group activities.

Peer Relationships

Once children begin to spend significant amounts of time among their peers, they must learn to create a satisfying place for themselves within the social group. Their greater appreciation of social rules and their increased ability to consider other people's points of view are essential resources for this developmental task. But no matter how sensitive or sophisticated they may be about social relations, there is no guarantee that they will be accepted by other children. In creating a life for themselves among peers, all children must learn to deal with issues of social status, come to terms with the possibility that they may not be liked, and deal with the peer conflicts that inevitably arise.

Peer Relations and Social Status

Whenever a group of children exists over a period of time, a social structure emerges. **Social structures** are complex organizations of relationships among individuals. Developmentalists describe children's social structures in a couple of ways: one focuses on degree of *dominance* (who does and does not hold power over group members); the other focuses on degree of *popularity* (who is liked or disliked).

Dominance As is true for many other species, dominance hierarchies contribute to the functioning of human social groups, including those of children (see Chapter 9, pp. 331–332). Dominance hierarchies are usually established through a repeated pattern of fighting or arguing and then making up (Pellegrini, 2006). Over time, individuals who are skilled at managing the conflict–reconciliation pattern establish dominance within the group (Hawley, Little, & Card, 2007). **Dominant children** are those who control "resources"—toys, play spaces, the determination of group activities, and so forth.

Although dominance hierarchies are evident even in preschool social groups (Pellegrini et al., 2007), there are critical moments in development when children work hard to negotiate their positions with each other. One such moment is the transition between elementary and middle school, when new social groupings are being formed. In a longitudinal study that followed more than 100 students from fifth through seventh grades, Andrew Pellegrini and Jeffrey Long (2002) found that, while bullying is used by elementary and middle school children to influence the dominance hierarchy, its incidence peaks during the sixth grade, the first year of middle school, when children are working to establish dominance in new social groups, and then diminishes significantly during the seventh grade, once the dominance patterns have been fully formed (see the box "Bullies and Their Victims").

Popularity Beyond their relative position in a dominance hierarchy, children acquire social status based on how well they are liked by their peers. The importance of being popular with peers increases substantially during middle childhood

Bullies and Their Victims

IN APRIL OF 1999, TWO TEENAGERS WITH automatic weapons entered their high school, massacred 15 individuals, and then killed themselves. It was widely speculated that they were social outcasts and may have been teased and taunted by their peers. The tragedy at Columbine turned a national spotlight not only on school violence but also on bullies and their victims. There has since been a flood of research directed toward identifying different forms of peer aggression, the factors that contribute to schoolchildren's aggressive behaviors, and the social and emotional consequences of being either the agent or the victim of physical or relational harm (Pellegrini & Long, 2002).

Bullies engage in unprovoked aggression intended to harm, intimidate, and/or dominate individuals who are unable to properly defend themselves because they are physically less strong or psychologically less resilient than their attackers. Bullying can be physical—pushing and hitting, for example—or verbal, as in teasing and name-calling. Children's access to communication technologies—cell phones and the Internet, in particular—creates a whole new world for bullies, who can now intimidate anytime, anywhere, through text messages and various social media such as

Facebook, in a new form of peer aggression known as *cyberbullying* (Tokunaga, 2010).

Because bullying is instrumental, that is, a means of controlling other people and getting one's way, developmentalists consider it a form of *proactive aggression* (Pellegrini et al., 2010). Proactive aggression is distinguished from *reactive aggression*, which is usually impulsive and displayed in response to a perceived threat or provocation (Polman et al., 2007). Research on aggression in middle childhood finds that proactive aggression may even be valued in some peer groups and provide a basis for friendship and group formation among middle school boys (Poulin & Boivin, 2000; Olthof, Goossens, Vermande, Aleva, & van der Meulen, 2011). In the same vein, some researchers argue that bullies often have quite well-developed social skills (Crick & Dodge, 1999; Sutton et al., 1999) and are sometimes among the boys considered to be most popular by their 11- to 12-year-old classmates (Rodkin et al., 2000). Although bullying may have some value in certain middle school peer relations, longitudinal research indicates that it predicts delinquency and violence in adulthood (Bender & Lösel, 2011).

A nationwide survey of schoolchildren conducted by the U.S. Department of Justice

(2007) found several patterns in bullying. As you can see in the table on the next page, boys are more likely than girls to report being threatened with harm and to experience physical forms of aggression such a being shoved or tripped. In contrast, girls are more likely than boys to report relational forms of aggression such as being made fun of or being the subject of rumors. Furthermore, the study found that bullying is reported more often by children from rural communities than by those from urban or suburban communities; and reports of bullying are highest among sixth-graders (the youngest group sampled for this study), and then drop off dramatically between seventh and eighth grade.

A bully will often repeatedly target the same child in his or her attacks, and a victimized child is often attacked by more than one bully. In middle childhood, victims of chronic bullying develop reputations among their peers as the kids most often teased, bullied, and "picked on" (Goodman et al., 2001). *Peer victimization* is the term used by developmentalists to describe the experiences of children who are chronically harassed, teased, and bullied at school. Victimized children often have a variety of social difficulties in addition to the mistreatment they receive directly from their peers. Some of these difficulties may predate the bullying and, in fact, may even play a part in eliciting it. In particular, a host of studies conducted in several North American, European, and Asian countries find that children who are bullied tend to lose their temper easily, have difficulty regulating their attention, and act in immature and dependent ways (Garner & Hinton, 2010; Tom, Schwartz, Chang, Farver, & Xu, 2010). The psychological consequences of peer victimization can be tragic and long-lasting. Depression, self-harm, and suicidal behavior have all been implicated as possible effects of persistent bullying (Undheim & Sund, 2011). Peer victimization decreases from the middle school years through adolescence not only because bullying decreases but also because children learn to ignore, avoid, and/or

Gideon Mendel/Corbis

Anna Hassan, a teacher at a large, inner-city school in London, England, deals with a playground bullying incident. Because children in England do not change schools during middle childhood, they do not go through the sixth-grade bullying peak observed in countries that transition children from elementary to middle schools.

(LaFontana & Cillessen, 2010), a fact that has led researchers to address a number of questions. Who are the popular children? Who are the outcast or excluded children? What effect does having a particular peer status have on a child's development? Researchers who study the relative social status of group members usually

Percentage of students ages 12–18 who reported being bullied at school, by types of bullying, and selected student and school characteristics: School year 2006–2007

Student or school characteristic	Were made fun of, called names, or insulted	Had rumors spread about them	Were threatened with harm	Were pushed, shoved, tripped, or spit on	Were made to do things they did not want to do	Were purposely excluded from activities	Suffered purposeful destruction of property
Total	21.0	18.1	5.8	11.0	4.1	5.2	4.2
Sex							
Male	20.3	13.5	6.0	12.2	4.8	4.6	4.0
Female	21.7	22.8	5.6	9.7	3.4	5.8	4.4
Grade							
6th	31.2	21.3	7.0	17.6	5.4	7.4	5.2
7th	27.6	20.2	7.4	15.8	4.1	7.7	6.0
8th	25.1	19.7	6.9	14.2	3.6	5.4	4.6
9th	20.3	18.1	4.6	11.4	5.1	4.5	3.5
10th	17.7	15.0	5.8	8.6	4.6	4.6	3.4
11th	15.3	18.7	4.9	6.5	4.2	3.9	4.4
12th	12.1	14.1	4.3	4.1	2.1	3.5	2.4
Urbanicity							
Urban	20.0	15.5	5.2	9.2	3.6	4.9	4.2
Suburban	21.1	17.4	5.7	11.2	4.1	5.0	4.0
Rural	22.1	24.1	7.0	13.1	5.1	6.3	4.9

Source: U.S. Department of Justice, 2007

retaliate against their aggressors (Pellegrini & Long, 2003; Smith & Monks, 2008).

The longitudinal research on bullies and victims has important implications for the timing and the content of prevention and intervention efforts. It would seem that the early elementary school years are a ripe time to introduce prevention measures that help children respond to bullying behaviors in ways that discourage further bullying. Intervention efforts, on the other hand, may be most effective if applied during the major social transition from primary to secondary schools (Goodman et al., 2001; Pellegrini et al., 2010). With the understanding that a major function of bullying is to establish status and relationships in the peer group, some researchers have suggested that schools devise ways to help children foster more varied and closer peer relationships as they move from the socially more intimate context of elementary school to the larger, hard-to-navigate social scene of secondary school.

The usual stereotype about bullies and dominance hierarchies is that they belong to the world of boys. However, as shown in the table and mentioned above, research calls this bias into question. Whereas boys may tend to engage in direct, physical aggression such as hitting, kicking, and pushing, girls often practice *relational aggression,* actions that threaten the relationships and social standing of their peers (Simmons, 2002). Common forms of relational aggression include making mean and derogatory comments, spreading rumors, or gossiping in ways intended to tarnish a peer's reputation (Crick, Ostrov, & Kawabata, 2007). Nicki Crick and her colleagues found that relational aggression, like more familiar forms of bullying, peaks during the sixth and seventh grades. It also seems to be used as a way to raise one's status within the peer system. Thus, girls who are particularly well-practiced in the art of relational aggression tend to be among the most popular. They have been called *alpha girls* in tribute to their position at the top of the dominance hierarchy. Crick and her colleagues suggest that relational aggression can be at least as damaging as more direct forms of aggression and should be taken just as seriously (Murray-Close, Ostrov, & Crick, 2007).

begin in one of two ways. Using a *nomination procedure,* they may ask children to name their friends or to name children whom they would like to sit near, play with, or work with. Using a *rating procedure,* they may ask children to rank every child in the group according to a specific criterion, such as popularity within the group

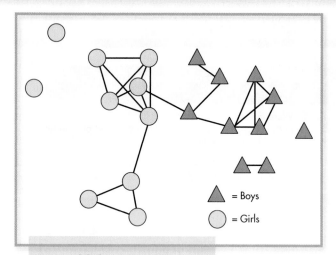

FIGURE 13.2 This sociogram shows the relationships among a group of fifth-grade boys and girls. Notice that the one boy who has a friendship with a girl has a friendship with two other boys but is not part of the larger group of boys, whereas the girl in this friendship is part of a group of girls. Two girls and one boy are social isolates. (Adapted from Gronlund, 1959.)

▲ = Boys

○ = Girls

or desirability as a friend or as a teammate in sports. Data obtained through these techniques can then be used to construct *sociograms*, graphic representations of each child's relationship to all others in the group (Figure 13.2).

As you can imagine, there has been an enormous amount of research on children's social status and its implications for development. What follows is a summary of that work, grouped according to the four main *popularity statuses* that have been identified (Asher & Coie, 1990; Ladd, 1999; Rubin, Bukowski, & Parker, 2006a).

Popular Children. *Popular children* are those who receive the highest numbers of positive nominations, or the highest rankings, from their peers. In general, popular children tend to be rated as more physically attractive than children with other statuses (Boyatzis et al., 1998; Langlois, 1986), and they seem more skilled at initiating and maintaining positive relationships. Kenneth Rubin and his colleagues comment that when popular children attempt to enter a group, "It is as if they ask themselves, 'What's going on?' and then, 'How can I fit in?'" They are also good at compromising and negotiating. Overall, their behavior appears to be socially competent (Rubin, Bukowski, & Parker, 2006a).

Rejected Children. *Rejected children* are those who receive few positive nominations, or receive low rankings, from their peers. They are actively disliked. Studies conducted in the United States, the Netherlands, and Korea find that some children are rejected because they are shy and withdrawn (Parke et al., 1997; Shin, 2007). These children are often aware of their social failure, an awareness that makes them lonelier and more distressed about their social relationships (Asher, Rose, & Gabriel, 2001, Crick & Ladd, 1993). The most common reason for rejection, however, is aggressive behavior; children quite naturally do not like to be around others who behave unpleasantly or hurt them (Dodge et al., 2003). Aggressive rejected children overestimate their social skills and competence and underestimate how much their peers dislike them (Bellmore & Cillessen, 2006; Hymel et al., 2002). They are also more likely to misinterpret various innocuous behaviors by peers (joking remarks, accidental bumping) as deliberate and hostile and to retaliate.

Once children are rejected, they may acquire a reputation as being someone that no one likes and may have a difficult time gaining acceptance by their peer group even if their behavior changes. Shelley Hymel and her colleagues found that when negative opinions about a child become general in a group, the child's reputation ("He is always hitting"; "She never gives anyone else a turn") can become self-perpetuating (Hymel et al., 1990). These researchers described a number of cases in which a peer group's expectations caused the members to interpret a child's behavior as aggressive or unfriendly even when, by objective standards, it was not. Such biased interpretations make the rejected child's task of winning acceptance more difficult and may even evoke the very behaviors (grabbing, hitting, tattling, or crying) that led to the child's being rejected in the first place.

Rejected children experience difficulties that extend beyond the classroom into everyday life. They show higher levels of delinquency, substance abuse, and psychological disturbances compared with children who are accepted by their peers. Not surprisingly, they are almost twice as likely to be arrested as juvenile delinquents (Kupersmidt et al., 2004).

Peer rejection is not only emotionally painful but is also associated with a number of difficulties that can extend well into the future, including delinquency, substance abuse, and psychological disturbances.

Neglected Children. *Neglected children* are those who receive few nominations of any kind. These children seem to be ignored by their peers rather than disliked. Neglected children, like rejected children, are less sociable than their peers, but they are neither aggressive nor overly shy and appear less concerned about their social status. A study conducted in Holland found that neglected children are more likely than rejected children to improve their social status among their classmates over the course of the school year (Cillessen et al., 1992). Neglected children also perform better academically than rejected children, are more compliant in school, and are better liked by their teachers (Wentzel & Asher, 1995).

Controversial Children. As the label suggests, *controversial children* are those who receive both positive and negative nominations. Controversial children tend to behave even more aggressively than rejected children. However, they compensate for their aggression by joking about it or by using other social and cognitive skills to keep their social partners from becoming angry enough to break off the relationship (Newcomb, Bukowski, & Pattee, 1993). Children who engage in high levels of relational aggression often generate a mixture of liking and dislike in their peers (Cillessen & Mayeux, 2004; Rose, Swenson, & Carlson, 2004). Like neglected children, controversial children tend not to be particularly distressed by their relative lack of social success. The reason may be that such children are usually liked by at least one other child—and this may be sufficient to prevent loneliness. As we discuss below, chronically friendless children are at risk for a variety of psychosocial problems (Ladd & Troop-Gordon, 2003).

Competition and Cooperation Among Peers

Spending significant time with one's peers creates conditions for both competition and cooperation, facets of social life that bear importantly on children's relationships with others. As you will see below, the extent to which children are competitive or cooperative in their interactions, and the effects of such interactions on peer relationships, depend on both the contexts and cultures in which they occur.

The Role of Context A classic series of studies by Muzafer and Carolyn Sherif (1956) provides the best evidence to date about the role of context in fostering cooperation and competition in children's social groups. In the most famous of these studies, 11-year-old boys, who were from similar backgrounds but were all strangers to one another, were divided into two groups and brought to two separate summer camps in Robbers Cave State Park in Oklahoma. To ensure that the boys at each encampment formed a cohesive group, the adults arranged for them to encounter problems they could solve only by cooperating. They provided the ingredients for each day's dinner, for example, but left it to the boys themselves to prepare and apportion the food. By the end of the week, friendships had formed and leaders had emerged within each group. Each group had adopted a name: the *Rattlers* and the *Eagles*.

When it was clear that both groups had formed a stable pattern of interactions, the adults let each group know about the other. The two groups soon expressed a keen desire to compete against each other, and the adults arranged for a tournament between the two, with prizes for the winners. On the first day of competition, the Eagles lost a tug-of-war with the Rattlers. Stung by their defeat, they burned the Rattlers' flag. In retaliation, the Rattlers seized the Eagles' flag. Scuffling and name-calling ensued. After 5 days in which hostility escalated, the experimenters took steps to reverse it by introducing a series of problems requiring cooperation between the groups. For example, they arranged for the food delivery truck to get stuck in mud (imagine kids at summer camp without food!). When efforts to push the truck failed, the boys came up with the idea of using their tug-of-war rope to pull the truck out, resulting in what the Sherifs (1956) described as "jubilation over the common success" (p. 323). After the two groups had banded together to solve several other problems requiring cooperation, the boys' opinions of each other changed significantly. Mutual respect largely replaced hostility, and several of the boys formed intergroup friendships.

As developmentalists interested in peer-group relations, the Sherifs intentionally manipulated the contexts of children's interactions in ways that encouraged competitive or cooperative behavior. But as a moment's reflection will no doubt reveal, such context manipulations by adults are far from unusual in children's lives. Take your own educational experiences as an example. If you attended school in a Western culture, it is likely that you were part of educational practices that foster interpersonal comparisons and competition in which children who show themselves better than their peers are publicly praised and rewarded: Their papers and tests are showcased on classroom bulletin boards; they make honor roll; and their parents display bumper stickers proclaiming their academic excellence.

In the face of growing criticism of competition in U.S. classrooms, some educators have made efforts to manipulate the contexts of children's schooling through *cooperative learning programs.* These programs, which focus on students' working together on projects, sharing information, studying together for tests, and developing respect for each other's particular strengths, are meant to foster children's appreciation for their peers' successes as well as their own. In a review of research on cooperative learning, Barry Schneider (2000) found evidence that when children care about each other's learning, they do better in school, engage in more prosocial behavior, and show improved relations with teachers and peers. It has been suggested that cooperative learning is particularly beneficial in classrooms where students have diverse cultural origins or ability levels (Klinger et al., 1998).

The Sherifs' classic experiment and the research on cooperative learning environments carry an important lesson. Cooperation and competition are not fixed characteristics of individuals or of groups but are heavily influenced by the context in which they occur. The research also carries an important but controversial message, namely, that competition is detrimental to peer group relationships, whereas cooperation nurtures relationships and children's sense of belonging. This message has been called into question, however, by research documenting cultural differences in the extent to which competition is valued and rewarded (Schneider et al., 2006).

The Role of Culture Most studies of cultural differences in children's tendencies to behave competitively or cooperatively with peers involve bringing children together to play games that have been specifically designed to distinguish between children's use of competitive or cooperative game strategies. In one such example, two children play a board game in which they move tokens toward a goal. In some instances, the player who reaches the goal first gets a toy as a prize. In other instances, one player is given a toy before the game begins and the children are told that if the child who was given the toy loses the game, the experimenter will take the toy away, and neither child will have a prize. Playing such games, children can, for example, play competitively, trying to maximize their own "wins" at the other child's expense and even choosing to compete when the only consequence for winning is to see the other player lose a toy. Alternatively, children can play cooperatively, allowing their opponents to win when there are no consequences for their own losses.

Using such experimentally designed games, researchers find that North American children tend to adopt competitive strategies, whereas children from Asia, Latin America, and other cultures that emphasize interdependence and the well-being of the group over individual success tend to adopt cooperative strategies (Kagan & Madsen, 1971; Shapira & Madsen, 1969; Domino, 1992).

At present there is no overarching explanation for which cultural factors in particular foster cooperation over competition. One leading possibility is that societies that value interdependence over independence also foster collaboration over competition (Kagitçibasi, 2003). However, a study of more than 1,000 preadolescent seventh-graders in Canada, Costa Rica, Cuba, and Spain suggests a more complicated picture. In this study, Barry Schneider and his colleagues (Schneider et al., 2006) reasoned that a cultural emphasis on interdependence or independence would tend to be reflected at the individual level in children's *basic social goals,* and that these goals would influence the extent to which children were inclined to be

Schools are important sources of cooperative and competitive experiences with peers.

Pacific Learning, Inc.

competitive in peer interactions. The researchers divided goals into three types, and to assess how strong each type was for the children, they had them fill out a questionnaire indicating the extent to which they agreed or disagreed with particular statements, such as:

1. *Ego-oriented goals*—"I feel really successful when I can do better than my friends."

2. *Task-oriented goals*—"I feel really successful when I keep practicing hard."

3. *Cooperation goals*—"I feel really successful when my friends and I help each other do our best."

The researchers also distinguished between two forms of competition, which they assessed through a second questionnaire.

1. *Hypercompetitiveness* (the desire to win at any cost as a means of maintaining feelings of self-worth, often with manifestations of aggressiveness)— "[Friend's name] and I often compare our school marks to see who did better, and he [she] gets upset if I do better in our tests or assignments."

2. *Nonhostile social comparison* (friendly competition with little emotional investment in who wins)—"[Friend's name] and I often play sports or games against each other; we see who's better, but we don't really care who wins."

As shown in Figure 13.3, there was much more hypercompetitiveness in the friendships of Spanish and Canadian children than there was in the friendships of the Costa Rican and Cuban children. The researchers also found significant gender differences, with boys of all the cultures scoring significantly higher than girls in hypercompetitiveness. On the other hand, there were no significant cultural differences in nonhostile social comparison. As expected, competitive behavior correlated strongly with children's social goals. Across all four cultures, children with high ego orientation also tended to be more hypercompetitive and less cooperative. Importantly, the researchers found significant cultural differences in the effects of hypercompetition on children's relationships. In particular, whereas friendly competition seemed to enhance the closeness of Latin American boys, hypercompetition correlated with

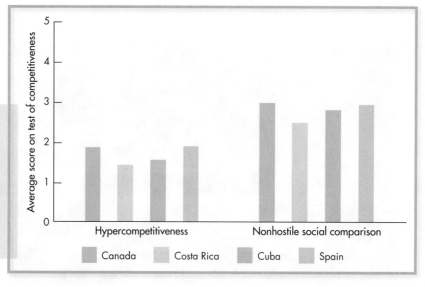

FIGURE 13.3 Hypercompetitiveness—that is, the desire to win at any cost—is significantly more common in the friendships of Canadian and Spanish children than in the friendships of Costa Rican and Cuban children. In contrast, nonhostile social comparison—that is, friendly competition—is not significantly different across the four cultures. (Adapted from Schneider et al., 2006.)

friendship termination. In the case of Canadian boys, a moderate amount of hyper-competition was associated with closer relationships, but higher levels threatened friendship bonds.

In short, this research suggests that certain kinds of competition among children are common across cultures and are not detrimental to peer relationships. It also suggests that even hypercompetitiveness may not necessarily be detrimental, depending in part on the culture in which it occurs.

Relations Between Boys and Girls

During middle childhood, children of all cultures spend a great deal of time in sexually segregated groups (Pellegrini & Long, 2003). Studies in the United States have found that when children are 6 years of age, roughly 68 percent choose a child of the same sex for a "best friend"; by the time children are age 12, the figure has grown to about 90 percent (Graham et al., 1998), prompting Eleanor Maccoby to propose that there are "two cultures of childhood" (Maccoby, 1998, p. 32). As shown in Figure 13.4, similar age differences have been found in non–Western cultures as well.

According to Maccoby, the tendency to aggregate with peers of the same sex strengthens throughout middle childhood because of gender differences in activity preferences. In particular, the *male-style play* preferred by boys includes high levels of physical activity, such as horseplay and play fighting, whereas the *female-style play* preferred by girls includes more cooperative and prosocial forms of play, such as clapping and jump-rope games.

As children increasingly play with same-sex peers, they amplify each other's gender-typed behavior, further socializing gender-typed activity preferences. Maccoby points out, however, that these two styles of play can be moderated depending on the extent of gender differentiation in the culture. That is, gender-typed play styles may be more subtle in children growing up in cultures that make few distinctions between males and females in terms of work, activities, and status, but more evident in children in cultures that draw strict lines around

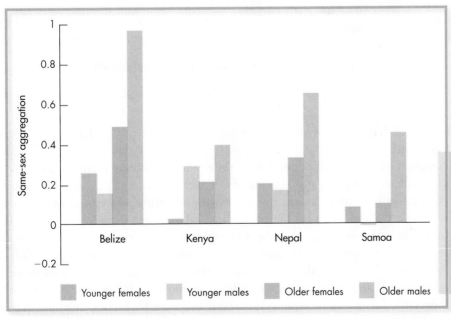

FIGURE 13.4 In many cultures throughout the world, the tendency to aggregate with peers of the same sex, first evident in early childhood, increases greatly during middle childhood, perhaps because boys' and girls' different preferences for styles of play becomes much more pronounced. (Adapted from Maccoby, 1998.)

In the Field Gender Politics on the Playground

Name:	Marjorie Goodwin
Education:	B.A. in Spanish (junior year in Spain), Lake Erie College; Ph.D. in anthropology, University of Pennsylvania
Current Position:	Professor of anthropology, University of California, Los Angeles
Career Objectives:	Study the culture and development of girls in the contexts of their relationships with each other and their position in society

MARJORIE GOODWIN, WHO DOES RESEARCH ON language, gender, and children's social organization, is taking notes during lunchtime at an elementary school in Southern California. The children are gulping down their food in order to rush off to play. They understand that whichever group is first to occupy a particular area—the soccer field, the jungle gym, the basketball courts—is the group allowed to use the space. But the competition for space isn't overwhelming; this is no free-for-all. Although girls might argue over who gets the hopscotch area first, and boys might quarrel over the basketball court, there are traditions about which groups gain access to different play areas. Research on children's play (Thorne, 1993)—and probably your own personal memories of your elementary school days—indicate that boys and girls occupy different territories on elementary school playgrounds. Boys control large spaces intended for team sports. They occupy the grassy soccer fields, baseball diamonds, and basketball courts. In contrast, the space controlled by girls is only a small portion of that controlled by boys, and tends to be cemented and closer to the school building.

But as Goodwin is about to discover, today is different. A group of fifth-grade girls who like to play soccer is beginning to challenge the idea that the playing fields are an exclusively male space (Goodwin, 2002). Today these girls have

Marjorie Goodwin.
Courtesy of Marjorie Goodwin

rushed through lunch in order to beat the boys to the soccer field. Once they have secured the space, they begin to organize their teams. Soon, however, two boys arrive, demanding their right to the field.

Amy: We have it today.
Paulo: We play soccer every day, okay?
Mark: It's more boys than girls.
Amy: So? Your point?
Mark: This is our field.

Amy: It's not your field. Did you pay for it? No. Your name is not written on this land.
Kathy: Mine is. K-A-T-H-Y [as she writes her name].

The boys move away, but return moments later with the male playground aide who confronts the girls:

Male aide: Girls. Go somewhere else! The boys are coming to play and you took over their field. I think I'm gonna go and tell the vice principal. . . . When the boys are coming out here to play soccer, okay? You have no right to kick them off the field. Listen, I've seen it happen more than once. . . . You can go over there and play soccer [pointing to the jungle gym area]. You girls can go anywhere to do what you're doing.
Laura: Why can't they go anywhere?

male and female behavior (see the box "In the Field: Gender Politics on the Playground").

Although middle childhood is a time when children increasingly seek out same-sex companions, the boundaries between boys and girls are far from impermeable. Boys and girls do interact with each other, sometimes in very amusing ways. Calling a boy on the telephone and leaving a pseudoromantic message on the family answering machine is one favorite border-crossing technique. Boys sometimes engage in more direct border crossing, such as pulling pigtails and snapping girls' bras. In addition, contact between boys and girls may be more frequent, open, and "normal" in the neighborhood than it is in the school setting, especially if there is a shortage of potential same-sex playmates. After being passed

Male aide: They can't go on the blacktop and play soccer. Somebody's gonna fall and hurt their knee.
Kathy: Well neither can we!

In her analysis of the dispute presented above, Goodwin argued that in negotiating access to the territory, the girls resisted and challenged not only the arguments of the boys ("Your name is not written on this land") and those of the male aide ("Why can't they go anywhere?") but also the very social structure of the playground. Historically the field had indeed belonged to boys. In all probability, this had been the case for generations of children attending the school.

True to his word, the aide summoned the vice principal, who, after hearing from all parties, formulated the problem in terms of exclusion, asking, "At school do we exclude anyone?" The girls responded with a long list of exclusionary practices typical of the boys' behavior: "They hog the ball"; "Boys are always team captains"; "They always pick boys first and then girls last." Apparently taking the girls' complaints to heart, the following year the school administrators instituted a rotating system for using the fields that allowed boys and girls equal access. Yet, despite the changes, Goodwin found that "boys continued to favor passing the ball to other boys; when they did pass to girls they did it with such force that girls often stopped playing. In addition, during the sixth grade, girls had to contend with boys grabbing their breasts in the midst of the game." The playground aides responsible for supervising the children's activities often looked on the boys' rejection of the girls on the playing field as part of a natural order. One even suggested that it prepared girls for their "appropriate" and "eventual" adult sex roles as sports spectators rather than participants.

Traditions by definition resist change. However, Goodwin's research indicates that some girls on some playgrounds are staging microrevolutions, challenging the status quo, and working to define a new moral order on their own terms. In addition to

At many schools, including this one in the United Kingdom, girls tend to play on small, paved places close to the school building, whereas boys tend to occupy large fields.

Photofusion Picture Library/Alamy

providing insight into transformation in cross-gender relations, Goodwin's research also challenges the idea, proposed by some, that girls, compared with boys, are less concerned about matters of justice and fairness, and instead tend to be more cooperative and focused on preserving harmony and cohesion (Gilligan, 1982; Maccoby, 1998; see Chapter 14). Goodwin argues that a narrow view of girls and women as nurturing and noncompetitive prevents us all—developmental scientists included—from seeing and studying girls and women as wielders of power and instruments of change (Goodwin, 2011). A broader view, Goodwin contends, permits the understanding that "we can not only obtain a better picture of children's worlds but also attempt to implement equity policies which promote children's fundamental democratic right to be spared oppression and humiliation in school" (Goodwin, 2006).

in the school playground by a boy who didn't even look at her, a sixth-grade girl confided to a researcher standing next to her, "He's one of my best friends." At the researcher's expression of puzzlement, the girl clarified, "We're friends in our neighborhood and at church, but in school we pretend not to know each other so we don't get teased" (Thorne, 1993, p. 50). However, these are exceptions to a fairly firm rule, and interactions with, or even proximity to, a member of the other sex can result in elaborate shows of having been contaminated and needing to engage in "cleansing rituals" to get rid of the "girl cooties" or the "boy germs." Alan Sroufe and his colleagues (1993) report that a boy at a day camp was seen leaving the girls' tent (where he had gone to retrieve his radio) and was bombarded with taunts from his peers like "Uuh, he's with the girls!" and "Did you

During middle childhood, children of all cultures begin to voluntarily spend a great deal of time in sexually segregated groups.

Yellow Dog Productions/Getty Images

kiss anyone, Charlie?" He had to chase and hit each taunter in turn to reestablish his place in the group.

From their own and others' observations of children in a variety of contexts in this same day camp, Sroufe and his coworkers abstracted a number of rules under which school-age children find it permissible to have contact with members of the other sex (Table 13.5). The researchers found that most children observed the rules for cross-sex contact; those who did not were generally unpopular with the other children, and also were judged by their counselors to be less socially competent than their peers. On occasion, the rules could be broken with social approval, as when the rule-breaking took the form of "raids" into enemy territory, accompanied by a lot of excitement. From time to time, for example, the boys would run through an area where the girls were playing and try to get the girls to chase them, or a couple of girls, shrieking with laughter, would threaten to kiss a boy.

table 13.5

Knowing the Rules: In What Circumstances Is It Permissible to Have Contact with the Other Gender in Middle Childhood?

Rule:	The contact is accidental.
Example:	You're not looking where you are going and you bump into someone.
Rule:	The contact is incidental.
Example:	You go to get some lemonade and wait while two children of the other gender get some. (There should be no conversation.)
Rule:	The contact is in the guise of some clear and necessary purpose.
Example:	You may say, "Pass the lemonade," to persons of the other gender at the next table. No interest in them is expressed.
Rule:	An adult compels you to have contact.
Example:	"Go get that map from X and Y and bring it to me."
Rule:	You are accompanied by someone of your own gender.
Example:	Two girls may talk to two boys, though physical closeness with your own partner must be maintained and intimacy with the others is disallowed.
Rule:	The interaction or contact is accompanied by disavowal.
Example:	You say someone is ugly or hurl some other insult or (more commonly for boys) push or throw something at the person as you pass by.

Source: Sroufe et al., 1993.

Friendship: A Special Type of Relationship

Harry Stack Sullivan (1953), an American psychiatrist, proposed that the formation of close, one-on-one relationships, which he called *chumships,* is key to the development of social skills and competencies during middle childhood. In Sullivan's words:

> If you will look very closely at one of your children when he finally finds a chum ... you will discover something very different in the relationship—namely, that your child begins to develop a new sensitivity to what matters to another person. And this is not in the sense of "what should I do to get what I want," but instead "what should I do to contribute to the happiness or to support the prestige and feeling of worth-whileness of my chum." So far as I have been ever able to discover, nothing remotely like this appears before the age of, say, 8½, and sometimes it appears decidedly later (pp. 245–246).

Sullivan believed that children's tendency to pick out one or a few other children with whom they feel this kind of special affinity is the childhood precursor of the need for interpersonal intimacy that will be called love when it is encountered again in adolescence. He further claimed that the failure to form such friendships in childhood creates a social deficit that is difficult to remedy later.

Sullivan's general view of the importance of friendships is widely shared by developmentalists who find that children with best friends score higher on measures of self-esteem and positive feelings of self-worth, whereas children with no friends tend to be timid, overly sensitive, and at risk for later psychological problems (Rubin, Bukowski, & Parker, 2006a; Ladd & Troop-Gordon, 2003). Expanding on Sullivan's early work, researchers have identified several developmental functions of friendships (Hartup, 1992; Parker et al., 2006). These functions include providing children with:

1. Contexts in which to develop many basic social skills, including communication, cooperation, and the ability to resolve conflicts;

2. Information about themselves, others, and the world;

3. Companionship and fun that relieve the stress of everyday life;

4. Models of intimate relationships characterized by helping, caring, and trust.

Given the importance of friendships for children's feelings of well-being and social success, developmentalists are naturally interested in understanding the processes through which children form and maintain close relationships with their peers.

Making Friends The old saying that "birds of a feather flock together" applies especially well to children's friendship choices. Children tend to pick as friends who are similar to themselves in age, ethnicity, sex, SES, and general skill level in various activities. Their friends are also likely to feel the same way about school as they do (children who enjoy school and get good grades tend to have friends who similarly enjoy school and get good grades) and to be interested in the same sports, music, movies, books, and so on (Rose & Asher, 2000). But other than noticing that certain peers are similar to themselves in appearance and background and have compatible interests, how, exactly, do children become close friends?

In a classic study of friendship formation, John Gottman (1983) arranged for pairs of children of the same age to meet and play together in one of the children's homes for three sessions within the space of a month. Each session was videotaped. The children, who were strangers to each other

Children tend to pick friends who are similar to themselves in sex, age, race, and general skill level.

at the start of the study, ranged from 3 to 9 years in age. In order to find out if the children became friends during the experiment, Gottman asked the host mothers to fill out a questionnaire at the end of the sessions that probed the strength and quality of the children's relationship. He then analyzed the tapes of the play sessions, comparing children who became friends with those who did not. Five aspects of the children's social interaction appeared to distinguish pairs who became friendly from those who did not.

1. *Common-ground activity.* The children who became friends were those who quickly found something they could do together. In addition, they explored their similarities and differences.

2. *Clear communication.* Children who became friends were likely to listen to each other, request clarification when they did not understand what the other said, and speak in ways that were relevant to the task at hand.

3. *Exchange of information.* Children who became friends both asked their partners for relevant information and provided such information to them.

4. *Resolution of conflicts.* Children who became friends gave good reasons when they disagreed with each other, and they were able to bring conflicts to a quick resolution.

5. *Reciprocity.* Children who became friends were likely to respond to their partner's positive behaviors with an appropriate positive contribution of their own.

Gottman's study sheds considerable light on how children become friends. The next question concerns how children maintain their friendships over time. Research indicates that during middle childhood, only about one-half of all close friendships are stable over the course of a school year (Bowker, 2004). What characteristics distinguish between friendships that endure over time and those that fall apart? And is the ability to keep friends any more or less important than the ability to make friends?

Keeping Friends

It makes sense that the reasons for one's initial choice of friends would have a bearing on whether the relationship is likely to endure. Indeed, a key characteristic of a lasting relationship is the degree to which two new friends are similar to each other at the start of their friendship. Developmentalists find that similarity promotes equality in the relationship, positive reinforcement, and cooperative interactions—all factors associated with friendship stability (Poulin & Chan, 2010). Thus, friend-keeping is enhanced when children share similar behavioral characteristics, even when those characteristics are maladaptive. For example, the stability of shy, withdrawn children's friendships is as high as that of nonshy peers *if* their friends are also shy and withdrawn (Rubin et al., 2006b).

The role of behavioral similarity in friendship stability is further illuminated in a short-term longitudinal study conducted by Wendy Ellis and Lynne Zarbatany (2007) that involved more than 600 children in fifth through eighth grades. Over the course of the first 3 months of a school year, the researchers collected information on the children's friendships, as well as on their behavioral characteristics, such as engaging in overt aggression (harming through physical or verbal actions such as hitting or threatening), engaging in relational aggression (harming by disrupting social relationships or self-esteem), and being bullied by peers. They found that behavioral similarity tended to predict friendship stability and that some of the most unstable relationships were those in which the children were behaviorally mismatched. For example, children's relationships were more stable when both friends scored either high or low on a measure of relational aggression than when they were mismatched on this measure. The same was true when the characteristic was that of being bullied. New friendships between girls who had not been bullied by peers and those who had been bullied tended to falter quickly. The researchers speculated that girls face negative social consequences for hanging out with unpopular (bullied) peers and may abandon these new friends at the first sign that their relationship with them may be diminishing their own social status. In contrast, when both girls were victims of bullying, the friendship was relatively stable, probably because the girls could provide each other with much-needed comfort and support with little risk of further drop in social status.

Importantly, the one exception Ellis and Zarbatany found to the pattern involved children who were high in measures of overt aggression. That is, when an aggressive child became friends with another aggressive child, the relationship was no more likely to endure than when the aggressive child became friends with a nonaggressive child. Although aggressive children had no trouble making new friends, they were at a distinct disadvantage in holding on to the friendships for any length of time.

A Cognitive-Developmental Approach

In addition to becoming skilled at making and keeping friends, during middle childhood, children develop a more sophisticated understanding of their friendships and the unique needs, motives, and goals of their friends. According to Robert Selman and his colleagues, this more complex understanding, which is a crucial ingredient for successful relationships, arises as a consequence of the higher levels of *perspective-taking* and declining *egocentrism* associated with the transition from preoperational to concrete-operational thinking (see Chapter 11, pp. 401–402). Based on extensive studies of children with and without friendship problems, Selman (1997) proposed that friendship involves three general spheres of influence that are affected by the development of perspective-taking: friendship understanding, friendship skills, and friendship valuing.

Friendship understanding refers to the child's developing knowledge of the nature of friendship. Selman describes children as young philosophers who have theories about how to make friends, sustain relationships, and manage conflicts. For example, an immature friendship philosophy, typical of preschoolers, is "a friend is someone who gives me toys." Somewhat more mature, and typical of the early elementary school years, is the idea that "a friend is someone who always does what you want." With increasing interpersonal understanding and decreasing egocentrism, children will eventually come to define friendships with reference to balancing, and even cherishing, different perspectives as a means of ensuring both personal autonomy and intimacy in relationships. (We discuss this aspect further in Chapter 15.)

The second influence on friendships, *friendship skills,* refers to the specific action strategies that children use in developing their relationships. Like friendship understanding, friendship skills become increasingly sophisticated over time. The action strategies used by preschoolers are often impulsive and focused on getting immediate needs met. In a conflict over a toy, for example, there may be grabbing and crying. In just a few years, however, children develop a capacity to take turns. Later, they manage conflicts by using complex strategies such as compromise, with each side agreeing to give up something in order to achieve a goal.

The final influence, *friendship valuing,* is the child's ability to make a personal commitment to a relationship and be emotionally invested and motivated to maintain it. As Selman (1997) observes, "to know friendship and practice friendship one must

social repair mechanisms Strategies that allow friends to remain friends even when serious differences temporarily drive them apart.

coregulation A form of indirect social control in which parents and children cooperate to reinforce the children's understandings of right and wrong, what is safe and unsafe, when they are not under direct adult control.

be involved in the process of being a good friend—one must take the risk of investing oneself in meaningful friendship experiences" (p. 44). To see the development of friendship valuing, consider a girl who breaks a play date with a close friend because a new acquaintance invited her to go to the circus. If the girl is in the early years of middle childhood, she may defend her decision in a way that is dismissive of the relationship, saying something like "Well, I love the circus." An older child would be more likely to consider her action in light of the relationship and the needs of her friend, reasoning "Alex's feelings may be hurt if I go to the circus with Janine, so I'll invite her for a sleepover this weekend." Selman argues that friendship valuing depends on children's increasing capacity to take responsibility for their own contributions to the friendship, and to see the personal consequences of their actions for the relationship.

Overall, middle childhood is a time during which children acquire a variety of resources for managing their relationships. This is particularly apparent when friends argue and fight. Whereas younger children rely on coercion to resolve their conflicts, as children progress through middle childhood they become aware of several alternatives. In a major review of research on children's conflict resolutions, Danielle Popp and her colleagues (2008) found that, in middle childhood, children are more aware of the importance of **social repair mechanisms**, strategies that allow friends to remain friends even when serious differences temporarily drive them apart. Examples of social repair mechanisms include negotiation, disengaging before a disagreement escalates into a fight, staying nearby after a fight to smooth things over, and minimizing the importance of a conflict once it is over. Each of these strategies increases the likelihood that when the conflict is over, the children will still be friends. Social repair mechanisms take on importance in middle childhood because of children's changed social circumstances. When no caregiver is present, children must settle conflicts on their own.

▲ APPLY :: CONNECT :: DISCUSS

Refer to the story of Cassie and Becca, at the beginning of the chapter. Using concepts presented in this section, explain what might have motivated Becca and Kelly's behavior toward Cassie.

The Influence of Parents

In addition to monumental shifts in the nature and influence of peer relations and friendships, middle childhood is a time of significant change in the relationship between children and their parents. As you will see, the new patterns of interaction that emerge in the family are felt also in other social arenas, including children's peer relationships.

Changing Expectations

As children grow older, the nature of parent–child interactions changes in a number of ways. For one thing, there is an overall decrease in overt expressions of affection (Collins et al., 1997). Parents no longer act as if their children are adorable; they expect them to behave themselves and perform appropriately. The children, for their part, are often embarrassed when their parents do show them open affection in public because they do not want to be "treated like a baby." For another, children are less likely to use coercive behaviors such as whining, yelling, or hitting; now they argue with their parents and point out their parents' inconsistencies.

In addition, parents are more severe with older children and are more critical of the mistakes they make (Maccoby, 1984). Two related factors combine to account for this change in parental standards and behavior as children enter middle childhood. First, parents all over the world believe that the children should now be more capable and responsible. Second, the strategies parents adopt to influence their children's good behavior and correct their bad behavior change as children's competence increases (Lamb & Lewis, 2005).

The precise ages at which parents expect children to be able to display behavioral competence in different areas vary across cultures. Jacqueline Goodnow and her colleagues asked Japanese, American, Australian, and Lebanese-born Australian mothers at what approximate age—before 4 years, between 4 and 6 years, or after 6 years—they expected children to be capable of each of 38 kinds of behavior (Goodnow et al., 1984). They found that Japanese mothers expected emotional maturity, compliance, and ritual forms of politeness from their children at an earlier age than mothers in the other three groups expected them from theirs. The American and Australian mothers, in contrast, expected their children to develop social skills and the ability to assert themselves verbally at a relatively early age. Finally, the Lebanese Australian mothers were distinctive in their willingness to let their children attain the needed competencies in their own good time, and their developmental timetables were usually later than those of the other groups. Despite cultural variations in the ages at which the various competencies were expected to be achieved, all the parents expected their children to master these basic competencies sometime during middle childhood.

For parents in economically developed countries, their children's school achievement is a major focus. Parents worry about how involved they should become in their child's schoolwork, what they should do if their child has academic problems, and how they should deal with any behavior problems their child may exhibit in school. Other matters of concern to parents during middle childhood include the extent to which they should monitor their children's social life and whether they should require their children to do house chores and, if so, what standards of performance to expect of them and whether to pay them (Goodnow, 1998). In less developed countries, where a family's survival often depends on putting children to work as early as possible, parents may be more likely to worry instead about their children's ability to take care of younger kin in the absence of adult supervision and to help with important economic tasks such as caring for livestock or tending a garden (Weisner et al., 2005).

As children grow older and are increasingly held responsible for themselves, parents attempt to influence their behavior by reasoning with them, appealing to their self-esteem ("You wouldn't do anything that stupid") or to their sense of humor, and arousing their sense of guilt. In many societies, when school-age children break rules, their parents are less likely to spank them than to deprive them of privileges or ground them (Lamb et al., 1999).

In sum, parents increasingly share their control over their children's lives with the children themselves (Collins & van Dulmen, 2006). Maccoby (1984) termed this sharing of responsibility **coregulation**. Coregulation is built on parent–child cooperation. It requires that parents prepare their children to act responsibly when adults are not present. Parents do this by reinforcing their children's understandings of right and wrong, what is safe and unsafe, and when they need to come to adults for help. For coregulation to succeed, children must be willing to inform their parents of their whereabouts, their activities, and their problems.

Although parent–child relationships change dramatically during the middle childhood years, parents continue to play an important and influential role in their children's lives and development.

This girl is being taught by her grandmother to weave in the tradition of her Padaung culture of Thailand. Given children's importance to the economy of Padaung families and communities, it is likely that parents, grandparents, and other adults raise their expectations for work performance when their children reach middle childhood.

Parents and Peers

While family life and peer relationships sometimes appear to be two separate social worlds, they are linked in several important ways. As we explained in our discussion of parents' roles in constructing children's *ecological niches* (see Chapter 2, pp. 71–72), parents have considerable power in determining the contexts in which their children spend their time. They choose, for example, the neighborhood in which they live and where their children go to school (and, hence, who their children have as potential playmates and schoolmates). They also provide or deny their children opportunities to interact with other children in specific activities during nonschool hours (Parke & Ladd, 1992), although this form of managing their children's social contacts with peers begins to decline during middle childhood (Schneider, 2000). The influence of parents on children's peer relations is also apparent in the way parents monitor where their children are, whom they are with, and what they are doing (Pettit et al., 2007). Children whose parents monitor them are more likely to engage in antisocial behavior and, in turn, to face rejection by their peers (see Ladd, 1999, for a review of this evidence).

In addition to these very direct ways of organizing their children's social lives, parents affect peer relationships indirectly by providing working models of the ways people should interact with each other. There is ample evidence that interactional patterns established between parents and children influence peer relations (Rubin et al., 2003). Aggressive behavior is a good case in point. As you saw in Chapter 9, parents may unwittingly encourage their children to behave aggressively when they themselves engage in coercive, power-assertive modes of socialization. Since aggressive behavior in children is associated with rejection by their peers, a number of researchers have focused on *coercive family interaction patterns* as a possible source of low social status in middle childhood (Granic, Hollenstein, Dishion, & Patterson, 2003).

In one such study, Thomas Dishion (1990) collected information on the social status of over 200 boys ages 9 and 10 by interviewing their teachers and classmates. Through interviews with the parents and the boys themselves, as well as home observations, he also obtained information about the children's family socialization patterns and their behavior in the family setting. Dishion found that the boys who were exposed to more coercive family experiences at home were the ones most likely to be rejected by their peers at school. These boys not only were more aggressive with their peers but also behaved badly in the classroom. Although boys from lower-income homes were more likely to fall within the rejected category, Dishion's data showed that socioeconomic class was not a direct cause of lower peer status or aggressive behavior. Rather, in accord with findings discussed in Chapter 10 (pp. 358–360), he found that poverty affected social status and behavior indirectly by increasing the general level of stress within the family. When parents coped well enough with the pressures of poverty to treat their children in a noncoercive way, the children were less likely to have low social status among their peers. These results were replicated and supplemented in a study conducted in the People's Republic of China (Chen & Rubin, 1994).

Children who have been maltreated are also at risk for peer rejection (Bolger & Patterson, 2001). In an effort to understand why, Kerry Bolger and Charlotte Patterson (2001) followed two groups of children across the elementary and middle school years. One group included a representative sample of more than 100 maltreated children; the other included an equal number of nonmaltreated children. Bolger and Patterson's results showed that children who are chronically maltreated, through either abuse or neglect, are at greater risk for becoming aggressive, which, as we have seen, places children at risk for peer rejection. In other words, maltreatment per se does not cause peer rejection. Instead, as shown in Figure 13.5, children's aggression mediates between maltreatment and rejection.

Alan Sroufe and his colleagues (Sroufe et al., 1999a, p. 258) have argued that children's relations with parents and peers are linked by a:

> . . . cascade effect wherein early family relationships provide the necessary support for effectively engaging the world of peers, which, in turn, provides the foundation for deeper and more extensive and complex peer relationships. Each phase supports the unfolding of subsequent capacities.

Whether or not this developmental cascade actually takes place depends critically on the stability of the environmental conditions and the extent to which they permit or disrupt parent–child interaction patterns. One very common example of such instability is the case of divorce.

Divorce

Between 40 and 50 percent of all marriages in the United States end in divorce, affecting more than 1 million children annually (U.S. Census Bureau, 2011; Centers for Disease Control and Prevention, 2006b). While the divorce rate in the United States is by far the highest in the world, the rate of divorce is rising rapidly in many places throughout the world, including in Asian, Eastern European, and other nations undergoing major social and economic transitions associated with globalization (Antonov & Medkov, 2007; Becker, 2007).

A range of problems has been associated with divorce. Children whose parents have divorced are twice as likely as children whose parents are still together to have problems in school, to act out, to be depressed and unhappy, to have lower self-esteem, and to be less socially responsible and competent (Amato, 2010; Sun & Li, 2002).

Divorce leads to several changes in children's life experiences that might be expected to contribute to these negative outcomes. First, divorce often brings changes in children's economic status. In the United States, the average income of single-parent families created by divorce or separation falls by 37 percent within 4 months of the breakup (U.S. Census Bureau, 2002). Moreover, nearly 25 percent of the custodial parents (more than 80 percent of whom are mothers) who are due child support receive no money at all from their former spouses, and roughly 30 percent receive only a portion of what is owed to them (Grail, 2009). As a consequence, about 25 percent of all custodial parents in 2007 found themselves living below the poverty threshold—twice the rate for the overall population. The changes in economic status often mean that after their parents divorce, children have to move away from their friends and neighbors to poorer neighborhoods with different schools and lower-quality child care. These changes are difficult for children to deal with.

Second, parents raising children alone are trying to accomplish by themselves what is usually a demanding job for two adults. Both fathers and mothers who have sole custody of their children complain that they are overburdened by the necessity of juggling child care and household and financial responsibilities by themselves (Amato, 2006). Divorce forces many parents to enter the workforce at the same time that they and their children are adapting to a new family configuration. In the United States, approximately 80 percent of custodial parents are in the labor force; most of them work full-time (Grail, 2009). Because of the many demands on their parents' time, children of divorce not only receive less guidance and assistance but also tend to lose out on important kinds of social and intellectual stimulation (Hetherington, Collins, & Laursen, 1999).

In studying the consequences of divorce, some developmentalists employ a *crisis model* that views divorce as a time-limited disturbance to which parents and children gradually adjust. Recently, however, developmentalists have created a *chronic*

FIGURE 13.5 Researchers have established that children who are chronically maltreated are often rejected by their peers. In their study, Bolger and Patterson found no direct relationship between maltreatment and peer rejection, as indicated by the broken orange arrow in this diagram. However, they found a significant relationship between maltreatment and aggressive behavior, and between aggressive behavior and peer rejection, as indicated by solid blue arrows, and thus concluded that maltreatment is an indirect cause of rejection that acts through the influence of aggressive behavior. (Adapted from Bolger & Patterson, 2001.)

strain model, which recognizes that ongoing hardships, including financial insecurity and continuing conflict between parents, may affect children's lives and adjustment for many years to come. Paul Amato (2006) has attempted to capture the insights of both models—representing both the short-term trauma associated with divorce and its long-term effects—with the *divorce-stress-adjustment perspective.* This more inclusive model views marital dissolution not as a discrete event but as a complex process that varies depending on the specific stressors and protective factors influencing the short- and long-term adjustment of the family as a whole and of its individual members.

Although it makes intuitive sense that the losses associated with the breakup of a family are the cause of the various behavioral and social problems exhibited by children of divorce, a number of studies that collected data about children before their parents divorced have cast doubt on this idea.

An alternative to the divorce-stress-adjustment perspective, in which child problems begin with the divorce itself, is the *selection perspective.* According to this model, most of the negative effects of family disruption may be accounted for by problems that predate the divorce (Sun & Li, 2008). Several large longitudinal studies indicate that long-standing dysfunctional family patterns and inherent characteristics of parents, such as antisocial personality traits, create unhealthy environments for children, thereby contributing to their adjustment problems (Hetherington, 2006; Sun & Li, 2008).

One effect of high rates of divorce is high rates of remarriage, resulting in "blended families." This photograph includes children from their parents' previous marriages who were blended into a new family.

Interestingly, the similarity in divorce rates among twin pairs is higher for monozygotic twins than for dizygotic twins, suggesting that a genetic component may be at work (D'Onofrio et al., 2007). That is, children from divorced families might be more troubled than those from intact families because they have inherited predispositions from their troubled parents that place them at greater risk for a variety of problems, including divorce (Vangelisti, Reis, & Fitzpatrick, 2002). According to these studies, the divorce itself has negligible effects on children's adjustments.

There is, of course, a range of individual differences in how children adjust to divorce. In his comprehensive review of research in the area, Amato identified factors that have been found to affect adjustment (Amato, 2010; Amato & Hohmann-Marriott, 2007). Factors that facilitate adjustment include active coping skills such as seeking social support; support from peers; and access to therapeutic interventions, including school-based support programs. Factors that impede adjustment include avoidant coping mechanisms, a tendency toward self-blame, and feelings of lack of control.

Amato, among others, realizes that research on the consequences of divorce fuels a contentious debate. Some see divorce as a source of a variety of social ills and child problems. Others, however, see it as a benign force that allows parents to seek happiness in new relationships and provides an escape for children otherwise trapped in dysfunctional families. On the strength of several decades of research, Amato concludes that "divorce benefits some individuals, leads others to experience temporary decrements in well-being that improve over time, and forces others on a downward cycle from which they might never fully recover" (Amato, 2000, p. 1285). Given the high divorce rates in the United States and the rising ones in other countries, continued research on the consequences of divorce remains a high priority.

▲ APPLY :: CONNECT :: DISCUSS

This section has presented evidence that coercive parenting practices are associated with the development of aggressive behavior and peer rejection in children. Review the previous section on peer relationships and suggest how parents might interact with children in ways that promote their ability to form successful friendships.

Reconsidering Middle Childhood

Sigmund Freud described the years of middle childhood as a period of *latency,* during which the sexual instincts that drive development lay dormant and the child experiences relative stability. Freud's idea that not much happens during middle childhood no doubt accounts for the lack of attention he devoted to the period. As documented in this and the previous two chapters, however, a host of significant changes occur between the ages of 6 and 12. Surveys of the world's cultures make it clear that adults everywhere assign 6- and 7-year-olds to a new social category, characterized by new responsibilities and by expectations for higher levels of independence, autonomy, and self-control.

Another universal characteristic of middle childhood is the rise of the peer group as a major context for development. For the first time, children must define their status within a group of relative equals without the intervention of adults. In many cultures, interactions with peers become coordinated, with games governed by rules serving as substitutes for adult control. The experience of negotiating these interactions and comparing themselves with peers contributes to children's mastery of the social conventions and moral rules that regulate their communities. Peer interactions also contribute to changing conceptions of self, providing crucial contexts within which children arrive at a new, more complex, and global sense of themselves.

The new cognitive capacities that develop at this time are less obvious than changes in the social domain but are no less important. As you saw in Chapters 11 and 12, thought processes in middle childhood become more logical, deliberate, and consistent. Children become more capable of thinking through actions and their consequences; they are able to engage in concentrated acts of deliberate learning in the absence of tangible rewards; they keep in mind the points of view of other people in a wider variety of contexts; and they learn to moderate their emotional reactions in order to facilitate smooth relations with their parents and their peers. As we have emphasized several times, these cognitive changes must be considered as both cause and effect of the social changes discussed in this chapter.

Least visible are the biological changes that underpin children's apparent new mental capacities and modes of social interaction. The fact that children are bigger, stronger, and better coordinated is obvious enough. But only recently has modern anatomical and neurophysiological research provided evidence of such subtle changes as the proliferation of brain circuitry, changing relations between different kinds of brain-wave activity, and the greatly expanded influence of the brain's frontal lobes. Without such biological changes, the cognitive and social changes we have reviewed would not be possible. By the same token, when children are severely deprived of experience, such biological changes are disrupted.

The existence of a universal pattern of changes associated with middle childhood in no way contradicts the fact that there are significant cultural variations in the particular ways that 6- to 12-year-old children's lives are organized. The beliefs and values of a culture shape and are transmitted through parenting practices and school curricula, as are particular expectations for age-appropriate behavior, duties, and responsibilities. Both interpersonal (family and peers) and institutional (schools) practices contribute to the *niche construction* of middle childhood, and position children for their next developmental step: adolescence.

SUMMARY

A New Sense of Self

- In middle childhood, there is a shift from self-concepts based on limited, concrete characteristics to more abstract, stable conceptions arrived at through social comparison.

- For Erikson, the crisis of middle childhood is that of industry versus inferiority. Positive self-esteem is associated with a sense of self as industrious.

- According to Harter, in middle childhood, self-evaluations become more differentiated, more integrated into an overall sense of self-worth, and more in keeping with judgments made by others. Children measure themselves against an "ideal self."

- High self-esteem may be linked to an authoritative parenting style. However, cross-cultural research suggests a more complicated picture of both self-esteem and the role of parenting practices.

Moral Development

- According to Piaget, in middle childhood there is a shift to autonomous morality, in which judgments of right and wrong are based on people's intentions rather than on the objective consequences of their behavior. Experience with rule-based games makes possible this shift and the emergence of self-governing peer groups.

- Kohlberg proposed six stages of moral reasoning, with children in middle childhood from heteronomous morality, based on authority and objective consequences, to instrumental morality, based on one's own and others' self-interests and equal exchange, and then to good-child morality, characterized by concern about others and their expectations and needs.

- Prosocial moral reasoning also becomes more sophisticated in middle childhood, with children showing more empathy and greater consideration of social norms.

- Social domain theory suggests that even young children distinguish between moral and social conventional domains, basing moral judgments on concepts of harm and welfare, a basis that shifts, over time, to more abstract concepts of justice and rights.

- The shift in moral reasoning from objective consequences to internal motives may be made possible by children's developing theories of mind, especially with respect to their increasing ability to interpret other people's behaviors in light of their mental states.

Peer Relationships

- Whenever a peer group forms, a social structure emerges. These structures are often described in one of two ways:

- In terms of dominance hierarchies, which are often influenced by bullying.

- In terms of relative popularity, with children often falling into one of four popularity statuses—popular, rejected, neglected, or controversial.

- Contexts may promote cooperation or competition in children's interactions. The extent, nature, and effects of competition may be influenced by culture.

- In middle childhood, gender differences in play style increase gender segregation, although the boundaries between boys and girls are far from impermeable.

- Friendship becomes important in middle childhood, and close friendships may contribute to self-esteem, providing models and contexts for developing social skills.

- Children tend to choose friends who are similar to themselves and with whom they interact well.

- Friendship stability is promoted by similarity, including in behavioral characteristics. Overly aggressive children have difficulty maintaining friendships.

- The changes in friendship of middle childhood may be possible because declining egocentrism and increased perspective-taking lead to increases in children's understanding of friendship, friendship skills, and commitment to friendships.

The Influence of Parents

- Parent–child interactions change in middle childhood, with parents expecting their children to display new behavioral competencies and increasingly sharing their control over their children's lives with their children.

- Parents affect their children's peer relationships both directly—by choosing neighborhoods, schools, and activities, and monitoring their children—and indirectly, by providing working models for interactions.

- Children whose parents divorce are more likely than other children to have problems in a range of areas. According to the divorce-stress-adjustment perspective, these problems stem from both the short-term trauma of divorce and its long-term effects. The selection perspective attributes problems not to divorce but to long-standing family patterns and to parents' characteristics that children have inherited.

Reconsidering Middle Childhood

- Around the world, despite considerable cultural variations, the ages of 6 and 7 mark the beginning of new responsibilities and expectations. Closely associated with these changes are the rise of the peer group as a context for development and new cognitive capacities.

Key Terms

industry versus inferiority, p. 466

social comparison, p. 467

self-esteem, p. 468

autonomous morality, p. 472

prosocial moral reasoning, p. 477

objective view of responsibility, p. 480

subjective view of responsibility, p. 480

social structures, p. 481

dominant children, p. 481

social repair mechanisms, p. 496

coregulation, p. 497

Major Milestones

	Physical Domain	Cognitive Domain	Social and Emotional Domain
What Develops...	• Rapid increase in height and weight, changing the requirements for food and sleep. • For boys, increase in muscle tissue, decrease in body fat. • For girls, increase in both muscle tissue and body fat. • Influx of hormones stimulates growth and functioning of reproductive organs. • Significant changes in brain regions associated with impulse control, decision making, and ability to multitask.	• Emergence of new forms of mental operations associated with scientific reasoning abilities. • Increased ability to think hypothetically. • Increase in working memory enables higher-level problem-solving strategies. • Increased decision-making skills. • Increased ability to use reasoning in making moral judgments.	• Compared with emotions in childhood, daily experience of positive emotions decreases and daily experience of negative emotions increases. • Increased ability to regulate emotions. • New bases for friendships, which, ideally, balance intimacy and autonomy needs. • Peer groups provide opportunities for exploring identity possibilities. • Gender-typed behaviors increase. • Increase in parent–child conflict in some but not all domains. • Emergence of a more coherent, stable sense of identity. • Emergence of sexual orientation and ethnic identities.
Sociocultural Contributions and Consequences...	• Access to nutritious food and health care lowers the age of pubertal onset for general populations. • Diets excessively high in fat that result in overweight and obesity may further lower the age of pubertal onset, as in low-income minority populations in the U.S. • Physical changes marking sexual maturity (breast development, facial hair, etc.) affect how peers, parents, and others interact with the child. • Cultural stereotypes regarding ideal body types may negatively impact girls' experience of normal weight gain and contribute to the development of eating disorders. • Some cultures mark pubertal onset with special rites and ceremonies.	• Emergence of various forms of reasoning and problem-solving skills is highly variable across cultures. • Social and emotional aspects of a context can substantially affect decision making. • Cultures vary in the extent to which they support the emergence of different moral standards and values. • Both parent and peer relationships and interaction styles can affect moral development.	• Parental warmth and behavior affect adolescent's developing emotion regulation ability. • Cultural expectations affect gender differences in the regulation and expression of emotion. • Cultural variation in support of developing autonomy. • Cultural differences in support of developing sexual orientation and ethnic-minority identities.

part V

Adolescence

Most of us look back on our adolescence and see it as a special time in our lives—a time that we still associate with intense friendships, dramatic and often embarrassing bodily changes, parents who were as maddening as they were supportive, experimentation with everything from sports and drama to drugs and alcohol, a feeling of freedom derived from such simple things as driving around in a car with friends. For some, adolescence was especially wonderful; for others, it was downright awful. But however we remember it, it is unlikely that any of us feel neutral about those few years that included such momentous events as the onset of reproductive maturity and that first, sexually charged kiss.

Puberty begins around the end of the first decade of life, with a cascade of biochemical events that alters the body's size, shape, and functioning. The most revolutionary of these alterations is the emergence of the ability to produce offspring—new human beings to carry forward the genetic and cultural heritages of the species. This biological fact has profound interpersonal implications. As their reproductive organs reach maturity, boys and girls begin to engage in new forms of social behavior because of emerging sexual attractions.

Although reproductive maturity is the biological signal of adulthood, most societies attempt to delay many social changes associated with adulthood, including marriage and parenting. In the United States and other industrialized countries, a gap of 7 to 9 years typically separates the biological changes of sexual maturity from the social roles that confer adult status. This lengthy period is necessary because it takes young people many years to acquire the knowledge and skills they will need to achieve independence and to contribute to their society. Nonetheless, some societies have only a brief delay between the beginnings of sexual maturity and adulthood (Whiting, Burbank, & Ratner, 1986). These are usually societies in which biological maturity occurs late by Western standards and in which the level of technology is relatively low. In such societies, by the time biological reproduction becomes possible, at about the age of 14 or 15, young people already know how to perform the basic tasks of their culture, such as farming, weaving cloth, preparing food, and caring for children.

In Chapter 14 we examine the advent of biological maturity, including both hormonal processes associated with reproduction and changes in the architecture of the brain that may contribute to adolescent behavior. We also explore the changes in intellectual functioning and moral reasoning that underpin the adolescent's ability to be an effective member of society. Chapter 15 concentrates on aspects of emotional and social life, including new abilities to regulate the intense emotions of adolescence, changing relationships with parents and peers, sexual relationships, and a changing sense of personal identity. We also examine the implications of adolescents' social and emotional development for their health and well-being, and overview recent theories and methods intended to promote positive youth development by establishing ties between adolescents and their communities and cultural institutions. Throughout, we will address the many ways that adolescence is a unique and essential time for establishing advanced ways of thinking and reasoning, healthy social and emotional relationships and identities, and acquiring the tools, practices, and traditions of culture.

Adolescents and Society

Historical Views

Adolescents in Modern Society

Biological Theories of Adolescent Development

G. Stanley Hall

Sigmund Freud

Modern Theories of Biological Development

Puberty

The Growth Spurt

Sexual Development

Brain Development

The Neuro-Hormonal System

The Timing of Puberty

Puberty and Health

Cognitive Development

Piaget's Theory of Formal Operations

Information-Processing Approaches

Sociocultural Approaches

Moral Development

Kohlberg's Theory of Moral Reasoning

Gilligan's Theory of Moral Reasoning

Parent and Peer Contributions to Moral Development

Cultural Variations in Moral Reasoning

The Relation Between Moral Reasoning and Moral Action

Implications

CHAPTER 14

Physical and Cognitive Development in Adolescence

There's all this crap about being accepted into a group and struggling and making an *effort to make friends and not being comfortable about your own self-worth as a human being. You're trying very hard to show everyone what a great person you are, and the best way to do that is if everyone else is drinking therefore they think that's the thing to do, then you might do the same thing to prove to them that you have the same values that they do and therefore you're okay. At the same time, the idea of peer pressure is a lot of bunk. What I heard about peer pressure all the way through school is that someone is going to walk up to me and say* "Here, drink this and you'll be cool." *It wasn't like that at all. You go somewhere and everyone else would be doing it and you'd think,* "Hey, everyone else is doing it and they seem to be having a good time—now why wouldn't I do this?" *In that sense, the preparation of the powers that be, the lessons that they tried to drill into me, they were completely off. They had no idea what we are up against.*

(Lightfoot, 1992, p. 240)

As this 16-year-old's rant about drinking or not drinking suggests, the complex developments of puberty are associated with major changes in the way young people think. New cognitive abilities launch adolescents into a world of complex problem solving, abstract thinking, and decision making that affects everything from their schoolwork to the way they think about themselves—as "cool" or otherwise. At the same time, however, adolescents have a reputation for exercising poor judgment and taking unreasonable risks, sometimes placing their health—and, on occasion, their lives—in great jeopardy.

As you know from previous chapters, the challenges facing individuals at any given period in development, and the challenges facing those who want to study and understand development, are deeply rooted in the views of society at a particular moment in history. So we begin our discussion of the physical and cognitive changes of adolescence by tracing the roots of current conceptions of adolescence. As you will see, many beliefs about adolescence have endured for thousands of years, whereas others relate to the issues and concerns of the modern world. These beliefs reflect the relationship between adolescents and society and influence the efforts of researchers and practitioners who want to understand adolescent development and devise strategies for promoting healthy developmental outcomes.

Adolescents and Society

The relationship between adolescents and society is no less complex than adolescent development itself. One source of this complexity is the fact that adolescents inhabit a gray, transitional area in between childhood and maturity. In some ways,

Michelle D. Bridwell/Photo Edit

Although higher levels of reasoning and problem solving emerge during adolescence, many teens engage in risky behaviors, including smoking cigarettes and drinking.

adolescents are pressed to be responsible, knowledgeable, independent, and adultlike; in other ways, they are encouraged to remain childlike and immature. For example, in some societies, adolescents may be urged to take on certain adult responsibilities but discouraged from mature sexual behavior. Societies guide their children through adolescence in various ways, depending on such factors as cultural beliefs and values and economic structures. However, virtually all societies recognize adolescence as an important transition that requires special attention.

Historical Views

The idea of a transitional period between childhood and adulthood is an ancient one, and many contemporary views of the problems and turmoil of adolescents are strikingly similar to views expressed millennia ago. Literature from the Middle Ages onward is filled with images of young people as passionate, sensual, and impulsive (Kiell, 1959; Violato & Wiley, 1990). In Chaucer's *Canterbury Tales,* for example, young squires are portrayed as seekers of high adventure, willing to take risks in love as well as in battle; Shakespeare's *Romeo and Juliet* depicts what is probably the most famous literary example of a teenage romance and suicide. The Greek philosopher Plato also wrote of the passions and perils of youth when he proposed what may well have been the first formal argument for a minimum drinking age:

[B]oys shall not taste wine at all until they are eighteen years of age . . . fire must not be poured upon fire, whether in the body or in the soul, until they begin to go to work—this is a precaution which has to be taken against the excitableness of youth; afterwards they may taste wine in moderation up to the age of thirty, but while a man is young he should abstain altogether from intoxication and from excess of wine. (*Laws, Book 2*)

Plato's student Aristotle also wrote about youthful passions and impulses and the unfortunate consequences they could lead to. However, he also viewed the period of adolescence as an especially fertile one for the development of new powers of thought, and suggested that individuals are not able to profit from "the education of reason" until they reach puberty.

The notion that adolescence is a period of both peril and promise—of emotional conflict and instability, as well as higher intellectual functioning—persisted into modern times. We will now consider how this notion came to prominence in contemporary societies.

Adolescents in Modern Society

In the late eighteenth and early nineteenth centuries, widespread interest in adolescence was sparked by two trends stemming from industrialization. One trend was increased urbanization and its related problems; the other was increased education.

Because industrialization generated wage-paying job opportunities, a great many young people flocked to the cities. Once in the cities, as child welfare advocates (among others) noted, many of these youths were not only joining the workforce, they were also getting into trouble (Addams, 1910; Kett, 1977). Adolescent drinking, sexual promiscuity, and card playing were identified as major social problems (Mintz, 2004). In response to the rising social problems created by adolescents, efforts were made to provide teenagers with organized services and structured activities that would occupy them during their leisure hours. Jane Addams, a founder of the famous Hull House of Chicago, which provided a wide range of services for the working class, initiated several programs designed specifically to deal with problems of youth—programs that were among the first of their type in United States. The Juvenile Protective Association, for example, was designed to prevent juvenile delinquency and was associated with the campaign that led to the establishment of the nation's first juvenile court (Polikoff, 1999). Addams also spearheaded the creation of the Juvenile Psychopathic Institute for the purpose of determining the degree to which juvenile delinquency is influenced by mental disorders.

Although increased industrialization is thought to have led to an increase in youth problems, it also created demands for more educated workers. Children were staying in school longer to prepare for the ever-increasing number of jobs that were available in the new industrial age. The massive expansion of education that took place during this period meant that high school attendance soared by over 700 percent between 1890 and 1918, and a new high school opened on average every day between 1900 and 1930 (Mintz, 2004). As education for adolescents became more extensive, educators were faced with the need to develop new ways of teaching that were appropriate to adolescents' advanced mental capacities. Likewise, as the adoption of adult roles and responsibilities was extended to the age of 18 or so, a host of new issues arose related to dating, work, and leisure activities. These issues affected family and peer relationships, as well as the young person's identity development.

In contemporary technologically advanced societies, prolonged education and delayed marriage and childbearing have expanded even further the years of transition from childhood to maturity. In the modern world, young people who are adults chronologically often continue to rely on their parents for support, engage in an extended period of identity exploration, and feel unprepared for the roles and responsibilities typically associated with adulthood. Does this description capture how you see yourself? If so, are you experiencing a prolonged adolescence or an entirely new stage of development? If you resist describing yourself as an "adolescent," you are not alone. Partly on the basis of how college students and slightly older young adults feel about themselves, some developmentalists have argued for the existence of a new stage of development. This stage carries the name **emerging adulthood**, which is meant to capture the unique developmental challenges facing many individuals between the ages of 18 and 25 in technologically advanced societies (Arnett, 2007; Kins & Beyers, 2010). Although the term is relatively recent, the idea behind it—that changing social conditions have set the stage for the emergence of a distinctive new period in the life cycle—was suggested decades ago (Keniston, 1963; Parsons, 1963).

Kenneth Keniston, in particular, proposed that the term "youth" be used to describe individuals in their late teens and early 20s who are coming of age in rapidly changing societies (1963). He argued that societies undergoing fast-paced technological change also experience a high degree of social, political, and cultural change as they adapt to these new technologies. Such societies tend to value innovation over tradition. As a consequence, the connections that once bound generations together are weakened: The knowledge and values of the parent generation feel less relevant to their children's interests and concerns. According to Keniston, under such conditions, youth turn to each other, rather than to their elders, to sort out fundamental identity issues. They create their own "youth culture" separate and distinct from the culture of the prior generation. The cultural discontinuity between generations contributes to a number of attitudes and behaviors that Keniston

Jane Addams founded the famous Hull House of Chicago, which provided a variety of programs intended to deal with problems of youth living in the city.

emerging adulthood The name of what some developmentalists propose is a new stage of development facing many individuals between the ages of 18 and 25 in technologically advanced societies.

observed in youth, including their sense of powerlessness to make a personal difference in their societies and their lack of interest and involvement in politics. Regardless of the specific label used to describe the period, it is widely agreed that the economic and social conditions of modern life have prolonged the transition to adulthood for many adolescents (Côté & Bynner, 2008), complicating development in a variety of areas, including family relationships, sexuality and romantic relationships, and the transition from school to work.

Clearly, the development and life experiences of young people are closely anchored to changes taking place in their societies. For just this reason, the scientific study of adolescence has undergone important changes over the course of time. In the section below, we explore theories and research that focus on the biological development of adolescence. We begin with the contributions of two early theorists—G. Stanley Hall and Sigmund Freud—and then turn our attention to the evolutionary and ethological approaches that they helped to inspire.

▲ APPLY :: CONNECT :: DISCUSS

Provide some personal examples of how social and cultural pressures to be both childlike and adultlike affected your adolescence. To what extent might these examples be associated with contemporary social and cultural issues facing adolescents and their families?

Biological Theories of Adolescent Development

In Chapter 1, we explained that early theories of children's development were heavily influenced by Darwin's theory of evolution. In the case of adolescence, this influence is readily apparent in the attention that developmentalists paid to the relationship between adolescent behavior and the survival of the species.

G. Stanley Hall

G. Stanley Hall, the first president of the American Psychological Association and a major figure in the shaping of developmental psychology, was instrumental in promoting the idea that understanding the unique qualities of adolescence was essential to understanding the proper education and counseling of adolescents, as well as to understanding the evolution of the species (Cairns, 1998; Hall, 1904). Two key features of his theory continue to influence modern thinking and research (Arnett & Cravens, 2006; White, 1991).

The more influential feature of Hall's theory is the notion that adolescence is a time of heightened emotionality and oppositions: stratospheric highs and deep depressions, boundless self-confidence and nagging insecurity, astounding generosity and equally astounding selfishness. In Hall's view, adolescence is a time of "storm and stress," attributable to "raging hormones" associated with the biological processes of puberty. Although contemporary research indicates that the relationship between adolescent hormonal levels and emotions is more complex than Hall suggested, there is compelling evidence that the increase in major depression during adolescence is driven at least in part by hormonal changes (Martel, Klump, Nigg, Breedlove, & Sisk, 2009; Hyde, Mazulis, & Abramson, 2008).

The second key feature of Hall's theory that remains influential is the idea that the stage of adolescence is the consequence of evolutionary processes. Consistent with most other theorists of his time, Hall believed that the developing child passes

G. Stanley Hall (1844–1924).

Bettmann/Corbis

through stages that correspond to the evolutionary steps of the species, beginning with the primitive, animal-like stage of infancy, and progressing toward the civilized, mature stage of modern adults. According to Hall, middle childhood corresponds to an ancient period of human evolution when reason, morality, feelings of love toward others, and religion were underdeveloped. He believed that it is only when they reach adolescence that young people go beyond the biologically predetermined past to create new ways of thinking and feeling. As a consequence, Hall believed, adolescence is more flexible and creative than any other period of development. For this reason, Hall asserted (as many others have) that adolescents are literally the future of our species.

Sigmund Freud

You may recall from Chapter 1 (p. 16) that Freud's psychodynamic theory reflects a largely biological position with respect to the sources of development. Freud viewed adolescence as a distinctive stage because it is the time during which human beings become capable of fulfilling the biological imperative to reproduce themselves, and sexual intercourse becomes a major motive of behavior. Accordingly, he considered adolescence to be the beginning of the *genital stage,* the final stage in his theory of psychosexual development.

Like Hall, Freud emphasized both storm and stress and evolutionary processes as major features of the stage. In Freud's theory, the emotional storminess associated with adolescence is the culmination of a psychological struggle among the three components of personality—the id, the ego, and the superego (see Chapter 9, p. 318). As Freud saw it, the upsurge in sexual excitation that accompanies puberty reawakens primitive instincts, increases the power of the id, and upsets the psychological balance achieved during middle childhood. This imbalance produces psychological conflict and erratic behavior. The main developmental task of adolescence is therefore to reestablish the balance of psychological forces by reintegrating them in a new and more mature way that is compatible with the individual's new sexual capacities.

The theoretical perspectives of Hall and Freud have had a lasting impact on developmental science, particularly on the study of the biological and social foundations of adolescence. Although there is currently some dispute regarding the extent to which adolescence is necessarily a period of stress and conflict (Lerner et al., 2011), it is widely accepted that adolescents are especially prone to argue with their parents, engage in risky and rebellious behaviors, experience mood fluctuations, and generally think and act in creative, imaginative ways.

Modern Theories of Biological Development

Modern biological approaches to adolescence emphasize how development is influenced by the evolutionary history of our species. A feature of adolescence that has received a lot of recent attention in this respect is the **growth spurt**, the rapid change in height and weight that marks the onset of puberty and the processes that culiminate in the capacity to sexually reproduce. Interestingly, it seems that human beings are the only primate species that experience a spurt of growth after early childhood (Locke & Bogin, 2006; Leigh, 2001). Figure 14.1 shows the speed of growth from birth to maturity for females in the United States and for captive female chimpanzees (Walker et al., 2006). As you can see, for girls, the *takeoff velocity,* when growth first begins its radical surge, begins at around 7½ years of age (for boys, takeoff velocity is closer to 10½ years of age). In contrast, the speed of growth of the female chimpanzees continues to decline in a relatively straight line over the course of time.

growth spurt A rapid change in height and weight that signals the onset of puberty.

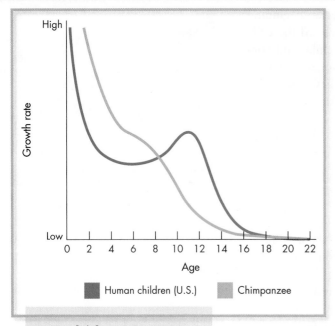

FIGURE 14.1 Compared with other primate species, the human species is markedly delayed in reaching physical maturity, and experiences a spurt of growth during adolescence.

Figure 14.1 illustrates another interesting species difference that has captured the attention of developmentalists: the slow rate of growth of humans relative to that of other primate species (Charnov, 2004). As you can see in the figure, although the speed of growth decreases substantially in both species, it remains dramatically slower in humans than in chimpanzees, until the adolescent growth spurt. Thus, in our species, the onset of puberty and the capacity to reproduce is radically delayed compared with its onset in our evolutionarily closest relatives.

Given that evolution operates to maximize species survival through reproduction, it would seem to follow that the sooner human beings started producing offspring, the better. So why the delay in reaching reproductive maturity? Evolutionary theorists have argued that delayed maturation in humans actually contributes to our reproductive success (see the box on the Pumé foragers for another example of the relationship between maturation and reproductive success). Energy that would be spent on rapid physical development is instead diverted to disease prevention (McDade, 2003) and to other functions that give humans time to develop the complex brain associated with capacities such as language, sophisticated problem solving, and an extraordinary ability to make and use the tools of culture. Moreover, from a biocultural perspective, the phenotype of delayed maturation confers significant reproductive advantages to our species "by allowing the adolescent to learn and practice adult economic, social, and sexual behavior before reproducing" (Bogin, 1999, p. 216).

▲ APPLY :: CONNECT :: DISCUSS

From a biocultural perspective, why might it be advantageous to develop advanced social, economic, and cognitive skills and abilities prior to, rather than after, reaching sexual maturity?

Puberty

Puberty refers to the series of biological developments that transforms individuals from a state of physical immaturity into a state in which they are biologically mature and capable of sexual reproduction. Generally taking 3 to 4 years to complete, puberty begins with a chemical signal from the hypothalamus, which "tells" the pituitary gland to make more growth hormones (Traggiai & Stanhope, 2003; Grumbach & Styne, 2002). These hormones stimulate growth throughout the body, with some of them stimulating the development and functioning of the *gonads,* or ovaries and testes. In the following discussion, we will first look at the physical changes of puberty and will then turn our attention to how adolescents react to these radical changes affecting their bodies.

The Growth Spurt

As noted, one of the first visible signs of puberty is the onset of the growth spurt, during which boys and girls grow more quickly than at any other time since they were babies (Kontulainen et al., 2007). Over the 2 to 3 years that the growth spurt

puberty The series of biological developments that transforms individuals from a state of physical immaturity into one in which they are biologically mature and capable of sexual reproduction.

Early Maturation and Reproductive Success: The Case of the Pumé Foragers

THE OLD SAYING THAT "THE EXCEPTION proves the rule" has very recently become relevant to understanding the adolescent growth spurt and its role in species evolution. In particular, two anthropologists, Karen Kramer and Russell Greaves, recently discovered a dramatic exception to the familiar pattern found in industrialized and developing nations in which physical growth slows considerably during middle childhood and then enters the growth spurt characteristic of pubertal onset, with peak height and weight velocities staggered by a year or two. The pattern doesn't hold for the Pumé, an isolated people living in the forest of southwestern Venezuela. In contrast to the typical pattern, Kramer and Greaves found that Pumé girls continue to grow at a fairly even pace throughout middle childhood and adolescence, with no evidence of entering a growth spurt, and achieve peak height and weight velocities at considerably earlier ages than their Western counterparts do. Their skeletal growth is particularly strong and steady, with peak height velocity beginning several years ahead of both peak weight velocity and the age of the first menstrual period. On average, by the time of her first period, a Pumé girl will have achieved 93 percent of her adult stature and 70 percent of her adult weight.

What might account for these unique patterns of growth among the Pumé? Kramer and Greaves suggest that they are a consequence of evolutionary processes that operate to prepare girls for early childbearing under conditions of nutritional stress and short life expectancy. Pumé children grow up, mature, and begin to have children of their own under conditions of severe nutritional stress (they eat reasonably well during the dry season but struggle not to starve during the wet season). One

of the most startling indicators of the Pumé's harsh developmental circumstances is their life expectancy—a scant 30 years, with almost half of all Pumé children dying before reaching puberty (Coale & Demeny, 1983). On average, Pumé girls begin bearing children when they are 15.5 years old. Such early childbearing is common when life expectancy is short (Migliano, Vinicius, & Lahr, 2007). But while we might simply expect an earlier growth spurt, such an energy-expensive developmental pattern would be extremely risky for the Pumé; girls who entered the growth spurt during the nutrition-poor rainy season would likely suffer delayed maturation, limiting their reproductive success. On the other hand, if the physical body, especially the important pelvic structures of the skeletal system, is underdeveloped, early childbirth can have dire, life-threatening consequences for both mother and baby. Consequently, girls who are genetically disposed not to an adolescent growth spurt but to strong

and steady skeletal growth throughout middle childhood and adolescence, well in advance of the first period, are physically better prepared for early childbearing under conditions of vastly fluctuating food availability. (Unlike weight, height is considerably less sensitive to nutritional fluctuations.) In general, at the time her first baby is born, a Pumé girl will have achieved 97 percent of her adult height and 84 percent of her adult weight. From a biocultural perspective, girls who develop according to these patterns can be expected to have more surviving offspring who, in turn, will pass on to subsequent generations the propensity for early maturation and reproductive success.

The unique patterns of Pumé reproductive maturation stand as an example of the remarkable ability of the human species to adapt to vastly different and swiftly changing environments. They also illustrate the essential role of developmental variation to the overall success of our species (see Chapter 2).

Growing up under especially harsh developmental conditions, including severe nutritional stress, Pumé girls typically begin having children around 15.5 years of age. Their physical growth is unique: Rather than undergoing a growth spurt during adolescence, the bodies of Pumé girls grow steadily throughout middle childhood and adolescence.

Russell D. Greaves, Ph.D.

lasts, up to 45 percent of skeletal growth takes place, and up to 37 percent of total bone mass may be accumulated (Whiting et al., 2004; Ballabriga, 2000). A boy may grow as much as 9 inches taller, and a girl, as much as 6 to 7 inches taller. Although adolescents continue to grow throughout puberty, they reach 98 percent of their adult height by the end of their growth spurt (Sinclair & Dangerfield, 1998).

The rate of growth during adolescence varies for different parts of the body, prompting James Tanner (1978) to quip, "A boy stops growing out of his trousers (at least in length) a year before he stops growing out of his jackets" (p. 69). As a result of asynchronous growth patterns, many adolescents develop a gangly appearance and become awkward in their movements.

Changes in physical size are accompanied by changes in overall shape. Girls develop breasts, and their hips expand. Boys undergo a marked increase in muscle development and shoulder width, and a decrease in body fat, giving them a more muscular and angular appearance than that of girls, who continue to have a higher ratio of fat to muscle and hence continue to have a rounder, softer look (Bogin, 1999).

Most boys not only *appear* to be stronger than girls at the end of puberty, they *are* stronger. Before puberty, boys and girls of similar size differ little in strength. But by the end of puberty, boys can exert more force per ounce of muscle than girls of the same size. Boys can also exercise for longer periods. They develop relatively larger hearts and lungs, which give them higher blood pressure when their heart muscles contract, a lower resting heart rate, and a greater capacity for carrying oxygen in the blood (oxygen in the blood neutralizes the chemicals that lead to fatigue during physical exercise) (Weisfeld & Janisse, 2005). In general, the aerobic power associated with the cardiovascular and muscular systems peaks earlier for females, but is of greater magnitude in males (Geithner et al., 2004).

The physiological differences between males and females may help to explain why males have traditionally been the warriors, hunters, and heavy laborers throughout human history. They also help to explain why most superior male athletes can outperform superior female athletes. In some important respects, however, females exhibit greater physical prowess than males do. On average, they are healthier, live longer, and are better able to tolerate long-term stress (Weisfeld & Janisse, 2005).

Sexual Development

The sexual development of many species, including our own, involves two distinctive components. The first component is the maturation of **primary sex characteristics**, also known as the reproductive organs or gonads, which consist of the egg-producing ovaries, in the case of females, and the sperm-producing testes, in the case of males. The second component of sexual development is the emergence of **secondary sex characteristics**—outward traits, such as breasts and facial hair, that distinguish males from females in a species but are not part of the reproductive system. Let's take a closer look at these two critical components of sexual maturation.

Primary Sex Characteristics During puberty, the sexual organs grow and become functional. Essential to reproduction, they provide not only the raw material (eggs/ova and sperm) for constructing new life but also produce hormones—primarily *estrogen* and *testosterone*—that play a fundamental role in the individual's development. While estrogen is generally associated with females, and testosterone with males, both are present in the two sexes and both are present before the onset of puberty, although in different amounts.

During puberty, testosterone in boys increases to 18 times the level it was in middle childhood, stimulating the testes to manufacture sperm cells and the prostate to produce semen, the fluid that carries the sperm cells (Bogin, 1999). A boy's first ejaculation, also known as **semenarche**, typically occurs spontaneously during sleep and is often called a nocturnal emission. For the first year or so after semenarche, the boy's sperm will be less numerous and less fertile than they will be in his later adolescent years and in early adulthood (Katchadourian, 1977).

primary sex characteristics The organs directly involved in reproduction.

secondary sex characteristics The anatomical and physiological signs that outwardly distinguish males from females.

semenarche The first ejaculation. Ejaculation often occurs spontaneously during sleep and is called a nocturnal emission.

In the case of girls, estrogen undergoes an eightfold increase during puberty (Malina & Bouchard, 1991). In conjunction with progesterone, another important hormone, estrogen stimulates the ovaries to release ova into the fallopian tubes. When conception does not take place, menstruation occurs. A girl's first menstrual period, also known as **menarche**, usually occurs relatively late in puberty, about 18 months after her growth spurt has reached its peak velocity, or upper limit. Similar to the boy's period of relative infertility, the girl's early menstrual periods tend to be irregular, and often occur without ovulation—the release of a mature egg. Regular ovulation typically begins about 12 to 18 months after menarche (Bogin, 1999). During all of this, the uterus is growing, and the vaginal lining thickens. Importantly, the pelvic inlet, the bony opening of the birth canal, does not reach adult size until most girls are about 18 years of age, which makes childbirth more difficult and potentially more dangerous for young adolescents (Bogin, 1999).

menarche The first menstrual period.

Secondary Sex Characteristics Unlike primary sex characteristics, which are directly involved in reproduction and largely hidden from view, secondary sex characteristics play an important role in communicating an individual's status as a reproductively mature male or female (Figure 14.2). Their communicative function lies in the fact that they are easily observed by others. Some of nature's most dramatic secondary sex characteristics belong to males: the great shaggy mane of the lion; the elegant if entirely impractical plumage of the peacock. Regardless of species, ethologists maintain that secondary sex characteristics are essential to reproductive success because they signal biological readiness for reproduction and trigger sexually relevant responses in others—flirting, for example in our own species.

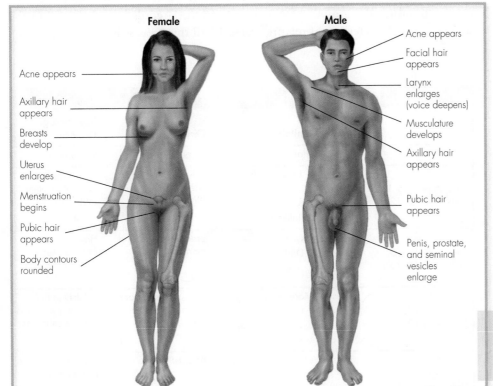

FIGURE 14.2 The hormonal changes that accompany puberty cause a wide variety of physical changes both in males and in females. (Adapted from Netter, 1965).

These photographs underscore the dramatic secondary sex characteristics that emerge as a consequence of reaching reproductive maturity. The colorful face of the mandrill and the shaggy mane of the lion communicate that these males are biologically prepared for reproduction.

The development of secondary sex characteristics in boys and girls follows a fairly predictable sequence. As shown in Table 14.1, the first signs that boys are entering puberty include growth of the testes, a thickening and reddening of the scrotal sac containing the testes, and the appearance of pubic hair. These changes usually occur about 3 years before a boy reaches the peak of his growth spurt. When the growth spurt begins, the boy's penis begins what will be a 2-year period of growth. Halfway into this period, the ejaculation of semen becomes possible. Another noticeable change concerns the deepening of the boy's voice. In late puberty, testosterone stimulates the growth of the larynx and vocal cords, which results in the deeper voice characteristic of mature males. Until this process is complete, a boy's

table 14.1

Tanner's Stages of Pubertal Development

Stage	Boys: Genitalia	Girls: Breasts	Boys and girls: Pubic hair
I	Prepubertal	Prepubertal	Prepubertal
II Boys: Age 12.5–14.5 Girls: Age 10–12	Testes: A bit larger (first sign in boys) Scrotum: Red Penis: Childlike still	Breast: Small bud, widened areola (first sign in girls)	Boys: Scant at base of scrotum Girls: Scant on labia majora
III Boys: Age 13–15 Girls: Age 11–13	Testes: Larger Scrotum: Darker Penis: Increases in length	Breasts: Larger and more elevated	Hair curlier and coarser, moving towards thighs
IV Boys: Age 13.5–15.5 Girls: Age 12–14	Testes: More enlargement Scrotum: More darkening Penis: Now increases in circumference	Breasts: Secondary mound of areola from body	Adult-type hair covering genitalia but not on thighs
V Boys: Age 14–18 Girls: Age 14–18	Testes, scrotum, and penis all adult	Breasts: Adult shape and size	Adult-type hair that extends to inner thighs

Source: Tanner, 1998

voice may crack and squeak, to the embarrassment of the boy and the amusement of his family and friends.

In the case of girls, the onset of sexual maturity is usually marked by the appearance of a small rise around the nipples called the breast bud. Pubic hair appears a little later, just before the girl enters her growth spurt. The breasts continue to grow throughout puberty as a function of both the development of mammary glands (the source of milk) and the increase of adipose (fatty) tissue, which gives them their adult shape.

Clearly, the sexual development of the human body is a dramatic and complex process. Less obvious, but just as important, are the radical changes that take place in the adolescent brain.

Brain Development

Until fairly recently, it was believed that most changes in the brain take place well before adolescence. However, new technologies such as magnetic resonance imaging (MRI) provide evidence that the brain remains a work in progress through adolescence and into early adulthood.

Although the brain, which has attained 90 percent of its adult weight by the age of 5, grows very little in size during adolescence (Sinclair & Dangerfield, 1998), recent longitudinal MRI studies point to complex changes in its organization and functioning (Durston & Casey, 2006; Gogtay et al., 2004). Two areas of the brain—the cerebral cortex and the limbic system—have received a good deal of scientific attention because of the significant roles they may play in adolescent behavior (see Figure 14.3).

"I think I'll be more relaxed once my secondary sex characteristics kick in."

Cerebral Cortex Changes The cerebral cortex continues to develop into early adulthood (Luciana, 2010). Neuroscientists have paid particular attention to changes in the frontal lobes of the cortex, which have emerged fairly recently in the brain evolution of our species and are associated with a number of advanced behaviors and processes, including memory, decision making, reasoning, impulse control, and the ability to multitask. Residing directly behind your forehead is an especially interesting frontal lobe structure called the **prefrontal cortex**, which is thought to contribute to a host of abilities that involve controlling and regulating one's thoughts, feelings, and behaviors. As noted in Chapter 11, these abilities are collectively referred to as *executive function* (see p. 413).

prefrontal cortex A frontal lobe structure that is thought to contribute to a host of abilities that involve controlling and regulating one's thoughts, feelings, and behaviors.

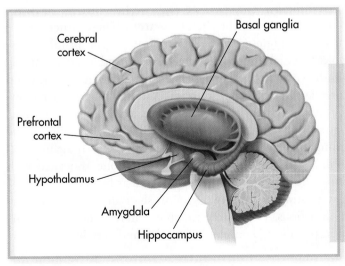

FIGURE 14.3 During adolescence, significant changes occur in the cortex, especially the prefrontal cortex, and in the limbic system. In evolutionary terms, the cortex is a fairly recent development for our species, and is associated with executive function, that is, the ability to control thoughts, feelings, and behaviors. The limbic system, which includes the amygdala, hippocampus, basal ganglia, and hypothalamus, evolved earlier than the cortex in our species, and is associated with the expression and interpretation of emotions.

(a)   (b)

FIGURE 14.4 These images are composites derived from brain scans of normally developing (a) children and adolescents and (b) adolescents and adults. The red areas indicate where there is both an increase in the size of the brain and a decrease in gray matter. As you can see, there are substantially more areas of red in the adolescent and adult image, most of which are concentrated in the frontal area of the brain associated with complex cognitive processes. The fact that areas of the brain are growing even though their gray matter is decreasing suggests that the growth is most likely due to an increase in white matter.

Some developmentalists, as well as parents, speculate that immaturities in the adolescent cerebral cortex contribute to risky behavior and poor decision making.

"Young man, go to your room and stay there until your cerebral cortex matures."

Results from MRI studies show that changes in the prefrontal cortex are of two kinds (Figure 14.4). One concerns the amount of white matter; the other, the amount of gray matter. White matter, you will remember, is made up of dense concentrations of myelin, the insulating substance that coats axons and thereby enhances communication between neurons (see p. 127 for review). Longitudinal studies indicate that white matter increases fairly steadily from childhood to early adulthood (Shaw et al., 2008), suggesting that during adolescence the brain is continuing on its course toward greater efficiency.

The story regarding gray matter, the neuronal cell bodies with their dendrites and axons, is a bit more complicated. In contrast to the steady increase of white matter throughout adolescence, gray matter first increases and then decreases. Since the amount of gray matter is believed to reflect the number of neural connections, or synapses, these changes in gray matter during adolescence suggest a spurt of synapse production, or synaptogenesis, in early puberty followed by a reduction in synapses, or synaptic pruning, in late adolescence. Neuroscientists believe that pubertal hormones may trigger the overproduction of synapses in adolescence (Giedd & Gordon, 2010). They base their speculation on the fact that peak amounts of gray matter occur in early puberty, when hormone production is at its highest, and that gray matter reaches a peak rate of growth in females about one year earlier than it does in males, consistent with the pattern of pubertal hormonal activity.

This spurt of synaptogenesis, followed by a period of synaptic pruning, parallels the pattern of brain development during infancy (see Chapter 4, p. 129). As you may recall from our earlier discussion, it is believed that the surge of synapse formation prepares the brain to learn and respond to a great variety of experiences that might be encountered by the developing individual. If the individual does not have experiences that stimulate the functioning of particular synapses, those synapses atrophy and die off, which decreases the amount of gray matter in the brain, leading to more efficient neural functioning (Bramen et al., 2011).

Limbic System Changes Notwithstanding the significance of changes to the cerebral cortex during adolescence, it has been recently pointed out that important developments occur in other, evolutionarily older parts of the brain as well (Casey et al., 2010; Whittle et al., 2008). Positioned deep beneath the cortex and above the brain stem are several brain structures, including the *amygdala,* the *hippocampus,* the *basal ganglia,* and the *hypothalamus* (see Figure 14.3), that are often referred to collectively as the **limbic system**. These structures are known to also undergo myelination and synaptic pruning during adolescence, although they do so earlier and less dramatically than do the cortical changes described above. Because these brain structures are associated more with emotion than with reasoning, the limbic system is often described as the "emotion brain" (in contrast to the cerebral cortex, which some have dubbed the "reasoning brain"). Neuroscientists, however, warn against distinguishing too sharply between two brains, one associated with emotions, the other with reasoning, primarily because of evidence suggesting that the two systems share in, or cooperate on, certain functions. For example, some limbic structures are involved in processing complex memories, and certain areas of the cortex are essential to understanding and interpreting emotional events and experiences (LeDoux, 2012).

Although the details of these synaptic changes are far from clear, developmentalists believe that they represent evidence of the brain's capacity to adapt to, and be shaped by, the individual's experiences (Toga, Thompson, & Sowell, 2006; Lenroot & Giedd, 2011). From the child hunter–gatherer's lessons in distinguishing edible from poisonous plants to the Buddhist youth's spiritual awakening, such neural flexibility and responsiveness is highly adaptive when you consider the vast landscape of experiences made possible by different cultures, families, neighborhoods, peer groups, and so forth. It is important to understand, however, that the brain responds to negative experiences as well as to opportunities for learning and positive adaptation. For example, some researchers have argued that the radical surge in gray matter during early adolescence makes the brain not only highly responsive to learning opportunities but also especially vulnerable to the effects and addictive properties of drugs, alcohol, and tobacco (Nasrallah et al., 2011).

Brain and Behavior Stirring the most recent excitement over the interplay of cortical and limbic brain structures is research suggesting a strong link between brain development and adolescent behavior, especially risk-taking behavior. Developmentalists have long argued that risky behavior may be related to an enhanced motivation for greater independence and new experiences, which emerges not only in our own adolescence but during the adolescence of many other mammalian species as well. Neuroscientists have suggested that this behavioral transition toward novelty-seeking and adventurousness is associated with the developing limbic system and is likely necessary for procreation, as well as for the learning of tasks and skills essential to mature functioning. However, the drive for novelty also increases exposure to potential danger. And because the cortex—the neurological seat of impulse control, decision making, and reasoning—remains immature through early adulthood, the developing organism is particularly vulnerable to negative outcomes. In the case of the human child, such outcomes include substance abuse, unprotected sex, inflicting harm on others, injuries, and death (Somerville, Jones, & Casey, 2010).

Research conducted with both human and nonhuman species suggests that adolescent risk-taking declines in late adolescence and early adulthood as the cortex matures and executive function improves, increasing the individual's ability to control the way he or she thinks, feels, and acts in particular situations (Steinberg, 2010; Van Leijenhorst et al., 2010). As you will learn in Chapter 15, many nonneurological factors are also known to influence adolescent risk-taking, including the tolerance of such behavior by the individual's culture and family and the involvement of peers in such behavior. The recent research on brain development and adolescent behavior adds an important piece to the puzzle of why adolescents are especially attracted to novelty and risk.

An important question for developmental neuroscientists concerns the role of pubertal hormones in facilitating brain development during adolescence. The brain is a major target of pubertal hormones (Lenroot & Giedd, 2010; Peper et al., 2010). Indeed, pubertal hormones have important *organizing effects* on the brain, meaning that they trigger structural brain changes. As we have noted, evidence suggests that pubertal hormones may affect synaptogenesis. Hormones also appear to affect synaptic pruning and myelination. In the early phase of puberty, increases in cerebral white matter seem to be triggered by elevated levels of *luteinizing hormone,* the

limbic system A group of brain structures, including the amygdala, hippocampus, basal ganglia, and hypothalamus. Because these brain structures are associated more with emotion than with reasoning, the limbic system is often described as the "emotion brain" (in contrast to the cerebral cortex, which some have dubbed the "reasoning brain").

hypothalamic-pituitary-gonadal (HPG) axis A circuit that extends from the brain to the sex organs (testes or ovaries) and back again; activated in adolescence, the HPG regulates the hormones that affect the body's growth and functions.

hypothalamus A brain structure, located just above the brain stem, that performs a number of important tasks, including the regulation of hunger, thirst, and sexual desire, and connects the nervous system to the endocrine system.

endocrine system A network of hormone-secreting glands associated with changes in the individual's mood, metabolism, and growth. The glands associated specifically with puberty include the pituitary gland, the thyroid gland, the adrenal glands, and the sex glands (gonads).

precursor of the sex hormones, which we describe below (Peper et al., 2008). A bit later, when sex hormones begin to surge, gray matter decreases in the frontal and parietal brain areas. The complex relationship between neurological changes and various pubertal hormones underscores the dynamic nature of brain development, and the importance of hormones to the developing individual, a topic that we will now address in more detail.

The Neuro-Hormonal System

It has been known for decades that puberty involves the activation of the so-called **hypothalamic-pituitary-gonadal (HPG) axis**, a circuit that extends from the brain to the sex organs (testes or ovaries) and back again and that is responsible for regulating the hormones that affect the body's growth and functions. The anatomical components of this circuit are shown in Figure 14.5. At the top of the circuit is the **hypothalamus**, a brain structure about the size of an almond, located just above the brain stem. The hypothalamus is a jack-of-all-trades that performs a number of important tasks, including the regulation of hunger, thirst, and sexual desire. One of the most important functions of the hypothalamus is to connect the nervous system to the **endocrine system**, a network of hormone-secreting glands associated with changes in the individual's mood, metabolism, and growth.

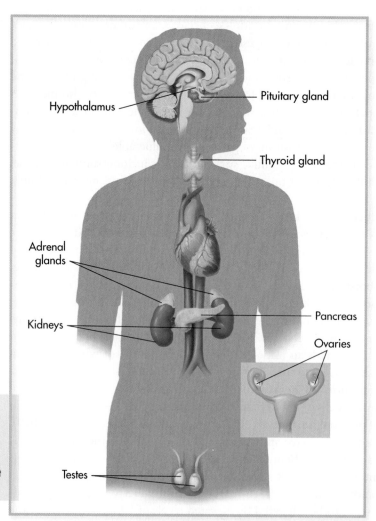

FIGURE 14.5 The hypothalamic-pituitary-gonadal (HPG) axis is a complex, interactive system involving the brain (hypothalamus and pituitary) and the sex glands. The activation of the HPG axis defines the onset of puberty.

The glands associated specifically with puberty include the *pituitary gland,* the *thyroid gland,* the *adrenal glands,* and the *sex glands (gonads).*

The anatomical components (the hypothalamus and glands) of the HPG axis form a highly complex system of hormonal communication associated with the onset of puberty. Specifically, puberty begins when the hypothalamus increases its production of *gonadotropin-releasing hormone (GnRH),* stimulating the pituitary gland to release hormones called *gonadotropins.* The gonadotropins travel to the sex glands, where they trigger the production of estrogens and androgens, which are the two classes of **sex hormones**. Most of the changes observed during puberty are due to *estradiol,* which is an estrogen, and *testosterone,* which is an androgen. Completing the circuit, the sex hormones travel through the bloodstream and communicate with special hormone-perceiving receptors located throughout the body, including in the skeletal system, where they contribute to bone strength and growth, and the brain, where they contribute to sex differences in the brain's neural pathways.

An important question for developmentalists is, What condition or set of conditions activates the HPG circuit, triggering the onset of puberty? Until very recently, it was thought that the developing person's energy store, or amount of body fat, was critical. The gradual increase in body fat that occurs over the course of childhood results in higher levels of **leptin**, a hormone that plays a key role in appetite and metabolism. Researchers believed that the cascade of hormones associated with pubertal onset is triggered when the levels of leptin reach a certain threshold in the hypothalamus. This belief is consistent with research demonstrating that puberty is delayed when adolescents are excessively thin as a consequence of illness, excessive exercise, eating disorders, or poverty. It is also consistent with the fact that, worldwide, adolescents from well-off communities begin puberty at earlier ages than do their counterparts living in underprivileged communities. (We will discuss these differences in more detail below.)

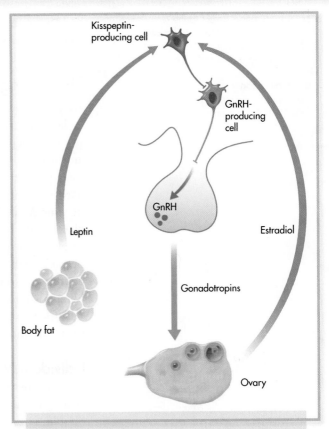

FIGURE 14.6 Scientists discovered recently that the hypothalamus produces a small protein, kisspeptin, that has a major role in the activation of the HPG axis. As shown here, in females, kisspeptin production is influenced by the level of leptin circulating in the body (leptin levels are associated with body fat), as well as the level of estradiol, a hormone produced by the ovaries. Kisspeptin stimulates the release of gonadotropin-releasing hormone (GnRH) from the hypothalamus, which stimulates the release of gonadotropins from the pituitary gland. In turn, the gonadotropins travel to the ovaries, stimulating them to produce sex hormones, primarily estrogens. (Modified from Roa et al., 2010, p. 92.)

Despite support for the notion that leptin triggers the activation of the HPG axis, a fascinating new discovery shows the story to be a bit more complicated. In what may well be the most significant breakthrough in pubertal science in the past three decades, researchers have discovered **kisspeptin**, a small protein produced by specialized cells in the hypothalamus of several mammalian species, including our own (Navarro & Tena-Sempere, 2011; Tena-Sempere, 2010). Kisspeptin production is influenced by leptin, as well as by circulating levels of estrogens and androgens, and plays a principal role in activating the HPG axis. Thus, puberty seems to be triggered not by any single factor but by a system of interacting neural and hormonal processes (see Figure 14.6).

The biological processes governing the onset of puberty are complex indeed. No less dramatic are their effects on the growing body. They are responsible for the maturation and functioning of the sex organs, and the visible bodily changes that announce to the world that the individual is now capable of reproduction. Our exploration of puberty now turns to consider the *timing* of these changes,

sex hormones Estrogens and androgens that circulate in the bloodstream and activate hormone-perceiving receptors located throughout the body.

leptin A hormone that plays a key role in appetite and metabolism.

kisspeptin A small protein that is produced by specialized cells in the hypothalamus and plays a key role in the activation of the HPG axis.

and the implications of timing for the individual's physical health, social relationships, and personal feelings.

The Timing of Puberty

As you know from your own observation, some children enter puberty earlier or later than most of their peers. In addition to individual variations in the timing of puberty, there are significant variations across generations, ethnic groups, and nations. For example, it is likely that you entered puberty at an earlier age than your same-sex grandparent, and perhaps even earlier than your same-sex parent. If you are African American, you probably reached puberty before most of your Asian American peers; if you were born and raised in South Korea, the chances are high that you reached puberty well in advance of your North Korean counterparts. It is important to understand the sources of such variations because they are associated with a number of physical, social, and psychological conditions, some of which are entirely normal, others of which signal an underlying pathology and are therefore matters of great concern. In this section, we will focus on individual and group (e.g., generational, ethnic) variations related to health and disease.

Individual Variation It is not uncommon for adolescents to wonder (and worry) whether the changes occurring in their body and bodily functions are all as they should be. Many of their concerns focus on the timing of pubertal events. Should certain of their body parts be bigger, or not so big, at this or that stage? Is their menstruation or first ejaculation early or late compared with that of their peers? Can pubertal events somehow be hurried along or delayed? As suggested above, whether an individual's pubertal development is early, on time, or late can only be determined in comparison with the development of a group of similar individuals. For example, in order to determine whether the initial appearance of facial hair on a particular Japanese boy is occurring at the "normal" time, one would have to know when most other Japanese boys begin to show facial hair. As a general rule, **early maturation** occurs when a pubertal event (or set of events) emerges before the 3rd percentile of the normal range. The growth of a boy's facial hair would be considered "early" if less than 3 percent of boys his age have grown facial hair, and the remaining 97 percent have not yet begun to enter this particular pubertal event. Similarly, **late maturation** occurs when a pubertal event emerges after the 97th percentile of the normal range (Brämswig & Dübbers, 2009).

Consider, as an example, the average ages and normal ranges of pubertal developments in boys and girls of White European descent shown in Table 14.2. In this population, early maturation is generally defined as the development of sexual characteristics before the age of 8 years in girls and 9 years in boys (Stanhope & Traggiai, 2004; Deligeorooglou & Tsimaris, 2010). Late maturation, for this particular population, is defined as the absence of pubertal signs after the age of 13.3 years in girls and 14 in boys. As you will shortly see, there can be very real and lasting social and psychological consequences for boys and girls who mature significantly earlier or later compared with their

table 14.2

Chronological age at the onset of pubertal development in girls and boys (Tanner stages)

	Parameter	Mean (years)	Normal range (years)
Girls	PH	10.4	8.0–12.6
	B	10.9	8.5–13.3
	PHV	12.2	10.2–14.2
	Menarche	13.4	11.2–15.6
Boys	G	11.2	8.2–14.2
	Testicular volume (≥ 3 mL)	11.9	10.1–13.7
	PH	12.2	9.2–15.2
	Spermarche	13.4	11.7–15.3
	PHV	13.9	12.3–15.5

PH = development of pubic hair; B = breast development; PHV = peak height velocity (the time when longitudinal growth during puberty is fastest); G = genital development
Source: Brämswig & Dübbers, 2009.

peers. However, moderately early or late maturation usually poses no long-term health risks.

Genetic factors play a significant role in the timing of puberty. Indeed, the age at which a child's parents entered puberty is one of the strongest predictors of the age of pubertal onset for the child (Belsky et al., 2007). Evidence that pubertal onset is closer for monozygotic twins than for dizygotic twins provides further support for the role of heredity in sexual maturation (Mustanski, Viken, Kaprio, Pulkkinen, & Rose, 2004). Other sources of variation, as we have noted, are gender and ethnicity (African American girls, for example, mature earlier than all other groups in the United States; see p. 525 [Chumlea et al., 2003; Herman-Giddens, 2006]). Variation in the timing of puberty can also arise from certain physical and emotional stressors such as family dysfunction and exposure to violence and war (Koziel & Jankowska, 2002; Belsky et al., 2007). Recent research, much of it conducted with nonhuman species, indicates that exposure to certain environmental chemicals such as DDT, lead, and phthalates (common in plastic bottles) may disrupt the endocrine system and alter the normal onset and course of sexual maturation (reviewed in Toppari & Juul, 2010).

In contrast to normal variations in pubertal timing discussed above, **precocious puberty** is a serious condition that involves the activation of the HPG axis before the age of 8 in girls and 9 in boys. As shown in Table 14.3, precocious puberty is associated with predispositions to a number of diseases, including cancer, diabetes, and overweight (Stanhope & Traggiai, 2004). It has an estimated prevalence rate of between 1:5000 and 1:10,000 and is 5 to 10 times more common in girls than in boys (Carel & Léger, 2008). Interestingly, higher rates of precocious puberty are found in foreign adopted and migrant children in the United States, perhaps due to a rapid increase in fat mass resulting from a switch in diet and eating patterns (Parent et al., 2003).

Regardless of the factors underpinning the early sexual maturation of one child or the late pubertal onset of another, the timing of puberty can be a psychological burden or an asset, depending on whether the child's maturing is early or late relative to that of peers and whether the child is male or female. If you were an early-maturing girl, or knew one, you may remember being acutely aware of some of the consequences of being "off time" in relation to your peers. Early-maturing girls can be magnets of unwanted sexual attention from older boys; they may have trouble sharing the trials and tribulations of puberty with their less mature girlfriends; and their parents, teachers, and even peers may expect more mature behavior from them despite the likelihood that their intellectual and emotional abilities are relatively less developed than their bodies would suggest. If you can think of other social or psychological consequences of girls' early sexual maturation, it is likely that they, too, are negative rather than positive. Indeed, the past two decades have produced a wealth of studies documenting the difficulties experienced by girls who mature early. Although most girls weather the storms of early maturation without lasting problems, many develop depressive disorders, eating disorders, anxiety, and poor self-image—all associated with their early pubertal onset (Graber, Nichols, & Brooks-Gunn, 2010; Mendle, Turkheimer, & Emery, 2007; Rudolph & Troop-Gordon, 2010). Early-maturing girls are also at risk for having problems in school, engaging in delinquent behaviors, abusing drugs and alcohol, and having sex at earlier ages compared with girls whose pubertal development is "on time" or late. In the United States, such effects have

precocious puberty A serious condition that involves the activation of the HPG axis before the age of 8 in girls and 9 in boys.

table **14.3**
Risks Associated with Early Puberty
• Increased adolescent risk-taking behavior
• Shorter adult stature
• Increased adult BMI, waist circumference, and adiposity
• Increased risk of adult-onset diabetes (owing to elevated BMI)
• Increased cardiovascular disease
• Increased risk of premenopausal breast cancer
• Increased mortality
(Adapted from Ahmed, Ong, & Dunger, 2009)

been found across multiple ethnic groups, including European Americans, African Americans, and Mexican Americans (Lynne et al., 2007; Ge, Brody, Conger, & Simons, 2006).

Early maturation is quite a different story for boys. Compared with their on-time and late-maturing counterparts, early-maturing boys tend to be more popular with peers and, in stark contrast to girls, generally pleased with their changing bodies (Weichold et al., 2003). As we discussed earlier, the growth spurt in muscle mass coupled with physiological changes to the respiratory and circulatory systems result in a more athletic body capable of higher levels of athletic performance. Given that athletic ability in boys and men is highly prized in many cultures, it is little wonder that boys are eager to develop physically and usually adjust well if development occurs relatively early. However, despite these apparent benefits, researchers point out that early-maturing boys share some risk factors with their female counterparts, including delinquency, substance abuse, and academic problems.

Researchers have pointed to several possible reasons why early-maturing youths are at risk for engaging in such problem behaviors. One explanation, which we address more fully in Chapter 15, relates to changes in friends and peer-group affiliations. In particular, when youths become sexually mature at relatively early ages, they may begin to form friendships with older peers or become involved with deviant peer groups, exposing themselves to contexts that promote risk-taking or rebelliousness (Ge et al., 1996; Rudolph, 2008; Weichold et al., 2003). A second, related explanation is that although their bodies are mature, and they may be experiencing hormone-related impulses and desires, their powers of reason may be relatively unsophisticated and childlike. Indeed, pubertal development and cognitive development seem to be largely unrelated (Giedd et al., 2006). Early sexual maturation is also associated with lower self-control and less emotional stability, as measured by psychological tests. The degree of adult supervision is yet another possible explanation for the relationship between early maturation and problem behavior. Compared with on-time and late maturers, early-maturing boys and girls are subject to less monitoring by parents and teachers (Silbereisen & Kracke, 1997).

Altogether, research on individual variation in pubertal timing suggests that understanding why one child might enter puberty earlier or later than another, or respond to the timing of his or her own puberty with anxiety and depression or with satisfaction and well-being, requires understanding how pubertal development intersects with the personal history and current context of the child in question.

Population Variation Developmentalists are interested not only in variations in pubertal timing that take place at the level of the individual; they are also interested in such variations as they occur in whole populations. Studies devoted to examining population differences in pubertal onset have been conducted in hundreds of countries and over the course of several centuries; their numbers may very well run into the thousands. What accounts for this extensive and enduring interest? The answer lies in the fact that the average age of sexual maturation is strongly associated with the health of the general population. In particular, sexual maturation, as well as other physical developments, can be significantly delayed in populations that suffer widespread malnutrition and exposure to disease as a consequence of poor medical care. Consider Figure 14.7, which shows the average age of menarche for girls growing up in urban and rural environments in several

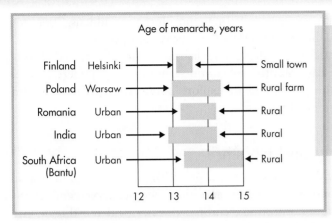

Age of menarche, years

FIGURE 14.7 Complex interactions between genetic and environmental factors result in large regional differences in the average age of pubertal onset. In general, puberty begins earlier in urban than in rural areas. (From Tanner, 1978.)

different countries. (Most studies of population variation rely on menarche to gauge pubertal onset because, unlike ejaculation, it is not tied to sexual behavior yet is readily observable and reasonably memorable [Herman-Giddens, 2007].) The differences are dramatic, and are more so in some countries than in others. Cross-national differences raise several important questions: Why does menarche occur earlier in some countries than in others? Why are the rural/urban differences relatively small in some countries (Finland, for example) but quite large in others (such as India and South Africa)? Identifying the factors that affect the onset of puberty would help developmentalists understand these national differences, and might help policy makers identify areas of the world in need of greater levels of health care.

In addition to cross-national differences, the age at which puberty is reached has also undergone striking historical changes. The **secular trend** refers to a pattern of decline in the average age of puberty that has occurred across all social, ethnic, and economic populations in industrialized countries and, to a lesser extent, in developing countries. For a time, the secular trend in both industrialized and developing countries was taken as evidence of good health. In industrialized countries, for example, the average age of menarche dropped from about 16 years in the mid-1800s to about 13 years in the 1960s (Parent, Teilmann, Juul, et al., 2003), presumably due to increased access to food, prenatal and child care, immunizations, and medicines and technologies that combat infectious diseases. Likewise, the downward trend in pubertal onset in developing countries is likely due to better nutrition and quality health care (Pawloski, Ruchiwit, & Pakapong, 2008; Ying-Xiu & Shu-Rong, 2008).

Since the 1960s, the secular trend has continued in industrialized countries, although at a slower rate than that observed between the mid-1800s and mid-1900s. This was demonstrated in a study of a nationally representative sample of girls in the United States who were surveyed 10 years apart in the late 1980s and 1990s. The study found that the average age of pubertal onset had declined from 12.09 to 12.06 for Black girls, from 12.24 to 12.09 for Mexican American girls, and from 12.57 to 12.52 years for (non-Hispanic) White girls (1999–2002 NHANES data, analyzed in Anderson & Must, 2005). Although these differences may seem slight, researchers argue that they are nonetheless highly meaningful. In particular, there is grave concern that the factors underpinning the trend have changed from positive ones, such as improved nutrition and access to health care, to ones that are decidedly unhealthy, including "overnutrition" associated with overweight and obesity, declining physical activity, and chemical pollution in the

secular trend A pattern in which the average age of puberty in industrialized countries declines across decades.

table 14.4
Earlier puberty: Theories and speculations
• Genetic differences among racial/ethnic groups
• Overweight and obesity; decreased physical activity
• Pre- and postnatal exposure to endocrine-disrupter chemicals
• Infant soy-based formulas
• Girls born small for gestational age
• Stress, absent fathers, unrelated males in the household
• Effects of different types of diet
• Exogenous hormones
• Hypersexualization of culture
Source: Herman-Giddens, 2007, p. 245.

environment (see Table 14.4, and Herman-Giddens, 2006, for review). Given the number of health and psychological problems associated with early sexual maturation (discussed above), it is clearly essential to continue monitoring pubertal onset across the globe, and to explore connections to genetic and environmental factors.

Puberty and Health

Worldwide, adolescence is a period of relatively good health. Compared with children and older people, adolescents experience fewer infections, chronic diseases, and life-threatening illnesses (WHO, 2008). Nevertheless, the astronomical growth rates of adolescence place new demands on the body, and developmentalists have recently begun to focus attention on the unique needs of adolescents for adequate nutrition, sleep, and physical activity.

Nutrition The body's total nutrient needs are greater during adolescence than at any other time in life. These needs are especially great during the growth spurt; in fact, it has been estimated that at the peak of the growth spurt, the body needs twice the nutrients that it needs at other points during adolescence. Optimal nutrition during adolescence is essential not only for achieving full growth potential but also for preventing a number of diseases in later life, including heart disease, cancer, and osteoporosis (Stang & Story, 2005). Unfortunately, as shown in Table 14.5, the average diet of adolescents, at least in the United States, is low in essential vitamins and minerals and high in fats and sugars.

The importance of a healthy diet to adolescent development cannot be over-emphasized. Vitamins and minerals, for instance, are known to influence essential physiological processes. Here are just a few examples:

table 14.5			
Nutrients of Concern in the Average Diet of Adolescents in the United States			
Nutrient Intakes		**Females**	**Males**
Lower-than-Recommended Intakes	**Vitamins**		
	Folate	✓	✓
	Vitamin A	✓	
	Vitamin E	✓	✓
	Vitamin B$_6$	✓	
	Minerals		
	Calcium	✓	✓
	Iron	✓	
	Zinc	✓	
	Magnesium	✓	✓
	Other		
	Fiber	✓	✓
Higher-than-Recommended Intakes	**Total fat**	✓	✓
	Saturated fat	✓	✓
	Sodium	✓	✓
	Cholesterol		✓
	Total sugars		✓
Source: Data from Stang & Story, 2005.			

- *Zinc* is vital for gene expression, and plays a role in sexual maturation. Only two-thirds of adolescents in the United States get enough zinc. Major sources include red meat, shellfish, and whole grains.

- *Vitamin A* contributes to reproduction, general growth, and the functioning of the immune system. It is also important to normal vision. In the United States, only two-thirds of adolescents consume the recommended amount of Vitamin A. In developing countries, as many as 500,000 children go blind each year because of Vitamin A deficiencies (Russell, 2001). Major sources of this nutrient include milk, cheese, and carrots.

- *Folate* is a mineral that plays a significant role in biological processes affecting DNA. Women who have folate deficiencies and become pregnant are at risk for having babies with neural tube defects such as spina bifida (McDowell et al, 2008). Men with low folate levels often have chromosomal abnormalities in their sperm (Young et al., 2008). Largely as a result of a 1998 FDA regulation requiring that certain food products be fortified with folic acid, folate blood levels have risen considerably for all age groups in the United States. Nevertheless, adolescents 12 to 19 years of age have lower folate levels than any other age group. Common sources of folate include cereal, orange juice, milk, and bread.

ICONS: Peacekeeping in a Virtual Classroom

IMAGINE THAT YOU AND A TEAM OF classmates are representing Nigeria at a conference table that includes teams of delegates from 10 other countries. This international committee is meeting to develop guidelines for how the United Nations should respond to outbreaks of genocide and politicide—that is, to mass murder committed against members of, respectively, an ethnic or political group. In the past, the international community has responded slowly and unsystematically, often simply standing by while brutal campaigns against a targeted group continued unchecked. Your committee is charged with proposing answers to the following questions: What guidelines should dictate when it is appropriate for the international community to commit peacekeeping forces to a specific conflict? How should a decision about when and how to commit such forces be made? Should international forces be involved in ending conflicts or limited to only keeping an existing peace?

The scenario described above is typical of the hypothetical situations given to high school and college students involved in a special project created at the University of Maryland. The International Communications and Negotiation Project (ICONS) uses computer networks and peer collaboration to create learning environments in which students reason about deep political issues concerning human rights and the global environment. In ICONS, students pretend to be diplomats from different countries and negotiate solutions to problems with other student-diplomats. Students on the same team (Nigeria, for example), meet face-to-face, but they interact with the other teams through computers. Each team needs to present a unified front when it negotiates with the other teams, which encourages team members to work toward a common perspective and fosters identification with the country they represent. For example, in the test conference shown in the figure, delegate teams from Brazil, Ireland, and Nigeria have developed group statements regarding issues such as how to define individuals who have been persecuted within their native country,

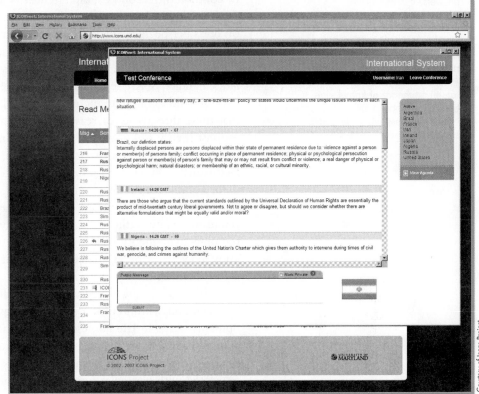

Courtesy of Icons Project

the possiblity of cultural bias in the Universal Declaration of Human Rights, and the authority of the United Nations to intervene in the internal affairs of countries experiencing civil war or genocide.

Although ICONS was originally designed simply to engage students in simulated international negotiation about political issues, it has captured the attention of developmentalists interested in how knowledge is co-constructed in social contexts. They have examined how students build political expertise on an issue in the course of interacting with teammates and other student teams (Torney-Purta, 1996). In general, they find that, over time, students generate increasingly sophisticated problem solutions. In the course of discussion—agreeing, disagreeing, clarifying goals, suggesting revisions, and justifying positions—students are increasingly able to take into account multiple political, economic, and humanitarian vari-

ables and the perspectives of different countries. In the terms of sociocultural theory, this sort of collaborative problem solving serves to scaffold the development of knowledge and contributes to a process through which student-diplomats are transformed from novices to experts. A central feature of the process is the creation of a "community of learners" (Rogoff et al., 2005) in which members feel responsibility toward each other and toward their common goals. Indeed, a survey tapping into the student-diplomats' sense of community found that 90 percent of the project participants reported moderate or high levels of identification with the country they represented. On the final day of her involvement in the project, one student remarked sadly, "It's really too bad; next week there won't be any [computer] messages for us as Nigerian diplomats. We'll have to go back to just being students" (Torney-Purta, 1996; p. 216).

3. So here were all these theorists and theories and stuff—and hell, I said, "These are *games*, just *games* and everybody makes up their own rules! So it's gotta be bullshit." But then I realized "What else have we got?" and now every time I get into a thing I set out to learn all its rules, 'cause that's the only way I can tell whether *I'm* talking bullshit.

objectivist theory of knowledge A belief that knowledge involves an accumulation of objective facts and "definite answers."

subjectivist theory of knowledge A belief that there is no absolute truth because truth can change depending on one's perspective.

evaluativist theory of knowledge A belief that although truth can change, it is nevertheless subject to particular standards of evaluation—the "rules of the game."

The first example reflects an **objectivist theory of knowledge**, that is, a belief that knowledge involves an accumulation of objective facts and "definite answers." In contrast, the second example reflects a **subjectivist theory of knowledge**, according to which there is no absolute truth because truth can change depending on one's perspective. Finally, the third example expresses an **evaluativist theory of knowledge**, in which it is recognized that although truth can change, it is nevertheless subject to particular standards of evaluation—the "rules of the game" (Hallett, Chandler, & Krettenauer, 2002; Gottlieb & Mandel Leadership Institute, 2007).

Most studies of epistemic reasoning in late adolescence and early adulthood find that these three types of reasoning form a developmental hierarchy, with an objectivist theory of knowledge emerging first, followed by a subjectivist theory and then by an evaluativist theory. However, recent studies have found that cultural factors may influence epistemic development, with some cultures emphasizing one theory of knowledge over another (Hofer, 2008; Tabak & Weinstock, 2008). Cultures that value tradition, for example, may believe that knowledge resides in, and is transmitted by, authority figures (worldly or spiritual), thereby tending to support the objectivist theory of knowledge. Other cultures, in contrast, may believe that knowledge must be evaluated in terms of scientific standards, thereby supporting the evaluativist theory of knowledge.

In light of the high degree of variability of formal-operational thinking both between and within cultures, as well as evidence that additional cognitive developments occur in late adolescence and early adulthood, modern researchers have argued that the study of advanced intellectual development should shift from focusing on a general stage of formal operations to looking at specific forms of reasoning associated with particular types of tasks and cultural practices.

Information-Processing Approaches

Whereas in the Piagetian view the advances in adolescents' cognition result from global, qualitative change, information-processing theorists believe that adolescents' expanded cognitive abilities are better explained as the result of the continuing development of various cognitive structures and processes. In particular, information-processing approaches emphasize how adolescents' ability to think systematically arises from the increased capacity of their working memory and from their ability to apply more powerful problem-solving strategies with increasing reliability (Case, 1998; Markovits & Lortie-Forgues, 2011). In problem solving, increased memory capacity makes it possible to coordinate several different factors at once, keep intermediate results in mind, and come up with a solution that is comprehensive and consistent.

Adolescent decision making is an area of special interest to developmentalists because it has far-reaching consequences for adolescents' health and well-being. Knowledge about how adolescents make decisions regarding risk-taking behavior, for example, may help educators, policy makers, and child advocates in addressing such problems as juvenile crime, suicide, pregnancy, automobile accidents, and sexually transmitted infections (Boyer & Byrnes, 2009; Keating & Halpern-Felsher, 2008). Likewise, the complexity of adolescent thinking is relevant to important legal issues. It is, for example, at the heart of debates about whether adolescents who commit crimes should be tried as adults (Grisso et al., 2003) and about whether adolescents should be allowed to undergo medical procedures, including abortions, without the consent of a parent. The decision-making abilities of adolescents are also relevant to the question of whether they are capable of giving *informed consent* (see Chapter 1, p. 42) to participate in research projects (Halpern-Felsher & Cauffman, 2001).

In their review of research on decision-making competence, Bonnie Halpern-Felsher and Elizabeth Cauffman (2001) identified five steps that are commonly associated with effective decision making.

1. Identify possible decision options.

2. Identify possible risks and benefits associated with each option.

3. Evaluate the desirability of each consequence.

4. Assess the likelihood of each consequence.

5. Decide on the best course of action by combining the information obtained in the previous steps according to a decision rule.

In an effort to examine variation in decision making in children's daily lives, Halpern-Felsher and Cauffman presented sixth- to twelfth-graders and young adults with decision-making scenarios in which they were asked to help a peer solve a problem. The problems included whether the peer should undergo a medical procedure (medical domain), should participate in a research project (informed-consent domain), or should live with the mother or the father after a divorce (family domain). For example, the following dilemma was presented for the medical domain: "I've been thinking about having this operation. It won't make me healthier or anything, but I'd like to have it because it would make me look better since I've always had this ugly thing like a bump on my cheek. I could have an operation to remove it. I'm trying to decide whether to have the operation, and I can't decide. Do you think I should have the operation?" (p. 262).

The participants were played a tape of the dilemmas and instructed to provide their advice out loud. The researchers then coded their responses, looking for whether or not the participants mentioned options (e.g., "Are there treatments other than surgery?"), risks (e.g., "You could be scarred by the operation"), benefits (e.g., "You could be happy with the results of the surgery"), long-term consequences (e.g., "In the long run, you might feel better about yourself"), and applying a decision rule ("Have you gotten a second opinion?").

Overall, the researchers found that the young adults demonstrated significantly higher levels of decision-making competence than did the adolescents, being more likely than adolescents, especially the sixth- to eighth-graders, to employ all five of the decision-making steps listed above. However, noting that many adolescents in the study displayed high levels of competence, the researchers argue that it is difficult to identify an age boundary between immature and mature decision making, and they caution against making hard-and-fast legal or social policies based solely on age or competence. It is particularly difficult, they contend, to justify withholding certain medical treatments (for HIV infection, for example) because adolescents do not fully understand the implications of the treatment. "In such cases," the researchers believe, "the benefits of extending health-care access may outweigh the risks" (Halpern-Felsher & Cauffman, 2001, p. 272).

In the work we have just described, adolescents were presented with hypothetical problems in artificial settings. As we will discuss in Chapter 15, making decisions in a laboratory can be quite different from making them in emotionally charged and socially meaningful "real life" settings.

Sociocultural Approaches

Like information-processing theorists, developmentalists who examine adolescent thinking from a sociocultural perspective focus mainly on specific forms of thinking used in particular problem-solving situations. In addition, however, sociocultural

Sociocultural approaches focus on how social interactions, relationships, and cultural norms contribute to intellectual development and learning. It is likely that these boys, thoroughly engrossed in their books, receive a lot of support from family, teachers, and peers for excelling at school.

theorists emphasize how the means of solving problems are influenced and guided by the social interactions of the participants (Subrahmanyam & Greenfield, 2008; Rogoff, 2003).

From a sociocultural perspective, games provide an ideal setting for exploring the development of complex reasoning skills in adolescence. As you may recall from our discussion in Chapter 13 (pp. 472–473), games typically include material and symbolic tools of culture, provide a means of transmitting cultural values and norms, and often involve quite sophisticated forms of reasoning. In addition, many games are highly social, requiring players to coordinate goals and strategies with each other. Using a Vygotskian sociocultural approach, Na'ilah Nasir has explored reasoning in the context of a game of strategy popular in many African American communities—dominoes (Nasir, 2005).

In the version of the game used in Nasir's study, pairs of individuals play in teams against one another. Each player selects 7 dominoes from the total set of 28 tiles set facedown. The faces of the dominoes are divided into halves, each of which is embossed with 0 to 6 dots, or pips. Whoever draws the double-6 tile (the one with 6 pips in each half) places it faceup on the board, and the game begins. If the next player has a domino with 6 pips at one end, the player lays the 6 end against one side of the first domino. The game then proceeds with the players taking turns similarly "matching" their pips with those that have been laid down. If a match can't be made, the player must "pass." If, after a domino is played, the sum of all the end dominoes is a multiple of five, then the player receives those points; if the sum is not a multiple of five, no points are scored. Playing the game well involves scoring points by making the right sorts of matches (resulting in multiples of five), assisting one's partner to make matches, and blocking matches of opponents, thereby preventing them from scoring (successful blocking requires keeping track of the opponent's passes, which provide clues to the possible matches available).

As you can see, dominoes can be a complexly strategic game involving the ability to calculate various point values associated with different possible moves, remembering earlier moves by partners and opponents, thinking hypothetically about possible future moves, and making inferences about how to help or hinder those possibilities through one's own game play. Nasir's analysis documents fascinating transformations in domino play from childhood to adolescence. As we would expect from Piagetian research, adolescents were much more adept at generating and evaluating the point value of possible moves—for themselves, as well as for their partner and opponents—than were younger children, who were primarily concerned with the matching of ends. Likewise, adolescents were also much more skilled than younger children in using information about previous moves and passes to anticipate and make inferences about future possible moves of opponents and partners. However, the Vygotskian approach adopted by Nasir emphasized how individuals sought and received help from other players in ways that scaffolded their developing knowledge of the game and their mastery of various scoring, blocking, and partner-assisting strategies. Consider the following examples, the first involving elementary school students, the second, high school students (Nasir, 2005, pp. 13, 20):

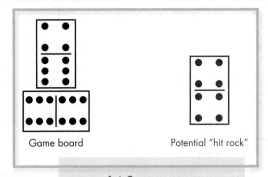

Game board   Potential "hit rock"

FIGURE 14.9 Popular in many African American communities, the game of dominoes calls on complex formal-operational reasoning skills.

> It's David's turn and he's not sure which domino to play. He holds out the 6-0 toward his partner, Tyrell, saying, "Man, put that down there, dog." An opponent responds with "Where?" Tyrell says, "It goes right there!" and plays the domino for David.
>
> Latrisha and Deondre are playing against James and Aaron. Deondre begins the game with the double 6. Aaron follows the play with the 6–4 [Figure 14.9]. James immediately criticizes this play by saying "What you doin' over there, man?" criticizing Aaron for leaving open the possibility of the other team playing the 4–4 (known as the "hit rock") and scoring 20 points. Latrisha chimes in, affirming James's criticism, "He lucky I ain't got the hit rock. I sho' would tax your butt."

From a Vygotskian perspective in which intellectual development is emphasized not as a solitary process but as one that emerges in the course of social participation, these types of social interactions are critical to the learning process. Whether responding to a peer's uncertainty (like David's) or mistake (like Aaron's), adolescents are often able to engage each other in new forms of thinking and acting. Just as social participation contributes to intellectual development, intellectual development, as we will see below, contributes to the adolescent's social participation, by affecting moral reasoning and behavior.

▲ APPLY :: CONNECT :: DISCUSS

Consider the various forms of reasoning described in this section: formal operations, postformal operations, and decision making. To what extent are they relevant to reasoning in everyday contexts? Should schools emphasize the development of some forms rather than others? Why?

Moral Development

Regardless of their theoretical orientation, developmentalists agree that adolescence is a time during which issues of moral behavior take on special importance for young people, typified by such questions as, What is right? What is wrong? What principles should I base my behavior on and use to judge the behavior of others? Evidence suggests that the processes used to think about such questions, like those used to think about science problems, undergo important changes between the ages of 12 and 19 years (Moshman, 2011; Turiel, 2002).

Kohlberg's Theory of Moral Reasoning

As we noted in Chapter 13 (pp. 473–477), the study of moral development has been greatly influenced by Lawrence Kohlberg, who proposed that moral reasoning may progress across three broad levels, each consisting of two stages (Table 14.7

summarizes these levels and stages). As they develop from one stage to the next, children make more-complex analyses both of moral obligations among individuals and of moral obligations between individuals and their social groups.

Recall that, according to Kohlberg, at the start of middle childhood, moral reasoning is at the *preconventional level* (stages 1 and 2), with children judging the rightness or wrongness of actions purely in light of their own wants and fears. Toward the end of middle childhood, children attain the first stage of the *conventional level*,

table 14.7

Kohlberg's Six Moral Stages

Level and Stage	What Is Right	Reasons for Doing Right	Social Perspective
Level I—Preconventional			
Stage 1—Heteronomous morality	• Adherence to rules backed by punishment; obedience for its own sake.	• Avoidance of punishment.	Egocentric point of view.
Stage 2—Instrumental morality	• Acting to meet one's own interests and needs and letting others do the same.	• To serve one's own needs or interests.	Concrete individualistsic perspective: right is relative, an equal exchange.
Level II—Conventional			
Stage 3—Good-child morality	• Living up to others' expectations.	• The need to be a good person in one's own eyes and those of others.	Perspective of the individual sharing feelings, agreements, and expectations with others.
Stage 4—Law-and-order morality	• Fulfilling the actual duties to which one has agreed. • Upholding laws, except in extreme cases in which they conflict with other fixed social duties. • Contributing to society, group, or institution.	• To keep the institution going as a whole. • What would happen "if everyone did it"? • The imperative of conscience to meet one's defined obligations (easily confused with stage 3 belief in rules and authority).	Perspective of an individual in relation to the social group: takes the point of view of the system that defines roles and rules.
Level III—Postconventional, or Principled			
Stage 5—Social-contract reasoning	• Being aware that people hold a variety of values and opinions, most of which are relative to the group that holds them. • Upholding rules in the interest of impartiality and because they are the social contract. • Upholding universal values and rights, such as life and liberty, regardless of the majority opinion.	• A sense of obligation to the law because of one's social contract to make and abide by laws for the welfare of all and for the protection of all people's rights. • A feeling of contractual commitment, freely entered upon, to family, friendship, trust, and work obligations. • Concern that laws and duties be based on rational calculation of overall utility, "the greatest good for the greatest number."	Prior-to-society perspective: Perspective of a rational individual aware of values and rights prior to social attachments and contracts.
Stage 6—Universal ethical principles	• Following self-chosen ethical principles because they are universal principles of justice: the equality of human rights and respect for the dignity of human beings as individual persons. • Judging laws or social agreements by the extent to which they rest on such principles. • When laws violate principles, acting in accordance with the principle.	• A belief in the validity of universal moral principles. • A sense of personal commitment to those principles.	Perspective of a moral point of view from which social arrangements derive: Perspective is that of any rational individual recognizing the nature of morality or the fact that persons are ends in themselves and must be treated as such.

Source: Adapted from Kohlberg, 1976.

Concerned about the welfare of their society, these South Korean university students are participating in a political protest.

stage 3, in which they begin to make moral judgments in terms of their relationships with others, taking into account shared feelings, expectations, agreements, and standards of right and wrong, especially those shared with people whom they are close to (see p. 477). Kohlberg called stage-3 reasoning "good-child morality" because he believed that for individuals in this stage, being moral means living up to the expectations of one's family and other significant people in one's life.

In adolescence, moral reasoning at stage 4, the second stage of the conventional level, begins to appear, although stage 3 remains the dominant mode of moral reasoning until people reach their mid-20s (Figure 14.10) (Colby et al., 1983). Reasoning at stage 4 is like that at stage 3 except that its focus—the social perspective from which judgments are made—shifts from relations between individuals to relations between the individual and the larger society. People who reason at stage 4 believe that society has legitimate authority over individuals, and they feel an obligation to accept its laws, customs, and standards of decent behavior. Moral behavior from this point of view is behavior that upholds the law, maintains the social order, and contributes to the group. For this reason, stage-4 reasoning is also called "law-and-order morality" (Brown & Herrnstein, 1975, p. 289).

Kohlberg believed that moral thinking at stages 3 and 4 depends on a partial ability to engage in formal-operational reasoning—specifically, it requires the ability to consider simultaneously the various existing factors relevant to moral choices (Kohlberg, 1984). People who are reasoning at stages 3 and 4, however, are still reasoning concretely insofar as they do not yet simultaneously consider all possible relevant factors or form abstract hypotheses about what is moral.

With the transition from stage 4 to stage 5 comes another basic shift in the level of moral judgment. Reasoning at the *postconventional* (or *principled*) level requires people to go beyond existing social conventions to consider more abstract principles of right and wrong. Reasoning at stage 5, called *social contract reasoning,* is based on the idea of a society as bound by a social contract designed and agreed upon by the group to serve the needs of its members. People

FIGURE 14.10 Mean percentage of U.S. citizens at each of Kohlberg's stages of moral reasoning at different ages. (Adapted from Colby et al., 1983.)

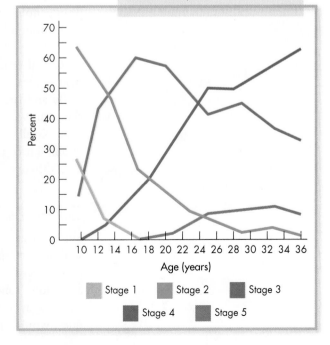

These teens were arrested on suspicion of planning to sell guns for money and drugs. Despite evidence that teenagers lack adult moral reasoning and decision-making skills, they are often tried as adults in U.S. courts of law.

still accept and value the social system, but instead of insisting on maintaining society as it is, they are open to democratic processes of change and to continual exploration of possibilities for improving the existing social order. Recognizing that laws are sometimes in conflict with moral principles, they become creators as well as maintainers of laws. Kohlberg found that stage 5 moral reasoning never appears before early adulthood and then only rarely.

To reach stage 6 in Kohlberg's system, the stage of *universal ethical principles,* the individual must make moral judgments in accordance with ethical principles that he or she believes transcend the rules of individual societies—principles of the equality of human rights and respect for the dignity of human beings as individuals. From this perspective, laws are valid only insofar as they rest on these principles. Kohlberg and his colleagues failed to observe stage-6 reasoning in their research on moral dilemmas, and Kohlberg eventually concluded that this stage is more usefully thought of as a philosophical ideal than as a psychological reality. Nonetheless, there are examples of people who have put their lives at risk because of moral beliefs guided by stage-6 reasoning. Such was the case during World War II, when many European gentiles attempted to protect Jews from the Nazi efforts to exterminate them, even though being caught would have resulted in their own execution. According to Samuel and Pearl Oliner (1988), most of these individuals were motivated by ethical principles that they believed apply to all of humanity, the hallmark of stage-6 moral reasoning.

By and large, research confirms that children and adolescents progress through the sequence of moral reasoning proposed by Kohlberg (Rest et al., 1999). However, Kohlberg's approach is not without its difficulties (Moshman, 2011; Turiel, 2002). Three important critiques address specific limitations associated with Kohlberg's theory.

Gilligan's Theory of Moral Reasoning

Since her car accident, Tara had been in a persistent vegetative state, kept alive by sophisticated medical machinery. Her case became headline news in Canada when doctors refused the request of Tara's family to disconnect her life-support system and allow Tara to die. Emotionally charged arguments emerged on both sides of the issue as the case went to court. Some insisted that acceding to the family's request would violate Tara's right to life; others insisted that failing to do so would violate her right to die with dignity. At one point in the hotly debated and highly publicized drama, Tara's older sister, Kim, was interviewed by the press. "Everyone is talking about rights—the right to life; the right to die. It's become a big legal thing," said Kim. "But this isn't about rights at all. It's about my sister, and about our family, and how we take care of each other. I wish people could see that, and feel some compassion for what we're going through."

One of the most strident criticisms of Kohlberg's theory is that its conception of the nature of morality is too narrow. Taking a different approach to moral reasoning, Carol Gilligan (1982) asserted that Kohlberg's theory reflects a **morality of justice**—that is, a morality that emphasizes issues of rightness, fairness, and equality. As Kim illustrated in her comments to the press, the debate regarding her sister's right to life, or right to die with dignity, reflects a morality of justice orientation. However, from Gilligan's perspective on moral development, Kohlberg's emphasis on justice neglects a key dimension of moral reasoning and action that Gilligan termed the **morality of care**. This second dimension focuses on relationships, compassion, and social obligations—just the sort of issues that Kim said were being overlooked in the case of her sister.

Gilligan's work inspired a great deal of debate, not because of her conception of a morality of care but because of her claim, based on largely anecdotal evidence, that there is a gender difference in moral orientation, with girls and women being oriented to the morality of care, and boys and men being oriented toward the morality of justice (Moshman, 1999). More systematic research with predominantly White U.S. adolescents and with African American adolescents has found few gender differences in moral reasoning (Turiel, 1998; Walker et al., 1995; Weisz & Black, 2003). Despite the lack of evidence for strong gender differences, Gilligan's conception of a morality of care provides a broader, more inclusive view of moral reasoning than Kohlberg's original formulation, and has helped to orient researchers to the broader contexts of moral development and judgment.

morality of justice A morality that emphasizes issues of rightness, fairness, and equality.

morality of care A morality that stresses relationships, compassion, and social obligations.

Parent and Peer Contributions to Moral Development

Kohlberg maintained that parents have a minimal role in the moral development of their children and that peer interactions are essential to promoting moral growth (Walker et al., 2000). This is due, he argued, to the differences in power inherent in the two types of relationships. Because children are under the unilateral authority of their parents, they are not inclined to try to understand their parents' point of view when it differs from their own or to negotiate and compromise on issues of disagreement. As you know from the previous discussion of sociocognitive conflict, intense engagement with alternative points of view can be a strong impetus to attaining higher levels of reasoning. Kohlberg believed that the more mutual and cooperative nature of peer relationships provides a more fertile context for moral development. Indeed, research indicates that both the quantity and quality of peer relationships, including the number of close friendships, amount of participation in social activities, and leadership status, are significantly related to moral reasoning in adolescence (Schonert-Reichl, 1999).

Be that as it may, developmentalists have challenged Kohlberg's idea that parents have little impact in the moral realm (Carlo, Mestre, Samper, Tur, & Armenta, 2011; Walker, 2007). Research finds that authoritative, democratic, responsive parenting is generally associated with higher levels of moral maturity in children (Pratt et al., 2003). A longitudinal study by Lawrence Walker and his colleagues (2000), for example, found that, in discussions of moral issues, adolescents' parents provided higher levels of reasoning than did adolescents' peers. In addition, when parents employed a "gentle Socratic method" of asking their teenagers questions that stimulate critical thinking, their children's moral maturity was advanced. There were, however, conditions in which peers were found to be effective in spurring adolescents' moral maturity. In particular, and consistent with the notion of socio-cognitive conflict, peer interactions that were turbulent and conflict-ridden were associated with the development of higher moral levels. The upshot is that both parent and peer relationships were highly influential in moral development, but each type of relationship contributed in distinctive ways.

Cultural Variations in Moral Reasoning

Like studies showing cross-cultural variability in formal-operational reasoning, studies using Kohlbergian dilemmas (such as the Heinz dilemma) reveal significant differences between cultural groups in moral reasoning (Kohlberg, 1969; Turiel, 2008). Although there are some exceptions (Shweder et al., 1987), most studies show that people who live in relatively small, technologically unsophisticated communities, have primarily face-to-face interactions with others, and have not received extensive schooling that exposes them to ways of life other than their own rarely reason beyond stage 3 on Kohlberg's scale (Figure 14.11). Most often they justify their moral decisions at the level of stage 1 or 2, although people in roles of special responsibility may reason at stage 3 (Snarey, 1995).

Kohlberg suggested that cultural differences in social stimulation produce differences in moral reasoning. However, several developmentalists have argued that Kohlberg's stage sequence, particularly in the higher stages, contains built-in value

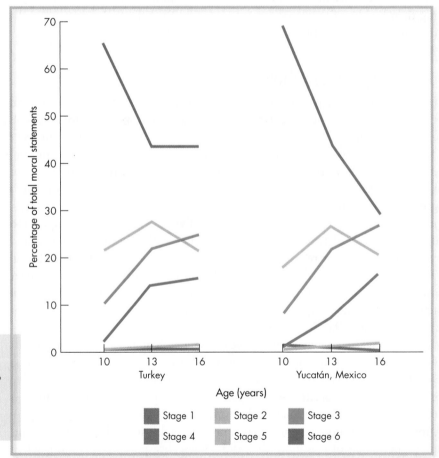

FIGURE 14.11 This figure reflects trends in the moral judgments of boys in small, isolated villages in two nations. Note the continuing high incidence of stage 1 responses even by 16-year-olds. (From Kohlberg, 1969.)

judgments that reflect the moral views of Western culture and democracy. Are we really to believe, such critics ask, that people who grow up in a traditional village in a developing country and reason at stage 2 of Kohlberg's sequence are less moral than the residents of a city in an industrially advanced country (Shweder et al., 2002)?

Kohlberg (1984) denied that cultural differences in performance on his dilemmas leads to the conclusion that some societies are more moral than others. He echoed the classical position of modern anthropology that cultures should be thought of as unique configurations of beliefs and institutions that help the social group adapt to both local conditions and universal aspects of life (Boas, 1911; Geertz, 1984). In this view, a culture in which stage 3 is the height of moral reasoning would be considered "morally equivalent" to a culture in which some people reason at stage 5 or 6, even though the specific reasoning practices could be scored as less "developed" according to Kohlberg's criteria.

Nevertheless, other approaches to moral reasoning have produced results that depart markedly from those obtained using Kohlberg's methods. Cross-cultural studies have reported that by adulthood, a shift from conventional to postconventional moral reasoning is quite widespread if not universal (Gielen & Markoulis, 2001). In cases in which differences appear between countries, the level of education provided to the populations in question appears to be the critical factor.

Using their *social domain theory,* which emphasizes the need to separate moral issues from issues involving social convention and personal choice (see Chapter 13, pp. 478–479), Elliot Turiel and his colleagues also provide evidence that the pattern of development for moral reasoning, defined in terms of justice and rights, is universal across cultures. The areas in which cultural differences *do* appear tend to be those related to social conventions and personal choice, the importance of obedience to authority, and the nature of interpersonal relations (Turiel, 2002; Wainryb, 1995).

An extensive study by Cecilia Wainryb provides an excellent example of how moral reasoning is culturally universal while reasoning in other social domains is culturally specific. Wainryb compared judgments about social conflicts given by a large sample of Israeli 9- to 17-year-olds. Half the participants were Jews from a secular, Westernized part of the Israeli population. The other half were from Druze Arabic villages, where the cultural norms emphasize hierarchical family structures, fixed social roles, and severe punishment for violating traditional duties and customs. The study pitted questions about justice and personal choice against questions about authority and interpersonal considerations (Table 14.8).

Wainryb found no cultural or age differences in response to questions involving justice. For example, an overwhelming percentage of participants at all ages said that a boy who saw someone lose money should return it, even though the boy's father said to keep the money, a conflict with authority. Jewish children were slightly more likely than Druze children to choose personal considerations over interpersonal considerations, but the variability within each cultural group was far larger than the variation between them. The only really significant cultural difference was that Jewish children were much more likely than Druze children to assert personal rights over authority—a result in line with the hierarchical family structure in Druze culture, in which obedience to authority is a central value.

In a similar vein, Joan Miller and her colleagues found that while people from India and the United States may differ in where they draw the line between moral infractions and personal conventions, members of both groups distinguish between the two (Miller & Schaberg, 2003). For example, people from India and the United

table 14.8
Items Pitting One Kind of Consideration Against Another

Justice versus Authority (J–A)

Hannan and his father were shopping and they saw that a young boy inadvertently dropped a 10-shekel bill.

J   Hannan told his father that they should return the money to the boy.

A   His father told him to keep it.

Justice versus Interpersonal (J–I)

On a field trip, Kobby realized that the school did not provide enough soft drinks for all the children.

I   Kobby had to choose between taking two drinks for his two younger brothers who were very thirsty, or

J   Alerting the teachers so that the drinks could be distributed equally among all children.

Personal versus Interpersonal (P–I)

Dalya was invited to a party.

P   She was looking forward to going there with her friends.

I   Her young sister sprained her ankle and asked Dalya to stay home with her and keep her company.

Personal versus Authority (P–A)

Anat loves music.

P   She wants to participate in an after-school music class.

A   Her father does not like music; he tells her not to participate in the music class and to take another class instead.

Source: Wainryb, 1995.

States judged the violation of dress codes in terms of social conventions, not moral issues; and members of both societies judged theft to be a moral issue, not a matter of social convention. These studies suggest that by dividing up questions of morality into separate domains, it is possible to obtain a more subtle picture of cultural influences on moral reasoning in which there are both universal and culture-specific elements.

The Relation Between Moral Reasoning and Moral Action

At some points in your life, you have probably acted in ways that violated your moral principles—you may have lied to your parents, cheated on an exam, betrayed a friend's confidence, or stolen someone's property. In adolescence (as in childhood; see Chapter 13, pp. 471–480), the links between moral reasoning and moral action are not particularly close, prompting developmentalists to examine factors that contribute to the variability in moral behavior—that is, why young people sometimes make moral choices in accordance with their moral principles and sometimes do not (Nucci, 2004a).

In some cases, societal standards and expectations contribute to variability in moral behavior. For example, studies of cheating among U.S. high school students generally find that it is widespread and is heavily influenced by school norms and the attitudes of teachers and friends (McCabe, 1999). High school students seem to be less guilt-stricken than college students, and more apt to blame others—schools, teachers, and society—for their dishonesty (Anderman & Murdock, 2007). As a participant in Donald McCabe's study explained, one reason that cheating is common is because there is no threat of being caught:

> I don't know if it's just our school, but like everybody cheats. Everyone looks at everyone else's paper. And the teachers don't care; they let it happen . . . . The students keep on doing it because they don't get in trouble (p. 683).

However, even in the absence of an obvious deterrent, some students expressed ambivalence about their behavior:

> I guess the first time you do it, you feel really bad, but then you get used to it. You keep telling yourself you're not doing anything wrong . . . . Maybe you might know in your heart that it's wrong, but it gets easier after a while to handle it" (p. 682).

Over time, cheating takes its toll in ways that can be easily discerned by students: "I'm at the point now where I don't know nothing. . . . If I don't cheat, I just fail" (p. 682).

A factor that helps adolescents to act morally is their increasing ability to understand the plight of others and to reason prosocially (Carpendale, Hammond, & Lewis, 2010). Indeed, studies of Brazilian and North American adolescents show strong correlations between sympathy, perspective-taking skills, and prosocial reasoning (Eisenberg et al., 2001). And as we discuss in Chapter 15, moral behavior is also tied to identity issues and the degree to which individuals are motivated to lead exemplary moral lives.

Yet another way to examine the relationship between moral reasoning and behavior is to approach it from the perspective of social domain theory. In the same way that this theory has proved useful in accounting for cross-cultural variability in moral reasoning, it provides insight into the relationship between adolescents' moral reasoning and their moral actions. In particular, the behaviors that researchers (and parents, as we discuss in Chapter 15) define as "moral" may not be defined as such by adolescents. An example comes from a study of the relationship between moral reasoning and risky behavior. Tara Kuther and Ann Higgins-D'Alessandro (2000) found that, compared with adolescents who report lower levels of drugs and alcohol use, those who report higher levels are more likely to see their risky behaviors as personal decisions rather than as moral or conventional decisions. The researchers suggested that directors of drug and alcohol intervention programs take heed of this tendency and encourage youth to explore their views of the personal-choice, social convention, and moral realms and examine their behavior in light of each realm.

According to a 2009 national survey, over a third of adolescents admitted to having used their cell phone to cheat on tests and about a quarter of those surveyed didn't think there was anything wrong in such behavior.

▲ APPLY :: CONNECT :: DISCUSS

Suppose you want to facilitate moral development in juvenile delinquents participating in a counseling program. How would you go about this from a Kohlbergian perspective? How would you do this from the perspective of social domain theory? In each case, consider whether your intervention programs would be most effective if carried out with teens individually, or in family or peer groups.

Implications

Bodily changes that signal sexual maturity; wholly new ways of thinking, deciding, and processing information; a new sense of what constitutes morally appropriate behavior—all of these are significant changes that are part of the transitions of adolescence. But however private and personal these changes may be, the expectations, technologies, and institutions of an adolescent's culture provide maps for the journey toward maturity. In the following chapter, we explore the social and emotional developments that interweave with the physical and cognitive changes we have been examining.

SUMMARY

Adolescence is characterized by remarkable changes in physical and intellectual development, presenting challenges whose specifics depend on the particular society.

Adolescents and Society

- Virtually all societies recognize adolescence as an important transition requiring special attention. In philosophy and literature through the ages, adolescence has been seen as a period of unique peril and promise.

- Industrialization led to increased attention to adolescence because it led to urban youth problems and to a need for a more educated workforce.

- Prolonged education and delayed marriage and childbearing are common in many contemporary societies. Consequences for young people include increasing reliance on parents for support, an extended period of identity exploration, and feelings of being unprepared for the roles and responsibilities of adulthood.

Biological Theories of Adolescent Development

- G. Stanley Hall saw adolescence as a time of "storm and stress" and as evolutionarily corresponding to a period beyond the biologically predetermined past, with adolescents thus representing the future of the species.

- Sigmund Freud saw adolescence as the beginning of the genital stage of psychosexual development and its main task as reestablishing the balance among the id, ego, and superego that was upset by the upsurge of sexual excitation at puberty.

- Modern biological approaches focus on evolutionary implications of such aspects as delayed maturation followed by the growth spurt at puberty, an evolutionarily advantageous pattern that is unique to humans.

Puberty

- Puberty refers to the biological developments that lead to physical maturity and the capacity for reproduction.

- The growth spurt is one of the first signs of puberty.

- In girls, the development of primary sex characteristics, or reproductive organs, includes the maturation of the ovaries, which leads to ovulation, typically beginning after menarche, the first menstrual period. In boys, it includes the maturation of the testes, which leads to sperm production and to semenarche, the first ejaculation. Development of secondary sex characteristics, beginning with breast buds in girls and pubic hair in both sexes, provides evidence that puberty is underway.

- Significant brain developments in adolescence include changes to the cortex and limbic system. The cortex, especially the prefrontal cortex, which is associated with higher forms of reasoning and decision making, undergoes a period of rapid synaptic growth and pruning. The limbic system, associated with the experience and interpretation of emotions, undergoes a period of myelination and synaptic pruning.

- The timing of puberty, earlier for girls than for boys, varies widely as a result of complex interactions between genetic and environmental factors. Caloric intake may be among the crucial environmental factors, as a certain level of body fat may be required for the onset of puberty; thus, nutritional improvements may have led to the secular trend of decline over the decades in the average age of puberty. However, "overnutrition," that is, diets excessively high in calories, has been identified as a source of recent trends toward earlier pubertal onset in many industrialized and developing countries.

- Although adolescence is generally a time of good health, its astronomical growth rates place new demands on the body, creating special needs for nutrition, sleep, and physical activity—needs that all too often are not fully met.

- Puberty has profound social and psychological consequences, which are influenced by cultural beliefs and values. For cultural reasons, puberty may tend to be more psychologically difficult for girls than for boys, especially if its timing is early rather than on time or late.

Cognitive Development

- According to Piaget, adolescence is marked by the emergence of a capacity for formal-operational thinking, for relating sets of relationships to each other. Formal-operational thinkers can reason by systematically manipulating variables and can use hypothetical-deductive reasoning, judging an argument based on logical form alone.

- Sociocognitive conflict—cognitive conflict rooted in social experience—may be particularly useful for promoting formal-operational thinking. Rather than being a universal stage, formal-operational thinking appears to depend on certain experiences and to not be consistently used by those who can use it.

- Epistemic development, involving how individuals reason about the nature of truth and knowledge, takes different forms during adolescence: the objectivist theory of knowledge; the subjectivist theory of knowledge; and the evaluativist theory of knowledge.

- Information-processing approaches attribute adolescents' more systematic thinking to increased capacity in working memory and to the use of more powerful problem-solving strategies.

- Sociocultural approaches demonstrate the role of social interactions in scaffolding the development of adolescent thinking.

Moral Development

- According to Lawrence Kohlberg, moral reasoning at stage 4 ("law-and-order morality") appears during adolescence, although reasoning at stage 3 ("good-child morality") remains more typical. Kohlberg believed that postconventional reasoning (based on principles) is relatively rare.

- Carol Gilligan argued that Kohlberg had emphasized a morality of justice at the expense of a morality of care.

- Although Kohlberg's approach showed significant differences between cultures in members' moral reasoning, cross-cultural studies taking other approaches suggest that differences between cultures are few and that the shift to postconventional reasoning is widespread. Social domain theory, one such approach, shows the importance of separating issues of morality from issues of social convention and personal choice.

- Parents and peers make important but distinct contributions to adolescents' moral development.

- Adolescents' actions do not always accord with their morals, perhaps reflecting inconsistent societal standards, as well as whether adolescents perceive particular behaviors as being in the domain of morality, social convention, or personal choice. Perspective-taking and prosocial reasoning encourage moral behavior.

Key Terms

emerging adulthood, p. 509

growth spurt, p. 511

puberty, p. 512

primary sex characteristics, p. 514

secondary sex characteristics, p. 514

semenarche, p. 514

menarche, p. 515

prefrontal cortex, p. 517

limbic system, p. 518

hypothalmic–pituitary–gonadal (HPG) axis, p. 520

hypothalamus, p. 520

endocrine system, p. 520

sex hormones, p. 521

leptin, p. 521

kisspeptin, p. 521

early maturation, p. 522

late maturation, p. 522

precocious puberty, p. 523

secular trend, p. 525

formal operations, p. 530

hypothetical-deductive reasoning, p. 533

sociocognitive conflict, p. 533

epistemic development, p. 534

objectivist theory of knowledge, p. 536

subjectivist theory of knowledge, p. 536

evaluativist theory of knowledge, p. 536

morality of justice, p. 543

morality of care, p. 543

CHAPTER

15

Emotional Development in Adolescence
The Experience of Emotions
Regulating Emotions

Relationships with Peers
Friendships
Cliques and Crowds
Peer Pressure and Conformity
Romantic Relationships

Sexual Relationships
Learning About Sex
The Sexual Debut

Relationships with Parents
Adolescent–Parent Conflicts
Parental Influences Beyond the Family

Identity Development
The "I" and the "Me"
Achieving a Mature Identity
Forming an Ethnic Identity
Forming a Sexual Identity
Identity and Culture

Adolescent Health and Well-Being
Emotional Health
Sexual Health
Positive Youth Development

Reconsidering Adolescence

Social and Emotional Development in Adolescence

Jason, 13, knows he is an easy target for bullies at his middle school. His small *stature hinders him from retaliating against the taller, heavier boys who tease him. He prefers to wear skinny jeans and black zip-up hoodies, fashion choices that induce comments like "emo" or "gay" from classmates. He has an affinity for comic books and Xbox games such as* Halo *and* Call of Duty, *and for pursuing these hobbies, other kids call him a loser. Jason says he has been ostracized and was once punched in the neck at school, but the peer torment does not end when he enters the comfort of his home, on the weekends, or during summer vacations. Last year, he says, he became a victim of cyberbullying—vicious, incessant, viral attacks through text messages, e-mails, and Facebook posts that have both replaced and supplemented traditional schoolyard bullying. "It's really horrifying the next day after the message has been sent around, and you're the laughingstock of the school," Jason says. "You have no idea why or what's funny." Jason tried following the crowd last year.*

When gray shorts and red T-shirts became trendy, he wore them to school. Still, the bullies haunted him online. They called him dumb, although he's an honor student. They made fun of his thin frame. Jason says he contemplated not joining Facebook. But he says that would have been useless, because bullies continued to write negative comments about him in mass group messages behind his back. "There's nothing I can really do," he said. Until a few weeks ago, Jason's mother was unaware that students attacked her son online. "It's just hard in general, because I feel like my hands are tied," she said. "I don't know what to do. I don't want anyone to retaliate against him. I don't want him to get into trouble." As Jason started eighth grade this year, the cyberbullying has subsided, probably because the kids found someone new to pick on, he says.

"Before all this happened, I would try to change myself," he said. "Now I see that I like myself and I enjoy myself, and I think that if they don't like me, they don't appreciate me, then I'm strong enough to say I don't need to talk to that person."

(Adapted from Chen, 2010)

As you likely know from high-profile incidents reported in the press, cyberbullying can be deadly. The tweeting, streaming, posting, and sexting not only of words but also of images and videos has substantially expanded the social networks of adolescents, as well as the capacity for some of them to inflict social humiliation on peers. In Chapter 13, you were introduced to some of the developmental features of middle childhood that converge to create a "perfect storm" for both the propensity to bully and the propensity to be profoundly hurt when bullied. In this chapter you will learn about the emergence of new developmental features that contribute to a variety of social and behavioral changes during adolescence, including the decline in bullying. These features include developing abilities to control impulses, to understand the emotional and psychological experiences of others, to resist peer pressure, and to have a clear and stable sense of self. Jason captures a number of these features when he recounts his transition from trying to change himself to fit in, to

Whether they grow up in Vermont in the United States or Tierra del Fuego in Argentina, adolescents increasingly turn to each other to share ideas, feelings, and experiences.

feeling good about himself and having the strength to dismiss peers who may not like or appreciate him for who he is.

In this chapter, we examine the new feelings, relationships, and ways of interacting with family and friends that are typical of adolescence and that mark a new beginning in adolescents' sense of themselves and their place in the world. Adolescence is a time of seeking answers to fundamental questions of identity: Who am I? Who will I become? What do I want? How do I fit in?

We begin our examination by exploring adolescents' emotional development, focusing on the different types of feelings that adolescents experience and how they come to express and control them. We then shift our attention to adolescents' changing relationships—with friends, romantic partners, sexual partners, and family. Our third topic is identity development and its relationship to adolescents' social lives and cultures. Finally, we consider adolescents' health and well-being, including health problems and diseases that typically emerge in adolescence, as well as approaches to positive youth development.

Emotional Development in Adolescence

Adolescence is widely regarded as a period fraught with emotional highs and lows and with behavior that is often driven by impulse rather than rational thought. You know from Chapter 14 that adolescents' reputation for emotional intensity, instability, and flaming passion was well established as early as Plato's day. (Recall his warning against adolescents' consumption of wine: "Fire must not be poured upon fire.") Two thousand years later, Freud described the adolescent as a "boiling cauldron of desire." Needless to say, these images of adolescence are as vivid today as they ever were.

In this section, we take the age-old notion of adolescence as an emotional rollercoaster ride punctuated with impulse-driven behavior and hold it up to the light of scientific analysis. Is it true that adolescents experience especially intense emotions and dramatic mood swings? If so, why, and how is emotional stability eventually achieved as adolescents mature? Is it true that adolescents' behavior is exceptionally impulsive? If it is, how can behavioral impulsivity be reconciled with the significant advances that occur in adolescents' cognitive development and reasoning? In addressing these questions, we will continue the approach we used in examining emotional development during infancy and childhood, distinguishing between how emotions are experienced and how they are controlled and regulated (see Chapters 6, 9, and 13).

The Experience of Emotions

Many believe that peaks and valleys of emotional experience are a defining feature of adolescence. However, as you know from our discussions regarding infants and children, the study of emotional experiences poses significant challenges for researchers. Consequently, it is difficult to document whether, and to what extent, adolescence is the emotional roller coaster that so many believe it to be.

The effective study of emotional development in adolescence requires research tools that provide access to adolescents' emotional lives. One such tool is the **experience sampling method (ESM)**, in which research participants carry electronic pagers that beep at random intervals, signaling that it is time for them to fill out a brief report on their current feelings (Csikszentmihalyi & Larson, 1987). Although the ESM is time-intensive and disruptive for participants (typically, the pager beeps every 1 to 2 hours, 15 hours per day, for a week or more), it has been praised for its *ecological validity* (see Chapter 1, p. 35) (Silk, Steinberg, & Morris, 2003). It has also generated a wealth of information about the types and intensities of adolescents' emotions, the situations in which they occur, and the extent to which they are related to gender, age, pubertal status, and psychological problems (Eisenberg et al., 2005; Larson & Richards, 2000; Silk et al., 2003).

In general, ESM studies find strong evidence for the idea that emotional states change in type and intensity throughout the adolescent years. Reed Larson and his colleagues conducted a comprehensive, longitudinal study using ESM data collected from 220 participants over a period spanning early to late adolescence (Larson et al., 2002). When the participants were signaled by their pagers, they rated their emotional states (happy–unhappy; cheerful–irritable, friendly–angry) on a 7-point scale. Twice a year, they also filled out questionnaires about whether they had experienced major life events, including stressful events, during the past 6 months. The researchers found that more than 70 percent of the time, the participants reported experiencing positive emotions. However, they also found some interesting changes in the participants' emotional life between early and late adolescence:

- On average, daily emotions became less positive between early adolescence and middle adolescence (10th grade) and remained relatively low through late adolescence; in other words, average happiness decreased during adolescence (Figure 15.1).

- The decline in average happiness was due in part to a decrease in intense positive emotions but due mostly to an increase in negative emotions.

- Throughout adolescence, girls tended to have more positive emotions on average than boys did, as shown in Figure 15.1.

- Stressful life events were associated with equal amounts of negative emotion throughout adolescence, suggesting that there was no time during which adolescents were particularly emotionally sensitive or reactive to major life events.

- Over the course of adolescence, emotions became less intense and emotional ups and downs became less frequent.

In general, research suggests that an emotional roller coaster may be a poor metaphor for adolescent emotional life. There

experience sampling method (ESM) Tool used by developmentalists in which study participants, when signaled by electronic pagers at random intervals, fill out brief reports on their feelings. ESM has been used to study adolescents' emotional lives.

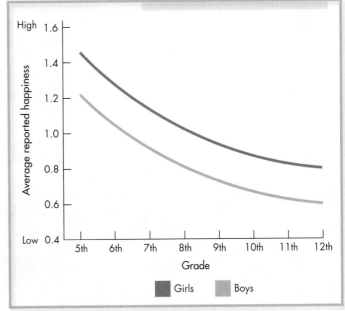

FIGURE 15.1 In general, girls report higher levels of happiness than do boys, although happiness declines for both girls and boys over the course of adolescence. (From Larson et al., 2002.)

sensation-seeking The desire to participate in highly arousing activities; it is especially common in early and mid-adolescence.

does not seem to be a particular time when adolescents are hypersensitive to stressful events, and the intensity and fluctuations of emotion seem to decrease over time.

Regulating Emotions

One of the primary explanations for why emotions become less intense and more stable over the course of adolescence is that teenagers become better able to control and regulate them, as well as the behaviors they might inspire (Steinberg, 2005). When his mom complains yet again that Josh's tongue-piercing looks gross and makes him sound like he has a speech impediment, Josh may retreat to fume in his room rather than lash out in fury, "It's my @#$#% tongue, and I'll do what I want to it!" Or when Marisha's friends are heading out to party, she may stay home to study chemistry, not because she is passionate about the subject (she hates it, actually) but because she wants to do well on tomorrow's exam.

Both Josh and Marisha are acting against impulse and inhibiting certain behaviors that would very likely lead to unsatisfying consequences. In addition, Marisha is persisting on a task (studying chemistry) despite a total lack of desire to do so, and in the face of a much more attractive alternative (partying). *Impulse control, inhibition,* and *persistence* are among the main features of emotion regulation, and they underlie the abilities to "down regulate" negative emotions (as Josh did when he cooled his fury) and "up regulate" positive ones (as Marisha did when she mustered enthusiasm for studying). Adolescents who have difficulty regulating their emotions, especially negative emotions, are more likely to experience depression, anger, and a variety of social and behavior problems (Hughes, Gullone, & Watson, 2011; Cooper et al., 2003).

As you may recall from earlier chapters, regulating emotions involves a complex interplay of biological and sociocultural processes. In adolescence, these processes interact in a unique way that has recently become of considerable interest to developmentalists.

Biological Processes As discussed in Chapter 14, adolescence includes two significant biological events that occur on different timetables: (1) an influx of pubertal hormones during early adolescence, and (2) a spurt in brain growth apparently triggered by hormones in early adolescence but not complete until late adolescence. Several studies suggest that pubertal hormones are associated with emotional intensity and may account for adolescents' **sensation-seeking**, or desire to participate in highly arousing activities (Martin et al., 2002; see Figure 15.2). In Chapter 14, we noted that novelty-seeking (sensation-seeking) seems to be a common feature in adolescents in many mammalian species, and this fact has led some developmentalists to argue that it may play an instrumental role in encouraging youths

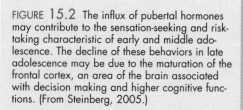

FIGURE 15.2 The influx of pubertal hormones may contribute to the sensation-seeking and risk-taking characteristic of early and middle adolescence. The decline of these behaviors in late adolescence may be due to the maturation of the frontal cortex, an area of the brain associated with decision making and higher cognitive functions. (From Steinberg, 2005.)

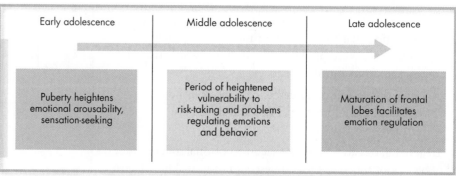

Early adolescence	Middle adolescence	Late adolescence
Puberty heightens emotional arousability, sensation-seeking	Period of heightened vulnerability to risk-taking and problems regulating emotions and behavior	Maturation of frontal lobes facilitates emotion regulation

to leave their families to join with peers for the purpose of exploring new territory and selecting mates (Spear, 2007, 2009). The infusion of hormones occurs at a time when the brain is undergoing considerable development, especially in regions of the frontal lobes associated with higher mental processes such as decision making, judgment, and impulse control (see p. 517). Some developmentalists, including Laurence Steinberg, have speculated that in early adolescence there is a gap between intense emotions triggered by pubertal hormones and the brain's ability to regulate those emotions (Figure 15.3). As a consequence, until the maturation of the frontal lobes is complete, the adolescent is especially vulnerable to risk-taking, recklessness, and emotional problems (Steinberg, 2005).

The possible link between brain development and adolescents' unique vulnerability to risky decision making was explored in a recent study comparing adolescents' and adults' decisions made under different social conditions (Gardner & Steinberg, 2005; Steinberg et al., 2008). The study involved a computerized driving game that presented opportunities for taking risks, such as driving through a yellow light in order to get more points for moving the car farther down the road. Participants were randomly assigned to one of two conditions—playing the game alone or playing while two friends were watching and giving advice. The adults in both conditions played similarly. In contrast, adolescents who played with friends present were much more likely than those who played alone to risk crashing the car by driving through yellow lights.

It seems, then, that adolescents may be more easily swayed by the social and emotional features of decision-making contexts than adults are. This is consistent with the argument that adolescents are hormonally "primed" for emotionally intense experiences but lack commensurate emotion-regulation abilities due to the fact that their brains—the frontal lobes in particular—are not yet fully mature.

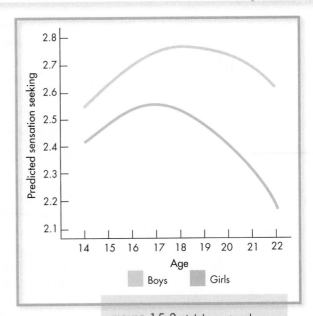

FIGURE 15.3 Adolescent males are much more likely than their female counterparts to engage in sensation-seeking behaviors. However, individuals of both genders appear particularly vulnerable to sensation-seeking within a window of time during which pubertal hormones are on the rise and maturation of the frontal lobes is incomplete. (Romer & Hennessy, 2007.)

Social Processes While biological processes may very well influence the maturity of adolescents' emotional responses, most developmentalists agree that the ways adolescents regulate their emotions depend importantly on the social and cultural contexts in which the adolescents develop. In particular, they depend on family interaction patterns and on social expectations regarding the expression of emotion.

Families play a critical role in how adolescents learn to manage their feelings. Consistent with research conducted on younger children (see Chapter 10, pp. 348–350), studies of adolescents find that warm, supportive parenting is associated with the ability to regulate one's feelings, whereas a family history of emotional negativity increases adolescents' negative emotions and aggressive behaviors, which can spill over into their peer relationships and contribute to social rejection (Kim et al., 2001).

In a longitudinal study that followed children from 9 to 13 years of age, Nancy Eisenberg and her colleagues explored the relationships between the emotional quality of parent–child interactions, adolescents' abilities to regulate their emotions, and adolescents' behavioral problems such as aggression (Eisenberg et al., 2005). The longitudinal design allowed the researchers to discover an interesting pattern: Parents' emotional warmth and expression of positive emotions during their children's mid-elementary school years (when the children were about 9 years old) predicted higher levels of children's emotion regulation 2 years later (early adolescence), which in turn predicted fewer behavioral problems 2 years after that (middle adolescence).

In addition to examining the role of family, developmentalists have explored how adolescents' gender affects their regulation of emotion. It is widely believed that males and females are socialized to manage their emotional expressions in vastly different ways. In particular, girls and women are considered to be "more emotional" than boys and men—that is, they are believed to experience emotions more intensely and to communicate them more willingly, presumably due to social conventions and cultural expectations that represent females as emotionally nurturing and expressive and males as independent and self-reliant.

Gender differences in crying provide an interesting example of the impact of sociocultural factors on adolescents' emotion regulation. Although boy and girl babies cry with equal frequency, gender differences in crying emerge in early childhood, with boys crying less often than girls, and become larger over the course of childhood (Brody, 2000; Jansz, 2000; Tilburg, Unterberg, & Vingerhoets, 2002). The ever-widening gender gap becomes particularly notable during adolescence, when boys cry much less frequently than girls do (girls' crying is relatively stable through adolescence; Tilburg et al., 2002). Several studies suggest that expectations, and sociocultural factors generally, underpin gender differences in crying. For example, one study of adolescents found that on measurements of shame, boys scored higher than girls on only one item: "I feel shame when I cry" (Truijers & Vingerhoets, 1999; cited in Tilburg et al., 2002). In addition, it seems that boys are more likely to cry if their parents are accepting of emotional expression and therefore less likely to reinforce cultural stereotypes (Bronstein et al., 1996).

Other evidence that gender differences in the expression of depressed emotions may be related to gender-role socialization comes from an observational home study in which adolescents and their mothers were videotaped as the adolescents took a math test that the researchers had designed and put on a computer (Cox, Mezulis, & Hyde, 2010). The adolescents first went through sets of practice problems, which had been designed to be within their abilities. Then came the test, which had been designed to ensure failure. After the test had been completed and the computer had revealed the test-taker's low score, the adolescents and their mothers discussed the test and the adolescents' disappointing performance. The researchers found that mothers of boys were less likely than mothers of girls to encourage their children's expression of negative emotion. This was particularly true for mothers who scored high on a test of how much they adhered to traditional gender roles, as measured by items such as, "I would not allow my son to play with dolls," and "Men who cry have weak character" (p. 846; see Figure 15.4).

To investigate the expression of the complex interplay between emotion and social expectations in boys and girls, Archana Singh-Manoux studied 9th- and 11th-grade adolescents in India and England (Singh-Manoux, 2000). The adolescents were asked to describe a situation that led to an experience of fear, shame, or sadness. They were then asked a series of questions regarding the intensity of the emotion, whether they shared their emotional experience with others, and for how long the experience had preoccupied them. In both cultures, girls were more likely than boys to share their emotional experiences with others and to be preoccupied with them longer. However, the intensity of the emotions was greater for girls than for boys only in England; in India, boys reported more intense emotions than did girls. Furthermore, on most measures, the differences between boys and

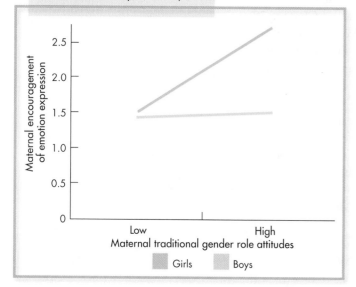

FIGURE 15.4 Mothers who tend to endorse traditional gender roles are significantly more likely to encourage the expression of emotions in daughters than in sons. (Cox, Mezulis, & Hyde, 2010.)

girls were much greater in England than in India. This may be due to different cultural conceptions of adolescence: In India, adolescents are considered older children rather than young men and women. Consequently, social pressures to act masculine or feminine may emerge later for Indian teenagers than for their English counterparts.

Altogether, research provides ample evidence that the experience and regulation of emotions undergo substantial change over the course of adolescence and are influenced by both biological and sociocultural factors. These changes have important implications for adolescents' relationships with peers, family, and sexual partners, topics that we address below.

The extent to which boys and girls differ in the expression of emotions depends importantly on their culture's conceptions of what is appropriate behavior for males and females. In some Asian cultures, it is considered impolite for girls to laugh without covering their mouths. The same convention does not apply to boys.

▲ APPLY :: CONNECT :: DISCUSS

In general, girls are considered "more emotional" than boys. Evaluate this belief in light of research on gender differences in emotional experience and emotion regulation.

Relationships with Peers

As children enter adolescence, their social activities and relationships with peers undergo several major changes. First, the sheer amount of time spent with peers increases dramatically, to the point where high school students spend twice as much time with their friends as they do with their parents or other adults (Csikszentmihalyi & Larson, 1984; Fuligni & Stevenson, 1995). Second, compared with younger children, adolescents are more mobile and better able to avoid the watchful eyes of parents and other authorities, so their peer activities are more likely to go unsupervised. As you will see, not only does the amount of time spent with peers change but so, too, does the nature of peer interactions and relationships. Peer groups increase in size and diversity during adolescence, and friendships and other close relationships increase in intensity. When exploring the nature of these changes and the implications they have for other areas of adolescent growth and adjustment, developmentalists tend to distinguish between adolescents' *close relationships* with friends and romantic partners and their *peer networks,* that is, their connections to groups of teens that may include casual acquaintances as well as good friends. As we discuss below, each type of relationship has different functions and fulfills different needs in adolescents' social and emotional development.

Friendships

In general, a **friendship** refers to a close relationship between two individuals. As you saw in previous chapters, the friendships of young children are often based on such shifting and transitory factors as playing with the same toys or being on the same sports team. Several large-scale studies conducted in the United States and other industrialized countries document the changing basis of friendships as children enter adolescence (Berndt, 2007; De Goede, Branje, & Meeus, 2009; Schneider et al., 2005). In contrast to the apparently superficial characteristics that bind younger children together, the characteristics that adolescents see as fundamental to their friendships are reciprocity, commitment, and equality (Hartup, 1998; Larsen, 1996). *Reciprocity,* the give-and-take of close relationships, includes emotional sharing as well as the sharing of interests and activities; *commitment* refers to the loyalty and trust between friends; and *equality* to the equal distribution of power among them.

friendship A close relationship between two individuals. Friendships in adolescence are characterized by reciprocity, commitment, and equality.

intimacy A sense of close connection between two individuals, resulting from shared feelings, thoughts, and activities.

autonomy The ability to assert one's own needs in a relationship.

homophobia A fear of homosexuality. Homophobia may diminish intimacy among adolescent males.

Developmental Functions of Friendships The dyadic friendships of adolescence serve two significant developmental functions: intimacy and autonomy—the yin and yang of social life (Selman et al., 1997). If you were asked which of the two is more salient in friendship, you would likely say **intimacy**, which, as defined by Selman, is "the gratifying connection between two individuals through some combination of shared feelings, thoughts, and activities" (Selman et al., 1997, p. 32). However, as Selman and his colleagues have demonstrated in numerous studies of normally developing and psychosocially disturbed children and adolescents, in healthy relationships, intimacy is balanced with **autonomy**—the ability to govern the self and assert one's own needs. Indeed, unhealthy friendships can place a child at significant risk, depending on whether the scales tip more toward intimacy or autonomy. Selman and his colleagues point out, for example, that the inability to assert one's needs without jeopardizing friendship intimacy contributes to a child's willingness to bow to peer pressure. On the other hand, an excess of autonomy can also be problematic—for example, bullying one's peers into risky behaviors.

Evidence from various studies indicates that close, well-balanced friendships have a positive influence on adolescents' social and personality development (Eccles, Brown, & Templeton, 2008). Adolescents who perceive their friends as supportive report fewer school-related and psychological problems, greater confidence in their social acceptance by peers, and less loneliness. Difficulty in making friends during adolescence is usually part of a broader syndrome of poor social adjustment often first apparent in early childhood (Pedersen et al., 2007).

Friendships and Gender While friends are important to both boys and girls during adolescence, there are differences in the quality of boys' and girls' friendships. In particular, research finds that girls' friendships are more intense and intimate (Brown, 2004). Several explanations have been offered. Thomas Berndt and Lonna Murphy (2002), for example, suggest that male adolescent friendships are less intimate because, compared with teenage girls, teenage boys are less trusting of their friends and, consequently, less likely to share the emotional details of their lives with them. Indeed, the study of Indian and English adolescents described earlier indicates that boys in both cultures tend to share more superficial aspects of emotionally charged experiences with friends, whereas girls are more likely to share their feelings (Singh-Manoux, 2000). Consider, for example, 13-year-old Michael's description of how boys discuss sex and sexual arousal "more openly" than girls:

> I think guys can speak about it [sex] more openly with each other from what I've seen from the girls in my school. They usually keep to themselves about it instead of talking about it, whereas guys can be more open with it. We talk about girls and wet dreams. . . . With guys you can just say, "Oh, I saw this really good-looking chick on TV and I cracked a boner."

Although Michael describes boys as more open with each other regarding these highly sensitive subjects, his language suggests that humor may be used to diffuse the emotional intensity of shared events. Indeed, Michael goes on to suggest that his friends keep some of their most deeply significant emotional experiences to themselves:

> [But] I've got a friend of mine whose mom died a few years ago and he never brought it up in school and even now he rarely talks about it. I've got another friend of mine whose dad is in the hospital with a disease and he never talks about that. (Martino & Pallotta-Chiarolli, 2003, p. 65)

Yet another explanation proposed for why the friendships of boys are less intimate than those of girls is that **homophobia**—a fear of homosexuality—prevents adolescent males from demonstrating or admitting to strong feelings of intimacy toward their male friends (Raymond, 1994). An ethnographic study of Australian boys and young men found evidence that they carefully monitored and policed the levels of intimacy in their relationships in order to avoid being perceived as homosexual (Martino & Pallotta-Chiarolli, 2003). Consider the following discussion between a researcher (Maria) and 16-year-old Darren who, although heterosexual, had been called gay because of the perceived closeness of his male friendships (p. 67):

> Maria: How do you feel about that [being labeled gay for having close friendships with other boys]?
> Darren: It's weird but I wouldn't know how to explain it. It [being called "gay"] gives you a shock.
> Maria: And do you find that you change the way you talk to some guys?
> Darren: Yes, exactly. I wouldn't bring up some subjects, I would just try and keep away from it.

In addition to differences in intimacy, the friendships of boys and girls differ in their degree of competition (Schneider et al., 2005), with girls' friendships tending to be less competitive. Among boys, friendly competition (as opposed to hyper-competitiveness, which is marked by higher levels of aggression) is usually enjoyed and may even increase the closeness of relationships. The higher level of competition in boys' friendships suggests that boys and girls have different relationship "goal orientations." Specifically, girls appear to focus more on *communal goals,* which emphasize relationship enhancement and cooperation, whereas boys appear to focus more on *agentic goals,* which emphasize dominance and self-interest (Saragovi et al., 2002; Rudolph & Conley, 2005). Such gender differences in goal orientation, of course, fit Western cultural conceptions of females as oriented more toward connectedness and intimacy and males more toward independence and autonomy.

Cliques and Crowds

A friendship is the smallest unit of peer interaction, a group of two. As children move into adolescence, two additional, more inclusive kinds of peer groups become prominent— *cliques* and *crowds.* Adolescent cliques and crowds are significant social groups in societies that group children by age for the purpose of education. In such societies, adolescents spend a lot of time with each other and consequently learn to establish and maintain relationships with groups of peers. Cliques and crowds differ in size as well as in the developmental functions that they serve (Figure 15.5).

In general, **cliques** are small and intimate and have the function of serving adolescents' emotional and security needs (Henrich et al., 2006). A clique typically includes five to seven members who are relatively good friends (Brown, 2004). Dexter Dunphy (1963), one of the first researchers to study cliques and crowds, noted that cliques are about the size of a family and serve a similar emotional function as an "alternative center of security" (p. 233). Furthermore, cliques have an internal structure that usually includes a leader who tends to be more mature and more socially connected compared with the other members of the group. In early adolescence, clique members are usually of the same gender, but by middle adolescence, mixed-gender cliques are common. Most

clique A group of several young people that remains small enough to enable its members to be in regular interaction with one another and to serve as the primary peer group.

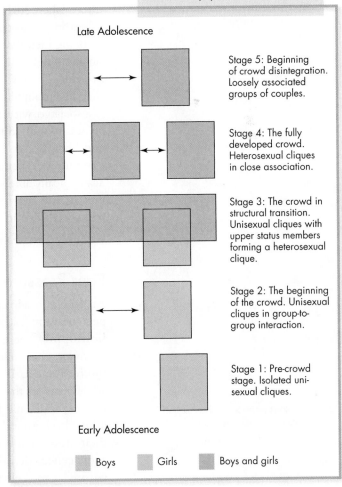

FIGURE 15.5 Stages of adolescents' social relationships from early to late adolescence, according to Dexter Dunphy.

Late Adolescence

Stage 5: Beginning of crowd disintegration. Loosely associated groups of couples.

Stage 4: The fully developed crowd. Heterosexual cliques in close association.

Stage 3: The crowd in structural transition. Unisexual cliques with upper status members forming a heterosexual clique.

Stage 2: The beginning of the crowd. Unisexual cliques in group-to-group interaction.

Stage 1: Pre-crowd stage. Isolated unisexual cliques.

Early Adolescence

Boys Girls Boys and girls

Simone Joyner / Getty Images

This crowd of Blink-182 fans probably includes a number of cliques—smaller groups of good friends who came to the concert together and will depart together. According to Dunphy, the crowd serves the important function of providing opportunities for adolescents to meet new people and develop new relationships.

adolescents belong to several different cliques, and their association with them may depend on the particular setting. For example, an adolescent may be a member of one clique in science class, another during sports practice, and still another in the neighborhood on the weekends.

A **crowd** is a larger group of friends and acquaintances that emerges when cliques interact, as they might at a big party or get-together. In contrast to the emotional functions of cliques, crowds appear to provide opportunities to meet new people, explore one's social identity (Barber, Eccles, & Stone, 2001), and develop new relationships, especially romantic relationships.

The importance of crowds to adolescents' exploration of identity comes especially from the fact that crowds typically have public identities of their own, that is, reputations for engaging in certain types of behaviors and having particular values, norms, and goals (Brown & Klute, 2003). Crowd reputations are apparent in stereotyped labels such as "jocks," "brains," "loners," "druggies," and "nerds" (Brown & Klute, 2003; Eckert, 1995). In schools with a diverse ethnic population, ethnic labels ("African Americans," "Latinos," "Asians," etc.) are also common (Brown & Huang, 1995). As names such as "jocks," "brains," and "druggies" indicate, crowds vary in the extent to which their norms and values conform to those of the adult community. Other labels, such as "normal" and "outcast," indicate how the crowd's norms and values adhere to those of the adolescent community.

Being identified as a member of a particular crowd may have a significant impact on an adolescent's social status, depending on the local peer culture. For example, as a rule, "brains" occupy a status somewhere between the elite groups and groups that are unpopular. However, in some peer cultures, poor academic achievement is associated with high levels of popularity—as is the case where aggressive, low-achieving individuals are highly popular (Rodkin et al., 2000; Estell et al., 2002)—and "brains" are disparaged. Similarly, in some working-class African American communities, being labeled as a "brain" can lead to being ostracized, causing many academically able young people try to mask their abilities (Ogbu, 1997). In general, crowds and the way they are categorized help adolescents learn about the alternative social identities that are available to them and strongly influence whom they are likely to meet and spend time with (Brown et al., 1994).

Peer Pressure and Conformity

An aspect of adolescent social relationships that has been extensively examined is peer pressure and conformity (Brown et al., 2008). Conformity, also known as **homophily**, refers to the degree to which friends are similar to each other in their behavior, their taste in clothes and music, and their goals and aspirations for the future (Kandel, 1978; Kandel & Chen, 2000; Furman & Simon, 2008). Although adolescents in the United States are more mobile than younger children, attend larger schools, and have more opportunities to meet peers of other social classes and ethnic backgrounds, their close friends tend to be even more similar to them than their close friends in elementary school were, a trend that continues throughout adolescence (Berndt & Keefe, 1995). High school friends are particularly likely to be similar in their values, their views of school, their academic achievement, and

crowd A large, reputation-based and mixed-gender social network observed when cliques interact.

homophily The degree to which friends are similar to each other.

their dating and other leisure-time activities (Berndt & Murphy, 2002; Patrick et al., 2002). They also tend to feel the same way about drug use, drinking, and delinquency (Solomon & Knafo, 2007; Tani et al., 2001; Urberg et al., 1998).

Selection and Socialization In a year-long seminal study of homophily in adolescent friendships, Denise Kandel (1978) focused on the areas of drug use, educational goals, and delinquency. Her findings suggested that two developmental processes are involved in the establishment of homophily: selection and socialization. Through *selection,* adolescents target others as potential friends, seeking out teenagers who seem similar to them in important traits and behaviors, especially those that are relevant to the adolescent's social reputation. Hockey players are more likely to hang out with other hockey players; delinquents, with other delinquents; good students, with other good students; and so on. Once selection has done its job, socialization comes into play. Through *socialization,* socially significant behaviors are modeled and reinforced in the course of ongoing interactions. Socialization accounts for the tendency of individuals to become increasingly more alike—to show higher levels of behavioral agreement—as their relationships develop over time. For example, studies have found that children who are at risk for antisocial behavior and who become friendly with delinquent peers are likely to become delinquent themselves (Monahan, Steinberg, & Cauffman, 2009).

Conformity and Deviance For decades, developmentalists have worried that it may be unhealthy for adolescents to spend excessive time with their peers, removed from the observation and control of adults. Frederic Thrasher (1927) argued as much in his classic study of more than 1,300 Chicago gangs in existence during the early years of the 1900s. The problem, he argued, was not due to the nature of the boys who joined the gangs, many of which began as neighborhood play groups. Gangs became problematic only when they functioned without supervision and opportunities to participate in socially acceptable activity. In a similar vein, Urie Bronfenbrenner (1970) made the point that "if children have contact only with their own age-mates, there is no possibility for learning culturally established patterns of cooperation and mutual concern" (p. 121).

It is an open question whether adolescents, left entirely to their own devices, would create a "Lord of the Flies" society, in which cooperation and concern for others would be overshadowed by self-interested, deviant behavior. There is, however, plenty of evidence to support the notion that deviancy can be socialized in the context of peer relationships (Blanton & Burkley, 2008). For example, Thomas Berndt and Keunho Keefe (1995) asked a large group of seventh- and eighth-graders in the fall and the spring of the school year to identify their friends and to describe any disruptive behaviors they engaged in. They found that boys and girls whose friends engaged in a high level of disruptive behavior in the fall reported an increase in the level of their own disruptive behavior in the spring, with the girls being more susceptible to such influence. Other studies show that if an adolescent's close friends smoke cigarettes, drink alcohol, use illegal drugs, are sexually active, or break the law, sooner or later the adolescent is likely to follow suit, as we discuss in more detail later in the chapter (Kandel & Chen, 2000; Reed & Roundtree, 1997).

Thomas Dishion and his colleagues proposed the concept of *deviancy training* to account for the homophily of antisocial behavior among adolescent peers (Dishion, Véronneau, & Meyers, 2010). **Deviancy training** occurs when friends respond to talk about rule-breaking and other deviant forms of behavior by laughing or reacting in other positive ways. This process was documented in a series of longitudinal studies in which boys were videotaped as they engaged in discussions with friends.

deviancy training Positive reactions to discussions of rule-breaking.

Adolescent gangs have been studied since the early 1900s. Modern developmentalists have focused on understanding the risk factors associated with gang involvement, as well as the social processes involved in deviant behavior.

The researchers coded the discussion sessions for "deviant talk" and whether it was reinforced. They found that deviancy training in discussions at age 13 or 14 predicted increased violent behavior, as well as the initiation of tobacco, alcohol, and marijuana use, by age 15 or 16 (Dishion et al., 1999).

Peer processes similar to deviancy training have been blamed for the surprising finding that group counseling and therapy for delinquent adolescents may, in some circumstances, do more harm than good (Dishion et al., 1999). In two experimentally controlled intervention studies, adolescents involved in group counseling, compared with those in other types of intervention, had higher rates of delinquency and deviant behavior up to 3 years after the termination of the counseling sessions (Dishion et al., 1999). Thus it appears that in the group setting, the teens mutually reinforced positive attitudes about delinquent behavior. This is a good lesson in the importance of scientific research in planning and understanding counseling and intervention practices. It also underscores the importance of designing and using developmentally appropriate therapies. Therapeutic strategies that are effective with adults may backfire when used with adolescents.

Romantic Relationships

In many cultures, a key function of the peer group is to provide an avenue to romantic relationships (Connolly, Furman, & Konarski, 2000; Furman & Simon, 2008). It has been noted, in fact, that romantic relationships are central to adolescents' sense of belonging and group status.

Dexter Dunphy argued that the process of developing romantic relationships takes place through a series of stages, as shown in Figure 15.5 (p. 559): The same-sex cliques of early adolescence give way to the mixed-sex crowds of mid-adolescence, which gradually disintegrate as members become involved in romantic relationships. Contemporary work generally supports the stages that Dunphy proposed and also marks mid-adolescence as a major turning point during which nearly 50 percent of adolescents report involvement in relatively intense romantic relationships (Feiring, 1996; Kuttler & La Greca, 2004; but see the box "Friends with Benefits" for an exception to this pattern).

Although these studies provide convincing evidence of a stagelike process, there are important cultural and historical variations in adolescent romantic relationships (Berndt & Savin-Williams, 1993; Brown et al., 1994). On the basis of the data he collected in the late 1950s, Dunphy reported that the crowd disintegrated into couples who were going steady or were engaged to get married. Fifty years later, this pattern may continue in some parts of the world, but it does not appear to be generally characteristic of contemporary industrialized societies. Instead, marriage is often postponed until several years after the initiation of sexual activity. In addition, adolescents typically do not stop hanging out with their friends once they become involved in romantic relationships (Connolly et al., 2004). Thus, romantic relationships take place alongside other peer relationships, creating a context in which adolescents must maneuver between relationships with their friends and their romantic partners. Developmentalists have found that adolescents often feel neglected when their friends start dating, particularly in

Romantic relationships become increasingly important during the adolescent years. In addition to providing opportunities for exploring intimacy and identity, romantic relationships are important to adolescents' sense of belonging and group status.

Name:	Benoit Denizet-Lewis
Education:	B.A. from the Medill School of Journalism, Northwestern University
Current Position:	Book author; contributing writer to the *New York Times Magazine*
Career Objectives:	Publish books and articles on youth culture, addiction, sex, and sexuality

"BEING IN A REAL RELATIONSHIP JUST COMPLICATES everything," says 16-year-old Brian. "You feel obligated to be all, like, couple-y. And that gets really boring after a while. When you're friends with benefits, you go over, hook up, then play video games or something. It rocks."

Brian's view reflects that of many, mostly White, suburban teens, for whom "hooking up" is more common than dating. Although it can encompass anything from kissing to sexual intercourse, and is often associated with oral sex, for most adolescents, "hooking up" refers to sexual encounters with a partner who is no more than a friend. Friends with whom one hooks up regularly are "friends with benefits."

Benoit Denizet-Lewis was among the first to call attention to this new type of friendship (Denizet-Lewis, 2004). With an educational background in journalism and sociology, and a keen interest in cultural issues, Denizet-Lewis spent several months hanging out and communicating online with nearly 100 high school students. What he found and reported on sent parents, teachers, counselors, and researchers scrambling to understand what was becoming a growing trend in adolescent sexual relationships.

Denizet-Lewis first met his teen informants online, at Internet sites popular with high school and college students, such as sites for placing personal profiles and chat rooms for flirting and, on occasion, arranging hook-ups. (Many informants indicated that hooking up with someone from your own school can be risky, and sought out partners from neighboring schools and towns.) Through online and face-to-face interviews with teens, Denizet-Lewis examined the world of adolescent casual sex in a way

Benoit Denizet-Lewis.

Benoit Denizet-Lewis / Patrick Lentz

that has thus far eluded the questionnaire and survey efforts of researchers. In addition to documenting the increasing popularity of hooking up, he found, for example, that although many teens have had romantic relationships, they find them complicated, often painful, and not at all necessary when one has close friends of the opposite sex who can be counted on for "benefits." As one teen explained, "A lot of guys get in relationships just so they can get steady [expletive]. But now that it's easy to get sex outside of relationships, guys don't need relationships." According to another informant, however, the relationship between friends with benefits can be a bit more complicated than it appears. On the day that Denizet-Lewis met Melissa, she was distressed because her friend with benefits had just broken up with her. "How is that even possible?" she asked. "The point of having a friend with benefits is that you won't get broken up with, you won't get hurt. He told me online that he met a girl that he really likes, so now, of course, we can't hook up anymore."

Despite the apparent enthusiasm for no-strings-attached sex, Denizet-Lewis found plenty of evidence that hooking up may have a downside. For one thing, it can jeopardize one's reputation and interfere with developing more serious relationships: "You have to be careful," said one boy. "I have this huge crush on this girl who knows a lot of the girls I know, and I don't want her to find out that I hook up a lot and think I'm dirty." Indeed, feeling "dirty," disappointed, confused, and guilty were common consequences of hooking up, especially for teens who wanted or expected more from the relationship. Another significant issue is the possible gender asymmetry in who actually benefits from being friends with benefits. Denizet-Lewis pointed out that a recurrent theme in his interviews was whether the sexual desires and satisfactions of boys overshadowed those of girls. The girls he spoke with voiced varying opinions. One said, "If I ask a guy to come over to my house and hook up, I'm the one benefiting because I'm the one who wants to. . . . It's not just about pleasing the guy." But another girl disagreed: "I feel like women have less power today. It's not just that the guy often doesn't respect the girl or the girl's sexuality, but the girl sometimes doesn't really respect and validate herself. . . . I think a lot of times girls are really self-destructive."

The adolescents interviewed by Denizet-Lewis make it abundantly clear that norms regarding sexual behavior and relationships are undergoing significant changes within the peer group. They also reveal the extent to which such changes invite reflection on other aspects of their lives, including how they think and feel about themselves.

In addition to its many other uses, the computer provides teens with Web sites where they can post personal profiles, chat, flirt, and, on occasion, arrange to "hook up."

Image Source Ltd. / dir.net

the early phases of new romantic relationships (Roth & Parker, 2001; Shulman & Seiffge-Krenke, 2001).

Ami Kuttler and Annette La Greca explored the complications of managing romantic and friend relationships in an ethnically diverse sample of adolescent girls (2004). They found that casual dating may actually enhance feelings of closeness with best friends because it provides opportunities to share and discuss intimate subjects regarding romance and sexuality. In addition, casual daters generally relied more on their best friends than on their dating partners for companionship, affection, and support. In contrast, girls who indicated that they were involved in "serious" romantic relationships reported less companionship with best friends, presumably because they spent less time with friends than with their romantic partners and tended to rely more on their romantic partners for their emotional needs. However, all girls, regardless of the seriousness of their romantic relationships, reported higher levels of conflict and pressure with their romantic partners than with their best friends.

Romantic relationships may evolve differently within different cultural subgroups. In the United States, for example, Black adolescents are less likely than White adolescents to have romantic experiences, although when they do, they are more likely to be involved in steady relationships. Black adolescents who have steady relationships are also more likely to cohabit in early adulthood than are White youths (Meier & Allen, 2009). It also appears that male gangs in economically depressed neighborhoods actively discourage involvement in significant relationships and often ridicule members who have them (Anderson, 1990). And given that most, presumably heterosexual adolescent peer groups generally disapprove of homosexual relationships, as we will discuss below, it is likely that peer influences are quite different in the formation of gay and lesbian relationships.

In addition, cultures vary widely in the extent to which they support and provide opportunities for the development of romantic relationships (Dhariwal et al., 2009). In many Middle Eastern cultures, particularly those influenced by Islamic religious traditions, dating is either carefully monitored by adults or actively discouraged (Mahdi, 2003). In Iraq, for example, even casual contact between adolescent boys and girls can have dire social consequences, as 16-year-old Samira reports:

> Yes, of course I would like to be able to speak with boys and get to know how they think about girls, but this is getting more and more difficult. I have heard some cases where a boy tried to drag a girl to speak with him by claiming that he was in love with her. But the truth is that he just wanted to show his friends that he had "a sexual affair" with her. This is a very dangerous thing to say about a girl in Iraq. Such incidents would mean that the girl has desecrated her family's honor—something for which she might be severely punished by her father or her brother. It would also mean that her chances of getting a husband become very slim. (Al-Ali & Hussein, 2003, p. 48)

⏏ APPLY :: CONNECT :: DISCUSS

How does Dunphy's distinction between cliques and crowds fit your own adolescent experience of peer groups? Reflect on the social structure of your high school and try to map out the different crowd types and the different cliques within them. How do the concepts of homophily, selection, and socialization apply?

Sexual Relationships

Your virginity is what determines whether you're a man or a boy in the eyes of every teenage male. Teenage men see sex as a race: the first one to the finish line wins. In high school, virginity is a self-demeaning label that you want nothing more than to get rid of. . . . It is much tougher for women. . . . A woman who has lots of sex at a young age is considered a slut. Women who don't have sex at all are considered prudes. The double standard is a trap for females.

—Jeff, 16, in W. Pollack, *Real Boys' Voices*, 2000

The step from being a virgin to being sexually active is a significant one. As expressed in Jeff's commentary on the relationship between sexual behavior and gender, the emergence of sexual behavior extends far beyond the physical act to include a host of social influences and cultural meanings (Peplau et al., 1999). In many cultures, sexuality is not a frequent topic of conversation between adolescents and their parents, peers, or school counselors. Nor are adolescents openly provided with opportunities to explore their sexuality. Martha Nussbaum (2010) argues that Western culture, including its scholars, associates strong feelings of shame with the body and its sexual behaviors and desires and is therefore reluctant to have sexuality addressed in an open manner. (It was, in fact, the inherent conflict between the human body's sexual drives and appetites and society's sanctions against their expression that inspired Freud's theory of psychosexual development.) According to some developmentalists, cultural ambivalence about sex may also account for why researchers have neglected to explore adolescent sexual experiences and sexual-identity development as a normal part of growing up, focusing instead only on problems associated with adolescent sexuality (Savin-Williams, 2008).

Indeed, as we discuss below, much of the information that adolescents receive about sexual behavior takes the form of warnings about potential negative outcomes, including unwanted pregnancy and **sexually transmitted infections (STIs)** (discussed fully on pp. 593–595). As you will see, there are enormous cultural and historical differences in how adolescents are educated about sex, including when they are expected to become sexually active, how they should have sex, and with whom.

> **sexually transmitted infections (STIs)** Infections typically acquired through sexual contact. Organisms causing infections can be transmitted through semen, vaginal fluid, blood, and other body fluids.

Learning About Sex

Q: how do u kno if u hve a sti?
A: if u hve sex u can get a sti chlamydia gonorrhea = no symptoms most of the time dropin get chcked

As you may know, adolescents can now use their cell phones to learn about sex and their sexual health. San Francisco's Department of Public Health, for example, has set up a text-messaging service aimed at teens living in areas of the city where the incidence of teen pregnancy and sexually transmitted infections is especially high. The service responds to inquiries with information, referrals, or advice on a variety of sexual issues that teens can select from a list of common concerns such as, *if ur condom broke, if u think ur pregnant,* and *if ur not sure u want to have sex* (Levine et al., 2008). During the first 25 weeks of service (April–October, 2006), the Department of Public Health received more than 4,500 inquiries—ample evidence that text messaging is a feasible way for at-risk adolescents to seek and receive information regarding sexual and reproductive health.

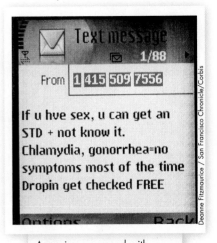

Agencies concerned with sexual health are using text messaging services to respond to adolescents' questions about pregnancy prevention and sexually transmitted infections.

At the annual Father–Daughter Purity Ball in Colorado Springs, Colorado, Hannah signs a contract promising to remain a virgin until she marries, while her father, who promises to defend her virginity, looks on. Events like this reflect the abstinence-only approach to sex education.

Adolescents learn about sexuality from a variety of sources—parents, peers, media, and special educational and counseling programs that have been devised by schools and public health agencies (Sutton et al., 2002). Likewise, adolescents learn about sexuality through several social processes, including observation, imitation, and explicit instruction. Like contexts of learning in general, the contexts of learning about sex can range from casual and subtle to rigorous and formal. Family conventions regarding touching and nudity, media depictions of sexual behavior, sex-education courses, and debates in the popular press regarding "abstinence-only" versus "comprehensive" sex education all contribute to young people's construction of an understanding of themselves as sexual beings.

In some cultures, like the Kaguru of Tanzania, knowledge of sexual behavior is communicated in the course of elaborate initiation ceremonies (Beidelman, 1997). Extensive ethnographic studies by Thomas Beidelman indicate that direct communication between Kaguru parents and their children about sexual matters is strictly forbidden. However, the stories, riddles, and songs that young children are taught are very often colored with allusions to sex and sexuality, and most of the songs taught to pubescent boys and girls at initiation involve instruction about sexual organs and sexual relations, communicated mainly through metaphor. Here are two examples (from Beidelman, 1997, p. 198):

Chimudodo chilimo, chidodo cilenga dilenga chitunge ne dikami.

Translation: The small, small mouth makes milk and water.

Explanation: This song explains that the penis is capable of both urinating and ejaculating semen. Kaguru sometimes describe semen as a kind of nurturant milk. Semen not only produces children but is also thought to foster the maturation of girls, who should have frequent intercourse if they want to develop a full, feminine figure.

Mang'ina sena mahusi-husi, galonda mbolo gabaka mafuta.

Translation: Your mothers are conniving to take a penis and anoint it with oil.

Explanation: Women are said to lubricate men's penises with oil before intercourse. Some Kaguru say that a woman should pass down her oil container to her daughter. It is as much a material embodiment of her personhood as a bow and arrow or a shotgun is for a man.

Although information about sexuality is often transmitted more explicitly in technologically advanced societies, there is a great deal of family, ethnic, and cultural variability in the nature of information taught and the manner in which it is transmitted. Studies of how mothers in the United States communicate with their adolescent children about sexuality and AIDS, for example, find significant differences that affect adolescents' knowledge of sexual matters. In one study, it was found that adolescents whose mothers dominated conversations with them about AIDS were less knowledgeable about AIDS 2 years later than were adolescents whose mothers had been more interactive in their conversations (Boone et al., 2003).

Research has also uncovered interesting ethnic differences in family communication patterns about sexual matters. For example, Eva Lefkowitz and her colleagues (Lefkowitz et al., 2000) discovered that when discussing sexuality and AIDS with their children, Hispanic (or Latina) American mothers were more likely to dominate the conversation than were European American mothers, who demonstrated greater responsiveness to their children's comments and questions. The finding that the Hispanic American mothers in this study tended to dominate the discussions is consistent with cultural expectations that children will be respectful and obedient toward their parents (Huynh & Fuligni, 2008).

There are also striking cultural differences among technologically advanced societies in the way sexuality is taught. In many European countries, adolescent sex is considered a normal part of development rather than a problem to be prevented, and adolescents have easy access to contraceptives, confidential health care, and comprehensive (rather than abstinence-only) sex education. According to a recent study of more than 30 European countries, those with low levels of adolescent pregnancy, childbearing, and STIs were characterized by societal acceptance of sexual activity among young people and the ready availability of comprehensive and balanced information about sexuality, pregnancy, and prevention of STIs, as well as an emphasis on teenage relationships and responsibility (Guttmacher Institute, 2011).

In contrast, teenage sex is considered by many in the United States to be risky and potentially harmful as a source of unintended pregnancies and STIs. This view is reflected in the rise of abstinence-only programs and the "virginity pledge" movement, which encourage youths to remain virgins until marriage. At its high point, approximately 23 percent of adolescent females and 16 percent of adolescent males were estimated to have taken this pledge (Bearman & Brückner, 2001). However, research indicates that pledgers are no different from nonpledgers in the ages at which they begin genital play, oral sex, and vaginal intercourse (Bersamin et al., 2005). They do differ from nonpledgers in one respect, however: They are less likely to practice safe sex (Rosenbaum, 2009).

The Sexual Debut

As you can see in Figure 15.6, the average age at which adolescents first engage in sexual intercourse varies considerably across the globe. There are also some interesting cultural differences between boys' and girls' sexual debut. For example, in the United States and most Western European cultures, boys tend to first have sexual intercourse at slightly earlier ages than girls do. However, the situation is reversed in many other countries, sometimes radically so (Centers for Disease Control and Prevention, 2004). In Ethiopia, the median age of first intercourse

FIGURE 15.6 Median age at first intercourse (age by which half of the population becomes sexually active). (From Wellings et al., 2006.)

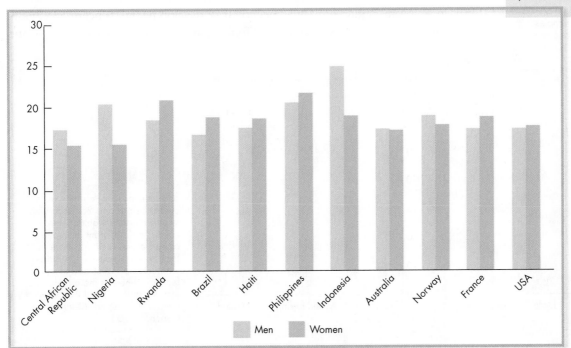

<table>
<tr><td colspan="5">table 15.1</td></tr>
<tr><td colspan="5">Percent of Adolescents and Young Adults Reporting Ever Having Had Various Sexual Experiences</td></tr>
</table>

Sexual Experience	Age 14–15	16–17	18–19	20–24
Males				
Masturbated alone	67.5	78.9	88.1	91.8
Masturbated with partner	6.7	20.3	49.3	54.5
Received oral from female	13.0	34.4	59.4	73.5
Received oral from male	1.6	3.2	8.8	9.3
Gave oral to female	8.3	20.2	60.9	70.9
Gave oral to male	1.6	2.8	10.1	9.3
Vaginal intercourse	9.9	30.3	62.5	70.3
Inserted penis into anus	3.7	6.0	9.7	23.7
Received penis in anus	1.0	0.9	4.3	10.8
Females				
Masturbated alone	43.3	52.4	66.0	76.8
Masturbated with partner	9.0	19.7	38.6	46.9
Received oral from female	3.8	6.6	8.0	16.8
Received oral from male	10.1	25.8	62.0	79.7
Gave oral to female	5.4	8.0	8.2	14.0
Gave oral to male	12.8	29.1	61.2	77.6
Vaginal intercourse	12.4	31.6	64.0	85.6
Received penis in anus	4.3	6.6	20.0	39.9

(Adapted from Herbenick et al., 2010)

is 15½ years for girls and 18½ years for boys; in Nepal, it is 16½ for girls and 18½ for boys. Cross-cultural variations in the adolescent sexual debut are likely due to a variety of biological and cultural factors, including the age of pubertal onset, social norms, age of marriage, and cultural practices regarding sexuality.

As you can see in Table 15.1, which is based on the largest study of sexual behavior ever conducted in the United States (Herbenick et al., 2010), the proportion of U.S. adolescents and young adults who have had various sexual experiences increases gradually between 14 and 24 years of age. The table also shows interesting gender differences over time. In particular, the proportion of males reporting ever having had vaginal intercourse increases from 10 to 70 percent between the ages of 14 and 24, whereas it increases for girls from 12 to 85 percent.

How do adolescents feel about their first experience of sexual intercourse? In the United States, research on this question has found that boys tend to report more positive feelings about first intercourse than do girls (Figure 15.7). For example, in a nationwide study, more than 10,000 young adults between 18 and 24 years of age were asked how much they had wanted to have sex at the time they had their first sexual experience (Abma, Martinez, & Copen, 2010). Very few young men said that they really had not wanted to have intercourse at the time; in contrast, young women were much more likely to report either that they had not wanted to have sex at the time or that they had had mixed feelings about it. Many girls are less positive about their initial experience of intercourse for a good reason: They were coerced into having sex. About 60 percent of the girls who had sex before they were 15 years old say that they did so involuntarily (Guttmacher Institute, 2006). Cultural attitudes, such as those expressed by Jeff at the start of this section, likely also play a role in adolescents' feelings about their early sexual experiences.

Beyond findings like these, researchers' knowledge of adolescents' first sexual experiences is remarkably thin. Only recently have developmentalists begun to explore areas such as adolescents' sexual desires (Tolman, Impett, Tracy, & Michael, 2006) and

Percent of never-married females and males 15–17 years of age who have ever had sexual intercourse (U.S. 1988–2002 data).

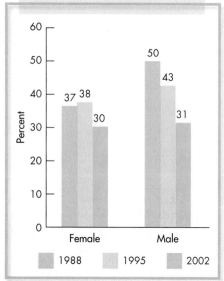

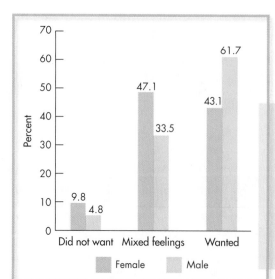

FIGURE 15.7 Percent of males and females who reported intercourse before age 20, according to whether they wanted intercourse, did not want intercourse, or had mixed feelings. More females than males either did not want intercourse or had mixed feelings, whereas more males than females reported that they wanted intercourse. (Abma, Martinez, and Copen, 2010.)

Teenage Pregnancy

EACH YEAR, ABOUT 7 PERCENT OF all U.S. teenage females—roughly 750,000—become pregnant. This is one of the highest teenage pregnancy rates among developed countries—more than twice that of Canada or Sweden, for example (McKay & Barrett, 2010). However, teenagers in the United States are no more sexually active than those in the other countries surveyed, so it seems clear that American adolescents use contraception far less often than do adolescents in other developed countries (Santelli, Sandfort, & Orr, 2008). For example, surveys conducted between 2001 and 2003 with tens of thousands of adolescents in Europe and the United States found that whereas condom use among U.S. adolescents was only slightly lower than that of European adolescents (around 75 percent), the use of birth-control pills by U.S. girls (11 percent) was less than half that of European girls (Godeau et al., 2008). One reason for the difference in contraceptive use may be that adults in many other industrialized countries have a more realistic view of the likelihood of teenage sexual activity and thus better prepare their adolescent children for dealing with their sexuality, whereas in the United States, sex education, for example, is still controversial in many communities, and can include approaches of questionable effectiveness, such as those with an abstinence-only emphasis (Blinn-Pike et al., 2008; McCarthy & Grodsky, 2011).

Researchers have identified a number of risk factors that increase the probability of teen pregnancy, including living in a low-SES home or in a disorganized or dangerous neighborhood, or having a mother who also became pregnant during her teen years (Miller et al., 2001). Risk is also associated with ethnicity. Pregnancy rates for African American and Hispanic teens, for example, are nearly 3 times higher than that of White teens (Kost, Henshaw, & Carlin, 2010). Biological factors,

including timing of pubertal development, also affect teen pregnancy risk.

One of the most significant risk factors for teen pregnancy is the age difference between sexual partners (Manlove et al., 2007). Indeed, more than one in four babies born to 15- to 17-year-old mothers were fathered by men who were at least 5 years older than the mothers.

The vast majority of teen pregnancies that occur in the United States are unintended, and nearly 30 percent end in voluntary abortions (Kost, Henshaw, & Carlin, 2010). However, researchers point out that "unintended" can have several meanings. For teenage girls who are mired in poverty, grow up in communities in which teen pregnancy is common, and see few opportunities to advance themselves in other ways, pregnancy may be a means of establishing a role for themselves. As one teen mother reported, "Most of my friends do have their babies. It seems like most of them are lost and that seems like the only thing—they feel needed, and I figure that is why they get pregnant, because they want to be needed" (Moran, 2000, p. 225).

Race, social class, education, and the strength of religious beliefs all affect a teenager's decision about whether or not to have and keep her child (Coley & Chase-Lansdale, 1998). African American teenagers are more likely than European American teenagers to become single mothers. According to government statistics, 83 percent of the teenagers who give birth come from poor or low-income families (National Center for Health Statistics, 2003). The more education a pregnant teenager's mother has (which is an indirect measure of her social class) and the better the teenager is doing in school, the more likely she is to decide to terminate the pregnancy. However, teenagers with strong religious convictions are likely to have and keep their babies, no matter what their race or social class (Eisen et al., 1983).

While many of the negative outcomes that follow from teenage pregnancy, such as poverty and low educational achievement, also precede pregnancy (as many as one-third of all teen mothers drop out of school before they become pregnant; Hoffman, 2006), teenage childbearing serves to further limit the futures of girls who are already disadvantaged. Compared with women who delay their childbearing, women who give birth while in their teens are, on average, more likely to drop out of school, to divorce, to continue to have children outside of marriage, to change jobs more frequently, to be on welfare, and to have health problems (Coley & Chase-Lansdale, 1998). They are also more likely to have low-birth-weight babies who are susceptible to illness and infant mortality.

Despite these grim findings, not every girl who bears a child while still in her teens ends up quitting school or living in poverty. Longitudinal studies of mothers who became pregnant as teenagers have found that some of these women eventually complete high school and become economically self-sufficient. Long-term success for these women was predicted by their being at grade level when they become pregnant, coming from smaller families that were not on welfare, and knowing that their family had high expectations for their future (Furstenberg et al., 1992).

There have been a number of efforts to reduce the probability of teenage pregnancy. Responding to the disproportionately high rates of teen pregnancy among economically disadvantaged African Americans, several Afrocentric educational programs have been developed. The aim of these programs is to instill pride and a sense of self-determination in girls of African descent. One such program, A Journey Toward Womanhood, encourages African American teenagers to explore different cultures and the role of women in history, and to develop interpersonal communication skills, job skills, self-confidence, and self-respect. Teens who participated in the program were more likely than nonparticipants to delay the onset of sexual behavior and to use contraception when they did engage in sexual intercourse (Dixon et al., 2000). Research on the effectiveness of these programs indicates that a focus on reproductive education alone is insufficient to affect adolescents' behaviors. To be effective, programs must examine the meaning of sexual behavior and pregnancy within broader social and economic contexts of adolescents' lives.

LaTanya, 19, and her daughter Jameelah, 10 months, attend a rally to support teen pregnancy prevention programs and education programs for teen mothers.

AP Photo / Patricia McDonnell

their social motives for engaging in sexual activity (O'Sullivan & Meyer-Bahlberg, 2003). The sexual experiences of sexual-minority youth (lesbians, gays, bisexuals, transsexuals) have likewise only recently begun to be studied (Savin-Williams & Diamond, 2004; Savin-Williams & Ream, 2007). One explanation for this is that sexuality research reflects the biases of the larger culture. In the United States, for example, the prevailing view that teen sex is categorically problematic because it can lead to unwanted pregnancy, STIs, abortions, dropping out of school, and so forth, may lead researchers to focus their attention on identifying risk and protective factors associated with, and the negative consequences of, having sex (Savin-Williams & Diamond, 2004; see the box "Teenage Pregnancy"). It is worth noting, however, that the vast majority of adolescents usually practice "safe sex," at least with respect to condom use. A national survey of condom use found that 79 percent of 14- to 17-year-olds reported using a condom during their most recent vaginal intercourse (Reece, Herbenick, Schick, Sanders, Dodge, & Fortenberry, 2010)

▲ APPLY :: CONNECT :: DISCUSS

Watch a few television shows that are popular among adolescents and young adults that feature teens or young adults as central characters (e.g., *Degrassi, True Blood, Pretty Little Liars, Gossip Girls*). How do they depict sexual relationships and communication about sex? How do they depict the social and physical (pregnancy, STIs) consequences of sex?

Relationships with Parents

The increasing time that adolescents spend with their peers and romantic partners and the increasing importance they place on these relationships inevitably change the relationships between adolescents and their parents. In fact, the amount of time that adolescents in the United States spend with their families drops by approximately 50 percent between the fifth and ninth grades (Larson & Richards, 1991). At the most general level, adolescents become more distant from their parents and more likely to turn to peers than to parents for support and advice on questions about how to conduct themselves in a wide range of contexts (Figure 15.8; Steinberg & Silk, 2002; Meeus, 2003). Furthermore, parents of adolescents are likely to be undergoing significant life changes of their own. They are reaching an age when they probably have increased responsibilities at work; their own parents are aging and may need special care; and their physical powers are beginning to decline. Given the stress that both parents and their adolescent children feel, it is not surprising that conflicts arise between them (Steinberg & Duncan, 2002). However, extensive research shows that the specifics of such conflicts, and, more generally, the ways in which parent–child relationships change, depend on a host of factors.

Adolescent–Parent Conflicts

When developmentalists describe adolescence as a period of "storm and stress," they are usually thinking about the conflicts between adolescents and their parents. Indeed, the parent–adolescent relationship is thought by many to reflect the basic dilemma of adolescence—teenagers are caught between two worlds, one of childhood dependence, the other of adult responsibility.

On the basis of a review of a large number of studies, Brett Laursen and his colleagues found that both the frequency and the intensity of

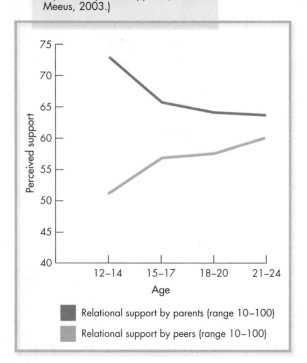

FIGURE 15.8 Although teens generally perceive their parents as highly supportive through their adolescence and early adulthood, their perception of support declines gradually across these years. In contrast, teens' perceptions of the support they receive from peers increases gradually across these years, but remains lower than perceptions of parent support. (From Meeus, 2003.)

Perceived support

Age

■ Relational support by parents (range 10–100)

■ Relational support by peers (range 10–100)

conflict between parents and adolescents change over the course of adolescence, peaking early in adolescence and then decreasing (Laursen & Collins, 2009). A longitudinal study suggested that this pattern depended importantly on the family context (Shanahan et al., 2007). Following siblings who were relatively close in age as they moved from middle childhood to adolescence, the researchers found the expected pattern for the older child—conflict peaked during early adolescence and then declined. For the younger sibling, however, conflict peaked during middle childhood—that is, as their older sibling transitioned to adolescence, not as they themselves transitioned. The researchers speculated that the younger sibling may be caught in the middle between the older sibling and the parents—swept up in conflict while trying to support or protect the older brother or sister.

When conflicts do arise, they can evoke strong feelings. Very often, however, adolescent–parent conflict is inspired by seemingly trivial matters such as household responsibilities and privileges, dating and curfews, involvement in athletics, financial independence, and perceived privacy invasions (Hawk, Keijsers, Hale, & Meeus, 2009). Arguments over "big issues," such as religion and politics, are much less common (Holmbeck, 1996).

Many parent–adolescent conflicts emerge as a result of parents and adolescents differing in their understanding of what constitutes the domain of "personal space" (Nucci, 1996; Turiel, 2010). As you may remember from the discussion of social domain theory in Chapters 9 and 13, people distinguish among three domains— the moral, the social conventional, and the personal—but may differ in how they distinguish among them. Conflicts between parents and adolescents often relate to differences in where they draw boundaries between the social conventional and personal domains. A parent who insists, for example, that an adolescent dress in a socially appropriate way and an adolescent who insists that dress is a matter of personal choice are disputing the boundaries of the social conventional and the personal (Milnitsky-Sapiro, Turiel, & Nucci, 2006; Smetana, 2006).

Research on parent–adolescent relationships in different ethnic groups shows broad cultural differences in where the boundaries between domains are drawn (Smetana, 2008; Smetana & Gettman, 2006). Judith Smetana has found, for example, that compared with middle-class European American families, middle-class African American families have relatively restricted definitions of what constitutes the adolescent's personal jurisdiction. Even so, negotiating the boundary of authority is still a significant source of parent–adolescent conflict for African American families. It seems that conflicts over "little things" represent deeper disagreements about the major issues of growing up—the power to decide for oneself and to take responsibility for oneself.

Smetana argues that African American families' parenting practices can be better described in terms of social domain theory than by such global terms as authoritarian or parent-centered. According to social domain theory, parents' expectations for obedience will vary from one domain of action to the next. This also suggests that parent–adolescent conflict need not characterize the entire relationship; rather, it is confined to certain areas where the authority to have one's way in the face of contentious issues is in dispute. Few adolescents take issue with parents' authority in the domain of moral action but will challenge it when it is applied to how they dress or color their hair.

This mother is helping her son prepare for his Bar Mitzvah, a Jewish ritual celebrating coming of age. Although she may continue to play an important role in her son's adolescence, her sphere of influence may shrink as he spends more time away from home with his peers.

Parental Influences Beyond the Family

Although conflicts between parents and their adolescent children may be stormy, they rarely lead to a serious breakdown in relations (Schneider & Stevenson, 1999). It seems clear that parents continue to play a very important role in their children's

table 15.2

Sample Items Measuring Relationships Between 6th- and 7th-Graders and Their Parents

How does each of the following questions and statements apply to your situation?

Parental Strictness

My parents want me to follow their directions even if I disagree with them.

I have to ask my parents' permission to do most things.

My parents worry that I am up to something they won't like.

Decision-Making Opportunities

How often do you take part in family decisions concerning yourself?

My parents encourage me to give my ideas and opinions even if we might disagree.

Parental Monitoring

When you go out at night, do you have a curfew?

When you are late getting home, do you have to call home?

Do your parents warn you it is dangerous to go out alone?

Source: Fuligni & Eccles, 1993.

---

lives. This continuing influence extends well beyond providing shelter, food, and advice. For example, a major study of more than 600 German adolescents and their parents indicated that adolescents whose parents demonstrate warmth, engage in discussions concerning academic and intellectual matters, and have high expectations for academic performance have better achievement in school than do peers whose parents are less warm and involved (Juang & Silbereisen, 2002). Similarly, research on parents' role in shaping adolescents' occupational aspirations indicated that in both the African American and European American samples studied, positive identification with parents was strongly related to adolescents' valuing of academics (Jodl et al., 2001). Parents also influence with whom their adolescent children interact, including the kinds of crowds with which their children are likely to become associated (Stuart, Fondacaro, Miller, Brown, & Brank, 2008; Holmbeck, Paikoff, & Brooks-Gunn, 1995).

In a study of sixth- and seventh-graders, Andrew Fuligni and Jacqueline Eccles (1993) asked young adolescents to answer a questionnaire about their parents' strictness, what opportunities they themselves had to make decisions on their own, and the extent to which their parents monitored their behavior (Table 15.2). The questionnaire also asked about the extent to which the adolescents turned to peers rather than to their parents for support, as well as about their adjustment to junior high school.

The researchers found that the extent to which the adolescents spent time with their peers and turned to them for advice depended on how their parents' behavior toward them changed in response to their growing up. Children who perceived their parents as becoming stricter as they progressed into adolescence turned to their peers to a greater extent than did those who felt that their parents included them in family decisions and encouraged them to express their ideas. At the same time, a certain degree of monitoring appeared to reduce adolescents' tendency to turn to peers. Children whose parents, for example, set a curfew for them and asked them to call if they were going to be late coming home were less peer-oriented than were those whose parents did not monitor their behavior. Similarly, adolescents in both the United States and China report experiencing more positive emotions, and better academic performance, when they perceive their parents as supporting their developing autonomy (Wang, Pomerantz, & Chen, 2007).

Studies of family communication patterns tell a similar story. In intensive clinical research into the family dynamics of both normally developing and troubled adolescents, Stuart Hauser and his colleagues (1991) identified two patterns of family interactions, constraining and enabling. *Constraining interactions* limit and restrict communication through detachment, lack of curiosity, and other forms of discouragement. In contrast, *enabling interactions* facilitate and enhance communication through explaining, empathizing, expressing curiosity, and encouraging mutual problem solving. The researchers argue that parents who promote enabling interactions enhance healthy psychological and identity development in their adolescents by "making the family environment safe for the adolescent to risk 'trying out' new ideas and perspectives, or expressing new feelings" (p. 27).

In a comprehensive review of research on the influence of parenting styles on adolescent behavior, Grayson Holmbeck and his colleagues (Holmbeck et al., 1995) reported that the developmental outcomes for adolescents are most favorable when parents:

1. Set clear standards for behavior.

2. Enforce rules in ways that are firm but not coercive.

3. Discipline their children in a consistent way.

4. Explain the basis for their decisions.

5. Permit real discussion of contentious issues.

6. Monitor their adolescents' whereabouts without being overprotective.

7. Foster a warm family environment.

8. Provide information and help their adolescents develop social skills.

9. Respond flexibly to their children as they develop.

You may recognize this pattern as consistent with the authoritative parenting style described in Chapter 10 (p. 349). Indeed, the analysis presented above parallels the findings of other studies showing that adolescent children of authoritative parents are more competent in school and less likely to get into trouble than are their peers from authoritarian or permissive families (Steinberg, 2001). Moreover, the positive influence of authoritative parenting applies whether the adolescents in question are classified as "jocks," "druggies," "nerds," or "brains" (Brown & Huang, 1995). Effective parenting may even extend to the adolescents' friends, indirectly supporting improved school performance and behavior as an indirect result of the effective parenting of their friends' parents (Fletcher et al., 1995).

On the whole, current evidence strongly supports the notion that adolescents' conflicts with their parents increase relative to middle childhood, while their feelings of family solidarity and warmth decrease (Collins & Laursen, 2006). Some adolescents really do break away and establish relationships outside the family that remove them from their parents both physically and emotionally, but the more common pattern is for adolescents and their parents to negotiate a new form of interdependence that grants the adolescent increasingly equal rights and more nearly equal responsibilities.

▲ APPLY :: CONNECT :: DISCUSS

Your 16-year-old daughter announces that she intends to leave home and school in order to join a spiritual community that encourages its members to "find themselves" by working toward the common good. As an informed and sensitive parent, you recognize this as an expression of developing autonomy but, for obvious reasons, believe it would be a terrible mistake for her to pursue such a plan at this point in her life. Keeping in mind the evidence presented in this section on effective parenting, write your daughter a letter about what you think of her plan.

Identity Development

"Who are you?" said the Caterpillar.

Alice replied, rather shyly, "I—I hardly know, sir . . . at least I know who I was when I got up this morning, but I think I must have been changed several times since then."

(Lewis Carroll, Alice's Adventures in Wonderland)

Despite having fallen down a rabbit hole into a fantasy world, Alice's confusion about who she is underscores one of the most challenging tasks and significant accomplishments of adolescence—the formation of a coherent and stable identity. **Identity development** is the process through which individuals achieve a sense of who they are, what moral and political beliefs they embrace, the sort of occupation

identity development The process through which individuals achieve a sense of who they are and of their moral and political beliefs, their career preferences, and their relationship to their culture and community.

saturated self A self full to the brim with multiple "me's" that have emerged as a consequence of needing to conform to social roles and relationships that demand different, and sometimes contradictory, selves.

exploration According to Marcia, the process through which adolescents actively examine their possible future roles and paths.

commitment According to Marcia, individuals' sense of allegiance to the goals, values, beliefs, and occupation they have chosen.

they wish to pursue, and their relationship to their communities and culture. In this section, we will explore various paths of identity development and their relationship to adolescents' families, friends, and culture.

The "I" and the "Me"

As discussed in Chapter 9, in attempting to understand the full scope of what an identity is, and the processes through which it is formed, developmentalists have found it useful to distinguish between two interlocking components of the self: the "I" and the "me." The *me-self*, you will recall, is the *object self*, which includes social roles and relationships ("I am a student"; "I am Tenisha's fiancé"); material possessions ("I drive an eco-friendly Prius"), traits ("I am ambitious"), and other features that can be objectively known (age, family, school, religion, and so forth). In contrast, the *I-self* is the *subject self*, the part of the self system that reflects on, guides, and directs the object self. According to Harter (1999, p. 6), the I-self includes:

- *Self-awareness,* an appreciation of one's internal states, needs, thoughts, and emotions
- *Self-agency,* the sense of authorship over one's thoughts and actions
- *Self-continuity,* the sense that one remains the same person over time
- *Self-coherence,* the sense that one is a single, integrated, and bounded entity

Some contemporary developmentalists maintain that the self is a story about who one is. If so, then the me-self is the character in that story, and the I-self is the author and storyteller (Nakkula & Toshalis, 2006).

Adolescents often seek out heroes to adulate and imitate. Dressed as Lady Gaga, these girls await the Monster Ball tour in Guadalajara, Mexico.

Identity theorists have long maintained that social and historical contexts play a pivotal role in how a person's self develops. A child growing up in a traditional society isolated from the modern world, for example, may have a relatively clearly defined path of identity development as a consequence of the limited number of social role possibilities. In contrast, aspects of the modern world have created new challenges and opportunities for understanding oneself in relation to one's society and culture. Kenneth Gergen (1991) has suggested that self-coherence is difficult to achieve in technologically advanced societies in which mass communications have dramatically accelerated and multiplied our relations to each other and to our communities. According to Gergen, modern society has resulted in a **saturated self**—a self full to the brim with multiple "me's" that have emerged as a consequence of needing to conform to a dizzying whirl of social roles and relationships that demand different, and sometimes contradictory, selves. The appearance of "multiple selves" in the self-descriptions of adolescents makes it necessary for them to deal with the fact that they are, in some sense, different people in different contexts. It is at this point that the question of personal authenticity—"Who is the real me?"—becomes particularly compelling, and, perhaps, anxiety provoking (Harter, 2006a).

Achieving a Mature Identity

The possibility that adolescents may be troubled by the feeling of multiple selves makes the search for one's "true self" one of the dominant developmental themes of adolescence (Meeus & de Wied, 2007). As we discussed in Chapter 1,

Erik Erikson believed that the quest for identity is a life-long task through which individuals achieve a coherent understanding of themselves in relation to their societies. Although the identity quest is lifelong, its challenges come to a climax during adolescence, when young people must deal with biological pressures to become sexually active and social pressures to adopt culturally valued roles and beliefs. According to Erikson (1968a), in order to successfully navigate these multiple pressures (regarding, for example, occupational goals, intimate relationships, social and political values, and religious beliefs), the adolescent has to integrate a stable sense of self across various roles and responsibilities, creating a unified sense of identity. Adolescents who fail this developmental task lack a vision of what their role is or might be. For Erikson, then, the crisis of adolescence is one of *identity versus role confusion.*

The popularity of Erikson's ideas created a demand for an assessment method that could both depict an identity in the process of being formed and provide quantitative measures of the different states of identity formation (Kroger, Martinussen, & Marcia, 2010; Marcia, 2002) (for a description of another assessment method, see the box "From Diaries to Facebook"). In an early and influential effort at such an assessment method, James Marcia (1966) focused on two factors identified by Erikson as essential to achieving a mature identity: exploration and commitment. **Exploration** refers to the process through which adolescents actively examine their possible future roles and paths in life, think about the choices their parents have made, and begin to search for alternatives that they find personally satisfying. **Commitment** refers to individuals' personal involvement in, and allegiance to, the goals, values, beliefs, and future occupation that they have adopted for themselves.

On the basis of interviews with male college students about their choice of occupation and beliefs about politics and religion, Marcia (1966, 2002) identified four patterns of coping with the task of identity formation that arise from four possible patterns of exploration and commitment (Figure 15.9):

1. *Identity achievement.* Adolescents who display this pattern have gone through a period of decision making about their choice of occupation, their political commitment, their religious beliefs, and so on, and are now actively pursuing their own goals. When asked about their political commitment, for example, they might respond with such answers as "I've thought it over, and I've decided to support the _____ party. Their program is the most sensible one for the country to be following." When asked about their occupational aspirations, they might say "It took me quite a while to figure it out, but now I really know what I want to try for a career."

2. *Foreclosure.* Young people who display this pattern are also committed to occupational and ideological positions, but they show no signs of having gone through a period of exploration. Instead, they have just adopted the values, beliefs, and aspirations of their parents. They respond to questions about their political beliefs with such answers as "I really never gave

In many cultures, adolescent identity development is complicated by the multiple identity possibilities that exist within the peer group and the larger culture.

FIGURE 15.9 When the combinations of Erikson's two factors in identity formation—exploration and commitment—are considered together, the result is the four patterns of adolescent identity formation proposed by Marcia.

		Commitment	
		No	Yes
Exploration	No	Identity diffusion	Foreclosure
	Yes	Moratorium	Identity achievement

politics much thought. Our family always votes for the _____ party, so that's how I vote." In the area of occupational choice, a typical answer might be "My parents decided a long time ago what I should take in school or go into for a career and I'm following through on their plans."

3. *Moratorium*. This pattern is displayed by adolescents actively engaged in a process of exploration. They might answer questions about their political beliefs by saying, "I'm not sure about my political beliefs, but I'm trying to figure out what I can truly believe in." Likewise, in reponding to questions about their future occupation, they might say "I'm still trying to decide how capable I am as a person and what jobs or school programs will be right for me."

From Diaries to Facebook

IF YOU HAVE EVER KEPT A DIARY OR JOURnal or written intimate letters to a close friend or lover, then you can probably appreciate how such personal documents can provide researchers with unique and important insights into the identity development of adolescents, as well as allowing them to "witness" emotions and issues of a personal nature that adolescents seldom reveal to adults. Probably the most well-known teenage diary is the one written by Anne Frank over the 2-year period in which she and her family, who were Jewish, hid in secret attic rooms to escape Nazi persecution during World War II. In the diary, Anne describes her puberty, her sexual awakening, and her changing relationships with family and peers. Viewed through the lens of developmental theory, diaries such as hers can provide a record of adolescents' cognitive and emotional growth (Haviland & Kramer, 1991; Magai & Haviland-Jones, 2002).

In addition to being viewed as a record of experience and development, diary and journal writing can be viewed as an experience in its own right—one that may be helpful in dealing with the identity issues and complex feelings that accompany adolescence. Would Anne have kept such a detailed account of her most personal thoughts and feelings if she had had easy access to friends with whom she could easily talk and share secrets? Did her regular retreat into the privacy of her diary provide her with much-needed personal "space" in the cramped quarters of the attic? On the basis of an analysis of diaries written between the late 1950s and early 1970s by 10- to 14-year-old girls, Barbara Crowther (1999) suggested that writing in a private diary can make a very public statement about independence and individuality. She noted, for example, that the keeping of a diary is rarely kept secret, and that girls will often make a big deal about it, putting warnings such as "Strictly Private—No Entry" on the diary covers. Such warnings, while appearing to be about ensuring privacy, are also a declaration: "I have ideas, feelings, opinions that are my own." Writing a diary, from Crowther's perspective, can be a way of establishing a sense of personal autonomy.

It is interesting to speculate about how the study of personal documents will change as a consequence of technological advances. The Internet has already enabled the construction of entirely new types of personal documents, from the personal Web page and blogs to the currently more popular social networking sites such as Facebook and MySpace. Unlike diaries, which can be intensely private, these new electronic documents are radically public and interactive, accessible to literally billions of people, any of whom may comment on the documents' contents. And whereas diaries are evolving records that preserve past entries, contributing to, or at least reflecting, a continuous self, Web pages and network postings may reflect something closer to Gergen's saturated self. That is, these personal digital expressions can be entirely rewritten to present an entirely different self—or selves—to the world.

According to a recent report by the Pew Internet & American Life Project, Internet content creation by teenagers continues to grow, with 73 percent of Internet-using teens creating and posting material on social networking Web sites (Lenhart, Madden, Smith, Purcell, Zickuhr & Rainie, 2011). Given the explosion of social networking, we might reasonably ask what purpose it serves. For many adolescents, social networking provides a tool for keeping in touch with friends. When a researcher asked teens why they joined MySpace, one

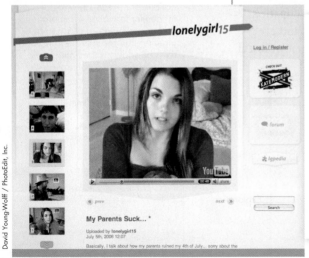

David Young-Wolff / PhotoEdit, Inc.

Although eventually revealed as a hoax, "lonelygirl15" was the screen name for a teenage video blogger on YouTube whose postings attracted the attention of millions. The fictional blogger, 15-year-old Bree, began by posting details of personal experiences typical of adolescence. When the video blogs took a turn toward soap-opera drama, the blog was investigated and found to be a fake, with Bree being played by an actress, Jessica Lee Rose.

4. *Identity diffusion.* Adolescents who manifest this pattern have neither explored nor committed to identity possibilities. They are likely to take a cynical attitude toward the issues confronting them, so they may answer questions about political commitment by declaring, "I stopped thinking about politics ages ago. There are no parties worth supporting." Regarding occupational choices, a typical response might be, "I'm really not interested in finding the right job; any job will do. I'll just do whatever is available."

Other researchers have extended Marcia's methods to incorporate additional domains of experience, including family life, friendships, dating, and sex roles (Luyckx et al., 2005; Grotevant, 1998). In general, the research has shown that identity achievement increases with age, whereas diffusion and moratorium decrease (Figure 15.10;

responded, "cuz that's where my friends are." When asked about what they did on such sites, another said, "I don't know. . . . I just hang out" (boyd, 2007, p. 9) Beyond its more obvious social functions, social networking presents teens with opportunities for self-expression and exploring the nature of one's relationship with others. This is particularly apparent in online profiles that are created and modified according to changing experiences, relationships, and peer reactions to posted material. Indeed, even the size and shifting content of one's online "friends" can be both used and interpreted as signs of social status and general "coolness." As described by one teen (boyd, 2007, p. 14):

As a kid, you used your birthday party guest list as leverage on the playground. "If you let me play I'll invite you to my birthday party." Then, as you grew up and got your own phone, it was all about someone being on your speed dial. Well today it's the MySpace Top 8. It's the new dangling carrot for gaining superficial acceptance. Taking someone off your Top 8 is your new passive aggressive power play when someone pisses you off.

Another teen points to the emotional distress that can accompany social networking activity:

MySpace always seems to caus way too much drama and i am so dang sick of it. im

sick of the pain and the hurt and the tears and the jealousy and the heartache and the truth and the lies. . . it just SUCKS!

In addition to the drama, the public displays of social networking clearly encourage a high degree of self-reflection that developmentalists consider the hallmark of the I-self. Unfortunately, these new electronic diary forms are ephemeral, making it difficult for developmentalists to find and analyze them after they have served their authors' adolescent purposes.

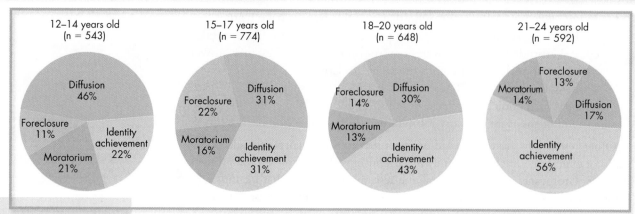

FIGURE 15.10 The proportion of identity statuses change across the adolescent years such that most individuals in the United States have an achieved identity by the time they reach their early 20s. (From Meeus, 2003.)

Meeus, 2003). The increase in identity achievement and the decrease in diffusion are both steady trends over the period from the years before high school to the late college years (Kroger, Martinussen, & Marcia, 2010; Moshman, 1998).

Because identity achievement is considered so important to normal adolescent development, researchers have given special effort to identifying factors that facilitate or complicate identity formation for adolescents growing up in different contexts and cultures.

Forming an Ethnic Identity

Ethnic identity refers to an enduring sense of oneself as a member of a particular ethnic group, including the feelings and attitudes one holds regarding one's membership in that group. The process of identity formation can be complicated for ethnic-minority and immigrant children (Quintana et al., 2006; Phinney, 2010). First, in cases in which the values, beliefs, and customs of the minority group differ from those of the majority population, ethnic-minority youth face the task of reconciling two different identities—one based on their own cultural heritage, the other based on that of the majority group. In effect, they have at least twice as much psychological work to do. Second, these young people often face prejudice, discrimination, and accompanying barriers to economic opportunity, all of which further complicate their task.

Multicultural influences are pervasive in many parts of the world, creating a special challenge for adolescents who may feel the tug of both traditional and modern beliefs, values, and expectations of behavior.

Stages of Ethnic-Identity Formation As you saw in Chapter 9 (pp. 313–315), ethnic-identity development is well underway by middle childhood, when ethnic-minority children know particular characteristics of their ethnic group and have developed basic attitudes about their ethnicity. During middle childhood and adolescence, children in ethnic-minority groups move through three additional stages of ethnic-identity formation (Cross, 2003; Ong, Fuller-Rowell, & Phinney, 2010). Although researchers apply different labels to these stages, they agree on the basic content of each stage and the general kinds of experiences associated with movement from one stage to the next. In this discussion, we have adopted the labels suggested by Jean Phinney (2008) because she explicitly links the stages to the processes of exploration and commitment discussed above.

Stage 1: Unexamined Ethnic Identity. In this stage, children tend to accept and show a preference for the cultural values of the majority culture in which they find themselves. This acceptance may include a negative evaluation of their own group (see

ethnic identity A sense of oneself as a member of a particular ethnic group.

Chapter 9, pp. 314–315). In some cases, this stage appears to correspond to Marcia's category of foreclosure, because the person refuses to consider the relevant issues and adopts the views of others unquestioningly. One Mexican American boy told Phinney, "I don't go looking for my culture. I just go by what my parents say and do, and what they tell me to do, the way they are" (p. 68). In other cases, the failure to examine questions of ethnic identity is more similar to identify diffusion. For example, an African American girl remarked, "Why do I need to learn about who was the first Black woman to do this or that? I'm just not too interested" (p. 68).

Stage 2: Ethnic Identity Search.

Movement beyond stage 1 is often initiated by a shocking experience in which the young person is rejected or humiliated because of his or her ethnic background. The specifics of such encounters are quite varied (Cross, 2003; Fordham & Ogbu, 1986). A minority student who does extremely well on tests may be accused of cheating simply because the teacher assumes that members of the student's ethnic group are incapable of such work; or a boy and girl who have been friends for years may be forbidden to socialize with each other romantically because they have different skin colors, ethnic backgrounds, or religious affiliations. However, a shocking encounter is not necessary for young people to begin pondering their ethnic identity: for some, this move into stage 2 is precipitated simply by a growing awareness that the values of the dominant group may not be beneficial to ethnic minorities.

In stage 2, young people show an intense concern for the personal implications of their ethnicity and often engage in an active search for information about their group. They are likely to become involved in social and political movements in which ethnicity is a core issue. They may also experience intense anger at the majority group and glorify their own ethnic heritage.

Signithia Fordham and John Ogbu (1986) describe cases in which African American adolescents go through a process of *oppositional identity formation,* rejecting the patterns of dress, speech, mannerisms, and attitudes associated with European American society and adopting an identity that opposes them. These researchers believe that the process of oppositional identity formation provides one of the major explanations for the school failure of African American children. For many of these young people, who feel automatically shut out of the economic opportunities of the majority culture, successful identity formation requires that they look upon the academic activities of school as irrelevant to their lives. Evidence suggests that similar identity processes are at work in the development of adolescents of many minority groups in the United States (Phinney, 2008).

Stage 3: Ethnic-Identity Achievement.

Individuals who achieve a mature ethnic identity have resolved the conflicts characteristic of stage 2 and now have a secure self-confidence in their ethnicity and a positive self-concept (Cross, 2003). Researchers have found that mature ethnic identity may be a protective factor against particular risks (LaFromboise et al., 2006). An example comes from a study of 434 seventh-grade students living in a large Southwestern city who self-identified as American Indian: Students who had a greater sense of ethnic pride also had stronger antidrug norms (Kulis, Napoli, & Marsiglia, 2002).

Family and Community Influences

Naturally, developmentalists have been interested in identifying the factors that may facilitate ethnic-identity formation. In a study of immigrant Armenian, Vietnamese, and

Responding to an increasingly multiethnic population, schools and communities provide opportunities to celebrate the cultural heritage of young people. This girl is demonstrating Korean drumming at her school's "International Day."

Michael J. Doolittle / The Image Works

Mexican families, Jean Phinney and her colleagues found that identity formation is strongest when the native language is maintained in the home and when adolescents spend significant amounts of time with peers who share their ethnic heritage (Phinney & Ong, 2002). Positive ethnic-identity formation also seems to be fostered when parents deliberately uphold cultural traditions in the home and instruct their children in them.

Many families that immigrate to the United States settle in established communities that share their ethnic heritage. For example, families who move from Mexico to the Southwest may become part of a Mexican American community that has existed for generations. In such communities, it may be relatively easy for children, including in immigrant families, to develop a positive ethnic identity if their peers, family, and community embrace familiar cultural traditions. Increasingly, however, Mexican and other Latino immigrants are settling in areas without established Latino communities—for example, in Maine, Indiana, Arkansas, Alabama, Tennesse, South Carolina, and North Carolina (U.S. Census, 2011). This situation creates new identity challenges both within the developing Latino community and within the settled community of long-time residents who have little understanding of Latino cultures.

In an ethnographic study, Karen Grady (2002) documents how a group of Latino students, predominantly Mexican, whose families had recently settled in rural Indiana came to develop a sense of shared identity. The students had been marginalized and isolated in the high school, when English proficiency tests had placed most of them together in lower-track and ESL classes with limited bilingual resources and teaching personnel. Most of the "instruction" involved completing unchallenging worksheets. After a while, the students established their own routines for occupying the day. Specifically, they worked on lowrider art, a contemporary art form that combines a variety of ethnic themes (religious symbols, pre-Columbian motifs, symbols of the Mexican revolution) into a celebration of Mexican and Latino heritage (Figure 15.11). One girl, Xochitl, told Grady that she got her ideas for her art from *Lowrider* magazine, commenting, "I like to read that magazine because it talks about my culture and I feel so proud when I read that my people are doing good things and not going out in the streets and selling drugs or getting into trouble" (p. 176). The students' artwork was soon the talk of the school, and the art teacher incorporated the art form into her curriculum in much the same way that she included Greco-Roman art and Impressionism, requiring students to learn the symbolic meanings of its images. Grady argues that through lowrider art, the students were able to make themselves visible to the rest of the students, and to others in the dominant culture, as members of an ethnic group with its sources of pride and a remarkable history.

FIGURE 15.11 Popular among U.S. adolescents of Hispanic descent, lowrider art often includes symbols of both American and Mexican culture.

Danny Villescas / The Castro Collection

Ethnicity and Peer Culture In addition to family and community influences, ethnic-identity development is also influenced by peer culture. This is nowhere more apparent than in the case of hip-hop culture. From its beginnings in gangsta rap, through its expansion into B-boying, MC'ing, DJ'ing, graffiti, and styles of dress and speech, hip-hop has expressed the damage and injustice of growing up poor—especially Black and poor—in the inner cities of the United States (Dyson, 1995; Richardson & Scott, 2002; Chang, 2005). Researchers of hip-hop argue that it constitutes a genuine culture that influences the formation of identity among adolescents, particularly those of African and Latino descent. A striking example is Murray Forman's (2002) ethnographic study of Somali immigrant adolescents, which documents how these minority youth expand the frontiers of their own identity through the medium of hip-hop.

Since the early 1990s, Somalis have immigrated to the United States in unprecedented numbers to escape the political violence and oppression of their homeland. Uprooted from their traditional ways of life and transplanted to an entirely foreign environment, Somali adolescents face a clash of cultures. Moreover, upon their arrival in North America, "being Black" becomes a salient identity issue; cultural codes of race are simply not relevant in Somalia, where virtually the entire population is Black. According to Forman, an important means of coping with this cultural transition is to try to find a sense of self and belonging in peer groups. Hip-hop, Forman argues, provides an important vehicle by which Somali adolescents can understand the racial basis of their new social status because it generates an awareness of Blackness and the situation of Black urban youth: "There is a sense of comfort—even a sense of security—in the students' identification with hip hop" (2002, p. 110).

As you can see, in many ways the development of ethnic identity follows a similar course to the development of identity in general. Developmentalists point out, however, that ethnic-identity development is unique in some very important respects (Phinney, 2010; Côté, 2009). Unlike general identity development, which is believed to involve a certain degree of choice (of occupations, spiritual beliefs, political positions, and so on), one cannot choose one's ethnic heritage. In addition, as underscored by Forman's research, one's ethnic heritage can take on different degrees of salience, depending on its relation to other groups in the community. The unique issues of choice (or lack thereof) and salience also apply to the process of forming a sexual identity.

Music and dance play important roles in adolescent identity development and peer culture. Originated by African American teenagers in the 1970s, breakdancing swept the North American continent and crossed the oceans, affecting youth culture throughout the world.

Forming a Sexual Identity

> I was truly happy before my mind understood what it was to be sexual at all. My troubles began when my body began changing and when my intellect began understanding those changes and the feelings they caused. Parties were great in middle school until I became sexual. An innocent game of spin-the-bottle among friends was a lot of fun. . . . Things got tougher, however, when one of my oversexed and underexperienced adolescent friends would suggest that we play a game of "French" spin-the-bottle. It sent a shiver up my spine and caused my stomach to contract to the size of a pea. When we entered high school . . . I wasn't comfortable. I just couldn't bring myself to talk about girls and all of the other stuff that high school guys talked about. I did, however, more often than not, awkwardly participate in the talks about girls and sex. However, in the back of my mind was the ever-present feeling that I wasn't normal, and that I must change.
>
> (Anonymous, reflecting on his growing awareness of his homosexuality, in Garrod et al., 1999).

If identity can be defined as an answer to the question "Who am I?", then sexual identity development can be defined as answering the question "Who am I as a sexual being?" More specifically, **sexual identity** refers to an individual's understanding of himself or herself as heterosexual, homosexual (gay or lesbian), or bisexual (Horn, Kosciw, & Russell, 2009). However, as you might imagine, it simply does not happen

sexual identity An individual's understanding of himself or herself as heterosexual, homosexual, or bisexual.

More than 6,000 high school students participated in the annual Gay Straight Youth Pride Celebration that took place in Massachusetts.

that young heterosexual people discover and declare to the world (or themselves), "I'm straight!" (Striepe & Tolman, 2003). Instead, as is clearly suggested by the young man quoted above, developing a sexual identity can be particularly pressing and complicated for **sexual-minority (LGBT) youth**, that is, adolescents who develop an identity as lesbian, gay, bisexual, or transgendered. Large national samples of adolescents indicate that by age 19, over 8 percent of males and females have had same-sex attractions or relationships (Russell & Joyner, 2001). Interestingly, whereas most females who report same-sex attractions also "identify" themselves as lesbian or bisexual, fewer than 2 percent of males "identify" themselves as gay or bisexual (Garofalo et al., 1999).

Adolescents seem to go through a series of stages in the process of defining themselves as gay, lesbian, or bisexual (Ferrer-Wreder et al., 2002; Troiden, 1993). Richard Troiden developed the following stage model of forming a sexual-minority identity. As you read through the stage descriptions, notice how the questions of personal authenticity, self-continuity, and self-coherence that are key to identity formation are additionally complicated for sexual-minority youths:

Stage 1: Sensitization; Feeling Different. Like the young man quoted at the start of this section, during early adolescence many sexual-minority youths begin to experience a feeling of being "different."

Stage 2: Self-Recognition; Identity Confusion. With puberty, they may realize that they are attracted to members of the same sex and begin to label such feelings as "gay," "lesbian," "bisexual," "pansexual," or "omnisexual." This recognition can be the source of considerable inner turmoil and identity confusion. As one adolescent expressed it:

> You are confused about what sort of person you are and where your life is going. You ask yourself the questions "Who am I? Am I a homosexual? Am I really a heterosexual?" (Cass, 1984, p. 156)

By middle or late adolescence, sexual-minority youth begin to believe that they are probably LGBT because they are uninterested in the heterosexual activities of their peers. Many sexual-minority adults recall adolescence as a time when they were loners and social outcasts.

Stage 3: Identity Assumption. Some young people who have had same-sex sexual experiences and who recognize that they prefer sexual relations with members of their own sex do not openly acknowledge their preference. Many others, however, move from private acknowledgment of their LGBT orientation to disclosing it publicly, at least to other sexual-minority individuals. Young people who have achieved this level of LGBT identity deal with it in a variety of ways. Some try to avoid same-sex contacts and attempt to pass as heterosexual because they are afraid of being stigmatized. Others begin to align themselves with the LGBT community.

Stage 4: Commitment; Identity Integration. This final stage of sexual-minority identity is reached by those who have come to terms with their sexual orientation. They have experienced a fusion of their sexuality and emotional commitments, express satisfaction with their sexual orientation, and have "come out," that is, publicly disclosed their orientation.

sexual-minority (LGBT) youth Adolescents who develop identities as gays, lesbians, or bisexuals.

Troiden notes that commitment to an LGBT identity may vary from weak to strong, depending on such factors as the individual's success in forging satisfying personal relationships, being accepted by family members, and functioning well at work or in a career. Indeed, the social stigma, oppression, and threats to physical safety facing sexual-minority youth, along with fear of being rejected by parents, can make coming out a major challenge (Heights, 1999). Retrospective accounts of gay men indicate that "living a lie," "alienation and isolation," and "telling others" were significant issues in their adolescent experiences (Flowers & Buston, 2002). Nowadays, the ability to interact electronically with other sexual-minority youth may help adolescents cope with feelings of isolation and provide a safe forum for examining issues related to developing a sexual identity. As one young woman recalled her experience:

> Actually, over the Internet was when I had my first close encounter . . . there was this bisexual woman on the rave net. And she was very persuasive, and that was like when I was, "This is safe. This is the Internet. And I can do this—I can talk to her, and no one has to know." So that's when I started experimenting with the idea that maybe it's okay to accept all these feelings after all. And that's how it all started to come out, and that's when I started to come out.

(Reported in Addison & Comstock, 1998)

Table 15.3 illustrates the average age of first disclosure in a sample of 117 young adults who were approximately 20 years of age at the time of the study and who self-identified as gay, lesbian, or bisexual (Maguen et al., 2002). Two noteworthy patterns emerge from the data in the table: First, the average age of disclosure is similar across the subgroups; second, the subgroups are significantly different in the average age both of awareness of same-sex attractions and of acting on these attractions. These age differences are consistent with distinct patterns of experience found for the different subgroups. For example, lesbians are more likely than gay men to report sexual contacts with both males and females; moreover, they are more likely than gay men to have had their first sexual contact with a person of the other sex. The distinctive pattern that characterizes lesbians is consistent with arguments that sexual-minority women may be more likely than men to be attracted to both sexes, and that girls may be under more social pressure to date (Ellis et al., 2002; Savin-Williams & Diamond, 2004).

It has been pointed out that in most respects, the needs and concerns of youths with same-sex attractions are simply those of all youths: "Regardless of sexual orientation, youths need the love and respect of their parents, must negotiate their ongoing relationships as they move toward adulthood, are concerned with peer status, desire love and sex, and wonder about their future" (Savin-Williams, 2001, p. 6).

table 15.3

Milestones of Sexual-Minority Development (mean age)

Milestone	Gay (n = 53)	Lesbian (n = 34)	Bisexual (n = 25)
Became aware	9.6	10.9	13.2
Sexual contact	14.7	14.3	14.9
Same-sex contact	14.9	16.4	16.7
Disclosure	16.8	16.0	16.8

Source: Maguen et al., 2002.

Identity and Culture

Adolescents' perceptions of themselves as a member of a particular sexual minority or a particular ethnic group clearly affect their sense of identity. Might, then, their sense of identity develop in radically different ways depending on the particular culture in which they live? Many researchers have answered this question in the affirmative, arguing that a culture's values, beliefs, and patterns of life profoundly affect the identity development of its members (Markus & Kitayama, 2010; Shweder, 2007). For example, it is common for cultures to be considered along a continuum that describes the degree to which concepts of the self and identity are rooted either in the individual or in the social group (Greenfield et al., 2006; Kâğıtçıbaşı, 2007). At one end are cultures whose members see themselves primarily as individuals, as most middle-class Americans do. At the other end are cultures, such as Japan's, whose members see themselves primarily in relation to the larger social group. Members of the first kind of culture are said to perceive themselves as *independent;* members of the second kind, to perceive themselves as *interdependent.*

According to Hazel Markus and Shinobu Kitayama, people whose cultures encourage an **independent sense of self**—that is, individualistic cultures—are oriented to being unique, to promoting their individual goals, and to expressing their own thoughts and opinions. By contrast, people whose cultures emphasize an **interdependent sense of self**—that is, collectivist cultures—seek to fit into the group, to promote the goals of others (that is, of the group), and to develop the ability to "read" the minds of others by anticipating their emotions and needs.

As Markus and Kitayama point out, this difference in orientation to the self creates different sets of problems for the young person who is forging a unified sense of identity. For example, the American emphasis on the autonomous, independent self presupposes that identity formation is an individual, personal process. By contrast, in collectivist societies, an integral part of identity formation is conformance to, and acceptance by, the group. Thus adolescents in collectivist societies—particularly highly traditional collectivist societies—do not have to make many of the decisions and choices that American adolescents must face in order to resolve their identity. It makes little sense to assert that healthy identity formation requires adolescents to make a "commitment to a sexual orientation, an ideological stance, and a vocational choice" (Marcia, 1980, p. 160) in traditional collectivist societies in which marriages are arranged by the family, one's vocation is whatever one's father or mother does, and strict subordination to one's elders is a moral imperative (Grotevant, 1998). The most distinctive fact about identity formation in such societies is that it involves little of the cognitive deliberation and personal choice that play such large roles in accounts of identity formation in Western cultures. In societies with few distinct adult roles, a young person has few decisions to make.

In response to this view, Elliot Turiel (2002) has cautioned against grouping cultures into two broad categories—those that foster an independent sense of self versus those that foster interdependence. He argues that cultures, and the people who live in them, are much more diverse in their practices, struggles, and ambitions than can be captured by a two-category system. Even in America, it is unlikely that the "rugged individualist" could ever have "won the West"—much less survived it—in the absence of collectivist practices such as barn raising.

Following Erikson's influential theory, many contemporary developmentalists believe that identity is one of the most complex areas of adolescent development because it is so centrally tied to the child's developing relationship to community and culture. As such, identity development is influenced by the society's roles and categories, norms and moral codes, as well as the adolescent's emerging ability to make sense of them.

Indeed, some developmentalists, including Jack Martin and Bryan Sokol, have made the point that the diversity inherent to particular societies encourages advanced levels of *perspective-taking* through which adolescents and young adults imagine themselves not only from the perspective of particular others, as younger children do (see Chapter 8, p. 280), but also from the perspectives of various abstract social practices, conventions, and ideologies (Martin & Sokol, 2011; Martin, Sokol, & Elfers, 2008). For example, a young woman may imagine herself not only from the perspective of her particular math professor (as a good student who should go into engineering) or her mother (as someone who should come home for spring break and help paint the porch) but also from the abstract perspectives of what it means in her society to be and act as a

In Balinese society, tooth filing is a significant ceremony that marks the age of puberty. The ceremony involves a slight filing of the upper canine teeth, and is meant to eradicate symbolically the "wild" nature of the individual.

independent sense of self The sense of self encouraged by individualistic cultures, characterized by an orientation to being unique, promoting one's individual goals, and expressing one's thoughts and opinions.

interdependent sense of self The sense of self encouraged by collectivist cultures, characterized by an orientation to fitting into the group, promoting group goals, and developing the ability to understand the thoughts of others.

woman, an engineer, a responsible member of a family. Arguing that self-development is fundamentally a process of understanding ourselves through the perspectives of others—other people, practices, institutions, and belief systems—Martin and Sokol suggest that a mature identity entails an integration of diverse perspectives into a sense of self as unified and whole (Martin & Sokol, 2011).

Clearly, developing a coherent identity is a complex process. For some adolescents, this process is further complicated by social and emotional problems, as we discuss next.

▲ APPLY :: CONNECT :: DISCUSS

How does the distinction between an independent and an interdependent sense of self apply to your own sense of self?

Adolescent Health and Well-Being

As you have learned, the changes associated with adolescence have profound social and psychological consequences—not only for young people themselves but for their families, friends, and communites as well. Cultural beliefs, family values, and peer-group norms all contain changing, and sometimes conflicting, expectations about how adolescents should behave in their new, sexually mature bodies. And, of course, the adolescent body itself is undergoing enormous transformations in both external appearance and internal hormonal functioning and neural organization. Remarkably, most adolescents weather these stormy changes without lasting difficulties. For some, however, the challenges of adolescence pose significant problems for health and well-being, by either aggravating preexisting problems or creating conditions for the emergence of new problems which may or may not persist into adulthood.

Emotional Health

One of the most extensively studied topics of adolescence is the increase of social and emotional problems during this period (Steinberg, 2008). In general, developmentalists distinguish between two categories of emotional problems: internalizing problems and externalizing problems. **Internalizing problems**, which are more common in girls, include disturbances in emotion or mood such as depression, worry, guilt, and anxiety. **Externalizing problems**, which are more common in boys, include social and behavioral problems such as aggression and delinquency—ranging from the violation of age-appropriate social norms, such as skipping school and running away, to law-breaking behaviors such as drug use and vandalism (Graber, 2004; Farrington, 2004).

Developmentalists seeking to understand and help adolescents with social and emotional problems have focused on three broad questions: Why do these problems seem to erupt during adolescence? What are the differences between adolescents who develop these problems and those who do not? Why is it that when problems do arise, girls tend to have internalizing problems and boys externalizing problems?

Depression and Anxiety On the basis of decades of research conducted throughout the world, it is now widely accepted that there is a surge during adolescence in feelings of depression, sadness, and anxiety, and that it mostly affects girls (Costello et al., 2008; Twenge & Nolen-Hoeksema, 2002). Several studies have examined adolescents' **emotional tone**, or their sense of well-being versus depression and anxiety

internalizing problems Disturbances in emotion or mood such as depression, worry, guilt, and anxiety; more common in girls than in boys.

externalizing problems Social and behavioral problems such as aggression and delinquency; more common in boys than in girls.

emotional tone One's sense of well-being versus depression and anxiety.

(reviewed in Petersen et al., 1998). In general, findings show that for adolescents in the United States and many other countries, positive emotional tone increases throughout adolescence for boys but plateaus after early adolescence for girls. This pattern is reflected in Figure 15.12, which depicts results from a study conducted with several thousand Scottish children at 11, 13, and 15 years of age (Sweeting & West, 2003).

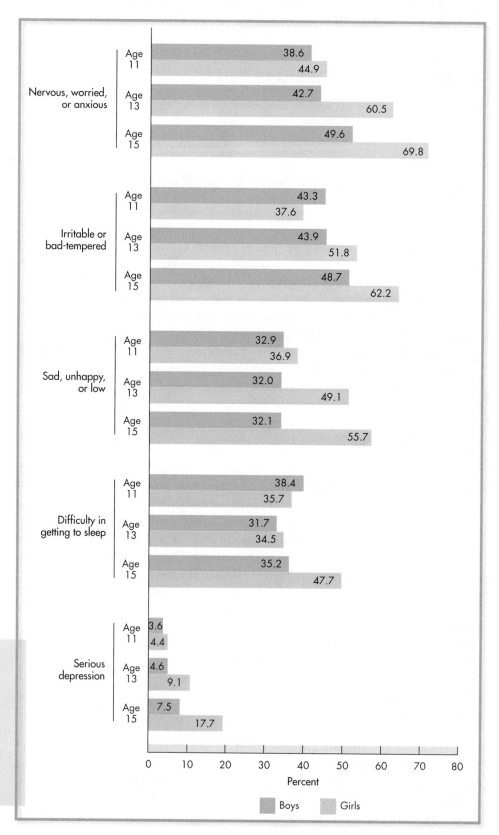

FIGURE 15.12 Consistent with research done in many other countries, results from a large national study of Scottish children found an increase in emotional distress for boys and girls between the ages of 11 and 15, as well as an ever-widening gender gap such that among 15-year-olds, girls are twice as likely as boys to experience serious depression. (From Sweeting & West, 2003.)

As the figure shows, there was an increasing gender difference in emotional distress, such that by the age of 15, girls were about twice as likely as boys to experience serious depression (Keenan et al., 2010). Similar trends have been found in Mexican adolescents (Borges et al., 2008).

Characterized by some combination of sadness, apathy, hopelessness, poor self-esteem, and trouble finding pleasure in activities that one used to enjoy, **depression** is one of the most common psychological problems of adolescence. The incidence of depression in adolescence depends on the number and severity of the symptoms. Virtually all adolescents (and adults, for that matter) experience episodes of sadness, or *depressed mood;* and approximately 25 percent of teens report regular bouts of feeling sad (Avenevoli & Steinberg, 2001). In contrast, approximately 16 percent of adolescent girls and 8 percent of boys meet the criteria for the more serious *depressive disorder* (Table 15.4 lists the criteria, set out by the American Psychiatric Association's *Diagnostic and Statistical Manual of Mental Disorders*).

A great deal of research has been devoted to identifying the causes of depression and to finding ways to prevent and treat it. One finding is that depression likely has a genetic component, given that the concordance rate of depression in monozygotic (MZ) twins is significantly higher than it is for dizygotic (DZ) twins (Glowinski, Madden, Bucholz, Lynskey, & Heath, 2003) and that one's risk of developing depression is elevated threefold if a biological parent has a history of depression (Weissman et al., 2005). Characteristics of the environment, such as poor peer relationships, excessive family conflict, and parental divorce, have also been implicated as risk factors for depression (Graber, 2004; Davila & Steinberg, 2006; Compas et al., 2010; Sheeber et al., 2007; see the box "Suicide Among Native American Adolescents" for a discussion of the relationship between culture and the most serious consequence of depression).

Notwithstanding the significance of each of these genetic and environmental risk factors, some of the most consistent and intriguing findings relate to the risk factors of puberty and gender (Conley & Rudolph, 2009; Mendle, Harden, Brooks-Gunn, & Graber, 2010). As we mentioned, gender differences in rates of depression are striking, with women being twice as likely as men to be diagnosed with the disorder. Interestingly, there is no gender difference in depression rates during childhood. Indeed, the overall gender difference in rates of depression seems largely due to surging rates for girls at the time of puberty (the rates for boys remaining fairly stable throughout adolescence and adulthood [Rudolph, Hammen, & Daley, 2006; Twenge & Nolen-Hoeksema, 2002]).

A number of additional explanations have been offered to account for the adolescent surge in depression and other internalizing problems, as well as for the large gender difference in their incidence. Accounting for the surge, some developmentalists point to the stresses associated with the host of biological and social changes we have previously noted, including with the chemistry of puberty, transitions to different schools, new friends and peer groups, increased family conflict, and increased pressure to achieve from parents and teachers (Compas, 2004).

As for gender differences in the surge, one explanation is suggested by our earlier discussions of gender differences in regulation of emotion and in intimacy orientation. Recall that girls appear to be more preoccupied with negative emotions than boys are and to be more focused on achieving and maintaining emotional closeness in their relationships. Given these differences, it is predictable that girls might react more negatively to the stressful events of adolescence than boys do, especially when those events involve conflict in relationships with parents,

table 15.4
DSM-IV Diagnostic Criteria for Major Depressive Disorder*

1. Depressed mood throughout most of the day
2. Reduced interest and pleasure in all or most activities
3. Significant changes in weight or appetite
4. Sleeping difficulties (too little or too much)
5. Psychomotor agitation or retardation
6. Fatigue or loss of energy
7. Excessive feelings of guilt or being worthless
8. Problems in reasoning, concentrating, or making decisions
9. Recurrent thoughts of death or suicide

*At least five of these symptoms must be present during a 2-week period.

depression An emotional state involving some combination of sadness, apathy, hopelessness, poor self-esteem, and trouble finding pleasure in activities that one used to enjoy. Depression is one of the most common psychological problems of adolescence, especially for girls.

Suicide Among Native American Adolescents

NATIVE AMERICAN ADOLESCENTS are at greater risk for killing themselves than are members of any ethnic or age group in the United States—indeed, the world (Dorgan, 2010; Kermayer, 1994). Michael Chandler, Chris Lalonde, and their colleagues are working to understand why (Chandler et al., 2003; Hallett, Chandler, & Lalonde, 2007). Their efforts have led them to evaluate suicide risk in light of the complex relationship between identity development and cultural change.

One identity issue that all adolescents must face is the problem of self-continuity. Self-continuity is understanding oneself as the same person throughout time, despite obvious internal or external changes. According to Chandler and his colleagues, without some way to understand that the self will continue in time regardless of change, it is difficult for adolescents to imagine themselves in the future and to work toward, or be invested in, their own future selves, and suicide might thus seem a more reasonable course of action than it would be otherwise.

In the process of studying adolescents of Western European and Native American descent, the research team identified cultural differences in the ways that adolescents solved the problem of self-continuity (Chandler et al., 2003). In particular, most adolescents of Western European descent gave essentialist accounts of self-continuity. That is, they believed that they were the same person across time and situations because some essential feature of their identity remained unchanged—their fingerprints, or basic personality structure, for example: "I have always been competitive. When I was little I wanted to win races, now I want to get the best grades" (p. 35). Native American adolescents, in contrast, gave narrative accounts

Children who grow up in tribes that preserve their cultural ceremonies and practices may be less vulnerable to suicide risk in adolescence.

of self-continuity, arguing that they were the same person across time because they were able to tell a story about their life experiences and relationships that linked together their past, present, and future selves.

These two distinct ways of understanding self-continuity reflect the two different cultural traditions. Western European cultural conceptions of self tend to emphasize largely stable and internal individual traits and attributes ("I have always been competitive"). Native American cultures, in contrast, and consistent with their storytelling traditions, tend to conceptualize the self in terms of the ever-

changing relationships and connections between the person and the world. What is particularly interesting in light of adolescent mental health issues is that the two ways of understanding self-continuity may result in profoundly different levels of suicide risk, especially under conditions of radical social change such as those affecting Native American communities.

Over the course of just a few generations, Native American cultures were crushed by the policies of the federal government. Tribal lands were taken, hunting and fishing practices were outlawed, families were broken up and relocated to reservations, and many Native American languages and cultural practices were suppressed to the point of extinction. In a manner of speaking, Native American stories have been silenced. For adolescents struggling to establish a narrative-based account of self-continuity, the consequences of having no cultural stories can be dire.

But how can it be determined that the higher rate of suicide among Native American adolescents is due to the devastation of Native American cultures and not to some other factor, such as genetic vulnerability to depression, for example? As it happens, Native American suicides are not equally distributed throughout all tribes. In many tribes, suicides are quite rare—in fact, much less common than the national average. In other tribes, in contrast, suicide rates are astoundingly high.

What accounts for these differences? According to Chandler and his colleagues, the answer lies in differences in the extent to which tribes have attempted to reconstruct their culture and reclaim their heritage. The researchers identified six cultural continuity factors that are present in the tribes with

peers, and romantic partners (Rudolph, 2002). A second, related explanation is that, compared with boys, girls are more concerned about how they are judged by others. Such "social–evaluative concerns" contribute to girls' being more competent in their interpersonal relationships but also more vulnerable to feelings of depression and anxiety (Rudolph & Conley, 2005).

In addition, some developmentalists believe that cultural values and stereotypes contribute to girls' greater ambivalence toward their changing bodies and thereby contribute to gender differences in depression and anxiety. In particular, girls' maturing bodies tend to be viewed as sexual objects to a greater extent than

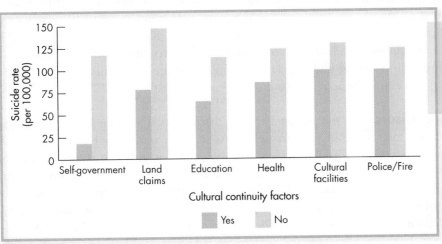

Native American tribes that engage in forms of cultural continuity and efforts to be self-determining have lower adolescent suicide rates than tribes whose cultural traditions have been eroded or lost.

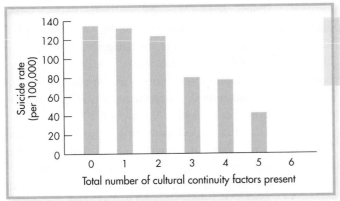

The effects of cultural continuity factors are cumulative; as the number of continuity factors rise, so does adolescents' protection from suicide risk.

lower suicide rates and lacking in tribes with higher suicide rates. As shown in the first figure, suicide rates are greatly reduced if the tribe is self-governing, fights legal battles to win back traditional lands, exercises some control over its own public health services, schools, and police and fire departments, and has built a facility for cultural activities.

It appears, moreover, that the effects of these cultural continuity factors are cumulative. That is, the presence of each additional factor further decreases suicide risk, as shown in the second figure.

Chandler's work demonstrates that tribal efforts to reclaim a cultural heritage can help provide adolescents with a safety net while

they work through the developmental task of establishing a sense of self-continuity. It also underscores the importance of understanding development in the context of culture and history (Hallett, Chandler & Lalonde, 2007).

boys' bodies do, making girls feel more self-conscious (Brooks-Gunn & Warren, 1989; Martin, 1996; Thorne, 1993). It may be that the sexualization of the female body also accounts for the different reactions that parents have to their sons' and daughters' development. In contrast to boys, who report that their parents grant them greater freedom as they become sexually mature, many girls report that their parents become more restrictive (Martin, 1996). The perception of higher levels of parental control may contribute to feelings of anxiety and depression to the extent that girls resent and attempt to resist parents' efforts to restrict their behavior.

Treatment options for adolescents suffering from depression and anxiety range from drug therapies to individual and family therapy. Research indicates that one of the most effective treatments is **cognitive-behavioral therapy (CBT)**, which is based on the theory that negative thoughts and/or poor coping behaviors may cause the adolescent to feel depressed and anxious (Kennard et al., 2009). CBT involves helping the adolescent to develop adaptive communication and problem-solving skills, monitor and regulate changing emotions, and schedule time for relaxing and enjoyable activities.

Eating Disorders

One pubertal change that carries significant consequences for emotional tone is the increase in weight. As we have noted, for boys, this increase comes largely from a gain in muscle mass, whereas for girls, the increase is largely the result of the addition of body fat, estimated to be, on average, a little more than 24 pounds over the course of adolescence (Bogin, 1999). These changes are perfectly normal but can carry very different psychological consequences for boys and girls, depending on cultural values and beliefs. For boys in many cultures, bulking up is valued—as an athletic advantage and as a step toward becoming "buff" and sexy. For girls, in contrast, the increase in fat can deviate from cultural ideals and thus be a source of significant psychological distress (Polivy & Herman, 2004). In the United States, for example, a thin, prepubertal body shape is the current ideal for women, an ideal reflected in everything from television, movie, and magazine images to dolls given to young girls (Dittmar, Halliwell, & Ive, 2006). In general, research finds that girls' exposure to media that directly or indirectly promotes thinness as the physical ideal is associated with the development of a negative body image that can persist over time (Groesz, Levine, & Murnen, 2002; Hausenblaus, Janelle, & Gardner, 2004).

It is now widely acknowledged that many adolescent girls who are dissatisfied with their bodies go on fad diets that may cut out entire classes of food such as fats or carbohydrates, or take drugs to suppress their appetite, or induce vomiting and take laxatives to avoid gaining weight. All of these practices endanger their health and, in extreme forms, can lead to eating disorders such as **anorexia nervosa**, or intentional self-starving, and **bulimia nervosa**, or cycles of "binge eating" followed by self-induced vomiting (Keel, Gravener, Joiner, & Haedt, 2010; Keel & Klump, 2003). A third disorder, often called **eating disorder not otherwise specified (EDNOS)**, is diagnosed when the criteria for anorexia or bulimia nervosa are not quite met. EDNOS is the most common diagnosis for adolescents with eating disorders (Golden et al., 2003).

The criteria most commonly used to diagnose anorexia nervosa and bulimia are shown in Table 15.5. When these criteria are applied, very few adolescents are diagnosed with eating disorders: Less than 1 percent of adolescents are diagnosed with anorexia, while approximately 3 percent are diagnosed with bulimia nervosa. However, this particular classification system is not entirely applicable to children and adolescents, the age groups during which eating disorders typically emerge (Miller & Golden, 2010). For example, wide variation in the adolescent growth spurt, the absence of menstrual periods in early puberty, and the unpredictability of menstrual periods immediately following menarche limit the application of the diagnostic criteria presented in the table. In addition, the developmental immaturity of children and adolescents may hinder their abilitiy to express abstract concepts such as self-awareness, motivation to lose weight, or feelings of anxiety or depression (Golden et al., 2003).

Furthermore, clinicians have long recognized the importance of identifying and treating children with "subthreshold" conditions (which include some, but not all, of the standard criteria), as well as children exhibiting other "disordered" behaviors

cognitive-behavioral therapy (CBT) A treatment for depression and anxiety that is based on the theory that these problems are related to negative thoughts and/or poor coping behaviors. CBT is designed to help the adolescent develop adaptive communication and problem-solving skills, monitor and regulate changing emotions, and schedule time for relaxing and enjoyable activities.

anorexia nervosa An eating disorder that involves intentional self-starving.

bulimia nervosa An eating disorder that involves cycles of "binge eating" followed by self-induced vomiting.

eating disorder not otherwise specified (EDNOS) An eating disorder that is diagnosed when the criteria for anorexia or bulimia nervosa are not quite met. EDNOS is the most common diagnosis for adolescents with eating disorders.

table 15.5	
DSM-IV Diagnostic Criteria for Anorexia and Bulimia Nervosa	
Condition	**DSM-IV Diagnostic Criteria**
Anorexia nervosa	A. Refusal to maintain body weight at or above a minimally normal weight for age and height B. Intense fear of gaining weight or becoming fat, even though underweight C. Disturbance in the way in which one's body weight or shape is experienced, undue influence of body weight or shape on self-evaluation, or denial of the seriousness of low body weight D. In postmenarcheal females, amenorrhea (absence of at least 3 consecutive menstrual cycles) *Specify Type* *Restricting type:* During current episode, individual has not regularly engaged in binge-eating (eating an excessive amount of food in a short time period) or purging (self-induced vomiting or the misuse of laxatives, diuretics, or enemas) *Binge-eating/purging type:* During current episode, individual has regularly engaged in recurrent binge-eating or purging

Bulimia Nervosa	A. Recurrent episodes of binge-eating characterized by:
	  i. Eating an excessive amount of food in a short period of time
	  ii. Feeling that one cannot stop eating or control what or how much one is eating
	
	B. Recurrent inappropriate compensatory behaviors to prevent weight gain, such as self-induced vomiting; misuse of laxatives, diuretics, enemas, or other medications; fasting; or excessive exercise
	
	C. Binge-eating and inappropriate compensatory behavior both occur on average at least twice a week for 3 months
	
	D. Self-evaluation is unduly influenced by body shape and weight
	
	E. This disturbance does not occur exclusively during episodes of anorexia nervosa

associated with eating that are not included in the standard description of anorexia nervosa and bulimia nervosa. Examples include *functional dysphagia,* in which food avoidance is associated with a fear of choking or vomiting, and *pervasive food refusal,* which involves refusal not only to eat but also to drink, walk, talk, or care for oneself (Nicholls, Chater, & Lask, 2000). Using a broader set of criteria for defining disordered eating behaviors, a recent 8-year longitudinal study conducted in a large U.S. city found that 12 percent of adolescent girls developed eating disorders (Stice, Marti, Shaw, & Jaconis, 2009).

The road to recovery from eating disorders can be long and difficult, with frequent relapses. This is especially true of anorexia nervosa. More than 20 percent of individuals diagnosed with anorexia nervosa continue to have an eating disorder many years later. In addition, these individuals frequently suffer from other psychiatric problems, including depression, anxiety, and substance abuse. Sadly, according to some reports, as many as 15 percent die either from complications related to their eating disorder or from committing suicide (see Miller & Golden, 2010, for review). Although there is less longitudinal research on individuals with bulimia nervosa and EDNOS, their recovery seems more promising, with 60 to 75 percent achieving good outcomes or full recovery (Keel, Gravener, Joiner, & Haedt, 2010; Herzog et al., 1999).

Delinquency and Other Externalizing Problems Like internalizing problems, externalizing problems seem to peak in adolescence. For both boys and girls, delinquent behaviors such as skipping school, stealing or destroying property,

getting into fights, and taking illegal drugs rise sharply between early and mid-adolescence, after which they decline (Dodge & Pettit, 2003; Storvoll & Wich-strom, 2002; Steinberg, 2008). However, the gender differences, which, as noted, are reversed from those of internalizing problems, are much greater than those of internalizing problems (Lahey et al., 2000). In fact, it has been estimated that boys account for 70 percent of all juvenile *person offenses* such as assault, robbery, ho-micide, and other crimes involving force or threat of force against persons (Puz-zanchera & Adams, 2011).

The incidence of delinquent behaviors during adolescence poses an important question: Is the increase due to the fact that a larger proportion of teens are in-volved, perhaps minimally, in behaviors such as skipping school, drinking alcohol, smoking pot, getting into fights, and so forth, or is it the case that a small number of teens become increasingly active in such behavior? Studies indicate that the in-crease reflects both factors—an increase in the number of teens involved and an increase in the involvement of specific individuals (Maccoby, 2004). For example, in a nationwide longitudinal study of Norwegian adolescents, more than 75 percent of all 15- to 16-year-old boys and girls reported some involvement in delinquent behaviors (with the percentage being somewhat higher for boys than for girls), but only 25 percent of boys and 15 percent of girls reported high levels of involve-ment (Storvoll & Wichstrom, 2002). This is consistent with other research indicat-ing that over 50 percent of all juvenile violent behaviors are perpetrated by only 6 percent of all adolescents, most of whom are also involved in other externalizing behaviors such as theft and the frequent use of drugs and alcohol (Dodge & Pettit, 2003; Moffitt et al., 2002).

Naturally, developmentalists are especially concerned about this small minority of adolescents who show high levels of delinquency, as well as about those who exhibit other serious forms of chronic externalizing problems. Adolescents in these groups account for the majority of referrals to outpatient adolescent mental health clinics and the largest proportion of placements in special education classes (re-viewed in Dodge & Pettit, 2003).

To shed light on these groups, a team of researchers studied approximately 1,000 individuals growing up in New Zealand, following them from birth to adulthood (Moffitt et al., 2002; Moffitt, 2007). The researchers identified two highly distinc-tive developmental patterns of externalizing problems. In one, called *adolescent onset,* externalizing problems emerged in adolescence and had a fairly brief time course, declining significantly in young adulthood. In the other, called *childhood onset,* or *life-course persistent,* high levels of aggression emerged in preschool and persisted throughout childhood and adolescence and into adulthood. Although boys out-numbered girls in both groups, the boy/girl ratio was much smaller (1.5 to 1) in the adolescent-onset group than in the childhood-onset group, in which boys out-numbered girls by a ratio of 10 to 1. Note that these results are similar to those of the Norwegian study described previously, in which gender differences were much greater for reports of high involvement in externalizing behaviors than for overall reports of involvement.

The developmental histories of adolescents who exhibit childhood-onset prob-lems are strikingly different from those of their adolescent-onset peers (Patter-son et al., 1989; Dodge et al., 2009). As shown in Figure 15.13, boys who go on to develop life-course-persistent problems such as substance use and addiction typi-cally have difficult temperaments and receive inconsistent parenting during early childhood (the developmental histories of life-course-persistent girls have not yet been well studied). In essence, by virtue of their difficult temperaments, these young boys are hard to handle, and their parents lack the skills necessary to cope

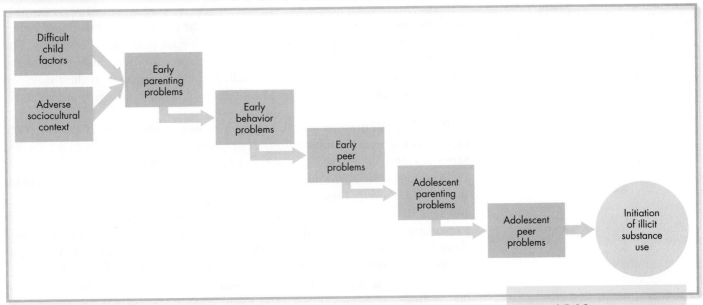

FIGURE 15.13 Research suggests that adolescent substance use may be rooted in a long history of interacting peer, family, and child temperament factors. (Adapted from Dodge et al., 2009.)

effectively with their behaviors. Instead, they tend to respond either by ignoring the boys' inappropriate and often aggressive behaviors, which fails to teach the boys social skills, including self-control, or by using excessive punishment, which, as described in Chapter 9, creates a family system in which parents and children are caught in a dynamic of escalating negative interactions. Both approaches increase the chances that, when such boys begin school, they are both aggressive and undersocialized. As a consequence, by middle childhood, they are often rejected by peers and performing poorly in school. By late childhood and adolescence, they typically form alliances with other deviant peers, who further reinforce their externalizing behaviors.

As noted above, there has been little research into how and why some girls develop externalizing problems. On the other hand, there has been a great deal of speculation as to why such problems are less common in girls than in boys. In general, most developmentalists maintain that the gender differences are largely due to an interaction of biological and sociocultural processes. As discussed in Chapter 9 (pp 330–331), boys and girls may have different biological predispositions to behave aggressively (Maccoby, 2004). Coupled with this are the considerable differences in the socialization of boys and girls, by parents as well as by peers (Zahn-Waxler & Polanichka, 2004). In particular, norm-violating behaviors are less tolerated in girls, and more often ignored in boys. Moreover, the *communal orientation* of girls discussed earlier would seem to further diminish their involvement in externalizing behaviors.

All told, evidence indicates that adolescence is a vulnerable period for the onset of social and emotional problems and that these problems are significantly affected by sociocultural norms and expectations.

Sexual Health

According to a 2008 report from the Centers for Disease Control and Prevention (CDC), about 25 percent of all 14- to 19-year-old girls in the United States have at least one sexually transmitted infection. Furthermore, of the approximately 19 million new infections that occur each year, nearly 50 percent have been contracted by young people ages 15 to 24, and the infection rates are on the rise for this age group (Weinstock et al., 2004). The statistics are even more alarming in the case

positive youth development (PYD) A general approach to adolescence that emphasizes the strengths and positive qualities of youths that contribute to their psychological health as well as to the welfare of their communities.

of ethnic-minority groups, all of which—with the exception of Asians and Pacific Islanders—have STI rates that are significantly higher than those of Whites. The costs of STIs are high. Apart from their consequences for individuals' physical and psychological well-being, the direct medical costs associated with their diagnosis and treatment are estimated to be $14.7 billion annually (Chesson et al., 2006).

Chlamydia With more than 1.2 million cases reported to the CDC in 2009, chlamydia is among the most commonly reported infectious diseases in the United States (Centers for Disease Control and Prevention, 2010). As shown in Figure 15.14, among females, the rate of infection is higher for 15- to 19-year-olds than for any other age group. Estimates are that chlamydia affects 1 in 7 adolescent females and 1 in 10 adolescent males. The infection rate for African American women is particularly startling—more than twice that of Hispanic women and more than 7 times that of European American women. Chlamydia often goes unreported, placing women at increased risk for pelvic inflammatory disease and infertility. Complications among infected men are rare but can include painful inflammation of the urethra.

Human Papillomavirus There are more than 40 different types of human papillomavirus (HPV), which affects the skin and mucous membranes in the genital areas of males and females. It is the most common sexually transmitted infection, with at least 50 percent of all men and women acquiring a form of the disease at some point in their lives (Centers for Disease Control and Prevention, 2010). However, HPV usually has no noticeable symptoms, so it often goes undiagnosed. Thus, although it is the most common STI, it is far from being the most commonly *reported* disease.

There are two general categories of HPV: "low risk" (wart causing), and "high risk" (cancer causing). Most infections are low risk, and are successfully eliminated within 2 years by the individual's immune system. Although both genital warts and cancers can be treated, there is no current treatment for the virus itself. Recently, however, a vaccine has been developed that protects girls and women from the HPV types that most often cause cancers and warts. It is recommended

FIGURE 15.14 Infection rates of chlamydia, one of the most commonly reported infectious diseases in the United States, peaks during the adolescent and early adulthood years. (From Centers for Disease Control and Prevention, 2010.)

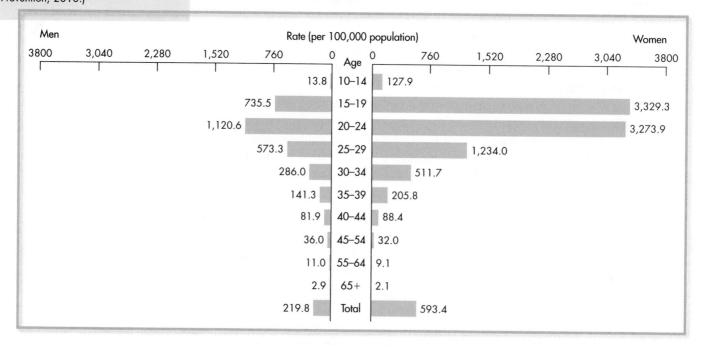

Men					Rate (per 100,000 population)		Women			
3800	3,040	2,280	1,520	760	0	Age	0	760	1,520	2,280	3,040	3800
					13.8	10–14	127.9			
	735.5					15–19					3,329.3
1,120.6						20–24					3,273.9
		573.3				25–29		1,234.0		
			286.0			30–34	511.7			
				141.3		35–39	205.8			
				81.9		40–44	88.4			
				36.0		45–54	32.0			
				11.0		55–64	9.1			
				2.9		65+	2.1			
				219.8		Total	593.4			

that girls be vaccinated when they reach 11 or 12 years of age, although all females under the age of 26 may profit from completing the vaccination series.

HIV/AIDS Human immunodeficiency virus (HIV) is the virus that causes acquired immunodeficiency syndrome (AIDS), a deadly disease that attacks the immune system, preventing it from combating infections. HIV is generally found in the blood and semen or vaginal fluid of infected individuals. Most HIV is contracted through anal, oral, or vaginal sex, or by sharing needles or syringes with an infected person, or prenatally or in infancy, by exposure through the uterine environment or breast milk.

In the United States, those under 25 years of age account for less than 15 percent of new HIV/AIDS cases diagnosed in a given year (Figure 15.15). However, because the virus has a long incubation period before symptoms occur, many individuals who contract the infection during their teen years may not be diagnosed until their 20s or 30s. It is estimated that 25 percent of infected individuals are unaware that they have contracted the virus.

As with other STIs, HIV/AIDS is especially prevalent in African American and Hispanic populations in the United States (Kaiser Foundation, 2008). In part this may be because the disease is concentrated primarily in large metropolitan areas in the United States, where there are large populations of these two groups. They may also be at greater risk because more African American and Hispanic youth become sexually active at earlier ages than do their European American counterparts (Figure 15.16), and the age of first intercourse itself predicts infection risk.

To date, there is no cure for AIDS, although significant strides have been made in managing symptoms of the disease and prolonging the lives of infected individuals. Consequently, health-care professionals and educators focus their attention on communicating the importance of disease prevention, for HIV/AIDS as well as for all other STIs. For sexually active youth, the consistent use of condoms is the most reliable means of STI prevention.

Positive Youth Development

Given that adolescents are generally healthier than any other age group, it is somewhat ironic that the lion's share of research on adolescent health and well-being has focused on illness and disease. Recently, however, many developmentalists have begun to balance the scales by defining a general approach to adolescence—**positive youth development (PYD)**—that emphasizes the strengths and positive qualities of youths that contribute to their psychological health as well as the welfare of their communities (Lerner, Phelps, Forman, & Bowers, 2009), As described by Jacqueline Lerner and her colleagues, the PYD perspective has its origins in the concept of the *plasticity* of development. As you may recall from earlier discussions, plasticity refers to the degree to which development is open to change and intervention as a consequence of specific experiences. Extending the notion of plasticity to

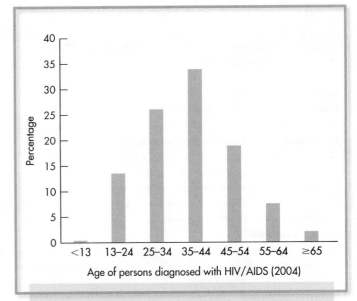

FIGURE 15.15 Because it can take many years before a person infected with HIV shows symptoms of the disease, many teens who contract the virus may not be diagnosed until their 20s or 30s. (From Centers for Disease Control and Prevention, 2008.)

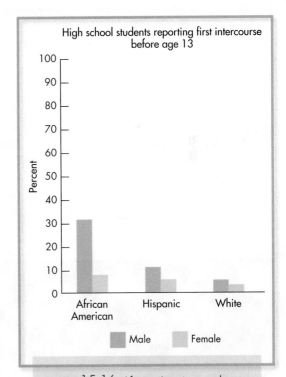

FIGURE 15.16 African American and Hispanic adolescents are more likely than their White counterparts to report having first intercourse before age 13. Early intercourse is known to be a risk factor for sexually transmitted infections. (From Centers for Disease Control and Prevention, 2004.)

table 15.6

Assets That Facilitate Positive Youth Development

Intellectual development

Critical thinking and reasoning skills

Good decision-making skills

In-depth knowledge of more than one culture

School success

Psychological and emotional development

Good mental health, including positive self-regard

Good emotional self-regulation and coping skills

Mastery motivation and positive achievement motivation

Sense of personal autonomy/responsibility for self

Prosocial and culturally sensitive values

Social development

Connectedness—perceived good relationships and trust with parents and peers

Attachment to institutions such as school, church, youth development programs

Commitment to civic engagement

Context characteristics

    Appropriate structure, including age-appropriate monitoring, clear and consistent rules, predictability

    Emotional support, including warmth, good communication, and responsiveness

    Prosocial norms, such as strong expectations for prosocial and moral behaviors, obligations for service

    Opportunity for efficacy and "mattering," such as involvement in practices that support autonomy, opportunities to demonstrate and acquire mastery in valued activities

(Adapted from Eccles, Brown, & Templeton, 2008)

adolescent development, the PYD approach examines individual strengths such as future-mindeness, optimism, honesty, and insight, as well as the role of youth programs, communities, and societies in both promoting such strengths and profiting from them.

Jacquelynne Eccles and her colleagues have been working to identify the personal and social assets that facilitate positive youth development. As shown in Table 15.6, they have identified assets within several domains, including intellectual development, psychological and emotional development, and social development. Although an adolescent can develop positively in the absence of some, or even many of the assets listed, Eccles argues that it is best to have at least some assets in each domain, and that the more the adolescent has, the greater the likelihood of positive development.

Research on what, exactly, promotes positive youth development has focused mostly on the influence of after-school programs such as 4-H, Big Brothers/Big Sisters, and Boy Scouts/Girl Scouts, which share in the common goal of learning and working with others for the betterment of self and community. In general, programs are most effective when they meet three criteria:

1. Allow for the development of positive adult–youth relationships that last at least 1 year.

2. Provide activities that promote skill building.

3. Provide opportunities to use skills.

Another important factor in the success of such programs is leadership. In general, research finds that the most successful adult program leaders are those who seek the input of the youths, follow the youths' lead, and push the youths toward higher levels of achievement (Larson & Walker, 2006; Larson, 2007).

In a study of how participation in an urban art project may contribute to positive development, Reed Larson and his colleagues traced a fascinating developmental pattern. Specifically, when youths were engaged in an internship that involved real-life challenges to plan and create murals for their communities, they progressed from an egocentric focus on their own ideas to developing strategies and skills for teamwork that were applied to accomplish their artful goals (Larson, 2007). Needless to say, this structured civic engagement not only bolstered the youths' positive development but also benefited the community in which they lived. The mutuality of positive youth and community development is at the heart of the PYD perspective: Youths thrive when they are meaningfully engaged in community affairs, and communities thrive when their youths are healthy, happy, and committed to the well-being of those around them.

These Penn State University students are participating in THON, an annual dance marathon that has raised $78 million since 1977 to combat childhood cancer. In addition to helping children with cancer, this sort of structured civic engagement contributes to these young adults' positive development.

Penn State IFC / Panhellenic Dance Marathon

▲ APPLY :: CONNECT :: DISCUSS

Your school board is once again seeking your assistance, this time to revamp its sex education program, which is considered outdated and out of touch with issues facing today's youth. The goal is to develop programs aimed at seventh-graders (12-year-olds) and tenth-graders (15-year-olds). Outline a general plan for each program. What topics should each program include? What "issues facing today's youth" should be addressed? Should boys and girls participate in the program together or separately? Explain how the program would take into account differences between 12- and 15-year-olds.

Reconsidering Adolescence

Evidence presented in this chapter, as well as in Chapter 14, indicates that the biocultural transition of adolescence universally involves dramatic transformation across the physical, cognitive, social, and emotional domains, and is often accompanied by conflict, anxiety, and uncertainty.

Compared with all other primate species, humans are radically delayed in reaching reproductive maturity. Many have argued that the delay is to allow the brain to develop areas associated with advanced processes—language, reasoning, decision making—required to make and use the sophisticated tools of human culture. Even so, at the onset of puberty, the frontal lobes are not sufficiently mature for the effective regulation of the surge of emotional intensity associated with the release of hormones, and poorly regulated emotions make the adolescent vulnerable to risk-taking, recklessness, and emotional problems.

While the onset and course of adolescence are heavily influenced by such biological factors, the many contexts of development—from the physical environment to cultural values and practices—also play significant roles in adolescent development. Thus, culture has played a role in the timing of the onset of puberty, as evidenced by the secular trend—the increasingly early pubertal onset associated with changes in the contexts of development across recent generations. In the past, the secular trend was attributed to increased access to nutritious food and health care. The continuing downward trend of the past few decades, however, has been associated with the rising tide of obesity and poor health, particularly among low-income minority populations in the United States, providing an unfortunate illustration of how phenotypic development is constrained by both biological and cultural processes.

Similarly, research provides strong evidence that the adolescent experience—how individuals navigate the passage to adulthood—is to a large extent structured by families, communities, and institutions, and dependent on cultural beliefs, values, and practices. For example, many of the questions that concern adolescents—Who am I? Who will I become? Who will be my mate? What is right and just?—may be less significant in cultures where identity, career, and social role possibilities are mapped out in advance according to long-standing cultural traditions, and where traditional beliefs and values are rarely open to question.

And then there is the issue of whether the cumulative cultural evolution of technologically advanced societies has created a context for the emergence of yet another way station between childhood and adulthood, a new stage of "emerging adulthood," in which the developing individual comes to terms with a kaleidoscopic array of possibilities—for identity, relationships, education, and ways of understanding the nature of truth and knowledge. But regardless of whether emerging adulthood proves to be a specific stage in the life course, we can be sure that the transition to adulthood reflects a special relationship between developing individuals and the cultures they will transform and carry into the future.

SUMMARY

Emotional Development in Adolescence

- Contrary to perceptions of adolescence as an emotional roller coaster, research indicates that over adolescence, ups and downs become less frequent and emotions less intense, although average happiness decreases.

- Decreased emotional intensity is in large part explained by increased emotional regulation. In early adolescence, the frontal lobes are not fully mature and may be unable to deal with hormonally triggered emotions, leaving adolescents vulnerable to risk-taking; later maturation of the frontal lobes facilitates emotional regulation. Emotional regulation also appears to be promoted by parental warmth and to be shaped by social expectations related to gender.

Relationships with Peers

- During adolescence, time spent with peers increases dramatically, peer groups become larger, and peer relationships become more important and intense.

- Adolescents seek friendships marked by reciprocity, commitment, and equality. Close friendships serve the functions of intimacy and autonomy and thus promote social and personality development. Girls' friendships are more intense and intimate than boys' friendships, with expressions of intimacy between boys curtailed perhaps by lack of trust, perhaps by homophobia; gender differences in relationship goals may also explain friendship differences.

- In addition to friendships, adolescent peer relations take the form of cliques—small, intimate peer groups that serve emotional and security needs—and crowds—larger groups that provide opportunities to meet people, to develop romantic relationships and, because different crowds have different reputations, to explore social identity.

- According to classic research by Dexter Dunphy, romantic relationships develop in a stagelike process in which same-sex cliques of early adolescence give way to mixed-sex crowds, which gradually give way to romantic relationships. Significant cultural variations exist, however, and in contemporary industrialized societies, marriage is postponed and romantic relationships take place alongside other peer relationships.

- Adolescent peer relationships tend to be characterized by high levels of homophily, or similarity in behaviors, tastes, views, and goals. A study by Denise Kandel showed homophily as resulting from two successive processes: selection, in which adolescents target as potential friends peers with whom they share similarities, and socialization, in which friends mutually model and reinforce significant behavior. Thus, deviancy can be socialized in the context of

peer relationships, in a process that has been labeled deviancy training.

Sexual Relationships

- The step from virginity to sexual activity is a significant one and is treated in different ways from culture to culture.

- Adolescents learn about sexuality from various sources—parents, peers, media, and educational programs—and there is great variability in what is taught and how it is taught.

- Greater societal acceptance of teenage sexuality may be linked to lower levels of teen pregnancy and STIs.

- Age at first intercourse varies considerably across countries and over time. Boys tend to report more positive feelings about first intercourse than do girls.

Relationships with Parents

- In intensity and frequency, parent–child conflict reaches a peak in early adolescence and then decreases. Conflicts tend to focus on such matters as responsibilities and curfews—seemingly trivial but related to major issues of growing up. They often reflect differences between parents' and adolescents' understanding of what belongs to the personal, as opposed to the social conventional, domain.

- Parents of adolescents generally continue to be an important influence in their children's lives and to be called on for advice, particularly if parents provide a safe environment for communication and have an authoritative parenting style. Over adolescence, parents and their teenagers typically negotiate a new form of interdependence.

Identity Development

- A key challenge of adolescence is that of forming a coherent, stable identity through the process of identity development. The self can be seen as consisting of two selves. One is a me-self, or object self, including roles and relationships, possessions, and characteristics; the other is an I-self, or subject self, reflecting on and guiding the object self. Contexts play a role in the development of self, and according to Kenneth Gergen, modern society has resulted in a saturated self—multiple me's—making the question of authenticity more pressing for adolescents.

- For Erik Erikson, the quest for identity, although lifelong, is particularly the task of adolescence. Focusing on exploration and commitment, the factors Erikson considered essential to achieving a mature identity, James Marcia identified four patterns young people fall into: identity achievement, with commitment following exploration; foreclosure, or commitment without exploration; moratorium, or active exploration with commitment not yet reached; and identity diffusion, with neither commitment nor exploration. Over the course of adolescence, there is an increase in achievement and a decrease in diffusion.

- Families can effectively promote identity development if they offer support and encourage exploration.

- The development of an ethnic identity can be more complicated for ethnic-minority youth, especially if their ethnic group's culture differs significantly from the majority culture or if the group faces prejudice. Jean Phinney has identified a process that leads from unexamined ethnic identity through an identity search to ethnic-identity achievement. Positive ethnic formation is easiest when families uphold cultural traditions and the ethnic group is well-established in the community.

- The development of sexual identity—individuals' understanding of themselves as heterosexual, gay or lesbian, or bisexual—can be especially pressing and complicated for sexual-minority youth. According to Richard Troiden's stage model, sexual-minority youth move from sensitization and feeling different, generally in early adolescence, through self-recognition and identity confusion and then identity assumption, before finally reaching, in many cases, commitment and identity integration.

- According to many developmentalists, identity development may be profoundly affected by cultural factors. For example, people whose culture encourages an independent sense of self may be oriented to promoting their individual goals and expressing their opinions; those whose culture is collectivist may be oriented to trying to fit in and to promoting group goals.

Adolescent Health and Well-Being

- For some individuals, the challenges of adolescence pose significant problems for health and well-being, by either aggravating preexisting problems or creating conditions for the emergence of new problems which may or may not persist into adulthood.

- Some emotional problems that may emerge during adolescence include internalizing problems, such as depression and anxiety, which are more common among girls, and externalizing problems, such as aggression and delinquency, which are more common among boys.

- Gender differences in the emergence of emotional problems are likely due to the biological and cultural factors that contribute to girls' concerns about how they are evaluated

by others, and boys' propensities to engage in aggressive behaviors.

- Depression is one of the most common psychological problems of adolescence. Risk factors associated with depression include biological inheritance (risk is elevated when a biological parent has a history of depression), as well as characteristics of the environment (poor peer relationships, family conflict) and cultural values and stereotypes (the sexualization of the female body).

- Cognitive behavior therapy (CBT) is one of the most effective treatments for depression. Based on the idea that negative thoughts and/or poor coping behaviors may cause a person to feel depressed and anxious, this approach involves helping the adolescent monitor and regulate his or her emotions and to develop adaptive communication and problem-solving skills.

- A girl's negative body image can result in the development of an eating disorder, such as anorexia nervosa (intentional self-starving), bulimia nervosa (cycles of "binge eating" followed by self-induced vomiting), or "eating disorder not otherwise specified" (EDNOS), when the criteria for diagnosing anorexia or bulimia are not quite met. Recovery from eating disorders is difficult, with relapses common; however, most individuals achieve good outcomes over time.

- Positive youth development (PYD) is a relatively new approach to adolescence that emphasizes the strengths and positive qualities of youth that contribute to their psychological health as well as to the welfare of their communities.

Reconsidering Adolescence

- Although humans are radically delayed in reaching puberty compared with other primate species, the frontal lobes of the human brain remain immature at the onset of puberty, perhaps contributing to adolescents' vulnerability to risk-taking and emotional problems.

- Culture, in addition to biology, plays a significant role in the onset and course of adolescent development. Increased access to health care and nutrition has resulted in the decline of pubertal onset in many countries. In many contemporary societies, overnutrition has further reduced the average age of pubertal onset.

- In societies in which education continues to be prolonged, and marriage and family delayed, adolescents confront an increasing array of possibilities for identity, occupation, and relationships, prompting some developmentalists to posit a new stage for late adolescents—emerging adulthood.

Key Terms

experience sampling method (ESM), p. 553

sensation-seeking, p. 554

friendship, p. 557

intimacy, p. 558

autonomy, p. 558

homophobia, p. 558

clique, p. 559

crowd, p. 560

homophily, p. 560

deviancy training, p. 561

sexually transmitted infections (STIs), p. 565

identity development, p. 573

saturated self, p. 574

exploration, p. 575

commitment, p. 575

ethnic identity, p. 578

sexual identity, p. 581

sexual-minority (LGBT) youth, p. 582

independent sense of self, p. 584

interdependent sense of self, p. 584

internalizing problems, p. 585

externalizing problems, p. 585

emotional tone, p. 585

depression, p. 587

cognitive-behavioral therapy (CBT), p. 590

anorexia nervosa, p. 590

bulimia nervosa, p. 590

eating disorder not otherwise specified (EDNOS), p. 590

positive youth development (PYD), p. 595

Appendix

Guide to Discussions of Specific Aspects of Development

Guide 1 Discussions of Physical Development

Period	Characteristic	Page Numbers
Early Infancy	Physical development in the first three months	124–126
	Maturation of the nervous system	126–130
	Brain development in first three months	128–130
	Infant sensory capacity	131–139
	Reflexes present at birth	141
	Development of reaching and grasping	144
	Maturation of sleeping patterns	150–153
Later infancy	Physical growth in the first two years	162–164
	Brain development in the first two years	165–168
	Fine motor skills	168–171
	Gross motor skills	171–175
	Control during elimination	175–177
Early childhood	The biological key to language	238–241
	Biological explanations of language acquisition	239–241
	Motor development	272–274
	Health and nutrition	274–276
	Brain maturation	276–277
Middle childhood	Patterns of growth	391–393
	Motor development	393–397
	Brain development	398–400
Adolescence	Biological theories	510–512
	Puberty	512–530

Guide 2 Discussions of Social Development

Period	Characteristic	Page Numbers
Early Infancy	Infant's preference for facelike figures	136–137
	Emergence of social smiling	205–206
	Infant sleeping arrangements	151–153
	Crying	155–157
	Coordination of infant's needs and caretaker's responses	141–143, 151, 153
Later infancy	Intersubjectivity	203–207
	Infant-caregiver relationship	207–208
	Self-recognition	224–225
	Self-reference	226
Early childhood	The environmental key to language	241–247
	Social explanations of language development	263
	Scripts	298–300
	Acquiring a sex-role identity	308–313
	Acquiring an ethnic or racial identity	313–315
	Personal identity	315–317
	Self-regulation	320–321
	Aggression	329–331
	Prosocial behavior	336–338
	Family origins and structure	345–348
	Parenting styles	348–351
	Relations with siblings	351–353
	Family diversity	351–358
	Distressed families	358–364
	Child care	364–369
	Effects of media	372–380
Middle childhood	Sociodramatic play	323–326
	Social organization of classroom instruction	439–442
	Rule-based games	402, 473
	Morality	471–480
	Peer relationships	481–496
	Influence of parents	496–500
	Sense of self	466–471
Adolescence	Peer relationships	557–562
	Romantic Relationships	562–564
	Relations with parents	569–573
	Identity development	573–585
	Social problems of adolescence	585–593

Guide 3 Discussions of Language Development

Period	Characteristic	Page Numbers
General	Biological key to language	238–241
	Environmental key to language	241–247
	Domains of language acquisition	247–255
	Explanations of language acquisition	261–267
Infancy	Language preferences at birth	223–224
	Intersubjectivity and social referencing	221–222
	Pointing	222
	Beginnings of speech: cooing, babbling, jargoning	223–224
Early childhood	Phonological development	248, 250
	Semantic development and first words	248–251
	Earliest vocabulary	251–253
	Pragmatic development	257–261
Middle childhood	The language of school	459–461

Guide 4 Discussions of Emotional Development

Period	Characteristic	Page Numbers
Early infancy	Evidence of temperament differences at birth	148–150
	Emotion in the first three months	201–205
	Crying and parents' responses	155–157
Later infancy	Theories of emotional development	203–210
	The onset of wariness	209–211
	Beginnings of attachment	207
	Explanations of attachment	207–209
	Patterns of attachment	207–210, 214, 220–221
	Self-conscious emotions	226–228
Early childhood	Regulation of emotions	326–329
	Aggression	329–335
	Empathy and understanding others	336–338
Middle childhood	Emotions and friendship	493–496
Adolescence	Experience of emotions	552–554
	Regulating emotions	554–557
	Emotional problems	585–593

Guide 5 Discussions of Cultural Influences on Development

Period	Characteristic	Page Numbers
General	Cultural explanations of language	252–253
	Family organization	344–347, 353–356
	Influence on community	369–371
Early infancy	Motor skills	168–175
	Sleeping arrangements	151
	Sleep schedules	151–153
	Nursing behaviors	153–154
Later infancy	Attachment	207–221
	Language	222–224
Early childhood	Role of language	238–253
	Scripts	298–301
	Unevenness of development	272, 300–301
	Acquiring a sex-role identity	307–313
	Acquiring ethnic and racial identity	313–315
	Internalization of adult standards	322–326
	Regulation of emotion	326–329
	Causes of aggression	329–335
	Family structure and roles	344–348
Middle childhood	Concrete operations	400–408
	Information processing and memory	409–414
	Intelligence	420
	Intelligence testing	420
	Schooling	431–435,437–445
	Moral reasoning	471–480
	Competition and cooperation among peers	485–489
Adolescence	Formal operations	530–536
	Formal operations and adolescent thinking	530–536
	Moral reasoning	539–547
	Friendships	557–559
	Romantic relationships	562–564
	Parent-child relations	569–573
	Identity formation	573–580
	Cultural Identity	583–585

Guide 6 Discussions of Cognitive Development

Period	Characteristic	Page Numbers
Early Infancy	Intermodal perception	136–139
	Piagetian substages 1 and 2	145, 146, 178
	Learning	146–148
	Piagetian substages 3 and 4	178–181
	Criticisms/challenges of Piaget's theory	177–178
	Appearance/stages of object permanence	181–187
	Perception of number	189–190
	Categorizing by perceptual features	190–192
	Memory	193–195
	Imitation	146, 180, 206
Later infancy	Piagetian substages 5 and 6	180–181
	Mastery of object permanence	181–184
	Generalized imitation	206
	Categorizing by conceptual features	190–192
	Attention and memory	192–195
Early childhood	Maturation of the brain	276–277
	Preoperational thinking	277–279
	Egocentrism	279–280
	Confusing appearance and reality	280–290
	Precausal reasoning	273–283
	Uneven levels of performance	284–285
	Information processing and memory	285–288
	Privileged domains	288–298
	Role of cultural context	298–301
	Empathy	336–337
Middle childhood	Brain development	398–400
	Concrete operations	400–408
	Information processing and memory	409–414
	Strategies	411–413
	Intelligence	420–425
	Culture and cognition	415, 418
	Learning to read	434, 439–441
	Learning mathematics	434–435, 441–443
	Learning disabilities	444–449
	Moral reasoning	471–480
	Peer relationships	485–489
Adolescence	Puberty brain development	517–518
	Formal operations and reasoning	530–534
	Morality	539–542

Glossary

A-not-B error A pattern of reacting in the object permanence task, in which the infant looks for the hidden object in location A, where the infant had previously found the object, instead of location B, where the infant has just observed it being hidden.

academic motivation The ability to try hard and persist at school tasks in the face of difficulties.

action Complex, coordinated behaviors.

adoption study A study that focuses on children who have been reared apart from their biological parents.

age of viability The age at which the fetus is able to survive outside the uterus.

allele The specific form of a gene that influences a particular trait.

allocaregiving Child care and protection provided by group members other than the parents, usually other relatives.

amnion A thin, tough, transparent membrane that holds the amniotic fluid, and surrounds the embryo.

anorexia nervosa An eating disorder that involves intentional self-starving.

Apgar scale A quick, simple test used to diagnose the physical state of newborn infants.

apprenticeship A form of education in which a young person learns a craft or skill by spending an extended period of time working for an adult master.

attachment The emotional bond that children form with their caregivers at about 7 to 9 months of age.

autobiographical memory A personal narrative that helps children acquire an enduring sense of themselves.

authoritarian parenting pattern Parenting style identified by Baumrind that focuses on enforcing obedience and conformity to traditional standards, including by use of punishment, and that is lacking in verbal give-and-take with children and in expression of warmth.

authoritative parenting pattern Parenting style identified by Baumrind in which parents set standards and limits for children but also encourage discussion and independence, and express warmth.

autism A biologically based condition that includes an inability to relate normally to other people and low scores on false-belief tasks.

autonomous morality The second and final stage of Piaget's theory of moral development in which right and wrong are defined according to internal motives and intentions rather than objective consequences.

autonomy The ability to assert one's own needs in a relationship.

autonomy versus shame and doubt For Erikson, the second stage of infancy, during which children develop a sense of themselves as competent to accomplish tasks or as not competent.

avoidant attachment The attachment pattern in which infants are indifferent to where their mother is sitting, may or may not cry when their mother leaves, are as likely to be comforted by strangers as by their mother, and are indifferent when their mother returns to the room.

axon The main protruding branch of a neuron; it carries messages to other cells in the form of electrical impulses.

babbling A form of vocalizing, beginning at around 7 months, in which infants utter strings of syllables that combine a consonant sound and a vowel sound.

Baldwin effect The role of cultural factors in determining which phenotypes are adaptive.

basic emotions Joy, fear, anger, surprise, sadness, disgust—universal emotions, expressed similarly in all cultures and present at birth or in the early months.

basic trust versus mistrust For Erikson, the first stage of infancy, during which children either come to trust others as reliable and kind and to regard the world as safe or come to mistrust others as insensitive and hurtful and to regard the world as unpredictable and threatening.

behaviorism Theories that focus on development as the result of learning, and on changes in behavior as a result of forming associations between behavior and its consequences.

biological drives Impulses to attempt to satisfy essential physiological needs.

bottom-up processing An approach to education that starts with teaching basic skills and, once they have been mastered, moves on to more complex tasks.

brain stem The base of the brain, which controls such elementary reactions as blinking and sucking, as well as such vital functions as breathing and sleeping.

Brazelton Neonatal Assessment Scale A scale used to assess a newborn's neurological condition.

bulimia nervosa An eating disorder that involves cycles of "binge eating" followed by self-induced vomiting.

canalized A trait that is canalized follows a strictly defined path, regardless of most environmental and genetic variations.

carriers Individuals who are heterozygous for a trait with a dominant and recessive allele and thus express only the characteristics associated with the dominant allele but may pass the recessive allele, including for a recessive disorder, on to their offspring.

causation When the occurrence of one event depends upon the occurrence of a prior event.

centration Young children's tendency to focus on only one feature of an object to the exclusion of all other features.

cephalocaudal pattern The pattern of development that proceeds from the head down.

cerebral cortex The brain's outermost layer. The networks of neurons in the cerebral cortex integrate information from several sensory sources with memories of past experiences, processing them in a way that results in human forms of thought and action.

child-care center An organized child-care facility supervised by licensed professionals.

chorion A membrane that surrounds the amnion and becomes the fetal component of the placenta.

chromosome A threadlike structure made up of genes. In humans, there are 46 chromosomes in every cell except sperm and ova.

chronology In language development, a simple story structure used by young children, in which they present a sequence of concrete events.

classical conditioning Learning in which previously existing behaviors come to be elicited by new stimuli.

cleavage The series of mitotic cell divisions that transform the zygote into the blastocyst.

clinical interview A research method in which questions are tailored to the individual, with each question depending on the answer to the preceding one.

clique A group of several young people that remains small enough to enable its members to be in regular interaction with one another and to serve as the primary peer group.

co-construction The shaping of environments through interactions between children and their caregivers, siblings, neighbors, and friends.

codominance Outcome in which a trait that is determined by two alleles is different from the trait produced by either of the contributing alleles alone.

coevolution The combined process that emerges from the interaction of biological evolution and cultural evolution.

cognitive-behavioral therapy (CBT) A treatment for depression and anxiety that is based on the theory that these problems are related to negative thoughts and/or poor coping behaviors. CBT is designed to help the adolescent develop adaptive communication and problem-solving skills, monitor and regulate changing emotions, and schedule time for relaxing and enjoyable activities.

cohort A group of persons born about the same time who are therefore likely to share certain experiences.

cohort sequential design A research design in which the longitudinal method is replicated with several cohorts.

collective monologues Communications in which young children each voice their own thoughts without attending to what the others are saying.

commitment According to Marcia, individuals' sense of allegiance to the goals, values, beliefs, and occupation they have chosen.

compensation A mental operation in which the child realizes that changes in one aspect of a problem are compared with and compensated for by changes in another aspect.

concrete operations In Piaget's terms, coordinated mental actions that allow children to mentally combine, separate, order, and transform concrete objects and events that children experience directly.

conditional response (CR) In classical conditioning, a response to the pairing of the conditional stimulus (CS) and the unconditional stimulus (UCS).

conditional stimulus (CS) In classical conditioning, a stimulus that elicits a behavior that is dependent on the way it is paired with the unconditional stimulus (UCS).

conservation of number Recognition of the one-to-one correspondence between sets of objects of equal number.

conservation of volume The understanding that the amount of a liquid remains unchanged when poured from one container into another that has different dimensions.

constructivist theory Piaget's theory, in which cognitive development results from children's active construction of reality, based on their experiences with the world.

continuity/discontinuity Addresses the extent to which development tends to be continuous, consisting of the gradual accumulation of small changes, and the extent to which it is discontinuous, involving a series of abrupt, radical transformations.

control group The group in an experiment that is treated as much as possible like the experimental group except that it does not participate in the experimental manipulation.

conversational acts Actions that achieve goals through language.

cooperative breeding In humans and certain other species, a system involving networks of support in which individuals other than parents contribute resources toward rearing the young.

coregulation A form of indirect social control in which parents and children cooperate to reinforce the children's understandings of right and wrong, what is safe and unsafe, when they are not under direct adult control.

correlation The condition that exists between two factors when changes in one factor are associated with changes in the other.

correlation coefficient The degree of association between factors, symbolized as r and ranging between -1.0 and $+1.0$.

critical period A period during which specific biological or environmental events are required for normal development to occur.

cross-sectional design A research design in which individuals of various ages are studied at the same time.

crowd A large, reputation-based and mixed-gender social network observed when cliques interact.

cultural modeling Culturally specific ways of telling stories.

cultural style A dominant way of thinking about and relating to the world that arises from a people's common historical experience.

culture Material and symbolic tools that accumulate through time, are passed on through social processes, and provide resources for the developing child.

cumulative cultural evolution The dynamic ongoing process of cultural change that is a consequence of variation that individuals have produced in the cultural tools they use.

decentration The cognitive ability to pull away from focusing on just one feature of an object in order to consider multiple features.

decoding The process of translating units of print into units of sound.

deferred imitation The imitation of an action observed in the past.

dendrite The protruding parts of a neuron that receive messages from the axons of other cells.

depression An emotional state involving some combination of sadness, apathy, hopelessness, poor self-esteem, and trouble finding pleasure in activities that one used to enjoy. Depression is one of the most common psychological problems of adolescence, especially for girls.

detachment For Bowlby, the state of indifference toward others experienced by children who have been separated from their caregiver for an extended time and have not formed a new stable relationship.

developmental science The field of study that focuses on the range of children's physical, intellectual, social, and emotional developments.

developmental stage A qualitatively distinctive, coherent pattern of behavior that emerges during the course of development.

deviancy training Positive reactions to discussions of rule-breaking.

differential emotions theory The view that basic emotions are innate and emerge in their adult form, either at birth or on a biologically determined timetable.

differential reinforcement In gender identification, the process by which girls and boys are rewarded for engaging in ways that are considered gender-appropriate in their culture.

dishabituation The term used to describe the process in which an infant's interest is renewed after a change in the stimulus.

disorganized attachment The insecure attachment pattern in which infants seem to lack a coherent method for dealing with stress.

They may behave in seemingly contradictory ways, such as screaming for their mother but moving away when she approaches. In extreme cases, they may seem dazed.

display rules A social or cultural group's informal conventions regarding whether, how, and under what circumstances emotions should be expressed.

dizygotic (DZ) twins Twins who come from two zygotes.

DNA (deoxyribonucleic acid) A long, double-stranded molecule that makes up chromosomes.

dominant allele The allele that is expressed when an individual possesses two different alleles for the same trait.

dominant children In reference to social hierarchies, those children who control "resources" such as toys, play spaces, and decisions about group activities.

dynamic systems theory A theory that addresses how new, complex systems of behavior develop from the interaction of less complex parts.

early maturation Refers to the occurrence of a pubertal event (or set of events) before the 3rd percentile of the normal range.

eating disorder not otherwise specified (EDNOS) An eating disorder that is diagnosed when the criteria for anorexia or bulimia nervosa are not quite met. EDNOS is the most common diagnosis for adolescents with eating disorders.

ecological inheritance Environmental modifications, as a result of niche construction, that affect the development of offspring and descendants.

ecological systems theory A theory focusing on the organization and interactions of the multiple environmental contexts within which children develop.

ecological validity The extent to which behavior studied in one environment (such as a psychological test) is characteristic of behavior exhibited by the same person in a range of other environments.

ectoderm Cells of the inner cell mass that develop into the outer surface of the skin, the nails, part of the teeth, the lens of the eye, the inner ear, and the central nervous system.

effortful control The inhibition of an action that is already under way.

ego In Freudian theory, the mental structure that develops out of the id as the infant is forced by reality to cope with the social world. The ego mediates between the id and the social world, allowing children to control and regulate behavior.

egocentrism In Piaget's terms, the tendency to "center on oneself," that is, to consider the world entirely in terms of one's own point of view.

elaboration A memory strategy that involves making connections between two or more things to be remembered.

elaborative style A form of talking with children about new events or experiences that enhances children's memories for those events and experiences.

Electra complex In Freudian theory, the process by which young girls blame their mother for their "castrated" condition, transfer their love to their father, and compete with their mother for their father's affection.

electroencephalography (EEG) A common physiological method used to evaluate infant sensory capacities, which involves attaching sensors to the baby's head and measuring changes in brain waves in response to the presentation of different stimuli.

embryonic period The period that extends from the time the organism becomes attached to the uterus until the end of the 8th week of pregnancy, when all the major organs have taken primitive shape.

emergent literacy Knowledge, skills, and attitudes that provide the building blocks for learning to read and write.

emergent numeracy Knowledge, skills, and attitudes that provide the building blocks for learning how to do math.

emerging adulthood The name of what some developmentalists propose is a new stage of development facing many individuals between the ages of 18 and 25 in technologically advanced societies.

emotion A feeling state that involves distinctive physiological reactions and cognitive evaluations, and motivates action.

emotion regulation Ways of acting to modulate and control emotions.

emotional tone One's sense of well-being versus depression and anxiety.

empathy Sharing another person's emotions and feelings.

endocrine system A network of hormone-secreting glands associated with changes in the individual's mood, metabolism, and growth. The glands associated specifically with puberty include the pituitary gland, the thyroid gland, the adrenal glands, and the sex glands.

endoderm Cells of the inner cell mass that develop into the digestive system and the lungs.

entity model of intelligence The belief that intelligence is a quality of which each person has a certain fixed amount.

epigenesis The process by which a new phenotypic form emerges through the interactions of the preceding form and its current environment.

epistemic development Refers to changes in how individuals reason about the nature of knowledge.

equilibration The main source of development, consisting of a process of achieving a balance between the child's present understanding and the child's new experiences.

ethnic identity An individual's sense of belonging to an ethnic group, and the feelings and attitudes that accompany the sense of group membership.

ethnic socialization Ethnic-based messages communicated to children.

ethnography The study of the cultural organization of behavior.

ethology An interdisciplinary science that studies the biological and evolutionary foundations of behavior.

evaluativist theory of knowledge A belief that although truth can change, it is nevertheless subject to particular standards of evaluation—the "rules of the game."

evolutionary theories Theories that explain human behavior in terms of how it contributes to the survival of the species and that look at how our evolutionary past influences individual development.

executive function Higher-level cognitive processes, such as aspects of cognition associated with supervising and controlling lower-level cognitive processes.

experience-dependent Development of neural connections that is initiated in response to experience.

experience-expectant Processes of brain development that seem to anticipate experiences that are universal in all normally developing members of our species.

experience sampling method (ESM) Tool used by developmentalists in which study participants, when signaled by electronic pagers at random intervals, fill out brief reports on their feelings. ESM has been used to study adolescents' emotional lives.

experiment In psychology, research in which a change is introduced into a person's experience and the effect of that change is measured.

experimental group The group in an experiment whose experience is changed as part of the experiment.

explicit instruction The social process in which children are purposefully taught to use the resources of their culture.

explicit memory The type of memory that is used to recall, without any clear reminder, absent objects and events.

exploration According to Marcia, the process through which adolescents actively examine their possible future roles and paths.

extended families Families in which not only parents and their children but other kin—grandparents, cousins, nieces and nephews, or more distant family relations—share a household.

externalizing problems Social and behavioral problems such as aggression and delinquency; more common in boys than in girls.

exuberant synaptogenesis A rapid growth in synaptic density that prepares the brain for a vast range of possible experiences.

false-belief task A technique used to assess children' theory of mind; children are tested on their understanding either of stories in which a character is fooled into believing something that is not true or of situations in which they themselves have been tricked into a false belief.

family child care Child care provided in someone else's home, that of either a relative or a stranger.

family structure The social organization of a family. Most commonly, the structure is nuclear or extended.

family study A study that compares members of the same family to determine how similar they are on a given trait.

fast mapping The way in which children quickly form an idea of the meaning of an unfamiliar word they hear in a familiar and highly structured social interaction.

fetal alcohol syndrome A syndrome found in babies whose mothers were heavy consumers of alcohol while pregnant. Symptoms include an abnormally small head and underdeveloped brain, eye abnormalities, congenital heart disease, joint anomalies, and malformations of the face.

fetal period The period that begins in the 9th week after conception, with the first signs of the hardening of the bones, and continues until birth.

fine motor skills Motor skills related to the development and coordination of small muscles, such as those that move the fingers and eyes.

Flynn effect The steady increase over the past 100 years in IQ test performance, an increase believed to support the environmental hypothesis of intelligence.

fontanels "Soft spots," or spaces, that separate the bones of the skull prenatally and in early infancy.

food-insecure Lacking enough food to ensure good health.

formal education The most structured type of explicit education, through which adults instruct the young in the specialized knowledge and skills of their culture.

formal operations In Piaget's terms, a kind of mental operation in which all possible combinations are considered in solving a problem. Consequently, each partial link is grouped in relation to the whole; in other words, reasoning moves continually as a function of a structured whole.

formats Recurrent socially patterned activities in which adult and child do things together.

friendship A close relationship between two individuals. Friendships in adolescence are characterized by reciprocity, commitment, and equality.

gender schema A mental model containing information about males and females that is used to process gender-relevant information.

gender segregation The term for the preference of girls to play with other girls, and of boys to play with other boys.

gene pool The total variety of genetic information possessed by a sexually reproducing population.

genes The segments on a DNA molecule that act as hereditary blueprints for the organism's development.

genotype The genetic endowment of an individual

germ cells The sperm and ova, which are specialized for sexual reproduction and have half the number of chromosomes normal for a species.

germinal period The period that begins at conception and lasts until the developing organism becomes attached to the wall of the uterus about 8 to 10 days later.

gestational age The amount of time between conception and birth. The normal gestational age is between 37 and 43 weeks.

grammar The rules of a given language for the sequencing of words in a sentence and the ordering of parts of words.

grammatical morphemes Words and parts of words that create meaning by showing the relations between other elements within the sentence.

gross motor skills Motor skills related to the development and coordination of large muscles; important for locomotion

growth charts Charts that show average values of height, weight, and other measures of growth, based on large samples of normally developing infants; the charts are used to evaluate an infant's development.

growth spurt A rapid change in height and weight that signals the onset of puberty.

habituation The process in which attention to novelty decreases with repeated exposure.

heredity The biological transmission of characteristics from one generation to the next.

heritability A measure of the degree to which a variation in a particular trait among individuals in a specific population is related to genetic differences among those individuals.

heterochrony Variability in the rates of development of different parts of the organism.

heterogeneity Variability in the levels of development of different parts of the organism at a given time.

heteronomous morality Piaget's term for young children's tendency to define morality in terms of objective consequences and externally imposed controls.

heterozygous Having inherited two genes of different allelic forms for a trait.

home child care Child care provided in the child's own home, primarily by a grandmother or other family member, while the parents are at work.

homophily The degree to which friends are similar to each other.

homophobia A fear of homosexuality. Homophobia may diminish intimacy among adolescent males.

homozygous Having inherited two genes of the same allelic form for a trait.

hostile aggression Aggression that is aimed at hurting another person physically, psychologically, or socially.

hypothalamic-pituitary-gonadal (HPG) axis A circuit that extends from the brain to the sex organs (testes or ovaries) and back again; activated in adolescence, the HPG regulates the hormones that affect the body's growth and functions.

hypothalamus A brain structure, located just above the brain stem, that performs a number of important tasks, including the regulation of hunger, thirst, and sexual desire, and connects the nervous system to the endocrine system.

hypothesis A possible explanation based on theory that is precise enough to be shown to be true or false.

hypothetical-deductive reasoning Reasoning that involves the ability to judge an argument entirely on the basis of its logical form, regardless of whether the argument is true.

id In Freudian theory, the mental structure present at birth that is the main source of psychological energy. It is unconscious and pleasure-seeking and demands that bodily drives be satisfied.

identification A psychological process in which children try to look, act, feel, and be like significant people in their social environment.

identity A mental operation in which the child realizes that a change limited to outward appearance does not change the substances involved.

identity development The process through which individuals achieve a sense of who they are and of their moral and political beliefs, their career preferences, and their relationship to their culture and community.

imitation The social process through which children learn to use their culture's resources by observing and copying the behaviors of others.

implantation The process by which the blastocyst becomes attached to the uterus.

implicit memory The ability to recognize objects and events that have been previously experienced.

incremental model of intelligence The belief that intelligence is something that can grow over time as one learns.

independent sense of self The sense of self encouraged by individualistic cultures, characterized by an orientation to being unique, promoting one's individual goals, and expressing one's thoughts and opinions.

industry versus inferiority According to Erikson's theory, the stage during which children judge themselves to be industrious and successfully meeting the new challenges posed by adults at home and school, or inferior and incapable of meeting such challenges.

infant-directed speech (or motherese or baby-talk) Speech that adults use with infants, characterized by high pitch, exaggerated intonation, clear boundaries between meaningful parts of utterance, and simplified vocabulary.

information-processing theories Theories that look at cognitive development in terms of how children come to process, store, organize, retrieve, and manipulate information in increasingly efficient ways.

initiative versus guilt According to Erikson's theory, the stage in early childhood during which children face the challenge of continuing to declare their autonomy and existence as individuals, but in ways that begin to conform to the social roles and moral standards of society.

inner speech According to Vygotsky, the internalization of egocentric speech that occurs during early childhood and allows individuals to mentally plan activities and solve problems.

institutional review boards (IRBs) Groups responsible for evaluating and overseeing the ethical soundness of research practices at an institution.

instructional discourse A distinctive way of talking and thinking that is typical in school but rarely encountered in everyday interactions in the community or home.

instrumental aggression Aggression that is directed at obtaining something.

Intelligence Quotient (IQ) The ratio of mental age to chronological age, calculated as $IQ = (MA/CA)100$.

intentionality The ability to engage in behaviors directed toward achieving a goal.

interdependent sense of self The sense of self encouraged by collectivist cultures, characterized by an orientation to fitting into the group, promoting group goals, and developing the ability to understand the thoughts of others.

intermodal perception The ability to perceive an object or event by more than one sensory system simultaneously..

internal working model A mental model that children construct as a result of their experiences with their caregivers and that they use to guide their interactions with their caregivers and others.

internalizing problems Disturbances in emotion or mood such as depression, worry, guilt, and anxiety; more common in girls than in boys.

intimacy A sense of close connection between two individuals, resulting from shared feelings, thoughts, and activities.

kinship studies Studies that use naturally occurring conditions provided by kinship relations to estimate genetic and environmental contributions to a phenotypic trait.

kisspeptin A small protein that is produced by specialized cells in the hypothalamus and plays a key role in the activation of the HPG axis.

kwashiorkor A potentially fatal form of malnutrition in which the diet is extremely low in protein.

language acquisition device (LAD) Chomsky's term for an innate language-processing capacity that is programmed to recognize the universal rules that underlie any particular language that a child might hear.

language acquisition support system (LASS) Bruner's term for the patterned behaviors and formatted events within which children acquire language. It is the environmental complement to the innate, biologically constituted LAD.

large for gestational age Babies whose weight at birth is above the 90th percentile of babies of the same sex who are the same gestational age.

late maturation Refers to the occurrence of a pubertal event after the 97th percentile of the normal range.

law of effect Thorndike's notion that behaviors that produce a satisfying effect in a given situation are likely to be repeated in the same or a similar situation, whereas behaviors that produce an uncomfortable effect are less likely to be repeated.

learning A relatively permanent change in behavior brought about by making associations between behavior and events in the environment.

leptin A hormone that plays a key role in appetite and metabolism.

limbic system A group of brain structures, including the amygdala, hippocampus, basal ganglia, and hypothalamus. Because these brain structures are associated more with emotion than with reasoning, the limbic system is often described as the "emotion brain" (in contrast to the cerebral cortex, which some have dubbed the "reasoning brain").

locomotion The ability to move around on one's own.

longitudinal design A research design in which data are gathered about the same group of people as they grow older over an extended period of time.

low birth weight The term used to describe babies weighing 5 pounds, 8 ounces (2500 grams) or less at birth, whether or not they are premature.

mastery orientation A way that children approach school tasks in which they are motivated to learned, to try hard, and to improve their performance.

material tools Cultural tools, including physical objects and observable patterns of behavior such as family routines and social practices.

media Forms of mass communication, including newspapers, magazines, books, comic books, radio, television, films, video games, and the Internet.

mediation The process through which tools organize people's activities and ways of relating to their environments.

meiosis The process that produces sperm and ova, each of which contains only half of the parent cell's original complement of 46 chromosomes.

memory span The number of randomly presented items of information that can be repeated immediately after they are presented.

memory strategies Specific actions used deliberately to enhance remembering.

menarche The first menstrual period.

mental modules Hypothesized innate mental faculties that receive inputs from particular classes of objects and produce corresponding information about the world.

mental operations In Piaget's theory, the mental process of combining, separating, or transforming information in a logical manner.

mesoderm The cells of the inner cell mass that give rise to the muscles, the bones, the circulatory system, and the inner layers of the skin.

metacognition The ability to think about one's own thought processes.

metamemory The ability to think about one's memory processes.

metaphor Use of a word in a way that draws a comparison between the thing the word usually refers to and some other, unrelated thing.

microgenetic design A research method in which individuals' development is studied intensively over a relatively short period of time.

mirror neurons Specialized brain cells that fire when an individual sees or hears another perform an action, just as they would fire if the observing individual were performing the same action.

mitosis The process of cell duplication and division that generates all the individual's cells except sperm and ova.

modeling In gender identification, the process by which children observe and imitate individuals of the same sex as themselves.

monozygotic (MZ) twins Twins who come from one zygote and therefore have identical genotypes.

morality of care A morality that stresses relationships, compassion, and social obligations.

morality of justice A morality that emphasizes issues of rightness, fairness, and equality.

morpheme The smallest unit of meaning in the words of a language.

motor drive The pleasure young children take in using their new motor skills.

mutation An alteration in the molecular structure of an individual's DNA.

myelin An insulating material that forms a sheath around certain axons and speeds the transmission of nerve impulses from one neuron to the next.

natural selection The process through which species survive and evolve, in which individuals with phenotypes that are more adaptive to the environmental conditions survive and reproduce with greater success than individuals with phenotypes are that less adaptive.

naturalistic observation Observation of the actual behavior of people in the course of their everyday lives.

nature The inherited biological predispositions of the individual.

neighborhood physical disorder A problem in distressed communities, including both physical deterioration (garbage on the streets, rundown buildings, etc.) and chaotic activity (crowding, high noise levels, etc.).

neural tube An embryonic structure that later develops into the brain and spinal cord.

neuron A nerve cell.

neurotransmitter A chemical secreted by a neuron sending a message that carries the impulse across the synaptic gap to the receiving cell.

niche construction The active shaping and modification of individuals' environments by the individuals' own behaviors, activities, and choices.

no-nonsense parenting Parenting characterized by a mix of high parental control—including punishment—and warmth, and associated especially with African American single mothers.

nuclear families Families consisting of parents (including single parents) and their children.

nurture The influences exerted on development by the individual's social and cultural environment and personal experiences.

object permanence The understanding that objects have substance, maintain their identity when their location is changed, and ordinarily continue to exist when out of sight.

objective view of responsibility An understanding that responsibility depends on objective consequences alone.

objectivist theory of knowledge A belief that knowledge involves an accumulation of objective facts and "definite answers."

objectivity (scientific) The requirement that scientific knowledge not be distorted by the investigator's preconceptions.

objectivity (Piagetian) The mental distancing made possible by decentration. Piaget believed the attainment of objectivity to be the major achievement of cognitive development.

Oedipus complex In Freudian theory, the desire young boys have to get rid of their father and take his place in their mother's affections.

ontogenetic adaptation Refers to a trait or behavior that has evolved because it contributes to survival and normal development; in one view, infant emotions are ontogenetic adaptations.

operant conditioning Learning in which changes in behavior are shaped by the consequences of that behavior, thereby giving rise to new and more complete behaviors.

organizational strategies Memory strategies in which materials to be remembered are mentally grouped into meaningful categories.

ossification A process through which new bone tissue is formed at the growth plates of long bones.

overextension The error of applying verbal labels too broadly.

perceptual scaffolding The way in which a familiar word serves as an anchor for learning new words that come immediately before or after it.

performance orientation A way of approaching school tasks in which students are motivated by their level of performance, ability, and incentives for trying.

permissive parenting pattern Parenting style identified by Baumrind in which parents express warmth but do not exercise control over their children's behavior.

personal distress A self-focused emotional reaction to another person's distress.

personal identity A person's sense of his or her self as persisting over time (I-self), as well as a sense of personal characteristics such as appearance and abilities that can be objectively known (me-self).

personality formation The process through which children develop their own unique patterns of feeling, thinking, and behaving in a wide variety of circumstances.

phallic stage In Freudian theory, the period beginning around the age of 3 or 4 years when children begin to regard their own genitals as a major source of pleasure.

phenotype The organism's observable characteristics that result from the interaction of the genotype with the environment.

phenotypic plasticity Refers to the degree to which the phenotype is open to influence by the environment, rather than determined by the genotype.

phonemes The smallest sound categories in human speech that distinguish meanings. Phonemes vary from language to language.

phonological development Learning to segment speech into meaningful units of sound.

placenta An organ made up of tissue from both the mother and the fetus that serves as a barrier and filter between their bloodstreams.

plasticity The degree to which, and the conditions under which, development is open to change and intervention.

playworld practice A type of classroom activity that is based on theories regarding the importance of play in intellectual development and involves students enacting and discussing various themes in children's literature.

polygenic inheritance Refers to the contribution of a variety of genes—sometimes very many—to a particular trait.

positive youth development (PYD) A general approach to adolescence that emphasizes the strengths and positive qualities of youths that contribute to their psychological health as well as to the welfare of their communities.

pragmatic development Learning the conventions that govern the use of language in particular social contexts.

precausal thinking Piaget's description of the reasoning of young children that does not follow the procedures of either deductive or inductive reasoning.

precocious puberty A serious condition that involves the activation of the HPG axis before the age of 8 in girls and 9 in boys.

preformationism The belief that adultlike capacities, desires, interests, and emotions are present in early childhood.

prefrontal area Part of the cortex that is located directly behind the forehead and is important to the development of voluntary behaviors.

prefrontal cortex A frontal lobe structure that is thought to contribute to a host of abilities that involve controlling and regulating one's thoughts, feelings, and behaviors.

preoperational stage According to Piaget, the stage of thinking between infancy and middle childhood in which children are unable to decenter their thinking or to think through the consequences of an action.

preterm The term for babies born before the 37th week of pregnancy.

prevention science An area of research that examines the biological and social processes that lead to maladjustment as well as those that are associated with healthy development.

primary circular reaction The term Piaget used to describe the infant's tendency to repeat pleasurable bodily actions for their own sake.

primary intersubjectivity Organized, reciprocal interaction between an infant and caregiver with the interaction itself as the focus.

primary sex characteristics The organs directly involved in reproduction.

privileged domains Cognitive domains that call on specialized kinds of information, require specifically designated forms of reasoning, and appear to be of evolutionary importance to the human species.

prosocial behavior Behavior such as sharing, helping, caregiving, and showing compassion.

prosocial moral reasoning The thinking that is involved in deciding whether to share with, help, or take care of other people when doing so may prove costly to oneself

protective factors Environmental and personal factors that are the source of children's resilience in the face of hardship.

protodeclaratives Early conversational acts whose purpose is to establish joint attention and sustain a dialogue.

protoimperatives Early conversational acts whose purpose is to get another person to do something.

proximodistal pattern The pattern of development that proceeds from the middle of the organism out to the periphery.

psychodynamic theories Theories, such as those of Freud and Erikson, that explore the influence on development and developmental stages of universal biological drives and the life experiences of individuals.

puberty The series of biological developments that transforms individuals from a state of physical immaturity into one in which they are biologically mature and capable of sexual reproduction.

public policies Governmental laws and programs such as those designed to promote the welfare of children and families.

realistic mathematics education An approach to mathematics education that focuses on developing the student's understanding of how math can be used to solve real-world problems.

recessive allele The allele that is not expressed when an individual possesses two different alleles for the same trait.

reciprocal teaching A method of teaching reading in which teachers and children take turns reading text in a manner that integrates decoding and comprehension skills.

reflex A specific, well-integrated, automatic (involuntary) response to a specific type of stimulation.

rehearsal The process of repeating to oneself the material that one is trying to remember.

relational aggression Indirect aggression intended to harm someone's friendships or exclude an individual from the group.

reliability The scientific requirement that when the same behavior is measured on two or more occasions by the same or different observers, the measurements be consistent with each other.

replicability The scientific requirement that other researchers can use the same procedures as an initial investigator did and obtain the same results.

representations Internal, mental symbols of experience; according to Piaget, the ability to form mental symbols emerges during sensorimotor substage 6.

research design The overall plan that describes how a study is put together; it is developed before conducting research.

resilience The ability to recover quickly from the adverse effects of early experience or persevere in the face of stress with no apparent special negative psychological consequences.

resistant attachment The attachment pattern in which infants stay close to their mother and appear anxious even when their mother is near. They become very upset when their mother leaves but are not comforted by her return. They simultaneously seek renewed contact with their mother and resist their mother's efforts to comfort them.

reversibility A mental operation in which the child realizes that one operation can be negated, or reversed, by the effects of another.

risk factors Personal characteristics or environmental circumstances that increase the probability of negative outcomes for children. Risk is a statistic that applies to groups, not individuals.

saturated self A self full to the brim with multiple "me's" that have emerged as a consequence of needing to conform to social roles and relationships that demand different, and sometimes contradictory, selves.

scale errors Young children's inappropriate use of an object due to their failure to consider information about the object's size.

school-cutoff strategy A means of assessing the impact of early education by comparing the intellectual performance of children who are almost the same age but begin schooling a year apart because of school rules that set a specific cutoff birthday date for starting school.

school engagement The thoughts, behaviors, and emotions that children have about school and learning.

scripts Event schemas that specify who participates in an event, what social roles they play, what objects they are to use during the event, and the sequence of actions that make up the event.

secondary circular reactions The behavior characteristic of the third substage of Piaget's sensorimotor stage, in which babies repeat actions to produce interesting changes in their environment.

secondary intersubjectivity A form of interaction between infant and caregiver, emerging at about 9–12 months, with communication and emotional sharing focused not just on the interaction but on the world beyond.

secondary sex characteristics The anatomical and physiological signs that outwardly distinguish males from females.

secular trend A pattern in which the average age of puberty in industrialized countries declines across decades.

secure attachment A pattern of attachment in which children play comfortably and react positively to a stranger as long as their mother is present. They become upset when their mother leaves and are unlikely to be consoled by a stranger, but they calm down as soon as their mother reappears.

secure base Bowlby's term for the people whose presence provides the child with the security that allows him or her to make exploratory excursions.

self-conscious emotions Emotions such as embarrassment, pride, shame, guilt, and envy, which emerge after 8 months with infants' growing consciousness of self.

self-esteem One's evaluation of one's own worth.

self-regulation The ability to control one's thoughts, emotions, and behaviors.

semantic development Learning meanings of words and of combinations of words.

semenarche The first ejaculation. Ejaculation often occurs spontaneously during sleep and is called a nocturnal emission.

sensation-seeking The desire to participate in highly arousing activities; it is especially common in early and mid-adolescence.

sensitive period A time in an organism's development when a particular experience has an especially profound effect.

sensorimotor stage Piaget's term for the stage of infancy during which the process of adaptation consists largely of coordinating sensory perceptions and simple motor behaviors to acquire knowledge of the world.

separation anxiety The distress that babies show when the person to whom they are attached leaves.

sex hormones Estrogens and androgens that circulate in the bloodstream and activate hormone-perceiving receptors located throughout the body.

sexual identity An individual's understanding of himself or herself as heterosexual, homosexual, or bisexual.

sexual-minority (LGBT) youth Adolescents who develop identities as gays, lesbians, or bisexuals.

sexually transmitted infections (STIs) Infections typically acquired through sexual contact. Organisms causing infections can be transmitted through semen, vaginal fluid, blood, and other body fluids.

small for gestational age Newborns whose birth weight falls in the lowest 10 percent for their gestational age because they have not grown at the normal rate.

social capital The resources that communities provide children and families, including not only schools, health services, and so on, but also social structures, expectations for behavior, and levels of trust and cooperation among community members.

social comparison The process of defining oneself in relation to one's peers.

social disorganization A problem in distressed communities, including weak social cohesion (lack of trust and connection among community members), poor neighborhood climate (fear related to crime and violence), and perceived racism.

social domain theory The theory that the moral domain, the social conventional domain, and the personal domain have distinct rules that vary in how broadly the rules apply, and what happens when they are broken.

social enhancement The most basic social process of learning to use cultural resources, in which resources are used simply because others' activities have made them available in the immediate environment.

social learning theories Theories that emphasize the behavior–consequences associations that children learn by observing and interacting with others in social situations.

social referencing Infants' tendency to look to their caregiver for an indication of how to feel and act in unfamiliar circumstances..

social repair mechanisms Strategies that allow friends to remain friends even when serious differences temporarily drive them apart.

social structures Complex organizations of relationships between individuals.

socialization The process by which children acquire the standards, values, and knowledge of their society.

sociocognitive conflict The term used by developmentalists to describe cognitive conflict that is rooted in social experience.

sociocultural theory The theory associated with Vygotsky that emphasizes the influence of culture on development.

sociodramatic play Make-believe play in which two or more participants enact a variety of related social roles.

socioeconomic status (SES) An indicator of social class based on factors such as income, education, and occupation.

socioemotional competence The ability to behave appropriately in social situations that evoke strong emotions.

somatic cells All the cells in the body except for the germ cells (the ova and sperm).

specific learning disabilities A term used to refer to the academic difficulties of children who fare poorly in school despite having normal intelligence.

spinal cord The part of the central nervous system that extends from below the waist to the base of the brain.

strange situation A procedure designed to assess children's attachment on the basis of their use of their mother as a secure base for exploration, their reactions to being left alone with a stranger and then completely alone, and their response when they are reunited with their mother.

subjective view of responsibility An understanding that responsibility depends on both intentions and consequences.

subjectivist theory of knowledge A belief that there is no absolute truth because truth can change depending on one's perspective.

superego In Freudian terms, the conscience. It represents the authority of the child's parents and sits in stern judgment of the ego's efforts to hold the id in check. It becomes a major force in the personality in middle childhood.

symbolic play Play in which one object stands for, or represents, another.

symbolic tools Cultural tools, such as abstract knowledge, beliefs, and values.

sympathy Feelings of sorrow or concern for another.

synapse The tiny gap between the axon of one neuron and the dendrite of another.

synaptic pruning The process of selective dying-off of nonfunctional synapses.

synaptogenesis The process of synapse formation.

syntactic bootstrapping Use of knowledge of grammar to figure out the meaning of new words.

systems theories Theories that envision development in terms of complex wholes made up of parts and that explore how these wholes and their parts are organized and interact and change over time.

temperament The term for the individual modes of responding to the environment that appear to be consistent across situations and stable over time. Temperament includes such characteristics as children's activity level, their intensity of reaction, the ease with which they become upset, their characteristic responses to novelty, and their sociability.

teratogens Environmental agents that can cause deviations from normal development and can lead to abnormalities or death.

tertiary circular reactions The fifth stage of the sensorimotor period, characterized by the deliberate variation of action sequences to solve problems and explore the world.

theory A broad framework or set of principles that can be used to guide the collection and interpretation of a set of facts.

theory of gradual differentiation The view that infants are born only with general emotional reactions, which differentiate into basic emotions over the first 2 years.

theory of mind Coherent theories about how people's beliefs, desires, and mental states combine to shape their actions.

theory theory The theory that young children have primitive theories about how the world works, which influence how children think about, and act within, specific domains.

top-down processing An approach to education that focuses on using skills to accomplish specific, meaningful tasks.

totipotent stem cells Cells that have the potential to grow into a complete embryo and, ultimately, a normal, healthy infant.

true dialogue A communication in which each person's utterances take into account the utterances of others.

twin study A study in which groups of monozygotic (identical) and dizygotic (fraternal) twins of the same sex are compared to each other and to other family members for similarity on a given trait.

umbilical cord A flexible helical structure containing blood vessels that connects the developing organism to the placenta.

unconditional response (UCR) In classical conditioning, the response, such as salivation, that is invariably elicited by the unconditional stimulus (UCS).

unconditional stimulus (UCS) In classical conditioning, the stimulus, such as food in the mouth, that invariably causes the unconditional response (UCR).

underextension The error of applying verbal labels too narrowly.

validity The scientific requirement that the data being collected actually reflect the phenomenon being studied.

violation-of-expectations method A test of mental representation in which the child is habituated to an event and then presented with possible and impossible variants of the event.

visual acuity Sharpness of vision.

visual preference technique A common behavioral method used to evaluate infant sensory capacities, which involves presenting two different stimuli at once to determine if the baby displays a preference by looking at one longer than the other.

X chromosome One of the two chromosomes that determine sex; in females, both members of the 23rd pair of chromosomes are X, and in males, one member of the 23rd pair is.

Y chromosome One of the two chromosomes that determine sex; in males, one member of the 23rd pair of chromosomes.

zone of proximal development For Vygotsky, the gap between what children can accomplish independently and what they can accomplish when interacting with others who are more competent.

zygote The single cell formed at conception from the union of the sperm and the ovum.

References

Abebe, T., & Aase, A. (2007). Children, AIDS and the politics of orphan care in Ethiopia: The extended family revisited. *Social Science & Medicine, 64,* 2058–2069.

Abbott, S. (1992). Holding on and pushing away: Comparative perspectives on an Eastern Kentucky child rearing practice. *Ethos, 20,* 33–65.

Abma, J. C., Martinez, G. M., & Copen, C. E. (2010). Sexual activity, contraceptive use, and childbearing, National Survey of Family Growth 2006–2008. *National Center for Health Statistics. Vital Health Statistics, 23*(30).

Abrams, R., Gerhardt, K., & Antonelli, P. J. (1998). Fetal hearing. *Developmental Psychobiology, 33,* 1–3.

Acebo, C., Sadeh, A., Seifer, R., Tzischinsky, O., Hafer, A., & Carskadon, M. A. (2005). Sleep/wake patterns derived from activity monitoring and maternal report for healthy 1- to 5-year-old children. *Sleep, 28,* 1568–1577

Adamson, L. B. (1995). *Communication development during infancy.* Madison, WI: Brown & Benchmarks.

Addams, J. (1910). *The spirit of youth and the city streets.* New York: Macmillan.

Addison, J., & Comstock, M. (1998). Virtually out: The emergence of a lesbian, bisexual, and gay youth cyberculture. In J. Austin & M. Willard (Eds.), *Generations of youth: Youth cultures and history in twentieth-century America.* New York: New York University Press.

Adolph, K. E., Karasik, L. B., & Tamis-LeMonda, C. S. (2010). Using social information to guide action: Infants' locomotion over slippery slopes. *Neural Networks, 23,* 1033–1042.

Ahmed, M. L., Ong, K. K., & Dunger, D. B. (2004). Childhood obesity and the timing of puberty. *Trends in Endocrinology & Metabolism, 20,* 237–242.

Ahnert, L., & Lamb, M. (2000). The East German child care system: Associations with caretaking and caretaking beliefs, children's early attachment and adjustment. *American Behavioral Scientist, 44,* 1843–1863.

Ahnert, L., & Lamb, M. (2003). Shared care: Establishing a balance between home and child care settings. *Child Development, 74,* 1044–1049.

Ahnert, L., Pinquart, M., & Lamb, M. E. (2006). Security of children's relationships with nonparental care providers: A meta-analysis. *Child Development, 77*(3), 664–679.

Ainsworth, M. D. S. (1967). *Infancy in Uganda: Infant care and the growth of love.* Baltimore, MD: Johns Hopkins University Press.

Ainsworth, M. D. S. (1982). Attachment: Retrospect and prospect. In C. M. Parkes & J. Stevenson-Hinde (Eds.), *The place of attachment in human behavior.* New York: Basic Books.

Ainsworth, M. D. S., & Bell, S. M. (1969). Some contemporary patterns of mother-infant interaction in the feeding situation. In A. Ambrose (Ed.), *Stimulation in early infancy.* New York: Academic Press.

Ainsworth, M. D. S., Bell, S. M., & Stayton, D. J. (1971). Individual differences in strange-situation behavior of one-year-olds. In H. R. Schaffer (Ed.), *The origins of human social relations.* New York: Academic Press.

Ainsworth, M. D. S., Blehar, M. C., Waters, E., & Wall, S. (1978). *Patterns of attachment: A psychological study of the strange situation.* Mahwah, NJ: Lawrence Erlbaum Associates

Ajia, O. (2007). Drumming up pride among post-war Burundi's street children. *UNICEF.* Retrieved from http://www.unicef.org/infobycountry/burundi_39331.html

Al-Ali, N., & Hussein, Y. (2003). Iraq. In A. Mahdi (Ed.), *Teen life in the Middle East.* Westport, CT: Greenwood Press.

Alastalo, H., Raikkonen, K., Pesonen, A.-K., Osmond, C., Barker, D. J. P., Kajantie, E., et al. (2009). Cardiovascular health of Finnish war evacuees 60 years later. *Annals of Medicine, 41*(1), 66–72.

Aldrich, C. A., & Hewitt, E. S. (1947). A self-regulating feeding program for infants. *Journal of the American Medical Association, 35,* 341.

Alencar, A. I., de Oliveira Siqueira, J., & Yamamoto, M. E. (2008). Does group size matter? Cheating and cooperation in Brazilian school children. *Evolution and Human Behavior, 29,* 42–48.

Allen, R. E., & Myers, A. L. (2006). Nutrition in toddlers. *American Family Physician 74,* 1527–1532.

Alexander, K., Quas, J., Goodman, G., Ghetti, S., Edelstein, R., Redlich, A. D., et al. (2005). Traumatic impact predicts long-term memory of documented child sexual abuse. *Psychological Science, 16,* 33–40.

Amato, P. (2000). The consequences of divorce for adults and children. *Journal of Marriage and the Family, 62,* 1269–1287.

Amato, P. R. (2006). Marital discord, divorce, and children's well-being: Results from a 20-year longitudinal study of two generations. In A. Clarke-Stewart & J. Dunn (Eds.), *Families count: Effects on child and adolescent development. The Jacobs Foundation series on adolescence* (pp. 179–202). New York: Cambridge University Press.

Amato, P. R. (2010). Research on divorce: Continuing trends and new developments. *Journal of Marriage and Family, 72,* 650–666.

Amato, P. R., & Hohmann-Marriott, B. (2007). A comparison of high- and low-distress marriages that end in divorce. *Journal of Marriage and Family. 69,* 621–638.

American Academy of Pediatrics. (2003). Policy statement. *Pediatrics, 112,* 424–430.

American College of Obstetricians and Gynecologists. (2009) Induction of labor. *Obstetrics & Gynecology. ACOG Practice Bulletin No. 107.* 114–386.

Ammerman, R. T., Kolko, D. J., Kirisci, L., Blackson, T. C., & Dawes, M. A. (1999). Child abuse potential in parents with histories of substance use disorder. *Child Abuse and Neglect, 23,* 1225–1238.

Anderman, E. M., Austin, C. C., & Johnson, D. (2001). The development of goal orientation. In A. Wigfield & J. S. Eccles (Eds.), *Development of achievement orientation* (pp. 197–221). San Diego: Academic Press.

Anderman, E. M., & Murdock, T. B. (2007) In E. M. Anderman & T. B. Murdock (Eds.), *Psychology of academic cheating* (pp. 1–5). San Diego, CA: Elsevier Academic Press.

Anderson, C. A., Shibuya, A., Ihori, N., Swing, E. L., Bushman, B. J., Sakamoto, A., Saleem, M. (2010). Violent video game effects on aggression, empathy, and prosocial behavior in Eastern and Western countries. *Psychological Bulletin, 136,* 151–173.

Anderson, D., & Kirkorian, H. (2006). Attention and television. In J. Bryant & P. Vorderer (Eds.), *Psychology of entertainment* (pp. 35–54). Mahwah, NJ: Lawrence Erlbaum Associates.

Anderson, E. (1990). *Streetwise: Race, class, and change in an urban community.* Chicago: University of Chicago Press.

Anderson, S. E., Bandini, L. G., & Must, A. (2005). Child temperament does not predict adolescent body composition in girls. *International Journal of Obesity, 29,* 47–53.

Anderson, S. W., Damasio, H., & Damasio, A. R. (2005). A neural basis for collecting behaviour in humans. *Brain: A Journal of Neurology, 128,* 201–212.

Anglin, J. M. (1993). Vocabulary development: A morphological analysis. *Monographs of the Society for Research in Child Development, 58*(10), 1–166.

Anglin, J. M. (1995). Classifying the world through language: Functional relevance, cultural significance, and category name learning. *International Journal of Intercultural Relations, 19,* 161–181.

Annie E. Casey Foundation. (2010). Kids Count Data Center. Retrieved from http://datacenter.kidscount.org/data/acrossstates/Rankings.aspx?ind=5938

Annis, R. C., & Corenblum, B. (1987). Effect of test language and experimenter race on Canadian Indian children's racial and self-identity. *Journal of Social Psychology, 126,* 761–773.

Antonov, A. I., & Medkov, V. M. (2007). Demographic processes in the countries of Eastern Europe, the CIS, and the Baltic: Trends in the 1990s and what we should expect in the next decade. In A. S. Loveless & T. B. Holman (Eds.), *The family in the new millennium: World voices supporting the "natural" clan: Vol. 1. The place of family in human society* (pp. 296–315). Westport, CT: Praeger Publishers/Greenwood Publishing Group.

Antonov, A. N. (1947). Children born during the siege of Leningrad in 1942. *Journal of Pediatrics, 30,* 250.

APA. (2000). *Diagnostic and statistical manual of mental disorders, fourth edition (DSM-IV).* American Psychiatric Association.

Apgar, V. (1953). A proposal for a new method of evaluation of the newborn infant. *Current Researches in Anesthesia and Analgesics, 32,* 260–267.

Apple, R. (2006). *Perfect motherhood: Science and childrearing in America.* New Brunswick, NJ: Rutgers University Press.

Arey, L. (1974). *Developmental anatomy* (7th ed.). Philadelphia, PA: Saunders Publishers

Ariel, J., & McPherson, D. (2000). Therapy with lesbian and gay parents and their children. *Journal of Marital and Family Therapy, 26,* 421–432.

Ariès, P. (1962). *Centuries of childhood.* Translated from the French by Robert Baldick. London: Cape.

Ariès, P. (1965). *Centuries of childhood: A social history of family life.* Oxford, England: Vintage Books.

Arnett, J. J. (2007). Child development perspectives. Special Issue: Emerging adulthood around the world. *Child Development Perspectives. Special Issue: Emerging adulthood around the world, 1,* 68–73.

Arnett, J. J., & Cravens, H. (2006). G. Stanley Hall's adolescence: A centennial reappraisal: Introduction. *History of Psychology, 9,* 165–171.

Arsenio, W. F. (2006). Happy victimization: Emotion dysregulation in the context of instrumental, proactive aggression. In W. F. Arsenio (Ed.), *Emotion regulation in couples and families: Pathways to dysfunction and health* (pp. 101–121). Washington, DC: American Psychological Association.

Arterberry, M. E., & Yonas, A. (2000). Perception of three-dimensional shape specified by optic flow by 8-week-old infants. *Perception and Psychophysics, 62,* 550–556.

Asendorph, J. (2002). Self-awareness, other-awareness, and secondary representation. In A. Meltzoff & W. Prinz (Eds.), *The imitative mind: Development, evolution, and brain bases.* Cambridge, England: Cambridge University Press.

Asher, S. R., & Coie, J. D. (Eds.). (1990). *Peer rejection in childhood.* New York: Cambridge University Press.

Asher, S. R., Rose, A. J., & Gabriel, S. W. (2001). Peer rejection in everyday life. In M. R. Leary (Ed.), *Interpersonal rejection* (pp. 105–142). London: Oxford University Press.

Ashford, K. B., Hahn, E., Hall, L., Rayens, M. K., Noland, M., & Ferguson, J. E. (2010). The effects of prenatal secondhand smoke exposure on preterm birth and neonatal outcomes. *Journal of Obstetetric, Gynecological and Neonatal Nursing, 39,* 525–535.

Astington, J. W. (1993). *The child's discovery of the mind.* Cambridge, MA: Harvard University Press.

Astington, J. W., & Filippova, E. (2005). Language as the route into other minds. In B. F. Malle & S. D. Hodges (Eds.), *Other minds: How humans bridge the divide between self and others* (pp. 209–222). New York: Guilford Press.

Atkinson, J. (1998). The "where and what" or "who and how" of visual development. In F. Simion & G. Butterworth (Eds.), *The development of sensory, motor and cognitive capacities in early infancy: From perception to cognition.* Hove, England: Psychology Press/Lawrence Erlbaum Associates.

Atkinson, R. C., & Shiffrin, R. M. (1968). Human memory: A proposed system and its control processes. In K. W. Spence & J. T. Spence (Eds.), *The psychology of learning and motivation: Advances in research and theory: Vol. 2.* Orlando, FL: Academic Press.

Atran, S. (1998). Folk biology and the anthropology of science: Cognitive universals and cultural particulars. *Behavioral & Brain Sciences, 21,* 547–609.

Au, T. K., Sidle, A. L., & Rollins, K. B. (1993). Developing an intuitive understanding of conservation and contamination: Invisible particles as a plausible mechanism. *Developmental Psychology, 29,* 286–299.

Aubrey, J. S., & Harrison, K. (2004, May). The gender-role content of children's favorite television programs and its links to their gender-related perceptions. *Media Psychology, 6*(2), 111–146.

Auyeung, B., Baron-Cohen, S., Ashwin, E., & Knickmeyer, R. (2009). Fetal testosterone predicts sexually differentiated childhood behavior in girls and in boys. *Psychological Science, 20,* 144–148.

Avenevoli, S., & Steinberg, L. (2001). The continuity of depression across the adolescent transition. *Advances in Child Development and Behavior, 28,* 139–173

Aviezer, O., & Sagi-Schwartz, A. (2008). Attachment and non-maternal care: Towards contextualizing the quantity versus quality debate. *Attachment & Human Development, 10,* 275–285.

Avis, J., & Harris, P. L. (1991). Belief-desire reasoning among Baka children: Evidence for a universal conception of mind. *Child Development, 62,* 460–467.

Aylward, G. P. (2005). Neurodevelopmental outcomes of infants born prematurely. *Journal of Developmental & Behavioral Pediatrics, 26,* 427–440.

Azmitia, M., & Hesser, J. (1993). Why siblings are important agents of cognitive development: A comparison of siblings and peers. *Child Development, 64,* 430–444.

Bahrick, L. E., Moss, L., & Fadil, C. (1996). Development of visual self-recognition in infancy. *Ecological Psychology, 8,* 189–208.

Bainbridge, J., Meyers, M. K., Tanaka, S., & Waldfogel, J. (2005, September). Who gets an early education? Family income and the enrollment of three- to five-year-olds from 1968 to 2000. *Social Science Quarterly, 86*(3), 724–745.

Bajanowski, T., Vege, Å., Byard, R., Krous, H., Arnestad, M., Bachs, L., et al. (2007). Sudden infant death syndrome (SIDS)—Standardised investigations and classification: Recommendations. *Forensic Science International, 165*(2–3), 129–143.

Ballabriga, A. (2000, March). Morphological and physiological changes during growth: An update. *European Journal of Clinical Nutrition, 54*(Suppl. 1), S1–S6.

Baillargeon, R. (1993). The object concept revisited: New directions in the investigation of infants' physical knowledge. In C. E. Granrud (Ed.), *Visual perception and cognition in infancy.* Hillsdale, NJ: Lawrence Erlbaum Associates.

Baillargeon, R. (2001). Infants' physical knowledge: Of acquired expectations and core principles. In E. Dupoux (Ed.), *Language, brain, and cognitive development: Essays in honor of Jacques Mehler* (pp. 341–361). Cambridge, MA: The MIT Press.

Baillargeon, R. (2002). The acquisition of physical knowledge in infancy: A summary of eight lessons. In U. Goswami (Ed.), *Blackwell's handbook of childhood cognitive development* (pp. 47–83). Oxford, England: Blackwell Publishing.

Baillargeon, R. (2004). Infants' physical world. *Current Directions in Psychological Science, 13,* 89–94.

Baillargeon, R., Zoccolillo, M., Keenan, K., Côté, S., Pérusse, D., Wu, H., et al. (2007). Gender differences in physical aggression: A prospective population-based survey of children before and after 2 years of age. *Developmental Psychology, 43,* 13–26.

Baker, J. L., Olsen, L. W., & Sorensen, T. I. (2008). Weight at birth and all-cause mortality in adulthood. *Epidemiology, 19,* 197–203.

Baker, S. A., Golinkoff, R. M., & Petitto, L.-A. (2006). New insights into old puzzles from infants' categorical discrimination of soundless phonetic units. *Language Learning and Development, 2*(3), 147–162.

Bakker, E., & Wyndaele, J. J. (2000). Changes in the toilet training of children during the last 60 years: The cause of an increase in lower urinary tract dysfunction? *BJU International, 86,* 248.

Bakker, R., Steegers, E. A., Obradov, A., Raat, H., Hofman, A., & Jaddoe, V. W. (2010). Maternal caffeine intake from coffee and tea, fetal growth, and the risks of adverse birth outcomes: The Generation R Study. *American Journal Clinical Nutrition, 91,* 1691–1698.

Bandura, A. (1997). Behavior theory and the models of man (1974). In J. M. Notterman (Ed.), *The evolution of psychology: Fifty years of the American Psychologist* (pp. 154–172). Washington, DC: American Psychological Association.

Barber, B., Eccles, J., & Stone, M. (2001). Whatever happened to the jock, the brain, and the princess? Young adult pathways linked to adolescent activity involvement and social identity. *Journal of Adolescent Research, 16,* 429–455.

Barber, B. K., Stoltz, H. E., & Olsen, J. A. (2005). Toward disentangling fathering and mothering: An assessment of relative importance. *Journal of Marriage and Family, 67,* 1076–1092.

Bard, K. (2004). What is the evolutionary basis for colic? *Behavioral and Brain Sciences, 27,* 459.

Bard, K. A., Todd, B., Bernier, C., Love, J., & Leavens, D. (2006). Self-awareness in human and chimpanzee infants: What is measured and what is meant by the mark and mirror test? *Infancy, 9,* 191–219.

Bargelow, P., Vaughn, B. E., & Molitor, N. (1987). Effects of maternal absence due to employment on the quality of infant-mother attachment in a low-risk sample. *Child Development, 58,* 945–953.

Barker, D., Osmond, C., Simmonds, S., & Wield, G. (1993). The relations of small head circumference and thinness at birth to death from cardiovascular disease in adult life. *British Medical Journal, 306,* 422–426.

Barker, D. J. P., Osmond, C., Forsén, T. J., Kajantie, E., Eriksson, J. G. (2005). Trajectories of growth among children who later develop coronary heart disease or its risk factors. *New England Journal of Medicine, 353,* 1802-9.

Baron-Cohen, S., Leslie, A. M., & Frith, U. (1986) Mechanical, behavioural, and intentional understanding of picture stories in autistic children. *British Journal of Developmental Psychology, 4,* 113–125.

Baron-Cohen, S., Leslie, A. M., & Frith, U. (2007). Does the autistic child have a 'theory of mind'? In B. Gertler & L. Shapiro (Eds.), *Arguing about the mind* (pp. 310–318). New York: Routledge/Taylor & Francis Group.

Barr, R. G., Konner, M., Bakeman, R., & Adamson, L. (1991). Crying in pKung San infants: A test of the cultural specificity hypothesis. *Developmental Medicine & Child Neurology, 33,* 601–610.

Barrett, J. (2001). Do children experience God as adults do? In J. Andressen (Ed.), *Religion in mind: Cognitive perspectives on religious belief, ritual, and experience.* Cambridge, England: Cambridge University Press.

Barrett, M. (1995). Early lexical development. In P. Fletcher & B. McWhinney (Eds.), *The handbook of child language* (pp. 362–392). Cambridge, MA: Blackwell Publishing

Bartlett, E. (1977). The acquisition of the meaning of color terms. In P. T. Smith & R. N. Campbell (Eds.), *Proceedings of the Sterling Conference on the psychology of language.* New York: Plenum Press

Barsalou, L. W. (2008, April). Cognitive and neural contributions to understanding the conceptual system. *Current Directions in Psychological Science, 17*(2), 91–95.

Barton, B. K., & Morrongiello, B. A. (2011). Examining the impact of traffic environment and executive functioning on children's pedestrian behaviors. *Developmental Psychology, 47,* 182–191.

Basow, S. A. (2006). Gender role and gender identity development. In J. Worell & C. D. Goodheart (Eds.), *Handbook of girls' and women's psychological health: Gender and well-being across the lifespan. Oxford series in clinical psychology* (pp. 242–251). New York: Oxford University Press.

Bates, E. (1999). On the nature and nurture of language. In E. Bizzi, P. Calissano, & V. Volterra (Eds.), *Frontiere della biologia* [Frontiers of biology]. Rome: Giovanni Trecanni.

Bates, E. (2005). Plasticity, localization, and language development. In S. T. Parker, J. Langer, & C. Milbrath (Eds.), *Biology and knowledge revisited: From neurogenesis to psychogenesis. The Jean Piaget symposium series* (pp. 205–253). Mahwah, NJ: Lawrence Erlbaum Associates.

Bates, E., Benigni, L., Bretherton, I., Camaioni, L., & Volterra, V. (1979). *The emergence of symbols: Cognition and communication in infancy.* New York: Academic Press.

Bates, E., Camaioni, L., & Volterra, V. (1975). The acquisition of performatives prior to speech. *Merrill Palmer Quarterly, 21,* 205–226.

Bates, E., O'Connell, B., & Shore, C. (1987). Language and communication. In J. D. Osofsky (Ed.), *Handbook of infant development* (2nd ed.). New York: Wiley.

Bates, E., & Roe, K. (2001). Language development in children with unilateral brain injury. In C. A. Nelson & M. Luciana (Eds.), *Handbook of developmental cognitive neuroscience.* Cambridge, MA: The MIT Press.

Bates, E., Thal, D., Finlay, B., & Clancy, B. (2002). Language development and its neural correlates. In I. Rapin & S. Segalowitz (Eds.), *Handbook of neuropsychology* (pp. 109–176). Amsterdam: Elsevier.

Bauer, I. (2001). *Diaper free! The gentle wisdom of natural infant hygiene.* Saltspring Is., BC, Canada: Natural Wisdom Press.

Bauer, P. J., & Fivush, R. (2010). Context and consequences of autobiographical memory development. *Cognitive Development, 25,* 303–308.

Bauer, P. J., Wiebe, S. A., Carver, L. J., Waters, J. M., & Nelson, C. (2003). Developments in long-term explicit memory late in the first year of life: Behavioral and electrophysiological indices. *Psychological Science, 14,* 629–635.

Baumer, S., Ferholt, B., & Lecusay, R. (2005). Promoting narrative competence through adult-child joint pretense: Lessons from the Scandinavian educational practices of playworld. *Cognitive Development, 20,* 576–590.

Baumrind, D. (1971). Current patterns of parental authority. *Developmental Psychology Monographs, 4(1, Part 2).*

Baumrind, D. (1980). New directions in socialization research. *American Psychologist, 35,* 639–652.

Baumrind, D., Larzelere, R. E., & Owens, E. B. (2010). Effects of preschool parents' power assertive patterns and practices on adolescent development. *Science and Practice, 10,* 157–201.

Bayley, N. (1993). *The Bayley scales of infant development.* San Antonio, TX: Psychological Corporation.

Bayliss, D. M., Jarrold, C., Baddeley, A. D., Gunn, D. M., & Leigh, E. (2005). Mapping the developmental constraints on working memory span performance. *Developmental Psychology, 41,* 579–597.

Bearce, K., & Rovee-Collier, C. (2006) Repeated priming increases memory accessibility in infants. *Journal of Experimental Child Psychology, 93,* 357–376.

Bearison, D. J., & Dorval, B. (2002). *Collaborative cognition: Children negotiating ways of knowing. (Advances in discourse processes).* Westport, CT: Ablex Publishing.

Bearman, P., & Brückner, H. (2001). Promising the future: Virginity pledges and first intercourse. *American Journal of Sociology, 106,* 859–911.

Becker, G. S. (2007). The role of the family in modern economic life. In A. S. Loveless & T. B. Holman (Eds.), *The family in the new millennium: World voices supporting the "natural" clan: Vol. 1. The place of family in human society* (pp. 3–11). Westport, CT: Praeger Publishers/Greenwood Publishing Group.

Beidelman, T. (1997). *The cool knife: Imagery of gender, sexuality, and moral educaion in Kaguru initiation ritual.* Washington, DC: Smithsonian Institution Press.

Belsky, J. (1993). Etiology of child maltreatment: A developmental ecological analysis. *Psychological Bulletin, 114,* 413–434.

Belsky, J. (2005). Attachment in ecological context. In K. Grossmann, K. Grossmann, & E. Waters (Eds.), *Attachment from infancy to adulthood.* New York: Guilford Press.

Belsky, J., & Pasco Fearon, R. M. (2008). Precursors of attachment security. In J. Cassidy & P. R. Shaver (Eds.), *Handbook of attachment: Theory, research, and clinical applications* (2 ed., pp. 295–316). New York: Guilford Press.

Belsky, J., Steinberg, L. D., Houts, R. M., Friedman, S. L., DeHart, G., Cauffman, E., et al. (2007). Family rearing antecedents of pubertal timing. *Child Development, 78,* 1302–1321.

Belkin, L. (2005, November 6). A doctor for the future. *New York Times Magazine.*

Bellmore, A. D., & Cillessen, A. H. N. (2006). Reciprocal influences of victimization, perceived social preference, and self-concept in adolescence. *Self and Identity 5*(3), 209–229.

Bemak, F., & Young, M. E. (1998). Role of catharsis in group psychotherapy. *International Journal of Action Methods, 50*(4), 166–184.

Bender, D., & Lösel, F. (2011). Bullying at school as a predictor of delinquency, violence and other anti-social behaviour in adulthood. *Criminal Behaviour and Mental Health, 21,* 99–106.

Bengtson, V. L. (2005). *Sourcebook of family theory and research.* Thousand Oaks, CA: Sage Publications.

Beran, M., & Beran, M. (2004). Chimpanzees remember the results of one-by-one addition of food items to sets over extended time periods. *Psychological Science, 15,* 94–99.

Bergen, D. (2011). Communicative actions and language narratives in preschoolers' play with "talking" and "non-talking" rescue heroes. In D. Sluss & O. Jarrett (Eds), *Investigating play in the 21st century* (pp. 229–249). New York: University Press of America.

Berger, S. E., & Adolph, K. E. (2003). Infants use handrails as tools in a locomotor task. *Developmental Psychology, 39*(3), 594–605.

Berkowitz, L. (2003). Affect, aggression and antisocial behavior. In R. Davidson, K. Scherer, & H. Goldsmith (Eds.), *Handbook of affective sciences.* Oxford, England: Oxford University Press.

Berland, J. (1982) *No five fingers are alike.* Cambridge, MA: Harvard University Press.

Bernal, J. F. (1972). Crying during the first few days and maternal responses. *Developmental Medicine and Child Neurology, 14,* 362–372.

Berndt, T. J. (2007). Children's friendships: Shifts over a half-century in perspectives on their development and their effects. In G. Ladd, *Appraising the human development sciences: Essays in honor of Merrill-Palmer Quarterly (Landscapes of childhood series).* Detroit, MI: Wayne State University Press.

Berndt, T. J., & Keefe, K. (1995). Friend's influence on adolescent's adjustment in school. *Child Development, 66,* 1312–1329.

Berndt, T. J., & Murphy, L. M. (2002). Influences of friends and friendships: Myths, truths, and research recommendations. In R. V. Kail (Ed.), *Advances in child development and behavior: Vol. 30* (pp. 275–310). San Diego: Academic Press.

Berndt, T. J., & Savin-Williams, R. C. (1993). Peer relations and friendships. In P. H. Tolan & B. J. Cohler (Eds.), *Handbook of clinical research and practice with adolescents.* New York: Wiley.

Bersamin, M., Walker, S., Waiters, E., Fisher, D., & Grube, J. (2005). Promising to wait: Virginity pledges and adolescent sexual behavior. *Journal of Adolescent Health, 36,* 428–436.

Berstein, J., Brocht, C., & Spade-Aguilar, M. (2000). *How much is enough? Basic family budgets for working families.* Washington, DC: Economic Policy Institute.

Bertenthal, B. I., Campos, J. J., & Kermoian, R. (1994). An epigenetic perspective on the development of self-produced locomotion and its consequences. *Current Directions in Psychological Science, 3*(5), 140–145.

Betancourt, T. S., Brennan, R. T., Rubin-Smith, J., Fitzmaurice, G. M., & Gilman, S. E. (2010). Sierra Leone's former child soldiers: A longitudinal study of risk, protective factors and mental health. *Journal of the American Academy of Child & Adolescent Psychiatry, 49,* 606–615.

Bettelheim, B. (1977). *The uses of enchantment: The meaning and importance of fairytales.* New York: Vintage Books.

Beuf, A. H. (1977). *Red children in white America.* Philadelphia: University of Pennsylvania Press.

Bialystok, E. (2001). *Bilingualism in development: Language, literacy, and cognition.* Cambridge, England: Cambridge University Press.

Bialystok, E., & Shapero, D. (2005). Ambiguous benefits: the effect of bilingualism on reversing ambiguous figures. *Developmental Science, 8,* 595–604.

Biancotti, J. C., Narwani, K., Buehler, N., Mandefro, B., Golan-Lev, T., et al. (2010). Human embryonic stem cells as models for aneuploid chromosomal syndromes. *Stem Cells, 28,* 1530–1540.

Biblarz, T. J., & Savci, E. (2010). Lesbian, gay, bisexual, and transgender families. *Journal of Marriage and Family, 72,* 480–497.

Biemiller, A., & Slonim, N. (2001). Estimating root word vocabulary growth in normative and advantaged populations: Evidence for a common sequence of vocabulary acquisition. *Journal of Educational Psychology, 93*(3), 498–520.

Bigelow, A. E. (1998). Infants' sensitivity to familiar imperfect contingencies in social interaction. *Infant Behavior and Development, 21,* 149–161.

Biggler, R. (1995). The role of classification skill in moderating environmental influences on children's gender stereotyping: A study of the functional use of gender in the classroom. *Child Development, 66,* 1440–1452.

Binet, A., & Simon, T. (1916). *The development of intelligence in children.* Vineland, NJ: Publications of the Training School at Vineland (reprinted by Williams Publishing Co., Nashville, TN, 1980.).

Binnie, L., & Williams, J. (2003). Intuitive psychology and physics among children with autism and typically developing children. *Autism, 7,* 173–193.

Bird, D., & Bird, R. (2005). Martu children's hunting strategies in the Western desert, Australia. In B. Hewlett & M. Lamb (eds.), *Hunter-gatherer childhoods: Evolutionary, developmental & cultural perspectives.* New Brunswick: Transaction Publishers.

Bjorklund, D., Dukes, C., & Brown, R. (2009). The development of memory strategies. In M. Courage & N. Cowan (Eds.), *The development of memory in infancy and childhood.* Hove, UK: Psychology Press.

Bjorklund, D. F., & Pellegrini, A. D. (2002). *The origins of human nature: Evolutionary developmental psychology.* Washington, DC: American Psychological Association.

Bjurström, E. (1994). *Children and television advertising.* Vallingby, Sweden: Konsumentverket.

Blachman, B. A., Schatschneider, C., Fletcher, J. M., Francis, D. J., Clonan, S. M., Shaywitz, B A., & Shaywitz, S. E. (2004).

Effects of intensive reading remediation for second and third graders and a 1-year follow-up. *Journal of Educational Psychology, 96,* 444–461.

Blair, C., Zelazo, P. D., & Greenberg, M. T. (2005). The measurement of executive function in early childhood. *Developmental Neuropsychology, 28*(2), 561–571.

Blair, P., Sidebotham, P., Berry, P., Evans, M., & Fleming, P. (2006). Major epidemiological changes in sudden infant death syndrome: A 20-year population-based study in the UK. *Lancet, 367,* 314–319.

Blake, J., & De Boysson-Bardies, B. (1992). Patterns in babbling: A cross-linguistic study. *Journal of Child Language, 19,* 51–74

Blakeslee, S. (2006, January 6). Cells that read minds. *New York Times.*

Blanton, H., & Burkley, M. (2008). Deviance regulation theory: Applications to adolescent social influence. In M. J. Prinstein & K. A. Dodge (Eds.), *Understanding peer influence in children and adolescents. Duke series in child development and public policy* (pp. 94–121). New York: Guilford Press.

Blicharski, T. Bon, M., & Strayer, F. (2011) *Origins of gender differences during the preschool years.* Paper presented as a part of the symposium, The sociogenesis of gender during early childhood (T. Blicharski, organizer), at the Annual Meeting of the Jean Piaget Society, Berkeley, CA.

Blinn-Pike, L. (2008). Sex education in rural schools in the United States: Impact of rural educators' community identities. *Sex Education, 8,* 77–92.

Block, C. C., Parris, S. R., Reed, K. L., Whiteley, C. S., & Cleveland, M. D. (2009). Instructional approaches that significantly increase reading comprehension. *Journal of Educational Psychology, 101,* 262–281.

Block, J., Scribner, R., & DeSalvo, K. (2004). Fast food, race/ethnicity, and income: A geographic analysis. *American Journal of Preventive Medicine, 27,* 211–217.

Bloom, L. (1973). *One word at a time: The use of single word utterances before syntax.* The Hague: Mouton.

Bloom, P. (2010, May 9). The moral life of babies. *New York Times Magazine.*

Blum-Kulka, Shoshana and Catherine E. Snow. (2002). *Talking to adults: The contribution of multiparty discourse to language acquisition.* Mahwah, N.J: Lawrence Erlbaum Associates.

Boaler, J. (2001). Mathematical modelling and new theories of learning. *Teaching Mathematics and Its Applications 20*(3), 121–127.

Boas, F. (1911). *The mind of primitive man.* New York: Macmillan.

Bock, J. (2005). Farming, foraging, and children's play in the Okavango Delta, Botswana. In A. D. Pellegrini & P. K. Smith (Eds.), *The nature of play: Great apes and humans* (pp. 254–281). New York: Guilford Press.

Bogin, B. (1999). *Patterns of human growth* (2nd ed.). New York: Cambridge University Press.

Bogin, B. (2001). *The growth of humanity.* New York: Wiley-Liss.

Bogin, B., Smith, P., Orden, A. B., Varela Silva, M. I., & Loucky, J. (2002). Rapid change in height and body proportions of Maya American children. *American Journal of Human Biology, 14,* 753–761.

Boland, A., Haden, C., & Ornstein, P. (2003). Boosting children's memory by training mothers in the use of an elaborative conversational style as an event unfolds. *Journal of Cognition and Development, 4,* 39–65.

Bolger, K., & Patterson, C. (2001). Developmental pathways from child maltreatment to peer rejection. *Child Development, 72,* 549–568.

Boo, K. (2006, February 6). A reporter at large: Swamp nurse. *The New Yorker,* p. 54.

Books, S. (2008). *Poverty and schooling in the U.S.: Contexts and consequences.* New York: Taylor & Francis.

Boone, T. L., Lefkowitz, E. S., Romo, L., Corona, R., Sigman, M., & Au, T. K. F. (2003). Mothers' and adolescents' perceptions of AIDS vulnerability. *International Journal of Behavioral Development, 27,* 347–354.

Borges, G., Medina-Mora, M. E., Benjet, C., Ruíz, J. Z., & Breslau, J. (2008). Descriptive epidemiology of depression in Latin America and Hispanics in the United States. In S. A. Aguilar-Gaxiola & T. P. Gullotta (Eds.), *Depression in Latinos: Assessment, treatment, and prevention* (pp. 53–71). New York: Springer.

Borke, H. (1975). Piaget's mountains revisited: Changes in the egocentric landscape. *Developmental Psychology, 11,* 240–443.

Bornstein, M. H., Cote, L. R., Maital, S., Painter, K., Park, S.-Y., Pascual, L., et al. (2004). Cross-linguistic analysis of vocabulary in young children: Spanish, Dutch, French, Hebrew, Italian, Korean, and American English. *Child Development, 75,* 1115–1139

Bornstein, M. H., & Putnick, D. L. (2007). Chronological age, cognitions, and practices in European American Mothers: A multivariate study of parenting. *Developmental Psychology, 43,* 850–864.

Bornstein, M. H. M., Clay; Arterberry, Martha E. (2011). Perception of object-context relations: Eye-movement analyses in infants and adults. *Developmental Psychology, 47,* 364–375.

Bortfeld, H., Morgan, J., Golinkoff, R., & Rathbun, K. (2005). Mommy and me: Familiar names help launch babies into speech-stream segmentation. *Psychological Science, 16,* 298–304.

Bos, H. M. W., Gartrell, N. K., van Balen, F., H, P., & Sandfort, T. G. (2008). Children in planned lesbian families: A cross-cultural comparison between the United States and the Netherlands. *American Journal of Orthopsychiatry, 78,* 211–219.

Bos, H. M. W., Sandfort, T. G. M., de Bruyn, E. H., & Hakvoot, E. M. (2008). Same-sex attraction, social relationships, psychosocial functioning, and school performance in early adolescence. *Developmental Psychology, 44,* 59–68.

Bos, H. M. W., & van Balen, F. (2008). Children in planned lesbian families. Stigmatisation, psychological adjustment and protective factors. *Culture, Health and Sexuality, 10,* 221–236.

Bos, H. M. W., van Balen, F., & van den Boom, D. C. (2007). Child adjustment and parenting in planned lesbian-parent families. *American Journal of Orthopsychiatry, 77,* 38–48.

Bottoms, B. L., Goodman, G. S., Schwartz-Kenney, B. M., & Thomas, S. N. (2002). Understanding children's use of secrecy in the context of eyewitness reports. *Law & Human Behavior, 26*(3), 285–314.

Bower, T. G. R. (1979). *Human development.* San Francisco: W. H. Freeman.

Bower, T. G. R. (1982). *Development in human infancy.* New York: W. H. Freeman.

Bowker, A. (2004). Predicting friendship stability during early adolescence. *Journal of Early Adolescence, 24,* 85–112.

Bowlby, J. (1969). *Attachment and loss: Vol. 1. Attachment.* New York: Basic Books.

Bowlby, J. (1973). *Attachment and loss: Vol. 2. Separation.* New York: Basic Books.

Bowlby, J. (1980). *Attachment and loss: Vol. 3. Loss, sadness, and depression.* New York: Basic Books.

Boyatzis, C. J., Baloff, P., & Durieux, C. (1998). Effects of perceived attractiveness and academic success on early adolescent peer popularity. *Journal of Genetic Psychology, 159,* 337–344.

Boyce, W., & Ellis, N. (2005). Biological sensitivity to context: An evolutionary-developmental theory of the origins and functions of stress reactivity. *Development & Psychopathology, 17,* 271–301.

boyd, d. (2007). Why youth ♥ social network sites: The role of networked publics in teenage social life. In D. Buckingham (Ed.), *Youth,* *identity, and digital media.* MacArthur Foundation Series on Digital Learning. Cambridge, MA: MIT Press.

Boyer, L. A., Lee, T. I., Cole, M. F., Johnstone, S. E., Levine, S. S., Jacob P. Zucker, J. P., et al. (2005, September 23). Core transcriptional regulatory circuitry in human embryonic stem cells. *Cell, 122*(6), 947–956.

Boyer, T., & Byrnes, J. (2009). Adolescent risk-taking: Integrating personal, cognitive, and social aspects of judgment. *Journal of Applied Developmental Psychology, 30,* 23–33.

Boykin, A. W., & Cunningham, R. T. (2001). The effects of movement expressiveness in story content and learning context on the analogical reasoning performance of African American children. *Journal of Negro Education, 70,* 72–83.

Bradley, C., McMurray, R., Harrell, J., & Deng, S. (2000). Changes in common activities of 3rd through 10th graders: The CHIC study. *Medicine and Science in Sports and Exercise, 32,* 2071–2078.

Bramen, J. E., Hranilovich, J. A., Dahl, R. E., Forbes, E. E., Chen, J., Toga, A. W., et al. (2011). Puberty influences medial temporal lobe and cortical gray matter maturation differently in boys than girls matched for sexual maturity. *Cerebral Cortex, 21,* 636–646.

Brämswig, J., & Dübbers, A. (2009). Störungen der pubertätsentwicklung. / Disorders of pubertal development. *Deutsches Ärzteblatt International, 106,* 295–304.

Brandon, P. (2004). The child care arrangements of preschool age children in immigrant families in the United States. *International Migration Review, 42,* 65–88.

Brauer, J., Anwander, A., & Friederici, A. D. (2011). Neuroanatomical prerequisites for language functions in the maturing brain. *Cerebral Cortex, 21,* 459–466.

Brazelton, T. B. (1984). *Neonatal behavioral assessment scale* (2nd ed.). London: Spastics International Medical Publications.

Bremner, J., Johnson, S., Slater, A., Mason, U., Foster, K., & Cheshire, A. (2005). Conditions for young infants' perception of object trajectories. *Child Development, 76,* 1029–1043.

Bretherton, I. (2005). In pursuit of the internal working model construct and its relevance to attachment relationships. In K. E. Grossmann, K. Grossmann, & E. Waters (Eds.), *Attachment from infancy to adulthood: The major longitudinal studies* (pp. 13–47). New York: Guilford Press.

Bretherton, I., & Munholland, K. (1999). Internal working models in attachment relationships: A construct revisited. In J. Cassidy & P. Shaver (Eds.), *Handbook of attachment: Theory, research and clinical applications.* New York: Guilford Press.

Bridges, K. (1932). Emotional development in early infancy. *Child Development, 3,* 324–334.

Brodersen, N. H., Steptoe, A., Williamson, S., & Wardle, J. (2005). Sociodemographic, developmental, environmental, and psychological correlates of physical activity and sedentary behavior at age 11 to 12. *Annals of behavioral medicine a publication of the Society of Behavioral Medicine, 29*(1), 2–11.

Brody, G. H. (1998). Sibling relationship quality: Its causes and consequences. *Annual Review of Psychology, 49,* 1–24.

Brody, G. H., & Murry, V. M. (2001). Sibling socialization of competence in rural, single-parent African American families. *Journal of Marriage and the Family 63,* 996–1008.

Brody, L. (2000). The socialization of gender differences in emotional expression: Display rules, infant temperament, and differentiation. In A. H. Fischer (Ed.), *Gender and emotion: Social psychological perspectives* (pp. 24–47). Cambridge, England: Cambridge University Press.

Bronfenbrenner, U. (1970). *Two worlds of childhood: U.S. and U.S.S.R.* New York: Russell Sage Foundation.

Bronson, G. W. (1991). Infant differences in rate of visual encoding. *Child Development, 62,* 44–54.

Bronson, G. W. (1994). Infants' transitions toward adult-like scanning. *Child Development, 65,* 1243–1261.

Bronson, G. W. (1997). The growth of visual capacity: Evidence from infant scanning patterns. *Advances in Infancy Research, 11,* 109–141.

Bronstein, P., Briones, M., Brooks, T., & Cowan, B. (1996). Gender and family factors as predictors of late adolescent emotional expressiveness and adjustment: A longitudinal study. *Sex Roles, 34,* 739–765.

Brooke, J. (1991, June 15). Cubato journal: Signs of life in Brazil's industrial valley of death. *New York Times,* Pt. 1, p. 2.

Brooks-Gunn, J., & Warren, M. (1989). Biological and social contributions to negative affect in young adolescent girls. *Child Development, 60,* 40–55.

Brotman, L. M., Gouley, K. K., Keng-Yen, H., & Kamboukos, D. (2007). Effects of a psychosocial family-based preventive intervention on cortisol response to a social challenge in preschoolers at high risk for antisocial behavior. *Archives of General Psychiatry, 64,* 1172.

Brown, A. L. (1997). Transforming schools into communities of thinking and learning about serious matters. *American Psychologist, 52*(4), 399–413.

Brown, A. L., Campione, J. C., Reeve, R. A., Ferrara, R. A., & Palincsar, A. S. (1992). Interactive learning and individual understanding: The case of reading and mathematics. In L. T. Landsmann (Ed.), *Culture, schooling, and psychological development.* Mahwah, NJ: Lawrence Erlbaum Associates.

Brown, A. L., Palincsar, A. S., & Armbruster, B. B. (1994). Instructing comprehension-fostering activities in interactive learning situations. In R. B. Ruddell & N. J. Unrau (Eds.), *Theoretical models and processes of reading* (pp. 757–787). Newark, DE: International Reading Association.

Brown, B. B. (1999). Measuring the peer environment of American adolescents. In S. L. Friedman & T. D. Wachs (Eds.), *Measuring environment across the life span.* Washington, DC: American Psychological Association.

Brown, B. B. (2004). Adolescents' relationships with peers. In R. M. Lerner & L. Steinberg (Eds.), *Handbook of adolescent psychology* (2nd ed., pp. 363–394). Hoboken, NJ: John Wiley & Sons.

Brown, B. B., Bakken, J. P., Ameringer, S. W., & Mahon, S. D. (2008). A comprehensive conceptualization of the peer influence process in adolescence. In M. J. Prinstein & K. A. Dodge (Eds.), *Understanding peer influence in children and adolescents. Duke series in child development and public policy* (pp. 17–44). New York: Guilford Press.

Brown, B. B., & Huang, B. (1995). Examining parenting practices in different peer contexts: Implications for adolescent trajectories. In L. J. Crockett & A. C. Crouter (Eds.), *Pathways through adolescence: Individual development in relation to social contexts* (pp. 151–174). Mahwah, NJ: Lawrence Erlbaum Associates.

Brown, B. B., & Klute, C. (2003). Friendships, cliques, and crowds. In Gerald R. Adams & M. D. Berzonsky (Eds.), *Blackwell handbook of adolescence* (pp. 330–348). Malden, MA: Blackwell Publishing.

Brown, G., Schoppe-Sullivan, S., Mangelsdorf, S., & Neff, C. (2010). Observed and reported supportive coparenting as predictors of infant-mother and infant-father attachment security. *Early Child Development and Care, 180,* 121–137.

Brown, G. L, McBride, B. A., Shin, N., & Bost, K. K. (2007). Parenting predictors of father-child attachment security: Interactive effects of father involvement and fathering quality. *Fathering, 5*(3), 197–219.

Brown, P. (2002). Everyone has to lie in Tzeltal. In S. Blum-Kulka & C. E. Snow (Eds.), *Talking to adults: The contribution of multiparty discourse to language acquisition* (pp. 241–275). Mahwah, NJ: Erlbaum.

Brown, R. (1973). *A first language: The early stages.* Cambridge, MA: Harvard University Press.

Brown, R., & Bellugi, U. (1964). Three processes in the child's acquisition of syntax. *Harvard Educational Review, 34,* 133–151.

Brown, R., & Herrnstein, R. J. (1975). *Psychology.* Boston: Little, Brown.

Bruer, J. T. (2001). A critical and sensitive period primer. In D. B. J. Bailey, J. T. Bruer, F. J. Symons, & J. W. Lichtman (Eds.), *Critical thinking about critical periods.* Baltimore, MD: Paul H. Brookes.

Bruer, J. T., & Greenough, W. T. (2001). The subtle science of how experience affects the brain. In D. B. Bailey, Jr., J. T. Bruer, F. J. Symons, & J. W. Lichtman (Eds.), *Critical thinking about critical periods* (pp. 209–232). Baltimore, MD: Paul H. Brookes.

Bruner, J. (1966), *Toward a theory of instruction.* New York: Norton.

Bruner, J. S. (1982). Formats of language acquisition. *American Journal of Semiotics, 1,* 1–16

Brunet, M., Guy, F., Pilbeam, D., Mackaye, H. T., Likius, A., et al. (2002). A new hominid from the Upper Miocene of Chad, Central Africa. *Nature, 418,* 145–151.

Bryant Ludden, A., & Wolfson, A. R. (2010). Understanding adolescent caffeine use: Connecting use patterns with expectancies, reasons, and sleep. *Health Education & Behavior, 37,* 330–342.

Bryant, P., & Nunes, T. (2011). Children's understanding of mathematics. In U. Goswami (Ed.), *The Wiley-Blackwell handbook of childhood cognitive development* (2nd ed., pp. 549–573). New York: Wiley-Blackwell.

Bullock, M. (1984). Preschool children's understandings of causal connections. *British Journal of Developmental Psychology, 2,* 139–142.

Bullock, M., & Gelman, R. (1979). Preschool children's assumptions about cause and effect: Temporal ordering. *Child Development, 50,* 89–96.

Bushnell, I. W. R. (2001). Mother's face recognition in newborn infants: Learning and memory. *Infant and Child Development, 10,* 67–74.

Buss, C., Davis, E., Muftuler, L., Head, K., & Sandman, C. (2010). High pregnancy anxiety during mid-gestation is associated with decreased gray matter density in 6–9-year-old children. *Psychoeuroendocrinology, 35,* 141–153.

Butler, R. (2005). Competence assessment, competence, and motivation between early and middle childhood. In A. Elliot & C. Dweck (Eds.), *Handbook of Competence and Motivation* (pp. 202–221). New York: Guilford.

Buttelmann, D., Call, J., & Tomasello, M. (2008). Behavioral cues that great apes use to forage for hidden food. *Animal Cognition, 11*(1), 117–128.

Butterworth, G. (2001). Joint visual attention in infancy. In G. Bremner & A. Fogel (Eds.), *Blackwell handbook of infant development. Handbooks of developmental psychology* (pp. 213–240). Malden, MA: Blackwell Publishers.

Butterworth, G., & Morissette, P. (1996). Onset of pointing and the acquisition of language in infancy. *Journal of Reproductive & Infant Psychology, 14,* 219–231.

Cairns, R. B. (1979). *Social development: The origins of interchanges.* New York: W. H. Freeman.

Cairns, R. B. (1998). The making of developmental psychology. In W. Damon & R. M. Lerner (Eds.), *Handbook of child psychology: Vol. 1. Theoretical models of human development* (5th ed.). New York: Wiley.

Calamaro, C. J., Mason, T. B., & Ratcliffe, S. (2009). Adolescents living the 24/7 lifestyle: Effects of caffeine and technology on sleep duration and daytime functioning. *Pediatrics,* e1005–e1010.

Calkins, S., & Degnan, K. (2005). Temperament in early development. In R. T. Ammerman (Ed.), *Comprehensive handbook of personality and psychopathology: Vol. 3. Child psychopathology.* Hoboken, NJ: John Wiley & Sons.

Cameron, N. (Ed.). (2002). *Human growth and development.* New York: Academic Press.

Campbell, D. (1997). *The Mozart effect: Tapping the power of music to heal the body, strengthen the mind, and unlock the creative spirit.* New York: Avon.

Campbell, F., Pungello, E., Miller-Johnson, S., Burchinal, M., & Ramey, C. (2001). The development of cognitive and academic abilities: Growth curves from an early childhood educational experiment. *Developmental Psychology, 37,* 231–242.

Campbell, S., Spieker, S., Burchinal, M., & Poe, M. (2006). Trajectories of aggression from toddlerhood to age 9 predict academic and social functioning through age 12. *Journal of Child Psychology and Psychiatry, 47*(8), 791–800.

Campos, J. J., Anderson, D. I., Barbu-Roth, M. A., Hubbard, E. M., & Hertenstein, M. J. (2000). Travel broadens the mind. *Infancy, 1,* 149–219.

Camras, L., A., Oster, H., Bakeman, R., Meng, Z., Ujiee, T., & Campos, J. J. (2007). Do infants show distinct negative facial expressions for fear and anger?: Emotional expression in 11-month-old European-American, Chinese, and Japanese infants. *Infancy, 11*(2), 131–155.

Caplan, N., Choy, M. H., & Whitmore, J. K. (1991). *Children of the boat people: A study of educational success.* Ann Arbor: University of Michigan Press.

Capps, R., Fix, M., Murray, J., Ost, J., Herwantoro, S., Zimmerman, W., et al. (2004). *Promise or peril: Immigrants, LEP students, and the No Child Left Behind Act.* Washington, DC: Urban Institute.

Carel, J.-C., & Léger, J. (2008). Precocious puberty. *The New England Journal of Medicine, 358,* 2366–2377.

Carey, S. (1978). The child as word learner. In M. Halle, J. Bresnan, & G. A. Miller (Eds.), *Linguistic theory and psychological reality.* Cambridge, MA: The MIT Press.

Carlo, G., Mestre, M. V., Samper, P., Tur, A., & Armenta, B. E. (2011). The longitudinal relations among dimensions of parenting styles, sympathy, prosocial moral reasoning, and prosocial behaviors. *International Journal of Behavioral Development, 35,* 116–124.

Carlo, G., Mestre, M. V., Samper, P., Tur, A., & Armenta, B. E. (2011). The longitudinal relations among dimensions of parenting styles, sympathy, prosocial moral reasoning, and prosocial behaviors. *International Journal of Behavioral Development, 35,* 116–124.

Carlson, S., Davis, A., & Leach, J. (2005). Less is more: Executive function and symbolic representation in preschool children. *Psychological Science, 16,* 609–616.

Carlson, V. J., & Harwood, R. L. (2003). Attachment, culture, and the caregiving system: The cultural patterning of everyday experiences among Anglo and Puerto Rican mother-infant pairs. *Infant Mental Health Journal, 24,* 53–73.

Carpendale, J., & Lewis, C. (2004). Constructing an understanding of mind: The development of children's social understanding within social interaction. *Behavioral and Brain Sciences, 27,* 79–151.

Carpendale, J. I. M., Hammond, S. I., & Lewis, C. (2010). The social origin and moral nature of human thinking. *Behavioral and Brain Sciences, 33,* 334.

Carpenter, M., Call, J., & Tomasello, M. (2002). A new false belief test for 36-month-olds. *British Journal of Developmental Psychology, 20*(3), 393–420.

Carskadon, M. A. (2011). Sleep in adolescents: the perfect storm. *Pediatric Clinics Of North America, 58,* 637–647.

Carskadon, M. A., Acebo, C., & Jenni, O. G. (2004). Regulation of adolescent sleep: implications for behavior. *Annals of the New York Academy of Sciences, 1021,* 276–291.

Case, R. (1998). The development of conceptual structures. In D. Kuhn & R. S. Siegler (Eds.), *Handbook of child psychology: Vol. 2. Cognition, perception and language* (5th ed., pp. 745–800). New York: Wiley.

Case, R. (1999). Conceptual development in the child and in the field: A personal view of the Piagetian legacy. In R. Case (Ed.), *Conceptual development: Piaget's legacy* (pp. 23–51). Mahwah, NJ: Lawrence Erlbaum Associates.

Case, R., Kurland, D. M., & Goldberg, J. (1982). Operational efficiency and growth of short-term memory span. *Journal of Experimental Child Psychology, 33,* 386–404.

Casey, B. J., Jones, R. M., Levita, L., Libby, V., Pattwell, S. S., Ruberry, E. J., et al. (2010). The storm and stress of adolescence: Insights from human imaging and mouse genetics. *Developmental Psychobiology, 52,* 225–235.

Caspi, A. (1998). Personality development across the life course. In W. Damon & N. Eisenberg (Eds.), *Handbook of child psychology: Vol. 3. Social, emotional, and personality development* (5th ed., pp. 311–388). New York: Wiley.

Caspi, A., Roberts, B. W., & Shiner, R. L. (2005). Personality development: Stability and change. *Annual Review of Psychology, 56,* 453–484.

Cass, V. C. (1984, May). Homosexual identity formation: Testing a theoretical model. *Journal of Sex Research, 20*(2), 143–167

Cassidy, T. (2005, December 4). Special care of early babies; New studies of neotatal brain development are changing the way hospitals manage premature births. *The Boston Globe,* p. 34.

Caughy, M., Campo, P., Randolph, S., & Nickerson, K. (2002). The influence of racial socialization practices on the cognitive and behavioral competence of African American preschoolers. *Child Development, 73,* 1611–1625.

Causey, K., Gardiner, A., & Bjorklund, D. (2008). Evolutionary developmental psychology and the role of plasticity in ontogeny and phylogeny. *Psychological Inquiry, 19,* 27–30.

Centers for Disease Control and Prevention. (2004). *National vital statistics report* (Vol. 52, No. 3, September, 18th, 2003). Washington, DC: Department of Health and Human Services.

Centers for Disease Control and Prevention. (2006a). *Births: Final data for 2004.* National Vital Statistics Report, 55.

Centers for Disease Control and Prevention. (2006b). *Births, marriages, divorces, and deaths: Provisional data for 2005.* National Vital Statistics Report, 54(20). Retrieved April 4, 2007, from http://www.cdc.gov/nchs/data/nvsr/nvsr54/nvsr54_20.pdf

Centers for Disease Control and Prevention. (2007). *Autism spectrum disorders overview.* Retrieved October 10, 2008, from http://www.cdc.gov/ncbddd/autism/overview.htm

Centers for Disease Control and Prevention. (2007). *Autism spectrum disorders overview.* Retrieved October 10, 2008, Retrieved from http://www.cdc.gov/ ncbddd/autism/overview.htm

Centers for Disease Control and Prevention. (2008). HIV/AIDS Fact Sheet. Retrieved from http://www.cdc.gov/hiv/resources/factsheets/PDF/youth.pdf

Centers for Disease Control and Prevention. (2009). Childhood overweight and obesity. Retrieved from http://www.cdc.gov/obesity/childhood/index.html

Centers For Disease Control And Prevention. (2010). *Sexually Transmitted Disease Surveillance 2009.* Atlanta: U.S. Department of Health and Human Services, Centers for Disease Control and Prevention.

Chaffin, M., Hanson, R., Saunders, B., Nichols, T., Barnett, D., Zeanah, C., Berliner, L., Egeland, B., Newman, E., et al. (2006). Report of the APSAC task force on attachment therapy, reactive attachment disorder, and attachment problems. *Child Maltreatment, 11,* 76–89.

Chan, A., Keane, R. J., & Robinson, J. S. (2001). The contribution of maternal smoking to preterm birth, small for gestational age and low birthweight among Aboriginal and non-Aboriginal births in South Australia. *Medical Journal of Australia, 174,* 389–393.

Chandler, M. J., Lalonde, C. E., Sokol, B. W., & Hallett, D. (2003, June). Personal persistence, identity development, and suicide: A study of Native and non-Native North American adolescents. *Monographs of the Society for Research in Child Development, 68*(2), vii–130.

Chandler, M. J., & Proulx, T. (2008). Personal persistence and persistent peoples: Continuities in the lives of individual and whole cultural communities. In F. Sani (Ed.), *Self-continuity: Individual and collective perspectives* (pp. 213–226). New York: Psychology Press.

Chandra, A., Mosher, W., Copen, C., & Sionean, C. (2011). *Sexual Behavior , Sexual Attraction , and Sexual Identity in the United States: Data From the 2006–2008 National Survey of Family Growth.* National Health Statistics Report Number 36. Retrieved from: www.cdc.gov/nchs/data/nhsr/nhsr036.pdf

Chang, F., Dell, G., & Bock, K. (2006). Becoming syntactic. *Psychological Review, 113,* 234–272.

Chang, J. (2005). *Can't stop won't stop: A history of the hip-hop generation.* New York: Picador.

Chang, J. C., Ye, L., & Kan, Y. W. (2006). Correction of the sickle cell mutation in embryonic stem cells. *Proceedings of the National Academy of Sciences, 103,* 1036–1040.

Chao, R. K. (1996). Chinese and European American mothers' beliefs about the role of parenting in children's school success. *Journal of Cross-Cultural Psychology, 27,* 403–423.

Charnov, E. (2004). The optimal balance between growth rate and survival in mammals. *Evolution and Ecological Research, 6,* 307–313.

Charpak, N., Ruiz-Pelaez, J. G., Figueroa de Calume, Z., &

Charpak, Y. (2001). A randomized, controlled trial of kangaroo mother care: Results of follow-up at 1 year of corrected age. *Pediatrics, 108*(5), 1072–1079.

Chavajay, P. (2008). Organizational patterns in problem solving among Mayan fathers and children. *Developmental Psychology, 44,* 882–888.

Chavajay, P., & Rogoff, B. (2002). Schooling and traditional collaborative social organization of problem solving by Mayan mothers and children. *Developmental Psychology, 38,* 55–66.

Chen, C., & Stevenson, H. W. (1988). Cross-linguistic differences in digit span of preschool children. *Journal of Experimental Child Psychology, 46,* 150–158.

Chen, M.-Y., James, K., & Wang, E. K. (2007). Comparison of health-promoting behavior between Taiwanese and American adolescents: a cross-sectional questionnaire survey. *International Journal of Nursing Studies, 44,* 59–69.

Chen, S. (2010). In a wired world, children unable to escape cyberbullying. Retrieved October 5, 2010, Retrieved from http://www.cnn.com/2010/LIVING/10/04/youth.cyberbullying.abuse/index.html

Chen, X., & Rubin, K. H. (1994). Family conditions, parental acceptance, and social competence and aggression in Chinese children. *Social Development, 3*(3), 269–290.

Chen, Z., & Siegler, R. S. (2000). Intellectual development in childhood. In R. J. Sternberg (Ed.), *Handbook of intelligence* (pp. 92–116). New York: Cambridge University Press.

Chess, S., & Thomas, A. (1996). *Temperament: Theory and practice.* New York: Brunner-Mazel.

Chesson, H. W., Gift, T. L., & Pulver, A. L. S. (2006). The economic value of reductions in gonorrhea and syphilis incidence in the United States, 1990–2003. *Preventive Medicine: An International Journal Devoted to Practice and Theory, 43*(5), 411–415.

Chi, M. T. H. (1978). Knowledge structures and memory development. In R. S. Siegler (Ed.), *Children's thinking: What develops?* Mahwah, NJ: Lawrence Erlbaum Associates.

Chirkov, V., & Ryan, R. (2001). Parent and teacher autonomy–support in Russian and U.S. adolescents. *Journal of Cross-Cultural Psychology, 32,* 618–635.

Chisholm, K. (1998). A three-year follow-up of attachment and indiscriminate friendliness in children adopted from Romanian orphanages. *Child Development, 69,* 1092–1106.

Chomsky, N. (1959). Review of verbal behavior by B. F. Skinner. *Language, 35,* 26–58.

Chomsky, N. (1980). Initial states and steady states. In M. Piatelli-Palmerini (Ed.), *Language and learning: The debate between Jean Piaget and Noam Chomsky.* Cambridge, MA: Harvard University Press.

Chomsky, N. (1988). *Language and problems of knowledge.* Cambridge, MA: The MIT Press.

Chomsky, N. (2006). *Language and mind* (3rd ed.). New York: Cambridge University Press.

Choudhury, S., Charman, T., & Blakemore, S. J. (2009). Mentalizing and development during adolescence. In M. D. Haan & M. R. Gunnar (Eds.), *Handbook of developmental social neuroscience* (pp. 159–174). New York: Guilford Press.

Christian, K., Bachnan, H. J., & Morrison, F. J. (2001). Schooling and cognitive development. In R. J. Sternberg & E. L. Grigorenko (Eds.), *Environmental effects on cognitive abilities* (pp. 287–335). Mahwah, NJ: Lawrence Erlbaum.

Christian, P. (2002). Maternal nutrition, health, and survival. *Nutritional Review, 60,* S59–S63.

Chu, N. F. (2005). Prevalence of obesity in Taiwan. *Obesity Review, 6,* 271–274.

Chudler, E. H. (2011). *Neuroscience for kids: The brain and language.* Retrieved October 15th, 2011, from http://faculty.washington.edu/chudler/lang.html

Chugani, H., Behen, M., Muzik, O., Juhász, C., Nagy, F., & Chugani, D. (2001). Local brain functional activity following early deprivations: A study of postinstitutionalized Romanian orphans. *NeuroImage, 14,* 1290–1301.

Chumlea, W. C., Dwyer, J., Bergen, C., Burkart, J., Paranandi, L., Frydrych, A., Cockram, D. B., et al. (2003). Nutritional status assessed from anthropometric measures in the HEMO study. *Journal of Renal Nutrition, 13,* 31–38

Cicchetti, D., & Toth, S. L. (1993). Child maltreatment research and social policy: The neglected nexus. In D. Cicchetti & S. L. Toth (Eds.), *Advances in applied developmental psychology series: Vol. 8. Child abuse, child development, and social policy.* Norwood, NJ: Ablex.

Cicchetti, D., & Toth, S. L. (1998). The development of depression in children and adolescents. *American Psychologist, 53,* 221–241.

Cicchetti, D., Toth, S. L., & Maughm, A. (2000). An ecological-transactional model of child maltreatment. In A. Sameroff, M. Lewis, & J. Miller (Eds.), *Handbook of developmental psychology* (2nd ed.). New York: Plenum.

Cillessen, A., & Mayeux, L. (2004). From censure to reinforcement: Developmental changes in the association between aggression and social status. *Child Development, 75,* 147–163.

Cillessen, A. H. N., Van IJzendoorn, H. W., Van Lieshorst, C. F. M., & Hartup, W. W. (1992). Heterogeneity among peer-rejected boys: Subtypes and stabilities. *Child Development, 63,* 893–905.

Clark, C. (2003). *In sickness and in play: Children coping with chronic illness.* New Brunswick, NJ: Rutgers University Press.

Clark, E. (2004). How language acquisition builds on cognitive development. *Trends in Cognitive Sciences, 8,* 472–478.

Clark, E. V. (1995). Later lexical development and word formation. In P. Fletcher & B. MacWhinney (Eds.), *The handbook of child language* (pp. 393–412). Oxford, England: Blackwell Publishing.

Clark, E. V. (2002). *First language acquisition.* Cambridge, UK: Cambridge University Press.

Clark, E. V. (2006). Color, reference, and expertise in language acquisition. *Journal of Experimental Child Psychology, 94,* 339–343.

Clark, E. V. (2008). What shapes children's language?: Child-directed speech, conventionality, and the process of acquisition. In E. V. Clark (Ed.), *Routes to language: Studies in honor of Melissa Bowerman* (pp. 233–254). New York: Psychology Press/Taylor & Francis.

Clark, E. V. (2010). Learning a language the way it is: Conventionality and semantic domains. In E.V. Clark (Ed.), *Words and the mind: How words capture human experience* (pp. 243–265). New York: Oxford University Press.

Clark, E. V., & Bernicot, J. (2008). Repetition as ratification: How parents and children place information in common ground. *Journal of Child Language, 35,* 349–371.

Clark, E. V., & Wong, A. D.-W. (2002). Pragmatic directions about language use: Words and word meanings. *Language in Society, 31,* 181–212.

Clark, K. B., & Clark, M. P. (1939). The development of consciousness of self and the emergence of racial identity in Negro pre-school schoolchildren. *Journal of Social Psychology, 10,* 591–599.

Clark, K. B., & Clark, M. P. (1950). Emotional factors in racial identification and preference in Negro children. *Journal of Negro Education, 19,* 341–350.

Clarke, A. M., & Clarke, A. D. B. (2000). *Early experience and the life path.* London: Jessica Kingsley.

Clarke-Stewart, A., & Koch, J. B. (1983). *Children: Development through adolescence.* New York: Wiley.

Clausson, B., Granath, F., Ekbom A., Lundgren, S., Nordmark, A., Signorello, L. B., et al. (2002). Effect of caffeine exposure during pregnancy on birth weight and gestational age. *American Journal of Epidemiology, 155,* 429–436.

Clearfield, M. W., Diedrich, F. J., Smith, L. B., & Thelen, E. (2006). Young infants reach correctly in A-not-B tasks: On the development of stability and perseveration. *Infant Behavior & Development, 29,* 435–444.

Clearfield, M. W., Dineva, E., Smith, L. B., Diedrich, F. J., & Thelen, E. (2009). Cue salience and infant perseverative reaching: Tests of the dynamic field theory. *Developmental Science, 12,* 26–40.

Coale, A., Demeny, P. (1983). *Regional model life tables and stable populations.* New York: Academic Press.

Cobb, P., Gravemeijer, K., Yackel, E., McClain, K., & Whitenack, J. (1997). Mathematizing and symbolizing: The emergence of chains of signification in one first-grade classroom. In D. Kirshner & J. A. Whitson (Eds.), *Situated cognition: Social, semiotic, and psychological perspectives* (pp. 151–234). Mahwah, NJ: Lawrence Erlbaum Associates.

Code of Federal Regulations, 34. §300.7[c][10]. (2006) Federal Definition/Criteria for Specific Learning Disabilities. Retrieved January 10, 2012, from http://dpi.wi.gov/sped/ldcriter.html

Coghlan, D., & Jacobs, C. (2005). Kurt Lewin on reeducation: Foundations for action research. *Journal of Applied Behavioral Science, 41,* 2005, 444–457.

Cohen, L. B. (2002). Extraordinary claims require extraordinary controls: Reply. *Developmental Science, 5*(2), 210–212.

Cohen, L. B., & Cashon, C. H. (2006). Infant cognition. In D. Kuhn, R. S. Siegler, W. Damon, & R. M. Lerner (Eds.), *Handbook of child psychology: Vol. 2. Cognition, perception, and language* (6th ed., pp. 214–251). Hoboken, NJ: Wiley.

Cohen, L. B., Chaput, H. H., & Cashon, C. H. (2002). A constructivist model of infant cognition. *Cognitive Development, 17,* 1323–1343.

Cohen, L. B., & Marks, K. S. (2002). How infants process addition and subtraction events. *Developmental Science, 5*(2), 186–201.

Coie, J. D., & Dodge, K. A. (1998). Aggression and antisocial behavior. In N. Eisenberg (Ed.), *Handbook of child psychology: Vol. 3. Social, emotional, and personality development* (5th ed., pp. 779–882). New York: Wiley.

Colby, A., & Kohlberg, L. (1987). *The measurement of moral judgment.* New York: Cambridge University Press.

Colby, A., Kohlberg, L., Gibbs, J., & Lieberman, M. (1983). A longitudinal study of moral development. *Monographs of the Society for Research in Child Development, 48* (1–2, Serial No. 200).

Cole, M. (1996). *Cultural psychology: A once and future discipline.* Cambridge, MA: The Belknap Press of Harvard University Press.

Cole, M. (2005). Cross-cultural and historical perspectives on the developmental consequences of education. *Human Development, 48,* 195–216.

Cole, M., & The Distributed Literacy Consortium. (2006). *The fifth dimension: An after-school program built on diversity.* New York: Russell Sage.

Coles, C. D., Goldstein, F. C., Lynch, M. E., Chen, X., Kable, J. A., Johnson, K. C., et al. (2011). Memory and brain volume in adults prenatally exposed to alcohol. *Brain and Cognition, 75,* 67–77.

Coley, R. L., & Chase-Lansdale, P. L. (1998). Adolescent pregnancy and parenthood. *American Psychologist, 53*(2), 152–166.

Collins, A. (2006). Cognitive apprenticeship. In A. Collins (Ed.), *The Cambridge handbook of the learning sciences* (pp. 47–60). New York: Cambridge University Press.

Collins, W. A. (2005). Commentary: Parsing parenting: Refining models of parental influence during adolescence. *Monographs of the Society for Research in Child Development, 70*(4), 138–145.

Collins, W. A., & Laursen, B. (2006). Parent-adolescent relationships. In P. Noller & J. A. Feeney (Eds.), *Close relationships: Functions, forms and processes* (pp. 111–125). Hove, England: Psychology Press/Taylor & Francis (UK).

Collins, W. A., Laursen, B., Mortensen, N., Luebker, C., & Ferreira, M. (1997). Conflict processes and transitions in parent and peer relationships: Implications for autonomy and regulation. *Journal of Adolescent Research, 12,* 178–198.

Collins, W. A., & van Dulmen, M. (2006). The significance of middle childhood peer competence for work and relationships in early adulthood. In A. C. Huston & M. N. Ripke (Eds.), *Developmental contexts in middle childhood: Bridges to adolescence and adulthood. Cambridge studies in social and emotional development* (pp. 23–40). New York: Cambridge University Press.

Colon, A., Colon, A., & Colon, P. (2001). *A history of children.* Westport, CT: Greenwood Press.

Colwell, J., Grady, C., & Rhaiti, S. (1995). Computer games, self-eteem, and gratification of needs in adolescents. *Journal of Community and Applied Social Psychology, 5,* 195–206.

Compas, B. E. (2004). Processes of risk and resilience: Linking contexts and individuals. In R. M.. Lerner & L. Steinberg (Eds.), *Handbook of adolescence,* 2nd ed. New York: John Wiley & Sons, Inc.

Compas, B. E., Champion, J. E., Forehand, R., Cole, D. A., Reeslund, K. L., Fear, J., et al. (2010). Coping and parenting: Mediators of 12-month outcomes of a family group cognitive–behavioral preventive intervention with families of depressed parents. *Journal of Consulting and Clinical Psychology, 78,* 623–634.

Comstock, G., & Scharrer, E. (2007). *Media and the American child.* New York: Elsevier.

Conboy, B. T., & Thal, D. J. (2006). Ties between the lexicon and grammar: cross-sectional and longitudinal studies of bilingual toddlers. *Child Development, 77,* 712–735.

Conchas, G. Q. (2001). Structuring failure and success: Understanding the variability in Latino school engagement. *Harvard Educational Review. Special Issue: Immigration and education, 71*(3), 475–504.

Conley, C. S., & Rudolph, K. D. (2009). The emerging sex difference in adolescent depression: Interacting contributions of puberty and peer stress. *Development and Psychopathology, 21,* 593–620.

Connolly, J., Craig, W., Goldberg, A., & Pepler, D. (2004). Mixed gender groups, dating, and romantic relationships in early adolescence. *Journal of Research on Adolescence, 14,* 185–207.

Connolly, K., & Dalgleish, M. (1989). The emergence of a tool using skill in infancy. *Developmental Psychology, 25,* 539–549.

Connolly, J., Furman, W., & Konarski, R. (2000). The role of peers in the emergence of heterosexual romantic relationships in adolescence. *Child Development, 71,* 1395–1408.

Connor, J. M., & Ferguson-Smith, M. A. (1993). *Essential medical genetics* (3rd ed.). Oxford, England: Blackwell Publishing.

Consortium for Longitudinal Studies (Ed.). (1983) *As the twig is bent . . . lasting effects of preschool programs.* Hillsdale, NJ: Erlbaum.

Cook, J. T., & Frank, D. A. (2008). Food security, poverty, and human development in the United States. *Annals of the New York Academy of Sciences, 1136,* 193–209.

Cooper, M., Wood, P., Orcutt, H., & Albino, A. (2003). Personality and the predisposition to engage in risky or problem behaviors during adolescence. *Journal of Personality and Social Psychology, 84,* 390–410.

Coopersmith, S. (1967). *The antecedents of self-esteem.* New York: W. H. Freeman.

Corbin, P. F., & Bickford, R. G. (1955). Studies of the electroencephalogram of normal children. *Electroencephalography and Clinical Neurology, 7,* 15–28.

Cordes, S., & Brannon, E. M. (2009). Crossing the divide: Infants discriminate small from large numerosities. *Developmental Psychology, 45,* 1583–1594.

Cormier, K., Mauk, C., & Repp, A. (1998). Manual babbling in deaf and hearing infants: A longitudinal study. In E. V. Clark (Ed.), *The Proceedings of the Twenty-Ninth Annual Child Language Research Forum* (pp. 55–61). Chicago: Center for the Study of Language and Information.

Correa-Chavez, M., & Rogoff, B. (2009). Children's attention to interactions directed to others: Guatemalan Mayan and European American patterns. *Developmental Psychology, 45,* 630–641.

Costello, D. (2000, June 9). Spanking makes a comeback. *Wall Street Journal.*

Costello, D. M., Swendsen, J., Rose, J. S., & Dierker, L. C. (2008, April). Risk and protective factors associated with trajectories of depressed mood from adolescence to early adulthood. *Journal of Consulting and Clinical Psychology, 76,* 173–183.

Costello, E. J., Compton, S. N., Keeler, G., & Angold, A. (2003, October). Relationships between poverty and psychopathology: A natural experiment. *Journal of the American Medical Association, 290,* 2023–2029.

Côté, J., & Bynner, J. M. (2008). Changes in the transition to adulthood in the UK and Canada: The role of structure and agency in emerging adulthood. *Journal of Youth Studies, 11,* 251–268.

Côté, J. E. (2009). Identity formation and self-development in adolescence. In R. M. Lerner & L. Steinberg (Eds.), *Handbook of adolescent psychology, Vol 1: Individual bases of adolescent development* (3rd ed.). Hoboken, NJ: John Wiley & Sons.

Cotton, A. (2006). Camfed founder receives Women of the Year award. Retrieved October 10, 2008, from http://uk.camfed.org/news/2006/03/08/marking-international-womens-day/#more-71

Courage, M. L., Reynolds, G. D., & Richards, J. E. (2006) Infants' attention to patterned stimuli: Developmental change from 3 to 12 months of age. *Child Development* 77(3), 680–695.

Courage, M. L., & Setliff, A. E. (2010). When babies watch television: Attention-getting, attention-holding, and the implications for learning from video material. *Developmental Review, 30,* 220–238.

Cowan, P. A. (1978). *Piaget: With feeling: Cognitive, social, and emotional dimensions.* New York: Holt, Rinehart and Winston.

Cox, S. J., Mezulis, A. H., & Hyde, J. S. (2010). The influence of child gender role and maternal feedback to child stress on the emergence of the gender difference in depressive rumination in adolescence. *Developmental Psychology, 46,* 842–852.

Cressman, V. L., Balaban, J., Steinfeld, S., Shemyakin, A., Graham, P., Parisot, N., & Moore, H. (2010). Prefrontal cortical inputs to the basal amygdala undergo pruning during late adolescence in the rat. *Journal of Comparative Neurology, 518,* 2693–2709.

Creveling, C. C., Varela, R. E., Weems, C. F., & Corey, D. M. (2010). Maternal control, cognitive style, and childhood anxiety: A test of a theoretical model in a multi-ethnic sample. *Journal of Family Psychology, 24,* 439–448.

Crewe, S. (2003). African-American grandparent caregivers: Eliminating double jeopardy in social policy. In T. Bent-Goodley (Ed.), *African-American social workers and social policy.* Binghamton, NY: Harworth Social Work Practice Press.

Crick, N. R., & Dodge, K. A. (1999). "Superiority" is in the eye of the beholder: A comment on Sutton-Smith and Swettenham. *Social Development, 8,* 128–131.

Crick, N. R., & Ladd, G. W. (1993). Children's perceptions of their peer experiences: Attributions, loneliness, social anxiety and social avoidance. *Developmental Psychology, 29,* 244–254.

Crick, N. R., Ostrov, J. M., & Kawabata, Y. (2007). Relational aggression and gender: An overview. In D. J. Flannery, A. T. Vazsonyi, & I. D. Waldman (Eds.), *The Cambridge handbook of violent behavior and aggression* (pp. 245–259). New York: Cambridge University Press.

Crosnoe, R. (2006, March). Health and the education of children from racial/ethnic minority and immigrant families. *Journal of Health and Social Behavior,* 47(1), 77–93.

Cross, W. E. (2003). Tracing the historical origins of youth delinquency and violence: Myths and realities about black culture. *Journal of Social Issues,* 59(1), 67–82.

Cross, W. E., & Cross, T. B. (2008). Theory, research, and models. In S. M. Quintana & C. McKown (Eds.), *Handbook of race, racism, and the developing child* (pp. 154–181). Hoboken, NJ: John Wiley & Sons.

Crowther, B. (1999). Writing as performance: Young girls' diaries. In R. Josselson & A. Lieblich (Eds.), *Making meaning in the narrative study of lives.* Thousand Oaks, CA: Sage Publications.

Csikszentmihalyi, M., & Larson, R. (1984). *Being adolescent: Conflict and growth in the teenage years.* New York: Basic Books.

Csikszentmihalyi, M., & Larson, R. (1987). The experience sampling method. *Journal of Nervous and Mental Disease, 175,* 526–536.

Cunningham, F. G., MacDonald, P. C., Gant, N. F., Leveno, K. J., Gilstrap, L. C., III, Hankins, G. D. V., & Clark, S. L. (2001). *Williams obstetrics* (21st ed.). Stamford, CT: Appleton & Lange.

Cunningham, S., Elo, I., Herbst, K., & Hosegood, V. (2010). Prenatal development in fural South Africa: Relationship between birth weight and access to fathers and grandparents. *Population Studies, 64,* 229–246.

Cunningham, W. A., & Zelazo, P. D. (2010). The development of iterative reprocessing: Implications for affect and its regulation. In W. A. Cunningham, Zelazo, Philip David (Ed.), *Developmental social cognitive neuroscience* (pp. 81–98). New York: Psychology Press.

Curtis, H. (1979). *Biology.* New York: Worth.

Curtiss, S., Fromkin, V., Krashen, S., Rigler, D., & Rigler, M. (1974). The Linguistic Development of Genie. *Language, 50,* 528–554.

Dahl, R. E., & Hariri, A. R. (2005). Lessons from G. Stanley Hall: Connecting new research in biological sciences to the study of adolescent development. *Journal of Research on Adolescence, 15,* 367–382.

Dahl, R. E., & Lewin, D. (2002). Pathways to adolescent health: Sleep regulation and behavior. *Journal of Adolescent Health, 31,* 175–184.

Daiute, C. (2010). *Human Development and Political Violence.* New York: Cambridge University Press.

Damon, W., & Hart, D. (1988). *Self-understanding in childhood and adolescence.* Cambridge, England: Cambridge University Press.

D'Angiulli, A., & Siegel, L. S. (2003). Cognitive functioning as measured by the WISC-R: Do children with learning disabilities have distinctive patterns of performance? *Journal of Learning Disabilities, 36,* 48–58.

Darwin, C. (1859/1958). *The origin of species.* New York: Penguin.

Darwin, C. (1872). *The expression of emotion in man and animals.* London: John Murray.

Dasen, P. R. (1972). Cross-cultural Piagetian research: A summary. *Journalm of Cross-Cultural Psychology, 3,* 29–39.

Dasen, P. R. (1973). Preliminary study of sensori-motor development in Baoule children. *Early Child Development & Care, 2,* 345–354.

David, H. P. (1981). Unwantedness: Longitudinal studies of Prague children born to women twice denied abortions for the same pregnancy and matched controls. In P. Ahmed (Ed.), *Pregnancy, childbirth, and parenthood.* New York: Elsevier.

Davidov, M., & Grusec, J. E. (2006). Untangling the links of parental responsiveness to distress and warmth to child outcomes. *Child Development, 77,* 44–58.

Davies, H. D., & Fitzgerald, H. E. (Eds.). (2008). *Obesity in childhood and adolescence:Vol. 1. Medical, biological, and social issues. Praeger perspectives: Child psychology and mental health.* Westport, CT: Praeger Publishers/Greenwood Publishing Group.

Davila, J., & Steinberg, S. J. (2006). Depression and romantic dysfunction during adolescence. In T. E. Joiner, J. S. Brown, & J. Kistner (Eds.), *The interpersonal, cognitive, and social nature of depression* (pp. 23–41). Mahwah, NJ: Lawrence Erlbaum Associates.

Davis, B. L., MacNeilage, P. F., Matyear, C. L., & Powell, J. K. (2000). Prosodic correlates of stress in babbling: An acoustical study. *Child Development, 71,* 1258-1275.

Davis, C., Yanasak, N., Allison, J., Tomporowski, P., et al. (2011). Exercise improves executive function and achievement and alters brain activation in overweight children: A randomized, controlled trial. *Health Psychology, 30,* 91–98.

Deák, G. O. (2006). Do children really confuse appearance and reality? *Trends in Cognitive Sciences, 10*(12), 546–550.

DeCasper, A. J., & Spence M. J. (1986). Prenatal maternal speech influences newborn's perceptions of speech sounds. *Infant Behavior and Development, 3,* 133–150.

De Goede, I. H. A., Branje, S. J. T., & Meeus, W. H. J. (2009). Developmental changes and gender differences in adolescents' perceptions of friendships. *Journal of Adolescence, 32,* 1105–1123.

Delaney, C. (2000). Making babies in a Turkish village. In J. S. DeLoache & A. Gottlieb (Eds.), *A world of babies: Imagined childcare guides for seven societies.* Cambridge, England: Cambridge University Press.

de Lemos, C. (2000). Questioning the notion of development: The case of language acquisition. *Culture & Psychology, 6*(2), 169–182.

Deligeoroglou, E., & Tsimaris, P. (2010). Menstrual disturbances in puberty. *Best practice research Clinical obstetrics gynaecology, 24,* 157–171.

DeLoache, J. (2011). Early development of the understanding and use of symbolic artifacts. In U. Goswami (Ed.), *Wiley-Blackwell handbook of childhood cognitive development* (2 ed.). Malden, MA: Blackwell.

DeLoache, J., Uttal, D., & Rosengren, K. (2005). Scale errors offer evidence for a perception-action dissociation early in life. *Science, 304,* 1027–1029.

Denham, S., Caverly, S., Schmidt, M., Blair, K., DeMulder, E., Caal, S., Hamada, H., & Mason, T. (2002). Preschool understanding of emotions: Contributions to classroom anger and aggression. *Journal of Child Psychology and Psychiatry, 43,* 901–916.

Denizet-Lewis, B. (2004, May 30). Friends, friends with benefits and the benefits of the local mall. *New York Times Magazine.*

Dennis, W., & Dennis, M. (1940). The effect of cradling practices upon the onset of walking in Hopi children. *Journal of Genetic Psychology, 56,* 77–86.

Dent-Read, C. (1997). A naturalistic study of metaphor development: Seeing and seeing as. In C. Dent-Read & P. Zukow-Goldring (Eds.), *Evolving explanations of development* (pp. 255–296). Washington, DC: American Psychological Association.

deRegnier, R.-A., Long, J. D., Georgieff, M. K., & Nelson, C. A. (2007). Using event-related potentials to study perinatal nutrition and brain development in infants of diabetic mothers. *Developmental Neuropsychology, 31*(3), 379–396.

Devaney, B. L., Ellwood, M. R., & Love, J. M. (1997). Programs that mitigate the effects of poverty on children. *The Future of Children, 7,* 88–112.

Devescovi, A., Caselli, M. C., Marchione, D., Pasqualetti, P., Reilly, J., & Bates, E. (2005). A cross-linguistic study of the relationship between grammar and lexical development. *Journal of Child Language, 32*(4), 759–786.

De Villiers, J. G., & De Villiers, P. A. (1978). *Language acquisition.* Cambridge, MA: Harvard University Press.

De Vries, J. I., Hay V. G., & Prechtl, H. F. (1982). The emergence of fetal behaviour. I. Qualitative aspects. *Early Human Development, 7,* 301–322.

de Vries, M. W., & de Vries, M. R. (1977). Cultural relativity of toilet training readiness: A perspective from East Africa. *Pediatrics 60,* 170.

De Vries, R. (1969). Constancy of genetic identity in the years three to six. *Monographs of the Society for Research in Child Development, 34* (Serial No. 127).

de Vrijer, B., Harthoorn-Lasthuizen, E. J., & Oosterbaan, H. P. (1999). The incidence of irregular antibodies in pregnancy: A prospective study in the region of the 's-Hertogenbosch. *Nederlands Tijdschrift voor Geneeskunde, 143,* 2523–2527.

Dewald, J. F., Meijer, A. M., Oort, F. J., Kerkhof, G. A., & Bögels, S. M. (2010). The influence of sleep quality, sleep duration and sleepiness on school performance in children and adolescents: A meta-analytic review. *Sleep Medicine Reviews, 14*(3), 179–189.

De Wolff, M., & van IJzendoorn, M. H. (1997). Sensitivity and attachment: A meta-analysis on parental antecedents of infant attachment. *Child Development, 68,* 571–591.

Dhariwal, A., Connolly, J., Paciello, M., Caprara, G. V. (2009). Adolescent peer relationships and emerging adult romantic styles: A longitudinal study of youth in an Italian community. *Journal of Adolescent Research 24,* 579–600.

Diamond, A. (1991). Neuropsychological insights into the meaning of object concept development. In R. Gelman (Ed.), *The epigenesis of mind: Essays on biology and cognition* (pp. 67–110). Mahwah, NJ: Lawrence Erlbaum Associates.

Diamond, A. (2000). Close interrelation of motor development and cognitive development and of the cerebellum and prefrontal cortex. *Child Development, 71,* 44–56.

Diamond, A. (2002a). A model system for studying the role of dopamine in prefrontal cortex during early development in humans. In M. H. Johnson & Y. Munakata (Eds.), *Brain development and cognition: A reader* (pp. 441–493). Malden, MA: Blackwell Publishing.

Diamond, A. (2002b). Normal development of prefrontal cortex from birth to young adulthood: Cognitive functions, anatomy, and biochemistry. In D. Stuss & R. Knight (Eds.), *Principles of frontal lobe functioning* (466–503). New York: Oxford University Press.

Diamond, A., & Amso, D. (2008). Contributions of neuroscience to our understanding of cognitive development. *Current Directions in Psychological Science, 17,* 26–40.

Dickens, W. T., & Flynn, J. R. (2006, October). Black Americans reduce the racial IQ gap: Evidence from standardization samples. *Psychological Science, 17*(10), 913–920.

Diener, M. L., Nievar, M. A., & Wright, C. (2003). Attachment security among mothers and their young children living in poverty: Associations with maternal, child, and contextual factors. *Merrill-Palmer Quarterly, 49*(2), 154–182.

Dietz, T. (2000). Disciplining children: Characteristics associated with the use of corporal punishment. *Child Abuse and Neglect, 24,* 1529–1542.

Dimant, R. J., & Bearison, D. J. (1991). Development of formal reasoning during successive peer interactions. *Developmental Psychology, 27,* 277–284.

Dishion, T. J. (1990). The family ecology of boys' peer relations in middle childhood. *Child Development, 61,* 874–892.

Dishion, T. J., McCord, J., & Poulin, F. (1999). When interventions harm. *American Psychologist, 54,* 755–764.

Dishion, T. J., & Patterson, G. R. (2006). The development and ecology of antisocial behavior in children and adolescents. In D. Cicchetti & D. J. Cohen (Eds.), *Developmental psychopathology: Vol. 3. Risk, disorder, and adaptation* (2nd ed., pp. 503–541). Hoboken, NJ: John Wiley & Sons.

Dishion, T. J., Véronneau, M.-H., & Myers, M. W. (2010). Cascading peer dynamics underlying the progression from problem behavior to violence in early to late adolescence. *Development and Psychopathology, 22,* 603–619.

Dittmar, H., Halliwell, E., & Ive, S. (2006). Does Barbie make girls want to be thin? The effect of experimental exposure to images of dolls on the body image of 5- to 8-year-old girls. *Developmental Psychology, 42,* 283–292.

Dixon, A. C., Schoonmaker, C. T., & Philliber, W. W. (2000). A journey toward womanhood: Effects of an Afrocentric approach to pregnancy prevention among African-American adolescent girls. *Adolescence, 35,* 425–429.

Do, J. T., Han, D. W., & Schöler, H. R. (2006). Reprogramming somatic gene activity by fusion with pluripotent cells. *Stem Cell Reviews, 2,* 257–264.

Dodge, K. A., Coie, J., & Lynam, D. (2006) Aggression and antisocial behavior in youth. In N. Eisenberg, W. Damon, & R. M. Lerner (Eds.), *Handbook of child psychology: Vol. 3. Social, emotional, and personality development* (6th ed., pp. 719–788). Hoboken, NJ: John Wiley & Sons.

Dodge, K. A., Greenberg, M. T., & Malone, P. S. (2008). Testing an idealized dynamic cascade model of the development of serious violence in adolescence. *Child Development, 79,* 1907–1927.

Dodge, K. A., Lansford, J. E., Burks, V. S., Bates, J. E., Pettit, G. S., Fontaine, R., & Price, J. M. (2003). Peer rejection and social information-processing factors in the development of aggressive behavior problems in children. *Child Development, 74,* 374–393.

Dodge, K. A., Malone, P. S., Lansford, J. E., Miller, S., & Pettit, G. S. (2009). A dynamic cascade model of the development of substance-use onset: I. Introduction. *Monographs of the Society for Research in Child Development, 74*, 1–31.

Dodge, K. A., & Pettit, G. S. (2003, March). A biopsychosocial model of the development of chronic conduct problems in adolescence. *Developmental Psychology. Special Issue: Violent children, 39*, 349–371.

Domino, G. (1992). Cooperation and competition in Chinese and American children. *Journal of Cross-Cultural Psychology, 23*, 456–467.

Dondi, M., Simion, F., & Caltran, G. (1999). Can newborns discriminate between their own cry and the cry of another newborn infant? *Developmental Psychology, 35*, 323–334.

D'Onofrio, B. M., Turkheimer, E., Emery, R. E., Harden, K. P., Slutske, W. S., Heath, A. C., et al. (2007). A genetically informed study of the intergenerational transmission of marital instability. *Journal of Marriage and Family, 69*, 793–809.

Dore, J. (1979). Conversational acts and the acquisition of language. In E. Ochs & B. B. Schieffelin (Eds.), *Developmental Pragmatics*. New York: Academic Press.

Dorgan, B. L. (2010). The tragedy of Native American youth suicide. *Psychological Services, 7*, 213–218.

Dossett, D., & Burns, B. (2000). The development of children's knowledge of attention and resource allocation in single and dual tasks. *The Journal of Genetic Psychology 16*(2), 216–234.

Douple, E. B., Mabuchi, K., Cullings, H. M., Preston, D. L., Kodama, K., Shimizu, Y., et al. (2011). Long-term radiation-related health effects in a unique human population: Lessons learned from the atomic bomb survivors of Hiroshima and Nagasaki. *Disaster Medicine and Public Health Preparedness, 5*, Suppl. 1:S122–133.

Draganova, R., Eswaran, H., Murphy, P., Lowery, C., & Preissl, H. (2007). Serial magnetoencephalographic study of fetal and newborn auditory discriminative evoked responses. *Early Human Development, 83*, 199–207.

Drewnowski, A., & Darmon, N. (2005). Food choices and diet costs: an economic analysis. *The Journal of nutrition, 135*, 900–904.

Driessen, R., Leyendecker, B., Schölmerich, A., & Harwood, R. (2010). Everyday experiences of 18- to 36-month-old children from migrant families: The influence of host culture and migration experience. *Early Child Development and Care, 180*, 1143–1163.

Dromi, E. (1999). Early lexical development. In M. Barrett (Ed.), *The development of language* (pp. 99–131). Philadelphia: Psychology Press/Taylor & Francis.

Dromi, E., & Zaidman-Zait. (2011). Interrelations between communicative behaviors at the outset of speech: Parents as observers. *Journal of child language, 38*, 101–120.

Drukker, M., & van Os, J. (2003). Mediators of neighbourhood socio-economic deprivation and quality of life. *Social Psychiatry and Psychiatric Epidemiology, 38*, 698–706

Dubois, L., Farmer, A., Girard, M., & Peterson, K. (2006). Preschool children's eating behaviors are related to dietary adequacy and body weight. *European Journal of Clinical Nutrition, 61*, 846–855.

Dufur, M. J., Howell, N. C., Downey, D. B., Ainsworth, J. W., & Lapray, A. J. (2010). Sex differences in parenting behaviors in single-mother and single-father households. *Journal of Marriage and Family, 72*, 113–130.

Duncan, G., & Raudenbush, W. (1999). Assessing the effects of context in studies of children and youth development. *Educational Psychology, 34*, 29–41.

Dunn, J. (1988). *The beginnings of social understanding*. Cambridge, MA: Harvard University Press.

Dunphy, D. C. (1963). The social structure of urban adolescent peer groups. *Sociometry, 26*, 230–246.

Durham, W. (1991). *Coevolution: Genes, culture, and human diversity*. Palo Alto, CA: Stanford University Press.

Durston, S., & Casey, B. J. (2006). What have we learned about cognitive development from neuroimaging? *Neuropsychologia. Special Issue: Advances in developmental cognitive neuroscience, 44*(11), 2149–2157.

Dweck, C. S. (1999). *Self-theories: Their role in motivation, personality, and development*. Philadelphia, PA: Psychology Press/Taylor & Francis.

Dweck, C. S., & Master, A. (2009). Self-theories and motivation: Students' beliefs about intelligence. In K. R. Wenzel & A. Wigfield (Eds.), *Handbook of motivation at school* (pp. 123–140). New York: Routledge/Taylor & Francis.

Dybdahl, R. (2001). Children and mothers in war: An outcome study of a psychosocial intervention program. *Child Development, 72*, 1214–1230.

Dyson, M. (1995) *Between god and gangsta rap*. New York: Oxford University Press.

Dyson, M. (2007). *Know what I mean? Reflections on hip-hop*, New York: Basic Civitas Books.

Eagly, A. H., & Koenig, A. M. (2006). Social role theory of sex differences and similarities: Implication for prosocial behavior. In K. Dindia & D. J. Canary (Eds.), *Sex differences and similarities in communication* (2nd ed., pp. 161–177). Mahwah, NJ: Lawrence Erlbaum Associates.

Eccles, J., Brown, B. V., & Templeton, J. (2008). A developmental framework for selecting indicators of well-being during the adolescent and young adult years. In B. V. Brown (Ed.), *Key indicators of child and youth well-being: Completing the picture* (pp. 197–236). Mahwah, NJ: Lawrence Erlbaum Associates.

Eckert, P. (1995). Trajectory and forms of institutional participation. In L. J. Crockett & A. C. Crouter (Eds.), *Pathways through adolescence: Individual development in relation to social contexts* (pp. 175–195). Mahwah, NJ: Lawrence Erlbaum Associates.

Eckes, T., & Trautner, H. (Eds.). (2000). *The developmental social psychology of gender*. Mahwah, NJ: Erlbaum.

Edvardsen, J., Torgersen, S., Roysamb, E., Lygren, S., Skre, I., Onstad, S., et al. (2008). Heritability of bipolar spectrum disorders. Unity or heterogeneity? *Journal of Affective Disorders, 106*, 229–240.

Egeland, G. M., Skjaerven, R., & Irgens, L. M. (2000). Birth characteristics of women who develop gestational diabetes: Population-based study. *British Medical Journal, 321*, 546–547.

Eggebeen, D. J. (2002). The changing course of fatherhood: Men's experiences with children in demographic perspective. *Journal of Family Issues, 23*, 486–505.

Eggebeen, D. J., Dew, J., & Knoester, C. (2010). Fatherhood and men's lives at middle age. *Journal of Family Issues, 31*, 113–130.

Eimas, P. D. (1985). The perception of speech in early infancy. *Scientific American, 252*(1), 66–72.

Eisen, M., Zellman, G. I., Leibowitz, A., Chow, W. K., & Evans, J. R. (1983). Factors discriminating pregnancy resolution decisions of unmarried adolescents. *Genetic Psychology Monographs, 108*, 69–95.

Eisenberg, N. (1992). *The caring child*. Cambridge, MA: Harvard University Press.

Eisenberg, N. (2010). Empathy-related responding: Links with self-regulation, moral judgment, and moral behavior. In N. Eisenberg (Ed.), *Prosocial motives, emotions, and behavior: The better angels of our nature* (pp. 129–148). Washington, DC: American Psychological Association.

Eisenberg, N., Eggum, N. D., & Edwards, A. (2010). Empathy-related responding and moral development. In William F. Arsenio & E. A.

Lemerise (Eds.), *Emotions, aggression, and morality in children: Bridging development and psychopathology* (pp. 115–135). Washington, DC: American Psychological Association.

Eisenberg, N., & Fabes, R. A. (2006). Emotion regulation and children's socioemotional competence. In L. Balter & C. S. Tamis-LeMonda (Eds.), *Child psychology: A handbook of contemporary issues* (2nd ed., pp. 357–381). New York: Psychology Press.

Eisenberg, N., Fabes, R. A., Murphy, B., Karbon, M., Smith, M., & Maszk, P. (1996). The relations of children's dispositional empathy–related responding to their emotionality, regulation, and social functioning. *Developmental Psychology, 32,* 195–209.

Eisenberg, N., Fabes, R. A., Shepard, S., Murphy, B., Jones, J., & Guthrie, I. (1998). Contemporaneous and longitudinal prediction of children's sympathy from dispositional regulation and emotionality. *Developmental Psychology, 34,* 910–924.

Eisenberg, N., Hofer, C., & Vaughan, J. (2007). Effortful control and its socioemotional consequences. In J. J. Gross (Ed.), *Handbook of emotion regulation* (pp. 287–306). New York: Guilford Press.

Eisenberg, N., Losoya, S., & Spinrad, T. (2003). Affect and prosocial responding. In R. Davidson, K. Scherer, & H. Goldsmith (Eds.), *Handbook of affective sciences.* Oxford, England: Oxford University Press.

Eisenberg, N., Spinrad, T. L., & Sadovsky, A. (2006). Empathy related responding in children. In M. Killen & J. G. Smetana (Eds.), *Handbook of moral development* (pp. 517–549). Mahwah, NJ: Lawrence Erlbaum Associates.

Eisenberg, N., Zhou, Q., Spinrad, T., Valiente, C., Fabes, R., & Liew, J. (2005). Relations among positive parenting, children's effortful control, and externalizing problems: A three-way longitudinal study. *Child Development, 76,* 1055–1071.

Eisenberg, N., Zhou, Q., & Koller, S. (2001). Brazilian adolescents' prosocial moral judgement and behavior: Relationships to sympathy, perspective taking, gender-role orientation, and demographic characteristics. *Child Development, 72,* 518–534.

Elder, G. H. J. (1998). The life course and human development. In W. Damon & R. M. Lerner (Eds.), *Handbook of child psychology: Vol. 1. Theoretical models of human development* (5th ed., pp. 939–992). New York: Wiley.

Elias, C., & Berk, L. (2002). Self-regulation in young children: Is there a role for sociodramatic play? *Early Childhood Research Quarterly, 17,* 216–238.

Ellis, B., & Bjorklund, D. (Eds.). (2005). *Origins of the social mind: Evolutionary psychology and child development.* New York: Guilford Press.

Ellis, S. A., & Gauvain, M. (1992). Social and cultural influences on children's collaborative interactions. In L. T. Winegar & J. Valsiner (Eds.), *Children's development within social context* (pp. 155–180). Mahwah, NJ: Lawrence Erlbaum Associates.

Ellis, S., & Siegler, R. S. (1997). Planning as a strategy choice, or why don't children plan when they should? In S. L. Friedman & E. K. Scholnick (Eds.), *The developmental psychology of planning: Why, how, and when do we plan?* (pp. 183–208). Mahwah, NJ: Lawrence Erlbaum Associates.

Ellis, S. J., Kitzinger, C., & Wilkinson, S. (2002). Attitudes towards lesbians and gay men and support for lesbian and gay human rights among psychology students. *Journal of Homosexuality, 44,* 121–138.

Ellis, W. E., & Zarbatany, L. (2007). Explaining friendship formation and friendship stability. The role of children's and friends' aggression and victimization. *Merrill-Palmer Quarterly, 53*(1), 79–104.

Elman, J. L., Bates, E. A., Johnson, M. J., Karmilof-Smith, A., Parsi, D., & Plunkett, K. (1996). *Rethinking innateness: A connectionist perspective on development.* Cambridge, MA: The MIT Press.

El-Sheikh, M., Buckhalt, J., Mize, J., & Acebo, C. (2006). Marital conflict and disruption of children's sleep. *Child Development, 77,* 31–43.

Emde, R. N., & Hewitt, J. K. (Eds.). (2001). *Infancy to early childhood: Genetic and environmental influences on developmental change.* New York: Oxford University Press.

Enfield, N. J., & Levinson, S. C. (2006). *Roots of human sociality: Culture, cognition and interaction* (Wenner-Gren International Symposium Series). Oxford, England: Berg Publishers. New York: Oxford University Press.

Enns, G. M., Koch, R., Brumm, V., Blakely, E., Suter, R., & Jurecki, E. (2010). Suboptimal outcomes in patients with PKU treated early with diet alone: Revisiting the evidence. *Molecular Genetics and Metabolism, 101,* 99–109.

Erdley, C., & Asher, S. (1999). A social goals perspective on children's social competence. *Journal of Emotional and Behavioral Disorders, 7*(3), 156–167.

Erikson, E. H. (1950). *Childhood and society.* New York: W. W. Norton.

Erikson, E. H. (1963a). *Childhood and society* (2nd ed.) New York: W. W. Norton.

Erikson, E. H. (1963b). *The challenge of youth.* New York: Doubleday.

Erikson, E. H. (1968a). *Identity: Youth and crisis.* New York: W. W. Norton.

Erikson, E. H. (1968b). Life cycle. In D. L. Sills (Ed.), *International encyclopedia of the social sciences: Vol. 9.* New York: Crowell, Collier.

Erickson, F., & Mohatt, G. (1982). Cultural organization of participation structures in two classrooms of Indian students. In G. Spindler (Ed.), *Doing the ethnography of schooling: Educational anthropology in action* (pp. 132–175). Prospect Heights, IL: Waveland Press.

Erikson, M. F., Sroufe, L. A., & Egeland, B. (1985). The relationship between the quality of attachment and behavior problems in preschool in a high-risk sample. *Monographs of the Society for Research in Child Development, 50,* 1–2, No. 209.

Eshleman, L. (2003) *Becoming a family: Promoting healthy attachments with your adopted child.* Dallas, TX: Taylor Publishing Company.

Estevez, P. A., Held, C. M., Holtzmann, C. A., Perez, C. A., Perez, J. P., Heiss, J., Garrido, M., & Peirano, P. (2002). Polysomnographic pattern recognition for automated classification of sleep-waking states in infants. *Medical and Biological Engineering and Computing, 40,* 105–113.

Estell, D. B., Farmer, T. W., Cairns, R. B., & Cairns, B. D. (2002). Social relations and academic achievement in inner-city early elementary classrooms. *International Journal of Behavioral Development, 26,* 518–528.

Evans, G. W. (2006.) Child development and the physical environment. *Annual Review of Psychology, 57,* 423–451.

Fabricius, W. V., & Hagen, J. W. (1984). Use of casual attributions about recall performance to assess metamemory and predict strategic memory behavior in young children. *Developmental Psychology, 20*(5), 975–987.

Fadiman, A. (1998). *The spirit catches you and you fall down: A Hmong child, her American doctors, and the collision of two cultures.* New York: Farrar, Straus & Giroux.

Fan, G. X., Qing, L. X., Jun, Y., & Mei, Z. (1999). Molecular studies and prenatal diagnosis of phenylkletonuria in Chinese patients. *Southeast Asian Journal of Tropical Medicine & Public Health, 30* (Suppl. 2), 63–65.

Fanaroff, A. A., & Martin, R. J. (Eds.). (1997). *Neonatal-perinatal medicine: Diseases of the fetus and infant.* St. Louis, MO: Mosby.

Fantz, R. L. (1961). The origins of form perception. *Scientific American, 204*(5) 66–72.

Fantz, R. L. (1963). Pattern vision in newborn infants. *Science, 140,* 296–297.

Farrington, D. (2004). Conduct disorder, aggression, and delinquency. In R. M. Lerner & L. Steinberg (Eds.), *Handbook of adolescent psychology* (2nd ed.). Hoboken, NJ: John Wiley & Sons.

Farver, J., Eppe, S., & Ballon, D. (2006). Acculturation and family characteristics that facilitate literacy development among Latino children. In M. Bornstein & L. Cole (Eds.), Acculturation and parent-child relationships: Measurement and development. Mahwah, NJ: Lawrence Erlbaum Associates.

Fauth, R. C., Leventhal, T., & Brooks-Gunn, J. (2007). Welcome to the neighborhood? Long-term impacts of moving to low-poverty neighborhoods on poor children's and adolescents' outcomes. *Journal of Research on Adolescence, 17,* 249–284.

Feinberg, I., & Campbell, I. G. (2010). Sleep EEG changes during adolescence: an index of a fundamental brain reorganization. *Brain and Cognition, 72,* 56–65.

Feinberg, I., March, J. D., Fein, G., Floyd, T. C., Walker, J. M., & Price, L. (1978). Period and amplitude analysis of 0.5-3 c/sec activity in NREM sleep of young adults. *Electroencephalography and Clinical Neurophysiology, 44*(2), 202–213.

Feiring, C. (1996). Lovers as friends: Developing conscious views of romance in adolescence. *Journal of Research on Adolescence, 7,* 214–224.

Feldman, D. H. (2004). Piaget's stages: The unfinished symphony of cognitive development. *New Ideas in Psychology, 22,* 175–231.

Fenson, L., Dale, P. S., Reznick, J. S., Bates, E., Thal, O. J., & Pettnick, S. J. (1994). Variability in early communicative development. *Monographs for Research in Child Development, 59*(5, Serial No. 242).

Ferholt, B., & Lecusay, R. (2010). Adult and child development in the zone of proximal development: Socratic dialogue in a playworld. *Mind, Culture, and Activity, 17,* 59–83.

Fernald, A. (1991). Prosody in speech to children: Prelinguistic and linguistic functions. In R. Vasta (Ed.), *Annals of child development: Vol. 8.* London: Kingley.

Fernald, A. (2001). Hearing, listening, and understanding: Auditory development in infancy. In G. Bremner & A. Fogel (Eds.), *Blackwell handbook of infant development* (pp. 35–70). Malden, MA: Blackwell Publishing.

Fernald, A., Perfors, A., & Marchman, V. (2006). Picking up speed in understanding: Speech processing efficiency and vocabulary growth across the 2nd year. *Developmental Psychology, 42*(1), 98–116.

Fernald, L. C., Gunnar, M. R. (2009). Poverty-alleviation program participation and salivary cortisol in very low-income children. *Social Science and Medicine, 68,* 2180—2189.

Fernandez, M., Blass, E., Hernandez-Reif, M., Field, T., & Miguel, S. (2003). Sucrose attenuates a negative electroencephaliographic response to aversive stimulus for newborns. *Journal of Developmental and Behavioral Pediatrics, 24,* 261–266.

Ferran, L. (2010). Michelle Obama: Let's Move Initiative battles childhood obesity. Retrieved from http://abcnews.go.com/GMA/Health/michelle-obama-childhood-obesity-initiative/story?id=9781473&page=1

Ferrer-Wreder, L., Lorente, C. C., Kurtines, W., Briones, E., Bussell, J., Berman, S., & Arrufat, O. (2002). Promoting identity development in marginalized youth. *Journal of Adolescent Research, 17,* 168–187.

Field, T. (2010). Postpartum depression effects on early interactions, parenting, and safety practices: A review. *Infant Behavior & Development, 33,* 1–6.

Field, T. M. (1979). Differential behavioral and cardiac responses of 3-month-old infants to a mirror and peer. *Infant Behavior & Development, 2*(2), 179–184.

Field, T. M., Diego, M., & Sanders, C. (2001). Exercise is positively related to adolescents' relationships and academics. *Adolescence, 36,* 106–110.

Field, T. M., Diego, M., Hernandez-Reif, M., & Fernandez, M. (2007a). Depressed mothers' newborns show less discrimination of other newborns' cry sounds. *Infant Behavior & Development, 30,* 431–435.

Fields, W. M., Segerdahl, P., & Savage-Rumbaugh, S. (2007). The material practices of ape language research. In J. Valsiner & A. Rosa (Eds.), *The Cambridge handbook of sociocultural psychology* (pp. 164–186). New York: Cambridge University Press.

Fiese, B., Gundersen, C., Koester, B., & Washington, L. (2011). Household food insecurity: Serious concerns for child development. *SRCD Social Policy Report, 25* (3), 1–19.

Fireman, G., & Kose, G. (2002, December). The effect of self-observation on children's problem solving. *Journal of Genetic Psychology, 163,* 410–423.

Fischer, K. W., & Yan, Z. (2002). The development of dynamic skill theory. In R. Lickliter & D. Lewkowicz (Eds.), *Conceptions of development: Lessons from the laboratory.* Hove, England: Psychology Press.

Fishbein, H. D. (1976). *Evolution, development and children's learning.* Pacific Palisades, CA: Goodyear.

Fisher, C., Klingler, S., & Song, H. (2006). What does syntax say about space? 2-year-olds use sentence structure to learn new prepositions. *Cognition, 101*(1), b19–b29.

Fivush, R., & Nelson, K. (2006, March) Parent-child reminiscing locates the self in the past. *British Journal of Developmental Psychology, 24*(1), 235–251.

Flavell, J. H. (1971). Stage-related properties of cognitive development. *Cognitive Psychology, 2,* 421–453.

Flavell, J. H. (2007). Theory-of-mind development: Retrospect and prospect. In G. W. Ladd (Ed.), *Appraising the human developmental sciences. Landscapes of childhood series* (pp. 38–55). Detroit, MI: Wayne State University Press.

Flavell, J. H., Flavell, E. R., Green, F. L., & Korfmacher, J. E. (1990). Do young children think of television images as pictures or real objects? *Journal of Broadcasting & Electronic Media, 34,* 339–419.

Flavell, J. H., Friedrichs, A. G., & Hoyt, J. D. (1970). Developmental changes in memorization processes. *Cognitive Psychology, 1,* 324–340.

Flavell, J. H., Green, F. L., & Flavell, E. R. (1986). Development of knowledge about the appearance-reality distinction. *Monographs of the Society for Research in Child Development, 51*(1, Serial No. 212).

Fletcher, A. C., Darling, N. E., Steinberg, L., & Dornbusch, S. (1995). The company they keep: Relation of adolescents' adjustment and behavior to their friends; perceptions of authoritative parenting in the social network. *Developmental Psychology, 31,* 300–310.

Flowers, P., & Buston, K. (2002). "I was terrified of being different": Exploring gay men's accounts of growing up in a heterosexist society. *Journal of Adolescence, 24,* 51–65.

Flykt, M., Kanninen, K., Sinkkonen, J., & Punamäki, R.-L. (2010). Maternal depression and dyadic interaction: The role of maternal attachment style. *Infant and Child Development, 19,* 530–550.

Flynn, E., & Siegler, R. (2007). Measuring change: Current trends and future directions in microgenetic research. *Infant and Child Development, 16,* 1135–1149.

Flynn, J. R. (1999). Searching for justice: The discovery of IQ gains over time. *American Psychologist, 54*(1), 5–20.

Flynn, J. R. (1984). The mean IQ of Americans: Massive gains 1932 to 1978. *Psychological Bulletin, 95,* 29–51.

Flynn, J. R. (2007). *What is intelligence? Beyond the Flynn effect.* New York: Cambridge University Press.

Fodor, J. (1983). *The modularity of mind.* Cambridge, MA: The MIT Press.

Fordham, S., & Ogbu, J. U. (1986). Black students' school success: Coping with the "burden of 'acting white.'" *Urban Review, 18*(3), 176–206.

Foreman, N., Fielder, A., Minshell, C., Hurrion, E., & Sergienko, E. (1997). Visual search, perception, and visual-motor skill in "healthy" children born at 27–32 weeks' gestation. *Journal of Experimental Child Psychology, 64*(1), 27–41.

Forman, M. (2002). Keeping it real: African youth identities and hip hop. In R. Young (Ed.), *Critical Studies, 19, Music, popular culture, identities.* New York: Rodopi.

Forsen, T., Eriksson, J., Tuomilehto, J., Reunanen, A., Osmond, C., & Barker, D. (2000). The fetal and childhood growth of persons who develop type 2 diabetes. *Annals of Internal Medicine, 133,* 176–182.

Forsyth, B. W. C. (1989). Colic and the effect of changing formulas: A double-blind, multiple crossover study. *Journal of Pediatrics, 115,* 521–552.

Forum on Child and Family Statistics (2011). America's children: Key indicators of well-being, 2011. Retrieved from http://www.childstats.gov/pdf/ac2011/ac_11.pdf

Fowler, A. (1990). Language abilities in children with Down syndrome: Evidence for a specific syntactic delay. In D. Cicchetti & M. Beeghly (Eds.), *Children with Down syndrome: A developmental perspective* (pp. 302–328). Cambridge, UK: Cambridge University Press.

Fox, S. E., Levitt, P., & Nelson, C. A. (2010). How the timing and quality of early experiences influence the development of brain architecture. *Child Development, 81,* 28–40.

Fraiberg, S. H. (1959). *The magic years: Understanding and handling the problems of early childhood.* New York: Scribner.

Frankel, K., & Bates, J. (1990). Mother-toddler problem solving: Antecedents in attachment, home behavior, and temperament. *Child Development, 61,* 810–819.

Franklin, A., Giannakidou, A., & Goldin-Meadow, S. (2011). Negation, questions, and structure building in a homesign system. *Cognition, 118*(3), 398–416.

Franzini, L. (2008). Self-rated health and trust in low-income Mexican-origin individuals in Texas. *Social Science & Medicine, 67,* 1959–1969.

Franzini, L., Caughy, M. O., Nettles, S. M., & O'Campo, P. (2008). Perceptions of disorder: Contributions of neighborhood characteristics to subjective perceptions of disorder. *Journal of Environmental Psychology, 28,* 83–93.

Franzini, L., & Fernandez-Esquer, M. E. (2006). The association of subjective social status and health in low-income Mexican-origin individuals in Texas. *Social Science & Medicine, 63,* 788–804.

Freed, K. (1983, March 14). Cubatao—a paradise lost to pollution. *Los Angeles Times,* pp. 1, 12, 13.

Freud, S. (1905/1953). Three essays on the theory of sexuality. In J. Strachey (Ed.), *The standard edition of the complete psychological works of Sigmund Freud: Vol. 7.* London: Hogarth Press.

Freud, S. (1920/1955). Beyond the pleasure principle. In J. Strachey (Ed.), *The standard edition of the complete psychological works of Sigmund Freud: Vol. 18.* London: Hogarth Press.

Freud, S. (1921/1949). Group psychology—The analysis of the ego. In J. Strachey (Ed.), *The standard edition of the complete psychological works of Sigmund Freud: Vol. 18.* London: Hogarth Press.

Freud, S. (1933/1964). *New introductory lectures in psychoanalysis.* New York: W. W. Norton.

Freud, S. (1940/1964). An outline of psychoanalysis. In J. Strachey (Ed.), *The standard edition of the complete psychological works of Sigmund Freud: Vol. 32.* London: Hogarth Press.

Friederici, A. D., Bahlmann, J., Heim, S., Schubotz, R. I., & Anwander, A. (2006). The brain differentiates human and non-human grammars: Functional localization and structural connectivity. *Proceedings of the National Academy of Sciences, 103,* 2458–2463.

Frith, U. (1989). *Autism.* Oxford, England: Oxford University Press.

Frith, U. (2003). *Autism: Explaining the enigma* (2nd ed.). Oxford, England.

Fry, D. P. (1988). Intercommunity differences in aggression among Zapotec children. *Child Development, 59,* 1008–1018.

Frye, D. (2000). Theory of mind, domain specificity, and reasoning. In K. J. Riggs & P. Mitchell, *Children's reasoning and the mind* (pp. 149–167). Hove, England: Psychology Press/Taylor & Francis.

Fuhs, M. W., & Day, J. D. (2011). Verbal ability and executive functioning development in preschoolers at Head Start. *Developmental Psychology, 47,* 404–416.

Fujioka, T., Trainor, L. J., & Ross, B. (2008). Simultaneous pitches are encoded separately in auditory cortex: An MMNm study. *Neuroreport: For Rapid Communication of Neuroscience Research, 19,* 361–366.

Fuligni, A. J., & Eccles, J. S. (1993). Perceived parent-child relationships and early adolescents' orientation toward peers. *Developmental Psychology, 29,* 622–632.

Fuligni, A. J., & Stevenson, H. W. (1995). Time use and mathematics achievement among American, Chinese, and Japanese high school students. *Child Development, 66,* 830–842.

Fullard, W., & Reiling, A. M. (1976). An investigation of Lorenz's babyness. *Child Development, 47,* 1191–1193.

Funk, J. B., Baldacci, H. B., Pasold, T., & Baumgardner, J. (2004). Violence exposure in real-life, video games, television, movies, and the internet: Is there desensitization? *Journal of Adolescence, 27,* 23–39.

Furman, W., & Simon, V. A. (2008). Homophily in adolescent romantic relationships. In M. J. Prinstein & K. A. Dodge (Eds.), *Understanding peer influence in children and adolescents. Duke series in child development and public policy* (pp. 203–224). New York: Guilford Press.

Furstenberg, F. F., Jr. (1998). Social capital and the role of fathers in the family. In A. Booth & A. C. Crouter (Eds.), *Men in families: When do they get involved? What difference does it make?* (pp. 295–301). Mahwah, NJ: Lawrence Erlbaum Associates.

Furstenberg, F. F., Jr., Hughes, M. E., & Brooks-Gunn, J. (1992). The next generation: The children of teenage mothers grow up. In M. Rosenheim & M. F. Testa (Eds.), *Early parenthood and coming of age in the 1990's.* New Brunswick, NJ: Rutgers University Press.

Gallego, M. A., Cole, M., & Laboratory of Comparative Human Cognition. (2000). Classroom culture and culture in the classroom. In V. Richardson (Ed.), *The Handbook of Research on Teaching.* Washington, DC: American Educational Research Association.

Galloway, A. T., Fiorito, L., Lee, Y., & Birch, L. L. (2005). Parental pressure, dietary patterns, and weight status among girls who are "picky eaters". *Journal of the American Dietary Association, 105,* 541–548.

Gallup, G. G. J. (1970). Chimpanzees: Self-recognition. *Science, 167,* 86–87.

Gammage, J. (2003, June 14). Bringing Jin Yu home. *The Philadelphia Inquirer.*

Garciaguirre, J. S., Adolph, K. E., & Shrout, P. (2007). Baby carriage: Infants walking with loads. *Child Development 78,* 664–680.

Gardner, H. (1983). *Frames of mind: The theory of multiple intelligences.* New York: Basic Books.

Gardner, H. (2006, September–October). On failing to grasp the core of MI theory: A response to Visser et al. *Intelligence, 34*(5), 503–505.

Gardner, M., & Steinberg, L. (2005). Risk-taking among adolescents, young adults, and adults: The role of peer influence. *Developmental Psychology, 41*(4), 625–635.

Gardner, W., & Rogoff, B. (1990). Children's deliberateness of planning according to task circumstances. *Developmental Psychology, 26,* 480–487.

Garner, P. W., & Hinton, T. S. (2010). Emotional display rules and emotion self-regulation: Associations with bullying and victimization in community-based after school programs. *Journal of Community & Applied Social Psychology, 20,* 480–496.

Garofalo, R., Wolf, R., Wissow, L., Woods, E., & Goodman, E. (1999). Sexual orientation and risk of suicide attempts among a representative sample of youth. *Archives of Pediatrics and Adolescent Medicine, 153,* 487–493.

Garrod, A., Smulyan, L., Powers, S., & Kilkenny, R. (Eds.). (1999). *Adolescent portraits: Identity, relationships, and challenges.* Boston: Allyn & Bacon.

Garrow, I., & Werne, J. (1953). Sudden apparently unexplained death during infancy: III. Pathological findings in infants dying immediately after violence, contrasted with those after sudden apparently unexplained death. *American Journal of Pathology, 29,* 833–851.

Gartrell, N., Deck, A., Rodas, C., Peyser, H., & Banks, A. (2005). The national lesbian family study: 4. Interviews with the 10-year-old children. *American Journal of Orthopsychiatry, 75,* 518–524.

Gartstein, M. A., Gonzalez, C., Carranza, J. A., Ahadi, S. A., & Ye, R. (2006). Studying cross-cultural differences in the development of infant temperament: People's Republic of China, the United States of America, and Spain. *Child Psychiatry and Human Development, 37,* 145–161.

Garvey, C., & Berndt, R. (1977). Organization of pretend play. *Catalog of Selected Documents in Psychology, 7,* 107.

Gaskins, S. (1999). Children's daily lives in a Mayan village: A case study of culturally constructed roles and activities. In A. Göncü (Ed.), *Children's engagement in the world: Sociocultural perspectives* (pp. 25–61). New York: Cambridge University Press.

Gates, G. J., & Romero, A. (2009). Parenting by gay men and lesbians: Beyond the current research. In E. Peters & C. M. Kamp Dush (Eds.), *Marriage and family: Perspectives and complexities.* New York: Columbia University Press.

Gau, S., & Soong, W. (2003). The transition of sleep-wake patterns in early adolescence. *Sleep, 26,* 449–454.

Ge, X., Brody, G. H., Conger, R. D., & Simons, R. L. (2006). Pubertal maturation and African American children's internalizing and externalizing symptoms. *Journal of Youth and Adolescence, 35,* 531–540.

Geary, D. (2006). Development of mathematical understanding. In D. Kuhn & R. S. Siegler (Eds.), *Handbook of child psychology: Vol. 2. Cognition, perception, and language* (6th ed., pp. 777–810). New York: Wiley.

Geary, D., Bow-Tomas, C., Lui, F., & Siegler, R. (1996). Development of arithmetical competencies in Chinese and American children: Influence of age, language, and schooling. *Child Development, 67,* 2022–2044.

Geers, A., Spehar, B., & Sedey, A. (2002, February). Use of speech by children from total communication programs who wear cochlear implants. *American Journal of Speech-Language Pathology, 11*(1), 50–58.

Geertz, C. (1984). From the native's point of view: On the nature of anthropological understanding. In R. Shweder & R. Levine (Eds.), *Culture theory.* Cambridge, England: Cambridge University Press.

Geiger, B. (1996). *Fathers as primary caregivers.* Westport, CT: Greenwood.

Georgieff, M. K., & Raghavendra, R. (2001). The role of nutrition in cognitive development. In C. A. Nelson and M. Luciana (Eds.), *Handbook of developmental cognitive neuroscience* (pp. 491–504). Cambridge, MA: The MIT Press.

Geithner, C. A., Thomis, M. A., Vanden Eynde, B., Maes, H. H., Loos, R. J., Peeters, M., et al. (2004, September). Growth in peak aerobic power during adolescence. *Medicine & Science in Sports & Exercise, 36*(9), 1616–1624.

Gelman, R. (1990). First principles affect learning and transfer in children. *Cognitive Science, 14,* 79–107.

Gelis, J. (1991). *History of childbirth.* Cambridge, England: Polity Press.

Gergen, K. J. (1991). *The saturated self: Dilemmas of identity in contemporary life.* New York: Basic Books.

Gershoff, E. T., & Aber, J. L. (2004, July). Editors' introduction: Assessing the impact of September 11th, 2001, on children, youth, and parents: Methodological challenges to research on terrorism and other nonnormative events. *Applied Developmental Science, 8*(3), 106–110.

Gertner, Y., Fisher, C., & Eisengart, J. (2006). Learning words and rules: Abstract knowledge of word order in early sentence comprehension. *Psychological Science, 17,* 684–691.

Geschwind, D. H., & Dykens, E. (2004). Neurobehavioral and psychosocial issues in Klinefelter syndrome. *Learning Disabilities Research & Practice, 19*(3) 166–173.

Giacoman, S. L. (1971). Hunger and motor restraint on arousal and visual attention in the infant. *Child Development, 42*(2), 605–614.

Gibson, E. J. (1988). Exploratory behavior in the development of perceiving, acting, and the acquiring of knowledge. *Annual Review of Psychology, 39,* 1–41.

Giedd, J. N., Clasen, L. S., Lenroot, R., Greenstein, D., Wallace, G. L., Ordaz, S., et al. (2006). Puberty-related influences on brain development. *Molecular and Cellular Endocrinology, 254–255*(3), 154–162.

Giedd, J. N., & Gordon, D. (2010). The teen brain: Primed to learn, primed to take risks. *The Dana Foundation's Cerebrum, 72,* 46–55.

Giedd, J. N., & Rapoport, J. L. (2010, Sep 9). Structural MRI of pediatric brain development: What have we learned and where are we going. *Neuron, 67,* 728–734.

Gielen, U. P., & Markoulis, D. C. (2001). Preference for principled moral reasoning: A developmental and cross-cultural perspective. In L. L. Adler & U. P. Gielen (Eds.), *Cross-cultural topics in psychology* (2nd ed., pp. 81–101). Westport, CT: Praeger.

Gilbert, S. F. (2001). Ecological developmental biology: Developmental biology meets the real world. *Developmental Biology, 233*(1), 1–12.

Giles, J., & Heyman, G. (2003). Preschoolers' beliefs about the stability of antisocial behavior: Implications for navigating social challenges. *Social Development, 12,* 182–197.

Gilligan, C. (1982). *In a different voice: Psychological theory and women's development.* Cambridge, MA: Harvard University Press.

Gilmore, C. K., & Spelke, E. S. (2008, June). Children's understanding of the relationship between addition and subtraction. *Cognition, 107,* 932–945.

Ginsburg, H. (1977). *Children's arithmetic.* New York: Van Nostrand.

Ginsburg, H. P. (2008). Challenging preschool education: Meeting the intellectual needs of all children. In B. Z. Presseisen (Ed.), *Teaching for intelligence* (2nd ed., pp. 212–229). Thousand Oaks, CA: Corwin Press.

Gittelsohn, J., Song, H.-J., Suratkar, S., Kumar, M. B., Henry, E. G., Sharma, S., et al. (2010). An urban food store intervention positively affects food-related psychosocial variables and food behaviors. *Health Education & Behavior, 37,* 390–402.

Glowinski, A. L., Madden, P. A. F., Bucholz, K. K., Lynskey, M. T., & Heath, A. C. (2003). Genetic epidemiology of self-reported lifetime DSM-IV major depressive disorder in a population-based twin sample of female adolescents. *Journal of Child Psychology and Psychiatry, 44,* 988–996.

Gluck, M. E., Venti, C. A., Lindsay, R. S., Knowler, W. C., Salbe, A. D., & Krakoff, J. (2009). Maternal influence, not diabetic intrauterine environment, predicts children's energy intake. *Obesity, 17,* 772–777.

Godeau, E., Gabhainn, W., Wignes, C., Ross, J., Boyce, W., & Todd, J. (2008). Contraceptive use by 15-year-old students at their last sexual intercourse: Results from 24 countries. *Archives of Pediatric Adolescent Medicine, 162,* 66–73.

Gogtay, N., Giedd, J., Lusk, L., Hayashi, K. I., Sreenstein, D., & Vaituzis, A. (2004). Dynamic mapping of human cortical development during childhood through early adulthood. *Proceedings of the National Academy of Sciences of the United States of America, 101,* 8174–8179.

Golden, N. H., Katzman, D. K., & Kreipe, R. E. (2003). Eating disorders in adolescents: A position paper of the Society for Adolescent Medicine. *Journal of Adolescent Health, 33,* 496–503.

Goldin-Meadow, S., & Mylander, C. (1998). Spontaneous sign systems created by deaf children in two cultures. *Nature, 391,* 279–281.

Goldin-Meadow, S., Mylander, C., & Franklin, A. (2007). How children make language out of gesture: Morphological structure in gesture systems developed by American and Chinese deaf children. *Cognitive Psychology, 55*(2), 87–135.

Goldin-Meadow, S., Özyürek, A., Sancar, B., & Mylander, C. (2009). Making language around the globe: A crosslinguistic study of homesign in the United States, China, and Turkey. In S. Goldin-Meadow, A. Özyürek, B. Sancar & C. Mylander (Eds.), *Crosslinguistic approaches to the psychology of language: Research in the tradition of Dan Isaac Slobin* (pp. 27–39). New York: Psychology Press.

Goldsmith, H. H., & Campos, J. J. (1982). Toward a theory of infant temperament. In R. N. Emde & R. Harmon (Eds.), *The development of attachment and affiliative systems.* New York: Plenum Press.

Golinkoff, R., & Hirsh-Pasek, K. (2006). Baby wordsmith: From associationist to social sophisticate. *Current Directions in Psychological Science, 15,* 30–33.

Golinkoff, R. M., Hirsh-Pasek, K., & Schweisguth, M. A. (1999). A reappraisal of young children's knowledge of grammatical morphemes. In J. Weissenborn & B. Hoehle (Eds.), *Approaches to bootstrapping: Phonological, syntactic, and neurophysiological aspects of early language acquisition.* Amsterdam and Philadelphia: John Benjamins.

Golinkoff, R. M., Mervis, C. B., & Hirsh-Pasek, K. (1994). Early object labels: The case for a developmental lexical principles framework. *Journal of Child Language, 21,* 125–155.

Golombok, S., & Hines, M. (2002). Sex differences in social behavior. In P. Smith & C. Hart (Eds.), *Blackwell handbook of childhood social development.* Malden, MA: Blackwell Publishing.

Goncu, A., & Gaskins, S. (2011). Comparing and extending Piaget's and Vtgotsky's understandings of play: Symbolic play as individual, sociocultural, and educational interpretation. In A. Pellegrini (Ed.), *The Oxford Handbook of the Development of Play.* New York: Oxford University Press.

Goodman, C., & Silverstein, M. (2006). Grandmothers raising grandchildren: Ethnic and racial differences in well-being among custodial and coparenting families. *Journal of Family Issues, 27,* 1605–1626.

Goodman, G. S. (2005). Wailing babies in her wake. *American Psychologist, 60*(8), 872–881.

Goodman, G. S. (2006). Children's eyewitness memory: A modern history and contemporary commentary. *Journal of Social Issues, 62*(4), 811–832.

Goodman, G. S., Emery, R. E., & Haugaard, J. J. (1998). Developmental psychology and the law: Divorce, child maltreatment, foster care, and adoption. In I. E. Sigel & K. A. Renninger (Eds.), *Handbook of child psychology: Vol. 4. Child psychology in practice* (5th ed., pp. 775–876). New York: Wiley.

Goodman, G. S., Hirschman, J. E., Hepps, D., & Rudy, L. (1991, January). Children's memory for stressful events. *Merrill-Palmer Quarterly, 37*(1), 109–157.

Goodman, G. S., & Melinder, A. (2007). Child witness research and forensic interviews of young children: A review. *Legal and Criminological Psychology 12*(1), 1–19.

Goodman, M. R., Stormshak, E., & Dishion, T. (2001). The significance of peer victimization at two points in development. *Applied Developmental Psychology, 22,* 507–526.

Goodnow, J. J. (1998). Beyond the overall balance: The significance of particular tasks and procedures for perceptions of fairness in distributions of household work. *Social Justice Research, 11,* 359–376.

Goodnow, J. J., Cashmore, J., Cotton, S., & Knight, R. (1984). Mothers' developmental timetables in two cultural groups. *International Journal of Psychology, 19,* 193–205.

Goodwin, M. H. (2002). Exclusion in girls' peer groups: Ethnographic analysis of language practices on the playground. *Human Development, 45*(6), 392–415.

Goodwin, M. H. (2006). *The hidden life of girls: Games of stance, status, and exclusion.* Oxford, England: Blackwell Publishing.

Goodwin, M. H. (2011). Engendering children's play: Person reference in children's conflictual interaction. In S. A. Speer & E. Stokoe (Eds.), *Conversation and gender* (pp. 250–271). New York: Cambridge University Press.

Goodman, M. R., & Rao, S. P. (2007). Grandparents raising grandchildren in a US-Mexico border community. *Qualitative Health Research, 17,* 1117–1136.

Goossens, L. (2001). Global versus domain-specific statuses in identity research: A comparison of two self-report measures. *Journal of Adolescence, 24,* 681–699.

Gopnik, A., & Meltzoff, A. N. (1997). *Words, thoughts, and theories.* Cambridge, MA: The MIT Press.

Gopnik, A., & Rosati, A. (2001). Duck or rabbit? Reversing ambiguous figures and understanding ambiguous representations, *Developmental Science, 4,* 175–183.

Gopnik, A., Wellman, H. M., Gelman, S. A., & Meltzoff, A. N. (2010). A computational foundation for cognitive development: Comment on Griffths et al. and McLelland et al. *Trends in Cognitive Sciences, 14,* 342–343.

Gordon, P. (2004, October 15). Numerical cognition without words: Evidence from Amazonia. *Science, 306,* 496–499.

Gordon, R. A., Savage, C., Lahey, B. B., Goodman, S. H., Jensen, P. S., Rubio-Stipic, M., et al. (2003). Family and neighborhood income: Additive and multiplicative associations with youths' well-being. *Social Science Research, 32,* 191–219.

Gormley, W., & Gayer, T. (2005). Promoting school readiness in Oklahoma: An evaluation of Tulsa's pre-K program. *Journal of Human Resources, 40,* 533–558.

Goswami, U. (Ed.). (2002). *Blackwell handbook of childhood cognitive development.* Oxford, England: Blackwell Publishing.

Goswami, U. (2008). *Cognitive development: The learning brain.* Hove, England: Psychology Press.

Gottardo, A., Chiappe, P., Siegel, L. S., & Stanovich, K. E. (1999). Patterns of word and nonword processing in skilled and less-skilled readers. *Reading & Writing, 11*(5–6), 465–487.

Gottlieb, A. (2000). Luring your child into this life: A Beng path for infant care. In J. S. DeLoache & A. Gottlieb (Eds.), *A world of babies: Imagined childcare guides for seven societies* (55–88). Cambridge, England: Cambridge University Press.

Gottlieb, A. (2005). *The afterlife is where we come from: The culture of infancy in West Africa.* Chicago: University of Chicago Press.

Gottlieb, E., & Mandel Leadership Institute. (2007) Learning how to believe: Epistemic development in cultural context. *Journal of the Learning Sciences, 16*(1), 5–35.

Gottlieb, G. (2002). Developmental-behavioral initiation of evolutionary change. *Psychological Review, 109*(2), 211–218.

Gottlieb, G., & Lickliter, R. (2007, January). Probabilistic epigenesis. *Developmental Science, 10,* 1–11.

Gottman, J. M. (1983). How children become friends. *Monographs of the Society for Research in Child Development, 48*(3, Serial No. 201).

Gotz, M., Lemish, D., Aidman, A., & Moon, H. (2005). *Media and the make-believe worlds of children.* Mahwah, NJ: Lawrence Erlbaum Associates.

Graber, J. A. (2004). Internalizing problems during adolescence. In R. M. Lerner & L. Steinberg (Eds.), *Handbook of adolescent psychology* (2nd ed.). Hoboken, NJ: John Wiley & Sons.

Graber, J. A., Nichols, T. R., & Brooks-Gunn, J. (2010). Putting pubertal timing in developmental context: Implications for prevention. *Developmental Psychobiology, 52,* 254–262

Grady, K. (2002). Lowrider art and Latino students in the rural Midwest. In S. Wortham, E. Murillo, & E. Hamann (Eds.), *Education in the new Latino diaspora.* Westport, CT: Ablex.

Graham, J. A., Cohen, R., Zbikowski, S. M., & Secrist, M. E. (1998). A longitudinal investigation of race and sex as factors in children's classroom friendship choices. *Child Study Journal, 28*(4), 245–266.

Grail, T. S. (2009). http://www.census.gov/prod/2009pubs/p60-237.pdf, Washington, D.C.: U.S. Department of Commerce, Census Bureau.

Granic, I., Hollenstein, T., Dishion, T. J., & Patterson, G. R. (2003). Longitudinal analysis of flexibility and reorganization in early adolescence: A dynamic systems study of family interactions. *Developmental Psychology, 39,* 606–617.

Gratier, M., Greenfield, P. M., & Isaac, A. (2009). Tacit communicative style and cultural attunement in classroom interaction. *Mind, Culture, and Activity, 16,* 296–316.

Greenberg, M. T., & Kusché, C. A. (2006). Building social and emotional competence: The PATHS curriculum. In S. Jimerson, A. Nickerson, M. J. Mayer, & M. J. Furlong (Eds.), *Handbook of school violence and school safety: From research to practice* (pp. 395–412). Mahwah, NJ: Lawrence Erlbaum.

Greenfield, P. M., Brazelton, T. B., & Childs, C. P. (1989). From birth to maturity in Zinacantan: Ontogenesis in cultural context. In V. Bricker & G. Gossen (Eds.), *Ethnographic encounters in southern Mesoamerica: Celebratory essays in honor of Evon Z. Vogt.* Albany: Institute of Mesoamerican Studies, State University of New York.

Greenfield, P. M., Keller, H., Fuligni, A., & Maynard, A. (2003). Cultural pathways through universal development. *Annual Review of Psychology, 54,* 461–490.

Greenfield, P. M., & Lyn, H. (2007). Symbol combination in Pan: Language, action, and culture. In D. A. Washburn (Ed.), *Primate perspectives on behavior and cognition* (pp. 255–267). Washington, DC: American Psychological Association.

Greenfield, P. M., Lyn, H., & Savage-Rumbaugh, E. S. (2008). Protolanguage in ontogeny and phylogeny: Combining deixis and representation. *Communication in Biological and Artificial Systems, 34,* 51.

Greenfield, P. M., Suzuki, L., & Rothstein-Fisch, C. (2006). Cultural pathways through human development. In K. Renninger, I. Sigel, W. Damon, & R. Lerner (Eds.), *Handbook of child psychology: Vol. 4. Child psychology in practice* (6th ed.). Hoboken, NJ: Wiley.

Greenough, W., Black, J., & Wallace, C. (1987). Experience and brain development. *Child Development, 58,* 539–559.

Greenspan, S. I. (2003). Child care research: A clinical perspective. *Child Development, 74,* 1064–1068.

Greenspan, S. I., & Shanker, S. (2004). *The first idea: How symbols, language and intelligence evolved from our primate ancestors to modern humans.* Cambridge, MA: Da Capo Press.

Gregor, J. A., & McPherson, D. A. (1966). Racial preference and ego identity among White and Bantu children in the Republic of South Africa. *Genetic Psychology Monographs, 73,* 218–253.

Griffin, P. (1983). Personal communication.

Grigorenko, E. L., Geissler, P., Wenzel, P. R., Okatcha, F., Nokes, C., Kenny, D. A., et al. (2001). The organization of Luo conceptions of intelligence: A study of implicit theories in a Kenyan village. *International Journal of Behavioral Development, 25,* 367–378.

Grisso, T., Steinberg, L., Woolard, J., Cauffman, E., Scott, E., Graham, S., et al. (2003). Juveniles' competence to stand trial: A comparison of adolescents' and adults' capacities as trial defendants. *Law and Human Behavior, 27*(4), 333–363.

Groeschel, S., Vollmer, B., King, M. D., & Connelly, A. (2010). Developmental changes in cerebral grey and white matter volume from infancy to adulthood. *International Journal of Developmental Neuroscience, 28,* 481–489.

Groesz, L. M., Levine, M. P., & Murnen, S. K. (2002). The effect of experimental presentation of thin media images on body satisfaction: A meta-analytic review. *International Journal of Eating Disorders, 31,* 1–16.

Grolnick, W. S., McMenamy, J. M., & Kurowski, C. O. (1999). Emotional self-regulation in infancy and toddlerhood. In L. Balter & C. S. Tamis-LeMonda (Eds.), *Child psychology: A handbook of contemporary issues.* Philadelphia: Psychology Press/Taylor & Francis.

Gronlund, N. E. (1959). *Sociometry in the classroom.* New York: Harper Brothers.

Grossmann, K., Grossmann, K. E., Kindler, H., & Zimmermann, P. (2008). A wider view of attachment and exploration: The influence of mothers and fathers on the development of psychological security from infancy to young adulthood. In K. Grossmann, K. E. Grossmann, H. Kindler & P. Zimmermann (Eds.), *Handbook of attachment: Theory, research, and clinical applications* (2 ed., pp. 857–879). New York: Guilford Press.

Grossman, T., Johnson, M. H., Farroni, T., & Csibra, G. (2007). Social perception in the infant brain: Gamma oscillatory activity in response to eye gaze. *Social Cognitive and Affective Neuroscience, 2,* 284–291.

Grotevant, H. D. (1998). Adolescent development in family contexts. In W. Damon & N. Eisenberg (Eds.), *Handbook of child psychology: Vol. 3. Social, emotional, and personality development* (5th ed., pp. 1097–1150). New York: Wiley.

Grumbach, M., & Styne, D. (2002). Puberty: Ontogeny, neuroendocrinology, physiology, and disorders. In P. Larsen, H. Kronenberg, S. Melmed, & K. Polonsky (Eds.), *Williams textbook of endocrinology* (10th ed., pp. 1509–1625). Philadelphia: Saunders.

Guest, A. M. (2007). Cultures of childhood and psychosocial characteristics: Self-esteem and social comparison in two distinct communities. *Ethos, 35,* 1–32.

Gunter, B., Oates, C., & Blades, M. (2005). *Advertising to children on TV: Content, impact and regulation.* Mahwah, NJ: Lawrence Erlbaum Associates.

Guralnick, M. J. (2005) Early intervention for children with intellectual disabilities: Current knowledge and future prospects. *Journal of Applied Research in Intellectual Disabilities, 18*(4), 313–324.

Guttler, F. (1988). Epidemiology and natural history of phenylketonuria and other hyperphenylalaninemias. In R. J. Wurtman & E. Ritter-Walker (Eds.), *Dietary phenylaline and brain function.* Boston: Birkhauser.

Guttmacher Institute. (2006). *Abortion in women's lives.* Retrieved April 25, 2007, Retrieved from http://www.guttmacher.org/pubs/2006/05/04/AiWL.pdf

Guttmacher Institute. (2011). Facts on American teens' sexual and rproductive health. Retrieved December 15th, 2011, Retrieved from http://www.guttmacher.org/pubs/FB-ATSRH.html#5

Haden, C. A., Ornstein, P. A., Eckerman, C. O., & Didow, S. M. (2001). Mother-child conversational interactions as events unfold: Linkages to subsequent remembering. *Child Development, 72,* 1016–1031.

Hagenauer, M., Perryman, J., Lee, T., & Carskadon, M. (2009). Adolescent changes in homeostatic and circadian regulation of sleep. *Developmental Neuroscience, 31,* 276–284.

Haith, M. M. (1980). *Rules that babies look by: The organization of newborn visual activity.* Mahwah, NJ: Lawrence Erlbaum Associates.

Haines, M. M., Stansfeld, S. A., Brentnall, S., Head, J., Berry, B., Jiggins, M., & Hygge, S. (2001, November). The West London Schools Study: The effects of chronic aircraft noise exposure on child health. *Psychological Medicine, 31,* 1385–1396.

Hakkarainen, P. (2004). Narrative learning in the fifth dimension. *Outlines: Critical Social Studies, 6,* 5–20.

Halberstadt, A., Denham, S., & Dunsmore, J. (2001). Affective social competence. *Social Development, 10,* 79–119.

Hall, G. S. (1904). *Adolescence.* New York: Appleton.

Hallett, D., Chandler, M. J., & Krettenauer, T. (2002). Disentangling the course of epistemic development: Parsing knowledge by epistemic content. *New Ideas in Psychology. Special Issue: Folk epistemology, 20,* 285–307.

Hallett, D., Chandler, M. J., & Lalonde, C. E. (2007). Aboriginal language knowledge and youth suicide. Cognitive Development, *22,* 392–399.

Halpern-Felsher, B., & Cauffman, E. (2001). Costs and benefits of a decision: Decision-making competence in adolescents and adults. *Applied Developmental Psychology, 22,* 257–273.

Halverson, H. M. (1931). An experimental study of prehension in infants by means of systemic cinema records. *Genetic Psychology Monographs, 10,* 107–286.

Hamlin, J. K., Wynn, K., & Bloom, P. (2007). Social evaluation by preverbal infants. *Nature, 450,* 557–559.

Hanawalt, B., & Kobialka, M. (Eds.). (2000). *Medieval practices of space.* Minneapolis: University of Minnesota Press.

Harden, K. P., Turkheimer, E., & Loehlin, J. C. (2007, March). Genotype by environment interaction in adolescents' cognitive aptitude. *Behavior Genetics, 37*(2), 273–283.

Hartshorn, K., Rovee-Collier, C., Gerhardstein, P., Bhatt, R. S., Wondoloski, T. L., Klein, P., Gilch, J., et al. (1998). The ontogeny of long-term memory over the first year-and-a-half of life. *Developmental Psychobiology, 32*(2), 69–89.

Harden, K. P., Turkheimer, E., & Loehlin, J. C. (2007). Genotype by environment interaction in adolescents' cognitive aptitude. *Behavior Genetics, 37,* 273–283.

Harlow, H. F. (1959). Love in infant monkeys. *Scientific American, 200*(6), 68–74.

Harlow, H. F., & Harlow, M. K. (1962). Social deprivation in monkeys. *Scientific American, 207*(5), 136–146.

Harlow, H. F., & Harlow, M. K. (1969). Effects of various mother-infant relationships on rhesus monkey behaviors. In B. M. Foss (Ed.), *Determinants of infant behavior: Vol. 4* (4th ed.). London: Methuen.

Harrington, M. (1963). *The Other America: Poverty in the United States.* New York: Touchstone.

Harrison, K., Bost, K., McBride, B., & Donovan, S. (2011). Toward a developmental conceptualization of contributors to overweight and obesity in childhood: The six-Cs model. *Child Development Perspectives, 5,* 50–58.

Hart, B., & Risley, T. R. (1999). *The social world of children learning to talk.* Baltimore: Brookes.

Hart, C., Young, C., Nelson, D., Jin, S., Bazarskaya, N., Nelson, L., et al. (1999). Peer contact patterns, parenting practices, and preschoolers' social competence in China, Russia, and the United States. In P. Slee & K. Rigby (Eds.), *Children's peer relationships* (pp. 3–30). London: Routledge.

Harter, S. (1982). The perceived competence scale for children. *Child Development, 53,* 87–97.

Harter, S. (1987). The determinants and mediational role of global self-worth in children. In N. Eisenberg (Ed.), *Contemporary topics in developmental psychology.* New York: Wiley.

Harter, S. (1998). The development of self-representation. In N. Eisenberg (Ed.), *Handbook of child psychology: Vol. 3. Social, emotional, and personality development* (5th ed., pp. 553–617). New York: Wiley.

Harter, S. (1999). *The construction of the self: A developmental perspective.* New York: Guilford Press.

Harter, S. (2006a). Developmental and individual difference-perspectives on self-esteem. In D. K. Mroczek & T. D. Little (Eds.), *Handbook of personality development* (311–334). Mahwah, NJ: Erlbaum.

Harter, S. (2006b). The development of self-esteem. In M. H. Kernis (Ed.), *Self-esteem issues and answers: A sourcebook of current perspectives* (pp. 144–150). New York: Psychology Press.

Harter, S., & Pike, R. (1984). The pictorial scale of perceived competence and social acceptance for young children. *Child Development, 55,* 1969–1982.

Hartup, W. W. (1992). Friendships and their developmental significance. In H. McGurk (Ed.), *Childhood social development: Contemporary perspectives.* London: Lawrence Erlbaum Associates.

Hartup, W. W. (1998). The company they keep: Friendships and their developmental significance. In A. Campbell & S. Muncer (Eds.), *The social child* (pp. 143–163). Hove, UK: Psychology Press/Erlbaum.

Hauck, F. R., Herman, S. M., Donovan, M., Iysau, S., Moore, C. M., Donoghue, E., et al. (2003). Sleep environment and the risk of sudden infant death syndrome in an urban population: The Chicago Infant Mortality Study. *Pediatrics, 111,* 1207–1214.

Hauck, R. F., & Tanabe, K. O. (2008). International trends in sudden infant death syndrome: Stabilization of rates requires further action. *Pediatrics, 122,* 660–666.

Hausenblas, H. A., Janelle, C. M., Ellis Gardner, R., & Focht, B. C. (2004). Viewing physique slides: Affective responses of women at high and low drive for thinness. *Journal of Social and Clinical Psychology, 23,* 45–60.

Hauser, G., Chitayat, D., Berbs, L., Braver, D., & Mulbauer, B. (1985). Peculiar odors in newborns and maternal pre-natal ingestion of spicy foods. *European Journal of Pediatrics, 144,* 403.

Hauser, M. D., & Chomsky, N. (2002). The faculty of language: What is it, who has it, and how did it evolve? *Science, 298,* 1569–1579.

Hauser, S., Powers, S., & Noam, G. (1991). *Adolescents and their families: Paths of ego development.* New York: Free Press.

Haviland, J. M., & Kramer, D. A. (1991). Affect-cognition relationships in adolescent diaries: The case of Anne Frank. *Human Development, 34*(3), 143–159.

Hawk, S., Keijsers, L., Hale, W. W., & Meeus, W. (2009). Mind your own business! Longitudinal relations between perceived privacy invasion and adolescent-parent conflict. *Journal of Family Psychology, 23,* 511–520.

Hawkins, A. J., Lovejoy, K. R., Holmes, E. K., Blanchard, V. L., & Fawcett, E. (2008). Increasing fathers' involvement in child care with a couple-focused intervention.

Hawley, P. H., Little, T. D., & Card, N. A. (2007, March). The allure of a mean friend: Relationship quality and processes of aggressive adolescents with prosocial skills. *International Journal of Behavioral Development, 31,* 170–180.

Haworth, C., & Plomin, R. (2010). Quantitative genetics in the era of molecular genetics: Learning abilities and disabilities as an example. *Journal of the American Academy of Child & Adolescent Psychiatry, 49*, 783–793.

Hayes, K., & Hayes, C. (1951). The intellectual development of a homeraised chimpanzee. *Proceedings of the American Philosophical Society, 95*, 105–109.

Haywood, K. M., & Getchell, N. (2005). *Life span motor development* (4th ed.). Champaign, IL: Human Kinetics.

Heath, S. B. (1983). *Ways with words: Language, life, and work in communities and classrooms.* Cambridge, England: Cambridge University Press.

Heckman, J. J., Moon, S. H., Pinto, R., Savelyev, P., & Yavitz, A. (2010). New cost-benefit and rate of return analysis for the Perry Preschool Program: A summary. In J. J. Heckman, S. H. Moon, P. S. Rodrigo Pinto, & A. Yavitz (Eds.), *Childhood programs and practices in the first decade of life: A human capital integration* (pp. 366–380). New York: Cambridge University Press.

Heifetz, S. A. (1996). The umbilical cord: Obstetrically important lesions. *Clinical Obstetric Gynecology, 39*, 571–587.

Heights, R. (1999). Identity development of homosexual youth and parental and familiar influences on the coming out process. *Adolescence, 34*, 597–601.

Heinsohn, R., & Double, M. (2004). Cooperate or speciate: New theory for the distribution of passerine birds. *Trends in Ecology and Evolution, 19*, 55–60.

Helland, T., Asbjornsen, A. E., Hushovd, E., & Hugdahl, K. (2008). Dichotic listening and school performance in dyslexia. *Dyslexia: An International Journal of Research and Practice, 14*, 42–53.

Helwig, C. C. (2008). The moral judgment of the child reevaluated: Heteronomy, early morality, and reasoning about social justice and inequalities. In C. Wainryb, J. G. Smetana, & E. Turiel. (Eds.), *Social development, social inequalities, and social justice.* Mahwah, NJ: Lawrence Erlbaum Associates.

Helwig, C. C., Yang, S., Tan, D., Liu, C., & Shao, T. (2011). Urban and rural Chinese adolescents' judgments and reasoning about personal and group jurisdiction. *Child Development, 82*, 701–716.

Henrich, J. (2004). Demography and cultural evolution: Why adaptive cultural processes produced maladaptive losses in Tasmania. *American Antiquity, 69*, 197–218.

Henrich, J., & Henrich, N. (2006). Culture, evolution and the puzzle of human cooperation. *Cognitive Systems Research. Special Issue: Cognition, Joint Action and Collective Intentionality, 7*(2–3), 220–245.

Herbenick, D., Reece, M., Schick, V., & Sanders, S. (2010). Sexual behavior in the United States: Results from a national probability sample of men and women ages 14–94. *Journal of Sexual Medicine, 7*, 255–265.

Herek, G. M. (2006). Legal recognition of same-sex relationships in the United States: A social science perspective. *American Psychologist, 61*(6), 607–621.

Herman-Giddens, M. E. (2006). Recent data on pubertal milestones in United States children: the secular trend toward earlier development. *International Journal of Andrology, 29*(1), 241–246;

Herman-Giddens, M. E. (2007). The decline in the age of menarche in the United States: should we be concerned? *Journal of Adolescent Health, 40*, 201–203.

Herrnstein, R. J., & Murray, C. (1994). *The bell curve: Intelligence and class structure in American life.* New York: Free Press.

Herzog, D. B., Dorer, D. J., Keel, P. K., Selwyn, S. E., Ekeblad, E. R., Flores, A. T., Greenwood, D. N., et al. (1999). Recovery and relapse in anorexia and bulimia nervosa: a 7.5-year follow-up study. *Journal of the American Academy of Child & Adolescent Psychiatry, 38*, 829–837.

Hespos, S. J., & Baillargeon, R. C. (2008). Young infants' actions reveal their developing knowledge of support variables: Converging evidence for violation-of-expectation findings. *Cognition, 107*, 304–316.

Hetherington, E. M. (1988). Parents, children, and siblings: Six years after divorce. In R. A. Hinde & J. Stevenson-Hinde (Eds.), *Relationships within families: Mutual influences.* Oxford, England: Oxford University Press.

Hetherington, E. M. (2006). The influence of conflict, marital problem solving and parenting on children's adjustment in nondivorced, divorced and remarried families. In A. Clarke-Stewart & J. Dunn (Eds.), *Families count: Effects on child and adolescent development. The Jacobs Foundation series on adolescence* (pp. 203–237). New York: Cambridge University Press.

Hetherington, E. M., Collins, W. A., & Laursen, E. (1999). Social capital and the development of youth from nondivorced, divorced and remarried families. In W. A. Collins (Ed.), *Relationships as developmental contexts* (pp. 177–209). Mahwah, NJ: Lawrence Erlbaum Associates.

Hewlett, B. S. (1992). The parent-infant relationship and socio-emotional development among Aka pygmies. In J. L. Roopnarine & D. B. Carter (Eds.), *Parent-child socialization in diverse cultures: Vol. 5* (pp. 223–244). Norwood, NJ: Ablex.

Hewlett, B., & Lamb, M. (2005). Emerging issues in the study of hunter-gatherer children. In B. Hewlitt & M. Lamb (Eds.), *Hunter-gatherer childhoods: Evolutionary, cultural and developmental perspectives.* New Brunswick, NJ: Transaction Publishers.

Hewlett, B. S., Lamb, M. E., Shannon, D., Leyendecker, B., & Schölmerich, A. (1998). "Culture and early infancy among central African foragers and farmers": Correction to Hewlett et al. (1998). *Developmental Psychology, 34*, 891.

Heywood, C. (2001). *A history of childhood: Children and childhood from medieval to modern times.* Malden, MA: Polity Press.

HHS/U.S. Department of Health and Human Services, (2003). Summary: Child Maltreatment 2003. Retrieved from http://www.acf.hhs.gov/programs/cb/pubs/cm03/summary.htm

Hickendorff, M., van Putten, C. M., Verhelst, N. D., & Heiser, W. J. (2010). Individual differences in strategy use on division problems: Mental versus written computation. *Journal of Educational Psychology, 102*, 438–452.

Hickling, A. K., & Wellman, H. M. (2001). The emergence of children's causal explanations and theories: Evidence from everyday conversation. *Developmental Psychology, 37*(5), 668–683.

Hicks, L. E., Langham, R. A., & Takenaka, J. (1982). Cognitive and health measures following early nutritional supplementation: A sibling study. *American Journal of Public Health, 72*, 1110–1118.

Hiebert, J., Stigler, J. W., Jacobs, J. K., Givvin, K. B., Garnier, H., Smith, M., et al. (2005). Mathematics teaching in the United States today (and tomorrow): Results from the TIMSS 1999 Video Study. *Educational Evaluation and Policy Analysis, 27*(2), 111–132.

Hindman, H. D. (2002). *Child labor: An American history.* Armonk, NY: Sharpe.

Hindmarsh, P. C., Geary, M. P., Rodeck, C. H., Kingdom, J. C., & Cole, T. J. (2008). Factors predicting ante- and postnatal growth. *Pediatric Research, 63*(1), 99–102.

Hirsh-Pasek, K., Golinkoff, R. M., Berk, L. E., & Singer, D. G. (2009). *A mandate for playful learning in preschool: Presenting the evidence.* New York: Oxford University Press.

Hodges, J., & Tizard, B. (1989a). IQ and behavioral adjustments of exinstitutional adolescents. *Journal of Child Psychology and Psychiatry, 30*, 53–75.

Hodges, J., & Tizard, B. (1989b). Social and family relationships of exinstitutional adolescents. *Journal of Child Psychology and Psychiatry, 30*, 77–97.

Hofer, B. (2008). Personal epistemology and culture. In M. Khine (Ed.), *Knowing, knowledge and beliefs: Epistemological studies across diverse culture* (pp. 3–22). New York: Springer Science + Business Media.

Hoff, E. (2001). *Language development.* Belmont, CA: Wadsworth

Hoff, E. (2006, March). How social contexts support and shape language development. *Developmental Review, 26*(1), 55–88.

Hoff-Ginsberg, E., & Tardiff, T. (1995). Socioeconomic status and parenting. In M. H. Bornstein (Ed.), *Handbook of parenting: Biology and ecology of parenting: Vol. 2* (pp. 161–188). Mahwah, NJ: Lawrence Erlbaum Associates.

Hoffman, S. (2006). By the numbers: The public costs of teen childbearing. Retrieved October 15th, 2011, Retrieved from www.thenationalcampaign.org/resources/pdf/pubs/btn_full.pdf

Holcroft, C. J., Blakemore, K. J., Allen, M. A., & Graham, E. M. (2003). Prematurity and neonatal infection are most predictive of neurologic morbidity in very low birthweight infants. *Obstetrics & Gynecology, 101,* 1249–1254.

Holden, G. W. (2002). Perspectives on the effects of corporal punishment: Comment on Gershoff (2002). *Psychological Bulletin, 128,* 590–595.

Holmbeck, G. N. (1996). A model of family relational transformations during the transition to adolescence: Parent-adolescent conflict and adaptation. In J. A. Graber & J. Brooks-Gunn (Eds.), *Transitions through adolescence: Interpersonal domains and context* (pp. 167–199). Mahwah, NJ: Lawrence Erlbaum Associates.

Holmbeck, G. N., Paikoff, R. L., & Brooks-Gunn, J. (1995). Parenting adolescents. In M. H. Bornstein (Ed.), *Handbook of parenting: Children and parenting: Vol. 1* (pp. 91–118). Mahwah, NJ: Lawrence Erlbaum Associates.

Holm-Denoma, J. M., Lewinsohn, P. M., Gau, J. M., Joiner, T. E., Jr., Striegel-Moore, R., & Otamendi, A. (2005, November). Parents' reports of the body shape and feeding habits of 36-month-old children: An investigation of gender differences. *International Journal of Eating Disorders, 38*(3), 228–235.

Holowka, S., & Petitto, L. A. (2002). Left hemisphere cerebral specialization for babies while babbling. *Science, 297*(5586).

Holsti, L., Grunau, R. V. E., & Whitfield, M. F. (2002). Developmental coordination disorder in extremely low birth weight children at nine years. *Journal of Developmental and Behavioral Pediatrics, 23,* 9–15.

Honwana, A. (2000). Children of war: Understanding war and war cleansing in Mozambique and Angola. Retrieved April 25, 2006, from http://cas.uchicago.edu/workshops/African/papers/honwana.htm

Hopkins, B., & Westen, T. (1988). Maternal handling and motor development: An intracultural study. *Genetic Psychology Monographs, 14,* 377–420.

Horn, S. S., Kosciw, J. G., & Russell, S. T. (2009). Special issue introduction: New research on lesbian, gay, bisexual, and transgender youth: Studying lives in context. *Journal of Youth and Adolescence, 38,* 863–866.

Horn, T. S. (Ed.). (2002). *Advances in sport psychology.* Champaign, IL: Human Kinetics.

Hoshower, L. M., Buikstra, J. E., Goldstein, P. S., & Webster, A. D. (1995). Artificial cranial deformation at the Omo M10 site: A Tiwanaku complex from the Moquegua Valley, Peru. *Latin American Antiquity, 6,* 145–164.

Hossain, Z., Roopnarine, J. L., Ismail, R., Hashmi, S., & Sombuling, A. (2007). Fathers' and mothers' reports of involvement in caring for infants in Kadazan families in Sabah, Malaysia. *Fathering, 5*(1), 58–72.

Hoven, C. W., Duarte, C. S., Wu, P., Erickson, E. A., Musa, G. J., & Mandell, D. J. (2004, October). Exposure to trauma and separation anxiety in children after the WTC attack. *Applied Developmental Science. 8*(4), 172–183.

Howe, N., Brody, M.-H., & Recchia, H. (2006). Effects of task difficulty on sibling teaching in middle childhood. *Infant and Child Development, 15*(5), 455–470.

Howe, N., Aquan-Assee, J., Bukowski, W. M., Lehoux, P. M., & Rinaldi, C. M. (2001). Siblings as confidants: Emotional understanding, relationship warmth, and sibling self-disclosure. *Social Development, 10,* 439–454.

Howell, S. (1984). Equality and hierarchy in Chewong classification. *Journal of the Anthropological Society of Oxford, 15*(1), 30–44.

Howes, C. (1999). Attachment relationships in the context of multiple caregivers. In J. Cassidy & P. R. Shaver (Eds.), *Handbook of attachment: Theory, research, and clinical applications* (pp. 671–687). New York: Guilford Press.

Hrdy, S. (2009). *Mothers and others: The evolutionary origins of mutual understanding.* Cambridge, MA: Harvard University Press.

Hrdy, S. B. (2007). Evolutionary context of human development: The cooperative breeding model. In C. A. Salmon & T. D. Shackelford (Eds.), *Family relationships: An evolutionary perspective* (pp. 39–68). New York: Oxford University Press.

Huang-Pollack, C. L., Carr, T. H., & Nigg, J. T. (2002). Development of selective attention: Perceptual load influences early versus late attentional selection in children and adults. *Developmental Psychology, 38,* 363–375.

Hubel, D., & Wiesel, T. (2004). *Brain and visual perception: The story of a 25-year collaboration.* New York: Oxford University Press.

Huelsken, C., Sodian, B., & Pickel, G. (2001). Distinguishing between appearance and reality in a dressing-up game—a problem of dual coding or preserving identity? *Zeitschrift für Entwicklungspsychologie und Paedagogische Psychologie, 33*(3), 129–137.

Hughes, C., Jafee, S., Happe, F., Taylor, A., Caspi, A., & Moffitt, T. (2005). Origins of individuals differences in theory of mind: From nature to nurture. *Child Development, 76*(2), 356–370.

Hughes, D. (2003). Correlates of African American and Latino parents' messages to children about ethnicity and race: A comparative study of racial socialization. *American Journal of Community Psychology, 31,* 15–33.

Hughes, D., & Chen, L. (1999). The nature of parents' race-related communications to children: A developmental perspective. In L. Balter & C. S. Tamis-LeMonda (Eds.), *Child psychology: A handbook of contemporary issues* (pp. 467–490). Philadelphia: Psychology Press.

Hughes, D., Rodriguez, J., Smith, E., Johnson, D. J., Stevenson, H. C., & Spicer, P. (2006, September). Parents' ethnic-racial socialization practices: A review of research and directions for future study. *Developmental Psychology, 42,* 747–770.

Hughes, E. K., Gullone, E., & Watson, S. D. (2011). Emotional functioning in children and adolescents with elevated depressive symptoms. *Journal of Psychopathology and Behavioral Assessment, 33,* 335–345.

Hughes, H., Graham-Bermann, S., & Gruber, G. (2001). Resilience in children exposed to domestic violence. In S. Graham-Bermann & J. Edleson (Eds.), *Domestic violence in the lives of children: The future of research, intervention and social policy.* Washington, DC: American Psychological Association.

Huizink, A. C., & Mulder, E. J. (2006). Maternal smoking, drinking or cannabis use during pregnancy and neurobehavioral and cognitive functioning in human offspring. *Neuroscience & Biobehavioral Reviews, 30,* 24–41.

Hulbert, A. (2003). *Raising America: Experts, parents, and a century of advice about children.* New York: Knopf.

Hunsley, M., & Thoman, E. B. (2002). The sleep of co-sleeping infants when they are not co-sleeping: Evidence that co-sleeping is stressful. *Developmental Psychobiology, 40,* 14–22.

Hurd, Y. L., Wang, X., Anderson, V., Beck, O., Minkoff, H., & Dow-Edwards, D. (2005). Marijuana impairs growth in mid-gestation fetuses. *Neurotoxicology and Teratology, 27,* 221–229.

Hurt, H., Betancourt, L. M., Malmud, E. K., Shera, D. M., Giannetta, J. M., Brodsky, N. L., et al. (2009). Children with and without gestational cocaine exposure: A neurocognitive systems analysis. *Neurotoxicology and Teratology, 31,* 334–341.

Hussong, A. M., Zucker, R. A., Wong, M. M., Fitzgerald, H. E., & Puttler, L. I. (2005). Social competence in children of alcoholic parents over time. *Developmental Psychology, 41,* 747–759.

Huttenlocher, P. R. (1994). Synaptogenesis in human cerebral cortex. In G. Dawson & K. W. Fischer (Eds.), *Human behavior and the developing brain.* New York: Guilford Press.

Hutto, D. D. (2008, April). *Folk psychological narratives: The sociocultural basis of understanding reasons.* Cambridge, MA: The MIT Press.

Huynh, V. W., & Fuligni, A. J. (2008, July). Ethnic socialization and the academic adjustment of adolescents from Mexican, Chinese, and European backgrounds. *Developmental Psychology, 44*(4), 1202–1208.

Hyde, J. S., Mezulis, A., & Abramson, L. (2008). The ABCs of depression: Integrating affective, biological, and cognitive models to explain the emergence of the gender difference in depression. *Psychological Review,* 291–313.

Hymel, S., Vaillancourt, T., McDougall, P., & Renshaw, P. D. (2002). Peer acceptance and rejection in childhood. In P. K. Smith & C. H. Hart (Eds.), *Blackwell handbook of childhood social development* (pp. 265–284). Malden, MA: Blackwell Publishing.

Hymel, S., Wagner, E., & Butler, L. J. (1990). Reputational bias: View from the peer group. In S. R. Asher & J. D. Coie (Eds.), *Peer rejection in childhood.* Cambridge, England: Cambridge University Press.

Iervolino, A. C., Hines, M., Golombok, S. E., Rust, J., & Plomin, R. (2005). Genetic and environmental influences on sex-typed behavior during the preschool years. *Child Development, 76,* 826–840.

Inagaki, K., & Hatano, G. (2002). *Young children's naive thinking about the biological world.* New York: Psychology Press.

Inagaki, K., & Hatano, G. (2006). Young children's conception of the biological world. *Current Directions in Psychological Science, 15,* 177–181.

Inhelder, B., & Piaget, J. (1958). *The growth of logical thinking from childhood to adolescence.* New York: Basic Books.

Inoue-Nakamura, N. (2001). Mirror self-recognition in primates: An ontogenetic and a phylogenetic approach. In T. Matsuzawa (Ed.), *Primate origins of human cognition and behavior* (pp. 297–312). New York: Springer-Verlag.

ISPCAN. (2006). *World perspectives on child abuse* (7th ed.). Chicago: National Society for the Prevention of Child Abuse and Neglect.

Itard, J. M. G. (1801/1982). *The wild boy of Aveyron.* New York: Appleton-Century-Crofts.

Ivey, P. (2000). Cooperative reproduction in Ituri Forest huntergatherers: Who cares for Efe infants? *Current Anthropology, 41,* 856–866.

Izard, C. E., Huebner, R. R., Risser, D., McGinnes, G. C., & Dougherty, L. M. (1980). The young infant's ability to produce discrete emotion expressions. *Developmental Psychology, 16,* 132–140.

Izard, C. E., Woodburn, E. M., & Finlon, K. J. (2010). Extending emotion science to the study of discrete emotions in infants. *Emotion Review, 2,* 134–136.

Izawa, E.-I., Yanagihara, S., Atsumi, T., & Matsushima, T. (2001). The role of basal ganglia in reinforcement learning and imprinting in domestic chicks. *Neuroreport: For Rapid Communication of Neuroscience Research, 12,* 1743–1747.

Jablonka, E., & Lamb, M. (2005). *Evolution in four dimensions.* Cambridge, MA: The MIT Press.

Jablonka, E., & Lamb, M. J. (2007). Precis of evolution in four dimensions. *Behavioral and Brain Sciences, 30,* 353–365.

Jackson, J. P., Jr. (2006). The historical context of the African American social scientist. *Monographs of the Society for Research in Child Development, 71*(1), 218–223.

Jackson, J. S., McCullough, W. R., & Gurin, G. (1997). Family, socialization environment, and identity development in Black Americans. In H. P. McAdoo (Ed.), *Black families* (3rd ed., pp. 251–266). Thousand Oaks, CA: Sage.

Jaeger, J. (2005). *Kids' slips: What young children's slips of the tongue reveal about language development.* Mahwah, NJ: Lawrence Erlbaum Associates.

Jaffe, J., Beebe, B., Feldstein, S., Crown, C. L., & Jasnow, M. D. (2001). *Monographs of the Society for Research in Child Development, 66*(2), vii–131.

Jaffee, S. R., Van Hulle, C., & Rodgers, J. L. (2011). Effects of non-maternal care in the first 3 years on children's academic skills and behavioral functioning in childhood and early adolescence: A sibling comparison study. *Child Development, 82*(4), 1076–1091.

Jahoda, G. (1980). Theoretical and systematic approaches in cross-cultural psychology. In H. C. Triandis & W. W. Lambert (Eds.), *Handbook of cross-cultural psychology: Vol. 1.* Boston: Allyn & Bacon.

James, D. (2010). Fetal learning: A critical review. *Infant and Child Development, 19,* 45–54.

James, D., Pillai, M., & Smoleniec, J. (1995). Neurobehavioral development in the human fetus. In J. P. Lecanuet & W. P. Fifer (Eds.), *Fetal development: A psychobiological perspective* (pp. 101–128). Mahwah, NJ: Lawrence Erlbaum Associates.

James, W. T. (1890). *The principles of psychology.* New York: Holt, Rinehart and Winston.

James, W. T. (1951). Social organization among dogs of different temperaments: Terriers and beagles reared together. *Journal of Comparative and Physiological Psychology, 44,* 71–77.

Jenkins, H. (Ed.). (1998). *The children's culture reader.* New York: New York University Press.

Janowsky, J. S., & Carper, R. (1996). Is there a neural basis for cognitive transitions in school-age children? In Arnold J. Sameroff & M. M. Haith (Eds.), *The five to seven year shift: The age of reason and responsibility.* Chicago: University of Chicago Press.

Jenni, O., Deboer, T., & Achermann, P (2006). Development of the 24-h rest-activity pattern in human infants. *Infant Behavior & Development, 29,* 143–152.

Jennings, K. D., & Dietz, L. J. (2003). Mastery motivation and goal persistence in young children. In M. H. Bornstein, L. Davidson, C. L. Keyes, K. A. Moore, & the Center for Child Well Being (Eds.), *Well-being: Positive development across the life course. Crosscurrents in contemporary psychology* (pp. 295–309). Mahwah, NJ, Lawrence Erlbaum Associates.

Jansz, J. (2000). Masculine identity and restrictive emotionality. In A. H. Fischer (Ed.), *Gender and emotion: Social psychological perspectives* (pp. 24–47). Cambridge, England: Cambridge University Press.

Jarrett, R. (2000). Voices from below: The use of ethnographic research for informing public policy. In J. Mercier, S. Garasky, & M. Shelly (Eds.), *Redefining family policy: Implications for the 21st century.* Ames, IA: Iowa State University Press.

Jia, G., Chen, J., & Kim, H. (2008). Bilingual vocabulary development among infants and toddlers with Chinese or Korean as home languages. Unpublished manuscript.

Jodl, K. M., Michael, A., Malanchuk, O., Eccles, J., & Sameroff, A. (2001). Parents' roles in shaping early adolescents' occupational aspirations. *Child Development, 72,* 1247–1265.

Joh, A., Sweeney, B., & Rovee-Collier, C. (2002). Minimum duration of reactivation at 3 months of age. *Developmental Psychobiology, 40*(1), 23–32.

John, V. P. (1972). Styles of learning—styles of teaching: Reflections on the education of Navajo children. In C. Cazden, V. P. John, & D. Hymes (Eds.), *Functions of language in the classroom* (pp. 331–343). New York: Teachers College Press.

Johnson, D. (2001). Parental characteristics, racial stress, and racial socialization processes as predictors of racial coping in middle childhood. In A. M. Neal-Barnett, J. Contreras, & K. Kerns (Eds.), *Forging links: African American children—clinical and developmental perspectives.* Westport, CT: Praeger

Johnson, D., Jaeger, E., Randolph, S., Cauce, A., Ward, J., & NICHD Early Child Care Research Network. (2001). Child care and children's peer interaction at 24 and 36 months: The NICHD Study of Early Child Care. *Child Development, 72,* 1478–1500.

Johnson, S., Amso, D., & Slemmer, J. (2003). Development of object concepts in infancy: Evidence for early learning in an eye-tracking paradigm. *Proceedings of the National Academy of Science, USA, 100,* 10568–10573.

Johnson, S. P., Amso, D., Frank, M., & Shuwairi, S. (2008). Perceptual development in infancy as the foundation of event perception. In S. P. Johnson, D. Amso, M. Frank, & S. Shuwairi (Eds.), *Understanding events: From perception to action* (pp. 65–95): Oxford University Press.

Jolly, A. (1999). *Lucy's legacy: Sex and intelligence in human evolution.* Cambridge, MA: Harvard University Press.

Jones, H. E. (2006). Drug addiction during pregnancy: Advances in maternal treatment and understanding child outcomes. *Current Directions in Psychological Science, 15*(3), 126–130.

Jones, R. E. (1997). *Human reproductive biology.* San Diego: Academic Press.

Jones, M., Yonezawa, S., Ballesteros, E., & Mehan, H. (2002). Shaping pathways to higher education. *Educational Researcher, 3,* 3–17.

Jones, S. M., & Zigler, E. (2002). The Mozart effect: Not learning from history. *Journal of Applied Developmental Psychology, 23*(3), 355–372.

Jordan, B. (1993). *Birth in four cultures: A cross-cultural investigation of childbirth in* Yucatan, Holland, Sweden, and the United States. Prospect Heights, IL: Waveland Press.

Jordan, K., & Brannon, E. (2006). The multisensory representation of number in infancy. *Proceedings of the National Academy of Sciences, 103,* 3486–3489.

Jordan-Young, R. (2010). *Brain storm.* Cambridge, MA: Harvard University Press.

Joseph, J. (2001). Separated twins and the genetics of personality differences: A critique. *American Journal of Psychology, 114*(1), 1–30.

Joseph, K. S., Liston, R. M., Dodds, L., Dahlgren, L., & Allen, A. C. (2007). Socioeconomic status and perinatal outcomes in a setting with universal access to essential health care services. *Canadian Medical Association Journal, 177,* 583–590.

Joshi, M. S., & MacLean, M. (1994). Indian and English children's understanding of the distinction between real and apparent emotion. *Child Development, 65,* 1372–1384.

Juang, L. P., & Silbereisen, R. K. (2002). The relationship between adolescent academic capability beliefs, parenting and school grades. *Journal of Adolescence, 25,* 3–18.

Jung, C. (1915). *The theory of psychoanalysis.* New York: Nervous and Mental Disease Publishing Company.

Jusczyk, P. W. (2001). Finding and remembering words: Some beginnings by English-learning infants. In E. Bates (Ed.), *Language development: The essential readings* (pp. 19–25). Malden, MA: Blackwell Publishing.

Justice, E., Lindsey, L., & Morrow, S. (1999). The relation of self-perceptions to achievement among African American preschoolers. *Journal of Black Psychology, 25,* 48–60.

Juston, A., Bickham, D., Lee, J., & Wright, J. (2007). From attention to comprehension: How children watch and learn from television. In N. Pecora, J. Murray, & E. Wartella (Eds.), Children and television: Fifty years of research. Mahwah, NJ: Lawrence Erlbaum Associates.

Jyoti, D. F., Frongillo, E. A., & Jones, S. J. (2005). Food insecurity affects school children's academic performance, weight gain, and social skills. *Journal of Nutrition, 135,* 2831–2839.

Kagan, J. (1981). *The second year: The emergence of self-awareness.* Cambridge MA: Harvard University Press.

Kagan, J. (2000). Human morality is distinctive. *Journal of Consciousness Studies, 7*(1–2), 46–48.

Kagan, J. (2001). Biological constraint, cultural variety, and psychological structures. In A. Harrington (Ed.), *Unity of knowledge: The convergence of natural and human science* (pp. 177–190). New York: New York Academy of Sciences.

Kagan, S., & Madsen, M. C. (1971). Cooperation and competition of Mexican, Mexican-American, and Anglo-American children of two ages under four instructional sets. *Developmental Psychology, 5,* 32–39.

Kağıtçıbaşı, Ç. (2003). Autonomy, embeddedness and adaptability in immigration contexts. *Human Development, 46*(2–3), 145–150.

Kağıtçıbaşı, Ç. (2007). *Family, self, and human development across cultures: Theories and applications* (2nd ed.). Mahwah, NJ: Lawrence Erlbaum Associates.

Kaiser Foundation. (2008, March). *HIV/AIDS policy fact sheet 2008.* Retrieved October 10, 2008, from http://www.kff.org/hivaids/upload/3029-09.pdf

Kalanda, B. F., van Buuren, S., Verhoeff, F. H., & Brabin, B. J. (2005). Catch-up growth in Malawian babies, a longitudinal study of normal and low birthweight babies born in a malarious endemic area. *Early Human Development, 81,* 841–850.

Kalkwarf, H. J., Zemel, B. S., Gilsanz, V., Lappe, J. M., Horlick, M., Oberfield, S., et al. (2007). The Bone Mineral Density in Childhood Study: Bone Mineral Content and Density According to Age, Sex, and Race. *Journal of Clinical Endocrinology & Metabolism, 92,* 2087–2099.

Kaltenbach, K., Berghella, V., Finnegan, L., & Woods, J. R., Jr. (1998). Opioid dependence during pregnancy: effects and management in substance abuse in pregnancy. *Obstetrics and Gynecology Clinics of North America, 25*(1), 139–152.

Kamara, A. I., & Easley, J. A. (1977). Is the rate of cognitive development uniform across cultures? A methodological critique with new evidence from Themne children. In P. R. Dasen (Ed.), *Piagetian psychology: Cross-cultural contributions.* New York: Gardner.

Kandel, D. (1978). Homophily, selection, and socialization in adolescent friendships. *American Journal of Sociology, 84,* 427–436.

Kandel, D. B., & Chen, K. (2000, May). Types of marijuana users by longitudinal course. *Journal of Studies on Alcohol, 61*(3), 367–378.

Kaplan, H., & Dove, H. (1987). Infant development among the Ache of Eastern Paraguay. *Developmental Psychology, 23,* 190–198.

Kaplan, H., Lancaster, J., Hill, K., Hurtado, M., & Robson, A. (2003). Embodied capital and the evolutionary economics of the human life span. *Population and Development Review 29*(3) Suppl., 152–182.

Kaptijn, R., Thomese, F., Van Tilburg, T. G., & Liefbroer, A. C. (2010). How grandparents matter: Support for the cooperative breeding hypothesis in a contemporary Dutch population. *Human Nature, 21,* 393–405.

Karmiloff, K., & Karmiloff-Smith, A. (2001). *Pathways to language: From fetus to adolescent*. Cambridge, MA: Harvard University Press.

Karsten, S. L., Sang, T.-K., Gehman, L. T., Chatterjee, S., Liu J., Lawless, G. M., et al. (2006). A genomic screen for modifiers of tauopathy identifies puromycin-sensitive aminopeptidase as an inhibitor of tauinduced neurodegeneration. *Neuron, 51,* 549–560.

Katchadourian, H. A. (1977). *The biology of adolescence*. San Francisco: W. H. Freeman.

Kaufman, J., & Zigler, E. (1989). The intergenerational transmission of child abuse. In D. Cicchetti & V. Carlson (Eds.), *Child maltreatment: Theory and research on the causes and consequences of child abuse and neglect*. Cambridge, England: Cambridge University Press.

Kaye, K. (1982). *The mental and social life of babies*. Chicago: University of Chicago Press.

Keating, D. (2004). Cognitive and brain development. In R. M. Lerner & L. Steinberg (Eds.), *Handbook of adolescent psychology* (2nd ed.). Hoboken, NJ: John Wiley & Sons.

Keating, D. P., & Halpern-Felsher, B. L. (2008). Adolescent drivers: A developmental perspective on risk, proficiency, and safety. *American Journal of Preventive Medicine, 35,* S272-S277.

Keel, P. K., Gravener, J. A., Joiner, T. E., Jr., & Haedt, A. A. (2010). Twenty-year follow-up of bulimia nervosa and related eating disorders not otherwise specified. *International Journal of Eating Disorders, 43,* 492–497.

Keel, P. K., & Klump, K. L. (2003). Are eating disorders culture-bound syndromes? Implications for conceptualizing their etiology. *Psychological Bulletin, 129,* 747–769.

Keenan, K., Hipwell, A., Chung, T., Stepp, S., Stouthamer-Loeber, M., Loeber, R., et al. (2010). The Pittsburgh girls study: Overview and initial findings. *Journal of Clinical Child and Adolescent Psychology, 39,* 506–521.

Keeney, T. J., Cannizzo, S. D., & Flavell, J. H. (1967). Spontaneous and induced verbal rehearsal in a recall task. *Child Development, 38,* 935–966.

Keller, H. (2003). Socialization for competence: Cultural models of infancy. *Human Development, 46*(5), 228–311.

Keller, H. (2011) Culture and cognition: Developmental perspectives. *Journal of Cognitive Education and Psychology, 10,* 3–8.

Keller, H., Borke, J., Chaudhary, N., Lamm, B., Kleis, A., et al. (2010). Continuity in parenting strategies: A cross-cultural comparison. *Journal of Cross-Cultural Psychology, 41,* 391–409.

Kelley, T. (2005, October 9). Toilet training at 6 months? Better take a seat. *New York Times.*

Kellman, P. J., & Banks, M. S. (1998). Infant visual perception. In R. Siegler & D. Kuhn (Eds.), *Handbook of child psychology: Vol. 2* (5th ed., pp. 103–146). New York: Wiley.

Kellogg, W. N., & Kellogg, L. A. (1933). *The ape and the child: A study of environmental influences upon early behavior*. New York: Whittlesey House.

Kelly, D. J., Liu, S., Lee, K., Quinn, P. C., & Pascalis, O. (2009). Development of the other-race effect during infancy: Evidence toward universality? *Journal of Experimental Child Psychology, 104,* 105–114.

Keniston, K. (1963). Social change and youth in America. In E. Erikson (Ed.), *Youth: Change and challenge*. New York: Basic Books.

Kennard, B. D., Clarke, G. N., Weersing, V. R., Asarnow, J. R., Shamseddeen, W., Porta, G., et al. (2009). Effective components of TORDIA cognitive–behavioral therapy for adolescentdepression: Preliminary findings. *Journal of Consulting and Clinical Psychology, 77,* 1033–1041.

Kermayer, L. (1994). Suicide among Canadian aboriginal people. *Transcultural Psychiatric Research Review, 31,* 3–57.

Kesmodel, U. (2001). Binge drinking in pregnancy: Frequency and methodology. *American Journal of Epidemiology, 154*(8), 777–782.

Kesner, J., & McKenry, P. (2001). Single parenthood and social competence in children of color. *Families in Society, 82,* 136–144.

Kett, J. F. (1977). *Rites of passage: Adolescence in America 1790 to the present*. New York: Basic Books.

Khan, I., Dekou, V., Hanson, M., Poston, L., & Taylor, P. (2004). Predictive adaptive responses to maternal high-fat diet prevent endothelial dysfunction but not hypertension in adult rat off-spring. *Circulation, 110,* 1097–1102.

Kiell, N. (1959). *The adolescent through fiction: A psychological approach*. New York: International Universities Press.

Killen, M., McGlothlin, H., & Lee–Kim, J. (2002). Between individuals and culture: Individuals' evaluations of exclusion from social groups. In H. Keller, Y. Poortinga, & A. Schoelmerich (Eds.), *Between biology and culture: Perspectives on ontogenetic development*. Cambridge, England: Cambridge University Press.

Killen, M., & Smetana, J. (2007, September). The biology of morality: Human development and moral neuroscience. *Human Development, 50*(5), 241–243.

Killen, M., & Smetana, J. G. (2010). Future directions: Social development in the context of social justice. *Social Development, 19,* 642–657.

Kim, E., Han, G., & McCubbin, M. A. (2007). Korean American maternal acceptance-rejection, acculturation, and children's social competence. *Family & Community Health, 30*(Suppl. 2), S33–S45.

Kim, I.-K., & Spelke, E. S. (1999). Perception and understanding of effects of gravity and inertia on object motion. *Developmental Science 2*(3), 339–362.

Kim, J. M. (1998). Korean children's concepts of adult and per authority and moral reasoning. *Developmental Psychology, 34,* 947–955.

Kim, J.-Y., McHale, S. M., Osgood, D. W., & Crouter, A. C. (2006). Longitudinal course and family correlates of sibling relationships from childhood through adolescence. *Child Development, 77,* 1746–1761.

Kim, K., Conger, R., Lorenz, F., & Elder, G. (2001). Parent-adolescent reciprocity in negative affect and its relation to early adult social development. *Developmental Psychology, 37,* 775–790.

Kim, S., Conway-Turner, K., Sherif-Trask, B., & Wolfolk, T. (2006). Reconstructing mothering among Korean immigrant working class women in the United States. *Journal of Comparative Family Studies, 37,* 43–65.

Kim, U., & Park, Y.-S. (2006). The scientific foundation of indigenous and cultural psychology: The transactional approach. In U. Kim, K.-S. Yang, & K.-K. Hwang (Eds.), *Indigenous and cultural psychology: Understanding people in context* (pp. 27–48). New York: Springer Science.

Kins, E., & Beyers, W. (2010). Failure to launch, failure to achieve criteria for adulthood? *Journal of Adolescent Research, 25,* 743–777.

Kirsh, S. (2006). *Children, adolescence and media violence: A critical look at research*. New York: Sage.

Kisilevsky, B. S., & Hains, S. M. (2010). Exploring the relationship between fetal heart rate and cognition. *Infant and Child Development, 19,* 60–75.

Kisilevsky, B. S., Hains, S. M., Lee, K. Muir, D. W., Xu, F., Fu, G., et al. (1998). The still-face effect in Chinese and Canadian 3- to 6-month-old infants. *Child Developmental Psychology, 34,* 629–639.

Kisilevsky, B. S., & Low, J. A. (1998). Human fetal behavior: 100 years of study. *Developmental Review, 18,* 1–29.

Kitamura, C., Thanavishuth, C., Luksaneeyanawin, S., & Burnham, D. (2002). Universality and specificity in infant-directed speech: Pitch modifications as a function of infant age and sex in a tonal and nontonal language. *Infant Behavior & Development, 2,* 372–392.

Klaczynski, P. A., & Cottrell, J. M. (2004). A dual-process approach to cognitive development: The case of children's understanding of sunk cost decisions. *Thinking & Reasoning, 10,* 147–174.

Klahr, D. (1989). Information-processing approaches. In R. Vasta (Ed.), *Annals of child development: Vol. 6. Six theories of child development: Revised formulations and current issues.* Greenwich, CT: JAI Press.

Klasen, F., Oettingen, G., Daniels, J., Post, M., & Hoyer, C. (2010). Posttraumatic resilience in former Ugandan child soldiers. *Child Development, 81,* 1096–1113.

Klaus, M. H., Kennell, J. H., & Klaus, P. H. (1995). *Bonding: Building the foundations of secure attachment and independence.* Reading, MA: Addison-Wesley.

Klemfuss, J. Z., & Ceci, S. (2009). Normative memory development and the child witness. In J. Z. Klemfuss & S. Ceci (Eds.), *The evaluation of child sexual abuse allegations: A comprehensive guide to assessment and testimony* (pp. 153–180). Hoboken, NJ: John Wiley & Sons.

Kline, M., & Boyd, R. (2010). Population size predicts technological complexity in Oceania. *Proceedings of the Royal Society (B), 277,* 2559–2564.

Klineberg, O. (1935). *Race differences.* New York: Harper & Row.

Klinger, J., Vaughn, B., & Schumm, J. (1998). Collaborative strategic reading during social studies and heterogeneous fourth-grade classrooms. *The Elementary School Journal, 96,* 275–293.

Knickmeyer, R., Wheelwright, S., Taylor, K., Raggatt, P., Hackett, G., & Baron-Cohen, S. (2005). Gender-typed play and amniotic testosterone. *Developmental Psychology, 41,* 517–528.

Kochanska, G., & Askan, N. (1995). Mother-child mutually positive affect, the quality of child compliance to requests, and prohibitions, and maternal control as correlates of early internalization. *Child Development, 66,* 236–254.

Kochanska, G., & Aksan, N. (2006). Children's conscience and self-regulation. *Journal of Personality, 74,* 1587–1617.

Kochanska, G., Philibert, R. A., & Barry, R. A. (2009). Interplay of genes and early mother-child relationship in the development of self-regulation from toddler to preschool age. *Journal of Child Psychology and Psychiatry, 50,* 1331–1338.

Kochukhova, O., & Gredebäck, G. (2007). Learning about occlusion: Initial assumptions and rapid adjustments. *Cognition, 105,* 26–46.

Kohlberg, L. (1966). A cognitive-developmental analysis of children's sex role concepts and attitudes. In E. E. Maccoby (Ed.), *The development of sex differences.* Palo Alto, CA: Stanford University Press.

Kohlberg, L. (1969). Stage and sequence: The cognitive-developmental approach to socialization. In D. A. Goslin (Ed.), *Handbook of socialization theory and research.* Chicago: Rand McNally.

Kohlberg, L. (1976). Moral stages and moralization: The cognitive-developmental approach. In J. Lickona (Ed.), *Moral development behavior: Theory, research and social issues.* New York: Holt, Rinehart and Winston.

Kohlberg, L. (1984). *The psychology of moral development: The nature and validity of moral stages: Vol. 2.* New York: Harper & Row.

Kokis, J., Macpherson, R., Toplak, M., West, R., & Stanovich, K. (2002). Heuristic and analytic processing: Age trends and associations with cognitive ability and cognitive styles. *Journal of Experimental Child Psychology, 83,* 26–52.

Kolata, G. (1986). Obese children: A growing problem. *Science, 232,* 20–21.

Konner, M. (1977). Evolution in human behavior development. In P. H. Leiderman, S. Tulkin, & A. Rosenfeld (Eds.), *Culture and infancy: Variations in human experience.* New York: Academic Press.

Konner, M. (2005). Hunter-gatherer infancy and childhood: The !Kung and others. In B. S. Hewlett & M. E. Lamb (Eds.), *Hunter-gatherer childhoods.* New Brunswick, NJ: Aldine Transaction.

Konner, M. (2010). *The evolution of childhood: Relationships, emotion, mind.* Cambridge, MA: Harvard University Press.

Kontulainen, S. A., Hughes, J. M., Macdonald, H. M., & Johnston, J. D. (2007). The biomechanical basis of bone strength development during growth. *Medicine and Sport Science, 51,* 13–32.

Koopmans-van Beinum, F. J., Clement, C. J., & van den Dikkenberg-Pot, I. (2001). Babbling and the lack of auditory speech perception: A matter of coordination? *Developmental Science, 4*(1), 61–70.

Korner, A. F., & Constantinou, J. C. (2001). The neurobehavioral assessment of the preterm infant: Reliability and developmental and clinical validity. In L. T. Singer & P. S. Zeskind (Eds.), *Biobehavioral assessment of the infant* (pp. 381–397). New York: Guilford Press.

Kost, K., Henshaw, S., & Carlin, L. (2010). U.S. teenage pregnancies, births and abortions: national and state trends and trends by race and ethnicity. Retrieved December 15th, 2011, from http://www.guttmacher.org/pubs/USTPtrends.pdf

Kostovic, I., & Jovanov-Milosevic, N. (2006). The development of cerebral connections during the first 20–45 weeks gestation. *Seminars in Fetal and Neonatal Medicine, 11,* 415–422.

Koyama, R., Takahashi, Y., & Mori, K. (2006). Assessing the cuteness of children: Significant factors and gender differences. *Social Behavior and Personality, 34,* 1087–1100.

Koziel, S., & Jankowska, E. A. (2002). Effect of low versus normal birthweight on menarche in 14-year-old Polish girls. *Journal of Paediatrics and Child Health, 38*(3), 268–271.

Krasnogorski, N. I. (1907/1967). The formation of artificial conditioned reflexes in young children. In Y. Brackbill & G. G. Thompson (Eds.), *Behavior in infancy and early childhood: A book of readings.* New York: Free Press.

Krcmar, M., & Vieira, E. T., Jr. (2005, June). Imitating life, imitating television: The effects of family and television models on children's moral reasoning. *Communication Research, 32*(3), 267–294.

Kreutzer, M. A., Leonard, S. C., & Flavell, J. H. (1975). An interview study of children's knowledge about memory. *Monographs of the Society for Research in Child Development, 40*(1, Serial No. 159).

Kroger, J., Martinussen, M., & Marcia, J. E. (2010). Identity status change during adolescence and young adulthood: A meta-analysis. *Journal of Adolescence, 33,* 683–698.

Kruger, A. C., & Konner, M. (2010). Who responds to crying?: Maternal care and allocare among the !Kung. *Human Nature, 21,* 309–329.

Kuhl, P. K. (2004). Early language acquisition: Cracking the speech code. *Nature Neuroscience Reviews, 5,* 831–843.

Kuhl, P. K., Stevens, E., Hayashi, A., Deguchi, T., Kiritani, S., & Iverson, P. (2006). Infants show a facilitation effect for native language phonetic perception between 6 and 12 months. *Developmental Science, 9*(2), F13–F21.

Kulis, S., Napoli, M., & Marsiglia, F. (2002). Ethnic pride, biculturalism, and drug use norms of urban American Indian adolescents. *Social Work Research, 26,* 101–112.

Kuo, Y.-L., Liao, H.-F., Chen, P.-C., Hsieh, W.-S., & Hwang, A.-W. (2008). The influence of wakeful prone positioning on motor development during the early life. *Developmental and Behavioral Pediatrics, 29,* 367–376.

Kupersmidt, J. B., Coie, J. D., & Howell, J. C. (2004). Resilience in children exposed to negative peer influences. In K. I. Maton, C. J. Schellenbach, B. J. Leadbeater, & A. L. Solarz (Eds.), *Investing in children, youth, families, and communities: Strengths-based research and policy* (pp. 251–268). Washington, DC: American Psychological Association.

Kushnir, T., & Gopnik, A. (2005, September). Young children infer causal strength from probabilities and interventions. *Psychological Science, 16*(9), 678–683.

Kusiako, T., Ronsmans, C., & Van der Paal, L. (2000). Perinatal mortality attributable to complications of childbirth in Matlab, Bangladesh. *Bulletin of the World Health Organization, 78*(5), 621–627.

Kuther, T., & Higgins-D'Alessandro, A. (2000). Bridging the gap between moral reasoning and adolescent engagement in risky behavior. *Journal of Adolescence, 23,* 409–422.

Kuttler, A., & La Greca, A. (2004). Linkages among adolescent girls' romantic relationships, best friendships, and peer networks. *Journal of Adolescence, 27,* 395–414.

Laberge, L., Petit, D., Simard, C., Vitaro, F., Tremblay, R., & Montplaisir, J. (2001). Development of sleep patterns in early adolescence. *Journal of Sleep Research, 10,* 59–67.

Laboratory of Comparative Human Cognition. (1983). Culture and cognitive development. In P. Mussen (Ed.), *Handbook of child psychology: Vol. 1. History, theory, and methods* (4th ed.). New York: Wiley.

Ladd, G. W. (1999). Peer relationships and social competence during early and middle childhood. *Annual Review of Psychology, 50,* 333–359.

Ladd, G. W., & Dinella, L. M. (2009). Continuity and change in early school engagement: Predictive of children's achievement trajectories from first to eighth grade? *Journal of Educational Psychology, 101,* 190–206.

Ladd, G. W., & Troop-Gordon, W. (2003). The role of chronic peer difficulties in the development of children's psychological adjustment problems. *Child Development, 74,* 1344–1367.

LaFontana, K. M., & Cillessen, A. H. N. (2010). Developmental changes in the priority of perceived status in childhood and adolescence. *Social Development, 19,* 130–147.

LaFromboise, T., Hoyr, D., Oliver, L., & Whitbeck, L. (2006). Family, community, and school influences on resilience among American Indian adolescents in the upper Midwest. *Journal of Community Psychology, 34,* 193–209.

Lagattuta, K. H., Nucci, L., & Bosacki, S. L. (2010). Bridging theory of mind and the personal domain: Children's reasoning about resistance to parental control. *Child Development, 81,* 616–635.

Lagercrantz, H., & Slotkin, T. A. (1986). The "stress" of being born. *Scientific American, 254,* 100–107.

Lahey, B. B., Schwab-Stone, M., Goodman, S. H., Waldman, I. D., Canino, G., Rathouz, P. J.; et al. (2000). Age and gender differences in oppositional behavior and conduct problems: A cross-sectional household study of middle childhood and adolescence. *Journal of Abnormal Psychology, 109,* 488–503.

Laland, K., Odling-Smee, J., & Feldman, M. (2000). Niche construction, biological evolution, and cultural change. *Behavioral and Brain Sciences, 23,* 131–175.

Lamb, M. E. (2010). How do fathers influence children's development? Let me count the ways. In M. E. Lamb (Ed.), *The role of the father in child development* (5 ed., pp. 1–26). New York: John Wiley & Sons.

Lamb, M. E., & Ahnert, L. (2006). Nonparental child care: Context, concepts, correlates, and consequences. In K. A. Renninger, I. E. Sigel, W. Damon, & R. M. Lerner (Eds.), *Handbook of child psychology: Vol. 4. Child psychology in practice* (6th ed., pp. 950–1016). Hoboken, NJ: John Wiley & Sons.

Lamb, M. E., Hwang, C. P., Ketterlinus, R. D., & Fracasso, M. P. (1999). Parent-child relationships: Development in the context of the family. In M. H. Bornstein & M. E. Lamb (Eds.), *Developmental psychology: An advanced textbook* (pp. 411–450). Mahwah, NJ: Lawrence Erlbaum Associates.

Lamb, M. E., & Lewis, C. (2005). The role of parent-child relationships in child development. In M. H. Bornstein & M. E. Lamb (Eds.), *Developmental science: An advanced textbook* (5th ed., pp. 429–468). Mahwah, NJ: Lawrence Erlbaum Associates.

Landau, B., & Gleitman, L. R. (1985). *Language and experience: Evidence from the blind child. Cognitive science series, 8.* Cambridge, MA: Harvard University Press.

Lander, K., Chuang, L., & Wickham, L. (2006). Recognizing face identity from natural and morphed smiles. *The Quarterly Journal of Experimental Psychology (2006), 59,* 801–808.

Lane, H. (1976). *The wild boy of Aveyron.* Cambridge, MA: Harvard University Press.

Langlois, J. H. (1986). From the eye of the beholder to behavioral reality: Development of social behaviors and social relations as a function of physical attractiveness. In C. P. Herman, M. P. Zanna, & E. T. Higgins (Eds.), *Physical appearance, stigma, and social behavior: The Ontario Symposium Vol. 3:* Mahwah, NJ: Erlbaum.

Langlois, J. H., Kalakanis, L., Rubenstein, A. J., Larson, A., Hallam, M., & Smoot, M. (2000). Maxims or myths of beauty? A meta-analysis and theoretical review. *Psychological Bulletin, 126,* 390–423.

Langlois, J. H., Ritter, J. M., Casey, R. J., & Sawin, D. B. (1995). Infant attractiveness predicts maternal behaviors and attitudes. *Developmental Psychology, 31,* 464–472.

Largo, R. H., Molinari, L., von Siebenthal, K., & Wolfensberger, U. (1996). Does a profound change in toilet-training affect development of bowel and bladder control? *Developmental Medicine and Child Neurology, 38,* 1106–1116.

Larsen, B. (1996). Closeness and conflict in adolescent peer relationships: Interdependence with friends and romantic partneter. In W. Bukowski, A. Newcomb, & W. Hartup (Eds.), *The company they keep: Friendship in childhood and adolescence.* New York: Cambridge University Press.

Larson, N., Neumark-Sztainer, D., Hannan, P. J., & Story, M. (2007). Family meals during adolescence are associated with higher diet quality and sihealthful meal patterns during young adulthood. *Journal of the American Dietetic Association, 107,* 1502–1510.

Larson, R., Moneta, G., Richards, M., & Wilson, S. (2002). Continuity, stability, and change in daily emotional experience across adolescence. *Child Development, 73,* 1151–1165.

Larson, R. W. (2007). From "I" to "we": Development of the capacity for teamwork in youth programs. In R. K. Silbereisen & R. M. Lerner (Eds.). *Approaches to positive youth development* (pp. 277–292). London: Sage.

Larson, R., & Richards, M. (1991). Daily companionship in late childhood and early adolescence: Changing developmental contexts. *Child Development, 62,* 284–300.

Larson, R., & Richards, M. (2000). *Changes in daily emotions associated with entry into adolescence for urban African Americans.* Paper presented at the biannual meeting of the International Society for the Study of Behavioral Development, Beijing, China.

Larson, R. W., & Walker, K. C. (2006). Learning about the "real world" in an urban arts youth program. *Journal of Adolescent Research, 21,* 244–268.

Laupa, M., Turiel, E., & Cowan, P. (1995). Obedience to authority in children and adults. In M. Killen & D. Hart (Eds.), *Morality in everyday life: Developmental perspectives* (pp. 131–165). Cambridge, England: Cambridge University Press.

Laursen, B., & Collins, W. A. (2009). Parent-child relationships during adolescence. In R. M. Lerner & L. Steinberg (Eds.), *Handbook of adolescent psychology, Vol 2: Contextual influences on adolescent development* (3rd ed., pp. 3–42). Hoboken, NJ: John Wiley & Sons.

Lave, J., & Wenger, E. (1991). *Situated learning: Legitimate peripheral practice.* New York: Cambridge University Press.

Lavezzi, A. M., Corna, M., Mingrone, R., & Matturri, L. (2010). Study of the human hypoglossal nucleus: Normal development and morpho-functional alterations in sudden unexplained late fetal and infant death. *Brain & Development, 32,* 275–284.

Lawlor, D. A., Davey Smith, G., Clark, H., & Leon, D. A. (2006). The associations of birthweight, gestational age and childhood BMI with type 2 diabetes: Findings from the Aberdeen Children of the 1950s cohort. *Diabetologia, 49,* 2614–2617.

Lawrence, J. A., & Valsiner, J. (2003, December). Making personal sense: An account of basic internalization and externalization processes. *Theory & Psychology, 13*(6), 723–752.

Leakey, M. D., & Hay, R. L. (1979). Pliocene footprints in the laetolil beds at Laetoli, northern Tanzania. *Nature, 278,* 317–323.

Lecanuet, J. P., Granier-Deferre, C., DeCasper, A., Hopkins, B., & Johnson, S. P. (2005). Are we expecting too much from prenatal sensory experiences? Prenatal development of postnatal functions. *Advances in infancy research* (pp. 31–49). Westport, CT: Praeger Publishers/Greenwood Publishing Group.

Lecanuet, J. P., Granier-Deferre, C., & DeCasper, A. J. (2005). Are we expecting too much from prenatal sensory experiences? In B. Hopkins & S. Johnson (Eds.), *Advances in Infancy Research* (pp. 31–49). London: Praeger.

Lecanuet, J. P., Graniere-Deferre, C., Jacquet, A-Y., & DeCasper, A. J. (2000). Fetal discrimination of low-pitched musical notes. *Developmental Psychobiology, 36*(1), 29–39.

Lecanuet, J.-P., & Jacquet, A.-Y. (2002). Fetal responsiveness to maternal passive swinging in low heart rate variability state: Effects of stimulation direction and duration. *Developmental Psychobiology, 40*(1), 57–67.

Lecanuet, J. P., & Schaal, B. (1996). Fetal sensory competencies. *European Journal of Obstetrics, Gynecology, and Reproductive Biology, 68,* 1–23.

Lederman, S. A., Rauh, V., Weiss, L., Stein, J. L., Hoepner, L. A., Becker, M., et al. (2004). The effects of the World Trade Center event on birth outcomes among term deliveries at three lower Manhattan hospitals. *Environmental Health Perspectives, 112,* 1772–1778.

LeDoux, J. (2012). Rethinking the emotional brain. *Neuron, 73,* 653–676.

Lee, B. H., Stoll, B. J., McDonald, S. A., Higgins, R. D., & National Institute of Child Health and Human Development Neonatal Research Network. (2006). Adverse neonatal outcomes associated with antenatal dexamethasone versus antenatal betamethasone. *Pediatrics, 117,* 1503–1510.

Lee, C. D. (2010). Every shut eye ain't sleep: Modeling the scientific from the everyday as cultural process. In C. Milbrath & C. Lightfoot (Eds.), *Art and human development* (pp. 139–166). New York: Psychology Press.

Lee, C. D., Rosenfeld, E., Mendenhall, R., Rivers, A., & Tynes, B. (2004). Cultural modeling as a frame for narrative analysis. In C. Daiute & C. Lightfoot (Eds.), *Narrative analysis: Studying the development of individuals in society.* Thousand Oaks, CA: Sage.

Lee, H. C., Green, C., Hintz, S. R., Tyson, J. E., Parikh, N. A., Langer, J., & Gould, J. B. (2010). Prediction of death for extremely premature infants in a population-based cohort. *Pediatrics, 126,* 644–650.

Lee, J. (2007). Two worlds of private tutoring: The prevalence and causes of after-school mathematics tutoring in Korea and the United States. *Teachers College Record, 109,* 1207–1234.

Lee, T., Hummer, D., Jechura, T., & Mahoney, M. (2004b, June). Pubertal development of sex differences in circadian function: An animal model. *Annals of the New York Academy of Sciences, 1021,* 262–275.

Lee, V. E., & Burkam, D. T. (2003). Dropping out of high school: The role of school organization and structure. *American Educational Research Journal, 40,* 353–393.

Lefeber, Y., & Voorhoeve, H. W. A. (1998). *Indigenous customs in childbirth and child care.* Assen, Netherlands: Von Gocum.

Lefkowitz, E., Romo, L., Corona, R., Au, T., & Sigman, M. (2000). How Latino American and European American adolescents discuss conflicts, sexuality, and AIDS with their mothers. *Developmental Psychology, 36,* 315–325.

Legare, C. H., Gelman, S. A., & Wellman, H. M. (2010). Inconsistency with prior knowledge triggers children's causal explanatory reasoning. *Child Development, 81,* 929–944.

Leigh, S. (2001). Evolution of human growth. *Evolutionary Anthropology, 10,* 223–236.

Leighton, D., & Kluckhohn, C. (1947/1969). *Children of the people; the Navaho individual and his development.* Cambridge, MA: Harvard University Press.

Lejeune, L., Anderson, D. I., Campos, J. J., Witherington, D. C., & Uchiyama, I. (2006). Responsiveness to terrestrial optic flow in infancy: Does locomotor experience play a role? *Human Movement Science, 25,* 4–17.

Lemerise, E., & Arsenio, W. (2000). An integrated model of emotion processes and cognition in social information processing. *Child Development, 71,* 107–118.

Lenhart, A., Madden, M., Smith, A., Purcell, K., Zickuhr, K., & Rainie, L. (2011). Teens, kindness and cruelty on social network sites. Retrieved December 15th, 2011, from http://pewinternet.org/Reports/2011/Teens-and-social-media.aspx

Lenneberg, E. H. (1967). *Biological foundations of language.* Hoboken, NJ: Wiley.

Lenroot, R., & Giedd, J. (2006). Brain development in children and adolescents: Insights from anatomical magnetic resonance imaging. *Neuroscience and Biobehaviorial Reviews, 30,* 718–729.

Lenroot, R., & Giedd, J. (2010). Sex differences in the adolescent brain. *Brain and Cognition, 72,* 46–55.

Lenroot, R. K., & Giedd, J. N. (2011). Annual Research Review: Developmental considerations of gene by environment interactions. *The Journal of Child Psychology and Psychiatry and Allied Disciplines, 52*(4), 429–441.

Lenroot, R. K., Schmitt, J. E., Ordaz, S. J., Wallace, G. L., Neale, M. C., Lerch, J. P., et al. (2009). Differences in genetic and environmental influences on the human cerebral cortex associated with development during childhood and adolescence. *Human Brain Mapping, 30,* 163–174.

Leoni, L. (1964). *Tico and the golden wings.* New York: Pantheon.

Lerner, J., Phelps, E., Forman, Y., & Bowers, E. (2009). Positive youth development. In R. Lerner & R. Steinberg (Eds.), *Handbook of Adolescent Psychology.* New York: John Wiley & Sons.

Lerner, R. M., Almerigi, J. B., Theokas, C., & Lerner, J. V. (2005), Positive youth development: A view of the issues. *The Journal of Early Adolescence, 25,* 110–116.

Lerner, R. M., Lerner, J., Bowers, E., Lewin-Bizan, S., Gestsdottir, S., & Urban, J. (2011). Thriving in childhood and adolescence: The role of self-regulating processes. *New Directions for Child and Adolescent Development, 133,* 1–97.

Lerner, R. M., Wiatrowski, M. D., Mueller, M. K., Napolitano, C. M., Schmid, K. L., et al. (2011). A Vision for the American juvenile system. In F. T. Sherman, F. H. Jacobs (Eds.), *Juvenile justice: Advancing research, policy, and practice.* (92–108). Hoboken, NJ: John Wiley & Sons.

Leslie, A. M. (1994). To MM, to BY, and agency: Core architecture and domain specificity. In L. A. Hirschfeld & S. Gelman (Eds.), *Mapping the mind: Domain specificity in cognition and culture.* New York: Cambridge University Press.

Leslie, A. M. (2002). Pretense and representation revisited. In N. L. Stein, P. J. Bauer, & M. Rabinowitz (Eds.), *Representation, memory, and development: Essays in honor of Jean Mandler* (pp. 103–114). Mahwah, NJ: Lawrence Erlbaum Associates.

Lester, B. M., Boukydis, C. Z., Garcia-Coll, C. T., Hole, W., & Peucker, M. (1992). Infantile colic: Acoustic cry characteristics, maternal perception of cry, and temperament. *Infant Behavior & Development, 15*, 15–26.

Lester, B. M., & Tronick, E. Z. (1994). The effects of prenatal cocaine exposure and child outcome. Special issue: Prenatal drug exposure and child outcome. *Infant Mental Health Journal, 15*, 107–120.

Levine, D., McCright, J., Dobkin, L., Woodruff, A., & Klausner, J. (2008). Sexinfo: A sexual health text messaging service for San Francisco youth. *American Journal of Public Health, 98*, 1–3.

LeVine, R. A. (1988). Human parental care: Universal goals, cultural strategies, individual behavior. *New Directions for Child Development, 40*, 3–12.

LeVine, R. A., Dixon, S., LeVine, S., Richman, A., Leiderman, P. H., Keefer, C. H., & Brazelton, T. B. (1994). *Child care and culture: Lessons from Africa.* New York: Cambridge University Press.

LeVine, R. A., LeVine, S. E., & Schnell, B. (2001). "Improve the women": Mass schooling, female literacy, and worldwide social change. *Harvard Educational Review, 71*(1), 1–50.

Levy, B. S., Wilkinson, F. S., & Marine, W. M. (1971). Reducing neonatal mortality rate with nurse-midwives. *American Journal of Obstetrics and Gynecology, 109*(2), e10-e18.

Levy, E. (1989). Monologue as development of the text-forming function of language. In K. Nelson (Ed.), *Narratives from the crib.* Cambridge, MA: Harvard University Press.

Lewis, M. (2001). Origins of the self-conscious child. In W. R. Crozier & L. E. Alden (Eds.), *International handbook of social anxiety: Concepts, research and interventions relating to the self and shyness* (pp. 101–118). New York: Wiley.

Lewis, M., & Brooks-Gunn, J. (1979). *Social cognition and the acquisition of self.* New York: Plenum Press.

Lewontin, R. (2001). *The triple helix: Gene, organism, and environment.* Cambridge, MA: Harvard University Press.

Liang, X., Fuller, B., & Singer, J. D. (2000). Ethnic differences in child care selection: The influence of family structure, parental practices, and home language. *Early Childhood Research Quarterly, 15*, 357–384.

Liaw, F.-R., Meisels, S. J., & Brooks-Gunn, J. (1995). The effects of experience of early intervention on low birth weight, premature children: The Infant Health and Development Program. *Early Childhood Research Quarterly, 10*, 405–431.

Liben, L., & Bigler, R. (2002). The developmental course of gender differentiation. *Monographs for the Society for Research in Child Development, 67*, 1–147.

Lickliter, R. (2007). The dynamics of development and evolution: Insights from behavioral embryology. *Developmental Psychobiology, 49*, 749–757.

Liddell, C. (2002). Emic perspectives on risk in African childhood. *Developmental Review, 22*, 97–116.

Liebal, K., Behne, T., Carpenter, M., & Tomasello, M. (2009). Infants use shared experience to interpret pointing gestures. *Developmental Science, 12*, 264–271.

Lightfoot, C. (1992). *The culture of adolescent risk taking.* New York: Guilford Press.

Lightfoot, C., & Bullock, M. (1990). Interpreting contradictory communications: Age and context effects. *Developmental Pychology, 26*, 830–836.

Lillard, A. (2006). The socialization of theory of mind: Cultural and social class differences in behavior explanation. In A. Antonietti, O. Sempio-Liverta, & A. Marchetti (Eds.), *Theory of mind and language in developmental contexts* (pp. 65–76). New York: Springer Science.

Lipsitt, L. P. (2003). Crib death: A biobehavioral phenomenon. *Current Directions in Psychological Science, 12*(5), 164–170.

Liu, D., Wellman, H. M., Tardif, T., & Sabbagh, M. A. (2008). Theory of mind development in Chinese children: A meta-analysis of false-belief understanding across cultures and languages. *Developmental Psychology, 44*, 523–531.

Liu, H.-M., Tsao, F.-M., & Kuhl, P. K. (2009). Age-related changes in acoustic modifications of Mandarin maternal speech to preverbal infants and five-year-old children: A longitudinal study. *Journal of Child Language, 36*, 909–922.

Liu, S., Quinn, P. C., Wheeler, A., Xiao, N., Ge, L., & Lee, K. (2010). Similarity and difference in the processing of same- and other-race faces as revealed by eye tracking in 4- to 9-month-olds. *Journal of Experimental Child Psychology, 108*, 180–189.

Locke, J. L., & Bogin, B. (2006). Language and life history: A new perspective on the development and evolution of human language. *Behavioral and Brain Sciences, 29*, 259–325.

Loehlin, J. C. (1992). *Genes and environment in personality development: Vol. 2.* Newbury Park, CA: Sage Publications.

Lonsdorf, E. V. (2007). The role of behavioral research in the conservation of chimpanzees and gorillas. *Journal of Applied Animal Welfare Science, 10*, 71–78.

Lopez, G. (2001). The value of hard work: Lessons on parent involvement from an (im)migrant household. *Harvard Educational Review, 71*, 416–437.

Lorenz, J. M. (2001). The outcome of extreme prematurity. *Seminars in Perinatology* (Philadelphia), *25*(5), 348–359.

Lorenz, K. (1943). Die Angebornen Formen mogicher Erfahrung. *Zeitschrift fur Tierpsychologie, 5*, 233–409.

Lorenz, K. (1966). *On aggression.* New York: Harcourt, Brace & World.

Love, J., Harrison, L., Sagi-Schwartz, A., van IJzendoorn, M., Ross, C., Ungerer, J., et al. (2003). Child care quality matters: How conclusions may vary with context. *Child Development, 74*, 1021–1033.

Low, J., & Hollis, S. (2003, March). The eyes have it: Development of children's generative thinking. *International Journal of Behavioral Development, 27*(2), 97–108.

Lozoff, B., Askew, G. L., & Wolf, A. W. (1996). Cosleeping and early childhood sleep problems: Effects of ethnicity and socioeconomic status. *Journal of Developmental and Behavioral Pediatrics, 17*, 9–15.

Luciana, M. (2010). Adolescent brain development: Current themes and future directions: Introduction to the special issue. *Brain and Cognition, 72*, 1–5.

Lundqvist, C., & Sabel, K.-G. (2000). Brief report: The Brazelton Neonatal Behavioral Assessment Scale detects differences among newborn infants of optimal health. *Journal of Pediatric Psychology, 25*, 577–582.

Luo, Y., & Baillargeon, R. (2005). Can a self-propelled box have a goal? Psychological reasoning in 5-month-olds. *Psychological Science, 16*, 601–608.

Luria, A. R. (1973). *The waking brain.* New York: Basic Books.

Luria, A. R. (1976). *Cognitive development: Its cultural and social foundations* (M. Lopez-Morillas & L. Solotaroff, Trans.). London: Harvard University Press.

Luria, A. R. (1981). *Language and cognition.* New York: Wiley.

Luster, T., & Haddow, J. L. (2005). Adolescent mothers and their children: An ecological perspective. In T. Luster & L. Okagaki (Eds.), *Parenting: An ecological perspective. Monographs in parenting* (2nd ed., pp. 73–101). Mahwah, NJ: Lawrence Erlbaum Associates.

Luthar, S., & Becker, B. (2002). Privileged but pressured? A study of affluent youth. *Child Development, 73*, 1593–1610.

Luthar, S., Cicchetti, D., & Becker, B. (2000). The construct of resilience: A critical evaluation and guidelines for future research. *Child Development, 71*, 543–562.

Lutz, C. (1987). Goals, events, and understanding Ifaluk emotion theory. In D. Holland & N. Quinn (Eds.), *Cultural models in language and thought.* Cambridge, England: Cambridge University Press.

Luyckx, K., Goossens, L., Soenens, B., Beyers, W., & Vansteenkiste, M. (2005). Identity statuses based on 4 rather than 2 identity dimensions: Extending and refining Marcia's Paradigm. *Journal of Youth and Adolescence, 34,* 605–618.

Lynne, S., Graber, J. A., Nichols, T., Brooks-Gunn, J., & Botvin, G. (2007). Links between pubertal timing, peer influences, and externalizing behaviors among urban students followed through middle school. *Journal of Adolescent Health, 40,* 181.e7–181.e13.

Lyon, T. D., Carrick, N., & Quas, J. A. (2010). Young children's competency to take the oath: Effects of task, maltreatment, and age. *Law and Human Behavior, 34,* 141–149.

Lyra, M. C. D. P. (2007). Modeling the dynamics of meaning construction: Appropriation of the home environment. *Culture & Psychology, 13,* 179–188.

MacCallum, F., & Golombok, S. (2004). Childen raised in fatherless families from infancy: A follow-up of children of lesbian and single heterosexual mothers at early adolesence. *Journal of Psychology and Psychiatry, 45,* 1407–1419.

Maccoby, E. E. (1984). Middle childhood in the context of the family. In W. A. Collins (Ed.), *Development during middle childhood: The years from six to twelve.* Washington, DC: National Academy Press.

Maccoby, E. E. (1998). *The two sexes.* Cambridge, MA: Harvard University Press.

Maccoby, E. E. (2003). The gender of child and parent as factors in family dynamics. In A. C. Crouter & A. Booth (Eds.), *Children's influence on family dynamics: The neglected side of family relationships* (pp. 191–206). Mahwah, NJ: Lawrence Erlbaum Associates.

Maccoby, E. E. (2004). Aggression in the context of gender development. In M. Putallaz & K. Bierman (Eds.), *Aggression, antisocial behavior, and violence among girls.* New York: Guilford Press.

Maccoby, E. E. (2007). Historical overview of socialization research and theory. In J. E. Grusec & P. D. Hastings (Eds.), *Handbook of socialization: Theory and research* (pp. 13–41). New York: Guilford Press.

MacDorman, M. F., & Mathews, T. J. (2008) Recent Trends in Infant Mortality in the United States. *NCHS data brief, 9.* Hyattsville, MD: National Center for Health Statistics.

MacDorman, M. F., & Singh, G. K. (1998). Midwifery care, social and medical risk factors, and birth outcomes in the USA. *Journal of Epidemiology & Community Health, 52*(5), 310–317. BMJ Group. Retrieved from http://eutils.ncbi.nlm.nih.gov/entrez/eutils/elink.fcgi?dbfrom=pubmed&id=9764282&retmode=ref&cmd=prlinks

MacFarlane, A. (1977). *The psychology of childbirth.* Cambridge, MA: Harvard University Press.

Magai, C., & Haviland-Jones, J. (2002). *The hidden genius of emotion: Lifespan transformations of personality.* Cambridge, England: Cambridge University Press.

Magnuson, K. A., & Waldfogel, J. (2005). Early childhood care and education: Effects on ethnic and racial gaps in school readiness. *The Future of Children, 15*(1), 169–196.

Magnuson, K. A., Lahaie, C., & Waldfogel, J. (2006). Preschool and school readiness of children of immigrants. *Social Science Quarterly, 87,* 1241–1262.

Magnuson, K., & Shager, H. (2010). Early education: Progress and promise for children from low-income families. *Children and Youth Services Review, 32,* 1186–1198.

Magolda, M. (2008). The evolution of self-authorship. In M. Khine (Ed.), *Knowing, knowledge and beliefs: Epistemological studies across diverse cultures* (pp. 45–64). New York: Springer Science + Business Media.

Maguen, S., Floyd, F., Bakeman, R., & Armistead, L. (2002). Developmental milestones and disclosure of sexual orientation among gay, lesbian, and bisexual youths. *Applied Developmental Psychology, 23,* 219–233.

Mahdi, A. (2003). *Teen life in the Middle East.* Westport, Connecticut: Greenwood Press.

Main, M., Hesse, E., & Kaplan, N. (2005). Predictability of attachment behavior and representational processes at 1, 6, and 19 years of age: The Berkeley Longitudinal Study. In K. E. Grossmann, K. Grossmann, & E. Waters (Eds.), *Attachment from infancy to adulthood: The major longitudinal studies* (pp. 245–304). New York: Guilford Press.

Main, M., & Solomon, J. (1990). Procedures for identifying infants as disorganized/disoriented during the Ainsworth strange situation. In M. Greenberg, D. Cicchetti, & E. M. Cummings (Eds.), *Attachment in the preschool years: Theory, research, and intervention* (pp. 121–160). Chicago: University of Chicago Press

Majnemer, A., & Barr, R. G. (2005). Influence of supine sleep positioning on early motor milestone acquisition. *Developmental Medicine & Child Neurology, 47*(6), 370–376.

Malchiodi, C. A., & Ginns-Gruenberg, D. (2008). Trauma, loss, and bibliotherapy: The healing power of stories. In C. A. Malchiodi (Ed.), *Creative interventions with traumatized children* (pp. 167–185). New York: Guilford Press.

Maleta, K., Virtanen, S., Espo, M., Kulmala, T., & Ashorn, P. (2003). Timing of growth faltering in rural Malawi. *Archives of Disease in Childhood, 88,* 574–578.

Malina, R. M. (1998). Motor development and performance. In S. J. Ulijaszek, F. E. Johnston, & M. A. Preece (Eds.), *The Cambridge encyclopedia of human growth and development* (pp. 247–250). Cambridge, England: Cambridge University Press.

Malina, R. M., & Bouchard, C. (1991). *Growth, maturation and physical activity.* Champaign, IL: Human Kinetics Books.

Malloy, L. C., & Quas, J. A. (2009). Children's suggestibility: Areas of consensus and controversy. In Kathryn Kuehnle & M. Connell (Eds.), *The evaluation of child sexual abuse allegations: A comprehensive guide to assessment and testimony* (pp. 267–297). Hoboken, NJ: John Wiley & Sons.

Mandler, J. M. (1998). Representation. In D. Kuhn & R. S. Siegler (Eds.), *Handbook of child psychology: Vol. 2. Cognition, perception and language* (5th ed., pp. 255–308). New York: Wiley.

Mandler, J. M. (2004). *The foundations of mind: Origins of conceptual thought.* Oxford, England: Oxford University Press.

Mandler, J. M. (2006). Actions organize the infant's world. In K. Hirsh-Pasek & R. M. Golinkoff (Eds.), *Action meets word: How children learn verbs.* New York: Oxford University Press.

Mandler, J. M. (2007). On the origins of the conceptual system. *American Psychologist, 62,* 741–751.

Mandler, J. M., & McDonough, L. (1993). Concept formation in infancy. *Cognitive Development, 8,* 291–318.

Mandler, J. M., & McDonough, L. (1996). Drinking and driving don't mix: Inductive generalization in infancy. *Cognition, 59,* 307–335.

Mandler, J. M., Scribner, S., Cole, M., & DeForest, M. (1980). Cross-Cultural Invariance in Story Recall. *Child Development, 51,* 19.

Manlove, J. S., Ryan, S., & Franzetta, K. (2007, February). Risk and protective factors associated with the transition to a first sexual relationship with an older partner. *Journal of Adolescent Health, 40*(2), 135–143.

Manstead, A. S. R. (1995). Children's understanding of emotion. In J. A. Russell & J. M. Fernandez-Dols (Eds.), *Everyday conceptions of emotion:*

An introduction to the psychology, anthropology and linguistics of emotion. Boston: Kluwer Academic Publishers.

Marcia, J. E. (1966). Development and validation of ego identity status. *Journal of Personality and Social Psychology, 3,* 551–558

Marcia, J. E. (1980). Identity in adolescence. In J. Adelson (Ed.), *Handbook of adolescent psychology.* New York:Wiley.

Marcia, J. E. (2002). Identity and psychosocial development in adulthood. *Identity, 2*(1), 7–28.

Margulies, S., & Thibault, K. (2000). Infant skull and suture properties: Measurements and implications for mechanisms of pediatric brain injury. *Journal of Biomechanical Engineering, 122,* 364–371.

Maric, J., Dunjic, B., Stojiljkovic, D., Britvic, D., & Jasovic-Gasic, M. (2010). Prenatal stress during the 1999 bombing associated with lower birth weight:A study of 3,815 births from Belgrade. *Archives of Women's Mental Health, 13,* 83–89.

Markovits, H., & Barrouillet, P. (2002). The development of conditional reasoning: A mental model account. *Developmental Review, 22,* 5–36.

Markovits, H., & Lortie-Forgues, H. (2011). Conditional reasoning with false premises facilitates the transition between familiar and abstract reasoning. *Child Development, 82,* 646–660.

Markovits, H., & St-Onge, M. J. (2009): Adolescents' and adults' internal models of conditional strategies for object conflict. *The Journal of Genetic Psychology, 170,* 135–150.

Markus, H. R., & Kitayama, S. (2010). Cultures and selves: A cycle of mutual constitution. *Perspectives on Psychological Science, 5,* 420–430.

Marlowe, F. (2005). Who tends Hadza children? In B. Hewlitt & M. Lamb (Eds.), *Hunter-gatherer childhoods: Evolutionary, cultural and developmental perspectives.* New Brunswick, NJ: Transaction Publishers.

Marshall, P. J., & Kenney, J. W. (2009). Biological perspectives on the effects of early psychosocial experience. *Developmental Review, 29,* 96–119.

Marsiglio, W., Amato, P., Day, R., & Lamb, M. (2000). Scholarship on fatherhood in the 1990s and beyond. *Journal of Marriage and the Family, 62,* 1173–1191

Martel, M. M. K., Kelly, Nigg, J. T., Breedlove, S. M., & Sisk, C. (2009). Potential hormonal mechanisms of attention-deficit/hyperactivity disorder and major depressive disorder: A new perspective. *Hormones and Behavior, 55,* 465–479.

Martin, C. A., Kelly, T. H., Rayens, M. K., Brogli, B. R., Brenzel, A., Smith, W. J., et al. (2002). Sensation seeking, puberty, and nicotine, alcohol and marijuana use in adolescence. *Journal of the American Academy of Child and Adolescent Psychiatry, 41,* 1495–1502.

Martin, C. B., Jr. (1998). Electronic fetal monitoring: A brief summary of its development, problems and prospects. *European Journal of Obstetrics & Gynecology and Reproductive Biology, 78,* 133–140.

Martin, C. H., & Halverson, C. F. (1981). A schematic processing model of sextyping and stereotyping in children. *Child Development, 52,* 1119–1134.

Martin, C. L., & Ruble, D. N. (2010). Patterns of gender development. *Annual Review of Psychology, 61,* 353–381.

Martin, J., & Sokol, B. (2011). Generalized others and imaginary audiences: A neo-Meadian approach to adolescent egocentrism. *New Ideas in Psychology, 29,* 364–375.

Martin, J., Sokol, B. W., & Elfers, T. (2008). Taking and coordinating perspectives: From prereflective interactivity, through reflective intersubjectivity, to metareflective sociality. *Human Development, 51,* 294–317.

Martin, J. A., Hamilton, B. E., Sutton, P. D., Ventura, S. J., Menacker, F., Kirmeyer, S., et al. (2009). Births: Final data for 2006, *National vital statistics reports* (Vol. 57). Hyattsville, MD: National Center for Health Statistics.

Martin, J. A., Kung, H. C., Mathews, T. J., Hoyert, D. L., Strobino, D. M., Guyer, B., et al. (2008). Annual summary of vital statistics: 2006. *Pediatrics, 121,* 788–801.

Martin, K. (1996). *Puberty, sexuality and the self: Boys and girls at adolescence.* New York: Routledge.

Martino, W., & Pallotta-Chiarolli, M. (2003). *So what's a boy?: Addressing issues of masculinity in Education.* London: Open University Press.

Mascolo, M. F., & Fischer, K. W. (1998). The development of self through the coordination of component systems. In M. D. Ferrari & R. J. Sternberg (Eds.), *Self-awareness: Its nature and development* (pp. 332–384). New York: Guilford Press.

Mascolo, M., Fischer, K., & Li, J. (2003). Dynamic development of component systems of emotions: Pride, shame and guilt in China and the United States. In R. Davidson, K. Scherer, & H. Goldsmith (Eds.), *Handbook of affective sciences.* Oxford, England: Oxford University Press.

Massey, C. M., & Gelman, R. (1988). Preschooler's ability to decide whether a photographed unfamiliar object can move itself. *Developmental Psychology, 24,* 307–317.

Mather, M. (2009). Children in immigrant families chart new path. Population Reference Bureau Reports on America. Retrieved from http://www.prb.org/pdf09/immigrantchildren.pdf

Matturri, L., Biondo, B., Suarez-Mier, M. P., & Rossi, L. (2002). Brain stem lesions in the sudden infant death syndrome:Variability in the hypoplasia of the arcuate nucleus. *Acta Neuropathology* (Berlin), *104,* 12–20.

Maurer, D., Mondloch, C. J., & Lewis, T. L. (2007). Effects of early visual deprivation on perceptual and cognitive development. *Progress in Brain Research, 164,* 87–104.

Maurer, D., O'Craven, K. M., Le Grand, R., Mondloch, C. J., Springer, M. V., Lewis, T. L., & Grady, C. L. (2007). Neural correlates of processing facial identity based on features versus their spacing. *Neuropsychologia, 45,* 1438–1451.

Maxwell, L. E., & Evans, G. W. (2000, March). The effects of noise on pre-school children's pre-reading skills. *Journal of Environmental Psychology, 20*(1), 91–97.

Maynard, A. E. (2008). What we thought we knew and how we came to know it: Four decades of cross-cultural research from a Piagetian point of view. *Human Development, 51,* 56–65.

Maynard, A. E., & Greenfield, P. M. (2003). Implicit cognitive development in cultural tools and children: Lessons from Maya Mexico. *Cognitive Development, 18,* 489–510.

McCabe, D. (1999). Academic dishonesty among high school students. *Adolescence, 34,* 681–687.

McCarthy, A., Hughes, R., Tilling, K., Davies, D., Smith, G. D., & Ben-Shlomo, Y. (2007). Birth weight; postnatal, infant, and childhood growth; and obesity in young adulthood: Evidence from the Barry Caerphilly Growth Study. *American Journal of Clinical Nutrition, 86,* 907–913.

McCarthy, B., & Grodsky, E. (2011). Sex and school: Adolescent sexual intercourse and education. *Social Problems, 58,* 213–234.

McCarty, M. E., Clifton, R. K., Ashmead, D. H., Lee, P., & Goubet, N. (2001). How infants use vision for grasping objects. *Child Development, 72,* 973–987.

McDade, T. (2003). Life history theory and the immune system: Steps toward a human ecological immunology. *Yearbook of Physical Anthropology, 46,* 100–125.

McDonald, P. G., te Marvelde, L., Kazem, A. J. N., & Wright, J. (2008). Helping as a signal and the effect of a potential audience during provisioning visits in a cooperative bird. *Animal Behaviour, 75,* 1319–1330.

McDowell, M., Lacher, D., Pfeiffer, C., Mulinare, J., & Piccianno, M. (2008). *Blood folate levels: The latest NHANES results.* (No. 6 NCHS Data Brief). Atlanta, GA: CDC/National Center for Health Statistics.

McElwain, N. L., & Booth-LaForce, C. (2006). Maternal sensitivity to infant distress and nondistress as predictors of infant-mother attachment security. *Journal of Family Psychology, 20*(2), 247–255.

McGloin, J. M., & Widom, C. S. (2001). Resilience among abuse and neglected children grown up. *Development and Psychopathology, 13*(4), 1021–1038.

McGraw, M. B. (1975). *Growth: A study of Johnny and Jimmy.* New York: Arno Press. (Original work published 1935)

McGuire, S. (2002). Nonshared environment research: What is it and where is it going? *Marriage & Family Review, 33*(1), 31–56.

McHale, S., & Crouter, A. (1996). The family contexts of children's sibling relationships. In G. H. Brody (Ed.), *Sibling relationships: Their causes and consequences.* Norwood, NJ: Ablex.

McKay, A., & Barrett, M. (2010). Trends in teen pregnancy rates from 1996–2006: A comparison of Canada, Sweden, U.S.A., and England/Wales. *The Canadian Journal of Human Sexuality, 19,* 43–52.

McKelvie, P., & Low, J. (2002). Listening to Mozart does not improve children's spatial ability: Final curtains for the Mozart effect. *British Journal of Developmental Psychology, 20,* 241–258.

McKenna, J. J. (1996) Sudden infant death syndrome in cross-cultural perspective: Is infant-parent cosleeping protective? *Annual Review of Anthropology, 25,* 201–216.

McKinney, C., & Renk, K. (2008, June). Differential parenting between mothers and fathers: Implications for late adolescents. *Journal of Family Issues, 29*(6), 806–827.

McKinney, M. L. (1998). Cognitive evolution by extending brain development: On recapitulation, progress, and other heresies. In J. Langer & M. Killer (Eds.), *Piaget, evolution, and development.* Mahwah, NJ: Lawrence Erlbaum Associates.

McLeod, N. M. H., Arana-Urioste, M. L., & Saeed, N. R. (2004, March). Birth prevalence of cleft lip and palate in Sucre, Bolivia. *The Cleft Palate—Craniofacial Journal, 41*(2), 195–198.

McLoughlin, G., Ronald, A., Kuntsi, J., Asherson, P., & Plomin, R. (2007, December). Genetic support for the dual nature of attention deficit hyperactivity disorder: Substantial genetic overlap between the inattentive and hyperactive-impulsive components. *Journal of Abnormal Child Psychology. 35*(6), 999–1008.

McLoyd, V. C. (1998b). Socioeconomic disadvantage and child development. *American Psychologist, 53*(2), 185–204.

McLoyd, V. C., & Smith, J. (2002). Physical discipline and behavior problems in African American, European American, and Hispanic children: Emotional support as a moderator. *Journal of Marriage and Family, 64,* 40–53.

McNeill, D. (1966). Developmental psycholinguistics. In S. Smith & G. A. Miller (Eds.), *The genesis of language: A psycholinguistic approach.* Cambridge, MA: The MIT Press.

McPhee, C. (1970). Children and music in Bali. In J. Belo (Ed.), *Traditional Balinese culture* (pp. 212–239). New York: Columbia University Press.

Meara, E. (2001). *Why is health related to socioeconomic status? The case of pregnancy and low birth weight.* Cambridge, MA: National Bureau of Economic Research.

Meeus, W. (2003). Parental and peer support, identity development and psychological well-being in adolescence. *Psychology: The Journal of the Hellenic Psychological Society, 10*(2–3), 192–201.

Meeus, W., & de Wied, M. (2007). Relationships with parents and identity in adolescence: A review of 25 years of research. In M. Watzlawik

& A. Born Aristi (Eds.), *Capturing identity: Quantitative and qualitative methods* (pp. 131–147). Lanham, MD: University Press of America.

Mehan, H. (1979). Learning lessons: Social organization in the classroom. *American Journal of Sociology, 87,* 244.

Mehan, H. (1984). Language and schooling. *Sociology of Education, 57*(3), 174–183.

Meier, A., & Allen, G. (2009). Romantic relationships from adolescence to young adulthood: Evidence from the National Longitudinal Study of Adolescent Health. *The Sociological Quarterly, 50,* 308–335.

Meléndez, L. (2005). Parental beliefs and practices around early self regulation: The impact of culture and immigration. *Infants & Young Children, 18,* 136–146.

Melot, A.-M., & Houde, O. (1998). Categorization and theories of mind: The case of the appearance/reality distinction. *Cahiers de Psychologie Cognitive/Current Psychology of Cognition 17*(1), 71–93.

Meltz, B. (2004, January 29). Nurturing an adopted child. *Boston Globe,* p. H1.

Meltzoff, A., & Borton, R. (1979). Intermodal matching by human neonates. *Nature, 282,* 403–404.

Meltzoff, A., & Decety, J. (2003). What imitation tells us about social cognition: A rapprochement between developmental psychology and cognitive neuroscience. *The Royal Society, 358,* 491–500

Meltzoff, A. N. (1988). Imitation of televised models by infants. *Child Development, 59,* 1221–1229.

Meltzoff, A. N. (2007). The 'like me' framework for recognizing and becoming an intentional agent. *Acta Psychologica. Special Issue: Becoming an intentional agent, 124*(1), 26–43

Mendle, J., Harden, K. P., Brooks-Gunn, J., & Graber, J. A. (2010). Development's tortoise and hare: Pubertal timing, pubertal tempo, and depressive symptoms in boys and girls. *Developmental Psychology, 46,* 1341–1353.

Mendle, J., Turkheimer, E., & Emery, R. E. (2007). Detrimental psychological outcomes associated with early pubertal timing in adolescent girls. *Developmental Review, 27,* 151–171.

Mennella, J., & Beauchamp, C. (1999). Experience with a flavor in mother's milk modifies the infant's acceptance of flavored cereal. *Developmental Psychobiology, 35,* 197–203.

Mennella, J., & Beauchamp, G. (2005). Understanding the origin of flavor preferences. *Chemical Senses, 30*(Suppl. 1), 242–243.

Mennella, J., Jagnow, C., & Beauchamp, G. (2001). Prenatal and postnatal flavor learning by human infants. *Pediatrics, 107,* 88–94.

Mesman, J., van IJzendoorn, M. H., & Bakermans-Kranenburg, M. J. (2009). The many faces of the Still-Face Paradigm: A review and meta-analysis. *Developmental Review, 29,* 120–162.

Meyers, S. (2001). *Everywhere babies.* San Diego: Harcourt.

Migliano, A. B., Vinicius, L., & Lahr, M. M. (2007). Life history trade-offs explain the evolution of human pygmies. *Proceedings of the National Academy of Sciences of the United States of America, 104,* 20216–20219.

Miller, B. C., Bgenson, B., & Galbraith, K. (2001). Family relationships and adolescent pregnancy risk: A research synthesis. *Developmental Review, 21,* 1–38.

Miller, C. A., & Golden, N. H. (2010). An introduction to eating disorders: Clinical presentation, epidemiology, and prognosis. *Nutrition in Clinical Practice, 25,* 110–115.

Miller, J. G., & Schaberg, L. (2003). Cultural perspectives on personality and social psychology. In T. Millon, & M. J. Lerner (Eds.), *Handbook of psychology: Vol. 5. Personality and social psychology* (pp. 31–56). New York: Wiley.

Miller, J. L., Macedonia, C., & Sonies, B. C. (2006). Sex differences in prenatal oral-motor function and development. *Developmental Medicine and Child Neurology, 48,* 465–470.

Miller, K. (1996). The effects of state terrorism and exile on the indigenous Guatemalan refugee children: A mental health assessment and an analysis of children's narratives. *Child Development, 67,* 89–106.

Miller, P. (1982) *Amy, Wendy and Beth: Learning language in south Baltimore.* Austin: University of Texas Press.

Miller, P. (2002). *Theories of developmental psychology* (4th ed.). New York: Worth.

Miller, P. J., Fung, H., & Mintz, J. (1996). Self-construction through narrative practices: A Chinese and American comparison of early socialization. *Ethos, 24,* 1–44.

Miller, P. J., Wang, S.-h., Sandel, T., & Cho, G. E. (2002). Self-esteem as folk theory: A comparison of European American and Taiwanese mothers' beliefs. *Parenting: Science and Practice, 2,* 209–239.

Mills, C. M., & Keil, F. C. (2004, January). Knowing the limits of one's understanding: The development of an awareness of an illusion of explanatory depth. *Journal of Experimental Child Psychology, 87,* 1–32.

Milnitsky-Sapiro, C., Turiel, E., & Nucci, L. (2006). Brazilian adolescents' conceptions of autonomy and parental authority. *Cognitive Development, 21*(3), 317–331.

Mintz, S. (2004). *Huck's raft: A history of American childhood.* Cambridge, MA: Cambridge University Press.

Mitchell, E. (1985). The dynamics of family interaction around home video games. *Marriage & Family Review. Special Issue: Personal computers and the family, 8,* 121–135.

Modell, J., & Elder, G. H. (2002). Children develop in history: So what's new? In W. Hartup & R. A. Weinberg (Eds.), *Child psychology in retrospect and prospect: In celebration of the 75th anniversary of the Institute of Child Development. The Minnesota symposia on child psychology* (Vol. 32, pp. 173–205). Mahwah, NJ: Lawrence Erlbaum Associates.

Modry-Mandell, K. L., Gamble, W. C., & Taylor, A. R. (2007, February). Family emotional climate and sibling relationship quality: Influences on behavioral problems and adaptation in preschool-aged children. *Journal of Child and Family Studies, 16*(1), 61–73.

Moffitt, T. E. (2007). A review of research on the taxonomy of life-course persistent versus adolescence-limited antisocial behavior. In D. J. Flannery, A. T. Vazsonyi, & I. D.Waldman (Eds.), *The Cambridge handbook of violent behavior and aggression* (pp. 49–74). New York: Cambridge University Press.

Moffitt. T. E., Caspi, A., Rutter, M., & Silva, P. A. (2002, November). Review of sex differences in antisocial behaviour: Conduct disorder, delinquency and violence in the Dunedin Longitudinal Study. *Psychological Medicine, 32*(8), 1475–1476.

Molina, J. C., Spear, N. E., Spear, L. P., Mennella, J. A., & Lewis, M. J. (2007). The International Society for Developmental Psychobiology 39th annual meeting symposium: Alcohol and development: Beyond fetal alcohol syndrome. *Developmental Psychobiology, 49*(3), 227–242.

Monahan, K. C., Steinberg, L., & Cauffman, E. (2009). Affiliation with antisocial peers, susceptibility to peer influence, and antisocial behavior during the transition to adulthood. *Developmental Psychology, 45,* 1520–1530.

Mondloch, C. J., & Desjarlais, M. (2010). The function and specificity of sensitivity to cues to facial identity: An individual-differences approach. *Perception, 39,* 819–829.

Mondloch, C. J., Lewis, T. L., Budreau, D. R., Maurer, D., Dannemiller, J. L., Stephens, B. R., & Kleiner-Gathercoal, K. A. (1999). Face perception during early infancy. *Psychological Science, 10,* 419–422.

Monk-Turner, E., Heiserman, M., Johnson, C., Cotton, V., & Jackson, M. (2010). The portrayal of racial minorities on prime time television: A replication of the Mastro and Greenberg study a decade later. *Studies in popular culture, 32.*

Moon, C., Cooper, R. P., & Fifer, W. P. (1993). Two-day-olds prefer their native language. *Infant Behavior Development, 16,* 495–500.

Moore, K. L., & Persaud, T. V. N. (1993). *The developing human: Clinically oriented embryology* (5th ed.). Philadelphia: Saunders.

Moore, K. L., & Persaud, T. V. N. (1998). *The developing human: Clinically oriented embryology.* Philadelphia: Saunders.

Moore, M. K., & Meltzoff, A. N. (2004). Object permanence after a 24-hr delay and leaving the locale of disappearance: the role of memory, space, and identity. *Developmental Psychology, 40,* 606–620.

Mora, J. O., & Nestel, P. S. (2000). Improving prenatal nutrition in developing countries: Strategies, prospects, and challenges. *American Journal of Clinical Nutrition, 71*(Suppl. 5), 1353S–1363S.

Moran, J. P. (2000). *Teaching sex:The shaping of adolescence in the 20th century.* Cambridge, MA: Harvard University Press.

Moore, M. K., & Meltzoff, A. N. (2008). Factors affecting infants' manual search for occluded objects and the genesis of object permanence. *Infant behavior development, 31*(2), 168–180.

Morelli, G. A., Rogoff, B., Oppenheim, D., & Goldsmith, D. (1992). Cultural variation in infants sleeping arrangements: Questions of independence. *Developmental Psychology, 28,* 604–613.

Morelli, G. A., Tronick, E., & Beeghly, M. (1999). *Is there security in numbers? Child care in a hunting and gathering community and infants' attachment relationships.* Albuquerque, NM: Society for Research in Child Development.

Morgan, G., & Woll, B. (Eds.). (2002). *Directions in sign language acquisition.* Philadelphia: John Benjamins.

Morgan, J. (1999). *When chickenheads come home to roost.* New York: Simon & Schuster.

Morokuma, S., Doria, V., Ierullo, A., Kinukawa, N., Fukushima, K., Nakano, H., et al. (2008). Developmental change in foetal response to repeated low-intensity sound. *Developmental Science, 11,* 47–52.

Morrison, F. J., Smith, L., & Dow-Ehrensberger, M. (1995). Education and cognitive development: A natural experiment. *Developmental Psychology, 31,* 789–799.

Morrongiello, B. A., Fenwick, K. D., Hillier, L., & Chance, G. (1994). Sound localization in newborn human infants. *Developmental Psychobiology, 27*(8), 519–538.

Morrow, C. E., Bandstra, E. S., Anthony, J. C., Ofir, A. Y., Xue, L., & Reyes, M. B. (2003). Influence of prenatal cocaine exposure on early language development: Longitudinal findings from four months to three years of age. *Journal of Developmental and Behavioral Pediatrics, 24*(1), 39–50.

Morton, S. M. B. (2006). Maternal nutrition and fetal growth and development. In P. Gluckman & M. Hanson (Eds.), *Developmental origins of health and disease* (pp. 98–129). New York: Cambridge University Press.

Moshman, D. (1998). Cognitive development beyond childhood. In D. Kuhn & R. S. Siegler (Eds.), *Handbook of child psychology: Vol. 2. Cognition, perception, and language* (5th ed., pp. 947–978). New York: Wiley.

Moshman, D. (1999). *Adolescent psychological development: Rationality, morality and identity.* Mahwah, NJ: Lawrence Erlbaum Associates.

Moshman, D. (2009). Adolescence. In U. Müller, J. I. M. Carpendale, & L. Smith (Eds.), *The Cambridge companion to Piaget* (pp. 255–269). New York: Cambridge University Press.

Moshman, D. (2011) *Adolescent rationality and development.* New York: Psychology Press.

Moss, N. E., & Carver, K. (1998). The effect of WIC and Medicaid on infant mortality—the United States. *American Journal of Public Health, 88,* 1354–1361.

Motch, S. (2009). *Palestine: A look inside.* Booklocker.com, Inc.

Müller, U. (2009). Infancy. In U. Müller (Ed.), *The Cambridge companion to Piaget* (pp. 200–228). New York: Cambridge University Press.

Müller, U., Sokol, B., & Overton, W. F. (1999). Developmental sequences in class reasoning and propositional reasoning. *Journal of Experimental Child Psychology, 74,* 69–106.

Mullis, I. V. S., Martin, M. O., & Foy, P. (with Olson, J. F., Preuschoff, C., Erberber, E., Arora, A., & Galia, J.). *TIMSS 2007 international mathematics report: Findings from IEA's trends in international mathematics and science study at the fourth and eighth grades.* Chestnut Hill, MA: TIMSS & PIRLS International Study Center, Boston College, 2008.

Munakata, Y., Casey, B., & Diamond, A. (2004). Developmental cognitive neuroscience: Progress and potential. *Trends in Cognitive Sciences, 8,* 122–128.

Murray, L., & Trevarthen, C. (1986, February). The infant's role in mother-infant communications. *Journal of Child Language, 13*(1), 1529.

Murray-Close, D., Ostrov, J. M., & Crick, N. R. (2007). A short-term longitudinal study of growth of relational aggression during middle childhood: Associations with gender, friendship intimacy, and internalizing problems. *Development and Psychopathology, 19*(1), 187–203.

Mustanski, B., Viken, R. J., Kaprio, J., Pulkkinen, L., & Rose, R. J. (2004). Genetic and environmental influences on pubertal development: Longitudinal data from 12–14 year-old twins. *Developmental Psychology, 40,* 1188–1198

Nadel, J. (2002). Imitation and imitation recognition: Functional use in preverbal infants and nonverbal children with autism. In A. Meltzoff & W. Prinz (Eds.), *The imitative mind: Development, evolution, and brain bases.* Cambridge, England: Cambridge University Press.

Nader, P., O'Brien, M., Houts, R., Bradley, R., Belsky, J., Crosnoe, R., et al. (2006). Identifying risk for obesity in early childhood. *Pediatrics, 118,* 594–601.

Nagler, J. (2002). Sudden infant death syndrome. *Current Opinion in Pediatrics, 14,* 247–250.

Nakkula M., & Toshalis, E. (2006). *Understanding youth: Adolescent development for educators.* Cambridge, MA: Harvard Education Press.

Nasir, N. (2005). Individual cognitive structuring and the sociocultural context: Strategy shifts in the game of dominoes. *Journal of the Learning Sciences, 14,* 5–34.

Nasrallah, N. A., Clark, J. J., Collins, A. L., Akers, C. A., Phillips, P. E., & Bernstein, I. L. (2011). Risk preference following adolescent alcohol use is associated with corrupted encoding of costs but not rewards by mesolimbic dopamine. *Proceedings of the National Academy of Sciences of the United States of America, 108,* 5466–5471.

National Center for Children in Poverty (2011). Who are America's Poor Children? Retrieved from http://www.nccp.org/publications/pub_1001.html

National Center for Education Statistics. (2004). *English language learner students in U.S. public schools: 1994 and 2000* (No. NCES 2004-035). Washington, DC: U.S. Department of Education.

National Center for Family Homelessness (2009). *State report card on child homelessness: America's youngest outcasts.* From http://www.homeless-childrenamerica.org/documents/rc_summary_001.pdf

National Center for Health Statistics. (2003). *Healthy people, 2000, review.* Hyattsville, MD: National Center for Health Statistics.

National Council of Teachers of Mathematics. (2000). *Principles and standards for school mathematics.* Reston, VA: National Council of Teachers of Mathematics.

National Institute on Deafness and Other Communication Disorders (2012). *Aphasia.* Retrieved from http://www.nidcd.nih.gov/health/voice/pages/aphasia.aspx#types

Navarro, V. M., & Tena-Sempere, M. (2011). Neuroendocrine control by kisspeptins: Role in metabolic regulation of fertility. *Nature Reviews Endocrinology, 8*(1), 40–53.

Nazzi, T., Kemler Nelson, D. G., Jusczyk, P. W., & Jusczyk, A. M. (2000). Six-month-olds' detection of clauses embedded in continuous speech: Effects of prosodic well-formedness. *Infancy, 1*(1), 123–147.

Needham, A., & Baillargeon, R. (1993). Intuitions about support in 4.5-month-old infants. *Cognition, 47*(2), 121–148.

Needham, A., Barrett, T., & Peterman, K. (2002). A pick-me-up for infants' exploratory skills: Early stimulated experiences reaching for objects using "sticky mittens" enhances young infants' object exploration skills. *Infant Behavior and Development, 25,* 279–295.

Nelson, C. A., & Bloom, F. E. (1997). Child development and neuroscience. *Child Development, 68,* 970–987.

Nelson, C. A., Moulson, M. C., & Richmond, J. (2006). How does neuroscience inform the study of cognitive development? *Human Development, 49,* 260–272.

Nelson, C. A., Zeanah, C. H., Fox, N. A. (2007). The effects of early deprivation on brain-behavioral development: The Bucharest Early Intervention Project. In D. Romer & E. F. Walker (Eds.), *Adolescent psychopathology Adolescent psychopathology and the developing brain: Integrating brain and prevention science* (pp. 85–91). New York: Oxford University Press.

Nelson, K. (1981). Social cognition in a script framework. In J. H. Flavell & L. Ross (Eds.), *Social cognitive development.* Cambridge, MA: Cambridge University Press.

Nelson, K. (2003). Co-constructing the cultural person through narratives in early childhood. In C. Daiute & C. Lightfoot (Eds.), *Narrative analysis: Studying the development of individuals in society.* New York: Sage Press.

Nelson, K. (2009). Narrative practices and folk psychology: A perspective from developmental psychology. *Journal of Consciousness Studies, 16,* 69–93.

Nelson, K., & Fivush, R. (2000). Socialization of memory. In E. Tulving & F. I. M. Craik (Eds.), *The Oxford handbook of memory* (pp. 283–295). London: Oxford University Press.

Nelson, K., & Shaw, L. (2002). Developing a socially shared symbolic system. In E. Amsel & J. Byrnes (Eds.), *Language, literacy, and cognitive development.* Mahwah, NJ: Lawrence Erlbaum Associates.

Nelson, K., Skwerer, D. P., Goldman, S., Henseler, S., Presler, N., & Walkenfeld, F. F. (2003). Entering a community of minds: An experimental approach to "theory of mind." *Human Development, 46,* 24–46.

Netter, F. H. (1965). *The CIBA collection of medical illustrations.* Summit, NJ: CIBA Pharmaceutical Products.

Neville, H. J. (2005). Development and plasticity of human cognition. In U. Mayr, E. Awh, & S. W. Keele (Eds.), *Developing individuality in the human brain: A tribute to Michael I. Posner. Decade of behavior* (pp. 209–235). Washington, DC: American Psychological Association.

Newberger, D. (2000). Down syndrome: Prenatal risk assessment and diagnosis. *American Family Physician, 15,* 825–837.

Newcomb, A. F., Bukowski, W. M., & Pattee, L. (1993). Children's peer relations: A meta-analytic review of popular, rejected, controversial and average sociometric status. *Psychological Bulletin, 113,* 99–128.

Newell, M. L., Coovadia, H., Cortina-Borja, M., Rollins, N., Gaillard, P., & Dabis, F. (2004). Ghent International AIDS Society (IAS) Working Group on HIV Infection in Women and Children. Mortality of infected and uninfected infants born to HIV-infected mothers in Africa: A pooled analysis. *Lancet, 364,* 1236–1243.

Newport, E. L., Bavelier, D., & Neville, H. J. (2001). Critical thinking about critical periods: Perspectives on a critical period for language acquisition. In E. Dupoux (Ed.), *Language, brain, and cognitive development: Essays in honor of Jacques Mehler* (pp. 481–502). Cambridge, MA: The MIT Press.

Newton, N., & Newton, M. (1972). Lactation: Its psychological component. In J. G. Howells (Ed.), *Modern perspectives in psycho-obstetrics*. New York: Brunner/Mazel.

Nguyen, D., Smith, L. M., Lagasse, L. L., Derauf, C., Grant, P., Shah, R., Arria, A., et al. (2010). Intrauterine growth of infants exposed to prenatal methamphetamine: Results from the infant development, environment, and lifestyle study. *The Journal of Pediatrics, 157,* 337–339. Retrieved from http://www.ncbi.nlm.nih.gov/pubmed/16951010

NICHD Early Child Care Research Network. (2002). Structure, process, outcome: Direct and indirect effects of caregiving quality on young children's development. *Psychological Science, 13,* 199–206.

NICHD Early Child Care Research Network. (2003a). Child care and common communicable illnesses in children aged 37 to 54 months. *Archives of Pediatrics and Adolescent Medicine, 157,* 196–201.

NICHD Early Child Care Research Network. (2003b). Does amount of time spent in child care predict socioemotional adjustment during the transition to kindergarten? Child Development, 74, 976–1005.

NICHD Early Child Care Research Network. (2003c). Does quality of care affect child outcomes at age 4? *Developmental Psychology, 39,* 451–469.

NICHD Early Child Care Research Network. (2004, January). Are child developmental outcomes related to before- and after-school care arrangements? Results from the NICHD study of early child care. *Child Development 75,* 280–295.

NICHD Early Child Care Research Network (2010). Study overview. Retrieved from http://www.nichd.nih.gov/research/supported/seccyd/overview.cfm

Nicholls, D., Chater, R., & Lask, B. (2000). Children into DSM don't go: A comparison of classification systems for eating disorders in childhood and early adolescence. *The International Journal of Eating Disorders, 28*(3), 317–324.

Nijhuis, J. G., Prechtl, H. F. R., Martin, C. B., & Bots, R. S. G. M. (1982). Are there behavioral states in the human foetus? *Early Human Development, 6,* 177–195.

Nkata, M. (2001). Perinatal mortality in breech delivery. *Tropical Doctor, 31*(4), 222–223.

Nord, M., Coleman-Jensen, A., Andrews, M., & Carlson, S. (2010). *Household food security in the United States, 2009* (Economic Research Report No. 108): United States Department of Agriculture.

Nsamenang, A. (2006). Human ontogenesis: An indigenous African view on development and intelligence. *International Journal of Psychology. Special Issue: The indigenous psychologies, 41*(4), 293–297.

Nucci, L. (1996). Morality and the personal sphere of actions. In E. Reed, E. Turiel, & T. Brown (Eds.), *Values and knowledge* (pp. 41–60). Mahwah, NJ: Lawrence Erlbaum Associates.

Nucci, L. (2004a). Social interaction and the construction of moral and social knowledge In J. I. M. Carpendale & U. Muller (Eds.), *Social interaction and the development of knowledge* (pp. 195–213). Mahwah, NJ: Lawrence Erlbaum Associates.

Nucci, L. (2004b). The promise and limitations of the moral self construct. In C. Lightfoot, C. LaLonde, & M. Chandler (Eds.), *Changing conceptions of psychological life*. Mahwah, NJ: Lawrence Erlbaum Associates.

Nucci, L. (2009). *Nice is not enough: Facilitating moral development*. Upper Saddle River, NJ: Merrill/Pearson Education.

Nucci, L., & Turiel, E. (2009). Capturing the complexity of moral development and education. *Mind, Brain, and Education, 3,* 151–159.

Nunes, T., & Bryant, P. (2009). Children's reading and spelling: Beyond the first steps. In T. Nunes & P. Bryant (Eds.), *Children's reading and spelling: Beyond the first steps*. Malden, MA: Wiley-Blackwell.

Nunes, T., Bryant, P., Evans, D., Bell, D., Gardner, S., et al. (2007). The contribution of logical reasoning to the learning of mathematics in primary school. *British Journal of Developmental Psychology, 25,* 147–166.

Nussbaum, M. (2010). *From disgust to humanity: Sexual orientation and constitutional law*. New York: Oxford University Press.

Nyiti, R. M. (1976). The development of conservation in the Meru children of Tanzania. *Child Development, 47,* 1122–1129.

Nyiti, R. M. (1982). The validity of "cultural differences explanations" for cross-cultural variation in Piagetian cognitive development. In D. A. Wagner & H. W. Stevenson (Eds.), *Cultural perspectives on child development*. San Francisco, CA: W. H. Freeman.

Oakes, L. M., & Cohen, L. B. (1990). Infant perception of a causal event. *Cognitive Development, 5,* 193–207.

Obleser, J., Meyer, L., & Friederici, A. D. (2011). Dynamic assignment of neural resources in auditory comprehension of complex sentences. *NeuroImage, 56,* 2310–2320.

O'Brien, M., Peyton, V., Mistry, R., Hruda, L., Jacobs, A., Caldera, Y., et al. (2000). Gender-role cognition in three-year-old boys and girls. *Sex Roles, 42,* 1007–1025.

Ochs, E. (1982). Talking to children in Western Samoa. *Language in Society, 11,* 77–104.

Ochs, E. & B. B. Schieffelin. (1984). Language acquisition and socialization: three developmental stories and their implications. In R. Shweder & R. Levine (eds.), *Culture theory: Essays on mind, self and emotion*, (276–320). New York: Cambridge University Press.

Ochs, E., & Schieffelin, B. (1995). The impact of language socialization or grammatical development. In P. Fletcher & B. MacWhinney (Eds.), *The handbook of child language*. Cambridge, MA: Blackwell Publishing.

Office of Head Start. (2010). Retrieved December 15th, 2011, from http://www.acf.hhs.gov/programs/ohs/about/fy2010.htm

Ogbu, J. U. (1997). Understanding the school performance of urban blacks: Some essential background knowledge. In H. J. Walberg & O. Reyes (Eds.), *Children and youth: Interdisciplinary perspectives* (pp. 190–222). Thousand Oaks, CA: Sage.

Ogden, C., & Carroll, M. (2010). Prevalence of obesity among children and adolescents: United States, Trends 1963–1965 through 2007–2008. Retrieved from http://www.cdc.gov/nchs/data/hestat/obesity_child_07_08/obesity_child_07_08.pdf

Ogden, C. L., & Flegal, K. M. (2010). Changes in terminology for childhood overweight and obesity. *National Health Statistics Reports,* (25), 1–5.

Okami, P., Weisner, T., & Olmstead, R. (2002). Outcome correlates of parent-child bedsharing: An eighteen-year longitudinal study. *Journal of Developmental and Behavioral Pediatrics, 23,* 244–253.

Olds, D. L. (2006). The nurse-family partnership: An evidence-based preventive intervention. *Infant Mental Health Journal, 27*(1), 5–25.

O'Leary, C. M., Nassar, N., Kurinczuk, J. J., de Klerk, N., Geelhoed, E., & Elliott, E. J. (2010). Prenatal alcohol exposure and risk of birth defects. *Pediatrics, 126,* 43–850.

Oliner, S. B., & Oliner, P. (1988). *The altruistic personality: Rescuers of Jews in Nazi Germany*. New York: Macmillan.

Olsen, B. R., Reginato, A. M., & Wang, W. (2000). Bone development. *Annual Review of Cell and Developmental Biology, 16,* 191–220.

Olson, K. (2007, February 18). Her autistic brothers. *New York Times Magazine,* 42–47.

Olson, K. R., & Dweck, C. S. (2009). Social cognitive development: A new look. *Child Development Perspectives, 3*, 60–65.

Olthof, T., Goossens, F. A., Vermande, M. M., Aleva, E. A., & van der Meulen, M. (2011). Bullying as strategic behavior: Relations with desired and acquired dominance in the peer group. *Journal of School Psychology, 49*, 339–359.

Ong, A. D., Fuller-Rowell, T. E., & Phinney, J. S. (2010). Measurement of ethnic identity: Recurrent and emergent issues. *Identity, 10*, 39–49.

Orioli, I. M., & Castilla, E. E. (2000). New associations between prenatal exposure to drugs and malformations. *American Journal of Human Genetics, 67*(4, Suppl. 2), 175.

Ornstein, P., & Haden, C. (2009). Developments in the study of memory development. In M. Courage & N. Cowan (Eds.), *The development of memory in infancy and childhood*. Hove, UK: Psychology Press.

Ornstein, P. A., Haden, C., & Hendrick, A. (2004). Learning to remember: Social-communicative exchanges and the development of children's memory skills. *Developmental Review, 24*, 374–395.

Ornstein, P. A., & Light, L. L. (2010). Memory development across the life span. In P. A. Ornstein & L. L. Light (Eds.), *The handbook of life-span development, Vol. 1: Cognition, biology, and methods*. Hoboken, NJ: John Wiley & Sons.

Ornstein, P. A., Shapiro, L. R., Clubb, P. A., Follmer, A., & Baker-Ward, L. (1997). The influence of prior knowledge on children's memory for salient medical experiences. In N. Stein, P. A. Ornstein, B. Tversky, & C. J. Brainerd (Eds.), *Memory for everyday and emotional events* (pp. 83–112).

Osofsky, J., & Fitzgerald, H. (Eds.). (2000). *Handbook of infant mental health. World Association for Infant Mental Health*. New York: Wiley.

Oster, H. (2005). The repertoire of infant facial expressions: An ontogenetic perspective. In J. Nadel & D. Muir (Eds.), *Emotional development*. Oxford, England: Oxford University Press.

Ostrer, H., Huang, H. Y., Masch, R. J., & Shapiro, E. (2007). A cellular study of human testis development. *Sexual Development 1*(5), 286–292.

Ostrov, J., & Crick, N. (2006). How recent developments in the study of relational aggression and close relationships in early childhood advance the field. *Journal of Applied Developmental Psychology, 27*, 189–192.

Ostrov, J., Gentile, D., & Crick, N. (2006). Media exposure, aggression and prosocial behavior during early childhood: A longitudinal study. *Social Development, 15*, 612–627.

O'Sullivan, L. F., & Meyer-Bahlberg, H. F. L. (2003, April). African American and Latina inner-city girls' reports of romantic and sexual development. *Journal of Social and Personal Relationships. Special Issue: Race/ethnicity and interpersonal relationships, 20*(2), 221–238.

Out, D., Pieper, S., Bakermans-Kranenburg, M. J., & van IJzendoorn, M. H. (2010). Physiological reactivity to infant crying: A behavioral genetic study. *Genes, Brain & Behavior, 9*, 868–876.

Padilla, A. (2006). Bicultural social development. *Hispanic Journal of Behavioral Sciences, 28*, 467–497.

Page-Goertz, S., McCamman, S., & Westdahl, C. (2001). Breastfeeding promotion. Top tips for motivating women to breastfeed their infants. *AWHONN Lifelines, 5*(1), 41–43.

Pak, S. (2010). The growth status of North Korean refugee children and adolescents from 6 to 19 years of age. *Economics and Human Biology, 8*, 385–395.

Paley, V. G. (1981). *Wally's stories*. Cambridge, MA: Harvard University Press.

Paley, V. G. (1984). *Boys & girls: Superheroes in the doll corner*. Chicago: The University of Chicago Press.

Palincsar, A. S., Spiro, R. J., Kucan, L., Magnusson, S. J., Collins, B., Hapgood, S., et al. (2007). Designing a hypermedia environment to support comprehension instruction. In D. S. McNamara (Ed.), *Reading comprehension strategies: Theories, interventions, and technologies* (pp. 441–462). Mahwah, NJ: Lawrence Erlbaum Associates.

Pan, B. A., & Snow, C. E. (1999). The development of conversational and discourse skills. In M. Barrett (Ed.), *The development of language* (pp. 229–250). Hove, England: Psychology Press.

Panksepp, J. (2010). The evolutionary sources of jealousy: Cross-species approaches to fundamental issues. In S. Hart & M. Legerstee (Eds.), *Handbook of jealousy: Theory, research, and multidisciplinary approaches* (pp. 101–120). Hoboken, NJ: Wiley-Blackwell.

Panksepp, J., & Smith-Pasqualini, M. (2005). The search for fundamental brain/mind sources of affective experience. In J. Nadel & D. Muir (Eds.), *Emotional Development*. Oxford, England: Oxford University Press.

Parent, A.-S., Teilmann, G., Juul, A., Skakkebaek, N. E., Toppari, J., & Bourguignon, J.-P. (2003). The timing of normal puberty and the age limits of sexual precocity: Variations around the world, secular trends, and changes after migration. *Endocrine Reviews, 24*, 668–693

Parent, C. Z., Tie-Yuan, Caldji, C., Bagot, R., Champagne, F. A., Pruessner, J., & Meaney, M. J., (2005). Maternal care and individual differences in defensive responses. *14*, 229–233.

Parke, R. D., & Buriel, R. (1998). Socialization in the family: Ethnic and ecological perspectives. In W. Damon & N. Eisenberg (Eds.), *Handbook of child development: Vol. 3. Social, emotional, and personality development* (5th ed., pp. 463–552). New York: Wiley.

Parke, R. D., & Ladd, G. W. (1992). Family-peer relationships. *Merrill-Palmer Quarterly, 40*, 1–20.

Parke, R. D., O'Neil, R., Spitzer, S., Isley, S., Welsh, M., Wang, S., et al. (1997). A longitudinal assessment of sociometric stability and the behavioral correlates of children's social acceptance. *Merrill-Palmer Quarterly, 43*, 635–662.

Parker, J. G., Rubin, K. H., Erath, S. A., Wojslawowicz, J. C., & Buskirk, A. A. (2006). Peer relationships, child development, and adjustment: A developmental psychopathology perspective. In D. Cicchetti & D. J. Cohen (Eds.), *Developmental psychopathology: Vol. 1. Theory and method* (2nd ed., pp. 419–493). Hoboken, NJ: John Wiley & Sons.

Parker, S. T. (2005). Piaget's legacy in cognitive constructivism, niche construction, and phenotype development and evolution. In S. T. Parker, J. Langer, & C. Milbrath (Eds.), *Biology and knowledge revisited: From neurogenesis to psychogenesis*. Mahwah, NJ: Lawrence Erlbaum Associates.

Parker, S. T., & McKinney, M. L. (1999). *Origins of intelligence: The evolution of cognitive development in monkeys, apes, and humans*. Baltimore, MD: Johns Hopkins University Press.

Parsons, T. (1963). Youth in the context of American society. In E. Erikson (Ed.), *Youth: Change and challenge*. New York: Basic Books.

Patrick, H., Anderman, L. H., & Ryan, A. M. (2002). Social motivation and the classroom social environment. In C. Midgley (Ed.), *Goals, goal structures, and patterns of adaptive learning* (pp. 85–108). Mahwah, NJ: Lawrence Erlbaum Associates.

Patterson, C. J. (2006, October). Children of lesbian and gay parents. *Current Directions in Psychological Science, 15*(5), 241–244.

Patterson, C. J. (2009). Children of lesbian and gay parents: Psychology, law, and policy. *American Psychologist, 64*, 727–736.

Patterson, C. J., & Riskind, R. G. (2010). To be a parent: Issues in family formation among gay and lesbian adults. *Journal of GLBT Family Studies, 6*, 326–340.

Patterson, G. R., DeBaryshe, B. D., & Ramsey, E. (1989). A developmental perspective on antisocial behavior. *American Psychologist, 44*(2), 329–335.

Patterson, G. R., Littman, R. A., & Bricker, W. (1967). Assertive behavior in young children: A step toward a theory of aggression. *Monographs of the Society for Research for Child Development, 32*(Serial No. 113).

Pavlov, I. P. (1927). *Conditioned reflexes.* Oxford, England: Oxford University Press.

Pawloski, L. R., Ruchiwit, M., & Pakapong, Y. (2008). A cross-sectional examination of growth indicators from Thai adolescent girls: Evidence of obesity among Thai youth? *Annals of Human Biology, 35,* 378–385.

Pecora, N., Murray, J. P., & Wartella, E. A. (Eds.). (2006). *Children and television: Fifty years of research.* Mahwah, NJ: Lawrence Erlbaum Associates.

Pedersen, S., Vitaro, F., Barker, E. D., & Borge, A. I. H. (2007). The timing of middle-childhood peer rejection and friendship: Linking early behavior to early-adolescent adjustment. *Child Development, 78,* 1037–1051.

Pelaez, M., Field, T., Pickens, J., & Hart, S. (2008). Disengaged and authoritarian parenting behavior of depressed mothers with their toddlers. *Infant Behavior & Development, 31*(1), 145–148.

Pellegrini, A. D. (2006). The development and function of rough-and-tumble play in childhood and adolescence: A sexual selection theory perspective. In A. Göncü & S. Gaskins (Eds.), *Play and development: Evolutionary, sociocultural, and functional perspectives. The Jean Piaget symposium series* (pp. 77–98). Mahwah, NJ: Lawrence Erlbaum Associates.

Pellegrini, A. D., & Long, J. (2002). A longitudinal study of bullying, dominance, and victimization during the transition from primary through secondary school. *British Journal of Developmental Psychology, 20,* 259–280.

Pellegrini, A. D., & Long, J. D. (2003). A sexual selection theory longitudinal analysis of sexual segregation and integration in early adolescence. *Journal of Experimental Child Psychology, 85*(3), 257–278.

Pellegrini, A. D., Long, J. D., Solberg, D., Roseth, C., & Dupuis, D. (2010). Bullying and social status during school transitions. In S. R. Jimerson, S. M. Swearer, & D. L. Espelage (Eds.), *Handbook of bullying in schools: An international perspective* (pp. 199–210). New York: Routledge/Taylor & Francis Group.

Pellegrini, A. D., Roseth, C. J., Mliner, S., Bohn, C. M., Van Ryzin, M., Vance, N., et al. (2007). Social dominance in preschool classrooms. *Journal of Comparative Psychology, 121,* 54–64.

Pelletier, D. L., & Frongillo, E. A. (2003). Changes in child survival are strongly associated with changes in malnutrition in developing countries. *Nutrition, 133,* 107–119.

Pellicano, E. (2010). Preview. The development of core cognitive skills in autism: A 3-year prospective study. *Child Development, 81,* 1400–1416.

Peltonen, K., Quota, S., El Sarraj, E., Punamäki, R. L. (2010). Military trauma and social development: The moderating and mediating roles of peer and sibling relations in mental health. *34,* 554–563.

Péneau, S., Rouchaud, A., Rolland-Cachera, M. F., Arnault, N., Hercberg, S., Castetbon, K. (2011). Body size and growth from birth to 2 years and risk of overweight at 7–9 years. *International Journal of Pediatric Obesity, 6,* 162–169.

Peper, J. S., Brouwer, R. M., Schnack, H. G., Van Baal, G. C. M., Van Leeuwen, M., Van Den Berg, S. M., Delemarre-Van De Waal, H. A., et al. (2008). Cerebral white matter in early puberty is associated with luteinizing hormone concentrations. *Psychoneuroendocrinology, 33,* 909–915.

Peper, J. S., Brouwer, R. M., van Leeuwen, M., Schnack, H. G., Boomsma, D. I., Kahn, R. S., et al. (2010). HPG-axis hormones during puberty: A study on the association with hypothalamic and pituitary volumes. *Psychoneuroendocrinology, 35,* 133–140.

Peplau, L. A., DeBro, S. C., Veniegas, R. C., & Taylor, P. L. (1999). *Gender, culture, and ethnicity: Current research about women and men.* Mountain View, CA: Mayfield.

Perrizo, K., & Pustilnik, S. (2006). Association between sudden death in infancy and co-sleeping. *American Journal of Forensic Medicine and Pathology, 27,* 169–172.

Perry, W. G. (1970) *Forms of intellectual and ethical development in the college years: A scheme.* New York: Holt, Rinehart, and Winston.

Persaud, T. V. N. (1977). *Problems of birth defects: From Hippocrates to thalidomide and after.* Baltimore, MD: University Park Press.

Petersen, A., Sarigiani, P., Leffert, N., & Camarena, P. (1998). Resilience in adolescence. In A. Schwartzberg (Ed.), *The adolescent in turmoil.* Westport, CT: Praeger.

Peterson, C. (2005). Mind and body: Concepts of human cognition, physiology and false belief in children with autism or typical development. *Journal of Autism and Developmental Disorders, 35,* 487–497.

Peterson, C., Jesso, B., & McCabe, A. (1999). Encouraging narratives in preschoolers: An intervention study. *Journal of Child Language, 26,* 49–67.

Peterson, C., & McCabe, A. (2004). Echoing our parents: Parental influences on children's narration. In M. W. Pratt & B. H. Fiese (Eds.), *Family stories and the life course, Across time and generations* (pp. 27–54). Mahwah, NJ: Lawrence Erlbaum Associates.

Pettit, G. S., Keiley, M. K., Laird, R. D., Bates, J. E., & Dodge, K. A. (2007). Predicting the developmental course of mother-reported monitoring across childhood and adolescence from early proactive parenting, child temperament, and parents' worries. *Journal of Family Psychology. 21,* 206–217.

Pettitt, D. J., Aleck, K. A., Baird, H. R., Carraher, M. J., Bennett, P. H., & Knowler, W. C. (1988). Congenital susceptibility to NIDDM. Role of intrauterine environment. *Diabetes, 37,* 622–628.

Petitto, L.-A. (2009). New discoveries from the bilingual brain and mind across the life span: Implications for education. *Mind, Brain, and Education, 3,* 185–197.

Petitto, L.-A, Katerlos, M., Levy, B. G., Gauna, K., Tétreault, K., & Ferraro, V. (2001). Bilingual signed and spoken language acquisition from birth: Implications for the mechanisms underlying early bilingual language acquisition. *Journal of Child Language, 28,* 453–496.

Phinney, J. S. (2006). Ethnic identity exploration in emerging adulthood. In J. J. Arnett & J. L. Tanner (Eds.), *Emerging adults in America: Coming of age in the 21st century* (pp. 117–134). Washington, DC: American Psychological Association.

Phinney, J. S. (2008). Ethnic identity exploration in emerging adulthood. In D. L. Browning (Ed.), *Adolescent identities: A collection of readings. Relational perspectives book series* (pp. 47–66). New York: The Analytic Press/Taylor & Francis Group.

Phinney, J. S. (2010). Understanding development in cultural contexts: How do we deal with the complexity? *Human Development, 53,* 33–38.

Phinney, J. S., & Baldelomar, O. A. (2011). Identity development in multiple cultural contexts. In J. S. Phinney & O. A. Baldelomar (Eds.), *Bridging cultural and developmental approaches to psychology: New syntheses in theory, research, and policy* (pp. 161–186). New York: Oxford University Press.

Phinney, J. S., & Ong, A. D. (2002). Adolescent-parent disagreements and life satisfaction in families from Vietnamese- and European-American backgrounds. *International Journal of Behavioral Development, 26*(6), 556–561.

Piaget, J. (1926). *The language and thought of the child.* New York: Meridian Books.

Piaget, J. (1929/1979). *The child's conception of the world.* New York: Harcourt Brace.

Piaget, J. (1930). *The child's conception of physical causality*. New York: Harcourt Brace.

Piaget, J. (1932/1965). *The moral judgment of the child*. New York: Free Press. (Original work published 1932)

Piaget, J. (1952a). *The child's conception of number*. New York: W. W. Norton.

Piaget, J. (1952b). *The origins of intelligence in children*. New York: International Universities Press.

Piaget, J. (1954). *The construction of reality in the child*. New York: Basic Books.

Piaget, J. (1965/1995). *Sociological studies*. New York: Routledge.

Piaget, J. (1966/1974). Need and significance of cross-cultural studies in genetic psychology. In J. W. Berry & P. R. Dasen (Eds.), *Culture and cognition: Readings in cross-cultural psychology*. London: Methuen.

Piaget, J. (1973). *The psychology of intelligence*. Totowa, NJ: Littlefield & Adams.

Piaget, J. (1977). *The development of thought: Equilibration of cognitive structure*. New York: Viking.

Piaget, J., & Inhelder, B. (1956). *The child's conception of space*. London: Routledge & Kegan Paul.

Piaget, J., & Inhelder, B. (1969). *The psychology of the child*. New York: Basic Books.

Piaget, J. & Inhelder, B. (1973). *Memory and intelligence*. New York: Basic Books.

Piatt, J. H., Jr. (2003). *Infant heads: Too big, too small, misshapen*. Retrieved July 29, 2006, from http://www.drexelmed.edu/documents/ped_neurosurgery/about_heads.pdf

Pick, A. D. (1997). Perceptual learning, categorizing, and cognitive development. In C. Dent-Read & P. Zukow-Golding (Eds.), *Evolving explanations of development: Ecological approaches to organism environment systems* (pp. 335–370). Washington, DC: American Psychological Association.

Pinelli, J., & Symington, A. (2001). Non-nutritive sucking for the promotion of physiologic stability and nutrition in preterm infants. *Cochrane Database of Systematic Reviews, 3*, CD001071.

Pinker, S. (1994) *The language instinct: How the mind creates language*. New York: Harper Collins.

Pinker, S. (2002). *The blank slate: The modern denial of human nature*. New York: Viking.

Pinker, S. (2007). *The stuff of thought: Language as a window into human nature*. New York: Viking.

Pinquart, M., & Teubert, D. (2006). Effects of parenting education with expectant and new parents: A meta-analysis. *Journal of Family Psychology, 24*, 316–327.

Pinquart, M., & Teubert, D. (2010). Effects of parenting education with expectant and new parents: A meta-analysis. *Journal of Family Psychology JFP Journal of the Division of Family Psychology of the American Psychological Association Division 43, 24* 316–327.

Pinto, D., Pagnamenta, A., Klei, L., Anney, R., & Merico, D. (2010). Functional impact of global rare copy number variation in autism spectrum disorders. *Nature, 466*, 368–372.

Pittman, R., & Oppenheim, R. W. (1979). Cell death of motoneurons in the chick embryo spinal cord. *Journal of Comparative Neurology, 187*(2), 425–446.

Pizzuto, E., Ardito, B., Caselli, M. C., & Volterra, V. (2001). Cognition and language in Italian deaf preschoolers of deaf and hearing families. In M. D. Clark, M. Marschark, & M. Karchmer (Eds.), *Context, cognition, and deafness* (pp. 49–70). Washington, DC: Gallaudet University Press.

Pleck, J. H., & Masciadrelli, B. P. (2003). Paternal involvement in U.S. residential fathers: Levels, sources, and consequences. In M. Lamb (Ed.), *The role of the father in development*. New York: Wiley.

Plumert, J. M., Kearney, J. K., Cremer, J. F., Recker, K. M., & Strutt, J. (2011). Changes in children's perception-action tuning over short time scales: Bicycling across traffic-filled intersections in a virtual environment. *Journal of Experimental Child Psychology, 108*, 322–337.

Pnevmatikos, D. (2002). Conceptual changes in religious concepts of elementary schoolchildren: The case of the house where God lives. *Educational Psychology, 22*(1), 93–112.

Polikoff, B. (1999). *With one bold act: The story of Jane Addams*. Chicago: Boswell Books.

Polivy, J., & Herman, C. P. (2004). Sociocultural idealization of thin female body shapes: An introduction to the special issue on body image and eating disorders. *Journal of Social and Clinical Psychology, 23*(1), 1–6.

Pollack, H. A., & Frohna, J. G. (2002). Infant sleep placement after the back to sleep campaign. *Pediatrics, 109*(4), 608–614.

Pollitt, E. (2001). Statistical and psychobiological significance in developmental research. *American Journal of Clinical Nutrition, 74*(3), 281–282.

Pollitt, E., Saco-Pollitt, C., Jahari, A., Husaini, M. A., & Huang, J. (2000). Effects of an energy and micronutrient supplement on mental development and behavior under natural conditions in undernourished children in Indonesia. *European Journal of Clinical Nutrition, 54*(2), S80–S90.

Pollock, D. (1999). *Telling bodies performing birth: Everyday narratives of childbirth*. New York: Columbia University Press.

Polman, H., de Castro, B. O., Koops, W., van Boxtel, H. W., & Merk, W. W. (2007, August). A meta-analysis of the distinction between reactive and proactive aggression in children and adolescents. *Journal of Abnormal Child Psychology. 35*(4), 522–535.

Pomerantz, E. M., Ruble, D. N., Frey, K. S., & Greulich, F. (1995). Meeting goals and confronting conflict: Children's changing perceptions of social comparison. *Child Development, 66*, 723–738.

Pontius, K., Aretz, M., Griebel, C., Jacobs, C., LaRock, K., et al. (2001). Back to sleep—Tummy time to play. *Newsletter of the Children's Hospital, 4*(4), 1–3.

Poole, D., & Lindsay, D. (2001). Children's eyewitness reports after exposure to misinformation from parents. *Journal of Experimental Psychology: Applied, 7*, 27–50.

Popp, D., Laursen, B., Kerr, M., Stattin, H., & Burk, W. K. (2008). Modeling homophily over time with an actor-partner interdependence model. *Developmental Psychology, 44*, 1028–1039.

Porter, R., & Winberg, J. (1999). Unique salience of maternal breast odors for newborn infants. *Neuroscience and Biobehavioral Reviews, 23*, 439–449.

Portes, A., & Rumbaut, R. (2001). *Legacies: The story of the second generation*. Berkeley: University of California Press.

Posada, G., Carbonell, O. A., Alzate, G., & Plata, S. J. (2004). Through Colombian lenses: Ethnographic and conventional analyses of maternal care and their associations with secure base behavior. *Developmental Psychology, 40*, 508–518.

Posner, M. I., Rothbart, M. K., Sheese, B. E., & Tang, Y. (2007). The anterior cingulate gyrus and the mechanism of self-regulation. *Cognitive, Affective, & Behavioral Neuroscience, 7*(4), 391–395.

Poulin, F., & Boivin, M. (2000). The formation and development of friendship in childhood: The role of proactive and reactive aggression. *Developmental Psychology, 36*, 233–240.

Poulin, F., & Chan, A. (2010). Friendship stability and change in childhood and adolescence. *Developmental Review, 30*, 257–272.

Poulin-Dubois, D., & Forbes, J. (2006). Word, intention, and action: A two-tiered model of action word learning. In K. Hirsh-Pasek & R. M.

Golinkoff (Eds.), *Action meets word: How children learn verbs* (pp. 262–285). New York: Oxford University Press.

Poulsen, P., Esteller, M., Vaag, A., & Fraga, M. F. (2007). The epigenetic basis of twin discordance in age-related diseases. *Pediatric Research, 61,* 38R–42R.

Powell, A., Shennan, S., & Thomas, M. G. (2009). Late pleistocene demography and the appearance of modern human behavior. *Science, 324,* 1298–1301.

Pratt, M. W., & Fiese, B. H. (Eds.). (2004). *Family stories and the life course: Across time and generations.* Mahwah, NJ: Lawrence Erlbaum Associates.

Pratt, M. W., Hunsberger, B., Pancer, S. M., & Alisat, S. (2003, November). A longitudinal analysis of personal values socialization: Correlates of a moral self-ideal in late adolescence. *Social Development, 12,* 563–585.

Prechtl, H. (1977). *The neurological examination of the full-term newborn infant* (2nd ed.). Philadelphia: Lippincott.

Preisser, D. A., Hodson, B. W., & Paden, E. P. (1988). Developmental phonology: 18–29 months. *Journal of Speech and Hearing Disorders, 53,* 125–130.

Prentice, A. M., & Jebb, S. A. (2003). Fast foods, energy density and obesity: A possible mechanistic link. *Obesity Review 4*(4), 187–194.

Prescott, E., & Jones, E. (1971). *Standards for day care centers for infants and children under 3 years of age.* Evanston, IL: American Academy of Pediatrics.

Pressley, M., & Hilden, K. (2006). Cognitive strategies. In D. Kuhn, R. S. Siegler, W. Damon, & R. M. Lerner (Eds.), *Handbook of child psychology: Vol. 2. Cognition, perception, and language* (6th ed., pp. 511–556). Hoboken, NJ: John Wiley & Sons.

Preyer, W. T. (1890). *The mind of the child . . . observations concerning the mental development of the human being in the first years of life.* New York: Appleton.

Pruden, S., Hirsh-Pasek, K., Golinkoff, R., & Hennon, E. (2006). The birth of words; Ten-month-olds learn words through perceptual salience. *Child Development, 77,* 266.

Pujol, J., Soriano-Mas, C., Ortiz, H., Sebastián-Gallés, N., Losilla, J., M., & Deus, J. (2006). Myelination of language-related areas in the developing brain. *Neurology, 66,* 339–343.

Puma, M., Bell, S., Cook, R., Heid, C., & Lopex, M. (2005). *Head Start impact study first year findings.* Washington, DC: U.S. Department of Health and Human Services.

Puzzanchera, C., & Adams, B. (2011). Juvenile arrests 2009. *Juvenile Offenders and Victims: National Report Series Bulletin, December, 2011.* Office of Juvenile Justice and Delinquency Prevention. Retrieved from http:// ojjdp.gov/publications/PubAbstract.asp?pubi=258483

Quas, J. A., Davis, E. L., Goodman, G. S., & Myers, J. E. B. (2007). Repeated questions, deception, and children's true and false reports of body touch. *Child Maltreatment, 12*(1), 60–67.

Quinn, P. C. (2002). Early categorization. In U. Goswami (Ed.), *Blackwell handbook of childhood cognitive development* (pp. 85–101). Oxford, England: Blackwell Publishing.

Quinn, P. C., & Eimas, P. D. (1996). Perceptual organization and categorization in young infants. In C. Rovee-Collier & L. P. Lipsitt (Eds.), *Advances in infancy research: Vol. 10* (pp. 1–36). Norwood, NJ: Ablex.

Quinn, P. C., Eimas, P. D., & Rosenkrantz, S. L. (1993). Evidence for representations of perceptually similar natural categories by 3-month-old and 4-month-old infants. *Perception, 22,* 463–475.

Quinn, P. C., Westerlund, A., & Nelson, C. A. (2006) Neural markers of categorization in 6-month-old infants. *Psychological Science 17*(1), 59–66.

Quintana, S. M., Aboud, F. E., Chao, R. K., Contreras-Grau, J., Cross, W. E., Jr., Hudley, C., et al. (2006). Race, ethnicity, and culture in child development: contemporary research and future directions. *Child Development, 77,* 1129–1141.

Racz, S. J., McMahon, R. J., & Luthar, S. S. (2011). Risky behavior in affluent youth: Examining the co-occurrence and consequences of multiple problem behaviors. *Journal of Child and Family Studies, 20,* 120–128.

Raeburn, P. (2005, August 14). A second womb. *New York Times Magazine,* p. 37.

Raikes, H., Luze, G., Brooks-Gunn, J., Raikes, H. A., Pan, B. A., Tamis-LeMonda, C. S, et al. (2006). Mother-child bookreading in low income families: Correlates and outcomes during the first three years of life. *Child Development, 77,* 924–953.

Rapoport, J. L., Castellanos, F. X., Gogate, N., Janson, K., Kohler, S., & Nelson, P. (2001). Imaging normal and abnormal brain development: New perspectives for child psychiatry. *The Australian and New Zealand Journal of Psychiatry, 35*(3), 272–281. Retrieved from http:// www.ncbi.nlm.nih.gov/pubmed/11437799

Rauch, F., & Schoenau, E. (2001). Changes in bone density during childhood and adolescence: An approach based on bone's biological organization. *Journal of Bone and Mineral Research, 16,* 597–604.

Rauscher, F. H., Shaw, G. L., & Ky, K. N. (1993). Music and spatial task performance. *Nature, 365,* 611.

Raymond, D. (1994). Homophobia, identity, and the meanings of desire: Reflections on the culture construction of gay and lesbian adolescent sexuality. In J. Irvine (Ed.), *Sexual cultures and the construction of adolescent identities* (pp. 115–150). Philadelphia: Temple University Press.

Read, M. (1960/1968). *Children of their fathers: Growing up among the Ngoni of Malawi.* New York: Holt, Rinehart & Winston.

Read, M. (1983). *Children of their fathers: Growing up among the Ngoni of Malawi.* New York: Irvington.

Reddy, V. (2005). Feeling shy and showing-off: Self-conscious emotions must regulate self-awareness. In J. Nadel & D. Muir (Eds.), *Emotional development* (pp. 183–204). Oxford, England: Oxford University Press.

Reece, M., Herbenick, D., Schick, V., Sanders, S., Dodge, B, & Fortenberry, J. D. (2010). Condom use rates in a national probability sample of males and females ages 14 to 94 in the United States. *Journal of Sexual Medicine, 7,* 266–276.

Reed, M. D., & Roundtree, P. W. (1997). Peer pressure and adolescent substance abuse. *Journal of Quantitative Criminology, 13*(2), 143–180.

Reichel-Dolmatoff, G., & Reichel-Dolmatoff, A. (1961). *The people of Aritama.* London: Routledge & Kegan Paul.

Relier, J.-P. (2001). Influence of maternal stress on fetal behavior and brain development. *Biology of the Neonate, 79*(3–4), 168–171.

Renz-Polster, H., & Buist, A. S. (2002). Being born by cesarean section increases the risk of asthma and hay fever as a child. *Journal of Investigative Medicine, 50,* 29a.

Repacholi, B. M., Meltzoff, A. N., & Olsen, B. (2008). Infants' understanding of the link between visual perception and emotion:"If she can't see me doing it, she won't get angry." *Developmental Psychology, 44,* 561–574.

Rest, J., Narvaez, D., Bebeau, M. l. J., & Thoma, S. J. (1999). *Postconventional moral thinking: A neo-Kohlbergian approach.* Mahwah, NJ: Lawrence Erlbaum Associates.

Reynolds, G. D., & Richards, J. E. (2007). Infant heart rate: A developmental psychophysiological perspective. In L. A. Schmidt & S. J. Segalowitz (Eds.), *Developmental psychophysiology* (pp. 106–117). New York: Cambridge Press.

Rice, C., Koinis, D., Sullivan, K., & Tager-Flusberg, H. (1997). When 3-year-olds pass the appearance-reality test. *Developmental Psychology, 33,* 54–61.

Rich, J. L. (2004, March). Play school. *Teacher Magazine, 15*(5), 40–45.

Richardson, J., & Scott, K. (2002). Rap music and its violent progeny: America's culture of violence in context. *The Journal of Negro Education, 71*(3), 175–192.

Richardson, K., & Norgate, S. H. (2006). A critical analysis of IQ studies of adopted children. *Human Development, 49,* 319–335.

Richerson, P., & Boyd, R. (2005). *Not by genes alone: How culture transformed human evolution.* Chicago: University of Chicago Press.

Richmond, J., & Nelson, C. A. (2007, September). Accounting for change in declarative memory: A cognitive neuroscience perspective. *Developmental Review, 27*(3), 349–373.

Rideout, V., & Hamel, E. (2006). *The media family: Electronic media in the lives of infants, toddlers, preschoolers, and their parents.* Menlo Park, CA: Kaiser Family Foundation.

Rideout, V., Roberts, D. F., & Foehr., U. G. (2005). *Generation M: Media in the lives of 8–18 year-olds.* Menlo Park, CA: Kaiser Family Foundation.

Rideout, V. J., Foehr, U. G., & Roberts, D. F. (2010). *Generation M2: Media in the lives of 8- to 18-year-olds.* Menlo Park, CA: Kaiser Family Foundation.

Ritz, B., Wilhelm, M., & Zhao Y. (2006). Air pollution and infant death in southern California, 1989–2000. *Pediatrics, 118,* 493–502.

Rivero, M. (2010). Maternal expression of communicative intentions and pragmatic fine tuning in early infancy. *Infant Behavior & Development, 33,* 373–386.

Rizzolatti, G., & Sinigaglia, C. (2010). Mirroring and making sense of others. *Nature Reviews Neuroscience, 11,* 264–274.

Roa, J., García-Galiano, D., Castellano, J. M., Gaytan, F., Pinilla, L., & Tena-Sempere, M. (2010). Metabolic control of puberty onset: New players, new mechanisms. *Molecular and Cellular Endocrinology, 324,* 87–94.

Robbins, W. J., Brody, S., Hogan, A. G., Jackson, C. M., & Greene, C. W. (Eds.). (1929). *Growth.* New Haven, CT: Yale University Press.

Roberts, D., Foehr, U., & Rideout, V. (2005, March). *Generation M: Media in the lives of 8–18 year-olds. A Kaiser Family Foundation study.* Menlo Park, CA: Henry J. Kaiser Family Foundation.

Robinson, J. L. (2000). Are there implications for prevention research from studies of resilience? *Child Development, 71*(3), 570–572.

Robinson, J. L., Emde, R. N., & Corley, R. P. (2001). Dispositional cheerfulness: Early genetic and environmental influences. In R. N. Emde & J. K. Hewitt (Eds.), *Infancy to early childhood: Genetic and environmental influences on developmental change* (pp. 163–177). New York: Oxford University Press.

Robinson, S. R., & Kleven, G. A. (2005). Learning to move before birth. In B. Hopkins & S. P. Johnson (Eds.), *Prenatal development of postnatal functions (Advances in infancy research)* (pp. 131–175). Westport, CT: Praeger Publishers/Greenwood Publishing Group.

Rochat, P. (2000). *The infant world: Self, objects, people.* Cambridge, MA: Harvard University Press

Rochat, P. (2009) *Others in Mind—Social origins of self-consciousness.* New York: Cambridge University Press.

Rochat, P., & Striano, T. (2002). Who's in the mirror? Self-other discrimination in specular images by four- and nine-month-old infants. *Child Development, 73,* 35–46.

Rodkin, P. C., Farmer, T. W., Pearl, R., & Van Acker, R. (2000). Heterogeneity of popular boys: Antisocial and prosocial configurations. *Developmental Psychology, 36*(1), 14–24.

Rogoff, B. (2003). *The cultural nature of human development.* Oxford, England: Oxford University Press.

Rogoff, B., Correa-Chávez, M., & Navichoc-Cotuc, M. (2005). A Cultural/Historical View of Schooling in Human Development. In D. B. Pillemer & S. H. White (Eds.), *Developmental Psychology and the Social Changes of Our Time* (pp. 225–263). New York: Cambridge University Press.

Rogoff, B., Moore, L., Najafi, B., Dexter, A., Correa-Chávez, M., & Solís, J. (2007). Children's development of cultural repertoires through participation in everyday routines and practices. In J. E. Grusec & P. D. Hastings (Eds.), *Handbook of socialization: Theory and research* (pp. 490–515). New York: Guilford Press.

Rogoff, B., & Waddell, K. J. (1982). Memory for information organized in a scene by children from two cultures. *Child Development, 53,* 1224–1228.

Romer, D., & Hennessy, M. (2007). A biosocial-affect model of adolescent sensation seeking: The role of affect evaluation and peer-group influence in adolescent drug use. *Prevention Science, 8,* 89–101.

Roosa, M. (2000). Some thoughts about resilience versus positive development, main effects versus interactions, and the value of resilience. *Child Development, 71,* 567–569.

Rose, A. J., & Asher, S. R. (2000) Children's friendships. In C. Hendrick & S. S. Hendrick (Eds.), *Close relationships: A sourcebook* (pp. 47–57). Thousand Oaks, CA: Sage Publications.

Rose, A. J., Swenson, L., & Carlson, W. (2004). Friendships of aggressive youth: Considering the influence of being disliked and of being perceived popular. *Journal of Experimental Child Psychology, 88,* 25–45.

Rose, L. T., & Fischer, K. W. (2009). Dynamic development: A neo-Piagetian approach. In L. T. Rose & K. W. Fischer (Eds.), *The Cambridge companion to Piaget* (pp. 400–421). New York: Cambridge University Press.

Rose, S. A., Feldman, J. F., & Jankowski, J. J. (2004). Infant visual recognition memory. *Developmental Review, 24,* 74–100.

Rose, S. A., Feldman, J. F., & Jankowski, J. J. (2009). Information processing in toddlers: Continuity from infancy and persistence of preterm deficits. *Intelligence, 37,* 311–320.

Rosen, W. D., Adamson, L. B., & Bakeman, R. (1992). An experimental investigation of infant social referencing: Mothers' messages and gender differences. *Developmental Psychology, 28*(6), 1172–1178.

Rosenbaum, J. (2009). Patient teenagers? A comparison of the sexual behavior of virginity pledgers and matched nonpledgers. *Pediatrics, 123,* e110-e120.

Rosenblatt, R. A., Dobie, S. A., Hart, L. G., Schneeweiss, R., Gould, D., Raine, T. R., et al. (1997). Interspecialty differences in the obstetric care of low-risk women. *American Journal of Public Health, 87*(3), 344–351.

Rosengren, K. S., & Brasswell, G. S. (2001). Variability in children's reasoning. In H. W. Reese and R. Kail (Eds.), *Advances in child development and behavior: Vol. 28* (pp. 2–41). New York: Academic Press.

Rosenstein, D., & Oster, H. (1988). Differential facial responses to four basic tastes in newborns. *Child Development, 59,* 1555–1568.

Rosenzweig, M. R. (1984). Experience, memory, and the brain. *American Psychologist, 39,* 365–376.

Ross, M. G., & Nyland, M. J. M. (1998). Development of ingestive behavior. *American Journal of Physiology, 43,* 879–893.

Roth, M., & Parker, J. (2001). Affective and behavioral responses to friends who neglect their friends for dating partners: Influences of gender, jealousy and perspective. *Journal of Adolescence, 24,* 281–296.

Rothbart, M. K. (2007). Temperament, development, and personality. *Current Directions in Psychological Science,* 207–212.

Rothbaum, F., & Kakinuma, M. (2004). Amae and attachment: Security in cultural context. *Human Development, 47,* 34–39.

Rothbaum, F., Weisz, J., Pott, M., & Morelli, G. (2000). Attachment and culture: Security in the United States and Japan. *American Psychologist, 55,* 1093–1104.

Rovee-Collier, C., & Giles, A. (2010). Why a neuromaturational model of memory fails: Exuberant learning in early infancy. *Behavioural Processes, 83,* 197–206.

Rovee-Collier, C., Hartshorn, K., & DiRubbo, M. (1999). Long-term maintenance of infant memory. *Developmental Psychobiology, 35,* 91–102.

Ruffman, T., Slade, L., & Redman, J. (2005). Young infants' expectations about hidden objects. *Cognition, 97,* 35–43.

Rubin, J. Z., Provezano, F. J., & Luria, Z. (1974). The eye of the beholder: Parents' view on sex of newborns. *American Journal of Orthopsychiatry, 44,* 512–519.

Rubin, K. H., Bukowski, W. M., & Parker, J. G. (2006a). Peer interactions, relationships, and groups. In N. Eisenberg, W. Damon, & R. M. Lerner (Eds.), *Handbook of child psychology: Vol. 3. Social, emotional, and personality development* (6th ed., pp. 571–645). New York: Wiley.

Rubin, K. H., Burgess, K. B., Kennedy, A. E., & Stewart, S. L. (2003). Social withdrawal in childhood. In E. J. Mash & R. A. Barkley (Eds.), *Child psychopathology* (2nd ed., pp. 372–406). New York: Guilford Press.

Rubin, K. H., Wojslawowicz, J. C., Rose-Krasnor, L., Booth-LaForce, C., & Burgess, K. B. (2006b). The best friendships of shy/withdrawn children: Prevalence, stability, and relationship quality. *Journal of Abnormal Child Psychology, 34*(2), 143–157.

Rubin, Z. (1980). *Children's friendships.* Cambridge, MA: Harvard University Press.

Rubinowitz, L. S., Rosenbaum, J. E., Dvorin, S., Kulieke, M., McCareins, A., & Popkin, S. (2000). *Crossing the class and color lines: From public housing to white suburbia.* Chicago: University of Chicago Press.

Ruble, D. N., & Martin, C. L. (1998). Gender development. In W. Damon & N. Eisenberg (Eds.), *Handbook of child development: Social, emotional, and personality development: Vol. 5* (pp. 933–1016). New York: Wiley.

Ruble, D. N., & Martin, C. L. (2002). Conceptualizing, measuring and evaluating the developmental course of gender differentiation. *Monographs of the Society for Research in Child Development, 67,* 148–166.

Rudolph, K. D. (2008). Developmental influences on interpersonal stress generation in depressed youth. *Journal of Abnormal Psychology, 117,* 673–679.

Rudolph, K. D., & Conley, C. (2005). The socioemotional costs and benefits of social-evaluative concerns: Do girls care too much? *Journal of Personality, 73*(1), 115–138.

Rudolph, K. D., Hammen, C., & Daley, S. E. (2006). Mood disorders. In D. A. Wolfe & E. J. Mash (Eds.), *Behavioral and emotional disorders in adolescents: Nature, assessment, and treatment* (pp. 300–342). New York, NY: Guilford Publications.

Rudolph, K. R., & Troop-Gordon, W. (2010). Personal-accentuation and contextual amplification models of pubertal timing predicting youth depression. *Development and Psychopathology, 22,* 433–451.

Ruel, M. T., & Menon, P. (2002). Child feeding practices are associated with child nutritional status in Latin America: Innovative uses of the demographic and health surveys. *Journal of Nutrition, 132*(6), 1180–1187.

Rumbaugh, D. M., Savage-Rumbaugh, E. S., & Sevcik, R. A. (1994). Biobehavioral roots of language: A comparative perspective on chimpanzee, child, and culture. In R. W. Wrangham, W. C. McGrew, F. B. M. de Waal, & P. G. Helthe (Eds.), *Chimpanzee cultures.* Cambridge, MA: Harvard University Press.

Rumbaugh, D. M., & Washburn, D. A. (2003). *Intelligence of apes and other rational beings.* New Haven, CT: Yale University Press.

Russell, R. (2001). New nicronutrient dietary reference intakes from the National Academy of Sciences. *Nutrition Today, 36,* 163–171.

Russell, S., & Joyner, K. (2001). Adolescent sexual orientation and suicide risk: Evidence from a national study. *American Journal of Public Health, 91,* 1276–1281.

Russell, S. T., Crockett, L. J., & Chao, R. K. (Eds.). (2010). *Asian American parenting and parent–adolescent relationships.* New York: Springer.

Rust, J., Golombok, S., Hines, M., & Johnston, K. (2000). The role of brothers and sisters in the gender development of preschool children. *Journal of Experimental Child Psychology, 77,* 292–303.

Ryan, R. R., Martin, A., & Brooks-Gunn, J. (2006). Is one good parent good enough? Patterns of mother and father parenting and child cognitive outcomes at 24 and 36 months. *Parenting: Science and Practice, 6,* 211–228.

Ryan, S. (2000). Examining social workers' placement recommendations of children with gay and lesbian adoptive parents. *Families in Society, 81,* 517–528.

Ruiz, S., Roosa, M., & Gonzales, N. (2002). Predictors of self-esteem for Mexican American and European American youths: A reexamination of the influence of parenting. *Journal of Family Psychology, 16,* 70–80.

Saarni, C. (2007). The development of emotional competence: Pathways for helping children to become emotionally intelligent. In R. Bar-On, J. G. Maree, & M. J. Elias (Eds.), *Educating people to be emotionally intelligent* (pp. 15–35). Westport, CT: Praeger Publishers/Greenwood Publishing Group.

Saarni, C. (2011). Emotional competence and effective negotiation: The integration of emotion understanding, regulation, and communication. In C. Saarni (Ed.), *Psychological and political strategies for peace negotiation: A cognitive approhach* (pp. 55–74). New York: Springer.

Saarni, C., Campos, J. J., Camras, L. A., & Witherington, D. (2006). Emotional development: Action, communication, and understanding. In N. Eisenberg, W. Damon, & R. M. Lerner (Eds.), *Handbook of child psychology: Vol. 3. Social, emotional, and personality development* (6th ed., pp. 226–299). Hoboken, NJ: John Wiley & Sons.

Sachs, J., Bard, B., & Johnson, M. (1981). Language learning with restricted input: Case studies of two hearing children of deaf parents. *Applied Psycholinguistics, 2,* 33–54.

Sadovsky, A., & Troseth, G. (2000). Aspects of young children's perceptions of gender-typed occupations. *Sex Roles, 42,* 993–1006.

Sagi, A., van IJzendoorn, M. H., Aviezer, O., Donnell, F., Koren-Karie, N., Joels, T., et al. (1995). Attachments in a multiple-caregiver and multiple-infant environment: The case of the Israeli kibbutzim. *Monographs of the Society for Research in Child Development, 60*(2–3), 71–91.

Sagi-Schwartz, A., & Aviezer, O. (2005). Correlates of attachment to multiple caregivers in kibbutz children from birth to emerging adulthood: The Haifa Longitudinal Study. In K. E. Grossmann, K. Grossmann, & E. Waters (Eds.), *Attachment from infancy to adulthood: The major longitudinal studies* (pp. 165–197). New York: Guilford Press.

Sai, F. Z. (2005). The role of the mother's voice in developing mother's face preference: Evidence for intermodal perception at birth. *Infant and Child Development, 14,* 29–50.

Sampaio, R. C., & Truwitt, C. L. (2001). Myelination in the developing human brain. In C. Nelson & M. Luciana (Eds.), *Handbook of developmental cognitive science* (pp. 35–44). Cambridge, MA: The MIT Press.

San Antonio, D. M. (2004). Adolescent lives in transition: How social class influences the adjustment to middle school. Albany, NY: State University of New York Press,

Sandberg, A., & Samuelsson, I. P. (2003). Preschool teachers' play experiences then and now. *Early Childhood Research and Practice, 5,* 1–19.

Sanson, A., Hamphill, S., & Smart, D. (2002). Temperament and social development. In P. Smith & C. Hart (Eds.), *Blackwell handbook of childhood social development*. Malden, MA: Blackwell Publishing.

Sapp, F., Lee, K., & Muir, D. (2000). Three-year-olds' difficulty with the appearance-reality distinction: Is it real or is it apparent? *Developmental Psychology, 36*(5), 547–560.

Saragovi, C., Aube, J., Koestner, R., & Zuroff, D. (2002). Traits, motives, and depressive styles as reflections of agency and communion. *Personality and Social Psychology Bulletin, 28,* 563–577.

Saltvedt, S., Almstrom, H., Kublickas, M., Valentin, L., Bottinga, R., Bui, T. H., et al. (2005). Screening for Down syndrome based on maternal age or fetal nuchal translucency: A randomized controlled trial in 39, 572 pregnancies. *Ultrasound in Obstetrics and Gynecology, 25*(6), 537–545

Salzarulo, P., & Ficca, G. (Eds.). (2002). *Advances in consciousness research: Vol. 38. Awakening and sleep-wake cycle across development*. Amsterdam: John Benjamins.

Sameroff, A. J. (1983). Developmental systems: Contexts and evolutions. In P. H. Mussen (Ed.), *Handbook of child psychology: Vol. 1. History, theory and methods*. New York: Wiley.

Sameroff, A. J., Bartko, W. T., Baldwin, A., Baldwin, C., & Seifer, R. (1998). Family and social influences on the development of child competence. In M. Lewis & C. Feiring (Eds.), *Families, risk, and competence* (pp. 161–186). Mahwah, NJ: Lawrence Erlbaum Associates.

Sameroff, A. J., & Haith, M. M. (1996). *The five to seven year shift: The age of reason and responsibility*. Chicago: University of Chicago Press.

Sameroff, A. J., Seifer, R., Baldwin, A., & Baldwin, C. (1993). Stability of intelligence from preschool to adolescence: The influence of social and family risk factors. *Child Development, 64,* 80–97.

SAMHSA. (2006). *Results from the 2005 National Survey on Drug Use and Health: Detailed Tables*. In: *Substance Abuse and Mental Health Services Administration*. Rockville, MD: Office of Applied Studies.

Santelli, J., Sandfort, T., & Orr, M. (2008). Transnational comparisons of adolescent contraceptive use: What can we learn from these comparisons? *Archives of Pediatrics Adolescent Medicine, 162,* 92–94.

Sarnecka, B., & Gelman, S. (2004). Six does not just mean a lot: Preschoolers see number words as specific. *Cognition, 92,* 329–352.

Sato, Y., Sogabe, Y., & Mazuka, R. (2010). Discrimination of phonemic vowel length by Japanese infants. *Developmental Psychology, 46,* 106–119.

Savage-Rumbaugh, E. S. (1993). How does evolution design a brain capable of learning language? *Monographs of the Society for Research in Child Development 58,* 243–252.

Savage-Rumbaugh, E. S., Toth, N., & Schick, K. (2007). Kanzi learns to knap stone tools. In D. A. Washburn (Ed.), *Primate perspectives on behavior and cognition* (pp. 279–291). Washington, DC: American Psychological Association.

Savin-Williams, R. C. (2001). A critique of research on sexual-minority youths. *Journal of Adolescence, 24,* 5–13.

Savin-Williams, R. C. (2008). Refusing and resisting sexual identity labels. In D. L. Browning (Ed.), *Adolescent identities: A collection of readings* (pp. 67–91). New York: Analytic Press/Taylor & Francis Group.

Savin-Williams, R. C., & Diamond, L. (2004). Sex. In R. M. Lerner & L. Steinberg (Eds.), *Handbook of adolescent psychology* (2nd ed.). Hoboken, NJ: John Wiley & Sons.

Savin-Williams, R. C., & Ream, G. L. (2007). Prevalence and stability of sexual orientation components during adolescence and young adulthood. *Archives of Sexual Behavior, 36,* 385–394.

Saxe, G. B. (2002). Children's developing mathematics in collective practices: A framework for analysis. *Journal of the Learning Sciences, 11*(2–3), 275–300.

Saxon, T. F., Gollapalli, A., Mitchell, M. W., & Stanko, S. (2002). Demand feeding or schedule feeding: Infant growth from birth to 6 months. *Journal of Reproductive and Infant Psychology, 20*(2), 89–100.

Scarr, S., & Salapatek, P. (1970). Patterns of fear development during infancy. *Merrill-Palmer Quarterly, 16*(1), 53–90.

Schachner, A., & Hannon, E. E. (2011). Infant-directed speech drives social preferences in 5-month-old infants. *Developmental Psychology, 47,* 19–25.

Schack-Nielsen, L., Larnkjaer, A., & Michaelsen, K. F. (2005). Long term effects of breastfeeding on the infant and mother. *Advances in Experimental Medicine and Biology, 569,* 16–23.

Schafer, G., & Plunkett, K. (1998). Rapid word learning by fifteen-month-olds under tightly controlled conditions. *Child Development, 69*(2), 309–320.

Scherf, K. S., Sweeney, J. A., & Luna, B. (2006, July). Brain basis of developmental change in visuospatial working memory. *Journal of Cognitive Neuroscience, 18*(7), 1045–1058.

Scheuermann, B. (2002). *Autism: Teaching does make a difference*. Belmont, CA: Wadsworth Thomson Learning.

Schick, B. (2006). Acquiring a visually motivated language: Evidence from diverse learners. In B. Schick, M. Marschark, & P. Spencer (Eds.), *Advances in the sign language development of deaf children*. New York: Oxford University Press.

Schlaggar, B., & Church, J. (2009). Functional neuroimaging insights into the development of skilled reading. *Current Directions in Psychological Sciences, 1*(18), 21–26.

Schlagmüller, M., & Schneider, W. (2002). The development of organizational strategies in children: Evidence from a microgenetic longitudinal study. *Journal of Experimental Child Psychology, 81*(3), 298–319.

Schmitt-Rodermund, E., & Silbereisen, R. K (2008, March). Well adapted adolescent ethnic German immigrants in spite of adversity: The protective effects of human, social, and financial capital. *European Journal of Developmental Psychology, 5*(2), 186–209.

Schneider, B. H. (2000). *Friends and enemies: Peer relations in childhood*. New York: Oxford University Press.

Schneider, B. H., del Pilar Soteras de Toro, M., Woodburn, S., Fulop, M., Cervino, C., Bernstein, S., et al. (2006). Cross-cultural differences in competition among children and adolescents. In X. Chen, D.C. French, & B. H. Schneider (Eds.), *Peer relationships in cultural context. Cambridge studies in social and emotional development* (pp. 310–338). New York: Cambridge University Press.

Schneider, B. H., & Stevenson, D. (1999). *The ambitious generation: America's teenagers, motivated, but directionless*. New Haven, CT: Yale University Press.

Schneider, B. H., Woodburn, S., del Pilar Soteras del Toro, M., & Udvari, S. J. (2005, April). Cultural and gender differences in the implications of competition for early adolescent friendship. *Merrill-Palmer Quarterly, 51*(2), 163–191.

Schneider, W. (2011). Memory development in childhood. In Usha Goswami (Ed.), *The Wiley-Blackwell handbook of childhood cognitive development (2nd edition)*. New York: Wiley-Blackwell.

Schneider, W., Gruber, H., Gold, A., & Opwis, K. (1993). Class expertise and memory for chess positions in children and adults. *Journal of Experimental Child Psychology, 56,* 328–349.

Schneider, W., Knopf, M., & Sodian, B. (2009). Verbal memory development from early childhood to early adulthood. In W. Schneider & M. Bullock (Eds.), *Human development from early childhood to early adulthood: Findings from a 20 year longitudinal study*. New York: Psychology Press.

Scholes, R. J. (1998). The case against phonemic awareness. *Journal of Research in Reading, 21*(3), 177–218.

Schonert-Reichl, K. A. (1999). Relations of peer acceptance, friendship adjustment, and social behavior to moral reasoning during early adolescence. *Journal of Early Adolescence, 19,* 249–279.

Schroeder, J. H., Desrocher, M., Bebko, J. M., & Cappadocia, M. C. (2010). The neurobiology of autism: Theoretical applications. *Research in Autism Spectrum Disorders, 4,* 555–564.

Schuetze, P., Eiden, R. D., & Edwards, E. P. (2009). A longitudinal examination of physiological regulation in cocaine-exposed infants across the first 7 months of life. *Infancy, 14,* 19–43.

Schuetze, P., Eiden, R. D., & Danielewicz, S. (2009). The association between prenatal cocaine exposure and physiological regulation at 13 months of age. *Journal of Child Psychology and Psychiatry, 50,* 1401–1409.

Schuler, M. E., & Nair, P. (1999). Frequency of maternal cocaine use during pregnancy and infant neurobehavioral outcome. *Journal of Pediatric Psychology, 24*(6), 511–514.

Schum, T. R., Kolb, T. M., McAuliffe, T., Simms, M. D., Underhill, R. L., & Marla, L. (2002). Sequential acquisition of toilet-training skills: A descriptive study of gender and age differences in normal children. *Pediatrics, 109*(3), e48.

Schwartz, S. J., Weisskirch, R. S., Zamboanga, B. L., Castillo, L. G., & Ham, L. S. (2011). Dimensions of acculturation: Associations with health risk behaviors among college students from immigrant families. *Journal of Counseling Psychology, 58,* 27–41.

Shweder, R. A., Goodnow, J. J., Hatano, G., LeVine, R. A., Markus, H. R., & Miller, P. J. (2006). The cultural psychology of development: One mind, many mentalities. In R. M. Lerner & W. Damon (Eds.), *Handbook of child psychology: Vol. 1. Theoretical models of human development* (6th ed., pp. 716–792). Hoboken, NJ: John Wiley & Sons.

Scribner, S., & Cole, M. (1981). *The psychology of literacy.* Cambridge, MA: Harvard University Press.

Sears, R. (1975). Your ancients revisited: A history of child development. In E. M. Hetherington (Ed.), *Review of child development research: Vol. 5.* Chicago: University of Chicago Press.

Segal, N. L. (1999). *Entwined lives: Twins and what they tell us about human behavior.* New York: Dutton/Penguin Books.

Segal, N. L., & Johnson, W. (2009). Twin studies of general mental ability. In Y. Kim (Ed.), *Handbook of behavior genetics* (pp. 81–99). New York: Springer.

Segall, M. H., Dasen, P., Berry, J. W., & Poortinga, Y. (1999). *Human behavior in global perspective: An introduction to cross-cultural psychology* (2nd ed.). Needham Heights, MA: Allyn & Bacon.

Segall, M. H., Ember, C., & Ember, M. (1997). Aggression, crime, and warfare. In J. W. Berry, M. H. Segall, & C. Kagitçibasi (Eds.), *Handbook of cross-cultural psychology: Vol. 3. Social and behavioral applications* (pp. 213–254). Boston: Allyn & Bacon.

Selman, R., Levitt, M., & Schultz, L. (1997). The friendship framework: Tools for the assessment of psychosocial development. In R. Selman, C. Watts, & L. Schultz (Eds.), *Fostering friendship: Pair therapy for treatment and prevention.* New York: Aldine de Gruyter.

Senghas, A. (2011). The emergence of two functions for spatial devices in Nicaraguan sign language. *Human Development, 53,* 287–302.

Senghas, R., Senghas, A., & Pyers, J. (2005). The emergence of Nicaraguan sign language: Questions of development, acquisition, and evolution. In S. T. Parker, J. Langer, & C. Milbrath (Eds.), *Biology and knowledge revisited: From neurogenesis to psychogenesis* (pp. 287–306). Mahwah, NJ: Lawrence Erlbaum Associates.

Serene, J. A., Ashtari, M., Szeszko, P. R., & Kumra, S. (2007). Neuroimaging studies of children with serious emotional disturbances: A selective review. *The Canadian Journal of Psychiatry / La Revue canadienne de psychiatrie, 52,* 135–145.

Serjeant, G. R., & Serjeant, B. E. (2001). *Sickle cell disease* (3rd ed.). Oxford, England: Oxford University Press.

Serpell, R. (2000). Intelligence and culture. In R. J. Sternberg and E. L. Grigorenko (Eds.), *Handbook of intelligence.* New York: Cambridge University Press.

Serpell, R., & Hatano, G. (1997). Education, schooling, and literacy. In J. W. Berry, P. R. Dasen, & T. S. Saraswathi (Eds.), *Handbook of cross-cultural psychology: Vol. 2.* Boston: Allyn & Bacon.

Serpell, R., & Haynes, B. P. (2004). The cultural practice of intelligence testing: Problems of international export. In R. J. Sternberg & E. L. Grigorenko (Eds.), *Culture and competence: Contexts of life success* (pp. 163–185). Washington, DC: American Psychological Association.

Shanahan, L., McHale, S. M., Osgood, D. W., & Crouter, A. C. (2007, May). Conflict frequency with mothers and fathers from middle childhood to late adolescence: Within- and between-families comparisons. *Developmental Psychology, 43*(3), 539–550.

Shapira, A., & Madsen, M. C. (1969). Cooperative and competitive behavior of kibbutz and urban children in Israel. *Child Development, 4,* 609–617.

Shapka, J. D., & Keating, D. P. (2005). Structure and change in self-concept during adolescence. *Canadian Journal of Behavioural Science, 37*(2), 83–96.

Shatz, M. (1978). Children's comprehension of question-directives. *Journal of Child Language, 5,* 39–46.

Shaver, P. & Cassidy, J. (2008). Handbook of attachment: theory, research, and clinical applications. New York: Guilford Press.

Shaw, D. S., Winslow, E. B., Owens, E. B., & Hood, N. (1998). Young children's adjustment to chronic family adversity: A longitudinal study of low-income families. *Journal of the American Academy of Child and Adolescent Psychiatry, 37*(5), 545–553.

Shaw, P., Greenstein, D., Lerch, J., Clasen, L., Lenroot, R., Gogtay, N., et al. (2006, March). Intellectual ability and cortical development in children and adolescents. *Nature, 440*(7084), 676–679.

Shaw, P., Kabani, N. J., Lerch, J. P., Eckstrand, K., & Lenroot, R. (2008). Neurodevelopmental trajectories of the human cerebral cortex. *Journal of Neuroscience, 28,* 432–443.

Sheeber, L. B., Davis, B., Leve, C., Hops, H., & Tildesley, E. (2007). Adolescents' relationships with their mothers and fathers: associations with depressive disorder and subdiagnostic symptomatology. *Journal of Abnormal Psychology, 116*(1), 144–154.

Sherif, M., & Sherif, C. W. (1956). *An outline of social psychology.* New York: Harper & Row.

Shin, Y. (2007). Peer relationships, social behaviors, academic performance and loneliness in Korean primary school children. *School Psychology International, 28*(2), 220–236.

Shinskey, J., & Munakata, Y. (2005). Familiarity breeds searching: Infants reverse their novelty preferences when reaching for hidden objects. *Psychological Science, 16,* 596–600.

Shonkoff, J., & Phillips, D. (Eds.). (2000). *From neurons to neighborhoods: The science of early childhood development.* Washington, DC: National Academy Press.

Shonkoff, J. P., Boyce, W. T., McEwen, B. S., (2009). Neuroscience, molecular biology, and the childhood roots of health disparities: Building a new framework for health promotion and disease prevention. *Journal of the American Medical Association, 301,* 2252–2259.

Shopen, T. (1980). How Pablo says "love" and "store." In T. Shopen & J. M. Williams (Eds.), *Standards and dialects in English.* Cambridge, MA: Winthrop.

Shostak, M. (1981). *Nissa: The life and words of a !Kung Woman.* Cambridge, MA: Harvard University Press.

Shulman, S., & Seiffge-Krenke, I. (2001). Adolescent romance: Between experience and relationships. *Journal of Adolescence, 24,* 417–428.

Shweder, R. A. (2007). An anthropological perspective: The revival of cultural psychology—some premonitions and reflections. In S. Kitayama & D. Cohen (Eds.), *Handbook of cultural psychology* (pp. 821–838). New York: Guilford Press.

Shweder, R. A., Goodnow, J. J., Hatano, G., LeVine, R. A., Markus, H. R., & Miller, P. J. (1998). The cultural psychology of development: One mind, many mentalities. In R. M. Lerner (Ed.), *Handbook of child psychology: Vol. 1. Theoretical models of human development* (5th ed., pp. 865–938). Hoboken, NJ: Wiley.

Shweder, R. A., Mahapatpa, M., & Miller, J. G. (1987). Culture and moral development. In J. Kagan & S. Lamb (Eds.), *The emergence of morality in young children.* Chicago: University of Chicago Press.

Shweder, R. A., Minow, M., & Markus, H. R. (Eds.). (2002). *Engaging cultural differences: The multicultural challenge in liberal democracies.* New York: Russell Sage Foundation.

Siegel, L. S. (2008, January–March). Morphological awareness skills of English language learners and children with dyslexia. *Topics in Language Disorders, 28*(1), 15–27.

Siegler, R. S. (1998). *Children's thinking* (3rd ed.). Upper Saddle River, NJ: Prentice Hall.

Siegler, R. S. (2005). Children's learning. *American Psychologist, 60,* 769–778.

Siegler, R. S., & Opfer, J. (2003). The development of numerical estimation: Evidence for multiple representations of numerical quantity. *Psychological Science, 14*(3), 237–243.

Silbereisen, R. K., & Kracke, B. (1997). Self-reported maturational timing and adaptation in adolescence. In J. Schulenberg, J. L. Maggs & K. Hurrelmann (Eds.), *Health risks and developmental transitions during adolescence* (pp. 85–109). New York: Cambridge University Press.

Silk, J., Steinberg, L., & Morris, A. (2003). Adolescents' emotion regulation in daily life: Links to depressive symptoms and problem behavior. *Child Development, 74,* 1869–1800.

Silva, K., Correa-Chavez, M., & Rogoff, B. (2010). Mexican-heritage children's attention and learning from interactions directed to others. *Child Development, 81,* 898–912.

Silva, L. M., Jansen, P. W., Steegers, E. A., Jaddoe, V. W., Arends, L. R., Tiemeier, H., et al. (2010). Mother's educational level and fetal growth: The genesis of health inequalities. *International Journal of Epidemiology, 39,* 1250–1261.

Simmons, R. (2002). *Odd girl out: The hidden culture of aggression in girls.* New York: Harcourt.

Simons, D. A., & Wurtele, S. K. (2010). Relationships between parents' use of corporal punishment and their children's endorsement of spanking and hitting other children. *Child Abuse & Neglect, 34,* 639–646.

Simons, L. G., & Conger, R. D. (2007). Linking motherfather differences in parenting to a typology of family parenting styles and adolescent outcomes. *Journal of Family Issues, 28,* 212–241.

Simpkins, S. D., Fredricks, J. A., Davis-Kean, P. E., & Eccles, J. S. (2006). Healthy mind, healthy habits: The influence of activity involvement in middle childhood. In A. C. Huston & M. N. Ripke (Eds.), *Developmental contexts in middle childhood: Bridges to adolescence and adulthood. Cambridge studies in social and emotional development* (pp. 283–302). New York: Cambridge University Press.

Simpson, J. A., Collins, W. A., Tran, S., & Haydon, K. C. (2007). Attachment and the experience and expression of emotions in romantic relationships: A developmental perspective. *Journal of Personality and Social Psychology, 92,* 355–367.

Sinclair, D. C., & Dangerfield, P. (1998). *Human growth after birth.* New York: Oxford University Press.

Singer, J. L. (2006). Epilogue: Learning to play and learning through play. In D. G. Singer, R. M. Golinkoff, & K. Hirsh-Pasek (Eds.), *Play = learning: How play motivates and enhances children's cognitive and social-emotional growth* (pp. 251–262). New York: Oxford University Press.

Singer, L. T., & Zeskind, P. S. (Eds.). (2001). *Biobehavioral assessment of the infant.* New York: Guilford Press.

Singh-Manoux, A. (2000). Culture and gender issues in adolescence: Evidence from studies on emotion. *Psicothema, 12*(Suppl. 1), 93–100.

Singleton, J. (Ed.). (1998). *Learning in likely places: Varieties of apprenticeship in Japan.* New York: Cambridge University Press.

Siqueland, E. R. (1968). Reinforcement patterns and extinction in human newborns. *Journal of Experimental Child Psychology, 6,* 431–432.

Sizun, J., & Westrup, B. (2004). Early developmental care for preterm neonates: A call for more research. *Archives of Disease in Childhood: Fetal and Neonatal Edition, 89,* 384–388.

Skinner, B. F. (1938). *The behavior of organisms.* New York: Appleton-Century-Crofts.

Skinner, B. F. (1953). *Science and human behavior.* New York: Macmillan.

Slater, S. J., Ewing, R., Powell, L. M., Chaloupka, F. J., & Johnston, L. D. (2010). The association between community physical activity settings and youth physical activity, obesity, and body mass index. *Journal of Adolescent Health, 47,* 496–503.

Slaughter, V., & McConnell, D. (2003). Emergence of joint attention: Relationships between gaze following, social referencing, imitation, and naming in infancy. *Journal of Genetic Psychology, 164,* 54–71.

Slobin, D. (2005). From ontogenesis to phylogenesis: What can child language tell us about language evolution? In S. T. Parker, J. Langer, & C. Milbrath (Eds.), *Biology and knowledge revisited: From neurogenesis to psychogenesis* (pp. 287–306). Mahwah, NJ: Lawrence Erlbaum Associates.

Smetana, J. G. (2006). Social-cognitive domain theory: Consistencies and variations in children's moral and social judgments. In M. Killen & J. G. Smetana (Eds.), *Handbook of moral development* (pp. 119–153). Mahwah, NJ: Lawrence Erlbaum Associates.

Smetana, J. G. (2008). Conflicting views of conflict. *Monographs of the Society for Research in Child Development, 73,* 161–168.

Smetana, J. G., & Gettman, D. C. (2006, November). Autonomy and relatedness with parents and romantic development in African American adolescents. *Developmental Psychology, 42*(6), 1347–1351.

Smith, A. M., Fried, P. A., Hogan, M. J., & Cameron, I. (2004). Effects of prenatal marijuana on response inhibition: An fMRI study of young adults. *Neurotoxicology and Teratology, 26*(4), 533–542.

Smith, K. (2002). *Who's minding the kids? Child care arrangements: Spring 1997.* Current Population Reports, P70–86, U.S. Census Bureau. Washington, DC: U.S. Government Printing Office.

Smith, P. K., & Monks, C. P. (2008). Concepts of bullying: Developmental and cultural aspects. *International Journal of Adolescent Medicine and Health, 20*(2), 101–112.

Smitsman, A. W. (2001). Action in infancy—Perspectives, concepts, and challenges: The development of reaching and grasping. In A. Fogel (Ed.), *Blackwell handbook of infant development* (pp. 71–98). Malden, MA: Blackwell Publishing.

Smotherman, W. P., & Robinson, S. R. (1996). The development of behavior before birth. *Developmental Psychology, 32,* 425–434.

Smyser, C. D., Inder, T. E., Shimony, J. S., Hill, J. E., Degnan, A. J., et al. (2010). Longitudinal analysis of neural network development in preterm infants. *Cerebral Cortex,* 2852–2862.

Smyth, C. M., & Bremner, W. J. (1998). Klinefelter syndrome. *Archives of Internal Medicine, 158,* 1309–1314.

Snarey, J. R. (1995). Cross-cultural universality of social moral development: A critical review of Kohlbergian research. *Psychological Bulletin, 97,* 202–232.

Snow, C. E. (1972). Mother's speech to children learning language. *Child Development, 43,* 549–565.

Snow, C. E. (1995). Issues in the study of input: Fine-tuning, universality, individual and developmental differences, and necessary causes. In P. Fletcher & B. MacWhinney (Eds.), *The handbook of child language.* Oxford, England: Blackwell Publishing.

Sokol, B. W., & Chandler, M. J. (2004). A bridge too far: On the relations between moral and secular reasoning. In J. I. M. Carpendale & U. Muller (Eds.), *Social interaction and the development of knowledge* (pp. 155–174). Mahwah, NJ: Lawrence Erlbaum Associates.

Solomon, S., & Knafo, A. (2007). Value similarity in adolescent friendships. In T. C. Rhodes (Ed.), *Focus on adolescent behavior research* (pp. 133–155). Hauppauge, NY: Nova Science Publishers.

Solomon, S. G. (2005). *American playgrounds: Revitalizing community space.* Lebanon, NH: University Press of New England.

Somerset, D. A., Moore, A., Whittle, M. J., Martin, W., & Kilby, M. D. (2006). An audit of outcome in intravascular transfusions using the intrahepatic portion of the fetal umbilical vein compared to cordocentesis. *Fetal Diagnosis and Therapy, 21*(3), 272–276.

Somerville, L. H., Jones, R. M., & Casey, B. J. (2010). A time of change: Behavioral and neural correlates of adolescent sensitivity to appetitive and aversive environmental cues. *Brain and Cognition, 72,* 124–133.

Sommer, K., Whitman, T., Gorkowski, J., & Gondoli, D. (2000). Prenatal maternal predictors of cognitive and emotional delays in children of adolescent mothers. *Adolescence, 35,* 87–112.

Sowell, E. R., Delis, D., Stiles, J., & Jernigan, T. L. (2001). Improved memory functioning and frontal lobe maturation between childhood and adolescence: A structural MRI study. *Journal of the International Neuropsychological Society, 7,* 312–322.

Sowell, E. R., Thompson, P. M., & Toga, A. W. (2007). Mapping adolescent brain maturation using structural magnetic resonance imaging. In D. Romer & E. F. Walker (Eds.), *Adolescent psychopathology and the developing brain: Integrating brain and prevention science* (pp. 55–84). New York: Oxford University Press.

Sowell, E. R., Trauner, D. A., Gamst, A., & Jernigan, T. L. (2002). Development of cortical and subcortical brain structures in childhood and adolescence: A structural magnetic resonance imaging study. *Developmental Medical Child Neurology, 44,* 4–16.

Spear, L. P. (2007). The developing brain and adolescent-typical behavior patterns: An evolutionary approach. In: D. Romer, & E. F. Walker (Eds.), *Adolescent psychopathology and the developing brain: Integrating brain and prevention science* (pp. 9–30). New York: Oxford University Press.

Spear, L. P. (2009). *The behavioral neuroscience of adolescence.* New York: W. W. Norton & Co.

Spearman, C. (1927). *The abilities of man.* New York: Macmillan.

Spelke, E. S. (2000). Core knowledge. *American Psychologist, 35,* 1233–1234.

Spelke, E. S., Breinlinger, K., Macomber, J., & Jacobson, K. (1992). Origins of knowledge. *Psychological Review, 99*(4), 605–632.

Spencer, M. B. (1988). Self-concept development. *New Directions for Child Development, 42,* 59–72.

Spencer, M. B. (2006). Revisiting the 1990 special issue on minority children: An editorial perspective 15 years later. *Child Development, 77,* 1149–1154.

Spencer, M. B., & Markstrom-Adams, C. (1990). Identity processes among racial and ethnic minority children in America. *Child Development, 61,* 290–310.

Spitz, H. H., Minsky, S. K., & Besselieu, C. L. (1985). Influence of planning time and first move strategy on Tower of Hanoi problem solving performance of mentally retarded young adults and nonretarded children. *American Journal of Mental Deficiency, 90*(1), 46–56.

Sreeramareddy, C. T., Joshi, H. S., Sreekumaran, B. V., Giri, S., & Chuni, N. (2006). Home delivery and newborn care practices among women in western Nepal: A questionnaire survey. BMC Pregnancy and Childbirth, 6, 27.

Sroufe, L. A., Carlson, E. A., Levy, A. K., & Egeland, B. V. (1999). Implications of attachment theory for developmental psychopathology. *Development & Psychopathology, 11*(1), 1–13.

Sroufe, L. A., Carlson, E., & Shulman, S. (1993). Individuals in relationships: Development from infancy through adolescence. In D. C. Funder, R. D. Parke, C. Tomlinson-Keasey, & K. Widaman (Eds.), *Studying life through time: Personality and development.* Washington, DC: American Psychological Association.

Sroufe, L. A., Coffino, B., & Carlson, E. A. (2010). Conceptualizing the role of early experience: Lessons from the Minnesota longitudinal study. *Developmental Review, 30,* 36–51.

Sroufe, L. A., Egeland, B., Carlson, E., & Collins, W. A. (2005). Placing early attachment experiences in developmental context. In K. E. Grossmann, K. Grossmann, & E. Waters (Eds.), *Attachment from infancy to adulthood: The major longitudinal studies* (pp. 48–70). New York: Guilford Publications.

Sroufe, L. A., & Fleeson, J. (1986). Attachment and the construction of relationships. In W. W. Hartup & Z. Rubin (Eds.), *Relationships and development.* Mahwah, NJ: Lawrence Erlbaum Associates.

Stallings, J., Fleming, A., Corter, C., Worthman, C., & Steiner, M. (2001). The effects of infant cries and odors on sympathy, cortisol, and autonomic responses in new mothers and nonpostpartum women. *Parenting: Science and Practice, 1*(1–2), 71–100.

Stang, J., & Story, M. (Eds.). (2005). *Guidelines for adolescent nutrition services.* Retrieved June 15, 2006, from http://www.epi.umn.edu/let/pubs/adol_book.shtm

Stanhope, R., & Traggiai, C. (2004). Precocious puberty (complete, partial). *Endocrine Development, 7,* 57–65.

Stauder, J. E., Molenaar, P. C., & Van Der Molen, M. W. (1999). Brain activity and cognitive transition during longitudinal event-related brain potential study. *Child Neuropsychology, 5,* 44–59.

Stearns, P. (2006). *Childhood in world history.* New York: Routledge.

Steele, R. G., Nesbitt-Daly, J. S., Daniel, R. C., & Forehand, R. (2005, December). Factor structure of the Parenting Scale in a low-income African American sample. *Journal of Child and Family Studies, 14*(4), 535–549.

Stein, A., Thompson, A., & Waters, A. (2005). Childhood growth and chronic disease: Evidence from countries undergoing the nutrition transition. *Maternal and Child Nutrition, 3,* 177–184.

Steinberg, L. (2001). We know some things: Parent-adolescent relationships in retrospect and prospect. *Journal of Research on Adolescence, 11,* 1–19.

Steinberg, L. (2005, February). Cognitive and affective development in adolescence. *Trends in Cognitive Sciences 9*(2), 69–74.

Steinberg, L. (2008, March). A social neuroscience perspective on adolescent risk-taking. *Developmental Review, 28*(1), 78–106.

Steinberg, L. (2010). A dual systems model of adolescent risk-taking. *Developmental Psychobiology, 52,* 216–224.

Steinberg, L., Albert, D., Cauffman, E., Banich, M., Graham, S., & Woolard, J. (2008). Age differences in sensation seeking and impulsivity as indexed by behavior and self-report: Evidence for a dual systems model. *Developmental Psychology, 44,* 1764–1778.

Steinberg, L., & Duncan, P. (2002). Work group IV: Increasing the capacity of parents, families, and adults living with adolescents to improve adolescent health outcomes. *Journal of Adolescent Health, 31*(Suppl. 6), 261–263.

Steinberg, L., Silk, J. S. (2002) Parenting adolescents. In M. H. Bornstein (Ed.) *Handbook of parenting: Vol. 1: Children and parenting (2nd ed.)* (pp. 103–133). Mahwah, NJ: Lawrence Erlbaum Associates.

Steiner, M., Attarbaschi, A., Konig, M., Nebral, K., Gadner, H., Haas, O. A., Mann, G., & Austrian Berlin-Frankfurt-Munster Group. (2005). Equal frequency of TEL/AML1 rearrangements in children with acute lymphoblastic leukemia with and without Down syndrome. *Journal of Pediatric Hematology/Oncology, 22*(1), 11–16.

Stennes, L. M., Burch, M. M., Sen, M. G., & Bauer, P. J. (2005). A longitudinal study of gendered vocabulary and communicative action in young children. *Developmental Psychology, 41*, 75–88.

Stern, D. N. (1977). *The first relationship.* Cambridge, MA: Harvard University Press.

Stern, D. N. (2002). *The first relationship: Infant and mother.* Cambridge, MA: Harvard University Press.

Stern, W. (1910). Abstracts of lectures on the psychology of testimony and on the study of individuality. *American Journal of Psychology, 21*, 273–282.

Stern, W. (1912). *Psychologische methoden der intelligenz-prufung.* Leipzig: Barth.

Sternberg, R. (1985). *Beyond IQ: A triarchic theory of human intelligence.* New York: Cambridge University Press.

Sternberg, R. J. (1990). *Metaphors of mind: Conceptions of the nature of intelligence.* New York: Cambridge University Press.

Sternberg, R. J. (2007, January). A systems model of leadership: WICS. *American Psychologist. Special Issue: Leadership, 62*(1), 34–42.

Sternberg, R. J., & Grigorenko, E. L. (2008). Ability testing across cultures. In L. A. Suzuki & J. G. Ponterotto (Eds.), *Handbook of multicultural assessment: Clinical, psychological, and educational applications* (pp. 449–470). San Francisco, CA: Jossey-Bass.

Stevens, J., Quittner, A. L., Zuckerman, J. B., & Moore, S. (2002). Behavioral inhibition, self-regulation of motivation, and working memory in children with attention deficit hyperactivity disorder. *Developmental Neuropsychology, 21*(2), 117–140.

Stevenson, H. W., & Stigler, J. W. (1992). *The learning gap: Why our schools are failing and what we can learn from Japanese and Chinese education.* New York: Summit.

Stevenson, H. W., Stigler, J. W., Lee, S., Lucker, G. W., Kitamura, S., & Hsu, C. (1985). Cognitive performance and academic achievement of Japanese, Chinese, and American children. *Child Development, 56*, 718–734.

Stevenson, R. (1977). *The fetus and newly born infant: Influence of the prenatal environment (2nd ed.).* St. Louis: Mosby.

Stice, E., Marti, C. N., Shaw, H., & Jaconis, M. (2009). An 8-year longitudinal study of the natural history of threshold, subthreshold, and partial eating disorders from a community sample of adolescents. *Journal of Abnormal Psychology, 118*, 587–597.

Stigler, J. W., Gallimore, R., & Hiebert, J. (2000). Using video surveys to compare classrooms and teaching across cultures: Examples and lessons from the TIMSS video studies. *Educational Psychologist, 35*(2), 87–100.

Steinberg, L., Albert, D., Cauffman, E., Banich, M., Graham, S., & Woolard, J. (2008). Age differences in sensation seeking and impulsivity as indexed by behavior and self-report: Evidence for a dual systems model. *Developmental Psychology, 44*, 1764–1778.

Stipek, D. (2001). Pathways to constructive lives: The importance of early school success. In A. C. Bower & D. J. Stipek (Eds.), *Constructive & destructive behavior: Implications for family, school, & society* (pp. 291–315). Washington, DC: American Psychological Association.

St. James-Roberts, I., Alvarez, M., Csipke, E., Abramsky, T., Goodwin, J., & Sorgenfrei, E. (2006). Infant crying and sleeping in London, Copenhagen, and when parents adopt a "proximal" form of care. *Pediatrics, 117*, 1146–1155.

St. James-Roberts, I., Conroy, S., & Wilshir, K. (1996). Bases for maternal perceptions of infant crying and colic behavior. *Archives of Disease in Childhood, 75*, 375–381.

Stoltz, H. E., Barber, B. K., & Olsen, J. A. (2005). Toward disentangling fathering and mothering: An assessment of relative importance. *Journal of Marriage and Family, 67*, 1076–1092.

Storvoll, E. E., & Wichstrom, L. (2002, April). Do the risk factors associated with conduct problems in adolescents vary according to gender? *Journal of Adolescence 25*(2), 182–202.

Stone, J. L., & Church, J. (1957). *Childhood and adolescence: A psychology of the growing person.* New York: Random House.

Stone, K. C., LaGasse, L. L., Lester, B. M., Shankaran, S., Bada, H. S., Bauer, C. R., et al. (2010). Sleep problems in children with prenatal substance exposure: The Maternal Lifestyle Study. *Archives of Pediatric and Adolescent Medicine, 164*, 452–456.

Stoltzfus, R. J., Kvalsvig, J. D., Chwaya, H. M., Montresor, A., Albonico, M., Tielsch, J. M., et al. (2001). Effects of iron supplementation and anthelmintic treatment on motor and language development of preschool children in Zanzibar: Double blind, placebo controlled study. *British Medical Journal, 323*, 1389–1393.

Strathearn, L., Gray, P. H., O'Callaghan, M. J., & Wood, D. O. (2001). Childhood neglect and cognitive development in extremely low birth weight infants: A prospective study. *Pediatrics, 108*(1), 142–151.

Stratton, K., Howe, C., & Battaglia, F. (1996). *Fetal alcohol syndrome: Diagnosis, epidemiology, prevention, and treatment.* Washington, DC: National Academy Press.

Straus, M. (2009) *Differences in corporal punishment in 32 nations and its relation to national differences in IQ.* Paper presented at the 14th International Conference on Violence, Abuse, and Trauma.

Strauss, R. (1999). Childhood obesity. *Current Problems in Pediatrics, 29*(1), 1–29.

Strauss, S., & Ziv, M. (2004). Teaching: Ontogenesis, culture, and education. *Cognitive Development, 19*, 451–456.

Strayer, F. F. (1991). The development of agonistic and affiliative structures in preschool play groups. In J. Silverberg & P. Gray (Eds.), *To fight or not to fight: Violence and peacefulness in humans and other primates.* Oxford, England: Oxford University Press.

Striano, T., & Rochat, P. (2000). Emergence of selective social referencing in infancy. *Infancy, 1*(2), 253–264.

Striano, T., Stahl, D., & Cleveland, A. (2009). Taking a closer look at social and cognitive skills: A weekly longitudinal assessment between 7 and 10 months of age. *European Journal of Developmental Psychology, 1*, 567–591

Striepe, M., & Tolman, D. (2003). Mom, Dad, I'm straight: The coming out of gender ideologies in adolescent sexual-identity development. *Journal of Clinical Child and Adolescent Psychology, 32*, 523–530.

Stross, B. (1973). Acquisition of botanical terminology by Tzeltal children. In M. S. Edmonson (Ed.), *Meaning in Mayan languages* (pp. 107–142). The Hague: Mouton

Stuart, J., Fondacaro, M., Miller, S. A., Brown, V., & Brank, E. M. (2008). Procedural justice in family conflict resolution and deviant peer group involvement among adolescents: The mediating influence of peer conflict. *Journal of Youth and Adolescence, 37*, 674–684.

Stunkard, A. J., Sorenson, T. I., Hanis, C., Teasdale, T. W., Chakraborty, R., Schull, W. J., & Schulsinger, F. (1986). An adoption study of human obesity. *New England Journal of Medicine, 314*, 193–198.

Suárez-Orozco, C., Bang, H. J., & Onaga, M. (2010). Contributions to variations in academic trajectories amongst recent immigrant youth. *International Journal of Behavioral Development, 34,* 500–510.

Suárez-Orozco, C., Suárez-Orozco, M. M., & Todorova, I. (2008). *Learning a new land: Immigrant students in American society.* Cambridge, MA: Harvard University Press.

Subbotsky, E. V. (1993). *The birth of personality: The development of independent and moral behavior in preschool children.* New York: Harvester Wheatsheaf.

Subrahmanyam, K., Garcia, E. C. M., Harsono, L. S., Li, J. S., & Lipana, L. (2009). In their words: Connecting on-line weblogs to developmental processes. *British Journal of Developmental Psychology, 27,* 219–245.

Subrahmanyam, K., & Greenfield, P. (2008). Online communication and adolescent relationships. *The Future of Children, 18,* 119–146.

Subrahmanyam, K., Kraut, R., Greenfield, P., & Gross, E. (2001). New forms of electronic media: The impact of interactive games and the Internet on cognition, socialization, and behavior. In D. Singer & J. Singer (Eds.), *Handbook of children and the media.* Thousand Oaks, CA: Sage.

Subrahmanyam, K., & Šmahel, D. (2011). Digital youth: The role of media in development. New York: Springer.

Sugiyama, L., & Chacon, R. (2005). Juvenile responses to household ecology among the Yora of Peruvian Amazonia. In B. Hewlitt & M. Lamb (Eds.), *Hunter-gatherer childhoods: Evolutionary, cultural and developmental perspectives.* New Brunswick, NJ: Transaction Publishers.

Sullivan, H. S. (1953). *The interpersonal theory of psychiatry.* New York: W. W. Norton.

Sullivan, J. A. (2000). Introduction to the musculoskeletal system. In J. A. Sullivan & S. J. Anderson (Eds.), *Care of the Young Athlete* (pp. 243–258). Rosemont, IL: American Academy of Orthopaedic Surgeons and American Academy of Pediatrics.

Sullivan, J. A., Anderson, S. J. (Eds.). (2000). *Care of the young athlete.* Rosemont, IL: American Academy of Orthopaedic Surgeons and American Academy of Pediatrics.

Sullivan, K., & Winner, E. (1993). Three-year-olds' understanding of mental states: The influence of trickery. *Journal of Experimental Child Psychology, 56*(2), 135–148.

Summerfield, D. (1999). A critique of seven assumptions behind psychological trauma programmes in war-affected areas. *Social Science and Medicine, 48,* 1449–1462.

Sunseth, K., & Bowers, P. G. (2002). Rapid naming and phonemic awareness: Contributions to reading, spelling, and orthographic knowledge. *Scientific Studies of Reading, 6*(4), 401–429.

Suomi, S. (1995). Influences of attachment theory on ethological studies of biobehavioral development in nonhuman primates. In S. Goldberg, R. Muir, & J. Kerr (Eds.), *Attachment theory: Social, developmental, and clinical perspectives* (pp. 185–202). Mahwah, NJ: Analytic Press.

Super, C. M. (1976). Environmental effects on motor development: A case of African infant precocity. *Developmental Medicine and Child Neurology, 18,* 561–567.

Super, C. M., & Harkness, S. (1972). The infant's niche in rural Kenya and metropolitan America. In L. Adler (Ed.), *Issues in cross-cultural research.* New York: Academic Press.

Super, C. M., & Harkness, S. (2002). Culture structures the environment for development. *Human Development, 45,* 270–274.

Sun, Y., & Li, Y. (2002). Children's well-being during parents' marital disruption process: A pooled time-series analysis. *Journal of Marriage and Family, 64,* 472–488.

Sun, Y., & Li, Y. (2008). Stable postdivorce family structures during late adolescence and socioeconomic consequences in adulthood. *Journal of Marriage and Family 70,* 129–143.

Suomi, S. J. (2000). A biobehavioral perspective on developmental psychopathology: Excessive aggression and serotonergic dysfunction in monkeys. In A. Sameroff, M. Lewis, & S. M. Miller (Eds.), *Handbook of developmental psychopathology* (2nd ed., pp. 237–256). Dordrecht, Netherlands: Kluwer Academic.

Susman, E. J. (2006). Psychobiology of persistent antisocial behavior: Stress, early vulnerabilities and the attenuation hypothesis. *Neuroscience & Biobehavioral Reviews, 30*(3), 376–389.

Susman, E. J., Nottelmann, E. D., Dorn, L. D., Inoff-Germain, G., & Chrousos, G. P. (1998). Physiological and behavioral aspects of stress in adolescence. In G. P. Chrousos, D. L. Loriaux, & P. W. Gold (Eds.), *Mechanisms of physical and emotional stress* (pp. 341–352). New York: Plenum Press.

Susman, E. J., Schmeelk, K. H., Ponirakis, A., & Gariepy, J. L. (2001). Maternal prenatal, postpartum, and concurrent stressors and temperament in 3-year-olds: A person and variable analysis. *Development and Psychopathology, 13*(3), 629–652.

Sutton, J., Smith, P. K., & Swettenham, J. (1999). Bullying and "theory of mind": A critique of the "social skills deficit" view of anti-social behavior. *Social Development, 8*(1), 117–127.

Suzuki, K., Minai, J., & Yamagata Z. (2007). Maternal negative attitudes towards pregnancy as an independent risk factor for low birthweight. *Journal of Obstetrics and Gynaecology Research 33,* 438–444.

Sweeney, J., & Bradbard, M., R. (1988). Mothers' and fathers' changing perceptions of their male and female infants over the course of pregnancy. *Journal of Genetic Psychology, 149*(3), 393–404.

Sweeney, N. M., Tucker, J., Reynosa, B., & Glaser, D. (2006). reducing hunger-associated symptoms: The midmorning nutrition break. *The Journal of School Nursing, 22,* 32–39.

Sweeting, H., & West, P. (2003). Sex differences in health at ages 11, 13 and 15. *Social Science & Medicine, 56,* 31–39.

Symington, A., & Pinelli, J. (2003). Developmental care for promoting development and preventing morbidity in preterm infants. *Cochrane Database of Systematic Reviews, 4,* CD001814.

Szkrybalo, J., & Ruble, D. N. (1999). "God made me a girl": Sex-category constancy judgments and explanations revisited. *Developmental Psychology, 35*(2), 392–402.

Tabacchi, G., Giammanco, S., La Guardia, M., & Giammanco, M. (2007). A review of the literature and a new classification of the early determinants of childhood obesity: From pregnancy to the first years of life. *Nutrition Research, 27,* 587–604.

Tabak, I., & Weinstock, M. (2008). A sociocultural exploration of epistemological beliefs. In M. S. Khine (Ed.), *Knowing, knowledge and beliefs: Epistemological studies across diverse cultures* (pp. 177–195). New York: Springer Science + Business Media.

Tager-Flusberg, H. (2007, December). Evaluating the theory-of-mind hypothesis of autism. *Current Directions in Psychological Science, 16*(6), 311–315.

Tallal, P. (2003). Language learning disabilities: Integrating research approaches. *Current Directions in Psychological Science, 12*(6), 206–211.

Tallal, P., Merzenich, M., Miller, S., & Jenkins, W. (1998). Language learning impairment: Integrating research and remediation. *Scandinavian Journal of Psychology, 39*(3), 197–199.

Tallal, P., & Rosen, G. D. (2006). Process faster, talk earlier, read better. In P. Tallal & G. D. Rosen (Eds.), *The dyslexic brain: New pathways in neuroscience discovery* (pp. 49–74). Mahwah, NJ: Lawrence Erlbaum.

Tani, C. R., Chavez, E. L., & Deffenbacher, J. L. (2001). Peer isolation and drug use among while non-Hispanic and Mexican American adolescents. *Adolescence, 36,* 127–139.

Tanner, J. M. (1978). *Fetus into man: Physical growth from conception to maturity.* Cambridge, MA: Harvard University Press.

Tanner, J. M. (1990). *Fetus into man: Physical growth from conception to maturity* (Rev. ed.). Cambridge, MA: Harvard University Press.

Tanner, J. M. (1998). Sequence, tempo, and individual variation in growth and development of boys and girls aged twelve to sixteen. In D. P. Harriet (Ed.), *Adolescent behavior and society: A book of readings* (5th ed., pp. 34–46). New York: McGraw-Hill.

Taylor, C. A., Manganello, J. A., Lee, S. J., & Rice, J. C. (2010). Mothers' spanking of 3-year-old children and subsequent risk of children's aggressive behavior. *Pediatrics, 125,* 1057–1065.

Taylor, P., Passel, J., Fry, R., Morin, R., Wang, W., Velasco, G., & Dockterman, D (2010). *The return of the multi-generational family household: A social and demographic trends report.* Washington, DC: Pew Research Center.

Taylor, P. D., McConnell, J., Khan, I. Y., Holemans, K., Lawrence, K. M., Asare-Anane, H., et al. (2005). Impaired glucose homeostasis and mitochondrial abnormalities in offspring of rats fed a fat-rich diet in pregnancy. *American Journal of Physiology: Regulatory, Integrative, and Comparative Physiology, 288,* 134–139.

Temple, C. M., & Sanfilippo, P. M. (2003). Executive skills in Klinefelter's syndrome. *Neuropsychologia, 41,* 1547–1559.

Tena-Sempere, M. (2010). Kisspeptin signaling in the brain: Recent developments and future challenges. *Molecular and Cellular Endocrinology, 314,* 164–169.

Tenenbaum, H. R., Callanan, M., Alba-Speyer, C., & Sandoval, L. (2002). The role of educational background, activity, and past experiences in Mexican-descent families' science conversations. *Hispanic Journal of Behavioral Sciences, 24*(2), 225–248.

Terplan, M., Smith, E. J., Kozloski, M. J., & Pollack, H. A. (2009). Methamphetamine use among pregnant women. *Obstetrics and Gynecology, 113,* 1285–1291.

Tessier, R., Charpak, N., Giron, M., Cristo, M., de Calume, Z. F., & Ruiz-Peláez, J. G. (2009). Kangaroo Mother Care, home environment and father involvement in the first year of life: A randomized controlled study. *Acta paediatrica, 98,* 1444–1450.

Tharp, R. G. (2005). Research in diversity and education: Process and structure in synthesizing knowledge. *Journal of Education for Students Placed at Risk, 10,* 355–361.

Thatcher, R. W. (1994). Cyclic cortical reorganization. In G. Dawson & K. W. Fischer (Eds.), *Human behavior and the developing brain.* New York: Guilford Press.

Thelen, E. (1995). Motor development: A new synthesis. *American Psychologist, 50,* 79–95.

Thelen, E. (2002). Self-organization in developmental processes: Can systems approaches work? In M. H. Johnson & Y. Munakata (Eds.), *Brain development and cognition: A reader* (2nd ed., pp. 336–374). Malden, MA: Blackwell Publishing.

Thelen, E., Fisher, D. M., & Ridley-Johnson, R. (2002). The relationship between physical growth and a newborn reflex. *Infant Behavior and Development, 25*(1), 72–85.

Thelen, E., Schoener, G., Scheier, C., & Smith, L. B. (2001). The dynamics of embodiment: A field theory of infant perseverative reaching. *Behavioral and Brain Sciences, 24*(1), 1–86.

Thelen, E., & Smith, L. B. (1998). Dynamic systems theory. In W. Damon & R. M. Lerner (Eds.), *Handbook of child psychology: Vol. 12* (5th ed., pp. 563–634). New York: Wiley.

Thiessen, E. D., Hill, E. A., & Saffran, J. R. (2005). Infant-directed speech facilitates word segmentation. *Infancy, 7,* 53–71.

Thoman, E. B., & Whitney, M. P. (1989). Sleep states of infants monitored in the home: Individual differences, developmental trends, and origins of diurnal cyclicity. *Infant Behavior & Development, 12,* 59–75.

Thomas, L. R., Donovan, D. M., Sigo, R. L. W., Austin, L., & Marlatt, G. A. (2009). The community pulling together: A tribal community-university partnership project to reduce substance abuse and promote good health in a reservation tribal community. *Journal of Ethnicity in Substance Abuse, 8,* 283–300.

Thomas, M., & Karmiloff-Smith, A. (2003). Modeling language acquisition in atypical phenotypes. *Psychological Review, 110,* 647–682.

Thompson, C. A., & Siegler, R. S. (2010). Linear numerical-magnitude representations aid children's memory for numbers. *Psychological Science, 21,* 1274–1281.

Thompson, G. B., & Nicholson, T. (Eds.). (1999). *Learning to read: Beyond phonics and whole language.* New York: Teachers College Press.

Thompson, R., & Einstein, F. (2010). Epigenetic basis for fetal origins of age-related disease. *Journal of Women's Health, 19,* 581–587.

Thompson, R. A. (1998). Early sociopersonality development. In N. Eisenberg (Ed.), *Handbook of child psychology: Vol. 3. Social, emotional, and personality development* (5th ed., pp. 25–104). New York: Wiley.

Thompson, R. A., & Newton, E. K. (2010). Emotion in early conscience. In R. A. Thompson & E. K. Newton (Eds.), *Emotions, aggression, and morality in children: Bridging development and psychopathology* (pp. 13–31). Washington, DC: American Psychological Association.

Thorne, B. (1993). *Gender play: Girls and boys in school.* New Brunswick, NJ: Rutgers University Press.

Thrasher, F. (1927). *The gang: A study of 1,313 gangs in Chicago.* Chicago: University of Chicago Press.

Tilburg, M., Unterberg, M., Tiemeier, H., Lenroot, R. K., Greenstein, D. K., Tran, L., Pierson, R., & Giedd, J. N. (2010). Cerebellum development during childhood and adolescence: A longitudinal morphometric MRI study. *NeuroImage, 49,* 63–70.

Tilburg, M., Unterberg, M., & Vingerhoets, A. (2002). Crying during adolescence: The role of gender, menarche, and empathy. *British Journal of Developmental Psychology, 20,* 77–87.

Tizard, B., & Hodges, J. (1978). The effect of early institutional rearing on the development of eight-year-old children. *Journal of Child Psychology and Psychiatry, 19,* 99–118.

Tizard, B., & Rees, J. (1975). The effect of early institutional rearing on the behavioral problems and affectional relationship of four-year-old children. *Journal of Child Psychology and Psychiatry, 16,* 61–73.

Toga, A. W., Thompson, P. M., & Sowell, E. R. (2006). Mapping brain maturation. *Trends in Neurosciences, 29*(3), 148–159.

Tokita, M., Kiyoshi, T., & Armstrong, K. N. (2007). Evolution of craniofacial novelty in parrots through developmental modularity and heterochrony. *Evolution & Development, 9*(6), 590–601.

Tokunaga, R. S. (2010). Following you home from school: A critical review and synthesis of research on cyberbullying victimization. *Computers in Human Behavior, 26,* 277–287.

Tolchinsky, L. (2006). The emergence of writing. In C. A. MacArthur, S. Graham, & J. Fitzgerald (Eds.), *Handbook of writing research* (pp. 83–95). New York: Guilford Press.

Tolman, D. L., Impett, E. A., Tracy, A. J., & Michael, A. (2006). Looking good, sounding good: Femininity ideology and adolescent girls' mental health. *Psychology of Women Quarterly, 30,* 85–95.

Tom, S. R., Schwartz, D., Chang, L., Farver, J. A. M., & Xu, Y. (2010). Correlates of victimization in Hong Kong children's peer groups. *Developmental Psychology, 31,* 27–37.

Tomasello, M. (1999). *The cultural origins of human cognition.* Cambridge, MA: Harvard University Press.

Tomasello, M. (2000). First steps toward a usage-based theory of language acquisition. *Cognitive Linguistics. Special Issue: Language Acquisition 11*(1–2), 61–82.

Tomasello, M. (2011). Language development. In U. Goswami Ed., *The Wiley-Blackwell handbook of childhood cognitive development* (2nd ed., pp. 239–257). Malden, MA: Blackwell.

Tomasello, M., & Hermann, E. (2010). Ape and human cognition: What's the difference? *Current Directions in Psychology Science, 19,* 3–8.

Toppari, J., & Juul, A. (2010). Trends in puberty timing in humans and environmental modifiers. *Molecular and Cellular Endocrinology, 324,* 39–44.

Torney-Purta, J. (1996). Conceptual change among adolescents using computer networks and peer collaboration in studying international political issues. In S. Vosniadou, E. De Corte, R. Glaser, & H. Mandl (Eds.), *International perspectives on the design of technology-supported learning environments.* Mahwah, NJ: Erlbaum.

Traggiai, C., & Stanhope, R. (2003, February). Disorders of pubertal development. *Best Practice and Research Clinical Obstetrics and Gynaecology, 17*(1), 41–56.

Travis, F. (1998). Cortical and cognitive development in 4th, 8th and 12th grade students: The contribution of speed of processing and executive functioning to cognitive development. *Biological Psychology, 48*(1), 37–56.

Tremblay, R., Nagin, D., Séguin, J., Zoccolillo, M., Zelazo, P., Boivin, M., et al. (2005). Physical aggression during early childhood: Trajectories and predictors. *Canadian Child and Adolescent Psychiatry Review, 14*(1), 3–9.

Tremblay, R. E. (2011). Origins, development, and prevention of aggressive behavior. In R. E. Tremblay (Ed.), *Origins, development, and prevention of aggressive behavior.* New York: Cambridge University Press.

Trevarthen, C. (1998). The concept and foundations of infant intersubjectivity. In S. Braten (Ed.), *Intersubjective communication and emotion in early ontogeny* (pp. 15–46). New York: Cambridge University Press.

Trevarthen, C. (2005). Action and emotion in development of cultural intelligence: Why infants have feelings like ours. In J. Nadel & D. Muir (Eds.), *Emotional development.* Oxford, England: Oxford University Press.

Trevarthen, C. (2009). The intersubjective psychobiology of human meaning: Learning of culture depends on interest for co-operative practical work-and affection for the joyful art of good company. *Psychoanalytic Dialogues, 19,* 507–518.

Trevarthen, C., & Reddy, V. (2007). Consciousness in infants. In M. Velmans & S. Schneider (Eds.), *The Blackwell companion to consciousness* (pp. 41–57). Malden, MA: Blackwell Publishing.

Triandis, H. C., McCusker, C., & Hui, C. H. (1990, November). Multimethod probes of individualism and collectivism. *Journal of Personality and Social Psychology, 59*(5), 1006–1020.

Troiden, R. R. (1993). The formation of homosexual identities. In L. D. Garnets & D. C. Kimmel (Eds.), *Psychological perspectives on lesbian and gay male experiences* (pp. 191–217). New York: Columbia University Press.

Tronick, E. (2005). Why is connection with others so critical? The formation of dyadic states of consciousness and the expansion of individuals' states of consciousness: Coherence governed selection and the cocreation of meaning out of messy meaning making. In J. Nadel & D. Muir (Eds.), *Emotional development* (pp. 293–315). Oxford, England: Oxford University Press.

Tronick, E. (2007). *The neurobehavioral and social-emotional development of infants and children (The Norton series on interpersonal neurobiology).* New York: W. W. Norton.

Tronick, E., & Reck, C. (2009). Infants of depressed mothers. *Harvard Review of Psychiatry, 17,* 147–156.

Troop-Gordon, W., & Ladd, G. W. (2005). Trajectories of peer victimization and perceptions of the self and schoolmates: Precursors to internalizing and externalizing problems. *Child Development, 76,* 1072–1091.

Troseth, G. L. (2003). Getting a clear picture: Young children's understanding of a televised image. *Developmental Science, 6,* 247–253.

Tuchmann-Duplessis, H. (1975). *Drug effects on the fetus.* Acton, MA: Publishing Science Group.

Tuchmann-Duplessis, H., David, G., & Haegel, P. (1971). *Illustrated human embryology: Vol. 1.* New York: Springer-Verlag.

Tucker, G. R. (1999). *A global perspective on bilingualism and bilingual education.* Washington, DC: ERIC Clearinghouse on Languages and Linguistics.

Tudge, J., Odero, D., Piccinini, C., Doucet, F., Sperb, T., & Lopes, R. (2006). A window into different cultural worlds: Young children's everyday activities in the United States, Brazil, and Kenya. *Child Development, 77,* 1446–1469.

Tulving, E., & Craik, F. I. M. (Eds.). (2000). *The Oxford handbook of memory.* London: Oxford University Press.

Tulviste, P. (1991). *The cultural-historical development of verbal thinking.* Commack, NY: Nova Science.

Turati, C., Di Giorgio, E., Bardi, L., & Simion, F. (2010). Holistic face processing in newborns, 3-month-old infants, and adults: Evidence from the composite face effect. *Child Development, 81,* 1894–1905.

Turiel, E. (1983). *The development of social knowledge: Morality and convention.* Cambridge, England: Cambridge University Press.

Turiel, E. (1998). The development of morality. In W. Damon & N. Eisenberg (Eds.), *Handbook of child psychology: Vol. 3. Social, emotional, and personality development* (5th ed., pp. 863–932). New York: Wiley.

Turiel, E. (2002). *The culture of morality.* Cambridge, England: Cambridge University Press.

Turiel, E. (2006). The development of morality. In N. Eisenberg, W. Damon, & R. M. Lerner (Eds.), *Handbook of child psychology: Vol. 3. Social, emotional, and personality development* (6th ed., pp. 789–857). Hoboken, NJ: John Wiley & Sons.

Turiel, E. (2008). Thought about actions in social domains: Morality, social conventions, and social interactions. *Cognitive Development, 23*(1), 136–154.

Turiel, E. (2010). Domain specificity in social interactions, social thought, and social development. *Child Development, 81,* 720–726.

Turnbull, E., Rothstein-Fisch, C., Greenfield, P. M., & Quiroz, B. (2001). *Bridging cultures between home and school.* Mahwah, NJ: Lawrence Erlbaum Associates.

Twenge, J. M., & Nolen-Hoeksema, S. (2002, November). Age, gender, race, socioeconomic status, and birth cohort difference on the children's depression inventory: A meta-analysis. *Journal of Abnormal Psychology, 111*(4), 578–588.

U.S. Census Bureau. (2002). *Statistical abstract of the United States: 2002* (122nd ed.). Washington, DC: U.S. Government Printing Office.

U.S. Census Bureau. (2003). *The foreign-born population: 2000.* Retrieved December 1, 2008, from http://www.census.gov/prod/2003pubs/c2kbr-34.pdf

U.S. Census Bureau. (2011). *Statistical abstract of the United States: 2012: Historical Statistics* (131st ed.). Washington, DC: U.S. Department of Commerce.

U.S. Department of Health & Human Services, *Administration on Children Youth & Families. Child Maltreatment 2007* (2009). Washington, DC: U.S. Government Printing Office.

U.S. Department of Labor, Bureau of Labor Statistics (2009). Women in the Labor Force: A Data Book (2009 edition). Retrieved from http://data.bls.gov/search/query/results?cx=013738036195919377644%3A6ih0hfrgl50&q=women+with+children

Underwood, M. (2002). Aggression among boys and girls. In P. Smith & C. Hart (Eds.), *Blackwell handbook of childhood social development.* Malden, MA: Blackwell Publishing.

Undheim, A. M., & Sund, A. M. (2011). Bullying—a hidden factor behind somatic symptoms? *Acta Paediatrica, 100,* 496–498.

UNESCO. (2004). *Global education digest 2004: Comparing education statistics across the world*. Montreal, Canada: UNESCO Institute for Statistics.

UNESCO. (2007). EFA Global Monitoring Report: Strong foundations: Early childhood care and education. Retrieved January 9, 2007, from http://unesdoc.unesco.org/images/0014/001477/147794E.pdf

UNICEF. (2003). *Prevention of mother-to-child transmission of HIV*.

UNICEF. (2009). *Tracking progress on child and maternal nutrition: A survival and development priority*. Atlanta, GA: Center for Disease Control.

United Nations Commission on Population and Development. (2005). *Trends in total migrant stock: The 2005 revision*. Retrieved October 18, 2008, from http://www.un.org/esa/population/publications/migration/UN_Migrant_Stock_Documentation_2005.pdf

United Nations Department of Economic and Social Affairs. (2005). *World youth report 2005*. Retrieved October 18, 2008, from http://www.un.org/esa/socdev/unyin/wpayinformation.htm#WYR2005

United Nations Department of Economic and Social Affairs. (2006). International migration 2006. Retrieved from http://www.un.org/esa/population/publications/2006Migration_Chart/Migration2006.pdf

United Nations General Security Council. (2011). Children and armed conflict. Retrieved from http://www.un.org/children/conflict/_documents/S2011250.pdf

United Nations Statistics Division. (2006). *Demographic Yearbook 2006*. New York: United Nations.

Urberg, K. A., Degirmencioglu, S. M., & Tolson, J. M. (1998). Adolescent friendship selection and termination: The role of similarity. *Journal of Social & Personal Relationships, 15*(5), 703–710.

Ursitti, F., Klein, J., & Koren, G. (2001). Confirmation of cocaine use during pregnancy: A critical review. *Therapeutic Drug Monitoring, 23*(4), 347–353.

Uzgiris, I. C., & Hunt, J. (1975). *Assessment in infancy: Ordinal scales of psychological development*. Champaign: University of Illinois Press.

Valdes, G. (1996). Con reseto: Bridging the distances between culturally diverse families and schools. New York: Teachers College Press.

Valentin, S. (2005). Commentary: Sleep in German infants: The cult of independence. *Pediatrics, 115*, 269–271.

Valian, V. (1999). Input and language acquisition. In W. C. Ritchie & T. K. Bhatia (Eds.), *Handbook of child language acquisition* (pp. 497–530). San Diego: Academic Press.

Valkenburg, P. M., & Peter, J. (2007). Online communication and adolescent well-being: Testing the stimulation versus the displacement hypothesis. *Journal of Computer-Mediated Communication, 12*(4), article 2.

Valsiner, J. (1998). Editorial: Culture and psychology on the move. *Culture & Psychology, 4*, 5–9.

Valsiner, J. (2005). Transformations and flexible forms: Where qualitative psychology begins. *Qualitative Research in Psychology, 4*(4), 39–57.

Valsiner, J. (2006). Developmental epistemology and implications for methodology. In R. M. Lerner & W. Damon (Eds.), *Handbook of child psychology: Vol. 1. Theoretical models of human development* (6th ed., pp. 166–209). Hoboken, NJ: John Wiley & Sons.

Valsiner, J. (2007). *Culture in minds and societies*. New York: Sage.

Valsiner, J., & Rosa, A. (2007). *The Cambridge handbook of sociocultural psychology*. New York: Cambridge University Press.

Valsiner, J., van Oers, B., Wardekker, W., Elbers, E., & van der Veer, R. (2009). Contextualizing learning: How activity theories can change our conventional research practices in the study of development. *Human Development, 52*, 69–76.

van De Beek, C., van Goozen, S. H. M., Buitelaar, J. K., & Cohen-Kettenis, P. T. (2009). Prenatal sex hormones (maternal and amniotic fluid) and gender-related play behavior in 13-month-old Infants. *Archives of Sexual Behavior, 38*, 6–15. Retrieved from http://www.ncbi.nlm.nih.gov/pubmed/18080735

Van Der Put, N. M., Thomas, C. M., Eskes, T. K., Trijbels, F. J., Steegers-Theunissen, R. P., Mariman, E. C., De Graaf-Hess, A., et al. (1997). Altered folate and vitamin B12 metabolism in families with spina bifida offspring. *QJM Monthly Journal of the Association of Physicians, 90*(8), 505–510.

Vanfraussen, K., Ponjaert-Kristoffersen, I., & Brewaeys, A. (2002). What does it mean for youngsters to grow up in a lesbian family created by means of donor insemination. *Journal of Reproductive and Infant Psychology, 20*, 237–252.

Vangelisti, A., Reis, H., & Fitzpatrick, M. (Eds.). (2002). *Stability and change in relationships*. Cambridge, England: Cambridge University Press.

von Hofsten, C. (1982). Eye-hand coordination in the newborn. *Developmental Psychology, 18*, 450–461.

von Hofsten, C. (1984). Developmental changes in the organization of prereaching movements. *Developmental Psychology, 20*, 378–388.

Van IJzendoorn, M. H., & Sagi-Schwartz, A. (2001). Cross-cultural patterns of attachment: Universal and contextual dimensions. In J. Cassidy & P. R. Shaver (Eds.), *Handbook of attachment: Theory, research, and clinical applications* (pp. 713–734). New York: Guilford Press.

Van IJzendoorn, M. & Sagi-Schwartz, A. (2008). Cross-cultural patterns of attachment: Universal and contextual dimensions. In J. Cassidy & P. Shaver (Eds.), *Handbook of Attachment: Theory, Research, and Clinical Applications (2nd edition)*, pp. 880–1020. New York: Guilford Press.

Van Leijenhorst, L., Gunther Moor, B., Op De Macks, Z. A., Rombouts, S. A. R. B., Westenberg, P. M., & Crone, E. A. (2010). Adolescent risky decision-making: neurocognitive development of reward and control regions. *NeuroImage, 51*, 345–355.

Van Mierlo, J., & Van den Bulck, J. (2004). Benchmarking the cultivation approach to video game effects: A comparison of the correlates of TV viewing and game play. *Journal of Adolescence, 27*, 97–111.

Van Wagner, V., Epoo, B., Nastapoka, J., & Harney, E. (2007). Reclaiming birth, health, and community: Midwifery in the Inuit villages of Nunavik, Canada. *Journal of Midwifery and Women's Health, 52*(4), 384–391.

Vartanian, L. R., Schwartz, M. B., & Brownell, K. D. (2007, April). Effects of soft drink consumption on nutrition and health: A systematic review and meta-analysis. *American Journal of Public Health, 97*(4), 667–675.

Vasquez, O. (2002). *La classe magica*. Mahwah, NJ, Lawrence Erlbaum Associates.

Ventura, S., & Hamilton, B. (2011). U.S. teenage birth rate resumes decline. *NCHS data brief, 58*. Hyattsville, MD: National Center for Health Statistics. Retrieved from http://www.cdc.gov/nchs/data/databriefs/db58.htm#findings

Verhoeven, M., Junger, M., van Aken, C., Deković, M., & van Aken, M., A. G. (2010). Mothering, fathering, and externalizing behavior in toddler boys. *Journal of Marriage and Family 72*, 307–317.

Viding, E., Jones, A. P., Frick, P. J., Moffitt, T. E., & Plomin, R. (2008, January). Heritability of antisocial behaviour at 9: Do callous unemotional traits matter? *Developmental Science, 11*(1), 17–22.

Vinden, P. G. (1998). Imagination and true belief: A cross-cultural perspective. In J. de Rivera & T. R. Sarbin (Eds.), *Believed-in imaginings: The narrative construction of reality*. Memory trauma, dissociation, and hypnosis series (pp. 73–85). Washington, DC: American Psychological Association.

Vinden, P. G. (2002). Understanding minds and evidence for belief: A study of Mofu children in Cameroon. *International Journal of Behavioral Development, 26*(5), 445–452.

Vintzileos, A. M., Ananth, C. V., Smulian, J. C., Scorza, W. E., & Knuppel, R. A. (2001). Do maternal-fetal medicine practice characteristics influence high-risk referral decisions by general obstetrician-gynecologists? *Journal of Maternal-Fetal Medicine, 10,* 112–115.

Vintzileos, A. M., Ananth, C. V., Smulian, J. C., Scorza, W. E., & Knuppel, R. A. (2002). Prenatal care black-white fetal death disparity in the United States: Heterogeneity by high-risk conditions. *Obstetrics and Gynecology, 99*(3), 483–489.

Violato, C., & Wiley, A. (1990). Images of adolescence in English literature: The middle ages to the modern period. *Adolescence, 25,* 253–264.

Volterra, V., Iverson, J., & Castrataro, M. (2006). The development of gesture in hearing and deaf children. In B. Schick, M. Marschark, & P. Spencer (Eds.), *Advances in the sign language development of deaf children* (pp. 46–70). New York: Oxford University Press.

von Hofsten, C. (1982). Eye-hand coordination in the newborn. *Developmental Psychology, 18*(3), 450–461.

von Hofsten, C. (1984). Developmental changes in the organization of prereaching movements. *Developmental Psychology, 20*(3), 378–388.

von Hofsten, C. (2001). On the early development of action, perception, and cognition. In F. Lacerda, C. von Hofsten, & M. Heimann (Eds.), *Emerging cognitive abilities in early infancy* (pp. 73–89). Mahwah, NJ: Lawrence Erlbaum Associates.

von Koss Torkildsen, J., Friis Hansen, H. F., Svangstu, J. M., Smith, L., Simonsen, H. G., Moen, I., & Lindgren, M. (2009). Brain dynamics of word familiarization in 20-month-olds: Effects of productive vocabulary size. *Brain and Language, 108,* 73–88.

Vurpillot, E. (1968). The development of scanning strategies and their relation to visual differentiation. *Journal of Experimental Child Psychology, 6,* 632–650.

Vygotsky, L. S. (1934/1986). *Thought and language.* Cambridge, MA: MIT Press.

Vygotsky, L. S. (1978). *Mind in society.* Cambridge, MA: Harvard University Press.

Wachs, T. D. (2000). *Necessary but not sufficient: The respective roles of single and multiple influences on individual development* (pp. 69–96). Washington, DC: American Psychological Association.

Wachs, T. D., & Bates, J. E. (2001). Temperament. In G. Bremmer & A. Fogel (Eds.), *Blackwell handbook of infant development: Vol. 12. Handbooks of developmental psychology* (pp. 465–501). Malden, MA: Blackwell Publishing.

Waddington, Conrad H. (1957). *The Strategy of the Genes.* London: Geo Allen & Unwin.

Wagner, D. A. (1974). The development of short-term and incidental memory: A cross cultural study. *Child Development, 48,* 389–396.

Wagner, D. A. (1978). Memories of Morocco: The influence of age, schooling, and environment on memory. *Cognitive Psychology, 10,* 1–28.

Wahlstrom, K. L. (2002). Accommodating the sleep patterns of adolescents within current educational structures: An uncharted path. In M. Carskadon (Ed.), *Adolescent sleep patterns: Biological, social, and psychological influences* (pp. 172–197). New York: Cambridge University Press.

Wainright, J. L., & Patterson, C. J. (2008). Peer relations among adolescents with female same-sex parents. *Developmental Psychology, 44,* 117–126.

Wainryb, C. (1995). Reasoning about social conflicts in different cultures: Druze and Jewish children in Israel. *Child Development, 66*(2), 390–401.

Wainryb, C. (2010). Resilience and risk: How teens experience their violent world, and what they learn—and lose—in the process. *Journal of Applied Developmental, 31,* 410–412.

Waldinger, R. J., Vaillant, G. E., & Orav, E. J. (2007). Childhood sibling relationships as a predictor of major depression in adulthood: A 30-year prospective study. *American Journal of Psychiatry, 164,* 949–954.

Walker, L. J. (2007). Progress and prospects in the psychology of moral development. In G. W. Ladd (Ed.), *Appraising the human developmental sciences: Essays in honor of Merrill-Palmer Quarterly. Landscapes of childhood series.* Detroit, MI: Wayne State University Press.

Walker, L. J., Hennig, K., & Krettenauer, T. (2000). Parent and peer contexts for children's moral reasoning development. *Child Development, 71,* 1033–1048.

Walker, L. J., Pitts, R. C., Henning, K. H., & Matsuba, M. K. (1995). Reasoning about morality and real-life moral problems. In M. Killen & D. Hart (Eds.), *Morality in everyday life: Developmental perspectives.* New York: Cambridge University Press.

Walker, R., Hill, K., Burger, O., & Hurtado, M. (2006). Life in the slow lane revised: Ontogenetic separation between chimpanzees and humans. *American Journal of Physical Anthropology, 129,* 577–583.

Walker, S., Irving, K., & Berthelsen, D. (2002). Gender influences on preschool children's social problem-solving strategies. *The Journal of Genetic Psychology, 163,* 197–209.

Walsh, W. (2002). Spankers and nonspankers: Where they get information on spanking. *Family Relations, 51,* 81–88.

Wandersman, A., & Florin, P. (2003). Community interventions and effective prevention. *American Psychologist, 58*(6–7), 441–448.

Wang, Q., Pomerantz, E. M., & Chen, H. (2007, September). The role of parents' control in early adolescents' psychological functioning: A longitudinal investigation in the United States and China. *Child Development, 78,* 1592–1610.

Wang, S.-H., & Baillargeon, R. (2008). Can infants be "taught" to attend to a new physical variable in an event category? The case of height in covering events. *Cognitive Psychology, 56,* 284–326.

Wang, S.-H, Baillargeon, R., & Brueckner, L. (2004). Young infants' reasoning about hidden objects: Evidence from violation-of-expectation tasks with test trials only. *Cognition, 93,* 167–198.

Wang, S.-H, Baillargeon, R., & Paterson, S. (2005). Detecting continuity violations in infancy: A new account and new evidence from covering and tube events. *Cognition, 95,* 129–173.

Wang, X., Zuckerman, B., Pearson, C., Kaufman, G., Chen, C., Wang, G., et al. (2002). Maternal cigarette smoking, metabolic gene polymorphism, and infant birth weight. *Journal of the American Medical Association, 287,* 195–202.

Ward, K. (1994). Genetics and prenatal diagnosis. In J. R. Scott, P. J. DiSaia, C. B. Hammond, & W. N. Spellacy (Eds.), *Dansforth's obstetrics and gynecology* (7th ed.). Philadelphia: J. B. Lippincott.

Ward, L. M., Hansbrough, E., & Walker, E. (2005). Contributions of music video exposure to black adolescents' gender and sexual schemas. *Journal of Adolescent Research, 20,* 143–166.

Ware, E. A., Uttal, D. H., Wetter, E. K., & DeLoache, J. S. (2006). Young children make scale errors when playing with dolls. *Developmental Science, 9*(1), 40–45.

Washburn, S. L. (2004). *Classification and human evolution.* New York: Routledge.

Watamura, S., Donzella, B., Alwin, J., & Gunnar, M. (2003). Morning-to-afternoon increases in cortisol concentrations for infants and toddlers at child care: Age differences and behavioral correlates. *Child Development, 74,* 1006–1020.

Waters, E., Hamilton, C., & Weinfield, N. (2000a) The stability of attachment security from infancy to adolescence and early adulthood: General introduction. *Child Development, 71,* 678–683.

Waters, E., Merrick, S., Treboux, D., Crowell, J., & Albersheim, L. (2000b). Attachment security in infancy and early adulthood: A twentyyear longitudinal study. *Child Development, 71,* 684–689.

Waters, H. S., & Waters, E. (2006). The attachment working models concept: Among other things, we build script-like representations of secure base experiences. *Attachment & Human Development. Special Issue: Script-like Attachment Representations and Behavior in Families and Across Cultures, 8*(3), 185–197

Watson, J. B. (1930). *Behaviorism.* Chicago: University of Chicago Press.

Waxman, S., & Leddon, E. (2011). Early word-learning and conceptual development: Everything had a name, and each name gave birth to a new thought. In U. Goswami (ed), *The Wiley-Blackwell handbook of childhood cognitive development* (2nd ed., pp. 180–209). Malden, MA: Blackwell.

Webb, S. J., Monk, C. S., & Nelson, C. A. (2001). Mechanisms of postnatal neurobiological development: Implications for human development. *Developmental Neuropsychology, 19*(2), 147–171.

Weikum, W. M., Vouloumanos, A., Navarra, J., Soto-Faraco, S., Sebastián-Gallés, N., & Werker, J. F. (2007). Visual language discrimination in infancy. *Science, 316* (5828), 1159.

Weinstock, H., Berman, S., & Cates, W., Jr. (2004). Sexually transmitted diseases among American youth: Incidence and prevalence estimates, 2000. *Perspectives on Sexual and Reproductive Health, 36*(1), 6–10.

Weinstock, M. (2005, July). The potential influence of maternal stress hormones on development and mental health of the offspring. *Brain, Behavior, and Immunity, 19*(4), 296–308.

Weisfeld, G. E., & Janisse, H. C. (2005). Some functional aspects of human adolescence. In B. J. Ellis & D. F. Bjorklund (Eds.), *Origins of the social mind: Evolutionary psychology and child development* (pp. 189–218). New York: Guilford Press.

Weisner, T. S., Matheson, C., Coots, J., & Bernheimer, L. P. (2005). Sustainability of daily routines as a family outcome. In A. E. Maynard & M. I. Martini (Eds.), *Learning in cultural context: Family, peers, and school. International and cultural psychology series* (pp. 41–73). New York: Kluwer.

Weiss, D., & Newport, E. (2006). Mechanisms underlying language acquisition: Benefits from a comparative approach. *Infancy, 92,* 241–257.

Weissman, M. M., Wickramaratne, P., Nomura, Y., Warner, V., Verdeli, H., Pilowsky, D. J., Grillon, C., et al. (2005). Families at high and low risk for depression: A 3-generation study. *Archives of General Psychiatry, 62,* 29–36.

Weisz, A. N., & Black, B. M. (2003). Gender and moral reasoning: African American youths respond to dating dilemmas. *Journal of Human Behavior in the Social Environment, 6*(3), 17–34.

Weitoft, G., Hern, A., Haglunk, B., & Rosen, M. (2003). Mortality, severe morbidity, and injury in children living with single parents in Sweden: A population-based study. *Lancet, 361,* 289–295.

Wellings, K., Martine, C., Slaymaker, E., Singh, S., Hodges, Z., Patel, D., et al. (2006). Sexual behaviour in context: A global perspective. *Lance, 368,* 1706–1728.

Wellman, F. (2011). Developing a theory of mind. In U. Goswami (Ed.), *The Wiley-Blackwell handbook of childhood cognitive development* (2 ed.). Malden, MA: Blackwell.

Wellman, H. M., & Gelman, S. A. (1998). Knowledge acquisition in foundational domains. In D. Kuhn & R. S. Siegler (Eds.), *Handbook of child psychology: Vol. 2. Cognition, perception, and language* (5th ed., pp. 523–574). New York: Wiley.

Wellman, H. M., Hickling, A. K., & Schult, C. A. (1997). Young children's psychological, physical, and biological explanations. In H. M. Wellman & K. Inagaki (Eds.), *The emergence of core domains of thought: Children's reasoning about physical, psychological, and biological phenomena* (pp. 7–26). San Francisco: Jossey-Bass.

Wells, G. (2007). The mediating role of discoursing in activity. *Mind, Culture, and Activity, 14*(3), 160–177.

Welsh, B. C., & Farrington, D. P. (2009). Early developmental prevention of delinquency and later offending: Prospects and challenges. *European Journal of Developmental Science, 3,* 247–259.

Wen, M., Cagney, K. A., & Christakis, N. A. (2005, September). Effect of specific aspects of community social environment on the mortality of individuals diagnosed with serious illness. *Social Science & Medicine, 61*(6), 1119–1134.

Wentzel, K. R., & Asher, S. R. (1995). The academic level of neglected, rejected, popular, and controversial children. *Child Development, 66,* 754–763.

Werker, J. F., Pegg, J. E., & McLeod, P. J. (1994). A cross-language investigation of infant preference for infant-directed communication. *Infant Behavior and Development, 17,* 323–333.

Whitaker, R. C., Wright, J. A., Pepe, M. S., Seidel, K. D., & Dietz, W. H. (1997). Predicting obesity in young adulthood from childhood and parental obesity. *New England Journal of Medicine, 337,* 869–873.

White, M. I. (2001). Children and families: Reflections on the "crisis" in Japanese childrearing today. In H. Shimizu & R. A. LeVine (Eds.), *Japanese frames of mind: Cultural perspectives on human development* (pp. 257–266). New York: Cambridge University Press.

White, S. H. (1996). The relationship of developmental psychology to social policy. In E. F. Zigler & S. L. Kagan (Eds.), *Children, families, and government: Preparing for the twenty-first century* (pp. 409–426). New York: Cambridge University Press.

White, S. H. (1991). Three visions of educational psychology. In L. Tolchinsky-Landsmann (Ed.), *Culture, schooling and psychological development* (pp. 1–38). Norwood, NJ: Ablex.

Whiteman, S. D., McHale, S. M., & Crouter, A. C. (2007, November). Competing processes of sibling influence: Observational learning and sibling deidentification. *Social Development, 16*(4), 642–661.

Whitehouse, A., Maybery, M. T., Hart, R., & Sloboda, D. M. (2010). Free testosterone levels in umbilical-cord blood predict infant head circumference in females. *Developmental Medicine and Child Neurology, 52,* 73–77.

Whiting, B. B., & Whiting, J. W. M. (1975). *Children of six cultures: A psycho-cultural analysis.* Cambridge, MA: Harvard University Press.

Whiting, J. W. M., Burbank, V. K., and Ratner. M. S., (1986). The duration of maidenhood across cultures. In J. B. Lancaster & B. A. Hamburg (Eds.), *School Age Pregnancy and Parenthood,* (pp. 273–302). New York: Aldine.

Whiting, J. W. M., & Child, I. L. (1953). *Child training and personality.* New Haven, CT: Yale University Press.

Whiting, S. J., Vatanparast, H., Baxter-Jones, A., Faulkner, R. A, Mirwald, R., & Bailey, D. A. (2004, March). Factors that affect bone mineral accrual in the adolescent growth spurt. *The Journal of Nutrition, 134*(3), 696S–700S.

Whittle, S., Yücel, M., Fornito, A., Barrett, A., Wood, S. J., Lubman, D. I., Simmons, J., et al. (2008). Neuroanatomical correlates of temperament in early adolescents. *Journal of the American Academy of Child & Adolescent Psychiatry, 47,* 682–693

WHO (World Health Organization). (2006). WHO child growth standards based on length/height, weight and age. *Acta Paediatrica, 95*(Suppl. 450), 76–85.

WHO (World Health Organization). (2009). Aids epidemic update. Retrieved from data.unaids.org/pub/report/2009/jc1700_epi_update_2009_en.pdf

WHO (World Health Organization). (2010). Resolution of the Sixty-third World Health Assembly, adopted 21 May, 2010, (WHA 63).

Marketing of food and nonalcoholic beverages to children. Retrieved from http://whqlibdoc.who.int/publications/2010/9789241500210_eng.pdf

WHO/UNAIDS/UNICEF. (2010). *Towards Universal Access: Scaling Up Priority HIV/AIDS Interventions in the Health Sector.* (Progress Report). Geneva, Switzerland: AUTHOR.

Wolfenstein, M. (1953). Trends in infant care. *American Journal of Orthopsychiatry, 23,* 120–130.

Woodruff-Pak, D. S., Logan, C. G., & Thompson, R. F. (1990). Neurobiological substrates of classical conditioning across the life-span. *Annals of the New York Academy of Sciences, 608,* 150–178.

Worchel, F. F., & Allen, M. (1997). Mothers' ability to discriminate cry types in low-birthweight premature and full-term infants. *Children's Health Care, 26*(3), 183–195.

Wigle, D. T., Arbuckle, T. E., Turner, M. C., Bérubé, A., Yang, Q., Liu, S., & Krewski, D. (2008). Epidemiologic evidence of relationships between reproductive and child health outcomes and environmental chemical contaminants. *Journal of Toxicology and Environmental Health Part B Critical Reviews, 11*(5–6), 373–517.

Wilcox, A. J., Baird, D. D., & Weinberg, C. R. (1999). Time of implantation of the conceptus and loss of pregnancy. *New England Journal of Medicine, 340,* 1796–1799.

Wilkening, F., & Cacchione, T. (2011). Children's intuitive physics. In U. Goswami (Ed.), *The Wiley-Blackwell handbook of childhood cognitive development* (2 ed.). Malden, MA: Blackwell.

Willford, J. A., Chandler, L. S., Goldschmidt, L., & Day, N. L. (2010). Effects of prenatal tobacco, alcohol and marijuana exposure on processing speed, visual-motor coordination, and interhemispheric transfer. *Neurotoxicology and Teratology, 32,* 580–588.

Wilson, B. J., Smith, S. L., Potter, W. J., Kunkel, D., Linz, D., Colvin, C. M., et al. (2002, March). Violence in children's television programming: Assessing the risks. *Journal of Communication, 52*(1), 5–35.

Wilson, E. O. (1975). *Sociobiology: The new synthesis.* Cambridge, MA: Harvard University Press.

Wilson, S. M., Olver, R. E., & Walters, D. V. (2007). Developmental regulation of lumenal lung fluid and electrolyte transport. *Respiratory Physiology and Neurobiology, 159*(3), 247–255.

Wimmer, H., & Hartl, M. (1991). Against the Cartesian view on mind: Young children's difficulty with own false beliefs. *British Journal of Developmental Psychology, 9,* 125–138.

Winner, E. (1998). *The point of words: Children's understanding of metaphor and irony.* Cambridge, MA: Harvard University Press.

Winnicott, D. W. (1971). *Playing and reality.* London: Tavistock.

Wolff, P. H. (1966). The causes, controls, and organization of behavior in the neonate. *Psychological Issues, 5,* 1–105.

Wozniak, R. H. (2009). Consciousness, social heredity, and development: The evolutionary thought of James Mark Baldwin. *American Psychologist: Charles Darwin and Psychology, 1809–2009, 64,* 93–101.

Wu, C., & Chao, R. K. (2005, November). Intergenerational cultural conflicts in norms of parental warmth among Chinese American immigrants. *International Journal of Behavioral Development, 29*(6), 516–523.

Wu, P., Robinson, C. C., Yang, C., Hart, C. H., & Olsen, S. F. (2002). Similarities and differences in mothers' parenting of preschoolers in China and the United States. *International Journal of Behavioral Development, 26,* 481–491.

Wynn, K. (1992). Addition and subtraction by human infants. *Nature, 358,* 749–750.

Xiong, X., Harville, E. W., Mattison, D. R., Elkind-Hirsch, K., Pridjian, G., & Buekens, P. (2008). Exposure to Hurricane Katrina, post-traumatic stress disorder and birth outcomes. *American Journal of Medical Science, 336,* 111–115.

Yang, C., & Hahn, H. (2002). Cosleeping in young Korean children. *Journal of Developmental & Behavioral Pediatrics, 23,* 151–157.

Yang, Q., Carter, H., Mulinare, J., Berry, R., Friedman, J., & Erickson, J. (2007). Race-ethnicity differences in folic acid intake in women of childbearing age in the United States after folic acid fortification: Findings from the National Health and Nutrition Examination Survey, 2001–2002. *American Journal of Clinical Nutrition, 85,* 1409–1416.

Yaman, A., Mesman, J., van IJzendoorn, M. H., Bakermans-Kranenburg, M. J., & Linting, M. (2010). Parenting in an individualistic culture with a collectivistic cultural background: The case of Turkish immigrant families with toddlers in the Netherlands. *Journal of Child and Family Studies, 19,* 617–628.

Yanai, J., Dotan, S., Goz, R., Pinkas, A., Seidler, F. J., Slotkin, T. A., & Zimmerman, F. (2008). Exposure of developing chicks to perfluorooctanoic acid induces defects in prehatch and early posthatch development. *Journal of Toxicology and Environmental Health, Part A, 71*(2), 131–133.

Yau, J., & Smetana, J. (2003). Conceptions of moral, social-conventional, and personal events among Chinese preschoolers in Hong Kong. *Child Development, 74*(3), 647–658.

Yerkes, R. M. (Ed.). (1921). *Psychological examining in the United States Army. Memoirs of the National Academy of Sciences, 15,* 1–890.

Yeung, W., Sandberg, J., Davis-Dean, P., & Hofferth, S. (2001). Children's time with fathers in intact families. *Journal of Marriage and the Family, 63*(1), 136–154.

Yinan, H. (2007). Infant born with birth defects every thirty seconds. *China Daily* Retrieved June 1, 2011, from http://www.chinadaily.com.cn/china/2007-10/30/content_6215074.htm

Ying-Xiu, Z., & Shu-Rong, W. (2008). Distribution of body mass index and the prevalence changes of overweight and obesity among adolescents in Shandong, China from 1985 to 2005. *Annals of Human Biology, 35*(5), 547–555.

Ylisaukko-oja, T., Alarcón, M., Cantor, R. M., Auranen, M., Vanhala, R., Kempas, E., et al. (2006). Search for autism loci by combined analysis of Autism Genetic Resource Exchange and Finnish families. *Annals of Neurology, 59*(1), 145–155.

Yorifuji, T., Tsuda, T., Inoue, S., Takao, S., & Harada, M. (2011). Long-term exposure to methylmercury and psychiatric symptoms in residents of Minamata, Japan. *Environment International, 37,* 907–913.

Yoshida, K. A., Iversen, J. R., Patel, A. D., Mazuka, R., Nito, H., & al., e. (2010). The development of perceptual grouping biases in infancy: A Japanese-English cross-linguistic study. *Cognition,* 356–361.

Yoshikawa, H. (2005). *Placing the first year findings of the National Head Start Impact Study in context.* Washington, DC: U.S. Department of Health and Human Services.

Yoshikawa, H., Rosman, E., & Hsueh, J. (2001). Variation in teenage mothers' experiences of child care and other components of welfare reform: Selection processes and developmental outcomes. *Child Development, 72,* 299–317.

Young, M., Miller, B., Norton, M., & Hill, E. (1995). The effect of parental supportive behaviors on life satisfaction of adolescent offspring. *Journal of Marriage and the Family, 57,* 813–822.

Young, S. S., Eskenazi, B., Marchetti, F. M., Block, G., & Wyrobek, A. J. (2008). The association of folate, zinc and antioxidant intake with sperm aneuploidy in healthy non-smoking men. *Human Reproduction, 23,* 1014–1022.

Zafeiriou, D. I., Tsikoulas, I. G., Kremenopoulos, G. M., & Kontopoulos, E. E. (1999). Moro reflex profile in high-risk infants at the first year of life. *Brain and Development, 21*(3), 216–217.

Zahn-Waxler, C., & Polanichka, N. (2004). All things interpersonal: Socialization and female aggression. In M. Putallaz & K. Bierman (Eds.), *Aggression, antisocial behavior, and violence among girls.* New York: Guilford Press.

Zeanah, C. H., Egger, H. L., Smyke, A. T., Nelson, C. A., & Fox, N. A. (2009). Institutional rearing and psychiatric disorders in Romanian preschool children. *The American Journal of Psychiatry, 166,* 777–785.

Zeifman, D. M. (2001). An ethological analysis of human infant crying: Answering Tinbergen's four questions. *Developmental Psychobiology, 39*(4), 265–285.

Zelazo, P. D., Müller, U. (2011) Executive function in typical and atypical development In U. Goswami (Ed.), *The Wiley-Blackwell handbook of childhood cognitive development (2nd ed.),* 574–603. New York: Wiley-Blackwell.

Zelazo, P. R. (1983). The development of walking: New findings and old assumptions. *Journal of Motor Behavior, 15,* 99–137.

Zeskind, P. S., & Lester, B. M. (2001). Analysis of infant crying. In L. T. Singer & P. S. Zeskind (Eds.), *Biobehavioral assessment of the infant* (pp. 149–166). New York: Guilford Press.

Zentella, A. (1997). *Growing up bilingual: Puerto Rican children in New York.* Walden, MA: Blackwell.

Zero to Three. (2003). *Choosing quality child care.* Retrieved April 4, 2007, from http://www.zerotothree.org/choosecare.htm

Zigler, E., & Styfco, S. (2008). America's Head Start Program: An effort for social justice. In C. Wainryb, J. Smetana, & E. Turiel (Eds.), *Social development, social inequalities, and social justice* (pp. 53–80). Mahwah, NJ: Lawrence Erlbaum.

Zigler, E., & Styfco, S. J. (2010). The hidden history of Head Start. In E. Zigler & S. J. Styfco (Eds.), *The hidden history of Head Start.* New York: Oxford University Press.

Zielinski, D. S., & Bradshaw, C. P. (2006, February). Ecological influences on the sequelae of child maltreatment: A review of the literature. *Child Maltreatment: Journal of the American Professional Society on the Abuse of Children, 11*(1), 49–62.

Zielinski, D. S., Eckenrode, J., & Olds, D. L. (2009). Nurse home visitation and the prevention of child maltreatment: Impact on the timing of official reports. *Development and Psychopathology, 21,* 441–453.

Zhou, Z., Peverly, S. T. & Lin J. (2005). Understanding early mathematical competencies in American and Chinese children. *School Psychology International 26,* 413–427.

Zigler, E. F., & Hall, N. W. (1989). Physical child abuse in America: Past, present, and future. In D. Cicchetti & V. Carlson (Eds.), *Child maltreatment: Theory and research on the causes and consequences of child abuse and neglect.* New York: Cambridge University Press.

Zukow-Goldring, P. (1995). Sibling caregiving. In M. Bornstein (Ed.), *Handbook of parenting: Vol. 3. Status and social conditions of parenting.* Mahwah, NJ: Lawrence Erlbaum Associates.

Name Index

Note: Page numbers followed by f indicate figures; those followed by t indicate tables.

Aase, A., 218
Abbott, S., 151
Abebe, T., 218
Aber, J. L., 376
Abma, J. C., 568, 568f
Abrams, R., 86
Abramson, L., 510
Acebo, C., 274
Achermann, P., 152
Adamson, L. B., 222, 223, 224
Addams, J., 508–509
Addison, J., 583
Adolph, K. E., 173
Ahmed, M. L., 523t
Ahnert, L., 213, 214, 215, 368
Aidman, A., 372
Ainsworth, J. W., 354
Ainsworth, M. D. S., 207, 210–211, 214
Ajia, O., 343
Aksan, N., 320, 321
Al-Ali, N., 564
Alba-Speyer, C., 297
Aldrich, C. A., 154
Alencar, A. I., 478
Aleva, E. A., 482
Alexander, K., 286
Allen, G., 564
Allen, M., 157
Allen, M. A., 115
Allen, R. E., 276
Almerigi, J. B., 3
Als, H., 143
Amato, P. R., 499, 500
American Academy of Pediatrics, 393
American College of Obstetricians and Gynecologists, 108
American Psychiatric Association (APA), 217
Ammerman, R. T., 362
Amso, D., 139, 184, 187
Ananth, C. V., 92
Anderman, E. M., 447, 546
Anderson, C. A., 380
Anderson, D., 167
Anderson, E., 564
Anderson, S. E., 525
Anderson, S. J., 273
Anderson, S. W., 33
Anderson, V., 98
Anglin, J. M., 236, 250, 264
Annan, K., 429

Annie E. Casey Foundation, 437
Annis, R. C., 314
Antonelli, P. J., 86
Antonov, A. I., 499
Antonov, A. N., 92
Anwander, A., 241
APA (American Psychiatric Association), 217
Apgar, V., 111, 112t
Apple, R., 5
Aquan-Assee, J., 352
Arana-Urioste, M. L., 249
Arey, L., 80f
Ariel, J., 358
Ariès, P., 5, 6, 346
Aristotle, 508
Armbruster, B. B., 440
Armenta, B. E., 543
Armistead, L., 583, 583t
Armstrong, K. N., 81–82
Arnault, N., 275
Arnett, J. J., 509, 510
Arsenio, W. F., 334
Arterberry, M. E., 135
Asendorph, J., 206
Asher, S., 335
Asher, S. R., 484, 485, 493
Ashford, K. B., 97
Ashmead, D. H., 144
Ashtari, M., 33
Ashwin, E., 85
Askew, G. L., 151
Astington, J. W., 291, 297
Atkinson, J., 134
Atkinson, R. C., 285f
Atran, S., 293
Atsumi, T., 10
Au, T. K., 289–290
Aubrey, J. S., 378
Austin, C. C., 447
Austin, L., 30
Auyeung, B., 85
Avenevoli, S., 587
Aviezer, O., 218
Avis, J., 297
Aylward, G. P., 114
Azmitia, M., 353

Bachnan, H. J., 450
Bahrick, L. E., 137
Baillargeon, R., 131, 184, 185, 186, 187, 188, 237, 289, 331
Bainbridge, J., 438
Baird, D. D., 81
Bajanowski, T., 155
Bakeman, R., 222, 583, 583t
Baker, J. L., 93
Baker, S. A., 223

Bakermans-Kranenburg, M. J., 156, 204, 220
Bakker, E., 176, 177
Bakker, R., 96
Baldelomar, O. A., 313
Baldwin, J. M., 8, 73
Ballabriga, A., 513
Ballon, D., 459
Bandini, L. G., 525
Bandura, A., 25–26
Bang, H. J., 356
Banks, A., 358
Banks, M. S., 135
Barber, B., 560
Barber, B. K., 213, 470
Bard, B., 244
Bard, K., 156, 156f
Bardi, L., 137
Bargelow, P., 215
Barker, D., 92, 99, 275
Baron-Cohen, S., 85, 293, 295
Barr, R. G., 156, 175
Barrett, J., 474, 475
Barrett, M., 253, 569
Barrett, T., 144
Barrouillet, P., 534
Barry, R. A., 320
Barsalou, L. W., 277
Bartlett, E., 253
Barton, B. K., 406
Basow, S. A., 117
Bates, E., 223, 240, 241, 241f, 254, 258, 266, 266f
Bates, J., 220
Bates, J. E., 148
Battaglia, F., 97
Bauer, I., 176
Bauer, P. J., 195, 307, 316
Baumer, S., 443
Baumrind, D., 333, 349–350, 470
Bavelier, D., 11
Bayley, N., 171
Bayliss, D. M., 409
Bearce, K., 148
Bearison, D., 534
Bearison, D. J., 533
Bearman, P., 567
Beauchamp, G., 138
Beck, O., 98
Becker, B., 363
Becker, G. S., 499
Behne, T., 222
Beidelman, T., 566
Belkin, L., 67
Bell, S. M., 214
Bellmore, A. D., 484
Bellugi, U., 246
Belsky, J., 213, 215, 220, 363, 523

Bemak, F., 335
Bender, D., 482
Bengtson, V. L., 40–41
Beran, M., 435
Bergen, D., 265
Berger, S. E., 173
Berk, L., 324
Berk, L. E., 322
Berkowitz, L., 329, 334, 334f
Berland, J., 131
Bernal, J. F., 154
Berndt, R., 280
Berndt, T. J., 557, 558, 560, 561, 562
Bernicot, J., 246
Bersamin, M., 567
Berstein, J., 359f
Besselieu, C. L., 406
Betancourt, T. S., 372
Bettelheim, B., 375
Beuf, A. H., 314
Beyers, W., 509
Bialystok, E., 244, 245
Biancotti, J. C., 63
Biblarz, T. J., 358
Bickford, R. G., 398, 398f
Biemiller, A., 236
Big Boi, 254
Bigelow, A. E., 225
Bigler, R., 311, 313
Binet, A., 9, 420, 421
Binnie, L., 294–295
Birch, L. L., 394
Bird, D., 389, 390
Bird, R., 389, 390
Bjorklund, D., 10, 23, 331, 412
Bjorklund, D. F., 8
Bjurström, E., 376
Blachman, B. A., 434
Black, B. M., 543
Blades, M., 376
Blair, C., 414
Blair, P., 154, 410
Blake, J., 224
Blakemore, K. J., 115
Blakemore, S. J., 33
Blakeslee, S., 206
Blanton, H., 561
Blicharski, T., 307, 307t, 330, 331t
Blinn-Pike, L., 569
Block, C. C., 441
Block, J., 527
Bloom, F. E., 130
Bloom, L., 252
Bloom, P., 227
Boaler, J., 442
Boas, F., 545

Bock, J., 390
Bock, K., 256
Bogin, B., 162, 164, 392, 511, 512, 514, 515, 590
Boivin, M., 482
Boland, A., 287, 288
Bolger, K., 498, 499f
Bon, M., 307, 307t, 330, 331t
Boo, K., 365
Books, S., 359
Boone, T. L., 566
Booth-LaForce, C., 214
Borges, G., 587
Borke, H., 280, 280f
Bornstein, M. H., 135, 252, 360
Bortfeld, H., 223
Borton, R., 139
Bos, H. M. W., 358
Bosacki, S. L., 319
Bost, K., 393
Bots, R. S. G. M., 87
Bottoms, B. L., 286
Bouchard, C., 515
Bower, T. G. R., 182f, 182–183
Bowers, E., 595
Bowers, P. G., 434
Bowker, A., 494
Bowlby, J., 141, 208–210, 220
Boyatzis, C. J., 484
Boyce, W., 14
Boyce, W. T., 358, 359
boyd, d., 577
Boyd, R., 54, 56, 73
Boyer, L. A., 84
Boyer, T., 536
Boykin, A. W., 459, 459f
Brabin, B. J., 164
Bradbard, M. R., 117
Bradley, C., 529
Bradshaw, C. P., 362, 363
Bramen, J. E., 518
Brämswig, J., 522, 522t
Brandon, P., 438
Branje, S. J. T., 557
Brank, E. M., 572
Brann, A., 115
Brannon, E., 189
Brannon, E. M., 190
Brasswell, G. S., 284
Brauer, J., 241
Braun-McDonald, B., 217
Brazelton, T. B., 112
Breedlove, S. M., 510
Breinlinger, K., 188
Bremner, J., 184
Brennan, R. T., 372
Bretherton, I., 220
Brewaeys, A., 358
Bridges, K., 202
Britvic, D., 89
Broca, P., 239

Brocht, C., 359f
Broderson, N. H., 529
Brody, G. H., 348, 351
Brody, L., 556
Brody, M.-H., 353
Bronfenbrenner, U., 27, 72, 343–344, 561
Bronson, G. W., 134, 135, 136, 136f
Bronstein, P., 556
Brooke, J., 103
Brooks-Gunn, J., 115, 213, 226, 358, 523, 572, 587, 589
Brotman, L. M., 367
Brown, A. L., 440, 441, 441f, 560, 562
Brown, B. B., 558, 559, 560, 573
Brown, B. V., 558, 596t
Brown, G. L., 213
Brown, P., 245
Brown, R., 246, 256f, 257t, 412, 541
Brown, V., 572
Brownell, K. D., 392
Brückner, H., 567
Brueckner, L., 185
Bruer, J. T., 11, 128
Bruer, T. J., 165
Bruner, J., 431
Bruner, J. S., 260, 263–264, 267
Brunet, M., 57
Bryant, P., 434, 435
Bryant Ludden, A., 528
Bucholz, K. K., 587
Buist, A. S., 110
Buitelaar, J. K., 85
Bukowski, W. M., 352, 485
Bullock, M., 283, 283f, 327
Burch, M. M., 307
Buriel, R., 355
Burkam, D. T., 439
Burkley, M., 561
Burns, B., 413
Bushnell, I. W. R., 137
Buss, C., 90
Buston, K., 583
Butler, R., 467
Buttelmann, D., 238
Butterworth, G., 222, 223
Bynner, J. M., 510, 581
Byrnes, J., 536

Cacchione, T., 289
Cagney, K. A., 371
Cairns, R. B., 331, 510
Calamaro, C. J., 528, 529
Calkins, S., 148, 150
Call, J., 238, 291
Callanan, M., 297
Caltran, G., 336
Camaioni, L., 258

Cameron, N., 391, 396
Campbell, D., 167
Campbell, F., 368
Campbell, I. G., 529
Campbell, S., 331
Campos, J. J., 31, 168, 172, 200, 222
Camras, L. A., 200, 201
Caplan, N., 458
Capps, R., 438, 454
Card, N. A., 481
Carel, J.-C., 523
Carey, S., 253
Carlin, L., 569
Carlo, G., 543
Carlson, S., 55
Carlson, V. J., 219
Carlson, W., 485
Carpendale, J., 351
Carpendale, J. I. M., 547
Carpenter, M., 222, 291
Carper, R., 398
Carr, T. H., 413
Carrick, N., 286
Carroll, L., 573
Carroll, M., 393, 394, 395
Carskadon, M. A., 528, 529
Carver, K., 92–93
Case, R., 285, 410, 410f, 536
Casey, B. J., 517, 518, 519
Cashon, C. H., 190
Caspi, A., 14, 350
Cass, V. C., 582
Cassidy, J., 213
Cassidy, T., 143
Castanon, I., 445
Castetbon, K., 275
Castilla, E. E., 96
Cauffman, E., 536–537, 561
Caughy, M., 315
Causey, K., 10, 23
Ceci, S., 286
Centers For Disease Control And Prevention, 99, 107, 108, 109–110, 113, 163f, 296, 394, 499, 567, 593, 594, 594f, 595, 595f
Chacon, R., 346
Chaffin, M., 217
Chan, A., 96, 494
Chandler, L. S., 97
Chandler, M. J., 459, 480, 536, 588–589
Chandra, A., 582, 583
Chang, F., 256
Chang, J., 580
Chang, J. C., 74
Chang, L., 482
Chao, R. K., 355
Chaput, H. H., 190
Charma, B., 429

Charman, T., 33
Charnov, E., 512
Charpak, N., 34
Chase-Lansdale, P. L., 569
Chater, R., 591
Chaucer, G., 508
Chavajay, P., 453, 455
Chen, C., 410
Chen, H., 572
Chen, J., 245
Chen, K., 560, 561
Chen, L., 315
Chen, P.-C., 175
Chen, S., 551
Chen, X., 498
Chen, Z., 288
Chess, S., 148, 149
Chesson, H. W., 594
Chi, M. T. H., 410–411
Child, I. L., 274
Chirkov, V., 470
Chisholm, K., 216
Chomsky, N., 262
Choudhury, S., 33
Choy, M. H., 458
Christakis, N. A., 371
Christian, K., 450
Christian, P., 91
Chu, N. F., 93
Chuang, L., 137
Chudler, E. H., 240f
Chugani, H., 168
Chumlea, W. C., 523
Church, J., 265, 446
Cicchetti, D., 363, 381, 382t
Cillessen, A., 485
Cillessen, A. H. N., 482, 484, 485
Clancy, B., 254
Clark, C., 324–325
Clark, E. V., 241, 246, 250, 254, 260, 264, 267
Clark, H., 92
Clark, K. B., 314
Clark, M. P., 314
Clarke, A. D. B., 14
Clarke, A. M., 14
Clarke-Stewart, A., 105f
Clausson, B., 96
Clearfield, M. W., 184, 186
Clement, C. J., 224
Clifton, R. K., 144
Coale, A., 513
Cobb, P., 442
Coghlan, D., 30
Cohen, L. B., 131, 190, 192
Cohen-Kettenis, P. T., 85
Coie, J., 330
Coie, J. D., 334, 484
Colby, A., 473, 541, 541f
Cole, M., 52, 310, 417, 418, 433, 440, 444–445, 453, 461

Cole, S., 310
Coles, C. D., 97
Coley, R. L., 569
Collins, A., 431
Collins, W. A., 350, 496, 497, 499, 571, 573
Colon, A., 381
Colon, P., 381
Compas, B. E., 587
Comstock, G., 374, 380
Comstock, M., 583
Conboy, B. T., 245
Conchas, G. Q., 454
Conger, R. D., 354
Conley, C., 559, 588
Conley, C. S., 587
Connelly, A., 126, 127
Connolly, J., 562
Connolly, K., 170
Connor, J. M., 65
Conroy, S., 157
Consortium for Longitudinal Studies, ., 437
Conway-Turner, K., 353
Cook, J. T., 275
Cooper, M., 554
Coopersmith, S., 469, 470
Coovadia, H., 100
Copen, C. E., 568, 568f
Corbin, P. F., 398, 398f
Cordes, S., 190
Corenblum, B., 314
Corey, D. M., 355
Corley, R. P., 70
Cormier, K., 224
Corna, M., 154
Correa-Chavez, M., 457
Cortina-Borja, M., 100
Costello, D., 333
Costello, D. M., 585
Costello, E. J., 359
Côté, J., 510, 581
Côté, J. E., 332
Cotton, A., 429
Cotton, V., 378
Cottrell, J. M., 534
Courage, M. L., 167, 193, 193f
Cowan, P. A., 88f, 292
Cox, S. J., 556, 556f
Craik, F. I. M., 272
Cravens, H., 510
Cremer, J. F., 397
Creveling, C. C., 355
Crewe, S., 346
Crick, N., 331, 377
Crick, N. R., 482, 483, 484
Crockett, L. J., 355
Crosnoe, R., 438
Cross, T. B., 313
Cross, W. E., 313, 578, 579
Crouter, A. C., 351

Crowther, B., 576
Csikszentmihalyi, M., 553, 557
Cunningham, F. G., 98, 105
Cunningham, R. T., 459, 459f
Cunningham, S., 114
Cunningham, W. A., 321
Curtis, H., 83f
Curtiss, S., 241

Dabis, F., 100
Dahl, R., 274
Dahl, R. E., 528
Daiute, C., 372
Daley, S. E., 587
Dalgleish, M., 170
Damasio, A. R., 33
Damasio, H., 33
Damon, W., 466, 467t
Dangerfield, P., 513, 517
D'Angiulli, A., 445
Danielewicz, S., 98
Darmon, N., 527
Darwin, C., 8, 58, 205, 331
Darwin, W., 8
Dasen, P. R., 180, 415
Davey Smith, G., 92
David, G., 81f
David, H. P., 90
Davidov, M., 213
Davies, H. D., 394
Davila, J., 587
Davis, A., 55
Davis, B. L., 224
Davis, C., 414, 414f
Davis, E., 90
Day, J. D., 413
Day, N. L., 97
Deák, G. O., 282
Deboer, T., 152
De Boysson-Bardies, B., 224
de Bruyn, E. H., 358
DeCasper, A. J., 86, 88
Decety, J., 206
Deck, A., 358
Degnan, K., 148, 150
De Goede, I. H. A., 557
Dekou, V., 93
Deković, M., 333
Delaney, C., 140
de Lemos, C., 248
Deligeoroglou, E., 522
Dell, G., 256
DeLoache, J., 276–277, 277f
Demeny, P., 513
Denham, S., 334
Denizet-Lewis, B., 563
Dennis, M., 174
Dennis, W., 174
Dent-Read, C., 254
de Oliveira Siqueira, J., 478
deRegnier, R.-A., 392

DeSalvo, K., 527
Devescovi, A., 256
De Villiers, J. G., 246t, 256
De Villiers, P. A., 246t, 256
De Vries, J. I., 87t
de Vries, M. R., 176
de Vries, M. W., 176
De Vries, R., 281, 281f
de Vrijer, B., 101
Dew, J., 354
Dewald, J. F., 528
de Wied, M., 574
De Wolff, M., 214
Dhariwal, A., 564
Diamond, A., 165, 184, 245, 277
Diamond, L., 570, 583
Dickens, W. T., 423
Diener, M. L., 214
Dietz, L. J., 447
Dietz, T., 333
Di Giorgio, E., 137
Dimant, R., 534
Dinella, L. M., 448–449
Dishion, T. J., 332, 498, 561, 562
The Distributed Literacy Consortium, 444
Dittmar, H., 590
Dixon, A. C., 569
Do, J. T., 82
Dodge, B., 570
Dodge, K. A., 330, 334, 482, 484, 592, 593f
Domino, G., 487
Dondi, M., 336
D'Onofrio, B. M., 500
Donovan, D. M., 30
Donovan, S., 393
Dore, J., 258
Dorgan, B. L., 588
Dorval, B., 533
Dossett, D., 413
Double, M., 347
Douple, E. B., 102
Dove, H., 174
Dow-Edwards, D., 98
Downey, D. B., 354
Draganova, R., 87
Drewnowski, A., 527
Driessen, R., 219
Dromi, E., 251, 251f, 253f
Drukker, M., 369, 371
Dübbers, A., 522, 522t
Dubois, L., 274
Ducote, C., 249
Dufur, M. J., 354
Dukes, C., 412
Duncan, G., 359
Duncan, P., 570
Dunger, D. B., 523t
Dunjic, B., 89
Dunn, J., 330, 337

Dunphy, D. C., 559, 559f, 562
Durham, W., 73
Durston, S., 517
Dweck, C. S., 447, 448, 468
Dybdahl, R., 372
Dykens, E., 66
Dyson, M., 580

Eagly, A. H., 310
Easley, J. A., 417
Eccles, J., 558, 560, 596, 596t
Eccles, J. S., 572, 572t
Eckenrode, J., 365
Eckert, P., 560
Eckes, T., 308
Edvardsen, J., 70
Edwards, A., 477
Edwards, E. P., 98
Egeland, B., 220
Egeland, G. M., 92
Eggebeen, D. J., 354
Egger, H. L., 220
Eggum, N. D., 477
Eiden, R. D., 98
Eimas, P. D., 132, 133f, 191
Einstein, A., 15
Einstein, F., 92, 93
Eisen, M., 569
Eisenberg, N., 327, 328, 336, 337, 338, 477–478, 547, 553, 555
Eisengart, J., 255
Elbers, E., 4
Elder, G. H. J., 29, 39
Elfers, T., 584
Elias, C., 324
Ellis, B., 331
Ellis, N., 14
Ellis, S. A., 418, 418f
Ellis, S. J., 583
Ellis, W. E., 494–495
Ellis Gardner, R., 590
Elman, J. L., 266
Elo, I., 114
El Sarraj, E., 352, 353f
El-Sheikh, M., 274
Emde, R. N., 14, 69, 70, 149, 150
Emery, R. E., 523
Enfield, N. J., 53
Enns, G. M., 65
Epoo, B., 109
Eppe, S., 459
Erdley, C., 335
Erickson, F., 460
Erikson, E. H., 16, 18, 228–229, 306–307, 466, 575
Erikson, M. F., 220
Eriksson, J., 92
Eshleman, L., 217
Estell, D. B., 560

Esteller, M., 71
Estevez, P. A., 152
Evans, G. W., 371

Fabes, R. A., 477
Fabricius, W. V., 412
Fadil, C., 137
Fadiman, A., 79
Fan, G. X., 65
Fanaroff, A. A., 102
Fantz, R. L., 135, 135f, 136, 136f, 137
Farrington, D., 585
Farrington, D. P., 439
Farver, J., 459
Farver, J. A. M., 482
Fauth, R. C., 358
Feinberg, I., 529
Feiring, C., 562
Feldman, D. H., 285
Feldman, J. F., 194, 194f
Fenson, L., 224, 252, 266
Ferguson, J. E., 97
Ferguson-Smith, M. A., 65
Ferholt, B., 443
Fernald, A., 132, 246, 266
Fernald, L. C., 359
Fernandez, M., 137
Ferran, L., 395
Ferrer-Wreder, L., 582
Ficca, G., 151, 152
Field, T. M., 204, 226, 529
Fields, W. M., 238
Fiese, B., 275
Fiese, B. H., 344
Filippova, E., 297
Finlay, B., 254
Fiorito, L., 394
Fireman, G., 406
Fischer, K., 326, 328
Fischer, K. W., 285, 301, 466
Fishbein, H. D., 68f, 128f
Fisher, C., 255, 256
Fisher, D. M., 174
Fitzgerald, H., 220
Fitzgerald, H. E., 394
Fitzmaurice, G. M., 372
Fitzpatrick, M., 500
Fivush, R., 272, 316
Flavell, J. H., 12, 281, 376, 407, 412
Fleeson, J., 220
Fletcher, A. C., 573
Florin, P., 380
Flowers, P., 583
Floyd, F., 583, 583t
Flykt, M., 214
Flynn, E., 41
Flynn, J. R., 423, 424f
Focht, B. C., 590
Fodor, J., 293

Foehr, U. G., 372, 374f, 380
Fondacaro, M., 572
Forbes, J., 254
Fordham, S., 579
Foreman, N., 115
Forman, M., 581
Forman, Y., 595
Forsen, T., 92
Forsyth, B. W. C., 157
Fortenberry, J. D., 570
Forum on Child and Family Statistics, 364–365
Fowler, A., 267
Fox, S. E., 129, 165
Foy, P., 457
Fraga, M. F., 71
Fraiberg, S. H., 309
Frank, A., 576
Frank, D. A., 275
Frank, M., 139
Frankel, K., 220
Franklin, A., 242–243
Franzini, L., 369, 370
Freed, K., 103
Freud, S., 16–18, 208, 286, 308, 309, 318, 474, 501, 511
Friederici, A. D., 240, 241
Frith, U., 2, 293, 295
Frohna, J. G., 155
Frongillo, E. A., 163, 275
Fry, D. P., 332
Frye, D., 284
Fuhs, M. W., 413
Fujioka, T., 277
Fuligni, A., 21, 455
Fuligni, A. J., 557, 566, 572, 572t
Fullard, W., 25
Fuller, B., 438
Fuller-Rowell, T. E., 578
Fung, H., 305
Funk, J. B., 377, 380
Furman, W., 560, 562
Furstenberg, F. F., Jr., 354, 360, 569

Gabriel, S. W., 484
Gaillard, P., 100
Gallego, M. A., 440, 461
Gallimore, R., 456
Galloway, A. T., 394
Gallup, G. G. J., 225
Gamble, W. C., 351
Gammage, J., 199
Garcia, E. C. M., 378
Garciaguirre, J. S., 173
Gardiner, A., 10, 23
Gardner, H., 421, 421t
Gardner, M., 555
Gardner, W., 405, 405f
Gariepy, J. L., 89
Garner, P. W., 482

Garofalo, R., 582
Garrod, A., 581
Garrow, I., 154
Gartrell, N. K., 358
Gartstein, M. A., 150
Garvey, C., 280
Gaskins, S., 33, 322
Gates, G. J., 357
Gau, S., 529
Gauvain, M., 418f
Gayer, T., 439
Ge, X., 524
Geary, D., 435
Geers, A., 242
Geertz, C., 545
Geiger, B., 213
Geithner, C. A., 514
Gelis, J., 107
Gelman, R., 283, 283f, 292, 292f
Gelman, S., 435
Gelman, S. A., 284, 284f, 290, 295
Genie, 241–242
Gentile, D., 377
Georgieff, M. K., 392
Gergen, K. J., 574
Gerhardt, K., 86
Gershoff, E. T., 376
Gertner, Y., 255
Geschwind, D. H., 66
Getchell, N., 396, 396f
Gettman, D. C., 571
Giacoman, S. L., 140
Giammanco, M., 394
Giammanco, S., 394
Giannakidou, A., 242–243
Gibbs, J., 541, 541f
Gibson, E. J., 170
Giedd, J., 276, 518, 519
Giedd, J. N., 129, 524
Gielen, U. P., 545
Gilbert, S. F., 83, 84, 85
Giles, A., 147, 194
Giles, J., 335
Gilligan, C., 491, 542–543
Gilman, S. E., 372
Gilmore, C. K., 435
Ginns-Gruenberg, D., 375
Ginsburg, H., 403f
Ginsburg, H. P., 435
Gittelsohn, J., 527
Glaser, D., 528
Gleitman, L. R., 256
Glowinski, A. L., 587
Gluck, M. E., 93
Godeau, E., 569
Gogtay, N., 129f, 399, 399f, 517
Goldberg, J., 410, 410f
Golden, N. H., 590, 591
Goldin-Meadow, S., 242–243, 243, 267

Goldschmidt, L., 97
Goldsmith, H. H., 31
Golinkoff, R. M., 223, 253, 254, 257, 322
Gollapalli, A., 155
Golombok, S., 307, 358
Goncu, A., 322
Gonzales, N., 470–471
Goodman, C., 346
Goodman, G. S., 286, 363
Goodman, M. R., 346, 482, 483
Goodnow, J. J., 497
Goodwin, M. H., 490–491
Goossens, F. A., 482
Goossens, L., 577
Gopnik, A., 13, 245, 252, 264, 295
Gordon, D., 518
Gordon, P., 435
Gordon, R. A., 363
Gormley, W., 439
Goswami, U., 284, 285, 414
Gottardo, A., 446
Gottlieb, A., 106, 123
Gottlieb, E., 536
Gottlieb, G., 11, 84
Gottman, J. M., 493–494
Gotz, M., 372
Goubet, N., 144
Graber, J. A., 523, 585, 587
Grady, K., 580
Graham, E. M., 115
Graham, J. A., 489
Graham-Bermann, S., 363
Grail, T. S., 499
Granic, I., 498
Granier-Deferre, C., 86, 88
Gratier, M., 455
Gravener, J. A., 590, 591
Gray, P. H., 115
Greaves, R., 513
Gredebäck, G., 187
Greenberg, M. T., 30, 414
Greenfield, P., 538
Greenfield, P. M., 21, 56, 238, 239, 415–416, 416f, 455, 458, 583
Greenough, W., 129
Greenough, W. T., 128, 165
Greenspan, S. I., 214, 237
Gregor, J. A., 314
Griffin, P., 251
Grigorenko, E. L., 419
Grisso, T., 536
Grodsky, E., 569
Groeschel, S., 126, 127, 127f
Groesz, L. M., 590
Grolnick, W. S., 326
Gronlund, N. E., 484f
Grossman, T., 132
Grossmann, K., 220

Grotevant, H. D., 577, 584
Gruber, G., 363
Grumbach, M., 512
Grunau, R. V. E., 115
Grusec, J. E., 213
Guest, A. M., 467, 468, 470, 471t
Gullone, E., 554
Gunnar, M. R., 359
Gunter, B., 376
Guralnick, M. J., 66
Gurin, G., 314
Guttler, F., 65
Guttmacher Institute, 567, 568

Hackett, G., 85
Haden, C., 287, 410, 411
Haedt, A. A., 590, 591
Haegel, P., 81f
Hagen, J. W., 412
Hagenauer, M., 528
Hahn, E., 97
Hahn, H., 151
Haines, M. M., 371
Hains, S. M., 86
Haith, M. M., 134, 135, 390
Hakkarainen, P., 443
Hakvoot, E. M., 358
Halberstadt, A., 327, 334
Hale, W. W., 571
Hall, G. S., 510–511, 528, 530
Hall, L., 97
Hall, N. W., 363
Hallett, D., 536, 588–589
Halliwell, E., 590
Halpern-Felsher, B. L., 536–537
Halverson, C. F., 312, 312f
Halverson, H. M., 170f
Hamel, E., 372, 373t
Hamilton, B., 360, 360f
Hamilton, B. E., 112
Hamilton, C., 220
Hamlin, J. K., 227
Hammen, C., 587
Hammond, S. I., 547
Hamphill, S., 306
Han, D. W., 82
Hanawalt, B., 6
Hannan, P. J., 394
Hannon, E. E., 132, 246
Hansbrough, E., 378
Hanson, M., 93
Harada, M., 102
Harden, K. P., 70, 587
Hariri, A. R., 528
Harkness, S., 153, 300
Harlow, H. F., 208, 209
Harlow, M. K., 209
Harney, E., 109
Harrington, M., 437
Harris, P. L., 297

Harrison, K., 378, 392, 393
Harsono, L. S., 378
Hart, B., 246
Hart, C., 113
Hart, D., 466, 467t
Hart, R., 85
Harter, S., 228, 316, 466, 468–469, 469f, 469t, 470, 574
Hartl, M., 291
Hartshorn, K., 194, 194f
Hartup, W. W., 493, 557
Harwood, R. L., 219
Hassan, A., 482
Hatano, G., 284, 292–293
Hauck, F. R., 154, 155
Hausenblas, H. A., 590
Hauser, G., 138
Hauser, M. D., 262
Hauser, S., 572
Haviland, J. M., 576
Haviland-Jones, J., 576
Hawk, S., 571
Hawkins, A. J., 213
Hawley, P. H., 481
Haworth, C., 69
Hay, R. L., 49
Hayes, C., 238
Hayes, K., 238
Haynes, B. P., 425
Haywood, K. M., 396, 396f
Head, K., 90
Heath, A. C., 587
Heath, S. B., 459
Heckman, J. J., 438
Heifetz, S. A., 83
Heights, R., 583
Heinsohn, R., 347
Heiserman, M., 378
Helland, T., 446
Helwig, C. C., 320, 478
Hendrick, A., 287
Hennessy, M., 555f
Henning, K. H., 543
Henrich, J., 56, 73, 559
Henrich, N., 73
Henshaw, S., 569
Herbenick, D., 568, 568t, 570
Herbst, K., 114
Hercberg, S., 275
Herek, G. M., 358
Herman, C. P., 590
Herman-Giddens, M. E., 523, 525, 526, 526t
Hermann, E., 55
Herrnstein, R. J., 422, 541
Herzog, D. B., 591
Hespos, S. J., 184, 185
Hesser, J., 353
Hetherington, E. M., 351, 499, 500
Hewitt, E. S., 154

Hewitt, J. K., 14, 69, 149, 150
Hewlett, B., 347
Hewlett, B. S., 156, 213
Heyman, G., 335
Heywood, C., 1
Hickendorff, M., 442
Hickling, A. K., 288, 295
Hicks, L. E., 93
Hiebert, J., 456, 457
Higgins-D'Alessandro, A., 547
Hilden, K., 411, 412
Hill, A., 49
Hill, E. A., 246
Hill, L., 254
Hillis, C. B., 9
Hindman, H. D., 7
Hindmarsh, P. C., 97
Hines, M., 307
Hinton, T. S., 482
Hirsh-Pasek, K., 254, 322
Hodges, J., 216, 218
Hodson, B. W., 248
Hofer, B., 534, 536
Hoff, E., 241, 245, 250
Hoff-Ginsberg, E., 34
Hoffman, M., 336
Hoffman, S., 569
Hofman, A., 96
Hohmann-Marriott, B., 500
Holcroft, C. J., 115
Holden, G. W., 362
Hollenstein, T., 498
Hollis, S., 408, 409f
Holmbeck, G. N., 571, 572
Holm-Denoma, J. M., 276
Holowka, S., 241
Holsti, L., 115
Honwana, A., 373
Hopkins, B., 174
Horn, S. S., 581
Horn, T. S., 396
Hosegood, V., 114
Hoshower, L. M., 125f
Hossain, Z., 213
Houde, O., 281, 282
Hoven, C. W., 376
Howe, C., 97
Howe, N., 352, 353
Howell, N. C., 354
Howell, S., 297
Howes, C., 213
Hrdy, S., 347
Hsieh, W.-S., 175
Huang, B., 560, 573
Huang, H. Y., 85
Huang, J., 93
Huang-Pollack, C. L., 413
Hubel, D., 129
Huelsken, C., 282
Hughes, C., 295
Hughes, D., 315, 469

Hughes, E. K., 554
Hughes, H., 363
Huizink, A. C., 97
Hulbert, A., 2, 5
Hunsley, M., 151
Hunt, J., 181
Hurd, Y. L., 98
Hurt, H., 98
Husaini, M. A., 93
Hussein, Y., 564
Hussong, A. M., 38
Huttenlocher, P. R., 276
Hutto, D. D., 306
Huynh, V. W., 566
Hwang, A.-W., 175
Hyde, J. S., 510, 556, 556f
Hymel, S., 484

Impett, E. A., 568
Inagaki, K., 284, 292–293
Inhelder, B., 20, 277, 280, 280f, 400–401, 401f, 402
Inoue, S., 102
Inoue-Nakamura, N., 225
Irgens, L. M., 92
Isaac, A., 455
ISPCAN, 362, 362t
Itard, J. M. G., 1–2
Ive, S., 590
Ivey, P., 33
Izard, C. E., 202, 202f
Izawa, E.-I., 10

Jablonka, E., 73, 138, 237, 267
Jackson, J. P., Jr., 314
Jackson, J. S., 314
Jackson, M., 378
Jacobs, C., 30
Jacobson, K., 188
Jaconis, M., 591
Jacquet, A.-Y., 86
Jaddoe, V. W., 96
Jaeger, J., 252
Jaffe, J., 360
Jagnow, C., 138
Jahari, A., 93
Jahoda, G., 415
James, D., 87, 88
James, W. T., 131, 331
Janelle, C. M., 590
Janisse, H. C., 514
Jankowska, E. A., 523
Jankowski, J. J., 194, 194f
Janowsky, J. S., 398
Jansz, J., 556
Jarrett, R., 347
Jasovic-Gasic, M., 89
Jebb, S. A., 395
Jenkins, H., 53
Jenni, O., 152
Jennings, K. D., 447

Jia, G., 245
Jodl, K. M., 572
Joh, A., 194
John, V. P., 418
Johnson, C., 378
Johnson, D., 315, 447
Johnson, M., 244
Johnson, M. H., 132
Johnson, S., 135, 187
Johnson, S. P., 139
Johnson, W., 70, 71
Joiner, T., 276
Joiner, T. E., Jr., 590, 591
Jolly, A., 141
Jones, E., 437
Jones, H. E., 99
Jones, M., 31
Jones, R. E., 102, 108
Jones, R. M., 519
Jones, S. J., 275
Jones, S. M., 167
Jordan, B., 107
Jordan, K., 189
Jordan-Young, R., 85
Joseph, J., 71
Joseph, K. S., 114
Joshi, M. S., 328
Jovanov-Milosevic, N., 127
Joyner, K., 582
Juang, L. P., 572
Jung, C., 309
Junger, M., 333
Jusczyk, A. M., 223
Jusczyk, P. W., 223
Justice, E., 314
Juston, A., 376
Juul, A., 523, 525
Jyoti, D. F., 275

Kagan, J., 38, 228
Kagan, S., 487
Kagitçibasi, Ç., 487, 583
Kaiser Foundation, 595
Kakinuma, M., 218
Kalanda, B. F., 164
Kalkwarf, H. J., 273
Kaltenbach, K., 99
Kamara, A. I., 417
Kan, Y. W., 74
Kandel, D., 561
Kandel, D. B., 560, 561
Kanninen, K., 214
Kaplan, H., 174, 389
Kaprio, J., 523
Kaptijn, R., 347
Karasik, L. B., 173
Karmiloff, K., 263
Karmiloff-Smith, A., 263, 267
Karsten, S. L., 296
Katchadourian, H. A., 514
Kaufman, J., 362

Kawabata, Y., 483
Kaye, K., 22, 153
Keane, R. J., 96
Kearney, J. K., 397
Keating, D. P., 38, 534, 536
Keefe, K., 560, 561
Keel, P. K., 590, 591
Keenan, K., 587
Keeney, T. J., 411
Keijsers, L., 571
Keil, F. C., 407, 407t, 408f
Keller, H., 21, 174, 350, 451, 455
Kelley, T., 176
Kellman, P. J., 135
Kellogg, L. A., 238
Kellogg, W. N., 238
Kelly, D. J., 137
Kemler Nelson, D. G., 223
Keniston, K., 509
Kennard, B. D., 590
Kennell, J. H., 111
Kenney, J. W., 128
Kermayer, L., 588
Kesmodel, U., 97
Kesner, J., 357
Kett, J. F., 508
Khan, I. Y., 93
Kiell, N., 508
Killen, M., 319, 479
Kim, E., 351, 356
Kim, H., 245
Kim, I.-K., 289
Kim, J. M., 478
Kim, J.-Y., 352f
Kim, K., 555
Kim, S., 353
Kim, U., 456
King, M. D., 126, 127
Kins, E., 509
Kirkorian, H., 167
Kisilevsky, B. S., 86, 87, 204
Kitamura, C., 246
Kitayama, S., 583, 584
Kiyoshi, T., 81–82
Klaczynski, P. A., 534
Klahr, D., 406f
Klasen, F., 372
Klaus, M. H., 111
Klaus, P. H., 111
Klein, J., 98
Klemfuss, J. Z., 286
Kleven, G. A., 87
Kline, M., 56
Klineberg, O., 422
Klinger, J., 486
Kluckhohn, C., 203
Klump, K., 510
Klump, K. L., 590
Klute, C., 560
Knafo, A., 561
Knickmeyer, R., 85

Knoester, C., 354
Knopf, M., 410
Knowler, W. C., 93
Knuppel, R. A., 92
Kobialka, M., 6
Koch, J. B., 105f
Kochanska, G., 320, 321
Kochukhova, O., 187
Koenig, A. M., 310
Kohlberg, L., 310–311, 473–477,
   476t, 539–542, 541, 541f,
   541t, 543, 544, 544f, 545
Kokis, J., 534
Kolata, G., 392
Kolb, T. M., 177
Konarski, R., 562
Konner, M., 23, 156, 213, 274,
   347
Kontulainen, S. A., 512
Koopmans-van Beinum, F. J.,
   224
Koren, G., 98
Kosciw, J. G., 581
Kose, G., 406
Kost, K., 569
Kostovic, I., 127
Koyama, R., 116
Koziel, S., 523
Kozloski, M. J., 99
Kracke, B., 524
Krakoff, J., 93
Kramer, D. A., 576
Kramer, K., 513
Krasnogorski, N. I., 146
Krcmar, M., 377
Krettenauer, T., 536
Kreutzer, M. A., 412
Kroger, J., 575, 578
Kruger, A. C., 156, 347
Kuhl, P. K., 133, 237, 246, 248
Kulis, S., 579
Kumra, S., 33
Kung, H. C., 93
Kuo, Y.-L., 175
Kupersmidt, J. B., 484
Kurland, D. M., 410, 410f
Kurowski, C. O., 326
Kusché, C. A., 30
Kushnir, T., 13
Kusiako, T., 110
Kuther, T., 547
Kuttler, A., 562, 564
Ky, K. N., 167

Laberge, L., 528
Laboratory of Comparative
   Human Cognition, 300, 440
Ladd, G. W., 38, 448–449, 484,
   485, 493, 498
LaFontana, K. M., 482
LaFromboise, T., 579

Lagattuta, K. H., 319
Lagercrantz, H., 110–111
La Greca, A., 562, 564
La Guardia, M., 394
Lahey, B. B., 592
Lahr, M. M., 513
Laland, K., 72
Lalonde, C. E., 588–589
Lamb, M., 73, 138, 237, 267,
   347, 368
Lamb, M. E., 213, 214, 215, 497
Landau, B., 256
Lander, K., 137
Lane, H., 1, 2
Langham, R. A., 93
Langlois, J. H., 116, 484
Lapray, A. J., 354
Largo, R. H., 175, 177
Larnkjaer, A., 124
Larsen, B., 557
Larson, N., 394
Larson, R., 553, 553f, 557, 570
Larson, R. W., 596
Larzelere, R. E., 333
Lask, B., 591
Laupa, M., 478
Laursen, B., 571, 573
Laursen, E., 499
Lave, J., 431
Lavezzi, A. M., 154
Lawlor, D. A., 92
Lawrence, J. A., 41
Leach, J., 55
Leakey, M. D., 49
Lecanuet, J.-P., 86, 88, 89
Lecusay, R., 443
Leddon, E., 250
Lederman, S. A., 89
LeDoux, J., 519
Lee, B. H., 113
Lee, C. D., 260, 260f, 460–461
Lee, J., 457
Lee, K., 282
Lee, P., 144
Lee, S. J., 333
Lee, T., 528
Lee, V. E., 439
Lee, Y., 394
Lee-Kim, J., 479
Lefeber, Y., 88
Lefkowitz, E., 566
Legare, C. H., 284, 284f
Léger, J., 523
Lehoux, P. M., 352
Leigh, S., 511
Leighton, D., 203
Lejeune, L., 168
Lemerise, E., 334
Lemish, D., 372
Lenhart, A., 576
Lenneberg, E. H., 224

Lenroot, R. K., 127, 276, 519
Leon, D. A., 92
Leonard, S. C., 412
Leoni, L., 339
Lerner, J., 595
Lerner, J. V., 3
Lerner, R., 511
Lerner, R. M., 3
Leslie, A. M., 190, 295
Lester, B. M., 98, 155, 156
Leventhal, T., 358
Levine, D., 565
Levine, M. P., 590
LeVine, R. A., 153, 348, 453
LeVine, S. E., 453
Levinson, S. C., 53
Levitt, P., 129, 165
Levy, B. S., 107
Levy, E., 235
Lewin, D., 274
Lewis, C., 351, 497, 547
Lewis, C. S., 443
Lewis, M., 226, 228
Lewontin, R., 72
Leyendecker, B., 219
Li, J., 326, 328
Li, J. S., 378
Li, Y., 499, 500
Liang, X., 438
Liao, H.-F., 175
Liaw, F.-R., 115
Liben, L., 311
Lickliter, R., 11, 84
Liddell, C., 218
Liebal, K., 222
Lieberman, M., 541, 541f
Liefbroer, A. C., 347
Light, L. L., 287
Lightfoot, C., 327, 507
Lillard, A., 297
Lindsay, D., 286
Lindsay, R. S., 93
Lin J., 456
Linting, M., 220
Lipana, L., 378
Lipsitt, L. P., 154
Little, T. D., 481
Liu, C., 478
Liu, D., 291
Liu, H.-M., 246
Liu, S., 137
Locke, J. L., 511
Loehlin, J. C., 70
Logan, C. G., 128
Long, J. D., 481, 482, 483, 489
Lonsdorf, E. V., 24
Lopez, G., 355
Lorenz, J. M., 115
Lorenz, K., 11, 25, 25f, 331
Lösel, F., 482
Losoya, S., 328

Love, J., 368
Low, J., 167, 408, 409f
Low, J. A., 87
Lozoff, B., 151
Luciana, M., 517
Luna, B., 410
Lundqvist, C., 112
Luo, Y., 237
Luria, A. R., 236, 239, 433
Luria, Z., 117
Luster, T., 361
Luthar, S., 363, 381
Lutz, C., 390
Lyn, H., 238, 239
Lynam, D., 330
Lynne, S., 524
Lynskey, M. T., 587
Lyon, T. D., 286
Lyra, M. C. D. P., 117

MacCallum, F., 358
Maccoby, E. E., 311, 350, 489,
    489f, 491, 497, 592, 593
MacDorman, M. F., 107
Macedonia, C., 87
MacFarlane, A., 86
MacLean, M., 328
MacNeilage, P. F., 224
Macomber, J., 188
Madden, M., 576
Madden, P. A. F., 587
Madsen, M. C., 487
Magai, C., 576
Magnuson, K. A., 438, 439
Magolda, M., 534
Maguen, S., 583, 583t
Mahdi, A., 564
Main, M., 211, 212, 220
Majnemer, A., 175
Malchiodi, C. A., 375
Maleta, K., 164f
Malina, R. M., 396, 515
Malloy, L. C., 286
Mandel Leadership Institute, 536
Mandler, J. M., 177, 181, 191,
    192, 195, 252, 417
Manganello, J. A., 333
Manlove, J. S., 569
Manstead, A. S. R., 327
Marchman, V., 266
Marcia, J. E., 575, 575f, 578, 584
Margulies, S., 125
Maric, J., 89
Marine, W. M., 107
Markoulis, D. C., 545
Markovits, H., 534, 536
Marks, K. S., 190
Markstrom-Adams, C., 314
Markus, H. R., 583, 584
Marla, L., 177
Marlatt, G. A., 30

Marlowe, F., 346
Marshall, P. J., 128
Marsiglia, F., 579
Marsiglio, W., 354
Martel, M. M., 510
Marti, C. N., 591
Martin, A., 213
Martin, C. A., 554
Martin, C. B., 87
Martin, C. B., Jr., 110, 134
Martin, C. H., 312, 312f
Martin, C. L., 309, 311, 312, 313
Martin, J., 447, 584, 585
Martin, J. A., 93, 112
Martin, K., 529, 589
Martin, M. O., 457
Martin, R. J., 102
Martinez, G. M., 568, 568f
Martino, W., 558, 559
Martinussen, M., 575, 578
Marts, L., 364
Masch, R. J., 85
Masciadrelli, B. P., 213
Mascolo, M., 326, 328
Mascolo, M. F., 466
Mash, C., 135
Mason, T. B., 528, 529
Massey, C. M., 292, 292f
Master, A., 447, 448
Mather, M., 354, 355f, 454
Mathews, T. J., 93, 107
Matsuba, M. K., 543
Matsushima, T., 10
Matturri, L., 154
Matyear, C. L., 224
Mauk, C., 224
Maughm, A., 382t
Mauk, C., 224
Maurer, D., 134
Maxwell, L. E., 371
Maybery, M. T., 85
Mayeux, L., 485
Maynard, A., 21, 455
Maynard, A. E., 415–416, 416f,
    451
Mazuka, R., 132
McAuliffe, T., 177
McBride, B., 393
McCabe, A., 259
McCabe, D., 546
McCamman, S., 153
McCarthy, A., 394
McCarthy, B., 569
McCarty, M. E., 144
McConnell, D., 222
McConnell, J., 93
McCullough, W. R., 314
McDade, T., 512
McDonald, P. G., 347
McDonough, L., 191
McDowell, M., 526
McElwain, N. L., 214

McEwen, B. S., 358, 359
McGloin, J. M., 363
McGlothlin, H., 479
McGraw, M. B., 172f
McGuire, S., 71
McHale, S. M., 351
McKay, A., 569
McKelvie, P., 167
McKenna, J. J., 151
McKenry, P., 357
McKinney, C., 354
McKinney, M. L., 180
McLeod, N. M. H., 249
McLeod, P. J., 132
McLoughlin, G., 70
McLoyd, V. C., 333, 359
McMahon, R. J., 363
McMenamy, J. M., 326
McNeill, D., 262
McPhee, C., 300
McPherson, D., 358
McPherson, D. A., 314
Meara, E., 114
Medkov, V. M., 499
Meeus, W. H. J., 557, 570, 570f,
    574, 577–578, 578f
Mehan, H., 440
Meier, A., 564
Meisels, S. J., 115
Meléndez, L., 152
Melinder, A., 286
Melot, A.-M., 281, 282
Meltz, B., 217
Meltzoff, A., 139, 206
Meltzoff, A. N., 177, 206, 206f,
    252, 264, 295
Mendel, J., 523
Mendle, J., 587
Mennella, J., 138
Menon, P., 163
Mesman, J., 204, 220
Mestre, M. V., 543
Meyer, L., 240
Meyer-Bahlberg, H. F. L., 570
Meyers, S., 142
Mezulis, A., 510
Mezulis, A. H., 556, 556f
Michael, A., 568
Michaelsen, K. F., 124
Migliano, A. B., 513
Miller, B. C., 569
Miller, C. A., 590, 591
Miller, J. G., 545
Miller, J. L., 87
Miller, K., 372
Miller, P., 33, 245
Miller, P. J., 305, 470
Miller, S. A., 572
Mills, C. M., 407, 407t, 408f
Milnitsky-Sapiro, C., 571
Minai, J., 90

Mingrone, R., 154
Minkoff, H., 98
Minsky, S. K., 406
Mintz, J., 305
Mintz, S., 5, 508, 509
Mitchell, E., 379
Mitchell, M. W., 155
Modell, J., 29
Modry-Mandell, K. L., 351
Moffitt, T. E., 592
Mohatt, G., 460
Molenaar, P. C., 399
Molina, J. C., 97
Molitor, N., 215
Monahan, K. C., 561
Mondloch, C. J., 137
Monk, C. S., 129
Monks, C. P., 483
Monk-Turner, E., 378
Moon, C., 132
Moon, H., 372
Moore, K. L., 94, 95f, 100t
Moore, M. K., 177
Moore, S., 165
Mora, J. O., 92
Moran, J. P., 569
Morelli, G., 218
Morelli, G. A., 151, 213
Morgan, G., 242
Morgan, J., 466
Mori, K., 116
Morissette, P., 223
Morokuma, S., 86
Morris, A., 553
Morrison, F. J., 450
Morrongiello, B. A., 132, 406
Morrow, C. E., 98
Morton, D. H., 67
Morton, S. M. B., 92
Moshman, D., 530, 533, 534,
    539, 542, 543, 578
Moskowitz, C., 296
Moss, L., 137
Moss, N. E., 92–93
Motch, S., 30
Moulson, M. C., 33
Muftuler, L., 90
Muir, D., 282
Mulder, E. J., 97
Müller, U., 177, 413, 533
Mullis, I. V. S., 457
Munakata, Y., 133, 186–187
Munholland, K., 220
Murdock, T. B., 546
Murnen, S. K., 590
Murphy, L. M., 558, 561
Murray, C., 422
Murray, J. P., 376
Murray, L., 204
Murray-Close, D., 483
Murry, V. M., 348, 351

Must, A., 525
Mustanski, B., 523
Myers, A. L., 276
Myers, M. W., 561
Mylander, C., 242, 243

Nadel, J., 206
Nader, P., 274
Nagler, J., 154
Nair, P., 113
Nakkula M., 574
Napoli, M., 579
Nasir, N., 538–539
Nasrallah, N. A., 519
Nastapoka, J., 109
National Center for Children in
    Poverty, 359, 359f
National Center for Education
    Statistics, 244
National Center for Family
    Homelessness, 359
National Center for Health
    Statistics, 569
National Council of Teachers of
    Mathematics, 441–442
National Institute on Deafness
    and Other Communication
    Disorders, 239
Navarro, V. M., 521
Nazzi, T., 223
Needham, A., 144, 188
Nelson, C. A., 33, 129, 130, 165,
    166, 191, 220
Nelson, K., 259, 272, 297, 298,
    299, 300, 316, 317
Nestel, P. S., 92
Netter, F. H., 515f
Neumark-Sztainer, D., 394
Neville, H. J., 11, 33
Newberger, D., 66f
Newcomb, A. F., 485
Newell, M. L., 100
Newport, E., 238
Newport, E. L., 11
Newton, E. K., 222, 227, 228,
    326
Newton, M., 156
Newton, N., 156
Nguyen, D., 99
NICHD Early Child Care
    Research Network, 215,
    367, 368, 439
Nicholls, D., 591
Nichols, T. R., 523
Nicholson, T., 434
Nievar, M. A., 214
Nigg, J. T., 413, 510
Nijhuis, J. G., 87
Nkata, M., 105
Noland, M., 97
Nolen-Hoeksema, S., 585, 587

Nord, M., 275, 275t
Norgate, S. H., 70
Nsamenang, A., 298, 301
Nucci, L., 319, 320, 479, 546,
    571
Nunes, T., 434, 435, 442
Nussbaum, M., 565
Nyiti, R. M., 417
Nyland, M. J. M., 87

Oakes, L. M., 190
Oates, C., 376
Obama, M., 394
Obleser, J., 240
Obradov, A., 96
O'Brien, M., 313
O'Callaghan, M. J., 115
Ochs, E., 245, 246, 263
O'Connell, B., 258
Office of Head Start, 437
Office of Juvenile Justice and
    Delinquency Prevention,
    592
Ogbu, J. U., 560, 579
Ogden, C., 393, 394, 395
Okami, P., 151
Olds, D. L., 365
O'Leary, C. M., 97
Oliner, P., 542
Oliner, S. B., 542
Olmstead, R., 151
Olsen, B., 206
Olsen, B. R., 273
Olsen, J. A., 213, 470
Olsen, L. W., 93
Olson, K., 296
Olson, K. R., 468
Olthof, T., 482
Olver, R. E., 87
Onaga, M., 356
Ong, A. D., 578, 580
Ong, K. K., 523t
Opfer, J., 435
Oppenheim, R. W., 87
Orav, E. J., 352
Orioli, I. M., 96
Ornstein, P. A., 286, 287, 410,
    411
Osmond, C., 92, 99
Osofsky, J., 220
Oster, H., 137, 203, 205
Ostrer, H., 85
Ostrov, J., 331, 377
Ostrov, J. M., 483
O'Sullivan, L. F., 570
Out, D., 156
Owens, E. B., 333
Özyürek, A., 242

Paden, E. P., 248
Padilla, A., 460

Page-Goertz, S., 153
Paikoff, R. L., 572
Pak, S., 392
Pakapong, Y., 525
Paley, V. G., 271, 317, 323,
    338–339
Palincsar, A. S., 440
Pallotta-Chiarolli, M., 558,
    559
Pan, B. A., 255
Panksepp, J., 201, 203
Parent, A.-S., 523, 525
Parent, C. Z., 367
Park, Y.-S., 456
Parke, R. D., 355, 484, 498
Parker, J., 564
Parker, J. G., 493
Parker, S. T., 73, 180
Parsons, T., 509
Pasco Fearon, R. M., 213
Paterson, S., 131
Patrick, H., 561
Pattee, L., 485
Patterson, C., 498, 499f
Patterson, C. J., 357, 358
Patterson, G. R., 332, 498, 592
Pavlov, I. P., 146
Pawloski, L. R., 525
Pecora, N., 376
Pedersen, S., 558
Pegg, J. E., 132
Pelaez, M., 204
Pellegrini, A. D., 8, 481, 482,
    483, 489
Pelletier, D. L., 163
Pellicano, E., 293
Peltonen, K., 352, 353f
Péneau, S., 275
Peper, J. S., 519, 520
Peplau, L. A., 565
Perfors, A., 266
Perrizo, K., 151
Perry, W. G., 534
Perryman, J., 528
Persaud, T. V. N., 94, 95f, 96,
    100t
Peter, J., 379
Peterman, K., 144
Petersen, A., 586
Peterson, C., 259, 288, 294–295
Petitto, L.-A., 223, 244, 245
Petitto, L. A., 241
Pettit, G. S., 93, 498, 592
Peverly, S. T., 456
Pew Research Center, 346
Peyser, H., 358
Phelps, E., 595
Philibert, R. A., 320
Phillips, D., 215, 321, 360
Phinney, J. S., 313, 578, 579,
    580, 581

Piaget, J., 19–21, 20, 35, 37, 144–146, 177, 178–183, 265, 277–278, 279–280, 280, 280f, 282–283, 284, 285, 286, 318–319, 400–401, 400–404, 401f, 402, 415, 472–473, 474, 533
Piaget, L., 179, 180
Piatt, J. H., Jr., 154
Pick, A. D., 425
Pieper, S., 156
Pike, R., 468
Pillai, M., 87
Pinelli, J., 143
Pinker, S., 247, 262
Pinquart, M., 213, 215, 365
Pinto, D., 296
Pittman, R., 87
Pitts, R. C., 543
Pizzuto, E., 242
Plage, D., 296
Plage, M., 296
Plato, 508
Pleck, J. H., 213
Plomin, R., 69
Plumert, J. M., 397
Plunkett, K., 254
Pnevmatikos, D., 474
Polanichka, N., 593
Polikoff, B., 509
Polivy, J., 590
Pollack, H. A., 99, 155
Pollack, W., 565
Pollitt, E., 40, 93
Pollock, D., 104
Polman, H., 482
Pomerantz, E. M., 467, 468, 572
Ponirakis, A., 89
Ponjaert-Kristoffersen, I., 358
Pontius, K., 175
Poole, D., 286
Popp, D., 496
Porter, R., 138
Portes, A., 356, 459
Posada, G., 218
Posner, M. I., 165
Poston, L., 93
Pott, M., 218
Poulin, F., 482, 494
Poulin-Dubois, D., 254
Poulsen, P., 71
Powell, A., 56
Powell, J. K., 224
Powell, K., 530
Pratt, M. W., 344, 543
Prechtl, H., 141
Prechtl, H. F. R., 87
Preisser, D. A., 248
Prentice, A. M., 395
Prescott, E., 437
Pressley, M., 411, 412

Preyer, G., 358
Preyer, W. T., 8, 9t
Proulx, T., 459
Provezano, F. J., 117
Pruden, S., 223, 254
Pujol, J., 165, 240, 276
Pulkkinen, L., 523
Puma, M., 437
Punamäki, R.-L., 214, 352, 353f
Purcell, K., 576
Pustilnik, S., 151
Putnick, D. L., 360
Pyers, J., 243

Quas, J. A., 286
Quinn, P. C., 191, 192
Quintana, S. M., 578
Quiroz, B., 458
Quittner, A. L., 165
Qumaluk, A., 109
Quota, S., 352, 353f

Raat, H., 96
Racz, S. J., 363
Raeburn, P., 143
Raggatt, P., 85
Raghavendra, R., 392
Rahman, R., 113f
Raikes, H., 436
Rainie, L., 576
Rao, S. P., 346
Rapoport, J. L., 33, 129
Ratcliffe, S., 528, 529
Rauch, F., 273
Raudenbush, W., 359
Rauscher, F. H., 167
Rayens, M. K., 97
Raymond, D., 559
Read, M., 107, 389
Ream, G. L., 570
Recchia, H., 353
Reck, C., 201
Recker, K. M., 397
Reddy, V., 199, 226
Redman, J., 184
Reece, M., 70, 570
Reed, M. D., 561
Rees, J., 216
Reginato, A. M., 273
Reichel-Dolmatoff, A., 258
Reichel-Dolmatoff, G., 258
Reiling, A. M., 25
Reis, H., 500
Relier, J.-P., 89
Renk, K., 354
Renz-Polster, H., 110
Repacholi, B. M., 206 Repp, A., 224
Rest, J., 542
Reunanen, A., 92
Reynolds, G. D., 193, 193f

Reynosa, B., 528
Rice, C., 282
Rice, J. C., 333
Rich, J. L., 444, 445
Richards, J. E., 193, 193f
Richards, M., 553, 553f, 570
Richardson, J., 580
Richardson, K., 70
Richerson, P., 54, 73
Richmond, J., 33, 165
Rideout, V. J., 372, 373t, 374f, 380
Ridley-Johnson, R., 174
Rigler, D., 241
Rinaldi, C. M., 352
Riskind, R. G., 357
Risley, T. R., 246
Ritz, B., 103
Rivero, M., 246
Rizzolatti, G., 205, 206
Roa, J., 521f
Robbins, W. J., 163f
Roberts, B. W., 14
Roberts, D. F., 372, 374f, 380
Robinson, J. L., 70, 381
Robinson, J. S., 96
Robinson, S. R., 87
Rochat, P., 222, 225, 226
Rodas, C., 358
Rodkin, P. C., 482, 560
Roe, K., 240, 241, 241f
Rogoff, B., 21, 40, 52, 54, 55, 167, 298, 300, 387, 405, 405f, 418, 431, 451, 452, 453, 457, 533, 535, 538
Rolland-Cachera, M. F., 275
Rollins, N., 100
Romer, D., 555f
Romero, A., 357
Ronsmans, C., 110
Roosa, M., 381, 470–471
Rosa, A., 52
Rosati, A., 245
Rose, A. J., 484, 485, 493
Rose, L. T., 285
Rose, R. J., 523
Rose, S. A., 194, 194f
Rosen, W. D., 222
Rosenbaum, J., 567
Rosenblatt, R. A., 110
Rosengren, K., 277f
Rosengren, K. S., 284
Rosenkrantz, S. L., 191
Rosenstein, D., 137
Rosenzweig, M. R., 130
Ross, B., 277
Ross, M. G., 87
Roth, M., 564
Rothbart, M. K., 149, 149t, 150
Rothbaum, F., 218
Rothstein-Fisch, C., 56, 458

Rouchaud, A., 275
Roundtree, P. W., 561
Rovee-Collier, C., 147, 148, 194
Rubin, J. Z., 117
Rubin, K. H., 484, 493, 494, 498
Rubin, Z., 336
Rubin-Smith, J., 372
Ruble, D. N., 309, 311, 312, 313
Ruchiwit, M., 525
Rudolph, K., 559, 588
Rudolph, K. D., 524, 587, 588
Rudolph, K. R., 523
Ruel, M. T., 163
Ruffman, T., 184
Ruiz, S., 470–471
Rumbaugh, D. M., 238
Rumbaut, R., 356, 459
Russell, R., 526
Russell, S., 582
Russell, S. T., 355, 581
Rust, J., 310
Ryan, R., 470
Ryan, R. R., 213
Ryan, S., 358

Saarni, C., 200, 326, 327, 328
Sabel, K.-G., 112
Sachs, J., 244
Saco-Pollitt, C., 93
Sadovsky, A., 310, 338, 477
Saeed, N. R., 249
Saffran, J. R., 246
Sagi, A., 218–219
Sagi-Schwartz, A., 218, 219f
Sai, F. Z., 139
St. James-Roberts, I., 156, 156f, 157
Salapatek, P., 172
Salbe, A. D., 93
Saltvedt, S., 65
Salzarulo, P., 151, 152
Sameroff, A. J., 15, 360, 381, 381f, 390
SAMHSA, 97, 98f
Sampaio, R. C., 276
Samper, P., 543
Samuelsson, I. P., 443
San Antonio, D. M., 369–370
Sancar, B., 242
Sandberg, A., 443
Sanders, S., 570
Sandfort, T. G. M., 358
Sandman, C., 90
Sandoval, L., 297
Sanfilippo, P. M., 66
Sanson, A., 306
Santelli, J., 569
Sapp, F., 282
Saragovi, C., 559
Sarnecka, B., 435
Sato, Y., 132

Savage-Rumbaugh, E. S., 52, 238, 239
Savage-Rumbaugh, S., 238
Savci, E., 358
Savin-Williams, R. C., 562, 565, 570, 583
Saxe, G. B., 22
Saxon, T. F., 155
Scarr, S., 172
Schaal, B., 86
Schaberg, L., 545
Schachner, A., 132, 246
Schack-Nielsen, L., 124
Schafer, G., 254
Scharrer, E., 374, 380
Scheier, C., 186
Scherf, K. S., 410
Scheuermann, B., 295
Schick, B., 242
Schick, K., 52
Schick, V., 570
Schieffelin, B., 245, 246, 263
Schlaggar, B., 446
Schlagmüller, M., 411
Schmeelk, K. H., 89
Schmitt-Rodermund, E., 454
Schneider, B. H., 486, 487–488, 488f, 498, 557, 559, 571
Schneider, W., 409, 410, 411
Schneiders, B., 418
Schnell, B., 453
Schoenau, E., 273
Schoener, G., 186
Schöler, H. R., 82
Scholes, R. J., 434
Schölmerich, A., 219
Schonert-Reichl, K. A., 543
Schroeder, J. H., 293
Schuetze, P., 98
Schuler, M. E., 113
Schult, C. A., 295
Schum, T. R., 77, 177
Schwartz, D., 482
Schwartz, M. B., 392
Schwartz, S. J., 459
Scorza, W. E., 92
Scott, K., 580
Scribner, R., 527
Scribner, S., 453
Sears, R., 9
Segal, N. L., 70, 71
Segall, M. H., 330, 332, 417
Segerdahl, P., 238
Seiffge-Krenke, I., 564
Selman, R., 495–496, 558
Sen, M. G., 307
Sendak, M., 258, 326, 375
Senghas, A., 243
Senghas, R., 243
Serene, J. A., 33
Serjeant, B. E., 74

Serjeant, G. R., 74
Serpell, R., 419, 425
Setliff, A. E., 167
Shager, H., 438
Shakespeare, W., 508
Shanahan, L., 571
Shanker, S., 237
Shao, T., 478
Shapero, D., 245
Shapira, A., 487
Shapiro, E., 85
Shapka, J. D., 38
Shatz, M., 258
Shaver, P., 213
Shaw, D. S., 381
Shaw, G. L., 167
Shaw, H., 591
Shaw, L., 259
Shaw, P., 276, 399, 399f, 518
Sheeber, L. B., 587
Shennan, S., 56
Sherif, C. W., 486
Sherif, M., 486
Sherif-Trask, B., 353
Shiffrin, R. M., 285f
Shin, Y., 484
Shiner, R. L., 14
Shinskey, J., 186–187
Shonkoff, J., 215, 321, 360
Shonkoff, J. P., 358, 359
Shopen, T., 251
Shore, C., 258
Shostak, M., 104
Shrout, P., 173
Shulman, S., 564
Shu-Rong, W., 525
Shuwairi, S., 139
Shweder, R. A., 151, 479, 544, 545, 583
Siegel, L. S., 445, 446
Siegler, R. S., 41, 285, 288, 406, 418, 435
Sigo, R. L. W., 30
Silbereisen, R. K., 454, 524, 572
Silk, J., 553
Silk, J. S., 570
Silva, K., 457
Silva, L. M., 114
Silverstein, M., 346
Simion, F., 137, 336
Simmonds, S., 99
Simmons, R., 465, 483
Simms, M. D., 177
Simon, T., 420, 421
Simon, V. A., 560, 562
Simons, D. A., 333
Simons, L. G., 354
Simpkins, S. D., 396, 397f
Simpson, J. A., 207
Sinclair, D. C., 513, 517
Singer, D. G., 322

Singer, J. D., 438
Singer, J. L., 472
Singer, L. T., 111, 112
Singh, G. K., 107
Singh-Manoux, A., 556, 558
Sinigaglia, C., 205
Sinkkonen, J., 214
Siqueland, E. R., 131f
Sisk, C., 510
Sizun, J., 143
Skinner, B. F., 19, 147
Skjaerven, R., 92
Slade, L., 184
Slater, S. J., 371
Slaughter, V., 222
Slemmer, J., 187
Slobin, D., 243
Sloboda, D. M., 85
Slonim, N., 236
Slotkin, T. A., 110–111
Smahel, D., 379
Smart, D., 306
Smetana, J. G., 319, 320, 479, 571
Smith, A., 576
Smith, A. M., 97
Smith, E. J., 99
Smith, J., 333
Smith, K., 346
Smith, L. B., 27, 186
Smith, P. K., 483
Smith-Pasqualini, M., 203
Smitsman, A. W., 169
Smoleniec, J., 87
Smotherman, W. P., 87
Smulian, J. C., 92
Smyke, A. T., 220
Smyser, C. D., 127
Snarey, J. R., 544
Snow, C. E., 245, 246, 255
Sodian, B., 410
Sogabe, Y., 132
Sokol, B. W., 480, 584, 585
Solomon, J., 211, 212
Solomon, S., 561
Solomon, S. G., 5
Somerset, D. A., 102
Somerville, L. H., 519
Sommer, K., 360
Sonies, B. C., 87
Soong, W., 529
Sorensen, T. I., 93
Sowell, E. R., 398, 410, 519
Spade-Aguilar, M., 359f
Spear, L. P., 555
Spearman, C., 421
Spelke, E. S., 188, 289, 435
Spence M. J., 88
Spencer, M. B., 30, 314
Spinrad, T. L., 328, 338, 477
Spitz, H. H., 406

Sreeramareddy, C. T., 107
Sroufe, L. A., 202, 220, 491–492, 492t, 499
Stallings, J., 156
Stang, J., 526, 526t
Stanhope, R., 512, 522, 523
Stanko, S., 155
Stauder, J. E., 399
Stearns, P., 7
Steegers, E. A., 96
Steele, R. G., 348
Stein, A., 275
Steinberg, L., 519, 553, 554, 554f, 555, 561, 570, 573, 585, 587, 592
Steinberg, S. J., 587
Steiner, M., 65
Stennes, L. M., 307
Stern, D. N., 134, 203
Stern, W., 286, 420
Sternberg, R. J., 418, 419, 422
Stevens, J., 165
Stevenson, D., 571
Stevenson, H. W., 410, 456, 557
Stevenson, R., 100t
Stice, E., 591
Stigler, J. W., 456
Stipek, D., 359
Stojiljkovic, D., 89
Stoltz, H. E., 213, 470
Stoltzfus, R. J., 93
Stone, J. L., 265
Stone, K. C., 97
Stone, M., 560
St-Onge, M. J., 536
Storvoll, E. E., 592
Story, M., 394, 526, 526t
Strathearn, L., 115
Stratton, K., 97
Straus, M., 333
Strauss, R., 394
Strauss, S., 353
Strayer, F. F., 307, 307t, 330, 331t, 332
Striano, T., 172, 222, 225, 226
Striepe, M., 582
Stross, B., 264
Strutt, J., 397
Stuart, J., 572
Stunkard, A. J., 392
Styfco, S. J., 437, 438
Styne, D., 512
Suárez-Orozco, C., 356
Suárez-Orozco, M. M., 356
Subbotsky, E. V., 478
Subrahmanyam, K., 378, 379, 538
Sugiyama, L., 346
Sullivan, H. S., 493
Sullivan, J. A., 273, 273f
Sullivan, K., 291

Summerfield, D., 373
Sun, Y., 499, 500
Sund, A. M., 482
Sunseth, K., 434
Suomi, S., 149, 209
Super, C. M., 153, 174, 300
Susman, E. J., 89, 524
Sutton, J., 482
Sutton, P. D., 112
Suzuki, K., 90
Suzuki, L., 56
Sweeney, B., 194
Sweeney, J., 117
Sweeney, J. A., 410
Sweeney, N. M., 528
Sweeting, H., 586, 586f
Swenson, L., 485
Symington, A., 143
Szeszko, P. R., 33
Szkrybalo, J., 311

Tabacchi, G., 394
Tabak, I., 536
Tager-Flusberg, H., 295
Takahashi, Y., 116
Takao, S., 102
Takenaka, J., 93
Tallal, P., 446–447
Tamis-LeMonda, C. S., 173
Tan, D., 478
Tanabe, K. O., 155
Tani, C. R., 561
Tanner, J. M., 69, 111, 128f, 163, 513, 516t, 525f
Tardiff, T., 34
Taylor, A. R., 351
Taylor, C. A., 333
Taylor, K., 85
Taylor, P., 93, 346f
Taylor, P. D., 93
Teilmann, G., 525
Temple, C. M., 66
Templeton, J., 558, 596t
Tena-Sempere, M., 521
Tenenbaum, H. R., 297
Terplan, M., 99
Tessier, R., 35
Teubert, D., 365
Thal, D., 254
Thal, D. J., 245
Tharp, R. G., 461
Thatcher, R. W., 398
Thelen, E., 27, 142, 144, 163, 174, 186
Theokas, C., 3
Thibault, K., 125
Thiessen, E. D., 246
Thoman, E. B., 151, 152
Thomas, A., 148, 149
Thomas, L. R., 30
Thomas, M., 267

Thomas, M. G., 56
Thomese, F., 347
Thompson, C. A., 288
Thompson, G. B., 434
Thompson, P. M., 519
Thompson, R., 92, 93
Thompson, R. A., 214, 222, 227, 228, 326, 327
Thompson, R. F., 128
Thorndike, E., 19
Thorne, B., 490, 491, 589
Thrasher, F., 561
Tilburg, M., 556
Tizard, B., 216, 218
Todorova, I., 356
Toga, A. W., 519
Tokita, M., 81–82
Tokunaga, R. S., 482
Tolchinsky, L., 434
Tolman, D. L., 568, 582
Tom, S. R., 482
Tomasello, M., 55, 222, 228, 238, 241, 250, 263, 264, 291
Toppari, J., 523
Torney-Purta, J., 534
Toshalis, E., 574
Toth, N., 52
Toth, S. L., 363, 381, 382t
Tracy, A. J., 568
Traggiai, C., 512, 522, 523
Trainor, L. J., 277
Trautner, H., 308
Travis, F., 410
Tremblay, R., 204
Tremblay, R. E., 329
Trevarthen, C., 199, 201, 203, 204, 221, 225
Triandis, H. C., 455t
Troiden, R. R., 582
Tronick, E., 201, 204
Tronick, E. Z., 98
Troop-Gordon, W., 38, 485, 493, 523
Troseth, G. L., 310, 376
Truwitt, C. L., 276
Tsao, F.-M., 246
Tsimaris, P., 522
Tsuda, T., 102
Tuchmann-Duplessis, H., 81f, 102
Tucker, G. R., 244
Tucker, J., 528
Tudge, J., 435–436, 436f
Tulving, E., 272
Tulviste, P., 452
Tuomilehto, J., 92
Tur, A., 543
Turati, C., 137
Turiel, E., 319, 320, 473, 478, 479, 539, 542, 543, 544, 545, 571, 584

Turkheimer, E., 70, 523
Turnbull, E., 458
Twenge, J. M., 585, 587

UNAIDS, 218, 218f
Underhill, R. L., 177
Underwood, M., 330
Undheim, A. M., 482
UNESCO, 430, 438, 438f
UNICEF, 92, 94f, 100, 275
United Nations Commission on Population and Development, 355
United Nations Department of Economic and Social Affairs, 353–354, 355f, 379
United Nations General Security Council, 372
United Nations Statistics Division, 361f
U.S. Census Bureau, 354, 365, 499, 580
U.S. Department of Health and Human Services (HHS), 363
U.S. Department of Health & Human Services, Administration on Children Youth & Families, 116
U.S. Department of Justice, 482, 483
U.S. Department of Labor, Bureau of Labor Statistics, 214
Unterberg, M., 556
Urberg, K. A., 561
Ursitti, F., 98
Uttal, D., 276, 277f
Uzgiris, I. C., 181

Vaag, A., 71
Vaillant, G. E., 352
Valdes, G., 246
Valentin, S., 151
Valian, V., 262
Valkenburg, P. M., 379
Valsiner, J., 4, 21, 29, 41, 52, 117, 141, 306
van Aken, C., 333
van Aken, M., 333
van Balen, F., 358
van Buuren, S., 164
van De Beek, C., 85
Van den Bulck, J., 380
van den Dikkenberg-Pot, I., 224
van der Meulen, M., 482
Van Der Molen, M. W., 399
Van der Paal, L., 110
Van Der Put, N. M., 91
van der Veer, R., 4
Vandross, L., 354
van Dulmen, M., 497

Vanfraussen, K., 358
Vangelisti, A., 500
van Goozen, S. H. M., 85
Van IJzendoorn, M. H., 156, 204, 214, 218, 219f, 220
Van Leijenhorst, L., 519
Van Mierlo, J., 380
van Oers, B., 4
Van Tilburg, T. G., 347
Van Wagner, V., 109
Varela, R. E., 355
Vartanian, L. R., 392
Vasquez, O., 460
Vaughn, B. E., 215
Venti, C. A., 93
Ventura, S., 360, 360f
Ventura, S. J., 112
Verhoeff, F. H., 164
Verhoeven, M., 333
Vermande, M. M., 482
Véronneau, M.-H., 561
Viding, E., 70
Vieira, E. T., Jr., 377
Viken, R. J., 523
Vinden, P. G., 297
Vingerhoets, A., 556
Vinicius, L., 513
Vintzileos, A. M., 92
Violato, C., 508
Vollmer, B., 126, 127
Volterra, V., 242, 258
von Hofsten, C., 144, 169
von Koss Torkildsen, J., 254
Voorhoeve, H. W. A., 88
Vurpillot, E., 413, 413f
Vygotsky, L. S., 21–22, 41, 201, 263, 265–266, 322, 353

Wachs, T. D., 148, 150
Waddell, K. J., 452
Waddington, Conrad H., 68, 71
Wagner, D. A., 451f, 451–452, 452f
Wahlstrom, K. L., 529
Wainright, J. L., 358
Wainryb, C., 372, 545, 546t
Waldfogel, J., 439
Waldinger, R. J., 352
Walker, E., 378
Walker, K. C., 596
Walker, L. J., 543
Walker, R., 511
Walker, S., 330
Walsh, W., 333
Walters, D. V., 87
Wandersman, A., 380
Wang, Q., 572
Wang, S.-H., 131, 185, 187
Wang, W., 273
Wang, X., 97, 98

Ward, K., 63
Ward, L. M., 378
Wardekker, W., 4
Ware, E. A. 276
Warren, M., 589
Wartella, E. A., 376
Washburn, D. A., 238
Washburn, S. L., 57
Watamura, S., 367
Waters, E., 213, 220
Waters, H. S., 213
Watson, J. B., 18, 19
Watson, S. D., 554
Waxman, S., 250
Webb, S. J., 129
Weems, C. F., 355
Weichold, K., 524
Weikum, W. M., 133
Weinberg, C. R., 81
Weinfield, N., 220
Weinstock, H., 593
Weinstock, M., 89, 536
Weisfeld, G. E., 514
Weisner, T., 151
Weisner, T. S., 497
Weiss, D., 238
Weissman, M. M., 587
Weisz, A. N., 543
Weisz, J., 218
Weitoft, G., 346, 356–357
Wellings, K., 567f
Wellman, F., 290
Wellman, H. M., 284, 284f, 288, 290, 295
Wells, G., 55
Welsh, B. C., 439
Wen, M., 371
Wenger, E., 431
Wentzel, K. R., 485
Werker, J. F., 132

Werne, J., 154
Wernicke, C., 239
West, P., 586, 586f
Westdahl, C., 153
Westen, T., 174
Westerlund, A., 191
Westrup, B., 143
Wetter, E. K., 276
Wheelwright, S., 85
Whitaker, R. C., 392
White, M. I., 457
White, S. H., 390, 510
Whitehouse, A., 85
Whiteman, S. D., 351
Whitfield, M. F., 115
Whiting, B. B., 344
Whiting, J. W. M., 274, 344, 505
Whiting, S. J., 513
Whitmore, J. K., 458
Whitney, M. P., 152
Whittle, S., 518
WHO (World Health Organization), 101, 124–125, 125f, 171, 274, 526
WHO/UNAIDS/UNICEF, 100, 101f
Wichstrom, L., 592
Wickham, L., 137
Widom, C. S., 363
Widome, R., 528
Wield, G., 99
Wiesel, T., 129
Wigle, D. T., 102
Wilcox, A. J., 81
Wild Boy of Aveyron, 1–2, 10
Wiley, A., 508
Wilhelm, M., 103
Wilkening, F., 289
Wilkinson, F. S., 107

Willford, J. A., 97
Williams, J., 294–295
Wilshir, K., 157
Wilson, B. J., 377
Wilson, E. O., 331
Wilson, S. M., 87
Wimmer, H., 291
Winberg, J., 138
Winner, E., 254, 291
Winnicott, D. W., 207
Witherington, D., 200
Wolf, A. W., 151
Wolfenstein, M., 6, 175
Wolff, P. H., 152, 152f
Wolfolk, T., 353
Wolfson, A. R., 528
Woll, B., 242
Wong, A. D.-W., 254
Wood, D. O., 115
Woodruff-Pak, D. S., 128
Worchel, F. F., 157
World Health Organization (WHO), 101, 124–125, 125f, 171, 274, 526
Wozniak, R. H., 73
Wright, C., 214
Wu, C., 355
Wu, P., 350
Wurtele, S. K., 333
Wyndaele, J. J., 176, 177
Wynn, K., 189, 189f, 227

Xiong, X., 89
Xu, Y., 482

Yamagata Z., 90
Yamamoto, M. E., 478
Yaman, A., 220
Yan, Z., 301
Yanagihara, S., 10

Yanai, J., 99, 102
Yang, C., 151
Yang, Q., 91
Yang, S., 478
Yau, J., 320
Ye, L., 74
Yerkes, R. M., 422, 423f
Yeung, W., 354
Yinan, H., 103
Ying-Xiu, Z., 525
Ylisaukko-oja, T., 296
Yonas, A., 135
Yorifuji, T., 102
Yoshida, K. A., 133
Yoshikawa, H., 361, 437
Young, M., 354
Young, M. E., 335
Young, S. S., 526

Zafeiriou, D. I., 141
Zahn-Waxler, C., 593
Zaidman-Zait, A., 251
Zarbatany, L., 494–495
Zeanah, C. H., 220
Zeifman, D. M., 156
Zelazo, P. D., 321, 413, 414
Zelazo, P. R., 142
Zentella, A., 246
Zero to Three, 366t
Zeskind, P. S., 111, 112, 155, 156
Zhao Y., 103
Zhou, Z., 456
Zickuhr, K., 576
Zielinski, D. S., 362, 363, 365
Zigler, E., 167, 362, 437, 438
Zigler, E. F., 363
Ziv, M., 353
Zuckerman, J. B., 165
Zukow-Goldring, P., 351

Subject Index

Note: Page numbers followed by f indicate figures; those followed by t indicate tables.

Abusive families, 361–363, 362t
Academic motivation, 447–448
Accommodation, in Piaget's theory, 20, 21, 144
Ache people, child-rearing practices of, 174–175
Acquired immunodeficiency syndrome (AIDS)
  in adolescence, 595, 595f
  children orphaned by, 429
  teaching children about, 566
  teratogenic effects of, 100–101, 101f
Action(s)
  coordinated, development of, 141–142, 142f, 144
  moral, moral reasoning related to, 546–547
  self-regulation of, 321–322
Action research, 30, 31
Activity
  chaotic, neighborhoods and, 371
  fetal, 87, 87t, 88f, 89
Activity level, temperament and, 148
Actual self, ideal self compared with, 469
Adaptability, temperament and, 148
Adaptation, in Piaget's theory, 20, 144
Addams, Jane, 508–509
Adolescence, 505–599
  biological theories of development in, 510–512
    of Freud, 511
    of Hall, 510–511
    modern, 511–512
  cognitive development in, 530–539
    information-processing approaches to, 536–537
    Piaget's theory of, 530–536, 531t
    sociocultural approaches to, 537–539, 539f
  emotional development in, 552–557
    experience of emotions and, 553f, 553–554

regulating emotions and, 554–557
  emotional health in, 585–593
    delinquency and other externalizing problems and, 585, 591–593, 593f
    depression and anxiety and, 585–590, 586f, 587t
    eating disorders and, 590–591, 591t
    suicide among Native Americans and, 588–589
  friendship in
    developmental functions of, 558
    gender and, 558–559
  identity development in. See Identity development
  moral development in. See Moral development, in adolescence
  parent-child relationships in, 570f, 570–573
    conflicts and, 570–571
    influences beyond family, 571–573, 572t
  peer relationships in. See Peer relationships, in adolescence
  positive youth development in, 595–596, 596t
  puberty and. See Puberty
  sexual health in, 593–595
  sexual relationships in, 564–570
    first sexual experiences and, 567f, 567–568, 568f, 568t, 570
    learning about sex and, 565–567
    teenage pregnancy and, 567, 569
  society and, 507–510
    historical views and, 508
    modern, 508–510
  teen mothers and, 360f, 360–361, 361f, 364–365
Adoption, 216
  by gay and lesbian couples, 358
Adoption studies, 70–71
Adrenal gland, 521

Adrenal hyperplasia, congenital, 85
Adrenaline, maternal stress and, 89
Adulthood, emerging, 509
Affiliative behaviors, 307
Affluence, families and, 363–364
Africa. See also specific countries and peoples
  education in, 429, 430f
  nomads of, lactose tolerance among, 74
African Americans
  chlamydia among, 594, 594f
  cultural style of, 459
  culture-sensitive instruction and, 460–461
  education and, 430
  ethnic identity and, 314–315, 580–581
  families of, 348, 351, 355, 357
  HIV/AIDS in, 595, 595f
  infant sleeping arrangements among, 151
  language and school success and, 459–460
  maternal nutrition and prenatal development among, 91
  narratives among, 260
  parent-child relationships in adolescence and, 571
  phenylketonuria in, 65
  puberty in, 522, 524
  romantic relationships in adolescence and, 564
  self-esteem among, 315
  sickle-cell anemia among, 74–75
  teenage pregnancy among, 569
Age. See also Adolescence; Early childhood; Infancy; Middle childhood
  gestational, 93
  parental expectations and, 496–497
  at puberty, 522–526
    individual differences in, 522t, 522–524, 523t
    population variation in, 524–526, 525f, 526t
    school-cutoff strategy and, 449–450

of sexual partners, teenage pregnancy among, 569
  of viability, 86
Agentic goals, friendship and, 559
Aggression
  bullying and, 482–483
    cyberbullying, 551
  in early childhood, 329–335
    causes and controls of, 331–335
    development of, 329–331, 330f, 331t
  friendships and, 495
  hostile, 329, 330
  instrumental, 330
  parenting and, 498
  proactive, 482
  reactive, 482
  relational, 331, 483
AIDS
  in adolescence, 595, 595f
  children orphaned by, 429
  teaching children about, 566
  teratogenic effects of, 100–101, 101f
Air pollution, 103
Aka people
  attachment among, 213
  infant crying among, 156
Alcohol, teratogenic effects of, 97, 97f
Alleles, 62
Allocaregiving, 347
Alpha girls, 483
Altruistic behavior, 327
Amish people, genetic disorders among, 67
Amnion, 82, 83f
Amniotic fluid, 82, 83f
  fetal swallowing of, 87
Amygdala, 518
Anal stage, 17, 17t
Analgesics, for childbirth pain, 108
Analytic intelligence, 422
Androgens, 85. See also Testosterone
Anemia
  Cooley's, 64t
  sickle-cell, 64t, 74f, 74–75
Anencephaly, 91
Anesthetics, for childbirth pain, 108

Angola, parenting and self-esteem and, 470
Anorexia nervosa, 590, 591t
A-not-B error, 183–184
Anxiety
in adolescence, 585–590, 586f, 587t
pregnancy, 90–91
Apgar scale, 111–112, 112t
Aphasia, 239
Appearance, reality distinguished from, in early childhood, 280–282, 281f
Applied research, 30, 31
Apprenticeship, 431
formal education compared with, 431–433
Approach-withdrawal, temperament and, 148
Arabic culture, moral development in, 545, 546t
Armenian Americans, ethnic identity among, 579–580
Asian Americans
families of, 355, 356
puberty in, 522
Asian cultures. See also specific groups
cooperation and competition among peers and, 487
emotion regulation in adolescence in, 557
sexually transmitted infections and, 594
Assimilation, in Piaget's theory, 20–21, 144
Attachment, 207–221
explanations of, 207–209
to fathers and others, 213
infant's appearance and, 116
patterns of, 210–213
later development and, 220–221
variations in, causes of, 214–220
phases of, 209–210
reactive attachment disorder and, 217
Attachment statuses, 211–213
"Attachment-in-the-making" phase of attachment, 210
Attention
increased control of, in middle childhood, 413, 413f
in infancy, 193f, 193–194, 194f
visual, 194

Attention span, temperament and, 148
Attitudes, maternal, prenatal development and, 90–91
Australia
autism in, 294–295
parental expectations in, 497
Tasmanian societies of, loss of aspects of culture of, 56
Australian Aborigine people
loss of aspects of culture of, 56
vocabulary of, 264
Australopithecus afarensis, 49, 50, 57, 73
Authoritarian parenting pattern, 349, 350t
Authoritative parenting pattern, 349, 350t
self-esteem and, 469–470
Autism
modularity theory and, 293–295, 294f, 295f
support for siblings and, 296
Autism Genome Project, 296
Autism spectrum disorder (ASD), 296
Autobiographical memory, 316–317
Autonomous morality, 319, 472–473
Autonomy, friendship and, 558
Autonomy versus shame and doubt stage, 17t, 229, 306
Avoidant attachment, 211
Axons, 126, 126f, 127

Babbling, 223–224, 237
Babinski reflex, 141t
Baby talk, 245–246
Babyness, adult response evoked by, 25, 25f
Baby-talk, 132, 245–246
Back to Sleep movement, 154, 175
Baganda people, pregnancy spacing among, 153
Balance sense, fetal, 86
Baldwin effect, 73
Balinese people, dancing among, 300
Basal ganglia, 518
Basic emotions, 201–203
Basic research, 30, 31
Basic trust versus mistrust stage, 17t, 228–229
Baule people, sensorimotor development in, 180

Bedouin people, lactose tolerance among, 74
Behavior
brain development and
in adolescence, 519–520
in infancy, 165–166
organization of, 140–148
coordinated action and, 141–142, 142f, 144
learning theories of, 146–148
Piaget's theory of, 144–146, 145t
reaching and, 144
reflexes and, 140–141, 141t
sequences of, 8
Behavior modification, 26
Behaviorism, 18–19, 23t
Belgium, violent video games in, 380
Beng people, childbirth and, 106
Big Brothers/Big Sisters, 596
Bilingualism, 244–245
Biocultural approach, 43. See also Biological factors; Culture; Genetics
Biological drives, 208
Biological factors
aggression and, 331–332, 332f
coevolution of culture and, 73–75
emotion regulation and, 554f, 554–555, 555f
inheritance of. See Genetics
in language development, 262–263
Biological theories of development in, adolescence, 510–512
Biology, cognitive development in, 291–293, 292f, 293f
Birth process. See Childbirth
Birth weight
low, 114–115
maternal nutrition and, 92
maternal stress and, 89
in United States, 111
Bodily-kinesthetic intelligence, 421t
Body cells, 60
Body mass index (BMI), 392–393
Body proportions, changes in, 162–163, 163f, 272–273, 273f
Bonobos, moral behavior in, 227
Bottom-up processing, 440

Boy Scouts/Girl Scouts, 596
Brain
imaging of, 33
brain development and, 399f, 399–400
physical activity and, 414
intersubjectivity and, 205–207, 206f
language and, 239–241, 240f, 241f
Brain activity
dyslexia and, 446, 447f
measurement of, 3
in middle childhood, 398, 398f
Brain development
in adolescence, 517f, 517–520
behavior and, 519–520
cerebral cortex changes and, 517–518, 518f
limbic system changes and, 518–519
in early childhood, 276–277, 277f
fetal, maternal nutrition and, 93
in infancy, 126–130, 165–168
behavior and, 165–166
brain structure and, 127–128, 128f
experience and, 128–130, 129f, 166–168
neurons and neuronal networks and, 126f, 126–127, 127f
intelligence and, 399
in middle childhood, 398f, 398–400, 399f
Brain stem, 127, 128f
Brainy-baby movement, 167
Brazelton Neonatal Assessment Scale, 112–113
Brazil
air pollution in, prenatal development and, 103
school readiness in, 435–436, 436f
Breakdancing, 581
Breeding, cooperative, 347
Broca's aphasia, 239
Broca's area, 239, 240, 240f, 242
Bubble blowing, 145
Bulimia nervosa, 590, 591t
Bullying, 482–483
cyberbullying, 551
Burundi, war orphans in, 343, 344

Caffeine, as teratogen, 96
Cambodia, cultural style of, 458–459
Cameroon, child-rearing practices in, 174
Canada. *See also specific cultural groups*
  bilingualism in, 245
  cooperation and competition among peers in, 487–489, 488f
  intersubjectivity in, 204
  premature births in, 114
  teenage pregnancy in, 569
Canterbury Tales (Chaucer), 508
Capture error, 184
Caregivers. *See also* Child care; Fathers; Mother(s); Parent(s)
  attachment to. *See* Attachment
  signs of interest in, infant following of, 222
Caribbean families, 347
Carriers, 62
Categorizing, in infancy, 190–192, 190f–192f
Causation, correlation compared with, 36
Cause-effect relationships, in infancy, 190
Central nervous system (CNS). *See also entries beginning with term* Brain
  structure of, 127–128, 128f
Centration, 279–284, 401
  distinction between appearance and reality and, 280–282, 281f
  egocentrism and, 279–280, 280f
  precausal reasoning and, 282–284, 283f, 284f
Centuries of Childhood (Ariès), 6
Cephalocaudal development, 84
Cerebral cortex, 128, 128f
  in adolescence, 517–518, 518f
  behavior and, 165–166
Cesarean delivery, 108–110
Chaotic activity, neighborhoods and, 371
Chewa people, definition of intelligence by, 419
Chewong people, language of, 297
Chicken pox, maternal, prenatal development and, 100t

Child care, 364–369
  child-care centers for, 366, 366t
  developmental effects of, 367–369
  family, 365–366
  home, 365
Child labor, 7
Child life specialists, 325
Childbirth, 104–111
  cultural variations in, 106–107
  stages of labor and, 105f, 105–106
  in United States, 104, 107–111
    baby's experience of birth and, 110–111
    medical interventions and, 108–110
    pain and medication and, 108
Child-care centers, 366, 366t
Child-rearing, poverty and, 359–360
Children
  historical beliefs about, 5–7, 6f
  in workforce, 7
Chimpanzees
  language in, 238–239
  tool use among, 24
China
  air pollution in, prenatal development and, 103
  board games in, 405
  emotional development in, 328, 329f
  group focus in, 305
  infant sleeping arrangements in, 151
  intersubjectivity in, 204
  mathematics achievement in, 456
  memory span in middle childhood in, 410
  moral development in, 478
  parents and peer relationships in, 498
  sex-role identity in, 310
  social smiling in, 203
  temperament in, 150
  toilet training in, 176
Chlamydia, 594, 594f
Chorion, 82, 83f
Chromosomes, 59
  sex, 61–62, 62f
Chronic model of divorce, 499–500
Chronic sleep deprivation, in adolescence, 528

Chronology, 259
Chumships, 493
Classical conditioning
  developing action and, 146–147, 147f
  toilet training and, 176
Classification, in concrete operational stage, 404
Classrooms. *See* Education; Instruction; School(s)
"Clear-cut attachment" phase of attachment, 210
Cleavage, in germinal period, 81f, 81–82
Cleft lip and palate, 249
Clinical interviews, 32t, 35, 37
Cliques, in adolescence, 559f, 559–560
Cocaine, teratogenic effects of, 98
Co-construction, 72, 306
Codominance, 62, 63f
Coercive family interaction patterns, 498
Coevolution, of culture and biology, 73–75
Cognitions, aggression and, 331–335, 334f
Cognitive development
  in adolescence, 530–539
    information-processing approaches to, 536–537
    Piaget's theory of, 530–536, 531t
    sociocultural approaches to, 537–539, 539f
  child care and, 367–368
  in early childhood, 277–301
    culture and, 298–301
    information-processing approaches to, 285f, 285–288
    preoperational, 277–285, 278t
    in privileged domains, 288–298
    guide to discussions of, A–5
  in infancy, 177–181
    sensorimotor development and, 178t, 178–181
  in middle childhood, 400–425
    individual differences in, 419–425
    information-processing approaches to, 409–414
    Piaget's theory of, 400–409, 401f
    social and cultural contexts and, 414–418

Piaget's theory of, 19–21, 20t, 23t
Cognitive theories, of language development, 264–267
Cognitive-behavioral therapy (CBT), 590
Cognitive-developmental theory
  of moral development in early childhood, 318–319
  of sex-role identity development, 308t, 310–311
Cohort(s), 39
Cohort sequential research design, 38t, 40–41, 41f
Collective monologues, 265
Collectivist cultural style
  education and, 455, 455t, 457–459, 459f
  identity and, 584
Color perception, in infancy, 135
Columbine shooting, 482
Commitment
  friendship and, 557
  identity formation and, 575
Communal goals, friendship and, 559
Communication. *See also* Language; Language development; Speech
  in infancy, 221–224
    beginnings of language comprehension and speech and, 223–224
    caregiver's signs of interest and, 222
    social referencing and, 222
  symbolic, 54–55
Communities, 369–371
  culture and, 369–370
  distressed, 370–371
  ethnic identity formation and, 579–580
  neighborhood physical disorder and, 371
  university-community partnerships and, 30–31
Compensation, conservation of volume and, 404
Competence
  sense of, development in middle childhood, 466
  socioemotional, 328
Competition, among peers, 485–489
  context and, 486–487
  culture and, 487–489, 488f

Conceptual development, in infancy, 181–192
  categorizing and, 190–192, 190f–192f
  cause-effect relationships and, 190
  counting and, 189f, 189–190
  object permanence and, 181–187, 182f, 183f
  understanding properties of physical world and, 187–188, 188f
Conceptual thinking, 177
Concrete individualistic social perspective, 476
Concrete operation(s), 401, 402t, 530
Concrete operational stage, 20t, 145t, 278, 400–409, 401f, 402t, 531t
  classification in, 404
  conservation in, 402–404, 403f
  limitations of concrete operations and, 408, 409f
  metacognition in, 406–408, 407t, 408f
  planning in, 405f, 405–406, 406f
Conditional response (CR), 146
Conditional stimulus (CS), 146
Conditioning
  classical, developing action and, 146–147, 147f
  operant, 19
    developing action and, 147f, 147–148
Confidentiality, in research, 42
Conflict
  parent-child, in adolescence, 570–571
  resolution of, friendships and, 494
  sociocognitive, 533–536
    post-formal-operational thinking and, 534–536
    variability in formal-operational thinking and, 534
Conformity, in adolescence, 560–562
  deviance and, 561–562
  selection and socialization and, 561
Congenital adrenal hyperplasia (CAH), 85
Consent, informed, 42
Conservation, 402–404
  culture and, 415–417, 416f

of number, 402–403, 403f
of volume, 403f, 403–404
Constraining interactions, in families, 572
Constructivist theory, 19–21, 20t, 23t. See also Piaget's theory
Contexts
  cooperation and competition among peers and, 486–487
  cultural. See Culture
  of development, 4, 343–385. See also Child care; Communities; Families; Media
    risk and resilience and, 380–382, 381f, 382t, 383t
  of learning, 431–433, 432t
Continuity/discontinuity, 10, 12f, 12–13
Control group, 34
Control processes, in early childhood, 286–287
Controversial children, 485
Conventional moral reasoning, 473–474, 476t, 477, 540t, 540–541
Conversational acts, 258–259
Cooing, 237
Cooley's anemia, 64t
Cooperation, among peers, 485–489
  context and, 486–487
  culture and, 487–489, 488f
Cooperative breeding, 347
Cooperative learning programs, 486
Coregulation, 497
Correlation, causation compared with, 36
Correlation coefficient, 36
Cortisol, maternal stress and, 89
Co-sleeping, 151
Costa Rica, cooperation and competition among peers in, 487–489, 488f
Côte d'Ivoire, sensorimotor development in, 180
Counting, in infancy, 189f, 189–190
Crawling, 171–172, 172f
Crawling reflex, 141t
Creative intelligence, 422
Creeping, 171–172, 172f
Crisis model of divorce, 499
Critical periods, 11

Cross-sectional research design, 38t, 39f, 39–40
Crowds, in adolescence, 560
Crying
  gender differences in, 556
  in infancy, 155–157, 156f
Cuba, cooperation and competition among peers in, 487–489, 488f
Cultural beliefs, about pregnancy, 79
Cultural bias, intelligence tests and, 424–425
Cultural context, unevenness of development and, 300–301
Cultural evolution, cumulative, 55–56
Cultural modeling, 260
Cultural scripts, 298–300
Cultural style
  education and, 455, 455t, 457–459, 459f
  identity and, 584
Cultural tools, 52–54, 53t
  material, 53
  symbolic, 53–54
Culture. See also Sociocultural theory; entries beginning with term Ethnic; specific cultural groups
  aggression and, 332
  attachment and, 218–220, 219f
  basic emotions and, 201
  coevolution of biology and, 73–75
  cognitive development and
    in early childhood, 298–301
    in middle childhood, 414–418
  complexity of, 55–56
  cooperation and competition among peers and, 487–489, 488f
  definition of, 52
  domain-specific cognitive development and, 297–298
  emotional regulation and, 328, 329f
  families and, 346, 346f
  family and school readiness and, 435–436, 436f
  guide to discussions of, A–4
  identity formation and, 583–585
  infant sleep/wake cycle and, 152–153

inheritance of, 51f, 51–56
  complexity of culture and, 55–56
  cultural tools and, 52–54, 53t
  special process of, 54
  symbols and language and, 54–55, 55f
intelligence tests and, 424–425
memory strategies and, 417–418
moral development in adolescence and, 544f, 544–546
parent-child relationships in adolescence and, 571
planning and, 418, 418f
sex-role identity development and, 308t, 312–313
sociocultural theory and, 21–22, 23t
"Culture-free" tests, 425
Culture-sensitive instruction, 460–461
Cumulative cultural evolution, 55–56
Cyberbullying, 551
Cystic fibrosis, 64t
Cytomegalovirus infection, maternal, prenatal development and, 100t

Data collection methods, 32t, 32–35, 37
  clinical interviews, 32t, 35, 37
  experiments, 32t, 34–35
  naturalistic observation, 32t, 33–34
Deafness, language development and, 224, 242–244
Death
  of children, historical records of, 6
  due to AIDS, 429
  fetal, maternal nutrition and, 92
  in infancy, 151, 154–155, 175
  SIDS and, 154–155, 175
  suicide among Native American adolescents and, 588–589
Decentration, 279, 337, 401
Decision making, adolescent, 536
Decoding text, 434
Deferred imitation, 180
Delayed transmission, 204
Delinquency, 591–593, 593f

Dendrites, 126, 126f
Denmark, infant crying in, 156
Dependent variable, 34
Depressed mood, 587
Depression, in adolescence, 585–590, 586f, 587t
Depressive disorder, 587
Detachment, 208
Development
  of brain. *See* Brain development
  cephalocaudal, 84
  cognitive. *See* Cognitive development
  conceptual. *See* Conceptual development
  contexts of, 4
  continuity/discontinuity and, 10, 12f, 12–13
  critical periods in, 11
  domains of, 3–4
  ego, 18
  emotional. *See specific entries beginning with term* Emotion
  of feeding behavior, 142
  identity. *See* Identity development
  individual differences and, 10, 14
  intellectual. *See* Cognitive development
  language. *See* Language development
  moral. *See* Moral development
  motor. *See* Motor development
  periods of, 3
  plasticity and, 10–11
  prenatal. *See* Pregnancy; Prenatal development
  proximodistal, 84
  sensory. *See* Sensory development
  sexual, 514–517
    primary sex characteristics and, 514–515
    secondary sex characteristics and, 515f, 515–517, 516t
  sources of, 10
  theories of. *See* Theories
Developmental research. *See* Research
Developmental science, 2–14
  central issues of, 10–14
  cultural and and historical forces shaping, 4–9

emergence of, 7–9, 8f, 9t
  interdisciplinary nature of, 2
  international nature of, 2
Developmental stages, 8, 12f, 12–13
Developmentalists, 3
Deviance, conformity and, 561–562
Deviancy training, 561–562
Diabetes, maternal, prenatal development and, 93, 100t
Diaper Free! The Gentle Wisdom on Natural Infant Hygiene (Bauer), 176
Diaper-free movement, 175, 176
Diaries, 576
Diet. *See* Nutrition
Differential emotions theory, 202f, 202–203
Differential reinforcement, 310
Differentiated language hypothesis, 244–245
Differentiation, of primary circular reactions, 145
Difficult babies, 148
Dishabituation, 132
Disorganized attachment, 211, 212
Display rules, 327–328
Distractibility, temperament and, 148
Distress, personal, 337–338
Distressed communities, 370–371
  economic disadvantage and, 370–371
  physical and social disorder and, 371
Distressed families, 358–364
  abuse and, 361–363, 362t
  affluence and, 363–364
  poverty and, 358–360, 359f
  teen mothers and, 360t, 360–361, 361f
Divorce, 499–500
Divorce-stress-adjustment perspective, 500
Dizygotic (DZ) twins, 61, 70
  depression in, 587
  growth patterns of, 391
DNA (deoxyribonucleic acid), 59, 59f
Domains of development, 3–4
Domain-specific cognitive development
  in biology, 291–293, 292f, 293f
  explanations for, 293–298

in physics, 289f, 289–290
  in psychology, 290–291
Dominant alleles, 62
Dominant children, 481
Dominican people, ethnic identity among, 315
Down syndrome, 64t, 65–66, 66f
  development in, 68
Drive(s), biological, 208
Drive reduction, attachment and, 208, 208f
Drugs
  for childbirth pain, 108
  as teratogens, 96–99
Dual-language learners (DLLs), 244–245
Duchenne muscular dystrophy, 64t
Dynamic systems approach, 186
Dynamic systems theory, 27, 142
Dyscalculia, 446
Dysgraphia, 446
Dyslexia, 446–447, 447f
Dysphagia, functional, 591

Early childhood, 235–269, 271–303, 305–341
  aggression in, 329–335
    causes and controls of, 331–335
    development of, 329–331, 330f, 331t
  brain development in, 276–277, 277f
  changing body proportions in, 272–273, 273f
  child care and, 364–369
    child-care centers for, 366, 366t
    developmental effects of, 367–369
    family, 365–366
    home, 365
  cognitive development in, 277–301
    culture and, 298–301
    information-processing approaches to, 285f, 285–288
    preoperational, 277–285, 278t
    in privileged domains, 288–298
  health in, 274–276
  identity development in, 306–317
    ethnic identity and, 313–315

personal identity and, 315–317
  sex-role identity and, 307t, 307–313, 308f, 308t
  language development in. *See* Language development
  moral development in, 317–320
    cognitive-developmental view of, 318–319
    psychodynamic view of, 318, 471–472
    social domain view of, 319t, 319–320
  motor development in, 273t, 273–274
  nutrition in, 274–276, 275f, 275t
  prosocial behavior in, 336–338
    empathy and, 336–337
    sympathy and, 337–338
  self-regulation in, 320–329
    of emotions, 326–329
    play and, 322–326
    of thought and action, 321–322
  sleep in, 274
  social groups in, 338–339
  truthfulness in, 286
Early maturation, 522, 523–524
Easy babies, 148
Eating disorder(s), 590–591, 591t
Eating disorder not otherwise specified (EDNOS), 590
Ecological inheritance, 72
Ecological niches, 498
Ecological systems theory, 27–29, 29f
Ecological validity, 35, 553
Ectoderm, 83, 83f
Education. *See also* Instruction; School(s)
  access to, 430, 454
  adolescence and, 508, 509
  cognitive consequences of, 449–454
  diversity and, 454–461, 455t
    culturally responsive classroom strategies and, 460–461
    culture of school and, 455, 455t, 457–459, 459f
    language and, 459–460
    mathematics achievement and, 456–457
  formal, 431. *See also* School(s)
  industrialization and, 7

Education (continued)
  research strategies for studying
      cognitive consequences of
      for assessing second-
      generation impact of
      schooling, 453–454
    for comparing schooled and
      nonschooled children,
      450–453
    school-cutoff strategy,
      449–450
EEG coherence, in middle
    childhood, 398
Efe people, child-rearing
    methods of, 33–34
Effortful control, 321
  temperament and, 149, 149t
Ego, 17, 318
Ego development, 18
Egocentric empathy, 336
Egocentrism
  in early childhood, 279–280,
      280f
  language development and,
      265
Elaboration, in middle
    childhood, 412
Elaborative style, in early
    childhood, 288
Electra complex, 309
Electroencephalography (EEG),
    131–132
  EEG coherence in middle
      childhood and, 398
Elimination, control of,
    175–177
Embryonic period, 81, 82–85
  embryonic growth during,
      83f, 83–84, 84t
  nutrition and protection
      during, 82–83, 83f
  sexual differentiation during,
      85
Emergent literacy, 433–434
Emergent numeracy, 433–434
Emerging adulthood, 509
Emotion(s)
  aggression and, 331–335, 334f
  basic, 201–203
  definition of, 200
  experience of, in adolescence,
      553f, 553–554
  ontogenetic adaptations, 203
  self-conscious, emergence of,
      226, 228
Emotion regulation, 201
  in adolescence, 554–557
    biological processes in,
      554f, 554–555, 555f

social processes in, 555–
      557, 556f
  in early childhood, 326–329
    culture and, 328, 329f
    emotional expression and,
      327–328
    feelings and, 326–327
    to maintain intersubjectivity,
      205
Emotional development
  in adolescence, 552–557
    emotional problems and,
      585–593
    experience of emotions
      and, 553f, 553–554
    regulating emotions and,
      554–557
  child care and, 368
  guide to discussions of, A–3
  in infancy, 200–221, 201f
    infant-caregiver relationship
      and. See Attachment;
      Infant-caregiver
      relationship
    intersubjectivity and brain
      and, 205–207, 206f
    social life and, 203–205
    theories of, 201–203
Emotional expression
  controlling, 327–328
  discontinuity of, 202
Emotional health, in
    adolescence, 585–593
  delinquency and other
      externalizing problems
      and, 585, 591–593, 593f
  depression and anxiety and,
      585–590, 586f, 587t
  eating disorders and, 590–
      591, 591t
  suicide among Native
      Americans and, 588–589
Emotional tone, 585–587
Empathy, in early childhood,
    336–337
Enabling interactions, in
    families, 572
Endocrine system, 520–521
Endoderm, 83, 83f
Endogenous scanning, in
    infancy, 134
Endogenous smiles, 203
England. See also United
    Kingdom
  adolescent friendship in,
      558
  display rules in, 327
  emotion regulation in
      adolescence in, 556–557

infant crying in, 156
  orphanage care in, 216–217
Entity model of intelligence,
    448
Environmental deprivation
  language development and,
      242–244
  in orphanages, 166, 168
Environmental factors
  depression and, 587
  language development and,
      241–247
  nature and nurture and, 10
  timing of puberty and, 524–
      526, 525f, 526t
Environmental hypothesis of
    intelligence, 422–424
Environmental teratogens,
    102–103
Epigenesis, 84
Epistemic development, 534
Equality, friendship and, 557
Equilibration, in Piaget's
    theory, 21
Erikson's psychodynamic
    theory, 17t, 18, 23t
  autonomy versus shame and
      doubt stage in, 17t, 229,
      306
  generativity versus stagnation
      stage in, 17t
  identity versus role confusion
      stage in, 17t, 575
  industry versus inferiority
      stage in, 17t, 466
  initiative versus guilt stage in,
      17t, 306–307
  integrity versus despair stage
      in, 17t
  intimacy versus isolation stage
      in, 17t
  trust versus mistrust stage in,
      17t, 228–229
Estradiol, 521
Estrogen, 514
Ethical standards, for research,
    42–43
Ethnic identity, 313–315
  formation of, 578–581
    family and community
      influences on, 579–
      580
    peer culture and, 580–581
    stages of, 578–579
Ethnic socialization, 314–315
Ethnicity. See also specific groups
  face perception in infancy
      and, 137
  family diversity and, 354–355

intelligence and, 422–424,
      423f, 424f
  SIDS and, 155
Ethnography, 33–34
Ethological theory, of
    attachment, 208–209, 209f
Ethology, 23, 25
  infant-parent attachment and,
      116
European Americans
  conservation in middle
      childhood among, 416
  ethnic identity and, 314
  families of, 344–345, 355
  infant sleeping arrangements
      among, 151
  language and school success
      and, 459–460
  maternal nutrition and
      prenatal development
      among, 91
  parenting and self-esteem and,
      470
  phenylketonuria in, 65
  planning in middle childhood
      among, 418, 418f
  puberty in, 522t, 522–523,
      524, 525
  romantic relationships in
      adolescence and, 564
  SIDS among, 155
  teenage pregnancy among,
      569
  temperament among, 148
Evaluativist theory of
    knowledge, 536
Evolution
  cultural, cumulative, 55–56
  families and, 346–347
  natural selection and, 58–59
Evolutionary theories, 23, 25, 25f
Executive function, 517
  in middle childhood, 413–
      414, 414f
Exogenous scanning, in infancy,
    134–135
Exosystem, 28, 28f, 343–344
Expectations
  parental, in middle childhood,
      496–497
  social, about newborns,
      116–117
Experience
  brain development in infancy
      and, 166–168
  object permanence and, 186–
      187, 187f
Experience sampling method
    (ESM), 553

Experience-dependent brain development processes, 130, 165, 277, 400
Experience-expectant brain development processes, 128–129, 129f, 165
Experiment(s), 32t, 34–35
Experimental group, 34
Explicit instruction, 54
Explicit memory, 195
Exploration, identity formation and, 575
Extended families, 345–346
Externalizing problems, 585, 591–593, 593f
Extraversion, temperament and, 149, 149t
Exuberant synaptogenesis, 129, 166
Eye movements, in infancy, 134–135
Eyeblink reflex, 140, 141t

Face perception, in infancy, 136f, 136–137
Facebook, 576
Factories Inquiries Committee (England), 7
False-belief task, 290–291
Families, 344–364. See also Fathers; Mother(s); Parent(s); Siblings
  attachment patterns and, 214
  biocultural origins of, 345–347
  culture and, 346, 346f
  distressed, 358–364
  emotion regulation and, 555
  evolution and, 346–347
  extended, 345–346
  gay and lesbian, 357–358
  identity formation and, 579–580
  immigrant, 353–356, 355f. See also specific groups
  nuclear, 345
  parenting practices and, 347–350
  school readiness and, 435–436, 436f
  siblings and, 351–353, 352f, 353f
  single-parent, 356–357
Family child care, 365–366
Family structure, 345
Family studies, 69–70
Famine, prenatal development and, 91–92
Fantasy play, 180

Fantasy role play, 472
Fast mapping, 254
Fathers, 354
  attachment to, 213
Feeding behavior
  development of, 142
  in infancy, 153–155
Feelings. See also Emotion(s)
  controlling, 326–327
Females. See also Gender; Mother(s); Pregnancy; entries beginning with term Sex or Sexual
  congenital adrenal hyperplasia in, 85
  sexual differentiation and, 85
  X chromosomes and, 61–62, 62f
  Y chromosomes and, disorders of, 64t, 66, 68
Female-style play, 489
Fetal alcohol syndrome, 97
Fetal period, 81, 85f, 85–89
  fetal activity during, 87, 87t, 88f, 89
  fetal learning during, 88f, 88–89
  sensory capabilities during, 86–87
Fetus, 85f
Fifth Dimension, 444–445
Figurative language, 254–255
Fiji, moral behavior in, 227
Fine motor skills
  in early childhood, 273t, 273–274
  in infancy, 168–171, 169f
    manual dexterity and, 170f, 170–171
    reaching and grasping and, 169f, 169–170, 170f
Finland
  instructional methods in, 443
  overweight in, 275
Flynn effect, 423
Folate, puberty and, 526
Fontanels, 125–126
Food insecurity, 275, 359
Foreclosure, 575–576
Formal education. See also Education; School(s)
  apprenticeship compared with, 431–433
Formal operational stage, 20t, 145t, 278, 402t, 530–536, 531t
  sociocognitive conflict and post-formal-operational thinking and, 534–536

variability in formal-operational thinking and, 534
Formats, language development and, 263–264
4-H, 596
France
  childbirth in, 107
  cultural rituals of, 51
  intersubjectivity in, 204
  overweight in, 274–275
Fraternal twins, 61, 70
  depression in, 587
  growth patterns of, 391
Free recall, 411
Freedom from harm, 42
Freudian theory, 16–18, 17t
  of adolescent development, 511
  of attachment, 208, 208f
  of moral development in early childhood, 318, 471–472
  of sex-role identity development, 308t, 308–309
Friends with benefits, 563
Friendship(s)
  in adolescence, 557–559
    developmental functions of, 558
    friends with benefits and, 563
    gender and, 558–559
  in middle childhood, 493–496
    cognitive-developmental approach to, 495–496
    forming, 493–494
    maintaining, 494–495
Friendship skills, 495
Friendship understanding, 495
Friendship valuing, 495–496
Frontal lobes, 128, 128f
Functional dysphagia, 591

Gambian families, 347
Games
  development of reasoning skills and, 538–539
  rule-based, moral development and, 472–473
Gangs, 561
Gay families, 357–358
Gay males, 558–559
Gender. See also entries beginning with term Sex or Sexual
  aggression and, 483
  crying and, in adolescence, 556

emotion regulation and, 556
  friendship and, in adolescence, 558–559
  motor development and, in middle childhood, 396, 397f
  peer relationships and, in middle childhood, 489f, 489–492, 492t
Gender schema theory, of sex-role identity development, 308t, 311–312, 312f
Gender segregation, 351
  aggression and, 330
Gene(s), 57
Gene pool, 63
Generativity versus stagnation, 17t
Genetic disorders, 63, 64t, 65–68
  in Plain People, 67
Genetics
  depression and, 587
  ecological inheritance and, 72
  genotype and, 57, 59, 71–72
  heritability and, 69–71
    estimating, 69
    studying, 69–71, 70t
  inheritance through sexual reproduction and, 59f, 59–62
  laws of genetic inheritance and, 62–63, 63f
  mutations and genetic abnormalities and, 63, 64t, 65–68
  natural selection and, 58–59
  nature and nurture and, 10
  niche construction and, 71–72
  phenotype and, 57–58, 68f, 68–69, 71–72
  timing of puberty and, 523
Genital herpes, prenatal development and, 100t
Genital stage, 17t, 511
Genotype, 57, 59, 71–72
Germ cells, 60–61, 61f
Germany
  child care in, 368
  infant sleeping arrangements in, 151
  parenting style in, 350
Germinal period, 81f, 81–82
  cleavage in, 81f, 81–82
  implantation in, 82
Gestational age, 93
Ghana, education in, 430

Gilligan's theory of moral reasoning, 542–543
Global empathy, 336
Globalization, nutrition and, 275
Goals
   agentic, friendship and, 559
   communal, friendship and, 559
God, children's ideas about, 474–475
Gonad(s), 85, 512, 521
Gonadal ridges, 85
Gonadotropin-releasing hormone (GnRH), 521
Gonorrhea, maternal, prenatal development and, 100t
Good-child morality, 540t, 541
Grammar development, 236, 247, 255–257
   meaning and, 255f, 255–256
Grammatical morphemes, 256–257
Graphemes, 434
Grasping, in infancy, 169f, 170, 170f
Grasping reflex, 141t
Gray matter, 127, 518
Greenland, toilet training in, 176
Gross motor skills
   in early childhood, 273, 273t
   in infancy, 168, 171f, 171–174
      creeping and crawling and, 171–172, 172f
      walking and, 172–174, 173f
Growth. See also Height; Weight
   in adolescence, 511–514, 512f
   of brain, in infancy, 127, 127f
   embryonic, 83f, 83–84, 84t
   in infancy, 124–125, 124–126, 125f, 162f, 162–164
   measuring, 124–125, 125f
   musculoskeletal, 164
   size and shape and, 162–164, 163f, 164f
   of skull, 125–126
   in middle childhood, 390–393, 391f, 391–393
Growth charts, 124, 125f
Growth plates, 273, 273f
Growth spurt, of puberty, 511–514, 512f
Gusii people, families of, 344–345, 351

Habitat
   existing, changes to, 72
   selection of, 72
Habituation, 132, 146
Hall's theory of adolescent development, 510–511
Harm, freedom from, 42
Hazara people, prosocial behavior among, 336
Head Start program, 437–438, 439
Health
   in early childhood, 274–276
      nutrition and, 274–276, 275f, 276t
      sleep and, 274
   emotional, in adolescence, 585–593
      delinquency and other externalizing problems and, 585, 591–593, 593f
      depression and anxiety and, 585–590, 586f, 587t
      eating disorders and, 590–591, 591t
      suicide among Native Americans and, 588–589
   genetic disorders and, 63, 64t, 67
   HIV/AIDS and
      in adolescence, 595, 595f
      children orphaned by, 429
      teaching children about, 566
      teratogenic effects of, 100–101, 101f
   maternal, prenatal development and, 99–104, 100t
   mental, 359
   poverty and, 359
   puberty and, 526–530
   sexual, in adolescence, 593–595
   teratogens and, 94–103, 95f, 96f
      drugs as, 96–99
      environmental, 102–103
      infections as, 99–101
      Rh incompatibility as, 101–102
Hearing
   fetal, 86–87
   in infancy, 132f, 132–133, 133f
Height
   in infancy, 162–164, 163f, 164f
   in middle childhood, 391–392

"Heinz dilemma," 474–475
Hemophilia, 64t
Hepatitis, maternal, prenatal development and, 100t
Heredity, 57
Heritability, 69–71
   estimating, 69
   studying, 69–71, 70t
Heroin, teratogenic effects of, 99
Heterochrony, 82
Heterogeneity, 82
Heteronomous morality, 319, 472, 475, 540t
Heterozygosity, 62
Hip-hop culture, 580–581
Hippocampus, 518
Hispanic Americans
   child-centered speech among, 246
   chlamydia among, 594, 594f
   ethnic identity among, 580
   families of, 356, 357
   HIV/AIDS in, 595, 595f
   maternal nutrition and prenatal development among, 91
   parenting and self-esteem and, 470–471
   preschool enrollment among, 439
   puberty in, 524, 525
   SIDS among, 155
   teaching children about HIV/AIDS and, 566
   teenage pregnancy among, 569
   theory theory and, 295, 297
HIV/AIDS
   in adolescence, 595, 595f
   children orphaned by, 429
   teaching children about, 566
   teratogenic effects of, 100–101, 101f
Hmong people, beliefs about pregnancy among, 79
Holland, childbirth in, 107
Home child care, 365
Home signing, 242
Homophily, in adolescence, 560–562
   deviance and, 561–562
   selection and socialization and, 561
Homophobia, 558–559
Homozygosity, 62
Hooking up, 563
Hopi people, child-rearing practices of, 174

Hormones
   maternal stress and, 89
   in puberty, 512, 514, 521, 521f
      brain development and, 519–520
   sexual differentiation and, 85
Hostile aggression, 329, 330
Hull House, 508–509
Human immunodeficiency virus (HIV)
   in adolescence, 595, 595f
   children orphaned by, 429
   teaching children about, 566
   teratogenic effects of, 100–101, 101f
Human papillomavirus (HPV), 594–595
Hypertension, maternal, prenatal development and, 100t
Hypothalamic-pituitary-gonadal (HPG) axis, 520f, 520–522, 521f
Hypothalamus, 518, 520
Hypotheses, 29
Hypothetical-deductive reasoning, 533

Id, 17, 318
Ideal self, actual self compared with, 469
Identical twins, 61, 70
   depression in, 587
   development of, 82
   growth patterns of, 391
Identification, 307
Identity, conservation of volume and, 404
Identity achievement, 575
Identity development, 573–585
   culture and, 583–585
   in early childhood, 306–317
      ethnic identity and, 313–315
      personal identity and, 315–317
      sex-role identity and, 307t, 307–313, 308f, 308t
   ethnic identity and, 578–581
   family and community influences on, 579–580
   peer culture and, 580–581
   stages of formation of, 578–579
   I-self and me-self and, 574
   mature identity and, 574–578, 575f, 578f

sex-role. *See* Sex-role identity development
sexual identity and, 581–583, 583t
Identity diffusion, 577
Identity formation, oppositional, 579
Identity versus role confusion stage, 17t, 575
Ifaluk people, transition to middle childhood in, 390
Illness. *See also* Health; *specific illnesses*
chronic, coping with through play, 324–325
Imitation, 54, 146
deferred, 180
Immigrant families, 353–356, 355f. *See also specific groups*
increased diversity of, 454–455, 455t
preschool enrollment among, 438–439
Implantation, 82
Implicit memory, 195
Imprinting, 11, 23, 25
Impulse control, 554
Inclusion, relation of, 404
Incremental model of intelligence, 448
Independent cultural style, education and, 455, 455t, 457–459, 459f
Independent sense of self, 584
Independent variable, 34
India
access to technology in, 379
adolescent friendship in, 558
board games in, 405
display rules in, 327–328
emotion regulation in adolescence in, 556–557
moral development in, 545–546
parenting style in, 350
toilet training in, 176
Individual differences, 10, 14
in cognitive development, in middle childhood, 419–425
Individualist cultural style
education and, 455, 455t, 457–459, 459f
identity and, 584
Indonesia, sex-role identity in, 312
Industrialization
adolescence and, 508, 509
beliefs about children and, 7

Industrialized countries. *See also specific countries*
childbirth in, 107
Industry versus inferiority stage, 17t, 466
Infancy, 123–159, 161–197, 199–231. *See also* Newborn(s)
arousal states in, 152, 152t
attachment in. *See* Attachment
attention in, 193f, 193–194, 194f
brain development in, 126–130, 165–168
behavior and, 165–166
brain structure and, 127–128, 128f
experience and, 128–130, 129f, 166–168
neurons and neuronal networks and, 126f, 126–127, 127f
cognitive development in, 177–181
sensorimotor development and, 178t, 178–181
communication in, 221–224
beginnings of language comprehension and speech and, 223–224
caregiver's signs of interest and, 222
social referencing and, 222
conceptual development in, 181–192
categorizing and, 190–192, 190f–192f
cause-effect relationships and, 190
counting and, 189f, 189–190
object permanence and, 181–187, 182f, 183f
understanding properties of physical world and, 187–188, 188f
crying in, 155–157, 156f
death in, 151, 154–155, 175
emotional development in, 200–221, 201f
attachment and. *See* Attachment
intersubjectivity and brain and, 205–207, 206f
social life and, 203–205
theories of, 201–203
feeding in, 153–155

hearing in, 132f, 132–133, 133f
memory development in, 194–195, 195f
moral behavior in, 227
motor development in, 168–177
control of elimination and, 175–177
of fine motor skills, 168–171, 169f
of gross motor skills, 168, 171f, 171–174
practice and, 174–175
organization of behavior in, 140–148
coordinated action and, 141–142, 142f, 144
learning theories of, 146–148
Piaget's theory of, 144–146, 145t
reaching and, 144
reflexes and, 140–141, 141t
physical growth in, 124–126, 162f, 162–164
measuring, 124–125, 125f
musculoskeletal, 164
size and shape and, 162–164, 163f, 164f
of skull, 125–126
prematurity and. *See* Premature infants
reaching in, 144
reflexes in, 140–141, 141t
self in, 224–228
sensory development in, 130–139, 139t
evaluation methods for, 131–132
of hearing, 132f, 132–133, 133f
of taste and smell senses, 137f, 137–138
of vision, 133–137
sleep in, 151–153, 152f, 152t
sleeping arrangements in, 151
smell sense in, 138
taste sense in, 137f, 137–138
temperament in, 148–150, 149t
unwanted infants and, 90
vision in, 133–137
color perception and, 135
face perception and, 136f, 136–137
pattern and object perception and, 135f, 135–136, 136f

visual acuity and, 134, 134f
visual scanning and, 134–135
Infant care, manuals on, 6–7
Infant growth restriction, 163–164
Infant-caregiver relationship, 207–221. *See also* Attachment
"Infant-directed speech," 132
Infant-directed speech, 245–246
Infections, as teratogens, 99–101
Influenza, maternal, prenatal development and, 100t
Information-processing theories, 26
of cognitive development, 285f, 285–288
in adolescence, 536–537
in middle childhood, 409–414
Informed consent, 42
in adolescence, 536
Inheritance
biological. *See* Genetics
cultural, 54–55
social processes of, 54
symbols and language and, 54–55
ecological, 72
Inhibition, emotion regulation and, 554
Initiative versus guilt stage, 17t, 306–307
Innatist hypothesis of intelligence, 422
Inner speech, 265–266
Institutional review boards (IRBs), 42
Instruction
by apprenticeship, 431
culture-sensitive, 460–461
medium of, apprenticeship versus formal instruction and, 432
playworld practice and, 443–444
realistic mathematics education and, 441–443
reciprocal teaching and, 440–441, 441f
Instructional design, classroom organization and, 439–444
Instructional discourse, 440
Instrumental aggression, 330
Instrumental morality, 475–477, 540t
Integration, of primary circular reactions, 145

Integrity versus despair stage, 17t
Intellectual development. *See* Cognitive development
Intelligence, 420–425
  brain development and, 399f, 399–400
  definition of, cultural variations in, 419
  entity model of, 448
  environmental hypothesis of, 422–424
  general, 421
  incremental model of, 448
  innatist hypothesis of, 422
  measurement of. *See* Intelligence tests
  multiple intelligences and, 421t, 421–422
  population differences in, 422–424, 423f, 424f
  sensorimotor, 177
Intelligence tests
  cultural bias and, 424–425
  historical background of, 9, 420
  IQ and, 420, 420f
Intensity of reaction, temperament and, 148
Intentionality, emergence of, 179
Interactive media, 378–380
  content of, 380
  form of, 378–380
Interdependent cultural style, education and, 455, 455t, 457–459, 459f
Interdependent sense of self, 584
Intermodal perception, 138–139, 139f
Internal working model, 210, 220
Internalization, 472
Internalizing problems, 585–591
International Communications and Negotiation project (ICONS), 535
Intersubjectivity
  primary, 203–207, 209, 237
    brain and, 205–207, 206f
    emotion regulation to maintain, 205
  secondary, 221–222, 237
    social referencing and, 222
Interviews, clinical, 32t, 35, 37
Intimacy
  in adolescence, 562–564
  friendship and, 558

Intimacy versus isolation stage, 17t
Intuitive physics, 289
Inuit people, childbirth and, 109
IQ scores, 420, 420f
I-self, 574
Islamic culture, romantic relationships in adolescence and, 564
Israel
  child rearing in *kibbutzim* in, 218–219
  moral development in, 545, 546t
Italy
  display rules in, 327
  infant sleeping arrangements in, 151

Japan
  household possessions in, 52
  infant sleeping arrangements in, 151
  interactive media in, 378–379
  material tools in, 53
  parental expectations in, 497
  phonemic distinction in, 133
  symbolic tools in, 53–54
Japanese macaque monkeys, cultural inheritance in, 51f, 51–52
Jargoning, 224, 237
Jewish culture
  moral development in, 545, 546t
  parent–child relationships and, 571
A Journey Toward Womanhood, 569
Juvenile Protective Association, 509

Kaguru people, learning about sex and, 566
Kaluli people, teaching of language among, 245
Kangaroo care, 34–35
Kenya
  school readiness in, 435–436, 436f
  toilet training in, 176
Kids Unlimited, 215
Kinship studies, 69, 71
Kipsigis people
  child-rearing practices of, 174
  infant sleep/wake behavior among, 152–153
Kisspeptin, 521, 521f

Klinefelter's syndrome, 64t, 66, 68
Knowledge base, expansion in middle childhood, 410–411
Kohlberg's theory of moral development
  in adolescence, 539–542, 540t, 541f, 544f, 544–545
  in middle childhood, 473–477, 476t
Korea
  infant sleeping arrangements in, 151
  mathematics achievement in, 456–457
  moral development in, 478
Kukatja people, transition to middle childhood in, 390
!Kung people
  attachment among, 213
  childbirth and, 104
  infant crying among, 156
  instruction among, 431
  number system of, 424–425
Kwashiorkor, 153

Labor. *See also* Childbirth
  induction of, 108
  stages of, 105f, 105–106
Lactose intolerance, evolution of, 73–74
Laetoli footprints, 49, 50, 75
Language
  in animals, 238–239
  brain and, 239–241, 240f, 241f
  domain-specific cognitive development and, 297
  education and, 459–460
  figurative, 254–255
  pidgin, 243
  power of, 236–237
  representation and, 180
Language acquisition device (LAD), 262
Language acquisition support system (LASS), 264
Language development, 235–269
  beginnings in infancy, 223–224
  bilingualism and multilingualism and, 244–245
  deafness and, 224
  domains of, 247–260
    grammar, 236, 247, 255–257

  phonological, 236, 247, 248, 250
  pragmatic, 236, 248, 257–260
  semantic, 236, 247, 250f, 250–255
  explanations of, 261–267
    biological, 262–263
    cognitive approaches and, 264–267
    social and cultural, 263–264
  guide to discussions of, A–3
  keys to, 238–247
    biological, 238–241
    environmental, 241–247
  mental retardation and, 366–367
  power of language and, 236–237
  progress of, 237t
The Language Instinct (Pinker), 262
Laotian people
  childbirth practices of, 80
  cultural style of, 458–459
Large for gestational age babies, 93
Late maturation, 522
Latin America, cooperation and competition among peers and, 487
Latinos/as. *See* Hispanic Americans
Law of effect, 19
Law-and-order morality, 540t, 541
Lead poisoning, 359
Learning, 146
  behaviorism and, 19
  contexts of, 431–433, 432t
  by explicit instruction, 54
  fetal, 88f, 88–89
  motivation to learn and, 447–448
  about sex, 565–567
  social learning theories and, 25–26
  by symbolic communication, 54–55
Learning disabilities, specific, 445–447, 447f
Learning theories, of developing action, 146–148
  classical conditioning and, 146–147, 147f
  operant conditioning and, 147f, 147–148
Lebanon, parental expectations in, 497

Length, fetal, 85f
Leptin, 521
Lesbian(s), 558–559
Lesbian families, 357–358
Let's Move! campaign, 394–395
Liberia, memory development in, 417, 418
Limbic system, in adolescence, 518–519
Linguistic intelligence, 421t
Lip, cleft, 249
Literacy, emergent, 433–434
Locomotion, 171. *See also* Crawling; Creeping; Walking
Logical thinking, in schooled versus nonschooled children, 451
Logical-mathematical intelligence, 421t
Longitudinal research design, 38t, 38–39
Long-term memory, in early childhood, 286–287
Low birth weight, 114–115 developmental consequences of, 114–115
Luo people, words for problem-solving abilities of, 419
Luteinizing hormone, brain development in adolescence and, 519–520

Macaque monkeys, cultural inheritance in, 51f, 51–52
Macrosystem, 28, 28f, 344
Magnetic resonance imaging (MRI), of brain, 33
Malaria, sickle-cell anemia and, 74–75
Malawi, infant growth in, 164
Malaysia, preschool in, 367
Males. *See also* Fathers; Gender; *entries beginning with term* Sex *or* Sexual
  gay, 357–358, 558–559
  sexual differentiation and, 85
  Y chromosomes and, 62, 62f
  disorders of, 64t, 66, 68
Male-style play, 489
Mali people, household possessions of, 52
Malnutrition, maternal, prenatal development and, 91–93, 94f
Manual dexterity, in infancy, 170f, 170–171
Marijuana, teratogenic effects of, 97–98, 98f

Mastery orientation, 447
Material tools, 53
Mathematics
  achievement in, cross-cultural comparison of, 456–457
  dyscalculia and, 446
  emergent numeracy and, 433–434
  precursors to learning, 434–435, 435f
  realistic mathematics education and, 441–443
Mayan people
  childbirth and, 107
  children's activities and, 33, 34
  conservation in middle childhood among, 415–416
  height in middle childhood among, 392
  infant sleeping arrangements among, 151
  language development among, 264
  memory development in, 418
  mothers' communication with infants among, 245
  teaching styles of, 453, 455, 457–458
Mbuti pygmy people, cultural rituals of, 51
Meaning, grammar and, 255f, 255–256
Media, 372, 373t, 374f, 374–380
  interactive, 378–380
    content of, 380
    form of, 378–380
  print, 374–375, 375f
  television, 375–378
    content of, 377–378
    form of, 376
Mediation, tools and, 54
Meiosis, 60–61, 61f
Memory
  autobiographical, 316–317
  development in infancy, 194–195, 195f
  explicit, 195
  implicit, 195
  in infancy, 194–195, 195f
  long-term, in early childhood, 286–287
  in middle childhood, 409–413
    expanded knowledge base and, 410–411
    improved memory strategies and, 411–412

metamemory and, 412–413
  speed and capacity of working memory and, 409–410, 410f
  object permanence and, 184
  in schooled versus nonschooled children, 451–452, 451f–452f
  short-term (working)
    in early childhood, 286–287
    increased speed and capacity in middle childhood, 409–410, 410f
Memory span, in middle childhood, 410
Memory strategies
  cultural variations in use of, 417–418
  in middle childhood, 411–412
Menarche, 515
Mennonites, genetic disorders among, 67
Mental health. *See also* Health, emotional
  poverty and, 359
Mental modules, 293
Mental operations, 278, 401
  conservation of volume and, 404
Mental retardation
  in Down syndrome, 65
  language development and, 366–367
  modularity theory and, 294
  in phenylketonuria, 65
Mercury, prenatal development and, 102
Me-self, 574
Mesoderm, 83, 83f
Mesosystem, 27–28, 28f, 343
Metacognition, in concrete operational stage, 406–408, 407t, 408f
Metacognitive skills, in schooled versus nonschooled children, 452–453
Metalinguistic skills, in schooled versus nonschooled children, 453
Metamemory, in middle childhood, 412–413
Metaphors, 254–255
Methadone, teratogenic effects of, 99
Methamphetamine, teratogenic effects of, 99
Methods of study, early focus on, 8

Mexican people. *See also* Hispanic Americans
  birthday celebrations of, 300
  infant sleeping arrangements and, 151
Micmac people, conservation in middle childhood among, 416
Microgenetic research design, 38t, 41–42
Microsystem, 27, 28f, 343
Middle childhood, 389–503
  brain development in, 398f, 398–400, 399f
  cognitive development in, 400–425
    individual differences in, 419–425
    information-processing approaches to, 409–414
    Piaget's theory of, 400–409, 401f
    social and cultural contexts and, 414–418
  executive function in, 413–414, 414f
  growth patterns in, 391f, 391–393
  increased control of attention in, 413, 413f
  moral development and. *See* Moral development
  motor development in, 393–397, 396f
    gender differences in, 396, 397f
    practice and, 396–397, 397f
  parent-child relationships in, 496–500
    changing expectations and, 496–497
    divorce and, 499–500
    peer relationships and, 498–499, 499f
  peer relationships and. *See* Peer relationships, in middle childhood
  school as context for development in. *See* School(s)
  social and emotional development in, 465–503
    moral development and. *See* Moral development
    peer relationships and. *See* Peer relationships, in middle childhood
    sense of self and, 466–471

Middle Eastern cultures, romantic relationships in adolescence and, 564
Middle Eastern nomads, lactose tolerance among, 74
Minamata disease, 102
Mirror neurons, 205–207
Miscarriage, maternal nutrition and, 92
Mission-oriented research, 30, 31
Mitosis, 60, 60f, 81
Modeling, 25, 310
 cultural, 260
Modularity theory, 293–295, 294f, 295f
Monozygotic (MZ) twins, 61, 70
 depression in, 587
 development of, 82
 growth patterns of, 391
Moral action, moral reasoning related to, 546–547
Moral development. See also Moral reasoning
 in adolescence, 539–547
  cultural variations in, 544f, 544–546
  Gilligan's theory of, 542–543
  Kohlberg's theory of, 539–542, 540t, 541f, 544f, 544–545
  moral action and moral reasoning and, 546–547
  parents and peers and, 543–544
 in early childhood, 317–320
  cognitive-developmental view of, 318–319
  psychodynamic view of, 318
  social domain view of, 319t, 319–320
 in middle childhood, 471–480
  Kohlberg's theory of, 473–477, 476t
  Piaget's theory of, 472–473
  prosocial moral reasoning and, 477–478
  social domain theory of, 478–479
  theories of mind and, 479–480
Moral reasoning. See also Moral development
 in adolescence, Kohlberg's theory of, 539–542, 540t, 541f, 544f, 544–545

conventional, 473–474, 476t, 477, 540t, 540–541
 Gilligan's theory of, 542–543
 Kohlberg's theory of, in adolescence, 539–542, 540t, 541f, 544f, 544–545
 moral action related to, 546–547
 postconventional, 473–474, 476t, 540t, 541–542
 preconventional, 473–474, 475–477, 476t, 540, 540t
 prosocial, 477–478
 theory of mind and, 479–480
Moral rules, 319t, 319–320
Morality
 autonomous, 319, 472–473
 of care, 543
 heteronomous, 319, 472, 475, 540t
 of justice, 543
Moratorium, 576
Moro reflex, 141, 141t, 143
Morphemes, 248, 250
 grammatical, 256–257
Mother(s)
 adolescent, 360f, 360–361, 361f, 364–365
 African American, no-nonsense parenting by, 348
 attachment to. See Attachment
 attitudes and stress of, prenatal development and, 89–91
 communication with infants, 244–245
 depression in, intersubjectivity and, 204–205
 nutrition of, prenatal development and, 91–94
 sensitivity of, attachment and, 219
 substitute, attachment and, 208, 208f, 209, 209f
 teratogenic effects and. See Teratogens
Motherese, 132, 245–246
Motivation
 apprenticeship versus formal instruction and, 431–432
 to learn, 447–448
Motives, hidden, 18
Motor development
 in early childhood, 273t, 273–274
  of fine motor skills, 273t, 273–274
  of gross motor skills, 273, 273t

in infancy, 168–177
  control of elimination and, 175–177
  of fine motor skills, 168–171, 169f
  of gross motor skills, 168, 171f, 171–174
  practice and, 174–175
 in middle childhood, 393–397, 396f
  gender differences in, 396, 397f
  practice and, 396–397, 397f
Motor drive, 273
Motor perseveration, 184
"Mozart effect," 167
Multilingualism, 244–245
Multiple intelligences, 421t, 421–422
Multipotent stem cells, 82
Mumps, maternal, prenatal development and, 100t
Musculoskeletal system, growth of, in infancy, 164
Musical intelligence, 421t
Mutations, 63
Myelin, 127
Myelination
 in early childhood, 276
 in middle childhood, 398
MySpace, 576–577

Naïve biology, 292
Naïve physics, 289
Naïve psychology, 290
Narratives, 259–260, 260f
Native Americans. See also specific groups
 families of, 354
 SIDS among, 155
 suicide among, 588–589
Natural selection, 58–59, 347
Naturalistic observation, 32t, 33–34
Nature, 10
Navajo people
 planning in middle childhood among, 418, 418f
 social smile and, 203
Nazi experiments, 42
Negation, conservation of volume and, 404
Negative affect, temperament and, 149, 149t
Neglected children, 485
Neglectful parenting, 349
Neighborhood(s). See Communities

Neighborhood physical disorder, 371
Nepal, childbirth in, 106–107
Neural tube, 91
Neurofibromatosis, 64t
Neuro-hormonal system, in adolescence, 520f, 520–522, 521f
Neuroimaging, 33
 brain development and, 399f, 399–400
 physical activity and, 414
Neuron(s), 126f, 126–127, 127f
 mirror, 205–207
Neuronal networks, 127
Neuroscience, 33
Neurotransmitters, 127
New Zealand, delinquency in, 592
Newborn(s), 111–115
 appearance of, 116
 baby's experience of birth and, 110–111
 features eliciting care, 25, 25f
 low birth weight and, 114–115
 parent-child relationship and, 115–117
 premature, 113f, 113–115
 social expectations about, 116–117
 viability of, assessing, 111–113
Newborn intensive care unit (NICU), 143
Ngoni people
 childbirth and, 107
 transition to middle childhood in, 389
Nicaragua, transition to middle childhood in, 390
Nicaraguan Sign Language, 243
Niche construction, 71–72
9/11 terrorist attack, 375–376
Nomination procedure, popularity and, 483
No-nonsense parenting, 348
North America. See also specific countries and groups
 bilingualism in, 244
 cooperation and competition among peers and, 487
 mothers' communication with infants in, 244–245
 teaching of grammar in, 246
North Korea
 height in middle childhood in, 392
 puberty in, 522

Norway
  delinquency in, 592
  skiing and skating in, 300
Nuclear families, 345
Number, conservation of, 402–403, 403f
Numeracy, emergent, 433–434
Nuremburg Code, 42
Nursing behavior, 153–155
Nurture, 10
Nutrition
  in early childhood, 274–276, 275f, 276t
  during embryonic period, 82–83
  maternal, prenatal development, 91–94
  puberty and, 526t, 526–528

Obesity, 392–393
  effort to combat, 394–395
  maternal, prenatal development and, 93
  parental attitudes toward, 276
Object(s)
  perception of, in infancy, 135f, 135–136
  transitional, 207
Object permanence, 179, 181–187, 182f, 183f
  A-not-B error and, 183–184
  dynamic systems approach and, 186
  experience and, 186–187, 187f
  memory and, 184
  perseveration and, 184
  violation-of-expectations method and, 185f, 185–186
Objective view of responsibility, 480
Objectivist theory of knowledge, 536
Objectivity, 31, 279
Observation
  naturalistic, 32t, 33–34
  Preyer's rules of, 8, 9t
Occipital lobes, 128, 128f
Oceania, variety of tools used by societies in, 56
Odawa Indian people, culture-sensitive instruction and, 450
Oedipus complex, 309
Oksapmin people, number concepts of, 21, 22
Ontogenetic adaptations, emotions as, 203

Operant conditioning, 19
  developing action and, 147f, 147–148
Operation Smile, 249
Oppositional identity formation, 579
Oral stage, 17t
Organizational strategies, in middle childhood, 411–412
Organizing effects, of pubertal hormones, 519
The Origin of Species (Darwin), 8
Orphanages, attachment patterns and, 216–218, 218f
Ossification
  during early childhood, 273, 273f
  during fetal period, 85f
Out-of-home care, attachment patterns and, 214–215
Ovaries, 85, 512, 612
Overextension, 252, 253t
Overnourishment, maternal, prenatal development and, 93
Overweight. See also Obesity
  maternal, prenatal development and, 93

Pacific Islanders, sexually transmitted infections and, 594
Pacifiers, for premature infants, 143
Padaung culture, parental expectations in, 497
Palate, cleft, 249
Palestine
  sibling relationships in, 352
  social policy in, 30
Parent(s). See also Fathers; Mother(s)
  attitudes toward food and eating, nutrition and, 276
  gay and lesbian, 357–358
  interdependent cultural style and, 458–459
Parent-child relationships
  in adolescence, 570f, 570–573
    conflicts and, 570–571
    influences beyond family, 571–573, 572t
  in middle childhood, 496–500
    changing expectations and, 496–497
    divorce and, 499–500
    peer relationships and, 498–499, 499f

Parenting, 347–350
  goals of, 348
  influence on adolescent behavior, 572–573
  moral development in adolescence and, 543–544
  no-nonsense, 348
  self-esteem and, 469–470
  styles of, 348–350, 350t
Parietal lobes, 128, 128f
Pattern perception, in infancy, 135–136, 136f
Peer relationships
  in adolescence, 557–564
    cliques and crowds and, 559f, 559–560
    conformity and, 560–562
    ethnic identity and, 580–581
    friendships and, 557–559
    moral development and, 544
    parent-child relationships and, 572
    peer pressure and conformity and, 560–562
    romantic relationships and, 562–564
  in middle childhood, 481–496
    competition and cooperation and, 485–489
    friendship and, 493–496
    gender and, 489f, 489–492, 492t
    parents and, 498–499, 499f
    social status and, 481–485
Peer victimization, 482–483
Perception
  of color, in infancy, 135
  of faces, in infancy, 136f, 136–137
  intermodal, 138–139, 139f
  of patterns and objects, in infancy, 135f, 135–136, 136f
Perceptual scaffolding, 223
Performance motivation, 447
Permissive parenting pattern, 349, 350t
Perry Preschool Program, 438
Perseveration, object permanence and, 184
Persistence
  emotion regulation and, 554
  temperament and, 148
Personal distress, 337–338

Personal identity, 315–317
Personal intelligence, 421t
Personal sphere, 319, 319t, 320
Personality, Freud's theory of, 17–18
Personality formation, 305–306
Personality structure, 316
Perspective-taking
  friendships and, 495–496
  identity and, 584–585
Peru, families in, 346
Pervasive food refusal, 591
Phallic stage, 17t, 309
Phenotype, 57–58, 68f, 68–69, 71–72
  variation in, natural selection and, 58
Phenotypic plasticity, 68f, 68–69
Phenylketonuria (PKU), 64t, 65
Phonemes, 132, 237, 434
Phonological awareness, 434
Phonological development, 236, 247, 248, 250
Phonological processing, 446
Physical activity, puberty and, 529–530
Physical deterioration, of neighborhoods, 371
Physical development. See also Brain development; Growth; Motor development
  guide to discussions of, A–1
Physics, cognitive development in, 289f, 289–290
Piaget's theory, 19–21, 20t, 23t
  of cognitive development
    in adolescence, 530–536, 531t
    in early childhood, 277–285, 278t
    in infancy, 177–181
    in middle childhood, 400–409, 401f, 402t, 415–417, 416f
  of developing action, 144–146, 145t
  of moral development
    in early childhood, 318–319
    in middle childhood, 472–473
Pidgin language, 243
Pima Indians, obesity and diabetes among, 93
Pituitary gland, 521
Placenta, 82–83, 83f
Plain People, genetic disorders among, 67

Planning
   in concrete operational stage,
      405f, 405–406, 406f
   in middle childhood, culture
      and, 418, 418f
Plasticity, 10–11, 128, 166–168
   phenotypic, 68f, 68–69
   positive youth development
      and, 595
Play
   coping with chronic illness
      through, 324–325
   self-regulation and, 322–326
   symbolic (fantasy, pretend),
      180
Playgrounds, early and modern,
   5
Playworld practice, 443–444
Pollution, teratogenic effects of,
   102–103
Polygenic inheritance, 63
Polygenic traits, 424
Popular children, 484
Popularity, 481–485, 484f
   controversial children and,
      485
   neglected children and, 485
   popular children and, 484
   rejected children and, 484
Popularity statuses, 484
Positive youth development
      (PYD), 595–596, 596t
Postconventional moral
      reasoning, 473–474, 476t,
      540t, 541–542
Poverty
   communities and, 370–371
   families in, 358–360, 359f
Practical intelligence, 422
Practice, motor development
      and
   in infancy, 174–175
   in middle childhood, 396–
      397, 397f
Pragmatic development, 236,
   248, 257–260
Preattachment phase of
      attachment, 209
Precausal reasoning, 282–284,
   283f, 284f
Precocious puberty, 523, 523t
Preconventional moral
      reasoning, 473–474, 475–
      477, 476t, 540, 540t
Preformationism, 6
Prefrontal cortex, 165, 517
Pregnancy. See also Prenatal
      development
   beliefs about, 79

shorter, emergence of, 58–59
   teenage, 567, 569
Pregnancy anxiety, 90–91
Premature infants
   causes of prematurity and,
      114
   developmental consequences
      of prematurity and,
      114–115
   kangaroo care for, 34–35
   massage for, 113
   NICU care for, 143
Prenatal development, 80–104.
   See also Pregnancy
   embryonic period of, 81,
      82–85
   fetal period of, 81, 85f, 85–89
   germinal period of, 81f,
      81–82
   maternal attitudes and stress
      and, 89–91
   nutrition and, 91–94
   teratogens and, 94–103, 95f,
      96f
      drugs as, 96–99
      environmental, 102–103
      infections as, 99–101
      Rh incompatibility as,
         101–102
Preoperational stage, 20t, 145t,
   277–285, 278t, 402t, 531t
   centration and, 279–284
      distinction between
         appearance and reality
         and, 280–282, 281f
      egocentrism and, 279–280,
         280f
      precausal reasoning and,
         282–284, 283f, 284f
      uneven levels of performance
         and, 284–285
Prereaching, 144, 169
Preschools, 437–439, 438f
Pretend play, 180
Preterm infants, 111. See also
      Premature infants
Prevention science, 380–382,
   381f, 382t, 383t
Primary intersubjectivity, 203–
   205, 209, 237
Primary sex characteristics,
      sexual development,
   514–515
Print media, 374–375, 375f
Privileged domains, cognitive
      development in, 288–298
   in biology, 291–293, 292f,
      293f
   explanations for, 293–298

in physics, 289f, 289–290
   in psychology, 290–291
Proactive aggression, 482
Problem solving, in infancy,
   180
Project Head Start, 437–438,
   439
Prosocial behavior, 327
   in early childhood, 336–338
      empathy and, 336–337
      sympathy and, 337–338
Prosocial moral reasoning,
   477–478
Protective factors, 381, 382t
Protestant Reformation, beliefs
      about children and, 6
Protodeclaratives, 258
Protoimperatives, 258
Proximodistal development, 84
Pseudowords, 446
Psychoanalysis, 16
Psychodynamic theories, 16–18
   of Erikson. See Erikson's
      psychodynamic theory
   of Freud. See Freudian
      theory
   of moral development in early
      childhood, 318
   of sex-role identity
      development, 308t,
      308–309
Psychology, cognitive
      development in, 290–291
Psychosexual stages, of Freud,
   17, 17t
Psychosocial stages, of Erikson,
   17t, 18. See also Erikson's
      psychodynamic theory
Puberty, 512–530
   brain development and, 517f,
      517–520
   growth spurt of, 511–514,
      512f
   health and, 526–530
   neuro-hormonal system and,
      520f, 520–522, 521f
   precocious, 523, 523t
   sexual development in,
      514–517
   timing of, 522–526
      individual differences in,
         522t, 522–524, 523t
      population variation in,
         524–526, 525f, 526t
Public policies, 382
Puerto Ricans
   child-centered speech among,
      246
   ethnic identity among, 315

maternal sensitivity and, 219
   temperament among, 148
Pumé people, early maturation
      and reproductive success
      in, 513
Punch and Judy, 480
Puritans, beliefs about children
      and, 6

Qalandar people, child-rearing
      practices of, 130–131
Qualitative change, 12
Quality of mood, temperament
      and, 148
Quantitative change, 12
Quechua people, child-care
      practices of, 73

Radiation, teratogenic effects
      of, 102
Rating procedure, popularity
      and, 483–484
Reaching, in infancy, 144, 169,
   169f
Reactive aggression, 482
Reactive attachment disorder
      (RAD), 217
Reading
   dyslexia and, 446–447, 447f
   emergent literacy and,
      433–434
   precursors to, 434
Realistic mathematics
      education, 441–443
Reality, appearance
      distinguished from, in early
      childhood, 280–282, 281f
Reality principle, 318
Reasoning
   games for exploring
      development of, 538–539
   hypothetical-deductive, 533
   by manipulating variables,
      531–533, 532f
   moral. See Moral reasoning
   precausal, 282–284, 283f,
      284f
Recessive alleles, 62
Recessive disorders, 63, 64t
Reciprocal relationship phase of
      attachment, 210
Reciprocal teaching, 440–441,
   441f
Reciprocity, friendship and, 557
Referential intentions, 250
Reflexes, in infancy, 140–141,
   141t
Rehearsal, in middle childhood,
   411–412

Reinforcement
  differential, 310
  in operant conditioning, 147
Rejected children, 484
Relation of inclusion, 404
Relational aggression, 331, 483
Reliability, 31
Religion
  beliefs about children and, 6
  children's ideas about God
    and, 474–475
Replicability, 31
Representation(s), 180–181
Representational thinking, 177
Research, 29–43
  action (mission-oriented),
    30, 31
  applied, 30, 31
  basic, 30, 31
  criteria for, 31–32
  data collection methods for,
    32t, 32–35, 37
    clinical interviews, 32t,
      35, 37
    experiments, 32t, 34–35
    naturalistic observation, 32t,
      33–34
  ethical standards for, 42–43
  goals of, 29–31
  research designs and, 37–42
    cohort sequential, 38t,
      40–41, 41f
    cross-sectional, 38t, 39f,
      39–40
    longitudinal, 38t, 38–39
    microgenetic, 38t, 41–42
Resilience, 381
Resistant attachment, 211
Reversibility, conservation of
  volume and, 404
Rh incompatibility, 101–102
Rhesus monkeys, attachment
  in, 208, 208f, 209, 209f
Rhythmicity, temperament and,
  148
Risk factors, 380–381, 382t
Risk-taking behavior, in
  adolescence, 519, 554f,
  554–555, 555f
Romanian orphanages,
  deprivation in, 166, 168,
  216
Romantic relationships, in
  adolescence, 562–564
Romeo and Juliet (Shakespeare),
  508
Rooting reflex, 141t
Rubella, teratogenic effects of,
  99–100

Rule(s)
  display, 327–328
  moral, 319t, 319–320
  of observation, of Preyer, 8, 9t
Rule-based games, moral
  development and, 472–473

Saturated self, 574
Scale errors, in early childhood,
  276–277, 277f
Scandinavian people, lactose
  tolerance among, 74
Schemas
  gender, 308t, 311–312, 312f
  in Piaget's theory, 20, 144
School(s), 429–463. See also
    Education; Instruction
  barriers to success in, 444–449
    motivational, 447–448
    specific learning disabilities
      as, 445–447, 447f
    student engagement and,
      448–449
  classroom social organization
    and, 439–444
  cooperative learning programs
    and, 486
  instructional design and,
    439–444
  problems posed to children
    in, 432, 432t
  readiness for, 348, 433–439
    family and, 435–436, 436f
    precursors to learning
      mathematics and, 434–
      435, 435f
    precursors to reading and
      writing and, 434
    preschools and, 437–439,
      438f
  start times of, 529
School engagement, 448–449
School-cutoff strategy, 449–450
Scripts, cultural, 298–300
Secondary intersubjectivity,
  221–222, 237
  social referencing and, 222
Secondary sex characteristics,
  sexual development, 514,
  515f, 515–517, 516t
Second-order operations, 530
Secular trend, in timing of
  puberty, 525
Secure attachment, 211
Sedatives, for childbirth pain,
  108
Selection, homophily and, 561
Selection perspective on
  divorce, 500

Selective dropout, 39
Self
  as agent, 226
  identity development in
    adolescence and, 574
  independent sense of, 584
  in infancy, 224–228
  interdependent sense of, 584
  in middle childhood, 466–
    471
    changing conceptions of self
      and, 466–468, 467t
    self-esteem and, 468–471,
      469f, 469t
  saturated, 574
Self-agency, 574
Self-awareness, 574
Self-coherence, 574
Self-concept, developmental
  model of, 466–468, 467t
Self-conscious emotions,
  emergence of, 226, 228
Self-continuity, 574
Self-efficacy, 25–26
Self-esteem, 468–471, 469f,
  469t
  foundations of, 469–471, 471t
Self-recognition, 225–226
Self-regulation, in early
  childhood, 320–329
  of emotions, 326–329
  play and, 322–326
  of thought and action,
    321–322
Semantic development, 236,
  247, 250f, 250–255
Semenarche, 514
Sensation-seeking, in
  adolescence, 519, 554f,
  554–555, 555f
Sensitive periods, 11, 166–168
Sensorimotor intelligence, 177
Sensorimotor stage, 20t, 144–
  146, 145t, 178–181, 278,
  402t, 531t
  beginning of symbolic
    representation substage
    of, 178t, 180–181
  coordination of secondary
    circular reactions substage
    of, 178t, 179
  exercising reflex schemas
    substage of, 145, 178t
  primary circular reactions
    substage of, 145–146,
    178t
  secondary circular reactions
    substage of, 178t,
    178–179

  tertiary circular reactions
    substage of, 178t,
    179–180
Sensory development
  fetal, 86–87
  in infancy, 130–139, 139t
    evaluation methods for,
      131–132
    of hearing, 132f, 132–133,
      133f
    of taste and smell senses,
      137f, 137–138
    of vision, 133–137
Sensory register, 286
Sequences of behavior, 8
Sex. See also Gender
  Freudian theory and, 16–17
  growth in infancy and, 164
Sex chromosomes, 61–62, 62f
Sex determination, 61–62, 62f
Sex glands, 85, 521
  development of, 512
Sex hormones, 85, 514, 521
Sex-linked chromosomal
  abnormalities, 66, 68
Sex-role identity development,
  307t, 307–313, 308f, 308t
  cognitive-developmental view
    of, 308t, 310–311
  cultural view of, 308t,
    312–313
  gender schema view of, 308t,
    311–312, 312f
  psychodynamic view of, 308t,
    308–309
  social learning view of, 308t,
    309–310, 310f
Sexual development, 514–517
  primary sex characteristics
    and, 514–515
  secondary sex characteristics
    and, 515f, 515–517,
    516t
Sexual differentiation, 85
Sexual health, in adolescence,
  593–595
Sexual identity, 581–583, 583t
Sexual relationships, in
  adolescence, 564–570
  first sexual experiences and,
    567f, 567–568, 568f,
    568t, 570
  learning about sex and,
    565–567
  teenage pregnancy and, 567,
    569
Sexual reproduction, genetic
  inheritance through, 59f,
  59–62

Sexually transmitted diseases (STDs), maternal, prenatal development and, 100t, 100–101, 101f
Sexually transmitted infections (STIs), 565
Sexual-minority (LGBT) youth, 582
Short-term memory
  in early childhood, 286–287
  increased speed and capacity in middle childhood, 409–410, 410f
Siblings, 351–353, 352f, 353f
Sickle-cell anemia, 64t, 74f, 74–75
Sickle-cell trait, 74
Sierra Leone, conservation in middle childhood in, 416
Sign language
  home sign, 242
  Nicaraguan, 243
Signifying, 461
Single-parent families, 356–357
Skeleton, ossification of
  in early childhood, 273, 273f
  in fetal period, 85f
Skull, growth in infancy, 125–126
Sleep
  in early childhood, 274
  puberty and, 528–529
Slow-to-warm-up babies, 148
Smell sense, in infancy, 138
Smiles
  endogenous, 203
  social, 203
Smoking, teratogenic effects of, 96–97
Social capital, 369
Social cohesion, 371
Social comparison, 467–468
Social control, in middle childhood, 465
Social development, guide to discussions of, A–2
Social disorganization, 371
Social domain theory, 478–479, 545
  of moral development in early childhood, 319t, 319–320
Social enhancement, 54
Social expectations, about newborns, 116–117
Social factors, aggression and, 332
Social groups, in early childhood, 338–339
Social intelligence, 421t

Social interaction, infant emotions and, 203–205
Social learning theories, 25–26
  of sex-role identity development, 308t, 309–310, 310f
Social networking, 576–577
Social organization, apprenticeship versus formal instruction and, 432
Social policy, action research and, 30
Social processes, emotion regulation and, 555–557, 556f
Social referencing, 172, 173, 222
Social relations, apprenticeship versus formal instruction and, 432
Social repair mechanisms, 496
Social smiles, 203
Social stereotypes, on television, 378
Social structures, 481–485
  dominance and, 481
  popularity and, 481–485, 484f
Social-contract reasoning, 540t, 541–542
Socialization, 305
  ethnic, 314–315
  homophily and, 561
Society for Research in Child Development, ethical standards devised by, 43
Sociocognitive conflict, 533–536
  post-formal-operational thinking and, 534–536
  variability in formal-operational thinking and, 534
Sociocultural theory, 21–22, 23t
  of cognitive development, in adolescence, 537–539, 539f
  of language development, 263–264
Sociodramatic play, 323–326
Socioeconomic status (SES). See also Poverty
  attachment patterns and, 214
  school readiness and, 435–436, 436f
Socioemotional competence, 328
Sociograms, 484, 484f
"Soft spots," 125–126

Somali immigrants, ethnic identity and, 581
Somatic cells, 60
South Africa, low birth weight in, 114
South Korea
  gross motor development in, 273
  height in middle childhood in, 392
  puberty in, 522
Spain, cooperation and competition among peers in, 487–489, 488f
Spatial intelligence, 421t
Specific learning disabilities, 445–447, 447f
Speech, inner, 265–266
Spina bifida, 91
Spinal cord, 127, 128f
Stage theories of development, 8
Stages of development, cognitive. See Piaget's theory
Stanford-Binet test, 9
Stem cells
  multipotent (adult), 82
  totipotent, 82
Stepping reflex, 141t, 142, 142f
Stillbirths, maternal nutrition and, 92
Still-face method, 204
Strange situation, 211
Stress, birth weight and, 89
Subjective view of responsibility, 480
Subjectivist theory of knowledge, 536
Sub-Saharan Africa
  orphans in, 218, 218f
  pregnancy spacing among, 153
Substitute mothers, attachment and, 208, 208f, 209, 209f
Sucking, fetal, 87
Sucking reflex, 140–141, 141t
Sudden infant death syndrome (SIDS), 154–155
  back to sleep movement and, 175
  infant sleeping arrangements and, 151
Suicide, among Native American adolescents, 588–589
Sukuma people, pregnancy spacing among, 153
Superego, 17–18, 318, 472

Supplemental food programs, for women, infants, and children, 92–93
Swaddling, 143, 157
Swallowing, fetal, 87
Sweden
  families in, 346, 356
  instructional methods in, 443
  teenage pregnancy in, 569
Switzerland, toilet training in, 175
Symbolic communication, 54–55
Symbolic play, 180
Symbolic tools, 53–54
Sympathy, in early childhood, 337–338
Synapses, 127
Synaptic pruning, 129, 129f, 166
  in adolescence, 518
  in early childhood, 276
  in middle childhood, 398
Synaptogenesis, 127
  in adolescence, 518
  exuberant, 129, 166
Syntactic bootstrapping, 256
Syphilis, maternal, prenatal development and, 100t
Systems theories, 26–29
  dynamic, 27
  ecological, 27–29, 29f

Tainae people, changelings and, 297
Taiwan
  adolescent sleep patterns in, 529
  language development in deaf children in, 243
  parenting and self-esteem and, 470
Takeoff velocity, 511
Tamagotchi, 378–379
Tanner's stages of pubertal development, 516t
Tanzania
  conservation in middle childhood in, 416
  families in, 346
Tasmanian societies, loss of aspects of culture of, 56
Taste sense, in infancy, 137f, 137–138
Tay-Sachs disease, 64t
Technological advances
  for brain activity measurement, 3
  fetal imaging and, 86

Teenage pregnancy, 567, 569
Television, 375–378
   content of, 377–378
   form of medium, 376
Temperament, 148–150, 149t, 306
Temporal lobes, 128, 128f
Teratogens, 94–103, 95f, 96f
   drugs as, 96–99
   environmental, 102–103
   infections as, 99–101
   Rh incompatibility as, 101–102
Testes, 85, 512
Testosterone, 85, 514, 521
Thalassemia, 64t
Thalidomide, 96
Theories, 15–29
   in developmental science, 15–16
   grand, 16–22
      behaviorist, 18–19, 23t
      constructivist, 19–21, 20t, 23t
      psychodynamic.
         See Erikson's psychodynamic theory
      sociocultural, 21–22, 23t
   modern, 22–23, 25–29
      evolutionary, 23, 25, 25f
      information-processing, 26
      social learning, 25–26
      systems, 26–29
   psychodynamic. See Freudian theory; Psychodynamic theories
Theory of gradual differentiation, 202
Theory of mind, 290–291
   moral reasoning and, 479–480
Theory theory, 293, 295, 297
Thinking. See also Moral reasoning; reasoning
   conceptual, 177
   precausal, 282–284, 283f, 284f
   representational, 177
   self-regulation of, 321–322
3-day measles, teratogenic effects of, 99–100
Threshold of responsiveness, temperament and, 148
Thyroid gland, 521
Tobacco, as teratogen, 96–97
Toilet training, 175–177
Tools, cultural, 52–54, 53t
   material, 53
   symbolic, 53–54

Top-down processing, 440
Totipotent stem cells, 82
Tower of Hanoi problem, 405f, 405–406, 406f
Toxemia, prenatal development and, 100t
Toxoplasmosis, maternal, prenatal development and, 100t
Transductive thinking, 282–283
Transitional objects, 207
Triangulation, 32
Trisomy 21, 64t, 65–66, 66f
   development in, 68
True dialogue, 265
Trust versus mistrust stage, 17t, 228–229
Truthfulness, in early childhood, 286
Turkey, newborn care in, 140
Turner syndrome, 64t
Twin(s)
   dizygotic (fraternal), 61, 70
      depression in, 587
      growth patterns of, 391
   genotype of, 58
   monozygotic (identical), 61, 70
      depression in, 587
      development of, 82
      growth patterns of, 391
Twin studies, 70, 71

Uganda, cognitive abilities in, 425
Ultrasound, fetal, 86
Umbilical cord, 83, 83f
Unconditional response (UCR), 146
Unconditional stimulus (UCS), 146
Unconscious, 18
Underextension, 253
Undernutrition
   maternal, prenatal development and, 91–93, 94f
   parental attitudes toward, 276
Unitary language hypothesis, 244
United Kingdom. See also England
   instructional methods in, 443
United Kingdom, instructional methods in, 443
United Nations Declaration of the Rights of the Child, 381, 383t

United States
   birth weight in, 111
   brainy-baby movement in, 167
   childbirth in, 104, 107–111
      baby's experience of birth and, 110–111
      medical interventions and, 108–110
      pain and medication and, 108
   childhood obesity in, 392–393
   complexity of speech in, 246
   conservation in middle childhood in, 417
   emotional development in, 328
   families of, 354
   heritability of height in, 69
   immigrants to, 355–356
   industrialization in, 7
   infant feeding schedules in, 153–154
   infant sleeping arrangements in, 151
   infant sleep/wake behavior in, 152–153
   intersubjectivity in, 204
   language development in, 264
   language development in deaf children in, 242–243
   maternal sensitivity in, 219
   mathematics achievement in, 456–457
   memory span in middle childhood in, 410
   moral development in, 545–546
   overweight in, 274
   parental expectations in, 497
   public policies in, 382
   school readiness in, 435–436, 436f
   teenage pregnancy in, 569
   temperament in, 150
   toilet training in, 176
Universal ethical principles, 540t, 542
University of California at San Diego, 31
University-community partnerships, 30–31
Utku people, moral behavior of, 227

Validity, 32
   ecological, 35, 553
Vernix caseosa, 111

Viability
   age of, 86
   of newborn, assessing, 111–113
Vietnam
   cultural style of, 458–459
   speech-language pathology in, 249
Vietnamese Americans, ethnic identity among, 579–580
Violation-of-expectations method, 185f, 185–186, 289
Violence, on television, 377–378
"Virginity pledge," 566, 567
Vision
   fetal, 86
   in infancy, 133–137
      color perception and, 135
      face perception and, 136f, 136–137
      pattern and object perception and, 135f, 135–136, 136f
      visual acuity and, 134, 134f
      visual scanning and, 134–135
Visual acuity, in infancy, 134, 134f
Visual attention, 194
Visual cliff, 172, 172f
Visual fixation, 194
Visual preference technique, 132
Visually guided reaching, 144
Vitamin A, puberty and, 526
Vocabulary
   earliest, 251f, 251–252
   growth spurt in, 253–254
   receptive, 252
Volume, conservation of, 403f, 403–404
Vygotsky's sociocultural theory, 21–22, 23t

Walking
   development of, 172–174, 173f
   upright, 57
Walpiri people, mothers' communication with infants among, 245
War, 372–373
   maternal nutrition and prenatal development during, 91–92
Wealth, families and, 363–364

Weight. *See also* Obesity; Overweight; Undernutrition
  at birth
    maternal nutrition and, 92
    maternal stress and, 89
  fetal, 85f
  genetic and environmental influences on, 392–393
  in infancy, 162–164, 163f, 164f
  in middle childhood, 392–393
Wernicke's aphasia, 239
Wernicke's area, 239, 240, 240f

West Africa. *See also specific groups*
  infant care in, 123
West Indian people, child-rearing practices of, 174
Western Europe, industrialization in, 7
Wharton's jelly, 83
Where the Wild Things Are (Sendak), 326, 375
White Americans. *See* European Americans
White matter, 127, 518
WIC program, 92–93
Wild Boy of Aveyron, 1–2, 10
Williams syndrome, 267
Word errors, 252–253, 253t

Working memory
  in early childhood, 286–287
  increased speed and capacity in middle childhood, 409–410, 410f
World Trade Center terrorist attack, 375–376
Writing
  dysgraphia and, 446
  emergent literacy and, 433–434
  precursors to, 434

X chromosomes, 61–62, 62f
  disorders of, 64t, 66, 68
  sexual differentiation and, 85

Y chromosomes, 62, 62f
  disorders of, 64t, 66, 68
  sexual differentiation and, 85

Zambia, education in, 429
Zapotec people, aggression among, 332
Zinc, puberty and, 526
Zincateco people, social expectations about infants among, 117
Zone of proximal development, 22, 353
  education and, 441
Zygote, 60, 80, 81, 81f